CONTRACT LAW LIBRARY

Misrepresentation, Mistake and Non-Disclosure

Third Edition

CONTRACT LAW LIBRARY

Misrepresentation, Mistake and Non-Disclosure

Third Edition

John Cartwright, B.C.L., M.A.
Professor of the Law of Contract, University of Oxford
Tutor in Law, Christ Church, Oxford
Professor of Anglo-American Private Law, University of Leiden
Solicitor

SWEET & MAXWELL THOMSON REUTERS

First Edition	2002	by John Cartwright
Second Edition	2007	by John Cartwright
Third Edition	2012	by John Cartwright

Published in 2012 by Sweet & Maxwell, 100 Avenue Road, London NW3 3PF part of Thomson Reuters (Professional) UK Limited (Registered in England & Wales, Company No 1679046.
Registered Office and address for service: Aldgate House, 33 Aldgate High Street, London EC3N 1DL)

For further information on our products and services, visit *www.sweetandmaxwell.co.uk*

Typeset by Letterpart Ltd, Reigate, Surrey

Printed and bound in Great Britain by CPI Group (UK) Ltd, Croydon, CR0 4YY.

No natural forests were destroyed to make this product; only farmed timber was used and re-planted.

A CIP catalogue record of this book is available for the British Library.

ISBN: 978-0-41404-955-0

Preface

In 2011, introducing their Consultation Paper on Consumer Redress for Misleading and Aggressive Practices, the English and Scottish Law Commissions wrote:

> "The current law of misrepresentations provides redress in most cases of consumer detriment but the problem is that the rights are fragmented, complex and unclear. We consider seven possible routes to a remedy that may apply where a trader has misled a consumer. Many of these causes of action depend on proving the trader was fraudulent or negligent, which is difficult in consumer cases. The definition of a misrepresentation is also overly complicated.
>
> Although the statutory remedies for misrepresentation in England and Scotland provide a good balance of protection, they are perceived as inaccessible. The remedies are uncertain and consumers rarely know what they are entitled to. Overall the current law confuses traders, consumers and their advisers alike and hinders private ordering."

Since the first edition of this book, its purpose has been to provide a path through the complexity of the law of misrepresentation, and in particular to cast light on the confusion of remedies available for misrepresentations and the overlapping (but not identical) rules for what counts as an actionable misrepresentation for the several remedies, and to assist the practitioner in the the search for the remedy which is both available and most suitable for the client. In the preface to the second edition it was suggested that review of the law of misrepresentation and non-disclosure would be welcome, but it was admitted that a general review was unlikely. It was therefore cheering to discover that, with a view to recommending private remedies for a consumer against a trader under the Consumer Protection from Unfair Trading Regulations 2008, the Law Commissions had been given the terms of reference (as set out in paragraph 1.15 of the 2011 Consultation Paper), inter alia:

> "to advise on a possible restatement and simplification of the law of misrepresentation, to make it more transparent and easier for businesses and consumers to understand and to remove unnecessary differences between the civil law and Regulations."

Unfortunately, the optimism that this heralded a general review of the law of misrepresentation was short lived: by paragraph 1.20 of the Consultation Paper the Law Commissions told us that they had already changed direction, and instead of undertaking a general review and simplification of the law of misrepresentation, they proposed to leave it largely untouched and instead to add a new set of remedies to provide private remedies for breach of the Regulations. So from the height of the welcome prospect of a review and simplification of the law, we return to the depths of an additional layer of complexity. Add to this the fact that, within the Law Commission's review of insurance law, a Bill is already before Parliament to change radically the law on misrepresentation and non-disclosure in consumer insurance contracts, and a Consultation Paper is promised during winter 2011–12 for business insurance contracts—which will add further layers of differences in the law for this particular type of contract by contrast with the general law—the picture is destined to become even more (in the words of the Law Commissions) "fragmented, complex and unclear".

This edition therefore continues the aim of giving a comprehensive but, it is hoped, clear and comprehensible path through the complexities of the subject. There have been thorough revisions of all the chapters to bring them as far as possible up to date in the light of developments, large and small, in the law. Over the last five years there has been no shortage of cases applying and refining the existing law. Case law has brought clarity and stability to some issues, such as the effectiveness of "no representation" and "non-reliance" clauses, the commercial interpretation of arbitration clauses in relation to disputes involving misrepresentation claims, abolition of expert immunity from liability in negligence, and confirmation that, in the light of the decision in *The Great Peace* rejecting rescission in equity for common mistake, there can be no rescission for unilateral mistake of fact. Some apparently clear decisions have also, however, thrown up doubts or new questions, such as whether it is really right to interpret the "common intention" for the purposes of rectification by a wholly objective test, and whether the breach of a duty of disclosure should give rise to a claim for damages in tort (and, if so, whether the development so far which allows a claim in the tort of deceit will spread to allow a claim under section 2(1) of the Misrepresentation Act 1967). It is also becoming clearer that the reaction elsewhere in the common law world to the decision in *The Great Peace* is rather cool, but for the moment it is being supported in the lower courts in England. There are also developments on the horizon. It has already been noted above that the law on misrepresentation and non-disclosure in relation to insurance contracts is under review, and the Consumer Insurance (Disclosure and Representations) Bill 2011 is discussed on the basis that it is likely to be enacted shortly after the publication of this book: further legislative reforms on business insurance contracts are more distant but will surely follow. And the Law Commission will continue its work to devise private remedies for breach of the Consumer Protection from Unfair Trading Regulations—whatever form they eventually take, the new remedies will have an impact on the operation of the existing law on misrepresentation (not as great an impact, perhaps, as the Trade Practices Act 1974 has had in Australia, but there may be lessons to be learned from the other common law jurisdictions in this as in other aspects of the law). The winds are also blowing from Europe. At the time of writing the Consumer Rights Directive had just been adopted by the European Parliament, but it is a watered-down, compromise document which no longer has the range and potential impact that it might have had. Now, however, we wait to see the outcome of the Commission's proposal for a Regulation to introduce an "Optional Instrument" of European contract law, which would have the potential to bring into English law a parallel set of model contract rules, which would introduce very different ideas in relation to the role of mistake and non-disclosure in contract. When the text of this edition was finalised, we had the Commission's revised draft of the "Feasibility study for a future instrument on European contract law" (see paras 1–05 and 17–54 of this book). Since the book went to press, we now have the Commission's proposal for a Regulation on a Common European Sales Law (COM(2011) 635), on which the Law Commission has already published its advice to the UK Government. These are, no doubt, long-term potential developments, and as in previous editions of this book the aim in this edition is not to make a detailed comparative study of its topics with proposals for reform, but to present the law as it is, for the adviser to see a clear picture of the solutions to the practical problems that arise in relation to claims of misrepresentation, mistake and non-disclosure. But it is also important to see the topic in perspective, and to realise where points are unclear or may yet become subject to review.

As always, I must acknowledge the friendly assistance and encouragement which I have received at every stage from the team at Sweet and Maxwell in the planning and execution of this new edition; I am also grateful to them for undertaking the compilation of the tables and the index.

John Cartwright
Christ Church
Oxford

Abbreviations: Books Referred to in the Text

All books are published in the UK unless otherwise indicated.

Allen	D.K. Allen, *Misrepresentation* (Sweet & Maxwell Ltd, 1988)
Anson	J. Beatson, A. Burrows and J. Cartwright, *Anson's Law of Contract* (29th edn, Oxford University Press, 2010)
Benjamin	M.G. Bridge (ed.), *Benjamin's Sale of Goods* (8th edn, Sweet & Maxwell Ltd, 2010)
Bowstead & Reynolds	P.G. Watts, *Bowstead & Reynolds on Agency* (19th edn, Sweet & Maxwell Ltd, 2010)
Burrows	A. Burrows, *Remedies for Torts and Breach of Contract* (3rd edn, Oxford University Press, 2004)
Burrows, Finn & Todd	J. Burrows, J. Finn and S. Todd, *Law of Contract in New Zealand* (3rd edn, LexisNexis NZ, Wellington, 2007)
Carter, Peden and Tolhurst	J.W. Carter, E. Peden and G.J. Tolhurst, *Contract Law in Australia* (5th edn, LexisNexis Butterworths, Chatswood NSW, 2007)
Cartwright	J. Cartwright, Unequal Bargaining, A Study of Vitiating Factors in the Formation of Contracts (Oxford University Press, 1991)
Charlesworth & Percy	C. Walton (ed.), *Charlesworth & Percy on Negligence* (12th edn, Sweet & Maxwell, 2010) with supplements

Cheshire, Fifoot and Furmston	M.P. Furmston, *Cheshire, Fifoot and Furmston's Law of Contract* (15th edn, Oxford University Press, 2006)
Chitty	H. Beale (ed.), *Chitty on Contracts* (30th edn, Sweet & Maxwell Ltd, 2008) with supplements
Clarke	M.A. Clarke, J.M. Burling and R.L. Purves, *The Law of Insurance Contracts* (6th edn, Informa Publishing, 2009)
Clerk & Lindsell	M.A. Jones and A.M. Dudgale (eds), *Clerk & Lindsell on Torts* (20th edn, Sweet & Maxwell Ltd, 2010) with supplements
Corbin	A.L. Corbin, *Corbin on Contract* (West, St. Paul, Minnesota, 1960) with supplements
Dugdale & Stanton	A.M. Dugdale and K.M. Stanton, *Professional Negligence* (3rd edn, Butterworths Tolley, 1998)
Emmet	J.T. Farrand and A. Clarke, *Emmet and Farrand on Title* (19th edn, Sweet & Maxwell Ltd, 1986) looseleaf
Farnsworth	E.A. Farnsworth, *Contracts* (4th edn, Aspen, New York, 2004)
Fridman	G.H.L. Fridman, *The Law of Contract in Canada* (5th edn, Carswell, Toronto, 2006)
Furmston	M. Furmston (ed.), *The Law of Contract (Butterworths Common Law Series)* (4th edn, LexisNexis Butterworths, 2010)
Goff & Jones	Lord Goff of Chieveley and G. Jones, *The Law of Restitution* (7th edn, Sweet & Maxwell Ltd, 2006) with supplements
Gore-Browne	A. Alcock (gen. ed.), *Gore-Browne on Companies* (45th edn, Jordan Publishing Ltd, 2004), looseleaf
Hodgin	R.W. Hodgin, *Professional Liability: Law and Insurance* (2nd edn, Informa Publishing Group Ltd, 1999)

Jackson & Powell	J.L. Powell, R. Stewart and the Hon Mr Justice Jackson (eds), *Jackson & Powell on Professional Liability* (6th edn, Sweet & Maxwell Ltd, 2006) with supplements
Jones and Goodhart	G. Jones and W. Goodhart, *Specific Performance* (2nd edn, Butterworths, 1996)
Lando and Beale	O. Lando and H. Beale, *Principles of European Contract Law Parts I and II* (Kluwer Law International, The Hague, 2000)
Lewison	K. Lewison, *The Interpretation of Contracts* (5th edn, Sweet & Maxwell Ltd, 2011) with supplements
McGregor	H. McGregor, *McGregor on Damages* (18th edn, Sweet & Maxwell Ltd, London, 2009) with supplements
Phipson	H.M. Malek (ed.), *Phipson on Evidence* (17th edn, Sweet & Maxwell Ltd, 2010)
Seddon and Ellinghaus	N.C. Seddon and M.P. Ellinghaus, *Cheshire and Fifoot's Law of Contract*, Australian Edition (9th edn, LexisNexis Butterworths, Chatsworth NSW, 2008)
Snell	J. McGhee, *Snell's Equity* (32nd edn, Sweet & Maxwell Ltd, 2010)
Spencer Brown (Misrepresentation)	K.R. Handley (ed.), *Spencer Bower, Turner and Handley: Actionable Misrepresentation* (4th edn, Butterworths, 2000)
Spencer Bower (Non-Disclosure)	A.K Turner and R.J. Sutton, *Spencer Bower, Turner and Sutton: Actionable Non-Disclosure* (2nd edn, Butterworths, 1990)
Stoljar	S.J. Stoljar, *Mistake and Misrepresentation* (Sweet & Maxwell, 1968)
Swann	J. Swann, *Canadian Contract Law* (LexisNexis Butterworths, Markham, Ontario, 2006)
Treitel	E. Peel (ed.), *Treitel, The Law of Contract* (13th edn, Sweet & Maxwell Ltd, 2011)

Waddams	S.M. Waddams, *Law of Contracts* (6th edn, Canada Law Book, Toronto, 2010)
Williston	W.H.E. Jaeger, *Williston on Contracts* (3rd edn, Baker Voorhis, Mount Kisco, New York, 1957 onwards)
Winfield & Jolowicz	W.V.H. Rogers, *Winfield & Jolowicz on Tort* (18th edn, Sweet & Maxwell Ltd, 2010)

OTHER SELECTED ABBREVIATIONS

CA	Companies Act
CCA	Court of Criminal Appeal
CPR	Civil Procedure Rules
Ct. Sess.	Court of Session
DCFR	Draft Common Frame of Reference
HCA	High Court of Australia
IH	Inner House, Court of Session
NYCA	New York Court of Appeals
NZCA	New Zealand Court of Appeal
OH	Outer House, Court of Session
PC	Privy Council
SCC	Supreme Court of Canada
Sup. Ct.	Supreme Court

TABLE OF CONTENTS

Part 2 MISTAKE

Part 3 NON-DISCLOSURE

TABLE OF CASES

Medcalf v Mardell (Wasted Costs Order); sub nom. Medcalf v Weatherill [2002] UKHL 27; [2003] 1 A.C. 120; [2002] 3 W.L.R. 172; [2002] 3 All E.R. 721; [2002] C.P. Rep. 70; [2002] C.P.L.R. 647; [2002] 3 Costs L.R. 428; [2002] P.N.L.R. 43; (2002) 99(31) L.S.G. 34; (2002) 152 N.L.J. 1032; (2002) 146 S.J.L.B. 175; [2002] N.P.C. 89 . . . . 5–49, 11–07
Melbourne Banking Corp Ltd v Brougham (No.2) (1881-82) L.R. 7 App. Cas. 307, PC (Aus) 4–10
Mercantile Credit Co Ltd v Garrod [1962] 3 All E.R. 1103 QBD 5–21
Mercantile Credit Co Ltd v Hamblin [1965] 2 Q.B. 242; [1964] 3 W.L.R. 798; [1964] 3 All E.R. 592; 108 S.J. 674 CA 13–57
Merrett v Babb [2001] EWCA Civ 214; [2001] Q.B. 1174; [2001] 3 W.L.R. 1; [2001] B.L.R. 483; (2001) 3 T.C.L.R. 15; 80 Con. L.R. 43; [2001] Lloyd's Rep. P.N. 468; [2001] P.N.L.R. 29; [2001] 1 E.G.L.R. 145; [2001] 8 E.G.C.S. 167; (2001) 98(13) L.S.G. 41; (2001) 145 S.J.L.B. 75 . . 6–32, 6–42
Mersey Steel and Iron Co v Naylor, Benzon & Co (1882) 9 Q.B.D. 648 CA 8–36
Merton LBC v Richards [2005] EWCA Civ 639; [2005] H.L.R. 44 4–11
Metall und Rohstoff AG v ACLI Metals (London) Ltd [1984] 1 Lloyd's Rep. 598; [1985] E.C.C. 502 CA (Civ Div) 5–42
Metall und Rohstoff AG v Donaldson Lufkin & Jenrette Inc [1990] 1 Q.B. 391; [1989] 3 W.L.R. 563; [1989] 3 All E.R. 14; (1989) 133 S.J. 1200 CA (Civ Div) 11–06
Midland Bank Plc v Greene [1994] 2 F.L.R. 827; [1995] 1 F.C.R. 365; (1995) 27 H.L.R. 350; [1994] Fam. Law 676; [1993] N.P.C. 152 Ch D . 4–13, 17–26
Midland Bank Trust Co Ltd v Hett, Stubbs & Kemp [1979] Ch.384; [1978] 3 W.L.R. 167; [1978] 3 All E.R. 571; [1955-95] P.N.L.R. 95; 121 S.J. 830 Ch D 3–46, 6–29, 6–41
Midland Great Western Railway of Ireland v Johnson (1858) 6 H.L.C. 798; 10 E.R. 1509 3–24
Mihalis Angelos, The. *See* Maredelanto Compania Naviera SA v Bergbau-Handel GmbH (The Mihalis Angelos) 3–24
Miljus (t/a A&Z Engineering) v Yamazaki Machinery UK Ltd [1997] 1 C.L.Y. 992 QBD (OR) 9–30
Miller Paving Ltd v B. Gottardo Construction Ltd (2007) 285 D.L.R. (4th) 568 15–32
Miller v Cannon Hill Estates Ltd [1931] 2 K.B. 113 KBD 8–05, 8–08
Ministry of Health v Simpson; sub nom. Diplock's Estate, Re [1951] A.C. 251; [1950] 2 All E.R. 1137; 66 T.L.R. (Pt. 2) 1015; 94 S.J. 777 HL 3–33
Ministry of Housing and Local Government v Sharp [1970] 2 Q.B. 223; [1970] 2 W.L.R. 802; [1970] 1 All E.R. 1009; 68 L.G.R. 187; (1970) 21 P. & C.R. 166; 114 S.J. 109 CA (Civ Div) 6–24, 6–39
Molyneux v Hawtrey [1903] 2 K.B. 487 CA 17–41
Monro v Bogdanor Urban District Council [1915] 3 K.B. 167 CA 11–20
Montmore International Ltd v Abbey Healthcare (festival) Ltd [2010] EWCA Civ 761; [2010] All E.R. (D) 62 11–17
Moorgate Mercantile Co Ltd v Twitchings [1977] A.C. 890 HL . . 10–23, 10–24, 10–28

TABLE OF STATUTES

TABLE OF STATUTORY INSTRUMENTS

TABLE OF EUROPEAN LEGISLATION

Treaties and Conventions

Directives

Regulations

TABLE OF FOREIGN STATUTES

CHAPTER 1

GENERAL INTRODUCTION

I. SCOPE OF THIS BOOK

Defects in formation of the contract. This book is concerned with certain problems[1] that can arise during the formation of a contract. After entering into a contract, one party may claim that he was misled by the other; or that he would not have entered into the contract if he had been given information by the other; or simply that he made a mistake in entering into the contract. These issues are closely linked because they all concern the claimant's misunderstanding about something which he says was relevant to his decision to enter into the contract—whether the misunderstanding was simply his own mistake, or was caused by the other party (misrepresentation) or at least should have been prevented by the other party (non-disclosure). Misrepresentation, mistake and non-disclosure can also be relevant in other contexts, but the focus in this book will be their impact during the negotiations for a contract, and the remedies which are in consequence available to one or both parties to the contract. **1–01**

Finding practical solutions. In one sense, the most fundamental of the topics discussed in this book is *mistake*. As we shall see, claims based on the defendant's misrepresentation or on his failure to disclose information both have at their heart a complaint that the **1–02**

[1] This book will not cover the whole range of problems (vitiating factors) that may arise during the formation of the contract, and which can impact on a party's decision to give his assent. For a detailed discussion of duress or undue influence exercised by the other party, see N. Enonchong, *Duress, Undue Influence and Unconscionable Dealing* (2005).

claimant entered into the contract under a mistake. However, we shall also see that English law does not give primary focus to the claim based on the mistake, but has developed rules relating to misrepresentation which offer the claimant a much more favourable route to obtaining a remedy—and a wider range of remedies. For this reason, in practice the claimant's first call is on the rules relating to misrepresentation. Only if he cannot find a satisfactory solution based on misrepresentation (either because he cannot establish a misrepresentation on which to found a remedy or, if there was a misrepresentation, because the remedies available on the facts for that misrepresentation are not adequate) will the claimant turn to the rules which might provide a remedy for his own mistake or the defendant's non-disclosure. For this reason, a significant proportion—the first Part—of this book is devoted to the remedies available for misrepresentation. Mistake and non-disclosure are considered in Parts II and III respectively.

Within each Part, the material is organised in ways which should enable the reader to identify the elements of a claim, and the remedies which are available. It will be helpful here, however, to set the scene by outlining the key elements of misrepresentation, mistake and non-disclosure, and the differences between them; and by giving a brief overview of the remedies that are available for each.

II. Distinguishing between Misrepresentation, Mistake and Non-Disclosure

1–03 **Misrepresentation and mistake.** Misrepresentation and mistake are generally treated entirely separately in English law,[2] although this tends to mask the fact that misrepresentation is really a sub-category of mistake: induced mistake. In a claim of misrepresentation the claimant asserts that the defendant communicated to him inaccurate information on which he relied; that is, by his statement the defendant caused him to make a mistake. The claimant will generally find it more advantageous to plead the misrepresentation than simply the mistake. Without showing that

[2] Chitty, Chs 5, 6; Furmston, Ch.4, ss.B, C; Treitel, Chs 8, 9; Anson, Chs 8, 9; Cheshire, Fifoot and Furmston, Chs 8, 9. An exception is Goff & Jones, Ch.9, which deals with both mistake and misrepresentation under the general heading 'Relief from Transactions Entered into Under a Mistake'.

the defendant committed a legal wrong, such as a tort or a breach of contract, there will be no claim for damages. Establishing the mistake shows only the claimant's own misunderstanding of the facts or other circumstances surrounding his entry into the contract, and without more the claimant cannot hold the defendant responsible for any loss caused by it; the misrepresentation, by contrast, may sometimes be actionable as a tort[3] or breach of contract.[4] If the claimant seeks to show that the contract is void, he may sometimes be able to do so by relying simply on the mistake; but even then the claim is not easy. The courts are reluctant to allow one party's mistake to vitiate a contract because it would undermine the other party's security of contract.[5] By contrast, where he can show that the mistake was induced by the other party's statement, and so can plead his claim not as mistake but as misrepresentation, the possibility of avoiding the contract is much greater: rescission of the contract is generally available as a remedy for misrepresentation.[6] Even where the misrepresentation was innocent, the fact that the defendant caused the mistake is sufficient to displace the argument that his security of contract be protected.[7] However, misrepresentation makes the contract only voidable, and not void.[8] Sometimes, therefore, in order to obtain an adequate remedy the claimant may need to rely on his mistake if he can thereby show that the contract was void, such as where rescission of the (voidable) contract has now become barred.[9]

Misrepresentation and non-disclosure. A claim for misrepresentation is based on the defendant's provision of false information to the claimant; a claim for non-disclosure is based on the **1–04**

[3] Deceit (below, Ch.5) or negligence (Ch.6), or a statutory claim under the Misrepresentation Act 1967 s.2(1) (Ch.7).

[4] Below, Ch.8.

[5] Below, paras 12–12 to 12–15.

[6] Below, Ch.4.

[7] Cartwright, esp. pp.103–104, Chs 10, 11. See also R. Bigwood, "Pre-Contractual Misrepresentation and the Limits of the Principle in *With v O'Flanagan*" [2005] C.L.J. 94 (misrepresentation as an "agency-responsible act on the part of a human 'misrepresentor' and not merely an 'event'"); *cf.*, however, para.4–27, n.126, below.

[8] Below, para.4–05.

[9] Below, paras 4–38, 12–19.

defendant's failure to provide information. The claim for non-disclosure is therefore fundamentally different from the claim for misrepresentation in that, as in the case of mistake, the claimant cannot say that his misunderstanding or lack of information was caused by the defendant. But the English courts have generally seen non-disclosure as closely related to misrepresentation, and some of the remedies available in a claim of misrepresentation are also available for non-disclosure. The courts are much more cautious in imposing liability for non-disclosure than for misrepresentation: it is much easier to find a (negative) duty not to provide false information than to find a (positive) duty to provide information. The starting-point is therefore that there is no duty to provide information to the other party during contractual negotiations, and therefore there is no general liability for non-disclosure.[10] There are, however, certain situations in which the courts will recognise the duty to disclose information in the formation of a contract, either because of the nature of the contract itself, or because of the pre-existing relationship between the negotiating parties.[11]

1–05 **Comparative approaches.** This book discusses the English law of misrepresentation, mistake and non-disclosure. From time to time mention is made of the approaches of other legal systems to similar issues; it is important to be clear from the outset about the significance of such comparative material.

Although it is rash to group together all civil law jurisdictions—even European civil law jurisdictions—since the detail of their approaches will inevitably differ, it is not unreasonable to generalise in relation to two significant matters that bear upon the subject of this book.[12] First, that the civil lawyer tends to view an alleged

[10] Below, Ch.16.

[11] Below, Ch.17.

[12] For a comparative study of European jurisdictions, see R. Sefton-Green (ed.), *Mistake, Fraud and Duties to Inform in European Contract Law* (2005). See also Lando and Beale, arts 1.102(1), 1.201, 2.301, 4.102 to 4.107, 4.112 to 4.119 and corresponding Comment and Notes; C. von Bar and E. Clive (eds), *Principles, Definitions and Model Rules of European Private Law: Draft Common Frame of Reference (DCFR), Full Edition* (Sellier, Munich, 2009), arts II.-3:101 to II.-3:109, II.-3:301, II.-7:101 to II.-7:205, II.-7:209 to II.-7:216, and corresponding Comments and Notes; Commission Expert Group on European Contract Law, "Feasibility study for a future instrument in European Contract Law" (3 May 2011), arts 8, 13–27, 45–46, 50–55; below, n.16; H. Kötz and A. Flessner, *European Contract Law*, Vol.1, trans. T. Weir, Ch.10, pp.196–208; J. Cartwright,

mistake about the subject-matter as a starting-point for the analysis of a challenge to the validity of the contract because the parties' will, or consent, is at the heart of the notion of contractual obligation. If the mistake was also induced—by, in particular, the other party's fraud—then this may strengthen the position. But the mistake itself can be a first point of analysis. Although the introduction of mistake into English law came through a recognition of civil law analogies,[13] the modern English law of mistake is far removed from the modern civil law. Secondly, modern civil law systems also differ from English law in that they are much more receptive to duties of good faith between parties during the negotiations for a contract. This has a particular significance for the acceptance of duties of disclosure.[14] A comparison with the approach taken by European civil jurisdictions to problems which arise in the English cases can illuminate the relevant issues, and can illustrate how another legal framework for contracting can deal with them.[15] But one should not be led too quickly into assuming that English law could adopt particular solutions by analogy with our continental European neighbours.

However, the current European project to produce a "Common Frame of Reference" for European contract law appears likely to result in an "Optional Instrument" which, given effect by a

"Defects of Consent in Contract Law" in A. Hartkamp, M. Hesselink, E. Hondius, C. Mak and E. du Perron (eds), *Towards a European Civil Code* (4th edn, 2011), p.537. For a comparison between English law and French law, see J. Cartwright, "Defects of Consent and Security of Contract: French and English Law Compared" in P. Birks and A. Pretto (eds), *Themes in Comparative Law in Honour of Bernard Rudden* (2002), p.153.

[13] In this instance, however, the principal analogy was Roman law: *Kennedy v The Panama, New Zealand and Australian Royal Mail Co Ltd* (1867) L.R. 2 Q.B. 580 at 587–588, although it is misleading to say that the English law as declared in that case was the same as the civil law: J. Cartwright, "The rise and fall of mistake in the English law of contract", in *Mistake, Fraud and Duties to Inform in European Contract Law*, above, n.12, at pp.67–71. For a history of the law and doctrines of mistake in English law, see C. MacMillan, *Mistakes in Contract Law* (2010).

[14] Below, para.16–04.

[15] For an example of judicial comparison, see *Shogun Finance Ltd v Hudson* [2003] UKHL 62, [2004] 1 A.C. 919 at [84]–[85] (Lord Millett: "it would be unfortunate if our conclusion proved to be different [from that in Germany]. Quite apart from anything else, it would make the contemplated harmonisation of the general principles of European contract law very difficult to achieve"); below, para.14–39.

Regulation, would constitute a self-standing set of contract law rules, common to all Member States and constituting a second regime of domestic contract law in each Member State, which can be chosen in cross-border transactions between, at least, business sellers and suppliers of goods contracting with consumers.[16] The feasibility study for a future instrument of European Contract Law which was published in May 2011 contained a number of provisions relevant to the topics considered in this book: a general duty to negotiate in accordance with good faith and fair dealing, breach of which gives rise to liability to pay damages for loss caused to the other party[17]; provisions for avoidance of the contract (and damages for loss suffered[18]) on the basis of mistakes[19] and fraud[20]; and a

[16] See the Commission's Green Paper on "Policy options for progress towards a European Contract Law for consumers and businesses" COM(2010) 348, 1.7.2010, in which Option 4 (a Regulation setting up an "Optional Instrument") appears to be the favoured instrument for European contract law. For the development of the idea of a European contract law and different ideas before the Green Paper about the form that it might take (in particular, a "toolbox"; an optional instrument; or a code of European contract law), see Parliament Resolution 26 June 1989, OJ 1989 C 158/400; Commission Communication on "European Contract Law" COM(2001) 398 (11.07.2001); Commission Communication: "A more coherent European contract law; an action plan" COM(2003) 68 (12.2.2003); Commission Communication on "European Contract Law and the revision of the *acquis*: the way forward" COM(2004) 651, 11.10.2004. The "Draft Common Frame of Reference" (above, n.12) was the product of an academic research project on a possible text for a Common Frame of Reference, covering contract, tort and other areas of private law and, in relation to contract, building largely on Lando and Beale. In 2010 the Commission established an Expert Group to develop a possible instrument of European contract law based on the DCFR: the Expert Group's "Feasibility study for a future instrument in European Contract Law" was published on 3 May 2011, comprising 189 articles which have the appearance of a self-standing code for contracts for the supply of goods or services. Following consultation on the Expert Group's document, the Commission worked on the feasibility study, and in August 2011 published a revised working draft with amendments both small and more significant, such as the removal of the general duty to negotiate in good faith and its associated remedy in damages. See now the Commission's proposal for a Regulation on a Common European Sales Law (COM (2011) 635); Preface, p. vii, above. For the current state of developments, see *http://ec.europa.eu/justice/contract*.

[17] The text of the Expert Group, above, n.16 art.27(2), (3); identical to DCFR, II.–3:301(2), (3); but deleted in the working draft published in August 2011; above, n.16.

[18] *ibid*., art.53, equivalent to DCFR, II.-7:214(1).

[19] *ibid*., art.45, developed from DCFR, II.–7.201; below, para.15–34, n.187.

range of mandatory duties to disclose information.[21] Many of these provisions would sit more comfortably with European civil codes than they do with the English common law.[22] Their impact in English law will depend on the form of implementation of the Common Frame of Reference, which is not yet clear; and even if it is introduced as an Optional Instrument, a separate set of rules that can be chosen by the parties within English law—a form of "mini contract code"—it would be technically separate from the rules of the existing English domestic contract law. One can, however, envisage some tension between two such different sets of contract law rules within a single jurisdiction, and it is not inconceivable that English judges, growing used to applying the different principles of the Optional Instrument, might see merit in developing the common law rules on such things as mistake and duties of disclosure to reduce the differences. Any such development is, however, not only contingent on the final form of the European developments themselves, but also highly speculative and in practice very distant.[23]

Nor can one assume that other common law systems take an approach identical to English law. In the following chapters examples will sometimes be given by way of contrast and comparison from the law in America, Australia, Canada, New Zealand and Singapore, and although the underlying notions of

---

[20] *ibid.*, art.46, developed from DCFR, II.–7:205; this includes fraudulent non-disclosure: *cf.* below, para.17–54, n.253.

[21] *ibid.*, arts 13–23 (both general duties applicable to all contracts for the supply of goods or services, and duties specific to distance or off-premises contracts); below, para.17–54.

[22] See, e.g. the materials cited above, n.12, and esp. the Comments contained in von Bar and Clive, *Principles, Definitions and Model Rules of European Private Law: Draft Common Frame of Reference (DCFR)* (above, n.12), vol.1, on each of the provisions mentioned in nn.17 to 20, above, which outline the relationship between the rules presented in the DCFR and national laws. For a comparison between the first published draft of the DCFR and English law, see S. Whittaker, "The 'Draft Common Frame of Reference': An Assessment commissioned by the Ministry of Justice, United Kingdom" (November 2008; available at *http://www.justice.gov.uk/publications/docs/Draft_Common_Frame_of_Reference__an_assessment.pdf* [Accessed 30 June 2011]).

[23] *cf.* J. Cartwright, "Interpretation of English Law in Light of the Common Frame of Reference" in H. Snijders and S. Vogenauer (eds), *Content and Meaning of National Law in the Context of Transnational Law* (Sellier, Munich, 2009), p.197.

contract in these jurisdictions may be closer to English law than the civilian systems, there are also some significant differences. For example, the High Court of Australia has taken a different view of the significance of the relationship between the common law and equitable doctrines of mistake,[24] and section 52 of the Trade Practices Act 1974,[25] by providing a general prohibition on misleading or deceptive conduct in trade or commerce, with private remedies for breach of this prohibition, has had a very great impact on the general law of contract and on misrepresentation in particular; and legislation in New Zealand has reformed radically (and, in many respects, simplified) the common law of mistake[26] and misrepresentation.[27]

In reviewing areas of private law, the Law Commission often considers the relevant law in other jurisdictions. For example, in formulating its preliminary proposals on how to provide private remedies for misleading and aggressive practices by a trader in breach of the Consumer Protection from Unfair Trading Regulations 2008,[28] the Law Commission[29] discussed the lessons that could be learnt from the law in Ireland, Australia, the United States and New Zealand, and the proposals contained in the Draft Common Frame of Reference.[30] It can be very instructive to make such comparisons; but the purpose of this book is more limited: not to survey the law with a view to comparison with other jurisdictions

---

[24] *Taylor v Johnson* (1982–1983) 151 C.L.R. 422, following, at least in relation to mistake about the terms of a written contract, the approach of Denning L.J. in *Solle v Butcher* [1950] 1 K.B. 671, CA, which has now been rejected in England: below, para.13–31.

[25] The 1974 Act has been renamed: see now s.18 of the Australian Consumer Law, Sch.2 to the Competition and Consumer Act 2010. There are also corresponding State and Territory provisions; and an equivalent provision in the Australian Securities and Investments Commission Act 2001 to cover misleading and other conduct by persons in relation to financial services. See generally below, para.7–48.

[26] Contractual Mistakes Act 1977.

[27] Contractual Remedies Act 1979.

[28] SI 2008/1277, implementing the Unfair Commercial Practices Directive 2005/29/EC; see below, para.7–48.

[29] Law Com. Consultation Paper No.199, *Consumer Redress for Misleading and Aggressive Practices* (2011), Pt 11.

[30] Above, n.12.

and to propose reform; rather, to assist the lawyer who needs to understand the present state of the law to find a way through its complexities.

PART 1

Misrepresentation

CHAPTER 2

INTRODUCTION: THE CLAIM FOR MISREPRESENTATION

I. SCOPE OF THIS PART

Pre-contractual misrepresentation. This Part of the book is concerned with liability for misrepresentation. Broadly, this means liability for false statements although "misrepresentation" includes more than false statements made through the medium of words[1]: it will cover cases in which the defendant is responsible for a falsehood communicated to the claimant, whether by words or conduct, and whether made by the defendant or by his agent, or by a third party in circumstances where the defendant is in law responsible for it. The scope of the inquiry must, however, be clear from the outset. It will not consider all potential liabilities to which a defendant may be subject as a result of a false statement: it is concerned only with civil liability and not criminal liability for statements; and within civil liability for misrepresentation the focus is on liability for misrepresentations made during the negotiations for a contract. The aim is to provide the tools to enable a claimant to analyse the remedies available to him where he has entered into a contract and seeks a remedy by reference to a misrepresentation made to him at or before the formation of the contract. The inquiry will go beyond liability within the remedies usually classified as "contractual": very often the law of tort can provide a useful remedy for a claimant in such circumstances. Remedies in tort for **2–01**

[1] Below, paras 3–03 to 3–04.

misrepresentation will therefore be considered, though only those torts which are generally useful for a claimant in the particular context with which this book is concerned.[2]

II. THE FOCUS ON INDIVIDUAL REMEDIES FOR MISREPRESENTATION

2–02 **A confusion of remedies.**[3] Most of the contract books dealing with misrepresentation begin by defining a "misrepresentation" and listing the requirements for an action based on misrepresentation, and then proceed to discuss the remedies available.[4] There are some difficulties with such an approach.[5] Even if we limit the context to pre-contractual misrepresentations, there is a wide range of remedies available at common law (both contract and tort), in equity, and under statute; and the rules for each of the remedies have been developed over the years without any real attempt by the

---

[2] The torts of deceit (below, Ch.5) and negligence (below, Ch.6) will be discussed in detail but not, for example, defamation, malicious falsehood or passing off where the claimant's action is for loss (whether injury to his reputation or economic loss) consequential upon a statement made by the defendant to a third party, rather than loss arising out of the claimant's entering into a contract as a result of a statement made by the defendant to him: see further below, para.5–02.

[3] Throughout this book the term "remedy" is used in a broad sense, to include not only judicial remedies but also non-judicial remedies (such as rescission, which may be effected by action of the claimant without an order of the court: below, para.4–18). Courses of action open to the representee such as refusing to perform his obligations under the contract and raising the misrepresentation as a defence to the representor's action under the contract, will also be considered.

[4] e.g. Spencer Bower (Misrepresentation), Chs 2–10, esp. Ch.2 (representation), Ch.6 (inducement and materiality); Chitty, paras 6–006 to 6–040 ("traditional rule" that the misrepresentation must be a false statement of fact, by or known to the other party which induced the representee to act; but distinctions are properly drawn within this for different remedies: see paras 6–012, 6–029, 6–030, 6–035); Furmston, Ch.4, s.B, esp. paras 4.24 (untrue positive statement of fact, made or adopted by a party to the contract), 4.39 to 4.40 (inducement, subsuming the requirement of materiality); Treitel, paras 9–003 to 9–013 (misrepresentation generally of fact), 9–016 to 9–027 (material, reliance); Anson, pp.301–306 (false representation of fact, addressed to the party misled, which induced the contract); Cheshire, Fifoot and Furmston, pp.332–341 (statement of fact which induced the contract) and Allen, pp.12–21 (material, unambiguous statement of fact which induced the representee to contract).

[5] Cartwright, pp.61–62.

judges or Parliament to devise a unified theory of misrepresentation. In consequence, there is not even a single meaning of the word "misrepresentation" which can be applied to all the remedies, and the requirements for the action vary from one remedy to another.[6] For example, the inquiry as to whether a duty of care is owed in the tort of negligence by a person making a pre-contractual careless misrepresentation[7] addresses questions different from those which are relevant if the claim is for rescission of the contract[8] or even for damages for the tort of deceit.[9] All three claims may be based on the same statement; but when considering the tort of negligence it is not normal to ask whether the statement was one of fact (by contrast with, say, a statement of opinion); whereas for the remedy of rescission of the contract the fact/opinion issue is regularly addressed.[10]

Dangers in assimilating the rules of different remedies. Lord Herschell in *Derry v Peek* warned against the danger of reading rules from one remedy across to another[11]: 2–03

> "I think it important that it should be borne in mind that . . .an action [of deceit] differs essentially from one brought to obtain rescission of a contract on the ground of misrepresentation of a material fact. The principles which govern the two actions differ widely. Where rescission is claimed it is only necessary to prove that there was misrepresentation; then, however honestly it may have been made, however free from blame the person who made it, the contract, having been obtained by misrepresentation, cannot stand. In an action of deceit, on the contrary, it is not enough to establish misrepresentation alone; it is conceded on all hands that something more must be proved to cast liability upon the defendant, though it has been a matter of controversy what additional elements are requisite. I lay stress upon this because observations made by learned judges in actions

[6] The Law Commission has recently proposed adding further remedies: the "right to unwind" the contract (similar, but not identical, to rescission), price discount, and damages for certain types of loss as remedies for certain breaches of the Consumer Protection from Unfair Trading Regulations 2008, SI 2008/1277, implementing the Unfair Commercial Practices Directive 2005/29/EC: see Law Com. Consultation Paper No.199, *Consumer Redress for Misleading and Aggressive Practices* (2011).

[7] Below, Ch.6.

[8] Below, Ch.4.

[9] Below, Ch.5.

[10] Below, para.6–12, n.62.

[11] (1889) 14 App. Cas. 337, HL, at 359–360.

> for rescission have been cited and much relied upon at the bar by counsel for the respondent. Care must obviously be observed in applying the language used in relation to such actions to an action of deceit. Even if the scope of the language used extend beyond the particular action which was being dealt with, it must be remembered that the learned judges were not engaged in determining what is necessary to support an action of deceit, or in discriminating with nicety the elements which enter into it."

In this passage Lord Herschell was considering in particular the different states of mind required for rescission and deceit; but his warning to be cautious in reading decisions concerning one remedy in relation to other remedies can usefully be taken as of general application. It will be necessary, in considering each remedy for misrepresentation, to look carefully at the rules which have been devised for the particular remedy; and this will be the approach followed in the following chapters. Chapter 3 will consider some elements which are common to many of the remedies. But after that, the elements of each remedy will be considered in detail, separately.

III. AN OVERVIEW OF THE REMEDIES FOR MISREPRESENTATION

2–04 **Categories of remedy.** Broadly, the remedies for misrepresentation fall into categories by type. Having discovered that the defendant's statement was false, the claimant may wish to be released from the contract into which he entered in reliance on it. Typically this means rescission of the contract *ab initio*, although sometimes the remedy of termination of the contract, which has only prospective effect, may be available and appropriate. If he has suffered loss as a result of his reliance on the statement, the claimant may wish to pursue a claim in damages, but there are different measures of damages and in order to know which claim to pursue the claimant needs to have an understanding of the different measures of damages and the circumstances in which each is available.

2–05 **Rescission of the contract.** Rescission is the avoidance of the contract *ab initio*. The contract is voidable, not void, and so the contract creates rights and obligations which remain valid unless and until it is rescinded; but rescission has the effect of retrospectively making the contract a nullity from the beginning so that the parties are placed back in the position as if there had been no contract. Any performance of the obligations which has taken place under the terms of the contract before rescission must be reversed. Rescission is a general remedy for pre-contractual misrepresentation, but it is subject to various limitations or "bars": rescission is no longer available (and so the contract remains valid and indefeasible) if, for example, it would prejudice the rights of innocent third parties, or if the reversal of performance (by way of restitution) is no longer possible. The remedy of rescission is discussed in Chapter 4.

Termination of the contract. Termination of the contract must be contrasted with rescission[12]: termination is a remedy under which the contract is not retrospectively avoided, but involves the discharge of only the future, unaccrued obligations of both parties under the contract. It is not a general remedy for pre-contractual misrepresentation but is sometimes available as a remedy for breach of contract, including, therefore, cases in which the defendant's statement has become a term of the contract and constitutes a breach of such a kind as entitles the claimant to terminate the contract. Since termination discharges the unaccrued obligations of both parties, it can allow the claimant to free himself to enter into an alternative contract with another party. In a case where he terminates the contract, the claimant will also be entitled to claim damages (on the contract measure[13]) for loss flowing from the breach, if he wishes to do so. He is not, however, required to do so, and may sometimes find that the most appropriate course of action is just to terminate the contract without making any claim for damages if he has no substantive loss to claim; or to terminate and claim damages on an alternative basis, such as in tort. The remedy of termination is discussed in Chapter 8. 2–06

Damages: the different measures. Where the claimant has suffered loss in consequence of his reliance on the defendant's statement he may seek to recover damages from the defendant to compensate that loss. Before he can do so, however, he must 2–07

[12] The terminology is, however, inconsistent and many cases and even some textbooks use "rescission" as the name of the remedy referred to in this book as "termination": below, para.8–35.

[13] Below, para.2–08.

establish a cause of action which entitles him to claim damages. This requires proof of the necessary elements of a wrong: a tort or a breach of contract, or a statutory claim to damages. But within the remedies in damages for the several causes of action, there are two basic measures of damages which by way of shorthand may be referred to as damages on the contract measure, and damages on the tort measure. Both involve the same basic principle: putting the claimant in the position in which he would have been if the wrong in question had not been committed.[14]

2–08 **Damages on the contract measure.** Damages on the contract measure[15] are designed to place the claimant, so far as money can do it, in the same position as if the contract had been performed rather than breached.[16] In the context of misrepresentation, if the claimant can establish that the defendant promised in the contract that his statement was true[17] this means that damages will be

[14] *Livingstone v Rawyards Coal Co.* (1880) 5 App. Cas. 25, HL (Sc.), at 39.

[15] Sometimes referred to as "loss of bargain" or "positive interest" or "expectation interest" or "performance interest" damages, and contrasted with "negative interest" or "reliance interest" damages, which may sometimes be awarded for breach of contract to cover the claimant's wasted expenditure: *Surrey County Council v Bredero Homes Ltd* [1993] 1 W.L.R. 1361 at 1369; but the "reliance" interest is only recoverable as long as it is not clear that the claimant would not have recouped the expenses if the contract had been properly performed, i.e. it is not available where it would in effect be providing the claimant with an escape from a bad bargain: *C. & P. Haulage v Middleton* [1983] 1 W.L.R. 1461, CA; *C.C.C. Films (London) Ltd v Impact Quadrant Films Ltd* [1985] Q.B. 16 at 32–33; *Omak Maritime Ltd v Mamola Challenger Shipping Co. Ltd* [2010] EWHC 2026 (Comm), [2010] 2 C.L.C. 194, esp. at [42], [55] (Teare J.: reliance losses are a species of expectation losses: there are not two principles at work, and both reliance and expectation losses are founded on, and are illustrations of, the fundamental principle in *Robinson v Harman*, below, n.16). For a third possible measure, designed to deprive the defendant of a gain rather than compensate the claimant's loss, see below, para.8–32, n.153. On these different measures of damages for breach of contract see generally, Chitty, paras 26–002 to 26–003; Furmston, para.8.4; Treitel, paras 20–021 to 20–037; Anson, pp.539–542; Burrows, Ch.2. The "reliance" interest is in substance like the tort measure, below.

[16] *Robinson v Harman* (1848) 1 Exch. 850 at 855, 154 E.R. 363 at 365 (Parke B.). For further discussion see below, paras 8–24 *et seq.*

[17] Sometimes a claim for breach of contract may instead be based on the defendant's promise that he took care in making the statement. In such cases the damages are calculated on a basis which is the same as the tort measure: below, para.8–26.

calculated to put the claimant in the financial position in which he would have been if the statement had been true.

The claimant will recover damages on the contract measure only[18] if he can establish a breach of contract. The circumstances in which such a claim can be made in the context of misrepresentation are discussed in Chapter 8.

Damages on the tort measure. Damages on the tort measure, by contrast, are designed not to fulfil the expectation created by the representation, but to compensate the claimant for the loss he has suffered by relying on it: they put back into the claimant's pocket what he once had, but no longer has, as a result of the tort. Where the claimant was induced by the misrepresentation to enter into a contract, very often this means that damages will be calculated to put him into the position as if he had not relied on it—that is, as if he had not entered into the contract. 2–09

Damages are awarded on the tort measure in claims in the torts of deceit and negligence, as well as under section 2(1) of the Misrepresentation Act 1967 and certain other statutory claims.[19] However, even if the same basic measure is used in each of these claims, this does not mean that there are no differences between them. The courts have developed rules which distinguish, in particular, between the torts of deceit and negligence not in the basic measure of damages but in the rules governing the scope of recoverable loss within that basic measure. Broadly speaking, a claimant who can recover in the tort of deceit[20] can recover the whole of his loss flowing from his reliance on the misrepresentation, whereas a claimant who is awarded damages in the tort of negligence may be able to recover only a more limited range of losses: those within the scope of the particular duty of care which the defendant owed,[21] and which were of a kind the defendant could reasonably have foreseen.[22] The detailed rules for the calculation of

[18] For the measure of damages under the Misrepresentation Act 1967 s.2(2), which may be calculated on a basis similar to the contract measure (but this is debatable) see below, para.4–71.

[19] e.g. Financial Services and Markets Act 2000 s.90: below, para.7–62.

[20] Or under the Misrepresentation Act 1967 s.2(1), in which the deceit measure is used, although this is controversial: below, para.7–33. See also the remedy under the Financial Services and Markets Act 2000 s.90: above, n.19.

[21] Below, para.6–55.

[22] Below, para.6–56.

damages in deceit, negligence and under section 2(1) of the Misrepresentation Act 1967 are discussed in Chapters 5, 6 and 7 respectively.

2–10 **Illustration of the difference between contract measure and tort measure damages.** A simple example may demonstrate the essential difference between the calculation of damages on the contract measure and on the tort measure.

> A, in selling his car to B, makes a misrepresentation about the age of the car. The car is 5 years old, but A tells B that it is 2 years old. B pays £5,000 for the car. The market value of a 2-year-old car which otherwise has the same characteristics as the car A is selling is £5,500. The market value of the actual car, however, given that it is in fact 5 years old, is £3,500.

If the statement about the age of the car was promised in the contract and damages are assessed on the contract measure, the question is: how much worse off is B immediately after the transaction than he would have been if the representation had been true? The answer is £2,000: he should have had a car worth £5,500 but in fact he has a car worth £3,500. If, however, the tort measure is applied the question is: how much worse off is B immediately after the transaction than he would have been if he had never relied on the statement—that is, if he had never bought the car? To this question the answer is £1,500: he started with £5,000 in his pocket, and has received in exchange a car worth only £3,500.

On the facts in this example the better claim is on the contract measure, and so if the claimant can establish both a breach of contract and a cause of action which carries the tort measure of damages, he would be advised to pursue the contract claim.[23] However, it will not always be so: on those facts the contract measure was better only because (on the assumption that the representation was true) the bargain was a good one for the

[23] Where the claimant can establish both a breach of contract and a tort (or another cause of action which gives an independent claim for damages on the tort measure, such as under the Misrepresentation Act 1967 s.2(1)), he has the choice between the separate measures of recovery. Contrast the case where a claimant may sometimes recover the "reliance interest", i.e. wasted expenditure, as damages for breach of contract: it may appear as though the claimant has a choice between damages on the contract and tort measures, but "reliance" damages are not available as a remedy for breach of contract where it would in effect be providing the claimant with an escape from a bad bargain: above, n.15.

claimant, and because on the very simple facts given there were no other issues as to recoverable loss that affected the choice between the contract and tort remedies. In a case where, even if the representation had been true, the bargain would still have been a bad one for the claimant, the contract measure is generally less favourable—such as if the example were varied as follows:

> A, in selling his car to B, makes a misrepresentation about the age of the car. The car is 5 years old, but A tells B that it is 2 years old. B pays £5,000 for the car. The market value of a 2-year-old car which otherwise has the same characteristics as the car A is selling is £4,500. The market value of the actual car, however, given that it is in fact 5 years old, is £3,500.

Here, the tort measure is the same as in the first example: £1,500. The change in the market value of the car *as it was promised to be* does not appear in the calculation of tort measure damages: that is a matter only for the contract measure. But the contract measure is now different from the first example: if the car had been of the age that A promised, B would have a car worth £4,500 and so the contract measure of damages would be £1,000, the difference between the value of what he was promised (£4,500) and what he received (£3,500). Here, the bargain is a bad bargain: B is paying more than the market value of the car, even on the assumption that its age is as warranted. And in those circumstances the tort measure would be greater than the contract measure.[24]

Choice of remedy. These examples show that it is important to analyse carefully how each available remedy would apply to the facts in hand, in order to enable the claimant to decide which is the most suitable remedy to pursue as his first line of argument.[25] Other factors may be relevant than those contained in the examples: in relying on the misrepresentation the claimant may have suffered a particular type of loss, or a range of consequential losses, which 2–11

[24] Burrows, pp.114–117, uses a variant on this example to argue that the approach of Lord Hoffmann in *South Australia Asset Management Corp. v York Montague Ltd* [1997] A.C. 191, below, para.6–55, is wrong.

[25] The claimant may include alternative claims in his particulars of claim, even if the alternatives depend on inconsistent facts, as long as he is not asserting that he believes that both sets of facts are true, and is merely affirming his honest belief that on either one set of facts or the other his case is made out: below, para.11–08.

may be recoverable only if he pursues a particular cause of action[26]; or he may prefer to pursue a cause of action which avoids being met by a defence which the defendant might otherwise have raised.[27] Sometimes the claimant may be restricted in his choice of remedies by the circumstances in which the misrepresentation was made. For example, the representor may not be the other party to the contract: if so, and unless the other party is in law responsible for the statement even though he did not make it himself,[28] the claimant cannot avoid the contract for misrepresentation,[29] and if he seeks to recover damages for loss suffered in consequence of his reliance on the misrepresentation, he will be limited to remedies in tort.[30] And a significant question for the claimant will be whether (if rescission and/or termination of the contract are available on the facts) he wishes to be released from the contract now that he has discovered the misrepresentation; or whether he is content to remain bound but to recover damages for his loss.[31] This is not to say that a claimant is necessarily restricted to a single remedy. Sometimes he may be able to obtain a combination of remedies, if he can establish the

[26] e.g. if he has suffered losses which the defendant might not reasonably have been able to foresee he is likely to wish to establish a claim not only on the tort measure but more particularly on the measure in the tort of deceit, since both the contract measure of damages (below, para.8–30) and the tort measure applied within the tort of negligence (below, para.6–56) restrict the recovery of damages by a test based on foreseeability of the kind of loss.

[27] e.g. if he establishes fraud and brings a claim in deceit he cannot be met by a defence of contributory negligence: below, para.5–31, which might apply in a claim for tort damages in negligence or under the Misrepresentation Act 1967 s.2(1): below, paras 6–48, 7–27.

[28] e.g. through the principles of agency, or where the contracting party is affected by knowledge or notice of a third party's misrepresentation: below, paras 4–72 to 4–78.

[29] In such a case the claimant may be driven to argue that the contract is void for his own mistake: above, para.1–03; below, para.12–19.

[30] i.e. the torts of deceit and negligence. Although the remedy under the Misrepresentation Act 1967 s.2(1) is damages on the tort measure, it is only available against the other contracting party, and not even against the agent of the contracting party personally if he made the misrepresentation: below, para.7–09.

[31] *Arnison v Smith* (1889) 41 Ch.D. 348, CA, at 371 (Cotton L.J.: "a man may affirm a contract and yet sue the person who by fraud induced him to enter into it"); *Production Technology Consultants Ltd v Bartlett* [1988] 1 E.G.L.R. 182, CA (affirmation of contract does not preclude claim for damages under the Misrepresentation Act 1967 s.2(1)). The judge in *Laureys v Earl* [2005] EWHC 2601 (QB), [2005] All E.R. (D) 96 (Nov) at [57], suggesting the contrary, appears to have confused the Misrepresentation Act 1967 s.2(1) and s.2(2).

elements of each on the facts of his case. There are, however, some logical and practical restrictions on the cumulation of remedies.

Cumulation of remedies: possible combinations. A claimant may at the same time obtain two remedies which are not logically inconsistent, and where the award of the two remedies does not involve double recovery of his loss. Most common, perhaps, is the award of damages on the tort measure with rescission of the contract.[32] Damages on the tort measure in a case of misrepresentation are generally designed to place the claimant in the position as if he had not entered into the contract[33]; rescission involves the avoidance of the contract *ab initio* and placing both parties back in the position as if there had been no contract.[34] There is therefore no logical inconsistency in allowing both concurrently, although if rescission is effected the claimant may (in consequence of the reversal of performance of both parties' obligations) recover some of what he has lost. For example, the purchaser of a car will return the car and recover the price when he rescinds the contract: he will therefore not be able to include within the quantification of his claim to damages the loss which is constituted by the difference between the price paid and the value of the car.[35] But he could claim any other losses which are recoverable on the tort measure, such as consequential losses he has suffered during the time he held the car under the contract which has now been rescinded. Certain other combinations of remedies are available: termination of the contract with an award of damages for breach of contract[36]; damages under both section 2(1) and section 2(2) of the Misrepresentation Act 2–12

[32] *Archer v Brown* [1985] Q.B. 401 at 415 (damages in the tort of deceit or under the Misrepresentation Act 1967 s.2(1), recoverable with rescission); see also below, para.4–17. In relation to an award under s.2(1), it seems that rescission of the contract will not undermine the claim for damages: although a prerequisite of a claim under s.2(1) is that the claimant "has entered into a contract after a misrepresentation has been made to him", this remains true even where the contract is rescinded. It would be different if there were no contract at all, e.g. if the contract were not simply voidable for misrepresentation but void for mistake: below, para.12–19.

[33] Above, para.2–09.

[34] Above, para.2–05.

[35] See the example above, para.2–10.

[36] Above, para.2–06. Both are based on the same breach of contract, and are naturally capable of being awarded together.

1967[37]; rescission with indemnity.[38] There is no logical inconsistency in awarding two different heads of tort measure damages, although there cannot be double recovery in respect of the same loss.[39]

2–13 **Cumulation of remedies: impossible combinations.** Certain combinations of remedies are, however, logically inconsistent and the claimant must elect between them. Rescission cannot be awarded with any remedy which presupposes that the contract remains in place beyond its formation[40]: damages for breach of contract cannot therefore be awarded if the contract is rescinded, since the obligation to pay damages under the contract requires the continued existence of the contract; nor can termination, which discharges the future, unaccrued obligations, but leaves the accrued obligations in place.[41] Damages on inconsistent measures cannot normally be awarded together, and so an award of both contract measure and tort measure damages would be impossible, since it would give the claimant both his financial equivalent of performance, and at the same time a financial release from the transaction

[37] Misrepresentation Act 1967 s.2(3) explicitly allows this. The remedies are consistent, for the same reasons given above in relation to the combination of rescission and tort measure damages: damages under s.2(1) are awarded on the tort measure; damages under s.2(2) are the court's award of damages in lieu of the rescission which the claimant sought. But, as with other combinations of remedy, s.2(3) makes clear that there can be no double recovery, although in this case the statute applies this rule in a particular way: it is the award of damages under s.2(2) that is to be taken into account in assessing the defendant's liability under s.2(1).

[38] The indemnity was devised in order to accompany rescission to give compensation for obligations incurred under the contract: below, para.4–17. Logically, an indemnity may also be obtained with an award of damages on the tort measure, although in practice this will not be ordered since the losses which are recoverable within the indemnity will normally be recoverable within the tort measure of damages: the tort measure will be the more extensive claim: *ibid.*

[39] e.g. for a negligent misrepresentation, actionable both in the tort of negligence and under the Misrepresentation Act 1967 s.2(1). Damages under the Act are on the same measure as in the tort of deceit and so will normally be the more extensive claim: below, para.7–33.

[40] An award of damages under the Misrepresentation Act 1967 s.2(1) presupposes that the claimant entered into a contract, but not that it remains in place: above, n.32.

[41] *Photo Production Ltd v Securicor Transport Ltd* [1980] A.C. 827, HL, at 849.

into which he entered in reliance on the misrepresentation.[42] An award of damages under section 2(2) of the Misrepresentation Act 1967 cannot be made together with rescission of the contract, simply because they are designed by the statute to be alternatives[43]; nor with an award of damages in the tort of deceit, since the court's discretion to make an award under the Act applies only where the representation is made "otherwise than fraudulently".[44]

Multiple defendants: contribution between co-defendants. 2–14
The representee may have a claim for damages against more than one defendant: either because he relied on more than a single representation, or because more than one person is in law responsible for the (single) representation on which he relied.[45] Where two or more defendants are jointly or severally liable for damage suffered by the claimant, the court will have jurisdiction under the Civil Liability (Contribution) Act 1978 to apportion between the co-defendants the damages payable.[46] Under the Act

---

[42] For a similar argument in relation to the award of damages for breach of contract so as to give both lost profits and wasted expenditure, see *Cullinane v British "Rema" Manufacturing Co. Ltd* [1954] 1 Q.B. 292, CA.

[43] *cf.* the statutory discretion under the Senior Courts Act 1981 (formerly Supreme Court Act 1981) s.50, for the Court of Appeal or High Court to award damages *in addition to* or in substitution for the equitable remedies of injunction and specific performance.

[44] An award of damages on the deceit *measure* is possible: damages under s.2(1) are awarded on the same measure as in the tort of deceit, and can be awarded with damages under s.2(2): above, para.2–12.

[45] e.g. a representation by an agent of the contracting party actionable against the agent personally in tort, but against the contracting party under the Misrepresentation Act 1967 s.2(1); below, para.7–09; and a misrepresentation in a prospectus or listing particulars may give rise to claims against a number of defendants under the Financial Services and Markets Act 2000 s.90; below, para.7–55. For clauses designed to exclude joint and several liability, see below, para.9–05, n.15.

[46] See generally Chitty, Ch.17; Clerk & Lindsell, Ch.4; Winfield & Jolowicz, Ch.21. For a claim for contribution under the Civil Liability (Contribution) Act 1978 s.1 there is a special limitation period of two years from the accrual of the right to recover contribution: see s.10. Time begins to run when there is a judgment or award which ascertains the quantum of the liability, and not merely its existence: *Aer Lingus Plc v Gildacroft Ltd* [2006] EWCA Civ 4, [2006] 1 W.L.R. 1173; or, where the parties settle the claim, from the date of the settlement agreement, even where the agreement is later embodied in a court order, unless the parties' agreement provided that it would not take effect until the order: *Knight v Rochdale Healthcare NHS Trust* [2003] EWHC 1831 (QB), [2004] 1 W.L.R. 371.

each pays such proportion of the total damages "as may be found by the court to be just and equitable having regard to the extent of that person's responsibility for the damage in question".[47]

Contribution is available only where the defendants are liable for the *same* damage,[48] and therefore the first issue is to identify the damage suffered by the claimant, or the categories of his loss, for which both defendants are liable. A sharp contrast in their respective liabilities can arise where one defendant is liable in deceit and the other in the tort of negligence, given the differences in the scope of liability in the two torts: for example, the test for remoteness of damage is narrower in negligence (only losses of a kind that the defendant could reasonably have foreseen[49]) than in deceit (all loss caused by the fraud, even if unforeseeable[50]); and the range of defences in the two torts is not identical: in particular, contributory negligence is not available in deceit,[51] but is available in negligence.[52] In *Nationwide Building Society v Dunlop Haywards (DHL) Ltd*[53] the first defendant was liable in deceit for losses suffered by the claimant in making loans to a company in reliance on fraudulently overstated valuations of the property; the second defendants, the claimant's solicitors, were liable in negligence in respect of the same transaction. The first defendant's liability was significantly greater (£15.5m) than the second defendant's liability (£13.2m) because, amongst other things, the first defendant was

[47] s.2(1).

[48] Civil Liability Contribution Act 1978 s.1(1). For a restrictive view of the test of "same damage", see *Royal Brompton Hospital NHS Trust v Hammond* [2002] UKHL 14, [2002] 1 W.L.R. 1397; *Niru Battery Manufacturing Co. v Milestone Trading Ltd (No.2)* [2003] EWHC 1032 (Comm), [2003] 2 All E.R. (Comm) 365 (no contribution between those liable for damages, and those liable in restitution); affirmed [2004] EWCA Civ 487, [2004] 2 Lloyd's Rep. 319; but doubted in *Charter Plc v City Index Ltd* [2007] EWCA Civ 1382, [2008] Ch. 313 (defendant's liability to make good loss arising from its knowing receipt of trust funds could be liability to make compensation in respect of damage within the 1978 Act). *Cf. Eastgate Group Ltd v Lindsey Morden Group Inc.* [2001] EWCA Civ 1446, [2002] 1 W.L.R. 642 (damage can be "the same" even if the amount of damages recoverable in each claim might vary according to the different causes of action).

[49] Below, para.6–56.

[50] Below, para.5–40.

[51] Below, para.5–31.

[52] Below, para.6–48.

[53] [2009] EWHC 254 (Comm), [2010] 1 W.L.R. 258.

liable for certain unforeseeable consequential losses. In addition, the second defendant had a defence of contributory negligence which was not available to the first defendant. Christopher Clarke J. held[54] that the "same damage" for which both defendants were responsible to the claimant was £13.2m.; but this should be reduced to take into account the claimant's contributory negligence,[55] which he took to be 50%: the resulting damage to be apportioned was therefore £6.6m.[56]

The 1978 Act requires the court to apportion the damages having regard to the extent of each defendant's responsibility for the damage in question.[57] The extent of a person's responsibility involves both the degree of his fault and the degree to which it contributed to the damage in question. If one of the co-defendants is liable in deceit, but the other is liable only in negligence, the fraudulent representee will not necessarily bear a greater proportion of the damages: a more serious fault having less causative impact on the representee's damage may represent an equivalent responsibility to a less serious fault which had a greater causative impact: it is a matter for the judge to decide in the light of all the facts.[58] However, in *Nationwide Building Society v Dunlop Haywards*

---

[54] *ibid.*, at [71]–[72].

[55] "It seems to me neither just nor equitable that the amount of contribution which [the second defendants] are to be ordered to make should be assessed by treating the damage for which both defendants are responsible as the totality of the claimant's loss, ignoring contributory negligence, when the only reason for ignoring it is that the claim against [the first defendant] is in deceit. To do so would be to visit on [the second defendant] the approach taken by the court, partly for reasons of deterrence, against fraudsters, when [the second defendants] are innocent of any fraud": *ibid.*, at [71].

[56] No further reduction was to be made on account of a limitation clause which the second defendants had in their contract with the claimant, since there was no similar clause on which the first defendants could have relied (even if, given their fraud, they could not in law have relied on it: below, paras 5–33, 9–13): ibid., at [73]–[75]. In fact, the claim against the second defendant had been settled for a lower sum than £6.6m; the issue arose on a claim by the second defendant against the first defendent to recoup a proportion of the damages it had paid to the claimant under the settlement.

[57] s.2(1); above, text to n.47.

[58] *Downs v Chappell* [1997] 1 W.L.R. 426, CA, at 445 (overruled on another point by *Smith New Court Securities Ltd v Scrimgeour Vickers (Asset Management) Ltd* [1997] A.C. 254, HL); *Standard Chartered Bank v Pakistan Shipping Corp. (No.2)* [1998] 1 Lloyd's Rep. 684 at 707, not decided on appeal at [2000] 1 Lloyd's Rep. 218, CA.

(DHL) Ltd[59] the relative proportions in which the damages were to be borne were 80% and 20% because the moral blameworthiness of the (fraudulent) first defendant and the causative potency of its agent's fraud were very much greater than that of the (negligent) second defendant.[60]

2–15 **Common law, equity and statute.** It will be evident from the brief account above that the remedies which may be sought by a claimant have different origins: some have been established by the common law; others by equity; others by statute. The remedy of rescission was known at common law, but only for fraud; equity developed the remedy of rescission also for non-fraudulent misrepresentations. Damages for loss may be claimed at common law—either in tort (deceit or negligence) or for breach of contract; but statute has added certain remedies in damages for misrepresentation, either general[61] or specific to particular types of contract.[62] Damages may also be awarded in equity if the misrepresentation constitutes a breach of an equitable duty.[63] In the following chapters

---

59 Above, n.53 at [77].

60 In sum, therefore: the first defendant's liability to the claimant was £15.5m; of this, £6.6m was liability which was shared with the second defendant; but of that £6.6m only 20% (£1.32m) was apportioned to the second defendant.

61 Misrepresentation Act 1967 s.2(1), s.2(2).

62 e.g. share subscriptions: Financial Services and Markets Act 2000 s.90; below, paras 7–49 *et seq*.

63 *Bristol & West Building Society v Mothew* [1998] Ch. 1, CA. There is not, however, a separate claim for damages for misrepresentation in equity. Claims in the torts of deceit or negligence (for the established category of negligent misstatement) are defined by reference to the misrepresentation. A claim for damages in equity is a claim for a breach of an equitable duty which happens to be committed by making a misrepresentation. Where the nature of the equitable duty is of the same essential nature as the equivalent common law duty, the courts will generally calculate the damages on the same basis as at common law: *Bristol & West Building Society v Mothew*, at 17. Other remedies, peculiar to equity, may also sometimes be claimed where the misrepresentation constitutes a breach of an equitable duty, such as an account of profits; again, though, this is not a remedy *for misrepresentation* in the sense discussed in this book: below, para.6–11, n.54. Particular examples of remedies being awarded in equity by way of damages or an account of profits will be given where appropriate in the following chapters, but detailed treatment of the general nature of equitable duties and remedies must be sought in other works, such as Snell; J. Mowbray, L. Tucker, N. Le Poidevin,

we shall order the discussion by reference to the principal separate remedies where the cause of action is based on a misrepresentation made by the defendant.

E. Simpson and J. Brightwell, *Lewin on Trusts* (18th edn, 2007 with supplements); J.E. Martin, *Hanbury and Martin*: *Modern Equity* (18th edn, 2009).

CHAPTER 3

ELEMENTS COMMON TO A CLAIM FOR MISREPRESENTATION

I. THE CORE PROBLEM: DEFINING ACTIONABLE STATEMENTS

Controlling the liability for statements. Not every false statement can give rise to liability; not even every false statement which causes loss or damage. 3–01

> "It is a blinding glimpse of the obvious to say that there must be a dividing line between statements that are actionable and those which are not.[1]"

This is true as a general proposition concerning liability for words: whether a seller's statement is only "sales talk" or is to be taken seriously as descriptive of the product[2]; whether a statement made in an advertisement is only an invitation to treat or has the force of an offer capable of becoming a contract by simple acceptance[3]; whether a statement made during negotiations was only made to give information to the other party or formed part of the bargain between the parties.[4] Sellers make statements about their own and their rivals' products which may well cause damage to the rival, or cause a purchaser to buy an inferior product, but it would open the doors to a flood of litigation if such claims were not adequately controlled.[5] And statements can be made very casually, and even carelessly, and their consequences can be far-reaching, but it would be too much to impose liability for the financial consequences of all such statements: "if the mere hearing or reading of words were held to create proximity, there might be no limit to the persons to whom the speaker or writer could be liable".[6]

3–02 **Common elements in misrepresentation claims.** As was made clear in Chapter 2,[7] there is no unity in the remedies for misrepresentation, not even a unity in the terminology: in particular, there is no single meaning of "misrepresentation" for all the remedies. It can, however, still be helpful to consider the elements which commonly feature in misrepresentation claims, whatever the

---

[1] *De Beers Abrasive Products Ltd v International General Electric Co. of New York Ltd* [1975] 1 W.L.R. 972 at 978 (Walton J.).

[2] Below, para.3–14.

[3] *Partridge v Crittenden* [1968] 1 W.L.R. 1204; *Carlill v Carbolic Smoke Ball Co.* [1893] 1 Q.B. 256, CA.

[4] Below, para.8–04.

[5] *White v Mellin* [1895] A.C. 154, HL, 164 (slander of goods); *Evans v Harlow* (1844) 5 Q.B. 624 at 631, 114 E.R. 1384 at 1387 (libel).

[6] *Hedley Byrne & Co. Ltd v Heller & Partners Ltd* [1964] A.C. 465, HL, at 534 (Lord Pearce: the tort of negligence); see also at 482–483 (Lord Reid). Within the tort of negligence, the emphasis is on the problem of statements causing financial loss; where the statement leads to physical harm, the courts may be less cautions in imposing liability: below, para.6–18. The factors which affect the courts' willingness to impose liability vary from one remedy to another.

[7] Above, para.2–02.

remedy sought, because the discussion will set the context for more detailed discussion of the several remedies in later chapters. The remedies for misrepresentation generally define actionable statements using such concepts as whether the statement was false, and was sufficiently clear to be actionable; whether the claimant was entitled in the circumstances to take the statement seriously and therefore to rely on it; whether he did in fact rely on it and suffer a consequence against which the remedy in question is designed to protect. What follows in this chapter must be read in the light of the warning, given earlier,[8] against unthinkingly assimilating the different remedies and the rules applicable to them. The rules which apply to each remedy will be discussed in detail in their proper place in later chapters. But, with that caveat, the elements common to misrepresentation claims can be explored.

II. THE STATEMENT

There must be a "statement". We are considering the remedies available for misrepresentation in which the inquiry is limited to those cases where a falsehood is communicated to the claimant. Generally it will be a statement made by or on behalf of the defendant; occasionally the statement may be made by some other person but the defendant has responsibility in law for it.[9] But in all cases there must be a statement made to the claimant.[10] We are not here considering cases of spontaneous mistake by the claimant, which is discussed in detail in Part II; nor those cases where the defendant did not communicate anything but *ought* to have 3–03

[8] Above, para.2–03.

[9] Below, paras 4–24, 5–07, 7–09.

[10] Or to his agent in circumstances in which the claimant can rely on it to seek a remedy. For the problem where the claimant's agent knows of the falsity of the statement, see below, para.5–27; and for claims in negligence where the statement is made to a third party but causes loss to the claimant, see below, para.6–24. A misrepresentation made to a machine acting on behalf of the claimant, rather than to an individual, can be actionable if the machine is set up to process information in a different way from that in which it would process the correct information: *Renault UK Ltd v Fleetpro Technical Services Ltd* [2007] EWHC 2541 (QB), [2007] All E.R. (D) 208 (Nov) at [122] (claim for deceit: the question was whether it is possible in law to find a person liable in deceit if the fraudulent misrepresentation alleged was made not to a human being, but to a machine: at [121]).

done—that is, duties of disclosure. The existence and scope of duties of disclosure, and the remedies for actionable non-disclosure, are considered in Part III.

3–04 **Misrepresentation by conduct.** The false statement need not, however, be made through the medium of words, whether written or oral. What is required is that a falsehood be communicated to the claimant; and this can be done by his interpretation of the defendant's actions as well as by his hearing or reading the defendant's words. A "nod or a wink, or a shake of the head, or a smile from the purchaser intending to induce the vendor to believe the existence of a non-existent fact" can be enough.[11] And other conduct not directed at the claimant as directly as a nod of the head but which has the effect of communicating to him a falsehood can equally well constitute a "misrepresentation", such as the act of the agents of a lessor of a flat in covering up patches of dry rot, which has been held to be a misrepresentation to prospective tenants about the state of the property for the purposes of the tort of deceit.[12] Most

---

[11] *Walters v Morgan* (1861) 3 De G. F. & J. 718 at 724, 45 E.R. 1056 at 1059 (Lord Campbell L.C., contrasting this with "simple reticence" which "does not amount to legal fraud, however it may be viewed by moralists").

[12] *Gordon v Selico Co. Ltd* [1985] 2 E.G.L.R. 79 at 83 (this issue was not challenged on appeal: [1986] 1 E.G.L.R. 71). See also *Schneider v Heath* (1813) 3 Camp. 506, 170 E.R. 1462 (ship put into water to hide from purchaser the fact that the bottom was wormeaten and the keel broken); *Gosling v Anderson* [1972] E.G.D. 709, CA, at 714 (non-disclosure left purchaser with impression that there would be no difficulty about planning permission); *Curtis v Chemical Cleaning and Dyeing Co.* [1951] 1 K.B. 805, CA, at 808 (Lord Denning: any behaviour, by words or conduct, is sufficient to be a misrepresentation if it is such as to mislead the other party about the existence or extent of an exemption clause in the contract. If it conveys a false impression, that is enough); *Ex p. Whittaker* (1875) L.R. 10 Ch. App. 446 (implied representation by person taking away goods bought earlier at auction, that he intended to pay for them); *Re Eastgate* [1905] 1 K.B. 465 at 467 (contractual undertaking to pay money carries implied representation that party giving undertaking honestly intends to make payment and therefore that he believes that he has or will have the means of doing so when payment becomes due); *Salmon Harvester Properties Ltd v Metropolitan Police Authority* [2004] EWHC 1159 (QB), [2004] All E.R. (D) 315 (May) (implied representation by defendant that it had, or would obtain, power to enter into contract); *Advanced Industrial Technology Corp. v Bond Street Jewellers Ltd* [2006] EWCA Civ 923, [2006] All E.R. (D) 21 (Jul) (person pawning item represents that he has title to it or authority to pawn it). There are various areas of the law where a statement, or the communication of a person's intentions, are

cases which reach the courts involve words, perhaps because a misrepresentation by words is the clearest form of false statement; there is a greater possibility for argument about the meaning which actions can be taken to have communicated.

The statement must be false. The statement, to be actionable as a *mis*representation, must be false. A true statement which causes loss, even a true statement which was made maliciously with a view to causing the recipient some harm, is not actionable as a misrepresentation. A representation may be true without being entirely correct, as long as it is substantially correct and the difference between what is represented and what is actually correct was not material—that is, it would not have been likely to induce a reasonable person in the position of the representee to enter into the contract.[13] Of course, it is not enough that the statement is false: the different remedies require other additional elements, such as a particular state of mind (fraud, for the tort of deceit) or a failure to fulfil a duty of care in making the statement (for the tort of negligence). But in all the remedies considered in the following **3–05**

required and a similar approach is naturally followed in cases which may be used as analogies here. For example, the communication of an acceptance can be constituted by conduct which conveys the acceptor's intentions: *Brogden v Metropolitan Railway Co.* (1877) 2 App. Cas. 666, HL, at 686; in criminal law a "deception" can be practised by misleading conduct: e.g. *R. v Barnard* (1837) 7 Car. & P. 784 (representation inherent in wearing an Oxford cap and gown); *DPP v Ray* [1974] A.C. 370, HL (representation of customer's means and intention to pay, inherent in ordering a meal in a restaurant), but note that the deception offences in Theft Act 1968 were replaced by the general offence of fraud by Fraud Act 2006 which does not require deception: below, para.5–25, n.107; a "false or misleading statement" under the Property Misdescriptions Act 1991 may be by conduct: *Lewin v Barratt Homes Ltd* [2000] 1 E.G.L.R. 77 (showing pictures of design, and a show house, constituted statement to prospective purchaser that it presently intended, and was able, to build houses to that design); and trade marks which constitute misrepresentations about goods cannot be enforced: *Newman v Pinto* (1887) 57 L.T. 31 (pictures on box containing cigars made in Germany misrepresented them as made in Havannah: "a lie may be told by a box, just as well as by the mouth of an individual": Bowen L.J. at 37).

[13] *Avon Insurance Plc v Swire Fraser Ltd* [2000] 1 All E.R. (Comm) 573 at [17] (Rix L.J., adopting the test set out in Marine Insurance Act 1906 s.20(4)); *Raiffeisen Zentralbank Österreich A.G. v Royal Bank of Scotland Plc* [2010] EWHC 1392 (Comm), [2011] 1 Lloyd's Rep. 123 at [149]. *Cf.* below, para.3–16 (test in Marine Insurance Act 1906 s.20(5) for representation as to a matter of *expectation or belief* may be different from common law).

chapters in this Part, the claimant is complaining that he has suffered an undesirable consequence (either some form of loss, or having entered into a contract he now regrets) as a result of the defendant's false statement.

3–06 **Objective interpretation.** In all cases of misrepresentation, the claimant must include in his particulars of claim the details of the misrepresentation on which he relies, and this will require him to give sufficient indication of the alleged inaccuracy in the statement.[14] It is therefore necessary, in analysing a claim for misrepresentation, to identify the false statement for which the defendant is responsible, and which was communicated to the representee. In most cases the falsehood and its communication to the representee can be easily identified from the defendant's words or actions. Sometimes, however, there is some doubt about the meaning which was, or might have been, conveyed to the representee. In such cases the courts need a test to interpret the words or conduct. The test which is generally applied in the construction of the communications between the parties when considering whether a contract has been formed is objective, viewing the communication from the perspective of a reasonable person in the position of the recipient of it.[15] Applied by analogy to misrepresentation, the test is whether: (a) the words or conduct in fact led the representee to believe the alleged false fact, and (b) it was reasonable for the representee to believe it from the words or conduct as he perceived them. Where there is a dispute over the meaning of a statement, this is the approach the courts should use in determining whether it is to be treated as a misrepresentation.[16] In

---

[14] CPR, Pt 16, PD 16, para.8.2; below, para.11–07.

[15] *Smith v Hughes* (1871) L.R. 6 Q.B. 597; *The Hannah Blumenthal* [1983] 1 A.C. 854, HL; *Centrovincial Estates plc v Merchant Investors Assurance Co.Ltd* [1983] Com. L.R. 158 ("It is a well-established principle of the English law of contract that an offer falls to be interpreted not subjectively by reference to what has actually passed through the mind of the offeror, but objectively, by reference to the interpretation which a reasonable man in the shoes of the offeree would place on the offer": Slade L.J. at 158); *MCI WorldCom International Inc. v Primus Telecommunications Inc.*, below, n.17. See generally below, Ch.13.

[16] *Smith v Chadwick* (1884) 9 App. Cas. 187, HL, at 190 (Earl of Selborne L.C.: the statement is untrue if the representee "was justified in understanding, and did understand it, in the sense [which is false]"; *cf.* Lord Blackburn at 201). There are other, related issues which require a different approach: for example, when the representor's state of mind is relevant, e.g. in a deceit claim, the meaning which

applying this test, the characteristics of the representee are important:[17] "The court may regard a sophisticated commercial party who is told that no representations are being made to him quite differently than it would a consumer".[18] Where the alleged misrepresentation was express, the question is how a reasonable person in the claimant's position would have understood the words used.[19] Where it is alleged that there was an implied representation,[20] the question is what a reasonable person would have inferred was being impliedly represented by the representor's words and conduct in their context.[21]

---

the representor *intended* his words or conduct to convey. And the inquiry as to whether there was *reliance* on the statement (below, para.3–52) may look only to the actual response by the representee to the statement, not whether his response was a reasonable one. But the core question of whether there was a misrepresentation at all (that is, whether the representor can be held to have made a statement which was in fact false) is to be tested by this objective rule of communication. *Cf. Krakowski v Eurolynx Properties Ltd* (1995) 183 C.L.R.563, HCA, discussing these different senses in which a statement might be interpreted for the tort of deceit.

[17] *MCI WorldCom International Inc. v Primus Telecommunications Inc.*, above, n.15 at [30] (Mance L.J., citing the first edition of this book, para.2.12 (now para.3–14, below): "whether there is a representation and what its nature is must be judged objectively according to the impact that whatever is said may be expected to have on a reasonable representee in the position and with the known characteristics of the actual representee... The position in the case of a fraudulent misrepresentation may of course be different"), followed by *Kyle Bay Ltd t/a Astons Nightclub v Underwriters Subscribing under Policy No.019057/08/01* [2007] EWCA Civ 57, [2007] 1 C.L.C. 164 at [30]–[31]; *Raiffeisen Zentralbank Österreich A.G. v Royal Bank of Scotland Plc*, above, n.13 at [81].

[18] *Raiffeisen Zentralbank Österreich A.G. v Royal Bank of Scotland Plc*, above, n.13 at [81] (Christopher Clarke J.).

[19] *I.F.E. Fund S.A. v Goldman Sachs International* [2006] EWHC 2887 (Comm), [2007] 1 Lloyd's Rep. 264 at [50], affirmed [2007] EWCA Civ 811, [2007] 2 Lloyd's Rep. 447; *Raiffeisen Zentralbank Österreich A.G. v Royal Bank of Scotland Plc*, above, n.13 at [82] (Christopher Clarke J.: "The answer to that question may depend on the nature and content of the statement, the context in which it was made, the characteristics of the maker and of the person to whom it was made, and the relationship between them").

[20] Below, paras 3–08, 3–17 to 3–18, 3–44.

[21] *I.F.E. Fund S.A. v Goldman Sachs International* above, n.19 at [50]; *Raiffeisen Zentralbank Österreich A.G. v Royal Bank of Scotland Plc*, above, n.13 at [85] (Christopher Clarke J.: "In evaluating the effect of what was said a helpful test is whether a reasonable representee would naturally assume that the true state of facts did not exist and that, had it existed, he would in all the circumstances necessarily have been informed of it: *Geest Plc v Fyffes Plc* [1999] 1 All E.R.

It is possible that, even when tested objectively, a statement could equally well be understood in different senses: it is simply ambiguous. It will then be for the representee to establish the meaning of the words which he actually understood; it is not enough for him simply to claim that one of the meanings was actionable, or to leave it to the court to decide the "ordinary" meaning.[22]

3–07 **Contextual interpretation.** The interpretation of communications is always dependent on their context,[23] and this is no less true for (mis)representations. If, for example, the statement which is alleged to have been a misrepresentation was made by the defendant in answer to a question put by the claimant, it may be necessary to construe the question in order to ascertain the true meaning of the answer. In *Sykes v Taylor-Rose*[24] the vendors of a house, who had recently discovered that a horrific murder had been committed in the house some years earlier, answered their purchaser's question, "Is there any other information which you think the buyer might have a right to know?" honestly, with a simple "No". This was held not to be a misrepresentation because, on construction,[25] the question required only an honest answer. If

(Comm) 672 at 683 *per* Colman J."); *Foodco UK LLP (t/a Muffin Break) v Henry Boot Developments Ltd* [2010] EWHC 358 (Ch) at [197] (Lewison J.). It has been suggested that the court may be less disposed to find an implied misrepresentation if the claim is under the Misrepresentation Act 1967 s.2(1), because of the measure of damages awarded under the Act: *Avon Insurance Plc v Swire Fraser Ltd* [2000] 1 All E.R. (Comm) 573 at [200]; *Raiffeisen Zentralbank Österreich A.G. v Royal Bank of Scotland Plc* at [85]; but this has also been doubted: *Cassa di Risparmio della Repubblica di San Marino S.p.A. v Barclays Bank Ltd* [2011] EWHC 484 (Comm), [2011] All E.R. (D) 189 (Mar) at [223]; below, para.7–33, n.135.

[22] *Smith v Chadwick* (1884) 9 App. Cas. 187, HL.

[23] "In law context is everything": *R. (on the application of Daly) v Secretary of State for the Home Department* [2001] UKHL 26, [2001] 2 A.C. 532 at [28] (Lord Steyn) (statutory construction); Lewison, para.5.12.

[24] [2004] EWCA Civ 299, [2004] 2 P. & C.R. 30.

[25] *ibid.*, at [16], [29]–[32]. The question was contained in the Law Society's standard form of pre-contract inquiries. *Cf. McMeekin v Long* [2003] 2 E.G.L.R. 81 (question in standard form about neighbour disputes "could not be expressed in clearer language": Astill J. at 82).

the claimant wishes to rely on an answer to his question, it is therefore incumbent upon him to make the question sufficiently clear.[26]

True, but misleading, statements. Sometimes a statement can have a hidden meaning which has to be discovered by a careful analysis. There can be a statement of fact which is hidden within what appears to be simply a statement of opinion.[27] Or a true statement of fact may contain further statements by implication which are false and therefore actionable. For example, a statement by a vendor's solicitor that he did not know of covenants affecting the land to be sold was literally true, but carried the (false) implication that he had investigated the title which would have disclosed the covenants in question.[28] And a statement at auction that vacant property to be sold had been recently occupied by a tenant at a particular rent was true, but carried the implication that the land was still capable of being let for that value—which was false, since the vendor had failed to find new tenants except at a **3–08**

---

[26] *Economides v Commercial Assurance Co. Plc* [1998] Q.B. 587, CA, at 599–600 (Simon Brown L.J.: "if insurers wish to place upon their assured an obligation to carry out specific inquiries or otherwise take steps to provide objective justification for their valuations, they must spell out these requirements in the proposal form"); *Sykes v Taylor-Rose*, above, n.24 at [28], [50]; *Cheltenham BC v Laird* [2009] EWHC 1253 (QB), [2009] I.R.L.R. 621 at [274] (poorly drafted medical questionnaire completed by employee on taking up employment: to be construed objectively; correct answer to either of two ambiguous meanings would be true; relevant that employee is a lay rather than a medical person; it is for the employer to make the form clear and unambiguous).

[27] Below, para.3–17.

[28] *Nottingham Patent Brick and Tile Co. v Butler* (1886) 16 Q.B.D. 778. The vendor had disclosed the covenants but the solicitor contradicted him, and the purchaser's reliance in such matters on the solicitor, rather than the vendor, was held to be reasonable. It is well established that a statement by a vendor of land, in response to pre-contract enquiries, that he is not aware of a defect in title carries with it an implied representation that he has taken reasonable steps to ascertain whether any exists: and therefore that he has made such investigations as could reasonably be expected to be made by or under the guidance of a prudent conveyancer: *William Sindall Plc v Cambridgeshire CC* [1994] 1 W.L.R. 1016 at 1027 (Hoffmann L.J.). This principle extends beyond statements as to title: *Clinicare Ltd v Orchard Homes and Developments Ltd* [2004] EWHC 1694 (QB), [2004] All E.R. (D) 244 (Jul) at [20]–[26] (representation that vendor was not aware of dry rot carried the implication that he had made such investigations as could reasonably by expected of him in order to reach this conclusion).

lower rent.[29] As in all cases of misrepresentation, it will be for the representee to plead the meaning on which he claims to have relied.

3–09 **Timing of the falsity; change of facts.** In most cases of actionable misrepresentation the statement can be shown to have been false at the time it was made, and it remained false thereafter. Sometimes, however, there can be changes in circumstances which affect this analysis. A statement might be true when it is made but circumstances change so that, if repeated by the time the representee acts on it, it would then be false. Or it might have been false when made but later things change so that it becomes true. In general terms, for each of the remedies available for misrepresentation the requirement is that the statement be false at the moment when it is acted upon by the representee. However, this varies within the different remedies, and the details will be considered for each remedy.[30]

3–10 **Change of law.** One particular problem connected with changed circumstances flows from the decision of the House of Lords in *Kleinwort Benson Ltd v Lincoln City Council*.[31] Where a misrepresentation of law is actionable, it will be necessary to show that the statement of law on which the claimant relies was a misrepresentation. As with all cases of misrepresentation the general question—as discussed in the previous paragraph—will be whether the statement was false at the time the representee acted on it. But in this respect misrepresentations of law raise more difficult issues than misrepresentations of fact. If the facts change after the representee acted on the statement, that does not affect his actions (nor, therefore, the remedies available to him). Changes of fact cannot have retrospective effect. But changes of law can. In a claim based on a

[29] *Dimmock v Hallett* (1866) 2 Ch. App. 21. See also *R. v Lord Kylsant* [1932] 1 K.B. 442, CCA (company prospectus contained statements which were perfectly true but omitted information about the company's affairs with the result that the prospectus, taken as a whole, gave a false impression of the position of the company: a criminal offence under the Larceny Act 1861, s.84), following *Peek v Gurney* (1873) L.R. 6 H.L. 377, HL, at 386 and *Aaron's Reefs Ltd v Twiss* [1896] A.C. 273, HL, at 281.

[30] Below, paras 4–27 (rescission); 5–11 (deceit); 7–14 (Misrepresentation Act 1967 s.2(1)).

[31] [1999] 2 A.C. 349.

misrepresentation of law,[32] if there is a later change of the relevant rule of law, it will be necessary to establish whether the change had retrospective effect to the point at which the representation was acted on; and, if so, whether this affects the claim. Retrospective changes by statute are rare, and whether a retrospective change affects a misrepresentation claim would be a question of the proper construction of the statute.[33] In *Kleinwort Benson* it was established by a majority of the House of Lords[34] that where a judicial decision changes a rule of law, the effect of the decision is retrospective[35]:

---

[32] For misrepresentation of law see below, paras 3–20 *et seq*.

[33] There is a presumption against retrospective effect: see J.S. Bell and G. Engle, *Cross: Statutory Interpretation* (3rd edn, 1995), pp.187–190. For an example of a statute which did have explicit retrospective effect, but which was held not to have the effect of retrospectively making a false statement of law into a true statement (which would then have deprived the representee of a remedy), see *Tofts v Pearl Life Assurance Co. Ltd* [1915] 1 K.B. 189, CA.

[34] Lord Browne-Wilkinson and Lord Lloyd dissenting. For a view that the majority's analysis is a correct assessment of the nature of judicial decision-making, see J.M. Finnis, "The Fairy Tale's Moral" (1999) 115 L.Q.R. 170; D. Sheehan, "What is a Mistake?" (2000) 4 L.S. 538; for a different view, see S. Meier and R. Zimmermann, "Judicial Development of the Law, *Error Iuris*, and the Law of Unjustified Enrichment—a View from Germany" (1999) 115 L.Q.R. 556; P. Birks, "Mistakes of Law" (2000) 53 C.L.P. 205 at pp.223–230; F.A.R. Bennion, "Consequences of an Overrule" [2001] P.L. 450; J. Beatson, "Unlawful Statutes and Mistakes of Law" in A. Burrows and A. Rodger (eds), *Mapping the Law* (2006) at pp.163–180; Goff & Jones, para.5–003. *Cf. Deutsche Morgan Grenfell Group Plc v Inland Revenue Commissioners* [2006] UKHL 46, [2007] 1 A.C. 558 at [23] (Lord Hoffmann: a judicial decision clearly changes the law retrospectively; "It may be that this involves extending the concept of a mistake to compensate for the absence of a more general condictio indebiti and perhaps it would make objectors feel better if one said that because the law was now deemed to have been different at the relevant date, he was *deemed* to have made a mistake. But the reasoning is based upon practical considerations of fairness and not abstract juridical correctitude".) See also M.M. Bigelow, "Mistake of Law as a Ground of Equitable Relief" (1885) 1 L.Q.R 298 at pp.312–313 (an early discussion: the American courts "are not agreed in the wisdom of pressing the theory to the dangerous extreme of overturning intermediate transactions founded on" an earlier judicial decision later overruled). An approach similar to that of the majority in *Kleinwort Benson* was taken in the context of a misrepresentation of law by Page Wood V.C. in *Rashdall v Ford* (1866) L.R. 2 Eq. 750 at 754–755.

[35] [1999] 2 A.C. 349 at 378–379 (Lord Goff). See also *Deutsche Morgan Grenfell Group Plc v Inland Revenue Commissioners*, above, n. 34.

> "when he states the applicable principles of law, the judge is declaring these to constitute the law relevant to his decision. Subject to consideration by appellate tribunals, and (within limits) by judges of equal jurisdiction, what he states to be the law will, generally speaking, be applicable not only to the case before him but, as part of the common law, to other comparable cases which come before the courts, whenever the events which are the subject of those cases in fact occurred . . . [W]hen the judges state what the law is, their decisions do, in the sense I have described, have a retrospective effect. That is, I believe, inevitable. It is inevitable in relation to the particular case before the court, in which the events must have occurred some time, perhaps some years, before the judge's decision is made. But it is also inevitable in relation to other cases in which the law as so stated will in future fall to be applied."

Any statements of the law which were made on the basis of the "old" rule of law are therefore now shown to have been misrepresentations, even though at the time they were accurate under the generally established rules of law.

3–11 **Correction of the misrepresentation.** Since the test for whether a statement is an actionable misrepresentation generally looks to whether it was false at the moment when it was acted upon by the representee, it follows that a misrepresentation which is made but is adequately corrected before the representee acts upon it is no longer actionable. In such a case it can be said either that there is no longer a misrepresentation, or that the representee in acting in the knowledge of the truth is no longer relying on the representation.[36] The correction may be made by the representor, or by a third party, or by the representee independently discovering the truth. But the correction must be sufficient to remove the effect of the original misrepresentation: a partial or inadequate statement is not sufficient.[37] Where, however, the true position appears clearly from the very terms of the contract which the representee claims to have

[36] *Assicurazioni Generali S.p.A.v Arab Insurance Group* [2002] EWCA Civ 1642, [2003] 1 All E.R. (Comm) 140 at [63]. On reliance, see below, paras 3–50 *et seq.*

[37] *Clinicare Ltd v Orchard Homes and Developments Ltd* [2004] EWHC 1694 (QB), [2004] All E.R. (D) 244 (Jul) at [28] (correction must cover any implied misrepresentation, as well as an express misrepresentation); *Morris v Jones* [2002] EWCA Civ 1790, [2002] All E.R. (D) 82 (Dec) at [14]–[16]; *Assicurazioni Generali S.p.A. v Arab Insurance Group*, above, n.36, at [64]. For correction of the misrepresentation in a claim in deceit, see below, para.5–10; and

been induced to enter into by the misrepresentation, the misrepresentation will have been "corrected" as long as the claimant is bound by those terms.[38]

III. STATEMENT OF FACT?

(1) A Statement on which the Representee was Entitled to Rely

"Entitlement to rely" as the underlying principle. In different contexts, and for each of the several remedies, different expressions are used to define actionable misrepresentations. Sometimes it is said that a misrepresentation will not be actionable because it was only a statement of opinion or law and not a statement of fact; or it was only "sales talk"; or it was not a statement that the defendant had any duty to be careful in making; or it was not reasonable in the circumstances for the claimant to have relied on the statement. Whichever expression is used, the courts are seeking to identify those statements on which the representee ought to be entitled to rely.[39] False words do not generally cause harm without the intervention of a person who acts upon them. In the context of pre-contractual misrepresentation it is usually the contracting party who receives the words, believes them, enters into the contract and then regrets it when he discovers the truth. That the representee *relied* on the misrepresentation is therefore a key requirement which will be discussed below.[40] But it is equally important to consider whether the representee was in the circumstances *entitled* to rely on the statement. This is not to suggest that there is, or ought to be, a single test for all remedies for misrepresentation: "was the statement one on which the claimant was entitled to rely?" This 3–12

under the Misrepresentation Act 1967 s.2(1), see below, para.7–13; and as a defence to liability under the Financial Services and Markets Act 2000, see below, para.7–59.

[38] *Peekay Intermark Ltd v Australia and New Zealand Banking Group Ltd* [2006] EWCA Civ 386, [2006] 2 Lloyd's Rep 511 at [43] (misrepresentation corrected by the terms of the contract which the claimant signed and by which he was bound although he did not read them: *L'Estrange v Graucob* [1934] 2 K.B. 394, CA, below, para.13–34, applied).

[39] See, e.g. *Raiffeisen Zentralbank Österreich A.G. v Royal Bank of Scotland Plc* [2010] EWHC 1392 (Comm), [2011] 1 Lloyd's Rep. 123 at [81], [86].

[40] Below, para.3–51.

may be the underlying principle but a practical test is necessary to apply it, and the rules for each of the several remedies for misrepresentation are, in substance, addressing this through various tests. Bearing this in mind, it will be easier to explore the remedies and their approaches to defining which statements are actionable.

3–13 **The practical requirement of a statement of "fact".** It is often said that a misrepresentation, to be actionable, must have been one of (present) fact; and "fact" is here commonly contrasted with belief or opinion, law, and future fact or intention.[41] This distinction has been applied in relation to only some of the remedies we shall consider in later chapters[42]; but in relation to those remedies it is firmly established as a general proposition.[43] It is necessary to explore in some detail the reasoning of the courts in those cases which have drawn the distinction between misrepresentations of fact and misrepresentations of opinion, law and intention. It will be seen that this requirement is based in general terms on the courts' desire to limit actionable misrepresentations to those on which a representee ought to be entitled to rely.

---

[41] Spencer Bower (Misrepresentation), Ch.2; Chitty, para.6–006; Furmston, paras 4.32 to 4.35; Treitel, paras 9–003 to 9–013; Anson, pp.301–305; Cheshire, Fifoot and Furmston, pp.332–335; Allen, p.12.

[42] In particular, to the remedies of rescission (below, para.4–25) and damages under the Misrepresentation Act 1967 s.2(1) (below, para.7–07). The rule is not applied as such in relation to damages in the tort of negligence (below, para.6–12), and is qualified in relation to the tort of deceit (below, para.5–08). The question whether a pre-contractual representation was incorporated into the contract so as to give rise to a claim for damages for breach of contract also proceeds along other lines (below, para.8–04). The distinction is also used for other purposes outside the scope of this book, but from which useful analogies can sometimes be drawn, e.g. whether a statement was one giving rise to criminal liability for obtaining property or pecuniary advantage by deception under the Theft Act 1968 ss.15 and 16 (for which "deception" meant deception "by words or conduct as to fact or as to law, including a deception as to the present intentions of the person using the deception or any other person": s.15(4); repealed and replaced by Fraud Act 2006 s.2(3): "'Representation' means any representation as to fact or law, including a representation as to the state of mind of (a) the person making the reperesentation, or (b) any other person").

[43] The requirement that the statement be of fact *and not law* has been subject to recent development: below, paras 3–34 *et seq*. But some of the books still include it in their general statement of the restriction on actionable misrepresentations.

(2) Statements of Fact Contrasted with "Sales Talk", Uncertain Statements and Statements of Opinion

Sales talk. Some statements made during the negotiations for a contract might be regarded as just "sales talk"[44]: either the statements are, on their face, assertions of fact but they are only exaggerations, "puffing the product" and not to be taken seriously[45]; or they are not sufficiently clear and precise to constitute actionable misrepresentations. The circumstances of the contract and its negotiations have to be considered as a whole in order to decide whether the statement is to be regarded as actionable,[46] and the core question is whether the representee was entitled to take the statement seriously and so to rely on it in deciding whether to enter into the contract.[47] 3–14

[44] Of course, it is not only in contracts of *sale* that such hyperbolic or vague statements can be made, but the expression "sales talk" is a useful generic description of such statements.

[45] Sometimes referred to as *simplex commendatio* ("mere praise") of the product: this was a principle accepted in Roman law where, in the absence of fraud, "what a seller says in praise [of the good he is selling] is not to be taken as assertion, nor as promise": D.4.3.37. See *Mallan v Radloff* (1864) 17 C.B.(N.S.) 588 at 597, 144 E.R. 236 at 239. The same distinction has been applied in criminal law, e.g. in cases of obtaining money by false pretences: *R. v Ardley* (1871) L.R. 1 C.C.R. 301 at 306; *R. v Bryan* (1857) Dears. & Bell 265 at 283, 169 E.R. 1002 at 1009 (Willes J., dissenting on the facts: the question was whether there was "such ordinary praise of the goods, *dolus bonus*, as that a person ought not to be taken in by it, or whether it was a misrepresentation of a specific fact material to the contract and intended to defraud"). The notion of *dolus bonus* had been used in Roman Law (D. 4.3.1.3) and is sometimes used in modern civil systems following the Roman usage: J. Ghestin, *Traité de droit civil, La formation du contrat* (3rd edn, L.G.D.J. Paris, 1993), para.564; H., L. and J. Mazeaud and F. Chabas, *Leçons de droit civil, Tome II, Vol.1, Obligations, théorie générale* (9th edn, Montchrestien, Paris, 1998), para.191; G. Alpa, *Istituzioni di Diritto Privato, Nozion* (3rd edn, U.T.E.T., Turin, 2001), XLV, para.8.

[46] The burden of proving that there is a sufficient statement or "misrepresentation" for the purposes of the remedy claimed lies on the claimant: *Kyle Bay Ltd t/a Astons Nightclub v Underwriters Subscribing under Policy No.019057/08/01* [2007] EWCA Civ 57, [2007] 1 C.L.C. 164 at [32] (Neuberger L.J., rejecting the argument that the onus is on the person making the statement to show why it should not be an actionable misrepresentation).

[47] This formulation was cited by Mance L.J. in *MCI WorldCom International Inc. v Primus Telecommunications Inc.* [2004] EWCA Civ 957, [2004] 2 All E.R. (Comm) 833 at [30].

> "In the kind of situation where one expects, as a matter of ordinary common experience, a person to use a certain amount of hyperbole in the description of goods, property or services, the courts will do what any ordinary reasonable man would do, namely, take it with a large pinch of salt. [The test is] whether a reasonable man would take the claim as being a serious claim or not.[48]"

In applying this test, it is of limited use to rely on decided cases[49]: the cases only illustrate the general approach and cannot be taken as precedents for future decisions, even where an earlier case involved a statement which appears to be identical to the case under consideration, because more than just the words must be considered. It is a broader question of whether, in the circumstances—including questions of the particular circumstances of the representor and the representee[50]—the words should have been taken by the representee as being spoken seriously and therefore could be relied on. However, some indications can be obtained from the cases as to how a court will approach the question.

If the statement is vague, and not objectively verifiable, it is more likely to be held not to be an actionable statement; it might then be characterised as an opinion rather than a statement of fact.[51] For example, in *Trower v Newcome*[52] a statement in auction particulars

[48] *De Beers Abrasive Products Ltd v International General Electric Co. of New York Ltd* [1975] 1 W.L.R. 972 at 978 (slander of goods in publicity pamphlet comparing defendant's product with claimant's product: arguable claim because pamphlet purported to present results of a scientific test to support statements. Walton J. made clear that his proposition applied more widely than the tort of slander of goods, to include "vague commendatory statements about goods or services on offer": *ibid.*).

[49] *J.J. Savage & Sons Pty Ltd v Blakney* (1970) 119 C.L.R. 435, HCA, at 442 ("estimated speed" of a motor boat engine was only a representation, not a contractual promise).

[50] Below, para.3–18.

[51] Below, para.3–15.

[52] (1813) 3 Mer. 704 at 705, 36 E.R. 270 at 271. *Cf. Scott v Hanson* (1826) 1 Sim. 13, 57 E.R. 483 (land, in fact imperfectly watered, described in auction particulars as "uncommonly rich water meadow": "nothing more than the loose opinion of the auctioneer, or vendor, as to the obvious quality of the land, upon which the vendee ought not to have placed, and cannot be considered to have placed, any reliance": Leach V.C. at 15, at 484; affirmed (1829) 1 Russ. & My. 128, 39 E.R. 49); *Johnson v Smart* (1860) 2 Giff. 151, 66 E.R. 64 (house, which the purchaser had not seen, described in auction particulars as "substantial and convenient": "a description so relative in its terms as to afford abundant opportunity for a conflict of evidence as to matters which are rather matters of

for the sale of an advowson that the "avoidance of this preferment is likely to occur soon" was not actionable: the representation was "so vague and indefinite that the Court could not take notice of it judicially . . . its only effect ought to have been to put the Defendant upon making inquiries respecting the circumstances under which the alleged voidance was likely to take place". And in *Dimmock v Hallett*[53] the description in auction particulars that a farm's land was "fertile and improvable" was "a mere flourishing description by an auctioneer"; and the statement that the land "may be . . . considerably improved at a moderate cost" "puts a purchaser on inquiry, and if he chooses to buy on the faith of such a statement without inquiry, he has no ground of complaint".[54] These statements were therefore not actionable.[55]

However, statements which appear similarly vague or commendatory can, in an appropriate context, be held to be actionable. The statement in a company's prospectus that "the directors and their friends have subscribed a large portion of the capital" could be a misrepresentation where the directors had taken "a very small portion indeed" or where they had taken none[56]: although the words "a large portion" are vague, there comes a point where, on the facts, a "portion" is so small that the statement is objectively verifiable as false. Statements by the agent of a vendor of a grocery business, to a purchaser who had no business expertise, that the business was "a little gold mine" and "one of the best businesses in town" were representations actionable in the tort of deceit.[57] And statements by a financial adviser which asserted that a financial plan was "a safe and sensible way" of raising funds were actionable where the

opinion than of fact": Stuart V.C. at 156, at 66, although he decided on the evidence of a surveyor that the house was not improperly or untruly described as substantial and convenient).

53 (1866) L.R. 2 Ch. App. 21.

54 *ibid.* at 27 (Turner L.J.).

55 The contract was, however, discharged on the basis of another misrepresentation as to the letting value of the farm.

56 *Henderson v Lacon* (1867) L.R. 5 Eq. 249 at 257.

57 *Easterbrook v Hopkins* [1918] N.Z.L.R. 428. See also *Senanayake v Cheng* [1966] A.C. 63, PC (business was "a gold mine": rescission).

claimants were not financially sophisticated people but had dealt with the financial adviser who was negligent in giving such advice.[58]

3–15 **Statements of opinion and belief.** "Sales talk" is sometimes thought to be different from statements of opinion, although the cases cited in the last section indicate that the dividing line, if it can be drawn at all, is very thin. But there has been much discussion in the cases about when statements can be characterised as statements of opinion or belief (which are not, at least in some contexts,[59] actionable), and statements of fact (which are). It could be said, broadly, that a statement of belief[60] is a statement of what the

---

[58] *Investors Compensation Scheme Ltd v West Bromwich Building Society (No.2)* [1999] Lloyd's Rep. P.N. 496 (claims, inter alia, of negligence against the financial adviser, and for rescission of the mortgage as against the mortgagee who had notice under the doctrine of *Barclays Bank Plc v O'Brien* [1994] 1 A.C. 180, HL, below para.4–77, of the adviser's actionable misrepresentation. The adviser said that the scheme was "completely safe", "a sure-fire winner," "would make [the investors] financially secure for the rest of their lives" and that there was no chance that they would lose their homes). *Cf. Esso Petroleum Co. Ltd v Mardon* [1976] Q.B. 801, CA, below, para.6–28. See also *Fordy v Harwood*, unreported, March 30, 1999, but transcript available on *http://www.bailii.org* as [1999] EWCA Civ 1134 (statement in magazine advertisement that vintage car was "absolutely mint" held to be misrepresentation of fact justifying rescission); *Andrews v Hopkinson* [1957] 1 Q.B. 229 (oral statement by second hand car salesman that a car was "a good little bus. I would stake my life on it. You will have no trouble with it": held actionable as warranty of quality); *Turner v Anquetil* [1953] N.Z.L.R. 952 (newspaper advertisement that piano was in "good order": held actionable as warranty of quality even though no further oral assurance given).

[59] Above, n.42.

[60] "Belief" is defined in the Oxford English Dictionary (2nd edn, 1989, and online version June 2011 *http://www.oed.com* [accessed 30 June 2011]) as: "Mental acceptance of a proposition, statement, or fact, as true, on the ground of authority or evidence; assent of the mind to a statement, or to the truth of a fact beyond observation, on the testimony of another, or to a fact or truth on the evidence of consciousness; the mental condition involved in this assent." American judges have defined belief as "that state of the mind otherwise expressed in the phrase of having a conviction of the truth respecting some subject of investigation or inquiry" (*Latrobe v J.H. Cross Co. Inc.* (1928) 29 F.2d 201); "'Belief' is necessarily based upon at least assumed facts" (*Cook v Singer Sewing Mach. Co.* (1934) 138 Cal.App. 418, 32 P.2d 430). For the approach of English judges to "belief" and "reasonable grounds for belief" in the context of deceit and other remedies for misrepresentation, see below, paras 5–14 and 7–25.

speaker subjectively considers to be true fact (whether or not the fact is as he believes it to be); and a statement of opinion[61] is a statement of what the speaker thinks to be a valid assertion based on a consideration of relevant available material but without having the certainty that it is necessarily an assertion of truth.

Whether a statement is one of belief/opinion or fact is not as straightforward as might first appear. The words used by the speaker will of course be relevant and will be the starting-point; but a representation is not necessarily one of opinion just because the speaker says "In my opinion . . ."; nor is it necessarily not one of opinion just because he does not explicitly qualify it as such. If the statement is made about something on which there is an inherent lack of certainty, and so differing views could reasonably be held about it, the statement is more likely to be characterised as one of opinion.[62]

Qualifications imposed by the speaker. Sometimes the speaker will attempt to make clear that his statement is not to be taken as one for which he accepts responsibility.[63] If his assertion is made 3–16

[61] "Opinion" was defined in the Oxford English Dictionary (2nd edn, 1989) as: "What one thinks or how one thinks about something; judgement resting on grounds insufficient for complete demonstration; belief of something as probable, or as seeming to one's own mind to be true, though not certain or established"; revised in 3rd edn, 2004 and online version June 2011 *http://www.oed.com* [accessed 30 June 2011] to "what or how one thinks about something; judgement or belief".

[62] *Irish National Insurance Co. Ltd v Oman Insurance Co. Ltd* [1983] 2 Lloyd's Rep. 453 at 462 (description of an item of insurance business as written on a "first loss" basis: held, opinion, because of disagreement within the insurance market about whether the business could be properly so described, even if one view was held by a minority within the market); *Anderson v Pacific Fire and Marine Insurance Co.* (1872) L.R. 7 C.P. 65 (statement in letter from freight owner's captain, passed on to insurers, that a place was "considered by the pilot here as a good and safe anchorage, and well sheltered" held opinion because the place "does not appear to have been a place very well known to either party. It was, so to speak, a questionable place. All the information the [insurer] has he obtains from a person who professes not to know anything about it:" Willes J. at 69).

[63] On the effect of clauses designed to qualify a statement or to exclude liability for it, see Ch.9.

only "to the best of his belief",[64] it will simply be a question of his honesty in making the statement[65]: "I believe x" is false if the speaker does not actually believe x: there is a misrepresentation of the fact of what he is thinking at the moment he makes the statement.[66] But it is not false just because x is not at that moment true: to say "x is true" and "I believe that x is true" are quite different statements.[67] In the context of insurance contracts this is made clear by statute. Section 20(5) of the Marine Insurance Act 1906[68] provides that: "A representation as to a matter of expectation or belief is true if it be made in good faith" and this has been held in the Court of Appeal to entail a test of honesty, and not to allow any further qualification such as an implied representation that the belief is held on reasonable grounds.

> "Once statute deems an honest representation as to a matter of belief to be true, I cannot see that there is scope for inquiry as to whether there were objectively reasonable grounds for that belief.[69]"

---

[64] The words "best of" do not add anything to the force of this statement, although this is a common form of words: *Roe v Bradshaw* (1866) L.R. 1 Exch. 106 at 109 (affidavit "to the best of belief" of the deponent).

[65] *Hummingbird Motors Ltd v Hobbs* [1986] R.T.R. 276, CA, at 280 (O'Connor L.J.; Kerr L.J. at 281 thought that such a statement also implies that the representor knows of no facts which are inconsistent with his statement of belief, on the authority of *Smith v Land and House Property Corp.* (1884) 28 Ch.D. 7, below, para.3–17; but he was clear that there is no necessary implication that the speaker has reasonable grounds for his belief: such an implication depends on "the facts and the position of the parties in relation to the subject-matter"); *cf. I.F.E. Fund S.A. v Goldman Sachs International* [2006] EWHC 2887 (Comm), [2007] 1 Lloyd's Rep. 264, below, n.88.

[66] *Brown v Raphael* [1958] Ch. 636, CA, at 641. Such a misrepresentation will inevitably be fraudulent.

[67] *Macdonald v Law Union Fire and Life Insurance Co.* (1874) L.R. 9 Q.B. 328 at 331.

[68] Which is treated by the courts as containing principles applicable to insurance contracts generally, and not restricted to contracts of marine insurance: *P.C.W. Syndicates v P.C.W. Reinsurers* [1996] 1 W.L.R. 1136, CA, at 1140. S.20 is however to be amended by the Consumer Insurance (Disclosure and Representations) Bill (which is passing through Parliament during 2011) to exclude consumer insurance contracts from its scope: below, para.17–06.

[69] *Economides v Commercial Assurance Co. Plc* [1998] Q.B. 587, CA, at 606 (Peter Gibson L.J.). Simon Brown and Peter Gibson L.JJ. rejected the view of Steyn J. (obiter) in *Highlands Insurance Co. v Continental Insurance Co. (Note)* [1987] 1 Lloyd's Rep. 109 to the effect that s.20(5) does not exclude the possibility of implied representations of reasonable grounds for the belief,

At least in cases outside those governed by this statute, however, it is possible for a statement which appears on its face to be one of opinion or belief to carry an implication of fact; often the implication that the speaker has reasonable grounds for holding the opinion or belief. In all cases the question will be whether, on a proper construction of the actual communication made by the particular representor to the particular representee, the representee was entitled to treat it as containing a statement of fact which could be relied on.[70]

although Simon Brown L.J. said at 599 that "what may at first blush appear to be a representation merely of expectation or belief can on analysis be seen in certain cases to be an assertion of a specific fact . . . And . . . there must be some basis for a representation of belief before it can be said to be made in good faith". Sir Iain Glidewell, however, at 609, decided the case on other grounds and was not prepared without further argument to conclude that Steyn J.'s view was wrong. But the decision of the majority may be open to question in so far as it appears to exclude all argument that a statement in an insurance proposal that "*x* is true to the best of my belief" might carry an implication of fact: it is arguable that in all cases the question ought to be whether the statement is in substance a question of fact, or of opinion/belief; and s.20(5) of the 1906 Act only applies to statements which are in substance statements of belief; what counts is whether, as it seems to the insurer, the proposer has significantly better knowledge or means of knowledge: see Clarke, para.22–2B2. The 1906 Act was not intended to change the common law, only to codify it: Sir W. Robson, Solicitor General, in the second reading in the House of Commons: *Hansard* HC Vol.155, col.421 (1906). *Cf.* also *Bank Leumi Le Israel B.M. v British National Insurance Co. Ltd* [1988] 1 Lloyd's Rep. 71 at 75, where Saville J. appeared to treat insurance contracts as subject to the normal common law principle that a statement of the future, i.e. "expectation" within s.20(5), could carry an implication of reasonable grounds for making the forecast: below, para.3–44. However, it may be more likely as a matter of *practice* that common form statements of belief in insurance proposals will be construed as such, rather than as carrying implications of fact.

70 *Pawson v Watson* (1778) 2 Cowp. 785 at 788, 98 E.R. 1361 at 1362 (Lord Mansfield: a statement of belief by insured to insurer, about something which is later proved to be false, the insured "knowing nothing about it, nor having any reason to believe the contrary" does not render the policy voidable because the insurer "then takes the risk upon himself"); *Sykes v Taylor-Rose* [2004] EWCA Civ 299, [2004] 2 P. & C.R. 30, above, para.3–07 (on construction, the question "Is there any other information which you think the buyer might have a right to know?" asked only for an honest reply: "the question itself makes no reference to a requirement for the belief to be based upon reasonable grounds and . . . I can see no reason why such an obligation should be imported. The question is intended to be answered by persons with no legal training and its words should be given their normal and ordinary meaning": Sir William Aldous at [28]).

3–17 **Statement of fact implied in statement of opinion.** A commonly cited proposition is in the judgment of Bowen L.J. in *Smith v Land and House Property Corporation*[71]:

> "it is often fallaciously assumed that a statement of opinion cannot involve the statement of a fact. In a case where the facts are equally well known to both parties, what one of them says to the other is frequently nothing but an expression of opinion. The statement of such opinion is in a sense a statement of a fact, about the condition of the man's own mind, but only of an irrelevant fact, for it is of no consequence what the opinion is. But if the facts are not equally known to both sides, then a statement of opinion by the one who knows the facts best involves very often a statement of a material fact, for he impliedly states that he knows facts which justify his opinion."

Different kinds of implied statement can be found within what appears to be a statement of opinion.

First, it might be said that every statement of opinion carries the implication that it is honestly held[72]; but this does not really add anything, since if the "opinion" is not honestly held, it is a misrepresentation to say that it is.[73]

Sometimes the words of opinion can carry the implication of an assertion of a specific fact. This is similar to a "half truth", where a (true) statement of fact carries an implication of a further statement of fact which is false.[74] But here it is a statement of opinion which hides an assertion of fact. For example, in *Smith v Land and House Property Corporation* a statement by the landlord freeholder, to a purchaser of the freehold, that the property was let to "a very desirable tenant" was held to carry an implied statement that nothing had occurred in the relations between the landlord and the tenant which could be considered to make the tenant an unsatisfactory one: and since the tenant had only "paid his last quarter's rent by driblets under pressure"[75] this was not true.

---

[71] (1884) 28 Ch.D. 7 at 15, cited in, e.g. *Bisset v Wilkinson* [1927] A.C. 177, PC, at 182; *Brown v Raphael*, above, n.66 at 642; *Esso Petroleum Co. Ltd v Mardon* [1976] Q.B. 801, CA, at 831.

[72] *Economides v Commercial Assurance Co. Plc*, above, n.69 at 598, 608–609.

[73] *Brown v Raphael*, above, n.66.

[74] Above, para.3–08.

[75] (1882) 28 Ch.D. 7 at 15–16. See also *Thomas Witter Ltd v TBP Industries Ltd* [1996] 2 All E.R. 573 at 594 (forecast of profits included implied representation that forecast was made on same basis as earlier forecasts).

There can also be a different form of implied statement of fact, as described in the extract from Bowen L.J.'s judgment in *Smith v Land and House*, quoted above: he says that in some cases, a statement of opinion carries the implication that the speaker knows facts which justify his opinion; and therefore there will be an actionable misrepresentation if either the speaker himself had no basis of information for coming to such an opinion, or the facts do not reasonably justify that opinion.[76]

Test for implied statement of fact. In deciding whether there is such an implied statement of fact, the question is what the representee was entitled to understand.[77] A key issue is the balance of information (or access to relevant information[78]) held by the representor and the representee respectively. If the representee has significantly less information than the representor about facts or other circumstances which are relevant to the "opinion" expressed, it is more likely that he will be held entitled to rely on the statement as being more than just an opinion.[79] A statement by the vendor of the reversion of a trust fund that "Estate duty will be payable on the death of the annuitant who is believed to have no aggregable estate" was held to be a misrepresentation entitling the purchaser to rescind the contract because, although the statement was made innocently,[80] 3–18

[76] *Credit Lyonnais Bank Nederland v Export Credit Guarantee Department* [1996] 1 Lloyd's Rep. 200 at 216 (statement by bank to the ECGD in support of proposal for credit for exporting companies, that the management of the companies was "respectable and trustworthy and had demonstrated that it was highly able and efficient", was a misrepresentation because it was made without the bank having any factual basis from which it could have drawn the conclusions); *Barings Plc (In Liquidation) v Coopers & Lybrand (No.2)* [2002] B.C.L.C. 410 at [44]–[52] (finance director of audit client making representations to auditors as to the financial statements which he had the responsibility for preparing and the financial records which he had the responsibility for keeping: implied representation that he had reasonable grounds for making the statements he did).

[77] *Brown v Raphael*, above, n.66 at 649.

[78] "It suffices for the application of the principle if it appears that between the two parties one is better equipped with information or the means of information than the other": *ibid.* at 642 (Lord Evershed M.R.).

[79] Bowen L.J. in *Smith v Land and House Property Corp.*, quoted above.

[80] It was inserted into the auction particulars by the managing clerk of the vendor's solicitors, who normally acted as a litigation clerk, and "without any comprehension of the meaning of the words": [1958] Ch. 636 at 637.

> "it would flow from the language used and would be intended to be understood by a reader of the particulars that persons who knew the significance of the matter and who were experienced and competent to look into it were expressing a belief founded upon substantial and reasonable grounds[81];"

the seller appeared to be in possession of (or have access to) all the relevant information about the annuitant's circumstances whereas the purchaser had no such information; and the particulars were expressed on their face to have been prepared by a well-known firm of solicitors of standing and repute.

Where, however, the representee has no reason to believe that a statement, couched in the language of belief or opinion, is made with any special basis of information or skill, the statement will be characterised as simply belief or opinion, and so will not be actionable. In *Bisset v Wilkinson*[82] the statement by the vendor of land to his purchasers that "if the place was worked as I was working it, with a good six-horse team, my idea [is] that it would carry two thousand sheep" was held to be only a statement of opinion, and therefore did not entitle the purchasers, who bought the land for use as a sheep farm, to rescind the contract of sale. Lord Merrivale stated the general test to be applied[83]:

> "the material facts of the transaction, the knowledge of the parties respectively, and their relative positions, the words of representation used, and the actual condition of the subject-matter spoken of, are relevant to the two inquiries necessary to be made: What was the meaning of the representation? Was it true?"

No doubt a vendor of land, when speaking about the land he is selling, will normally be held to be making statements of fact because the vendor is generally the better placed to know about the property. Here, however, the facts were against such an implication. Although the vendor was a sheep farmer, the land he was selling

---

81 *ibid.*, at 643.

82 [1927] A.C. 177, PC; *Smith v Price* (1862) 2 F. & F. 748, 175 E.R. 1268 (seller of damaged cargo of wine did not make statement of fact about its value or condition to buyer when "he had not any better means of knowledge of that matter than the [purchaser], nor perhaps so good. He had not seen the wines, nor did he pretend to have done so": Erle C.J. at 753, at 1269–1270, directing the jury).

83 *ibid.*, at 183.

had never been used as a single sheep farm: it was newly formed as a unit of land from one plot which was part of a farm on which he had kept sheep, and another plot which was good land but which had deteriorated, and which the vendor had not worked as a sheep farm; and the purchasers knew all this. The trial judge held that[84]

> "in ordinary circumstances, any statement made by an owner who has been occupying his own farm as to its carrying capacity would be regarded as a statement of fact... This, however, is not such a case. The [purchasers] knew all about [the plot of deteriorated land] and knew also what sheep the farm was carrying when they inspected it. In these circumstances... the [purchasers] were not justified in regarding anything said by the plaintiff as to the carrying capacity as being anything more than an expression of his opinion on the subject."

It should be noticed that the question is not simply what the representee *did* understand, but what he *should* understand the statement to mean, and therefore whether he was *entitled* to rely on it.[85]

Repetition of another person's statement. A question can sometimes arise as to whether a contracting party makes a representation when he simply passes on information which he has received from another person who is not involved in the transaction. The answer ought to lie in the principles already discussed in this section. If the party makes clear that he is simply passing on information which he believes to be true but for which he cannot vouch, then the question will be one of his honesty in making the statement.[86] But he may, by passing the information on, be taken as 3–19

---

[84] Quoted and approved by the Privy Council: [1927] A.C. 177 at 183–184. The judge also held, that the purchasers had failed to prove that the farm, if properly managed, was not capable of carrying two thousand sheep: see at 185.

[85] There are other statements in the case by the Privy Council referring to what meaning of the words spoken "was actually conveyed to" the representee (see [1927] A.C. 177 at 183), but the question should be whether the representee was entitled to understand the representation as one of fact on which he was therefore entitled to rely. In this, as generally when the question is the meaning of communications between parties negotiating for a contract, an objective test is applied: what was a person in the representee's position reasonably entitled to conclude? Above, para.3–06; below, para.13–12.

[86] Above, para.3–16; and subject always to the question of whether he can be allowed in law to disclaim responsibility for the statement: below, Ch.9.

having responsibility for it if in the circumstances the representee is entitled to take it as being made as an assertion of fact on which he is entitled to rely.

As always, a careful consideration of the particular context of the statement is crucial. For example, where information about a target company is passed on to a participant in the financing of the takeover by the bidding company's adviser, which arranges and underwrites that part of the financing, the question is what a reasonable participant would understand was the scope of the responsibility undertaken by the arranger in relation to the contents of the documents which are issued.[87] Where the relevant document identified the source of the information and made clear that the arranger has not independently verified it, there was no express representation and the only implied representation was that, in supplying the document, it was acting in good faith, that is, not knowingly putting forward information likely to mislead. It did not go so far as to carry the implication that the adviser was unaware of any facts showing that the information was or might be materially incorrect, which would be significantly wider, and would have potentially required the adviser to carry out an evaluation in order to decide what information it was required to disclose.[88]

However, in cases where insurers have passed on to reinsurers information about the facts relating to the risk which they have themselves received from the insured it has been held that, as between insurer and reinsurer, the statement of information is to be treated as one of fact, even though the parties know that the information is only being passed on and the insurer has no direct personal knowledge of the facts he describes. Applying the test discussed earlier in this section, it is a question of what the reinsurer could reasonably understand the words to mean; and the expectations of the insurance market are the key: it would be

[87] *I.F.E. Fund S.A. v Goldman Sachs International* [2006] EWHC 2887 (Comm), [2007] 1 Lloyd's Rep. 264 at [54].

[88] *ibid.*, at [57]–[60], distinguishing *Hummingbird Motors Ltd v Hobbs* [1986] R.T.R. 276, CA, above, n.65; affirmed [2007] EWCA Civ 811, [2007] 2 Lloyd's Rep. 447. The document also expressly negatived a duty to review or update the information: see further below, para.9–03, n.11.

"commercially unrealistic, and would be contrary to present understanding in the London market whereby reinsurers place reliance on a broker's presentation of 'Information' as recording statements of fact, unless qualifying language or the context indicates that a particular statement falls in a different category.[89]"

(3) Fact Contrasted with Law

(a) *The "misrepresentation of law" rule*

The "misrepresentation of law" rule and the "mistake of law" rule. Until recently it was well established that, for some remedies, a misrepresentation of law generally did not suffice. For this purpose "law" is contrasted with "fact". However, it has recently been held that there is now no such rule, although the key to this development lies not in the law of contract, but in the law of restitution. Much of the case law which is generally relied on to show the misrepresentation of law rule has been in the context of mistake, rather than misrepresentation; and in the context of claims in restitution for money had and received, rather than claims in contract. Traditionally it has been said that money paid under a mistake of fact may be recovered, whereas money paid under a mistake of law may not; that a mistake of law is not sufficient to found a claim to restitution. And that a mistake of law does not render a contract void, whereas a mistake of fact may do so. The link between mistake and misrepresentation has been discussed already[90]; and it is perhaps not surprising that the courts should have reasoned from the mistake of law rule to establish a similar rule for misrepresentation. Where the courts re-assess the mistake of law rule, it is natural for them in consequence to re-assess the misrepresentation of law rule. 3–20

---

[89] *Highlands Insurance Co. v Continental Insurance Co.* [1987] 1 Lloyd's Rep. 109 at 112 (Steyn J.: statement on slip headed "Information"). See also *Sirius International Insurance Corp. v Oriental Assurance Corp.* [1999] 1 All E.R. (Comm) 699 (broker's document, "we have been informed that..." held statement of fact). Sometimes, however, the way in which a statement is presented will make clear that it is only a statement of opinion which is being passed on: *Anderson v Pacific Fire and Marine Insurance Co.* (1872) L.R. 7 C.P. 65, above, para.3–16.

[90] Above, para.1–03.

3–21 **Recent developments in the "mistake of law" rule.** The most significant recent developments (both in England and in other jurisdictions) have been in the context of claims for restitution of money paid or in respect of services rendered under a mistake of law: in short, in this context, the law/fact distinction was abolished by the House of Lords in *Kleinwort Benson Ltd v Lincoln City Council*,[91] and in consequence there is no longer a rule against recovery of, for example, money paid under a mistake of law. The Court of Appeal[92] has held that the effect of the decision in *Kleinwort Benson* "now permeates the law of contract" with the result that there is no longer a mistake of law rule in contract, and has approved a decision at first instance[93] which held that the misrepresentation of law rule has not survived.

In spite of these developments, however, the law/fact distinction cannot be entirely forgotten. For the purposes of both mistake and misrepresentation, questions remain as to how to deal with misunderstandings of the law, and such questions cannot be answered without a clear picture of the mistake and misrepresentation of law rules as they had been developed before *Kleinwort Benson*. In this chapter we shall therefore discuss the distinction between law and fact, and the origins and supposed rationale of the distinction, with a view in particular to exploring the significance that should be attributed to misrepresentations of law. It is not possible to do so without drawing on all relevant types of case, whether in mistake or misrepresentation, restitution or contract. But the focus here will be on the misrepresentation of law rule; the significance of mistakes of law will be further explored in Part II.[94]

(b) *The law/fact distinction*

Although, as will be explained in the following section, it became well established in the cases that there is a distinction between mistakes (and misrepresentations) of law and of fact, the application

[91] [1999] 2 A.C. 349, discussed below, para.3–34.
[92] *Brennan v Bolt Burdon* [2004] EWCA Civ 1017, [2005] Q.B. 303 at [10] (Maurice Kay L.J.), discussed below, para.3–36.
[93] *Pankhania v Hackney LBC* [2002] EWHC 2441 (Ch), [2002] All E.R. (D) 22 (Aug), discussed below, para.3–37.
[94] Below, para 15–24.

of the distinction is not always as clear-cut as such a significant rule would suggest.[95] Some examples will show how the courts have approached the issue.

Interpretation of statutes. Some situations are clear. A mistake about the existence of a public general statute, for example, is a mistake of law.[96] But the construction of a known statute and its application to the facts can be more difficult. If the issue is characterised as being the interpretation of the statute in the light of established facts, then it will be a question of law[97]; if the mistake or misrepresentation is as to the underlying facts, on which the application of the statute depends, then it is a question of fact. But it can sometimes be difficult to predict how a court will characterise the issue. For example, in *Solle v Butcher*[98] a flat was repaired and improved after suffering war damage, and a new rent was agreed by the landlord and tenant which was in excess of that chargeable under statutes which controlled the rents chargeable on properties which had previously been subject to tenancies. A majority of the Court of Appeal held that there was a mistake of fact; Bucknill L.J. characterised the issue as "whether the flat had been so restored, altered and reconstructed as to destroy its identity" and so to take it outside the ambit of the statute.[99] But Jenkins L.J. dissented on the **3–22**

---

[95] P.H. Winfield, "Mistake of Law" (1943) 59 L.Q.R. 327.

[96] *Sharp Bros & Knight v Chant* [1917] 1 K.B. 771, CA (in ignorance of the enactment of the Increase of Rent and Mortgage Interest (War Restrictions) Act 1915, tenant continued to pay rent in excess of the amount which was set by the statute as the maximum a landlord could recover. Although this was a case of ignorance of the law there was still a *mistake*: the ignorance led to the tenant's "belief that he could not by law refuse to pay" the contractual rent: Warrington L.J. at 777).

[97] *National Pari-Mutuel Association Ltd v R.* (1930) 47 T.L.R. 110, CA (betting duty paid on interpretation of the Finance Act shown to have been in error by later decision of House of Lords on identical facts); *Oudaille v Lawson* [1922] N.Z.L.R. 259 (statement that rent chargeable on property was restricted by War Regulations: false, because Regulations did not apply to rents over £2 a week, whereas rent on property in question was £3 10s.: held misrepresentation of law; *cf. Solle v Butcher*, below, n.98); *Kiriri Cotton Co. Ltd v Dewani* [1960] A.C. 192, PC, at 201 (payment of premium for lease forbidden by legislation; it is not however entirely clear from the facts whether this was in ignorance of the statute or, as the Privy Council assume, on the basis of its misinterpretation).

[98] [1950] 1 K.B. 671, CA.

[99] *ibid.*, at 685; see also Denning L.J. at 695, who applied the law/"private rights" distinction from *Cooper v Phibbs*, below, para.3–25. *Cf. Laurence v*

basis that the mistake was one of law not fact: it was "simply a mistake as to the effect of certain public statutes on the contract made".[100]

3–23 **Mistakes and misrepresentations about the power to enter into transactions.** A number of cases have involved a mistake or misrepresentation as to a person's power to act or to enter into a transaction. It will be a question of fact if the issue is whether the person had received the grant of whatever powers are necessary to permit him to act, such as an agent's authority to act on his principal's behalf, in which the mistake is not as to the scope of an agent's powers in law, but only whether in fact he has been authorised by the alleged principal.[101] If, however, the mistake is as to whether on the basis of ascertained facts the authority is sufficient to empower the person to act or to enter into the transaction, then it will be a matter of law. On this basis statements by officers of a company that they have the power to bind the

---

Lexcourt Holdings Ltd [1978] 1 W.L.R. 1128 (representation that premises might lawfully be used as offices treated as representation of fact, apparently without argument to the contrary).

[100] *Solle v Butcher*, above, n.98, at 705. This may be the better view: the only purpose in asking whether the flat was still the same flat was to know whether it was a flat—a "dwelling house"—to which the statutes applied. *Cf. William Whiteley Ltd v R.* (1909) 101 L.T. 741 in which the question whether certain employees were "male servants" within the Revenue Act 1869 was held to be a question of law.

[101] *Beattie v Lord Ebury* (1872) L.R. 7 Ch. App. 777 at 800 (Mellish L.J., contrasting the agent's warranty of his authority, an issue of fact, with cases where the grant of the authority is clear but its legal scope is mistaken, and discussing *Cherry v Colonial Bank of Australasia* (1869) L.R. 3 P.C. 24: directors personally liable for misrepresentation to bank that their manager had power to draw cheques on company's account; implied representation that the manager's authority had been properly granted); Bowstead & Reynolds, para.9–069 (noting that, whilst the traditional view is that the warranty of authority will not be implied where the representation is one of law, the whole question of mistake of law is open to argument after the decision of HL in *Kleinwort Benson Ltd v Lincoln City Council*, below, n.103); Chitty, paras 31–101 to 31–103. However, in the cases such a situation has generally involved either the tort of deceit (fraudulent warranty of the fact that the authority has been granted) or a contractual warranty of authority, neither of which draws a formal distinction between statements of fact and statements of law.

company have been held to be misrepresentations of law.[102] Sometimes, mistakes of capacity to enter into transactions hinge on a (mistaken) interpretation of a statute, and for that reason also can be held to be mistakes of law, such as the question which has arisen in a number of recent cases as to whether a local authority has the power to enter into certain financial transactions.[103]

Interpretation of documents. One area in which the law/fact distinction appears to be rather unclear in its application is the interpretation of documents. One would expect the question of what the words of a document are to be a matter of fact, and the legal effect of those words to be a matter of law[104]; but sometimes the courts have held mistakes or misrepresentations about the effect of a document to be mistakes or misrepresentations of fact; and the distinction between what a document says, and what it means, is not always easy to draw. For example, a statement by the agent of a vendor of property that a deed of covenant relating to the land (which the purchaser had not seen) contained nothing which would interfere with the purchaser's putting the land to a particular use, was held to be a misrepresentation of fact.[105] **3–24**

---

[102] *ibid.* (obiter; *cf.* HL (1874) L.R. 7 H.L. 102); *Rashdall v Ford* (1866) L.R. 2 Eq. 750.

[103] *Kleinwort Benson Ltd v Lincoln City Council* [1999] 2 A.C. 349, HL, following the decision in *Hazell v Hammersmith and Fulham LBC* [1992] 2 A.C. 1, HL, as to the local authority's *vires* under the Local Government Act 1972, as well as its status as a council incorporated by Royal Charter; *Morgan Guaranty Trust Co. of New York v Lothian Regional Council*, 1995 S.C. 151, 1995 S.L.T. 299 (Local Government (Scotland) Act 1973). The decision in *West London Commercial Bank Ltd v Kitson* (1884) 13 Q.B.D. 360, CA, that a representation that a *private* Act of Parliament gave the company certain powers was a representation of fact, rather than a representation of law, should no longer be relied on: Treitel (11th edn, 2003), p.334.

[104] *Midland Great Western Railway of Ireland v Johnson* (1858) 6 H.L.C. 798, 10 E.R. 1509 ("construction of a contract is clearly a matter of law": Lord Chelmsford L.C. at 811, at 1514); *Ord v Ord* [1923] 2 K.B. 432 at 445–446 (mistake about meaning of the words "free of any deduction" in separation deed held mistake of law); *Rogers v Ingham* (1876) 3 Ch.D. 351, CA (construction of will); *Lewis v Jones* (1825) 4 B. & C. 506, 107 E.R. 1148 ("every man is supposed to know the legal effect of an instrument which he signs": Bayley J. at 512, at 1150).

[105] *Wauton v Coppard* [1899] 1 Ch. 92; distinguished in *Kyle Bay Ltd t/a Astons Nightclub v Underwriters Subscribing under Policy No.019057/08/01* [2007] EWCA Civ 57, [2007] 1 C.L.C. 164 at [35] (statement about the meaning of an

> "The agent was not asked by the claimant as to the construction of the deed, or on any question of law, but merely whether as a fact there were any covenants affecting the property, having regard to the purpose for which the plaintiff wanted it.[106]"

The agent's answer was based on his mistaken construction of the deed; but it was held as between the agent and the purchaser to be a representation of fact. And where purchasers of company stock sought to make the company directors liable for their misrepresentations about the stock, which they later found would not have the expected level of priority as against other stock issued by the company, there was a disagreement between the judges at first instance and in the Court of Appeal as to whether there was a representation of fact or of law. The Court of Appeal held that the purchasers' mistake was not as to what stock they were buying but as to the rights of priority that stock would give them against the company's assets: it was therefore a mistake of law.[107] Jessel M.R.,[108] however, had granted the purchasers their remedy, and had drawn attention to the difficulty of distinguishing between fact and law, and in particular that many statements are founded on assumptions or propositions of law but can none the less themselves in substance be statements of fact.

Sometimes the courts have held that, although a mistaken construction of a document is a mistake of law, it is still actionable on the basis that the mistake is as to the private rights of a party, rather than the general law.[109]

---

insurance policy was only a contention, not a misrepresentation, when made to claimant's agent who had relevant professional qualifications and experience and who had, or at least would reasonably have been taken to have, a copy of the policy).

[106] *ibid.*, at 97.

[107] *Eaglesfield v Marquis of Londonderry* (1876) 4 Ch.D. 693 at 711, 715, 717.

[108] *ibid.,* at 702–703. The CA in that case did not comment on Jessel M.R.'s analysis.

[109] *Earl Beauchamp v Winn* (1873) L.R. 6 H.L. 223, HL; *Daniell v Sinclair* (1881) 6 App. Cas. 181, PC; *Anglo-Scottish Beet Sugar Corp. Ltd v Spalding Urban DC* [1937] 2 K.B. 607 at 615–616 (parties making payments due under terms of original contract rather than varied terms of which they were unaware because those responsible in their respective organisations had not informed them of the variation; but this might as easily have been characterised as a mistake of fact); *cf. Cooper v Phibbs*, below, para.3–25.

A representation about the validity of a document to achieve a particular legal transaction will be a representation of law—such as the statement by an agent selling an insurance policy that the purchaser will acquire a valid policy, when a rule of law prevents it being valid for lack of insurable interest.[110]

A misrepresentation about the contents or meaning of a document which is made with a view to inducing a person to enter into a transaction must be distinguished from a misrepresentation, made before the document is executed, about the effect which that same document will have once executed. Then the issue is not one of misrepresentation as such, but of the scope of the legal obligations to which the person has agreed. The courts have found little difficulty in holding that such representations result in the signatory being bound only to the misrepresented terms, or to terms which have the legal effect that the representor promised they would have rather than the effect which the document by its language, strictly construed, imports.[111]

---

[110] *British Workman's and General Assurance Co. v Cunliffe* (1902) 18 T.L.R. 502, CA (fraudulent misrepresentation, although the headnote to the report suggests otherwise); *Harse v Pearl Life Assurance Co.* [1904] 1 K.B. 558, CA (innocent misrepresentation); *Hughes v Liverpool Victoria Legal Friendly Society* [1916] 2 K.B. 482, CA (fraudulent misrepresentation).

[111] *Hirschfeld v The London, Brighton and South Coast Railway Co.* (1876) 2 Q.B. 1 (fraudulent misrepresentation about legal effect of deed of release: obiter, and the law/fact distinction was argued but not applied by the court; it is not clear whether this was because the statement was fraudulent (which overrides the law/fact distinction: below, para.3–33) or because the distinction is irrelevant in the case of pre-contractual misrepresentations about the scope of that same contract); *Curtis v Cleaning and Dyeing Co.* [1951] 1 K.B. 805, CA (innocent misrepresentation about meaning of exemption clause: but on the interpretation of this case *cf. AXA Sun Life Services Plc v Harry Bennett & Associates Ltd* [2011] EWCA Civ 133 at [105]); *Horry v Tate & Lyle Refineries Ltd* [1982] 2 Lloyd's Rep. 416 (obiter; innocent misrepresentation about legal effect of contract settling claim against insurers). The law/fact distinction was not properly taken in either *Curtis* or *Horry*. *Cf. City and Westminster Properties (1934) Ltd v Mudd* [1959] Ch. 129 (collateral contract to give effect to landlord's pre-contractual representation about terms of the lease); *Vadasz v Pioneer Concrete (SA) Pty Ltd* (1995) 184 C.L.R. 102, HCA, below, para.4–13 (rescission of part to enable contract to be left with effect as represented). For the potential conflict of these cases with the parol evidence rule: see Treitel, paras 6–013 to 6–030, esp. paras 6–017, 6–029. The court will not correct a mistake as to legal effect by construction, but may sometimes rectify the contract: Lewison, para.9.03; below, para.13–42, n.169.

3–25 **Mistake or misrepresentation of "private rights".** Sometimes the courts have characterised what appears at first sight to be a mistake or misrepresentation of law as one of fact, on the basis that the rule applies only to issues of general law, and so mistakes or misrepresentations of private rights are to be treated as issues of fact for this purpose. The origins of this distinction are contained in the speech of Lord Westbury in *Cooper v Phibbs*, a case in which it was held that the question of the ownership of property of which the claimant took a lease, but which was found to belong to him already, was one of fact because the issue of his rights of ownership was one of his private rights. Lord Westbury said[112]:

> "It is said, '*Ignorantia juris haud excusat*;' but in that maxim the word '*jus*' is used in the sense of denoting general law, the ordinary law of the country. But when the word '*jus*' is used in the sense of denoting a private right, that maxim has no application. Private right of ownership is a matter of fact; it may be the result also of matter of law; but if parties contract under a mutual mistake and misapprehension as to their relative and respective rights, the result is, that that agreement is liable to be set aside as having proceeded upon a common mistake. Now, that was the case with these parties—the Respondents believed themselves to be entitled to the property, the Petitioner believed that he was a stranger to it, the mistake is discovered, and the agreement cannot stand."

---

[112] (1867) L.R. 2 H.L. 149, HL, at 170. In *Cooper* the mistake about ownership derived from an ambiguous statement in a private Act of Parliament: see at 162–164 (Lord Cranworth). However, although there is old authority that a mistake about a private Act is to be treated as one of fact rather than law (*West London Commercial Bank Ltd v Kitson*, above, n.103) this is not the basis of the decision in *Cooper*. For examples of other applications of Lord Westbury's distinction, see *Earl Beauchamp v Winn*, above, n.109 at 234 (mistake over construction of deed of grant); *Daniell v Sinclair*, above, n.109 (mistaken construction of mortgage deed); *Anglo-Scottish Beet Sugar Corp Ltd v Spalding Urban DC*, above, n.109 at 615–616 (mistake as to varied contract); *Solle v Butcher* [1950] 1 K.B. 671, CA, at 693–694 ("mistake" for equitable jurisdiction to rescind includes mistakes of fact and mistakes of private rights); *Nutt v Read* (2000) 32 H.L.R. 761, CA (common misapprehension that a wooden chalet could in law be let separately from the caravan site pitch on which it stood: consequential misapprehension "that a letting of [the] pitch did not include a letting of anything which could be described as a dwelling-house, so as to bring the letting within the Housing Act 1988 . . . all parties were hopelessly at sea about the true effect in law of their proposed transaction": Chadwick L.J. at 768). Cases which applied the independent equitable jurisdiction to rescind for mistake, set out by Denning L.J. in *Solle v Butcher*, must now be read in the light of its disapproval in *The Great Peace* [2002] EWCA Civ 1407, [2003] Q.B. 679, below, para.15–32.

The distinction between law and fact in this context can sometimes be quite difficult to draw. As Jessel M.R. pointed out in *Eaglesfield v Marquis of Londonderry*,[113] many statements about an individual and his circumstances are statements of fact, although they involve also questions of law:

> "It is not the less a fact because that fact involves some knowledge or relation of law. There is hardly any fact which does not involve it. If you state that a man is in possession of an estate of £10,000 a year, the notion of possession is a legal notion, and involves knowledge of law; nor can any other fact in connection with property be stated which does not involve such knowledge of law. To state that a man is entitled to £10,000 Consols involves all sorts of law."

The principle stated in relation to mistake in *Cooper v Phibbs* has been applied also to misrepresentations characterised as statements of "private rights" rather than of the general law.[114]

Mistakes and misrepresentations about available remedies. 3–26
A mistake or misrepresentation about the availability of a particular legal remedy will generally be held to be one of law—such as the belief (induced by incorrect advice from his lawyer) on the part of a person paying a disputed sum that the overpayment would be recoverable if it should later be found not to be due.[115] Or the mistaken belief of an insurer that, on the established facts, he had no right to repudiate the policy for non-disclosure and so to resist

[113] (1876) 4 Ch.D. 693 at 702–703; his decision on the facts of the case was reversed by the Court of Appeal: above, n.107.

[114] *André & Cie S.A. v Ets Michel Blanc & Fils* [1979] 2 Lloyd's Rep. 427, CA, at 431, 432; however, at 434 Geoffrey Lane L.J. disagreed that the representation in the case could be characterised as one of private rights, which highlights the difficulty sometimes in drawing the distinction. There is a view that *Cooper v Phibbs* is an illustration of a particular tendency of the former courts of equity to be more disposed to grant remedies for mistakes which the courts of common law would have characterised as mistakes of law and therefore not remedied: *Daniell v Sinclair* (1881) 6 App.Cas. 181, PC, at 190–191; Law Com. No.227, *Restitution: Mistakes of Law and Ultra Vires Public Authority Receipts and Payments* (1994), para.2.13. But this is not how the Court of Appeal viewed it in *André v Michel Blanc*. See also P.H. Winfield, "Mistake of Law" (1943) 59 L.Q.R. 327 at p.339, concluding that the *Cooper v Phibbs* principle is applicable at both common law and equity, although the nomenclature used by the courts varies.

[115] *Nurdin & Peacock Plc v D.B. Ramsden & Co. Ltd* [1999] 1 W.L.R. 1249.

payment under the policy.[116] If, however, the mistake about the remedy flows from a correct application of the law but an incorrect assumption of the relevant underlying facts, the mistake will be characterised as one of fact, such as where an insurer pays a claim under a policy forgetting that the insured has failed to make the latest payment of premium.[117]

3–27 **Foreign law.** It has long been held that questions of foreign law are to be treated as questions of fact within an English court for the purposes of procedure and evidence:

> "the Judge cannot look it up for himself in the books or take judicial notice of what he already knows; there must be proof of foreign law by a qualified witness.[118]"

This was also applied by the Court of Appeal in the context of misrepresentation in *André & Cie S.A. v Ets Michel Blanc & Fils*. Lord Denning M.R.[119] criticised the misrepresentation of law rule in

[116] *Bilbie v Lumley* (1802) 2 East 469, 102 E.R. 448. *Cf. Brisbane v Dacres* (1813) 5 Taunt. 143, 128 E.R. 641 (mistaken belief by ship's captain that he had a legal obligation to make payment to commanding admiral of freight charges on treasure he carried).

[117] *Kelly v Solari* (1841) 9 M. & W. 54, 152 E.R. 24. The contrast between this case and *Bilbie v Lumley* has been cited as an illustration of the unsatisfactory distinction between mistakes of law and mistakes of fact: *Kleinwort Benson Ltd v Lincoln City Council* [1999] 2 A.C. 349, HL, at 372.

[118] *Furness Withy (Australia) Pty Ltd v Metal Distributors (UK) Ltd (The Amazonia)* [1990] 1 Lloyd's Rep. 236, CA, at 245 (Staughton L.J.). At first instance Gatehouse J. had refused to hold that the mistake was to be treated as one of fact, on the basis that "As a matter of procedure, of course, the proof of foreign law is a question of fact, but that is simply an evidentiary requirement, it does not undermine the nature of the mutual mistake": [1989] 1 Lloyd's Rep. 403 at 408. *Lazard Brothers & Co. v Midland Bank Ltd* [1933] A.C. 289, HL, at 297–298. The treatment of foreign law as fact is pragmatic: it is still a matter for the judge rather than being a "jury issue"; and sometimes a decision on a foreign law in civil proceedings can be binding in future cases: Civil Evidence Act 1972, s.4(2); CPR, Pt 33, r.33.7; Phipson, paras 1–36, 1–42; Lord Collins of Mapesbury (ed.), *Dicey, Morris and Collins, The Conflict of Laws* (14th edn, 2010), Ch.9. The law of the EU is not foreign law for this purpose: Phipson, para.1–42.

[119] [1979] 2 Lloyd's Rep. 427 at 430–431. He would also have held that the misrepresentation was one of fact on the basis that it was a representation as to private rights, following *Cooper v Phibbs*, above, para.3–25, which was the basis on which Lawton L.J. rested his judgment. Geoffrey Lane L.J. at 434 also took the view that a misrepresentation of foreign law is to be treated as one of fact.

general terms, but, on the basis that the rule was still binding, he characterised the misrepresentation in the case (a misrepresentation of the law in the US) as a misrepresentation of fact for the purposes of the claim for rescission and damages under section 2(1) of the Misrepresentation Act 1967. Given its origin in the rules of evidence of the English courts it is has been held that the rule, even when applied to mistake and misrepresentation in contract, is one relating to law which is foreign to the *forum*. It is not a question of whether the law is foreign to one or both of the *parties*, and therefore there can be no argument that the purpose of the rule is to protect only those parties who (by being foreign to the legal system whose rules are in issue) do not have access to the legal rules of which they are mistaken or which are misrepresented to them.[120]

(c) *The origins and rationale of the distinction*[121]

"Ignorance of the law is no excuse". The rule denying liability for mistake and misrepresentation of law is sometimes stated in the form of the maxim "ignorance of the law is no excuse". This maxim was used in other contexts before the law/fact distinction was first developed for mistake and misrepresentation in contract and restitution. In particular, it was applied in the context of criminal law to make clear that liability did not depend on the defendant's knowledge that his acts constituted a crime.[122] But it was also used in the case which is generally regarded as the origin of the modern **3–28**

[120] *Furness Withy (Australia) Pty Ltd v Metal Distributors (UK) Ltd (The Amazonia)*, above, n.118 at 245 (mistake of Australian law held to be treated as fact in the English court, even where one party was Australian). In *André & Cie S.A. v Ets Michel Blanc & Fils* the parties were Swiss and French and the misrepresentation was as to US law, so this issue was not addressed.

[121] For discussion of the history of the "mistake of law" rule, and criticism of the rule, see the judgments of Lord Goff in *Woolwich Equitable Building Society v I.R.C.* [1993] A.C. 70, HL, at 164 and *Kleinwort Benson Ltd v Lincoln City Council* [1999] 2 A.C. 349, HL, at 367–372; Law Com. No.227, above, n.114, pp.9–11, 29–33; P. Birks, "Mistakes of Law" (2000) 53 C.L.P. 205 at pp.210–216.

[122] Hale, *History of the Pleas of the Crown*, Pt I, Ch.6; *Table-Talk of John Selden* (2nd edn, 1696), p.89. But it was also used in other contexts: see *Brett v Rigden* (1568) 1 Pl. Com. 340 at 342, 75 E.R. 516 at 520 (will to be interpreted on assumption that testator knew the law); *Manser's Case* (1584) 2 Co. Rep. 3a at 3b (misinterpretation of legal effect of documents). The "mistake of law" rule was also established in Roman law: D.22.6 (esp. Paul, at D.22.6.9), but see P. Birks, "Mistakes of Law", above, n.121 at p.214.

rule denying restitution of money paid under a mistake of law: *Bilbie v Lumley*,[123] which was decided in 1802 and was followed in later cases,[124] and soon became accepted as a general rule. It has been argued that the rule, based originally on the maxim "ignorance of the law . . .", is an accident and was an unfortunate development in the law of restitution and contract.[125] It is certainly inadequate to rest such a general rule on a maxim which belongs in another context,[126] and which says nothing about the policy reasons for drawing the distinction between mistakes (and misrepresentations) of fact and law. However, other justifications have also been cited for the rule, which show that there are real concerns about whether there might not be some inherent difference between mistakes of law and mistakes of fact which calls for caution to be exercised in granting remedies for mistakes of law.

---

[123] (1802) 2 East 469 at 472, 102 E.R. 448 at 449–450 (Lord Ellenborough, following an obiter dictum of Buller J. in *Lowry v Bourdieu* (1780) 2 Dougl. 468 at 471, 99 E.R. 299 at 300).

[124] Especially *Brisbane v Dacres* (1813) 5 Taunt. 143, 128 E.R. 641; *Kelly v Solari* (1841) 9 M. & W. 54, 152 E.R. 24. In *Wilson & McLellan v Sinclair* 1830 4 Wils. & S. 398 at 409 the House of Lords applied *Brisbane v Dacres* in Scottish law.

[125] Lord Wright of Durley, *Legal Essays and Addresses* (1939), p.xix; *Hydro Electric Commission of Township of Nepean v Ontario Hydro* (1982) 132 D.L.R. (3d) 193, SCC, at 201–211. But such criticism is probably too harsh; although there is evidence from 18th century cases that no distinction was drawn between mistakes of fact and of law for the purpose of the action for money had and received, it is likely that there was also a growing belief that the fact that a payment had been made under a mistake of law should render it irrecoverable: *Kleinwort Benson Ltd v Lincoln City Council* [1999] 2 A.C. 349, HL, at 371–372 (Lord Goff), 405–406 (Lord Hope of Craighead, giving examples of the use of the maxim in argument in civil law cases). For the final rejection of the rule, and the overruling of *Bilbie v Lumley*, see below, para.3–34.

[126] It has been said that the maxim belongs in contexts, such as the criminal law, where the defendant is accused of wrongdoing and seeks to escape responsibility by his ignorance of the law: see discussion by Lord Goff in *Kleinwort Benson Ltd v Lincoln City Council*, above, n.125 at 371; *Morgan Guaranty Trust Co.of New York v Lothian Regional Council* 1995 S.C. 151 at 164, 1995 S.L.T. 299 at 315 (Lord President Hope); *Lansdown v Lansdown* (1730) Mos. 364, 25 E.R. 441 (King L.C., quoted and applied by Denning L.J. in *Solle v Butcher* [1950] 1 K.B. 671, CA, at 693); *Hydro Electric Commission of Township of Nepean v Ontario Hydro*, above, n.125 at 204.

Equal access to the law. Lord Ellenborough in *Bilbie v Lumley*[127] thought that "every man must be taken to be cognizant of the law": that is, a presumption that everyone knows the law. But this is nothing more than a fiction which simply restates the general proposition that no one can plead mistake of law. When used in a contractual context, it is based on the supposition that both parties have equal access to the law, and so both can have equal knowledge of it.[128] This idea has been used to justify the rule[129] but cases have also recognised that parties do not in fact know the law.[130] It is unrealistic to expect every contracting party to be fully and accurately informed of every relevant question of law. The quantity and complexity of primary and secondary legislation speak against it[131]—to say nothing of the difficulties for the parties of answering with certainty questions of interpretation of statute and common law, particularly when the parties can be held to have been under a mistake of law because of a later judicial decision which has retrospective effect in changing the understanding of the law which was settled at the time the mistake was made.[132] It should also be noticed that, even if (contrary to what has already been said) the argument of equal access to the law might be thought to have some merit in the context of mistake on the basis that each party should take responsibility for checking his own assumptions about the law, such a justification of the rule should not be read across unthinkingly into misrepresentation, where one party has taken it upon himself to state a point of law relevant to the transaction.[133] 3–29

---

[127] Above, n.123 at 472, at 449.

[128] *André & Cie S.A. v Ets Michel Blanc & Fils* [1979] 2 Lloyd's Rep. 427, CA, at 431.

[129] *Rashdall v Ford* (1866) L.R. 2 Eq. 750 at 754–755.

[130] *West London Commercial Bank Ltd v Kitson* (1884) 13 Q.B.D. 360, CA, at 362; *Evans v Bartlam* [1937] A.C. 473, HL, at 479 (Lord Atkin: "I am not prepared to accept the view that there is in law any presumption that any one, even a judge, knows all the rules and orders of the Supreme Court"); *Kiriri Cotton Co. Ltd v Dewani* [1960] A.C. 192, PC, at 204.

[131] *Woolwich Equitable Building Society v I.R.C.* [1993] A.C. 70, HL, at 192; M. Furmston, "Ignorance of the law" (1981) 1 L.S. 37.

[132] *Kleinwort Benson Ltd v Lincoln City Council*, above, n.125 (Lord Browne-Wilkinson and Lord Lloyd dissenting on the question of whether there is in such cases a "mistake"); above, para.3–10.

[133] On this fundamental distinction between mistake and misrepresentation, see above, para.1–03; below, para.16–03; Cartwright, Ch.11.

3–30 **Security of transactions.** Another argument sometimes put in favour of the mistake and misrepresentation of law rule is based on the security of transactions. To allow remedies for mistake and misrepresentation of law would undermine transactions because it is too easy to make—or, at least, to claim to have made—such a mistake. This idea is of course in direct conflict with the alleged rationale that everyone can be presumed to know the law. But it is also contained in Lord Ellenborough's judgment in *Bilbie v Lumley*[134]: "Every man must be taken to be cognizant of the law; otherwise there is no saying to what extent the excuse of ignorance might not be carried. It would be urged in almost every case." This argument has particular force in relation to the *mistake* of law rule. Within the law of mistake in contract it is often said that there is a general policy, based on security of transactions, in favour of restricting remedies.[135] And although there is a wider recovery in restitution on the basis of mistake, it has been said in that context that allowing mistakes of law could be a particular threat to the security of transactions.[136] But a claim based on the other party's misrepresentation is treated within contract as quite different from mistake, and the objections based on security of contract fall away once the source of the mistake is the other party—who by his misrepresentation can be treated as having forfeited the right to the argument based on security of contract. Any reluctance, based on the argument of security of transactions, to grant remedies for misrepresentation of law therefore also ought to be significantly less strong than in the case of mistake of law.[137]

---

[134] Above, n.123 at 472, at 449–450. See also *Table-Talk of John Selden* (2nd edn, 1696), p.89: "Ignorance of the Law excuses no man; not that all Men know the Law, but because 'tis an excuse every Man will plead, and no man can tell how to confute him."

[135] See particularly *Bell v Lever Bros Ltd* [1932] A.C. 161, HL, at 224; *Associated Japanese Bank (International) Ltd v Crédit du Nord S.A.* [1989] 1 W.L.R. 255 at 264–265, 268; *Tamplin v James* (1880) 15 Ch.D. 215, CA, at 220–221; and see generally below, paras 12–12 to 12–15.

[136] *Rogers v Ingham* (1876) 3 Ch.D. 351, CA, at 356–357. The argument was discussed by Lord Goff in *Kleinwort Benson Ltd v Lincoln City Council*, above, n.125 at 371. Birks at first adopted this position: *Introduction to the Law of Restitution* (Oxford University Press, 1985, revised 1989), p.166, but later recanted: (2000) 53 C.L.P. 205 at p.216.

[137] Chitty, para.6–013, n.61.

Law as opinion. It is sometimes said that the rule that a false statement of law cannot be an actionable misrepresentation is a sub-species of the rule that statements of opinion are not to be treated as "misrepresentations": unlike fact, law is not something which can be stated with certainty; a statement of law is essentially the speaker's own assessment, or opinion, of what the law would say on the matter. **3–31**

> "He who expresses his views on law to another is in the same position as one who expresses his views on any other question of science, art, or business, and the inquiry as to whether, and to what extent, his statement is a representation is governed by the same considerations.[138]"

In the case of some statements of law this may well be a useful way to consider the issue, but not in all cases,[139] and although there are a few references in the cases[140] to this as an underlying reason for distinguishing law from fact, it is not the way that the courts in England which have applied the rule appear generally to have viewed it.

Action on a mistake or misrepresentation of law as "voluntary". **3–32**
Sometimes it has been said that a person who acts on a mistake or misrepresentation of law has no remedy because his action is "voluntary". This language, which was particularly common in the context of claims for restitution of payments under a mistake of law, is unfortunate. It may simply be a tautology, meaning no more than that no remedy should be granted for the mistake: that is, the mistake of law rule bars recovery, and for that reason the payment can be said to have been "voluntary".[141] But if it means that, knowing the facts but realising that there might be some inherent uncertainty about the law, the payor decides to accept the risk of whether his belief about the law is accurate rather than testing it in the courts, then it is simply an application of a more general

---

[138] Spencer Bower (Misrepresentation), para.36. See also Cheshire, Fifoot and Furmston, p.335; Allen, p.15; Chitty, para.6–013.
[139] Below, para.3–40.
[140] *Beattie v Lord Ebury* (1872) L.R. 7 Ch.App. 777 at 802; *Stewart Brothers v Kiddie* 1899 S.L.T. 92; *Solle v Butcher* [1950] 1 K.B. 671, CA, at 703.
[141] Birks, *Introduction to the Law of Restitution*, above, n.136, p.164. For an example of this usage see *Woolwich Equitable Building Society v I.R.C.* [1993] A.C. 70, HL, at 165.

principle which also underlies the rule that a compromise cannot be re-opened.[142] In either case, it is not a satisfactory explanation of the mistake of law rule, but is better used in the second sense described, as a general proposition which applies to any transaction entered into by a person who takes a risk as to some matter: it is not peculiar to the law/fact distinction.[143]

3–33 **Exceptions to the mistake of law rule: fraud and parties not in pari delicto.** Even before the House of Lords removed the law/fact distinction in the *Kleinwort Benson* case, it was not true that a mistake or misrepresentation of law could not found remedies in contract or restitution. The "mistake of law" rule is more accurately stated in terms that a mistake of law *of itself* does not give rise to a remedy; something more is required. It has sometimes been said that where there is a mistake or misrepresentation of law, the parties are to be treated as *in pari delicto*—equally at fault as regards the mistake—and so neither can plead it against the other unless there is something which displaces that equality between the parties. So if in the circumstances in which the mistake is made one party has a duty towards the other to protect him, the "protected" party may be able to rely on his mistake for a remedy, even if the mistake is one of law. Examples are where the other party has a statutory duty to ensure that the relevant rule of law is given effect,[144] or where he has fiduciary duties towards the "protected" party.[145] There is also a consistent line of authority that if the

---

[142] For an example of this approach, see *Rogers v Ingham*, above, n.136 at 358. In *Bilbie v Lumley*, above, n.123 at 470, at 449, Lord Ellenborough also referred to a person making payment under a mistake of law "voluntarily with a full knowledge of all the facts of the case" but claiming recovery "on account of his ignorance of the law" and it has been argued that he intended to lay down only a narrow rule that voluntary submission to a claim is binding on the payer: Law Com. No.227, below, n.158, para.2.4.

[143] *cf. Kelly v Solari* (1841) 9 M. & W. 54 at 59, 152 E.R. 24 at 26, where Parke B. applied the same rule to mistakes of fact.

[144] *Kiriri Cotton Co. Ltd v Dewani* [1960] A.C. 192, PC; *Re Cavalier Insurance Co. Ltd* [1989] 2 Lloyd's Rep. 430 at 450.

[145] *Rogers v Ingham*, above, n.136 at 355–356. *Cf. Ministry of Health v Simpson* [1951] A.C. 251, HL (persons entitled to distribution of property from deceased's estate have right, after exhausting claim against personal representatives, to claim directly against those to whom the personal representatives have by mistake wrongly distributed the estate: an equitable rule, which operates regardless of whether the personal representatives' mistake was of law or fact. The rule

mistake of law is induced by the other party's fraudulent misrepresentation, the fraud overrides whatever the policy grounds may be for the reluctance to grant remedies for mistakes of law[146]; and this is sometimes also said to be an example of the principle that the misrepresentation of law rule is displaced when the parties are not *in pari delicto*.[147]

The idea that the equality of the parties is disturbed by a fraudulent misrepresentation is significant. There are statements in the cases[148] which could have led the courts to the view that any misrepresentation of law is enough to displace the "mistake of law" rule; that is, the party who takes it upon himself to make a (false) statement of law deprives himself of relying on the mistake of law

---

pre-dates *Bibie v Lumley*: at 270); *Gibbon v Mitchell* [1990] 1 W.L.R. 1304 at 1310 (voluntary transaction can be set aside where it did not have the legal effect the disponor intended: no bar to rescission on the basis that the disponor acted under mistake of law, because the disposition was gratuitous, and equity would intervene where those who would benefit from the mistaken disposition "could not conscionably insist upon their legal rights under the deed"; further explained in *Pitt v Holt* [2011] EWCA Civ 197, [2011] 2 All E.R. 450 at [186]–[188], [204]–[210]).

[146] See, e.g. *Rashdall v Ford* (1866) L.R. 2 Eq. 750 at 754 (no remedy because innocent misrepresentation of law); *Hirschfeld v The London, Brighton and South Coast Railway Co.* (1876) 2 Q.B.D. 1 (fraudulent misrepresentation as to effect of deed of release; but see above, para.3–24, n.111); *British Workman's and General Assurance Co. Ltd v Cunliffe* (1902) 18 T.L.R. 502, CA (fraudulent misrepresentation of validity of insurance policy, although the headnote to the report is misleading: premiums recovered); *Harse v Pearl Life Assurance Co.* [1904] 1 K.B. 558, CA (innocent misrepresentation of validity of insurance policy: no recovery of premiums); *Hughes v Liverpool Victoria Legal Friendly Society* [1916] 2 K.B. 482, CA (fraudulent misrepresentation of validity of insurance policy: premiums recovered); *André & Cie S.A. v Ets Michel Blanc & Fils* [1979] 2 Lloyd's Rep. 427, CA, at 434. In criminal law, a "deception" within Theft Act 1968, ss.15, 16 could be as to fact or as to law: ss. 15(4), 16(3); now repealed and replaced by Fraud Act 2006, s.2(3) ("'representation' means any representation as to fact or law . . .").

[147] *Hughes v Liverpool Victoria Legal Friendly Society*, above, n.146 at 488, 492, 496; *Harse v Pearl Life Assurance Co.*, above, n.146 at 563, 564.

[148] See especially *Kiriri Cotton Co. Ltd v Dewani*, above, n.144 at 204: "If there is something more in addition to a mistake of law—if there is something in the defendant's conduct which shows that, of the two of them, he is the one primarily responsible for the mistake—[the payment] may be recovered back . . . [I]f the responsibility for the mistake lies more on the one than the other—because he has misled the other when he ought to know better—then again they are not in pari delicto and the money can be recovered back."

rule to resist the other party's claim to a remedy, just as a false statement of fact, even one made innocently, overrides the reluctance within the law of contract to grant remedies for mistakes of fact.[149] This argument supports the view that, if the mistake of law rule has for good reasons been abolished in contract, *a fortiori* the misrepresentation of law rule cannot survive.[150]

(d) Rejection of the "mistake of law" rule in restitution, and the law/fact distinction in other jurisdictions

3–34 **Rejection by the House of Lords of the "mistake of law" rule in restitution.** In *Kleinwort Benson Ltd v Lincoln City Council*[151] the House of Lords unanimously rejected the "mistake of law" rule in the context of restitution. The detail of the case does not concern us here, beyond noting that it was a claim for restitution of money paid by a bank to local authorities under the terms of interest rate swap contracts which were found to have been *ultra vires* the local authority and therefore void. The issue was therefore one of restitution, not contract; and the question was whether it was a bar to the bank's recovery that it had paid the money under a mistake of law (the mistake that the contracts were valid, rather than *ultra vires* the local authority). The most detailed discussion of the arguments is contained in the speech of Lord Goff,[152] who considered the history of the "mistake of law" rule, criticisms of it and its rejection in other jurisdictions, and proposed that the House should hold

---

[149] Above, para.1–03; below, para.15–08.

[150] Below, para.3–37.

[151] [1999] 2 A.C. 349. Lord Browne-Wilkinson and Lord Lloyd dissented on the question of whether there was a mistake at the time of payment (when the payment was made it was believed to be valid in law; the House of Lords later held in another similar case that it was unlawful and the majority in *Kleinwort Benson* held that the effect of that later judgment was retrospective to a time which included the time of the disputed payment).

[152] *ibid.*, at 367–375. The other main discussion is in the speech of Lord Hope at 405–407 discussing similarly issues of history, principle and comparative law and concluding (at 405) that "the mistake of law rule should no longer form part of English law". The other speeches (Lord Browne-Wilkinson, Lord Lloyd and Lord Hoffmann) concentrated on the question of whether there was a mistake at all (above, n.151), but agreed with Lord Goff on the rejection of the "mistake of law" rule.

> "that the mistake of law rule no longer forms part of English law ... English law should now recognise that there is a general right to recover money paid under a mistake, whether of fact or law, subject to the defences available in the law of restitution."

The result of this case, therefore, is that there is no longer a formal distinction drawn within the law of restitution between mistakes of fact and mistakes of law: the remedies (such as restitution of mistaken payments in an action for money had and received) flow from the *mistake*, not the mistake being one of fact.

Rejection of the law/fact distinction in restitution in other jurisdictions. The House of Lords in *Kleinwort Benson* was following a trend in other common law (and mixed) jurisdictions. Indeed, three years earlier the Court of Session had already taken the step for Scotland in a similar case.[153] The courts of Canada,[154] Australia[155] and South Africa[156] had also recently rejected the "mistake of law" rule; in New Zealand the rule had been abolished by statute as long ago as 1958.[157] And there had already been a proposal from the Law Commission in England to abrogate by statute the "mistake of law" rule in restitution.[158] 3–35

The law/fact distinction in contract. These reversals of the "mistake of law" rule were all in the particular context of the law of restitution, and have generally been made without even a hint from 3–36

---

153 *Morgan Guaranty Trust Co. of New York v Lothian Regional Council*, 1995 S.C. 151, 1995 S.L.T. 299, another case involving an *ultra vires* interest rate swap contract. The leading judgment was given by the Lord President—Lord Hope, who referred back to his own speech when he sat in the House of Lords in *Kleinwort Benson*.

154 *Air Canada v British Columbia* (1989) 59 D.L.R. (4th) 161, SCC, following an influential earlier dissenting judgment in *Hydro Electric Commission of Township of Nepean v Ontario Hydro* (1982) 132 D.L.R. (3d) 193, SCC, at 195–219.

155 *David Securities Pty Ltd v Commonwealth Bank of Australia* (1992) 175 C.L.R. 353, HCA.

156 *Willis Faber Enthoven (Pty) Ltd v Receiver of Revenue*, 1992 (4) S.A. 202.

157 Judicature Act 1908 (New Zealand), s.94A and B, inserted by the Judicature Amendment Act 1958, s.2.

158 Law Com. No.227, *Restitution: Mistakes of Law and Ultra Vires Public Authority Receipts and Payments* (1994). The Report, which contained a draft Bill, had been accepted by the Government but no date had been set for the introduction into Parliament of a Bill to implement it.

the judges as to whether there ought to be a consequential reform within the law of contract. In *Kleinwort Benson* the House of Lords spoke only of the rules of restitution, and based the whole reasoning for the reversal of the "mistake of law" rule on the internal logic of the developing principles of restitution.[159] And the courts in other jurisdictions which have reversed the "mistake of law" rule in restitution have also similarly failed to say whether their decisions might have any implications for the rules within contract.[160] However, these reforms within the law of restitution have formed a trigger for consequential developments in the law of contract, which would be consistent with the approach in other modern systems. The law/fact distinction in contract is not a distinction drawn in most modern civil systems,[161] nor in international restatements of law such as the Unidroit Principles,[162] the Principles of European Contract Law[163] or the Draft Common Frame of Reference.[164] Academic writers in Australia[165] suggested that the fact/law distinction should be reconsidered in contract, and this has been

[159] See especially [1999] 2 A.C. 349, HL, at 373 (Lord Goff: the impetus for the reform of the mistake of law rule in restitution flows from "the combined effect of two fundamental changes in the law: first, recognition that there exists a coherent law of restitution founded upon the principle of unjust enrichment, and second, within that body of law, recognition of the defence of change of position").

[160] See cases cited above, nn.154, 155, 156.

[161] K. Zweigert and H. Kötz, *An Introduction to Comparative Law* (3rd edn, trans. T. Weir, 1998), p.568 (in the context of the claim in restitution). The authors regard the common law rule as "remarkable": p.567. See also J. Ghestin, *Traité de droit civil, La formation ducontrat* (3rd edn, L.G.D.J., Paris, 1993), para.505; R. Rodière (ed.), *Les vices du consentement dans le contrat* (A. Pedone, Paris, 1977), paras 49, 69, 92, 108, 127 and 167.

[162] International Institute for the Unification of Private Law, *Principles of International Commercial Contracts* (3rd edn, UNIDROIT, Rome, 2010), Art.3.2.1.

[163] Lando and Beale, para.4.103.

[164] C. von Bar and E. Clive (eds), *Principles, Definitions and Model Rules of European Private Law: Draft Common Frame of Reference (DCFR), Full Edition* (Sellier, Munich, 2009), II.–7:201(1). The "Feasibility study for a future instrument in European Contract Law" (May 2011), developed from the Draft Frame of Reference by the Commission Expert Group on European Contract Law (above, para.1.05, n.16) provides in art.45(1) that a party "may avoid a contract for mistake of fact or law . . .".

[165] B. Sangha, "The Law/Fact Distinction in Contract: A Lawyer's Plaything?" (1994) 7 J.C.L. 113 (a valuable discussion although the conclusion, which favours the use of the doctrine of unconscionability, is peculiar to Australian

adopted by the New South Wales Supreme Court.[166] Canadian[167] and Scottish[168] writers have also supported a similar change. In New Zealand, where this area is governed by statute, there is no law/fact distinction in mistake in contract, although "misrepresentation" for the purposes of the statutory provisions is not defined and retains its common law meaning—including, therefore, the common law distinction between fact and law.[169]

In England, the Law Commission in its consideration of the mistake of law rule in restitution had expressly disclaimed any intention to deal with contractual issues, on the basis that contracts raise further issues such as sanctity of contract and re-allocation of contractual risk, which do not arise in restitution.[170] However, the courts have taken it as self-evident that the developments in restitution should be read across into the law of contract. In

---

law); Carter, Peden and Tolhurst, paras 18–10 (misrepresentation of law might be just opinion) and 20–09 (mistake); Seddon and Ellinghaus, paras 11.13 (misrepresentation) and 12.8 (mistake).

[166] *Clasic International Pty Ltd v Lagos* [2002] NSWSC 1155 at [43], adopting Seddon and Ellinghaus (8th edn, 2002, para.12.8; above, n.165) (mistake of law).

[167] Waddams, paras 393 and 421 (misrepresentation); Swann, p.572 (mistake); Fridman, p.259 (mistake). These authors cite the *Air Canada* case, above, n.154, as authority that the law/fact distinction has already been abolished in relation to mistake. The Ontario Law Reform Commission in its *Report on Amendment of the Law of Contract* (1987) proposed statutory abolition of the law/fact distinction within misrepresentation (p.242) and mistake (p.259).

[168] D.M. Walker, *The Law of Contracts and Related Obligations in Scotland* (3rd edn, 1995), writing before the decision in the *Morgan Guaranty* case, above, n.153, approved retention of the mistake of law rule for mistake in contract (para.14.49) but suggested that misrepresentations of law should be actionable (para.14.113). *The Stair Memorial Encyclopaedia, The Laws of Scotland* (Vol. 15, 1996) only addresses the issue in the context of restitution, in the light of the *Morgan Guaranty* case, and does not consider whether there might be any change to the mistake and misrepresentation of law rule in contract: see paras 17 to 26, 681. M. Hogg, *Obligations* (2nd edn, 2006), para.3.38 and H.L. MacQueen and J. Thomson, *Contract Law in Scotland* (2000), para.4.59 (but *cf.* para.4.60) still assumed that a misrepresentation must be of fact, not law.

[169] Burrows, Finn & Todd, para.11.2.1. The remedies for misrepresentation are contained in the Contractual Remedies Act 1979, ss.6, 7 (damages and cancellation of contract for misrepresentation). *Cf.*, on mistake, the Contractual Mistakes Act 1977, s.2 (mistake is of fact *or law*, although relief based on the mistaken interpretation of a contract is then expressly excluded by s.6(2)).

[170] Law Com. No.227, above, n.158, para.1.11. The Law Commission did not even mention the *misrepresentation* of law rule in contract.

Brennan v Bolt Burdon,[171] which concerned an alleged mistake of law, Bodey J. took the view that developments in restitution in England, Australia and Canada, the views of academic writers in England,[172] and a decision at first instance[173] in relation to the misrepresentation of law rule

> "more or less compel a conclusion that in the English law of contract the former distinction between mistakes of fact and mistakes of law no longer pertains. For a different approach to survive as between the law of restitution and the law of contract would seem illogical and difficult to justify."

The impact of this decision, and difficulties which arise in abolishing the mistake of law rule in contract, will be discussed further in Part II.[174]

3–37 **Abandonment of the misrepresentation of law rule.** In *Pankhania v Hackney LBC*[175] the judge held that the misrepresentation of law rule has not survived the decision in *Kleinwort Benson*:

> "Its historical origin is as an off-shoot of the 'mistake of law' rule, created by analogy with it, and the two are logically inter-dependent . . . The distinction between fact and law in the context of relief from misrepresentation has no more underlying principle to it than it does in the context of relief from mistake. Indeed, when the principles of mistake and misrepresentation are set side by side, there is a stronger case for granting relief against a party who has induced a mistaken belief as to law in another, than against one who has merely made the same mistake himself. The rules of the common law should, so far as possible, be congruent with one another, and based on coherent principle. The survival of the

[171] [2004] EWCA Civ 1017, [2005] Q.B. 303 at [26]. See also Maurice Kay L.J. at [10]: "Although the *Kleinwort Benson* case concerned a restitutionary claim rather than a contractual one, it cannot be doubted that its effect now permeates the law of contract".

[172] *Halsbury's Laws of England* (4th edn, 1999 reissue), Vol.32, para.11 [see now 5th edn, 2010, vol.77, para.11], and Chitty (29th edn, 2004), para.5–018 [this appears to be a misprint for para.5–042; see now 30th edn, 2008, para.5–054]. For further discussion, see D. Sheehan, "Vitiation of Contracts for Mistake and Misrepresentation of Law" [2003] R.L.R. 26.

[173] *Pankhania v Hackney LBC* [2002] EWHC 2441 (Ch), [2002] All E.R. (D) 22 (Aug), discussed below, para.3–37.

[174] Below, para.15–24.

[175] Above, n.173 at [57] (Rex Tedd Q.C.).

> 'misrepresentation of law' rule following the demise of the 'mistake of law' rule would be no more than a quixotic anachronism. Its demise rids this area of the law of a series of distinctions, such as the 'private rights' exception, whose principal function has been to distinguish the 'mistake of law' rule, and confine it to a very narrow compass, albeit not to extinguish it completely.[176]"

He therefore held that a misrepresentation of law was sufficient to form the basis of a claim for damages under section 2(1) of the Misrepresentation Act 1967.[177] It should be noticed that the judge rightly accepted that, if the mistake of law rule is to be abandoned in contract, *a fortiori* the misrepresentation of rule should be abandoned. Indeed, one might even argue that, even if there were reasons for retaining the mistake of law rule in contract, the misrepresentation of law rule might properly be abandoned: the inducement of a claimant's mistake by the defendant's misrepresentation might of itself override any policy reasons which would otherwise render the claimant's mistake of law insufficient to give rise to any remedy in contract.[178]

American law. Much of what has been said above about the development of thinking in the English and other Commonwealth courts about the law/fact distinction, in both restitution and contract, could equally well be said of the courts in America. Soon after *Bilbie v Lumley* the mistake of law rule was applied in American law in the context of a contract entered into with knowledge of the facts but under a mistake of law.[179] Some cases took an even stronger line than in England, and refused remedies for fraudulent misrepresentations of law.[180] But for a long time now **3–38**

---

[176] For the "private rights" exception see above, para.3–25.
[177] Below, Ch.7, and especially para.7–11.
[178] Above, para.3–33. The particular context of the decision in *Pankhania*—the Misrepresentation Act 1967 s.2(1)—poses, however, certain difficulties in relation to misrepresentations of law because of the language of the section: see below, para.7–11.
[179] *Shotwell v Murray*, 1 Johns Ch. N.Y. 512, 516 (1815).
[180] e.g. *O-So Detroit Inc v Home Insurance Co*, 973 F.2d 498 (1992) (US Court of Appeals, sixth circuit, applying Michigan law: insurance contract not voidable for fraudulent misrepresentation of law); *Nagashima v Busck*, 541 So.2d 783 (1989) (District Court of Appeal of Florida, holding that Florida law—contrary to the Restatement of Torts 2d, para.525 (below, n.183)—does not allow an action in deceit for fraudulent misrepresentations, but recommending that this be

it has been argued that the rule should be discarded, and although case law across the several States is not unanimous about it, the general approach is not to deny remedies, either in contract or restitution, simply because a mistake or misrepresentation was one of law, rather than fact[181]; and the Second Restatement of Contracts[182] does not deny remedies for mistake or misrepresentation based on the distinction between law and fact. However, the American sources do show an underlying unease in simply assimilating law and fact for the purposes of mistake and misrepresentation. So the Second Restatement of Contracts discusses misrepresentations of law in the section dealing with justified reliance[183]: for every misrepresentation, whether of law or fact, the rule is that the claimant must have been justified in relying on it if he is to have a remedy. But the implication is that it will be more likely that a misrepresentation of law did not justify reliance. And it is sometimes said that statements of law are closer in this respect to statements of opinion than to statements of fact. Following this line of thinking, the American courts have often concluded that statements of law are actionable when the representor is a person who has, or purports to have, expert or superior knowledge of the law, or owes fiduciary duties to the representee.[184]

reviewed); *The Seckinger-Lee Co. v Allstate Insurance Co.*, 32 F.Supp.2d 1348 (1998) (US District Court Georgia; misrepresentation of law not sufficient for action for fraud).

[181] Williston, paras 1581 to 1583; Corbin, paras 616, 618.

[182] para.151, comment *b* (mistake); para.170 (misrepresentation).

[183] para.170; Farnsworth (a Reporter for the Restatement of Contracts 2d) also placed his discussion of misrepresentation of law under the general heading that reliance must be justified: para.4.14. *Cf.* also Restatement of Torts 2d: fraudulent misrepresentation of law actionable in tort if reliance justifiable: para.525, comment *d*; para.545.

[184] Restatement of Contracts 2d, para.170, comment *b*; Williston, para.1495; Farnsworth, para.4.14. And see, e.g. *Seeger v Odell*, 115 P.2d 977 (1941) (Supreme Court of California); *Hackett v St Joseph Light & Power Co.*, 761 SW 2d 206 (1988) (Missouri Court of Appeals); *Sainsbury v Pennsylvania Greyhound Lines Inc.*, 183 F.2d 548 (US Court of Appeals Fourth Circuit, applying Maryland law: misrepresentation of law by other party a defence to enforcement of the contract, where representor a lawyer). The First Restatement of Contracts (in 1932) took a stronger line, that misrepresentations of law are always statements of opinion and therefore not actionable *unless* made by an expert, or fraudulently (para.474). Similarly the Restatement of Restitution (1937), para.55, took the

(e) *The future: assimilation with the rules for misrepresentations of opinion? Applying the underlying principle*

Misrepresentation of law cannot be fully assimilated with misrepresentation of fact. Although there is now a decision at first instance holding that the misrepresentation of law rule has been abandoned[185]—a decision which has been approved by the Court of Appeal in the context of the mistake of law rule[186]—it is still not sufficient simply to assimilate misrepresentations of law and misrepresentations of fact. Facts are inherently objectively verifiable; but in many cases the law is not—and it is too easy to dismiss all the explanations for the law/fact distinction that used to be employed to justify the old misrepresentation and mistake of law rule.[187] Even if there is no longer an absolute misrepresentation of law rule, we should not ignore the instinctive reaction of the old lawyers that there was a real difference between a party's misunderstanding of the facts relevant to his transaction, and a misunderstanding of the law. 3–39

"Law" and "opinion": an imperfect analogy. There is a view expressed occasionally in the cases, and more frequently in the textbooks, that statements of law are to be regarded as statements of opinion.[188] The analogy is sometimes useful but not perfect. It is not true that all statements of law are simply statements of opinion. A false statement such as "there is no law requiring a motor cyclist to wear a helmet", made in ignorance of the existence of the Motor Cycles (Protective Helmet) Regulations 1998,[189] would be a misrepresentation of law, but is not just a statement of opinion. On the other hand, a statement about a debatable interpretation of a 3–40

---

view that there should be no restitution for misrepresentation of law unless fraudulent or reliance on the representation was justified (such as one made by an expert).

[185] *Pankhania v Hackney LBC*, above, para.3–37.

[186] *Brennan v Bolt Burdon*, above, para.3–36 at [10] (*Pankhania* was a "lucid and trenchant judgment": Maurice Kay L.J.).

[187] Above, paras 3–28 to 3–33.

[188] Above, para.3–31.

[189] SI 1998/1807, reg.4(1).

known rule of law appears much closer to a statement of opinion.[190] But the characterisation of all such statements as representations of law has until now rendered them generally[191] not actionable in contract.

3–41 **The underlying principle: entitlement to rely on the statement.** It is suggested that the better approach, in the light of the abandonment by the courts of the formal law/fact distinction, will be not to look to the question of whether a statement was one of law or of fact but to address the question which in reality underlies the law/fact distinction as well as the fact/opinion distinction: whether the statement, in the circumstances in which it was made and the position of the parties, was one which the representee was entitled to take seriously and rely on without making his own inquiries. Parties and the courts will need guidance as to how to answer this question; but since this is in substance what the courts have been addressing in cases where they have drawn the distinction between statements of opinion and statements of fact,[192] the tools are already at their disposal. It is not simply an application of those cases, since there may be arguments peculiar to a misrepresentation of law which will continue to lead a court to the conclusion that no remedy should flow from it.[193] But it is right to draw on the approach used in those cases not because "law" can simply be identified with "opinion"; but because the courts can now take a step towards generalising the underlying purpose of these distinctions to identify

[190] e.g. cases referred to above, para.3–22. A submission or contention about what what the law is, or what a document means, is also not a "misrepresentation": *Kyle Bay Ltd t/a Astons Nightclub v Underwriters Subscribing under Policy No.019057/08/01* [2007] EWCA Civ 57, [2007] 1 C.L.C. 164 at [35].

[191] In the remedies in which the law/fact distinction has been drawn (above, para.3–13, n.42); and unless there is something to override the rule against relief for mistake of law, such as proof of the representor's fraud (above, para.3–33).

[192] Above, paras 3–14 to 3–19.

[193] e.g. misrepresentations as to the legal effect of an agreement: until now these have been generally excluded under the blanket of the "misrepresentation of law" rule: above, para.3–24. But even if misrepresentations of law are generally now to be allowed to give rise to remedies, the mistake or misrepresentation of the legal effect of an agreement might well continue not generally to be actionable since normally a party should take his own advice on the matter. Such a representation by a lawyer might, however, be actionable. *Cf.* the Contractual Mistakes Act 1977 (New Zealand), s.6(2) excluding mistakes in the interpretation of a contract from actionable mistakes of law.

the core question: whether a statement was one which should be actionable because it was made in circumstances where the representee was reasonably entitled to rely on it.

(4) (Present) Fact Contrasted with Future Fact or Intention

Fraudulent statement of intention. When it is said that a statement, to be actionable, must be one of fact, it means that the statement must be of present fact: not "future fact", that is, not a statement of what will happen in the future, nor a statement of what the speaker will do in the future. A statement of what will happen in the future is a representation of the speaker's *present* belief about *future* events. A statement of intention is a representation of the speaker's *present* plan for his *future* conduct. If he does not have that belief or that plan at the time he speaks, he is not telling the truth about his present state of mind. His representation can be characterised as a fraudulent representation of fact and therefore actionable[194]: 3–42

> "the state of a man's mind is as much a fact as the state of his digestion. It is true that it is very difficult to prove what the state of a man's mind at a particular time is, but if it can be ascertained it is as much a fact as anything else. A misrepresentation as to the state of a man's mind is, therefore, a misstatement of fact."

Honest statement of future fact or intention. An honest statement of what will happen in the future is quite different from a statement of fact. It is simply a prediction, not a representation. 3–43

> "A statement as to a future state of affairs can in itself neither be true nor false at the time it is made, since the future cannot be foretold.[195]"

---

[194] *Edgington v Fitzmaurice* (1885) 29 Ch.D. 459, CA, at 483 (Bowen L.J.) (deceit); *cf.* below, para.5–08; *East v Maurer* [1991] 1 W.L.R. 461, CA (deceit: vendor of hairdressing salon misrepresented his intention not to work after the sale at another local competing salon); *Goff v Gauthier* (1991) 62 P. & C.R. 388 (vendor of land falsely represented his intention to withdraw and send contract to another potential purchaser if purchaser did not exchange contracts forthwith, whereas he only intended to consider his position and did not have another definite purchaser).

[195] *Bank Leumi Le Israel B.M. v British National Insurance Co. Ltd* [1988] 1 Lloyd's Rep. 71 (Saville J.); *Beattie v Lord Ebury* (1872) L.R. 7 Ch. App. 777 at 804; *Inntrepreneur Pub Co. (C.P.C.) v Sweeney* [2002] EWHC 1060, [2002] 2

If it is a statement about what the speaker will do in the future, it is a promise, not a representation. If one party wishes to hold the other liable in the event that the prediction is not borne out by the facts as the future finds them, or the promise is not kept, he has the means available within the law to do so, but not within the rules of pre-contractual misrepresentations.[196] The mechanism provided by the law for remedying such mispredictions or promises is the contract itself. If a contract contains as a term guaranteeing that a future event will happen, or that the party will do some identified act, then there will be a breach of contract if that event does not happen, or if the party fails to keep his promise. Put this way, it ought to be clear that a person who receives a statement of future fact or intention ought generally not to be entitled to rely on it: if he wishes to obtain a remedy he should ask for a warranty in the contract to the effect that the fact will turn out as represented, or that the promise will be kept.[197]

E.G.L.R. 132 at 142–144; *Foodco UK LLP (t/a Muffin Break) v Henry Boot Developments Ltd* [2010] EWHC 358 (Ch) at [193] (Lewison J.: "Outside the realms of mythology and literature, no one can foretell the future. Even in those realms the prophecies of the Oracle of Delphi were always ambiguous, Cassandra was never believed, and the prophecies of the witches in Macbeth were downright obscure. The law has thus been wary of imposing liability for statements about the future").

[196] *British Airways Board v Taylor* [1976] 1 W.L.R. 13, HL, at 17 ("the distinction is a real one and requires to be respected"; Lord Wilberforce, discussing the distinction between a statement of fact and a contractual promise for the purposes of criminal liability under the Trade Descriptions Act 1968, s.14(1); that context however imports other considerations of policy in the interpretation of statements: *ibid.* The provision was repealed by the Consumer Protection from Unfair Trading Regulations 2008 (SI 2008/1277) Sch.4(1), para.1, and replaced by the prohibition of unfair commercial practices (see also below, para.7–71)). For a similar reluctance to allow a statement of intention to be binding under the doctrine of estoppel by representation, see *Jordan v Money* (1854) 5 H.L.C. 185 at 215–216, 10 E.R. 868 at 882, HL; below, para.10–22.

[197] Although no positive remedy will generally be given for a party's failure to fulfil an (unwarranted) promise as to his future action, there is authority that this may justify the court's refusal to exercise its discretion to grant specific performance of a contract when the "representee" raises this as a defence: *Lamare v Dixon* (1873) L.R. 6 H.L. 414; below, para.10–07. Sometimes, also, the doctrine of promissory or proprietary estoppel might be invoked to lend enforcement to such a representation as to future conduct: below, para.10–28.

Statement of fact implied in statement of intention. As with all representations, however, it is necessary to examine carefully any statement of the future facts or of intention, to ensure that there is no sufficient statement of (present) fact contained within it. If there is, then it might be an actionable representation. It has been held that a statement of future fact could contain an implication not only that the statement is made honestly, but also that it is made on reasonable grounds.[198] Although a statement of the likely future profits of a business may be simply a prediction (and therefore not actionable[199]) it can sometimes be construed as a statement of the existing profitability of the company—its present capacity to make a particular return—and therefore be characterised as a present fact,[200] or a statement that the representor had reasonable grounds of fact for making the prediction.[201] A statement which appears to 3–44

[198] *Bank Leumi Le Israel B.M. v British National Insurance Co.Ltd*, above, n.195 (but on the facts it was not pleaded that the statement as to the future was not made honestly, or on reasonable grounds); *The Mihalis Angelos* [1971] 1 Q.B. 164, CA, at 194, 197, 204–205 (vessel described in charterparty as "expected ready to load" on a particular date: settled meaning in this context that the owner honestly expects that the vessel will be ready to load on that date, and that his expectation is based on reasonable grounds: misrepresentation and breach of contractual condition); following *Samuel Sand & Co. v Keighley Maxted & Co.* (1922) 27 Com. Cas. 296, CA (contract for sale of goods to be shipped in vessel "expected ready to load" at a particular time). If, however, a statement of "expectation" is made to induce a party to enter into an *insurance* contract, the statement will be tested simply as to the speaker's honesty, and there can be no implication that it is made on reasonable grounds: Marine Insurance Act 1906 s.20(5), above, para.3–16 (but see doubts there discussed in n.69).

[199] *Bellairs v Tucker* (1884) 13 Q.B.D. 562 (statement in company prospectus that "the directors confidently believe that the profits will be more than sufficient to pay dividends of at least 50% on the nominal capital . . . and will exceed [the dividends payable by another related company]").

[200] *Smith v Chadwick* (1884) 9 App. Cas. 187, HL ("the present value of the turnover or output"); *Foodco UK LLP (t/a Muffin Break) v Henry Boot Developments Ltd* [2010] EWHC 358 (Ch) at [207] (Lewison J.: "while a forecast may carry with it an implicit representation about a present fact (e.g. that the forecaster believes the forecast or that he has taken reasonable care in making it) it is that implicit representation about a present fact rather than the forecast itself that constitutes the actionable representation").

[201] *Lancaster City Council v Unique Group Ltd*, unreported, December 15, 1995 (prediction of the likely gate receipts of "Crinkley Bottom" theme park to be opened at Morcambe: "a statement as to 'existing' earning potential is no more than a forecast by another name"; but there was implied into the statement a representation that the forecast was given on reasonable grounds. Held not a

be a promise of future action can sometimes be held to be a representation of the speaker's present policy with regard to such action, and is therefore actionable.[202] And a statement which appears to be simply an assertion of future facts, or a promise, can sometimes be held also to imply a specific fact which is therefore actionable.[203] This, then, is similar to the approach which was

---

sufficient statement of fact to be actionable under the Misrepresentation Act 1967 s.2(1), although this was doubted by Langley J. in *Sumitomo Bank Ltd v Banque Bruxelles Lambert S.A.* [1997] 1 Lloyd's Rep. 487 at 515 and disapproved by CA in *Nelson Group Services (Maintenance) Ltd v BG Plc* [2002] EWCA Civ 547, [2002] All E.R. (D) 205 (Apr); below, para.7–10); *Esso Petroleum Co. Ltd v Mardon* [1976] 1 Q.B. 801, CA (estimated "throughput", or "estimated annual consumption", of petrol station: held contractual warranty of care in making the estimate, and similar duty in the tort of negligence).

202 *Kettlewell v Refuge Assurance Co.* [1908] 1 K.B. 545, CA, at 550, 551 (statement by insurer's agent that if policy holder paid five years' premiums, she would then continue to be insured thereafter without having to pay further premiums: held misrepresentation of the "existing practice" of the insurance company). *Cf. Kleinwort Benson Ltd v Malaysia Mining Corp. Bhd.* [1989] 1 W.L.R. 379, CA, where a statement by the parent company to the bank that "it is our policy to ensure that the business of [a subsidiary] is at all times in a position to meet its liabilities to [the bank]" was only a statement of policy: no promise beyond this could be implied; *Limit No.2 Ltd v Axa Versicherung A.G.* [2008] EWCA Civ 1231, [2008] 2 C.L.C. 673 at [7] (Longmore L.J.: "The word 'policy' can in general import elements of both the present and the future and thus carries with it an element of ambiguity").

203 *Karberg's Case* [1892] 3 Ch. 1, CA (statement in prospectus inviting subscribers for shares in a new company referred to two persons as members of the "planned" council of administration of the company; held to imply (falsely) that the two persons had "so far approved of the project as to have authorized the publication of their names in the list"); *British Airways Board v Taylor* [1976] 1 W.L.R. 13, HL (whether false statement for the purposes of the Trade Descriptions Act 1968 s.14(1) (now repealed): written confirmation of a booking on a specified flight was not simply a promise of that seat, but implied a statement of fact—that the airline had taken steps to secure a seat on the designated flight: Lord Edmund-Davies at 24; or that there was no risk attached to the guarantee of a seat on the flight, whereas the airline deliberately operated a system of overbooking of seats: Lord Wilberforce at 17); and, for the purposes of criminal liability for obtaining property or pecuniary advantage by deception under the Theft Act 1968 ss.15 and 16 (later replaced in part by provisions in the Theft Act 1978; and repealed and replaced by new general offence of fraud by Fraud Act 2006), see *R. v Gilmartin* [1983] Q.B. 953, CA (delivery of a cheque implies that the existing state of facts is such that in the ordinary course the cheque will be met); *DPP v Ray* [1974] A.C. 370, HL (ordering a meal in a restaurant can carry implied representation that the customer has the means and intention of paying for it); *cf. Re Eastgate* [1905] 1 K.B. 465 (goods obtained on

described above[204] in relation to statements of opinion: normally such a statement is not actionable because the recipient is not entitled to rely on it. In the case of statements as to the future, this is because there is no more than a misprediction or an unwarranted promise. But the words of the statement must be considered carefully, to see whether there is more than this: and in particular whether the particular statement, in its particular context (looking therefore also at the particular positions of the parties, their knowledge and the interpretation which can reasonably be placed by the representee on the statement) can be characterised as one of fact, on which reliance can therefore properly be placed.

(5) Other Tests for Other Remedies

The distinction between fact and opinion/law/intention is not relevant for all remedies. As has already been made clear,[205] not all remedies for misrepresentation require the statement to have been one of fact. It has traditionally been said to be a requirement of rescission[206] and of the claim for damages under section 2(1) of the Misrepresentation Act 1967.[207] The claim for damages in the tort of deceit is sometimes said also to have this requirement but, given that proof of fraud generally undermines the objection to a statement not being one of fact even when the remedy sought is rescission,[208] it can be seen only as a qualified rule within deceit. And the requirement that a statement be one of fact has no place in the rules governing the tort of negligence, or claims for breach of contract based on the incorporation into the contract of a pre-contractual representation. 3–45

credit with no intention to pay for them: contract held voidable for fraudulent misrepresentation of intention to pay); *Lewin v Barratt Homes Ltd* [2000] 1 E.G.L.R. 77 (showing pictures of design, and a show house, constituted statement to prospective purchaser that nothing stood in the way of building houses to that design). Fraud Act 2006 s.2(4) makes clear that a representation may be express or implied.

[204] Above, paras 3–17 to 3–18.
[205] Above, para.3–13.
[206] Below, para.4–25.
[207] Below, para.7–11.
[208] Above, para.3–33; below, para.5–08.

3–46 **Alternative tests: the tort of negligence.** Within the tort of negligence, there is no requirement that an actionable statement be one of fact[209]; and the distinction between statements of fact and statements of opinion, law and intention is not generally discussed. Indeed, it is quite usual for statements of opinion[210] and law[211] to be actionable in this tort: the test is not based on whether the statement was one of fact, but on whether it was made carelessly, in breach of a duty to take care. This will be discussed in detail below[212]; but for the present purposes it is sufficient to notice that, within the test for a duty of care, a key question is whether the statement was made in circumstances where the particular claimant was reasonably entitled to rely on the statement, and on the representor's exercise of care in making it. It was put in the following way by Lord Morris of Borth-y-Gest in *Hedley Byrne & Co. Ltd v Heller & Partners Ltd*[213]:

> "if in a sphere in which a person is so placed that others could reasonably rely upon his judgment or his skill or upon his ability to make careful inquiry, a person takes it upon himself to give information or advice to, or allows his information or advice to be passed on to, another person who, as he knows or should know, will place reliance upon it, then a duty of care will arise."

The principle underlying the rule in other remedies that a statement be one of fact—that a misrepresentation is actionable where the representee's reliance on it was reasonable—is therefore to be seen even more clearly within the tort of negligence.

3–47 **Incorporation of representations as contractual terms.** When a claim is made for damages or termination for breach of contract

---

[209] *Hedley Byrne & Co. Ltd v Heller & Partners Ltd* [1964] A.C. 465, HL, at 528.
[210] e.g. *Esso Petroleum Co. Ltd v Mardon* [1976] Q.B. 801, CA.
[211] e.g. a solicitor's breach of the duty to his client exercise care in giving legal advice: *Midland Bank Trust Co. Ltd v Hett, Stubbs & Kemp* [1979] Ch. 384; Charlesworth & Percy, paras 9–213 *et seq*. See also *B.L. Holdings Ltd v Robert J. Wood & Partners* (1978) 10 B.L.R. 48, reversed on facts by CA at (1979) 12 B.L.R. 1 (architect's duty to advise on legal requirements for office development permit to enable planning permission for building to be effective).
[212] Below, Ch.6.
[213] Above, n.209 at 503. See also *Caparo Industries Plc v Dickman* [1990] 2 A.C. 605, HL, at 638.

arising out of a misrepresentation which was made before the contract was entered into, the question is not whether the misrepresentation was one of fact, but whether it was incorporated into the contract as a term: whether the representor promised, or can be taken to have promised, that the (pre-contractual) statement was true,[214] or that he had taken care in making the statement.[215] Indeed, it is not sufficient to show that the statement was one of fact: it must be shown that the parties intended the statement to be incorporated as a term of the contract.[216]

However, when considering whether there is evidence of such an intention, the courts' method of inquiry is sometimes similar to that when they are deciding whether a statement is really one of fact, or only one of opinion. In a contract of sale, for example, whether statements by the seller about what he is selling are merely representations or enter the contract as warranties can depend on the relative positions of the parties: a specialist seller who makes representations about matters within his expertise to a non-specialist buyer may be held to have guaranteed his statements in the contract.[217] And in asking whether a pre-contractual statement became a contractual warranty that the statement had been given with reasonable care, the Court of Appeal has similarly asked whether the statement was made by a party who held himself out as having special knowledge and skill, to a representee who could reasonably be expected to rely on him.[218] The court has drawn the explicit analogy with the cases which address the distinction between statements of fact and statements of opinion, whilst making clear that the test is, strictly, different: whether the parties

---

[214] *Heilbut, Symons & Co. v Buckleton* [1913] A.C. 30, HL; below, para.8–04.
[215] *Esso Petroleum Co. Ltd v Mardon*, above, n.210.
[216] *Heilbut, Symons & Co. v Buckleton*, above, n.214 at 50.
[217] *Dick Bentley Productions Ltd v Harold Smith (Motors) Ltd* [1965] 1 W.L.R. 623, CA (statement by specialist car dealer about the mileage of a car: the dealer had told the buyer that he was in a position to discover the history of the cars he was selling); *cf. Oscar Chess Ltd v Williams* [1957] 1 W.L.R. 370, CA (misrepresentation of age of car by non-specialist seller when selling to garage: held not guaranteed in the contract). For other cases, and more detailed analysis of the courts' approach in determining whether pre-contractual representations are incorporated into the contract, see below, paras 8–07 to 8–13.
[218] *Esso Petroleum Co. Ltd vMardon*, above, n.210, esp. at 818.

intended the representation to be incorporated into the contract. In *Esso Petroleum Co. Ltd v Mardon* Ormrod L.J. said[219]:

> "A representation of fact is much more likely to be intended to have contractual effect than a statement of opinion; so it is much easier to infer that in the former case it was so intended, and more difficult in the latter. Similarly, where statements of future fact or forecasts are under consideration, it will require much more cogent evidence to justify the conclusion that such statements were intended to be contractual in character. It is, therefore . . . not an answer to say, simply, that the statement relied upon was an expression of opinion or a forecast and therefore cannot be a warranty. In my view, following Lord Moulton in the *Heilbut, Symons* case, the test is whether on the totality of the evidence the parties intended or must be taken to have intended that the representation was to form part of the basis of the contractual relations between them.[220]"

IV. THE REPRESENTOR'S STATE OF MIND

3–48 **Different remedies require different states of mind.** There is no common requirement amongst the several remedies for misrepresentation with respect to the defendant's honest or dishonest state of mind. The tort of deceit, for example, requires proof of fraud on the part of the representor[221]; the remedy of rescission does not, although for certain purposes it can be to the representee's advantage to prove fraud even where he is seeking only rescission and not damages in deceit.[222]

3–49 **Intention that the representee act on the representation.** It is sometimes said[223] that all the remedies have a minimum requirement as to the defendant's state of mind: he cannot be held responsible for the consequences of his statement unless he intended the representee to act on it. This requirement should not, however, be viewed as a significant hurdle for the representee to overcome. It is usually stated most explicitly in relation to the tort of deceit, where the courts often couple it with the requirement to

219 Above, n.210 at 826. See also Lord Denning M.R. at 818 and Shaw L.J. at 830–831.

220 For *Heilbut, Symons & Co. v Buckleton* see above, n.214, at 50.

221 Below, para.5–13.

222 Below, para.4–30.

223 Spencer Bower (Misrepresentation), para.117.

prove the defendant's fraud,[224] and in that context it can be seen naturally to have a positive subjective content. However, in relation to the other remedies, it means only that the representor, in making the statement, realised that his statement would be received by the representee and that he might therefore act upon it. It serves more to define the range of potential claimants—defining those who are entitled to sue on the representation[225]; the statement was consciously directed at the claimant. It is closely linked to the requirements that the representation be one on which the claimant was entitled to rely[226]; and that the representee must have in fact relied upon it.[227]

V. RELIANCE; CAUSATION

The requirement of a causal link between statement and loss. 3–50
Whichever remedy is sought for misrepresentation, it will be necessary to establish an adequate link between the statement and the consequence from which the representee claims to be relieved. If the claim is for damages, the question is whether the statement caused the loss. If the claim is for rescission of a contract, the inquiry is as to the causal link between the statement and the claimant's entry into the contract. The language used in the different remedies, and the legal tests employed for them, will vary, but generally the issue is similar: it is an issue of the claimant's reliance on the statement, and whether the statement caused the harm in issue. A false statement, even one made fraudulently, will not be actionable as a misrepresentation by the person to whom it was addressed if it had no impact on his actions, nor otherwise caused him loss.[228]

---

224 Below, para.5–13.

225 Chitty, para.6–028.

226 Above, para.3–12. If the statement was merely sales talk, for example, the claimant will not be entitled to take it seriously and rely upon it; but equally the defendant will not have intended him to do so because although he addressed the statement to him, it was not in circumstances where he expected that he would take it seriously.

227 If the defendant expected that the claimant might rely on it, it will generally be "material": below, para.3–53.

228 *Horsfall v Thomas* (1862) 1 H. & C. 90, 158 E.R. 813 (deliberate concealment by seller of defect in gun not actionable because the buyer had not seen the cover-up). This case has been doubted on other grounds (*Smith v Hughes*

3–51 **"Reliance" as the core requirement.** It is often misleading to talk in terms of a statement having caused loss; at least, a statement "causes" loss in a different way from an act. A badly built wall may fall over and injure a passer-by. It is not difficult to see that the defective workmanship caused the injury. But if I advise you that a wall is safe, and you walk past it and it falls over, your injury is "caused" in a different way: you took my words, trusted them and yourself took an action which put you in a position in which you suffered damage. A statement affects the decision-making processes of the person who reads or hears it, and that person then takes his own action in the light of the statement.[229] For many of the remedies, therefore, rather than using the language of "causation", it is more usual to speak of the representee's *reliance* on the statement; by "reliance" we are focusing on this causal link between the statement and the representee's own actions which then gave rise to the harm of which he complains, whether it is entering into the contract or doing some other act which resulted in his suffering loss.

3–52 **Actual reliance distinguished from reasonable reliance.** We are here concerned with whether the representee actually relied on the statement, or can be taken to have done so; not whether it was reasonable for him to rely. The question of whether the reliance was reasonable will often be relevant, but as part of the prior question about whether the statement was actionable. So if the claim is in the tort of negligence, the test for the existence of a duty of care includes a consideration of whether the statement was one on which the claimant could rely, although there is then a separate issue (treated within that remedy as an issue of "causation") as to whether the claimant did in fact rely on it.[230] And for some remedies, such as

(1871) L.R. 6 Q.B. 597 at 605), but this point remains good. *Edgington v Fitzmaurice* (1885) 29 Ch.D. 459, CA, at 483 (Bowen L.J.: the misrepresentation must have been "actively present to his mind").

229 *Caparo Industries Plc v Dickman* [1990] 2 A.C. 605, HL, at 635–636; *Henderson v Merrett Syndicates Ltd* [1995] 2 A.C. 145, HL, at 180; *White v Jones* [1995] 2 A.C. 207, HL, at 272.

230 Below, paras 6–22, 6–53. There is also, within the tort of negligence, some inconsistency in the use of the word "reliance": to say that the claimant relied on the statement is an issue of causation; to say that the claimant relied on the defendant's skill and care is a different matter: see below, para.6–22.

rescission, we have already seen[231] that to ask whether the statement is actionable often in substance involves an inquiry into whether its content, and the context in which it was made, mean that the representee was entitled to rely on it; but beyond that there will be a separate issue as to whether the representee did rely on it in entering into the contract. There is also sometimes said to be a requirement that the representation be "material" in the sense that is was by its nature capable of having influenced the representee in entering into the contract, or in acting in such a way that he suffered the loss he claims to recover.[232] But even in cases where this applies there is still a separate question of whether the statement *actually* influenced the representee in entering into the contract.[233]

"Materiality" of the statement and proof of reliance. This is not, however, to say that it is irrelevant to ask whether the statement was material, and whether it was reasonable for the claimant to rely on the statement, when inquiring into whether he did in fact rely on it. The burden of proof of reliance is on the claimant.[234] But if a representation is such that it was likely that a person in the representee's position would rely on it, a court may find it easier to believe the representee's assertion that he did rely on it: the materiality of the statement is evidence that goes towards establishing reliance. Materiality is not necessary to establish reliance: the question is whether the court is satisfied that the 3–53

[231] Above, para.3–41.

[232] Below, para.3–53. One area in which there is undoubtedly a requirement that the statement be material is insurance contracts: Marine Insurance Act 1906 ss.18 (duty of disclosure of material circumstances), 20 (material misrepresentations). The principles contained in the Act apply to all insurance contracts, not only marine insurance: above, para.3–16, n.68, although ss.18 and 20 are to be amended by the Consumer Insurance (Disclosure and Representations) Bill (which is passing through Parliament during 2011) to exclude consumer insurance contracts from their scope: below, para.17–06. "Material" circumstances and representations are defined in ss.18(2) and 20(2) as those "which would influence the judgment of a prudent insurer in fixing the premium, or determining whether he will take the risk".

[233] *Pan Atlantic Insurance Co. Ltd v Pine Top Insurance Co. Ltd* [1995] 1 A.C. 501, HL, esp. at 549.

[234] *Pan Atlantic Insurance Co. Ltd v Pine Top Insurance Co. Ltd*, above, n.233; *Drake Insurance Plc v Provident Insurance Plc* [2003] EWCA Civ 1834; [2004] Q.B. 601 at [64], [137] (non-disclosure).

representee actually relied on the statement.[235] And materiality of the statement is not sufficient of itself to establish reliance. It was once said that there is an inference *in law* that a statement, if material, was relied on by the person to whom it was addressed.[236] But this has been rejected[237] in favour of a rule, now well established in the context of a range of remedies for misrepresentation,[238] that materiality of a statement raises an inference *in fact* that it was relied on. It was put by Jessel M.R. in *Mathias v Yetts*[239] in the context of the remedy of rescission:

> "if a man has a material misstatement made to him which may, from its nature, induce him to enter into the contract, it is an inference that he is induced to enter into the contract by it. You need not prove it affirmatively. The man who makes the material misstatement to induce the other to enter into the contract cannot be heard to say that he did not enter into it, to some

[235] *Museprime Properties Ltd v Adhill Properties Ltd* [1990] 2 E.G.L.R. 196 at 201–202 (rescission).

[236] *Redgrave v Hurd* (1881) 20 Ch.D. 1, CA, at 21 (Jessel M.R.). This was put in terms of a rebuttable presumption of law—rebuttable by proof of the representee's knowledge of facts contrary to the representation, or evidence from the representee's conduct that he did not rely.

[237] *Smith v Chadwick* (1884) 9 App. Cas. 187, HL, at 196; *Smith v Land and House Property Corp.* (1884) 28 Ch.D. 7, CA, at 16; *Pan Atlantic Insurance Co. Ltd v Pine Top Insurance Co.Ltd*, above, n.233 at 570; *Barton v County Natwest Ltd* [1999] Lloyd's Rep. Bank. 408, CA, at [54]–[55]; *Dadourian Group International Inc. v Simms* [2009] EWCA Civ 169, [2009] 1 Lloyd's Rep. 601 at [99], [101]. On the distinction between presumptions of law and presumptions of fact, see Phipson, paras 6–16 to 6–18.

[238] Including rescission and deceit. But this method of analysis has not been used in the tort of negligence: *cf. Bristol and West Building Society v Mothew* [1998] Ch. 1, CA, at 11 (Millett L.J.: "the society's claim is not for misrepresentation. Accordingly, questions of inducement and materiality are not relevant. Its claim lies in negligence, and the relevant concept is reliance"). In *Fitzroy Robinson Ltd v Mentmore Towers Ltd* [2009] EWHC 1552 (TCC), [2009] B.L.R. 505 at [111] Coulson J. held that under s.2(1) "reliance needs to be proved to the civil standard" and there is no inference of fact that the representee was induced by a material statement: this is, however, against the authorities: see below, para.7–20, n.71.

[239] (1882) 46 L.T. 497, CA, at 502. See also Sir James Hannen at 505 and Lindley L.J. at 507. Jessel M.R. here claimed only to be restating what he had said in *Redgravev Hurd* (above, n.236) and so can be read as his own retraction of the proposition that the inference is one of law (above, n.236). For the application of the same principle in the tort of deceit, see *Smith v Chadwick* (1882) 20 Ch.D. 27, CA, at 44–45 (Jessel M.R.), 75 (Lindley L.J.); (1884) 9 App. Cas. 187, HL, at 196.

> extent, at all events, on the faith of that statement, unless he can prove one of two things: either in fact that the man did not rely upon it, and made inquiries and got information which showed that the misstatement was untrue, and still went on with the contract, that is one thing; or else that he said, expressly or impliedly, 'I do not care what your representations are; I shall not inquire about them. I shall enter into the contract taking the risk'."

The weight which such an inference of fact can carry will depend on the circumstances of the contract: the degree to which action by the representee on the basis of the particular misrepresentation was likely, and the available evidence of other grounds for the representee's actions.[240] But in substance the effect of the rule is that, once a statement is shown to be material, the representor will have the burden of adducing evidence to rebut the inference that his representation was relied on by the representee.[241]

The difficulty of proving reliance; multiple causes. The courts' willingness to infer reliance from the materiality of a statement is a consequence of the difficulty which a representee faces in proving why he entered into a contract. 3–54

> "It is impossible so to analyze the operations of the human mind as to be able to say how far any particular representation may have led to the formation of any particular resolution, or the adoption of any particular line of conduct. No one can do this with certainty, even as to himself, still less as to another.[242]"

---

240 *Smith v Chadwick* (1884) 9 App. Cas. 187, HL, at 196. The representee may, however, discharge the burden of proof of reliance without himself giving evidence of his decision to enter into the contract: *Waltham Forest LBC v Roberts* [2005] H.L.R. 2 (fraudulent "inducement" of secure tenancy of dwelling-house for purpose of landlord's claim to possession under the Housing Act 1986 s.84(1), Sch.2, Ground 5, established by application of the test in *Smith v Chadwick* without evidence from the actual decision-maker).

241 *Redgrave v Hurd*, above, n.236 at 24; *Mathias v Yetts*, above, n.239 at 505, 508; *Barton v County Natwest Ltd*, above, n.237 at [58]; Goff & Jones, para.9–021; Treitel, para.9–027.

242 *Reynell v Sprye* (1852) 1 De G. M. & G. 660 at 708, 42 E.R. 710 at 728 (Lord Cranworth); *Arnison v Smith* (1889) 41 Ch.D. 348, CA, at 369 (Lord Halsbury L.C.: the effect on the reader of the various statements in a company's prospectus cannot be separated out from the effect produced by the whole document: "you cannot weigh the elements by ounces"). As Lord Cranworth's statement makes clear, however difficult it would be for a representee to prove his own reliance, it will be even more difficult to require the representor to prove that the representee

Using as the paradigm case the pre-contractual misrepresentation, the starting-point is clear: look for evidence that the statement caused the representee to enter into the contract—or, at least, was one of the causes. It is clear that the misrepresentation need not be the *sole* cause, or even the *predominant* cause of the decision to contract: the decision to enter into a contract is generally based on a range of motives and as long as any one of those motives is vitiated by the misinformation given by the other party, it is enough to undermine the whole transaction.[243]

There is some disagreement in the authorities, however, about how the test of causation should be applied in cases of multiple possible causes. Some say that, if it is shown that the claimant would, or might well, still have entered into the contract even if the misrepresentation had not been made,[244] the misrepresentation cannot (on the "but for" test of causation) have caused him to enter into the contract and therefore he has no remedy.[245] Others say that

did *not* rely on the statement—that is, the shift in the evidential burden to the representor is a significant disadvantage to him.

[243] *Attwood v Small* (1838) 6 Cl. & Fin. 232 at 502, 7 E.R. 684 at 785, HL; *Smith v Kay* (1859) 7 H.L.C. 750 at 775–776, 11 E.R. 299 at 310, HL; *Mathiasv Yetts*, above, n.239 at 502; *Edgington v Fitzmaurice* (1885) 29 Ch.D. 459, CA, at 481, 483, 485; *Bristol and West Building Society v Mothew*, above, n.238; *UCB Corporate Services Ltd v Williams* [2002] EWCA Civ 555, [2002] 3 F.C.R. 448 at [85]–[90] (Jonathan Parker L.J., drawing an analogy between undue influence and fraudulent misrepresentation); H.L.A. Hart and T. Honoré, *Causation in the Law* (2nd edn, 1985), pp.192–194; *cf. Assicurazioni Generali S.p.A.v Arab Insurance Group* [2002] EWCA Civ 1642, [2003] 1 All E.R. (Comm) 140 at [59] (it must be "an effective cause" but not the sole cause: Clarke L.J.), [218] (Ward L.J., doubting this language: "We must be careful not to be led back into the error that the cause has to be a decisive cause").

[244] The question is what the claimant would have done if the misrepresentation had not been made, rather than what he would have done if the representation had been true: *Raiffeisen Zentralbank Österreich A.G. v Royal Bank of Scotland Plc* [2010] EWHC 1392 (Comm), [2011] 1 Lloyd's Rep. 123 at [180], [187].

[245] *Smith v Kay*, above, n.243 at 776, at 310 (Lord Wensleydale: "where, unless it had been employed, the contract would never have been made"); *Assicurazioni Generali S.p.A. v Arab Insurance Group*, above, n.243 at [59] (Clarke L.J.: "If the insurer would have entered into the contract on the same terms in any event, the representation or non-disclosure will not, however material, be an effective cause of the making of the contract and the insurer or reinsurer will not be entitled to avoid the contract"); *Raiffeisen Zentralbank Österreich A.G. v Royal Bank of Scotland Plc*, above, n.244 at [173]; *Cassa di Risparmio della Repubblica di San Marino S.p.A. v Barclays Bank Ltd* [2011] EWHC 484 (Comm), [2011] All E.R. (D) 189 (Mar) at [233], [467].

if the representation was in fact present to the claimant's mind when he took the decision to enter into the contract and it did in fact contribute to his decision to contract, that is sufficient even if he would still have entered into the contract, and on the same terms, if the misrepresentation had not been made.[246] It is submitted that the latter approach is preferable, since as long as the misrepresentation in fact operated on the claimant's mind when he decided to enter into the contract he did in fact rely on it.[247] In any event, even if a strict "but for" test may be adopted in the case of innocent or negligent misrepresentations, it appears to be generally accepted that it is not appropriate where the misrepresentation was fraudulent, on the basis that, having intended to deceive, the defendant cannot be allowed to argue that his fraud did not achieve its object.[248]

The claimant's own fault. In some cases it has been argued that the representee could himself have discovered the truth, and that his failure to do so should count against him in his misrepresentation claim. The relevance of the claimant's "fault" will vary from one remedy to another. Generally it does not count against him: so he is not deprived of the remedy of rescission just because he had the means of discovering that the statement was false[249]; nor will the representee's own fault be counted against him in a claim for deceit.[250] But it may sometimes be possible to argue in a claim based on the tort of negligence that the claimant's own fault in failing to check the statement amounts to contributory 3–55

[246] *Edgington v Fitzmaurice*, above, n.243 at 481, 483.

[247] The "but for" test of causation is problematic in other contexts: Clerk & Lindsell, paras 2–09 *et seq*; Winfield & Jolowicz, paras 6–6 to 6–7.

[248] *UCB Corporate Services Ltd v Williams*, above, n.243 at [89]; *Ross River Ltd v Cambridge City Football Club Ltd* [2007] EWHC 2115 (Ch), [2008] 1 All E.R. 1004 at [202]; *Raiffeisen Zentralbank Österreich A.G. v Royal Bank of Scotland Plc*, above, n.244 at [198]; *Cassa di Risparmio della Repubblica di San Marino S.p.A. v Barclays Bank Ltd*, above, n.245 at [233]; Chitty, para.6–035. At least in a case of fraud, it is also sufficient if the representee was induced by the representation to persevere in a decision already reached: fresh positive action in reliance is not required: *Barton v County Natwest Ltd*, above, n.237 at [55]; *Raiffeisen Zentralbank Österreich A.G. v Royal Bank of Scotland Plc* at [199] (*Barton* is limited to fraud).

[249] Below, para.4–35.

[250] Below, para.5–31.

negligence.[251] Even in such cases, however, the issue of the claimant's fault does not deny that he relied on the misrepresentation. Within the general requirement for all the remedies that the misrepresentation must have been relied on—must have caused the loss—the question is whether the representee actually relied on the statement in taking action. If he did not trust what he was told but made his own inquiries about whether the statement was true, then he relied not on the statement, but on his own inquiries. Similarly, if he assumes statements to be correct for the purpose of entering into the contract, without necessarily believing them to be accurate and with the intention of investigating their accuracy and ramifications later, he has not been induced by the statements to enter into the contract.[252] In such cases, the claimant's failure to discover the truth once he has taken on the task of checking the statement, or his entry into the contract without first checking the accuracy of the statements which he has decided may or may not be accurate, counts against him: he has taken the risk. But if he did trust what he was told, and acted on it, that is sufficient to constitute reliance, even though he had the means of knowledge at his disposal.

> "The person who has made the misrepresentation cannot be heard to say to the party to whom he has made that representation, 'You chose to believe me when you might have doubted me, and gone further'.[253]"

This is so even where the representee deliberately chooses not to check the truth of the statement, although if he was on notice of the fact that the statement might not be true he will not be allowed to base his claim on it: but for this to apply, it seems that the representee must have had knowledge of facts from which he ought to have realised that the statement was false.[254]

3–56 **"Non-reliance" clauses.** It is not uncommon for commercial contracts to address the issue of reliance directly by defining the

---

[251] Below, para.6–48.

[252] *Kyle Bay Ltd t/a Astons Nightclub v Underwriters Subscribing under Policy No.019057/08/01* [2007] EWCA Civ 57, [2007] 1 C.L.C. 164 at [42] (Neuberger L.J.: an unusual case; "the approach of [the claimant] appears mystifying").

[253] *Redgrave v Hurd*, above, n.236 at 23 (Baggallay L.J.); *New Brunswick and Canada Railway Co. v Conybeare* (1862) 9 H.L.C. 711 at 743, 11 E.R. 907, HL, at 920.

[254] *Redgrave v Hurd*, above, n.236 at 21, 23.

scope of reliance. For example, in a contract for the sale of shares in a company, there may be express warranties and representations about the company and its business, together with a clause by which the purchaser purports to confirm that in entering into the contract he has not relied on any representation other than those express warranties and representations set out in the contract. The courts' approach to such clauses has varied,[255] but it has recently become accepted that the parties can be estopped by a term in their contract to the effect that the contract is entered into on the basis that there has been no reliance on pre-contractual representations.[256] Such clauses will be considered in detail in Chapter 9.

[255] *Thomas Witter Ltd v TBP Industries* [1996] 2 All E.R. 573 at 596–597 (whether or not a party relied on a representation is a matter of fact which cannot simply be displaced by a clause denying the fact of reliance); *E.A. Grimstead & Son Ltd v McGarrigan* [1999] All E.R. (D) 1163, CA; *Watford Electronics Ltd v Sanderson C.F.L. Ltd* [2001] EWCA Civ 317, [2001] 1 All E.R. (Comm) 696, CA, at [39]–[40] (estoppel by representation, but it is difficult for the party who made a misrepresentation to establish that he relied on the representee's representation of non-reliance in order to found the estoppel); below, para.9–03, n.8.

[256] *Peekay Intermark Ltd v Australia and New Zealand Banking Group Ltd* [2006] EWCA Civ 386, [2006] 2 Lloyd's Rep. 511 at [57] (Moore-Bick L.J.), accepted in a series of recent cases at first instance and the Court of Appeal: below, para.9–03, n.9.

CHAPTER 4

RESCISSION OF THE CONTRACT FOR MISREPRESENTATION[1]

I. THE NATURE OF THE REMEDY

(1) Rescission at Common Law and in Equity

The claim for rescission in the modern law. The claim for rescission of the contract for misrepresentation is generally now a claim for the remedy which was developed by the courts of equity during the nineteenth century. The detail of the history of the **4–01**

[1] Spencer Bower (Misrepresentation), Chs 14, 15; Chitty, paras 6–103 to 6–133; Furmston, paras 4.46 to 4.60; Treitel, paras 9–078 to 9–114; Anson, pp.311–320; Cheshire, Fifoot and Furmston, pp.352–361; Allen, pp.29–39; D. O'Sullivan, S. Elliott and R. Zakrzewski, The Law of Rescission, Ch.4 and Pts III–VI.

remedy need not concern us here[2] beyond noting some points necessary for a proper understanding of some of the older cases which are still relied on in the modern law of rescission.

4–02 **Rescission at common law.** Although it appears that in the early nineteenth century the common law remedy for misrepresentation was only damages, rescission being thought of then as only an equitable remedy,[3] during the century the common law courts accepted that a contract could be rescinded for misrepresentation. The contract was voidable at common law, at the instance of the representee; but the remedy of rescission was available only on proof of fraud.[4] This common law remedy of rescission was never further developed. Since the courts of equity developed a more general remedy of rescission which did not depend on proof of fraud,[5] claims are in practice[6] now made simply for "rescission" of

---

[2] D. Ibbetson, *A Historical Introduction to the Law of Obligations* (1999), pp.208–209, 234–236, 252; J. O'Sullivan, "Rescission as a Self-help Remedy: a Critical Analysis" [2000] C.L.J. 509 at pp.516 *et seq.*; R.P. Meagher, J.D. Heydon and M.J. Leeming, *Meagher, Gummow and Lehane's Equity: Doctrines and Remedies* (4th edn, Butterworths LexisNexis, Sydney, 2002), Ch.24.

[3] *Attwood v Small* (1838) 6 Cl. & Fin. 232 at 395, 444, 502, 7 E.R. 684 at 746, 764, 785, HL.

[4] *Cornfoot v Fowke* (1840) 6 M. & W. 358, 151 E.R. 450; *White v Garden* (1851) 10 C.B. 918, 138 E.R. 364; *Stevenson v Newnham* (1853) 13 C.B. 285, 138 E.R. 1208; *Clarke v Dickson* (1858) El. Bl. & El. 148, 120 E.R. 463; *Kennedy v The Panama, New Zealand and Australian Royal Mail Co. Ltd* (1867) L.R. 2 Q.B. 580 at 587; *cf. Redgrave v Hurd* (1881) 20 Ch.D. 1, CA, at 13 (Jessel M.R.: at common law rescission extended only to a misrepresentation where the representor knew it to be false, or was "reckless, and without care, whether it was true or false, and not with the belief that it was true", i.e. what Lord Herschell was later to define in *Derry v Peek* (1889) 14 App. Cas. 337, HL, below, para.5–14, as *fraud* for the purpose of a claim at common law for damages in the tort of deceit). The common law remedy of damages for misrepresentation in the tort of deceit also requires proof of fraud: see Ch.5.

[5] Below, para.4–04.

[6] e.g. *Dunbar Bank Plc v Nadeem* [1998] 3 All E.R. 876, CA, at 884. There were also other limitations on the common law remedy which made the development of the equitable remedy of rescission more attractive, such as the more limited machinery of the common law to achieve restitution: *Erlanger v New Sombrero Phosphate Co.* (1878) 3 App. Cas. 1218, HL, at 1278–1279, below, paras 4–53 to 4–54, and the greater ability under the rules of equity to recognise and enforce the representee's property rights in rescinding a contract under which property had passed at common law: below, para.4–10. There was authority that at common law it was not possible to obtain rescission of a deed under which a lease had

the contra[illegible] which is generally meant [illegible]e equitable remedy which will be dis[illegible] this chapter[illegible]r, the tendency to assimilate the common [illegible] rules hides some of the old distinctions between them which may not have entirely lost their significance in practice.[7]

Rescission in equity: the early law. During most of the 4–03
nineteenth century it was said, even by judges sitting in the courts of equity before the fusion of the jurisdictions of law and equity in the Judicature Acts, that rescission required proof of fraud.[8] But such statements must be viewed with caution. Many difficulties in reading the old cases, both those decided by the old common law courts and those decided by the courts of equity, flow from the different uses of terminology, and in particular "fraud" which at common law became settled in its definition only by the decision of the House of Lords in *Derry v Peek* in 1889.[9] But in the cases on rescission in the courts of equity in the nineteenth century, it is clear that the judges often used the word "fraud" in a very different sense from that used even then in the common law: it would be "fraudulent" in the eyes of equity to allow a representor, even one who was ignorant of the falsity of his words at the time he made the statement and at the time they were acted on by the representee, now to retain the benefit of the contract once the truth has been discovered.[10] This is not requiring any dishonest state of mind on

been granted; the proper remedy was in equity: *Feret v Hill* (1854) 15 C.B. 207 at 223–226, 139 E.R. 400 at 407–408. There is now no obstacle to rescission of a deed which created an interest in real property: *Hart v Swaine* (1877) 7 Ch.D. 42 (copyhold wrongly sold as freehold).

[7] e.g. the remedial consequences of rescission effected by act of party differ between the common law and equity: below, para.4–11. There is also still some confusion in the case law about the mechanics for rescission: below, para.4–18; J. O'Sullivan, "Rescission as a Self-help Remedy: a Critical Analysis" [2000] C.L.J. 509. See also S. Worthington, "The Proprietary Consequences of Rescission" [2002] R.L.R. 28 at pp.29–32.

[8] *Attwood v Small*, above, n.3; *Smith v Kay* (1859) 7 H.L.C. 750, 11 E.R. 299, HL. But sometimes it was clear that fraud (in the sense required at common law for deceit) was not required: *Duranty's Case* (1858) 26 Beav. 268 at 273–4, 53 E.R. 901 at 903 (Romilly M.R.).

[9] Below, para.5–14.

[10] *New Brunswick and Canada Railway Co. v Conybeare* (1862) 9 H.L.C. 711 at 724–726, 11 E.R. 907 at 913; *Reese River Silver Mining Co. v Smith* (1869) L.R. 4 H.L. 64 at 79; *Hart v Swaine* (1877) 7 Ch.D. 42 at 46–47.

the part of the representor at the time of the statement or at the time of the contract: it is simply saying that a representor who has caused the representee to contract by a false statement cannot be allowed to retain the contract. As a rationale of the remedy of rescission, attributing responsibility to the party who caused the other party's misunderstanding and therefore giving the mistaken party the choice to accept or decline the contract, it can be defended.[11] But it is misleading to use the word "fraudulent" to describe the statement, since in this and other remedies for misrepresentation the time at which the defendant's state of mind should be tested for the purpose of establishing a cause of action is the moment when the statement was acted on (or, sometimes, the earlier moment when the statement was made); not the later time of the claim.

4–04 **Rescission in equity: the modern law.** By 1881 the courts had abandoned the language of "fraud" in discussing the equitable remedy of rescission. In *Redgrave v Hurd*[12] Jessel M.R. said that earlier judges had sometimes explained the rationale of the remedy as resting on "moral fraud" in seeking to take advantage of a contract now known to have been entered into on the basis of a false statement, but he made clear that in the courts of equity it was not necessary to prove that the party who obtained the contract knew at the time when the representation was made that it was false. This contrasted with the position at common law, where fraud was necessary[13]; but since the Judicature Acts the rules of equity prevailed[14] and therefore all courts would apply the equitable rules and grant the equitable remedy of rescission for misrepresentation, without requiring the misrepresentation to have been made fraudulently. Moreover, when the definition of fraud was considered and settled by the House of Lords in *Derry v Peek* it was made clear beyond doubt by Lord Herschell that rescission did not depend on proof of fraud but was also available, in principle, for wholly innocent misrepresentations[15]:

---

[11] Below, para.4–24; Cartwright, pp.103–104.

[12] (1881) 20 Ch.D. 1, CA, at 12–13.

[13] Above, n.4.

[14] Supreme Court of Judicature Act 1873, s.25(11); see now Senior Courts Act 1981, s.49(1).

[15] (1889) 14 App. Cas. 337 at 359. There had been some suggestions in the earlier cases that the courts might be looking, if not for dishonesty, still for some fault on the part of the representor (beyond simply having made the

"Where rescission [on the ground of misrepresentation of a material fact] is claimed it is only necessary to prove that there was a misrepresentation; then, however honestly it may have been made, however free from blame the person who made it, the contract, having been obtained by misrepresentation, cannot stand."

(2) The Effect of Rescission

Contract voidable for misrepresentation.[16] Where the requirements of the remedy of rescission are satisfied, the contract is not void *ab initio*; it is voidable at the instance of the representee.[17] The contract was therefore, from its creation and until the moment of its 4–05

misrepresentation) before rescission could be granted in equity: *Pulsford v Richards* (1853) 17 Beav. 87 at 94, 51 E.R. 965 at 968. It has been clear beyond doubt since *Derry v Peek* that rescission is available for even wholly innocent misrepresentations, i.e. negligence is not necessary; and that for fraud the common law requires dishonesty, i.e. negligence is not sufficient: below, para.5–14.

[16] "Rescission" is the proper description for the remedy of avoidance in both common law and equity; it is therefore used also in such other cases as contracts voidable for duress (common law) or undue influence (equity). It is not appropriate to use "rescission" to describe the remedy granted to declare a *void* (not voidable) contract of no effect at common law since in a void contract there are no obligations (and therefore no contract) to rescind: *Bell v Lever Bros Ltd* [1932] A.C. 161, HL, at 190. For the proposal of the Law Commission to introduce a remedy of the "right to unwind" the contract (similar to rescission but to avoid the alleged confusing nature of the existing terminology) in its proposals to provide civil remedies for certain breaches of the Consumer Protection from Unfair Trading Regulations 2008, SI 2008/1277, implementing the Unfair Commercial Practices Directive 2005/29/EC, see Law Com. Consultation Paper No.199, *Consumer Redress for Misleading and Aggressive Practices* (2011), paras. 14–17 *et seq.*

[17] This was the rule at common law: *White v Garden* (1851) 10 C.B. 918, 138 E.R. 364; *Stevenson v Newnham* (1853) 13 C.B. 285 at 302, 138 E.R. 1208 at 1215; *Clarke v Dickson* (1858) El. Bl. & El. 148 at 154, 120 E.R. 463 at 466; and is the position which is clearly established in the modern law, which takes over the equitable rules of rescission: *Bristol and West Building Society v Mothew* [1998] Ch. 1, CA, at 22 (Millett L.J.); *Lonrho Plc v Fayed (No.2)* [1992] 1 W.L.R. 1 at 11 (Millett J.). There are occasional references in the older cases which appear to point to the contract being void for misrepresentation, e.g. *Pawson v Watson* (1778) 2 Cowp. 785 at 788, 98 E.R. 1361 at 1362 (Lord Mansfield: a material misrepresentation which induced an insurer to issue an insurance policy "makes the policy void"); *Carter v Boehm* (1766) 3 Burr. 1905 at 1909, 97 E.R. 1162 at 1164 (Lord Mansfield: non-disclosure: "the policy is void").

rescission, effective to create the rights and obligations which its terms provided. But at the moment of rescission the contract is made a nullity from the beginning: it is retrospectively avoided, and any performance already made under the terms of the contract is reversed, so that the parties are placed in the position in which they would have been had there been no contract. These effects require, however, some elaboration.

4–06 **Rescission is a retrospective remedy.** At the moment of rescission of the contract, the contract becomes avoided *ab initio*: it is to be as if there had been no contract. This retrospective aspect of the remedy is natural in the context of the English law of contract: the circumstances in which a contract is void or voidable are generally only where there was a defect in its formation.[18] In the case of misrepresentation there was a sufficient agreement between the contracting parties to form a contract (and so the contract was not void *ab initio*[19]), but on the representee's side it was based on a false assumption which was created or perpetuated by the representor's statement.[20] The remedy therefore operates back to the time at which the defect arose: the moment of formation. This retrospective remedy of rescission for misrepresentation is to be contrasted with the remedy—sometimes also referred to as "rescission" of the contract, but in this book generally called "termination" of the contract—which is available for some breaches of contract, and involves the future, unaccrued obligations being released without there being any disturbance of those obligations which, at the moment the remedy takes effect, have already accrued.[21]

[18] In particular mistake (void); duress (voidable); undue influence (voidable): Chitty, paras 1–080 to 1–082. For similar reasons, based on the absence of full, free and informed consent at the moment of formation, legal systems generally take the view that a defect in formation such as misrepresentation will give rise to a remedy which has the effect of nullifying the contract *ab initio*. However, unlike English law, some systems will give an *ab initio* remedy also for non-performance: G.H. Treitel, *Remedies for Breach of Contract* (1988), para.282.

[19] On the assumption, which is made throughout this chapter, that the representee's mistake which was induced by the representor's statement was not sufficient to render the contract void at common law for mistake, independently of the misrepresentation: above, para.1–03.

[20] Above, para.1–03.

[21] Below, para.8–35.

Only the representee can claim rescission. Since the basis of the representee's claim is that he was misled by the representor's statement, the remedy can be invoked only by the representee. A party cannot be allowed to rely on his own conduct in having brought about the other party's misunderstanding in order himself to escape the contract.[22] **4–07**

Rescission must be possible. Since rescission is retrospective, and requires the parties to reverse performance so as to return to the position in which they were when they entered into the contract, there can be problems in obtaining the remedy if such reversal of performance is not possible. This may happen because it is in law or as a matter of fact not possible for one of the parties to return what he received under the contract, such as where the subject-matter of the contract has been passed on to a third party, or has been used up. Such situations, which sometimes amount to "bars" to obtaining the remedy of rescission, are considered in detail below.[23] **4–08**

Rescission of an executed or partly executed contract. The mere fact that the contract has been partly or even fully performed by one or both parties is not a bar to rescission.[24] But in the case of a contract under which performance has been rendered, the effect of the reversal of that performance sometimes needs to be considered carefully. There is both a legal and a factual dimension to the avoidance of the contract. As a matter of law, the obligations which were created by and pursuant to the (voidable) contract must be annulled. As a matter of fact, the parties' physical performance of those obligations must be reversed. In a contract of sale, for **4–09**

[22] *Reese River Silver Mining Co. v Smith*, above, n.10 at 74 (Lord Hatherley L.C.: party cannot rely on his own fraud to avoid contract). The representee, if innocent, may also be himself under a *mistake* as to the facts he states; in such cases he may allege that the contract is void for mistake: above, para.1–03. But even then he will not be able to do so if he held the mistaken belief without any reasonable ground: *McRae v Commonwealth Disposals Commission* (1951) 84 C.L.R. 377, HCA, at 408; *Associated Japanese Bank (International) Ltd v Crédit du Nord S.A.* [1989] 1 W.L.R. 255 at 268; *The Great Peace* [2002] EWCA Civ 1407, [2003] Q.B. 679 at [76]–[80]; below, paras 15–22 to 15–23.

[23] Paras 4–52 (impossibility of restitution) and 4–59 (intervening third-party rights).

[24] Although there was some judicial authority before 1967 that performance of the contract might bar rescission, the Misrepresentation Act 1967, s.1(b), provides that it does not.

example, it will often happen that the representee has passed goods to the other party under the terms of the contract which is to be rescinded: rescission will normally require the goods to be returned (and the price, if already paid, to be repaid); but questions have arisen in the cases about the nature of the representee's rights to the property during the period that the contract is voidable (but has not yet been rescinded); and therefore the effect of the remedy on his property rights at the moment of rescission.

4–10 **The "equity to rescind"; property rights before rescission.** The fact that a contract was induced by misrepresentation does not prevent the transfer of legal property rights in goods delivered or land transferred pursuant to the (voidable) contract: on rescission of the contract the representee therefore obtains a revesting of the property.[25] The position as regards the *equitable* property rights in the goods delivered or land transferred has however been the subject of some controversy. A representee who has a right to the remedy of rescission under the rules set out later in this chapter is said to have an *equity to rescind*. Some authorities[26] hold that the

---

[25] *Stevenson v Newnham* (1853) 13 C.B. 285 at 302–303, 138 E.R. 1208 at 1215–1216. For the means by which the revesting of property is effected, see below, para.4–11. The revesting of legal title in the case of rescission of a contract of sale induced by fraudulent misrepresentation is well established; but for the view that this is a misinterpretation of the old authorities, and incorrect in principle, see W. Swadling, "Rescission, Property, and the Common Law" (2005) 121 L.Q.R. 123.

[26] e.g. *Stump v Gaby* (1852) 2 De G. M. & G. 623 at 630, 42 E.R. 1015 at 1018; *Gresley v Mousley* (1859) 4 De G. & J. 78 at 93, 45 E.R. 31 at 37; *Melbourne Banking Corp. Ltd v Brougham* (1882) 7 App. Cas. 307, PC, at 311; J. Mowbray, L. Tucker, N. Le Poidevin, E. Simpson and J. Brightwell, *Lewin on Trusts* (18th edn, 2008), para.3–39. Such a position has also been taken in the context of contracts voidable on grounds other than misrepresentation. In *Re Garnett* (1886) 33 Ch.D. 300, CA, at 306 Lindley L.J. held that the setting aside of a release by a residuary legatee of her rights under a will, which was entered into without independent advice and in ignorance of the value of the rights in question, "confers no new title. It removes an impediment to the enjoyment of a pre-existing title". And in the context of a contract voidable for undue influence, Cotton L.J. suggested that the transferor of property could recover "on the ground that it was property the beneficial interest in which she had never effectually parted with": *Allcard v Skinner* (1887) 36 Ch.D. 145, CA, at 172. In Australia, see *Daly v Sydney Stock Exchange Ltd* (1986) 160 C.L.R. 371, HCA, at 388–389 (duty of disclosure arising out of fiduciary relationship; it "may be that . . . [the transferor] had an equitable interest in the property from the beginning", but the

representee retains an equitable interest in the property, but others[27] deny this and hold that the whole property passes under the contract and that the equity to rescind does not constitute a retained right of property for the representee.

It may be possible to reconcile the cases by accepting that the equity to rescind does not give rise to a full equitable interest in the transferred property of the kind which would arise if the representee transferred the legal title to be held on trust for himself; but that after the transfer the representee retains rights which can be recognised as proprietary for some purposes.[28] The retained rights can be disposed of inter vivos[29] or by will[30] so that the recipient can invoke the right to rescission and therefore recover the full property

---

transferee does not hold as constructive trustee as long as the contract stands); *Latec Investments Ltd v Hotel Terrigal Pty Ltd* (1965) 113 C.L.R. 265, HCA, at 282–284, 290–291. The reasoning behind the idea that a voidable contract gives rise to a continuing equitable interest appears to be similar to the principle that a contract to transfer an interest in land creates an equitable interest where a court would grant specific performance of the contract to order the interest to be conveyed: an operation of the maxim that "Equity looks on that as done which ought to be done": *Walsh v Lonsdale* (1882) 21 Ch.D. 9, CA; Snell, para.5–030; *cf. Stump v Gaby*, above; R. Chambers, *Resulting Trusts* (1998), pp.174–175. However the cases are not exactly parallel because in the case of rescission for misrepresentation the right to rescind does not (apart from the Misrepresentation Act, s.2(2), below, para.4–61) depend on the exercise of the court's discretion; and it is a right which the representee can choose whether to exercise, not a right which the court can presume should be exercised.

[27] *Clough v London and North Western Railway Co.* (1871) L.R. 7 Exch. 26 at 32, 34; *Bristol and West Building Society v Mothew* [1998] Ch. 1, CA, at 22; *Barclays Bank Plc v Boulter* [1999] 1 W.L.R. 1919, HL, at 1925; *Twinsectra Ltd v Yardley* [1999] Lloyd's Rep. Bank. 438, CA, at 461–462 (reversed on different grounds [2002] UKHL 12; [2002] 2 A.C. 164); Snell, para.15–020.

[28] *Latec Investments Ltd v Hotel Terrigal Pty Ltd*, above, n.26 at 291; *Blacklocks v JB Developments (Godalming) Ltd* [1982] Ch. 183 at 196; *Lewin on Trusts*, above, n.26, para.7–27. For a most thorough discussion, see S. Worthington, "The Proprietary Consequences of Rescission" [2002] R.L.R. 28 (the classical model "suggests that the claimant has a mere equity prior to rescission, but that after rescission legal or equitable title to the underlying property revests in the respective parties. The model is supported by precedent, consistent with legal doctrine, and suited to commercial and public goals": at 67). For a different view, that the transferee of property under a voidable contract holds the recoverable property under a resulting trust, see R. Chambers, *Resulting Trusts*, Ch.7.

[29] *Dickinson v Burrell* (1866) L.R. 1 Eq. 337; *Gross v Lewis Hillman Ltd* [1970] Ch. 445, CA, at 460–461; *Melbourne Banking Corp Ltd v Brougham*, above, n.26.

[30] *Stump v Gaby*, above, n.26; *Gresley v Mousley*, above, n.26.

rights. And where registered land is transferred under a voidable contract the transferor's equity to rescind has effect from the time the equity arises—that is, from the time of the contract and therefore before rescission is effected—as an interest capable of binding successors to the registered title.[31]

However, it is clear that the transferee of property under a voidable contract does not hold the property as trustee during the period before the contract is rescinded, nor does he have fiduciary duties to the transferor in respect of his use of the property.[32] And, except in registered land, the equity to rescind is not treated as equivalent to an equitable interest when the issue is whether a later

---

[31] Land Registration Act 2002 s.116(b), which is declared "for the avoidance of doubt" and applies to "a mere equity", including the equity to rescind. A registered disponee who gives valuable consideration will take free of the equity unless it is protected by entry of a notice in the register, or as an overriding interest: *ibid.*, s.29; see E.H. Burn and J. Cartwright, *Cheshire and Burn's Modern Law of Real Property* (18th edn, 2011), pp.903–906. Before the 2002 Act it had already been held that an equity had the quality of a "right" capable of constituting an overriding interest and therefore binding a purchaser under the Land Registration Act 1925 s.70(1)(*g*) (rights of person in actual occupation of the land or in receipt of rents and profits: see now the Land Registration Act 2002 Sch.3, para.2; *Cheshire and Burn's Modern Law of Real Property*, pp.1105–1106); *Blacklocks v JB Developments (Godalming) Ltd*, above, n.28 (equity to rectify, rather than to rescind; but at 195–196 Judge Mervyn Davies used rescission cases interchangeably with cases involving rectification); *Nurdin & Peacock Plc v Ramsden & Co. Ltd* [1999] 1 E.G.L.R. 119 at 124–126; [1999] Conv. 421 (S. Pascoe). The point was left open by the CA in *Collings v Lee* [2001] 2 All E.R. 332 at 338. Statements by Lord Upjohn and Lord Wilberforce in *National Provincial Bank Ltd v Ainsworth* [1965] A.C. 1175, HL, at 1238, 1254 appeared to deny that an equity to rescind could bind a purchaser of the land. The earlier statement (obiter) of Upjohn J. in *Smith v Jones* [1954] 1 W.L.R. 1089 at 1091 that the equity to rectify did not bind a purchaser of unregistered land can be read as saying not that the equity does not have proprietary characteristics, but that the rules of notice operative in unregistered land would not apply to hold a purchaser bound by such an equity.

[32] *Lonrho Plc v Fayed (No.2)* [1992] 1 W.L.R. 1 at 11 (transferee of shares under contract voidable for fraud has no duty to transferor in respect of use of the shareholding for mounting takeover bid for the remaining shares); *Daly v Sydney Stock Exchange Ltd*, above, n.26 at 389; and in relation to the payment of money under a voidable contract see *Shalson v Russo* [2003] EWHC 1637, [2005] Ch. 281 at [108] (Rimer J., distinguishing at [109]–[111] and [118] contrary dicta of Lord Browne-Wilkinson in *Westdeutsche Landesbank Girozentrale v Islington LBC* [1996] A.C. 669 at 715–6, and of Bingham J. in *Neste Oy v Lloyds Bank Plc* [1983] 2 Lloyd's Rep. 658 at 665–6); *Lewin on Trusts*, above, n.26, para.7–27. *Cf. Collings v Lee*, above, n.31 at 337 (equitable interest retained where

purchaser takes priority over the earlier rights.[33] But an equity to rescind will bind the transferee's trustee in bankruptcy.[34]

Property rights after rescission. At the moment that rescission takes effect[35] the obligations created by the contract are avoided. The representee immediately regains those legal and equitable property rights that can be revested without further formality,[36] but if the nature of the property is such that a revesting of the legal title requires a particular formality, such as where land[37] or shares have 4–11

transferors did not intend to transfer property, but transferee acquired transfer of legal estate without their knowledge and consent and in breach of his fiduciary duty to them).

33 *Phillips v Phillips* (1862) 4 De G. F. & J. 208 at 218, 45 E.R. 1164 at 1167. The rule is that, where equities are equal, the earlier in time prevails; but the purchaser of an equitable interest takes priority over an earlier equity to rescind. In *Latec Investments Ltd v Hotel Terrigal Pty Ltd*, above, n.26 at 286, Taylor J. suggested that, rather than the equity to rescind being of a lesser right than an equitable interest, the result might follow because a representee requires "the assistance of a court of equity to remove an impediment to his title as a preliminary to asserting his interest". However, the exercise of the right to rescind for misrepresentation is not dependent upon a court order: below, para.4–18. In *registered* land an equity now has the same priority as an equitable interest: Land Registration Act 2002, s.116(b); above, n.31.

34 *Re Eastgate* [1905] 1 K.B. 465. Where however, *money* is transferred under a voidable contract, no proprietary rights are retained and therefore the representee has no priority in the representee's bankruptcy: *Re Goldcorp Exchange Ltd* [1995] 1 A.C. 74, PC, at 102–103; below, para.4–12.

35 For the mechanism by which rescission is effected, see below, para.4–18.

36 *Car and Universal Finance Co. Ltd v Caldwell* [1965] 1 Q.B. 525, CA; *Newtons of Wembley Ltd v Williams* [1965] 1 Q.B. 560, CA (rescission of a contract of sale of a car revested legal title to the car even though the representee had not yet taken possession of it). For the view that "the remedy of rescission, by which the unjust enrichment of the representor is prevented, though for historical and practical reasons treated in books on the law of contract, is a straightforward remedy in restitution", see *Whittaker v Campbell* [1984] Q.B. 318 at 327 (Robert Goff L.J.); and Goff & Jones, Ch.9. However, it is suggested that the better view is that rescission itself is properly viewed as a contractual remedy based on the defective consent of the representee, although the *consequences* of rescission (the revesting of property, etc.) are restitutionary: above, para.4–09; below, para.4–52.

37 For formalities relating to the transfer of interests in land, see *Cheshire and Burn's Modern Law of Real Property*, above, n.31, Ch.25. An assured or secure tenancy of a dwelling-house cannot be brought to an end without a court order, even if the landlord was induced by misrepresentation to grant it; the statutory regime for the protection of tenants excludes the common law remedy of rescission: *Islington LBC v Uckac* [2006] EWCA Civ 340, [2006] 1 W.L.R. 1303;

been transferred pursuant to a voidable contract, the representor holds the legal title on constructive trust for the representee.[38] The duties of the representor under such a trust are not the full fiduciary duties of an express trustee; they extend only to the property obtained by the contract and liable to be returned.[39]

The proprietary (and other remedial) consequences of rescission may depend, however, on whether the misrepresentation was fraudulent or not. At common law, the avoidance of a contract for fraud had the effect of revesting the legal title[40]; and this will be given similar effect in equity.[41] After rescission, which can be effected by act of party without a court order,[42] the representee therefore has sufficient title to sue a third party in possession of the goods in the tort of conversion. However, if the misrepresentation was not fraudulent, and so would not have been recognised at common law as sufficient to render the contract voidable, the effect of rescission by act of party will not revest legal title to property which has passed under the contract, but only equitable title.[43] And

---

but it is a ground for possession that the landlord was induced to grant the tenancy by a false statement made knowingly or recklessly, i.e. fraudulently, by the tenant or a person acting at the tenant's instigation: Housing Act 1985 Sch.2, Pt I, Ground 5 (amended by the Housing Act 1996 s.146) (secure tenancy: public sector); *Merton LBC v Richards* [2005] EWCA Civ 639, [2005] H.L.R. 44; Housing Act 1988 Sch.2, Pt II, Ground 17 (introduced by the Housing Act 1996 s.102) (assured tenancy: private sector). In practice, this ground is rarely used by private landlords, but may be more useful for a public sector or social landlord: [2005] 25 E.G. 191 (S. Murdoch). For a case where the rescission of a contractual tenancy deprived the tenant of statutory protection see, however, *Killick v Roberts* [1991] 1 W.L.R. 1146.

[38] *FAI General Insurance Co. Ltd v Ocean Marine Mutual Protection and Indemnity Association* [1998] L.R.I.R. 24 at 28 (Aus. N.S.W. Com. Div); *Alati v Kruger* (1955) 94 C.L.R. 216, HCA, at 224.

[39] *Lonrho v Fayed (No.2)* [1992] 1 W.L.R. 1 at 11 (Millett J., drawing an analogy with the constructive trusteeship of a vendor of property contracted to be sold); *Daly v Sydney Stock Exchange Ltd*, above, n.26 at 389–390. In *El Ajou v Dollar Land Holdings Plc* [1993] 3 All E.R. 717 at 734 Millett J. took the view that a representor holds property after rescission not on "some new model remedial constructive trust, but an old-fashioned institutional resulting trust".

[40] *Car and Universal Finance Co. Ltd v Caldwell*, above, n.36.

[41] *El Ajou v Dollar Land Holdings Plc*, above, n.39 at 734.

[42] Below, para.4–18.

[43] *Alati v Kruger*, above, n.38 at 224.

an equitable title, without possession of the goods, does not suffice to support a claim for conversion.[44]

The revesting of property rights may be treated as operating retrospectively to the time of the contract for limited purposes, such as to the extent necessary to provide the representee with a continuing proprietary base to sustain a claim to trace the property.[45] However, it does not operate to render unlawful the representor's dealings with the property during the period between the contract and its rescission.[46]

Property rights in relation to money paid under a voidable contract. It has been said that the principles discussed above do not apply in the same way where money is transferred under a contract which is voidable for misrepresentation: the whole property in the money passes and no property rights, legal or equitable, remain in the transferor; no property rights revest on rescission; the transferee must repay an equivalent sum, and the transferor's rights are merely personal; even after rescission, the representee therefore cannot claim priority in the representor's bankruptcy.[47] However, although upon rescission restitution *in specie* is not possible in the case of the payment of money, and therefore must be effected by repayment of an equivalent sum, this does not mean that rescission cannot have the effect of revesting in 4–12

---

44 *MCC Proceeds Inc. v Lehman Bros International (Europe)* [1998] 4 All E.R. 675; *Hounslow LBC v Jenkins* [2004] EWHC 315 (QB), [2004] All E.R. (D) 160 (Feb); Clerk & Lindsell, para.17–67; S. Green and J. Randall, *The Tort of Conversion* (2009), pp.103–106.

45 *Lonrho v Fayed (No.2)*, above, n.39 at 11 (Millett J.); *El Ajou v Dollar Land Holdings Plc*, above, n.39 at 734 (Millett J.); *Bristol and West Building Society v Mothew* [1998] Ch. 1, CA, at 22–23 (Millett L.J.); *Shalson v Russo*, above, n.32 at [122]. It has also been held that a tenancy can be rescinded even after its expiry, so that there is retrospectively no contract to found a protected tenancy to continue after the expiry of the contractual term: *Killick v Roberts*, above, n.37.

46 *Bristol and West Building Society v Mothew*, above, n.45 at 22–23.

47 *Re Goldcorp Exchange Ltd* [1995] 1 A.C. 74, PC, at 102–103. For the view that, even in the case of the transfer of goods under a contract voidable for fraudulent misrepresentation, rescission should not have the effect of revesting title, but should leave the defrauded vendor to join the queue of unsecured creditors, see W. Swadling, "Rescission, Property, and the Common Law" (2005) 121 L.Q.R. 123 at p.153.

the representee the property in money paid under the voidable contract, entitling him at least to trace it into assets into which it was subsequently applied.[48]

4–13 **Rescission of the whole contract; rescission of part of the contract.** The general rule is that if rescission operates, the contract is set aside in its entirety: it is not simply set aside as regards a limited part of the contract which was directly affected by the misrepresentation relied upon to claim the remedy. This rule has two dimensions.

First, the representee must rescind the whole contract or none of it: he cannot elect to rescind only the part affected by the misrepresentation, whilst retaining the advantages of the remainder of the contract.[49] Similarly, if the representee is unable to make restitution of part of the benefits obtained under the contract, he cannot rescind as regards the remaining part: if a contract cannot be rescinded *in toto* it cannot be rescinded at all.[50] In deciding whether it is possible for the parties to make restitution, the courts adopt a flexible approach[51] and can sometimes appear to grant remedies which give less than full rescission of the whole of the obligations undertaken in the contract.[52] However, the principle remains that, once a right to rescind is established (including, therefore, there being no impediment to rescission on the basis of impossibility of restitution) the contract can be rescinded only in its entirety.

Secondly, the representor cannot resist rescission of the whole of the contract if the representor has a valid claim to rescission. For example, where a wife was induced to enter into a charge over her

[48] *Shalson v Russo*, above, n.32 at [124]–[127] (Rimer J., explaining *Re Goldcorp Exchange Ltd*, above, n.47, and applying *Banque Belge pour l'Etranger v Hambrouck* [1921] 1 K.B. 321). This does not give the representee priority over third parties, such as chargees, who have dealt with the representor in good faith and for value before rescission is effected. But it might allow him to assert property rights as against other creditors: *Shalson v Russo* at [126].

[49] *Urquhart v Macpherson* (1878) 3 App. Cas. 831, PC, at 837–838; *United Shoe Machinery Co. of Canada v Brunet* [1909] A.C. 330, PC, at 340.

[50] *Sheffield Nickel and Silver Plating Co. Ltd v Unwin* (1877) 2 Q.B.D. 214 at 223; *Hunt v Silk* (1804) 5 East 449, 102 E.R. 1142.

[51] Below, paras 4–54 to 4–56.

[52] e.g. *Cheese v Thomas* [1994] 1 W.L.R. 129, CA (rescission for undue influence: claimant was required to bear proportionate share of fall in value of property with which his contractual payment to defendant had been bought, rather than recovering the whole sum paid).

interest in the matrimonial home to secure her husband's debts by a misrepresentation that her liability would be limited to a specified figure (whereas in fact the terms of the charge imposed on her unlimited liability), the entire charge was set aside at her request.[53] This view has not prevailed in Australia where the High Court, in a case involving a director who entered into a guarantee of his company's past and future indebtedness following a misrepresentation that the guarantee related only to future debts, allowed the director to rescind the guarantee only in so far as it related to past debts. It was said that to hold the guarantor to the extent of the company's future indebtedness was to do no more than to hold him to what he was prepared to undertake independently of any misrepresentation.[54] These cases are unusual, in that the misrepresentation relates not to a fact which bears on the subject-matter of the contract, but to the content of the obligations about to be undertaken in the contract itself. If the representee sought to rely on the misrepresentation to obtain not rescission of the contract but rectification of a written contract to reflect the terms as misrepresented[55] or (in the case of a contract not reduced to writing) to assert that the contract stood but on the basis of terms as misrepresented,[56] he may be entitled to do so. But where the

---

[53] *TSB Bank Plc v Camfield* [1995] 1 W.L.R. 430, CA, followed in *De Molestina v Ponton* [2002] 1 Lloyd's Rep. 271 at 288 on the basis that *Vadasz v Pioneer Concrete (SA) Pty Ltd*, below, n.54, cannot be accepted into English law since it is inconsistent with *Barclays Bank Plc v O'Brien* [1994] 1 A.C. 180, HL. In *Scales Trading Ltd v Far Eastern Shipping Co. Public Ltd* [2001] Lloyd's Rep. Bank. 29 at 34 the Privy Council, on an appeal from New Zealand, declined to decide between *TSB Bank Plc v Camfield* and *Vadasz v Pioneer Concrete (SA) Pty Ltd.* Where, however, a contract can be severed, it may be possible to avoid only one part: *Barclays Bank Plc v Caplan* [1998] 1 F.L.R. 532 (side-letter extending guarantee avoided for undue influence, although main guarantee still enforceable).

[54] *Vadasz v Pioneer Concrete (SA) Pty Ltd* (1995) 184 C.L.R. 102. The decision in *TSB Bank Plc v Camfield*, above, n.53, was expressly rejected at 115–116. See also L. Proksch, "Rescission on Terms" [1996] R.L.R. 71; A. Robertson, "Partial Rescission, Causation and Benefit" (2001) 17 J.C.L. 163.

[55] A fraudulent misrepresentation, or other unconscionable conduct in obtaining the contract in its written form, must be shown: *May v Platt* [1900] 1 Ch. 616 at 623; *Commission for the New Towns v Cooper (Great Britain) Ltd* [1995] Ch. 259, CA; below, paras.13–47 to 13–48 (rectification for unilateral mistake).

[56] An innocent misrepresentation as to the terms suffices: *Curtis v Chemical Cleaning and Dyeing Co.* [1951] 1 K.B. 805, CA (exemption clause incorporated only in its meaning as represented; for the interpretation, however, that the clause

representee seeks to rely on the misrepresentation to obtain rescission of the entire contract, it is submitted that the approach taken in the English courts is correct. It flows from the fact that the remedy of rescission of the contract for misrepresentation is not within the discretion of the court, but is available as of right to a representee who satisfies the requirements of the remedy set out later in this chapter.[57] As long as there is no impediment to rescission, such as the representee not being able and willing to make restitution of benefits obtained under the contract,[58] the representor has no choice but to submit to rescission of the entire contract.

4–14 **Severable contracts.** The rules stated in the preceding paragraph apply to entire contracts. If what appears to be a single contract should properly be construed as severable into separate contracts, rescission will be available of the whole of each separate contract which is affected by the relevant misrepresentation.[59] For example, a single insurance policy may be written so as to separate the risks into separate contracts, with the result that a misrepresentation with respect to one risk will vitiate only the contract relating to that risk.[60] And a composite insurance policy—a single insurance policy

---

was on the facts not incorporated, see *AXA Sun Life Services Plc v Harry Bennett & Associates Ltd* [2011] EWCA Civ 133 at [105] (Rix L.J.)).

[57] *TSB Bank Plc v Camfield*, above, n.53 at 438–439 (Roch L.J.); *Car and Universal Finance Co. Ltd v Caldwell* [1965] 1 Q.B. 525, CA, below, para.4–20. For a different view, see J. Poole and A. Keyser, "Justifying Partial Rescission in English Law" (2005) 121 L.Q.R. 273, who advocate a discretionary remedy of partial rescission, limited to the case where there is a non-fraudulent misrepresentation about the content of the obligations of the contract. This is designed to fulfil the contractual expectations of the parties, but depends on acceptance that rescission for non-fraudulent misrepresentation is a discretionary remedy; *cf.* below, para.4–18.

[58] Below, para.4–52; *Dunbar Bank Plc v Nadeem* [1998] 3 All E.R. 876, CA; *Midland Bank Plc v Greene* (1995) 27 H.L.R. 350 (charge over house by defendant and husband to secure purchase moneys for purchase and the husband's personal debts: undue influence by husband: court could not set aside charge in part, but would order that it be set aside in full if the defendant repaid the debt in respect of her own share in the property).

[59] *De Molestina v Ponton*, above, n.53.

[60] *cf. Printpak v AGF Insurance Ltd* [1999] 1 All E.R. (Comm) 466, CA (warranty as to operation of burglar alarm only applied to part of insurance policy dealing with theft risks, and so under the Marine Insurance Act 1906 s.33(3) discharged the insurer from liability under only that section); *The Litsion Pride*

which insures two or more persons with separate interests (such as the landlord and tenant of property)—will generally be treated as containing separate contracts, so that a pre-contractual misrepresentation by one insured will allow the insurer to rescind the policy only as far as it relates to that insured.[61] A contract for the allotment of shares in a company has also been held to be a severable contract, so that the shareholder could rescind in relation to the shares he still held where he had parted with part of the shareholding before discovering the fraud which induced him to take the shares.[62]

Rescission of chains of contracts and of related contracts. 4–15
Sometimes there will be a chain of contracts, such as where A sells goods to B, which B sells on to C. If B has a claim against A to rescind the first contract, its exercise is likely to be dependent on C first rescinding his contract with B, since it will generally be impossible for B to restore the goods as long as the contract with C is outstanding. However, if C is willing and able to rescind that contract, B is reinvested with the rights of property in the goods, so allowing the exercise of his right of rescission against A.[63] However, for each link in the chain of contracts the requirements of rescission must be satisfied and the remedy sought by the party with the right to it. So, to take a different example, if by a misrepresentation X induces Y to buy goods, and Y later transfers the goods to Z, Z's remedy of rescission is normally only available against Y. He has no right as against X to require him to take back the goods and hand over the purchase price he received from Y. The misrepresentation made by X to Y is spent when Y buys the

[1985] 1 Lloyd's Rep. 437 (extension of cover separate from original contract). There is more extensive authority in American law for severance of contracts for this purpose, e.g. *Hesselberg v Aetna Life Ins. Co.*, 102 F.2d 23 (1939); *Bethune v New York Underwriters Ins. Co.*, 98 F.Supp. 366 (1951).

[61] *New Hampshire Insurance Co. v MGN Ltd* [1997] L.R.L.R. 24, CA; *Arab Bank Plc v Zurich Insurance Co.* [1999] 1 Lloyd's Rep. 262.

[62] *Re The Mount Morgan (West) Gold Mine Ltd* (1887) 56 L.T. 622. It would be otherwise if the contract were for the transfer of shares of different descriptions, rather than in a single category of shares in the same company: *ibid.*, at 625 (Kay J.).

[63] *Abram Steamship Co. Ltd v Westville Shipping Co. Ltd* [1923] A.C. 773, HL(Sc.).

property, and Z must find a separate claim, based on Y's own misrepresentation to him, in order to rescind the contract with Y.[64]

Where there are two or more related contracts, each must normally be considered separately as regards any claim to rescission. So if a purchaser buys two separate items, under two separate contracts from the same vendor, e.g. separate lots at auction, a misrepresentation by the vendor as to one of the items will not normally allow the purchaser to rescind also the second contract, unless both parties knew and understood that the two contracts were interdependent.[65]

4–16 **Clauses which survive rescission.** Although rescission involves the contract being retrospectively avoided, certain clauses will survive rescission: the concept of avoidance *ab initio* does not compel the conclusion that the former existence of the contract is denied, or that it cannot be recognised for the purpose of working out the consequences of its avoidance.[66] So it has been held that an exclusive jurisdiction clause in a contract can be given effect notwithstanding the avoidance of the contract for misrepresentation.[67] Similarly, a clause requiring disputes to be

[64] *Gross v Lewis Hillman Ltd* [1970] Ch. 445, CA, at 460–461, 463. This is an illustration of the rule that rescission can be sought only by a party to the contract: *Sanctuary Housing Association v Baker* [1998] 1 E.G.L.R. 42, CA, at 44 (landlord's consent to assignment of lease obtained by fraud of tenant and proposed assignee; landlord entitled to rescission of the consent to assignment, but not to rescission of the assignment itself to which it was not party).

[65] *Holliday v Lockwood* [1917] 2 Ch. 47. However, even though rescission of the second contract is not available, a court may still refuse specific performance of it, and leave the purchaser to his remedy in damages: *ibid.*, at 57.

[66] *FAI General Insurance Co. Ltd v Ocean Marine Mutual Protection and Indemnity Association* [1998] Lloyd's Rep. I.R. 24 at 28 (Giles C.J., Aus. N.S.W. Com. Div.): "a contract avoided *ab initio* is not, in Newspeak, an uncontract". The same logic would therefore not apply to a *void* (as opposed to only *voidable*) contract: *Mackender v Feldia A.G.* [1967] 2 Q.B. 590, CA, at 602–603; but see *Harbour Assurance Co. (UK) Ltd v Kansa General International Insurance Co. Ltd* [1992] 1 Lloyd's Rep. 81 at 90–93 holding that an arbitration clause can extend to a claim to voidness of a contract, e.g. for mistake at common law; Arbitration Act 1996 s.7 (unless otherwise agreed by the parties, arbitration agreement is to be treated as distinct and is unaffected by invalidity of the substantive contract of which it forms part).

[67] *FAI General Insurance Co. Ltd v Ocean Marine Mutual Protection and Indemnity Association*, above, n.66 (the clause must, of course, on its proper construction extend to disputes over the claim to avoidance: *ibid.*, at 31);

submitted to arbitration can survive the avoidance.[68] And clauses in the contract which make other provision for the consequences of rescission ought also to have effect—such as limitation and exclusion clauses.[69]

Rescission, indemnity and damages. Upon rescission of the contract the parties must each return to the other what they have received under the contract: so on rescission of a contract of sale the buyer must return the goods, and the seller must return the price.[70] Rescission will therefore often restore the representee to his original financial position. However, if in connection with the contract he **4–17**

Mackender v Feldia A.G., above, n.66 at 603 (Diplock L.J., reserving his position in relation to a claim for fraud; Russell L.J. at 605 reserved his position in relation to a claim for both fraudulent and innocent misrepresentation). See also *Deutsche Bank AG v Asia Pacific Broadband Wireless Communications Inc.* [2008] EWCA Civ 1091, [2008] 2 C.L.C. 520 at [24], [29] (jurisdiction clause, like an arbitration clause (below, n.68), is a separable agreement from the agreement as a whole, and disputes about the validity of the contract must be resolved under the terms of the clause, unless the jurisdiction clause is itself under some specific attack (e.g. fraud alleged in relation specifically to the clause, or (perhaps) if the signatures to the agreement were alleged to be forgeries), but not merely if there is a plausible allegation that the contract in which the clause is contained is vitiated by mistake, misrepresentation, illegality, lack of authority or lack of capacity).

68 *Harbour Assurance Co. (UK) Ltd v Kansa General International Insurance Co. Ltd*, above, n.66 at 90–91: the clause must be sufficiently widely drawn to cover the dispute, but the "inexorable logic of *Mackender v Feldia A.G.*," above, n.66, means that an arbitration clause can even extend even to claims for fraudulent misrepresentation; [1993] QB 701 (CA). The House of Lords has said that the older authorities should no longer be relied on: in line with Arbitration Act 1996 s.7 (above, n.66), "the construction of an arbitration clause should start from the assumption that the parties, as rational businessmen, are likely to have intended any dispute arising out of the relationship into which they have entered or purported to enter to be decided by the same tribunal. The clause should be construed in accordance with this presumption unless the language makes it clear that certain questions were intended to be excluded from the arbitrator's jurisdiction": *Fiona Trust & Holding Corp. v Privalov* [2007] UKHL 40, [2007] 4 All E.R. 951 at [13] (Lord Hoffmann).

69 e.g. a clause excluding remedies in damages for the misrepresentation (but not excluding rescission of the contract). Such a clause would be subject to the statutory controls on exemption clauses, and in particular the Misrepresentation Act 1967 s.3 (as amended by the Unfair Contract Terms Act 1977 s.8); below, paras 9–19 to 9–30.

70 The goods must normally be returned *in specie*; but the buyer does not recover "his" money, just an equivalent sum: above, para.4–12.

has undertaken obligations to third parties, or has incurred expenses in favour of third parties, rescission will not of itself be sufficient to restore the representee to his original position. There are two possible remedies to deal with this: an indemnity, or damages.

The courts of equity allowed a representee to recover an "indemnity" to compensate him for the obligations undertaken or expenditure incurred in favour of third parties under the contract which is rescinded.[71] This is not a general remedy in damages. It is available only as an adjunct to the remedy of rescission, and is the consequence of setting aside the contract into which the claimant was induced to enter: he is not put back into his original (pre-contract) position unless he is relieved from the consequences and obligations which are the result of the contract which is set aside.[72] There is some disagreement in the cases about the scope of the indemnity. It certainly covers the cost of performing obligations which were created by the contract itself[73]; but it has sometimes been said to go beyond this and to cover the cost of performing any obligation which was entered into under the contract which is rescinded.[74] The better view seems to be that the representee will be entitled to be indemnified only in respect of the expenditure incurred under the terms of the contract itself,[75] although the term requiring that expenditure might be either an express term or an implied term.[76]

But if following rescission the representee has losses beyond those in respect of which he can claim an indemnity against the representor,[77] he must seek a remedy in damages to make good

[71] *Newbigging v Adam* (1886) 34 Ch.D. 582, CA; *Whittington v Seale-Hayne* (1900) 82 L.T. 49; *Brown v Smitt* (1924) 34 C.L.R. 160, HCA.

[72] *Newbigging v Adam*, above, n.71 at 589.

[73] *ibid.*, at 589 (Cotton L.J.), 593, 595 (Bowen L.J.).

[74] *ibid.*, at 596 (Fry L.J., who thought that in this he was agreeing with Cotton L.J. This seems, however, doubtful: *Whittington v Seale-Hayne*, above, n.71 at 51).

[75] *Whittington v Seale-Hayne*, above, n.71.

[76] Treitel, para. 9–075. Under the Partnership Act 1890 s.41, a party who rescinds the partnership contract on the ground of fraud or misrepresentation is entitled to, inter alia, an indemnity against the person guilty of the fraud or making the misrepresentation against the debts and liabilities of the firm to third parties for which he continues to be liable.

[77] e.g. in *Whittington v Seale-Hayne*, above, n.71, the claimants rescinded a lease of property used for a poultry breeding business which had been induced by a misrepresentation as to the condition of the premises. They were entitled to

those losses. If the representation was fraudulent, he may seek to recover damages from the representee in the tort of deceit[78]; if it was not fraudulent he may claim under section 2(1) of the Misrepresentation Act 1967,[79] or sometimes in the tort of negligence.[80] A claim to damages in tort is compatible with rescission of the contract, and the representee is therefore entitled to both rescission and damages if he can establish his claim to each under the respective rules of the remedies.[81] A claim to any remedy for breach of contract is not, however, compatible with rescission (since the one remedy asserts that there is a contract under which a remedy can be granted; the other seeks to nullify that contract). If, therefore, the representee has losses which he wishes to recover as damages for breach of contract,[82] he must elect between the claim to damages and rescission.

(3) The Mechanics of Rescission

Rescission by election of the representee, not by order of the court. No court order is necessary for rescission to take effect: "the right to set aside or rescind the transaction is that of the representee, not that of the court".[83] Rescission is effected[84] 4–18

---

recover as an indemnity the rates paid to the local authority and repairs to the property which were incurred in fulfilment of their obligations as tenants under the lease; but they could not recover the loss of their poultry stock and the losses incurred in running the business, since those were general losses and not costs which they were required by the terms of the lease to incur.

78 Ch.5.

79 Which gives a remedy of damages on the tort measure where the representor cannot prove that he honestly and on reasonable grounds believed his statement: Ch.7.

80 Ch.6.

81 *Archer v Brown* [1985] Q.B. 401 at 415. In practice, any sum recoverable as an *indemnity* will also be recoverable within damages on the tort measure; the remedy of the indemnity is therefore useful only when there is no independent claim to damages, i.e. a wholly innocent misrepresentation which does not even give rise to a claim under the Misrepresentation Act 1967 s.2(1).

82 Ch.8.

83 *TSB Bank Plc v Camfield* [1995] 1 W.L.R. 430, CA, at 438. See also *Reese River Silver Mining Co. v Smith* (1869) L.R. 4 H.L. 64, HL, at 73; *Abram Steamship Co. Ltd v Westville Shipping Co. Ltd* [1923] A.C. 773, HL (Sc.), at 781; *Alati v Kruger* (1955) 94 C.L.R. 216 at 224, HCA; *Horsler v Zorro* [1975] Ch. 302 at 310; *Drake Insurance Plc v Provident Insurance Plc* [2003] EWHC 109 (Comm), [2003] 1 All E.R. (Comm) 759 at [31] (reversed on different

"by an unequivocal act of election [by the representee] which demonstrates clearly that he elects to rescind [the contract] and to be no longer bound by it."

A court may of course become involved in determining a dispute between the representor and the representee as to whether there was a right to rescind, but if it decides that rescission was justified the court order does not constitute the rescission: it merely confirms that the earlier act of election by the representee did validly rescind the contract, and then gives effect to it and makes any appropriate consequential orders. Even if there was no sufficient act of election

---

grounds [2003] EWCA Civ 1834, [2004] Q.B. 601; see at [102]: insurer's avoidance is a unilateral act); *Shalson v Russo* [2003] EWHC 1637 (Ch), [2005] Ch. 281 at [122]; *Brotherton v Aseguradora Colseguros SA* [2003] EWCA Civ 705, [2003] 2 C.L.C. 629 at [27], [45]. Snell, para.15–012 (in a change to the position stated in 31st edn, 2005, para.13.13) says that, notwithstanding these decisions, the foundational authorities presuppose the parallel operations of different mechanisms at law (act of party) and in equity (rescission only by court order) and that the judicial mechanism developed in Chancery still continues to exist today. However, the modern cases there cited concerned rescission for undue influence, abuse of confidence and breach of fiduciary duty (and note *Johnson v E.B.S. Pensioner Trustees Ltd* [2002] EWCA Civ 164, [2002] Lloyd's Rep. P.N. 309 at [78] (Dyson L.J.: "*whatever the position in relation to a claim to rescind based on misrepresentation*, the right to rescission on grounds of undue influence, abuse of confidence or breach of fiduciary duty depends on the exercise of the discretion by the court to intervene in the enforcement of legal rights"; emphasis added)). The early cases which acknowledged rescission by act of party were in the common law—and limited, therefore, to rescission for fraudulent misrepresentation: above, para.4–02. But it has clearly become accepted in the modern law that rescission can be effected by act of party also in the case of non-fraudulent misrepresentation; and this appears to be assumed by the Misrepresentation Act 1967 s.2(2); below, n.86. For the proposal that the remedy of rescission should be effected by the court, rather than by the party concerned, see J. O'Sullivan, "Rescission as a Self-help Remedy: a Critical Analysis" [2000] C.L.J. 509; see also J. Poole and A. Keyser, "Justifying Partial Rescission in English Law" (2005) 121 L.Q.R. 273. See also D. O'Sullivan, S. Elliott and R. Zakrzewski, *The Law of Rescission* (2008), Ch.11, who conclude at para.11.105 that, even where rescission is effected in equity, it is only in the case of fraud that no court order is required (note, however, that the authors of this work maintain a rather strong non-fusionist stance to the law of rescission in general: see esp. Ch.10).

84 *Car and Universal Finance Co. Ltd v Caldwell* [1965] 1 Q.B. 525 at 531 (Lord Denning M.R., sitting as trial judge). See also *Reese River Silver Mining Co. v Smith*, above, n.83 at 73; *Abram Steamship Co. Ltd v Westville Shipping Co. Ltd*, above, n.83 at 781.

before the proceedings were begun, the plea in the action that the contract has been or should be set aside will suffice, and therefore any order of the court will relate back at the latest to that time.[85]

Since 1967 the court has had a statutory discretion to declare the contract subsisting and to award damages in lieu of rescission in certain circumstances.[86] This emphasises that, but for the statute, the court has no power to declare the contract subsisting when the representee has exercised his right to rescind.[87] And since rescission is available as of right to a representee who can show that the requirements of the remedy, set out later in this chapter, have been satisfied, the court has no general power to impose terms on the grant of the remedy.[88]

Form of election to rescind. The question, then, is what constitutes a sufficient "unequivocal act of election" by the representee. It is clear that a formal notice to the representor that the representee now treats the contract as rescinded will normally[89] 4–19

[85] *Reese River Silver Mining Co. v Smith*, above, n.83 at 73; *Clough v London and North Western Railway Co.* (1871) L.R. 7 Exch. 26 at 36; *TSB Bank Plc v Camfield*, above, n.83 at 438–439; *Alati v Kruger*, above, n.83 at 224.

[86] Misrepresentation Act 1967 s.2(2); below, para.4–61. The section only applies where the representation was made "otherwise than fraudulently".

[87] *TSB Bank Plc v Camfield*, above, n.83 at 960. The assertion of Jacob J. to the contrary in *Thomas Witter Ltd v TBP Industries Ltd* [1996] 2 All E.R. 573 at 586 (discussing rescission for fraudulent misrepresentation) appears to be mistaken.

[88] *TSB Bank Plc v Camfield*, above, n.83. But see *Killick v Roberts* [1991] 1 W.L.R. 1146, CA, at 1150 (Nourse L.J.: rescission is "an equitable remedy... sometimes granted only on terms"; but it is not clear that he was considering the issue discussed here, and it is true that in other contexts the remedy has been granted subject to terms, e.g. mistake: *Cooper v Phibbs* (1867) L.R. 2 H.L. 149; but see now below, paras 15–32 to 15–33). Sometimes it may appear that terms are being imposed, such as when a representor is required to compensate the representee for the use of a chattel which he received under the contract which is being rescinded. However, this is not the general exercise of an equitable discretion to impose terms on the award of the remedy but a determination by the court of one of the requirements of the remedy itself: that such compensation is necessary as part of the requirement of restitution: below, para.4–54.

[89] There is an exception in the case of a contract to take an allotment of new shares in a company where, in addition to indicating a desire to rescind, the shareholder must take steps to have his name removed from the register of shareholders: rescission of the allotment of shares will take place when an action for removal is begun: *Re Scottish Petroleum Co.* (1883) 23 Ch.D. 413, CA; *First National Reinsurance Co. Ltd v Greenfield* [1921] 2 K.B. 260; *Reese River Silver Mining Co. Ltd v Smith* (1869) L.R. 4 H.L. 64, HL; Gore-Brown, para.43[17]. If,

suffice and will take effect, at the latest, at the moment of its receipt by the representor. Similarly, any informal notice or any act by the representee which sufficiently communicates his decision to rescind will suffice.

4–20 **Rescission without actual communication to the representor.** The general rule is that there must be communication[90] to the representor, because the representor is entitled to treat the contract as continuing until he is made aware of the representee's intention to exercise the right to rescind.[91] There is one general exception to this: that in the case of a contract pursuant to which property is transferred, such as a contract for the sale of goods, it is sufficient for the transferor to retake possession of the property in order to rescind—even if the transferee is not yet aware of the transferor's act in retaking the property.[92] But the courts have sometimes been prepared to accept that an election is made without such communication or actual recaption of the property transferred.

however, the company has already forfeited the representee's shares because he has failed to pay calls due in respect of the allotment, he has then ceased to be a member and has become a mere debtor to the company, and he can rescind the contract in the usual way: *Aaron's Reefs Ltd v Twiss* [1896] A.C. 273, HL.

[90] Consistently with the general approach to the interpretation of communications between contracting parties, the question is not whether the representor actually realised that the representor was exercising his right to rescind, but whether he ought to have realised it, from what the representee said or did; *Scarf v Jardine* (1882) 7 App. Cas. 345, HL, at 361; *cf.* above, para.3–06.

[91] *Car and Universal Finance Co. Ltd v Caldwell* [1965] 1 Q.B. 525, CA, at 554; *Reese River Silver Mining Co. v Smith*, above, n.89 at 74.

[92] This was accepted as a general rule in *Car and Universal Finance Co. Ltd v Caldwell*, above, n.91, although Davies L.J. at 558 noted that there was no very clear authority to this effect; *Re Eastgate* [1905] 1 K.B. 465 (rescission effected by breaking into house of buyer, who had absconded, and retaking goods). It might be argued that generally recaption of the goods constitutes sufficient notice to the representor, just as posting a letter containing a formal notice of rescission through the representor's letter box might also be argued to be a sufficient communication without waiting for the representor to open the letter and read it; but on recaption of the goods in the absence of the representor the representee knows that the representor does not yet know of the rescission—yet the rescission dates from the moment of recaption. In *Car and Universal Finance Co. Ltd v Caldwell* at 555 Upjohn L.J. was not convinced that recaption can be treated as simply a method of communication. It appears therefore to be better thought of as a separate rule.

In *Car and Universal Finance Co. Ltd v Caldwell*,[93] Caldwell contracted to sell a car to Norris and was persuaded to allow Norris to take the car in return for a cheque which was not met when presented. Caldwell then immediately reported the fraud to the police and the Automobile Association, asking for their assistance in tracing Norris and the car. It was held by Lord Denning M.R. (sitting as the trial judge) and the Court of Appeal that Caldwell had successfully rescinded the contract by his action in attempting to trace Norris and recover the car. In consequence, a later contract of sale of the car did not operate to extinguish Caldwell's title to the car because the rescission had already revested the legal and equitable title in him.[94]

It is important to understand the limits of this decision. It is authority that, at least where the claim to rescind is based on a fraudulent misrepresentation, and the representor has deliberately absconded so that he cannot be contacted by the representee who wishes to exercise his right to rescind by the normal means of communicating his election, the representee is entitled to rescind by the best other overt means possible; and that Caldwell's attempt to trace the representor and the car by contacting the police and the Automobile Association satisfied this requirement on the facts. It does not undermine the general rule that rescission requires communication to the representor of the election to rescind or actual recaption of the property transferred. Statements in the judgment of Lord Denning might suggest a greater relaxation of the requirement of actual communication: in particular, he used as analogies other

---

93 Above, n.91; followed in *Newtons of Wembley Ltd v Williams* [1965] 1 Q.B. 560, CA (car obtained by fraud: sellers unable to communicate with buyer but took all possible steps to trace him, and notified Hire Purchase Information Bureau that the car was theirs. The trial judge was Davies L.J., and Sellers L.J. presided in the Court of Appeal—both had sat in the CA in *Caldwell*). *Cf.* however, in Scottish law, *MacLeod v Kerr* 1965 S.C. 253, Ct. Sess. (contract not avoided by representee's notification of fraud to police: "an invocation of the powers of the criminal authorities cannot possibly be the avoidance of a contract entered into under the civil law": at 259 (Lord Guthrie)).

94 For this principle, see below, para.4–60. Lord Denning M.R. held in the alternative that, if there had been no valid rescission by Caldwell before the later contract, the purchaser had notice of the earlier defect in title and so the later contract did not extinguish Caldwell's right to rescind. The CA disagreed with this second ground, but affirmed Lord Denning M.R.'s decision on the primary ground that rescission had been effected notwithstanding the absence of communication to the representor.

cases of election which do not require actual communication but are satisfied by any unequivocal act clearly evincing his election.[95] However, such analogies were rejected in the Court of Appeal[96] where the judges were careful to make clear that they regarded their decision as laying down only a limited exception to the general rule. Indeed, it is not helpful even to use as an analogy the rules for affirmation of the contract by the representee on discovering the misrepresentation.[97] In that case, the election to affirm may be evidenced by the representee's words or acts alone without requiring the words or acts to have been communicated to the representor. It can be justified because the representee's election operates only against his own interest: he deprives himself of his right to rescind, and as far as the representor is concerned the contract simply remains on foot. But in the case of an election to rescind, it ought not to be sufficient for the representee to exercise his election without communication to the representor, because the election deprives the representor of the benefit of the contract. Taking this argument further leads to a convincing rationale for the decision in *Caldwell*, and also shows where its limit should lie: the circumstances in which it is appropriate for the representee to rescind without actual communication to the representor are where the conduct of the representor has been such as to deprive himself of the right to require actual communication. This approach, in substance, underlies the judgments in *Caldwell*. Sellers L.J. said[98]:

> "in circumstances such as the present case the other contracting party, a fraudulent rogue who would know that the vendor would want his car back as soon as he knew of the fraud, would not expect to be communicated with

---

[95] Forfeiture by a lessor; ratification of an agent's acts by his principal; acceptance of a repudiation of a contract; affirmation of a contract: see [1965] 1 Q.B. 525 at 532. *Cf.* Lord Denning's general position in the formation of a contract that communications should be viewed from the perspective of an external observer, rather than from the more limited perspective of the other contracting party: *Solle v Butcher* [1950] 1 K.B. 671, CA, at 691; *Frederick E. Rose (London) Ltd v William H. Pim. Jnr & Co. Ltd* [1953] 2 Q.B. 450, CA, at 460; Cartwright, pp.21–24; below, para.13–07, n.14.

[96] [1965] 1 Q.B. 525 at 549–550, 556, 559.

[97] Below, para.4–39. See [1965] 1 Q.B. 525 at 550.

[98] [1965] 1 Q.B. 525 at 550–551. See also Upjohn L.J. at 555. Davies L.J. at 558–559 went further and suggested that there was a term implied into the contract between Caldwell and Norris that Caldwell would be entitled to rescind by the best possible means other than actual communication.

> as a matter of right or requirement, and would deliberately, as here, do all he could to evade any such communication being made to him. In such exceptional contractual circumstances, it does not seem to me appropriate to hold that a party so acting can claim any right to have a decision to rescind communicated to him before the contract is terminated. To hold that he could would involve that the defrauding party, if skilful enough to keep out of the way, could deprive the other party to the contract of his right to rescind, a right to which he was entitled and which he would wish to exercise, as the defrauding party would well know or at least confidently suspect."

This principle need not then be restricted to cases of fraudulent misrepresentation. It is true that it is in cases of fraud that it is most likely to apply, since it is then most likely that the representor will in fact abscond, and also then easiest to infer that by absconding he intended to avoid communication. The focus should not, however, be on the nature of the misrepresentation, but on the reason for the representee's inability to communicate with the representor: it is possible for a representor, though not fraudulent at the time of the contract, none the less later to take steps deliberately to avoid communication: the principle underlying *Caldwell* ought also then to be applicable.[99]

Another reason for wishing to restrict the application of the principle in *Caldwell* is its impact on the property rights of later innocent purchasers who can find that they have no title because of an effective earlier election to rescind.[100] However, this raises broader questions about the relative claims of innocent parties where there have been successive contracts of sale of goods, which

[99] The CA was careful to reserve its position in cases of non-fraudulent misrepresentation, and Sellers L.J. went so far as to doubt whether a representor would deliberately avoid communication after making a non-fraudulent misrepresentation: [1965] 1 Q.B. 525 at 551–552.

[100] Law Reform Committee Twelfth Report, *Transfer of Title to Chattels*, Cmnd. 2958 (1966), para.16, recommending that the *Caldwell* rule should be reversed, and that "unless and until notice of the rescission of the contract is communicated to the other contracting party an innocent purchaser from the latter should be able to acquire a good title". The Law Commission announced in 2005 that it would re-open this question in its Ninth Programme of Law Reform: Law Com. No.293 (2005), paras 3.51–3.57. However, because "the issues involved in this project remain controversial" it was deferred in the Tenth Programme of Law Reform: Law Com No.311 (2008), paras 4.2–4.4, for further consideration in the Eleventh Programme "to see whether the climate has become more conducive to tackling this long-standing problem."

ought to be addressed in the context of the property law issues which are involved.[101] When considering the question of whether the contract has been rescinded, the Court of Appeal in *Caldwell* properly took the view that it is the position of the two contracting parties which must be considered.[102]

II. ELEMENTS OF THE CLAIM

4–21 **Overview of the elements of the claim.** In general terms, the equitable[103] remedy of rescission is available to a representee who can show that a false representation was made to him by or on behalf of the other party to the contract; that *either* the representation was made fraudulently *or* it was a representation of fact; and that the representation acted as an inducement to his decision to enter into the contract.[104] Some of these elements have been discussed already in Chapter 3; in such cases references will be made back to detailed discussion in that chapter. Other elements of the representee's claim will be discussed in detail in this section.

4–22 **Establishing the elements of the claim gives rise to a prima facie right to rescind.** If he establishes these elements the representee has a prima facie right to rescind, subject only to the question of whether the defendant can show one or more of the "bars" to rescission discussed in the next section.

(1) The Representation

4–23 **The representation: words or conduct.** The representee must show that a falsehood was communicated to him—a representation, which will commonly be in the form of words spoken or written by

---

[101] Below, paras 4–60 and 14–39. The effect of the Sale of Goods Act 1979 s.25(1) appears to be that the buyer in good faith and without notice will be protected, even after the representor has rescinded the contract, since he takes from a seller who has obtained possession with the consent of the representor: *Newtons of Wembley Ltd v Williams*, above, n.93; Chitty, para.43–241; Benjamin, para.7–025.

[102] [1965] 1 Q.B. 525 at 551, 555.

[103] Above, para.4–02.

[104] It need not be shown that the terms of the contract were disadvantageous to the representee: *C.I.B.C. Mortgages Plc v Pitt* [1994] 1 A.C. 200, HL, at 209.

the representor but can equally well be the representee's interpretation of the meaning of the representor's conduct. It will be for the representee to plead the particular representation on which he relies for the remedy; and in the case of any dispute over the meaning of any words or conduct of the representor it appears that an objective test of interpretation, tested from the representee's perspective, should be used. These requirements were discussed in Chapter 3.[105]

Representation by or on behalf of the other party to the contract. The representation must normally be made by the other party to the contract. The usual principles of agency apply, and so a representation made by a person capable of binding the contracting party as his agent will found a claim to rescission of the contract.[106] But it is not generally sufficient if the representee receives the false information from a person outside the contract, for whom the other contracting party is not responsible.[107] In such a case, the representee can allege that he has made a *mistake* in entering into the contract, but there is no claim for misrepresentation. And the circumstances in which a party can successfully claim that the contract was vitiated for mistake are much more limited.[108] The remedy of rescission for misrepresentation is based on a rationale that the contracting party who misleads the other bears responsibility for causing the other's mistake and thereby risks losing the benefit of the contract, even where he was honest in making the false statement.[109] Where the mistake is caused by a third party for whom the contracting party is not responsible, there is no equity against the contracting party stronger than the claim based simply 4–24

105 Above, paras 3–04 to 3–06.

106 *Lynde v Anglo-Italian Hemp Spinning Co.* [1896] 1 Ch. 178 at 182–183 (statements by agent of company). On the question whether a claimant who was induced by a fraudulent misrepresentation of an undisclosed principal can avoid the contract made with the agent who did not know of the fraud, see *Garnac Grain Co. Inc. v H.M.F. Faure & Fairclough Ltd* [1966] 1 Q.B. 650 at 656 (Megaw J.: yes); left open by CA at 674 (Sellers L.J.), 679 (Danckwerts L.J.: "the authorities seem to me far from clear"), 686 (Diplock L.J.: "I should be sorry to think that the law permitted a fraudulent but undisclosed principal . . . to reap the fruits of his own fraud in inducing the other contracting party to enter into the contract with his agent"); not considered in HL: [1968] A.C. 1130 at 1133.

107 *Duranty's Case* (1858) 26 Beav. 268 at 270–1, 53 E.R. 901 at 901 (Romilly M.R.).

108 Above, para.1–03; below, Pt II.

109 Cartwright, pp.103–104.

on the mistake itself. We shall see later in this chapter[110] that there is a line of cases, mainly involving contracts of guarantee, in which misrepresentations made by third parties have sometimes entitled representees to rescind; but these cases have to be examined with some care and they are an exception to the general rule stated in this paragraph.

4–25 **Representation (if not fraudulent) of fact.** It is often said that, in order to rescind, the representee must show that the representation was one of fact—and fact is here contrasted with opinion, law and intention. The distinctions between statements of fact, opinion, law and intention were considered in detail in Chapter 3, and that discussion[111] should be read here. Similarly, as discussed in that chapter,[112] a statement which is only "sales talk", or which is not sufficiently clear and precise to be treated as a representation of fact, will not found a claim to rescission.

Where, however, the representation was fraudulent, the courts do not need to look beyond the statement itself. Although a fraudulent statement of opinion or intention can be immediately recharacterised as a false statement of the state of the representor's mind,[113] a fraudulent statement of law cannot be fully equated with a statement of either fact or opinion—yet it can still give rise to rescission.[114] It appears therefore that the better approach would be first to ask whether the statement was made fraudulently or not. If fraudulent, that suffices. But if it was not made fraudulently, there will be a further stage in the analysis, to establish that the statement is properly to be characterised as one of fact, rather than one of opinion, law or intention—a statement on which the claimant was entitled to rely.[115]

4–26 **The representation must be false.** Only a *mis*representation—a false statement—can give rise to the remedy of rescission. The representee must show the meaning on which he relies for his claim

[110] Below, paras 4–72 to 4–78.
[111] Above, paras 3–12 to 3–44.
[112] Above, para.3–14.
[113] Above, paras 3–16, 3–42.
[114] Above, para.3–33. Although the courts have now accepted that a misrepresentation of law can give rise to remedies, the law/fact distinction cannot be entirely disregarded: above, para.3–39.
[115] Above, paras 3–18, 3–41, 3–44.

and that the statement, so interpreted, was false at the relevant time. If, therefore, he alleges that there is a hidden (false) meaning in an apparently true statement the representee must plead it.[116]

The timing of the falsity: the time of the contract. Changed facts between the statement and the contract. For the remedy of rescission, the question is whether the representation was false at the time when the representee relied on it in entering into the contract. No doubt most misrepresentations which give rise to rescission will have been false when made and will remain false thereafter. But it can happen that the circumstances surrounding the formation of a contract change, so that a statement which was true when made becomes false thereafter, or vice versa. **4–27**

If a statement was false when made but circumstances change so that, if repeated, it would have been true by the time the contract was concluded, there can be no remedy.[117] At the time of entering into the contract, the representee makes in fact no mistake, and therefore suffers no prejudice.

But a statement which was true when made but which would be false if repeated at the time of the contract at first sight raises more difficult questions since there are, in essence, two innocent parties—the representor who, let us assume, honestly made a statement which was accurate at the time, and the representee who has now entered into a contract in reliance on a statement which was by then false; and the question is which party should bear the risk of the relevant circumstances changing between the time of the statement and the time of the contract.

In general, the risk falls on the representor. The cases are not entirely unanimous about the reasoning behind it, but the rule is clearly established that if a statement was made which was capable of being later relied on by the representee (and so, for example, it was not by its language limited to the facts as they stood at the time

---

[116] Above, para.3–08. But it has been said that a representation need only be *substantially* true (it is not strictly construed and need not be strictly complied with) to avoid a claim to rescission: the courts take a less strict view of representations in this respect than of contractual warranties: *With v O'Flanagan* [1936] Ch. 575, CA, at 581.

[117] *cf. Gross v Lewis Hillman Ltd* [1970] Ch. 445, CA, at 458–459 (quoting the judgment of the trial judge to this effect, although the CA interpreted the statement differently, and therefore found a misrepresentation); *Briess v Woolley* [1954] A.C. 333, HL, at 353–354 (concerning, however, the tort of deceit).

it was made), and was not withdrawn or corrected before the time of the contract, its truth or falsehood is tested at the time of the contract, not at the time it was made. In *With v O'Flanagan*[118] the vendor of a medical practice told the purchaser, during negotiations, that the practice was "doing at the rate of £2,000 a year". That was true. But during the following period of four months before the contract was concluded the practice declined because of the vendor's illness, and by the time of the contract hardly any patients were attending the practice. If the representation had been repeated,[119] it would therefore plainly have been false. It was held that the purchaser could rescind the contract. Lord Wright M.R. gave two different reasons for so holding: either the vendor had a duty to communicate the changed circumstances[120]; or the representation was to be treated as a continuing representation

[118] Above, n.116.

[119] There was in fact another, later representation by the vendor's agents two weeks before the contract, in response to the purchaser's expression of concern about the practice, to the effect that a *locum tenens* who was looking after the practice was doing so satisfactorily. This representation was not, however, relied on by the purchaser in his claim to rescission: *With v O'Flanagan*, above, n.116 at 577.

[120] *With v O'Flanagan*, above, n.116 at 583, relying on *Davies v London & Provincial Marine Insurance Co.* (1878) 8 Ch.D. 469 at 474–475; *Re Scottish Petroleum Co.* (1883) 23 Ch.D. 413, CA and *Traill v Baring* (1864) 4 De G.J. & Sm. 318 at 329. But "there is no duty to keep the counterparty constantly updated, still less to keep him informed about the ins and outs of negotiations with third parties. The duty is to communicate a change of circumstance which the representor knows has falsified a previous representation where the falsity exists at the date when the contract is concluded. What matters is the state of affairs at the date when the contract is concluded, and the representation is acted upon": *Foodco UK LLP (t/a Muffin Break) v Henry Boot Developments Ltd* [2010] EWHC 358 (Ch) at [212] (Lewison J.).

whose truth was tested at the time of the contract.[121] Romer, L.J. put the issue narrowly in the form in which it had been pleaded by the representee[122]:

> "The only principle invoked by the appellant in this case is as follows. If A with a view to inducing B to enter into a contract makes a representation as to a material fact, then if at a later date and before the contract is actually entered into, owing to a change of circumstances, the representation then made would to the knowledge of A be untrue and B subsequently enters into the contract in ignorance of that change of circumstances and relying upon that representation, A cannot hold B to the bargain. There is ample authority for that statement and, indeed, I doubt myself whether any authority is necessary, it being, it seems to me, so obviously consistent with the plainest principles of equity."

So stated, the decision does not go further than a case of a change of circumstances which is known to the representor—that is, where his failure to disclose the changed circumstances is not merely a misrepresentation, but a fraudulent one. The judgment of Lord Wright M.R. did not make an express limitation to this effect. The cases on which he relied[123] were all cases involving allegations of failure to disclose changed circumstances which the representor had known about. But he noted that there might not always be fraud in the strict sense[124]:

> "nowadays the Court is more reluctant to use the word 'fraud' and would not generally use the word 'fraud' in that connection because the failure to disclose, though wrong and a breach of duty, may be due to inadvertence or a failure to realise that the duty rests upon the party who has made the representation not to leave the other party under an error when the representation has become falsified by a change of circumstances. This

---

[121] *ibid.*, at 584, relying on statements in *Smith v Kay* (1859) 7 H.L.C. 750 at 769, 11 E.R. 299 at 307 (Lord Cranworth) and *Brownlie v Campbell* (1880) 5 App. Cas. 925 at 950 (Lord Blackburn), although Lord Blackburn's statement was aimed not at changes of facts but at the representor's later discovery of the truth of the facts he has already (innocently) misrepresented. See also *Re an Arbitration between Marshall and Scottish Employers' Liability and General Insurance Co. Ltd* (1901) 85 L.T. 757 at 758 (Wright J.: declarations by insured on proposal form for insurance policy are declarations continuing to the execution of the policy).

[122] *ibid.*, at 586. The third judge, Clauson J., simply agreed.

[123] Above, nn.120 and 121.

[124] [1936] Ch. 575 at 584–585, commenting particularly on a statement of Lord Blackburn in *Brownlie v Campbell*, above, n.121 at 950.

> question only occurs when there is an interval of time between the time when the representation is made and when it is acted upon by the party to whom it was made, who either concludes the contract or does some similar decisive act; but the representation remains in effect and it is because that is so, and because the court is satisfied in a proper case on the facts that it remained operative in the mind of the representee, that the Court holds that under such circumstances the representee should not be bound."

It is not yet clear on the authorities whether a representation constitutes a *mis*representation for the purposes of the remedy of rescission if it was true when made, but without the representor's knowledge has become false before it is relied upon by the representee.[125] The better view is surely that the principle should not be limited to cases where the representor can be shown to have known of the changed circumstances. The question is whether there was a false statement relied on by the representee in entering into the contract. If a statement was made which was capable of being relied on even after a period of time during which the negotiations have lasted, and it is in fact by then false, it is a *mis*representation which can found a claim to rescission. This may seem harsh to a representor; but the remedy of rescission is available for even innocent misrepresentations, so it is not inconsistent with the underlying rationale of the remedy—to allow a party to avoid a contract where he was induced by the other party to misunderstand some fact relevant to his decision to contract.[126] And it will always be a matter of construction of the representation whether it was

[125] R. Bigwood, "Pre-Contractual Misrepresentation and the Limits of the Principle in *With v O'Flanagan*" [2005] C.L.J. 94 at p.99.

[126] This argument was criticised by Bigwood, above, n.125 at pp.118–125, who argues (at p.121) that "the legal concept of 'misrepresentation' presupposes a human 'misrepresentor', which *ex hypothesi* assumes a jural agent that was responsible, in agency-responsibility terms, for the conveyance of the erroneous information upon which the other party relied and of which he now complains", and (at p.122, n.94) that the argument in the text fails to "address the question of what it means, in agency-responsibility terms, to be a misrepresentor (as opposed to simply being a party to, or a victim of, a causative pre-contractual mistake)". Whilst noting (at p.123, n.95) that his argument based on agency-responsibility does not require legal negligence on the part of the representor, Bigwood asserts (at p.105) that "in order to qualify as a misrepresentation, the *creation* of the claimant's *mis*understanding must in some relevant sense be the product of 'voluntary choice' on the part of the alleged misrepresentor, or otherwise within his 'potential' or 'control'"; and that this is not satisfied until the representor knows of the falsity and fails to correct it. However, it is submitted that the

capable of being relied on after the time gap during which the facts have changed;[127] a party can always make clear that his statement is only to be taken as referring to the facts as they stand when the statement is made.

Whether the claim arising out of the changed circumstances can be based on the statement being *fraudulent* is an entirely different matter: for that, of course, it must at least be shown that the representor had the necessary state of mind about the falsity of the statement to satisfy the normal test for fraud. But the difficulty with *With v O'Flanagan* and the earlier cases on which it rests is that it tends not to keep sufficiently separate two legally distinct questions: Was there a misrepresentation? Was it made fraudulently?[128]

Change of represented intention between statement and contract. If the statement relied on to found a claim for rescission was a statement of the representor's intention one might expect the approach to be that discussed above: that is, if the statement is capable of being relied on in entering into the contract but the representor's intention, though first honestly stated, has **4–28**

argument in the text is better supported by the scope of innocent misrepresentation, and the line drawn between mistake and misrepresentation, in English law. Bigwood (at p.123) objects to the consequence that this would have for other jurisdictions, such as New Zealand, where an innocent misrepresentation gives rise to damages. See further above, paras 1–03, 1–05. Clarke, para.22–2A2, in the context of statements by applicants for insurance, also prefers Bigwood's analysis.

127 *Bank of Tokyo-Mitsubishi U.F.J. Ltd v Başkan Gida Sanayi Ve Pazarlama A.S.* [2009] EWHC 1276 (Ch), [2009] All E.R. (D) 308 (Jun) at [1015] (Briggs J.: "To treat one-off trade references as continuing representations would give rise to risks of grave injustice to the providers of those references, since they would be required, as it were, to remember thereafter what they had said, to keep a track on the underlying facts relevant to the reference, and to monitor the progress of the negotiations, so as to know whether a duty to alert the representee to a change of facts still had any practical content. That would in my judgment impose an entirely unreasonable burden on the provider of a gratuitous trade reference"); but *cf. Belfairs Management Ltd v Sutherland* [2010] EWHC 2276 (Ch), [2010] All E.R. (D) 59 (Sep) at [11] (Norris J.: "a statement of fact once made is likely to have a continuing effect — until the transaction is completed, or until the form of the transaction is changed so that the statement ceases to be material, or until some other event occurs which means that the statement ceases to be operative on the mind of the hearer").

128 The difficulties over the question of whether there is fraud in such a case are discussed in relation to the tort of deceit: below, para.5–17.

changed by the time of the contract, it becomes a false statement which therefore gives rise to the remedy. Since representations of intention are only actionable when they are fraudulent[129] the questions of whether the representation is false and actionable, and whether it is fraudulent, are here unavoidably interlinked.

The decision in *Traill v Baring*[130] is authority that the normal rule should apply. P, a life assurance society, had a risk of £3,000 which it wished to reinsure. It proposed to R that R should reinsure £1,000, telling R that another company, V, had agreed to take £1,000 and that P intended to retain the balance of the risk (£1,000). Later, but before the contract of reinsurance was concluded with R, P decided to reinsure the whole balance of £2,000 with V and did in fact enter into that contract with V.[131] It was held that R could avoid its contract with P on the basis of the uncommunicated change of intention by P as to the insurance of the balance of the risk.

However, in *Wales v Wadham*[132] it was held that the rule in *With v O'Flanagan*[133] does not apply to changes of intention. There, during their negotiations over the financial arrangements for their divorce, a wife made statements to her husband that she did not intend to remarry; she had also often told him during the marriage that she objected in principle to remarriage after divorce. But before the arrangements were concluded and embodied in a consent order, she secretly agreed to remarry another man. The husband was not, however, allowed to challenge the order on the basis that the

---

[129] Above, para.3–43.

[130] (1864) 4 De G.J. & S. 318, 46 E.R. 941.

[131] At first instance Stuart V.C. (under the name *Trail v Baring* (1864) 4 Giff. 485 at 490, 66 E.R. 797 at 800) had decided that it was not simply a change of intention, because the reinsurance with V had actually been effected by the time of the contract between P and R. However, it is clear in the decision of the Lords Justices that the principle is applied on the assumption that it was a representation of intention which had changed: (1864) 4 De G. J. & S. 318 at 326, 330, 46 E.R. 941 at 945, 946.

[132] [1977] 1 W.L.R. 199. This was a case at first instance, and therefore bound by the decision in *Traill v Baring* (which was not, however, cited), although *Wales v Wadham* received a brief note of approval on this issue from the House of Lords in *Livesey v Jenkins* [1985] A.C. 424 at 439. *Cf. Dietz v Lenning Chemicals Ltd* [1969] 1 A.C. 170 (HL) (consent order settling claim under Fatal Accidents Acts 1846–1959 by widow for herself and her young child set aside for innocent misrepresentation where widow (identified as such in the originating summons) had remarried by date of consent order).

[133] Above, para.4–27.

agreement should be rescinded for misrepresentation. Although Tudor Evans J. distinguished *With* on the basis that, as a matter of law, it did not apply to changes of intention, it might not have been necessary for him so to hold. The case may be better understood by seeing the judge's interpretation of the facts: he said[134] that the wife made honest statements of her intention, which were aimed at attempting to save her marriage; and she had not represented that she would never change her mind.

If a statement of intention, properly construed, simply states a current intention and contains no suggestion that the intention will not change in the future, it may more easily be construed as a statement which can be relied on only as to the representor's intention at the time of the statement: it is not to be seen as a *continuing* representation as easily as can a statement of fact.[135] But a statement of intention which goes further than this, and contains the suggestion that it can be relied on as a continuing intention as to the representor's future conduct, ought to be capable of founding a claim for rescission where the intention changes before the time of the contract and so, if restated, would be fraudulent and therefore actionable.[136]

---

[134] Above, n.132 at 211.

[135] For another example of such an interpretation of a statement of intention, see *Tudor Grange Holdings Ltd v Citibank N.A.* [1992] Ch. 53 at 67–68. See also *Limit No.2 Ltd v Axa Versicherung A.G.* [2008] EWCA Civ 1231, [2008] 2 C.L.C. 673 at [26] (Longmore L.J.: "A representation of intention cannot last for ever; it only relates to the time when it is made; there must come a time when it is spent").

[136] Another reason for the courts' reluctance to allow statements of intention to have the same continuing nature as statements of fact may be their reluctance to allow statements of intention to operate as misrepresentations at all: the representee should insist on a contractual promise if he wishes to hold the representor to a statement as to the future: above, para.3–43; *Tudor Grange Holdings Ltd v Citibank N.A.*, above, n.135. But given that a fraudulent statement of intention can give rise to rescission for misrepresentation, there seems no reason why a similar *fraudulent* change of intention cannot. For a change of intention which falsified a continuing representation for the purposes of a claim in the tort of deceit, see *Slough Estates Plc v Welwyn Hatfield DC* [1996] 2 E.G.L.R. 219. And in Australia, see *Jones v Dumbrell* [1981] V.R. 199 (following *Traill v Baring*, above, n.130, but emphasising that the representor was fraudulent in not disclosing the changed intention, and intended the earlier (and now false) statement to continue to operate).

(2) The Representor's State of Mind

4–29 **Fraud not required for rescission.** For the equitable remedy of rescission there is no requirement that the representation have been made fraudulently: even a wholly innocent misrepresentation suffices.[137]

4–30 **Advantages of proving fraud.** If, however, the representee is able to establish that the representor was fraudulent in making the statement on which he relies to rescind the contract, there may be certain advantages for other elements of his claim.[138] In particular, he is not then required to show that the statement was of fact, as opposed to opinion, law or intention[139]; it might be easier to establish his reliance on the statement by dispensing him from establishing that the statement was material,[140] and by removing any argument that he might still have entered into the contract if the

---

137 *Redgrave v Hurd* (1881) 20 Ch.D. 1, CA, at 12; *Derry v Peek* (1889) 14 App. Cas. 337, HL, at 359 (Lord Herschell, quoted above, para.4–04). At common law, only a fraudulent misrepresentation rendered the contract voidable: above, para.4–02. In relation to insurance contracts, under the *Insurance: Conduct of Business Sourcebook* issued by the Financial Services Authority (ICOBS, 8.1) an insurer must not unreasonably reject a claim (including by terminating or avoiding a policy); and a rejection of a consumer policyholder's claim is unreasonable, except where there is evidence of fraud, if it is for, inter alia, non-negligent misrepresentation of a fact material to the risk. See also the *Conduct of Business Sourcebook* (COBS) 17.1.3, which applies similar provisions to long-term care insurance contracts. Under the Consumer Insurance (Disclosure and Representations) Bill, which is expected to be enacted during 2012 (implementing Law Com No.319, *Consumer Insurance Law: Pre-Contract Disclosure and Misrepresentation* (2009): see further below, para.17–06) an individual taking out a consumer insurance contract will have only a duty of reasonable care not to make a misrepresentation to the insurer before the contract is entered into or varied; the insurer will no longer have a right to avoid the contract for wholly innocent misepresentation, but may still avoid the contract for fraud, or if the misrepresentation was careless and the insurer (if the consumer had complied with his duty of care) would not have entered into the contract on any terms.

138 *Whittaker v Campbell* [1984] Q.B. 318 at 327. If the contract is a secure or assured residential tenancy, rescission is not available but the fact that the landlord was induced to grant the tenancy by a fraudulent statement may entitle him to obtain an order for possession: above, para.4–11, n.37.

139 Above, para.4–25.

140 *Smith v Kay* (1859) 7 H.L.C. 750, 11 E.R. 299; below, para.4–33.

misrepresentation had not been made[141]; for the purposes of notifying the representor of his election to rescind time runs from his discovery of the fraud,[142] rather than from the time of the contract; the court may be more disposed, in case of doubt, to find that restitution of benefits received under the contract is still possible, or to award allowances in lieu of restitution[143]; and the court will have no discretion to refuse rescission and award damages in lieu.[144] He may also be able to rescind on proof of fraud where there is a term in the contract which validly excludes that remedy for negligent or innocent misrepresentation.[144a] He will also, of course, be able to claim damages in the tort of deceit—concurrently with obtaining rescission, if he so wishes and can establish the relevant losses.[145]

4–31 **Pleading and proving fraud.** Fraud must, however, be pleaded expressly and is not easily established. The difficulties of a claim of fraud are considered in detail in relation to the tort of deceit.[146]

(3) Reliance by the Representee

4–32 **The representation must have been an inducement to the representee's decision to contract.** This requirement has already been discussed in Chapter 3.[147] In brief, there must be a causal link between the representor's statement and the representee's decision to enter into the contract: that is, he must have relied on the

[141] Below, para.4–34.
[142] Or, perhaps, from the time he ought to have discovered it, if it is by his fault that he failed to do so: below, para.4–50.
[143] Below, para.4–55.
[144] Misrepresentation Act 1967 s.2(2), which applies only where the misrepresentation was made "otherwise than fraudulently": below, para.4–62.
[144a] *Erlson Precision Holdings Ltd (formerly GG132 Ltd) v Hampson Industries Plc* [2011] EWHC 1137 (Comm) at [41]. A clause cannot exclude liability for a party's own fraud: below, para.9–13.
[145] For the tort of deceit, see Ch. 5; and for the advantages for a damages claim of establishing a right to damages on the fraud measure, see below, paras 5–35 to 5–44, 7–33.
[146] Below, paras 5–46 to 5–49.
[147] Above, paras 3–50 to 3–56.

statement at the moment of contracting.[148] It need not, however, be shown that the statement was the only cause, or the main cause of the representee's decision: it is sufficient if it is *a* cause.[149]

4–33 **"Materiality" of the statement; proof of reliance.** Although judges have often referred to a requirement that the representation be "material" in the sense that a reasonable person would have relied on it,[150] the better view appears to be that as a general rule[151] this is not a separate requirement, and the question is whether the representee in fact relied upon it in entering into the contract.[152] But if the statement is material, it is easier to establish that the representee relied on it: the materiality of a statement raises an inference of fact that the representee, the other contracting party to whom it was addressed, relied on it; this places on the representor the burden of adducing evidence to rebut the inference.[153]

---

[148] Above, para.3–51. If the representee has required a pre-contractual statement to be confirmed in the contract as a warranty, that can show his reliance on it for the purpose of a claim for rescission: *Thomas Witter Ltd v TBP Industries Ltd* [1996] 2 All E.R. 573 at 595.

[149] *Attwood v Small* (1838) 6 Cl. & Fin. 232 at 502, 7 E.R. 684 at 785, HL; above, para.3–54.

[150] e.g. *Matthias v Yetts* (1882) 46 L.T. 497, CA, at 502; Treitel, paras 9–016 to 9–019. If "materiality" means not this, but that the misrepresentation was one which could be taken seriously—it is not, for example, just sales talk—then this is certainly a relevant requirement: see above, para.3–14.

[151] An area in which there is undoubtedly a requirement that the statement be material is insurance contracts; see also Clarke, para.22–3A. Under the Marine Insurance Act 1906 s.20(1) an insurer may avoid the contract for a material misrepresentation made by the assured or his agent; and (s.20(2)) a representation is material which would influence the judgment of a prudent insurer in fixing the premium, or determining whether he will take the risk. This applies to insurance contracts generally, and is not restricted to contracts of marine insurance: *PCW Syndicates v PCW Reinsurers* [1996] 1 W.L.R. 1136, CA, at 1140, although s.20 is to be amended by the Consumer Insurance (Disclosure and Representations) Bill (which is passing through Parliament during 2011) to exclude consumer insurance contracts from its scope: above, n.137; below, para.17–06.

[152] *Museprime Properties Ltd v Adhill Properties Ltd* [1990] 2 E.G.L.R. 196 at 201–202, adopting the view set out in Goff & Jones (3rd edn, 1986), p.168 (now 6th edn, 2002, para.9.022). For a different view, see Treitel, para.9–019; *Re A Company (No.001946 of 1991)* [1991] B.C.L.C. 737 at 746–747 (but Harman J. appears even there to link the lack of materiality to the consequent inability to prove reliance).

[153] *Mathias v Yetts* above, n.150 at 502; above, para.3–53.

It is sometimes said that if a misrepresentation was fraudulent it need not be shown to be material.[154] Indeed, in *Smith v Kay*[155] Lord Chelmsford said:

> "can it be permitted to a party who has practised a deception, with a view to a particular end, which has been attained by it, to speculate upon what might have been the result if there had been a full communication of the truth?"

But this statement is still concerned with proof of the representee's reliance on the statement, and might be better viewed not as a rule particular to fraud,[156] but as evidence of the courts' general approach to hold that, where the representor intended the representee to act on the statement and enter into the contract, then he cannot be heard to deny the representee's claim that he did act on it. On this basis, the court may more easily establish, as a matter of fact, that the representee relied on the representation if either there is evidence that the representor intended to induce the contract, or the representation was such that, objectively, it was likely to have that effect. But the core requirement is proof of reliance in fact on the misrepresentation.

"But for" causation. The representee is not required to show that he would not have entered into the contract had the representation not been made. The evidence may, however, show that he *would* or *might well* still have entered into the contract, even if the misrepresentation had not been made. In such a case one might argue that the representation did not cause him to enter into the contract, because "but for" the misrepresentation he would still have entered into the same contract, or suffered the same loss.[157] On **4–34**

[154] Treitel, para.9–017, relying on *Smith v Kay*, below, n.155.
[155] (1859) 7 H.L.C. 750, 11 E.R. 299.
[156] *Cf. Ross River Ltd v Cambridge City Football Club Ltd* [2007] EWHC 2115 (Ch), [2008] 1 All E.R. 1004 at [241] (Briggs J.: "in a case where fraudulent material misrepresentations have been deliberately made with a view (as I find) improperly to influence the outcome of the negotiation of the contact in favour of the maker and his principal, by an experienced player in the relevant market, there is the most powerful inference that the fraudsman achieved his objective, at least to the limited extent required by the law, namely that his fraud was actively in the mind of the recipient when the contract came to be made").
[157] Chitty, para.6–035; *Assicurazioni Generali SpA v Arab Insurance Group* [2002] EWCA Civ 1642, [2003] 1 All E.R. (Comm) 140 at [59]; *Raiffeisen*

the other hand, it is still true to say that the misrepresentation, if present to his mind and acting as one of the factors he took into account in making his decision, did in fact cause the representee to enter into the contract, and that he should still be permitted to base his claim to rescind upon the representation.[158] At least in relation to fraudulent representations the courts have indicated that they will not deny the representee the right to rescind on this ground.[159]

4–35 **The representee's ability to discover the truth.** The representee is not deprived of the right to rescind just because he could have discovered the truth about the representor's statement—even where it might have been reasonable to expect him to make enquiries and discover the truth. There is no equivalent in the remedy of rescission to the defence of contributory negligence in a claim for damages in tort.[160] This was made clear in *Redgrave v Hurd* where Baggallay L.J. said[161]:

Zentralbank Österreich A.G. v Royal Bank of Scotland Plc [2010] EWHC 1392 (Comm), [2011] 1 Lloyd's Rep. 123 at [173].

[158] *Edgington v Fitzmaurice* (1885) 29 Ch.D. 459, CA, at 481, 483.

[159] *UCB Corporate Services Ltd v Williams* [2002] EWCA Civ 555, [2002] 3 F.C.R. 448 at [85]–[90] (Jonathan Parker L.J., drawing an analogy between undue influence and fraudulent misrepresentation). Chitty, para.6–035 assumes that this is a rule peculiar to fraudulent misrepresentations, intended to deter fraud; followed in *Ross River Ltd v Cambridge City Football Club Ltd*, above, n.156 at [202]; see also *Raiffeisen Zentralbank Österreich A.G. v Royal Bank of Scotland Plc*, above, n.157 at [198]; and see generally above, para.3–54.

[160] In equity "the effect of false representation is not got rid of on the ground that the person to whom it was made has been guilty of negligence": *Redgrave v Hurd* (1881) 20 Ch.D. 1, CA, at 14 (Jessel M.R.). For the application of the doctrine of contributory negligence in a claim for damages in the tort of negligence, see below para.6–48; and under the Misrepresentation Act 1967 s.2(1), see below para.7–27. It might be argued that the earlier cases, e.g. *Reynell v Sprye* (1852) 1 De G. M. & G. 660, 42 E.R. 710, which developed the rule that the representee's negligence does not defeat the claim to rescission, did so in the particular context of fraudulent misrepresentation—and contributory negligence is not a defence to a claim for fraud: below, para.5–31. However, the decision in *Redgrave v Hurd* is unequivocal, since the plea of fraud was there rejected: see (1881) 20 Ch.D. 1 at 12.

[161] Above, n.160 at 23. He went on to make clear that it would be different if there were "certain circumstances of suspicion, which might put a person upon inquiry" and would therefore create a duty for the representee to check the truth of the statement. See also *Attwood v Small*, above, n.149 at 502–503, at 785–786; *Reynell v Spyre*, above, n.160 at 710, at 729; *Goldsmith v Rodger* [1962] 2 Lloyd's Rep. 249, CA (seller of a boat relied on buyer's statements about the state

> "The person who has made the misrepresentation cannot be heard to say to the party to whom he has made that representation, 'You chose to believe me when you might have doubted me and gone further.' The representation once made relieves the party from an investigation, even if the opportunity is afforded."

And even if the representee makes some inquiries, but fails to pursue them with reasonable diligence and so fails to discover the truth, he is not necessarily prevented from rescinding.[162] The question is always whether he relied on the statement. If it can be shown that in fact he did rely on it he can rescind even though he might have been expected to discover the truth of the statement. But if the representee's attempts to inquire into the truth demonstrated that he was relying on his own enquiries *rather than* the statement, rescission will not be available; not because of any doctrine of fault on the representee's part, but because one of the requirements of the remedy—reliance on the statement by the representee—is not satisfied.[163]

"Non-reliance" clauses. Contractual clauses which attempt to limit or negative the reliance by the representee on a statement made by the representor, or limit the legal consequences of such reliance, are considered in Chapter 9. **4–36**

No requirement that the consequences of misrepresentation be substantial. Once it is shown that the representee relied on the statement in entering into the contract, the contract may—subject to the application of any bars[164] to rescission—be rescinded. There is no requirement that the consequences of the misrepresentation must have been serious for the representee,[165] who can therefore take **4–37**

---

of the boat). P.S. Atiyah, *The Rise and Fall of Freedom of Contract*, p.772, thinks that *Redgrave v Hurd* involved "such a remarkable want of due precaution on the part of the buyer that the actual decision may well be of dubious validity".

[162] *ibid.*, at 17 (Jessel M.R.); at first instance Fry J. had thought that the representee's fault prevented rescission.

[163] *Attwood v Small*, above, n.149.

[164] Below, paras 4–38 to 4–71.

[165] *Cf.* the rule in Canada that that rescission of an *executed* contract for innocent misrepresentation is available only if the misrepresentation is "substantial"—if it gave rise to an *error in substantialibus*: Waddams, para.424; Fridman, p.300, criticising the rule; Swann, p.553, suggesting that the Canadian courts are now likely to be more relaxed as regards this requirement given that rescission is an

advantage of a misrepresentation in order to rescind a contract even where his motives in rescinding are not related to the particular misrepresentation which founds the claim; and where the consequences of the misrepresentation are relatively minor in the context of the contract as a whole. The only exception to this is contained in section 2(2) of the Misrepresentation Act 1967 under which a court has discretion, but only in cases where the statement was not fraudulent, to declare the contract subsisting and award damages in lieu of rescission in cases which will include relatively minor misrepresentations.[166]

III. LIMITS TO THE REMEDY

4–38 **The representor's rebuttal of the representee's prima facie right to rescind: the "bars" to rescission.** Once the representee has established a prima facie right to rescind in accordance with the rules set out in the previous section, the representor may seek to show that rescission is not available because of one or more established "bars" to rescission. These are[167]: (1) that the

---

equitable discretionary remedy). The authorities in England suggesting that execution of the contract constituted a bar to rescission were superseded by the Misrepresentation Act 1967 s.1(b); below, n.167. See also, in New Zealand, the Contractual Remedies Act 1979, s.7 ("cancellation" of the contract for misrepresentation only where the effect of the misrepresentation is substantially to change the contractual benefits and burdens). The position in New Zealand before this Act was to restrict rescission of a contract for the sale of goods on the ground of innocent misrepresentation to a case where the effect of the misrepresentation was that there was a complete difference in substance between the thing bargained for and the thing obtained, so as to constitute a failure of consideration: *Riddiford v Warren* (1901) 20 N.Z.L.R. 572, NZCA, following *Kennedy v The Panama, New Zealand and Australian Royal Mail Co. Ltd* (1867) L.R. 2 Q.B. 580; *Holmes v Burgess* [1975] 2 N.Z.L.R. 311 at 317.

[166] For the detail of the Misrepresentation Act 1967 s.2(2), see below, paras 4–61 to 4–71.

[167] There was some authority before 1967 that, in the case of non-fraudulent misrepresentation, rescission would be barred where the misrepresentation has become a term of the contract, or where the contract has been performed, but the Misrepresentation Act 1967 s.1 removed these bars to rescission. For the retention of these rules under the common law in Australia, but their abolition in certain states, see Carter, Peden and Tolhurst, paras 18–54 to 18–56; Seddon and Ellinghaus, paras 11.61 to 11.65 (arguing that abolition should follow in the other states). For an account of the position before the 1967 Act, see Tenth Report of the Law Reform Committee, *Innocent Misrepresentation*, Cmnd.1782 (1962),

representee has elected to affirm the contract; (2) that the representee has delayed too long in seeking rescission; (3) that restitution of benefits conferred under the contract, a necessary part of the implementation of rescission, is impossible; (4) that the rights of an innocent third party would be prejudiced by rescission; and (5) that the court should be persuaded to exercise its discretion under section 2(2) of the Misrepresentation Act 1967 to refuse rescission and award damages instead. These bars to rescission will be discussed in detail in this section.

(1) Affirmation of the Contract

The representee may elect to affirm or rescind. Since misrepresentation renders the contract not void but voidable at the instance of the representee,[168] it gives the representee an election[169]: the right to decide whether to rescind or not. The right to rescind, and the means by which the election to rescind is exercised, have already been discussed.[170] If the representee elects not to rescind, he affirms the contract. As long as the representee has not yet elected to exercise either his right to rescind or his right to affirm the contract, and as long as none of the other bars to rescission discussed later in this section have arisen, the election remains exercisable and the contract remains on foot but voidable.[171] 4–39

Affirmation is irrevocable. Once the representee has elected to affirm the contract, his affirmation is irrevocable. An election, once 4–40

paras 3 to 9 and 16. The Law Reform Committee had proposed that contracts for the sale or other disposition of an interest in land, apart from contracts for short leases, should not be capable of rescission after execution: paras 6 and 7.

168 Above, para.4–05.

169 This is an example of the general doctrine of election: *The Kanchenjunga* [1990] 1 Lloyd's Rep. 391, HL, at 398; *Clough v London and North Western Railway Co.* (1871) L.R. 7 Exch. 26 at 34–35. Authorities dealing with election in contexts other than rescission for misrepresentation can therefore be relevant although it is always important to consider whether the context in which election is considered carries particular implications for the interpretation of the rules of the doctrine; see also K.R. Handley, *Estoppel by Conduct and Election*, below, n.177.

170 Above, paras 4–18 to 4–20.

171 *Clough v London and North Western Railway Co.*, above, n.169 at 34, 35.

made, is final and binding.[172] However, affirmation bars only the remedy of rescission and leaves open other remedies, such as a claim for damages in deceit.[173]

4–41 **Affirmation not based on agreement or estoppel.** Affirmation is the representee's unilateral election between two mutually inconsistent rights (to rescind, or to accept, the contract). It is not of itself a contract, nor is it based on an express or implied agreement between the representor and the representee: no consideration is therefore required from the representor to make the election binding.[174] Nor is it based on the principles of estoppel,[175] although there can be circumstances where the representee, though he has not actually affirmed, might none the less be estopped from denying that he has.[176]

4–42 **The test for affirmation.** A representee has made his election to affirm the contract when, with sufficient knowledge of his right of election, he has shown clearly by his words or conduct that he has elected to affirm. It would of course be sufficient for a representee to make a clear statement to the effect that "I know I have the right to rescind; but I have decided not to exercise it". But in order to understand what will constitute affirmation short of such a statement, it is necessary to consider what level of knowledge of the right to rescind is necessary on the part of the representee before he can be held to have made the election; and what conduct on his part, short of such a clear statement, will suffice.

4–43 **Knowledge required.** In general terms, the doctrine of election [177] applies in the context of a contract when a state of affairs comes into existence in which one party becomes entitled to exercise a right, such as the right to rescind, and has to choose whether to exercise the right or not. The general rule for election is therefore

[172] *The Kanchenjunga*, above, n.169 at 398; *Scarf v Jardine* (1882) 7 App. Cas. 345, HL, at 360; Com. Dig. Election, C.2.
[173] *Arnison v Smith* (1889) 41 Ch.D. 348, CA, at 371 (Cotton L.J.); above, para.2–12
[174] *The Kanchenjunga*, above, n.169 at 398.
[175] *ibid.*, at 399; *Peyman v Lanjani* [1985] Ch. 457, CA, at 493, 500.
[176] Below, para.4–45.
[177] See generally, K.R. Handley, *Estoppel by Conduct and Election* (2006), Ch.14, esp. para.14–026.

that "his election ... has to be an informed choice, made with knowledge of the facts giving rise to the right".[178] In the context of rescission for misrepresentation, the representee cannot be held to have affirmed the contract if he did not have at least knowledge of the falsity of the statement which gives rise to the right to rescind.[179] But it appears that it may not be sufficient for him to know of the falsity, if he did not also appreciate that the falsity of the statement entitled him to rescind: that is, before he can be held to have affirmed the contract, the representee must have realised that he had a remedy available, which he has chosen not to claim. This follows from the decision of the Court of Appeal in *Peyman v Lanjani*,[180] where May L.J. said[181]:

> "I do not think that a party to a contract can realistically or sensibly be held to have made this irrevocable choice between rescission and affirmation unless he has actual knowledge not only of the facts of the serious breach of the contract by the other party which is the precondition of his right to choose, but also of the fact that in the circumstances which exist he does have that right to make that choice which the law gives him."

This case was concerned not with the remedy of rescission in equity for misrepresentation, but an express right, contained in a contract for the assignment of a lease, of "rescission"[182] for an irremovable

[178] *The Kanchenjunga*, above, n.169 at 399.

[179] In the light of the cases discussed in this section, actual knowledge ought to be necessary. In *Re Royal British Bank* (1859) 3 De G. & J. 387, 44 E.R.1317 it was held that a representee who had the means of knowledge that a representation was false would be barred from claiming rescission. But it is better, in light of the modern cases, to ask in a case where knowledge cannot sufficiently be proved whether the representee is none the less estopped from denying affirmation: below, para.4–45. *Cf.* below, para.4–50 (constructive notice of fraud in the context of lapse of time as bar to rescission).

[180] [1985] Ch. 457, CA.

[181] *ibid.*, at 494. See also Stephenson L.J. at 487 and Slade L.J. at 500. *Scarf v Jardine*, above, n.172 at 360–361. See also *Donegal International Ltd v Zambia* [2007] EWHC 197 (Comm), [2007] 1 Lloyd's Rep. 397 at [467] (Andrew Smith J.: "I would, if this part of the case had turned upon the affirmation argument, have concluded that he had the requisite knowledge, including, given that he is a lawyer, knowledge of the right to rescind").

[182] For the confusion of terminology between "rescission" and "termination" when the claim is for a breach of contract, and the meaning to be attributed to a right of "rescission" for defects in title under standard form contracts for the sale of an interest in land, such as that in *Peyman v Lanjani*, see below, paras 8–35 to 8–37.

defect of the assignor's title to the lease; and in coming to its decision on this point the Court of Appeal drew on cases of election and waiver in a range of different contexts. But they made clear that they saw the principle as equally applicable to the case of rescission for misrepresentation.[183]

4–44 **Conduct sufficient to constitute affirmation.** Affirmation may be effected by words or by the representee's conduct[184]: the question is whether he has sufficiently shown that he has elected not to claim his right to rescind. The question is not whether the representee in fact intended to show it: as in general where there is a question in contract as to whether a person intended to communicate something, his intention is tested not subjectively but objectively, viewing his words and conduct from the position of the party to whom the communication is addressed. This is borne out by the speech of Lord Blackburn in *Scarf v Jardine*[185]:

> "The principle, I take it, running through all the cases as to what is an election is this, that where a party in his own mind has thought that he would choose one of two remedies, even though he has written it down on a memorandum or has indicated it in some other way, that alone will not bind him but so soon as he has not only determined to follow one of his remedies but has communicated it to the other side in such a way as to lead the opposite party to believe that he has made that choice, he has completed his election and can go no further and whether he intended it or not, if he has done an unequivocal act—I mean an act which would be justifiable if he had elected one way and would not be justifiable if he had elected the other way—the fact of his having done that unequivocal act to the knowledge of the persons concerned is an election."

[183] The clearest statement is at [1985] Ch. 457 at 494 (May L.J.) but all three judges used authorities involving rescission *ab initio* for misrepresentation.

[184] Com. Dig. Election, C1; *Clough v London and North Western Railway Co.*, above, n.169 at 34–35.

[185] Above, n.172 at 360–361; *Peyman v Lanjani*, above, n.180 at 488. For the general approach to objectivity, see above, para.3–06; below, paras 13–08 to 13–19; Cartwright, Ch.1; and see in particular Lord Blackburn's general approach to objective interpretation of communications in the formation of a contract: *Smith v Hughes* (1871) L.R. 6 Q.B. 597 at 607 (as Blackburn J.); below, para.13–09.

Generally the representee communicates to the representor his election to affirm. But this is not strictly necessary[186]; and so, for example, it has been held that a shareholder in a company affirms his contract to take shares where, after discovering the truth about misrepresentations in the prospectus pursuant to which he subscribed for the shares, he keeps the shares and exercises acts of ownership over them inconsistent with rescission of the contract—such as receiving dividends, and selling or attempting to sell the shares.[187] And a purchaser of a lorry following a misrepresentation as to its condition affirmed the contract where he continued to use it beyond the period necessary to test it and discover the defects in it. [188] However, if the representee is only considering his position and has not yet acted so as to show that he has elected to rescind, it is not sufficient to establish affirmation.[189] Nor do actions by the

[186] *Car and Universal Finance Co. Ltd v Caldwell* [1965] 1 Q.B. 525 at 532 (Lord Denning M.R. sitting as the trial judge), 550 (Sellers L.J.). There is less significance in communication to the representor than in the case of an election to rescind, where the election deprives the representor of rights in the contract: above, para.4–20.

[187] *Re Hop and Malt Exchange and Warehouse Co.* (1866) L.R. 1 Eq. 483; *Hudson's Case* (1849) 2 De G. & J. 275, 44 E.R. 994; *cf. Aaron's Reefs Ltd v Twiss* [1896] A.C. 273, HL (no affirmation). See generally Gore-Browne, para.43[17].

[188] *Long v Lloyd* [1958] 2 All E.R. 402, CA (drawing an analogy on the facts with "acceptance" of goods defeating the right to reject under the Sale of Goods Act 1893 (now 1979) ss.11 and 35). However, the language of the judgment does not adequately distinguish the bars of affirmation and lapse of time (see at 407–408) and it is better not to use the test for the "acceptance" of goods as an analogy with affirmation: the right to reject goods can be lost by "acceptance" without the representee having knowledge of the right to rescind sufficient to bar his claim to rescission by affirmation: *Peyman v Lanjani* [1985] Ch. 457, CA, at 483; Treitel, para.9–111. It may be more appropriate to draw an analogy between "acceptance" of goods and the bar to rescission based on lapse of time in a case of non-fraudulent misrepresentation: below, para.4–48.

[189] *Laurence v Lexcourt Holdings Ltd* [1978] 1 W.L.R. 1128 at 1139 (lessee remained in possession of property for one year after discovering the lessor's misrepresentations about the purposes for which the property could lawfully be used: during the period the lessee negotiated with the lessors about possible alternative leasehold arrangements to solve the problem: held entitled to rescind when the negotiations broke down); *Senanayake v Cheng* [1966] A.C. 63, PC, at 78–79 (partner who had bought shares following misrepresentation that business was "a gold mine" discovered true state of affairs but continued to act as partner, including summoning and attending partners' meeting, for some two months thereafter held still entitled to rescind: it would not have been prudent for her to

representee which are minor in the context of the continuing contract necessarily show that he has affirmed it.[190]

4–45 **The representee may be estopped from denying affirmation.** Even if it cannot be shown that the representee has affirmed the contract, in accordance with the principle discussed earlier in this section, it might still sometimes be possible to show that he is estopped from denying affirmation.[191] The usual principles of estoppel will apply here: and so the questions will be whether the representee has by his words or conduct led the representor to believe that he has abandoned his right to rescind the contract, and whether the representor has relied to his detriment on that belief. It is always important to keep this claim to estoppel quite separate from the claim of affirmation itself, in which the principles are quite different. We have seen that, for affirmation, actual knowledge of the right to rescind is necessary, whereas a representor might be estopped from denying affirmation even when he did not have the knowledge necessary for affirmation itself.[192] But for affirmation, the mere communication to the representor is sufficient; for the estoppel, there is the additional requirement of the representor's reliance before he can hold the representee to have affirmed the contract which the representee did not in fact intend to affirm.[193]

4–46 **Affirmation must be of the whole contract, not part.** If the representee affirms the contract, he must affirm it in its entirety. He

act precipitately and she was entitled to explore the state of the business and possible solutions for it with the other partners).

190 *Abram Steamship Co. Ltd v Westville Shipping Co. Ltd* [1923] A.C. 773, HL (Sc.) (company took assignment of a contract to have ship built following misrepresentations about the progress on the construction, but after discovering truth gave its assent to a minor alteration in the design of the ship in response to request by the shipbuilders: held still entitled to recind the contract of assignment as against the assignor).

191 *Peyman vLanjani*, above, n.180 at 488, 493, 501.

192 *Coastal Estates Pty Ltd v Melevende* [1965] V.R. 433, Sup. Ct. Victoria, adopted in *Peyman v Lanjani* above, n.180 at 494.

193 *Habib Bank Ltd v Tufail* [2006] EWCA Civ 374, [2006] All E.R. (D) 92 (Apr) at [15].

cannot affirm one part, and claim to rescind another part, unless what appears to be a single contract can be severed into separate contracts.[194]

Pleading affirmation. It is for the representor to plead affirmation in order to bar the prima facie right to rescission which the representee has already established. As regards the detail of the pleading, in *Peyman v Lanjani* Slade L.J. said[195]: 4–47

> "If A wishes to allege that B, having had a right of rescission, has elected to affirm a contract, he should in his pleadings, so it seems to me, expressly allege B's knowledge of the relevant right to rescind, since such knowledge will be an essential fact on which he relies. The court may, and no doubt often will, be asked to order A to give further and better particulars of the allegation (see RSC Ord. 18, r. 12(4)).[196] In many cases the best particulars that A will be able to give will be to invite the court to infer knowledge from all the circumstances. However strong that prima facie inference may be, it will still be open to the court at the trial, after hearing evidence as to B's true state of mind, to hold on the balance of probabilities that he did not in fact have the requisite knowledge. In the latter event A's plea that B has elected will fail.[197]"

(2) Lapse of Time

Non-fraudulent misrepresentation: rescission barred by lapse of a reasonable time from the contract. There is no statutory limitation period for a claim for rescission for misrepresentation. But, although it is doubted by some writers,[198] it appears that 4–48

[194] *United Shoe Machinery Co. of Canada v Brunet* [1909] A.C. 330, PC, at 340; *West v National Motor and Accident Insurance Union Ltd* [1955] 1 Lloyd's Rep. 207, CA. For the possibility of severance of what appears to be a single contract into separate contracts, see also above, para.4–14.

[195] Above, n.180 at 500–501.

[196] ["Further and better particulars" no longer exist under the Civil Procedure Rules 1998. However, a court may order a party to provide further information under CPR, Pt 18. On procedure generally, see Ch.11.]

[197] Although it might still be arguable, on the facts, that the representee is *estopped* from denying that he has affirmed: above, para.4–45.

[198] Furmston, para.4.56; Snell (31st edn, 2005), para.13.16 suggested that lapse of time should never be seen as an independent bar to rescission, and can only ever be evidence of waiver or affirmation. This passage is deleted, and no mention is now made of lapse of time, in 32nd edn (2010), para.15–013; nor is *Leaf v International Galleries*, below, n.199 now cited in the book. However, for

rescission will cease to be available for a non-fraudulent misrepresentation if the representee delays too long after the time of the contract[199] before claiming the remedy. The underlying rationale of this bar to rescission was said by Jenkins L.J. in *Leaf v International Galleries*[200] to be based on the finality of transactions:

> "contracts such as this cannot be kept open and subject to the possibility of rescission indefinitely . . . I think that, at all events, it behoves the purchaser either to verify, or, as the case may be, to disprove the representation within a reasonable time, or else stand or fall by it. If he is allowed to wait five, ten, or twenty years and then reopen the bargain, there can be no finality at all."

This contains two aspects: that the bar is based on a general policy of finality of transactions; but also that his delay counts against the representee in the sense that he does not deserve to maintain the right to rescind if he fails to act within a reasonable time. This second aspect is important for understanding how the courts apply the bar.

4–49 **Meaning of "reasonable time".** The length of time within which the representee must rescind cannot be stated with precision, because what is "reasonable" must be determined in the light of the particular contract.[201] The quotation from the judgment of Jenkins L.J. in the preceding paragraph suggests that the representee is

---

a similar account of the equitable doctrine of laches, on which this bar to rescission is said to rest, see Snell (32nd edn), para.5–019.

199 *Leaf v International Galleries* [1950] 2 K.B. 86, CA (representee did not discover misrepresentation for five years but time already expired: below, para.4–49). If, however, the representee is under a legal disability, time will presumably run against him only after the disability is lifted: *Ernest v Vivian* (1863) 33 L.J. Ch. 513 at 518 (time for defence of laches ran against a minor from date of majority); *cf.*, by analogy, the Limitation Act 1980, s.28, under which time runs from the lifting of the disability except where the right of action first accrued to another person not under a disability.

200 *Leaf v International Galleries*, above, n.199 at 92. See also Evershed M.R. at 94.

201 The Law Commission, in its proposals to provide civil remedies for certain breaches of the Consumer Protection from Unfair Trading Regulations 2008 SI 2008/1277, proposes that there should be a fixed time, such as 3 months, within which the "right to unwind" the contract (their new remedy, similar to rescission) can be exercised, but that following that period (or if the right to unwind has been lost for other reasons) the claimant should be entitled to a discount on the price

expected to make inquiries into the representation—to check that the basis on which he contracted is as he thought.[202] On this basis, the time to which the representee is entitled will depend on the nature of the contract, its subject-matter and the representations that were made. In the case of a contract to purchase a perishable commodity, or where the nature of the subject-matter and the representation in issue are such that the representee ought easily to have been able to discover the truth soon after the contract was concluded, the time within which he is expected to exercise his right to rescind will be relatively short. But if it is reasonable for him to remain in ignorance for an extended period, he may be able still to rescind after that time.[203]

No direct analogy can be drawn with the limitation periods contained in the Limitation Act 1980.[204] In *Leaf v International*

paid: see Law Com. Consultation Paper No.199, *Consumer Redress for Misleading and Aggressive Practices* (2011), paras 14.21 *et seq.*

[202] See also Denning L.J., [1950] 2 K.B. 86 at 91; *Torrance v Bolton* (1872) L.R. 8 Ch. App. 118 at 124 (James L.J.: "a right to a reasonable time to ascertain his position, and to take advice from persons capable of advising him as to what he ought to do"); *Long v Lloyd* [1958] 2 All E.R. 402, CA, at 407 (purchaser of lorry entitled to time to test the lorry to check that it corresponded with its description).

[203] *Re Reese River Silver Mining Co.* (1867) L.R. 2 Ch. App. 604 (contract in August to purchase shares in a company on the basis of misrepresentations about its business in Nigeria: representee first learned from a company report at the end of December that the representation might be false, and was still entitled to wait until some weeks later for further information about the company before rescinding); *Adam v Newbigging* (1888) 13 App. Cas. 308, HL, at 320 (representee not required to act to rescind before his "suspicions were awakened" about the falsehood of the statement).

[204] The time periods in respect of issues arising out of contracts are mainly set in relation to damages claims, e.g. a period of six years from the date on which the cause of action accrued in the case of actions founded on simple contract (s.5). This is much longer than is generally likely to be held appropriate for rescission, the claim to which is more closely analogous to the right to reject goods for breach, for which the timescale is quite short: *Leaf v International Galleries*, above, n.199 at 90–91 (Denning L.J.); below. And the test for what constitutes a "reasonable time" within which the election to rescind must be exercised is narrower than the test in the Limitation Act 1980, s.32(1)(c), which allows an extension of the statutory limitation periods where the action is for relief from the consequences of a mistake, so that "the period of limitation shall not begin to run until the plaintiff has discovered the . . . mistake . . . or could with reasonable diligence have discovered it": *Peco Arts Inc. v Hazlitt Gallery Ltd* [1983] 1 W.L.R. 1315 at 1323–1324 (purchaser of a copy of a work of art which was mistaken for an original was entitled to rely on the expert opinion of those who

Galleries[205] Denning L.J. compared the bar of lapse of time in the remedy of rescission with the buyer's "acceptance" of defective goods under a contract of sale, which bars his right to reject the goods—and thought that, where the buyer of a painting which was falsely represented to be a Constable[206] would have been held to have accepted it because of a lapse of a reasonable time[207] since the contract had been concluded, he must equally be held to be too late to rescind for misrepresentation because "innocent misrepresentation is much less potent than a breach of condition, and a claim to rescission for innocent misrepresentation must at any rate be barred when a right to reject for breach of condition is barred". Since, however, the question of whether a representee still has the right to rescind or has been barred by lapse of time is one of fact, depending on the particular contract and the misrepresentation in issue, it is generally not helpful to rely on analogies with other remedies.

4–50 **Fraudulent misrepresentation: time runs from discovery of the fraud.** It is often said that lapse of time operates as a bar only to rescission for non-fraudulent misrepresentation; lapse of time may be evidence of affirmation of the contract in a case of fraud, but does not of itself bar rescission.[208] It is clear that, in a case of fraud, time does not run against the representee as long as he remains, without any fault on his part, in ignorance of the fraud.[209] But it

advised her at the time of the purchase, and who valued it later for insurance purposes, so she could not "with reasonable diligence have discovered" the mistake until it was pointed out by a later valuer more than 11 years after the purchase: Webster J. distinguished *Leaf v International Galleries* as a case involving rescission for misrepresentation and therefore governed by the general principles of laches and not the Limitation Act 1980).

205 Above, n.199 at 90–91, followed in *Long v Lloyd* [1958] 1 W.L.R. 753, CA. In *Leaf*, five years had passed from the time of the contract to the time when the buyer discovered that the painting was not a Constable, and sought to rescind the contract. "That, I need hardly say, is much more than a reasonable time" (Denning L.J. in *Leaf*: *ibid.*).

206 For discussion of whether the seller really thought it was a painting by *John* Constable, see Treitel, 11th edn (2003), p.293, n.71.

207 Sale of Goods Act 1893 (now Sale of Goods Act 1979) s.35; the buyer is deemed to accept the goods when, inter alia, "after the lapse of a reasonable time, he retains the goods without intimating to the seller that he has rejected them".

208 Treitel, para.9–113; Chitty, para.6–127; Furmston, para.4.56 (who does not even admit lapse of time in relation to innocent misrepresentation: above, n.198).

209 *Rolfe v Gregory* (1865) 4 De G. J. & S. 576 at 579, 46 E.R. 1042 at 1044; *Armstrong v Jackson* [1917] 2 K.B. 822 at 830.

seems preferable to say that time does run against the representee, even in a case of a fraudulent misrepresentation, but then only from the time he *discovered* it (or, perhaps, ought to have discovered it, if it is by his fault that he failed to do so).[210] The theoretical bases of affirmation[211] and lapse of time[212] are quite distinct, and although the representee's inaction after discovery of the fraud might generally be good evidence of his intention to affirm the contract, there seems no reason why it should not separately—and, indeed, more easily—be held to constitute a bar to rescission simply by virtue of the passage of more than a reasonable time for his action resulting in the fact that he no longer deserves to invoke the remedy.[213] Otherwise, by reserving his right to rescind (and so negativing affirmation), the representee could keep open the right to rescind beyond a reasonable time from discovery of the fraud; even in the case of fraud this appears to be unduly favourable to the representee.

Successor in title bound by time already run against predecessor. If the nature of the contract is such that the claimant can assert a right to rescind based on a representation made to a predecessor in title, the claimant can be in no better position than his predecessor and therefore takes subject to any time which has already run and which will continue to run notwithstanding the change in title.[214] 4–51

[210] In *Redgrave v Hurd* (1881) 20 Ch.D. 1, CA, at 13, Jessel M.R. spoke of delay counting "from the time by which due diligence the fraud might have been discovered", drawing an analogy with the rule in the statutes of limitation (see now the Limitation Act 1980, s.32(1)). *Cf. Re Royal British Bank* (1859) 3 De G. & J. 387 at 431–432, 44 E.R. 1317 at 1335, above, para.4–43, n.179 (representee with "means of knowledge" of fraud barred by affirmation: perhaps better viewed as case of lapse of time).

[211] Above, para.4–41.

[212] Above, para.4–48.

[213] *Ernest v Vivian* (1863) 33 L.J. Ch. 513 (fraud: delay of five years constituted laches); *Erlanger v New Sombrero Phosphate Co.* (1878) 3 App. Cas. 1218, HL, at 1279 (Lord Blackburn: "a Court of Equity requires that those who come to it to ask its active interposition to give them relief, should use due diligence, after there has been such notice or knowledge as to make it inequitable to lie by").

[214] *Ernest v Vivian*, above, n.213 at 517 (purchaser of lease which was voidable for fraud bound by time already passed against predecessor: even if purchaser had no knowledge of fraud he would still be bound by the (continuing) lapse of time which started when his predecessor had knowledge).

(3) Impossibility of Restitution

4–52 **Restitution must be possible.** Rescission of the contract for misrepresentation involves the contract being retrospectively avoided, and any performance already made under the terms of the contract being reversed, so that the parties are placed in the position in which they would have been had there been no contract.[215] In principle, therefore, a necessary precondition to rescission being available is that performance of the contract can in fact be reversed: and so, for example, the representee must be able to give back to the representor whatever he received under the contract.[216] As Crompton J. said in *Clarke v Dickson*[217]:

> "When you enunciate the proposition that a party has a right to rescind, you involve in it the qualification, if the state of things is such that he can rescind. If you are fraudulently induced to buy a cake you may return it and get back the price; but you cannot both eat your cake and return your cake."

4–53 **Narrower view of the old courts of common law to this bar.** The older cases in which this bar to rescission was applied must be viewed with some care, because the approach taken by the old courts of common law was more restrictive than that of the courts of equity—more restrictive, therefore, than the modern cases since

---

[215] Above, para.4–05. Since in English law rescission is possible only of the whole contract, and not of part only, it is not possible to solve a problem of impossibility of restitution by allowing rescission of only those obligations performance of which can be reversed: above, para.4–13; *cf.*, in Australia, *Vadasz v Pioneer Concrete (SA) Pty Ltd* (1995) 184 C.L.R. 102, HCA. Nor has English law developed a general principle of restitution by money-equivalent; *cf.* Commission Expert Group's "Feasibility study for a future instrument in European Contract Law" (May 2011; above, para.1–05, n.16), arts 176(1), 177(1) (where contract avoided for (inter alia) mistake or fraud, each party is obliged to return what he has received from the other party; if what was received cannot be returned, restitution is made by paying its monetary value).

[216] "The rule is stated as requiring the restoration of both parties to the *status quo ante*, but it is generally the defendant who complains that restitution is impossible": *Spence v Crawford* [1939] 3 All E.R. 271, HL (Sc.), at 289 (Lord Wright).

[217] (1858) El. Bl. & El. 148 at 152, 120 E.R. 463 at 465, in argument. However, for the rule that an insurer who avoids the contract of insurance on the basis of the insured's fraud need not repay the premium, at least where he raises the misrepresentation as a defence to the insured's claim under the policy, see below, para.10–11, n.49.

it is the equitable rules for rescission that are now applied.[218] At common law, it was held that rescission was only available if the representee could return *in specie* what he had received, without any change in its nature. It appears even to have been assumed that rescission would be barred if the representor had made use of whatever he had received under the contract without causing any physical deterioration.[219] A reason for this narrow view was that the common law had limited machinery available to adjust the rights of the parties in the event of rescission where one party had received a benefit under the contract which would not be disgorged by the reversal of performance: it was therefore thought to be preferable to refuse rescission, and leave the representee to his remedy in damages in the tort of deceit[220] which would deal with all the financial consequences of the misrepresentation.[221]

More flexible approach of the old courts of equity; the modern approach. However, the courts of equity, which did not award damages, had other remedies available such as ordering that an account be taken of any benefit received by the representee and an appropriate sum be paid over as part of the process of rescission. This provided more appropriate solutions for some of the cases in which the common law courts felt unable to rescind a contract. The modern approach to this bar to rescission has taken, and developed, 4–54

[218] Above, para.4–04.

[219] *Hunt v Silk* (1804) 5 East 449, 102 E.R. 1142 (contract to grant lease not capable of rescission *for breach* because tenant had gone into possession and paid premium; cited as equally applicable to rescission for misrepresentation in, e.g. *Clarke v Dickson*, above, n.217; *Spence v Crawford*, above, n.216 at 283–284, 290; *Abram Steamship Co. v Westville Shipping Co.* [1923] A.C. 773, HL (Sc.), at 782. It is not obvious that the principles applicable to rejection for breach must be identical to rescission for misrepresentation; nor that, even if there was no total failure of consideration in *Hunt v Silk* so as to entitle the tenant to recover sums paid, the lease was itself incapable of rescission by the tenant returning the property in the same physical state in which he received it).

[220] Since it was, in any event, only in cases of fraud that the common law recognised that he had a right to rescind: above, para.4–02. For the tort of deceit, see Ch.5.

[221] *Erlanger v New Sombrero Phosphate Co.*, above, n.213 at 1278–1279; *Clarke v Dickson*, above, n.217; *Alati v Kruger* (1955) 94 C.L.R. 216, HCA, at 223–224.

the equitable rules. The most often cited statement of principle is found in the judgment of Lord Blackburn in *Erlanger v New Sombrero Phosphate Co.*[222]:

> "a Court of Equity could not give damages, and, unless it can rescind the contract, can give no relief. And, on the other hand, it can take accounts of profits, and make allowance for deterioration. And I think the practice has always been for a Court of Equity to give this relief whenever, by the exercise of its powers, it can do what is practically just, though it cannot restore the parties precisely to the state they were in before the contract."

It is therefore necessary to explore how this principle is applied in the modern cases.

4–55 **"Impossibility" less easy to establish in cases of fraud.** In applying the bar of "impossibility of restitution", the courts will take account of whether the representation was fraudulent or not. This does not mean that the bar is not available for fraud if it is really impossible on the facts for restitution to be effected.[223] But the courts are more reluctant to find that restitution is impossible in a case of fraud. In *Spence v Crawford* [224] Lord Wright, discussing the test set out by Lord Blackburn in Erlanger, said:

> "Lord Blackburn is careful not to seek to tie the hands of the court by attempting to form any rigid rules. The court must fix its eyes on the goal of doing 'what is practically just'. How that goal may be reached must depend on the circumstances of the case, but the court will be more drastic in exercising its discretionary powers in a case of fraud than in a case of innocent misrepresentation... There is no doubt good reason for the distinction. A case of innocent misrepresentation may be regarded rather as one of misfortune than as one of moral obliquity. There is no deceit or intention to defraud. The court will be less ready to pull a transaction to pieces where the defendant is innocent, whereas in the case of fraud the

[222] *Erlanger v New Sombrero Phosphate Co.*, above, n.213; cited in, e.g. *Lagunas Nitrate Co. v Lagunas Syndicate* [1899] 2 Ch. 392, CA, at 456; *Spence v Crawford*, above, n.216 at 278–279, 288; *Alati v Kruger*, above, n.221 at 223–224.

[223] See, e.g. *Thomas Witter Ltd v TBP Industries Ltd* [1996] 2 All E.R. 573 at 588; *Society of Lloyd's v Leighs* [1997] C.L.C. 1398, CA; *Crystal Palace F.C. (2000) Ltd v Dowie* [2007] EWHC 1392 (QB), [2007] I.R.L.R. 682.

[224] Above, n.216 at 288–289; see also Lord Thankerton at 279–280; *Lagunas Nitrate Co. v Lagunas Syndicate*, above, n.222 at 423, 433–434.

> court will exercise its jurisdiction to the full in order, if possible, to prevent the defendant from enjoying the benefit of his fraud at the expense of the innocent plaintiff."

In the same case Lord Thankerton put the point more narrowly; he said[225] that a fraudulent representor "is not entitled in bar of restitution to found on dealing with the subject purchased, which he has been enabled by his fraud to carry out".

No rule can be deduced from the cases as to how the courts will use the principle that they will seek to prevent a fraudulent representor from succeeding in a defence of impossibility of restitution: so much depends on the facts of each case.[226] However, it appears that this principle will be used as part of the analysis in the modern law.[227]

---

[225] *ibid.*, at 281. He went on (at 281–282) to give as a possible example (but without deciding it) a case where a contract for the purchase of shares enabled the purchaser (the representor) to gain "ample control" over a company, and he had since disposed of other shares in the company so that he would now lose control if he were required to hand back the contracted shares pursuant to rescission of the contract: the purchaser might be able to resist rescission if he was innocent in his misrepresentation, but not if he was fraudulent. Lord Atkin and Lord Russell agreed with Lord Thankerton's speech; Lord Macmillan agreed with both Lord Thankerton and Lord Wright.

[226] *ibid.*, at 281.

[227] In *O'Sullivan v Management Agency and Music Ltd* [1985] Q.B. 428, CA, at 455, Dunn L.J. took the view that the principle stated in *Spence v Crawford* applied equally to cases of "constructive fraud" in equity, including claims based on undue influence or breach of fiduciary duty where the defendant seeks to resist rescission of a voidable transaction on the basis of impossibility of restitution; see also Fox L.J. at 466. Indeed, it is in cases of undue influence and breach of fiduciary duty that the modern cases have developed most significantly the rules for impossibility of restitution following Lord Blackburn's speech in *Erlanger v New Sombrero Phosphate Co.*: see also *Cheese v Thomas* [1994] 1 W.L.R. 129, CA (but there the defendant was an "innocent fiduciary" and the jurisdiction was exercised accordingly: see at 138); *Investors Compensation Scheme Ltd v West Bromwich Building Society* [1999] Lloyd's Rep. P.N. 496 at 542–544 (misrepresentation and undue influence); *Mahoney v Purnell* [1996] 3 All E.R. 61; below, n.232. In so far as such cases have relied on the fact that there was a breach of fiduciary duty in order to justify their leaning heavily in favour of finding equitable remedies (such as orders for compensation or adjustment of the losses to be borne by the parties) to enable rescission to proceed, they can be used equally to support a claim for rescission for misrepresentation but should perhaps be equated to claims for fraudulent misrepresentation, rather than non-fraudulent.

4–56 **Examples of rescission not barred because the court exercises equitable jurisdiction.** Although rescission might formerly have been barred at common law because, before rescinding, the representee had made use of property transferred pursuant to the contract, there will be no such automatic bar under the equitable principles which the courts now apply. The courts will assess a suitable sum to compensate the representor for the use of the property by the representee in the mean time; and if there is any deterioration in the property as a result of the use, monetary compensation will be ordered alongside rescission.[228] Similarly, an account may be ordered of any profits made by a party under the contract which is to be rescinded[229]; or where one party has rendered services to the other or has made payments or undertaken other obligations under the contract the court may award compensation in such amount as it thinks just and equitable as a condition of rescission.[230] The jurisdiction to order compensation as a condition of rescission based on the fact that restitution would otherwise be impossible appears to be similar to, but wider than, the jurisdiction to order payment to the representor of an indemnity in equity to reimburse him for such sums as he has disbursed in performance of the very terms of the contract which is being rescinded.[231] It is a broad jurisdiction, more akin to awarding

---

[228] *Alati v Kruger* (1955) 94 C.L.R. 216, HCA (purchase of business, and possession of business premises, by representee under contract voidable for fraud: rescission subject to payment of representor's lost rent during period of occupation and for business stock used up before rescission).

[229] *O'Sullivan v Management Agency and Music Ltd*, above, n.227.

[230] *Guinness Plc v Saunders* [1990] 2 A.C. 663, HL, at 698–699 (Lord Goff: a "just allowance" could be made for services rendered under contract voidable for breach of fiduciary duty); *Spence v Crawford*, above, n.216 (rescission subject to payment of compensation to representor in respect of obligations performed and costs incurred under the contract); *O'Sullivan v Management Agency and Music Ltd*, above, n.227 (undue influence and breach of fiduciary duty: rescission of contracts between composer/singer and manager on condition that defendant wrongdoer give up profits received, net of tax paid on those profits, but be compensated for work performed under the contract based on reasonable remuneration including a profit element because claimant's career had benefited significantly from their work. Only simple interest awarded because money on which award based had been used for claimant's benefit, as well as defendant's). On the question of the extent to which cases decided on the basis of undue influence and breach of fiduciary duty can be relied on in a case of misrepresentation, see above, n.227.

[231] Above, para.4–17.

damages to compensate for loss generally, and in the context of undue influence has been held to extend to a case where the wrongdoing party has made no profit from the contract (and therefore an account is not appropriate), but the claimant requires to be compensated for the net value of what he surrendered under the contract but which will not be restored to him in financial terms on rescission.[232]

Rescission will not be barred simply because property which was transferred under the contract, and which has to be returned, has decreased in value;[233] *a fortiori* where the decrease in value is directly related to the misrepresentation on which rescission is based.[234] The question is whether the property can, in substance, still be returned: only, therefore, if there has been such a change in its nature that it cannot be said to be possible to return what was received under the contract, will the bar be applied.[235] It has even been said that rescission of a contract of sale of quoted shares ought

---

[232] *Mahoney v Purnell*, above, n.227, relying on *O'Sullivan v Management Agency and Music Ltd*, above, n.227 (claimant transferred shares in business to son-in-law for undervalue: by the time of rescission, shares valueless: rescission, on payment to claimant of value of shares transferred). However, it might be argued that restitution really was impossible here since the company was now in liquidation; below, n.238. But May J. relied heavily on the authorities on compensation in equity for breach of fiduciary duty. On the extent to which this can be read across to claims for misrepresentation, see above, n.227.

[233] *Armstrong v Jackson* [1917] 2 K.B. 822 (fraud: rescission of contract to purchase shares which had fallen in value from nearly £3 at the time of the contract to 5 shillings a share by the time of the claim: rescission still possible: "the market valuation of the shares has greatly dropped, but the shares are the same shares"; McCardie J. at 828).

[234] *Adam v Newbigging* (1888) 13 App. Cas. 308, HL; *Spence v Crawford*, above, n.216 at 279.

[235] *cf. Cheese v Thomas*, above, n.227 (agreement between claimant and his great-nephew to contribute to purchase of house in shares 43:40; rescission for great-nephew's undue influence, although he was an "innocent fiduciary" and not morally reprehensible. Property had been sold at a loss. Both parties required to bear proportionate share (43:40) of loss: this was not a contract to transfer property (in which restoration of property would be ordered notwithstanding decrease in value) but contract to pay money for joint venture in which losses, as well as profits, must be taken into account on rescission: see Sir Donald Nicholls V.C. at 40–43); noted at [1994] L.M.C.L.Q. 330 (J. Mee); (1994) 110 L.Q.R. 173 (M. Chen-Wishart); *Investors Compensation Scheme Ltd v West Bromwich Building Society* [1999] Lloyd's Rep. P.N. 496 at 544–545 (rescission of contract under which claimants mortgaged their homes and received sums which were to be invested: practical justice did not necessarily require repayment of whole

still to be possible even after the specific shares purchased have been sold, since other identical shares can be purchased on the market and the defrauded purchaser can offer substantial restitution.[236]

4–57 **Examples of rescission barred because of impossibility of restitution.** Where, however, the court is not satisfied that it is possible for restitution to be effected as part of the process of rescission, even with a consequential order in the exercise of the equitable jurisdiction described in the last section, rescission will be barred and the claimant will be left to pursue any other remedies he has available.[237]

The most common circumstances in which the courts have found rescission barred are where restitution is impossible because the property cannot be returned—either at all, or because even though it appears still possible to return the property, its essential character has changed since the time it was transferred under the contract.[238]

amount borrowed on mortgage: the whole package of the borrowing plus the intended investment of the borrowed money had to be considered for each claimant).

[236] *Smith New Court Ltd v Scrimgeour Vickers (Asset Management) Ltd* [1997] A.C. 254, HL, at 263 (Lord Browne-Wilkinson). This was a case of fraud, which might therefore attract the more generous rule discussed above, para.4–55; but it was in any event obiter, since the claim for rescission was not pursued in the case, and goes beyond what has been applied in other cases. If such an argument were to be accepted, it would be important to set its limits. In substance, it would allow restitution of an equivalent thing, rather than restitution *in specie*; but it could apply only where there is no difference whatsoever between the equivalent and the original thing transferred under the contract: the other party cannot be required to take something by way of restitution that is not identical to that which he delivered under the contract.

[237] In particular, damages if he can establish a loss and a cause of action: for damages in deceit (in cases of fraudulent misrepresentation), see Ch.5; for damages in tort or under statute for careless misrepresentation see Chs 6 and 7; and for damages for breach of contract, see Ch.8.

[238] *Western Bank of Scotland v Addie* (1867) L.R. 1 Sc. & Div. 145, HL (Sc.) (shares in unincorporated association had changed since contract by virtue of the association's incorporation as a company); *Clarke v Dickson* (1858) El. Bl. & El. 148, 120 E.R. 463 (shares in partnership later incorporated as limited company). Although these are old cases, it seems likely that the result on this issue would still apply under the modern application of the *Erlanger* principle. *Cf. Thomas Witter Ltd v TBP Industries Ltd* [1996] 2 All E.R. 573 (contract for sale of business: rescission for fraudulent misrepresentation not possible because, although the business had been kept separate from the representee's other assets,

Rescission will also be barred where it could not unravel the transaction in its entirety, and would leave the representee in a better position than before the contract, and a better position than the contract had contemplated.[239]

The rule that rescission will be barred of a contract under which property has passed once a third party has acquired rights in the property for value and without notice of the earlier defect in title[240] could also be seen as a particular illustration of the bar based on impossibility of restitution: the later purchaser's rights take priority and provide a legal impediment to the ability of the representor to restore the property, and therefore to make restitution.[241] However, the cases dealing with intervening third party rights are generally viewed as a separate bar, and will be discussed in the next section.

---

it was unrealistic because of changes of key staff to regard it as the same business; and third parties, such as mortgagees of the business assets, would also be affected); *Sheffield Nickel and Silver Plating Co. Ltd v Unwin* (1877) 2 Q.B.D. 214 (contract by which director gave up shares and patent rights to company not capable of rescission for fraudulent misrepresentation by the director, because although the shares still existed the nature of the businesses carried on by the company had changed and one of the patent rights had been disposed of); *Lagunas Nitrate Co. v Lagunas Syndicate* [1899] 2 Ch. 392, CA (rescission of contract to transfer nitrate works could not be rescinded after the property had changed its nature by being worked); *Pilmer v The Duke Group Ltd* [2001] H.C.A. 31, (2001) 75 A.L.J.R. 1067 at [44] (no longer possible to rescind contracts for allotment of new shares for takeover once takeover complete); *Rayden v Edwardo Ltd* [2008] EWHC 2689 (Comm), at [41] (sale of shares could not be reversed where claimants had thereby ceased to be involved in running company and underlying business had changed substantially in nature). It must, however, be borne in mind in reading some of the older cases that the courts might now sometimes take a less strict view of the concept of "impossibility" of restitution: above, para.4–54.

239 *Murad v Al-Saraj* [2004] EWHC 1235 (Ch), [2004] All E.R. (D) 463 (May) at [298] (Etherton J.; rescission of contract for property joint venture would leave representees as sole shareholders of company in which property was vested and therefore sole beneficiaries of revenue and capital profits from the transaction; this would in effect re-write the commercial deal. The remedy should instead be an order against the fraudulent representor for an account of profits; on this see CA at [2005] EWCA Civ 959, [2005] All E.R. (D) 503 (Jul); below, para.5–43).

240 Below, para.4–60.

241 See also *Crystal Palace F.C. (2000) Ltd v Dowie* [2007] EWHC 1392 (QB), [2007] I.R.L.R. 682 at [216] (compromise agreement to terminate employment contract, entered into on basis of employee's fraudulent misrepresentations, could not be rescinded because it would require original employment contract to be revived and that would not be just to the employee's new employer).

4–58 **Rescission barred where it involves the court acknowledging an illegal or immoral contract.** Where the court's assistance is required in order to effect rescission, but rescission would involve the court ordering the re-transfer of an illegal business, rescission will be refused.[242] This is similar to the rule that rescission will not be available where restitution is impossible, together with the general rule that a court will not allow a claimant a remedy which requires him to rely on an illegal contract.[243]

(4) Intervening Third-Party Rights

4–59 **Rescission is barred if third parties would be prejudiced.** Rescission will generally be barred if it would prejudice the rights of third parties.[244] For example, a contract between a Lloyd's Name and certain Lloyd's companies authorising the companies to enter into settlements on behalf of the Name could not be rescinded for fraudulent misrepresentation because rescission would affect third parties with whom settlements had been entered into.[245] And after a company becomes insolvent, it is too late to rescind a contract to take an allotment of shares in the company because rights of the company's creditors (which crystallised on the insolvency) would be prejudiced by capital being withdrawn from the company by the reversal of the allotment.[246]

---

[242] *The Siben (No.2)* [1996] 1 Lloyd's Rep. 35 at 62–63 (rescission would have involved the court ordering the re-transfer of a business of which a significant part was the provision of prostitutes).

[243] On illegality in contract see generally R.A. Buckley, *Illegality and Public Policy* (2nd edn, 2009); Chitty, Ch.16; Treitel, Ch.11; *Tinsley v Milligan* [1994] 1 A.C. 340, HL, at 370.

[244] *Thomas Witter Ltd v TBP Industries Ltd*, above, n.238 at 588 (where Jacob J. suggested that the burden of proof that third parties would be affected did not lie on the party seeking to establish the bar).

[245] *Society of Lloyd's v Leighs* [1997] C.L.C. 1398, CA.

[246] *Oakes v Turquand* (1867) L.R. 2 H.L. 325, HL; *Tennent v City of Glasgow Bank* (1879) 4 App. Cas. 615, HL (Sc.); *Re Hull and County Bank* (1880) 15 Ch.D. 507; *Re Scottish Petroleum Co.* (1882) 23 Ch.D. 413, CA. *Cf. Senanayake v Cheng* [1966] A.C. 63, PC, at 80 (contract to buy share in partnership could still be rescinded even after insolvency of partnership because pre-dissolution liability of each partner to third parties unaffected); *Adam v Newbigging* (1888) 13 App. Cas. 308, HL. *Cf.* also *Load v Green* (1846) 15 M. & W. 216, 153 E.R. 828; *Re Eastgate* [1905] 1 K.B. 465 (trustee in bankruptcy of an insolvent *individual* takes subject to the right to rescind, so rescission of contract entered into with

Sale of property to a purchaser without notice of the defect in the contract. Since a contract induced by misrepresentation is only voidable, and not void, the legal property rights in goods delivered or land transferred pursuant to the contract can pass to the transferee, although the property rights are liable to be revested in the transferor upon rescission.[247] However, in the case of a contract relating to goods,[248] if before rescission is effected the goods have been transferred to a person who for value acquired rights[249] in them in good faith and without notice of the facts giving rise to the defect in earlier contract, it is too late to rescind.[250] This rule is contained in the Sale of Goods Act 1979 in relation to the transfer 4–60

individual not barred by his insolvency). Treitel para.9–107 sees a conflict between these last two cases and the company cases, but there is surely no conflict since the issue is whether a contract *with* the individual binds the trustee in bankruptcy; the company cases are not cases *with* the company, but *to take shares in it*. On the steps required to rescind a contract of allotment of shares, see above, para.4–19, n.89.

247 Above, para.4–11.

248 In the case of a land, the position varies according to whether or not the land is registered. In unregistered land, the equity to rescind is not binding on a purchaser of the legal title or equitable title without notice; a later purchaser of even an equitable interest in the property can therefore defeat the right: *Phillips v Phillips* (1862) 4 De G. F. & J. 208 at 218, 45 E.R. 1164 at 1167; *Latec Investments Ltd v Hotel Terrigal Pty Ltd* (1965) 113 C.L.R. 265, HCA, at 286. Where the title is registered a registered disponee who gives valuable consideration will take free of the equity unless it is protected by entry of a notice in the register, or as an overriding interest: above, para.4–10, n.31.

249 Typically, a purchaser, although it may be a transferee of a limited interest, such as a pledgee: *Whitehorn Brothers v Davison* [1911] 1 K.B. 463, CA.

250 If, however, the second contract is itself first rescinded so as to revest the property in the first transferee, rescission of the first contract again becomes possible: above, para.4–15. In *Car and Universal Finance Co. Ltd v Caldwell* [1965] 1 Q.B. 525, above, para.4–20, the contract was held to have been rescinded, even without actual communication to the representor, before a sale of the car to a subsequent purchaser without notice of the earlier defective contract. The timing of rescission can therefore be crucial to the rights of the relevant parties (the original representee, and the later purchaser); for criticism of this effect of the *Caldwell* rule relating to rescission without notice to the representor, see above, para.4–20, n.100. For another case where rescission was effected before a later sale to a purchaser without notice, see *Newtons of Wembley Ltd v Williams* [1965] 1 Q.B. 560, CA; and for a case where the bar operated, see *MacLeod v Kerr*, 1965 S.C. 253, Ct. Sess.

of title under a contract for the sale of goods,[251] but a similar general rule had already been established by the courts before statute intervened.[252] It is the representee who has the burden of proving that the defendant had notice of the misrepresentation which made the prior contract voidable, or was not in good faith, when he purchased the property.[253]

(5) Misrepresentation Act 1967, Section 2(2)

4–61 **Statutory discretion to award damages in lieu of rescission.** In s.2(2) of the Misrepresentation Act 1967 the courts[254] were given a new, statutory discretion to refuse rescission and to award damages instead. The terms of the subsection are as follows[255]:

---

[251] Sale of Goods Act 1979, s.23. By s.61(3) the purchaser is in good faith if he is in fact honest, whether or not he may be negligent. These provisions replaced those first enacted as the Sale of Goods Act 1893, ss.23 and 62(2) respectively.

[252] *Cundy v Lindsay* (1878) 3 App. Cas. 459, HL, at 463–464; *White v Garden* (1851) 10 C.B. 919, 138 E.R. 364; *Babcock v Lawson* (1880) 5 Q.B.D. 284, CA, at 286. The rule does not, though, apply to contracts which are *void* because no rights in the property pass under the void contract, so the later purchaser himself acquires no rights: *Cundy v Lindsay*; see also above, para.1–03. In *Car and Universal Finance Co. Ltd v Caldwell* [1965] 1 Q.B. 525 at 533, Lord Denning M.R., sitting as the trial judge, appears to have thought that a person has notice for the purposes of this rule if he actually knows of the defect in title, or has a suspicion and refrains from asking questions, but not if he is just blundering or negligent. However, "good faith" and "notice" are not synonymous, and it may be that a court will allow some degree of constructive notice, whilst being reluctant to adopt the full equitable doctrine of notice into commercial dealings: R.M. Goode, *Commercial Law* (4th edn, 2010), p.464; K.C. Sutton, *The Law of Sale of Goods in Australia and New Zealand* (2nd edn, Law Book Co, Sydney, 1974), pp.271–274.

[253] *Whitehorn Brothers v Davison*, above, n.249, criticised in Benjamin, para.7–029, but approved in *Barclays Bank Plc v Boulter* [1999] 1 W.L.R. 1919, HL, at 1925. It has, however, been held that where the question is not whether the defendant had notice of the defect in the earlier contract, but whether in the chain of contracts between the representee and the defendant there was a contract to a party who had notice of the defect in title and which therefore prevented the defendant subsequently obtaining rights in the goods, the burden of proof lies on the defendant, since he must show that he has a better right through his own purchase of the goods than the claimant's original title: *Thomas v Heelas*, unreported, November 27, 1986, CA.

[254] The subsection expressly applies to arbitration as well as to proceedings before a court, but for convenience reference will be made only to the exercise of the discretion by a court. An Employment Appeal Tribunal has doubted whether

> "*2.*—(2) Where a person has entered into a contract after a misrepresentation has been made to him otherwise than fraudulently, and he would be entitled, by reason of the misrepresentation, to rescind the contract, then, if it is claimed, in any proceedings arising out of the contract, that the contract ought to be or has been rescinded, the court or arbitrator may declare the contract subsisting and award damages in lieu of rescission, if of opinion that it would be equitable to do so, having regard to the nature of the misrepresentation and the loss that would be caused by it if the contract were upheld, as well as to the loss that rescission would cause to the other party."

If the subsection does not apply, and if the representee establishes the right to rescind in accordance with the rules set out earlier in this chapter, the court has no discretion to refuse rescission.[256] The detail of this subsection needs to be considered in order to understand the circumstances in which the discretion arises and the basis on which the courts are entitled to exercise it.

Discretion only in the case of non-fraudulent misrepresentations. The subsection applies only where the representee "has entered into a contract after a misrepresentation has been made to him otherwise than fraudulently." The subsection therefore applies to claims to rescind based on wholly blameless,[257] as well as negligent, misrepresentation; but not to fraudulent misrepresentation. If, therefore, a representee wishes to exercise the right to rescind for misrepresentation and to avoid any risk of the 4–62

---

the subsection applies to an industrial tribunal (now an employment tribunal: Employment Rights (Dispute Resolution) Act 1998 s.1(1)): *BAA Plc v Quinton*, unreported, October 22, 1992.

255 In Australia, South Australia and the Australian Capital Territory took s.2(2) as a model for their own similar legislation: Misrepresentation Act 1972 (SA), s.7(3); Law Reform (Misrepresentation) Ordinance 1977 (ACT), s.5, later replaced by Civil Law (Wrongs Act) 2002 (ACT), s.175: Carter, Peden and Tolhurst, para.18–75; Seddon and Ellinghaus, para.11.72.

256 Above, para.4–18.

257 This is clear from a comparison with s.2(1) and s.2(3): unlike s.2(2), s.2(1) excludes from its ambit cases where the representor can prove "that he had reasonable ground to believe and did believe up to the time the contract was made that the facts represented were true" (that is, it does not apply to the blameless representor: see below, para.7–25); and s.2(3) deals with the overlap of cases between s.2(1) and s.2(2), but is drafted on the explicit basis that it is possible to be liable under s.2(2) without being liable under s.2(1): *William Sindall Plc v Cambridgeshire CC* [1994] 1 W.L.R. 1016, CA, at 1037; *Thomas Witter Ltd v TBP Industries Ltd* [1996] 2 All E.R. 573 at 589–590.

court exercising its discretion under s.2(2), he will have an incentive to attempt to prove fraud in order to remove the statutory discretion altogether.[258]

4–63 **Not applicable to cases of non-disclosure.** Since the subsection applies only where a "misrepresentation has been made to" the representee, it has been held that it covers only cases of active misrepresentation, and not cases of non-disclosure.[259] Cases of "half-truth" or where silence communicates a falsehood[260] would, however, be included since they are regarded as "misrepresentations" for the purpose of other remedies at common law and in equity.

4–64 **Discretion where the representee "would be entitled... to rescind".** The discretion arises where the representee "would be entitled, by reason of the misrepresentation, to rescind the contract". This appears to require that there be a right to rescission, under the rules set out in the earlier part of this chapter, so that the court is presented with a choice: to order or confirm the rescission as claimed (in which cases the court cannot award damages under s.2(2))[261]; or to refuse it and to award damages instead.[262] This is

[258] *UCB Corporate Services Ltd v Thomason* [2005] EWCA Civ 225, [2005] 1 All E.R. (Comm) 601 at [47] (withdrawal of allegation of fraud "deprived [the claimant] of a straightforward way of insisting that the [contract] should be rescinded": Brooke L.J.). On the difficulties of proving fraud, see below, para.5–46.

[259] *Banque Keyser Ullmann S.A. v Skandia (UK) Insurance Co. Ltd* [1990] 1 Q.B. 665 at 790 on similar wording in the Misrepresentation Act 1967, s.2(1); applied to s.2(2) in *Ramphul v Toole* unreported, March 17, 1989, CA. For a question whether this interpretation might be revised in the light of the decision in *Conlon v Simms* [2006] EWCA Civ 1749, [2008] 1 W.L.R. 484, see below, para. 17–45. On non-disclosure generally, see Pt III.

[260] Above, para 3–08.

[261] There may, of course, be other claims for damages, such as under the Misrepresentation Act 1967 s.2(1); but these are not discretionary.

[262] Under the language of the subsection the court must award damages if it exercises the discretion to refuse rescission. But that will depend on the representee establishing a loss suffered by virtue of the misrepresentation if he remains bound by the contract, and if there is no such loss there will be no award of damages: *Bank Negara Indonesia 1946 v Taylor*, unreported, January 26, 1995, CA; *cf. William Sindall Plc v Cambridgeshire CC*, above, n.257 at 1038 (loss at time of trial was nil). On the principles of assessment of damages under s.2(2), see below, para.4–71.

the interpretation placed on the subsection by Cantley J. in *Alton House Garages (Bromley) Ltd v Monk*.[263] In that case, the seller of a Rolls Royce Corniche misrepresented facts about the car, including the fact that it had a verifiable service history. In consequence of there being no service record, the value was reduced by £3,500. The purchasers sought, inter alia,[264] damages under s.2(2) of the Misrepresentation Act even though, by the time of the action, they had affirmed the contract with knowledge of the misrepresentation and had even sold the car to a third party. Cantley J. took the view that he had no discretion under s.2(2):

> "It should be noted that the sub-section says 'would be entitled to rescind the contract' not 'would have been entitled'. The sub-section also says that this jurisdiction arises if it is claimed that the contract ought to be rescinded, not 'ought to have been or could have been rescinded'. It seems to me that this sub-section is dealing with the situation at the time when the court is being asked to exercise its discretion to declare the contract subsisting and award damages in lieu of rescission. The court is given a judicial discretion to choose, on equitable grounds, between rescission and damages in lieu of rescission. If the party claiming rescission is not entitled to rescission, there is no such choice. If this new jurisdiction can be invoked merely be making a hopeless claim that the contract ought to be rescinded we are getting nearer to the days of the old legal fiction than we have been for some time."

Statements in other cases appear to be based on a similar assumption: the courts check first whether rescission is available before seeking to exercise the jurisdiction under s.2(2).[265] However, in *Thomas Witter Ltd v TBP Industries Ltd*[266] Jacob J. decided he

---

[263] Unreported, July 31, 1981.

[264] According to the judge, they claimed damages "on every conceivable alternative ground"; they succeeded in their claim for damages for breach of contract (either a term of the contract as to the description of the car; or a collateral warranty as to the service history); alternatively under the Misrepresentation Act 1967 s.2(1). The judge thought that the claim under s.2(2) was brought "vainly, if all else fails".

[265] e.g. *Atlantic Lines & Navigation Co. Inc. v Hallam Ltd, The Lucy* [1983] 1 Lloyd's Rep. 188 at 201–202; and the point was conceded by the representee in *Alman v Associated Newspapers Group Ltd*, unreported, June 20, 1980.

[266] Above, n.257 at 590–591; (1995) 111 L.Q.R. 385 (H. Beale). The reasoned judgment of Cantley J. in *Alton House Garages (Bromley) Ltd v Monk* was not cited, although *Atlantic Lines & Navigation Co. Inc. v Hallam Ltd, The Lucy* and *Alman v Associated Newspapers Group Ltd*, above, n.265, were.

had discretion to award damages under the subsection where rescission had been available but was barred by the time of the hearing:

> "the power to award damages under section 2(2) does not depend upon an extant right to rescission—it only depends upon a right having existed in the past. Whether it depends upon such a right existing at any time, or depends upon such a right subsisting at the time when the representee first claims rescission, I do not have to decide . . . In principle, however, I would have thought that it is enough that at any time a right to rescind subsisted. It is damages in lieu of that right (even if barred by later events or lapse of time) which can be awarded."

In coming to this decision Jacob J. thought that the subsection was sufficiently ambiguous[267] to entitle him to enquire into what had been said in Parliament during the passage of the Act; and he discovered that the Solicitor-General had given an example, in the House of Commons, of how clause 2(2) of the then Bill might be used to award damages to the purchaser of a house where the contract could no longer be rescinded because of impossibility of restitution.[268]

However, although the decision of Jacob J. is attractive in that it gives greater flexibility to a judge to award damages even where there is no other available claim,[269] it is suggested that the more natural reading of the subsection is that of Cantley J.; and that if Parliament had intended to provide such a radical new remedy in damages for all cases of innocent misrepresentation, it would have done so in clearer terms.[270] More recently, in *Government of*

---

267 *Pepper (Inspector of Taxes) v Hart* [1993] A.C. 593, HL.

268 *Hansard*, HC Vol.741, cols 1388–1389 (February 20, 1967).

269 In *Thomas Witter Ltd v TBP Industries Ltd* the representee also succeeded under the Misrepresentation Act 1967 s.2(1), and Jacob J. held that the measure of damages did not, on the facts, differ between the two claims. But since s.2(2) extends to wholly innocent misrepresentations where there would be no claim for damages in tort or under s.2(1), the consequences of Jacob J.'s interpretation of s.2(2) could be very significant.

270 The decision of the CA in *William Sindall Plc v Cambridgeshire CC* [1994] 1 W.L.R. 1016 is not conclusive: although the court there found it unnecessary to consider s.2(2) because they first decided that the representee had no right to rescind, it was a case where he had never had a right to rescind (because there was, on the facts, no actionable representation), not a case where an earlier right to rescind had become barred.

Zanzibar v British Aerospace (Lancaster House) Ltd, Judge Jack Q.C. took this view, and declined to follow the earlier decision of Jacob J.[271]:

> "section 2(2) gives the court a discretionary power to hold the contract to be subsisting and to award damages where it would otherwise be obliged to grant rescission or to hold that the contract had been rescinded by the representee. The court does not have that power, and does not need to have that power, where rescission is no longer available."

Discretion even where contract already rescinded. The subsection applies where it is claimed "that the contract ought to be *or has been* rescinded". Since rescission is a remedy which can be effected by act of the representee without the need for a court order [272] it will often happen that, by the time the court hears the case, the representee has already taken sufficient steps to rescind the contract. If the court decides not to exercise its discretion under s.2(2), the rescission will date from the earlier sufficient act of the representee, which will simply be confirmed as valid by the order of the court. But if the court does exercise its discretion it will, in effect, resurrect the contract by retrospectively annulling the earlier rescission.[273] 4–65

[271] [2000] 1 W.L.R. 2333 at 2343. Judge Jack Q.C. thought that the section was sufficiently clear; and if not then the doubt should be resolved by reference to the Tenth Report of the Law Reform Committee, *Innocent Misrepresentation*, Cmnd.1782 (1962), paras 11 and 12, and statements by Lord Gardiner L.C. introducing the Bill into the House of Lords (*Hansard*, HL Vol. 274, cols 921 *et seq.* (May 17, 1966)) and not, as had Jacob J. in *Thomas Witter*, by relying on the statement of the Solicitor-General which "was an extempore answer given a little after 3 o'clock in the morning". Judge Humphrey Lloyd Q.C. in *Floods of Queensferry Ltd v Shand Construction Ltd* [2000] B.L.R. 81 at 91–93 similarly thought the subsection sufficiently clear; and Rex Tedd Q.C. in *Pankhania v Hackney LBC* [2002] EWHC 2441 (Ch), [2002] All E.R. (D) 22 (Aug) at [76] also preferred the approach taken in the *Zanzibar* case. The Australian legislation, modelled on s.2(2) (above, n.255) applies "where . . . a person has rescinded, or is entitled to rescind, the contract . . .": this assumes, perhaps even more clearly than s.2(2), that at the time of the hearing the party representee has not yet lost the right to rescind: Seddon and Ellinghaus, para.11.72.

[272] Indeed, even if the first claim is in the proceedings, it is generally the claim which constitutes the rescission, rather than the later order; above, para.4–18.

[273] *Atlantic Lines & Navigation Co. Inc v Hallam Ltd, The Lucy*, above, n.265 at 202 (Mustill J.: "there are some formidable difficulties in the practical application of this discretion to a case where the Court is not asked to order rescission as a direct and immediate remedy, but is invited to validate a rescission which has

4–66 **Burden of proof.** Since s.2(2) sets out the conditions which must apply and matters to which the court must have regard for the exercise of the discretion, no special case has to be shown before the court awards damages under the subsection. However, on the broader question of the burden of proof in the application of the subsection, it is the party seeking to persuade the court to exercise the discretion to refuse rescission who must establish the case for that exercise.[274] In addition, the party who claims damages in the event that rescission is refused must establish a substantial loss if damages are to be awarded under the subsection.[275]

4–67 **The width of the discretion; the range of factors a court may consider.** The discretion is wide. The three specific factors for the exercise of the discretion, given in the subsection,[276] are not the only factors a court may take into account: the general rule in s.2(2) is that the court exercises the discretion "if of opinion that it would be equitable to do so".[277]

4–68 **Factors in exercise of the discretion: (1) the nature of the misrepresentation.** The court is required to have regard to "the nature of the misrepresentation". It is under this head that a court might take the view that the misrepresentation, though it was a reason for the representee's decision to contract, was none the less

already been effected as a measure of self-help"). The avoidance of the contract is itself, in effect, voidable by the court by application of its discretion under s.2(2) but presumably, on the analogy of a voidable contract, if the rescission is annulled retrospectively this will not make unlawful anything done by the representee during the period he had validly rescinded (such as his recaption and use of property which had been transferred under the contract). The difficulty of application of the discretion in such a case will no doubt be one factor considered by the court in deciding how to exercise the discretion.

[274] *British & Commonwealth Holdings Plc v Quadrex Holdings Inc*, unreported, April 10, 1995, CA, contrasting the stricter rules for the exercise of the discretion to award damages in addition to or in substitution for the equitable remedies of injunction and specific performance.

[275] *UCB Corporate Services Ltd v Thomason* [2005] EWCA Civ 225, [2005] 1 All E.R. (Comm) 601 (no loss established, so no damages awarded although rescission refused under s.2(2)); *Huyton S.A. v Distribuidora Internacional de Productos Agricolas S.A.* [2003] EWCA Civ 1104, [2003] 2 Lloyd's Rep. 780 at [5].

[276] Below, paras 4–68, 4–69 and 4–70.

[277] *William Sindall Plc v Cambridgeshire CC*, above, n.270 at 1042–1043 (Evans L.J.).

relatively insignificant in the context of the whole contract and so it would not be right for the whole contract to fall if the award of damages under the subsection would provide a suitable remedy. This is certainly the kind of situation in the mind of the Law Reform Committee, which proposed the remedy which became s.2(2) of the Misrepresentation Act 1967.[278] A court might also, under this head, take into account the culpability of the representor, and be more disposed to exercise its discretion to maintain the contract in the case of a wholly blameless representation.[279]

Factors in exercise of the discretion: (2) the loss that refusal of rescission would cause the representee. The court must have regard to "the loss that would be caused by [the misrepresentation] if the contract were upheld". This refers to the loss which would be suffered by the representee; by implication, such loss will form the basis of the award of damages if the court then proceeds to exercise its discretion and declare the contract subsisting.[280] The basis on which this calculation is made is considered below.[281] 4–69

---

278 Law Reform Committee Tenth Report, above, n.271, paras 11 to 13; *William Sindall Plc v Cambridgeshire CC*, above, n.270 at 1036 (Hoffmann L.J.: "in the context of a £5m sale of land, a misrepresentation which would have cost £18,000 to put right and was unlikely seriously to have interfered with the development or resale of the property was a matter of relatively minor importance"); see also Evans L.J. at 1043; *Atlantic Lines & Navigation Co. Inc. v Hallam Ltd, The Lucy*, above, n.265 at 202 (Mustill J.: the representation was "of quite a trivial nature: at most it could be said to have tipped the scale, rather than striking to the root of the bargain"). In other common law jurisdictions there is similar concern to avoid rescission where it would be too drastic in comparison with the limited significance of a misrepresentation and its consequences: for New Zealand, see the Contractual Remedies Act 1979, ss.7–9 ("cancellation" of the contract—the (non-retrospective) remedy for both breach and misrepresentation—is not available unless either parties have expressly or impliedly agreed that truth of representation is essential to representee, or effect of misrepresentation is substantial: s.7(4); Burrows, Finn & Todd, para.18.2.2); and in Canada, see *Guarantee Co. of North America v Gordon Capital Corp.* (1999) 178 D.L.R. (4th) 1, SCC, at [44] (where misrepresentation incorporated into the contract, requirement that misrepresentation be "substantial", "material" or go "to the root of the contract"); and Waddams, para.424 (in case of executed contract, rescission is available only if the misrepresentation is "substantial").

279 *William Sindall Plc v Cambridgeshire CC*, above, n.270 at 1043.

280 *ibid.*, at 1036–1037, 1043. If there is a loss which cannot be quantified in money, it may be a reason for refusing to exercise the discretion and so to allow rescission: *Northcote Housing Association v Dixon* [2001] All E.R. (D) 452

4–70 **Factors in exercise of the discretion: (3) the loss that rescission would cause the representor.** The court must also have regard to "the loss that rescission would cause to the [representor]". So a court is likely to declare the contract subsisting where the consequences of rescission would be disproportionate when balanced against the loss which the representee would suffer if rescission is refused but which is then compensated by an award under s.2(2).[282] It should be noted, however, that it is not sufficient that there is a relatively small loss which could easily be compensated in money terms, if there are wider considerations to justify the court's refusing to declare the contract subsisting. For example, even though the consequences of a misrepresentation by an insured to an insurer might be compensated by an order that the insured pay the insurer the additional premium which he might have been expected to pay had he told the truth, s.2(2) is unlikely to be applied in this context because (particularly in commercial insurance contracts) an insurer's right to avoid a contract for misrepresentation fulfils an important "policing" function in ensuring disclosure.[283]

4–71 **Measure of damages.** The Misrepresentation Act does not specify the measure of damages that a court will award under s.2(2): it simply says that the court has the discretion to "award damages in lieu of rescission, if of opinion that it would be

(Nov) (housing association entitled to rescind lease procured by misrepresentation: if rescission were refused, association would suffer "(i) the loss of one property from its stock for allocation to eligible candidates, thus impeding it to that extent in its function of providing housing to qualifying persons, and (ii) the public interest damage to its reputation and to its undertaking in permitting false applications from ineligible candidates to prosper, causing more deserving candidates to be relegated" which could not be assessed in terms of damages).

281 Para.4–71.

282 *William Sindall Plc v Cambridgeshire CC*, above, n.270.

283 *Highlands Insurance Co. v Continental Insurance Co.* [1987] 1 Lloyd's Rep. 109, 118; *Ramphul v Toole*, unreported, March 17, 1989, CA; *H.I.H. Casualty and General Insurance Ltd v Chase Manhattan Bank* [2001] EWCA Civ 1250, [2001] 2 Lloyd's Rep. 483 at [116]. Note that under the Consumer Insurance (Disclosure and Representations) Bill, which is expected to be enacted during 2012, the insurer's right to rescind a *consumer* insurance contract for misrepresentation is to be limited to fraudulent and some careless misrepresentations, and the consumer's duty of disclosure is to be removed: above, para.4–29, n.137; below, para.17–06.

equitable to do so", having regard to certain factors. If these words are read strictly, it appears that the broad discretion is as to the award of damages, not as to the quantum.[284] That is, if the court exercises its discretion, the damages should be calculated on a principled basis. The question, however, is: what principle? The words of the subsection itself which indicate the answer are "loss that would be caused by [the misrepresentation] if the contract were upheld". This suggests that the purpose of the damages is to compensate the claimant for not being allowed to exercise his right to rescind: that is, damages to put him in the position in the financial position in which he would have been if the contract had been rescinded.[285] This points more towards the tort measure of damages than the contract measure.[286]

The full tort measure does not, however, seem appropriate. It cannot have been intended that damages be calculated on the same

---

[284] *cf.* language in other statutes where the calculation of the proportion of loss to be borne by a party is itself explicitly within the discretion of the court: Law Reform (Contributory Negligence) Act 1945, s.1(1); Civil Liability (Contribution) Act 1978, s.2(1).

[285] McGregor, para.41–062; Cartwright, p.101. A counter-argument (adopted in the earlier editions of this book) suggesting that it is not appropriate to award damages to put the claimant in the financial position in which he would have been if the contract had been rescinded, was put by Hoffmann L.J. in *William Sindall Plc v Cambridgeshire CC*, below, n.294 at 1037–1038 (relying on the Law Reform Committee, Tenth Report, above, n.271): that the purpose of s.2(2) is to allow the court to impose a remedy in damages which avoids the harsh consequences for the representor that rescission, if permitted, would entail; and this purpose would be undermined by an award of damages calculated so as to be a financial equivalent to rescission. However, the reasons for refusing rescission are not simply based on the *financial* harshness of that remedy above, paras 4–68, 4–70.

[286] For the difference between these two basic measures, see above, paras 2–07 to 2–10; and for the similarity of purpose of rescission and damages on the tort measure, see para.2–12. It is also consistent with an award under s.2(2) of a basic tort measure of damages (or, at least, it is prima facie inconsistent with a basic contract measure) that s.2(3) allows a combination of damages under both s.2(1) and s.2(2), since the measure of an award under s.2(1) is without doubt the tort measure: above, para.2–12, n.37. Treitel, para.9–071, without discussion of the decision in *William Sindall*, suggests that the damages under s.2(2) are really *sui generis*.

Damages under s.2(2) may in an appropriate case be zero: *UCB Corporate Services Ltd v Thomason* [2005] EWCA Civ 225; [2005] 1 All E.R. (Comm) 601 (no loss established, so no damages awarded although rescission refused under s.2(2)).

basis as in the tort of deceit, since this is the basis of calculation of damages under s.2(1), and the Act makes clear in s.2(3) that there is no necessary correlation between the measure of an award under s.2(1) and an award under s.2(2). It would be possible for the damages to be calculated on the basis of the tort measure but without some of the harsher consequences of a claim in deceit.[287] But since the tort measure of damages looks, broadly, to restoring in financial terms the *status quo ante* of the representor,[288] the full tort measure would not seem to be the appropriate measure for s.2(2). The purpose of the award of damages should be limited to the financial equivalent of rescission: the representee should only be compensated for such part of his overall loss as is attributable to the misrepresentation itself,[289] and not any wider losses which might be recoverable in a tort claim which flow from having entered into the contract.[290]

It certainly seems inappropriate to award the normal contractual measure of damages under s.2(2). In the context of misrepresentation, damages in contract are to fulfil the expectations created by the representation[291]; but in a claim under the subsection the representee relies on no warranty, no contractual promise made by the representor that his statement is true. Given the reluctance of the courts to find implied warranties as to the truth of a pre-contractual representation[292] one might have expected the Act to be clearer in

---

[287] In particular, the rule for remoteness of damage: below, para.5–40. Treitel, para.9–072, suggests that under s.2(2) no consequential losses at all might be recoverable.

[288] Above, para.2–09.

[289] e.g. in the case of property transferred under a contract, the reduction in value (as against price paid) caused by the misrepresentation.

[290] Particularly since s.2(2) can give a remedy in damages against a representor who has no liability in tort or under s.2(1): above, para.4–62. It is tolerably clear from the Act itself that s.2(2) only covers the loss which flows from the misrepresentation, whereas s.2(1) covers the loss which flows from entering into the contract: *William Sindall Plc v Cambridgeshire CC*, below, n.294 at 1037. Even though losses which flow from a general fall in the market values after the date of the contract might sometimes be recoverable in a tort claim (below, para.6–55) such losses will not be covered by a claim under s.2(2) because they do not flow from the misrepresentation itself: *William Sindall Plc v Cambridgeshire CC* at 1044.

[291] Below, para.8–24.

[292] Below, para.8–04.

its wording if such a consequence was intended.[293] However, the judgments in *William Sindall Plc v Cambridgeshire CC*,[294] although obiter and not unequivocal, lean towards the view that damages are to be calculated on a basis similar to damages for breach of contract, rather than damages in tort. Evans L.J.[295] preferred the view that the contract measure applies under s.2(2), which is to be measured either by the cost of remedying the defect, or by the reduced market value attributable to the defect—the "difference in value between what the plaintiff was misled into believing that he was acquiring and the value of what he in fact received". And Hoffmann L.J. similarly thought that the appropriate award was to compensate the representee for the loss he has suffered on account of the property not having been what it was represented to be.[296]

(6) Exclusion and Limitation Clauses

Contractual clauses which purport to exclude or limit the right to rescind are considered in Chapter 9.

[293] Treitel, para.9–071, n.360, points out that an amendment in Standing Committee to the clause of the Bill which became s.2(2), so as to make clear that the contractual basis was to apply, was withdrawn without discussion; but no conclusion can be drawn from this. See also McGregor, para.41–067, emphasising that it cannot be right, where there is no warranty, that a claimant can claim the benefit of his bargain.

[294] [1994] 1 W.L.R. 1016 at 1037–1038, 1044–1046 (obiter, since it was held that on the facts there was no right to rescind).

[295] *ibid.*, at 1044–1046. Russell L.J. simply agreed with both Hoffmann L.J. and Evans L.J. The circumstances are to be tested, and the damages assessed, at the date of the hearing when the court would otherwise order rescission (or confirm an earlier rescission by the representee): *ibid.*, at 1044; *cf.* at 1038 (Hoffmann L.J., who is more equivocal on the timing, as between the earlier rescission and the date of trial).

[296] *ibid.*, at 1037. The ceiling for damages is the sum which would be awarded on a claim for damages for breach of a warranty that the statement was true; but Hoffmann L.J. expressly left open the question of when damages under s.2(2) might be less, e.g. perhaps consequential losses which would be recoverable in a claim for breach of warranty might not be included in an award under s.2(2): Treitel, para.9–072. For emphatic criticism of *William Sindall* see McGregor, paras 41–065 to 41–070. In *Floods of Queensferry Ltd v Shand Construction Ltd* [2000] B.L.R. 81 at 94, however, Judge Humphrey Lloyd Q.C. preferred to follow the CA in *William Sindall*.

IV. MISREPRESENTATIONS BY THIRD PARTIES

4–72 **The problem of third-party misrepresentations.** Where the claimant has entered into a contract in reliance on a misrepresentation it will commonly be the other party or his agent who made the misrepresentation: each contracting party normally provides information relevant to the other's decision to enter into the contract. In this case the arguments in favour of allowing rescission are clear. From the claimant's perspective: he has been misled, and his consent was therefore given on a basis which turns out to have been false—the consent was defective. And it was the other party, who seeks to take the benefit of the contract, who misled him. Even where the representation was made innocently, the representee's argument in favour of rescission is good because the other party still caused the defect of consent.[297] Sometimes, however, the false information is provided by a third party to the contract, for whom the other contracting party has no responsibility.[298] In such a case the argument from the claimant's perspective is similar to the first case: although he was misled by a third party he was still misled, and so his consent was defective. However, from the other party's point of view, this second situation is radically different. He did not cause the defect of consent, so why should he lose the benefit of the contract?

4–73 **The starting-point: the misrepresentation must be by or on behalf of the other party.** The courts begin from the position set out above: that where the misrepresentation is made by a third party, the representee cannot on that ground avoid it.[299] The claimant may have remedies against the third party: typically, this will require him to establish a claim in tort against the third party, and so he must show that the representation was made fraudulently in order to sustain a claim in the tort of deceit, or that it was made without reasonable care in breach of a duty owed in the tort of negligence.[300] A wholly innocent misrepresentation by a third party

[297] Above, para.4–24, para.1–03; Cartwright, pp.103–104.

[298] Where the representor is the other party's agent acting within the scope of his agency, the other party is treated as having made the misrepresentation: above, para.4–24.

[299] *Pulsford v Richards* (1853) 17 Beav. 87 at 95, 51 E.R. 965 at 968.

[300] Below, Chs 5 (deceit) and 6 (negligence). Misrepresentation Act 1967 s.2(1) applies only between contracting parties: below, paras 7–05, 7–09.

will therefore normally leave the representee without remedy: he cannot avoid the contract against the other contracting party, and has no claim for damages against the representor.

Misrepresentation which causes an actionable mistake. Misrepresentation is, in effect, induced mistake: the defendant makes a false statement which the claimant believes and relies upon in entering into the contract.[301] Where, therefore, the misrepresentation is made by a third party, it might give rise to remedies for mistake. However, English law is reluctant to allow a party to rely on his mistake to render the contract void, so it will be relatively rare that this will provide the claimant with a remedy.[302] 4–74

Misrepresentation by third party of which the other party has knowledge or notice. The courts have accepted that the representee may avoid the contract on the basis of a misrepresentation made by a third party where the other party has knowledge of it at the time of the contract. The other party is entitled reasonably to rely on the claimant's apparent consent as being full and informed consent; but where he has knowledge that this apparent consent was not in fact full and informed he cannot so rely, and he is in no better position than if he had himself made the misrepresentation.[303] The acceptance by the courts that a contract can be avoided by a party on the basis of a misrepresentation made by a third party, but of which the other contracting party has knowledge, raises some significant questions which have not yet been satisfactorily answered, or even properly addressed, in the cases. How far does this principle extend? Does it only apply where the contracting party has actual knowledge of the third party's misrepresentation? And how does it fit with the established approach to mistake and duties of disclosure in the formation of a contract? 4–75

[301] Above, para.1–03.

[302] Above, para.1–03; below, paras 12–12 to 12–15.

[303] *Royal Bank of Scotland Plc v Etridge (No.2)* [2001] UKHL 44, [2002] 2 A.C. 773 at [144] (Lord Scott, discussing both misrepresentation and undue influence by third parties). *Cf. Bradford Third Equitable Benefit Building Society v Borders* [1941] 2 All E.R. 205, HL, at 220 (knowingly taking advantage of a fraudulent misrepresentation made by a third party can constitute the tort of deceit; below, para.5–07).

4–76 **Knowledge and notice.** There are relatively few cases in this area, and many of those which have discussed the issue have focused on undue influence, rather than misrepresentation, by third parties. But it appears now to be established that a misrepresentation by a third party will allow the representee to avoid the contract where the other contracting party had actual knowledge or actual notice of it at the time of the contract; but in cases to which the principle of *Barclays Bank Plc v O'Brien*[304] applies a contracting party may be affected by *constructive notice* of the third party's misrepresentation. This position was accepted by the House of Lords in *Royal Bank of Scotland Plc v Etridge (No.2)*.[305] What will constitute actual knowledge or actual notice? In other contexts it has been held that actual knowledge or actual notice extends in law to cases where the person has wilfully shut his eyes to the obvious, or has wilfully and recklessly failed to make such inquiries as an honest and reasonable man would make[306]; and it seems likely that

---

304 [1994] 1 A.C. 181, HL; below, para.4–77.

305 Above, n.303 at [40] (Lord Nicholls: "knowledge is required"), [144] (Lord Scott: *O'Brien* covers the case where "there had been no actual knowledge of the third party's undue influence of misrepresentation but merely knowledge of facts or circumstances that, if investigated, might have led to actual knowledge"). See also *Cobbett v Brock* (1855) 20 Beav. 524, 52 E.R. 706 (Romilly M.R.: "The real question is this: assume that a fraud was committed by the husband, did the Plaintiffs know of that fraud?"); *Kempson v Ashbee* (1874) L.R. 10 Ch. App. 15 at 21 (the question as whether the contract "was obtained under such exercise [of undue influence] as that the knowledge of it can be imputed to the Defendant"); *Talbot v Von Boris* [1911] 1 K.B. 854, CA, at 863 ("where the alleged duress is that of a person other than the person contracted with, it must be shewn that the duress by which the contract was procured was known to the plaintiff when he entered into the contract"); *Lynde v Anglo-Italian Hemp Spinning Co.* [1896] 1 Ch. 178 at 183 (contract with company voidable "where the company can be held affected, before the contract is complete, with the knowledge that it is induced by misrepresentations—as, for example, when the directors on allotting shares, know, in fact, that the application for them has been induced by misrepresentations"). See also N. Enonchong, *Duress, Undue Influence and Unconscionable Dealing* (2006), para.23–005 (constructive notice "as a tool to deal with the difficult problem of third party undue influence (or other wrongdoing)" was introduced by *O'Brien*).

306 *Commission for the New Towns v Cooper (Great Britain) Ltd* [1995] Ch. 259, CA, at 281 (rectification for unilateral mistake; below, para.13–47), applying categories discussed by Peter Gibson J. in *Baden v Société Générale pour Favoriser le Développement du Commerce et de l'Industrie en France S.A.* [1993] 1 W.L.R. 509 at 575–576 (constructive trusteeship). See also *Economides v Commercial Assurance Co. Plc* [1998] Q.B. 587, CA, at 601–602, 607

this will similarly be adopted here.[307] However, a person does not have not actual knowledge or actual notice of facts where he has only knowledge of circumstances which would indicate the facts to an honest and reasonable man, or knowledge of circumstances which would put an honest and reasonable man on inquiry. These are instances of constructive notice; and whether constructive notice is sufficient depends on the scope of the decision in *Barclays Bank Plc v O'Brien*.

Constructive notice under *Barclays Bank v O'Brien*. In a long line of cases[308] the courts have considered the problem of third-party misrepresentation in a particular factual context: where a person (usually a wife) has been induced to stand as surety in favour of a bank for a debtor (usually her husband) by the undue influence or misrepresentation of the debtor. The surety has sought to be released from the obligation she has undertaken in favour of the bank, although the bank did not itself apply the undue influence, or make the misrepresentation. In *Barclays Bank Plc v O'Brien*[309] the House of Lords sought to settle this area of the law, and in doing so laid down a test under which the wife would be able to set the transaction aside against the bank if the bank had actual or constructive notice of the facts establishing the undue influence or misrepresentation. And a bank would be put on inquiry, and would be required then to take certain steps to satisfy itself that the wife entered into the obligation freely and in knowledge of the true facts, where (a) the transaction was on its face not to the financial advantage of the wife, and (b) there was a substantial risk that the husband had committed a wrong (such as misrepresentation) against the wife. This test was subject to further refinement and explanation 4–77

(Nelsonian blindness equivalent to actual knowledge for purposes of duty of disclosure under the Marine Insurance Act 1906, s.18; below, paras 17–11, 17–12).

[307] In *Royal Bank of Scotland Plc v Etridge (No.2)*, above, n.303 at [144] Lord Scott relied on *Commission for the New Towns v Cooper (Great Britain) Ltd*, above, n.306.

[308] In *Barclays Bank Plc v O'Brien* [1994] 1 A.C. 180, HL, at 185 Lord Browne-Wilkinson noted that the problem had "given rise to reported decisions of the Court of Appeal on no less than 11 occasions in the last eight years"; and the decision of the House of Lords in *Royal Bank of Scotland Plc v Etridge (No.2)*, above, n.303, involved consolidated appeals on eight cases which had been heard in the Court of Appeal after *O'Brien*.

[309] Above, n.308.

by the House of Lords in *Royal Bank of Scotland Plc v Etridge (No.2)*,[310] from which it appears that the *O'Brien* principle, under which a contracting party is affected not only by actual notice but also by constructive notice of a misrepresentation by a third party, applies only to the kind of case of which *O'Brien* was itself an example: that is, surety contracts.[311] Lord Nicholls said[312] that what makes surety contracts different is that, at least in the case of non-commercial guarantees, they are one-sided: the guarantor obtains no benefit, and the bank knows it. In fact, this seems to be a decision of policy, intended to establish a balance between the bank and the surety: to allow the surety to raise misconduct by the debtor as a ground for not being bound by the contract, but to provide certainty for banks by giving them clear procedures to follow to ensure that, even if the surety's position is to be given greater protection in this context than under the general rules of contract, the bank can take reasonable steps to minimise the risk that it will be unable to enforce the surety contract, but at the same time to

---

310 Above, n.303.

311 *Royal Bank of Scotland Plc v Etridge (No.2)*, above, n.303 at [40]–[43] (Lord Nicholls), [144], [146] (Lord Scott). The detail of the *O'Brien* test was redefined so that, e.g. a bank will be put on inquiry of the risk of misrepresentation and undue influence where the relationship between the surety and the debtor is non-commercial: at [87] (Lord Nicholls); and the House gave further guidance on the steps the bank must take once it is put on inquiry. In the case of misrepresentation by the husband, the bank is able to correct the problem by providing the wife with accurate information. In Scotland, the *O'Brien* principle has also been accepted by the House of Lords but again only in the context of surety contracts: *Smith v Governor and Company of the Bank of Scotland*, 1997 S.C. 111 (see in particular Lord Jauncey at 115–116). See also *Donegal International Ltd v Zambia* [2007] EWHC 197 (Comm), [2007] 1 Lloyd's Rep. 397 at [464] (Andrew Smith J.: no legal basis for claim to rescind settlement contract on basis of third party's misrepresentation: "This case is far removed from the sort of tripartite transaction considered in *Barclays Bank Plc v O'Brien*"); *Royal Bank of Scotland Plc v Chandra* [2011] EWCA Civ 192, [2011] All E.R. (D) 35 at [32] (Patten L.J.: "equity will intervene in respect of guarantees which have been procured by misrepresentation (including innocent misrepresentations) in the same way that it will set aside guarantees procured by an exercise of undue influence. The two are not the same, although in certain cases they may overlap").

312 *Royal Bank of Scotland Plc v Etridge (No.2)*, above, n.303 at [43].

minimise the risk that the surety is entering into the contract in consequence of the debtor's misconduct.[313]

The (unresolved) conflict with *Smith v Hughes*. There is a potential conflict between the rules set out above and the established approach to mistake and duties of disclosure in the formation of a contract. The courts are reluctant to allow a party to rely on his own mistake to avoid the contract.[314] And it was made clear in *Smith v Hughes*[315] that a unilateral mistake about the subject-matter, even if known by the other party, does not of itself affect the validity of a contract, and that there is no general duty of disclosure: **4–78**

> "even if the vendor was aware that the purchaser thought that the article possessed that quality, and would not have entered into the contract unless he had so thought, still the purchaser is bound, unless the vendor was guilty of some fraud or deceit[316] upon him, and . . . a mere abstinence from disabusing the purchaser of that impression is not fraud or deceit; for, whatever be the case in a court of morals, there is no legal obligation on the vendor to inform the purchaser that he is under a mistake, not induced by the act of the vendor."

If a contracting party makes a mistake as a result of being given false information by a third party, he cannot normally rely on the misrepresentation by the third party as against his other contracting party.[317] However, according to the principle discussed earlier in this chapter, if the other party has actual knowledge or actual notice of the third party's misrepresentation, the claimant may avoid the contract. The courts which have established each of these rules have not considered the other rules. The court in *Smith v Hughes* decided that a contract is valid and enforceable against a party who made a

[313] For the social and policy context, and the attempt to balance the competing interests of the bank and the surety, see *ibid.*, at [34]–[41] (Lord Nicholls).
[314] Above, paras 1–03 and 4–24; below, paras 12–12 to 12–15.
[315] (1867) L.R. 6 Q.B. 597 at 607 (Blackburn J.); below, paras 15–10, 15–11 and 16–04.
[316] [It was natural for Blackburn J. to speak in terms of *fraudulent* misrepresentation because in 1867 it was not yet clear that a contract is voidable for non-fraudulent misrepresentations; and the extension to non-fraudulent misrepresentations was made in equity, whereas the court in *Smith v Hughes* was a common law court; *cf.* above, para.4–03.]
[317] Above, para.4–24.

mistake about the subject-matter,[318] even where the other party knew of the mistake, just as long as he did not cause it. But that court did not consider what the position would be if the contracting party knew of the mistake which was caused by a third party's misrepresentation. But nor did the House of Lords in *Barclays Bank Plc v O'Brien* or *Royal Bank of Scotland Plc v Etridge (No.2)* consider whether their acceptance of the rule that a contracting party can be affected by notice of a third party's misrepresentation might conflict with the general rule that knowledge of the other party's mistake is not sufficient to avoid the contract. Strictly, the cases can be reconciled: *Smith v Hughes* deals only with mistake, and not with misrepresentation. And *O'Brien* and *Etridge* do not go so far as to say that one party's knowledge of the other party's mistake is sufficient to render the contract voidable: they still assume that the ground of avoidance arises not from the party's mistake, but from the fact that he has been induced by a misrepresentation (even though a third party's misrepresentation). But it is unsatisfactory that the relationship between these rules has not been noticed by the judges in the recent cases. If the courts wish to maintain the strictness of the mistake rules, and the reluctance to impose duties of disclosure—that is, to maintain the position set out in *Smith v Hughes*—then it may be necessary for them to revisit the whole question of whether a contracting party's knowledge or notice of a third party's misrepresentation should be allowed to avoid the contract. But if they are prepared to move to a general rule that a party should be affected by knowledge of defects in the other party's consent—that is, to choose the position set out in *Etridge*—then the authority of *Smith v Hughes* in this respect may not survive.

[318] A mistake about the terms of the contract, however, attracts a different rule, because if the parties are not in agreement about the terms, the contract may be void if one party's misunderstanding cannot be overridden by the objective test for the formation of a contract: below, Ch.13. For the distinction between a mistake about the terms, and a mistake about the subject-matter, see below, para.15–02.

CHAPTER 5

LIABILITY IN TORT FOR MISREPRESENTATION: I — FRAUDULENT MISREPRESENTATION[1]

I. THE TORT OF DECEIT

Damages in the tort of deceit for fraudulent misrepresentation. 5–01
The action of deceit was developed by the courts of common law[2] to provide a remedy in damages for a person who has suffered loss by acting on a statement which was made to him fraudulently. The core of the action of deceit is *fraud* on the part of the representor, by which the claimant was *deceived*: this has been clear since the late eighteenth century.[3] During the course of the nineteenth century

[1] Clerk & Lindsell, Ch.18; Winfield & Jolowicz, paras 11–2 to 11–15; Spencer Bower (Misrepresentation), Chs 11 and 12; H. Carty, *An Analysis of the Economic Torts* (2nd edn, 2010), Ch.9; Chitty, paras 6–042 to 6–066; Furmston, paras 4.61 to 4.64; Treitel, paras 9–029 to 9–032, 9–062, 9–065, 9–067 to 9–068; Anson, pp.320–323; Cheshire, Fifoot and Furmston, pp.341–343, 364–365; Allen, pp.39–45.

[2] There is no such thing as an equitable action for deceit: *Arkwright v Newbold* (1881) 17 Ch.D. 301 at 320.

[3] The case most commonly cited as the origin of the tort in the modern law is *Pasley v Freeman* (1789) 3 T.R. 51, 100 E.R. 450 (fraudulent misrepresentation of a third party's creditworthiness, which caused the representee to extend credit and suffer losses; Grose J. dissented); *Derry v Peek* (1889) 14 App. Cas. 337, HL, at 363. For the problems in relation to representations of credit which were caused by the decision in *Pasley v Freeman*, and which provoked Lord

there was some debate about the exact meaning of "fraud" for the purposes of this tort, but in 1889 this debate was definitively settled by the House of Lords in *Derry v Peek*,[4] and since then the tort has remained in substance unchanged.[5] The most significant developments have been around the tort of deceit, rather than in it: the tort of negligence[6] has been developed to allow a representee to claim damages for loss sustained as a consequence of a statement which was made not fraudulently but only negligently; and under the Misrepresentation Act 1967[7] a new remedy of damages on the same measure[8] as the tort of deceit was given to a party who enters into a contract following a pre-contractual misrepresentation where the representor cannot prove that he had reasonable ground to believe, and did believe, that his representation was true. The development of these other remedies has taken away the need for a representee to rely on the tort of deceit as the single source of a remedy in damages in tort for misrepresentation. But the remedy remains available if the representee can establish its requirements—including, in particular, that the representor was fraudulent[9]—and claims in deceit are not infrequent in the modern law reports.[10]

5–02 **Deceit contrasted with other torts imposing liability for false statements.** The interest protected by the tort of deceit is the representee's financial interest which is damaged as a consequence of his reliance on a statement made to him fraudulently by the

Tenterden's Act, see below, para.5–30. For history of the tort of deceit, see Allen, pp.1–3; Ibbetson, *A Historical Introduction to the Law of Obligations*, pp.84–85; J.H. Baker, *An Introduction to English Legal History* (4th edn, 2002), pp.331–333, 336–337, 356.

[4] (1889) 14 App. Cas. 337; below, para.5–14.

[5] There were developments of the tort during the 20th century: not on the essential nature of the tort, but such things as a clarification of the rules relating to recoverable loss; below, para.5–35.

[6] Ch.6.

[7] Misrepresentation Act 1967 s.2(1); below, paras 7–03 to 7–47.

[8] This point is controversial: below, para.7–33.

[9] For the difficulties of proving fraud, see below, para.5–46.

[10] For some reasons why a claimant might still find it advantageous to establish fraud on the part of the representor, see above, para.4–30; below, paras 5–36, 5–37, 5–40, 5–42 and 5–43.

defendant. This tort therefore focuses on the economic loss[11] suffered by the representee who is deceived by the fraudulent representor.

A representor may be liable in other contexts, under the rules of other torts, for making a false statement. He may maliciously make false statements to third parties about the claimant's products, causing to the claimant by indirect means such loss as loss of business and loss of business reputation. Such a statement might give rise to liability in the tort of malicious falsehood[12] but it does not fall within the tort of deceit because it does not involve the claimant being "deceived".[13] Or the representor may knowingly make a false statement directly to the claimant calculated to cause him some personal harm, such as psychiatric injury: such a statement might give rise to a claim in tort, but it is not the tort of deceit.[14] And there are other torts in which a person may be liable for making false statements but without fraud, such as in the tort of defamation (where the interest protected is the claimant's reputation; and there is no requirement of fraud) or negligence (where again there is no requirement of fraud, although an economic interest similar to that protected by the tort of deceit can be covered) or passing off (where the claimant's business goodwill is

[11] Other losses can, however, also be recovered: below, para.5–44.

[12] *Ratcliffe v Evans* [1892] 2 Q.B. 524, CA; Clerk & Lindsell, Ch.23; Winfield & Jolowicz, paras 12.72–12.77.

[13] *T.J. Larkins & Sons v Chelmer Holdings Pty Ltd* [1965] Qd. R. 68 (architect's fraudulent statement to building owner not actionable in deceit by building contractor who suffered loss when owner withheld payment of money due).

[14] *Wilkinson v Downton* [1897] 2 Q.B. 57 (see especially Wright J. at 58: the *injuria* here is different from that covered by the tort of deceit; the claimant's economic losses were however covered by the tort of deceit: *ibid.*); *Janvier v Sweeney* [1919] 2 K.B. 316, CA; *Wong v Parkside Health N.H.S. Trust* [2001] EWCA Civ 1721, [2003] 3 All E.R. 932; *Wainwright v Home Office* [2003] UKHL 53; [2004] 2 A.C. 406 at [36]–[47]. In *P v B (Paternity: Damages for Deceit)* [2001] 1 F.L.R. 1041 at 1046, however, Stanley Burnton J. thought that *Wilkinson v Downton* and *Janvier v Sweeney* might be cases of deceit, showing the "generality and flexibility of the tort of deceit". See (2001) 117 L.Q.R. 571 (R. Bagshaw). But whilst physical harm is within the scope of deceit (below, para.5–36), that tort protects the loss caused by the representee's reliance on the representation; here the physical harm is caused more directly by the impact of the words, and is therefore more akin to tresspass to the person, although the place (if any) of *Wilkinson v Downton* in the modern law is unresolved: Clerk & Lindsell, para.15–14; H. Carty, *An Analysis of the Economic Torts* (2nd edn, 2010), p.193.

protected against misrepresentations likely to lead the public to believe that the defendant's goods or services are the goods or services of the claimant[15]). These other torts are not, for the most part, covered in any detail in this book, since they are dealing with issues arising out of misrepresentation which fall outside the scope of the book.[16] Cases of negligent statements on which the representee relies and suffers loss, which are within the scope of the book, are discussed in Chapter 6.

5–03 **Deceit not limited to pre-contractual misrepresentations.** The tort of deceit requires that the representee, being deceived by the representor's fraudulent statement, act on it and thereby suffer loss. Typically such act will involve his entering into a transaction which is disadvantageous to him: often he acts on the representation by entering into a contract. This is not a necessary requirement; and it is certainly not necessary that any disadvantageous contract into which he enters should be one which is with, or which directly benefits, the representor.[17] The gist of the tort is the loss caused to the representee by the deceit; not the benefit conferred on the

[15] Clerk & Lindsell, Ch.26; Winfield & Jolowicz, paras 18–44 to 18–52.

[16] Above, para.2–01.

[17] In *Pasley v Freeman* (1789) 3 T.R. 51, 100 E.R. 450, which is generally regarded as the origin of the modern tort of deceit, the action of deceit was extended beyond the case where the claimant and defendant were parties to a contract: Allen, p.2. And for a case where the claimant was not party to a contract with the defendant, see *Langridge v Levy* (1837) 2 M. & W. 519, 150 E.R. 863; affd. 4 M. & W. 337, 150 E.R. 1458 (gun bought from defendant by claimant's father, misrepresented to be safe, exploded and injured claimant). The tort of deceit extends to statements made in the context of domestic arrangements, even if the relationship between the representor and representee would not normally give rise to a contract because of the absence of intention to create legal relations: *P v B (Paternity: Damages for Deceit)*, above, n.14 (man could sue woman with whom he had lived for losses incurred in consequence of woman's fraudulent misrepresentation that he was the father of her child); (2001) 117 L.Q.R. 571 (R. Bagshaw); followed in *A v B* [2007] EWHC 1246 (QB), [2007] 2 F.L.R. 1051; *cf. Hulton v Hulton* [1916] 2 K.B. 642 (no action of deceit by husband against wife because of general rule against actions in tort between spouses; this would now be reversed by Law Reform (Husband and Wife) Act 1962, s.1). For reluctance in Australia to allow an action of deceit in this context, see *Magill v Magill* [2006] HCA 51, (2006) 226 C.L.R. 551, criticised at (2007) 123 L.Q.R. 337 (K.R. Handley). Under Companies Act 2006 s.463 no persons (directors or others) are liable to any person except the company for untrue or misleading statements in

representor.[18] But the tort extends to the case where one party to a contract fraudulently makes a false statement to the other party during the pre-contractual negotiations, and the representee enters into the contract in reliance on the statement. It is therefore no obstacle to a claim in deceit, that the parties have a contract which might also be a source of remedies for the misrepresentation which the claimant cites as the basis of his claim in deceit.[19]

Cumulation with other remedies. The general question of which remedies for misrepresentation can be cumulated has already been discussed.[20] In brief, it is possible for a representee to obtain rescission of the contract, as well as damages in the tort of deceit, if he can establish that the rules of both remedies are satisfied on the facts.[21] But it will generally not be possible for him to obtain an award of damages in deceit concurrently with an award of damages for breach of contract: although his claim may be made in the alternative, in the end he must elect which basis of loss to assert.[22] Nor, of course, may he obtain double compensation of any item of loss by recovering in more than one claim for tort damages. 5–04

directors' reports and directors' remuneration reports, even where the misrepresentations are fraudulent—a questionable exclusion: Gower and Davies *Principles of Modern Company Law* (8th edn, 2008), para.21–27.

[18] *Pasley v Freeman*, above, n.3 at 62, at 456. On the question whether the defendant can be made to make restitution of a profit made through his deceit, see below, para.5–43.

[19] *Archer v Brown* [1985] Q.B. 401. The concurrence of remedies in tort and contract, and the entitlement of the claimant generally to elect to pursue the remedy or remedies which are most favourable to his interest, was affirmed in the context of the tort of negligence in *Henderson v Merrett Syndicates Ltd* [1995] 2 A.C. 145, HL. But there was already no doubt before that case that, where there was a fraudulent pre-contractual misrepresentation, the representee was entitled to pursue either his remedy in tort, or his remedies under the contract; see, e.g. *Heilbut Symons & Co. v Buckleton* [1913] A.C. 30, HL; Winfield, *The Province of the Law of Tort* (1931), p.68; and for the historical origins of deceit in contractual warranties, see books cited above, n.3. In New Zealand the statutory remedy in damages for pre-contractual misrepresentation (Contractual Remedies Act 1979, s.6: damages as if the representation were a term of the contract) has expressly displaced the claim in the tort of deceit: s.6(1)(b); Burrows, Finn & Todd, para.11.2.7.

[20] Above, paras 2–11 to 2–13.

[21] *Archer v Brown*, above, n.19.

[22] Above, para.2–13; below, para.11–08.

II. ELEMENTS OF THE CLAIM IN THE TORT OF DECEIT

5–05 **Overview of the elements of the claim.** In general terms, the representee may recover damages in the tort of deceit if he can show that a false representation was made to him by or on behalf of the defendant; that the representation was made fradulently; that the defendant intended him to act on it; and that the representation was an inducement to his own action as a result of which he suffered the loss which he claims. Some of these elements have been discussed already in Chapter 3; in such cases reference will be made back to the detailed discussion in that chapter. Other elements of the representee's claim, and issues which arise because of the peculiarity of the tort of deceit and its basis in a claim of fraud, will be discussed in detail in this section. The defences which can be raised by a defendant once the representee has established the elements of his claim, the quantification of the damages recoverable in the tort of deceit, and the particular difficulties of proving a claim based on fraud, will be discussed in later sections of this chapter.

(1) The Representation

5–06 **The representation: words or conduct.** To succeed in the tort of deceit the representee must show that a misrepresentation was made to him: that is, a falsehood was communicated to him by which he was deceived.[23] Such communication may generally be through the medium of words spoken or written to him; but it can equally well be in the representee's interpretation of the meaning of the defendant's conduct.[24]

---

23 A person cannot therefore sue in deceit "in respect of representations which were not made to them directly or to an agent and in reliance upon which they did not act, being unaware of them. I regard that as obvious": *Chagos Islanders v Attorney General* [2003] EWHC 2222 (QB); *The Times*, October 10, 2003 at [364] (Ouseley J.). The Court of Appeal would, however, have been willing to allow argument as to whether a representation to a third party could constitute deceit "if only because the possibility of such an enlargement of the kinds of situation giving rise to a cause of action in deceit was a question of principle which deserved the attention of the court": [2004] EWCA Civ 997; *The Times*, September 21, 2004 at [37]. Such an enlargement would, however, fundamentally change the nature of the tort.

24 *Bradford Third Equitable Benefit Building Society v Borders* [1941] 2 All E.R. 205, HL, at 211; *Gordon v Selico Co. Ltd* [1985] 2 E.G.L.R. 79 (this issue was not challenged on appeal: [1986] 1 E.G.L.R. 71).

The test for whether a misrepresentation has been made is in general terms the same as in other remedies for misrepresentation.[25] The courts have sometimes laid particular emphasis, when discussing this tort, on the requirement that the defendant must have made an *active* misrepresentation, and have said that is not sufficient that a defendant knowingly stood by and allowed the claimant to persevere in his misunderstanding.[26] We shall see in Chapter 17 that certain recent decisions suggest that there may now be liability in deceit for loss caused by a fraudulent breach of a duty of disclosure.[27] But it is in any event clear that a partial statement, which conveys a falsehood by virtue of what is omitted to be said, will suffice.[28] So will conduct which communicates a falsehood, such as the concealment by a landlord of defects in the property he is letting by actively taking steps to cover up the defects and so to communicate to a prospective tenant that the property is sound.[29]

Representation by or on behalf of the defendant.[30] The representation which founds a claim in the tort of deceit must be 5–07

[25] Above, para.3–03.

[26] *Peek v Gurney* (1873) L.R. 6 H.L. 377, HL, at 391, 403; *Arkwright v Newbold* (1881) 17 Ch.D. 301, CA, at 318, 320; *Aaron's Reefs Ltd v Twiss* [1896] A.C. 273, HL, at 281; *Bradford Third Equitable Benefit Building Society v Borders*, above, n.24 at 211, 220. The contrast is most commonly made with the remedy of rescission, which can sometimes be a remedy for breach of a duty of disclosure.

[27] Below, para.17–37: *Conlon v Simms* [2006] EWHC 401 (Ch), [2006] 2 All E.R. 1024 at [202], affirmed on this point at [2006] EWCA Civ 1749, [2008] 1 W.L.R. 484 at [130]. See also *Brownlie v Campbell* (1880) 5 App. Cas. 925, HL, at 950. In *Bradford Third Equitable Benefit Building Society v Borders*, above, n.24 at 220 Lord Wright said that a person could be liable who learns of another's misrepresentation and "knowingly uses the delusion created by the fraud in the injured party's mind in order to profit by the fraud": this is not simple fraudulent non-disclosure, since it presupposes that a third party made a misrepresentation; but it goes beyond the established core case of deceit where the defendant himself fraudulently deceives the claimant.

[28] *Peek v Gurney*, above, n.26 at 403; *Aaron's Reefs Ltd v Twiss*, above, n.26 at 281. See also *R. v Lord Kylsant* [1932] 1 K.B. 442, CCA (criminal offence under the Larceny Act 1861 s.84).

[29] *Gordon v Selico Co. Ltd*, above, n.24. For a representation of honest intention to pay money implied from a contractual undertaking to pay, see *Re Eastgate* [1905] K.B. 465 at 467, applied in *Amalgamated Metal Trading Ltd v Department of Trade and Industry*, *The Times*, March 21, 1989 and *John Hudson and Co. Ltd v Oaten*, unreported, June 19, 1980, CA.

[30] Bowstead & Reynolds, para.8.185.

one for which the defendant is in law responsible. Therefore if he made the representation himself, or through the medium of an agent,[31] or if he manifestly approves and adopts a representation made by a third party,[32] he is responsible for it and is liable in deceit if the other elements of the claim against him are established. Even if a person signs a document in a representative capacity, such as a company director or an employee signing on behalf of his company or employer, he is still personally liable in deceit if he makes the representation[33] with the necessary fraudulent intention. There will, however, be a question as to whether his principal is also liable.[34]

The case of a representation by an agent must be analysed quite carefully, and the defendant's primary liability and his vicarious liability must be distinguished. If the defendant authorises his agent to make the representation, the defendant will be primarily liable in the tort of deceit if the other elements of the claim are satisfied—in particular, if the defendant himself has the necessary (fraudulent) intent. The agent who in fact makes the representation may also be

---

[31] *Cornfoot v Fowke* (1840) 6 M. & W. 358 at 370–371, 151 E.R. 450 at 455.

[32] *Bradford Third Equitable Benefit Building Society v Borders*, above, n.24 at 211 (Viscount Maugham, although this was not established on the facts); see also at 220 (Lord Wright, above, n.27).

[33] *cf.*, however, *G.E. Commercial Finance Ltd v Gee* [2005] EWHC 2056 (QB), [2006] 1 Lloyd's Rep. 337 at [103], where Tugendhat J. put the hypothetical case of "a young unqualified assistant to a chartered accountant who is the finance director of a large company. The assistant is asked to fax to the bank some figures given to him by the director. The assistant does so, signing the fax in his own name. Does that count as a representation to the bank by the assistant personally? In other words, does that make the assistant a representor?"

[34] *Standard Chartered Bank v Pakistan National Shipping Corp. (Nos 2 and 4)* [2002] UKHL 43, [2003] 1 A.C. 959, reversing CA which, in considering whether the director/employee had assumed a personal liability for the statement made on behalf of the company/employer, applied the test used by the House of Lords in the context of a director's liability in negligence, in *Williams v Natural Life Health Foods Ltd* [1998] 1 W.L.R. 830, HL; and asked whether, judged objectively, the director/employee conveyed directly or indirectly to the claimant that he assumed a personal responsibility towards the claimant: [2000] 1 Lloyd's Rep. 218 at 235 (Aldous L.J.). In the House of Lords this reasoning was rejected in relation to fraud. Lord Hoffmann said at [22], "no one can escape liability for his fraud by saying, I wish to make it clear that I am committing this fraud on behalf of someone else and I am not to be personally liable". The reasoning of the Court of Appeal had also been criticised in *Noel v Poland* [2001] 2 B.C.L.C. 645 (Toulson J.); *SX Holdings Ltd v Synchronet Ltd* [2001] C.P. Rep. 43, CA; *Daido Asia Japan Co. Ltd v Rothen* [2002] B.C.C. 589 (Lawrence Collins J.); (2000) 116 L.Q.R. 525 (P. Watts).

a tortfeasor in his own right, if he has taken responsibility for the representation, and if he too has the necessary intent.[35] But the defendant's liability here is different from the case where he is held vicariously liable for the agent's statement: then he is responsible in law to meet the representee's claim for damages not because he himself made the representation with the necessary intent, but because the elements of the claim are satisfied as against the agent, and the defendant is responsible for those acts done by his agent in the course of his agency. The circumstances in which a defendant can be vicariously liable for the fraud of his agent or employee are considered further below.[36]

The representation need not be of "fact". It is often said that the representation, to be actionable in the tort of deceit, must be one of fact.[37] It was seen in Chapter 3 that, as a general rule, the fraud of the representor overrides the policy reasons for distinguishing between a statement of fact and a statement of opinion, law or intention.[38] Although the rule can be kept intact by recharacterising fraudulent statements of opinion, law, and intention into statements of fact,[39] it is suggested that the better approach for the tort of **5–08**

---

35 Liability in deceit is not limited to the contracting parties, or to a party who has benefited by the fraud: above, para.5–03. Whether the agent has sufficient resources to justify a claim against him personally will depend on his circumstances.

36 Below, para.5–21.

37 e.g. *Bradford Third Equitable Benefit Building Society v Borders*, above, n.24 at 211; the editors of Clerk & Lindsell used to assert this: (18th edn, 2000), para.15–05; but now say that the representation may be of fact or law: (20th edn, 2010), para.18–05. However, at para.18–15 this is attributed to the development of the law following *Kleinwort Benson Ltd v Lincoln City Council* [1999] 2 A.C. 349, HL, above, para.3–34; whereas it is arguable that even before that decision a fraudulent misrepresentation (whether of law or not) was actionable in deceit: above, para.3–33

38 Above, para.3–33.

39 Clerk & Lindsell, paras 18.11–18.14 (implied statements of fact in fraudulent statements of intention or opinion); Winfield & Jolowicz, para.11–7 ("a misstatement of law ought to be a sufficient misstatement of fact for the purposes of deceit provided at least that the parties are not on equal footing with respect to knowledge of the law or to general intelligence"). *Cf.* R.F.V. Heuston and R.A. Buckley, *Salmond & Heuston on the Law of Torts* (21st edn, 1996), pp.370–371 ("the term 'fact' . . . is used to include everything except a promise").

deceit[40] would be to discard altogether the rule that the representation be one of fact, and simply to say that the tort applies to any fraudulent statement which was intended to be acted upon by the representee.

5–09 **The representation must be false.** The representee must have been deceived by the representation: the statement must therefore have been false. It is for the representee to allege and prove the meaning on which he relies for his claim that the statement was false.[41] The approach to be taken by a court in interpreting a representation, particularly in a case where there is any doubt over its meaning, was discussed in Chapter 3[42]; in general terms, a court should adopt a test of interpretation of the representation based on its reasonable interpretation from the perspective of the representee.[43] The court must also be satisfied that the representee in fact so interpreted the representation before it can accept that he relied on it.[44] It should be emphasised that this is addressing only the question of how the representation should be interpreted for the purposes of deciding whether it was false, and the representee's reliance on it. When the question is whether the defendant was fraudulent, a subjective test of the meaning he intended the representation to convey is applied.[45]

5–10 **Correction of the misrepresentation.** If, after making a misrepresentation but before the representee has acted upon it, the representor seeks to disclose the truth and therefore to remove the effect the false statement has already had on the representee's mind, he must do so clearly. An attempt to correct the falsity which does not put the representee in the position of knowing the true facts will not be sufficient. In principle, the question ought to be whether the representee ought reasonably to have realised the truth, after the

[40] The same approach is suggested for the remedy of rescission: above, para.4–25.

[41] *Smith v Chadwick* (1884) 9 App. Cas. 187, HL; below, para.11–11.

[42] Above, para.3–06.

[43] For the interpretation of the representation in the tort of deceit, see in particular *Smith v Chadwick* (1884) 9 App. Cas. 187, HL.

[44] Below, para.5–24.

[45] Below, para.5–18. For these different senses in which a statement might be interpreted in a case of fraud, see *Krakowski v Eurolynx Properties Ltd* (1995) 183 C.L.R. 563, HCA.

attempted correction had been made. But since the first statement has already had its operative effect, it is not an easy task for the defendant to show that his correction has removed the effect of his earlier statement: and the burden lies squarely on him to show it.[46] However, a correction addressed sufficiently to the claimant's agent who has authority to receive information will constitute a sufficient correction.[47]

Timing of the falsity: the time of reliance by the representee. Changed facts between statement and reliance. For a claim in the tort of deceit, the question is whether the representation was false at the time the representee acted on it in such a way as to cause the loss he claims. If the representation was false when made but would be true if repeated at the time the representee acted upon it, there is no misrepresentation, and therefore no claim in deceit.[48] If, however, the representation was true when made but would be false if repeated at the time the representee acted upon it, there will be a misrepresentation for the purposes of the tort as long as the statement was not so limited as to be taken to refer to the facts only as they stood when the statement was made.[49] But the focus is then not on this element of the representee's claim, but on the question of whether the defendant was fraudulent in failing to correct his earlier statement. For this, a subjective test is used: the defendant is liable only if his failure to correct the statement was dishonest.[50] 5–11

"Materiality" of the representation.[51] In the context of the tort of deceit the courts commonly require a misrepresentation to have been material before it can give rise to damages,[52] but it has 5–12

---

[46] *Arnison v Smith* (1889) 41 Ch.D. 129, CA, at 370, 371.

[47] *Foodco UK LLP (t/a Muffin Break) v Henry Boot Developments Ltd* [2010] EWHC 358 (Ch) at [207] (Lewison J., applying to the context of deceit dicta in *Strover v Harrington* [1988] Ch. 390 at 409–410 (Misrepresentation Act 1967 s.2(1)).

[48] *Briess v Woolley* [1954] A.C. 333, HL, at 353; *Ship v Croskill* (1870) L.R. 10 Eq. 73.

[49] For this issue in relation to the remedy of rescission of the contract, for which fraud is not required, see above, para.4–27.

[50] Below, para.5–17.

[51] Above, paras 3–52 to 3–53.

[52] *Smith v Chadwick*, above, n.41 at 190, 200–201; *Angus v Clifford* [1891] 2 Ch. 449, CA, at 469. The "materiality" of a statement is closely linked to the representee's reliance on it. If the misrepresentation achieved the representor's

sometimes been said that a representee will not be allowed to deny that his misrepresentation was material if, as must be shown in order to establish a claim in deceit,[53] it was one on which he intended the representee to act and the representee did so act.[54] But as in other remedies for misrepresentation, the courts also use the statement's materiality as evidence of the representee's reliance on it.[55]

(2) The Representor's State of Mind

5–13 **Two elements: fraud as to the truth of the statement; and intention that it be acted upon.** To establish a claim in the tort of deceit the representee must show that the representor was fraudulent, in the sense that he did not honestly believe that his representation was true; and that he intended the representee to act upon the statement. In this sense, the tort is one of intention; simple lack of care does not suffice, either as to the truth of the statement, or as to the realisation that the statement might have the consequence that a person in the representee's position might suffer harm by acting on it. In any claim in the tort of deceit, therefore, the enquiry into the defendant's state of mind is a very significant element—and one which the courts require to be proved strictly.[56]

---

intended result—including, therefore, the representee's reliance on it—the representor is not to be heard to deny that the representation was material. But when the question is whether the representee did rely on it, the fact that the representation was objectively material (in the sense that it was likely to be relied on by a person in the representee's position) is relevant. When considering "materiality" in this sense, it is therefore perhaps better not to regard it as an independent requirement. See also *Barings Plc (In Liquidation) v Coopers & Lybrand (No.2)* [2002] B.C.L.C. 410 at [117] (Evans-Lombe J.: "I should incline to the view that materiality is at most an aspect of proving inducement and is not a separate requirement", relying on *Pan Atlantic Insurance Co. Ltd v Pine Top Insurance Co. Ltd* [1995] 1 A.C. 501 at 533 (Lord Mustill)). See further above, paras 3–53 and 4–33.

53 Below, para.5–19.

54 *Smith v Kay* (1859) 7 H.L.C. 750 at 759, 11 E.R. 299 at 303, HL.

55 Below, para.5–25.

56 Below, para.5–46. A claim for damages under s.2(1) of the Misrepresentation Act 1967 is by contrast significantly easier to establish since, broadly, it requires the representee to establish the elements of the tort of deceit *apart from* the defendant's fraud; the burden is then thrown on the representor of establishing that he had reasonable ground to believe, and did believe, that his representation was true. A claim under the statute is therefore much more likely to be relied

The meaning of "fraud": *Derry v Peek*. The meaning of "fraud" was settled by the House of Lords in 1889 in *Derry v Peek*.[57] In the recent years before that decision some judges had assumed that a false statement could be actionable in deceit where the representor could be shown only to have failed to take reasonable care as to the truth of the statement.[58] But this was decisively[59] rejected by the House of Lords, and it was made clear that deceit requires proof that the representor did not honestly believe his statement.[60] 5–14

upon by a representee who falls within the terms of the section, and for whom a claim in deceit would not bring significant additional advantages: below, para.7–47. *Cf. Doe v Skegg* [2006] EWHC 3746 (Ch), [2006] All E.R. (D) 250 (Oct) at [33] (claim under s.2(1) and in deceit, perhaps because claimant thought exemplary damages more likely to be awarded if there is a finding of fraud).

57 (1889) 14 App. Cas. 337.

58 *Smith v Chadwick* (1882) 20 Ch.D. 27, CA, at 44 (Jessel M.R.), 73 (Cotton L.J.), but *cf.* Lindley L.J. at 75; *Arnison v Smith* (1889) 41 Ch.D. 348, CA, at 371 (Cotton L.J.); *Peek v Derry* (1887) 37 Ch.D. 541, CA (Cotton L.J., Sir James Hannen and Lopes L.J.). Kekewich J. in *Glasier v Rolls* (1889) 42 Ch.D. 436 applied the test set out by the Court of Appeal in *Peek v Derry*, but this was reversed on appeal (Cotton, Fry and Lopes L.JJ.) after the decision of the House of Lords in *Derry v Peek*: *ibid.* Some of the difficulty here appears to have arisen because the courts of equity had adopted a broader definition of "fraud" for the purposes of the remedy of rescission in this period: above, para.4–03 (it later became clear that there was no need at all for fraud to be established for rescission: above, para.4–04). In *Derry v Peek*, above, n.57 at 347 Lord Bramwell explained Jessel M.R.'s dictum in *Smith v Chadwick*, above, on the basis that "his knowledge of actions of deceit was small, if any". See also *Le Lievre v Gould* [1893] 1 Q.B. 491, CA, at 500 (Bowen L.J., explaining how the confusion over the meaning of fraud arose from the decisions of equity judges); *Nocton v Lord Ashburton* [1914] A.C. 932, HL, at 953 (Lord Haldane L.C.: "In Chancery the term 'fraud' ... came to be used to describe what fell short of deceit, but imported breach of a duty to which equity had attached its sanction"); *Heilbut Symons & Co. v Buckleton* [1913] A.C. 30, HL, at 48–49 (Lord Moulton: tendency on the "Chancery side of the Court" to extend deceit to cover innocent misrepresentation parallel to the extension of the collateral warranty "on the Common Law side of the Court"; *cf.* below, paras 8–04 and 8–06). But *cf. Redgrave v Hurd* (1881) 20 Ch.D. 1, CA, at 13 (Jessel M.R.: a very different statement of the meaning of fraud for the purposes of rescission at common law, consistent with the decision of the House of Lords in *Derry v Peek*).

59 *Angus v Clifford* [1891] 2 Ch. 449, CA, at 463–464, 470.

60 The defendant must in this sense be "dishonest" with regard to the truth of his statement, but it is not necessary that he be "dishonest" as that word is used in the criminal law: *Standard Chartered Bank v Pakistan National Shipping Corp. (No.2)* [2000] 1 Lloyd's Rep. 218, CA, at 224. For a detailed discussion of the different senses of "dishonesty" (in criminal law, and in other areas of civil law),

Unreasonableness of belief on the part of the representor may be evidence of fraud, but it is not of itself sufficient.[61] Lord Herschell summed up the rule[62]:

> "First, in order to sustain an action of deceit, there must be proof of fraud, and nothing short of that will suffice. Secondly, fraud is proved when it is shewn that a false representation has been made (1) knowingly, or (2) without belief in its truth, or (3) recklessly, careless whether it be true or false. Although I have treated the second and third as distinct cases, I think the third is but an instance of the second, for one who makes a statement under such circumstances can have no real belief in the truth of what he states. To prevent a false statement being fraudulent, there must, I think, always be an honest belief in its truth. And this probably covers the whole ground, for one who knowingly alleges that which is false, has obviously no such honest belief. Thirdly, if fraud be proved, the motive of the person guilty of it is immaterial. It matters not that there was no intention to cheat or injure the person to whom the statement was made."

The essence of the tort is therefore fraud: and the core issue in a claim is whether the representee can show that the representee did not honestly believe the representation. He was fraudulent if he knew it was false; or suspected it might not be true; or was reckless as to its truth. But if he had a positive, honest belief in the truth of the statement, however unreasonable that belief might have been,[63] he is not fraudulent and so cannot be held liable in deceit. So, too, if he knew the truth but it was not present to his mind when he made the statement and so he had forgotten it, or did not realise the significance of the information he had at his disposal, he is not dishonest for the purposes of the tort of deceit.[64] And it must be remembered that it is for the representee to prove the representor's

---

see also *Twinsectra Ltd v Yardley* [2002] UKHL 12, [2002] 2 A.C. 164, esp. at [26]–[37] (Lord Hutton), [114]–[134] (Lord Millett, dissenting).

[61] *Derry v Peek*, above, n.57 at 352, 369.

[62] *ibid.*, at 374.

[63] "As for the element of dishonesty, the leading cases are replete with statements of its vital importance and of warnings against watering down this ingredient into something akin to negligence, however gross": *A.I.C. Ltd v I.T.S. Testing Services (UK) Ltd (The Kriti Palm)* [2006] EWCA Civ 1601, [2007] 2 C.L.C. 223 at [256] (Rix L.J.); English law does not generally equate gross negligence with fraud: below, para. 9–15.

[64] *ibid.*, at 348; *British & Commonwealth Holdings Plc v Quadrex Holdings Inc.*, unreported, April 10, 1995, CA. If, however, he remembers or discovers the truth and realises its significance before the representee has acted on the statement, he may become fraudulent: below, para.5–17.

dishonesty—his lack of honest belief in the truth of the statement; not for the representor to prove his honest belief.[65]

"Recklessness" as to the truth. The representor will be fraudulent if he made the statement "recklessly, careless whether it be true or false".[66] It is important to notice that Lord Herschell does not here say that a representor is fraudulent if he fails to take care—is negligent—whether his statement is true. Negligence is not dishonesty: and the House of Lords in *Derry v Peek* was at pains to emphasise that negligence is not sufficient for deceit. "Recklessness" involves not caring whether the statement is true: an indifference to the truth.[67] **5–15**

Motive irrelevant. If the representor made a false statement without honestly believing it to be true, and intended the representee to act upon it,[68] he cannot escape liability by pleading that he had a good motive for the deception: "it matters not that there was no intention to cheat or injure the person to whom the statement was made".[69] A white lie is still a lie for the purposes of the tort of deceit. However, the motive for making the false statement can be relevant evidence in showing whether it was fraudulent,[70] or whether there was an intention that the representee should act upon it.[71] **5–16**

---

[65] Below, para.5–46.

[66] Lord Herschell in *Derry v Peek*, above, para.5–14.

[67] *Angus v Clifford*, above, n.59 at 471 (Bowen L.J.); *Le Lievre v Gould*, above, n.58 at 501 (Bowen L.J.); *Thomas Witter Ltd v TBP Industries Ltd* [1996] 2 All E.R. 573 at 585–587.

[68] Below, para.5–19.

[69] Lord Herschell in *Derry v Peek*, above, para.5–14; *Peek v Gurney* (1873) L.R. 6 H.L. 377, HL, at 409; *Smith v Chadwick* (1884) 9 App. Cas. 187, HL, at 201; *Bradford Third Equitable Benefit Building Society v Borders* [1941] 2 All E.R. 205, HL, at 211.

[70] *Barings Plc (In Liquidation) v Coopers & Lybrand (No.2)* [2002] EWHC 461 (Ch), [2002] 2 B.C.L.C. 410 at [62] (Evans-Lombe J.: "in trying to decide whether a person made a statement which he must have known to be false (or which satisfied the other tests [for establishing the tort of deceit]), it must be relevant to consider why he should have done so. A man is more likely knowingly to make a false statement if he has some reason for doing so").

[71] *Tackey v McBain* [1912] A.C. 186, PC (company's agent falsely stated to chairman of Shanghai Stock Exchange that the company had not received news relevant to the value of the company's property in Sumatra; claimant as holder of shares acted on this and suffered loss. But no deceit: although the agent knew the

5–17 **The timing of the fraud; changes of facts, or discovery of truth, between statement and reliance.** The time at which the elements of the claim in deceit are tested is the time at which the representation was acted on by the representee[72]: that, therefore, is the time at which the defendant must be shown to have been fraudulent. If there is a period of time between the statement and the representee's action on it, no difficulty will normally arise where the representor was fraudulent when he made the statement: it would be unusual for a representor to be able to convince a court that his fraud—his absence of honest belief in the truth of the statement—did not continue to the relevant time.[73] But, as has been seen already,[74] it is possible for a claim to be based on a statement which by its language constitutes a continuing representation and which was true when it was made—and was made honestly—but which would be false if repeated by the time the representee acts upon it. Similarly, a representor may make a statement which is false, but at the time he believes it to be true, and so he was not fraudulent; but he later discovers the falsity. In such cases the question is whether the representor can be shown to have become fraudulent by the time of the contract. For this to be established, the representee will have to show not only that the representor knew of the relevant change (he has discovered the change in the facts, or he has discovered that he has already made a false statement), but also that his knowledge is sufficient to make him fraudulent: he must realise the significance of the change for the statement he has already made.[75] Lord Blackburn put it in this way in *Brownlie v Campbell*[76]:

---

statement was false, it was made to keep the matter confidential for the company, and there was no intention to affect dealings in the shares). See also below, para.5–19.

[72] *Briess v Woolley* [1954] A.C. 333, HL, at 353–354.

[73] Although the burden of proof of the representor's fraud at the relevant time is on the representee (below, para.5–46) if the representee discharges that burden in relation to the time at which the statement was made it will in practice be for the representor to show that his fraudulent state of mind did not continue.

[74] Above, para.5–11.

[75] Approved in *Abu Dhabi Investment Co. v H. Clarkson & Co. Ltd* [2007] EWHC 1267 (Comm), [2007] All E.R. (D) 448 (May) at [232]; in *Foodco UK LLP (t/a Muffin Break) v Henry Boot Developments Ltd* [2010] EWHC 358 (Ch) at [214] as being also consistent with *With v O'Flanagan* [1936] Ch. 575 at 584 (Lord Wright M.R.) and *Krakowski v Eurolynx Properties Ltd* (1995) 183 C.L.R. 563, HCA, at [36]; and in *Windsor & District Housing Association v Hewitt*

"when a statement or representation has been made in the *bona fide* belief that it is true, and the party who has made it afterwards comes to find out that it is untrue, and discovers what he should have said, he can no longer honestly keep up that silence on the subject after that has come to his knowledge, thereby allowing the other party to go on, and still more, inducing him to go on, upon a statement which was honestly made at the time when it was made, but which he has not now retracted when he has become aware that it can be no longer honestly persevered in."

Subjective interpretation of the representation. There can sometimes be a disagreement about the meaning of a representation. Before a representee can found his claim in deceit upon a representation, particularly one where the meaning is disputed, he must establish the sense in which he understood it and acted upon it[77]; and in determining the meaning of the representation a court may consider how it would reasonably be interpreted: its objective meaning.[78] However, in addition, before the representor can be held to have been fraudulent it must be shown that the representor knew the falsity, or was reckless as to the truth, of the statement in the meaning that he intended to be understood or knew that it would or might be so interpreted. The objective meaning of the representation may well be relevant evidence as to whether the representor can be believed in his claim that he did not realise that his words 5–18

[2011] EWCA Civ 735 at [18] (Longmore L.J., noting that before a judge embarks on the inquiry into whether the representor remembers his earlier statement there must be some basis for supposing that the representor may have forgotten it).

[76] (1880) 5 App. Cas. 925 at 950. See also *British & Commonwealth Holdings Plc v Quadrex Holdings Inc.*, above, n.64; *Fitzroy Robinson Ltd v Mentmore Towers Ltd* [2009] EWHC 1552 (TCC), [2009] B.L.R. 505 (failure by architects to inform client that, shortly before contract, its project team leader had resigned). *Cf.* however *Arkwright v Newbold* (1881) 17 Ch.D. 30, CA, 325, 329 (CA, obiter, not prepared to say that persons issuing a prospectus would be liable in an action of deceit if they do not mention a fact coming to their knowledge before the allotment of shares which falsifies a statement in the prospectus). For a change in the facts falsifying an earlier true statement, see *With v O'Flanagan* [1936] 1 Ch. 575 (rescission: above, para.4–27). Cases dealing with this issue in relation to the remedy of rescission must however be used with caution here, since there is no requirement of fraud (in the sense used in *Derry v Peek*) for rescission: *ibid.* ; and for a change of intention which falsified a continuing representation, see *Slough Estates Plc v Welwyn Hatfield DC* [1996] 2 E.G.L.R. 219.

[77] Below, para.5–24.

[78] Above, para.5–12.

would be so interpreted.[79] But the test of fraud is subjective: the interpretation of the representation within the test of fraud is therefore also subjective.[80]

5–19 **Intention that the representation be acted upon by the representee.** It must be shown that the representor intended the representee to act on the representation in the manner which resulted in damage to him.[81] The representor need not know the representee individually: it is sufficient if he intended that a person in the position of the representee should act on the representation.[82] The damage which is the basis of the representee's claim need not

[79] *Arnison v Smith* (1889) 41 Ch.D. 348, CA, at 368–369 (Lord Halsbury L.C.: "the Defendants cannot be heard to say that they did not know the popular meaning of the words they used . . . they discussed the terms of the prospectus, took advice upon it, and every one of them must have known that the statement was, taking its words in their ordinary sense, untrue"); *cf. Derry v Peek*, above, n.57 at 369 (Lord Herschell).

[80] *Akerhielm v De Mare* [1959] A.C. 789, PC, at 805; *Angus v Clifford*, above, n.59 at 466 (Lindley L.J.: representor who "did not see the effect, or dream that the effect of what he was saying could mislead" would be careless, not fraudulent); *Gross v Lewis Hillman Ltd* [1969] 3 All E.R. 1476, CA; *Barton v County NatWest Ltd* [1999] Lloyds Rep. Bank. 408, CA; *Bank of Tokyo-Mitsubishi U.F.J. Ltd v Başkan Gida Sanayi Ve Pazarlama A.S.* [2009] EWHC 1276 (Ch), [2009] All E.R. (D) 308 (Jun) at [1002] (Briggs J., referring to this paragraph); *Maple Leaf Macro Volatility Master Fund v Rouvroy* [2009] EWHC 257 (Comm), [2009] 1 Lloyd's Rep. 475 at [327] (Andrew Smith J., referring to this paragraph); *Krakowski v Eurolynx Properties Ltd* (1995) 183 C.L.R. 563, HCA, at 577; *John McGrath Motors (Canberra) Pty Ltd v Applebee* (1964) 110 C.L.R. 656 at 659–660, HCA.

[81] *Bradford Equitable Building Society v Borders* [1941] 2 All E.R. 205, HL, at 211; *Barton v County NatWest Ltd*, above, n.80 at 419–420. This does not however require the representor to intend to induce the *specific* action taken by the representee in reliance on the misrepresentation: *Goose v Wilson Sandford & Co.* [2001] Lloyd's Rep. P.N. 189, CA, at 201–202; *Mead v Babington* [2007] EWCA Civ 518, [2007] All E.R. (D) 226 (May) at [16].

[82] *Bradford Equitable Building Society v Borders*, above, n.81 at 211 (Viscount Maugham: "a class of persons which will include the plaintiff"); *Swift v Winterbotham* (1873) L.R. 8 Q.B. 244 at 253 (Quain J.: credit reference given to bank but passed on to bank's customer who relied on it); *Richardson v Silvester* (1873) L.R. 9 Q.B. 34 (advertisement in public newspaper); *Peek v Gurney*, above, n.69 (company prospectus intended to be acted on by any who were induced by it to take allotment of shares, but did not extend to those who later bought shares in the market); *Andrews v Mockford* [1896] 1 Q.B. 372, CA (company prospectus which, on proper construction, was intended to be acted on not only by those taking initial allotment of shares, but also those who bought in

have been intended, in the sense that the extent of recoverable losses is not limited to that which was intended.[83] And it is important to keep separate the representor's intention and his motive: his motive need not have been to cheat or injure the representee.[84] But it must have been the representor's intention that his statement would cause an act of reliance of the kind which the representee has established.[85]

Proof of the intention that the statement be relied on is again proof of a subjective state of mind on the part of the representor. However, as is common in other areas of law where an element of a claim requires a person's "intention" to be established,[86] a court may in an appropriate case infer the necessary intention from a consideration of the natural consequences of the person's actions. In a claim in deceit, a court may look at the natural consequences of the statement to decide whether it is satisfied, as a matter of fact, that the representor intended them.[87]

---

the market); *Abu Dhabi Investment Co. v H. Clarkson & Co. Ltd* [2008] EWCA Civ 699, [2008] All E.R. (D) 354 (Jun) at [33], approving this sentence.

83 Below, para.5–40.

84 *Derry v Peek*, above, n.57 at 374; *Bradford Equitable Building Society v Borders*, above, n.81 at 211; above, para.5–16. But the representor's motive may be relevant to the proof of his intention: *Tackey v McBain*, above, n.71.

85 *Way v Hearn* (1862) 13 C.B. (N.S.) 292 at 305, 143 E.R. 117 at 122 (fraud "not committed with a view to [the] transaction" which formed the basis of the claim); *Peek v Gurney*, above, n.69; *Andrews v Mockford*, above, n.82. For a similar issue in the tort of negligence, where the duty is owed in respect of the reliance by the representee on the statement for a *purpose* which the defendant ought to have foreseen, see below, para.6–20. In negligence the gist is not fraud, so there the representee's action in reliance need not have been intended, but only a reasonably foreseeable consequence of the statement.

86 e.g. *R. v Moloney* [1985] A.C. 905, HL, at 928–929 (criminal law; murder); Phipson, para.16–10.

87 *Richardson v Silvester* (1873) L.R. 9 Q.B. 34 at 36; *Smith v Chadwick* (1884) 9 App. Cas. 187, HL, at 190. For a related but separate question of when a representee can show that his actual reliance should be inferred because it was a natural consequence of the statement (the statement was in this sense "material"), see below, para.5–25. In *Goose v Wilson Sandford & Co.*, above, n.81, the CA said that if a fraudulent misrepresentation is found to have been made it will give rise to a rebuttable presumption of fact that the representor intended the representee to act in reliance on it. However, this seems to be based on a misreading of cases, such as *Barton v County NatWest Ltd* [1999] Lloyd's Rep. Bank. 408, CA, at 421, in which the issue was not proof of the defendant's intention that the representee rely on the statement, but proof of the representee's *actual* reliance.

5–20 **Multiple defendants: proof of fraud as regards each separate defendant.** Where there is a claim in deceit against multiple defendants, it is important to consider the honesty or dishonesty of each defendant separately. Apart from cases of agency or vicarious liability[88] in which a person might be responsible in law for the fraud of another, the general rule is that for any single defendant all the elements of the tort must be proved before he can be liable: therefore he can only be liable in deceit if he was himself fraudulent.[89]

5–21 **Misrepresentation by agents or employees.** The questions which arise in the case of a misrepresentation made not by the defendant, but by his agent or employee, have been mentioned already.[90] A little more detail is necessary here, to examine how the courts analyse the issue with particular reference to the need to show fraud before a claim in deceit is established. Three separate cases can be addressed (in each case assuming that the statement is made to the representee who then acts on it and suffers loss):

(1) The defendant, D, authorises the statement to be made by his agent or employee, A. D knows that it is false. In this case there is no difficulty in establishing D's liability in deceit. He is clearly fraudulent for the purposes of his primary liability under the tort: the fact that he uses an agent to make the statement does not prevent it being his representation for the purposes of the tort.[91] If A also knows that the statement is false, or at least does not honestly believe that it is true, he too will be liable personally in deceit.

(2) D does not know that A is making the statement. A, who makes the statement, knows that it is false. Here D is not liable as a primary tortfeasor in deceit, because he does not personally have the necessary fraudulent state of mind. But the elements of the tort are satisfied as regards A, who is therefore personally liable in deceit. Whether D is liable, not as a primary tortfeasor but vicariously, depends on the application

88 Above, para.5–07; below, para.5–22.

89 *Angus v Clifford* [1891] 2 Ch. 449, CA, at 473–474.

90 Above, para.5–07.

91 Above, para.5–07; *Cornfoot v Fowke* (1840) 6 M. & W. 358, 151 E.R. 450.

of the normal rules of agency and vicarious liability: if A made the statement in the course of his employment or within the scope of his authority as agent, then D is liable.[92] It makes no difference that D was not himself fraudulent, nor that (if such is the case) D did not gain personally by A's tort.[93]

(3) D does not know that A is making the statement. A, who makes the statement, does not know that it is false. But D does know the circumstances which make the statement false: that is, if D had known that the statement was being made, he would have known that it was false. The tort of deceit is not here committed at all. Neither D nor A has the necessary fraudulent state of mind. Even on the assumption that A's statement was made in the course of his agency or employment, the fact that D *would* have had the necessary state of mind had he known that the statement was being made does not make him in fact fraudulent:

> "You cannot add an innocent state of mind to an innocent state of mind and get as a result a dishonest state of mind.[94]"

---

[92] *Lloyd v Grace, Smith & Co.* [1912] A.C. 716, HL; *Udell v Atherton* (1861) 7 H. & N. 172, 158 E.R. 437. On the scope of agency, see *Briess v Woolley* [1954] A.C. 333, HL; *Armagas Ltd v Mundogas S.A.* [1986] A.C. 717, HL; *Mercantile Credit Co. Ltd v Garrod* [1962] 3 All E.R. 1103 (liability for fraud of partner); *Alliance & Leicester Building Society v Edgestop Ltd* [1993] 1 W.L.R. 1462 at 1479–1480; *Credit Lyonnais Bank Nederland N.V. (now Generale Bank Nederland N.V.) v Export Credits Guarantee Department* [2000] 1 A.C. 486, HL (where employee is a joint tortfeasor, employer liable only if all the features of the wrong which are necessary to make the employee liable occurred in the course of the employment); *Dubai Aluminium Co. Ltd v Salaam* [2002] UKHL 48, [2003] 2 A.C. 266 (liability for partner's dishonest assistance). For the liability of the principal for his fraudulent agent, see Bowstead & Reynolds, paras 8–063 to 8–066, 8–177 to 8–190 (esp. 8–180, 8–185). For the general principles of vicarious liability in tort, see Clerk & Lindsell, Ch.6; Winfield & Jolowicz, Ch.20.

[93] *Lloyd v Grace, Smith & Co.,* above, n.92, explaining dicta in *Barwick v English Joint Stock Bank* (1867) L.R. 2 Exch. 259 and *Mackay v Commercial Bank of New Brunswick* (1874) L.R. 5 P.C. 394.

[94] *Armstrong v Strain* [1951] 1 T.L.R. 856 at 872 (Devlin J.); affirmed [1952] 1 K.B. 232, CA, explaining dicta in *London County Freehold and Leasehold Properties Ltd v Berkeley Property and Investment Co. Ltd* [1936] 2 All E.R. 1039, CA; *Cornfoot v Fowke*, above, n.91. *Cf.* also *S. Pearson & Co. Ltd v Dublin Corp.* [1907] A.C. 351, HL, at 359 (Earl of Halsbury): "it matters not in

5–22 **Liability for procuring and inducing another to commit the tort of deceit.** Where the defendant did not, directly or through an agent, make the fraudulent misrepresentation, he may still be liable as a joint tortfeasor with the person who does commit the tort of deceit if the latter committed the tort pursuant to a common design between the two of them that it be committed,[95] or if the defendant procured and induced that person to commit the tort.[96] The mere fact that a person is a director of a company does not by itself render him liable for torts committed by the company, even where he is involved in the commission of the acts which render the company liable in deceit. But it is possible for a director to be liable for ordering or procuring tortious acts to be done by his company.[97]

(3) Reliance by the Representee

5–23 **The representation must have been an inducement to the representee's action.** This requirement was discussed in Chapter 3,[98] and what was said there applies in general terms equally to the tort of deceit. The tort is not complete on proof of the defendant's

---

respect of principal and agent (who represent but one person) which of them possesses the guilty knowledge or which of them makes the incriminating statement" (similarly, Lord Loreburn L.C. at 354): this does not admit liability where neither party has the necessary fraudulent state of mind, nor is it authority that an innocent agent would be responsible for his principal's fraud. It only covers the principal's liability in using an innocent agent (case (1), above): *Anglo-Scottish Beet Sugar Corp. Ltd v Spalding Urban DC* [1937] 2 K.B. 607; *Egger v Viscount Chelmsford* [1964] 3 All E.R. 401 at 411; *Stratford Borough v J.H. Ashman (N.P.) Ltd* [1960] N.Z.L.R. 503, NZCA, at 520–521.

[95] *Dadourian Group International Inc. v Simms* [2009] EWCA Civ 169, [2009] 1 Lloyd's Rep. 601 at [84]. There may also be liability in the tort of conspiracy where there is a combination or agreement between two or more persons to injure or to use the unlawful means of fraudulent misrepresentations: *Kuwait Oil Tanker Co. SAK v Al Bader* [2000] 2 All E.R. (Comm) 271 at [129]; *London Allied Holdings Ltd v Lee* [2007] EWHC 2061 (Ch), [2007] All E.R. (D) 153 (Sep) at [252]; *Clerk & Lindsell*, paras 24–95 *et seq.*, esp. paras 24–98, 24–102 (fraud as unlawful means), 24–104 to 24–111 (conspiracy to injure).

[96] *Standard Chartered Bank v Pakistan National Shipping Corp. (No.2)* [2000] 1 Lloyd's Rep. 218, CA, at 235; *Daido Asia Japan Co. Ltd v Rothen* [2002] B.C.C. 589 at [42]–[43]. This is a general rule of law, unaffected by the reversal of the decision in *Standard Chartered Bank v Pakistan National Shipping Corp. (No.2)* by the HL at [2002] UKHL 43, [2003] 1 A.C. 959.

[97] *ibid.*

[98] Above, para.3–50.

fraud in making a false representation: it must also be acted upon by the representee.[99] A causal link is therefore required between the representor's statement and the representee's decision to act in such a way as to cause the loss he claims. But the representation need not be shown to be the only cause, or the main cause of the representee's decision: it is sufficient if it is *a* cause.[100]

Representee's interpretation of the statement. The representee must have relied on the representation in the meaning that the court is satisfied is false. If this is not shown, the false statement which is the basis of the claim cannot be held to have caused the 5–24

[99] *Briess v Woolley*, above, n.92 at 353; *Diamond v Bank of London and Montreal Ltd* [1979] Q.B. 333, CA, at 349 (tort commited when and where the representee acts upon the representation, even if damage which forms the basis of claim in deceit is suffered at a later time and in a different place). *Cf. Attwood v Small* (1838) 6 Cl. & Fin. 232 at 448, 7 E.R. 684 at 765 (Lord Brougham, discussing rescission for fraudulent misrepresentation, but also damages at common law for fraud: "general fraudulent conduct signifies nothing . . . it must be shown that the attempt [to overreach] was made, and was made with success, *cum fructu*"). The cause of action is complete when the representee acts on the fraudulent representation, even if there may be an arguable case that the loss has been fully recouped or mitigated: that is a matter which only goes to the assessment of damages, not the cause of action, and therefore summary judgment can be given in a claim of deceit on proof of reliance without requiring in addition proof of loss: *4 Eng Ltd v Harper* [2007] EWHC 1568 (Ch) at [50]; *cf.* below, para.6–46 (cause of action in tort of negligence not complete without proof of loss).

[100] *Attwood v Small*, above, n.99 at 502, at 785 (Lord Wynford); *Barton v County NatWest Ltd* [1999] Lloyd's Rep. Bank. 408, CA, at 421. It is sufficient if the representation caused the representee to persevere in a decision he had already reached: *ibid.*, applying *Australian Steel & Mining Corp. Pty Ltd v Corben* [1974] 2 N.S.W.L.R. 202. Even if the evidence shows that the claimant would still have entered into the contract if the misrepresentation had not been made, it is possible to hold that he did in fact rely upon it as long as it was present to his mind and acting as one of the factors he took into account in making his decision to enter into the contract: *UCB Corporate Services Ltd v Williams* [2002] EWCA Civ 555, [2002] 3 F.C.R. 448 at [89] (Jonathan Parker L.J); and the fact that the representation was fraudulent and was intended to influence the other party in entering into the contract allows the courts more easily to infer that the representation was in the representee's mind when he contracted: *Ross River Ltd v Cambridge City Football Club Ltd* [2007] EWHC 2115 (Ch), [2008] 1 All E.R. 1004 at [202], [241] (rescission for fraud). The test for causation of loss may, however, be different: see below, para.5–38. The approach to causation may differ as between fraudulent and non-fraudulent misrepresentations: above, para.3–54

representee's loss. No doubt in most cases there will be no real difficulty here. But if there is any doubt or ambiguity about the meaning to be attributed to a statement, the claimant must establish that he subjectively interpreted the representation in the sense in which the court holds that it was false.[101]

5–25 **Proof of reliance.** Once it is clear that the representee interpreted the representation in its false meaning, the question is whether the representee was in fact influenced by it. It is not necessary for the representee to give oral evidence to this effect and, indeed, oral evidence and cross-examination may not be conclusive because of the difficulty everyone has of explaining the impact on him of any particular representation, amongst the other factors which caused him to act.[102] A broader enquiry is therefore necessary and if the representation was "material"[103] in the sense that it is of such a nature that it would be likely to induce a person in the representee's position to take the action he claims he took, the court is entitled to infer that the representation was an inducement to his action, unless the representor can show the contrary. The materiality of the statement places on the representor the burden of adducing evidence to rebut the inference.[104]

If the claim in deceit arises out of facts which also give rise to criminal liability on the part of the representor, and the representor has already been convicted of an offence which required proof of

---

[101] *Smith v Chadwick* (1884) 9 App. Cas. 187, HL; *Arkwright v Newbold* (1881) 17 Ch.D. 301, CA, at 324–325; *Krakowski v Eurolynx Properties Ltd* (1995) 183 C.L.R. 563, HCA, at 577; above, para.5–18.

[102] *Arnison v Smith* (1889) 41 Ch.D. 348, CA, at 369; *Smith v Chadwick* (1884) 9 App. Cas. 187, HL, at 196.

[103] On whether the representation must be "material" as an independent requirement in the tort of deceit, see above, para.5–12.

[104] *Smith v Chadwick* (1882) 20 Ch.D. 27, CA, at 44–45; (1884) 9 App. Cas. 187, HL, at 196; *Arnison v Smith*, above, n.102 at 369; *Barton v County NatWest Ltd*, above, n.100 at 421–424 (where, however, Morritt L.J. and Roch L.J. both assumed that such a reversal of the burden of proof arises only in cases of fraud; but this is not so: above, para.3–53); *Dadourian Group International Inc. v Simms* [2009] EWCA Civ 169, [2009] 1 Lloyd's Rep. 601 at [99], [101]; *Parabola Investments Ltd v Browallia Cal Ltd* [2009] EWHC 901 (Comm), [2009] 2 All E.R. (Comm) 589 at [106] (Flaux J.: where the evidence is that had the claimant known the true position he would have acted differently, that in itself demonstrates that the fraudulent misrepresentation was actively present to the his mind to a sufficient extent to establish inducement).

the relevant reliance by the representee, then the fact of conviction will be admissible in evidence to establish, amongst other things,[105] the representee's reliance in the claim for damages in the tort of deceit.[106] A conviction for the crime of fraud by false representation under section 2 of the Fraud Act 2006 will not be sufficient for this purpose, however, because it does not require proof that the representee was deceived.[107]

Representee's ability to discover the truth. If the representee relied on the false statement it is not a bar to his claim to damages in deceit that he could have discovered the truth.[108] Contributory negligence is not a defence to a claim in deceit.[109] The fact that he asks questions of the representor but is put off the scent by false replies certainly does not prevent him saying that he relied on the statement.[110] However, if the representee makes some inquiries into the truth of the statement, he may be held to have relied not on the statement but on his own inquiries. It will be a question of fact whether he can still be held to have relied on the statement.[111] 5–26

---

[105] Below, para.5–46.

[106] Civil Evidence Act 1968, s.11; *Alliance & Leicester Building Society v Edgestop Ltd* [1993] 1 W.L.R. 1462 at 1478 (conviction for procuring the execution of a valuable security by deception under the Theft Act 1968, s.20(2), which was repealed and replaced by new general offence of fraud by Fraud Act 2006; but see below, n.107).

[107] Certain other defences of deception, formerly contained in the Theft Act 1968, were replaced by the new general offence of fraud under the Fraud Act 2006 s.1, focusing now on the defendant's dishonesty rather than whether the fraud achieved its object of deceiving the intended victim: J. Parry, *Arlidge and Parry on Fraud* (3rd edn, 2007), paras 4–166, 4–167. The offence of obtaining services dishonestly under Fraud Act 2006 s.11 does, however, require the dishonesty to have achieved its object.

[108] *Attwood v Small*, above, n.99 at 502–503, at 785; *Director of the Central Railway Company of Venezuela v Kisch* (1867) L.R. 2 H.L. 99, HL, at 120–121. For attempts by the representor to correct his misrepresentation, see above, para.5–10; *Flack v Pattinson* [2002] EWCA Civ 1762, [2002] All E.R. (D) 31 (Dec) (correct information given earlier by third party did not, on facts, preclude finding that claimant relied on defendant's misrepresentation).

[109] Below, para.5–31.

[110] *Attwood v Small*, above, n.99 at 503, at 785–786; *The Siben (No.2)* [1996] 1 Lloyd's Rep. 35; for the similar rule in the case of rescission (even where there is no fraud) see *Redgrave v Hurd* (1881) 20 Ch.D. 1, CA, above, para.4–35.

[111] *Holmes v Jones* (1907) 4 C.L.R. 1692, HCA; *Smith v Chadwick*, above, n.104.

5–27 **Knowledge of representee's agent.** Where the representee's agent knows that the representation is false or otherwise has relevant information about the facts which give the true state of affairs, but does not communicate the relevant information to the representee, the question is whether the knowledge of the agent is to be imputed to the representee. If the relevant information was acquired by the agent in the course of his work for the representee, it will be so imputed.[112] But if the knowledge was acquired outside the course of the work for the representee, it has been held that it will not be imputed to the representee, and so will not be a bar to the representee's action in deceit.[113]

5–28 **"Non-reliance" clauses.** Contractual clauses and non-contractual notices which attempt to limit or negative the reliance by the representee on a statement made by the representor, or limit the legal consequence of such reliance, are considered in Chapter 9.[114]

III. DEFENCES

5–29 **Defences limited by the policy against relief from fraud.** Once the representee has established the elements of a claim in deceit, it is for the representor to raise any defence on which he seeks to rely. However, the defences available to a defendant who has been shown to be fraudulent are very limited by contrast, for example, with the defences available in a case of misrepresentation actionable in the tort of negligence.[115] This is consistent with the general reluctance to allow a representor to escape the consequences of his fraudulent conduct.[116]

---

[112] Bowstead & Reynolds, paras 8.207–8.209.

[113] *Wells v Smith* [1914] 3 K.B. 722 at 725–726 (Scrutton J: in such a case "a man who tells a lie to another cannot protect himself by saying 'Your agent should have warned you of my lie'"); *Renault UK Ltd v Fleetpro Technical Services Ltd* [2007] EWHC 2541 (QB), [2007] All E.R. (D) 208 (Nov) at [128].

[114] For the particular problems which such clauses present for a claim based on fraud see below, paras 9–13, 9–14.

[115] Below, para.6–47.

[116] See also, in furtherance of this policy, above, paras 3–33 and 5–08 (fraud overrides the concern to limit statements to one of fact); 4–30 (bars to rescission more limited in case of fraud); below, para.5–40 (recoverable damages potentially more extensive because of fraud). For a general discussion of the policy, see *Smith New Court Securities Ltd v Scrimgeour Vickers (Asset*

Absence of writing: Lord Tenterden's Act. Under the Statute of Frauds Amendment Act 1828 ("Lord Tenterden's Act") s.6: **5–30**

> "No action shall be brought whereby to charge any person upon or by reason of any representation or assurance made or given concerning or relating to the character, conduct, credit, ability, trade, or dealings of any other person, to the intent or purpose that such other person may obtain credit, money, or goods upon,[117] unless such representation or assurance be made in writing, signed by the party to be charged therewith."

This section was enacted to prevent evasion of the Statute of Frauds, which provides[118] that no action shall be brought on a contract of guarantee unless the contract, or a memorandum or note of it, is in writing[119] signed by the defendant or his agent. After the decision in *Pasley v Freeman*[120] opened up the possibility of a

---

Management) Ltd [1997] A.C. 254, HL, at 279–280; *South Australia Asset Management Corp. v York Montague Ltd* [1997] A.C. 191, HL, at 215–216.

117 ["The words of the clause . . . are . . . clearly inaccurate, probably from a mistake in the transcriber into the Parliamentary roll. We must make an alteration in order to complete the sense, and must either transpose some words, and read the sentence as it if were 'to the intent or purpose that some other person may obtain money or goods upon credit', or interpolate others, and read it as if it were 'to the intent or purpose to obtain credit, money, or goods on such representation'": *Lyde v Barnard* (1836) 1 M. & W. 101 at 115, 150 E.R. 363 at 369, Parke B., preferring the former alteration as being narrower and therefore more probably closer to Lord Tenterden's object in drafting the Statute: below. *Cf.* Lord Abinger C.B., *ibid.*, at 123, at 372, suggesting that the inaccuracy resulted from the draftsman's failure to strike out the whole of the word "thereupon" which might have appeared in an earlier draft.]

118 Statute of Frauds 1667 s.4, which has been partly repealed by the Law of Property Act 1925 s.207, Sch.7, the Statute Law Revision Act 1948 and the Law Reform (Enforcement of Contracts) Act 1954 s.1, but is still in force in relation to contracts of guarantee.

119 "In a modern context, the section will clearly be satisfied if the representation is contained in an email, provided that the email includes a written indication of who is sending the email. It seems that it is not enough that the email comes from a person's email address without his having 'signed' it in the sense of either including an electronic signature or concluding words such as 'regards' accompanied by the typed name of the sender of the email: see the decision of HHJ Pelling QC (sitting as a High Court Judge) in *Pereira Fernandes v Mehta* [2006] 1 WLR 1543 [e-mail for purposes of Statute of Frauds 1677 s.4]": Flaux J., *Lindsay v O'Loughnane* [2010] EWHC 529 (QB), [2010] All E.R. (D) 200 (Mar) at [95].

120 (1789) 3 T.R. 51, 100 E.R. 450; above, para.5–01, n.3.

claim in the tort of deceit against one who fraudulently misrepresented a person's creditworthiness and thereby induced the claimant to extend credit and suffer loss, it became common practice, where there was no guarantee in writing, to use the representation which would, but for the Statute of Frauds, have been enforceable as a guarantee, in order to found a claim in deceit. Lord Tenterden's Act was introduced to provide a similar defence of absence of writing in the case of such an action.[121]

Because of this legislative history, it has been held that the defence under Lord Tenterden's Act applies only to fraudulent misrepresentations.[122] It is not therefore a defence to an action in the tort of negligence[123] or for breach of a contractual duty to take care in making the statement.[124] Although it has been held that the

---

[121] *Banbury v Bank of Montreal* [1918] A.C. 626, HL, at 639, 692–693, 711–712; *Lyde v Barnard*, above, n.117 at 103, 107, 114, 118, at 364, 365–366, 368, 370; *Tatton v Wade* (1856) 18 C.B. 371 at 381, 139 E.R. 1413 at 1417 (Pollock C.B. reporting Lord Tenterden's own statement of motive for introducing s.6). The section provides a defence to enforceability of the claim based on the representation, but does not destroy the cause of action itself: *Amalgamated Metal Trading Ltd v Department of Trade and Industry*, *The Times*, March 21, 1989. *Cf.* the equivalent provision in Scotland, the Mercantile Law (Scotland) Amendment Act 1856 s.6, which provides that unwritten representations and assurances as to credit "shall have no effect": *Clydesdale Bank Ltd v J. & G. Paton* [1896] A.C. 381, HL (Sc.). The Act is generally raised as a defence to claims based on express oral representations, but applies equally to *implied* representations as to credit: *John Hudson and Co. Ltd v Oaten*, unreported, June 19, 1980, CA. A representation implied into an appropriately signed document satisfies the Act; but a representation by conduct alone does not: *Contex Drouzhba Ltd v Wiseman* [2007] EWCA Civ 1201, [2008] B.C.C. 301 at [10], [12].

[122] *Banbury v Bank of Montreal*, above, n.121. In addition to the origins of the Act and its relation to the tort of deceit, there is a second strand of reasoning: that an action for breach of contract or in the tort of negligence is not an action by which a person is "charge[d] . . . upon or by reason of" the representation: it is not the representation but the breach of duty which is the cause of action; *ibid.*, at 713; *W.B. Anderson & Sons Ltd v Rhodes (Liverpool) Ltd* [1967] 2 All E.R. 850 at 865. The defence does not, however, apply only to a claim in the tort of deceit, but also extends to any claim which in substance is founded on a fraudulent misrepresentation: *Haslock v Fergusson* (1837) 7 Ad. & E. 86, 112 E.R. 403 (money had and received).

[123] *W.B. Anderson & Sons Ltd v Rhodes (Liverpool) Ltd*, above, n.122.

[124] *Banbury v Bank of Montreal*, above, n.121.

defence is available to a claim under s.2(1) of the Misrepresentation Act 1967,[125] this may be open to debate.[126]

The defence is available where the claim in deceit is based on an unwritten representation made to the claimant by the defendant (or, where the defendant is a company, by a duly authorised agent of the company acting in the course of his duties in the business of the company[127]) about the creditworthiness of a third party,[128] which was intended to induce,[129] and did induce,[130] the claimant to extend credit, make a loan or provide goods to that third party. The statute refers to statements as to the third party's "character, conduct,

---

[125] *UBAF Ltd v European American Banking Corporation* [1984] Q.B. 713, CA.

[126] Below, para.7–30.

[127] A company is a "person" within s.6, and so may raise the defence in an action: *Hirst v West Riding Union Banking Co. Ltd* [1901] 2 K.B. 560, CA; *Banbury v Bank of Montreal*, above, n.121 at 708, 713–714. Her Majesty's Government may also, if sued in deceit, seek to raise the defence under Lord Tenterden's Act: *Amalgamated Metal Trading Ltd v Department of Trade and Industry*, above, n.121. Since a company can only act through a human agent, the signature of an agent can be a signature of the company for the purposes of s.6: *UBAF Ltd v European American Banking Corp.*, above, n.125 at 724–725 (doubted, however, in Spencer Bower (Misrepresentation), para.195). In other cases, however, the signature of an agent is not included by Lord Tenterden's Act and is therefore not sufficient to prevent the operation of the defence of which the underlying purpose is that a person shall not be charged with fraud unless his own signature is attached to the document which evidences the fraud: *Williams v Mason* (1873) 28 L.T. 232; *Banbury v Bank of Montreal*, above, n.121 at 713; see also at 707. The equivalent provision in Scotland, the Mercantile Law (Scotland) Amendment Act 1856, s.6, by contrast, does allow the signature of an agent to defeat the defence.

[128] This may include a representation about the creditworthiness of a partnership of which the defendant is himself a partner: *Devaux v Steinkeller* (1839) Bing. N.C. 84, 133 E.R. 33; and a representation about the creditworthiness of a company of which the defendant is himself a director (but a letter or contract signed by the director on behalf of the company, containing expressly or impliedly the representation of creditworthiness, will satisfy the Act): *Contex Drouzhba Ltd v Wiseman*, above, n.121.

[129] It is irrelevant that the defendant might also have had another ulterior purpose or motive: *Clydesdale Bank Ltd v J. & G. Paton*, above, n.121; and it is irrelevant whether or not the defendant intended to benefit from the statement: *Pearson v Seligman* (1883) 48 L.T. 842, CA.

[130] To avoid the operation of the defence, the written representation need not be the sole inducement as long as it was a substantial inducement: *Tatton v Wade* (1856) 18 C.B. 371, 139 E.R. 1413. On the general question of inducement and reliance, see above, para.3–50; para.5–23.

credit, ability, trade, or dealings", but this has been interpreted as extending only to statements which go to his credit.[131]

5–31 **Contributory negligence not a defence.** Although contributory negligence is a defence to most torts, even those in which the defendant's liability is not itself necessarily based on proof of negligence,[132] it is not available as a defence to deceit. Contributory negligence was not a defence to deceit at common law before 1945[133]; and the House of Lords has confirmed that the Law Reform (Contributory Negligence) Act 1945 has made no change in this respect.[134]

---

131 *Diamond v Bank of London and Montreal Ltd* [1979] Q.B. 333, CA, at 347, 350–351; *Bishop v Balkis Consolidated Co. Ltd* (1890) 25 Q.B.D. 512, CA (certification by company of title to shares was not a representation of seller's credit even though it induced the claimant to advance money for purchase of shares). There can sometimes be difficulties of interpretation: see *Lyde v Barnard*, above, n.117 (Lord Abinger C.B. and Gurney B. applied the statute to a representation as to the encumbrances on the third party's property, but Alderson and Parke BB. disagreed and limited it to representations as to the personal credit and trustworthiness of the third party); *Swann v Phillips* (1838) 8 Ad. & E. 457 at 460–461, 112 E.R. 912 at 913 (representation that title deeds to property were in defendant's possession: a representation as to credit only if the words constituted an assurance that the claimant could therefore safely make a loan). For an implied representation by a company that it intended to pay for goods it contracted to purchase, which was in consequence an (implied) representation as to the company's credit by a director who procured that misrepresentation, see *John Hudson and Co. Ltd v Oaten*, above, n.121.

132 Clerk & Lindsell, paras 3–51 to 3–57; *Caswell v Powell Duffryn Associated Collieries Ltd* [1940] A.C. 152, HL (breach of statutory duty).

133 There appeared to be no case in which this point was addressed by way of *ratio decidendi* but since deceit is a tort where the defendant intended to cause the claimant to rely on the statement and suffer loss, it followed that the defence was not available: *Quinn v Leathem* [1901] A.C. 495, HL, at 537 (Lord Lindley: "The intention to injure the plaintiff negatives all excuses"); Glanville Williams, *Joint Torts and Contributory Negligence* (1951), para.55; Law Revision Committee, Eighth Report, Cmd.6032 (1939), p.18; *Alliance & Leicester Building Society v Edgestop Ltd* [1993] 1 W.L.R. 1462 at 1474.

134 *Standard Chartered Bank v Pakistan National Shipping Corp. (Nos 2 and 4)* [2002] UKHL 43, [2003] 1 A.C. 959 at [10]–[18] (Lord Hoffmann), approving the majority of the CA in that case, and three decisions to the same effect at first instance: *Alliance & Leicester Building Society v Edgestop Ltd*, above, n.133 (Mummery J.: deceit, both primary liability and vicarious liability); *Corporación Nacional del Cobre de Chile v Sogemin Metals Ltd* [1997] 1 W.L.R. 1396 (Carnwath J.: conspiracy involving bribery, but the judge discussed in detail the case of deceit and followed Mummery J.'s decision in *Alliance & Leicester v*

Illegality.[135] If a representee can establish the elements of the claim in deceit without having to rely upon or plead any 5–32

Edgestop); *Nationwide Building Society v Thimbleby & Co.* [1999] Lloyd's Rep. P.N. 359 (Blackburne J.: deceit). The 1945 Act allows a defence based on the "fault" of the claimant (s.1(1)); and, in the case of a claimant, "fault" is defined (s.4) as "negligence, breach of statutory duty or other act or omission" which gives rise at common law to a defence of contributory negligence: *Standard Chartered Bank v Pakistan National Shipping Corp. (Nos 2 and 4)*, above, at [11]. The claimant's contributory *deceit* is similarly not a defence: Clerk & Lindsell, para.3–60. In the US the Restatement of Torts (Second) does not allow contributory negligence as a defence to intentional torts generally (para.481) or deceit in particular (para.545A); but the Restatement of the Law Third, Torts: Apportionment of Liability (2000), para.1 comment *b.* does not take this position. The contributory negligence legislation in Commonwealth countries, based on the UK legislation, has received varying interpretation in relation to the tort of deceit: in Australia, C. Sappideen and P. Vines, *Fleming's The Law of Torts* (10th edn, Thomson Reuters Australia, Pyrmont N.S.W., 2011), para.25.50, n.47, say that contributory negligence is not a defence under apportionment legislation but cite no Australian cases; there is conflicting authority in New Zealand: S. Todd (ed.), *The Law of Torts in New Zealand* (5th edn, Thomson Brookers, Wellington, 2009), para.15.2.07 (but notice that in New Zealand a claim in deceit can lie only against a third party, and not against the other contracting party: Contractual Remedies Act 1979, s.6(1)(b), above, para.5–03, n.19); and contributory negligence has been applied to a claim in deceit in Canada: *Andersen v Stevens* (1981) 125 D.L.R. (3d) 736 (Sup. Ct. British Columbia); A.M. Linden, *Canadian Tort Law* (8th edn, LexisNexis Butterworths, Markham, Ontario, 2006), pp.104–106. For contributory negligence as a defence to a claim under the Misrepresentation Act 1967 s.2(1), where different policy considerations apply, see *Gran Gelato Ltd v Richcliff (Group) Ltd* [1992] Ch. 560, below, para.7–27.

[135] For the general approach to illegality as a defence in tort, see Clerk & Lindsell, paras 3–02 to 3–43; Winfield & Jolowicz, paras 25–18 to 25–25; Charlesworth & Percy, paras 4.248–4.253. In 2001 the Law Commission published provisional proposals for reform: Consultation Paper No.160, *The Illegality Defencein Tort*; but in 2010 it decided that no legislative reform is appropriate because it would be difficult to devise and draft a broad statutory scheme that would be an improvement on the current law, and in relation to most types of claim it is open to the courts to develop the law in ways that would render it considerably clearer, more certain and less arbitrary; the judiciary should base their decisions directly on the policies that underlie the illegality defence and explain their reasoning accordingly: Consultation Paper No.189, *The Illegality Defence: a Consultative Report* (2009), paras 1.13–1.14; confirmed in Law Com No.320, *The Illegality Defence* (2010), Pt.3, in which the Law Commission noted that, since the Consultative Report, the House of Lords had already begun to move in this direction in its decisions in *Gray v Thames Trains Ltd* [2009] UKHL 33, [2009] 1 A.C. 1339 and *Stone & Rolls Ltd v Moore Stephens* [2009] UKHL 39, [2009] 1 A.C. 1391, below, para.6–49.

illegality—to which, for example, he was party with the representor—his claim is not affected by the illegality.[136] This is so even if his act of reliance on the statement involves his entering into a contract which was tainted with illegality.[137] If the fraud consists of the representor inducing the representee to enter into a contract which, unbeknown to the representee, will be illegal, then there is no objection to allowing the representee to pursue a claim in deceit for the consequences of this illegality.[138]

5–33 **Exclusion and limitation clauses.** An exclusion or limitation clause in a contract with the representee will not generally protect the representor against an action in deceit. Such clauses are considered in Chapter 9.[139]

5–34 **Limitation periods.** Actions for damages in tort cannot normally be brought (that is, a claim form cannot be issued[140]) after the expiration of six years from the date on which the cause of action accrued.[141] However, where, as in a claim in deceit, an action is based on the fraud of the defendant, the limitation period does not begin to run until the claimant has discovered the fraud or could with reasonable diligence have discovered it.[142]

[136] *Standard Chartered Bank v Pakistan Shipping Corp. (No.2)* [2000] 1 Lloyd's Rep. 218, CA, at 232 (Aldous L.J., relying on the general principle of *Tinsley v Milligan* [1994] 1 A.C. 340 in which Lord Goff, Lord Keith and Lord Browne-Wilkinson disapproved the approach, used in the context of a claim in deceit in *Saunders v Edwards* [1987] 1 W.L.R. 1116, CA, that whether illegality operated as a defence depended upon whether it would "affront public conscience" to allow the claim). Ward L.J. agreed at 236. The reasoning and analysis of Evans L.J. at 229–230 was somewhat different. See also *Daido Asia Japan Co. Ltd v Rothen* [2002] B.C.C. 589 at [21]–[23].
[137] *The Siben (No.2)* [1996] 1 Lloyd's Rep. 35 at 63.
[138] *Shelley v Paddock* [1980] Q.B. 348, CA; the parties were not *in pari delicto*: Lord Denning M.R. at 356. Brandon L.J. had doubts about the result but did not dissent: at 357. For fraud overriding the normal rule that a misrepresentation of law is not actionable, on the basis of the principle that the parties are then not *in pari delicto*, see above, para.3–33.
[139] For the application of exclusion and limitation clauses to fraudulent misrepresentations, see para.9–13.
[140] Below, para.11–05.
[141] Limitation Act 1980, s.2.
[142] *ibid.*, s.32(1)(a). A claimant does not "discover" a fraud until he has material sufficient to enable him properly to plead it: *Law Society v Sephton* [2004] EWCA Civ 1627, [2005] Q.B. 1013 at [110]; and the burden of proof lies on the

IV. THE DAMAGES RECOVERABLE[143]

Principles of award of damages in deceit. In *Smith New Court Securities Ltd v Scrimgeour Vickers (Asset Management) Ltd*,[144] the House of Lords discussed in some detail the principles of an award of damages in deceit. The speeches of Lord Browne-Wilkinson and Lord Steyn in that case should be the first point of reference for any question as the measure of loss recoverable in an action of deceit. The details will be discussed in the following paragraphs, together with points which did not arise in *Smith New Court* but which are settled by other authority; in summary, damages in deceit are 5–35

claimants to establish that they *could not* have discovered the fraud: *Paragon Finance Plc v D.B. Thakerar & Co.* [1999] 1 All E.R. 400 at 418. The limitation period will also be delayed where any fact relevant to the claimant's right of action has been deliberately concealed from him by the defendant, until the claimant has discovered the concealment or could with reasonable diligence have discovered it: Limitation Act 1980 s.32(1)(b). Where the defendant's concealment of facts is subsequent to the accrual of the cause of action, the full limitation period begins to run only after the claimant has discovered, or should have discovered, the concealment: *Sheldon v R.H.M. Outhwaite (Underwriting Agencies) Ltd* [1996] A.C. 102, HL, criticised by the Law Commission in Consultation Paper No.151, *Limitation of Actions* (1998), paras 8.17 to 8.20.

In 2001 the Law Commission recommended reform of the law of limitation of actions: Law Com. No.270 (2001), to introduce a single, core limitation regime which would apply to most claims for a remedy for a wrong, including claims in deceit: a primary limitation period of three years starting from the date on which the claimant knows, or ought reasonably to know: (a) the facts which give rise to the cause of action; (b) the identity of the defendant; and (c) if the claimant has suffered injury, loss or damage or the defendant has received a benefit, that the injury, loss, damage or benefit was significant; and a long-stop limitation period of 10 years, starting from the date of the accrual of the cause of action or (for those claims in tort where loss is an essential element of the cause of action) from the date of the act or omission which gives rise to the cause of action. Although the long-stop limitation period would normally apply in claims of deceit, here as in any other claim the long-stop period would be extended where the defendant has concealed relevant facts, but only if the concealment was dishonest: Law Com. No.270 at paras 3.143 to 3.145. Moreover, concealment would only suspend the long-stop and would not start time running again. The Government accepted the Report in principle in July 2002, and in 2008 it was announced that provisions on the subject would be included within a proposed Civil Law Reform Bill. However, in 2009 the Government announced that the limitation reforms would not, after all, be taken forward: Law Com. No.323, *Annual Report 2009–10*, paras 3.12 to 3.15.

143 McGregor, paras 41–002 to 41–040.

144 [1997] A.C. 254, HL.

awarded to compensate the representee for all the loss which can properly be said to have been caused by his reliance on the fraudulent misrepresentation, subject always to the representee's duty to mitigate his loss after he discovers the fraud. If the representation caused him to enter into a transaction, the damages reflect the actual loss caused by entry into the transaction; and the starting-point for this calculation is the basic tort measure of damages, not the contract measure: the remedy in deceit does not protect the representee in respect of his positive interest in the bargain.[145]

5–36 **Proof of loss.** Damages in deceit are given to compensate the representee's loss.[146] "Loss" here is typically economic loss, since the paradigm case of deceit involves the representee being induced by the fraud into an unprofitable contract.[147] However, it also extends to other forms of tangible loss—damage to property,[148] loss

---

[145] *Smith New Court*, above, n.144 at 263–265, 282, approving *Doyle v Olby (Ironmongers) Ltd* [1969] 2 Q.B. 158 (where the CA reversed the trial judge's award on the contract measure); *East v Maurer* [1991] 1 W.L.R. 461, CA, below, para.5–39; *Parabola Investments Ltd v Browallia Cal Ltd* [2010] EWCA Civ 486, [2011] Q.B. 477, below, para.5–39; *Parna v G. & S. Properties Ltd* (1969) 5 D.L.R. (3d) 315 (CA Ontario, affirmed on liability rather than on the measure of damages, at (1970) 15 D.L.R. (3d) 336, SCC); *New Zealand Refrigerating Co. Ltd v Scott* [1969] N.Z.L.R. 30. For the basic measure of calculation of damages in contract ("bargain" or "expectation" interest) and tort ("negative" or "reliance" interest), see above, paras 2–07 to 2–10.

[146] This is the basis on which the judgments in *Smith New Court*, above, n.144, proceed. But for the statement that "damages for fraud are frequently a restitutionary remedy", see *South Australia Asset Management Corp. v York Montague Ltd* [1997] A.C. 191, HL, at 215 (Lord Hoffmann). This presumably means that the *effect* of an award of damages in deceit might often be to deprive the defendant of a benefit, not that it is in principle intended to remedy unjust enrichment. The only way in which a representee's profit will normally be in issue is as an element in a claim for exemplary damages (as to which see below, para.5–42). But, such a claim apart, the defendant's profit is not an element of the damages claim in deceit: *cf.* the facts of *Mafo v Adams* [1970] 1 Q.B. 548, CA. On the question whether the defendant can be made to make restitution of a profit made through his deceit, see below, para.5–43.

[147] Above, para.5–03.

[148] *Mullett v Mason* (1866) L.R. 1 C.P. 559 (value of five cows which died from disease caught by contact with a sixth cow, fraudulently misrepresented to be free from infectious disease).

of property[149] and physical injury[150]—but may also include intangible losses, such as damages for personal distress.[151] But if the representee can show no loss flowing from his reliance on the misrepresentation, he will have no claim for substantial compensatory damages.[152] A court may, however, be reluctant to conclude that no loss flowed from a fraud which achieved its end and will inquire carefully to ascertain whether there is any loss, direct or consequential, caused by the representee's action on the statement. For example, where a representee is induced to buy goods by a fraudulent misrepresentation about their quality but the goods are in fact worth at least what the representee paid for them, and maybe even more, there is still a claim in deceit if the representee has

---

[149] *Smith Kline & French Laboratories Ltd v Long* [1989] 1 W.L.R. 1, CA; *Mafo v Adams*, above, n.146 (representee induced to give up a flat of which he had security of tenure and protection by statutory rent control: "in the circles in which these parties move possession of such a flat is one of the most significant rights of property that any of them ever see in their lives": Widgery L.J. at 557).

[150] *Langridge v Levy* (1837) 2 M. & W. 519, 150 E.R. 863; affirmed 4 M. & W. 337, 150 E.R. 1458 (gun, misrepresented to be safe, exploded and injured claimant); *Burrows v Rhodes* [1899] 1 Q.B. 816 (claimant induced by fraudulent misrepresentation to take part in hostilities which were, unknown to him, illegal: suffered physical injury and was taken prisoner); *Banks v Cox* [2002] EWHC 2166 (Ch), [2002] All E.R. (D) 376 (Oct) (£10,000 awarded for depressive illness: not simply a claim for injured feelings). For a different kind of case, in which the defendant is liable in tort for knowingly making a false statement calculated to cause physical harm, see *Wilkinson v Downton* [1897] 2 Q.B. 57, above, para.5–02, n.14.

[151] Below, para.5–44.

[152] *Smith v Chadwick* (1884) 9 App. Cas. 187, HL, at 195–196; *McConnel v Wright* [1903] 1 Ch. 546, CA, at 554–555 (claim under the Directors Liability Act 1890, which was assessed on the same basis as the tort of deceit: below, paras 7–16, 7–33 and 7–62); *Holmes v Jones* (1907) 4 C.L.R. 1692, HCA, at 1709 (if the contract into which the representee is induced to enter is profitable, there may be no loss to claim in deceit); *Latkter v General Guarantee Finance Ltd* [2001] EWCA Civ 875. But *cf. Clef Aquitaine S.A.R.L. v Laporte Materials (Barrow) Ltd* [2001] Q.B. 488, CA (not necessary to prove the contract was itself loss-making if claimant shows that, but for the fraud, he would have entered into a different and more favourable transaction, with either the defendant or some third party); *London Allied Holdings Ltd v Lee* [2007] EWHC 2061 (Ch), [2007] All E.R. (D) 153 (Sep) at [253] (loss may be reduced if claimant has proprietary claims relating to money or other property handed over pursuant to the fraud, e.g. under a constructive trust).

consequential losses, such as the costs associated with having the goods put into the state in which he thought he was buying them.[153]

5–37 **Calculation of loss; timing.** In all claims of deceit the question is what loss was suffered by the representee consequent upon his reliance on the fraudulent misrepresentation. Where, therefore, the representee's reliance consists of his entering into a contract, he will recover the losses which he suffers as a result of entering into that contract. The recoverable loss is not limited to that part of the loss which flows from the fact that the statement was false.[154]

If the representee is induced by the fraud to enter into a transaction such as the purchase of property, the starting point for the calculation of damages will be to assess the difference in value between what he paid and what he received. That reflects the amount by which he is out of pocket—the basic measure of damages in tort.[155] And often it will be appropriate to select the date of the transaction as the date on which to assess those values. But that is not a rule, and it may be appropriate to select a later date: the question is how properly to value the financial loss suffered by the

---

153 *Hornal v Neuberger Products Ltd* [1957] 1 Q.B. 247, CA ("I confess that I do not look kindly on a defendant who, having got the plaintiff to buy a machine by knowingly telling him an untruth, afterwards says he suffered no damage": Denning L.J. at 260); *cf. Smith Kline & French Laboratories Ltd v Long*, above, n.149 (where representee is permanently deprived of goods in consequence of the deceit, measure of loss is not representee's cost of replacing them but, as in the tort of conversion, the market value of the goods: "it does not lie in the mouth of the defendant to suggest that the owner might not have found a purchaser or hirer [of the goods]": Slade L.J. at 10. In *Smith New Court*, above, n.144 at 282, Lord Steyn noted criticism of the decision in *Smith Kline v Long* by A. Burrows, *Remedies for Torts and Breach of Contract* (2nd edn, 1994), pp.173–174 (now 3rd edn, 2004, p.256), but declined to comment further).

154 *Smith New Court*, above, n.144 at 283 (Lord Steyn: on this point *Downs v Chappell* [1997] 1 W.L.R. 426, CA, was overruled). *Cf.* the tort of negligence in which the recoverable loss is defined by reference to the scope of the duty broken; so in a case where the defendant's duty was limited to taking reasonable care in providing accurate information, damages for breach of that duty cover only the consequences for the representee of the statement being inaccurate: *South Australia Asset Management Corporation v York Montague Ltd* [1997] A.C. 191, HL, below, para.6–55. At 216–217 Lord Hoffmann made clear that he did not intend his judgment on this principle to extend to the tort of deceit; see also *Smith New Court*, above, at 265 (Lord Browne-Wilkinson); *Slough Estates Plc v Welwyn Hatfield District Council* [1996] 2 E.G.L.R. 219 at 245.

155 Above, para.2–09.

representee by his reliance on the representor's fraudulent misrepresentation, in this example the loss suffered from entering into the transaction to purchase the property.[156] This has significance where there is a change in the value of the property, usually a reduction in the value for which the representee seeks to hold the representor responsible.[157] If the representee is free to dispose of the property and so to crystallise the loss, then he may normally be expected to do so and the loss will be calculated at the time he could have made the disposal. But if he is locked into holding the property, in the sense that he cannot reasonably be expected to dispose of it, or cannot dispose of it at all, it will be held that any subsequent decrease in the value of the property is recoverable, as long as there is no other intervening cause of the decrease in value which breaks the chain of causation between the fraud and the loss.[158] In *Smith*

---

[156] *Smith New Court*, above, n.144 at 265–266, 283–284, rejecting a number of older cases in so far as they had been regarded as laying down a rule that, in the case of property purchased pursuant to a fraudulent misrepresentation, the measure of damages was the difference in price paid and value received at the date of acquisition. See also *Parabola Investments Ltd v Browallia Cal Ltd* [2010] EWCA Civ 486, [2011] Q.B. 477 at [34] (instances given in *Smith New Court* are illustrative rather then exclusive).

[157] *cf.*, however, *Great Future International Ltd v Sealand Housing Corp.* [2002] EWHC 2454 (Ch), [2002] All E.R. (D) 28 (Dec) (claimant chose to retain property and sue for damages valued at date of acquisition, not taking into account later increase in value: "I do not see why in justice the Defendants should be entitled to claim or seek credit for any increase in the value of the Shares arising over the period that they concealed their fraud and harassed and delayed the Claimants when seeking to enforce their rights in the courts and to salvage their investment": at [29] (Lightman J.)).

[158] *Smith New Court*, above, n.144 at 266, 285; *Standard Chartered Bank v Pakistan National Shipping Corp.* [2001] EWCA Civ 55, [2001] 1 All E.R. (Comm) 822; *SX Holdings Ltd v Synchronet Ltd* [2001] C.P. Rep. 43, CA (arguable that claimant which had allowed defendant to take over control of a company's business pending completion of contract for sale of 51% shareholding became locked into transaction and it was reasonable to continue to press for completion rather than to seek to take back control); *Banks v Cox* [2002] EWHC 2166 (Ch), [2002] All E.R. (D) 376 (Oct) (claimants locked into loss-making business by their own and the defendants' financial position); *4 Eng Ltd v Harper* [2008] EWHC 915 (Ch), [2009] Ch. 91 at [55] (loss flowing from investment in company which had gone into administration continued until trial because administration prevented claimant from recovering funds on discovery of fraud); *Parabola Investments Ltd v Browallia Cal Ltd*, above, n.156 (loss of use of funds continued after fraud discovered).

New Court[159] Smith was induced by a fraudulent misrepresentation made by the vendor to purchase shares in a company on which it was later discovered that a major fraud had (before Smith's purchase of the shares) been committed. This resulted in a catastrophic reduction in the market value of the shares, and Smith made a significant loss on its later sale of the shares. Although the vendor's fraudulent misrepresentation was not about a fact which had any bearing on the reason for the later reduction in the value of the shares in the company,[160] Smith was held entitled to recover from the representor the whole of its loss: the causative influence of the fraud was not significantly attenuated or diluted by other causative factors acting simultaneously with or subsequent to the fraud.[161] And Smith was locked into the transaction because of the circumstances in which it bought them: the whole loss therefore

---

This is, in substance, applying the normal rules of mitigation and causation in assessing the recoverable loss. For a break in causation by a representee's decision not to crystallise the loss by selling a business bought in consequence of a fraudulent misrepresentation, see *Downs v Chappell* above, n.154 at 437 (overruled on another point by *Smith New Court*: above, n.154). If, by the time the representee realises the property or (without realising it) brings a claim for damages, its value has recovered, the rise in value ought to reduce the representee's recoverable loss. Where a strict market value test is applied, there might in some areas of the law be an argument, based on the principle *res inter alios acta*, that the claimant's ability to reduce his own loss ought not to reduce the damages paid by the defendant for his wrong, e.g. where a purchaser achieves a sub-sale of defective goods: *Slater v Hoyle and Smith* [1920] 2 K.B. 11, CA; Chitty, para.26–117. But the principle applied in deceit is the broader test of ascertaining the representee's loss: *Smith New Court*, above, n.144 at 284 (Lord Steyn); *cf. South Australia Asset Management Corp. v York Montague*, above, n.154 at 217–218 (Lord Hoffmann: rise in property market can reduce or remove completely the claimant's loss where the claim is based on careless valuation of property).

[159] Above, n.144.

[160] The representor (an employee of the vendor, who was also a director of the vendor's brokers) told Smith that it was bidding against two other parties who were interested in purchasing the shares: this was false, and it caused Smith to bid higher than it might otherwise have done. But the catastrophic fall in the value of the shares was caused by internal fraud in the company, of which neither the representor nor Smith knew: "Unknown to everybody, on that date [the sale to Smith], the shares were already pregnant with disaster": [1997] A.C. 254 at 267 (Lord Browne-Wilkinson).

[161] Below, para.5–38.

flowed from Smith's acquisition consequent upon the misrepresentation, and not from its decision to retain the shares.[162] On these facts the effect of this was to place on the vendor the whole risk of the particular loss which was suffered.[163] But the result highlights the fact that the purpose of damages in deceit is not simply to remedy the representee's loss which flows from the statement being false: as has already been made clear, it remedies the loss which flows from the reliance on the statement—here, entering into a share purchase contract which turned out (even for quite other reasons) to be inherently a loss-making contract.

Causation. The normal principles of causation apply in deceit, **5–38**
and so it must be shown that there is a sufficient continuing causal link between the misrepresentation and the loss which the representee claims to have suffered as a result of his reliance on it. This will be a question of fact; judges ask such questions as whether the representation was a substantial factor in producing the result, or whether in common sense terms there is a sufficient causal connection.[164]

---

[162] The purchase by Smith was of over 28 million shares in the company, bought not as a "bought deal"(in which it would normally have sold the shares on to its institutional clients shortly thereafter), but as a "market making risk" (with a view to holding them and only selling them as and when the opportunity might arise): see [1997] A.C. 254 at 268, 272, 285. Where the claimant is not locked in but simply takes some time to discover the misrepresented facts, and the decrease in value is in consequence delayed, the claim is still good: *Twycross v Grant* (1877) 2 C.P.D. 469 at 544–545, approved by Lord Steyn in *Smith New Court*, above, n.144 at 279; *Naughton v O'Callaghan* [1990] 3 All E.R. 191 (assessment of damages under the Misrepresentation Act 1967 s.2(1)).

[163] It should be noted that where the representee rescinds a contract induced by misrepresentation the effect can be similar: here, if rescission had been available Smith could have obtained the return of the purchase price, on returning the shares (and the reduction in the value of the shares would not be a bar to rescission, particularly in a case of fraudulent misrepresentation: above, paras 4–55 and 4–56). However, rescission was not pursued in this case because the shares had been disposed of (on which, however, see Lord Browne-Wilkinson [1997] A.C. 254 at 262; above, para.4–56, n.236).

[164] *Smith New Court*, above, n.144 at 284–285 (Lord Steyn: this the correct approach, although it "hardly amounts to an intellectually satisfying theory of causation"); *Chester v Afshar* [2004] UKHL 41, [2005] 1 A.C. 134 at [83] (Lord Hope: "An appeal to common sense when determining issues of causation is valuable in the right context . . . On its own common sense, and without more guidance, is no more reliable as a guide to the right answer in this case than an

The courts have drawn a distinction between the test for causation in relation to the claimant's reliance on the misrepresentation, and the test for causation in relation to the loss he suffers in consequence of that reliance. Even if it the evidence shows that the claimant would still have entered into the contract if the misrepresentation had not been made, it is possible to hold that he did in fact rely upon it as long as it was present to his mind and acting as one of the factors he took into account in making his decision to enter the contract.[165] However, the fact that the claimant might have acted differently had he not been induced by the misrepresentation is relevant to question of whether his loss was caused by the misrepresentation.[166]

5–39 **Lost potential profits.** When a court assesses loss for the purposes of a claim in deceit, it compares the representee's actual

appeal to the views of the traveller on the London Underground"). See also *Barings Plc (In Liquidation) v Coopers & Lybrand (No.2)* [2002] B.C.L.C. 410 at [124]–[148], applying to deceit the test in *Galoo Ltd v Bright Grahame Murray* [1994] 1 W.L.R. 1360, CA, below, para.6–54: "There are respects in which the rules as to causation and remoteness in deceit differ from those in negligence, but the basic appeal to common sense and the distinction between cause and occasion of the loss apply to both" (Evans-Lombe J., at 136). On causation in tort generally, see Clerk & Lindsell, Ch.2; Winfield & Jolowicz, paras 6–2 to 6–15. In *Smith New Court, ibid.*, Lord Steyn suggested that a *subsequent* fraud, resulting in the fall in the share price, would have broken the causative influence of the representor's fraud; *Twycross v Grant*, above, n.162 at 544–545 (Cockburn C.J.: horse catches disease after purchase: not taken into account; contrasted with latent disease inherent in the horse's system at time of purchase). *Cf. St Paul Travelers Insurance Co. Ltd v Okporuah* [2006] EWHC 2107 (Ch), [2006] All E.R. (D) 58 (Aug) at [57] (fraud practised by joint tortfeasors in obtaining money from bank; no break in chain of causation when one tortfeasor by later dishonest act misappropriated the money).

165 Above, para.5–23.

166 *UCB Corporate Services Ltd v Williams* [2002] EWCA Civ 555, [2002] 3 F.C.R. 448 at [89] (Jonathan Parker L.J, relying on *Downs v Chappell*, above, n.154). This has the curious consequence that a claimant may be able to rescind the contract for a fraudulent misrepresentation (see above, paras 3–54, 4–34), even though he cannot show that the loss he suffered from entering into the contract was caused by the misrepresentation for the purposes of a claim in the tort of deceit. *Cf. Cassa di Risparmio della Repubblica di San Marino S.p.A. v Barclays Bank Ltd* [2011] EWHC 484 (Comm), [2011] All E.R. (D) 189 (Mar) at [233] (where Hamblen J. declined to resolve the defendant's argument that a fraudulent representation must cause a loss to create a cause of action and to do so it must cause the entry into the contract from which the loss is said to arise).

financial position with the position in which he would have been if the representation had not been made. If the representee has been induced by the fraud to purchase an asset which has made him a loss, that loss is recoverable. But he may also in an appropriate case be able to argue that, as a result of entering into the transaction, he has lost the opportunity to make profits in the mean time. In an action of deceit[167] a representee cannot recover damages based on the profits that he would have made if the representation had been true: that is the normal measure of damages in contract, not tort.[168] But he can be heard to say that his financial position at the time of assessment is reduced by virtue of the fact that, had he not been misled by the representation, he would in the meantime have used his money, time and energy to make other profits: he pleads (and must prove) the hypothetical profitable business in which he would have engaged but for the deceit.[169] However, although the actionable head of loss must be proved on the balance of

---

[167] Similarly in a claim of negligence: below, para.6–58.

[168] Above, paras 2–08 and 2–09.

[169] *East v Maurer* [1991] 1 W.L.R. 461, CA (purchaser of unprofitable hairdressing business entitled to damages in deceit to include profits which the representee herself might have expected to make in another hairdressing business bought for a similar sum: profits of the actual business relevant only as evidence of what the profits of the hypothetical business might have been), approved in *Smith New Court*, above, n.144 at 282 (Lord Steyn); *4 Eng Ltd v Harper* [2008] EWHC 915 (Ch), [2009] Ch. 91; *Parabola Investments Ltd v Browallia Cal Ltd* [2010] EWCA Civ 486, [2011] Q.B. 477 (lost profits may include claim for period after fraud discovered); *Clef Aquitaine S.A.R.L. v Laporte Materials (Barrow) Ltd* [2001] Q.B. 488, CA (claimant induced by misrepresentation to enter into profitable contract, but could claim damages based on the different and *more* profitable transaction into which it would have entered but for the fraud). For criticism, see J. Poole and J. Devenney, "Reforming Damages for Misrepresentation" [2007] J.B.L. 269. An award of interest under the Senior Courts Act 1981 s.35A, for the period from the accrual of the cause of action will enable the claimant to be protected to some degree against the loss of use of his capital, but if he can prove a greater actual loss than the court might award as interest he will seek to do so: *Parabola Investments Ltd v Browallia Cal Ltd*, above, at [55], relying on, inter alia, *Sempra Metals Ltd v Inland Revenue Commissioners* [2007] UKHL 34, [2008] A.C. 561. However, only simple interest is normally awarded: compound interest may be awarded where money has been obtained and retained by fraud, but not where the claim is only for damages for loss caused by reliance on the fraudulent misrepresentation: *Black v Davies* [2005] EWCA Civ 531, [2005] All E.R. (D) 78 (May) at [87], explaining *President of India v La Pintada Compania Navigacion S.A.* [1985] A.C. 104 (HL) and *Westdeutsche Landesbank Girozentrale v Islington LBC* [1996] A.C. 669

probability, the quantification of the loss may involve a different exercise, in which the court estimates the loss by making the best attempt it can to eveluate the chances, great or small (unless those chances amount to no more than remote speculation), taking all significant factors into account.[170]

5–40 **Remoteness of damage.** In deceit the representee recovers all the losses (calculated on the principles described in this section) which flowed directly from his reliance on the fraudulent misrepresentation. Although in many other torts a defendant's liability is limited to those losses which he could reasonably have foreseen at the time of committing the tort,[171] there is no such limitation in deceit. This wider rule, which appears to apply generally to torts of intention, was justified by Lord Denning M.R.[172]:

> "The defendant is bound to make reparation for all the actual damage directly flowing from the fraudulent inducement. The person who has been defrauded is entitled to say: 'I would not have entered into this bargain at all but for your representation. Owing to your fraud, I have not only lost all the money I paid you, but, what is more, I have been put to a large amount of extra expense as well and suffered this or that extra damages.' All such damages can be recovered: and it does not lie in the mouth of the fraudulent person to say that they could not reasonably have been foreseen."

(HL). On the award of interest generally, see S. Sime and D. French (eds), *Blackstone's Civil Practice 2011*, Ch.62.

170 *Parabola Investments Ltd v Browallia Cal Ltd*, above, n.169 at [23] (Toulson L.J.); see also *4 Eng Ltd v Harper*, above, n.169 at [44].

171 For negligence, see below, para.6–56. For remoteness of damage in tort generally, see Clerk & Lindsell, paras 2–133 to 2–178; Winfield & Jolowicz, paras 6–16 to 6–41; J. Cartwright, "Remoteness of Damage in Contract and Tort: a Reconsideration" [1996] C.L.J. 488.

172 *Doyle v Olby (Ironmongers) Ltd* [1969] 2 Q.B. 158, CA, at 167, noted at (1969) 32 M.L.R. 556 (Treitel). Although Lord Mustill in *Smith New Court*, above, n.144 at 269 thought that the *ex tempore* judgments in *Doyle v Olby* should not generally be relied on ("there are instances when more is required in the way of analysis"), and for the future *Smith New Court* itself should be used as the source of authority, it is clear that, as regards the test for remoteness of damage in deceit, *Doyle v Olby* was approved by the House of Lords: see *Smith New Court* at 266–267, 282. See also *Kuwait Airways Corp. v Iraqi Airways Co. (Nos 4 and 5)* [2002] UKHL 19, [2002] 2 A.C. 883 at [101] ("The more culpable the defendant the wider the area of loss of which he can fairly be held responsible": Lord Nicholls of Birkenhead, referring to the discussion by Lord Steyn in *Smith New Court* at 279–285).

Mitigation. The normal rules of mitigation apply. The representee will therefore be unable to recover from the representor any part of his loss which the representor can prove[173] that the representee would not have suffered if he had taken such steps as he ought reasonably to have taken in order to avoid or reduce his loss.[174] However, in the case of deceit, there is no duty to mitigate until the representee has discovered the fraud: until he has this knowledge it is not reasonable to expect him to take steps to reduce the loss he has suffered.[175] The standard of "reasonable behaviour" expected of a representee by way of mitigation of his loss in a deceit action is no different from that expected of the claimant in any other action in tort or breach of contract, although the application of the rule will depend on the particular circumstances in which the representee finds himself placed as a result of the fraud.[176] 5–41

Exemplary damages.[177] In principle exemplary damages can be awarded in an action of deceit, although such an award is 5–42

[173] The burden lies on the representor to show not only that the representee failed in some respect to act reasonably, but also that his failure did in fact lead to an element in his loss which he could have avoided had reasonable steps been taken: *Standard Chartered Bank v Pakistan National Shipping Corp.* [2001] EWCA Civ 55, [2001] 1 All E.R. (Comm) 822 at [38]–[39].

[174] *Smith New Court*, above, n.144 at 285. For mitigation generally in tort, see Clerk & Lindsell, paras 28–08 to 28–11. Causation and mitigation are two sides of the same coin: if damage has been caused or exacerbated by the claimant's unreasonable conduct or inaction, then to that extent it has not been caused by the defendant's tort or breach of contract: *Standard Chartered Bank v Pakistan National Shipping Corp.*, above, n.173 at [41]; *The Elena D'Amico* [1980] 1 Lloyd's Rep. 75 at 88.

[175] *Smith New Court*, above, n.144 at 266.

[176] *Standard Chartered Bank v Pakistan National Shipping Corp. (Assessment of Damages)* [1999] 1 Lloyd's Rep. 747 at 759–760 (Toulson J.), rejecting the suggestion by McLachlin J. in *Canson Enterprises Ltd v Boughton & Co.* (1991) 85 D.L.R. (4th) 129, SCC, at 161–162 that, in cases of deceit and breach of fiduciary, a claimant "will not be required to act in as reasonable and prudent a manner as might be required in negligence or contract"; *Invertec Ltd v De Mol Holding B.V.* [2009] EWHC 2471 (Ch), [2009] All E.R. (D) 120 (Oct) at [383]–[385] (Arnold J.: contract for purchase of company share capital induced by fraudulent mispresentations: purchaser not locked in but could have rescinded the contract or allowed the company to go into administration or liquidation; the "decision to keep [the company] trading was not a reasonable attempt at mitigation, but a commercial gamble").

[177] For exemplary damages in tort generally, see Clerk & Lindsell, paras 28–137 to 28–151; Winfield & Jolowicz, paras 22–9 to 22–12; McGregor, Ch.11; A.

exceptional. The purpose of exemplary damages is to punish the defendant,[178] an award over and above the normal award of damages whose purpose is to compensate the claimant for his loss. In recent years there had been some doubt whether an award of exemplary damages was restricted to certain particular causes of action—in effect, to a limited range of torts[179]; and given that there had been no case in which exemplary damages had been awarded in deceit there was doubt about whether this tort fell within those torts in respect of which such an award could be made.[180] However, the House of Lords has held that there is no such restriction,[181] and so an award of exemplary damages may be made in a claim in deceit if

---

Burrows, *Remedies for Torts and Breach of Contract* (3rd edn, 2004), pp.410–429. The Law Commission proposed reform in Law Com. No.247, *Aggravated, Exemplary and Restitutionary Damages* (1997), but the Government decided not to take forward the Law Commission's proposals for legislation on exemplary damages, suggesting that "it may be that some further judicial development of the law in this area might help clarify the issues": *Hansard*, HC Vol.337, col.502 (November 9, 1999). In *Kuddus v Chief Constable of Leicestershire Constabulary* [2001] UKHL 29, [2002] 2 A.C. 122, the House of Lords was divided on the merits of the use of exemplary damages in tort.

[178] *Rookes v Barnard* [1964] A.C. 1129, HL, at 1221, 1227–1228. *Aggravated damages* are, by contrast, designed to compensate the claimant for the aggravated suffering and injury which are caused by the particular manner in which the defendant has committed the tort (*ibid.*, at 1221) and can be awarded in deceit, e.g. to compensate the representee for his injured feelings: *Archer v Brown* [1985] 1 Q.B. 401 at 426; below, para.5–44.

[179] The question turned on whether the House of Lords in *Cassell & Co. Ltd v Broome* [1972] A.C. 1027 could be taken to have decided that its earlier decision in *Rookes v Barnard*, above, n.178, was based on the assumption that exemplary damages were restricted to those causes of action in respect of which there was already authority for such an award. The CA in *A.B. v South West Water Services Ltd* [1993] Q.B. 507, CA (public nuisance) had taken the view that there was such a restriction.

[180] For: *Mafo v Adams* [1970] 1 Q.B. 548, CA, at 558–559 (Widgery L.J., but accepting that such an award will be rare). Against: *ibid.*, at 554–555 (Sachs L.J. The third judge in the case, Plowman J., simply agreed with the order proposed by Sachs and Widgery L.JJ., without commenting on the issue of exemplary damages: at 559); *Cassell & Co. Ltd v Broome* [1972] A.C. 1027, HL, at 1076, 1080 (Lord Hailsham L.C.), 1131 (Lord Diplock); *Metall und Rohstoff A.G. v ACLI Metals (London)* [1984] 1 Lloyd's Rep. 598, CA, at 612 (Purchas L.J.). In *Archer v Brown* [1985] 1 Q.B. 401, Peter Pain J. reviewed the authorities, and concluded at 423 that "the door . . . is open" but decided that it was "unnecessary . . . to decide whether to plunge through it" because on the facts no award of exemplary damages was appropriate.

[181] *Kuddus v Chief Constable of Leicestershire Constabulary*, above, n.177.

the case fulfils the general requirements for such an award.[182] Exemplary damages may be awarded in two categories of case: where there has been oppressive, arbitrary or unconstitutional action by the servants of the government; and where the defendant's conduct was calculated by him to make a profit for himself which may well exceed the compensation payable to the claimant.[183] It is perhaps natural that the courts should have contemplated the possibility of an award of exemplary damages in deceit: there are other rules within deceit which, by comparison with other torts, impose a heavier liability on the representor for the very reason that he was fraudulent.[184] However, it should be remembered that most deceits are punishable by the criminal law and so it will generally be better to leave punishment to the criminal process.[185]

Restitution of profits made through deceit. It has been said that a claimant may obtain restitution of benefits gained from committing the tort of deceit,[186] although this is not well attested by 5–43

[182] *Banks v Cox* [2002] EWHC 2166 (Ch), [2002] All E.R. (D) 376 (Oct) at [13] (Lawrence Collins J.). See *Parabola Investments Ltd v Browallia Cal Ltd* [2009] EWHC 901 (Comm), [2009] 2 All E.R. (Comm) 589 at [205] (Flaux J.: "as my own researches and enquiries have revealed, exemplary damages have been awarded in cases of deceit, primarily in the case of fraudulent insurance claims by insureds dealt with in the county courts").

[183] *Rookes v Barnard*, above, n.178 at 1226 (Lord Devlin). In *Kuddus v Chief Constable of Leicestershire Constabulary* the House of Lords was not asked to rule on whether the categories set out by Lord Devlin should be further developed, although Lord Nicholls at [67] thought that, in addition to the profit motive on the part of the defendant, a malicious motive ought also to be sufficient to make an award of exemplary damages available.

[184] Above, paras 5–08, 5–29 and 5–40.

[185] *Archer v Brown*, above, n.178 at 425. Although exemplary damages are in principle available in deceit, it would be inappropriate to make such an award where the representee has already been punished: *ibid.*, at 423. See also *Parabola Investments Ltd v Browallia Cal Ltd*, above, n.182, at [206] (Flaux J.: "I do have serious doubts as to the appropriateness of an award of exemplary damages against a defendant, even in a case of fraud, where the basis for that defendant's liability is vicarious liability", following doubts expressed in *Kuddus v Chief Constable of Leicestershire Constabulary*, above, n.177 at [47] (Lord Mackay) and [126]–[137] (Lord Scott)).

[186] Goff & Jones, para.36–005; *Murad v Al-Saraj* [2004] EWHC 1235, [2004] All E.R. (D) 463 (May) at [342] (Etherton J.).

the authorities.[187] What can certainly be said is that any claim for disgorgement of the defendant's profits, as such, is not a claim in the tort of deceit, but must be based on some other cause of action. In *Murad v Al-Saraj*[188] the defendant was made to account to the other parties to a property joint venture for profits he made in circumstances where he induced the other parties to participate with him by fraudulently misrepresenting the price for which the property was to be bought, and the nature and scale of his own contribution. The trial judge[189] held that the parties were in a fiduciary relationship, and the defendant was liable to account for breach of his fiduciary duty; but also said[190] that the claimants were entitled to an account of the profit "by reason of Mr Al-Saraj's actionable deceit". However, in the Court of Appeal it was made clear that the basis of the award was the breach of fiduciary duty[191]:

---

[187] Goff & Jones, above, n.186, rely on two cases from the early 19th century, in both of which the defendant was held liable to pay for goods which he had received following a fraudulent sale (induced by the defendant) to an accomplice who had not himself paid for them: *Hill v Perrott* (1810) 3 Taunt. 274, 128 E.R. 109; *Abbotts v Barry* (1820) 2 Brod. & B. 369, 129 E.R. 1009; discussed by G. Virgo, *Principles of the Law of Restitution* (2nd edn, 2006), pp.473–474. Other writers assert that the claimant *ought* to be able to elect to claim restitution of the defendant's profits, rather than damages in the tort of deceit: see J. Edelman, *Gain-Based Damages* (2004), pp.141–143, noting that the authorities support claims for restitution for broader "fraudulent" conduct, such as bribes, but that there is little English authority on the tort of deceit itself; Virgo, above, p.475. Burrows, *The Law of Restitution* (3rd edn, 2010), pp.659–662, is cautious in balancing the arguments for and against a general claim for restitution for torts, and at p.657 cites *Halifax Building Society v Thomas* [1996] Ch. 217 as casting doubt on whether restitution is available for the tort of deceit.

[188] [2005] EWCA Civ 959, [2005] W.T.L.R. 1573.

[189] Above, n.186, at [324] *et seq*.

[190] *ibid*., at [347].

[191] Above, n.186, at [46] (Arden L.J.). The fraud was relevant, however, in the calculation of the profits for which the defendant could be made to account. Although the equitable remedy to account does not depend on fraud or lack of good faith, the existence of a fraudulent intent is relevant to the question of the allowances to be made on taking the account: *ibid*., at [68], [84]. See also *Renault UK Ltd v Fleetpro Technical Services Ltd* [2007] EWHC 2541 (QB), [2007] All E.R. (D) 208 (Nov) at [152]–[157] (Judge Seymour Q.C., noting a different observation by Clarke L.J. in *Murad v Al-Saraj* at [164], but preferring the interpretation, based on Arden L.J.'s judgment, that the remedy of account is not available in the case of a claim based on fraudulent misrepresentation, but only on the basis of a fiduciary relationship); and *cf.* (in claim not in deceit but for account of profits in case of an unlawful cartel) *Devenish Nutrition Ltd v*

> "It would be tempting to jump to the conclusion from paragraph 347 of the judge's judgment . . . that in this case the judge took the novel step of awarding the equitable remedy of account for the common law tort of deceit (*cf. Attorney-General v Blake*[192]), but that is not in my judgment the true interpretation of the judge's judgment. The judge gave a remedy of account because there was a fiduciary relationship. For wrongs in the context of such a relationship, an order for an account of profits is a conventional remedy. The Murads considered that that remedy would be more beneficial to them because, if they were awarded damages at common law, they would simply be entitled to recover the difference between the profit share to which they agreed and that which they would have negotiated if the true position had been disclosed to them."

Damages for intangible losses. The losses which may be claimed by the representee in an action of deceit extends to intangible losses. Awards of damages in deceit have included sums to compensate a representee for the physical inconvenience and unpleasantness consequent on the way in which he and his family were by fraud deprived of their home[193]; for being "very deeply upset" when he lost a substantial sum and became unemployed after relying on a statement which had led him wrongly to believe that he would acquire a significant shareholding in a company and become a director[194]; and for the mental and physical suffering of a representee who lost money and her furniture after relying on a statement that she would acquire title to property abroad, and who discovered the fraud when she arrived to take possession of the 5–44

Sanofi-Aventis S.A. [2008] EWCA Civ 1086, [2009] Ch. 390 at [2], [4] (Arden L.J.: CA is precluded by decision in *Stoke-on-Trent CC v W. & J.Wass Ltd* [1988] 1 W.L.R. 1406, CA, from awarding account of profits in tort except where claimant entitled to property or a property right is entitled to sue for interference in the exceptional circumstances discussed by Lord Nicholls in *Attorney General v Blake* [2001] A.C. 268; Tuckey L.J. agreed at [156], but this limitation was rejected by Longmore L.J. at [145]).

[192] [2001] 1 A.C. 268, HL [below, para.8–32, n.153].

[193] *Mafo vAdams*, above, n.180 (£100, including aggravated damages: at 558).

[194] *Archer v Brown*, above, n.178 at 413–414: there was no evidence that he was actually ill, but "he lived through a nightmare and was deeply affected by it". The sum awarded under this head should be "moderate" (see Peter Pain J. at 426: aggravated damages of £500 awarded). See also *Kinch v Rosling* [2009] EWHC 286 (QB), [2009] All E.R. (D) 54 (Mar) at [18]–[19] (£10,000 as general damages for humiliation, distress and anxiety suffered by successful businessman who became bankrupt following deceit).

property.[195] Such losses are of course difficult to quantify. The authorities are unanimous that damages for inconvenience and disappointment can properly be awarded in an action of deceit, but the award should be moderate.[196] It should not, however, be regarded as simply a conventional award, but should bear some relation to the particular circumstances of the case.[197]

5–45 **Contribution between co-defendants.** Where a representee is liable in deceit jointly or severally with another defendant for damage suffered by the claimant—whether the co-defendant's liability is also in deceit, or is based on some other cause of action such as negligence or breach of contract—the court will, as in all cases of joint or several liability, have jurisdiction under the Civil Liability (Contribution) Act 1978 to apportion between the co-defendants the damages payable.[198]

V. ALLEGING AND PROVING FRAUD

5–46 **Burden of proof: the civil standard.** An action in the tort of deceit is a civil action, and therefore the normal rules of civil law actions apply for the standard of proof: the elements of the tort must be proved on the balance of probabilities.[199] But it is necessary to separate out the different elements of the tort, to see how a court will approach the question of proof. As regards the questions whether the alleged statement was made, whether it was objectively false,[200] and what loss the representee has proved he has in fact

---

195 *Shelley v Paddock* [1979] Q.B. 120; affirmed [1980] Q.B. 348, CA: there was no medical evidence, but the judge awarded damages by analogy with damages for loss of reputation in libel (£500 awarded under this head). On this analogy, see also *Saunders v Edwards* [1987] 1 W.L.R. 1116 at 1135.

196 *Saunders v Edwards*, above, n.195 at 1128; and see the cases cited above, nn.193, 194 and 195.

197 *ibid.* (Kerr L.J.: "There is no reason, for instance, why the same sum should be awarded for a spoiled holiday as for the disappointment, as here, of a couple buying a particular flat when getting married and then having a baby, in reliance on having a roof terrace of which they were fraudulently deprived": in such a case a sum higher than the £500 awarded by the judge would have been appropriate).

198 Above, para.2–14.

199 And not on the criminal standard, which requires proof "beyond reasonable doubt": Phipson, para.6.09.

200 Above, para.5–09.

suffered, the courts will treat the issue in the same manner as if they were considering other civil law remedies for the same, alleged statement—indeed, it will often be the case that a representee brings a claim under more than one head, and it would be unacceptable for a judge to say, for example, that he found that the statement was made for the purposes of one remedy, but not for the purposes of another.[201] And it has already been seen that, as regards the question whether the representee relied on the statement, the courts will readily infer reliance if the statement was one which, objectively, was likely to be relied on by a person in the representee's position.[202] Again, this is a test which is applied not only in deceit; and it would be equally unacceptable for a judge to hold that the representee relied on the representation when seeking rescission, but did not rely on it when claiming damages in deceit.[203] However, when it comes to the question which is at the heart of the claim in deceit—the fraudulent state of mind of the representor—the courts take a more cautious approach. There is no doubt that the burden of proof of the defendant's fraud lies on the claimant.[204] Again, the question of whether the representor's fraud is proved is tested by reference to the single civil standard of proof on the simple balance of probability; but in applying this test the courts take into account the consideration that the more serious the allegation is, the greater the proof needed to persuade a court that it can be satisfied that the allegation is established: the very gravity of an allegation of fraud is a circumstance which has to be weighed in the scale in deciding as to the balance of probabilities.[205] In an appropriate case, however, it is possible for the court to infer fraud on the basis of the evidence.[206]

---

201 *Hornal v Neuberger Products Ltd* [1957] 1 Q.B. 247, CA, at 258, 266. Statements in the judgments in this case appear not to keep sufficiently separate the questions of proof of the different elements of the tort.

202 Above, para.5–25.

203 For the similar inference of reliance in rescission, see above, para.4–33.

204 *Derry v Peek* (1889) 14 App. Cas. 337, HL, at 374; *Glasier v Rolls* (1889) 42 Ch.D. 436, CA, at 458.

205 *Smith New Court Securities Ltd v Scrimgeour Vickers (Asset Management) Ltd* [1997] A.C. 254, HL, at 274 (Lord Steyn), following the approach in *Re H (Minors) (Sexual Abuse: Standard of Proof)* [1996] A.C. 563, HL, at 586–587; *Hornal v Neuberger Products Ltd*, above, n.201 at 258, 263–264, 266, applying in the context of deceit the approach of Denning L.J. in *Bater v Bater* [1951] P. 35, CA, at 37 (proof of cruelty in divorce proceedings); *LPMG Ltd v Stapleford Commercials Ltd* [2006] EWHC 3753 (Ch), [2006] All E.R. (D) 196 (Jul) at [86]

It is possible for a representor to be held liable in deceit yet acquitted of a related *criminal* charge because the proof of his fraud is insufficient for the criminal law. But a criminal conviction, based on facts which are necessary to establish the civil claim, is admissible evidence of those facts in the civil action.[207]

5–47 **The claim.** The practice and procedure of actions based on misrepresentation are considered in detail in Chapter 11. But it should be noted here that in a claim of deceit it is particularly important that the allegation of fraud be clearly made: the defendant must know that this case is made against him, and the basis of fact on which it is alleged, in order to be able to mount his defence

---

(where serious allegation of dishonesty is made, court will start from basis that it is inherently improbable that such an act had occurred: cogent evidence required to persuade the court that fraud had in fact taken place). For more recent emphasis by HL (explaining *Re H (Minors)*, above) that there is only one civil standard of proof, on the balance of probability, see *Re B (Children) (Care Proceedings: Standard of Proof)* [2008] UKHL 35, [2009] 1 AC 11 at [13] (Lord Hoffmann), [62] (Baroness Hale), applied to deceit in *Dadourian Group International Inc. v Simms* [2009] EWCA Civ 169, [2009] 1 Lloyd's Rep. 601 at [32]. *Cf. Ahmed v Addy* [2004] EWHC 1465 (QB), [2004] All E.R. (D) 308 (Jun) where Mackay J., purporting to rely on *Hornal v Neuberger Products Ltd*, said at [3]: "Because of the nature of these allegations, involving as they do not an isolated fraudulent representation but a sustained campaign of deceit and forgery, I ought not to find in favour of the Claimant unless I am satisfied to the criminal standard that his claim is proved". In a claim for exemplary damages (see above, para.5–42) the court may require particularly strong evidence before making an award: it has been said that the courts must be careful to see that the case for punishment is as well established as in other penal proceedings: *Mafo v Adams* [1970] 1 Q.B. 548, CA, at 556.

206 *Connolly Ltd v Bellway Homes Ltd* [2007] EWHC 895 (Ch), [2007] All E.R. (D) 182 (Apr) at [131], [137] (Stephen Smith Q.C.) (figure given as estimate was "so far wide of the mark" that the court could infer dishonesty or deceit; "beyond the bounds of any genuine estimate of the average achievable sale price based on the enquiries he had made and the advice he had received").

207 Civil Evidence Act 1968, s.11; *Alliance & Leicester Building Society v Edgestop Ltd* [1993] 1 W.L.R. 1462 at 1478 (conviction for procuring the execution of a valuable security by deception under the Theft Act 1968, s.20(2), which was repealed and replaced by Fraud Act 2006). Note, however, that the new general offence of fraud under the Fraud Act 2006 s.1 focuses on the defendant's dishonesty and does not require proof that the victim of the fraud was deceived: above, para.5–25, n.107. The offence of obtaining services dishonestly under Fraud Act 2006 s.11 does, however, require the dishonesty to have achieved its object.

properly.[208] An amendment alleging fraud will be allowed in an appellate court only if the defendant has had the opportunity of defending himself, not only by the arguments of his counsel on appeal, but by giving evidence in his own defence specially directed to the charge made in the amendment.[209]

Method of trial. Although civil claims are normally now tried by judge alone,[210] where fraud is alleged[211] a party to an action to be heard in the Queen's Bench Division[212] or a county court may apply for the action to be tried by jury: and in such circumstances there will be a jury trial unless the court is of opinion that the trial requires any prolonged examination of documents or accounts or any scientific or local investigation which cannot conveniently be made with a jury.[213] In effect, therefore, there is a presumption of a jury trial in claims in the tort of deceit.[214] **5–48**

Costs in an action alleging fraud. A claim of fraud will generally substantially increase the complexity of an action, and **5–49**

---

[208] Below, para.11–07.
[209] *Bradford Third Equitable Benefit Building Society v Borders* [1941] 2 All E.R. 205, HL, at 218–219. For amendments to the statement of case, see below, para.11–10.
[210] There is a power for a court to order trial by jury in civil cases in either the Queen's Bench Division of the High Court (Senior Courts Act 1981, s.69(3)) or a county court (County Courts Act 1984, s.66(2)), but it is not normally exercised: *H v Ministry of Defence* [1991] 2 Q.B. 103, CA.
[211] "Fraud" here means actionable deceit and is not a more general reference to dishonesty: *Barclays Bank Ltd v Cole* [1967] 2 Q.B. 738, CA (on the similar wording of the Administration of Justice (Miscellaneous Provisions) Act 1933, s.6(1)(a)); *Grant v Travellers Cheque Associates Ltd, The Times*, April 19, 1995, CA (County Courts Act 1984, s.66).
[212] If the action is brought in another Division the defendant has no right to demand trial by jury, nor to require the action to be transferred to the Queen's Bench Division merely on the ground that he wants trial by jury. But the court may exercise its discretion under CPR, Pt 30, r.30.5 to order transfer to the Queen's Bench Division if it thinks the case suitable for trial by jury and if transfer will give effect to the overriding objective under CPR, Pt 1, r.1.1, of enabling the court to deal with the case justly: *Stafford Winfield Cook & Partners Ltd v Winfield* [1981] 1 W.L.R. 458 (a decision under the old RSC, Ord.4, r.3, applying a test of whether the case is "of a nature such that the interests of justice require the transfer to be made").
[213] Senior Courts Act 1981, s.69(1); County Courts Act 1984, s.66(3).
[214] Queen's Bench Guide 2007, para.9.3.1 (Jury list).

consequently its cost. Before the introduction of the Civil Procedure Rules it was established that if a representee alleged fraud but failed to establish it, those additional costs of the action would normally fall on him, even if he succeeded in his claim for damages on other grounds.[215] And if the judge was satisfied that the representee could have recovered substantially the same sum as he was awarded in the action by a significantly less expensive method, such as commercial arbitration, he might order the representee to bear the whole of the costs of the action.[216] However, under the Civil Procedure Rules there is no provision for a special rule in cases where fraud claims are successfully defended, and the court must exercise its discretion within the terms set out in the Rules[217] which form a complete code as to the principles upon which costs are to be awarded.[218]

---

[215] *Bellotti v Chequers Developments Ltd* [1936] 1 All E.R. 89; *Anderson v Thornton* (1853) 8 Exch. 425, 155 E.R. 1415; *Forester v Read* (1870) L.R. 6 Ch. App. 40; *Parker v McKenna* (1874) 10 Ch. App. 96. A barrister who drafts an allegation of fraud without having material of such a character as to lead responsible counsel to conclude that serious allegations could be based upon it may be personally liable for wasted costs: *Medcalf v Mardell* [2002] UKHL 27, [2003] 1 A.C. 120; below, para.11–07, n.36.

[216] *Jurgensen v F.E. Hookway & Co. Ltd* [1951] 2 Lloyd's Rep. 129 at 148–149.

[217] Under CPR, Pt 44, r.44.3 and r.44.5 the starting-point is that the unsuccessful party will be ordered to pay the costs of the successful party, but the court has a discretion to make a different order (r.44.3(2)); and in exercising its discretion the court takes into account, inter alia, the parties' conduct before and during the proceedings, and whether it was reasonable for a party to raise or pursue a particular allegation (r.44.3(5), 44.5(3)). On the general approach to costs under the CPR, by comparison with the old earlier practice, see I. Grainger and M. Fealy, *The Civil Procedure Rules in Action* (2nd edn, 2000), Ch.24; D. Greene, *The New Civil Procedure Rules* (1999), Ch.29. On practice and procedure generally, see below, Ch.11.

[218] *Cheltenham BC v Laird* [2010] EWCA Civ 847, [2010] All E.R. (D) 50 (Feb) at [20] (Thomas L.J.). See, e.g. *National Westminster Bank Plc v Kotonou* [2006] EWHC 1785 (Ch) at [18], affirmed [2007] EWCA Civ 23, [2007] C.P. Rep. 22 (split costs order where defendant, who was successful but lost on certain distinct issues, made wholly unnecessary, extravagant and untrue allegations of fraud which put the claimant to considerable additional and unnecessary expense); *National Westminster Bank Plc v Rabobank Nederland* [2007] EWHC 1742 (Comm), [2008] 1 All E.R. (Comm) 243 (costs on indemnity basis granted against defendant who had conducted litigation in an unreasonable or inappropriate manner, including pursing counterclaim for fraud that was deeply flawed and highly speculative).

"The principles set out in the Rules must be applied to cases of fraud, taking into account the particular features of a fraud case but in the light of the general principles set out. A court simply cannot depart from the clear terms of these Rules or circumscribe the way in which the Rules state the discretion is be exercised by devising [a special rule for fraud cases]. In a fraud case the Rules enable the judge to make what is a just order where the party who has successfully defended a claim seeks his costs. They plainly permit a judge to have regard to the fact that a defendant has defended himself or herself against a serious allegation with serious consequences. A judge can, in such circumstances, reflect in the order as to costs a degree of latitude which reflects the way in which a defendant defends such a claim. However, the extent, if any, of that latitude must be a matter which can only be judged in the individual circumstances of any particular case and there can be no general rule."

CHAPTER 6

LIABILITY IN TORT FOR MISREPRESENTATION: II—NEGLIGENT MISREPRESENTATION[1]

[1] Clerk & Lindsell, Chs 8 and 10; Winfield & Jolowicz, paras 11–16 to 11–35; Charlesworth & Percy, esp. Chs 2 and 9; Spencer Bower (Misrepresentation), Ch.22; Chitty, paras 6–067, 6–078 to 6–089; Furmston, para.4.68; Treitel, paras 9–030 to 9–038, 9–066, 9–069; Cheshire, Fifoot and Furmston, pp.343–347, 365–366; Dugdale & Stanton, Chs 7 and 8; Jackson & Powell; Hodgin, Ch.2 (J. Holyoak); R. Buckley, *The Law of Negligence* (4th edn, 2005), esp. Ch.4; C. Witting, *Liability for Negligent Misstatements* (2004).

I. THE TORT OF NEGLIGENCE

(1) No General Liability for "Careless" Statements

6–01 **The courts' caution in imposing liability for careless statements causing economic loss.** The courts have encountered some difficulty in formulating appropriate rules for liability in tort for careless statements. Some account of the historical development of this area of the law is necessary to understand the current position. This will be given briefly below[2] and although the law has now progressed to a position where there are established tests for the circumstances in which the courts will admit liability for careless statements, it must be borne in mind that their starting-point has been to assume that there is no *general* liability. That is, it is not true that a claimant can in general recover all loss caused by the defendant's careless statement.[3] In Chapter 5 we saw that the tort of deceit was established in its modern form by the late eighteenth century; and that since then it would be true to say that there is a general duty of honesty in speaking. Loss to the claimant which results from a failure of honesty is in principle recoverable. The same is not, however, true of negligent statements. The courts' caution comes from three separate directions: they are more cautious in imposing liability for negligence than for dishonesty; they are more cautious in imposing liability for words than for acts; and they are more cautious in allowing recovery for economic loss than for physical harm. When words are spoken dishonestly, with a view to the representee acting on them and suffering loss, the fraud overrides other considerations and the courts give a remedy through the tort of deceit. But once the element of fraud is eliminated and the speaker is honest, though careless, the picture changes: there is

---

[2] Below, paras 6–06 to 6–11.

[3] For the different approach of other legal systems to this issue, see K. Zweigert & H. Kötz, *An Introduction to Comparative Law* (3rd edn, 1998), Ch.40, contrasting the English, German and French approaches to liability for, amongst other things, statements and economic loss in tort; W.H. Van Boom, H. Koziol and C.A. Witting (eds), *Pure Economic Loss* (Springer-Verlag, Vienna, 2004); M. Bussani and V. Palmer (eds), *Pure Economic Loss in Europe* (2003); V.V. Palmer and M. Bussani, *Pure Economic Loss: New Horizons in Comparative Law* (2009)

no general duty not to be careless. The search is for when, and why, there should be a special duty to take care in speaking.[4]

Negligence contrasted with deceit. The claim in negligence is based on the defendant's failure to take reasonable care, rather than an intentional wrong. Where a defendant intends to cause the claimant's loss, there is little to be said against the claimant having a general right to recover all that loss; and so, in the context of liability for misrepresentations, the tort of deceit has long provided a remedy for the claimant's losses flowing from the defendant's fraud.[5] But in negligence the defendant's tort consists of failing to meet up to the objective standard of conduct expected of him, and therefore extends to cases where his state of mind was honest.[6] He could have foreseen the kind of harm he might cause. But to hold him liable for the full range of losses which he could have foreseen is too harsh. It took the English and Scottish courts until 1932[7] to begin to find suitable tests to generalise the circumstances in which a defendant might be liable in tort for the foreseeable consequences of failing to take care. And not until 1963[8] did the House of Lords generalise a liability in negligence for statements. 6–02

Words contrasted with acts. Even when they took the tort of negligence into the context of statements, the courts still felt that there was a greater difficulty in imposing liability for words than for acts. It is not always easy to distinguish words from acts[9]; and some 6–03

[4] *Hedley Byrne & Co. Ltd v Heller & Partners Ltd* [1964] A.C. 465, HL, at 534; *Nocton v Lord Ashburton* [1914] A.C. 932, HL, at 947; *White v Jones* [1995] 2 A.C. 207, HL, at 273–274.

[5] Above, Ch.5. Because of the dishonesty of the defendant the remedy in deceit goes so far as to allow recovery of all the loss caused by the fraudulent misrepresentation, even if the particular items of loss were not intended or even foreseeable: above, para.5–40.

[6] Below, para.6–42. In practice, "negligence" is used as a description of cases where the defendant honestly (unintentionally) made a misrepresentation, and so is contrasted with fraudulent statements in the tort of deceit although, strictly speaking, the defendant's subjective state of mind is not in issue in a claim in negligence.

[7] *Donoghue v Stevenson* [1932] A.C. 562, HL(Sc.).

[8] *Hedley Byrne & Co. Ltd v Heller & Partners Ltd*, above, n.4; below.

[9] For example, if a purchaser or a mortgagee relies on an incorrect valuation of property, is the claim based on the valuer's lack of care in undertaking the valuation (act) or his misstatement of value which is the culmination of his

recent cases have attempted to break down the words/acts distinction within negligence.[10] But in taking forward the step of formulating a general test for liability in tort for careless words, the House of Lords in *Hedley Byrne & Co. Ltd v Heller & Partners Ltd*[11] clearly regarded this as a separate test from that for liability for careless acts. The reason was the need to keep a tight control on the liability because, in short, the potential scope of harm which might be caused by words is so great. Lord Pearce said[12]:

> "Words are more volatile than deeds. They travel fast and far afield. They are used without being expended and take effect in combination with innumerable facts and other words. Yet they are dangerous and can cause vast financial damage."

And Lord Reid said[13]:

---

careless valuation (words)? See *Glanzer v Shepard*, 135 N.E. 275 (1922, NYCA: defendants, public weighers, issued inaccurate certificate of weight of goods which caused loss to claimant by overpayment for their purchase) at 276–277 (Cardozo J.): "here the defendants are held, not merely for careless words, but for the careless performance of a service—the act of weighing—which happens to have found in the words of a certificate its culmination and its summary. The line of separation between these diverse liabilities is difficult to draw. It does not lose for that reason its correspondence with realities. Life has relations not capable always of division into inflexible compartments. The molds expand and shrink." It should however be noted that Cardozo J. was emphasising that there was a careless act underlying the inaccurate certificate, to bring the case more clearly within the rules of liability in tort for negligence—which in 1922 were already ahead of the development in England but still had a good deal further to go. See also *Ultramares Corp. v Touch*, 174 N.E. 441 (1931, NYCA), below, n.17. Even in *Hedley Byrne* the House of Lords saw that there was not always a clear line to draw between words and acts: e.g. a bottle of hair wash which is dangerous because (a) it has a misleading label (words) or (b) it has been negligently made up (act): see [1964] A.C. 465 at 508 (Lord Hodson). This points towards the conclusion that there can be no firm distinction that careless acts are in principle actionable but careless statements are not. But it does not mean that the *test* for liability should be the same in both cases; nor does it deny that the courts need to be cautious in how they draw the test for negligent statements.

10 Below, para.6–11.

11 Above, n.4.

12 *ibid.*, at 534.

13 *ibid.*, at 482–483. At 482 Lord Reid said that *Donoghue v Stevenson*, above, n.7, "is a very important decision, but I do not think that it has any direct bearing on this case".

> "Apart altogether from authority, I would think that the law must treat negligent words differently from negligent acts . . . The most obvious difference between negligent words and negligence acts is this. Quite careful people often express definite opinions on social or informal occasions even when they see that others are likely to be influenced by them; and they often do that without taking that care which they would take if asked for their opinion professionally or in a business connection . . .
>
> Another obvious difference is that a negligently made article will only cause one accident, and so it is not very difficult to find the necessary degree of proximity or neighbourhood between the negligent manufacturer and the person injured. But words can be broadcast with or without the consent or the foresight of the speaker or writer. It would be one thing to say that the speaker owes a duty to a limited class, but it would be going very far to say that he owes a duty to every ultimate 'consumer' who acts on those words to his detriment . . .
>
> So it seems to me that there is good sense behind our present law that in general an innocent but negligent misrepresentation gives no cause of action. There must be something more than the mere misstatement . . . ."

Economic loss contrasted with physical damage. As shown by the extracts from the judgments of Lord Pearce and Lord Reid in *Hedley Byrne* in the previous paragraph, the courts were also mindful of the wide range of economic losses which might be caused by a careless statement. Words tend to cause economic losses more then physical damage, because the words do not themselves cause the loss; it is the representee's use of the words which causes him to suffer loss,[14] often by entering into a transaction which he later complains has resulted in his suffering economic loss. There can be cases in which the representee's reliance on the words places him in physical danger, or exposes him to the risk of damage to his property; then the limit of the damage is containable to the physical harm involved, and in any event the courts generally look more favourably on physical interests as more obviously deserving greater protection.[15] Even before *Hedley Byrne* the courts had felt able to impose liability for negligent statements 6–04

[14] Above, para.3–51.

[15] *Hedley Byrne*, above, n.4, at 536–537; *Home Office v Dorset Yacht Co. Ltd* [1970] A.C. 1004, HL, at 1027; *Murphy v Brentwood DC* [1991] 1 A.C. 398, HL, at 487 (Lord Oliver: "The infliction of physical injury to the person or property of another universally requires to be justified. The causing of economic loss does not. If it is to be categorised as wrongful it is necessary to find some factor beyond the mere occurrence of the loss and the fact that its occurrence could be foreseen").

causing physical injury.[16] But there is real scope for a claim for significant economic losses suffered in reliance on a careless statement; and this was the nature of the claim in *Hedley Byrne* itself where an advertising agent, relying on a credit reference given by a bank about one of its customers, entered into contracts on behalf of the customer under which it took personal responsibility but was later unable to obtain reimbursement because the customer became insolvent. *Hedley Byrne* makes clear that there is no objection in principle to allowing recovery of economic loss in the tort of negligence; but the circumstances in which recovery is to be permitted have to be controlled very carefully.

6–05 **The basic concern: indeterminate liability.** Similar concerns were also expressed in the American cases during the period of development of the tort of negligence in the US. A dictum which is very commonly cited in the English cases is that of Cardozo J.[17]: there is a risk of "liability in an indeterminate amount for an indeterminate time to an indeterminate class". This was an early attempt in America to articulate the need for caution in allowing liability in negligence for economic loss caused by a claimant's reliance on a misrepresentation.[18] Both the American courts[19] and

[16] *Clayton v Woodman & Son (Builders) Ltd* [1962] 2 Q.B. 533 (Salmon J., revsd on the facts [1962] 1 W.L.R. 585, CA), below, para.6–18; *cf. Clay v A.J. Crump & Sons Ltd* [1964] 1 Q.B. 533, CA (decided two months after the decision of the House of Lords in *Hedley Byrne).*

[17] *Ultramares Corp. v Touche*, 174 N.E. 441 at 444 (1931); cited (inter alia) in *Hedley Byrne*, above, n.4 at 537; *Candler v Crane, Christmas & Co.* [1951] 2 K.B. 164, CA, at 183, 203–204; *Ross v Caunters* [1980] Ch. 297 at 309; *Junior Books Ltd v Veitchi Co. Ltd* [1983] 1 A.C. 520 (H.L.(Sc.)) at 532; *Al Saudi Banque v Clark Pixley* [1990] Ch. 313 at 330; *Caparo Industries Plc v Dickman* [1990] 2 A.C. 605, HL at 621; *Customs & Excise Commissioners v Barclays Bank Plc* [2006] UKHL 28, [2007] 1 A.C. 181 at [74]; *Stone & Rolls Ltd v Moore Stephens* [2009] UKHL 39, [2009] 1 A.C. 1391 at [202]. In Canada: *Winnipeg Condominium Co. No.36 v Bird Construction Co.* (1995) 121 D.L.R. (4th) 193, SCC, at 217; *Hercules Managements Ltd v Ernst & Young* (1997) 146 D.L.R. (4th) 577, SCC, at 592. In Australia: *Bryan v Maloney* (1995) 182 C.L.R. 109, HCA, at 618, 632. In New Zealand: *Scott Group Ltd v McFarlane* [1978] 1 N.Z.L.R. 553 at 571 (NZCA).

[18] The dictum is now so often quoted that it is easy to lose sight of its context: it was a case, decided in 1931 (and therefore even before *Donoghue v Stevenson* [1932] A.C. 562), in which the issue was whether the defendants, a firm of "public accountants", i.e. broadly, auditors, were liable to the claimant which lent money to a company in reliance on the defendants' negligent certification that the

the English courts[20] have moved on to allow recovery in such circumstances, but only on the basis of the careful application of control mechanisms to regulate the scope of liability; and in formulating these control mechanisms the courts on both sides of the Atlantic have always borne in mind the general problems which have been discussed in this section.

(2) Development of Liability in Tort for Careless Statements

Early influence of *Derry v Peek*. Towards the end of the nineteenth century there were cases which suggested that there might be liability in tort for careless, as opposed to deliberate, misrepresentation. For example, in *Cann v Willson*[21] Chitty J. held that a valuer was liable in negligence for the loss suffered by a mortgagee for whom—at the mortgagor's request—he carelessly prepared a defective valuation. And the Court of Appeal in *Peek v Derry*[22] held company directors liable in the tort of deceit for misrepresentations in their company's prospectus which they honestly believed but without having reasonable grounds for that belief: that is, broadly speaking, negligence.[23] But this latter decision was reversed by the House of Lords in *Derry v Peek*,[24] and the House of Lords' judgments were immediately interpreted by the 6–06

company's accounts presented a true and correct view of the company's financial condition. Cardozo J.'s judgment contains a thorough discussion of the difficulties of allowing liability in negligence in such a case—and the wider consequences which would then follow. On the modern answer in English law to the actual question raised in *Ultramares*, see *Caparo Industries Plc v Dickman* [1990] 2 A.C. 605, HL, below, para.6–33.

[19] F.V. Harper, F. James Jr and O.S. Gray, *The Law of Torts* (3rd edn, 2006 with supplement), para.7.6.

[20] Below, paras 6–16 *et seq.*

[21] (1888) 39 Ch.D. 39, extending to the case of careless statements the principles shown in cases such as *George v Skivington* (1869) L.R. 5 Ex. 1 in which liability had already been imposed in negligence for dangerous products. Chitty J. preferred the ground of negligence, but he would also have found fraud on the basis of the decision of the CA in *Peek v Derry* (1887) 37 Ch.D. 541. This latter point was certainly overturned by the decision of the House of Lords in *Derry v Peek*, which reversed the CA on the basis that fraud requires dishonesty: above, para.5–14.

[22] (1887) 37 Ch.D. 541.

[23] *cf.* the liability under the Misrepresentation Act 1967 s.2(1); and the Financial Services and Markets Act 2000 s.90; below, Ch.7.

[24] (1889) 14 App. Cas. 337; see generally Ch.5.

Court of Appeal as authority that there could be no general liability for negligent misrepresentation, even outside the tort of deceit. The strongest decision in this respect was *Le Lievre v Gould*,[25] where it was held that a surveyor who carelessly issued certificates about the progress being made on a building project did not owe a duty to mortgagees who then advanced funds to the builder in reliance on the certificates. All three judges in the Court of Appeal emphasised the limited circumstances in which a person owed a duty to take care to one with whom he had no contractual relationship, and they relied on *Derry v Peek* as showing that there could be no general liability for negligent words. Bowen L.J. rejected the argument that

> "a man is responsible for what he states in a certificate to any person to whom he may have reason to suppose that the certificate may be shewn . . . the law of England does not go to that extent: it does not consider that what a man writes on paper is like a gun or other dangerous instrument, and, unless he intended to deceive, the law does not, in the absence of contract, hold him responsible for drawing his certificate carelessly.[26]"

Cann v Willson[27] was overruled.

6–07 ***Derry v Peek* limited to a decision on deceit.** The immediate reaction to *Derry v Peek* therefore appears to have been to accept it as establishing not only that the tort of deceit requires proof of dishonesty but also that, such dishonesty apart, there is no general liability for statements: no general duty in respect of careless statements, at least outside the context of cases where the duty

---

[25] [1893] 1 Q.B. 491, CA. Similarly clear statements were made in *Angus v Clifford* [1891] 2 Ch. 449, CA, at 463–464 (Lindley L.J.), 470 (Bowen L.J.) and *Low v Bouverie* [1891] 3 Ch. 82 at 100 (Lindley L.J.: no general duty; liability only if there is a "legal obligation" on the representor to give the representee the correct information), 105 (Bowen L.J.), 112 (Kay L.J.). Bowen L.J. in *Le Lievre v Gould*, above, at 503, went so far as to say "I have myself stated, until I am almost tired at doing so, and I have no doubt that other judges are equally tired at, exactly what *Derry v Peek* did decide and did not decide. I elaborated the same point at great length in *Angus v Clifford* and *Low v Bouverie*".

[26] *ibid.*, at 502. See also Lord Esher M.R. at 498 and A.L. Smith L.J. at 504. The reference to a "gun or other dangerous instrument" is to a category of liability in negligence which was already established; *cf. George v Skivington*, above n.21. See also *Scholes v Brook* (1891) 63 L.T. 837 (valuer of property not liable to mortgagee for negligent valuation if no contract).

[27] Above, n.21. *Cann v Wilson* was not cited or mentioned in the speeches in the House of Lords in *Derry v Peek*.

could attach to a contractual relationship between claimant and defendant. During the twentieth century, however, cases arose in which the courts sought to explore the possibility of extending liability to careless statements. But in order to do so, *Derry v Peek* had to be distinguished: even at the time of the most significant general development, the decision in *Hedley Byrne* in 1963, the House of Lords still regarded itself as bound by its own previous decisions.[28]

Nowhere in the judgments in *Derry v Peek* was it said explicitly that there was no liability for careless statements outside the scope of liability between contracting parties. The whole focus of the appeal, the point of law which formed the subject of the decision, was the test to be applied in the tort of deceit. For example, Lord Herschell said[29]:

> "I cannot assent to the doctrine that a false statement made through carelessness, and which ought to have been known to be untrue, of itself renders the person who makes it liable to an action *for deceit*. This does not seem to me by any means necessarily to amount to fraud, without which *the action* will not, in my opinion, lie."

So the later cases, which sought to avoid the restriction which *Derry v Peek* at first sight appeared to place on their freedom to develop the law, distinguished it as being applicable only to the tort of deceit, and having decided nothing (or, at least, nothing which bound the later judges) about liability in negligence.[30]

---

[28] This rule was changed in 1966 by Practice Statement (Judicial Precedent) [1966] 1 W.L.R. 1234, HL. In *Hedley Byrne,* therefore, the House also had to distinguish carefully the earlier decision in *Robinson v National Bank of Scotland Ltd*, 1916 S.C. (HL(Sc.)) 154 (no duty of care owed by bank making representations of creditworthiness of its customers in response to a request by another bank).

[29] (1889) 14 App. Cas. 337 at 373 (emphasis added). Indeed, at 360 Lord Herschell also referred "for the purpose of putting it aside" to a class of cases where "a person within whose special province it lay to know a particular fact, has given an erroneous answer to an inquiry made", such as *Burrowes v Lock* (1805) 10 Ves. Jun. 470, 32 E.R. 927.

[30] One can understand why the CA in the early cases held that the decision in *Derry v Peek* excluded liability in negligence for misrepresentations, at least in the kind of case which was represented by the facts of *Derry v Peek* itself. The cause of action (deceit, negligence, etc.) need not be pleaded; the claimant in *Derry v Peek* was required to plead the facts giving rise to his claim for damages, and the court has the duty to give the remedy if the facts disclose a cause of

6–08 ***Nocton v Lord Ashburton*: duties arise from fiduciary relationships, as well as from contract.** The first stage of development came in the decision of the House of Lords in *Nocton v Lord Ashburton*,[31] where a solicitor was held liable to compensate his client for losses incurred by acting on the solicitor's advice. The facts were unusual: the solicitor had a personal interest in the client's transaction on which he was giving advice. The House of Lords rejected the argument that *Derry v Peek* bound them to hold that the solicitor owed no duty to the client.[32] *Derry v Peek* was a decision only on the elements necessary to establish a claim in deceit, and did not hold that there could not be liability for careless misrepresentation if the misrepresentation was made by a person who owed a special duty to the claimant independently of the general duty to be honest which is sanctioned by the tort of deceit.[33] And such special duties arose not only out of contracts—a duty of care to a co-contractant giving rise to damages in tort, as well as in contract, for the contractual failure to take care[34]—but also where there was a relationship of the kind recognised historically by the courts of equity as imposing on one party the duty to look to the interests of the other. In short, a fiduciary relationship can include the obligation on the fiduciary to take care in making representations to the person to whom he owes his fiduciary duties.[35] The decision in *Nocton v Lord Ashburton* is not clear and unequivocal

action; if fraud is alleged but not established, the court should still give judgment for the claimant if the facts which are proved disclose a cause of action: *Swinfen v Lord Chelmsford* (1860) 5 H. & N. 890 at 921, 157 E.R. 1436 at 1449, quoted in *Nocton v Lord Ashburton* [1914] A.C. 932, HL, at 968. So the denial of the remedy in *Derry v Peek* ought to show that the HL believed that there was no cause of action, not simply that there was no cause of action in deceit. The later courts were however able to distinguish it.

[31] Above, n.30. This still pre-dates the generalisation of liability in negligence which followed the decision of the HL in *Donoghue v Stevenson* [1932] A.C. 562.

[32] There was no fraud, and so the action of deceit did not lie. On this point the CA had reversed the trial judge and found fraud but the HL restored the trial judge's decision: see [1914] A.C. 932 at 945, 966, 976.

[33] *ibid.*, at 946–947, 955, 969–971, 978.

[34] *ibid.*, at 956, 964.

[35] *ibid.*, at 950, 955–956 (Viscount Haldane L.C., emphasising the solicitor's financial interest in the transaction as giving rise to the special duty on the facts), 963–965 (Lord Dunedin), 970 (Lord Shaw, referring to Lord Herschell's statements in *Derry v Peek* about cases where a claim would lie without proof of fraud: above, n.29). It is necessary to find within the particular fiduciary relationship a duty which has been broken by virtue of the fiduciary's having

on some important points, e.g. it is not clear that the nature of the duty arising from the fiduciary obligations is identical in content to the common law duty in negligence.[36] And the remedy given was compensation, but this was not necessarily calculated in the same way as damages at common law for negligence.[37] But the decision reasserted the principle that there were situations, outside the tort of deceit, where a claimant could recover compensation for loss suffered by reliance on a misrepresentation, and therefore it gave a new perspective on the decision in *Derry v Peek*.

Development between *Nocton v Lord Asburton* and *Hedley Byrne*. It is important to remember that the modern tort of negligence was in the early stages of development in this period. So it should not be a surprise to find that the development of liability for careless statements was itself slow. Even after the tort began to be more developed in general as a result of the decision in *Donoghue v Stevenson*[38] in 1932, the decision of the Court of Appeal in *Le Lievre v Gould*[39] was held still to govern the question of liability for careless statements.[40] The acknowledgement in *Nocton v Lord Ashburton* that a duty of care could be imposed on a representor by virtue of his fiduciary relationship with the representee gave the courts the tools to develop the modern law of 6–09

made a misrepresentation: *ibid.*, at 950 (Viscount Haldane L.C., approving the decisions in *Angus v Clifford* [1891] 2 Ch. 449, CA, and *Low v Bouverie* [1891] 3 Ch. 82, CA).

[36] The HL appeared to think that they were applying not the common law concept of negligence, but the equitable rules for a fiduciary's duty—and therefore the duty was not limited to one of reasonable care: see [1914] A.C. 932 at 956–957, 963, 965.

[37] *ibid.*, at 958, 965. For the view that, in the developed law, a claim for compensation in equity for breach of a duty of care would be calculated on the same basis as common law damages, see *Bristol & West Building Society v Mothew* [1998] Ch. 1, CA, at 17. But on the question of whether a *separate* claim in equity for compensation survives in a case where there is a duty of care in the developed tort of negligence, see *Henderson v Merrett Syndicates Ltd* [1995] 2 A.C. 145, HL, at 205; below, n.54.

[38] [1932] A.C. 562, HL.

[39] [1893] 1 Q.B. 491.

[40] *Old Gate Estates Ltd v Toplis & Harding & Russell* [1939] 3 All E.R. 209; *Candler v Crane, Christmas & Co.* [1951] 2 K.B. 164, CA (Denning L.J., dissenting, thought at 176–178 that *Le Lievre* had been overtaken by *Nocton v Lord Ashburton* and *Donoghue v Stevenson*. The HL eventually in *Hedley Byrne*, below, para.6–10, took Denning L.J.'s position).

liability in tort for negligent misrepresentation, but the tools were not put to immediate use. The question was how flexibly the courts would use the test based on fiduciary duties. The language of the judgments in *Nocton v Lord Ashburton*[41] could have led to a restrictive test: that the duty would arise only where there was a relationship which was characterised in equity as fiduciary, and even in 1951 this appears to have been the Court of Appeal's view.[42] But in 1959 Salmon J. held that a bank owed fiduciary obligations to a customer in giving advice about investment; it therefore owed a duty of care in the tort of negligence arising out of that fiduciary duty.[43] This was a strained interpretation of the accepted principles of fiduciary relationships, and appears to have been done by Salmon J. explicitly in order to bring the facts of the case within the authorities so that he could find a duty of care.[44]

6–10 **Generalised duties in respect of statements: *Hedley Byrne*.** In 1963 the House of Lords took the decisive step. Building on the earlier decisions of the House of Lords[45] but overruling those

[41] Above, para.6–08.

[42] *Candler v Crane, Christmas & Co.,* above, n.40 (Denning L.J. dissenting).

[43] *Woods v Martins Bank Ltd* [1959] 1 Q.B. 55 at 72. The judge emphasised at 70 that each case must be analysed on its facts to see whether there is a relationship which gives rise to the duty: "the nature of [a banker's] business must in each case be a matter of fact and, accordingly, cannot be treated as if it were a matter of pure law". Salmon J. in *Clayton v Woodman & Son (Builders) Ltd* [1962] 2 Q.B. 533, above, n.16, also extended the liability for statements to cover claims in respect of physical damage.

[44] *Hedley Byrne* [1964] A.C. 465, HL, at 510–511. Indeed, the key sentence, "In my judgment, a fiduciary relationship existed between the claimant and the defendants" ([1959] 1 Q.B. 55 at 72) does not appear in the judgment of Salmon J. first published at [1958] 3 All E.R. 166 at 174 and [1958] 1 W.L.R. 1018 at 1032, and therefore appears to have been added by the judge, in revising the judgment, to bring the case more explicitly and unchallengeably within the principle of *Candler v Crane, Christmas & Co.,* above, n.40.

[45] By which they were still bound: above, n.28. The decisions principally relied on were *Nocton v Lord Ashburton*, above, n.30, and *Robinson v National Bank of Scotland Ltd*, above, n.28, a case which appears not to have been relied upon in England, at least, since it was decided but in which Viscount Haldane spoke words (at 157) on which the House of Lords relied in *Hedley Byrne* to show that he had not intended his judgment in *Nocton v Lord Ashburton* to limit the scope of duties of care in tort to fiduciary relationships in the narrow sense: see [1964] A.C. 465, HL, at 485–486, 502, 512, 523, 536.

cases[46] in the lower courts which had held that the duty in the tort of negligence was limited to relationships based on contract or fiduciary duties, they generalised the test: it was not necessary for there to be a fiduciary relationship of the kind historically recognised in equity. The language of the different judgments varies[47]; but broadly, a "special duty"[48] would arise to impose a duty of care on a person making a statement—giving information or advice—if there was a "special relationship" between the parties, a relationship wider than the narrow category of relationships defined as "fiduciary" in equity, but still limited in scope[49]; where one party "takes it upon himself" to make the statement and knows or ought to know that the recipient will receive the statement and rely on it[50]; or the representor "assumes a responsibility" to the representee in relation to the statement.[51] The decision on the facts in *Hedley Byrne* was that the defendant owed no duty of care, because he had

[46] *Candler v Crane, Christmas & Co.,* above, n.40 (Denning L.J.'s dissenting judgment was approved). *Le Lievre v Gould*, above, n.39 may have been correct on its facts, but was disapproved on the limited test it applied, and in particular was disapproved in so far as it had wrongly overruled *Cann v Willson* (1888) 39 Ch.D. 39, above, n.21. Cases in which the reasoning depended on the disapproved test from *Le Lievre v Gould* were also thereby overruled, e.g. *Old Gate Estates Ltd v Toplis & Harding & Russell*, above, n.40; *Heskell v Continental Express Ltd* [1950] 1 All E.R. 1033 at 1041–1042 (Devlin J.; see Lord Devlin in *Hedley Byrne* [1964] A.C. 465 at 532).

[47] For the test for a duty of care in the developed law, based on *Hedley Byrne* and later cases, see below, para.6–19. See also R. Buxton, "How the Common Law Gets Made: *Hedley Byrne* and Other Cautionary Tales" (2009) 125 L.Q.R. 60 at pp.61–68.

[48] This is a phrase taken from *Nocton v Lord Ashburton* and used in *Hedley Byrne*, above, n.44 at 509, 515, 525, 540.

[49] *ibid.*, at 486, 505, 525, 539. Lord Devlin at 525 noted that this language, taken from *Nocton v Lord Ashburton* [1914] A.C. 932, HL, at 956, was also used by Lord Thankerton in *Donoghue v Stevenson* [1932] A.C. 562, HL, at 603 to describe the relationship necessary to impose a duty of care in that case. As such, the language is descriptive but does not provide a workable test.

[50] *ibid.*, at 502–503, 514.

[51] *ibid.*, at 483, 486, 494, 529 (Lord Devlin: a relationship "equivalent to contract"), 539–540.

expressly disclaimed his liability: he had negatived any "assumption of responsibility".[52] But the speeches are authoritative as to when a duty of care will arise.[53]

6–11 **Later development of the principles established in *Hedley Byrne*.** The modern law of liability in tort[54] for careless statements therefore runs from the decision of the House of Lords in *Hedley Byrne*. The explanation, development and refinement of the law in this area through later cases will be discussed in detail below. But it should here be mentioned that there has been an attempt to develop the principles of *Hedley Byrne* beyond the sphere of statements, and to treat it as authority not simply for negligent statements giving rise to economic loss, but also more generally for the negligent performance of other services in such a way as to cause economic loss; that is, it is used as a guide also to the circumstances in which a person can be liable in tort for the economic loss caused by his careless acts.[55] This step forward in the use of *Hedley Byrne* as authority was taken by the House of Lords

---

[52] On the controls on such disclaimers since the enactment of the Unfair Contract Terms Act 1977, see below, para.6–51 and Ch.9.

[53] *W.B. Anderson & Sons Ltd v Rhodes (Liverpool) Ltd* [1967] 2 All E.R. 850 at 857.

[54] The duty of care in tort has been developed from the category of duties owed by fiduciaries (in the narrow sense); but where the defendant is in a fiduciary relationship with the claimant there are not two separate duties of care, but only one: "the liability of a fiduciary for the negligent transaction of his duties is not a separate head of liability but the paradigm of the general duty to act with care imposed by law on those who take it upon themselves to act for or advise others"; it is therefore not appropriate for a separate claim to be made on the basis of breach of fiduciary duty of care, concurrently with the claim in tort: *Henderson v Merrett Syndicates Ltd* [1995] 2 A.C. 145 at 205. On concurrence of duties in contract and tort, see below, para.6–29. And for the view that, even if the claim is brought in equity for breach of a duty of care, the measure of damages awarded will be the same as in an action based on the tort of negligence, see *Bristol & West Building Society v Mothew* [1998] Ch. 1, CA, at 17. However, the duty of care is to be distinguished from the proscriptive duties which are special to fiduciaries, whose core obligation is loyalty: a fiduciary may act loyally, but incompetently, and so be in breach of the duty of care but not the fiduciary duty: *Bristol & West Building Society v Mothew* at 17; *Hilton v Barker Booth & Eastwood* [2005] UKHL 8, [2005] 1 W.L.R. 567 at [29]; Snell, para.7–009; J.E. Martin, *Hanbury and Martin: Modern Equity* (18th edn, 2009), para.23–008.

[55] Or omissions to act: see *White v Jones* [1995] 2 A.C. 207, HL.

in *Henderson v Merrett Syndicates Ltd*.[56] In that case, in applying *Hedley Byrne* outside the context of careless statements, emphasis was placed on the need to show the defendant's "assumption of responsibility"[57] towards the claimant, rather than the other language[58] used in *Hedley Byrne* to describe the source of the special relationship under which the defendant's duty arose in favour of the claimant. This use of *Hedley Byrne* outside the context of statements need not concern us, since claims for economic loss consequent on careless acts (or failure to act), by contrast with claims based on careless statements (or failure to speak), are outside the scope of the book. No attempt will therefore be made here to explore in detail this aspect of the limits of the *Hedley Byrne* principle, nor to consider the difficulties which arise in the courts' attempt to define a general test for the duty of care in respect of economic loss caused by careless acts and omissions.[59] But in so far as the House of Lords has identified a principle which emerges from *Hedley Byrne* and which therefore inevitably casts light on the proper interpretation of *Hedley Byrne* itself, even when considered as authority for its particular context of careless statements, the recent cases (and the emphasis on the principle of the defendant's "assumption of responsibility") will be discussed.[60]

---

[56] [1995] 2 A.C. 145, HL, at 178–181 (Lord Goff, with whom the other members of the House agreed). Lord Goff had also very recently stated this principle in his judgment in *Spring v Guardian Assurance Plc* [1995] 2 A.C. 296, HL, at 317–319, below, paras 6–24 to 6–25 and 6–40 (although there the issue was liability for a careless statement, albeit one not addressed to the claimant). For earlier indications in the HL that *Hedley Byrne* could apply outside the context of careless statements, see *Junior Books Ltd v Veitchi Co. Ltd* [1983] A.C. 520 at 546; *D. & F. Estates Ltd v Church Commissioners for England* [1989] A.C. 177 at 215; *Murphy v Brentwood DC* [1991] 1 A.C. 398 at 466, 481.

[57] Above, n.51.

[58] Above, nn.49 and 50.

[59] For such a discussion, see Winfield & Jolowicz, paras 5–34 to 5–38; K. Barker, "Unreliable Assumptions in the Modern Law of Negligence" (1993) 109 L.Q.R. 461. And see the detailed consideration by the House of Lords in *Customs & Excise Commissioners v Barclays Bank Plc* [2006] UKHL 28, [2007] 1 A.C. 181, noted at [2008] L.M.C.L.Q. 258 (M. Stiggelbout), and the discussion in the context of a claim by a house owner against a builder in relatation to alleged defects in the building giving rise to economic loss, in *Robinson v P.E. Jones (Contractors) Ltd* [2011] EWCA Civ 9, [2011] B.L.R. 206.

[60] Below, para.6–25.

II. ELEMENTS OF THE CLAIM IN THE TORT OF NEGLIGENCE

6–12 **Overview of the elements of the claim.** In general terms, the representee may recover damages in the tort of negligence if he can show that, in respect of the loss which he has suffered, the defendant owed him a duty to take reasonable care in making the representation; that the representee was in breach of that duty by failing to take reasonable care; and that in consequence of the breach of duty he has suffered loss of a kind that is within the scope of the duty and is not too remote. This remedy differs from the other principal remedies for misrepresentation: here, the claim is based on the representor's failure to fulfil a duty of care in making the representation, not simply the falsity of the statement.[61] A representation may be false without having been made negligently. The terms of the inquiry are therefore different from those in relation to such remedies as rescission and the tort of deceit; the general elements of a claim in misrepresentation, discussed in Chapter 3, are not often raised directly in a claim in negligence.[62] And the tort of negligence is not aimed specifically at misrepresentations—indeed, we have already seen[63] that it was extended to cover misrepresentations only cautiously during the later twentieth century. Any discussion of the elements of the claim in negligence for misrepresentation must therefore look more generally to the elements of a claim in the tort of negligence. These elements will be discussed in this section, although the focus will be

---

61 *Banbury v Bank of Montreal* [1918] A.C. 626, HL, at 713; *Hedley Byrne & Co. Ltd v Heller & Partners Ltd* [1964] A.C. 465, HL, at 511; *W. B. Anderson & Sons Ltd v Rhodes (Liverpool) Ltd* [1967] 2 All E.R. 850 at 865.

62 And so, for example, the law/fact/opinion distinction is not raised, at least not in the same terms (nor the same language of analysis) as in a claim for rescission: above, paras 3–13 to 4–25; see, e.g. *Hagen v ICI Chemicals & Polymers Ltd* [2002] I.R.L.R. 31 at [98]–[103] (Elias J.: no rigid distinction between statements of fact, opinion and intention for the tort of negligence). And although the reliance of the representee on the careless statement is a requirement for the tort of negligence, it is not approached in the same way as in rescission or deceit (where the court may infer reliance from the materiality of the representation: above, paras 3–53, 4–33 and 5–25; below, para.6–53). This is not to say that there is no underlying unity of principle in the courts' approach to the remedies for misrepresentation: simply that the language of the cases—stating the formal elements of the claim—is different here. For discussion of some of the common threads uniting the remedies, see above, paras 3–45 to 3–47.

63 Above, paras 6–06 to 6–11.

the application of the elements of the claim to a case involving careless statements. The defences which can be raised by the defendant once the representee has established the elements of his claim, and the quantification of the damages recoverable in the tort of negligence, will be discussed in later sections in this chapter.

(1) Duty of Care

(a) *General principles*

The test for a duty of care: categorisation of duties. The claimant in an action of negligence will seek to show that his case falls within the principles of an established category of duty; that is, a situation in which the courts have held that a duty of care is owed by a person in the defendant's position to a person in the claimant's position. If he can point to no such established category, he will seek to argue from an existing category or categories, or from general principle, that a duty should be recognised in his case.[64] This test is essentially an application of the general rules of precedent: the question is whether the case in hand falls within the authority of an earlier case or line of cases; or, if not, whether an extension should be made to the existing authorities to impose a duty. Through the cases the courts have developed lines of authorities which can broadly be characterised as separate *categories* of case; and the case law which makes up those authorities contains the principles according to which duties of care are imposed within the several categories. A claimant may therefore be able to show that his case is indistinguishable from an earlier case in which a duty was held to exist; if so, he simply relies on that authority. But commonly he will need to argue more widely, that his case is either a concrete[65] example of a duty falling within the 6–13

[64] *Caparo Industries Plc v Dickman* [1990] 2 A.C. 605, HL, at 618, 628, 635, adopting into English law the approach set out by Brennan J. in *Sutherland Shire Council v Heyman* (1985) 157 C.L.R. 424, HCA, at 481. For later applications of this test in the English cases, see, e.g. *X v Bedfordshire CC* [1995] 2 A.C. 633, HL, at 751, 762; *Henderson v Merrett Syndicates Ltd* [1995] 2 A.C. 145, HL, at 182; *Stovin v Wise* [1996] A.C. 923, HL, at 948–949; *Barrett v Enfield LBC* [2001] 2 A.C. 550, HL, at 556, 564.

[65] For this distinction between a "notional duty", i.e. a duty which applies to a general class of relationship and damage, and the "factual duty" which arises on the facts of a case, see Clerk & Lindsell, para.8–06.

principles of an accepted category, or that it should be recognised as an extension from an established category. The court will then be called upon to consider the principles of the category or categories relied upon; and to ask such questions as whether it is "fair, just and reasonable" to impose a duty in the claimant's case. But in taking a decision to extend the law to a new case the court is then establishing a new category, or sub-category, of case[66]:

---

[66] *Barrett v Enfield LBC* [2001] 2 A.C. 550, HL, at 556, 559–560 (Lord Browne-Wilkinson). This has not always been the approach; and in particular during the last quarter of the 20th century much effort was devoted by the courts to thinking and re-thinking the general question of by what reasoning a duty should be held to (or not to) exist on any given set of facts. For a general account of the development—in particular, from *Anns v Merton LBC* [1978] A.C. 728, HL, to *Caparo Industries Plc v Dickman* [1990] 2 A.C. 605, HL, and *Murphy v Brentwood DC* [1991] 1 A.C. 398, HL—see Winfield & Jolowicz, Ch. 5; Clerk & Lindsell, paras 8–12 to 8–28; Charlesworth & Percy, paras 2–13 to 2–25. In brief, Lord Wilberforce in *Anns* had said (at 751–752) that, in deciding whether a duty of care exists, it is not necessary to bring the facts of the case within those of previous situations in which a duty of care has been held to exist; a general test was instead to be applied, under which a duty arose if there was a sufficient relationship of proximity that the defendant ought to have realised that his carelessness might be likely to cause damage to the claimant, and if there were no considerations which ought to negative or reduce or limit the scope of the duty or the persons to whom the duty is owed or the damages recoverable. Following this decision the courts first tended to apply Lord Wilberforce's test in such a way as to expand the range of duties and therefore to expand the tort of negligence, before the HL in the mid- to late-1980s began to curb its application by reinterpreting it as allowing a duty only where it was "just and reasonable" to do so (e.g. *Governors of the Peabody Donation Fund v Sir Lindsay Parkinson & Co. Ltd* [1985] A.C. 210, HL, at 241), where there was no existing authority for or against the category of duty in question (e.g. *The Aliakmon* [1986] A.C. 785, HL, at 815), and focusing more closely on the particular relationship of the parties to ask whether a duty should be imposed (e.g. *Yuen Kun Yeu v Att-Gen of Hong Kong* [1988] A.C. 175, PC, at 194). Finally, in *Caparo v Dickman*, they rejected the approach based on a general test altogether in favour of the principle of categorisation of cases. *Anns* was overruled on its facts in *Murphy v Brentwood DC*, above, in which the "general test" was also again criticised: see Lord Keith at 461 and Lord Oliver at 487–488. The language of a duty based on "foreseeability", "proximity" and it being "fair, just and reasonable" survives in the modern cases, but it is best used to describe and explain the circumstances in which a duty exists (or should by analogy be created) rather than as a formal test to apply: see *Caparo Industries Plc v Dickman*, above, n.64 at 618, 628, 633; *James McNaughton Paper Group Ltd v Hicks Anderson & Co.* [1991] 2 Q.B. 113, CA, at 123–124; *Law Society v KPMG Peat Marwick* [2000] 1 All E.R. 515 at

> "questions of public policy and the question whether it is fair and reasonable to impose liability in negligence are decided as questions of law. Once the decision is taken that, say, company auditors though liable to shareholders for negligent auditing are not liable to those proposing to invest in the company (see the *Caparo Industries* case[67]), that decision will apply to all future cases of the same kind. The decision does not depend on weighing the balance between the extent of the damage to the plaintiff and the damage to the public in each particular case."

Scope of the duty. It is not sufficient simply to say that A owes B a duty of care without defining that duty: the scope of a duty is not indeterminate, but is characterised by reference to the kind of loss which the claimant might suffer in consequence of the kind of activity in respect of which the defendant owes him the duty. This was made clear by the House of Lords in *Caparo Industries Plc v Dickman*[68] where the scope of an auditor's duty in certifying a company's accounts was characterised by reference both to the purpose for which the auditor gave the certificate and the kind of **6–14**

520–522; *Customs & Excise Commissioners v Barclays Bank Plc* [2006] UKHL 28, [2007] 1 A.C. 181 at [6], [35], [53], [71]–[72], [93].

In cases dealing with claims for economic loss the courts have identified three different approaches to identifying a duty of care: (a) the "assumption of responsibility" test (below, para.6–25); (b) the "threefold test" of "foreseeability", "proximity" and "fair, just and reasonable"; and (c) the incremental approach, based on analogy. See, e.g. *Bank of Credit and Commerce International (Overseas) Ltd v Price Waterhouse* [1998] B.C.C. 617, CA, at 631–635, where Sir Brian Neill thought that all three were useful in looking at a case for which there was no existing authority; and that if applied correctly each would yield the same result; Clerk & Lindsell, paras 8–98 to 8–99. In *Customs & Excise Commissioners v Barclays Bank Plc*, HL took a similar approach but were not entirely unanimous as to whether they preferred to focus on the "assumption of responsibility" test, or the threefold test; *cf. Van Colle v Chief Constable of the Hertfordshire Police* [2008] UKHL 50, [2009] 1 A.C. 225 at [42] (Lord Bingham: the threefold *Caparo* test is currently the most favoured), quoted by Lord Hope in *Mitchell v Glasgow CC* [2009] UKHL 11, [2009] 1 A.C. 874 at [22].

[67] [1990] 2 A.C. 605.

[68] Above, n.67. For the detail of this case, see below, para.6–20. See also *Mitchell v Glasgow CC* [2009] UKHL 11, [2009] 1 A.C. 874 at [26] (Lord Hope: local authority's duty to tenant in exercise of contractual duties as landlord was separate from whether it owed duty to warn about risk of injury from another tenant).

loss which a successful claimant might suffer in consequence of the certificate being inaccurate. Lord Bridge said[69]:

> "It is never sufficient to ask simply whether A owes B a duty of care. It is always necessary to determine the scope of the duty by reference to the kind of damage from which A must take care to save B harmless."

6–15 **Examples of accepted categories of duty.** In identifying an accepted category of duty into which the claimant's case falls one must consider a range of factors: the kind of activity undertaken by the defendant; whether the claimant was the kind of person to whom the defendant, in undertaking this activity, owed a duty; the kind of loss suffered by the claimant, viewed not only in broad terms (physical damage, economic loss, etc.) but also in more detail, to see whether the particular kind of loss, and the way in which the claimant suffered it, were within the scope of a duty owed to him by the defendant. For example, it is clearly accepted that a manufacturer of products owes a duty in certain circumstances to the ultimate consumer of the products but that duty only extends to physical harm, and not to the cost of repair or replacement of the defective product (economic loss).[70] It is in respect of claimants' economic losses that the courts have found most difficulty in defining defendants' duties of care, and therefore it is in cases of economic loss that there has been most discussion of the scope and limits of duties of care in negligence.[71] But although

---

[69] *ibid.*, at 627, following a dictum of Brennan J. in *Sutherland Shire Council v Heyman*, above, n.64 at 487. See also Lord Oliver at 651 and Lord Jauncey at 661. This approach was also restated and applied by the House of Lords in *South Australia Asset Management Corp. v York Montague Ltd* [1997] A.C.191, below, para.6–55; see esp. Lord Hoffmann at 211–212.

[70] *Donoghue v Stevenson* [1932] A.C. 562, HL. There is no *general* duty in respect of the consumer's economic losses of replacement or repair of the product: *Muirhead v Industrial Tank Specialities Ltd* [1986] Q.B. 507, CA. The duty under *Donoghue v Stevenson* extends also to repairers (*Haseldine v C.A. Daw & Son Ltd* [1941] 2 K.B. 343, CA) and in certain circumstances to sellers of secondhand products (*Andrews v Hopkinson* [1957] 1 Q.B. 229): in effect, these were extensions of the *Donoghue* duty to new situations by analogy with the duty owed to manufacturers (and the principles underlying that category of duty), although at the time the courts did not use the language of "extension of existing categories by analogy"; above, n.66.

[71] There is a particular concern based on indeterminate liability: above, paras 6.03 and 6.05. See, in relation to economic losses caused by a defendant's careless acts, *D. & F. Estates Ltd v Church Commissioners for England* [1989]

cases of physical harm appear at first sight to be less difficult,[72] it is still necessary even there to consider carefully, in accordance with the principles discussed in this section, the proper scope of the defendant's duty. And so if the claimant suffers physical damage in

---

A.C. 177, HL; *Murphy v Brentwood DC* [1991] 1 A.C. 398, HL; *Department of the Environment v Thomas Bates & Son* [1991] 1 A.C. 499, HL. It is not possible to treat "economic loss" as a single category of loss: the question here, as always in the tort of negligence, should be whether the particular kind of (economic) loss, suffered by a claimant in consequence of the particular kind of careless act (or omission) of the defendant, can give rise to a duty which has acceptable and principled limits and, under the test currently adopted for expansion of duties of care into new areas (above, para.6–13), whether the case in hand can be regarded as a principled extension by analogy from another, accepted category of duty. This is, in substance, what was attempted by the House of Lords in *Henderson v Merrett Syndicates Ltd*, above, para.6–11, building on *Hedley Byrne* and taking it into cases of economic loss caused otherwise than by reliance on the defendant's statements; see also, in Australia, *Bryan v Maloney* (1995) 182 C.L.R. 609, HCA (builder can owe duty of care to purchaser in respect of diminution of value to house caused by his careless workmanship: the scope of the duty was closely defined at 630), distinguished in *Woolcock Street Investments Pty Ltd v CDG Pty Ltd* (2004) 78 A.L.J.R. 628, HCA (the claimant's "vulnerability"—his inability to protect himself from the consequences of the defendant's want of reasonable care—is an important requirement in cases where there is a duty of care to avoid economic loss: at [23], [80], [212]; the majority did not decide whether doubt should be cast on *Bryan v Maloney*: at [35]; but *cf.* Callinan J. at [211]); in Canada, *Canadian National Railway Co. v Norsk Pacific Steamship Co.* [1992] 1 S.C.R. 1021, SCC, disagreeing on the scope and strength of the rule excluding recovery of economic loss in negligence; *Winnipeg Condominium Corp. No.36 v Bird Construction Co.* (1995) 121 D.L.R. (4th) 193, SCC (building contractors and architect can owe duty of care to purchaser in respect of costs of repair of building which is dangerous because of careless design/workmanship: duty limited to dangerous defects); see also *Privest Properties Ltd v Foundation Co. of Canada Ltd* (1995) 128 D.L.R. (4th) 577; *Martel Building Ltd v Canada* (2000) 193 D.L.R. (4th) 1, SCC (generally no duty of care between commercial parties in conducting negotiations); in New Zealand, *Invercargill City Council v Hamlin* [1996] A.C. 624, PC (local authority can owe duty of care to purchaser of building in respect of inspections during construction); *Riddell v Porteous* [1999] N.Z.L.R. 1, NZCA (builder can owe similar duty); in Singapore: *R.S.P. Architects Planners & Engineers v Ocean Front Pte Ltd* [1996] 1 S.L.R. 113 (developer owed duty to management corporation in relation to faulty construction of common property); *Spandeck Engineering (S.) Pte Ltd v Defence Science & Technology Agency* [2007] SGCA 37 (reviewing the English and Singaporean cases on economic loss generally, and reasserting a general two-stage test based on *Anns v Merton LBC*, above, n.66).

[72] *Caparo Industries Plc v Dickman*, above, n.64 at 655; *Murphy v Brentwood DC*, above, n.71 at 487.

consequence of the defendant's careless acts the scope of any duty owed will be affected by the question of whether the damage was suffered directly or indirectly—for example, if it was caused by third parties over whom the defendant had (or ought to have had) control; and whether imposing a duty is consistent with other relevant factors, such as the matrix of contractual rights in the context of which the defendant's careless act was performed.[73]

Our concern, however, is with the circumstances in which the courts will admit a duty of care in the case of representations. It is therefore necessary to consider in some detail how the courts have taken into the context of representations their general approach to the identification of a duty of care in the tort of negligence.

(b) *Application of general principles to representations*

6–16 **The principles set out in *Hedley Byrne*.** The basic approach taken by the House of Lords in *Hedley Byrne & Co. Ltd v Heller & Partners Ltd*[74] has been described above.[75] It was said that a duty to take care in making a statement can arise where there is a "special relationship" between the defendant and the claimant; where the defendant "takes it upon himself" to make the statement and knows or ought to know that the claimant will rely on the statement; or where the defendant "assumes a responsibility" to the claimant in relation to the statements. Since the decision in *Hedley Byrne* in

[73] *Home Office v Dorset Yacht Co. Ltd* [1970] A.C. 1004, HL; *Smith v Littlewoods Organisation Ltd* [1987] A.C. 241, HL; (damage caused by third parties); *Norwich City Council v Harvey* [1989] 1 W.L.R. 828, CA (careless act by subcontractor causing damage by fire to claimant's property: no duty because inconsistent with allocation of responsibilities in the building contract and subcontract, under which the claimant had the duty to insure against fire). See also *Marc Rich & Co. A.G. v Bishop Rock Marine Co. Ltd* [1996] A.C. 211, HL (careless certification of a ship led to the loss of the claimant's cargo when ship sank: no duty owed by certifier to cargo owner because, even though loss of property was foreseeable, duty was not fair, just and reasonable in the circumstances); *Mitchell v Glasgow CC* [2009] UKHL 11, [2009] 1 A.C. 874 (local authority landlord had no duty to warn tenant (T1) about action it was taking in relation to another tenant (T2) and consequential risk of physical harm to T1 from T2: foreseeability of physical harm not sufficient to create duty, and local authority had not assumed responsibility to T1 in relation to the risk of injury).

[74] [1964] A.C. 465.

[75] For detailed references to the judgments in *Hedley Byrne* see above, para.6–10 and notes to that paragraph.

1963 it has been accepted that a representor may owe a duty in tort to take reasonable care not to cause economic loss to a claimant who relies on his statement. But the test itself has been re-worked and re-stated by the House of Lords in a number of cases, and it is the later cases which explain the scope of the principles which originated in the speeches in *Hedley Byrne*. The most significant general discussion of the scope of the duty established in *Hedley Byrne* is found in the speeches in *Caparo Industries Plc v Dickman*[76]: this case, and the approach taken there by the House of Lords to the categorisation of duties of care in negligence for misrepresentation, will be discussed below.[77] The application of this approach to pre-contractual representations, and the particular contexts in which representors have been held to owe duties of care in respect of their statements, will be discussed in the following sections.[78]

Development since *Hedley Byrne*; the test in *Caparo v Dickman*. 6–17
In *Caparo v Dickman* the House of Lords reviewed *Hedley Byrne* and the cases which had followed it. In the course of this review, Lord Bridge and Lord Oliver summarised the general principles which could be deduced; and it is these statements of the general principles which have come to be regarded as the approach to follow: later judges have often applied the tests stated in *Caparo*, rather than *Hedley Byrne* itself.[79]

---

[76] Above, n.64.

[77] Below, paras 6–17 *et seq*.

[78] Below, paras 6–27 *et seq*. and 6–30 *et seq*.

[79] In *James McNaughton Papers Group Ltd v Hicks Anderson & Co.* [1991] 2 Q.B. 113, CA, at 124, Neill L.J. declined to look behind *Caparo*, but preferred instead to apply as a test the guidance set out there in Lord Oliver's speech. See also *Morgan Crucible Co. Plc v Hill, Samuel & Co. Ltd* [1991] Ch. 295, CA, at 317–318; *Machin v Adams* (1997) 84 B.L.R. 79, CA, at 93, 98; *Andrew v Kounnis Freeman* [1999] 2 B.C.L.C. 641, CA, at 650; *Law Society v KPMG Peat Marwick* [2000] 1 All E.R. 515 at 520, [2000] 1 W.L.R. 1921 at 1928, CA. In some of the more recent cases there has been a resurgence of judicial reliance on *Hedley Byrne*, not in relation to the tests there applied for liability in respect of statements, but in order to look through *Hedley Byrne* to a more general approach to liability in respect of economic loss for careless performance of services: above, para.6–11. When the issue is liability for negligent statements, however, it appears better to continue to regard *Caparo v Dickman* as the best authority to begin the analysis of the categorisation of duties of care in negligence.

Lord Oliver, whilst regarding negligent statements or advice as "a separate category displaying common features from which it is possible to find at least guidelines" by which a test for the duty of care can be deduced,[80] then went on to identify four distinct types of case: physical injury caused directly to the person who relies on the statement, or to a third person; and economic loss suffered directly by the person who relies on the statement, or by a third person.[81]

6–18 **Statement causing physical injury to the person or damage to property.** The cases involving a duty of care not to cause physical injury or damage to property by careless statements can be dealt with quite briefly. It has already been noticed that, even before the decision in *Hedley Byrne*, the courts had taken the step of extending *Donoghue v Stevenson*[82] to the case of a careless statement which caused physical injury to the person who relied on the statement.[83] Lord Oliver in *Caparo v Dickman* thought that it would similarly be possible for a duty to be owed in respect of injuries caused to third

[80] [1990] 2 A.C. 605 at 635. In drawing statements together into a single category Lord Oliver emphasised that what unites liability for careless statements—and distinguishes it from liability for careless acts—is that "the damage which may be occasioned by the spoken or written word is not inherent. It lies always in the reliance by somebody upon the accuracy of that which the word communicates and the loss or damage consequential upon that person having adopted a course of action upon the faith of it". On this, see above, para.3–51.

[81] *ibid.*, at 636. These may be regarded as sub-categories, or in substance separate categories of duty: Lord Oliver said that "it must not be assumed that because they display common features of reliance and foreseeability they are necessarily in all respects analogous". He also left open the possibility that there might be more categories than these four: *ibid.* If Lord Oliver did not intend to include damage to property within his four categories (all his examples are either personal injury or purely economic harm) then this should surely be added; however, the case of damage to property is generally treated as close to personal injury for the purposes of establishing a duty of care: below. For a duty on the police to give accurate information to a prison about the date of a prisoner's arrest (a duty extending to damages to compensate for loss of liberty where the prisoner was wrongly detained beyond his committed term of imprisonment), see *Clarke v Crew* (1999) 149 N.L.J. 899, CA; *cf. Kirkham v Chief Constable of the Greater Manchester Police* [1990] 2 Q.B. 283, CA (police duty to warn prison of known suicide risk in prisoner).

[82] [1932] A.C. 562, HL.

[83] *Clayton v Woodman & Son (Builders) Ltd* [1962] 2 Q.B. 533; above, para.6–04.

parties by statements—such as a doctor's negligent advice on the telephone to a parent, which causes the parent to give the wrong treatment to his or her sick child.[84] There will be relatively little difficulty in establishing a duty in respect of physical injury. The statement does not itself cause the physical injury, but the representee's reliance on the statement gives rise to the physical harm. In cases of physical injury, both injury to the person and damage to property, the courts regard such a duty as being generally based on foreseeability of the harm if care is not taken; and cases whose origin (or origin by analogy) lies in the line of cases at which *Donoghue v Stevenson* itself is the head can be used as authority for a duty, or as the basis of arguments by analogy for a duty.[85] In the case of physical injury consequent on a careless statement, therefore, the question will generally be whether the representor should have foreseen that the representee would rely on the statement and that the claimant's personal injury or damage to his property might result—whether or not the claimant is himself the representee.

Statement causing economic loss to the representee. The careless statement which causes economic loss to the representee as 6–19

[84] [1990] 2 A.C. 605 at 636. Lord Oliver's other examples were the negligent mis-labelling of a dangerous medicine, and the architect's negligent instruction to a bricklayer to remove the keystone of an archway (as in *Clayton v Woodman & Son (Builders) Ltd*, above, n.83).

[85] In *Caparo v Dickman*, above, n.84 at 636 Lord Oliver said that in the cases of physical injury which he discussed (above, n.84) "it is not easy to divorce foreseeability simpliciter and the proximity which flows from the virtual inevitability of damage if the advice is not followed". See also *Perrett v Collins* [1998] 2 Lloyd's Rep. 255, CA (person giving certificate of aircraft airworthiness owed duty to passengers he should have had in contemplation as likely to be injured if certificate given carelessly); *Customs & Excise Commissioners v Barclays Bank Plc* [2006] UKHL 28, [2007] 1 A.C. 181 at [31] (Lord Hoffmann). Sometimes, however, a duty will be denied where, although the physical harm was foreseeable, it is none the less not fair, just or reasonable to impose a duty, e.g. *Marc Rich & Co. A.G. v Bishop Rock Marine Co. Ltd*, above, n.73; or where there is no sufficient relationship of proximity, e.g. *Sutradhar v Natural Environment Research Council* [2006] UKHL 33, [2006] 4 All E.R. 490 (British Geological Survey, testing water from Bangladesh and issuing report about its quality, did not owe duty to individual in Bangladesh who claimed to have suffered arsenic poisoning as a result of Bangladeshi authorities not having taken steps to ensure drinking water not contaminated; the defendants had no control over, or responsibility for, the supply of drinking water in Bangladesh).

a consequence of his reliance on it is the core case with which we are concerned. This was the case for which *Hedley Byrne* was itself the authority; it was also the situation which arose in *Caparo v Dickman*, where the question was whether the auditors of the company owed a duty of care to a purchaser of shares in the company who claimed to have relied on the auditors' audit and certification of the company's accounts. Lord Oliver in *Caparo v Dickman*[86] drew from *Hedley Byrne* the following general statement of principle:

> "the necessary relationship between the maker of a statement or giver of advice ('the adviser') and the recipient who acts in reliance upon it ('the advisee') may typically be held to exist where (1) the advice is required for a purpose, whether particularly specified or generally described, which is made known, either actually or inferentially, to the adviser at the time when the advice is given; (2) the adviser knows, either actually or inferentially, that his advice will be communicated to the advisee, either specifically or as a member of an ascertainable class, in order that it should be used by the advisee for that purpose; (3) it is known either actually or inferentially, that the advice so communicated is likely to be acted upon by the advisee for that purpose without independent inquiry; and (4) it is so acted upon by the advisee to his detriment."

The key elements here[87] in establishing a duty of care are that the defendant should have known[88] the purposes for which his

[86] *Caparo v Dickman*, above, n.84 at 638, drawing also on the dissenting judgment of Denning L.J. in *Candler v Crane, Christmas & Co.* [1951] 2 K.B. 164, CA, above, n.40, which was approved by the House of Lords in *Hedley Byrne*; and *Smith v Bush* [1990] 1 A.C. 831, HL, below, para.6–22. Lord Oliver thought that his propositions were consistent with *Glanzer v Shepard*, 135 N.E. 275 (NYCA, 1922) and *Ultramares Corp. v Touche*, 174 N.E. 441 (NYCA, 1931), above, n.9. He did not claim that his statement was conclusive or exclusive, but it has been applied as a general test in later cases: see above, n.79. See also Lord Bridge at [1990] 2 A.C. 620–621.

[87] The fourth element listed by Lord Oliver (actual reliance by the representee) is surely not part of the test for the duty of care; it is necessary for the defendant's liability, but the actual reliance is part of the proof of causation of the claimant's loss from the statement: below, para.6–53. Lord Bridge's statements of the general test for the duty of care ([1990] 2 A.C. 620–621) do not include a reference to actual reliance.

[88] Throughout the test the question is whether the defendant had "knowledge, actual or inferential", i.e. he knew or ought to have known: see Lord Oliver at 638 ("such knowledge as would be attributed to a reasonable person placed as the [defendant was] placed").

statement might be used; that the claimant was a person who he should have realised might use it for that purpose; and that the claimant would rely on it without taking independent advice.

The purpose of the statement. The scope of the defendant's duty may be defined by reference to the purpose of his statement: that is, if the defendant makes his statement for a particular purpose, then he may owe a duty in respect only of such losses as are suffered by the claimant within the scope of that purpose. In *Caparo v Dickman* this point was crucial: the defendants' statement was an auditor's certification of the company's accounts under the Companies Act 1985[89]; and the House of Lords examined the legislation and concluded that its purpose was to protect the shareholders as a body, to enable them to exercise control over the company in general meeting; not to provide information for individual shareholders or debenture holders or those outside the company to enable them to take investment decisions. The duty of care was therefore owed to the shareholders as a body, not to individuals.[90] **6–20**

The statutory context for the defendants' statement in *Caparo v Dickman* provided the courts with a mechanism to determine the scope of the duty of care. In most cases of misrepresentation there is no such statutory context,[91] but the question, in principle, is the

---

[89] Companies Act 1985 ss.236, 237; see now Companies Act 2006 ss.495, 498.

[90] *Caparo v Dickman*, above, n.84 at 625–627, 629, 650–654, 661–662; applied in *Mann v Coutts & Co.* [2003] EWHC 2138 (Comm), [2004] 1 All E.R. (Comm) 1 at [178]–[193] (purpose of letter issued by bank); *Man Nutzfahrzeuge A.G. v Freightliner Ltd* [2007] EWCA Civ 910, [2007] 2 C.L.C. 455 (auditor did not owe special audit duty to parent company in respect of consequences of fraudulent statements made by audited company's financial controller as to accuracy of accounts).

[91] But for other examples see *Yuen Kun Yeu v Att-Gen of Hong Kong* [1988] A.C. 175, PC (scope of duties owed by Commissioner of Deposit-taking Companies defined by reference to Ordinance under which he acted); *Law Society v KPMG Peat Marwick* [2000] 1 W.L.R. 1921, CA (accountant reporting to Law Society under Solicitors Act 1974, s.34); *Jain v Trent Strategic Health Authority* [2009] UKHL 4, [2009] 1 A.C. 853 (health authority making inaccurate statements to magistrate for cancellation of nursing home registration under Registered Homes Act 1984 s.30 did not owe duty to proprietors of home because purpose of statutory power was to protect residents); *Desmond v Chief Constable of Nottinghamshire Police* [2011] EWCA Civ 3, [2011] Fam. Law. 358 (police providing information as required by Police Force Act 1997 to Criminal Records Bureau for issue of enhanced criminal record certificate: no common law duty to subject of reference). See also *Stovin v Wise* [1996] A.C. 923, HL (general

same: what was the purpose for which the statement was made? It has therefore been held that a defendant who provides *information* for the purpose of enabling the claimant to decide upon a course of action owes a duty only in respect of the consequences of that information being inaccurate, and not for other losses which the claimant might suffer as a result of transactions into which he enters in reliance on the information; whereas a defendant who provides *advice* as to what course of action the claimant should take will be held to owe a wider duty, which extends to the consequences to the claimant of his acting on that advice.[92] And even in the case of a statutory audit under the Companies Act, it is open for a claimant to argue that an auditor's certification, on the facts, was given not simply for the narrow statutory purposes of the audit but for wider purposes and therefore the duty extends to those wider purposes.[93] It is clear that the defendant does not owe a duty to a claimant simply because he could have foreseen that the claimant might act on the statement and suffer the loss: such a test would be far too wide, and would have imposed liability in *Caparo v Dickman* itself.[94] The search for the "purpose" of the statement as a means of defining the scope of the duty is in reality just another aspect of the broad questions of the extent of the duty which the defendant can be held to have undertaken; and whether the claimant was justified in relying on the statement in the way that he did.[95]

---

principles for existence of duty of care where defendant exercising statutory powers). Even if there is a relevant statutory context which might define the scope of duty in relation to a statement, the defendant may incur a wider scope of duty if he takes it upon himself to go beyond the statutory requirements: *Hagen v ICI Chemicals & Polymers Ltd* [2002] I.R.L.R. 31 at [93] (employer, with duty to give prescribed information to trades unions or employee representatives under the Transfer of Undertakings (Protection of Employment) Regulations 1981, giving more extensive information directly to individual employees for them to consider).

92 *South Australia Asset Management Corp. v York Montague Ltd* [1997] A.C.191 at 214. On this case and the measure of damages recoverable in cases of negligent "information" or "advice", see below, para.6–55.

93 Below, para.6–33.

94 [1990] 2 A.C. 605 at 631–632, 643 (Lord Oliver: it would "open up a limitless vista of uninsurable risk for the professional man"), 655 (Lord Jauncey).

95 *cf.* below, para.6–22.

Foreseeability of the identity of the claimant; chains of communications. The claimant must be a person who the defendant ought to have realised would rely on the statement: that is, the claimant must show not only that the defendant owed a duty, but that the duty was owed *to him*. But this does not mean that the defendant must know the identity of the claimant: it is sufficient if he knows him as "a member of an ascertainable class"[96]: the claimant is the kind of person who the defendant ought to realise would rely on the statement. In *Hedley Byrne* itself the defendant bank which gave the credit reference on one of its customers did not know the name of the person for whom the information was required: the enquiry came through a correspondent bank, and it was sufficient that the defendant should have known that it was required for a customer of the correspondent bank, for the purposes of extending credit.[97] 6–21

A greater difficulty arises where the statement is made to A with a view to A relying on it for a particular purpose, but it is passed on by A to B who relies on it. This may happen either because B is substituted for A; or because B relies on the statement in addition to A. An example of the first case would be where a property valuation is made for A, whom the valuer knows is contemplating lending funds on the security of the property, but after the report has been

---

[96] *Caparo v Dickman*, above, n.84 at 638 (Lord Oliver); see also at 621 (Lord Bridge).

[97] [1964] A.C. 465, HL, at 493–494; *Nightingale FinanceLtd v White & Co.* [1997] E.G.C.S. 183 (statements made to a limited class, of which one member was then entitled to rely on it and claim that a duty was owed to him directly). See also *Wild v National Bank of New Zealand Ltd* [1991] 2 N.Z.L.R. 454 (company not yet in existence at the time the statement was made: duty owed in respect of pre-incorporation representation where the representor knew that it would be a company yet to be formed, such as the claimant, that would rely on it); *M.G.B. Printing and Design Ltd v Kall Kwik UK Ltd* [2010] EWHC 624 (QB), [2010] All E.R. (D) 18 (Apr) at [24] (pre-incorporation statement but defendant always knew and contemplated that the company when incorporated would have the benefit of the advice); *Niru Battery Manufacturing Co. v Milestone Trading Ltd* [2002] EWHC 1425, [2002] 2 All E.R. (Comm) 705 at [66]; affirmed [2003] EWCA Civ 1446, [2004] Q.B. 985 (inspection company, though instructed by seller, is aware that its certificate is likely to be required for presentation to the buyer or a bank as part of the documents against which payment is to be made, so buyer is the person whom the inspection company should have in contemplation as the person most likely to be affected by any error in the certificate); followed by *AIC Ltd v ITS Testing Services (UK) Ltd* [2005] EWHC 2122 (Comm), [2006] 1 Lloyd's Rep. 1 at [14], [183].

prepared it is in fact B, rather than A, who lends the funds after receiving a copy of the report from A. In such a case it might be held, depending on the facts, that the valuation was aimed only at A personally and so B was not entitled to rely on it; but a court might be prepared to hold that the substitution of B for A does not change the scope of the duty, which was intended to be owed to the person who lent the funds (that is, who relied on it for the particular transaction for which the valuation was prepared).[98] In the case where B relies on the statement in addition to A, it will be more difficult to show that the duty extends also to B: B then has a separate interest in the statement, and may well rely on it for a purpose different from A's reliance, or in a capacity different from A's. It is possible that a duty will be owed to B as well as to A, but it must be shown that B was a person who the defendant realised would also be likely to receive and act upon the statement for his own purposes.[99]

---

[98] The cases on this particular issue are mixed: for a duty to B, see *Assured Advances Ltd v Ashbee & Co.* [1994] E.G.C.S. 169; against a duty to B, see *Secured Residential Funding Plc v Nationwide Building Society* [1997] E.G.C.S. 138; *Barex Brokers Ltd v Morris Dean & Co.* [1999] P.N.L.R. 344, CA (duty owed only to original lender not to an assignee). If A can be held simply to have been acting as agent for B, his undisclosed principal, a duty can be owed directly to B through the agency of A: *Secured Residential Funding Plc v Nationwide Building Society* [1998] E.G.C.S. 64.

[99] *Smith v Eric S. Bush* [1990] 1 A.C. 831, HL (valuer, instructed by mortgagee, owed duty on facts also to purchaser/mortgagor to whom valuer's report was in substance communicated and who paid for it, even though it was not actually passed on). The HL emphasised that there must be a probability (not merely foreseeability or a possibility) that the statement would be passed on to the purchaser who would rely on it in deciding to proceed with the purchaser: at 847, 848, 865, 871; and that the duty was owed only to the first purchaser who would receive and rely on the statement, and not to future purchasers: at 865. *Cf. Machin v Adams* (1997) 84 B.L.R. 79, CA (architect's certificate of state of completion of building works, addressed to owner of property; duty did not extend to purchaser of property to whom certificate was shown, and who claimed to have relied on it in deciding to proceed with purchase); *Omega Trust Co. Ltd v Wright Son & Pepper* [1997] 1 E.G.L.R. 120, CA (valuation of property addressed to one potential lender also passed onto second, undisclosed lender who lent 60% of the total loan: no duty on facts to second lender because of a disclaimer, limiting the duty to the valuer's "client", which was reasonable under the Unfair Contract Terms Act 1977; see also below, Ch.9); *Shankie-Williams v Heavey* [1986] 2 E.G.L.R. 139, CA (damp rot surveyor instructed for one flat did not owe duty to potential purchaser of adjoining flat to whom report was later shown); *Precis (521) Plc v William M. Mercer Ltd* [2004] EWCA Civ 114, [2005]

Foreseeability that the claimant would not act without taking independent advice; reasonable reliance. According to Lord Oliver's statement of general principle it must also be shown that the defendant should have realised that his statement was likely to be acted upon by the claimant for the purpose for which it was intended, *without independent inquiry.* This part of the test takes us to the heart of the matter. In substance, it means that the defendant should have realised that the claimant would rely on his care in making the statement, and would rely on the statement itself,[100] rather than taking his own steps to verify it. Looked at from the claimant's point of view, it means that the claimant will assert that, in the circumstances in which the statement was made, he was entitled to rely on the statement. The reasonableness of reliance by the claimant is therefore an element in the analysis of whether the defendant should have expected him so to rely.[101] 6–22

In *Smith v Eric S. Bush*,[102] for example, the valuer instructed by a mortgagee to value a house, knowing that the valuation would probably be relied upon by the prospective purchaser/mortgagor of the house, was held to owe a duty of care to the mortgagor, in carrying out the valuation. But the House of Lords made clear that the duty arose on the facts because the mortgagor's reliance on the valuation was reasonable. It was a purchase of a:

P.N.L.R. 28 (actuary, producing report for company on its pension fund, owed no duty to purchaser of company's shares to whom report was later passed on: purpose of report (above, para.6–20) was internal management of the fund and not review for third party's purposes, and although actuary knew that there was a corporate transaction in contemplation, it had no pre-existing relationship with the purchaser and did not assume responsibility to it).

[100] These are two very different senses of "reliance": to say that the claimant relied on the statement is an issue of causation: below, para.6–53; to say that the claimant relied on the defendant's skill is part of the test for a duty, but of itself it is hardly a satisfactory test: *cf.* below, para.6–25, n.125.

[101] *James McNaughton Paper Group Ltd v Hicks Anderson & Co.* [1991] 2 Q.B. 113, CA, at 126–127. This is the parallel, in the context of statements, of the principle in *Donoghue v Stevenson* [1932] A.C. 562, HL, that where a manufacturer can expect intermediate examination of his product, he does not owe a duty of care to the ultimate consumer: *McInery v Lloyds Bank Ltd* [1974] 1 Lloyd's Rep. 246, CA, at 254 (claimant should have consulted his own lawyers to check statement made by bank manager). For the possibility of contributory negligence by the claimant in relying on the statement without taking steps to verify it, see below, para.6–48.

[102] Above, n.99.

> "dwelling house of modest value in which it is widely recognised by surveyors that purchasers are in fact relying on their care and skill."

The result might well be different in the case of a valuation of a different kind of property, such as industrial property, large blocks of flats or very expensive houses, or even residential houses or flats of modest value where the purpose of the purchase is for commercial letting rather than owner-occupation,[103] because then the general expectation of the behaviour of purchasers would be different; and prudence would require the purchaser to obtain his own, independent valuation and survey.[104]

In *Patchett v Swimming Pool and Allied Trades Association Ltd*[105] a trade association made statements on its website to the effect that its members were "fully vetted before being admitted to membership, with checks on their financial record", and that only their registered pool installers belonged to their "bond and warranty scheme" which protected clients against insolvency of the contractor. This was held by a majority of the Court of Appeal not to give rise to a duty of care in favour of a member of the public who consulted the website and employed a swimming pool contractor whose name and details were on the website but who was only an

---

[103] *Scullion v Bank of Scotland (trading as Colleys)* [2011] EWCA Civ 693, [2011] All E.R. (D) 126 (Jun) at [47]–[54] (buy-to-let purchase of small residential property different from the ordinary residential house purchase of *Smith v Bush*: even if it was foreseeable on facts that purchaser would rely on the valuation, it was not just and equitable that valuer should be liable, because buy-to-let is essentially commercial in nature, the buy-to-let market has developed since *Smith v Bush*, a buy-to-let purchaser is as interested in rental value as capital value, and a valuation prepared for a mortgagee naturally focuses on capital value: so no inherent likelihood that buy-to-let purchaser would rely on valuation provided to a mortgagee); *Wilson v D.M. Hall & Sons* [2005] P.N.L.R. 22, OH (bank's valuer did not owe duty to experienced businessman undertaking commercial property development).

[104] *Smith v Eric S. Bush*, above, n.99 at 859–860 (Lord Griffiths); see also Lord Templeman at 854 and Lord Jauncey at 872. For other cases in which a duty of care has been denied because it was not reasonable in the circumstances for the claimant to rely, see *Williams v Natural Life Health Foods Ltd* [1998] 1 W.L.R. 830, HL, at 837 (director of company did not assume personal responsibility for advice given by his company); *Fashion Brokers Ltd v Clarke Hayes* [2000] Lloyd's Rep. P.N. 398, CA (solicitor not entitled to rely on information about permitted use of premises given by unidentified person at local authority over the telephone).

[105] [2009] EWCA Civ 717, [2010] 2 All E.R. (Comm) 138.

affiliate member of the trade association and so was not covered by the warranty scheme, but who became insolvent before the pool was completed. The fact that the statement was on a website was not of itself determinative: the normal principles of negligence apply.[106] But on the facts, no duty arose because the website invited readers to apply for an "information pack and members list": when read as a whole, the website urged the reader to make independent inquiry.[107]

Duty not limited to statements made in the course of the representor's business or profession. It was held, by a majority, by the Privy Council in *Mutual Life Ltd v Evatt*[108] that a duty of care could normally[109] arise only if the defendant's statement was made in the ordinary course of his business or profession; that is, if the defendant either carries on the business or profession of giving such advice or making such statements, or at least has held himself out to the claimant as possessing the skill and competence of one who is in such a business or profession.[110] The Privy Council therefore held that a statement made on behalf of a company about the financial stability of an associated company was not capable of giving rise to a duty of care to the representee who then took investment decisions on the basis of the advice received, since the representor company was not in the business of giving such 6–23

[106] *ibid.*, at [40] (Lord Clarke M.R.: "some websites are interactive and it may be possible . . . to conclude in particular circumstances that a duty is owed"); [42] (Scott Baker L.J.: "no different legal principles apply to misrepresentations on a website than to those anywhere else in the public domain").

[107] *ibid.*, at [31], [43]. Smith L.J. dissented on the basis that the website did not suggest to the reader that it was necessary to obtain the information pack in order to make a further check on the credentials of the members listed on the website, and that, objectively construed, the website invited reliance on the qualities inherent in membership without further inquiry: at [55], [57].

[108] [1971] A.C. 793 (Lord Diplock, Lord Hodson and Lord Guest). Lord Reid and Lord Morris, who sat in the House in *Hedley Byrne*, dissented and (at 813) disagreed with the construction placed by the majority in *Mutual Life* on passages taken from their speeches in *Hedley Byrne*.

[109] The majority left open the possibility that other particular factors might give rise to the duty, such as the defendant having a financial interest in the transaction upon which he gives advice: *ibid.*, at 809, referring to *W.B. Anderson & Sons Ltd v Rhodes (Liverpool) Ltd* [1967] 2 All E.R. 850. It does not, however, appear that Cairns J. in that case thought that it was the defendant's financial interest that created the duty: see at 857, 862.

[110] *ibid.*, at 805–806, 809.

financial advice. However, in their dissenting judgment Lord Reid and Lord Morris preferred the view that the defendant need not be, nor hold himself out as being, in a business or profession which involves making statements of the kind relied on to found the claim. In their view, a duty did arise on the facts because the statement was made on a business occasion—that is, it was not merely a casual or social context, but an occasion when the representee, knowing that the representor had access to relevant information on which to give advice as to the associated company's financial position, was reasonably entitled to rely on the advice; and the representor knew that the advice would be relied on. This latter approach, emphasising the core issue of whether the representee was reasonably entitled to rely on the statement, and whether the representor ought to have realised that he would so rely, is the better approach; and this is the view that has in general been adopted by the courts in England.[111]

---

[111] For criticism in the CA of the judgment of the majority in *Mutual Life Ltd v Evatt*, see *Esso Petroleum Co. Ltd v Mardon* [1976] Q.B. 801 at 827 (statements by petrol company to prospective tenant of petrol station about likely throughput, and therefore profitability: duty owed, but the representor there had a financial interest, so the decision of the majority in *Evatt* might in any event have covered the case: see argument by claimant's counsel at 814); *Howard Marine and Dredging Co. Ltd v A. Ogden & Sons (Excavations) Ltd* [1978] Q.B. 574 at 591, 600. In the HL the point was left open by Lord Oliver in *Caparo Industries Plc v Dickman* [1990] 2 A.C. 605 at 637 (auditors' certification of accounts was in any event covered by the judgment of the majority in *Evatt*); and in *Spring v Guardian Assurance Plc* [1995] 2 A.C. 296 at 320 Lord Goff also did not need to decide the issue but pointed out that the decision of the Privy Council is not binding on the House, and "has attracted serious criticism, particularly in the light of the formidable dissenting opinion of Lord Reid and Lord Morris" (reference given by former employer to prospective employer: "the skill of preparing a reference in respect of an employee falls as much within the expertise of an employer as the skill of preparing a bank reference fell within the expertise of the defendant bank in *Hedley Byrne* itself": *ibid.*). See also *Lennon v Commissioner of Police of the Metropolis* [2004] EWCA Civ 130, [2004] 1 W.L.R. 2594 at [25]–[28] (personnel officer in Metropolitan Police Service owed duty of care to police officer by assuming responsibility in giving advice about financial consequences of transfer to another force; irrelevant that she was not a professional adviser, nor employed to give advice to others in the Service about terms and conditions of service, service allowances or transfers). For a case where a friend was liable for giving careless advice about the quality of a second-hand car, because in the circumstances he acted as the buyer's agent in inspecting the car and went beyond a purely social or informal relationship to one

Statement causing economic loss to a third party.[112] In *Caparo v Dickman*[113] Lord Oliver characterised the case of a careless statement which causes economic loss to a third party as a different category, or sub-category, of duty. In such a case the defendant makes a statement to X; X relies upon it, but it is the claimant, rather than X, who suffers the loss. Even if the defendant owes a duty to X under the principles discussed earlier in this section,[114] that is not sufficient here. X can sue only in respect of his own loss; a duty must be owed directly to the claimant if he is to have a claim for his own loss. But the statement is not made to the claimant; so the language of the test for the duty of care under *Hedley Byrne* and *Caparo v Dickman*, used for the more straightforward case of a statement addressed to a person who then relies on it for his own purposes and himself suffers loss as a result, is not here suitable. One would expect as the starting point, if such a duty is to be held to exist in favour of a third party, that the statement made to X must satisfy all the elements of the test described in the earlier paragraphs of this section, except for the requirement that X must himself have suffered loss: so the defendant ought never to owe a duty to the third party unless he knew or ought to have known that the statement, made to X, would be relied upon by X for a particular purpose. But then there is a further difficulty. If the defendant were to owe a duty directly to any person whom he could foresee would suffer loss as a result of X's reliance—even any person whom he could foresee would be likely, or very likely, to suffer such loss[115]—the net would be spread far too wide. More is necessary to show the direct link of a duty of care owed by the defendant directly 6–24

of business where the buyer was relying on his skill and judgment, see *Chaudhury v Prabhakar* [1988] 3 All E.R. 718, CA.

[112] C. Witting, "Justifying Liability to Third Parties for Negligent Misstatements" (2000) 20 O.J.L.S. 615.

[113] [1990] 2 A.C. 605 at 636. Lord Oliver cited *Ross v Caunters* [1980] Ch. 297 and *Ministry of Housing and Local Government v Sharp* [1970] 2 Q.B. 223, CA, below, but did not discuss these cases further.

[114] There is no necessary link between a duty owed to X and a duty owed to the third party; the latter duty can exist without the former: *Spring v Guardian Assurance Plc* [1995] 2 A.C. 296 at 320.

[115] *cf.* the emphasis on the higher likelihood of reliance and loss in cases of a statement passed on to a third party: *Smith v Bush*, above, n.99. But the case there addresses a different issue: it is the likely *reliance* by that third party which provides an acceptable limiting factor for the range of potential claimants. Here, there is loss by the third party, but no reliance.

to the claimant. And in the absence of a factor such as the reliance by the claimant on the statement, it is extremely difficult to devise an appropriate test which will be generally applicable: it is therefore an area in which a careful and precise categorisation of cases[116] to establish duties of care will be necessary.

There are only a few reported cases involving such duties to third parties. In *Ministry of Housing and Local Government v Sharp*[117] the employee of a local authority who conducted a search of the local land charges register was held to owe a duty of care to persons who had registered charges in the register, so that when the employee carelessly failed to disclose in a search conducted for a purchaser of land that the claimant had registered a charge, with the effect that the purchaser took free of the charge, the claimant was entitled to sue for the loss that it suffered by no longer being able to enforce the charge. In *Ross v Caunters*[118] a solicitor who negligently failed properly to advise his client on the formalities necessary to execute a will, with the result that one intended beneficiary was unable to take a legacy because her husband had witnessed the will, was held to owe a duty of care directly to that beneficiary and therefore was liable to compensate her for the lost legacy. In *Spring v Guardian Assurance Plc* the House of Lords held that an employer or former employer, giving a reference on the character and abilities of his employee to a prospective future employer, can[119] owe a duty to the employee to take reasonable care in preparing the reference; and in such a case the employee is

[116] Above, para.6–13.

[117] [1970] 2 Q.B. 223, CA.

[118] [1980] Ch. 297 (Megarry V.C.), following *Ministry of Housing v Sharp*, above, and preferring to treat the facts as giving rise to an application of *Donoghue v Stevenson* [1932] A.C. 562, HL, rather than an extension of *Hedley Byrne*. The case, like *Ministry of Housing v Sharp*, was described by Lord Oliver in *Caparo v Dickman* [1990] 2 A.C. 605 at 636 as giving rise to "certain difficulties of analysis"; but in *White v Jones* [1995] 2 A.C. 207, HL, the duty was extended to the case where a solicitor negligently failed to draw up a will. The reasoning of the members of the House in *White v Jones* varied, and indeed Lord Keith and Lord Mustill dissented. But the case appears to confirm that, to be workable, the case of the solicitor's duty to a third party beneficiary under a will must be characterised as a separate category of duty and closely defined; and that it need not be limited to a duty in respect of advice or other statements: see below, para.6–25.

[119] For the circumstances in which such a duty will be owed, and for the scope of such a duty, see below, para.6–40.

entitled to claim damages if the reference is inaccurate and negligently prepared and he suffers loss as a result of the prospective employer relying on it and deciding not to employ him. In so holding,[120] the House of Lords devised a new category of case, drawing it from *Hedley Byrne* and *Caparo v Dickman*. In *Gorham v British Telecommunications Plc*[121] an insurance company in giving advice to its customer in relation to insurance provision for pension and life cover was held to owe a duty of care not only to the customer but also to the customer's wife and infant dependants whose interests were central to the purpose of the customer's venture into insurance.

In each of these cases it was possible to impose a duty of care because there was a limited range of potential claimants, and the defendant should have realised that the particular claimant, rather than the representee, would inevitably lose if the statement was inaccurate. The claimant was not just a collateral third party, who might suffer economic loss as the ripples of the consequences of the defendant's carelessness spread; the claimant was a person directly involved in the particular transaction into which the representee entered in reliance on the statement. In *Ministry of Housing and Local Government v Sharp* and *Spring v Guardian Assurance Plc* the claimant was a person with whom the defendant had had prior dealings, and therefore there could, in a sense, be said to be a pre-existing relationship involving reliance and care owed by the

---

[120] [1995] 2 A.C. 296, HL. The reasoning of each member of the House was not identical. Lord Goff (at 316–317) thought that the case was covered by *Hedley Byrne* itself, when properly interpreted as authority for a general principle of *assumption of responsibility*: above, para.6–11, below, para.6–25; Lord Lowry (at 325) agreed with Lord Goff on this point. Lord Slynn (at 332, 335) and Lord Woolf (at 342, 344) thought that the existing authorities did not cover the case, but using principles taken from *Hedley Byrne* and *Caparo v Dickman*, as well as the general language of "foreseeability", "proximity" and whether the duty would be "fair just and reasonable" (above, para.6–13) they devised and stated a test applicable to employers' references. Lord Keith dissented, on the basis that such a duty would be contrary to public policy, since it would cut across the defence of qualified privilege in the tort of defamation. *Cf. West Wiltshire DC v Garland* [1995] Ch. 297, CA (district auditors making report on local government officers under the Local Government Finance Act 1982 did not owe duty to officers under principle of *Spring v Guardian Assurance Plc* because the Act made clear that auditors should be free, short of bad faith, to criticise an officer without fear of exposing themselves to action for negligence).

[121] [2000] 1 W.L.R. 2129, CA, following *White v Jones*, above, n.118.

defendant to the claimant. Indeed, in these cases the defendant was under a duty to make the statement.[122] And in *Ross v Caunters* and *Gorham v British Telecommunications Plc* although there was no such prior relationship between the solicitor and the beneficiary, or between the insurance company and the infant dependants, the purpose of the transaction was to confer a benefit on a defined class of named individuals, including the claimant. These general features which link the cases do not of themselves amount to a satisfactory test for the duty of care. But they explain why the courts were prepared to impose a duty, and they are factors which a court will be likely to consider in future, different cases when deciding whether a new duty can be held to be owed by analogy with one or more of the existing categories.[123]

6–25 **"Assumption of responsibility".** There have, however, been some recent attempts to unite the cases under a generalised principle: that the basis of a defendant's duty to the claimant in respect of the economic loss he suffers is the defendant's

---

[122] In *Sharp* the statement was made under the Land Charges Act 1925, s.17(1), in response to a search of the local land charges register; in *Spring* the reference was required to be given under the Life Assurance and Unit Trust Regulatory Organisation (LAUTRO) rules. However, this statutory or regulatory context is not sufficient to define the duty (see above, para.6–20) since, at least in the case of *Spring*, it appears unlikely that the purpose of the regulatory requirement under the LAUTRO rules was to protect an individual employee in Spring's position.

[123] A doctor giving a medical report to a prospective employer on a job applicant who is not his patient does not owe a duty to the applicant: *Kapfunde v Abbey National Plc* [1999] I.C.R. 1, CA; nor does a doctor owe a duty to the patient's employer who suffers loss when the employee cannot continue his work: *West Bromwich Albion FC Ltd v El-Safty* [2005] EWHC 2866, [2006] P.N.L.R. 18 ("Should a consultant for example advising a Rooney or a Beckham or a Flintoff have a potential tortious liability to their club/county or England for negligent treatment—a liability running to many millions of pounds?" Royce J. at [64]); affirmed [2006] EWCA Civ 1299, [2007] P.I.Q.R. P7. And an insurance investigator, reporting on the causes of a fire, does not owe a duty to the insured whose claim is rejected: *South Pacific Manufacturing Co. Ltd v New Zealand Security Consultants & Investigations Ltd* [1992] 2 N.Z.L.R. 282, NZCA, approved *Spring v Guardian Assurance Plc* at 323–324 and 350. But a former employer who sends an e-mail containing negligent mis-statements to its employee's new employer, resulting in the employee being dismissed, does owe a duty to the former employee, even though this is not a "reference" as such and so is not covered by *Spring v Guardian Assurance Plc*, above, n.120, or any other authority: *McKie v Swindon College* [2011] EWHC 469 (QB), [2011] I.R.L.R. 575.

assumption of responsibility in favour of the claimant for the task he undertook. This principle was drawn from *Hedley Byrne* by Lord Goff in *Spring v Guardian Assurance Plc*[124] and applied to explain the basis of the duty to the employee who suffered loss in consequence of, but not by virtue of his own reliance on, the defendant's statement.[125] It was then immediately adopted by the House of Lords in *Henderson v Merrett Syndicates Ltd*[126] and other cases have also adopted the language of this test.[127] In essence, the

---

[124] Above, n.120.

[125] It is understandable why Lord Goff emphasised this aspect of the test in *Hedley Byrne*, above, para.6–10. In the context of a duty owed in respect of a statement, where the claimant relies on the statement and himself suffers loss, it is equally possible to use language based on the claimant's likely reliance and the defendant's *assumption of responsibility* arising from his foresight of that reliance. But in a case where there is no such reliance by the claimant—either because (as in *Spring v Guardian Assurance Plc*) the claimant suffers loss as a third party in consequence of a statement or (as in *White v Jones*, below, para.6–41) there is no statement at all, but the test is extended to cover acts and omissions, as well as words—the emphasis has to shift to the defendant's assumption of responsibility. See also J. Cartwright, "Liability in Negligence: New Directions or Old?" (1997) 13 Const. L.J. 157 at pp.159–162.

[126] [1995] 2 A.C. 145, HL (Lord Goff; the other members of the House of Lords agreed with his analysis).

[127] In the context of statements: *Williams v Natural Life Health Foods Ltd* [1998] 1 W.L.R. 830, HL (no personal assumption of responsibility by director for statements made by company); *Peach Publishing Ltd v Slater & Co.* [1998] B.C.C. 139, CA (assurance by accountant to purchaser of company that unaudited accounts were accurate: no duty on facts); *W v Essex CC* [1999] Fam. 90, CA (assurances by council to foster parents that no sexual abuser would be placed with them; rvsd on question of striking out: [2001] 2 A.C. 592); *Electra Private Equity Partners v KPMG Peat Marwick* [2000] B.C.C. 368, CA (auditor may assume responsibility to potential investor for accuracy of audit work). In other contexts: *Swinney v Chief Constable of Northumbria* [1997] Q.B. 464, CA (assumption of responsibility by police to informer to preserve confidentiality); *Invercargill City Council v Hamlin* [1996] A.C. 624 at 642, PC (builder's duty to subsequent purchaser based on assumption of responsibility and reliance: following *Bryan v Maloney* (1995) 182 C.L.R. 109, HCA, above, para.6–15, n.71); *Elguzouli-Daf v Metropolitan Police Commissioner* [1995] Q.B. 335, CA (Crown Prosecution Service owes no duty to particular defendant in absence of assumption of responsibility). However, even if an "assumption of responsibility" is sufficient to give rise to a duty of care in relation to economic loss, it is not a necessary test: *Customs & Excise Commissioners v Barclays Bank Plc* [2006] UKHL 28, [2007] 1 A.C. 181 at [4] (Lord Bingham); and although it has come to be seen as the "touchstone" or the "core" of claims for economic loss, this is too

test is to be objective[128]: viewing the words and actions of the defendant, can he be taken to have assumed a responsibility to the claimant to take care in performing the task in respect of which it is alleged that he was careless and caused the claimant's loss; and was the claimant reasonably entitled to rely[129] on the assumption of responsibility by the defendant? This test was devised expressly to take the decision in *Hedley Byrne* beyond the sphere of liability for careless statements: to that extent, it is beyond the scope of this book, although it has also sometimes been used in the context of statements[130] to consider whether a defendant's duty extends to the particular claimant who relies on his statements. However, where the direct authority of *Caparo Industries Plc v Dickman* is applicable, it is submitted that the statement in that case of principles for the existence and scope of a duty of care in respect of negligent statements[131] is to be preferred because it was devised particularly for the context of a statement made to a person who relies on it. But even in such a case it is equally possible to describe the defendant's duty as based on the responsibility he has assumed towards the claimant, by virtue of his making a statement which he knows the claimant will probably rely on for a particular purpose: the tests of "known reliance" and "assumption of responsibility" in such a case are two sides of the same coin.[132]

---

simple: *ibid.*, at [35]–[37] (Lord Hoffmann: it is a "slogan"), [49]–[53] (Lord Rodger: not "*the* touchstone"), [83], [93] (Lord Mance: "a core area" but "there is no single common denominator").

[128] *Henderson v Merrett Syndicates Ltd*, above, n.126 at 181; *Williams v Natural Life Health Foods Ltd*, above, n.127 at 835; *Customs & Excise Commissioners v Barclays Bank Plc*, above, n.127, at [5], [73]. But before there can be in law an assumption of responsibility the defendent must have had a choice: *Customs & Excise Commissioners v Barclays Bank Plc*, above (no duty owed by bank to third party to take reasonable care to comply with terms of freezing injunction affecting customer's account: the court order does not create a duty of care; see esp. Lord Hoffmann at [38]–[39]); *Desmond v Chief Constable of Nottinghamshire Police* [2011] EWCA Civ 3, [2011] Fam. Law. 358 at [48] (police providing information as required by Police Force Act 1997 to Criminal Records Bureau for issue of enhanced criminal record certificate have no choice: no assumption of responsibility).

[129] *Williams v Natural Life Health Foods Ltd*, above, n.127 at 837.

[130] Above, n.127.

[131] Above, para.6–19.

[132] *Bank of Credit and Commerce International (Overseas) Ltd v Price Waterhouse* [1998] B.C.C. 617, CA, at 634–635; *Perre v Apand Pty Ltd* (1999) 73

Duty to speak? The general question of when, and why, a duty to speak will arise will be discussed in Part III. But it should be noted here that, under the development of the *Hedley Byrne* principle made in *Henderson v Merrett Syndicates*,[133] a defendant can owe a duty to exercise reasonable care which extends to the duty to give information or advice, as well as the duty to take care that any information or advice actually given is accurate. Here again the emphasis is on the assumption of responsibility by the defendant rather than the reliance by the claimant.[134] 6–26

(c) Duties of care between parties to a contract

The tort of negligence in a contractual setting. The principles for the establishment of a duty of care discussed above are the general principles of the tort of negligence in relation to statements. Although the existence of a contract between the claimant and defendant might once have been a significant factor in establishing a duty owed by the defendant to take care in giving information or advice to the claimant,[135] the tort of negligence developed during the twentieth century so as to become general and independent of 6–27

A.J.L.R. 1190, HCA, at 1196 (Gaudron J.); *Esanda Finance Corp. Ltd v Peat Marwick Hungerfords* (1997) 188 C.L.R. 241, HCA, at 264.

[133] Above, para.6–25.

[134] *Henderson v Merrett Syndicates Ltd*, above, n.126 at 181 (Lord Goff, discussing a professional's assumption of responsibility to take positive steps for his client: liability for negligent omissions as much as negligent acts of commission); *Mitchell v Glasgow CC* [2009] UKHL 11, [2009] 1 A.C. 874 at [29] (Lord Hope: duty to warn of potential physical injury from criminal act of third party arises only where defendant assumed responsibility for safety); see also *Hamilton v Allied Domecq Plc* [2007] UKHL 33, 2007 S.C.(H.L.) 142 at [19]–[23] (no "voluntary assumption of responsibility" so no duty to speak, applying *Banque Keyser Ullmann S.A. v Skandia (U.K.) Insurance Co. Ltd* [1990] 1 Q.B. 65, CA, at 794–795). For examples, see *Credit Lyonnais S.A. v Russell Jones & Walker* [2002] EWHC 1310 (Ch), [2003] P.N.L.R. 2 (solicitor's duty to inform client of relevant matters discovered whilst carrying out instructions); *John D. Wood Ltd v Knatchbull* [2002] EWHC 2822 (QB), [2003] P.N.L.R. 17 (estate agent's duty to inform client of marketing of neighbouring property at higher price, thus depriving client of opportunity to obtain a better sale price); *H.I.H. Casualty & General Insurance Ltd v J.L.T. Risk Solutions Ltd* [2007] EWCA Civ 710, [2007] 2 C.L.C. 62 (insurance broker's post-placement duty).

[135] Above, para.6–08.

contract. *Donoghue v Stevenson*[136] established that a defendant could owe a duty to a claimant in addition to, but independently of, any contractual duties he owed to a third party. And when the tort of negligence was extended in *Hedley Byrne*[137] to the context of statements giving rise to economic loss, it was in a case where there was no contract between the parties. The question arises, however, of whether and how the general principles for a duty in the tort of negligence can be applied where there is such a contract. Two separate cases need to be considered: where the duty in tort is alleged to be owed in relation to statements made in the pre-contractual phase; and where the duty in tort is concurrent with a duty owed in the contract itself.

6–28 **Duty of care in making pre-contractual statements.** It was not until 1976 that the Court of Appeal in England[138] had the

[136] [1932] A.C. 562, HL.
[137] Above, para.6–10.
[138] For early cases in Canada and New Zealand which applied the principles of *Hedley Byrne* to pre-contractual statements, see *Sealand of the Pacific Ltd v Ocean Cement Ltd* (1973) 33 D.L.R. (3d) 625; *Capital Motors Ltd v Beecham* [1975] 1 N.Z.L.R. 576 (both of which were cited by Lord Denning in *Esso v Mardon*, below, n.140 at 820); for later cases see *Carman Construction Ltd v Canadian Pacific Railway Co.* (1982) 136 D.L.R. (3d) 193 SCC (no liability on facts); *Central Trust Co. v Rafuse* (1986) 31 D.L.R. (4th) 481, SCC; *B.G. Checo International Ltd v British Columbia Hydro & Power Authority* (1993) 99 D.L.R. (4th) 577, SCC; *Walker, Hobson & Hill Ltd v Johnson* [1981] 2 N.Z.L.R. 532. In New Zealand, the Contractual Remedies Act 1979, s.6, removed the common law actions in tort for fraudulent and negligent misrepresentation in respect of pre-contractual misrepresentations, and replaced them with a statutory right to damages as if the representation were a term of the contract; Burrows, Finn & Todd, para.11.2.7. In Australia, see *Johnson v South Australia* (1980) S.A.S.R. 1 at 26 (reversed on different grounds, (1982) 42 A.L.R. 161), applying *Esso Petroleum Co. Ltd. v Mardon*, below, n.140 but note that in Australia cases are commonly now brought under the (federal) Trade Practices Act 1974, s.52 (now s.18 of the Australian Consumer Law, Sch.2 to the Competition and Consumer Act 2010) or corresponding State and Territory legislation; below, para.7–48). The Scottish courts were slow to follow the other commonwealth jurisdictions: *Eastern Marine Services (and Supplies) Ltd v Dickson Motors Ltd*, 1981 S.C. 355, OH: action for delict founded on misrepresentations inducing contract still required proof of fraud, on the authority of *Manners v Whitehead* (1898) 1 F. 171. In *Ferguson v Mackay*, 1985 S.L.T. 94, OH, Lord Wylie (obiter) thought that *Manners v Whitehead* should be restricted to its particular facts, and that the developments in the law of negligence in the later 20th century meant that a duty of care could be found between contracting parties. The rule in *Manners v*

opportunity to hold that the duty of care, under the principles set out in *Hedley Byrne*, could be owed by one party to another in respect of statements made during the negotiations for a contract.[139] In *Esso Petroleum Co. Ltd v Mardon*[140] a representative of Esso gave inaccurate information[141] to Mr Mardon, a prospective tenant of a new petrol station: it overstated the likely throughput of the petrol station, which induced Mr Mardon to agree to take a lease. The Court of Appeal held that Esso had given a contractual warranty that they were making the throughput estimate with reasonable care; but that there was also a duty of reasonable care in tort under the principles of *Hedley Byrne*.[142] Although *Hedley Byrne* was a case in which there was no contract, actual or prospective between the parties, its principle was not limited to such a case, but could

---

Whitehead was abolished by the Law Reform (Miscellaneous Provisions) (Scotland) Act 1985 s.10(1), which provides that a party induced to enter into a contract by a negligent misrepresentation made by or on behalf of the other party shall not be disentitled from recovering damages by reason only that the misrepresentation is not fraudulent. See also Gloag and Henderson, *The Law of Scotland* (12th edn, ed. Lord Coulsfield and H.L. MacQueen, 2007), para.6–35; J. Thomson, *Delictual Liability* (4th edn, 2009), para 4.14, criticising the misapplication of the 1985 Act by the Lord Ordinary (Carloway) in *Hamilton v Allied Domecq Plc* 2001 SC 829, OH (who had held at [17] that the Act had made a negligent misrepresentations actionable without needing to prove a *Hedley Byrne* special relationship, the position which is adopted by W.W. McBryde, *The Law of Contract in Scotland* (3rd edn, 2007), para.15–77).

139 There is no general duty of care between parties negotiating for a contract. In *Martel Building Ltd v Canada* (2000) 193 D.L.R. (4th) 1, SCC held that there is in general no duty of care in conducting commercial negotiations apart from cases within the established categories of duty such as negligent misrepresentation, and no new category should be developed for the conduct of pre-contractual negotiations. See also *Holman Construction Ltd v Delta Timber Co. Ltd* [1972] N.Z.L.R. 1081; *Walford v Miles* [1992] 2 A.C. 128 at 138, HL (Lord Ackner: duty to carry on negotiations in good faith is inherently repugnant to the adversarial position of the parties when involved in negotiations. Each party to the negotiations is entitled to pursue his or her own interest, so long as he avoids making misrepresentations).

140 [1976] Q.B. 801, CA.

141 The estimate of the station's throughput had originally been accurate; but after the estimate was made the local planning authority required the station to be built "back to front", so that its entrance was not on the main road. But the throughput estimate was not revised and therefore inaccurate information was given to Mr Mardon.

142 This was therefore a case of concurrent duties (of identical scope, as the CA held) in contract and tort: below, para.6–29.

extend to the duty in tort to take reasonable care in making pre-contractual statements. Lord Denning M.R. said[143]:

> "It seems to me that *Hedley Byrne & Co. Ltd v Heller & Partners Ltd*, properly understood, covers this particular proposition: if a man, who has or professes to have special knowledge or skill, makes a representation by virtue thereof to another—be it advice, information or opinion—with the intention of inducing him to enter into a contract with him, he is under a duty to use reasonable care to see that the representation is correct, and that the advice, information or opinion is reliable. If he negligently gives unsound advice or misleading information or expresses an erroneous opinion, and thereby induces the other side into a contract with him, he is liable in damages."

If the contract which is concluded makes clear that the rights and liabilities between the parties are to be only those which have their origin in the contract itself, then such a pre-contractual duty may be negatived.[144] And if, in the circumstances of the negotiations, the party making the statement is entitled to assume that the other party is being separately advised about the subject-matter of the statement, he may owe no duty of care in relation to it.[145] But under the approach stated by Lord Denning it appears that there will very often be a duty of care in relation to statements made during the pre-contractual phase. Whether such a duty in the tort of negligence will be of significant assistance to a claimant, however, is another matter: the remedy of damages under section 2(1) of the Misrepresentation Act 1967 will generally provide a more effective remedy for a claimant in respect of pre-contractual careless statements.[146]

---

143 Above, n.140 at 820. See also Ormrod L.J. at 827–828 and Shaw L.J. at 832–833.

144 *ibid.*, at 832–833 (Shaw L.J.). This is subject to any restriction on the parties' freedom to agree terms which have the effect of excluding remedies in respect of pre-contractual representations: below, Ch.9.

145 *Inntrepreneur Pub Co. (CPC) v Sweeney* [2002] EWHC 1060, [2002] 2 E.G.L.R. 132 at 142 (landlord of public house did not owe duty to advise prospective tenant about legal implications of lease where it had made a contribution towards tenant's fees to his own solicitor).

146 Below, Ch.7. The remedy under the Misrepresentation Act 1967 was not available in *Esso v Mardon* because the representation on which Mr Mardon founded his claim was made in 1963: [1976] Q.B. 801 at 817, 827, 832. In New Zealand the statutory remedy in damages for pre-contractual misrepresentation

Concurrent duties of care in contract and tort. After considerable debate in the courts, particularly during the last quarter of the twentieth century,[147] it was finally settled by the House of Lords in *Henderson v Merrett Syndicates Ltd,*[148] that a defendant may owe a duty of care in tort to a claimant with whom he has a contractual relationship. The contract does not automatically carry parallel tortious duties;[149] but the contract and its terms are of course relevant to the question of whether a duty of care (and, if so, what duty) arises in tort. If a duty is found by applying the normal principles of tort, it can exist concurrently with the contractual duties and the claimant is entitled to take advantage of the remedy which is most advantageous to him.[150] The concurrence of duties in contract and tort in respect of pre-contractual representations is therefore now beyond dispute.[151] **6–29**

(Contractual Remedies Act 1979, s.6: damages as if the representation were a term of the contract) has expressly displaced the claim in the tort of negligence: s.6(1)(b).

[147] In particular, see *Midland Bank Trust Co. Ltd v Hett, Stubbs & Kemp* [1979] Ch. 384, where Oliver J. reviewed the arguments and earlier authorities in the light of the development of the tort of negligence in *Hedley Byrne*, and concluded in favour of allowing concurrent liability in the case of a solicitor's duty to his client; and *Tai Hing Cotton Mill Ltd v Liu Chong Hing Bank Ltd* [1986] A.C. 80, where the Privy Council had discouraged the search for duties in tort where the parties were in a contractual relationship. The cases, both before and after *Tai Hing Cotton Mill*, and the arguments of principle in the debate for and against concurrent duties in contract and tort, were summarised by Lord Goff in *Henderson v Merrett Syndicates Ltd* [1995] 2 A.C. 145 at 184–194.

[148] Above, n.147.

[149] *Robinson v P.E. Jones (Contractors) Ltd* [2011] EWCA Civ 9, [2011] B.L.R. 206 at [77], [94].

[150] *Henderson v Merrett Syndicates Ltd*, above, n.147 at 193–194. For concurrence of duties in negligence and for breach of statutory duty, see *West Wiltshire DC v Garland* [1995] Ch. 297; and for concurrence in negligence and defamation, see *Spring v Guardian Assurance Plc* [1995] 2 A.C. 296.

[151] *Esso Petroleum Co. Ltd v Mardon* was itself a significant judgment in settling the matter in favour of concurrence of actions, since it provided Court of Appeal authority on which Oliver J. in *Midland Bank Trust Co. Ltd v Hett, Stubbs & Kemp*, above, n.147 at 428–433, was able to rely to hold that concurrence was now accepted. As discussed above, para.6–28 and below, paras 7–46 to 7–47, after the enactment of the Misrepresentation Act 1967 s.2(1), the decision in *Esso* may not often be invoked to impose liability in tort on the other contracting party for pre-contractual misrepresentations, but it is still a significant authority on the point as well as on the question of when there will be an implied contractual warranty of reasonable care in making pre-contractual representations: below,

Where the claimant and defendant are in a contractual relationship, the significance of the contractual context to the determination of the existence and scope of a concurrent duty in tort should not be underestimated. If the law of tort is characterised[152] as the general law out of which the parties have freedom[153] to contract, then any duty in tort which would otherwise arise on the facts must be affected by the express and implied terms of the contract: the tort duty may therefore be limited in scope, or excluded altogether, by the contract.[154] In a case where the tort duty arises out of the very same facts by virtue of which the concurrent contractual obligation was created, it is likely that the scope of the duties in contract and tort will be substantially identical. For example, if there are concurrent duties in respect of pre-contractual representations then

---

para.8–15. For the concurrence of common law and *equitable* duties of care, see above, para.6–08 n.37 and para.6–11 n.54.

152 *Henderson v Merrett Syndicates Ltd*, above, n.147 at 193–194; *Robinson v P.E. Jones (Contractors) Ltd*, above, n.149 at [79] (Jackson L.J.): "the distinction between contract and tort/delict is essentially the same in both civil law and common law. It was originally articulated by Roman jurists (see [Gaius's] Institutes, 3.88) and it remains the case that (a) contracts and (b) the law of tort are separate sources of obligations. Contractual obligations are negotiated by the parties and then enforced by law because the performance of contracts is vital to the functioning of society. Tortious duties are imposed by law (without any need for agreement by the parties) because society demands certain standards of conduct".

153 Subject of course to specific statutory limitations to the contrary: below, Ch.9.

154 *Henderson v Merrett Syndicates Ltd*, above, n.147 at 193–194; *Titan Steel Wheels Ltd v Royal Bank of Scotland Plc* [2010] EWHC 211 (Comm), [2010] 2 Lloyd's Rep 92 at [89]. See the general discussion by Colman J. in *BP Plc v Aon Ltd* [2006] EWHC 424 (Comm), [2006] 1 All E.R. (Comm) 789 at [165] *et seq.*, e.g. at [166]: "If there is a contract binding between the claimant and defendant, it may exclude liability in tort. If there is no contract binding between them, but instead a chain of contracts by which they are indirectly linked, the existence of the chain and the character of the contracts which comprise it may prevent the defendant's conduct being reasonably understood as the kind of representation necessary to found liability in negligence". For the question whether A can owe a duty to C in tort where A and C have intentionally structured their relationships so that there is no direct contractual duty between A and C, but separate duties between A and B, and B and C, see *Riyad Bank v Ahli United Bank (UK) Plc* [2006] EWCA Civ 780, [2006] 1 C.L.C. 1007; at [47] Neuberger L.J. held that this is the same essential question as in the case of a direct contract between A and C: whether, in relation to the advice he gave, the adviser assumed responsibility to the claimant, in the light of the contractual context.

the duty in tort to take care in making statements may be indistinguishable in content from the contractual warranty that care will be taken in making those same statements.[155] Or the duty in tort of a professional—such as a surveyor[156] or solicitor[157]—to take reasonable care in giving advice to his client may be indistinguishable in content from his contractual duty to give the same advice. Since the scope of the duty in tort in respect of statements can itself be defined by the purposes for which the statements were made, the contractual context is inextricably linked with the creation of the duty of care. In relation to the nature of the claimant's interest which is protected by the respective duties in contract and tort, therefore, there will in such cases be no significant difference and the basic measure of loss recoverable in the contract and tort actions will often be the same.[158] This is not however to deny that there might sometimes be significant advantages for a claimant in pursuing one of the (concurrent) claims rather than the other.[159]

---

[155] *Esso Petroleum Co. Ltd v Mardon*, above, para.6–28.

[156] *South Australia Asset Management Corp. v York Montague Ltd* [1997] A.C. 191, HL.

[157] *cf. Midland Bank Trust Co. Ltd v Hett, Stubbs & Kemp*, above, n.147 (although on the facts the negligence alleged was not in giving wrong information, but the solicitor's nonfeasance: *ibid.*, at 435).

[158] *Esso Petroleum Co. Ltd v Mardon*, above, n.140 at 821 (Lord Denning M.R.: the duty in contract, being only one of reasonable care in making the statement, was identical to the duty in the tort of negligence, so the damages are in both cases calculated on the measure normally used in a tort claim); *South Australia Asset Management Corp. v York Montague Ltd*, above, n.156 at 211 and 216 (Lord Hoffmann: the scope of the valuer's duty in both contract and tort was only one of reasonable care and skill: the measure of damages follows from the scope of the duty). For further discussion of the measure of damages in the tort of negligence, see below, paras 6–52 *et seq.*; and in contract, see below, paras 8–24 *et seq.*

[159] For example, as between actions in contract and tort on any given set of facts there might be (a) different limitation periods, e.g. as in *Henderson v Merrett Syndicates* itself, the tort action might still be available when the contract action is barred, below, paras 6–50 and 8–21; (b) different defences available, e.g. contributory negligence, although not where the content of the contract and tort duties are identical: *Forsikringsaktieselkapet Vesta v Butcher* [1989] A.C. 852 at 858 *et seq.* (CA; the issue was not taken to HL); (c) different rules for the extent of recoverable losses, e.g. remoteness rules, although it is doubtful whether this should be so in a case of concurrence of actions: J. Cartwright, "Remoteness of Damage in Contract and Tort: A Reconsideration" [1996] C.L.J. 488 at pp.500–504; (d) different rules of procedure, e.g. where the claimant requires service out of the jurisdiction: below, para.11–06. For general discussion of the

(d) *Particular categories of duty in respect of statements*

6–30 **The authority of particular cases.** It is proposed now to discuss briefly some of the decided cases involving statements in which a duty of care in negligence has been accepted or rejected by the courts. It is important to appreciate the authority of such cases. As has already been made clear,[160] the previous cases are crucial as providing lines of authority from which the principles for categories of duty can be demonstrated. The general approach for the duty of care in respect of statements will be that discussed above,[161] and can be considered from different angles: Should the defendant have realised that the claimant was likely to rely on his statement for a particular purpose?[162] In making the statement did he undertake responsibility in favour of the claimant, and if so for what?[163] Was the claimant reasonably entitled to rely on the statement and on the defendant's skill and care in making it?[164] But within the cases dealing with the duty in respect of statements, there are groups of cases which can be considered to assist a future court in deciding how to define the duty of care. It should not however be assumed simply because, for example, there is authority for a particular duty of care owed by an auditor or a valuer, that this authority should be applied unthinkingly to all cases involving auditors or valuers. In every case it is necessary to consider the purpose of the statement and the circumstances in which it is made, and to measure this against the factors in the authorities which have established the category of duty relied upon.

6–31 **Relevance of the particular professional context.** Duties of care in the tort of negligence are not limited to those exercising particular professions or callings,[165] but it is in relation to the exercise of professions or callings that the duty to exercise care in

---

issues raised by allowing concurrence of actions in contract and tort, see *Henderson v Merrett Syndicates Ltd* [1995] 2 A.C. 145, HL, at 185–186; P. Cane, *Tort Law and Economic Interests* (2nd edn, 1996), pp.129–148.

160 Above, para.6–13.

161 Above, paras 6–19 *et seq.*

162 Above, para.6–20.

163 Above, para.6–25.

164 Above, para.6–22.

165 Above, para.6–23.

giving information or advice typically arises.[166] In assessing the existence and scope of such duties, it is therefore crucial to consider the particular context of the profession or calling involved, including the scope of activities and responsibility that is generally expected within the profession itself. This is not necessarily a limiting factor for the duty, since it is possible for a defendant to extend his duty to a particular claimant beyond the duties normally expected of a particular professional.[167] But in examining the authorities in order to categorise the accepted duties of care, it is helpful to begin by separating the duties according to their several professional contexts.

Agents, employees and company directors. Often a statement is made by one person on behalf of, or in the name of, another. It may be made by an agent or employee on behalf of his principal or employer: the bank clerk makes the statement on behalf of the bank[168]; the surveyor makes the statement in the name of his firm.[169] Or a professional may make a statement on behalf of his client: the solicitor makes the statement to the party with whom his client is proposing to contract; or the vendor's estate agent makes the statement to the potential purchaser. Normally there is no issue about the personal liability of the agent or employee, since the natural recourse is against the principal in whose name the statement was made. But occasionally such a question does arise, such as where the statement was made on behalf of a principal who is now insolvent, and so the only substantial recourse is against the **6–32**

[166] *Caparo Industries Plc v Dickman* [1990] 2 A.C. 605, HL, at 619.
[167] e.g. an auditor may go beyond the functions of an auditor and owe a wider duty in relation to his audit statements: below, para.6–33, n.195; or a solicitor may go beyond his normal duties to his client and undertake a duty to a third party such as his client's opponent: below, para.6–32, n.177. Where one professional holds himself out as competent to carry out services normally within the scope of another professional's services, his duties will normally be measured by reference to the standards of the latter profession: *cf. Prince Jefri Bolkiah v KPMG* [1999] 2 A.C. 222, HL (accountants carrying out litigation support services including tasks normally carried out by solicitors); *Frost v James Finlay Bank Ltd* [2002] EWCA Civ 667, [2002] Lloyd's Rep. P.N. 473 (on facts, bank did not hold itself out as offering insurance services and so did not assume responsibility of an insurance broker).
[168] *Hedley Byrne & Co. Ltd v Heller & Partners* [1964] A.C. 465, HL.
[169] *Smith v Eric S. Bush* [1990] 1 A.C. 831, HL.

person who made the statement.[170] In all cases the analysis of the duty of care in respect of the statement requires an answer to the question: with whom did the claimant have a "special relationship" within the principle of *Hedley Byrne* and *Caparo Industries Plc v Dickman*? Or, in other words, who was it that assumed a responsibility to the claimant in giving him the information or advice on which he relied? Even though the information or advice might have been passed through the medium of an agent or employee, the necessary relationship exists with only the principal where it is only the principal who holds himself out as having the skill or expertise on which the claimant is entitled to rely. But it is possible for there also to be a special relationship with the agent or employee, if on the facts he held himself out to the claimant as having the necessary skill and expertise in offering the information or advice and as undertaking personal responsibility for the statement.[171]

So it has been held that a firm of estate agents, acting for a vendor of property, can owe a duty to the purchaser if the

[170] *McCullagh v Lane Fox & Partners Ltd* [1996] 1 E.G.L.R. 35, CA, at 42. Another, quite separate, case is where the agent did not in fact have the authority to bind the principal. This has generally been dealt with as a matter of contract, under which the "agent" is in breach of his warranty of authority: Bowstead & Reynolds, paras 9–060 to 9–062. For a view, however, that this should now be covered by the tort of negligence, see T. Faulkner, "Breach of an Agent's Warranty of Authority" (2000) 74 A.L.J. 465.

[171] *Williams v Natural Life Health Foods Ltd* [1998] 1 W.L.R. 830, HL, at 835, 836–837. Lord Steyn at 835 made clear that this principle was applicable equally to statements made by agents, employees and company directors. See also *Gran Gelato Ltd v Richcliff (Group) Ltd* [1992] Ch. 560 at 570; *Smith v Eric S. Bush* [1990] 1 A.C. 831, HL (mortgagee's valuer owed duty of care to mortgagor); *Resolute Maritime Inc v Nippon Kaiji Kyokai* [1983] 1 W.L.R. 857 at 861 (agent not liable to other party under the Misrepresentation Act 1967 s.2(1); but there can be a duty in the tort of negligence); *J. Jarvis & Sons Ltd v Castle Wharf Developments Ltd* [2001] EWCA Civ 19, [2001] Lloyd's Rep. P.N. 308 (employer's quantity surveyors can owe duty to building contractor in relation to statements made during tender stage, but no liability on facts because contractor was experienced and could not be said to have relied on defendant's statements); *Merrett v Babb* [2001] EWCA Civ 214, [2001] Q.B. 1174; leave to appeal to House of Lords refused: [2001] 1 W.L.R. 1859 (employed surveyor personally liable); *John W. Pryke v Gibbs Hartley Cooper Ltd* [1991] 1 Lloyd's Rep. 602 at 616 (insurance broker may have personal liability in insurance market to underwriters, in respect of non-disclosure under the Marine Insurance Act 1906 s.19, and misrepresentations if responsibility assumed).

representative of the firm who made statements to the purchaser knew that his statements would be relied on by the purchaser in entering into the contract.[172] And the employees of insurance brokers have been held to owe duties personally to the assignee of the benefit of insurance policies where they were the individuals who made misrepresentations, and failed to make relevant disclosures, which allowed the insurers to avoid the policies.[173] And although one might expect to start from a general proposition that where an adviser to one party to an arm's length transaction gives advice to that party, his duty is prima facie to that party alone, it is possible for a duty to be owed to the other party where, on the facts, there is a sufficient link between the task the adviser has undertaken to perform and the course of action on which the advisee can be foreseen to be likely to embark, so as to satisfy the test for the imposition of a duty of care.[174]

However, a solicitor, when performing duties for his client, does not normally owe a duty to a third party,[175] such as the person with whom his client is proposing to enter into a conveyancing transaction,[176] or his client's opponent in adversarial litigation.[177] It

[172] *McCullagh v Lane Fox & Partners Ltd*, above, n.170 (but no duty on facts because of disclaimer of responsibility).

[173] *Punjab National Bank v De Boinville* [1992] 1 W.L.R. 1136, CA (not a case directly under *Hedley Byrne*, because the statements were not made to the claimant, but it still illustrates the general principle of employee's personal liability). "It is not every employee of a firm or company providing professional services that owes a personal duty of care to the client; it depends what he is employed to do." The employees were here personally liable because they "were evidently entrusted with the whole or nearly the whole of the task which their employers undertook": *ibid.*, at 1154 (Staughton L.J.). *Cf. John W. Pryke v Gibbs Hartley Cooper Ltd*, above, n.171 (duty of broker to underwriters).

[174] *Machin v Adams* (1997) 84 B.L.R. 79, CA, at 99, referring to the general approach to a duty of care set out in *Henderson v Merrett Syndicates Ltd* [1995] 2 A.C. 145, above, para.6–25. In the context particularly of liability for statements, the test generally used is that set out in *Caparo v Dickman* [1990] 2 A.C. 605, HL, above, para.6–19.

[175] *White v Jones* [1995] 2 A.C. 207, HL, at 256.

[176] *Gran Gelato Ltd v Richcliffe (Group) Ltd*, above, n.171; see also *Cemp Properties (UK) Ltd v Dentsply Research & Development Corp.* [1989] 2 E.G.L.R. 205 at 207.

[177] *Al-Kandari v J.R. Brown & Co.* [1988] Q.B. 665, CA, at 672. See also *A & J Fabrication (Batley) Ltd v Grant Thornton* [1999] Lloyd's Rep. P.N. 863 (liquidator's solicitor does not owe duty to company's creditor, even the major creditor who is funding the liquidator, in absence of direct assumption of

has been said[178] that this particularly restrictive rule in relation to solicitors may be based on the special role of a solicitor and grounds of policy relating to that role; but it is clear that a solicitor may undertake a duty to his client's opponent where he steps outside his general role as his client's solicitor and accepts responsibilities towards the opponent.[179]

---

responsibility); *Business Computers International Ltd v Registrar of Companies* [1988] Ch. 229 (debtor presenting winding-up petition does not owe duty to company in relation to service of process or other steps in proceedings); *Elguzouli-Daf v Metropolitan Police Commissioner* [1995] Q.B. 335, CA (Crown Prosecution Service does not owe duty to defendant in relation to conduct of his case in absence of assumption of responsibility); *Customs and Excise Commissioners v Barclays Bank Plc* [2006] UKHL 28, [2007] 1 A.C. 181 (bank does not owe duty to party who has obtained freezing order); *Jain v Trent Strategic Health Authority* [2009] UKHL 4, [2009] 1 A.C. 853 at [29]–[35] (Lord Scott, discussing and approving earlier cases); *Desmond v Chief Constable of Nottinghamshire Police* [2011] EWCA Civ 3, [2011] Fam. Law. 358 (police own no duty to party arrested but not charged in relation to information later provided for issue of enhanced criminal record certificate by Criminal Records Bureau).

178 *McCullagh v Lane Fox & Partners Ltd*, above, n.170 at 44 (Hobhouse L.J.). The caution in holding a solicitor liable to his client's opponent is not based simply on a conflict of interest; but note that Rule 3 ("Conflicts of interests") of the Solicitors' Code of Conduct 2007 prohibited a solicitor from acting for both parties in certain conveyancing transactions at arm's length and in certain mortgage transactions. The 2007 Code is being replaced by the Solicitors Regulation Authority Code of Conduct 2011, which is structured around mandatory Principles rather than a list of prescriptive rules, but in which acting for two buyers competing for a residential property where there is a conflict of interest is given as a specific example ("indicative behaviour": IB(3.13)) which would tend to show that a solicitor has not achieved the outcomes required by Chapter 3 of the Code ("Conflicts of interests") and will therefore contravene the Principles. The Code is available on *http://www.sra.org.uk*. See also *Hilton v Barker Booth & Eastwood* [2005] UKHL 8, [2005] 1 W.L.R. 567 (decision on the earlier Practice Rule 6 of the Law Society's Guide for the Professional Conduct of Solicitors (8th edn, 1999)). It is particularly in the context of conveyancing transactions that the courts have been reluctant to impose such duties in tort: *Gran Gelato Ltd v Richcliff (Group) Ltd*, above, n.171. See also *Dean v Allin & Watts* [2001] EWCA Civ 758, [2001] 2 Lloyd's Rep. 249 at [33] (where to the knowledge of both parties a solicitor is retained by one party and there is a conflict of interest between the client and the other party to the transaction, the court should be slow to find that the solicitor has assumed a duty of care to the other party, for such an assumption is ordinarily improbable).

179 *Al-Kandari v J.R. Brown & Co.,* above, n.177 (solicitors for husband gave implied undertaking to wife to retain husband's passport: duty to take care to keep passport in their possession and inform her if they no longer had it; husband

Although normally a company director does not undertake personal responsibility for advice given in the name of the company, even where he controls the company and personally plays a significant part in the production of the advice,[180] if the claimant approached the director for his advice because he was the person in the company with the relevant special knowledge and skill he may be held to have undertaken a personal responsibility to the claimant in offering the advice.[181] In all cases, therefore, it is important to look at the particular facts on which the duty is alleged to have been based and to apply the test for the duty of care; in the context of statements, therefore, to ask whether the particular defendant—employee, agent or director, or their respective principals—knew that the claimant would be likely to rely on the statement for a particular purpose without verifying it independently; whether the claimant was entitled so to rely on the statement; and whether the defendant can be taken to have undertaken responsibility to the claimant in making the statement.

---

had wife kidnapped, and absconded abroad with children); *Dean v Allin & Watts*, above, n.178 (solicitor acting for borrower owed duty to lender whom he knew or should have known was relying on him to provide effective security for loan and where lender and borrower had common interest in the security being effective); *Allied Finance and Investments Ltd v Haddow & Co.* [1983] N.Z.L.R. 22, NZCA (mortgagor's solicitors owed duty to mortgagee in making statements that documents had been effectually executed by mortgagor and that there were no other charges affecting the security).

180 *Williams v Natural Life Health Foods Ltd*, above, n.171, where there were no personal dealings between the claimant and the director; *Noel v Poland* [2001] 2 B.C.L.C. 645 (statements by chairman of insurance agency to underwriting Name were made as chairman on behalf of the company and not personally). The fact that a director has duties under the regulatory regime contained in the Financial Services and Markets Act 2000 and the Listing Rules does not mean that he can be taken necessarily to have assumed a responsibility in tort towards those affected by his failure to comply with those duties: *Partco Group Ltd v Wragg* [2002] 1 Lloyd's Rep. 320 at [22], affirmed [2002] EWCA Civ 594, [2002] 2 Lloyd's Rep. 343.

181 *The Thomas Saunders Partnership v Harvey* (1989) 30 Con. L.R. 103 (director assured architects and building owner that his company's flooring was suitable for use in new computer centre; held personally liable in deceit and negligence for owner's economic losses in being provided with a sub-standard floor).

6–33 **Accountants and auditors.**[182] There has been very considerable litigation in recent years concerning the duties owed by accountants and auditors.[183] Before the scope of an accountant's duty of care

[182] Clerk & Lindsell, paras 10–195 to 10–209; Jackson & Powell, Ch.15; Dugdale & Stanton, paras 8.02 to 8.05; Hodgin, Ch.5 (A. McGee); Charlesworth & Percy, paras 9–23 to 9–49; Gore-Browne, Ch.37B. Under CA 2006 ss.532–538 a company may enter into an agreement with its auditor to limit the amount of liability owed to the company in respect of any negligence, default, breach of duty or breach of trust, occurring in the course of the audit, of which the auditor may be guilty in relation to the company (s.534). Each such liability limitation agreement can apply only for a single year, and its contents may be regulated by regulations. In other respects it is immaterial how the agreement is framed, and the limit may be by reference to a sum of money, or to a formula (s.535), but it cannot have the effect of limiting the auditor's liability to less than such amount is fair and reasonable in all the circumstances of the case, having regard to the auditor's responsibilities under CA 2006 Pt.16, the nature and purpose of the auditor's contractual obligations to the company, and the professional standards expected of him (s.537). The effect of this provision is to reverse the automatic rule of joint liability, below, para.6–63, for the particular case of auditors' liability; it implements the Government's White Paper on Company Law Reform (Cm.6456, March 2005), para.3.5. On 30 June 2008 the Financial Reporting Council published guidance on liability limitation agreements: (2008) 29 Company Lawyer 304. The guidance is available on *http://www.frc.org.uk*. See generally P.E. Morris, "Contractual Limitations on the Auditor's Liability: An Uneasy Combination of Law and Accounting" (2009) 72 M.L.R. 607 noting at p.624 that uptake of liability limitation agreements is likely to be slow, and that they cannot be used by companies which are also listed on stock markets in the US.

[183] In addition to the cases cited in this section, see, in Australia: *Esanda Finance Corp. Ltd v Peat Marwick Hungerfords* (1997) 188 C.L.R. 241, HCA (auditor owed no duty to financiers who relied on audited accounts in entering into transactions with company); *Pilmer v The Duke Group Ltd* [2001] H.C.A. 31, (2001) 75 A.L.J.R. 1067 (accountants preparing report on value of shares in target company owed duty only to the company which retained them, and not to its shareholders); in Canada: *Hercules Managements Ltd v Ernst & Young* (1997) 146 D.L.R. (4th) 577, SCC (auditor owes no duty to shareholders: in Canada the general test of *Anns v Merton LBC* [1978] A.C. 728, above, para.6–13, n.66, is applied; but although the reliance by shareholders on a corporate audit was foreseeable and therefore there was a prima facie duty of care, this was negated by policy considerations, since the purpose of the audit was to enable the shareholders *collectively* to exercise control over the directors); in New Zealand: *Scott Group Ltd v McFarlane* [1978] 1 N.Z.L.R. 553, NZCA (auditor may owe duty of care to likely bidder for the company; this was however decided when the *Anns v Merton* test, above, was generally applied in England and New Zealand, and the narrower view of *Caparo v Dickman*, below, has now been taken in New Zealand: S. Todd (ed.), *The Law of Torts in New Zealand* (5th edn, Thomson

can be established, it is important to identify the function he held himself out as undertaking, since this bears directly on the question of the scope of duty (if any) for which he can be held to have undertaken responsibility, and the extent to which it was reasonable for the claimant to rely on his statement.[184]

If his function was to provide general accountancy services he will owe a duty, to the person to or for whom he provides those services, to take reasonable care in accordance with the standards generally expected of a qualified accountant.[185] For example, this can extend to the duty to give financial advice about the wisdom of entering into a transaction[186]; or it can require the accountant to take care in providing financial information similar to the duty undertaken by a valuer or surveyor.[187] The range of persons to whom the duty is owed will depend on the facts; there will generally be a duty to the claimant in tort, concurrently with the

---

Reuters, Wellington, 2009), para.5.8.05). It is important to notice that much of this litigation has been in the context of applications to strike out statements of case under CPR, Pt 3, r.3.4 (formerly RSC, Ord.18, r.19) as disclosing no reasonable grounds for bringing (or defending) the claim. In such cases the court must decide only whether a claim is at least arguable, on the basis of the facts as pleaded; it does not decide that there is a good claim on the facts, which can only be established if the claim then proceeds to trial. The court will strike out a claim only in a clear and obvious case, where the legal basis of the claim is unarguable or almost uncontestably bad; and is particularly reluctant to do so where the legal viability of a cause of action is sensitive to the facts, which can be established only at trial: *X v Bedfordshire County Council* [1995] 2 A.C. 633 at 693–694. Actions of negligence against auditors and other professional advisers engaged by a third party are a notable example of fact-sensitive cases where the law is still in a state of transition and in which courts should normally take particular care before determining the matter against the claimant before the full facts are known: *Electra Private Equity Partners v KPMG Peat Marwick* [2000] B.C.C. 368, CA, at 387 (following *Coulthard v Neville Russell* [1998] 1 B.C.L.C. 143, CA, at 155); *Equitable Life Assurance Society v Ernst & Young* [2003] EWCA Civ 1114, [2003] 2 B.C.L.C. 603 at [40], [106]–[107]; *Independents' Advantage Insurance Co. Ltd v Cook* [2003] EWCA Civ 1103, [2004] P.N.L.R. 3 at [15]–[17]. There is therefore a danger in assuming, from some of the reported cases, that accountants and (especially) auditors' liability is greater than it might in reality be.

184 Above, para.6–20.

185 On the question of the standard of care expected, see below, para.6–44. An accountant also owes duties of confidence to his client: *Prince Jefri Bolkiah v KPMG* [1999] 2 A.C. 222, HL.

186 *Siddell v Smith Cooper & Partners* [1999] Lloyd's Rep. P.N. 79, CA.

187 *Killick v PricewaterhouseCoopers* [2001] 1 B.C.L.C. 65.

contractual duties arising out of the accountant's retainer.[188] And if the accountant's dealings with a person by whom he is retained are such that he knows that his advice will be received and acted on directly by other identified individuals (such as directors or shareholders in the case of a retainer by a company), then he may also owe duties directly to those individuals.[189]

If, however, the accountant's function is limited to acting as auditor, then the scope of his duty, and the range of persons to whom he owes his duty, will be circumscribed by the purposes of the audit. In *Caparo Industries Plc v Dickman*[190] the House of Lords held that the purpose of an audit made under sections 236 and 237 of the Companies Act 1985[191] is to inform the members of the company—the shareholders[192]—about the financial position of the company as contained in the accounts prepared by the directors so that the members can collectively, in general meeting, exercise their rights over the company. The audit statement would be available to a much wider range of persons, since the company's audited accounts are publicly available. But even though it was foreseeable that the audit statement would be relied on by investors in, and lenders to, the company, no duty was owed to them—not even to existing shareholders in so far as they claimed to have relied on the statement in making further investment in the company, since the *capacity* in which they were owed a duty was not their individual

188 Above, para.6–29.

189 *Siddell v Smith Cooper & Partners*, above, n.186; *Christensen v Scott* [1996] 1 N.Z.L.R. 273, NZCA (arguable that accountants acting as general business advisers owed duty of care to directors and shareholders who had separate interest from company). Where, however, the breach of duty owed to the shareholder results in damage only to the value of his shareholding or other losses which reflect losses for which the company itself could have sued, he may have no loss to assert separately from the company: *cf. Prudential Assurance Co. Ltd v Newman Industries Ltd (No.2)* [1982] Ch. 204, CA; *Johnson v Gore Wood & Co.* [2002] 2 A.C. 1, HL, at 35–36, 51, 61–62; *Webster v Sandersons Solicitors* [2009] EWCA Civ 830, [2009] P.N.L.R. 37; Gore-Browne, paras 18[34], 18[35]; C. Mitchell, "Shareholders' Claims for Reflective Loss" (2004) 120 L.Q.R. 457. Similarly, where an employee's loss is reflective only of the company's loss: *John v PricewaterhouseCoopers*, unreported, April 11, 2001 (Ferris J.) at [219] (employee's salary was 99% of company's net income).

190 [1990] 2 A.C. 605.

191 See now Companies Act 2006 ss.495, 498.

192 And the directors: *Equitable Life Assurance Society v Ernst &Young*, above, n.183 at [123].

capacity, but as one of the class of shareholders for whose benefit the audit statement was made. This decision depended on a consideration of the particular statutory provisions pursuant to which the defendant auditors had certified the accounts[193]; any audit made for other purposes will similarly depend on the proper construction of the purposes of the audit.[194]

However, even if an auditor's statement is made within a statutory audit and therefore with a scope of duty which is limited by reference to the purposes of the audit, it is possible for him either in making the audit statement itself, or later by his repetition of it, to go beyond simply the function of auditor and thereby to owe a duty to a wider class of persons who receive and rely on the statement.[195]

---

[193] [1990] 2 A.C. 605 at 625–626, 630–632, 649–650, 652–654, 660–662. Nor does the duty extend to the company's creditors: *Al Saudi Banque v Clark Pixley* [1990] Ch. 313, approved in *Caparo Industries Plc v Dickman* at 662; nor its employees, even a key employee on whose talents the prosperity of the company depends and who was to be rewarded by the receipt of most of the company's net income: *John v PricewaterhouseCoopers*, above, n.189 at [215]. *Al Saudi Banque v Clark Pixley* was distinguished in *Independents' Advantage Insurance Co. Ltd v Cook* [2003] EWCA Civ 1103, [2004] P.N.L.R. 3, below, n.195. See also *Man Nutzfahrzeuge A.G. v Freightliner Ltd* [2007] EWCA Civ 910, [2007] 2 C.L.C. 455 (auditor did not owe special audit duty to parent company in respect of consequences of fraudulent statements made by audited company's financial controller as to accuracy of accounts).

[194] See *West Wiltshire DC v Garland* [1993] Ch. 409 (district auditors conducting audit under the Local Government Finance Act 1982 owe duty to local authority but not to individual officers of local authority; this point was not challenged on appeal: [1995] Ch. 297 at 304, CA); *Law Society v KPMG Peat Marwick* [2000] 1 W.L.R. 1921, CA (accountants producing annual report on firm of solicitors, which the solicitors were required under the Solicitors Act 1974 s.34 to deliver to Law Society, owed duty to the Society in its capacity as trustee of the "compensation fund"—a fund set up under a statutory scheme to be applied for the purpose of compensating clients defrauded by solicitors). The statutory context may also limit the *scope* of the duty (its content): *Deloitte Haskins and Sells v National Mutual Life Nominees Ltd* [1993] A.C. 774, PC (auditor appointed under the Securities Act 1978 s.50 [New Zealand] in respect of trustee for unsecured depositors with a company: duty under statute limited to duty to report when aware of matters, not to investigate and form an opinion). For the liability of an accountant under the Financial Services and Markets Act 2000 s.90 for information included in a prospectus or listing particulars, see below, para.7–55.

[195] *ADT Ltd v Binder Hamlyn* [1996] B.C.C. 808 at 830 (May J.: "it is accepted as possible for an auditor to assume a wider duty of care in special cases. But having regard to the general principles these cases must be such that the purpose

In *Caparo v Dickman* itself Lord Oliver made clear that his decision, limiting the auditor's duty to the shareholders, would not apply in "a case where accounts are audited specifically for the purpose of submission to a potential investor".[196] In such a case the auditor's function is not simply to report to the company's members, but to provide information for an individual investor to use in order to make his investment decision; that is, a known individual would be likely to rely on the statement for a known purpose, and so a duty can be owed under the general principles of *Hedley Byrne* and *Caparo v Dickman*.[197]

---

of the audit work has been widened so that it is no longer confined to the statutory one. The essential fact is in all these situations is that the auditor ought in all the circumstances to have regarded himself as carrying out the audit for the claimant's purposes as well as the company's"; approved *Electra Private Equity Partners v KPMG Peat Marwick* [2000] B.C.C. 368, CA at 404). For such a wider duty to be owed, it is not necessary that the auditor have a positive intention that the third party rely on it, although an express intention will more strongly support the existence of the duty: *Royal Bank of Scotland Plc v Bannerman Johnson Maclay*, 2005 1 S.C. 437, IH, at [49]–[50]. See also *Independents' Advantage Insurance Co. Ltd v Cook* [2003] EWCA Civ 1103, [2004] P.N.L.R. 3 at [20] (claim that it was common practice in the travel industry, as the defendants knew, for audited accounts to be provided to third parties for the purpose of obtaining bond facilities and other financial support: arguable that this took facts outside *Al Saudi Banque v Clark Pixley*, above, n.193, and that duty was owed to such third party: strike-out refused).

196 [1990] 2 A.C. 605 at 650.

197 Above, para.6–19; *Morgan Crucible Co. Plc v Hill Samuel & Co. Ltd* [1991] Ch. 295, CA (duty arguable where, during contested take-over and after identified bidder has emerged, directors and financial advisers of target company choose to make express representations with a view to influencing conduct of bidder); *Galoo Ltd v Bright Grahame Murray* [1994] 1 W.L.R. 1360, CA, at 1381–1382 (if auditor is expressly made aware that a particular identified bidder will rely on the audited accounts or other statements approved by the auditor, and intends that the bidder should so rely, the auditor will be under a duty of care to the bidder); *Bank of Credit and Commerce International (Overseas) Ltd v Price Waterhouse* [1998] B.C.C. 617, CA (auditor of one subsidiary company could owe duty to sister subsidiary company which had its own separate auditors if, on the facts, the two subsidiaries were interdependent to the point that they operated as a single business); *Electra Private Equity Partners v KPMG Peat Marwick*, above, n.195 (company's auditors can owe duty to investor where they provide audit information to accountants employed by bidder to investigate on suitability of investment knowing it will be used by the accountants in preparing report which would itself then be relied on by the investor). For a possible duty of care owed by auditors to the company's directors, see *Coulthard v Neville Russell* [1998] B.C.C. 359, CA (allegation that auditors failed to warn that loans made by

The principles discussed in this paragraph are particular applications of the general approach for the existence and scope of a duty of care. In all cases the underlying question is whether the defendant held himself out as undertaking responsibility for his statement in favour of the claimant, and (to consider the matter from the claimant's perspective) whether the claimant was entitled to rely on the statement and on the defendant's skill and care in making it. The duty which might otherwise be owed by an accountant or auditor might be negatived or reduced if, on the facts, the defendant does not hold himself out as making a statement on which the claimant is entitled to rely. So if an accountant produces accounts which he labels as "draft" accounts, and reasonably expects that the person to whom he provides them will make other enquiries or take independent advice, he will owe no duty.[198] And there can be a temporal limit to a duty of care: for example, in relation to an audit, even if a claimant is owed a duty of care by the auditor, and therefore is entitled to rely on the auditor's statement, such reliance may be reasonable only until the auditor would normally expect his statement about the company's financial circumstances to be superseded by the next audit statement—usually, the following year.[199]

Architects and other building designers.[200] The scope of duty owed by an architect, or another building designer,[201] will depend 6–34

company would be contrary to the Companies Act 1985, s.151, resulting in directors being disqualified). All these cases were decisions on applications to strike out; *cf.* above, n.183.

198 *James McNaughton Paper Group Ltd v Hicks Anderson & Co.* [1991] 2 Q.B. 113, CA.

199 *JEB Fasteners Ltd v Marks Bloom & Co.* [1981] 3 All E.R. 289 at 300–301 (this aspect of the judgment was not discussed in the CA [1983] 1 All E.R. 583); *cf. Galoo Ltd v Bright Grahame Murray* [1994] 1 W.L.R. 1360, CA.

200 Clerk & Lindsell, paras 10–182 to 10–194; D.L. Cornes, *Design Liability in the Construction Industry* (4th edn, 1994); Jackson & Powell, Ch.9; Dugdale & Stanton, paras 8.12 to 8.19; Hodgin, Ch.3 (I. Yule); S. Furst and Sir V. Ramsey, *Keating on Construction Contracts* (8th edn, 2006), Ch.13; Atkin Chambers, *Hudson's Building and Engineering Contracts* (12th edn, 2010), Ch.2.

201 e.g. an engineer, or even a contractor or subcontractor, who undertakes design responsibilities in relation to a building or part of a building, whether a new building or another project such as refurbishment or redevelopment of an existing building.

on the person to whom he is alleged to have owed the duty, and the scope of the task he has undertaken for that person.

In favour of his client, an architect or other designer will generally owe a duty, concurrently with his contractual duties,[202] to take reasonable care to perform the tasks he undertakes to the standards expected of his profession.[203] This duty will normally be owed in respect of physical damage caused to the client's other property, such as where defective design of an extension to a building causes physical damage to the existing structure. But, being based on the architect's assumption of responsibility to the client,[204] it may also extend to the economic losses which the client suffers by virtue of the defendant's failure to fulfil his duty of care, such as the costs of obtaining new designs, and such demolition and re-construction of the building as may be necessary in the light of the defendant's breach of duty.[205]

---

[202] Above, para.6–29; *Gable House Estates Ltd v Halpern Partnership* (1995) 48 Con. L.R. 1; *Bellefield Computer Services v E. Turner & Sons Ltd* [2002] EWCA Civ 1823, [2003] 1 Lloyd's Rep. P.N. 53 at [73]. The assumption in *Lancashire and Cheshire Association of Baptist Churches Inc v Howard & Seddon Partnership* [1993] 3 All E.R. 467 at 477, below, n.212, that the architect's duty in tort would only arise if there were an identifiable *statement* by the designer as to his design is now too restrictive in the light of *Henderson v Merrett Syndicates Plc* [1995] 2 A.C. 145, above, para.6–25.

[203] The duty in negligence will be only a duty of care; and so even if the contract contains higher duties, e.g. to design a building which is fit for a particular purpose, the duty in tort does not extend so far: *Greaves & Co. (Contractors) Ltd v Baynham Meikle & Partners* [1975] 1 W.L.R. 1095, CA, at 1101 (design & build contractor's contractual obligations of fitness for purpose and reasonable care). But the level of duty in tort—the care which the defendant can be held to have undertaken—will be set taking into account any relevant holding-out by the defendant that he has a particular expertise or skill: *Bolam v Friern Hospital Management Committee* [1957] 1 W.L.R. 582 at 586 (medical negligence); *Greaves & Co. (Contractors) Ltd v Baynham Meikle & Partners*, above.

[204] *cf. Robinson v P.E. Jones (Contractors) Ltd* [2011] EWCA Civ 9, [2011] B.L.R. 206 at [74]–[75], [81]–[83], [92]–[94], drawing a distinction between a professional provider of services (such as an architect) who normally assumes responsibility to the client, and a building contractor, who does not.

[205] In *Payne v John Setchell Ltd* [2002] P.N.L.R. 7 at [30], however, Judge Humphrey Lloyd Q.C. held that an architect was not to be distinguished from the builder: both provide services in the course of the construction process and for both the duty extends normally only to physical damage: "If any liability for such economic loss is to arise it must be for other reasons, e.g. as a result of advice or statements made upon which reliance is placed in circumstances which create a relationship where there is in law to be an assumption of the responsibility for

In *Pirelli General Cable Works Ltd v Oscar Faber & Partners*[206] consulting engineers who accepted responsibility for design of a chimney were assumed to owe a duty in tort to their client in respect of defects in the chimney which resulted from defective design and specification of materials in the construction of the chimney. The principal issue in the case was however one of limitation, and the House of Lords held that the action was statute barred: the date at which the action accrued was when damage to the chimney came into existence, not when it was discovered or could have been discovered.[207] This raises a fundamental issue within the law of negligence: since the duty is owed in respect of a particular kind of loss,[208] it is vital to identify the true nature of the loss which is the gist of the action. It was assumed in *Pirelli* that the relevant loss was the physical damage to the chimney, even though that was not damage to property separate from the property for the design of which the defendant had undertaken responsibility.[209] Although *Pirelli* has not yet formally been departed from by the House of Lords (or, now, the Supreme Court), it is submitted that the better view is that the gist of such an action is the economic loss suffered by reason of the diminution of value of the property by reason of the defect; the time at which the claim arises is therefore the time at which the defect is such that a reasonable building owner would take steps to have it remedied.[210]

---

loss—i.e. within the principle of *Hedley Byrne v Heller*." *Cf. Bellefield Computer Services v E. Turner & Sons Ltd*, above, n.202 at [76] (May L.J. noting that the borderline between design work and construction work is blurred); *Robinson v P.E. Jones (Contractors) Ltd*, above, n.204 at [51].

[206] [1983] 2 A.C. 1, HL.

[207] The chimney was constructed in 1969; cracks developed no later than April 1970, which could not with reasonable diligence have been discovered before October 1972; and the claimants actually discovered the cracks in November 1977 and issued their writ in October 1978.

[208] Above, para.6–14.

[209] In the case of careless acts, the general rule is that loss is sustained, and so the cause of action accrues, only when damage is caused to the person or to *other* property: *Murphy v Brentwood DC* [1991] 1 A.C. 398, HL; *Nitrigin Eireann Teoranta v Inco Alloys Ltd* [1992] 1 W.L.R. 499.

[210] *Invercargill City Council v Hamlin* [1996] A.C. 624, PC, at 648–649, expressly disapproving *Pirelli* for the law of New Zealand. The Privy Council left open the question of how *Pirelli* should continue to apply in England. *Pirelli* continues, however, to be applied as binding by the lower courts in England: *New Islington and Hackney Housing Association Ltd v Pollard Thomas and Edwards Ltd* [2001] B.L.R. 74 at 83; *Abbott v Will Gannon & Smith Ltd* [2005] EWCA Civ

The scope of the architect's duty depends, however, on a close analysis of what he undertook to do. An architect who designs a structure may hold himself out as giving advice as to the proper method of construction of the structure, on which the client is entitled to rely, so that the client can hold the architect liable to pay for the cost of remedying defects if the advice is given carelessly.[211] But if the architect submits designs simply to enable the client to consider them in the light of the accommodation which a proposed building would offer and its appearance, both aesthetically and functionally, he may not be held to have made through his plans any statement about the technical qualities of the proposed building; and so the client may not be entitled to rely on the architect as advising on such technical matters which therefore will not fall within the scope of the duty he has undertaken.[212] An architect may also undertake tasks which go beyond the design of the building, such as the day-to-day supervision of the building project, and certification of the progress of the works and their completion and of payments due to the contractor. In such cases the scope of his duty in the tort of negligence should be determined by reference to the type of activity he undertakes.[213]

198, [2005] P.N.L.R. 30. *Pirelli* was rejected in Canada in *City of Kamloops v Nielsen* [1984] 2 S.C.R. 2 (SCC), (1984) 10 D.L.R. (4th) 641.

[211] *Pirelli General Cable Works Ltd v Oscar Faber & Partners*, above, n.206, as interpreted by Lord Keith in *Murphy v Brentwood DC*, above, n.209 at 466 (Lord Keith).

[212] *Lancashire and Cheshire Association of Baptist Churches Inc v Howard & Seddon Partnership*, above, n.202 at 477 (submitting the plans was neither an express nor an implied statement of the technical qualities of the building).

[213] The architect will generally owe a duty of care to the client, concurrently with his contractual duties, in relation to the performance of the tasks he undertakes: *Wessex Regional Health Authority v HLM Design Ltd* (1995) 71 B.L.R. 32 (architect owes duty of care in tort and contract to client in respect of sums overpaid to building contractor as result of client's reliance on architect's over-certification of extension of time and of sums payable under building contract); *Valerie Pratt v George J. Hill Associates* (1987) 38 B.L.R. 25, CA (architect owed duty to client in relation to statement during tender process that contractor was reliable, and in relation to certification of sums due to contractor under building contract); *Sutcliffe v Thackrah* [1974] A.C. 727, HL (architect issuing interim certificates owed duty to client to act fairly between client and contractor, but not as an arbitrator so not immune from suit); *Nye Saunders and Partners v Alan E. Bristow* (1987) 37 B.L.R. 92, CA (architect in breach of duty by overestimating cost of project); *B.L. Holdings Ltd v Robert J. Wood & Partners* (1978) 10 B.L.R. 48, rvsd however on facts by (1979) 12 B.L.R. 1, CA

An architect may owe a duty to third parties in respect of foreseeable damage caused to them or their property.[214] But it will be more difficult to show that he owes a duty to third parties in respect of purely economic loss. The English courts[215] have been reluctant to hold that those involved in the production of a defective building owe duties in tort[216] even to their clients for the costs of

---

(architect's duty to advise on legal requirements for office development permit to enable planning permission for building to be effective).

214 *Targett v Torfaen BC* [1992] 3 All E.R. 27, CA (local authority's liability, as landlord which designed and constructed building, for tenant's personal injury); *Clayton v Woodman & Son (Builders) Ltd* [1962] 2 Q.B. 533 (architects' liability for personal injury to workman to whom they gave careless instructions about work to be carried out on site structure); *Clay v A.J. Crump & Sons Ltd* [1964] 1 Q.B. 533, CA (architect liable to workman injured on site by structure which architect had told demolition contractors could safely be left standing).

215 Other common law jurisdictions have in recent years declined to take such a restrictive approach, e.g. in Australia, *Bryan v Maloney* (1995) 182 C.L.R. 609, HCA (builder can owe duty of care to purchaser in respect of diminution of value to house caused by his careless workmanship: the scope of the duty was closely defined at 630), but see *Woolcock Street Investments Pty Ltd v CDG Pty Ltd* (2004) 78 A.L.J.R. 628, HCA, where the the majority left open at [35] the question of the correctness of *Bryan v Maloney*: but *cf.* Callinan J. at [211] (there is reason to question the correctness of *Bryan*), and McHugh J. at [71] (*Bryan v Maloney* does not apply to commercial premises. The majority at [17], however, did not think it appropriate to draw a bright line between dwellings and other buildings, instead focusing on the claimant's "vulnerability"); in Canada, *Winnipeg Condominium Corp. No.36 v Bird Construction Co.* (1995) 121 D.L.R. (4th) 193, SCC (building contractors and architect can owe duty of care to purchaser in respect of costs of repair of building which is dangerous because of careless design/workmanship: duty limited to dangerous defects); *Privest Properties Ltd v Foundation Co. of Canada Ltd* (1995) 128 D.L.R. (4th) 577; in New Zealand, *Invercargill City Council v Hamlin* [1996] A.C. 624, PC (local authority can owe duty of care to purchaser of building in respect of inspections during construction); *Riddell v Porteous* [1999] N.Z.L.R. 1, NZCA (builder can owe similar duty); *Rolls-Royce New Zealand Ltd v Carter Hold Harvey Ltd* [2004] N.Z.C.A. 97 (a very useful review of the Australian, American, Canadian, English and New Zealand authorities on defective buildings at [70]–[130]).

216 There is, however, a potential liability under the Defective Premises Act 1972 s.1, which imposes a duty on every person who takes on work for or in connection with the provision of a dwelling (whether the dwelling is provided by the erection, conversion or enlargement of a building): the duty is owed both to the person to whose order the dwelling is provided and to every person who acquires an interest in the dwelling, and is a duty to see that the work is done in a workmanlike or professional manner, with proper materials, so that as regards the work the dwelling will be fit for habitation when completed. This therefore imposes duties on designers as well as those involved in the construction process

remedying the defects.[217] So a builder does not normally owe such a duty to a later purchaser[218] or a tenant[219] of the property he builds. In principle, the question will be whether the architect can be taken to have undertaken a responsibility not only to his client, but also to a third party, such as a purchaser.[220]

---

itself; and extends to a duty to compensate for the economic losses flowing from the dwelling being unfit for habitation (including the cost of repair): see, e.g. *Bole v Huntsbuild Ltd* [2009] EWCA Civ 1146, (2009) 127 Con. L.R. 154. The existence of this statutory duty was relied upon by the House of Lords in *Murphy v Brentwood DC*, above, n.209 at 457, 472, 480–481, 491–492 and 498 as indicating that the common law of negligence need not (or even should not) be developed to cover such losses. The duty under the 1972 Act does not apply in the case of a dwelling built under an approved scheme (such as the National House-Building Council's schemes): s.2. But no such approved schemes have been in force for the purposes of the 1972 Act since March 31, 1979: Sir V. Ramsey and S. Furst, *Keating on Construction Contracts* (8th edn, 2008), para.15.001, although there still appear to have been relatively few reported cases under s.1 of the Defective Premises Act.

[217] *Robinson v P.E. Jones (Contractors) Ltd* [2011] EWCA Civ 9, [2011] B.L.R. 206 at [81]–[83], [92].

[218] *Murphy v Brentwood DC* [1991] 1 A.C. 398, HL (local authority owed no duty to purchaser of house in respect of economic loss resulting from latent defects in construction, because builder would owe no such duty).

[219] *Department of the Environment v Thomas Bates & Son Ltd* [1991] 1 A.C. 499, HL.

[220] In *Ketteman v Hansel Properties Ltd* [1987] A.C. 189, HL, architects owed a duty to first purchasers of houses which they had designed, where the houses developed cracks because of defective foundations. However, this was a case decided under the same assumption as (and following) *Pirelli General Cable Works Ltd v Oscar Faber & Partners*, above, n.206, that the gist of the claim was physical damage to the houses rather than the economic loss suffered by the owner. See also *Independent Broadcasting Authority v EMI Electronics Ltd* (1980) 14 B.L.R. 1, HL (structural engineers who as nominated sub-contractors designed a television mast were assumed by House of Lords to owe duty of care to employer in respect of their design, as well as in respect of assurances about stability of mast given directly to employer). There is also a reluctance to hold that the architect owes duties in respect of economic loss to persons other than his client during the building process: *Pacific Associates Inc. v Baxter* [1990] 1 Q.B. 993, CA (consulting engineer employed by client to supervise work did not owe duty directly to contractor in absence of assumption of responsibility). For duties in respect of physical damage to third parties during the building process, however, see above, n.214. See also *Bellefield Computer Services v E. Turner & Sons Ltd*, above, n.202 at [75] (May L.J., reserving the question whether or to what extent the scope of an architect's duty of care to a subsequent owner or occupier could extend to loss unassociated with physical damage).

Banks and other lenders.[221] A bank may owe a duty of care in tort to its customer, concurrently with the duties it owes in contract.[222] The scope of the duty of care will depend on the task the bank holds itself out as performing for the particular customer.[223] If the bank offers advice, such as financial advice to the customer on which the bank knows or ought to know that the customer will rely in taking his investment decisions, then the scope of the duty may extend to the consequences of the customer's entering into transactions in reliance on the advice.[224] The bank may undertake a general, continuing retainer in relation to giving such advice,[225] in which case the duty will extend appropriately, and may embrace the duty positively to offer advice in the light of changed market conditions. Or the only advice sought and offered may be in relation to a particular investment, in which case the duty will be limited to the particular transaction. But the relationship between a bank[226] and its customer is not of itself one where the banker owes duties to look to the customer's interests: it does not give rise to fiduciary duties on the bank, and indeed it is generally an arm's length relationship.[227] So if the customer or a potential customer approaches the bank with a proposition, such as a request for a loan, the bank owes no duty to advise the applicant as to the 6–35

---

221 Sir P. Cresswell and others (ed.), *Encyclopaedia of Banking Law*, Division C5; Dugdale & Stanton, paras 8.06 to 8.11; Charlesworth & Percy, paras 9–80 to 9–94.

222 The reluctance of the Privy Council in *Tai Hing Cotton Mill Ltd v Liu Chong Hing Bank Ltd* [1986] A.C. 80 at 107 to embark on an investigation as to whether in the relationship of banker and customer it is possible to identify tort, as well as contract, as a source of the obligations owed by one to the other, has now been superseded by the preference of the House of Lords in *Henderson v Merrett Syndicates Ltd* [1995] 2 A.C. 145 to allow, or even encourage, the finding of concurrent duties in contract and tort: see esp. at 186–187.

223 *Woods v Martins Bank Ltd* [1959] 1 Q.B. 55 at 70.

224 *South Australia Asset Management Corp. v York Montague Ltd* [1997] A.C. 191, HL, at 214.

225 *Woods v Martins Bank Ltd*, above, n.223.

226 A building society owes no higher duty than a bank: the relationship between a building society and its members does not in this respect carry additional privileges for the member or impose additional obligations on the society: *Investors Compensation Scheme Ltd v West Bromwich Building Society* [1999] Lloyd's Rep. P.N. 496 at 525.

227 *Lloyd's Bank Ltd v Bundy* [1975] Q.B. 326, CA, at 347 (Sir Eric Sachs), applied in *National Westminster Bank Plc v Morgan* [1985] A.C. 686, HL, at 708–709 (undue influence).

terms, effect or commercial prudence of his proposition.[228] But if a representative of the bank chooses to give advice—if he advises him on the effect of the terms of the loan,[229] or if he advises on the financial viability of a project which the bank is to finance,[230] or if he makes statements predicting the likely outcome of the application for a loan when it is received by his bank's head office[231]—then he will owe a duty to take reasonable care in making such statements if he knows or ought to know that the applicant will rely on them.

A bank may also owe a duty of care to a person who is not a customer or potential customer, if it gives information or advice to a person who it knows will rely on the accuracy of the information for a particular purpose; and on general principles[232] the duty will extend to the losses suffered by the claimant within the scope of the known purpose. For example, where a bank gives information about the creditworthiness of one of its own customers to a person it knows is considering extending credit to the customer, the bank may be held to have assumed a responsibility to the person asking for the information, unless the circumstances in which the information is given make clear that no such responsibility is being assumed.[233]

---

228 *Investors Compensation Scheme Ltd v West Bromwich Building Society*, above, n.226; *Williams and Glyn's Bank Ltd v Barnes* [1981] Com. L.R. 205 at 207.

229 *Cornish v Midland Bank Plc* [1985] 3 All E.R. 513, CA.

230 *Verity v Lloyds Bank Plc* [1995] C.L.C. 1557.

231 *Box v Midland Bank Ltd* [1979] 2 Lloyd's Rep. 391 at 399 (the appeal to the CA [1981] 1 Lloyd's Rep. 434 was only as to costs).

232 Above, para.6–14.

233 *Hedley Byrne & Co. Ltd v Heller & Partners* [1964] A.C. 465, HL (where the duty was negatived by an express disclaimer of responsibility); below, para.6–40. On the ability to disclaim responsibility after the passing of the Unfair Contract Terms Act 1977, see below, Ch.9. The bank does not however owe a duty to a third party to take reasonable care to comply with terms of freezing injunction affecting a customer's account, because the court order does not create a duty, and the bank in being notified of it does not assume a responsibility to the third party: *Customs & Excise Commissioners v Barclays Bank Plc* [2006] UKHL 28, [2007] 1 A.C. 181.

Expert witnesses. An expert who acts on behalf of one of the parties in civil litigation[234] will generally owe a duty of care to his client, concurrently with his contractual duties arising from his retainer.[235] The scope of the duty will depend on the scope of the instructions given by the client. However, the expert witness who is retained to act for a client in relation to litigation also owes a duty to the court,[236] and until recently it had been assumed that expert witnesses benefited from immunity from suit in relation to any claim for negligence by the client in relation to evidence given in court, and advice given in relation to court proceedings.[237] The Supreme Court has now abolished this special immunity,[238] and therefore any claim against an expert will now be based simply on the general principles of negligence.[239] **6–36**

Financial advisers. A financial adviser may owe a duty of care to his client, concurrently with any duties he owes in contract.[240] As in the case of all professionals, the scope of the financial adviser's duty will depend on the services he holds himself out as undertaking. If he is an independent financial adviser, he will **6–37**

---

234 A so-called "friendly expert": *Jones v Kaney* [2011] UKSC 13, [2011] 2 W.L.R. 823 at [71] (Lord Collins J.S.C.).

235 *Jones v Kerney*, above, n.234 at [88] (LordKerr J.S.C.), [95] (Lord Dyson J.S.C.).

236 Ibid., at [96]–[99]; this duty overrides any obligation to the client: CPR r.35.3(2).

237 *Palmer v Durnford Ford* [1992] Q.B. 483; *Stanton v Callaghan* [1998] Q.B. 75, CA (immunity in preparing joint expert witness statement for use in legal proceedings). For an account of the history of the immunity, and the authorities relating directly to expert witnesses, see *Jones v Kaney*, above, n.234 at [11]–[26] (Lord Phillips P.S.C.)

238 *Jones v Kaney*, above, n.234 (a seven-judge court; Lord Hope D.P.S.C. and Baroness Hale J.S.C. dissenting). This brings expert witnesses into line with barristers, whose immunity from suit in negligence in relation to court proceedings was abolished in *Arthur J.S. Hall & Co. v Simons* [2002] 1 A.C. 615, below, para.6–41, n.290. Witnesses *of fact* continue to enjoy immunity: *cf. Jones v Kaney* at [50], [65]–[66].

239 In tort or contract. The absolute privilege enjoyed by expert witnesses in respect of claims in defamation remains: *Jones v Kaney*, above, n.234 at [62], [72].

240 *Henderson v Merrett Syndicates Ltd* [1995] 2 A.C. 145, HL. The financial adviser may either be retained by the client by contract to give advice, or may act on the basis that he receives commission not from the client but from the parties with whom investments are placed.

typically owe a duty to exercise reasonable care and skill to advise the client about the range of investments which are suitable for the client's circumstances. Where, however, he holds himself out as giving advice only on a particular company's investment products, or a limited range of investments, his duty will not be to advise comprehensively but only in relation to that company's products or to that limited range of investments, although this may extend to a duty to advise the client not to enter into unsuitable investments.[241] Where the purpose of the investment is to enable the client to confer benefits on third parties, such as the client's dependants after his death, the adviser may also owe a duty directly to the third parties, but the duty in such a case can only be to exercise reasonable care to advise the client in relation to the provision of the benefits which the client intends to confer on the third parties, and not to protect the third parties' position more generally.[242]

6–38 **Insurance brokers.**[243] An insurance broker may owe a duty of care to the insured, his client, concurrently with the duties he owes in contract.[244] The duty will extend to taking reasonable care to

241 *Gorham v British Telecommunications Plc* [2000] 1 W.L.R. 2129, CA, at 2143–2144 (Pill L.J., discussing the duties of an insurance adviser, below, para.6–38).

242 *ibid.*, at 2142. The decision in *Gorham v British Telecommunications Plc* is an extension of the decision in *White v Jones* [1995] 2 A.C. 207, HL, below, para.6–44, n.286 to a case where the third parties, the client's dependants, failed to receive the benefits under a life insurance policy which the client had intended them to receive, and (as in *White v Jones*) hinged upon the fact that the client, after his death, could no longer remedy the failure to confer the benefit and so if the third party had no direct claim there would be a lacuna in which the only person who might have a valid claim [the deceased] had suffered no loss, and the only person who had suffered a loss [the third party] had no claim: *Gorham v British Telecommunications Plc*, above, n.241 at 2140 (Pill L.J.). Except in such a case it appears that it will be relatively rare for such a duty to be held to be owed to intended third-party beneficiary of an investment; but see *Richards v Hughes* [2004] EWCA Civ 266, [2004] P.N.L.R. 35 at [28] (Peter Gibson L.J.: chartered accountant had strong arguable case that he owed duty only to client and not to intended third party beneficiaries of trust on which he advised as investment scheme, but third parties' claim not bound to fail).

243 Clerk & Lindsell, paras 10–212 to 10–231; Jackson & Powell, Ch.16; Dugdale & Stanton, paras 8.26 to 8.32; Hodgin, Ch.8; Clarke, Ch.9; Charlesworth & Percy, paras 9–168 to 9–182.

244 *Youell v Bland Welch & Co. Ltd (The "Superhulls Cover" Case) (No.2)* [1990] 2 Lloyd's Rep. 431 at 459, approved *Henderson v Merrett Syndicates Ltd*,

fulfil such tasks as he has held himself out as performing on the insured's behalf[245]: and may therefore in an appropriate case include duties in relation to advice offered by the broker as to the suitability of insurance cover and the choice between alternative policies.[246] It has also been held by extension that a broker may owe a duty to a specific person who he knew was later to become an assignee of the benefit of the policy,[247] and that a managing agent at Lloyd's may owe a duty to a Name who is a member of a syndicate

---

above, n.240 at 182; *BP Plc v Aon Ltd* [2006] EWHC 424 (Comm), [2006] 1 All E.R. (Comm) 789 ("the proper professional standards of an insurance broker on the London and European markets": Colman J. at [181]). The duty does not depend on there being a contract, but in most cases there will be a contractual relationship between the broker and the insured. There is normally no duty of care not to make negligent misstatements implicit in the relationship of insurer and insured or proposer (and so no duty owed by either to the other): *H.I.H. Casualty and General Insurance Ltd v Chase Manhattan Bank* [2001] EWCA Civ 1250, [2001] 2 Lloyd's Rep. 483 at [59]–[74] (Rix L.J., who used as part of his argument the fact that most insureds have an insurance broker to look to in the case where an unsuitable insurance has been purchased).

245 [2007] EWCA Civ 710, [2007] 2 C.L.C. 62.

246 The regulatory context will be relevant to the scope of duties owed at common law: *cf. Jones v Environcom Ltd* [2010] EWHC 759 (Comm), [2010] P.N.L.R. 27 at [53]–[53] (FSA Insurance Conduct of Business Handbook demonstrated that broker must take reasonable steps to ensure that proposed policy is suitable for client's needs; this included advising client of duty of disclosure because "By definition, a policy which is voidable for non-disclosure is not suitable" (David Steel J.)). Where the broker acts only on behalf of a particular insurance company or holds himself out as offering advice only in relation to a limited range of insurance companies or policies, his duty will not be to advise comprehensively but may be limited to advising the client not to enter into unsuitable policies: *Gorham v British Telecommunications Plc*, above, n.241 at 2143–2144 (Pill L.J.). The time at which actionable damage is suffered in such a case will normally be the time when the claimant enters into an unsuitable insurance policy. *Cf. Iron Trade Mutual Insurance Co. Ltd v J.K. Buckenham Ltd* [1990] 1 All E.R. 808; *Islander Trucking Ltd v Hogg Robinson & Gardner Mountain (Marine) Ltd* [1990] 1 All E.R. 826. For the duty owed by a broker to advise the client about the availability of reinsurance cover in the market (which went beyond the duty simply to obtain cover), see *Aneco Reinsurance Underwriting Ltd v Johnson & Higgins Ltd* [2001] UKHL 51, [2002] 1 Lloyd's Rep. 157.

247 *Punjab National Bank v De Boinville* [1992] 1 W.L.R. 1138, CA; the extension was, on the facts, to a case where the future assignee "actively participates in giving instructions for the insurance to the broker's knowledge": *ibid.*, at 1154 (Staughton L.J.).

under the management of the agents.[248] Furthermore, if an insurance broker makes statements on behalf of his client to a third party who he knows is relying on him to take care in making the statement, he may owe a duty directly to that third party—such as where a broker confirms to a purchaser of property from his client that the property is adequately insured and the purchaser (to the broker's knowledge) in reliance on that confirmation advances funds to the purchaser but the property is lost without adequate insurance cover having been effected.[249]

An insurance adviser may also owe a duty of care directly to his client's dependants where the client seeks advice in relation to making provision for the dependants after his death.[250] Such duty is however limited to not giving negligent advice to the client which adversely affects the dependants' interests as the client intends them to be; it does not extend to ensuring that the dependants are properly provided for.[251]

6–39 **Local authorities and other public bodies.**[252] The position of local authorities and other public bodies as regards the imposition of duties of care in respect of statements made by their officers or employees is naturally affected by the public law context. But at the level of the careless performance of the authority's public powers and duties, the approach to the duty of care is still consistent with the general approach taken for the establishment of a duty of care in negligence. In *X v Bedfordshire County Council* Lord Browne-Wilkinson said[253]:

---

[248] *Henderson v Merrett Syndicates Ltd*, above, n.240 at 182 (either "an analogy from the categories of relationship already recognised as falling within the principle in *Hedley Byrne* or by a straight application of the principle stated in the *Hedley Byrne* case itself": Lord Goff).

[249] *Banque Paribas (Suisse) SA v Stolidi Shipping Co. Ltd* [1997] 2 C.L.Y. 3818.

[250] *Gorham v British Telecommunications Plc*, above, n.241.

[251] *ibid.*, at 2142 (Pill L.J.).

[252] For a detailed discussion of the liability of public authorities in negligence, see Clerk & Lindsell, Ch.14; R.A. Buckley, *The Law of Negligence* (4th edn, 2005), Ch.12; Dugdale & Stanton, Ch.9; H.W.R. Wade and C.F. Forsyth, *Administrative Law* (10th edn, 2009), pp.648–662; P.P. Craig, *Administrative Law* (6th edn, 2008), paras 29–004 to 29–020.

[253] [1995] 2 A.C. 633 at 739. In *Stovin v Wise* [1996] A.C. 923 at 947, Lord Hoffmann said that "In the case of positive acts . . . the liability of a public authority in tort is in principle the same as that of a private person but may be

> "the question whether there is such a common law duty and if so its ambit, must be profoundly influenced by the statutory framework within which the acts complained of were done. The position is directly analogous to that in which a tortious duty of care owed by A to C can arise out of the performance by A of a contract between A and B. In *Henderson v Merrett Syndicates Ltd*[254] your Lordships held that A (the managing agent) who had contracted with B (the members' agent) to render certain services for C (the Names) came under a duty of care to C in the performance of those services. It is clear that any tortious duty of care owed to C in those circumstances could not be inconsistent with the duty owed in contract by A to B. Similarly, in my judgment a common law duty of care cannot be imposed on a statutory duty if the observance of such common law duty of care would be inconsistent with, or have a tendency to discourage, the due performance by the local authority of its statutory duties."

A local or other public authority can owe a duty of care in the tort of negligence, including a duty in relation to statements made by its officers and employees[255]; but, in deciding whether such a duty exists on any given set of facts, the courts must inquire into the purpose for which the relevant statement was made and the context in which it was made (in particular, if the statement was made pursuant to a statutory power or duty, the purposes for which that power or duty was to be exercised); and they must consider the proper scope of responsibility which the authority can be taken to have been assuming towards the claimant in making the statement and whether it would be fair, just and reasonable to admit the alleged duty.[256]

---

restricted by its statutory powers and duties". See also *Gorringe v Calderdale MBC* [2004] UKHL 15, [2004] 1 W.L.R. 1057.

254 [1995] 2 A.C. 145.

255 See, e.g. *Minister of Housing and Local Government v Sharp* [1970] 2 Q.B. 223, above, para.6–24 (council clerk carelessly issuing inaccurate information about registered local land charges); *Welton v North Cornwall DC* [1997] 1 W.L.R. 570, CA (environmental health officer employed by local authority owed duty of care when acting outside scope of food safety legislation in wrongly advising claimant to make alterations to her kitchen: 90% of the work was unnecessary and the kitchen plan on which he insisted was ill-conceived, inappropriate and less efficient than the previous layout).

256 *cf. Murphy v Brentwood DC* [1991] 1 A.C. 398, HL (local authority, through its inspector, certifying plans and calculations for building does not owe duty to purchaser in respect of consequential defects in the building; and may not even owe duty to person injured by defects, given the context of the public law statutory purpose of supervising compliance with building regulations: see at 457, 463, 479 and 492); *Harris v Evans* [1998] 1 W.L.R. 1285, CA (Health and

6–40 **Referees.** A referee makes a statement, usually consisting of both factual information and the referee's opinion, about the person who is the subject of the reference. Common forms of reference are credit references, where the statement relates to the financial stability of the subject; and employment references, where the statement relates to the qualities of the subject to perform the duties of a particular job. In the case of references, there are two separate duties to consider: the duty to the recipient of the reference, and the duty to the subject of the reference.

The duty to the *recipient of the reference* will be in issue where the recipient relied on it but seeks later to claim that the reference was inaccurate and given carelessly, and that in so relying he has suffered loss. It was established in *Hedley Byrne & Co. Ltd v Heller & Partners Ltd*[257] that a bank, giving a credit reference about one of its customers to a person who it knows is likely to rely on the reference in dealing with, and entering into financial liabilities on behalf of, the customer can owe a duty of care to the recipient of the reference.[258] But the existence and scope of the duty of care cannot be determined without a careful consideration of the precise circumstances in which the reference was given; and it must be asked what task the referee undertook.[259] A referee may make it clear that he is not undertaking responsibility for the accuracy of the reference,[260] or the reference may be given in circumstances where the recipient is not entitled to assume that the referee is undertaking responsibility for it, such as a statement made informally or on a social occasion.[261] Or it may be clear that the statements can be taken as giving information or an opinion of only a limited scope,

Safety Executive inspector exercising powers under the Health and Safety at Work etc. Act 1974 in advising local authorities about safety of crane to be used by claimant in bungee jumping business did not owe duty to claimant, having regard to the purpose of the Act).

257 [1964] A.C. 465; above, para.6–10.

258 There was no duty on the facts, because of a disclaimer; but the duty would not have been affected by the fact that the information was passed to the claimant through its own bankers.

259 A bank normally assumes a duty only to provide a reference as to the credit of its named customer: it does not represent that the person with whom the claimant is dealing *is* the customer: *Gold Coin Joaillers S.A. v United Bank of Kuwait Plc*, *The Times*, November 4, 1996, CA.

260 *Hedley Byrne*, above, n.257. For the validity of a disclaimer of responsibility after the Unfair Contract Terms Act 1977, see Ch.9.

261 *ibid.*, at 482–483.

such as where an employment reference is given by a person who has only a social acquaintance with the subject, and so (as the recipient knows) has only a limited basis for forming his opinion.[262] If a referee holds himself out as only passing on information which he has obtained from another person, without himself expressing any personal opinion on, or certifying the accuracy of, that information, then his duty will be limited to taking reasonable care to ensure that the information is passed on accurately.[263] The duty will extend only to the consequences suffered by the claimant within the scope of the duty. If the duty is to take care to provide accurate information in the reference, the defendant is liable for the foreseeable consequences of the information being inaccurate.[264] But usually the scope of the duty will be limited to a particular transaction which the referee knows the recipient is likely to enter into in reliance on the reference: the recipient cannot therefore necessarily claim that losses he suffers in entering into other, later transactions with the subject of the reference are also within the scope of the duty.[265]

The duty to the *subject of the reference* will be in issue where the recipient relies[266] on it but in so doing causes loss not to himself but to the subject: typically, therefore, the reference causes him not to extend credit to the subject, or not to employ him. This is an example of a category of duty which does not fit within the general pattern of the cases based on *Hedley Byrne* and *Caparo Industries Plc v Dickman*, since the reliance by the recipient on the statement

---

262 *cf. Spring v Guardian Assurance Plc* [1995] 2 A.C. 296, HL, at 336 (Lord Slynn, discussing however the duty not to the recipient of the reference but to its subject).

263 *HIT Finance Ltd v Cohen Arnold & Co.* [2000] Lloyd's Rep. P.N. 125 (credit reference).

264 *South Australia Asset Management Corp. v York Montague Ltd* [1997] A.C. 191, HL, at 214.

265 *Conister Trust Plc v London Trust Bank Plc*, unreported, February 25, 2000 (P. Mott Q.C.: credit reference given in respect of one transaction was still on the facts operative in relation to later transaction, although later losses irrecoverable as flowing from claimant's contributory negligence. The judge, whilst relying on *South Australia Asset Management Corp. v York Montague Ltd*, above, n.264, treated these issues however as matters of causation and remoteness rather than of the scope of the duty of care).

266 There can be no claim without actual reliance by a third party: *Legal and General Assurance Society Ltd v Kirk* [2001] EWCA Civ 1803, [2002] I.R.L.R. 124.

causes loss not to him but to a third party, and as such it has been approached more cautiously by the courts.[267] There do not appear to be reported cases dealing with this in the context of credit references but in *Spring v Guardian Assurance Plc*[268] the House of Lords held, by a majority,[269] that a former employer could owe a duty to his former employee to take reasonable care when providing a reference to a potential employer. It appears that, generally, an employer will owe such a duty to his employee by virtue of their present or past employment relationship. Lord Goff said[270]:

> "The employer is possessed of special knowledge, derived from his experience of the employee's character, skill and diligence in the performance of his duties while working for the employer. Moreover, when the employer provides a reference to a third party in respect of his employee, he does so not only for the assistance of the third party, but also, for what it is worth, for the assistance of the employee. Indeed, nowadays it must often be very difficult for an employee to obtain fresh employment without the benefit of a reference from his present or a previous employer. It is for this reason that, in ordinary life, it may be the employee, rather than a prospective future employer, who asks the employer to provide the reference; and even when the approach comes from the prospective future employer, it will (apart from special circumstances) be made with either the express or the tacit authority of the employee . . . Furthermore, when such a reference is provided by an employer, it is plain that the employee relies upon him to exercise due skill and care in the preparation of the reference before making it available to the third party."

Key elements in the employer's assumption of responsibility to the employee are that the employee has expressly or impliedly requested the employer to make the statement; that the employer is

[267] Above, para.6–24. One issue which arises in such a case is the quantification of loss. In *Spring v Guardian Assurance Plc*, below, n.268, the issue of quantification of damages was remitted to the Court of Appeal. But Lord Lowry at 327 said that the claimant only had to establish that by reason of the negligence "he has lost a reasonable chance of employment (which would have to be evaluated) and has thereby sustained loss . . . He does not have to prove that, but for the negligent reference, [the recipient of the reference] *would* have employed him".

[268] [1995] 2 A.C. 296.

[269] Lord Keith dissented, on the basis that to accept such a duty would cut across the defence of qualified privilege in the tort of defamation.

[270] [1995] 2 A.C. 296 at 319. For statements in the other judgments showing a similar assumption that, in the normal case of an employment reference, a duty of care arises, see at 335 (Lord Slynn) and 345 (Lord Woolf).

in a position to influence the recipient's decision because of his special knowledge of the employee's past conduct; and that the employee relies on the employer to take care in making the statement because, as the employer knows, the employee's future depends upon it. But the context in which the reference is given must be considered carefully before the existence and scope of the duty can be settled. The duty might not exist, or might exist with a more attenuated scope if, for example, the referee is only a social acquaintance rather than a former employer, or if he is not a recent employer and makes clear his limited ability to give information relevant to the recipient's decision.[271] The duty does not necessarily extend to giving a full and comprehensive reference: it is to take reasonable care in giving a reference which is true, fair and accurate, and in order to determine the fairness of the reference it is necessary to have regard to the whole of the reference and its surrounding context.[272]

The duty is not limited to the employment relationship: it will extend to a reference given to a future employer about a person who was employed under a contract for services, such as a consultancy arrangement, rather than an employment contract.[273] But whether a statement made about a claimant in other contexts will attract the duty will depend on an extension of the category of duty which is illustrated by the decision of the House of Lords in *Spring v Guardian Assurance Plc*, and this involves a close consideration of the reasons for the imposition of the duty in *Spring* itself and whether the new case is sufficiently analogous to justify an extension, as well as the broader question of whether admitting such an extension would be fair, just and reasonable.[274]

---

[271] *Spring v Guardian Assurance Plc*, above, n.268 at 336.

[272] *Bartholomew v Hackney LBC* [1999] I.R.L.R. 246, CA; *Cox v Sun Alliance Life Ltd* [2001] EWCA Civ 649, [2001] I.R.L.R. 448; *Kidd v Axa Equity & Law Life Assurance Society Plc* [2000] I.R.L.R. 301.

[273] *Spring v Guardian Assurance Plc*, above, n.268 at 341.

[274] Above, para.6–13. Two possible general arguments relevant to the question of whether such an extension would be "fair, just and reasonable" were disposed of in *Spring v Guardian Assurance Plc*, above, n.268: it is not of itself an objection to say that admitting a duty in the tort or negligence would cut across the defence of qualified privilege in the tort of defamation (see at 324, 325, 334–335, 350–351; Lord Keith dissented on this point); nor is it contrary to Art.10 of the European Convention for the Protection of Human Rights and Fundamental Freedoms, which was not "intended to shield a negligent defendant in an action based on negligence . . . Freedom of speech is not to be identified with freedom

6–41 **Solicitors and barristers.**[275] A solicitor will generally owe a duty of care to his client, concurrently with his contractual duties arising from his retainer.[276] The scope of the duty[277] will depend on the

---

to . . . damage negligently" (Lord Lowry at 326; see also Lord Slynn at 336 and Lord Woolf at 352). The detail of the novel case will therefore have to be considered: see, e.g. *West Wiltshire DC v Garland* [1995] Ch. 297, CA (district auditors making report on local government officers under the Local Government Finance Act 1982 do not owe duty to officers under principle of *Spring v Guardian Assurance Plc* because the Act makes clear that auditors should be free, short of bad faith, to criticise an officer without fear of exposing themselves to action for negligence). In *Spring v Guardian Assurance Plc* the reference was given pursuant to regulatory rules of the insurance industry within which all the parties were working; and in particular LAUTRO r.3.5(2) which required insurers to satisfy themselves of their representatives' good character before employing them; and required those giving references to make "full and frank disclosure of all matters which are believed to be true" ([1995] 2 A.C. 296 at 306). But it was held that the duty to make full and frank disclosure to the prospective employer was not inconsistent with a duty of care to the employee: [1995] 2 A.C. 296 at 324, 326–327, 339–340, 345). A doctor giving a medical report to a prospective employer by way of assessment of a medical questionnaire completed by a prospective employee does not owe a duty to the prospective employee: *Kapfunde v Abbey National Plc* [1999] I.C.R. 1, CA. Nor does an insurance investigator reporting on the causes of a fire to an insurance company owe a duty to the insured whose claim is rejected: *South Pacific Manufacturing Co. Ltd v New Zealand Security Consultants & Investigations Ltd* [1992] 2 N.Z.L.R. 282, NZCA, approved in *Spring v Guardian Assurance Plc* at 323–324 and 350. See also *Desmond v Chief Constable of Nottinghamshire Police* [2011] EWCA Civ 3, [2011] Fam. Law. 358 at [48] (police providing information as required by Police Force Act 1997 to Criminal Records Bureau for issue of enhanced criminal record certificate have no choice but to do so: no assumption of responsibility and so no duty to subject of reference).

275 Clerk & Lindsell, paras 10–105 to 10–153; Jackson & Powell, Chs 11 and 12; Dugdale & Stanton, paras 8.34 to 8.42; Hodgin, Ch.9 (M. Mildred); Charlesworth & Percy, paras 9–95 to 9–106 and 9–213 to 9–301.

276 *Henderson v Merrett Syndicates Ltd* [1995] 2 A.C. 145, HL, at 181–182; *Midland Bank Trust Co. Ltd v Hett, Stubbs & Kemp* [1979] Ch. 384; *Hedley Byrne & Co. Ltd v Heller & Partners Ltd* [1964] A.C. 465, HL, at 530. He will also owe fiduciary duties, the content of which is not limited to a duty *of care*: *Nocton v Lord Asburton*, above, para.6–08; *Bristol and West Building Society v Mothew* [1998] Ch. 1, CA, at 16–1; *Longstaff v Birtles* [2001] EWCA Civ 1219, [2002] 1 W.L.R. 470; *Hilton v Barker Booth & Eastwood* [2005] UKHL 8, [2005] 1 W.L.R. 567 at [28]–[31]; below, paras 17–33 to 17–34.

277 As with other professionals, the duty may extend to the provision of services as well as the provision of advice—that is, the duty is not limited to a duty in respect of statements: *Henderson v Merrett Syndicates Ltd*, above, n.276, at 180. The scope of the duty in tort will be set by the terms of the contractual retainer:

instructions given by the client, and the task for which the solicitor assumes responsibility to the client. The retainer may be specific to a particular transaction or for the provision of a particular piece of advice; or it may be more general and therefore may carry a higher responsibility to keep the client's position under review and take positive steps to inform him and offer him further advice as circumstances change.[278] In all cases the duty is to take such care as is reasonable given the professional skill which the solicitor holds himself out as having.[279]

A solicitor may also owe a duty of care to persons with whom he has no contractual relationship.[280] It is possible, for example, that another person's interests are closely interwoven with his client's interests, and the solicitor gives advice knowing that the other person will also rely on it for a particular purpose,[281] with the result that he will be taken to have assumed a similar responsibility to that other person.[282] But where the other party is independently

---

White v Jones [1995] 2 A.C. 207, HL, at 256; *Credit Lyonnais S.A. v Russell Jones & Walker* [2002] EWHC 1310 (Ch), [2003] P.N.L.R. 2.

278 *Credit Lyonnais S.A. v Russell Jones & Walker*, above, n.277. *Cf. Littlewood v Radford* [2009] EWCA Civ 1024, [2010] 1 P. & C.R. 18 at [57]–[59] (Rimer L.J.: "If a professional person gives clear advice on a particular point to his client as to the need to take a particular step by a particular time, there cannot be any general principle that he is under a duty to keep repeating that advice", but here the contractual retainer required the defendant [a surveyor] to remind the claimant of procedural deadline given the importance of the deadline, and that she was an inexperienced client, and "just the sort of client who could be expected to rely on a professional adviser such as [the defendant] to remind her").

279 *Bolam v Friern Hospital Management Committee* [1957] 1 W.L.R. 582 at 586 (medical negligence).

280 For the assumption that a solicitor who receives instructions from an impostor who fraudulently claims to be the owner of property owes a duty of care to the real owner (and so, for example, has the duty to confirm the instructions directly with the person for whom he purported to act, and to confirm the client's identity), see *Nouri v Marvi* [2009] EWHC 2725 (Ch), [2010] P.N.L.R. 7 at [6]–[7] (the claim failed on other grounds; affirmed at [2010] EWCA Civ 1107, [2011] P.N.L.R. 7).

281 The principal elements necessary to establish a duty of care in relation to advice, in *Caparo Industries Plc v Dickman* [1990] 2 A.C. 605; above, para.6–19.

282 *Johnson v Gore Wood & Co.* [1999] B.C.C. 474, CA (arguable that solicitors acting for company also owed duty to shareholder who was the alter ego of the company, and with whom as representing the company they had direct dealings, where they gave advice knowing that the shareholder, as well as the company, would act on it. The appeal to HL at [2002] 2 A.C. 1 was argued on other issues. For further steps in the case, see *Johnson v Gore Wood & Co.* [2003] EWCA Civ

represented, or has interests opposed to his client, the solicitor will not normally owe such a duty unless he steps outside his general role as his client's solicitor and accepts responsibilities towards the opponent.[283] It has also been held that a solicitor can owe a duty of care to the person whom his client intended to be a beneficiary of his will, where that person fails to receive the benefit as a result of the solicitor's careless advice (or failure properly to advise)[284] or careless performance (or failure properly to perform)[285] his duties to his client. This is however an exceptional case[286] and it must not be assumed that a solicitor will generally owe a duty of care to the

---

1728, [2003] All E.R. (D) 58 (Dec), where CA considered the scope of the solicitors' duty under the principle of *South Australia Asset Management Corp. v York Montague Ltd* [1997] A.C. 191, below, para.6–55).

[283] For the particular reluctance to hold a solicitor liable to his client's opposite party in a conveyancing transaction or his opponent in adversarial litigation, see above, para.6–32.

[284] *Ross v Caunters* [1980] Ch. 297 (failure to advise client that the spouse of a named beneficiary must not witness the will).

[285] *White v Jones* [1995] 2 A.C. 207, HL (failure to draw up new will before client died).

[286] The reasoning in *White v Jones*, above, n.285, is varied and appears to provide no *ratio decidendi* beyond the particular kind of situation covered in the case. In the judgments of the majority, Lord Goff (at 268), in order "to fashion a remedy to fill a lacuna in the law" held that the solicitor's assumption of responsibility to his client should be "held in law to extent to the intended beneficiary who (as the solicitor can reasonable foresee) may, as a result of the solicitor's negligence, be deprived of the legacy in circumstances in which neither the testator nor his estate will have a remedy against the solicitor"; Lord Browne-Wilkinson (at 275–276) extended *Hedley Byrne* to a new category, and held that the solicitor assumed a responsibility directly to the intended beneficiaries because (inter alia) their economic well-being was dependent on the solicitor's proper discharge of his duty to the client, but he also agreed with Lord Goff's reasons; Lord Nolan (at 295) thought that the duty arose on the facts because of the actual dealings directly between the solicitor (who was the family solicitor) and the intended beneficiaries; but he also agreed with the reasons given by Lord Goff and Lord Browne-Wilkinson. Lord Keith (at 251) and Lord Mustill (at 290) dissented, on the basis that to admit such a duty was not an extension of the existing case law but the introduction of an entirely new duty; and that such a duty should not be admitted. The only reasoning which attracted a majority view was therefore that of Lord Goff, which was restricted to the facts of the particular type of case: see *Carr-Glynn v Frearsons* [1999] Ch. 326, CA, at 335 (Chadwick L.J.). It has, however, been applied in the analogous case of an insurance broker's duty to his client's dependants who failed to receive an intended benefit under a pension and life insurance policy: *Gorham v British Telecommunications Plc* [2000] 1 W.L.R. 2129, CA.

person whose interests will be damaged by the careless performance of (or omission to perform) his duties to his client.[287]

A barrister may also owe a duty of care towards the person for whom he exercises his professional skill.[288] There is generally no direct contract between the lay client and the barrister,[289] so the duty is generally exclusively in tort, rather than concurrently with contract. It used to be thought that no duty was owed to the client in relation to the barrister's performance of his duties as advocate, although this has been rejected.[290]

---

[287] *Clarke v Bruce Lance & Co.* [1988] 1 W.L.R. 881, CA (solicitor advising client about proposed dealing with property in his lifetime owes no duty of care to prospective beneficiary under client's then-will who may be prejudicially affected), approved by Lord Goff in *White v Jones*, above, n.285 at 256. *White v Jones* was applied and extended (but still in the context of a solicitor's duty to an intended beneficiary to ensure that effect was given to the testator's testamentary intentions) in *Carr-Glynn v Frearsons*, above, n.286 and *Martin v Triggs Turner Bartons* [2009] EWHC 1920 (Ch), [2010] P.N.L.R. 3; but further extension was rejected in *Worby v Rosser* [1999] Lloyd's Rep. P.N. 972, CA (solicitor owes no duty to intended beneficiaries to ensure testator has testamentary capacity) and *Gibbons v Nelsons* [2000] Lloyd's Rep. P.N. 603 (solicitor owed no duty where he did not know the benefit the client-testator intended to confer and the person or class of persons on whom the benefit was to be conferred). The Court of Appeal in *Johnson v Gore Wood & Co.,* above, n.282, relied on *White v Jones* but this was not necessary since on the facts there were direct dealings with the claimant, to whom a duty could be established under *Caparo Industries Plc v Dickman* [1990] 2 A.C. 605. See also *Richards v Hughes* [2004] EWCA Civ 266, [2004] P.N.L.R. 35 (chartered accountant had strong arguable case that he owed duty only to client and not to intended third-party beneficiaries of trust on which he advised as investment scheme, but third-parties' claim not bound to fail. "The implications of *White v Jones* are being explored case by case": Peter Gibson L.J. at [25]); *Rind v Theodore Goddard* [2008] EWHC 459 (Ch), [2008] P.N.L.R. 24 (not unarguable that solicitors owed duty of care to claimant as residuary beneficiary of client's estate in relation to advice which triggered inheritance tax charge on client's death).

[288] *Saif Ali v Sydney Mitchell & Co.* [1980] A.C. 198, HL.

[289] The formal rule that a barrister could not enter into a contract for the provision of his services was abolished by the Courts and Legal Services Act 1990 s.61. By custom, however, the barrister still looks to the solicitor, rather than the lay client, for payment of his fees: see Bar Standards Board, Code of Conduct, Annexe G2 (March 24, 2001, amended November 17, 2001) for an authorised form of contractual terms on which barristers may offer their services to solicitors.

[290] *Arthur J.S. Hall & Co. v Simons* [2002] 1 A.C. 615, HL (the seven members of the House were unanimous in holding that advocates no longer enjoy immunity from suit in respect of their conduct of civil proceedings; the majority

6–42 **Surveyors and valuers.**[291] A surveyor or valuer of property will commonly be engaged by contract to carry out his survey or valuation. He will usually owe a duty of care in tort, concurrently with his contractual duties, to his client, and the scope of his duty in tort will be set by reference to the contract: it will depend on the task which he has undertaken to perform, and any other relevant terms of the contract (such as exclusion clauses).[292]

The surveyor or valuer may also owe a duty of care to a person, other than his client, who he knows will probably rely on his report in relation to a particular transaction.[293] For example, in *Smith v Eric S. Bush*[294] a surveyor, engaged by a mortgagee to report on the value of a house in order to enable the mortgagee to decide whether to grant a mortgage on it, was held to owe a duty of care also to the mortgagor who he knew would probably also rely on the report, without taking independent advice, in deciding whether to purchase the house. Such a case is, in reality, just an application of the normal principles for the establishment of a duty of care in relation to advice,[295] and a crucial factor will be whether the claimant, who

(Lords Steyn, Browne-Wilkinson, Hoffmann and Millett) held that there was also no immunity in respect of their conduct of criminal proceedings).

[291] Clerk & Lindsell, paras 10–154 to 10–181; Jackson & Powell, Ch.10; Dugdale & Stanton, paras 8.43 to 8.49; Hodgin, Ch.10 (J. Murdoch); Charlesworth & Percy, paras 9–304 to 9–335. For the personal liability of an employed surveyor, see *Merrett v Babb* [2001] EWCA Civ 214, [2001] Q.B. 1174; above, para.6–32.

[292] *Henderson v Merrett Syndicates Ltd* [1995] 2 A.C. 145; above, para.6–29. The surveyor owes duty of care (in contract, as well as in tort) in carrying out valuation, but the *contractual* retainer carries an inherent unqualified obligation to inspect and value the right property: *Platform Funding Ltd v Bank of Scotland Plc* [2008] EWCA Civ 930, [2009] Q.B. 426. For the impact of exclusion clauses see *Smith v Eric S. Bush*, below, n.294, and below, Ch.9. When the claimant uses a valuation for a purpose different from that for which the valuer prepared it, the question is whether the actual use was outside the purposes for which the valuer should have reasonably contemplated it would be used: *Western Trust & Savings Ltd v Strutt & Parker* [1998] 3 E.G.L.R. 89, CA.

[293] For the question whether a surveyor who prepares a valuation for one lender owes a duty to a different or substitute lender, see above, para.6–21.

[294] [1990] 1 A.C. 831, HL. For a case where an accountant, appointed by the directors of a company to value its shares for the purpose of setting the price at which a shareholder's shares were to be compulsorily acquired pursuant to the company's Articles, owed a duty to the shareholder in the conduct of the valuation, see *Killick v PricewaterhouseCoopers* [2001] 1 B.C.L.C. 65.

[295] *Caparo Industries Plc v Dickman* [1990] 2 A.C. 605; above, para.6–19.

was not the surveyor's client, was nonetheless entitled to rely on the surveyor's advice. In *Smith v Eric S. Bush* the case was strengthened by the fact that the mortgagor paid for the valuation; and that it was a "dwelling house of modest value in which it is widely recognised by surveyors that purchasers are in fact relying on their care and skill". But in a case where larger sums are at stake, such as in the financing of industrial property, large blocks of flats or very expensive houses, or even residential houses or flats of modest value where the purpose of the purchase is for commercial letting rather than owner-occupation,[296] it might not be reasonable for a purchaser to rely on his financier's valuer, and he might be expected to obtain his own survey.[297]

If the surveyor or valuer undertakes only to provide information on the property, or its value, in order to assist the claimant to decide whether to enter into a transaction relating to the property, his duty will extend only to the consequences of the information being inaccurate.[298] So if the claimant is a mortgagee, it will be the financial consequence to the claimant of the fact that his security is of less value than he believed—that is, typically, when he enforces his security the loss he suffers by reason of the lower value of the security; and so this loss cannot exceed the difference between the inaccurate valuation and the correct value.[299] Or if the claimant is the purchaser, it will normally be the difference between the price paid on the basis of the inaccurate valuation and the actual (accurate) value of the property received.[300] If, however, the

[296] *Scullion v Bank of Scotland (trading as Colleys)* [2011] EWCA Civ 693, [2011] All E.R. (D) 126 (Jun) at [47]–[54], above, para.6–22, n.103 (buy-to-let purchase of small residential property different from the ordinary residential house purchase of *Smith v Bush*); see also *Wilson v D.M. Hall & Sons* [2005] P.N.L.R. 22, OH (bank's valuer did not owe duty to experienced businessman undertaking commercial property development.

[297] [1990] 1 A.C. 831 at 859–860 (Lord Griffiths); see also Lord Templeman at 854 and Lord Jauncey at 872. Correspondingly, it might also be reasonable in such cases for surveyors to exclude or limit their duty to the purchasers; for the question of limitation of surveyors' duties of care, see below, Ch.9.

[298] *South Australia Asset Management Corp. v York Montague Ltd* [1997] A.C. 191, HL, at 214.

[299] *ibid.*; *Nykredit Mortgage Bank Plc v Edward Erdman Group Ltd (No.2)* [1997] 1 W.L.R. 1627, HL.

[300] *ibid.*, at 216; *Nykredit Mortgage Bank Plc v Edward Erdman Group Ltd (No.2)*, above, n.299 at 1630. Even though the loss may only be realised at a later stage, it is in law sustained when the purchaser parts with his money and receives

surveyor or valuer undertakes in addition to provide advice on the property market more generally with a view to assisting the claimant to decide whether and which property to buy, his duty may extend to the consequences of the claimant's entering into the transaction, which might be significantly higher, such as where the claimant's losses are increased by fluctuations in the property market.[301]

(2) Breach of Duty

6–43 **Standard of care.** Once the claimant has established that the defendant owed him a duty to take care in making his statement, he must show that the defendant broke that duty: that is, that in making the statement he fell below the standard of care imposed on him by the duty. The duty is only one of reasonable care: a duty to take such care as a reasonable person would take in the defendant's position. It is not a duty to be accurate.[302] So a defendant who owes a duty may make a false statement and yet still not be liable in

in exchange property worth less than the price he paid: *ibid*; or, more particularly, when he irrevocably enters into the transaction which embodies that loss for him—typically, the contract to purchase: *Byrne v Hall Pain & Foster* [1999] 1 W.L.R. 1849, CA. The limitation period therefore runs from that time. Where the purchase is in order to let the property ("buy-to-let"), and the surveyor has given advice on both the purchase price and the rent that could be achieved, the duty extends to the consequences of the overstatement of the rental value of the property, as well as of the overstatement of the market (capital) value, but this does not cover all revenue losses suffered by purchaser in buying the flat: *Scullion v Bank of Scotland (trading as Colleys)* above, n.296 at [62]–[68] (obiter, because there was no duty of care). In the case of a lender whose security is less valuable than he believed, the position is more difficult because he suffers a loss only from the first moment (which may be the moment the mortgage is executed, or it may be later, or it may be never) that the value of rights acquired under the mortgage—the borrower's covenant and the true value of the overvalued property—is less than the amount of money he lent plus interest at a proper rate: *Nykredit Mortgage Bank Plc v Edward Erdman Group Ltd (No.2)*, above, at 1631. For the quantification of recoverable loss in negligence, see further below, paras 6–52 *et seq.*; and for limitation of actions, below, para.6–50.

[301] *ibid.*, at 214.

[302] The basic obligation of a professional in contract, as well as in tort, is an obligation of reasonable care and skill, and special facts or clear language are required to impose a stricter obligation in the contract: *Platform Funding Ltd v Bank of Scotland Plc*, above, n.292 at [48].

negligence if the claimant cannot show that in failing to give correct advice or accurate information he fell below the standard of reasonable care.

Setting the standard of care. The standard of care will depend upon the nature and scope of the task which the defendant undertook, and which therefore gave rise to the duty. The general test is the standard of care which would have been expected of an ordinary skilled person performing that task and exercising the skill which the defendant held himself out as exercising. Where the task falls within the normal tasks of a particular profession, this will generally mean the standard of care expected within that profession for the performance of that task. So an accountant, an architect, a solicitor or a surveyor will be tested by the standards generally expected within their respective professions.[303] But it is not a question of whether every member of the profession would have thought that the defendant's conduct was acceptable. Often there are differing views within a profession as to how a task should properly be performed. The defendant is not negligent as long as his performance of the task met standards regarded as acceptable by a responsible body of the relevant professional opinion.[304] In some **6–44**

---

303 *Greaves & Co. (Contractors) Ltd v Baynham Meikle & Partners* [1975] 1 W.L.R. 1095 at 1101 (Lord Denning M.R.); *Lloyd Cheyham & Co. Ltd v Littlejohn & Co.* [1987] B.C.L.C. 303 at 313 (Statements of Standard Accounting Practice ("SSAPs") are strong evidence of proper standards for accountants. Since 1990 the Accounting Standards Board has issued Financial Reporting Standards, which have replaced many SSAPs; Statements of Recommended Practice ("SORPs") are also issued as specialist standards for particular industries or sectors. See generally the Accounting Standards Board website: *http://frc.org.uk/asb*). Where, however, there is no recognisable profession, the nature of the expert evidence which will be acceptable depends on what tasks the defendant had undertaken to perform: *Pride Valley Foods Ltd v Hall & Partners (Contract Management) Ltd* (2000) 16 Const. L.J. 424 at [140] (no recognisable profession of project managers).

304 *Bolam v Friern Hospital Management Committee* [1957] 1 W.L.R. 582 at 586 (medical negligence). McNair J.'s direction to the jury in this case has been adopted as the test in other professional contexts, as the standard applicable both in the tort of negligence and (in the absence of a term imposing a higher standard) in contract: *Greaves & Co. (Contractors) Ltd v Baynham Meikle & Partners*, above, n.303 (structural engineers: implied contractual term); *G + K Ladenbau (UK) Ltd v Crawley & de Reya* [1978] 1 W.L.R. 266 at 282 (solicitor). It is not, strictly, conclusive for a defendant to show that his conduct was acceptable within the profession, since a court can hold that the profession's opinion was not

cases, particularly in cases of statements of opinion, there is inevitably no single correct statement, but a range of acceptable statements, such as where a surveyor advises on the value of property. In such cases, the defendant is not negligent as long as his valuation fell within the acceptable margins of differing opinion.[305]

6–45 **Evidence of breach of duty.** Once the standard of care required of the defendant has been established, a question of law, the question of whether the defendant was in breach of his duty when he made his statement is one of fact. The court must measure the defendant's conduct against the standard. The burden of establishing the breach lies on the claimant.[306] Where the question is whether a defendant has fallen below the standard required of a particular profession, evidence will generally[307] be required from an expert witness qualified to attest to the relevant professional standards. It will therefore not be appropriate to rely on expert

supportable at all; but this will be very rare: *Bolitho v City and Hackney H.A.* [1998] A.C. 232 at 243, HL; *Edward Wong Finance Co. Ltd v Johnson Stokes & Master* [1984] A.C. 296, PC (Hong Kong solicitors negligent in following conveyancing procedures commonly practised by the profession locally).

305 *South Australia Asset Management Corp. v York Montague Ltd*, above, n.298 at 221; *Platform Home Loans Ltd v Oyston Shipways Ltd* [1996] 2 E.G.L.R. 110 at 112–113 (Jacob J.: "valuation is an art and not a science, but it is not astrology"). But for the purpose of assessing damages once the defendant has been found to be negligent, the court must still decide what the "correct" valuation would have been—the figure most likely to have been put forward by a reasonable valuer, which will generally be the mean figure of the acceptable range: *South Australia Asset Management Corp. v York Montague Ltd*, above, at 221.

306 There is an exception where the claimant can show that the defendant has been convicted of a criminal offence the elements of which establish that the defendant was negligent in making the statement which is now the subject of the civil claim: Civil Evidence Act 1968, s.11.

307 *Worboys v Acme Investments Ltd* (1969) 4 B.L.R. 133 at 139, CA (architects); *Investors in Industry Commercial Properties Ltd v South Bedfordshire DC* [1986] 1 All E.R. 787 at 808–809, CA (architects: this point does not appear in the extract of the judgment reported at [1986] Q.B. 1034)).

evidence of an architect or a civil engineer to establish the standards expected of a surveyor[308] or an engineer to establish the standards expected of an architect.[309]

(3) Damage

The claimant must prove damage. The claimant must establish, as an element of his claim, that he has suffered loss or damage which was within the scope[310] of the defendant's duty and which was caused by the defendant's breach of that duty. The tort of negligence is not complete until the claimant has suffered damage; the cause of action therefore accrues, and the limitation period begins to run,[311] at the first moment at which such recoverable damage is suffered. The rules which govern the range of recoverable losses and the quantification of damages for negligent misrepresentation are discussed in Section IV of this chapter.[312] 6–46

III. DEFENCES

Defences generally available in the tort of negligence. A number of defences are available in the tort of negligence.[313] Those most commonly raised in claims based on careless statements are the claimant's contributory negligence; expiry of the limitation period barring the claimant's action; and the exclusion or limitation of the defendant's liability by a contractual term or a non-contractual notice. 6–47

---

[308] *Whalley v Roberts & Roberts* [1990] 1 E.G.L.R. 164; *Sansom v Metcalfe Hambleton & Co.* [1998] 2 E.G.L.R. 103, CA.

[309] *Investors in Industry Commercial Properties Ltd v South Bedfordshire DC*, above, n.307.

[310] Above, para.6–14.

[311] Below, para.6–50.

[312] Below, paras 6–52 to 6–62.

[313] For general treatment of all the defences, including *volenti non fit injuria*, as well as those discussed in this section, see Clerk & Lindsell, Ch.3; Winfield & Jolowicz, paras 6–42 to 6–55, Ch.25, paras 26–7 to 26–26; Charlesworth & Percy, Ch.4.

6–48 **Contributory negligence.**[314] The defence of contributory negligence is available in the tort of negligence[315] where the claimant suffers damage as a result partly of his own fault and partly of the fault of the defendant. In such a case the court reduces the damage to such extent as it thinks just and equitable having regard to the claimant's share in the responsibility for the damage.[316] This defence is therefore open to a defendant in a claim based on negligent misrepresentation. A claimant may be held to be contributorily negligent in relation to his own acts or omissions which, together with his reliance on the defendant's statement, caused his overall loss.[317] But it will generally not be possible to hold the claimant contributorily negligent simply by reason of his reliance on the defendant's statement. The duty of care will normally arise only where the defendant contemplates that the claimant will rely on his statement without taking independent advice, and it must be reasonable for the claimant so to rely.[318] It will therefore be relatively rare to find that, as a matter of fact, the duty was owed and broken and caused the claimant's loss, and yet the claimant was negligent in relying on the statement without taking further steps to verify it.[319] But it is possible for contributory negligence to be found on such a basis.[320]

---

[314] Clerk & Lindsell, paras 3–44 to 3–83; Winfield & Jolowicz, paras 6–42 to 6–55; Charlesworth & Percy, paras 4–03 to 4–72.

[315] And in other torts: Law Reform (Contributory Negligence) Act 1945 s.4 (definition of "fault"); Clerk & Lindsell, paras 3–51 to 3–64; Winfield & Jolowicz, para.6–44; but not in the tort of deceit: above, para.5–31; nor other intentional torts such as assault and battery: *Co-Operative Group (C.W.S.) Ltd v Pritchard* [2011] EWCA Civ 329, [2011] All E.R. (D) 312 (Mar). For contributory negligence as a defence to a claim for breach of contract, see below, para.8–20.

[316] Law Reform (Contributory Negligence) Act 1945 s.1(1).

[317] *Platform Home Loans Ltd v Oyston Shipways Ltd* [2000] 2 A.C. 190, HL (property overvalued by defendant; but Jacob J. held contributory negligence (at 20% in total) because claimant mortgagee (a) pursued imprudent lending policy in advancing as much as 70% of value of security in non-status loan in excess of £1 million, and (b) failed to follow their own usual procedures for insisting on details from borrower re-mortgaging property of when and for what price he purchased the property).

[318] Above, para.6–22.

[319] *JEB Fasteners Ltd v Marks Bloom & Co.* [1981] 3 All E.R. 289 at 297 (reliance on auditor's certificate of accounts. This point is unaffected by the appeal in the case [1983] 1 All E.R. 583, or later developments in auditors' liability, above, para.6–33); *Gran Gelato Ltd v Richcliff (Group) Ltd* [1992] Ch.

A particular problem can arise where the claimant in reliance on the defendant's careless statement suffers a loss only part of which falls within the scope of the defendant's duty of care, but there is also a finding of contributory negligence against the claimant.[321] The context in which this has arisen[322] is where a mortgagee lends on the basis of a security which has been negligently overvalued by the defendant; but in due course the loss suffered by the mortgagee is increased by other factors, typically the fall in the property market, beyond that attributable to the difference between the correct and the inaccurate valuation. The loss for which the defendant is liable is only that attributable to the incorrect valuation, and not the market fall; but it has been held by the House of Lords[323] that in such a case, where there is also a successful plea

---

560 at 574 (claim in negligence and under the Misrepresentation Act 1967 s.2(1), below, para.7–27. The juxtaposition of these two claims appears to have led Nicholls V.C. to speak in terms of the defendant having *intended* the claimant to rely on the statement, but this places the test too high in the tort of negligence).

[320] *Cavendish Funding Ltd v Henry Spencer & Sons Ltd* [1998] 1 E.G.L.R. 104 (claimants at fault by relying on property valuation to advance funds on mortgage without checking its accuracy where they also had a significantly lower valuation from another valuer); *Platform Home Loans Ltd v Oyston Shipways Ltd*, above, n.317 (reliance by mortgagee on valuation without making its own usual checks on original purchase date and price of the property which would have cast doubt on the valuation); *Barings Plc (In Liquidation) v Coopers & Lybrand (Issues Re Liability)* [2003] EWHC 1319, [2003] P.N.L.R. 34 (auditors liable for failure to detect management failures; damages reduced significantly to reflect management failures); *Speshal Investments Ltd v Corby Kane Partnership Ltd* [2003] EWHC 390 (Ch), [2003] All E.R. (D) 31 (Mar) (prudent lender would have realised that the valuer may be unreliable: 20% contributory negligence).

[321] *South Australia Asset Management Corp. v York Montague Ltd* [1997] A.C. 191, HL.

[322] *ibid*; *Nykredit Mortage Bank Plc v Edward Erdman Group Ltd (No.2)* [1997] 1 W.L.R. 1627, HL; *Platform Home Loans Ltd v Oyston Shipways Ltd*, above, n.317.

[323] *Platform Home Loans Ltd v Oyston Shipways Ltd*, above, n.317. In a powerful dissent, Lord Cooke of Thorndon took the view that the language of the Law Reform (Contributory Negligence) Act 1945 (and in particular s.1(2) read with s.1(1)) clearly contemplated that the reduction was to be applied to the sum which would have been recoverable if the claimant had not been contributory negligent: that is, only that loss which falls within the scope of the defendant's breach of duty. The objection of the majority to this approach was that it would involve the claimant's fault being discounted twice, since part of the claimant's own fault as held by the trial judge (above, n.317) was directed to its imprudence in over-lending; but this was already taken into account in the limitation of

of contributory negligence, the reduction of damages for contributory negligence should be applied to the total loss, and only then should it be asked whether the resulting quantum of damages falls within the scope of the defendant's duty.

6–49 **Illegality.**[324] The basis of the defence of illegality in tort has been subject to some debate in recent years, and the Law Commission has identified a range of policy rationales for the defence.[325]

---

recoverable loss to that attributable to the defendant's over-valuation (see Lord Hobhouse of Woodborough at 211–212 and Lord Millett at 213). The difficulties here might better be addressed by asking in every case the question: *in what respect* was the claimant at fault? If the claimant can recover only for such loss as flows from the defendant's negligent valuation, then his contributory negligence should be relevant only in cases where it impacts on that loss. If his own fault—over-lending beyond what the market can bear—relates to another aspect of his loss which is already dealt with in the basic test for recovery of damage (*South Australia Asset Management Corp. v York Montague Ltd*, below, para.6–55) then that should be excluded altogether from the assessment of the claimant's contributory negligence. This, in substance, appears to be the view of Lord Millett in *Platform Home Loans Ltd v Oyston Shipways Ltd*, above, n.317 at 213–214. For discussion of this case, see (1999) 115 L.Q.R. 527 (J. Stapleton); (1999) 62 M.L.R. 281 (T. Dugdale); [1999] L.M.C.L.Q. 355 (D. McLauchlan); (2000) 8 Tort L.Rev. 85 (D. Howarth).

324 Clerk & Lindsell, paras 3–02 to 3–43; Winfield & Jolowicz, paras 25–18 to 25–25; Charlesworth & Percy, paras 4–248 to 4–253. The Law Commission has undertaken a lengthy review of the illegality defence in contract, tort, unjust enrichment and trusts, but concluded that, in the areas of contract, unjust enrichment and tort, no legislative reform is appropriate because it would be difficult to devise and draft a broad statutory scheme that would be an improvement on the current law, and in relation to most types of claim it is open to the courts to develop the law in ways that would render it considerably clearer, more certain and less arbitrary; the judiciary should base their decisions directly on the policies that underlie the illegality defence and explain their reasoning accordingly: Consultation Paper No.189, *The Illegality Defence: a Consultative Report* (2009), paras 1.13–1.14; confirmed in Law Com No.320, *The Illegality Defence* (2010), Pt.3, in which the Law Commission noted that, since the Consultative Report, the House of Lords had already begin to move in this direction in its decisions in *Gray v Thames Trains Ltd* [2009] UKHL 33, [2009] 1 A.C. 1339 and *Stone & Rolls Ltd v Moore Stephens* [2009] UKHL 39, [2009] 1 A.C. 1391, below.

325 The "six main ones" are "(1) furthering the purpose of the rule which the claimant's illegal behaviour has infringed; (2) consistency; (3) the need to prevent the claimant profiting from his or her own wrong; (4) deterrence; (5) maintaining the integrity of the legal system; and (6) punishment": Consultation Paper No.189, above, n.324, para.2.5.

However, in *Stone & Rolls Ltd v Moore Stephens*[326] the House of Lords held by a majority that the defence was available to the auditors of a company against whom the company brought an action for the auditors' negligent failure to discover fraud which was perpetrated on the company by the person who was its sole directing mind and will and the beneficial owner, and for whose fraud the company was primarily (and not only vicariously) liable. This decision will not apply where the persons for whose benefit the duty exists—in the case of a statutory company audit, the shareholders collectively[327]—are not all responsible for the illegality,[328] and so where innocent shareholders are involved the company's claim against the auditors will normally not be met by the illegality defence.[329]

Limitation of actions.[330] The basic rule is that an action founded on tort—including, therefore, an action in negligence—cannot be 6–50

[326] [2009] UKHL 39, [2009] 1 A.C. 1391.
[327] *Caparo Industries Plc v Dickman* [1990] 2 A.C. 605; above, para.6–33.
[328] The members of the majority differed in their reasoning: Lord Phillips took the view that the sole person for whose benefit the duty was owed was the fraudster as beneficial owner of the company ([2009] UKHL 39, [2009] 1 A.C. 1391 at [86]); Lords Walker and Brown based their decision on the fact that the company was a "one man company" which was jointly (and primarily, not secondarily) liable for the fraud and so could not itself bring a claim for its loss without being met by the illegality defence (at [174], [201]). Lord Scott and Lord Mance dissented.
[329] *Stone & Rolls Ltd v Moore Stephens*, above, n.324 at [203] (Lord Brown). For a recent plea of illegality in a different context, see *Scullion v Bank of Scotland Plc* [2010] EWHC 572 (Ch), [2010] All E.R. (D) 181 (Mar) at [111]—[112] (claim by purchaser of property against valuer where value of property was overstated in mortgage application: if purchaser had been fraudulent in misleading mortgagee, his fraudulent conduct would be so intimately connected to his claim against valuer that the Court should refuse to permit him to make the claim; but fraud was not, on the facts, established; but CA later held that there was no claim because no duty of care: [2011] EWCA Civ 693, [2011] All E.R. (D) 126 (Jun), above, para.6–22, n.103).
[330] Clerk & Lindsell, Ch.32; Winfield & Jolowicz, paras 26–7 to 26–26; Charlesworth & Percy, paras 4–137 to 4–237; D.W. Oughton, J.P. Lowry and R.M. Merkin, *Limitation of Actions* (1998), Ch.18. In 2001 the Law Commission recommended reform of the law of limitation of actions: Law Com. No.270 (2001), to introduce a single, core limitation regime which would apply to most claims for a remedy for a wrong, claims for the enforcement of a right and claims for restitution: a primary limitation period of three years starting from the date on which the claimant knows, or ought reasonably to know (a) the facts which give

brought (that is, a claim form cannot be issued[331]) after the expiration of six years from the date on which the cause of action accrued.[332] In a claim for negligence, other than a claim for

rise to the cause of action; (b) the identity of the defendant; and (c) if the claimant has suffered injury, loss or damage or the defendant has received a benefit, that the injury, loss, damage or benefit was significant; and a long-stop limitation period of 10 years, starting from the date of the accrual of the cause of action or (for those claims in tort where loss is an essential element of the cause of action, such as negligence) from the date of the act or omission which gives rise to the cause of action. This proposed regime would apply to claims in negligence, except claims for personal injury where the court would have a discretion to disapply the primary limitation period, and no long-stop limitation period would apply. The long-stop limitation period would not run where the defendant has concealed relevant facts, but only if the concealment was dishonest. The Government accepted the Report in principle in July 2002, and in 2008 it was announced that provisions on the subject would be included within a proposed Civil Law Reform Bill. However, in 2009 the Government announced that the limitation reforms would not, after all, be taken forward: Law Com. No.323, *Annual Report 2009–10*, paras 3.12 to 3.15.

[331] Below, para.11–05.

[332] Limitation Act 1980, s.2. For the special time-limit in actions (including actions in negligence) for damages for personal injuries, see s.11. Most actions for negligent misrepresentation, being generally actions for damages to compensate economic loss, will fall under s.2. For a claim to contribution under the Civil Liability (Contribution) Act 1978, s.1, below, para.6–63, there is a special time-limit of two years from the accrual of the right to recover contribution: see s.10. For extension of limitation periods in cases of the claimant's disability, see s.28. The limitation period will also be delayed where any fact relevant to the claimant's right of action has been deliberately concealed from him by the defendant, until the claimant has discovered the concealment or could with reasonable diligence have discovered it: *ibid.*, s.32(1)(b). For the purposes of s.32(1)(b) the deliberate commission of a breach of duty in circumstances in which it is unlikely to be discovered for some time amounts to deliberate concealment of the facts involved in that breach of duty: s.32(2). S.32 deprives the defendant of a limitation defence (i) when he takes active steps to conceal his own breach of duty after he has become aware of it; and (ii) where he is guilty of deliberate wrongdoing and conceals or fails to disclose it in circumstances where it is unlikely to be discovered for some time. But it does not deprive a defendant of a limitation defence where he is charged with negligence if, being unaware of his error or that he has failed to take proper care, there has been nothing for him to disclose: *Cave v Robinson Jarvis & Rolf* [2002] UKHL 18, [2003] 1 A.C. 384 at [25]. See also *Williams v Fanshaw Porter & Hazelhurst* [2004] EWCA Civ 157, [2005] 1 W.L.R. 3185 at [14] (Park J.: s.32(1)(b) does not require that the defendant must have known that the concealed fact was relevant to the right of action, but for the concealment to be deliberate the fact must either be a fact which it was the defendant's duty to disclose to the claimant or one

damages for personal injuries, this period will if necessary be extended to the period of three years from the date when the claimant first had sufficient knowledge of the possibility of bringing his claim: broadly, this means the date when he had knowledge of the material facts about the damage in respect of which he claims; the identity of the defendant or any other person for whom the defendant is to be held responsible; and that the damage was attributable in whole or in part to the act or omission which is alleged to constitute negligence.[333] But in no case may an action for damages for negligence (other than an action for damages for personal injuries) be brought after the expiration of 15 years from the date on which the defendant last committed an act or omission alleged to form the basis of the claim.[334]

It is therefore crucial to identify the "accrual of the cause of action", which first sets the limitation period running. Since the cause of action in negligence is complete only when the claimant suffers recoverable damage,[335] the running of the limitation period hinges on the proper identification of actionable damage; and this in

which the defendant would ordinarily have disclosed in the normal course of his relationship with the claimant, but which he consciously decided not to disclose. Mance L.J. at [37]–[39] left open the question whether the defendant must realise that the fact has some relevance to an actual or potential claim against him). Where the defendant's concealment of facts is subsequent to the accrual of the cause of action, the full limitation period begins to run only after the claimant has discovered, or should have discovered, the concealment: *Sheldon v R.H.M. Outhwaite (Underwriting Agencies) Ltd* [1996] A.C. 102, HL. Under the new limitation regime proposed by the Law Commission, above, n.330, only dishonest concealment would prevent the long-stop limitation period from running, and concealment would only suspend the long-stop and would not start time running again.

333 s.14A, explained in *Haward v Fawcetts* [2006] UKHL 9, [2006] 1 W.L.R. 682. There is a special period of limitation under s.11 for claims for damages for personal injuries. In effect, the limitation period will be extended under s.14A only where the claimant acquires the relevant knowledge of the facts to bring his claim after the third anniversary of the damage first being suffered (that is, more than three years from the start of the regular limitation period of six years from accrual of the cause of action). S.14A does not apply to an action to which s.32(1)(b), above, n.332, applies: s.32(5).

334 s.14B. This applies even if the cause of action has not yet then accrued or if, although the cause of action has accrued, the claimant still does not have sufficient knowledge of the facts to start the extended limitation period of s.14A running: see s.14B(2). S.14B does not apply to an action to which s.32(1)(b), above, n.332, applies: s.32(5).

335 Above, para.6–42.

turn is linked back to the duty of care itself, since the scope of recoverable damage is defined by the duty.[336] In most cases with which we are concerned in this book—duties of care in respect of economic loss[337] caused by reliance on negligent statements—it is therefore necessary to identify the first moment at which the claimant suffered economic loss which falls within the scope of the breach of duty on which the claimant rests his claim.[338] In many cases this will not be contentious; but sometimes care is required to identify the damage.[339] For example, where the claimant relies on a negligent statement by purchasing an asset or entering into a disadvantageous contract, the loss will often be suffered at the moment of the purchase or the contract even if the valuation of the loss may be contingent on future events.[340] But where a lender

---

336 Above, para.6–14.

337 For negligent statements giving rise to physical harm, either to the person or to property, see above, para.6–18. Where the claim is for damages for personal injuries, the limitation period is governed by separate rules: above, n.332.

338 In the case of successive breaches of duty, or a continuing breach of duty, a fresh cause of action will accrue on each occasion that the claimant first suffers damage from each successive breach or each act or omission which constitutes a continuing breach of the duty: *Darley Main Colliery Co. v Mitchell* (1886) 11 App. Cas. 127, HL (cause of action in respect of land subsidence accrued only on damage, so limitation ran from each event of damage). In such a case, where there is a delay in issuing the claim form the claimant may seek to rely on damage flowing from one of the later acts or omissions constituting a breach in order to show that his claim is brought within the limitation period.

339 *Havenledge Ltd v Graeme John & Partners* [2001] Lloyd's Rep. P.N. 223, CA (solicitors negligent in failing to advise claimant to obtain mining engineer's report on property before purchasing it: significant differences between all three members of CA as to when cause of action arose: on purchase (Buxton L.J.), when significant sums spent on developing the property (Pill L.J.), or on actual disruption to claimant's business (Sir Anthony Evans)).

340 *McCarroll v Statham Gill Davis* [2003] EWCA Civ 425, [2003] P.N.L.R. 25 (singer entering into disadvantageous recording contract under which he might be (and later was) summarily expelled from rock group: there was an actual loss when the agreement was made); *Watkins v Jones Maidment Wilson* [2008] EWCA Civ 134, [2008] P.N.L.R. 23 (entry into contract, even if initially beneficial, involved losing chance of negotiating a better agreement); *Shore v Sedgwick Financial Services Ltd* [2008] EWCA Civ 863, [2008] P.N.L.R. 37 (investment in pension scheme); *Axa Insurance Ltd v Akther & Darby* [2009] EWCA Civ 1166, [2010] 1 W.L.R. 1662 (entry into insurance policies); *Williams v Lishman, Sidwell, Campbell & Price Ltd* [2010] EWCA Civ 418, [2010] P.N.L.R. 25 (investment in pension scheme: but no decision on effect of Limitation Act 1980 s.32(1) where losses both concealed and unconcealed if

advances funds on security which, as a result of the defendant's careless valuation, is inadequate, the lender's loss is not necessarily suffered at the moment the funds are advanced to the borrower. The valuer's duty extends to the economic losses suffered by the lender as a result of the valuation being inaccurate[341]; but as long as the actual value of the property (that is, the property with the *correct* valuation), together with the value of the borrower's covenant,[342] are at least equal to the amount of the loan plus interest for the time being owing on the loan, the lender has no loss. But as soon as the value of the security (including the value of the borrower's personal covenant) falls below that amount, the loss is suffered and the cause of action in negligence accrues, even though it might not yet be known to the lender.[343]

The defendant must include in his defence details of the expiry of any relevant limitation period on which he relies.[344] Once the issue is raised, the burden on a claimant is to show that, on the balance of probabilities, his cause of action accrued on a day within the period of limitation.[345] However, once the claimant has shown that relevant damage was suffered within the requisite period of

concealed loss suffered first); *Pegasus Management Holdings S.C.A. v Ernst & Young* [2010] EWCA Civ 181, [2010] P.N.L.R. 23 at [81]–[82] (claimant entering into wrong transaction suffers damage by not receiving what he ought to have received). By contrast, a contingent liability is not as such damage until the contingency occurs: *Law Society v Sephton & Co.* [2006] UKHL 22, [2006] 2 A.C. 543, distinguishing *Nykredit Mortage Bank Plc v Edward Erdman Group Ltd (No.2)*, below, n.343.

341 *South Australia Asset Management Corp. v York Montague Ltd* [1997] A.C. 191, HL; above, para.6–42.

342 For the difficulties involved in valuing the borrower's covenant, see *DnB Mortgages v Bullock & Lees* [2000] 1 E.G.L.R. 92, CA; *Eagle Star Insurance Co. Ltd v Gale & Power* (1955) 166 E.G. 37; *London & South of England Building Society v Stone* [1983] 1 W.L.R. 1242, CA.

343 *Nykredit Mortage Bank Plc v Edward Erdman Group Ltd (No.2)* [1997] 1 W.L.R. 1627, HL. But in a case where the lender does not have sufficient knowledge of the material facts in order to initiate his action, he may be able to rely on s.14A of the Limitation Act 1980, above, n.333, to extend the limitation period to the period of three years from the time when he does have such knowledge: *Mortgage Corp. v Lambert & Co.* [1999] 3 E.G.L.R. 59; *Hamlin v Edwin Evans* [1996] 2 E.G.L.R 106, CA; *Lloyds Bank Plc v Crosse & Crosse* [2001] EWCA Civ 366, [2001] P.N.L.R. 34.

344 CPR, Pt 16, PD 16, para.13.1.

345 *London Congregational Union Inc v Harriss & Harriss* [1988] 1 All E.R. 15 at 30, CA; *Lloyds Bank Plc v Crosse & Crosse*, above, n.343 at [41].

limitation, the burden may shift to the defendant to adduce evidence to show that the apparent accrual within the limitation period was misleading.[346]

6–51 **Exclusion and limitation clauses.** A defendant may seek to exclude or limit his liability in negligence by a contractual exclusion clause or a non-contractual notice; and the clause or notice may seek to achieve this in various ways—such as by negativing the defendant's assumption of responsibility to the claimant, and so preventing the duty arising[347]; or by excluding or limiting the remedy which would otherwise be available. The effect of such clauses and notices, and the limits on their effectiveness through such controls as the Unfair Contract Terms Act 1977, are discussed in Chapter 9.

IV. THE DAMAGES RECOVERABLE

6–52 **Principles of award of damages within the tort of negligence.** Damages are awarded in the tort of negligence to compensate the claimant for the loss he suffered in consequence of the defendant's negligence. The tort is not complete without proof of actionable damage and in order to recover substantial damages the claimant must prove his loss. The claimant will however recover only such loss as he can show falls within the scope of the defendant's duty on which he relies to found his claim; and which was caused by breach of that duty, and was not too remote. These principles, together with other aspects of the award of damages in the tort of negligence, will be discussed in the following paragraphs.[348]

---

346 *ibid.*, at 30, 34, CA; *DnB Mortgages v Bullock & Lees*, above, n.342; *Cartlege v E. Jopling & Sons Ltd* [1963] A.C. 758 at 784. Under the new limitation regime proposed by the Law Commission, above, n.330, the burden of proof of the primary limitation period would be on the claimant, but the defendant would have the burden of proving other defences, including the long-stop limitation period.

347 *Hedley Byrne & Co. Ltd v Heller & Partners Ltd* [1964] A.C. 465, HL; above, para.6–10 (non-contractual notice); *I.F.E. Fund SA v Goldman Sachs International* [2007] EWCA Civ 811, [2007] 2 Lloyd's Rep. 449 at [28]; *Titan Steel Wheels Ltd v Royal Bank of Scotland Plc* [2010] EWHC 211 (Comm), [2010] 2 Lloyd's Rep. 92 at [89]–[91].

348 For a detailed treatment, see McGregor.

Causation; reliance. The defendant is liable only for the loss he caused. In most claims in negligence for misrepresentation the claimant asserts that he relied on the statement, in the sense that he received and acted upon the defendant's statement in such a way that he then suffered the loss claimed.[349] Proof of such reliance is therefore an element in the proof of causation of damage: if it cannot be shown that the claimant relied on the statement in taking the action consequent upon which he claims to have suffered loss, he will not have established a causal link between the statement and the loss.[350] In applying this test, the courts have asked whether the statement influenced the claimant's conduct to a material degree, and whether it played a real and substantial (though not necessarily decisive) part in inducing the claimant to act.[351] The burden of proof of reliance is on the claimant.[352] **6–53**

[349] For cases where a statement might be actionable in negligence where the claimant suffers loss other than by his own reliance on it, see above, para.6–24.
[350] *Rushmer v Mervyn Smith (t/a Mervyn E. Smith & Co.)* [2009] EWHC 94 (QB), [2009] Lloyd's Rep. P.N. 41 (guarantor of loans to bank did not believe the profit figure stated in accounts, so did not rely; but no duty owed in any event).
[351] *JEB Fasteners Ltd v Marks Bloom & Co.* [1983] 1 All E.R. 583, CA; *Mann v Coutts & Co.* [2003] EWHC 2138 (Comm), [2004] 1 All E.R. (Comm) 1 at [199]–[201], applying also *Avon Insurance Plc v Swire Fraser Ltd* [2000] 1 All E.R. (Comm) 573 (a decision on the Misrepresentation Act 1967 s.2(1)), and *Assicurazioni Generali SpA v Arab Insurance Group* [2002] EWCA Civ 1642, [2003] 1 All E.R. (Comm) 140, where Clarke L.J. said at [59] that it must be "an effective cause" but not the sole cause; and at [218] Ward L.J., doubting this language: "We must be careful not to be led back into the error that the cause has to be a decisive cause". For a detailed discussion of reliance, see also *Hagen v ICI Chemicals & Polymers Ltd* [2002] I.R.L.R. 31 at [105]–[132] (Elias J.).
[352] The approach taken in other remedies, such as rescission, where the court may infer the claimant's reliance once it is shown that the statement is objectively material in the sense that a reasonable representee would have relied on it in the circumstances (above, para.3–53), has not been adopted in the tort of negligence: *Bristol and West Building Society v Mothew* [1998] Ch. 1, CA, at 11. In other contexts the House of Lords has recently created exceptions to the normal rules of causation: *Fairchild v Glenhaven Funeral Services Ltd* [2002] UKHL 22, [2003] 1 A.C. 32; *Barker v Corus UK Ltd* [2006] UKHL 20, [2006] 2 A.C. 572; *Sienkiewicz v Greif (UK) Ltd* [2011] UKSC 10, [2011] 2 W.L.R. 523 (employer's liability for personal injury caused by one of two or more separate exposures to the same agent (in these cases, asbestos dust) or agents acting in substantially the same way, each of which materially increases risk of injury, including the case where the only occupational exposure was small, and alternative exposure was environmental); *Chester v Afshar* [2004] UKHL 41, [2005] 1 A.C. 134 (surgeon liable for failure to warn of risks involved in operation where risk materialised

6–54 **Limits on recoverable loss: "effective cause".** However, even if it can be shown that the claimant relied on the defendant's statement, it does not necessarily follow that the defendant is responsible for all the losses which the claimant suffered. The test of causation, in both contract and tort, is notoriously difficult to formulate,[353] and the courts often resort to a test of "common sense"[354] in asking whether a particular item of loss, suffered by a claimant, can be said to have had a sufficient causal link with the defendant's wrongdoing. But in general terms, before the courts are prepared to hold that a particular item of the claimant's loss was in fact caused by the defendant's negligence they will require the breach of duty still to have been an "effective" or "dominant" cause of the loss, rather than simply an "occasion" for the loss.[355] For example, an auditor's failure to discover the company's insolvency, and his consequential inaccurate audit certificate about the company's financial state, may result in the company continuing to trade and investors continuing to invest in, or lend to, the company; but those later losses may be held not to have been caused by the audit certificate which merely provided the opportunity for the company to continue to trade and incur the losses.[356]

---

and patient injured, even though patient would have had the operation (but on a different occasion) anyway). These cases do not affect the area with which this chapter is concerned. *Cf. Beary v Pall Mall Investments* [2005] EWCA Civ 415, [2005] P.N.L.R. 35 (financial adviser's failure to advise about alternative investment, although claimant would still not have invested in it: causation not established. See Dyson L.J. at [38]: "The suggestion that the established principles of causation should be rejected in all cases of negligent financial advice is breathtakingly ambitious, contrary to authority and, in my view, wrong"); *White v Paul Davidson & Taylor* [2004] EWCA Civ 1511, [2005] P.N.L.R. 15 (claimant would not have acted differently if solicitor had given proper advice; *Fairchild* and *Chester v Afshar* do not apply to professional negligence of lawyers or accountants: Arden L.J. at [40]–[42]).

353 Clerk & Lindsell, Ch.2; R.A. Buckley, *The Law of Negligence* (4th edn, 2005), para.3.01; McGregor, Ch.6. For the test of causation in the tort of deceit, see above, para.5–38.

354 Above, para.5–38, n.164.

355 *Galoo Ltd v Bright Grahame Murray* [1994] 1 W.L.R. 1360, CA, at 1374.

356 *ibid*. Such a case might now be argued also on the basis that the later losses were not within the scope of the duty: below, para.6–55. *Galoo* was cited in the House of Lords in *South Australia Asset Management Corp. v York Montague Ltd* [1997] A.C. 191, but not referred to in the judgments. See also *Green v Turner* [1999] P.N.L.R. 28 (vendor's duty in making statements to purchaser about time within which transaction could be finalised and title registered was limited to the

Loss within the scope of the duty. It is important to remember that a purely factual view of causation is not sufficient because the true test is not whether the claimant's loss was caused by his reliance on the defendant's statement, but whether his loss was caused by the defendant's breach of duty. Given that a defendant owes a duty of care not in the abstract, but in respect of a particular loss which the claimant might suffer,[357] it is natural in any assessment of the recoverable damages to ask whether, or to what extent, the loss in fact suffered by the claimant was that kind of loss against which the defendant was under a duty to protect the claimant: that is, whether the loss which was in fact suffered by the claimant was loss within the scope of the defendant's duty of care.[358] This approach was confirmed by the House of Lords in *South Australia Asset Management Corp. v York Montague Ltd*[359] 6–55

---

purpose of inducing purchaser to enter contract, and not to enable purchaser to make subsequent investment decisions in relation to the land); *Dainty v Reynolds*, unreported, November 28, 2000, CA (trading losses flowing from negligent advice by agricultural consultant as to how a farming business should be conducted would be recoverable: *Galoo* distinguished); *Cossey v Lonnkvist* [2000] Lloyd's Rep. P.N. 885, CA (breach of contract by accountant: claimant's loss for unprofitable business not recoverable, under either *Galoo* or *South Australia Asset Management Corp. v York Montague Ltd*: see Sedley L.J. at [66], [67], [71]; Sir Anthony Evans dissenting). See also *Equitable Life Assurance Society v Ernst & Young* [2003] EWCA Civ 1114, [2003] 2 B.C.L.C. 603 at [133] (Brooke L.J.: "the facts of [*Galoo*] were idiosyncratic. Since, ex hypothesi, the company was insolvent, the losses suffered by continuing to trade were really suffered by the creditors (or by the company's parent), and so, although the case was not argued in that way, the real question may well have been whether the auditors owed any duty to the creditors (see Lord Hoffmann's lecture to the Chancery Bar Association, June 15, 1999, *Common Sense and Causing Loss*, pp.22–23)".

357 Above, para.6–14.

358 McGregor, paras 6–130 to 6–135.

359 [1997] A.C. 191, a decision in the HL on three separate cases, although up to the level of the Court of Appeal there had been also other cases which had since been settled (and the consolidated litigation is often known by the name of one of the settled cases: *Banque Bruxelles Lambert S.A. v Eagle Star Insurance Co. Ltd* [1995] Q.B. 375); and there are also a number of other similar reported cases, all arising out of the very significant fall in the property market during the early 1990s: see, e.g. *Platform Home Loans Ltd v Oyston Shipways Ltd* [2000] 2 A.C. 190, HL. The High Court of Australia has declined to follow the analysis in *South Australia Asset Management Corp. v York Montague Ltd*, and has held that in such a case the valuer can be responsible for the whole of the loss, including that part which flowed from the fall in market values: *Kenny & Good Pty Ltd v*

where the liability of property valuers for negligently providing inaccurate valuations was held to extend only to that part of the loss suffered by mortgagees, who relied on the valuations in making loans on (therefore) inadequate security, which flowed from the inaccuracy of the valuations. Where the mortgagees suffered more extensive losses as a consequence of the fall in the property market in the time between their making the advance and realising their security, that part of their loss was irrecoverable not because it was not in fact a consequence of their relying on the defendant's negligent statement (it was); nor because it was separable as other loss independently caused by a separate event (it was not)[360]; but simply because the duty did not extend to loss of that kind. On the facts, the duty was only a duty to provide accurate information about the property's value: the measure of damages was therefore the loss attributable to the inaccuracy of the information which the claimant suffered by reason of entering into the transaction on the assumption that the information was correct. The measure of damages would be different if the scope of the duty was wider: if the duty was not simply to provide information but a duty to advise the claimant as to what course of action to take; or if the defendant gave a warranty about the accuracy of the information.[361]

MGICA (1992) Ltd (1999) 73 A.J.L.R. 901. For commentaries on *South Australia Asset Management Corp.,* see (1997) 113 L.Q.R. 1 (J. Stapleton); [1997] C.L.J. 19 (J. O'Sullivan); [1998] Conv. 57 (J. Allinson); (1998) 61 M.L.R. 68 (J. Wightman); E. Peel, "SAAMCO Revisited" and R. Butler, "SAAMCO in Practice" in A. Burrows and E. Peel (eds), *Commercial Remedies* (2003) at pp.55–90; Burrows, *Remedies for Torts and Breach of Contract* (3rd edn, 2004), pp.109–122; and for discussion of the approach of the High Court of Australia, see (2000) 8 Tort L.Rev. 7 (A.M. Dugdale), p.183 (J. Murdoch); (2000) 116 L.Q.R. 1 (D.W. McLaughlan and C.E.F. Rickett).

360 *Nykredit Mortgage Bank Plc v Edward Erdman Group Ltd (No.2)* [1997] 1 W.L.R. 1627, HL, at 1638; *Platform Home Loans Ltd v Oyston Shipways Ltd* [2000] 2 A.C. 190, HL, at 208.

361 [1997] A.C. 191 at 214 (duty to advise: the adviser's duty extends to taking reasonable care to consider all the potential consequences of the course of action and, if negligent, will be responsible for all the foreseeable loss which is a consequence of that course of action having been taken), 216 (warranty of accuracy: damages (in contract) to put the claimant in the position as if the information had been accurate: see also below, para.8–25). For other cases, in other contexts, applying the principle stated in *South Australia Asset Management Corp. v York Montague Ltd*, see *Aneco Reinsurance Underwriting Ltd v Johnson & Higgins Ltd* [2001] UKHL 51, [2002] 1 Lloyd's Rep. 157 (insurance broker owed duty not simply to obtain reinsurance cover but to advise on

availability of cover in the market); *Bristol and West Building Society v Mothew* [1998] Ch. 1, CA (solicitor's duty to mortgagee in making statements about mortgagor's financing arrangements); *Green v Turner*, above, n.356; *Intervention Board for Agricultural Produce v Leidig* [2000] Lloyd's Rep. P.N. 144, CA (Board's representative wrongly told farmer he needed no quota to produce cream without paying levy; duty only to give information not to advise on farmer's career and business, so Board liable only to pay for levy during the years the farmer produced cream without quota but only until time when inaccuracy of information was corrected: *Esso Petroleum Co. Ltd v Mardon* [1976] Q.B. 801 distinguished on basis that there the information was fundamental to the claimant's decision to enter into the petrol station venture whereas here the farming venture was already underway before the misrepresentation was made); *Lloyds Bank Plc v Crosse & Crosse* [2001] EWCA Civ 366, [2001] P.N.L.R. 34 (solicitor in breach of duty of care in advising lender whether property had good and marketable title was in position analogous to a valuer, since the duty related to value and saleability of the property, so duty did not extend to all losses from loan transaction but only losses flowing from overvaluation in light of defendant's breach of duty); *Bristol and West Building Society v Fancy & Jackson* [1997] 4 All E.R. 582 (solicitors advising in relation to property transactions: scope of duty and therefore recoverable damage depended on the particular duty undertaken and broken); *Portman Building Society v Bevan Ashford* [2000] Lloyd's Rep. Bank. 96, CA (solicitor in breach of duty to lender for not disclosing borrower's second mortgage on property: liable for whole of lender's loss); *Cottingham v Attey Bower & Jones* [2000] Lloyd's Rep. P.N. 591 (solicitor in breach of duty to provide information about building regulations consent to client purchasing a house: liable only for absence of information and not losses flowing from defects in building); *Johnson v Gore Wood & Co.* [2003] EWCA Civ 1728, [2003] All E.R. (D) 58 (Dec) (scope of solicitor's duty to client); *Weston v Gribben* [2005] EWHC 2953 (Ch), [2005] All E.R. (D) 304 (Dec) (Foreign and Commonwealth Office may owe duty of care to third parties who suffer loss in reliance on document to which it has affixed apostille); *Andrews v Barnett Waddingham* [2006] EWCA Civ 93, [2006] P.N.L.R. 24 (actuaries advising on the Policyholders Protection Act 1975 did not owe duty in respect of loss suffered when investment failed in circumstances not covered by the 1975 Act); *Rushmer v Mervyn Smith (t/a Mervyn E. Smith & Co.)* [2009] EWHC 94 (QB), [2009] Lloyd's Rep. P.N. 41 (auditor's duty to company did not extend to guarantor); *Haugesund Kommune v Depfa ACS Bank* [2011] EWCA Civ 33, [2011] 1 C.L.C. 166 (scope of lawyer's duty to provide information about legal nature of transaction and counterparty's capacity to enter into it did not extend to losses suffered when counterparty had insufficient funds to make restitution when transaction held invalid). In assessing damages in such cases the judge must apply the test set out in Lord Hoffmann's judgment, without any gloss: *Bristol and West Building Society v Mothew*, above, at 27 (Staughton L.J.). For the application of the principle in *South Australia Asset Management Corp. v York Montague Ltd* to a case of several tortfeasors who are liable for the same

6–56 **Remoteness of damage.** In negligence, as in many torts,[362] a defendant's liability is limited to those losses which are of a kind he could reasonably have foreseen at the time of committing the tort—that is, at the time of the act or omission which constitutes his breach of duty.[363] If, therefore, the claimant suffers losses consequential upon the breach of duty which on an application of this test are too remote, those losses are irrecoverable.[364]

6–57 **Calculation of loss; timing.** Damages in negligence are calculated to compensate the claimant for his loss flowing from the breach of duty—that is, by how much his wealth is diminished by reason of the breach of duty.[365] This therefore links back to the nature of the duty itself; and in the case of negligent misrepresentation, where the defendant's duty was to take care to provide

---

damage but not in respect of the same *scope* of duty, see *Ball v Banner* [2000] Lloyd's Rep. P.N. 569 (rvsd on diff. grounds by CA: unreported, June 30, 2000).

[362] But not deceit: above, para.5–40.

[363] For the application of the test of remoteness of damage in the tort of negligence, see Clerk & Lindsell, paras 2–141 to 2–178; Charlesworth & Percy, paras 5–01 to 5–41; Winfield & Jolowicz, paras 6–16 to 6–41. The leading case is *The Wagon Mound* [1961] A.C. 388, PC (recovery limited to losses of a kind reasonably foreseeable) supplemented by *Hughes v Lord Advocate* [1963] A.C. 837, H.L.(Sc.) (irrelevant that the damage, caused by a known source of danger, occurs in an unforeseeable way, or is of an unforeseeable extent). For rules relating to the claimant's particular physical ("egg-shell skull") or economic ("impecuniosity") susceptibility, see Winfield & Jolowicz, paras 6–32, 6–33; *Lagden v O'Connor* [2003] UKHL 64, [2004] 1 A.C. 1067 in which HL departed from its earlier decision in *Liesbosch Dredger v Edison S.S.* [1933] A.C. 448, and so now allows a claimant to recover for the consequences of his impecuniosity.

[364] Under the approach in *Caparo Industries Plc v Dickman* [1990] 2 A.C. 605, HL, above, para.6–14 and *South Australia Asset Management Corp. v York Montague Ltd* [1997] A.C. 191, HL, above, para.6–55, the duty of care in negligence is itself defined by reference to the range of losses against which the defendant owes a duty of care to protect the claimant. The "kind" of loss which is in principle recoverable is therefore already defined before the question of remoteness of damage is addressed, and so the remoteness test, if it is not to be seen in this tort as simply the other side of the "duty" test without an independent function, must be used to distinguish between recoverable and irrecoverable "kinds" of damage in a more precise form than the duty test. For further discussion, see J. Cartwright, "Remoteness of Damage in Contract and Tort" [1996] C.L.J. 488.

[365] Contrast the measure of damages in cases of breach of contract, e.g. where there is a warranty that the statement is true—where the measure is the difference between the claimant's actual financial position and the position in which he

accurate information, the recoverable damage in the event of breach is based on the foreseeable consequences to the claimant of the information being wrong: one therefore compares the loss which he has actually suffered with what his position would have been if he had not acted on the assumption that the information was accurate. Where the duty was to advise the claimant as to his course of action, the recoverable damages will extend to the foreseeable loss which is a consequence of the course of action having been taken.[366]

There is no absolute general rule about the timing of the assessment of damages. Where the loss caused by the breach can be quantified as soon as it is suffered, that will normally be the appropriate time to value it. For example, it is well established that where a claimant purchases defective property in reliance on inaccurate information provided by the defendant, his loss accrues at the moment of acquisition,[367] and that the damages are normally[368] to be valued by the difference between the price paid and the actual market value of the property at the date at of purchase.[369] But continuing consequential losses after the primary

---

would have been if the statement had been true: *South Australia Asset Management Corp. v York Montague Ltd*, above, n.364 at 216; above, para.2–08; below, para.8–25.

366 *South Australia Asset Management Corp. v York Montague Ltd*, above, n.364 at 214, 216.

367 Or, rather, it is technically the date when he commits himself by contract to purchase it: *Byrne v Hall Pain & Foster* [1999] 1 W.L.R. 1849, CA.

368 This is not an absolute rule: *Keydon Estates Ltd v Eversheds LLP* [2005] EWHC 972 (Ch), [2005] P.N.L.R. 40.

369 *Philips v Ward* [1956] 1 W.L.R. 471, CA (surveyor); *Ford v White & Co.* [1964] 1 W.L.R. 885 (solicitor); *Perry v Sidney Phillips & Son* [1982] 1 W.L.R. 1297, CA (surveyor); *Watts v Morrow* [1991] 1 W.L.R. 1421, CA (surveyor); *Gardner v Marsh & Parsons* [1997] 1 W.L.R. 489, CA (surveyor); *Patel v Hooper & Jackson* [1999] 1 W.L.R. 1972, CA (surveyor). The claims are sometimes made in contract, sometimes in tort; but the content of the obligation (reasonable care and skill) is identical. Sometimes the measure of damages is put differently in the judgments: the difference between the fair value of the property if it had been in the condition described in the defendant's report and its value in its actual condition; but on the assumption that the price paid by the claimant was the fair value of the property as reported, the calculation is identical. This is the proper measure even where (a) the claimant in fact spent money repairing the defects, since to award the cost of repair would in effect be compensating for breach of warranty: *Watts v Morrow*, above; and (b) even if the claimant in fact later avoids the loss altogether as long as the later avoidance of loss resulted not from conduct, either of the claimant or of a third party, which flowed inexorably

loss has crystallised will still be recoverable; and very often the calculation of damages is bound to be affected by the extent to which loss in the future still has to be estimated at the date of trial.[370]

6–58 **Lost potential profits.** In an action of negligence a representee cannot recover damages based on the profits that he would have made if the representation had been true: that is the normal measure of damages in contract, not tort. But if he can show that his financial position at the time of assessment is reduced by virtue of the fact that, had he not been misled by the representation, he would in the mean time have used his money, time and energy to make other profits, those hypothetical lost profits (which must be pleaded and proved) are recoverable.[371]

---

from the original transaction and could properly be seen as part of a continuous course of dealing with the situation in which the claimant originally found himself: *Hussey v Eels* [1990] 2 Q.B. 227, CA (claimants obtained planning permission for demolition and re-sold to developers); *Gardner v Marsh & Parsons*, above (defect in property, of which claimant purchased lease, remedied by landlord under terms of covenant to repair: Peter Gibson L.J. dissented on basis that the claimants had effectively mitigated their loss by procuring the remedying of the defects by the landlord); *Primavera v Allied Dunbar Assurance Plc* [2002] EWCA Civ 1327, [2003] P.N.L.R. 12 (purchase of retirement fund at a loss which was effectively extinguished by time of trial by steps taken by claimant which were on his own account and therefore he did not have to give credit for the increase. Had the fund further decreased (rather than increased) in value during the period, he would not have been able to claim that additional loss against the defendant).

[370] *South Australia Asset Management Corp. v York Montague Ltd*, above, n.364 at 220. Where the claimant delays in incurring expenditure to remedy the damage, and so ultimately increases the cost of the remedy, the increased cost might still be recoverable where the delay was reasonable (for reasons which can include the commercial (financial) difficulties faced by the claimant in making the expenditure at an earlier date): *Dodd Properties Ltd v Canterbury City Council* [1980] 1 W.L.R. 433, CA; and see mitigation, below, para.6–60. Even where the primary loss is calculated as the difference between the price paid and the actual value of the property, in cases such as those discussed in n.369, above, the costs of alternative accommodation whilst the repairs are being carried out may still be recoverable: *Patel v Hooper & Jackson*, above, n.369.

[371] *South Australia Asset Management Corp. v York Montague Ltd*, above, n.364 at 216–217 (explaining *Swingcastle Ltd v Alastair Gibson* [1991] 2 A.C. 223, HL); *Esso Petroleum Co. Ltd v Mardon* [1976] Q.B. 801, CA, at 821–822, 829–830; *Keydon Estates Ltd v Eversheds LLP*, above, n.368. For a similar principle in the tort of deceit, see above, para.5–39; and see *Parabola Investments*

Loss of a chance. Where, in consequence of the defendant's breach of duty, the claimant has lost the *chance* of obtaining a particular benefit, he may be able to claim damages based on the lost benefit reduced to reflect the value of the chance.[372] He must be able to show on the balance of probabilities that he would have at least attempted to secure the advantage, the loss of which is the 6–59

Ltd v Browallia Cal Ltd in which the trial judge and CA relied on cases involving claims in negligence as well as claims in deceit: [2009] EWHC 901 (Comm), [2009] 2 All E.R. (Comm) 589 at [148] (*Esso Petroleum Co. Ltd v Mardon*, above); [2010] EWCA Civ 486, [2011] Q.B. 477 at [41], [44] (*Hungerfords v Walker* (1989) 171 C.L.R. 125 (HCA)). An award of interest under s.35A of the Supreme Court Act 1981 for the period from the accrual of the cause of action will enable the claimant to be protected to some degree against the loss of use of his capital, but if he can prove a greater actual loss than the court might award as interest he will seek to do so: *Parabola Investments Ltd v Browallia Cal Ltd*, above, at [55], relying on, inter alia, *Sempra Metals Ltd v Inland Revenue Commissioners* [2007] UKHL 34, [2008] A.C. 561. On the award of interest generally, see S. Sime and D French (eds), *Blackstone's Civil Practice 2011*, Ch.62.

[372] There are now many examples in the cases, which generally follow *Allied Maples Group Ltd v Simmons & Simmons* [1995] 1 W.L.R. 1602, CA: e.g. *Hartle v Laceys* [1999] Lloyd's Rep. P.N. 315, CA (claimant lost 60% chance of selling property before burden of restrictive covenant registered against it: damages payable by negligent solicitor reduced by 40%); *Lloyds Bank Plc v Parker Bullen* [2000] Lloyd's Rep. P.N. 51 (bank lost chance of negotiating better terms for lending, valued at 15% of the loss it actually suffered on inadequate security); *Thomas Eggar Verrall Bowles v Rice* [1999] All E.R. (D) 1509 (claimant lost chance of bidding for stock at auction through negligent failure of defendant solicitors to inform him of date of auction: damages of the profit he could have made, reduced by 30% to reflect 70% chance of succeeding in the auction); *Motor Crown Petroleum Ltd v S.J. Berwin & Co.* [2000] Lloyd's Rep. P.N. 438, CA (claimant lost chance of challenging local plan, and so lost 40% chance of succeeding in appeal against refusal of planning permission: loss of chance was an issue of quantification, not of causation); *Equitable Life Assurance Society v Ernst & Young* [2003] EWCA Civ 1114, [2003] 2 B.C.L.C. 603 (mutual life insurance company claimed that auditors' negligence resulted in directors not having information on which they would have acted to put company up for sale: striking-out action, so no decision on facts, nor evaluation of the chance claimed); *Perkin v Lupton Fawcett* [2008] EWCA Civ 418, [2008] P.N.L.R. 30 (solicitors liable for 20% chance that claimant client would have obtained properly drafted warranty from other party in negotiations and so would have reduced losses); *Joyce v Bowman Law Ltd* [2010] EWHC 251 (Ch), [2010] P.N.L.R. 22 (licensed conveyancer liable for 29% chance that claimant would have made higher profit from development); *Dennard v Pricewaterhousecoopers LLP* [2010] EWHC 812 (Ch), [2010] All E.R. (D) 192 (Apr) (valuer liable for 75% chance that claimants would have obtained higher sale price of shares).

subject-matter of his claim; but where the claim depends on the hypothetical conduct of a third party—such as the willingness of a third party to enter into a contract for the purchase of an asset at an acceptable price—the test is not what would have happened on the balance of probabilities, but whether the claimant has lost a real or substantial (as distinct from a merely speculative or fanciful) chance. If this is established, the court will evaluate the chance which can range from a small (but not merely fanciful) chance to something approaching certainty.[373] In short, therefore, the claimant must establish (on the balance of probabilities) that he has a loss—that he has lost a chance. But the chance may itself be less than 50 per cent: this is a matter of quantification of the loss.

6–60 **Mitigation.** The normal rules of mitigation apply to claims in the tort of negligence: the claimant will be unable to recover from the defendant any part of his loss which he would not have suffered if he had taken such steps as he ought reasonably[374] to have taken in order to avoid or reduce his loss.[375] Since the test of mitigation depends on what a reasonable person in the claimant's position would have done, the duty to mitigate arises only when the claimant knows of the breach of duty, and so is in a position to decide how to respond to it. And even if the action taken by a claimant in properly

[373] *Equitable Life Assurance Society v Ernst &Young*, above, n.372 at [83] (Brooke L.J., relying on *Kitchen v Royal Air Force Association* [1958] 1 W.L.R. 563 at 575–576 and *Allied Maples Group Ltd v Simmons & Simmons* [1995] 1 W.L.R. 1602 at 1611–1614). These principles are not affected by the decision in *Gregg v Scott* [2005] UKHL 2, [2005] 2 A.C. 176, where HL held (by a bare majority) that damages were not recoverable where doctor's negligence in delayed diagnosis resulted in patient's chance of recovery being reduced from 42% to 25%; the patient was already more likely than not to die, so the doctor did not (on the balance of probabilities) cause the loss (the prospect of being cured): see at [17]–[19] (Lord Nicholls, dissenting), [72], [82] (Lord Hoffmann), [117] (Lord Hope, dissenting), [218] (Baroness Hale).

[374] *Hussey v Eels*, above, n.369 (purchaser of house subject to subsidence had no duty to mitigate by securing planning permission, re-selling to developers and moving, although this was one course of action they could take if they so chose).

[375] *Esso Petroleum Co. Ltd v Mardon*, above, n.371 at 821–822, 829, 833.

attempting to mitigate his loss in fact results in the loss being increased, that additional loss will still be recoverable.[376]

Damages are compensatory. Damages in the tort of negligence are designed to compensate the claimant's losses. Although exemplary damages can in principle be awarded for any tort, the criteria for such an award will not generally be satisfied in the tort of negligence.[377] 6–61

Damages for intangible losses. The losses which may be claimed in an action of negligence may extend to intangible losses. In particular, in a number of cases claimants have been awarded damages to compensate for the distress and discomfort of living in a house in a deplorable condition which they had bought following a negligently inaccurate survey,[378] or for the relative discomfort in having to live in less desirable rented accommodation until the uninhabitable property bought as a result of the defendant's 6–62

---

[376] *ibid.* (lessee of petrol station making losses under lease induced by negligent misrepresentation: entry into substitute lease, under which he continued to make losses, was reasonable attempt to mitigate, so continuing losses were also recoverable).

[377] Exemplary damages are awarded in two categories of case: where there has been oppressive, arbitrary or unconstitutional action by the servants of the government; and where the defendant's conduct was calculated by him to make a profit for himself which may well exceed the compensation payable to the claimant: *Kuddus v Chief Constable of Leicestershire Constabulary* [2001] UKHL 29, [2002] 2 A.C. 122. *Cf.* the tort of deceit: above, para.5–42. Presumably a case could be made for an award of exemplary damages in an action of negligence where the defendant has weighed the cost of avoiding harm and negligently taken the risk, which materialises. The law on punitive damages in the US differs significantly from that in England, but *cf.* the facts of *Grimshaw v Ford Motor Co.,* 119 Cal.App.3d 757 (1981) (punitive damages awarded to victim of explosion of Ford Pinto car where management aware of crash tests showing vulnerability of the Pinto's fuel tank to rupture at low speed rear impacts with consequent significant risk of injury or death of the occupants by fire, and where "Ford could have corrected the hazardous design defects at minimal cost but decided to defer correction of the shortcomings by engaging in a cost-benefit analysis balancing human lives and limbs against corporate profits. Ford's institutional mentality was shown to be one of callous indifference to public safety": at 813–4).

[378] *Perry v Sidney Phillips & Son*, above, n.369 (claim in negligence and for breach of contract).

negligent valuation could be sold.[379] However, compensation for such losses must be modest, not excessive,[380] and is limited to the distress or inconvenience caused by the *physical*[381] consequences of the breach and not, for example, for the tension or frustration of a person who is involved in a legal dispute in which the other party refuses to meet its liabilities, because such aggravation is experienced by almost all litigants.[382]

6–63 **Contribution between co-defendants.** Where a representee is liable in negligence jointly or severally with another defendant for damage suffered by the claimant, whether the co-defendant's liability is also in negligence or is based on some other cause of action such as deceit or breach of contract, the court will, as in all cases of joint or several liability, have jurisdiction under the Civil

---

379 *Patel v Hooper & Jackson*, above, n.369 (negligence and breach of contract)

380 *Perry v Sidney Phillips & Son*, above, n.369 at 1303 (Lord Denning M.R., relying on cases decided in contract. Damages under this head were to be payable for a period during which it was reasonable for the claimant not to carry out repairs. The actual quantum of damages was left to be assessed by an Official Referee). For examples of awards in other cases, see *Patel v Hooper & Jackson*, above, n.369 (five years living in alternative inferior accommodation: £2000 for each claimant, husband and wife); *Watts v Morrow*, above, n.369 (six months living in house before and during remedial works: £750 for each claimant, husband and wife); *Roberts v J. Hampson & Co.* [1990] 1 W.L.R. 94 at 106 (disruption to young couple who could not bring their new baby to the home until remedial works had been carried out: they had instead to live with the wife's mother. "There is no suggestion that they were not welcome there, although there were the usual discords": £1,500 awarded); *Hipkins v Jack Cotton Partnership* [1989] 2 E.G.L.R. 157 (£750 for inconvenience of living with the mother of one of the claimants while remedial work carried out); *Farley v Skinner* [2001] UKHL 49, [2002] 2 A.C. 732 (£10,000 awarded as damages for breach of contract for noise against surveyor who was engaged to inspect and report on property to be occupied mainly at weekends and holidays, where the property was near an airport and the client had a particular concern about noise: see below, para.8–33).

381 *cf. Farley v Skinner*, above, n.380 at [85] (Lord Scott: "physical" means "a sensory (sight, touch, hearing, smell etc) experience": claim in contract).

382 *Perry v Sidney & Son*, above, n.369 at 1307. See also *Watts v Morrow*, above, n.369 at 1439–1441 (surveyor's liability in contract); *Hayes v James & Charles Dodd* [1990] 2 All E.R. 815, CA, at 823 (solicitor's liability in contract); *Hutchinson v Harris* (1978) 10 B.L.R. 19, CA, at 37, 46 (architect's liability in contract: no damages for distress because work was done to enable claimant not to live in the property but to let it for profit).

Liability (Contribution) Act 1978 to apportion between the co-defendants the damages payable.[383]

V. OTHER REMEDIES IN DAMAGES FOR NEGLIGENT MISREPRESENTATION

Comparison with Misrepresentation Act 1967 section 2(1). 6–64
Under this provision there is another remedy in damages, calculated on the tort measure, for misrepresentations which are (in substance) negligent. The detail of the remedy is discussed in Chapter 7, where there is also a detailed comparison with the tort of negligence.[384] Broadly, the remedy under section 2(1) of the Misrepresentation Act 1967 is more restricted in its application, since it is only available to one contracting party against the other contracting party, whereas the tort of negligence applies to all cases where a claimant can establish a duty of care, including actions between contracting parties.[385] But in those case where section 2(1) applies it is more attractive for the claimant since the elements of his claim are easier to establish than the elements of the tort of negligence; the burden of proving (in substance[386]) absence of negligence lies on the defendant (rather than, as in the tort of negligence, the burden of proving breach of duty lying on the claimant); and in certain circumstances the remedy of damages under the section might be more extensive than the remedy in negligence.[387] It is therefore clear that, where the claimant has a cause of action under section 2(1), it is unlikely to be of any benefit to him to pursue any action he may have in the tort of negligence.[388] But the tort will be used

---

383 Above, para.2–14. For the application of this where the scope of the co-defendants' duties is different under the principle of *South Australia Asset Management Corp. v York Montague Ltd*, above, para.6–55, see *Ball v Banner* [2000] Lloyd's Rep. P.N. 569 (rvsd by CA on diff. grounds: unreported, June 30, 2000). Under the Companies Act 2006 ss.532–538 a company may agree to limit its auditors' liability in such a way as to make them liable for only their own share of the damage, rather than jointly and severally liable for the whole damage: above, para.6–33, n.182.

384 Below, paras 7–45 to 7–47.

385 Above, paras 6–27 to 6–29.

386 s.2(1) does not refer to "negligence" but that is, in substance, what it covers: below, para.7–24.

387 Below, para.7–33.

388 *Cemp Properties (UK) Ltd v Dentsply Research & Development Corp. (No.1)* [1989] 2 E.G.L.R. 192 at 196.

where the Act is not available; in particular, where the claimant and the defendant are not parties to a contract.[389]

[389] In *Esso Petroleum Co. Ltd v Mardon* [1976] Q.B. 801, CA, the action was brought in tort because the Act did not apply to the misrepresentation, which was made in 1963: see at 817.

CHAPTER 7

STATUTORY LIABILITY FOR MISREPRESENTATION

I. DIFFERENT FORMS OF STATUTORY LIABILITY

Specific and general liabilities. Statutory liability for misrepresentation may take different forms. The liability may be defined by reference to specific circumstances: that is, a person making statements in some defined context may have a statutory duty to give accurate information, or to make the statement with care, and therefore be liable if the information is inaccurate, or given without the requisite care. Or there may be a general liability for false statements, which applies to all contracts, and is not restricted to contracts of a particular kind or to those entering into contracts in a 7–01 particular factual context. English law knows of both specific and general liabilities for misrepresentation. For example, directors and others involved in the publication of information inviting the public to subscribe for a new issue of shares have long owed duties, imposed by statute, in relation to the accuracy of that information.[1] But since 1967[2] there has also been a general provision, which applies to all contracts without restriction of context, by which one contracting party may be liable to the other for inaccurate statements made during the negotiations. In this chapter the general liability, because of its great significance, will be discussed before the specific liabilities, although it should be noted that the general liability, contained in section 2(1) of the Misrepresentation Act 1967, was itself developed by analogy with one of the specific liabilities.[3]

7–02 **Civil and criminal liabilities.** Statute may impose either criminal or civil sanctions, or both, for a false statement. In this book, however, we are generally concerned only with the civil liabilities which arise from making false statements; statutes which give rise only to criminal sanctions will therefore not be discussed in detail.[4]

II. GENERAL LIABILITY: SECTION 2(1) OF THE MISREPRESENTATION ACT 1967[5]

(1) Elements of the Claim Under Section 2(1)

7–03 **Overview of the elements of the claim.** Section 2(1) of the Misrepresentation Act 1967 provides as follows:

---

[1] Below, para.7–50.
[2] Misrepresentation Act 1967 s.2(1); below, paras 7–03 *et seq*.
[3] The liability of directors for information in their company's prospectus: see below, para.7–16. There is a real question about whether this was an adequate analogy, or whether the legislature, in extending directors' liabilities to (in effect) all contracts, was imposing too wide a liability. See the speech of Lord Wilberforce during the Second Reading debate on the Misrepresentation Bill on May 17, 1966, *Hansard*, HL Vol.274, Cols 950–951.
[4] Below, para.7–71.
[5] P.S. Atiyah and G.H. Treitel, "Misrepresentation Act 1967" (1967) 30 M.L.R. 369 (an excellent contemporary critique of the Act, although some of the points made in the article have been explained or superseded by later developments); Spencer Bower (Misrepresentation), Ch.13; Chitty, paras 6–068 to 6–077; Furmston, para.4.67; Treitel, paras 9–039 to 9–044, 9–060, 9–066; Anson,

> "**2.**—(1) Where a person has entered into a contract after a misrepresentation has been made to him by another party thereto and as a result thereof he has suffered loss, then, if the person making the misrepresentation would be liable to damages in respect thereof had the misrepresentation been made fraudulently, that person shall be so liable notwithstanding that the misrepresentation was not made fraudulently, unless he proves that he had reasonable ground to believe and did believe up to the time the contract was made that the facts represented were true."

In general terms, the representee may recover damages under this provision if he can show that he entered into a contract with the defendant; that the defendant made a misrepresentation to him before the contract; that he suffered loss as a result; and that the defendant would have been liable to pay damages if he had been fraudulent. These elements will be discussed in detail in this section. The defences which can be raised by the defendant once the representee has established the elements of the claim (both the specific defence set out in the statute, and general defences), the

---

pp.325–328; Cheshire, Fifoot and Furmston, pp.347–350, 366–367. The provisions of the Act discussed in this chapter do not extend to Scotland: s.6(3). For the Scottish solution to the need for a remedy in damages for a non-fraudulent misrepresentation by one contracting party to the other, see the Law Reform (Miscellaneous Provisions) (Scotland) Act 1985, s.10(1); above, para.6–28, n.138. In Australia, South Australia and the Australian Capital Territory took s.2(1) as a model for their own similar legislation: Misrepresentation Act 1972 (SA), s.7(1),(2); Law Reform (Misrepresentation) Ordinance 1977 (ACT), s.4, later replaced by Civil Law (Wrongs Act) 2002 (ACT), s.174, but the Australian enactments deal explicitly with some matters which have caused difficulties of interpretation in the UK statute (but not the measure of damages, which are also based on the "fiction of fraud": below, paras 7–16, 7–33); Carter, Peden and Tolhurst, paras 18–74 to 18–78; Seddon and Ellinghaus, para.11.92 to 11.101 (noting at para.11.101 that earlier proposals in other jurisdictions within Australia to follow the ACT legislation are not now necessary because the law of misrepresentation has been transformed by the misleading conduct legislation: Trade Practices Act 1974, s.52(1) [the 1974 Act was renamed on 1 January 2011: see now s.18 of the Australian Consumer Law, Sch.2 to the Competition and Consumer Act 2010]; below, para.7–48). For different solutions in New Zealand, see Burrows, Finn & Todd, paras 11.2 (Contractual Remedies Act 1979 s.6: innocent or fraudulent misrepresentation inducing entry into a contract: damages as if the representation were a term of the contract, i.e. as if it were true, and displacing claim to damages in deceit or negligence), 11.3 (Fair Trading Act 1986, s.9: liability for misleading or deceptive conduct in trade, which is similar to the Australian legislation but does not have quite the same impact because of the directness and simplicity of the Contractual Remedies Act 1979 s.6: see para.11.3.1; below, para.7–48).

quantification of the damages recoverable in such a claim, and the question of how a claim under section 2(1) relates to other remedies in damages for misrepresentation, will be discussed in later sections of this chapter.

7–04 **The Law Reform Committee, Tenth Report.**[6] The Misrepresentation Act 1967 was enacted to implement[7] the Tenth Report of the Law Reform Committee, which had been asked in 1959 to consider "whether any alterations were necessary or desirable in the law relating to innocent misrepresentation and the remedies available for such misrepresentation." The recommendation which is particularly relevant here is as follows[8]:

> "Where a person has, either by himself or his agent, induced another to enter into a contract with him (including a contract relating to land) by an untrue representation made for the purpose of inducing the contract he should be liable in damages for any loss suffered in consequence of the representation unless he proves that up to the time the contract was made he (or his agent, if the representation was made by him) believed the representation to be true and had reasonable grounds for his belief."

It is clear that section 2(1) was modelled closely on this recommendation which, together with the discussion in the Report leading to it,[9] is relevant to an understanding of the form in which the section was drafted.

(a) *The remedy is limited to contract*

7–05 **Pre-contractual misrepresentation.** The remedy is available only where the claimant "has entered into a contract after[10] a

[6] Cmnd.1782 (1962). The full text of the report is reproduced as Appendix B in Spencer Bower (Misrepresentation).

[7] *Hansard*, HL Vol.274, Col.922 (Lord Gardiner L.C., introducing in the House of Lords the Second Reading debate on the Misrepresentation Bill, May 17, 1966. Lord Gardiner had (as Gerald Gardiner Q.C.) been a member of the Law Reform Committee and signatory to the Report).

[8] paras 18, 27(5). For other recommendations of the Report and their implementation in the Misrepresentation Act 1967, see above, paras 4–38, n.167 (removal of bars to rescission); 4–61 to 4–71 (damages in lieu of rescission); below, para.9–19, n.75 (limit on effectiveness of exclusion clauses).

[9] paras 17 and 18.

[10] *Leofelis S.A. v Lonsdale Sports Ltd* [2008] EWCA Civ 640, [2008] E.T.M.R. 63 at [141] (Lloyd L.J.: it may be that damages under s.2(1) are not recoverable

misrepresentation has been made to him by another party thereto". Although, in substance,[11] section 2(1) provides a remedy based on the tort of deceit but under which damages on the tort measure are payable for negligent misrepresentation, the statutory claim is limited to the context of pre-contractual misrepresentations—unlike the torts of deceit and negligence themselves, which apply to statements irrespective of whether they are made between contracting parties.

In section 2(1) the word "contract" has its ordinary meaning. If, therefore, the transaction into which the claimant and defendant enter is not a contract, then statements made by the defendant before the transaction cannot give rise to a claim under this provision.[12]

The section applies to all contracts. Section 2(1) simply refers to "a contract"; there are no limitations in the Act as to the type of contract to which it relates.[13] The remedy of damages under this 7–06

---

in respect of a misrepresentation which is made in a contract, as distinct from one which is made before the contract is entered into: a draft containing the misrepresentation may be no more than a statement that, if and when the contract is entered into by all relevant parties, the particular party will make the statements in question).

[11] Below, para.7–33.

[12] *Rushton v Worcester City Council* [2001] EWCA Civ 367, [2002] H.L.R. 9 at [57] (in purchase by council house tenant under the right to buy provisions of the Housing Act 1985 no contract is entered into between claimants and council: claimants' right to transfer of the freehold is created by and derived from the 1985 Act, so the Misrepresentation Act 1967 s.2(1) cannot apply).

[13] The Law Reform Committee made clear in its recommendation (above, para.7–04) that the remedy should apply even in the case of contracts relating to land, because there had been some doubt whether a contract for the sale of land should be capable of rescission for misrepresentation after it had been executed, and the Law Reform Committee proposed formalising that rule in relation to the remedy of rescission: see paras 6, 7, 27(1). However, this restriction on the remedy of rescission was not adopted in the Act, which applies throughout to all contracts, regardless of subject-matter: above, para.4–38, n.167. In *H.I.H. Casualty and General Insurance Ltd v Chase Manhattan Bank* [2001] EWCA Civ 1250, [2001] 2 Lloyd's Rep. 483 at [51] the defendant reserved the right to argue in the House of Lords that the Misrepresentation Act 1967 does not apply to insurance contracts; this argument was not however pursued in the following appeal and Lord Bingham at [5] clearly assumed that the Misrepresentation Act 1967 s.2(1) applies to such a contract (note, however, that, in the case of consumer insurance contracts, the Consumer Insurance (Disclosure and Representations) Bill, which is expected to be enacted during 2012 (below, para.7–72,

section is therefore a general remedy for all cases of pre-contractual misrepresentation regardless of context.

(b) *The representation*

7–07 **"Misrepresentation" not defined.** There is no definition of "misrepresentation" in the Act. It has been said[14] that the word must therefore be taken to have its common law meaning. Although there is no single meaning of "misrepresentation" for the purpose of all the remedies discussed in this book,[15] it has been generally assumed in the cases that for the purposes of section 2(1) a "misrepresentation" bears the core meaning common to most remedies: a false statement, by words or conduct (but not silence), of fact which is sufficiently certain to be relied upon by the representee excluding, therefore, statements of opinion and intention, and "sales talk" or "mere puffs".[16]

7–08 **The representation: words or conduct.** As with all remedies for misrepresentation, it is necessary for a claim under section 2(1) that the defendant should have communicated to the claimant[17] a falsehood: typically, this will be by words (that is, literally, a statement) but it may equally be by conduct. For example, it has been held that where a husband entered into a contract to sell a house to the claimant without the consent of his wife who jointly

n.309), would replace any existing duty owed by a consumer insured to the insurer with a new duty to take reasonable care not to make a misrepresentation to the insurer (and its associated limited remedies)). There is also an overlap with the Financial Services and Markets Act 2000 s.90, below, paras 7–51, 7–64, which could have been avoided: Gore-Browne, para.43[5].

14 *André & Cie S.A. v Ets Michel Blanc & Fils* [1979] 2 Lloyd's Rep. 427, CA, at 434 (Geoffrey Lane L.J.: "it is plain from the title to the Act that it is an Act to amend the law relating to innocent misrepresentation . . . So it seems to be based upon the assumption that the common law rules shall be the foundation of the amendments which the Act proposes"); Atiyah and Treitel, above, n.5, p.369.

15 Above, paras 2–02, 3–02.

16 Atiyah and Treitel, above, n.5, p.369; below, para.7–10. For misrepresentations of law, see below, para.7–11.

17 The representation may be made to a third person but in circumstances in which it was intended to be acted on by the claimant (the other party to the contract): the words "to him" in s.2(1) do not narrow the class of persons who would be representees at common law: *Cheltenham BC v Laird* [2009] EWHC 1253 (QB), [2009] I.R.L.R. 621 at [326] (Hamblen J., applying *Peek v Gurney* (1873) L.R. 6 H.L. 377, HL, at 413 (deceit); above, para.5–19).

owned the house, the husband had by his conduct made a false representation to the claimant that he was the owner of the house and therefore able to sell it.[18] As with other remedies for misrepresentation, a "half-truth"—a partial statement which conveys a falsehood by virtue of what is omitted—will suffice.[19]

Representation by or on behalf of the other party. Where the misrepresentation is made by the contracting party personally, it is clear that section 2(1) can apply to make him personally liable. But where the misrepresentation is made by an agent of the contracting party acting in the course of his actual or ostensible authority, who is liable under the section: the agent, the contracting party, or both? It has been held in such a case that the principal is liable under the section for a statement made by his agent,[20] but the agent is not personally liable.[21] Any liability of the agent must be established on other grounds, such as in the torts of deceit[22] or negligence.[23] Although this appears to be settled, at least in the lower courts,[24] the arguments surrounding it are still worth considering since some issues remain to be resolved. The section provides (emphasising the key words): 7–09

> "Where a person has entered into a contract after a misrepresentation has been made to him *by another party thereto* and as a result thereof he has suffered loss, then, if *the person making the misrepresentation* would be liable to damages in respect thereof had the misrepresentation been made fraudulently, *that person* shall be so liable notwithstanding that the

[18] *Watts v Spence* [1976] Ch. 165 at 175.

[19] *Gosling v Anderson* [1972] E.G.D. 709, CA, at 714. For the question whether s.2(1) also extends beyond active misrepresentations to the breach of a duty of disclosure, see below, para.17–45.

[20] *ibid.*

[21] *Resolute Maritime Inc v Nippon Kaiji Kyokai, The Skopas* [1983] 1 W.L.R. 857, followed in *Cemp Properties (UK) Ltd v Dentsply Research & Development Corp.* [1989] 2 E.G.L.R. 205 at 207; *Morin v Bonhams & Brooks Ltd* [2003] EWHC 467, [2003] 2 All E.R. (Comm) 36 at [42]–[43]. See also *McCullagh v Lane Fox & Partners Ltd* [1996] 1 E.G.L.R. 35, CA, at 42–43.

[22] Above, Ch.5.

[23] Above, Ch.6.

[24] For cases at first instance which appear to accept the point, see *Gran Gelato Ltd v Richcliff (Group) Ltd* [1992] Ch. 560 at 570; *Phoenix International Life Sciences Inc. v Rilett* [2001] B.C.C. 115 (receiver an agent of the company, and arguably not converted by Insolvency Act 1986, s.44(1)(b), into principal contracting party for the purposes of the Misrepresentation Act 1967 s.2(1)).

> misrepresentation was not made fraudulently, *unless he proves that he had reasonable ground to believe and did believe up to the time the contract was made that the facts represented were true.*"

The liability is borne by the "person making the misrepresentation". If read literally, this could suggest that it is the agent who is liable—at least, if the draftsman has deliberately shifted the language from "party" to "person" to emphasise this. But it is not clear that the shift in language was intended to carry this meaning.[25]

A contrary argument would be that the use of the word "person" in the section is intended not to refer to the human person making the statement, but to the legal person—that is, the contracting party acting through his agent. On this view, the statute simply assumes the principles of agency. This is consistent with a statement by the Lord Chancellor in the Second Reading of the Bill,[26] and it is clear that the Law Reform Committee itself, in proposing the reform, had intended the principal to be liable for the agent's statement.[27] It is perhaps unfortunate that the draftsman of the Act did not follow more closely the language of the recommendation of the Committee in this respect.

A further issue is how the closing part of section will be interpreted in a case of agency. Under the section the defendant who makes a pre-contractual misrepresentation is liable "unless he proves that he had reasonable ground to believe and did believe" that he spoke the truth: that is, unless the defendant proves that he was both honest and reasonable in believing the statement to be true.[28] In a case of a statement by an agent, whose state of mind is relevant? Is it the agent, or the principal, or both, who must have been honest and have had reasonable grounds for the belief in the statement being true? It surely will make more sense for the agent's state of mind to be tested here: it is he who made the statement—the principal might not even know that the statement is being made by

[25] *Resolute Maritime Inc v Nippon Kaiji Kyokai*, above, n.21 at 3, accepting that the shift in language might be simply for the purposes of euphony (one cannot speak of "another *person* thereto"); and when read with s.2(3), where the word "person" in also used, that term might be intended throughout the section to include the principal in a case of a statement by an agent.

[26] *Hansard*, HL Vol.274, Col.955 ("there is no need for the Bill to deal with questions of agency as the ordinary law of agency will apply").

[27] Above, para.7–04 ("Where a person has, either by himself or his agent, induced . . . he should be liable in damages . . .").

[28] Below, para.7–23.

his agent—and only the agent's honesty and the grounds of his belief can sensibly be assessed in this context.[29] Indeed, this is the way in which the Law Reform Committee proposed it,[30] and again it is regrettable that the draftsman of the Act did not follow the language of the Committee's recommendation to make this clear. As the language of the Act stands, it is possible for a court to decide that, if the liability is only that of the principal, and therefore it is the principal to whom the section refers as the "person" making the representation, so too what matters is the principal's state of mind and, therefore, the information available to the principal, rather than to the agent, to decide whether he had reasonable grounds for belief in the truth of the statement.

An alternative approach would be to hold that the section does indeed impose liability on the human "person" making the statement—the agent—if he does not honestly and on reasonable grounds believe the truth of it. The question then would be how to hold the principal liable, since the references to the "person . . . liable" would then be to the agent, and not to the principal; but it would be strange to hold that the agent is liable but the principal is not. If the section were seen for what, in substance, it is, a statutory tort, the answer would be to attribute liability back to the principal by the doctrine of vicarious liability.[31] What is clear is that, however the section is construed, the courts must be creative in their interpretation to achieve a sensible answer to all the cases which might arise: and these difficulties would all have been avoided if the language of the Law Reform Committee had been adopted.

---

[29] *Howard Marine & Dredging Co. Ltd v A. Ogden & Sons (Excavations) Ltd* [1978] Q.B. 574, CA (enquiry into whether agent, who made misrepresentation, had reasonable ground for his belief); *Cassa di Risparmio della Repubblica di San Marino S.p.A. v Barclays Bank Ltd* [2011] EWHC 484 (Comm), [2011] All E.R. (D) 189 (Mar) at [289] (for defendant to prove that the relevant individuals had an honest and reasonable belief in the truth of the representations they were making).

[30] Above, para.7–04 ("unless he proves that up to the time the contract was made he (or his agent, if the representation was made by him) believed the representation to be true and had reasonable grounds for his belief").

[31] Vicarious liability is not confined to common law wrongs, but applies also to breaches of statutory obligations which give rise to civil liability in damages: *Majrowski v Guy's and St Thomas's NHS Trust* [2006] UKHL 34, [2007] 1 A.C. 224.

7–10 **Representation of fact?** The section imposes liability for a "misrepresentation" which, though not made fraudulently, would give rise to liability in damages if it had been made fraudulently (that is, in the tort of deceit).[32] In the tort of deceit fraudulent misrepresentations of intention, law and opinion are actionable[33]; it might be thought that all such misrepresentations are therefore within the scope of section 2(1) of the Misrepresentation Act. However, although it has indeed been held that a statement of intention can be brought within the section,[34] one might have thought that the section is limited to misrepresentations of fact. This is not simply because there would otherwise be a much wider liability for misrepresentations of opinion and intention which would, in effect, involve ascribing to the word "misrepresentation" a meaning which it does not generally bear at common law[35]; but also because the language of the section itself shows that the draftsman had in mind the restricted meaning of "misrepresentation", as a misrepresentation of fact. The closing words of the section refer to the defendant proving that he believed, on reasonable grounds, "that the *facts represented* were true," and this makes sense only if the actionable representations for the purposes of the section are restricted to representations of fact.[36]

---

[32] For further discussion of this "fiction of fraud", see below, para.7–16.

[33] Above, para.5–08.

[34] *Avon Insurance Plc v Swire Fraser Ltd* [2000] 1 All E.R. (Comm) 573 (Rix J.: statements about how underwriter and brokers intended to undertake underwriting in the following year; but the claim failed on other grounds). In *Thake v Maurice* [1986] Q.B. 644 at 659 Peter Pain J. at first instance appears to have assumed that a claim might have been available under s.2(1) because the defendant surgeon's statement about the effect of a vasectomy operation was a statement of an established medical fact, not a promise as to the future. See also *Inntrepreneur Pub Co. (CPC) v Sweeney* [2002] EWHC 1060, [2002] 2 E.G.L.R. 132 at [62] ("misrepresentation" in s.2(1) does not include statements of future fact, or predictions).

[35] *André & Cie S.A. v Ets Michel Blanc & Fils* [1979] 2 Lloyd's Rep. 427, CA, at 435 (obiter: misrepresentation of foreign law). See also *Springwell Navigation Corp. v J.P. Morgan Chase Bank* [2010] EWCA Civ 1221, [2010] 2 C.L.C. 705 at [119] (Misrepresentation Act 1967 is concerned with fact, not opinion, so claimant has to establish that statement of opinion carries implied statement of fact that the speaker had reasonable grounds for holding the opinion).

[36] *Lancaster City Council v Unique Group Ltd*, unreported, December 15, 1995 (representation of opinion). Where, however, the statement of opinion carries an implied representation that the representor knows of facts which justify his opinion, s.2(1) can apply: *Nelson Group Services (Maintenance) Ltd v BG Plc*

Representation of law. Until recently it was held that a misrepresentation of law was not sufficient to found a claim under section 2(1), on the basis that for the purposes of the section "misrepresentation" had the same meaning as at common law, which generally excluded misrepresentations of law.[37] However, the courts have now abandoned the formal distinction between misrepresentations of law and misrepresentations of fact[38]; and in *Pankhania v Hackney LBC*[39] the judge held that, in the light of these general developments, a misrepresentation of law is now sufficient to form the basis of a claim for damages under section 2(1) of the Misrepresentation Act 1967.[40] This decision sits somewhat uncomfortably with the closing words of the subsection,[41] but it is understandable that the draftsman of the Act made reference to "facts represented" since at the time of its enactment that was the commonly accepted meaning of "misrepresentation" at common law, and it is equally understandable that the courts today should seek to interpret the Act so as to make it consistent with the general law on pre-contractual misrepresentation.[42] 7–11

[2002] EWCA Civ 547, [2002] All E.R. (D) 205 (Apr), approving Langley J. in *Sumitomo Bank Ltd v Banque Bruxelles Lambert S.A.* [1997] 1 Lloyd's Rep. 487 at 515.

[37] *André & Cie S.A. v Ets Michel Blanc & Fils*, above, n.35, at 435.

[38] For a general discussion of the "mistake of law" and the "misrepresentation of law" rules, and their abandonment by the courts in the contexts of both restitution and contract, see above, paras 3–20 to 3–41.

[39] [2002] EWHC 2441 (Ch), [2002] All E.R. (D) 22 (Aug) (Rex Tedd Q.C.), approved in *Brennan v Bolt Burdon* [2004] EWCA Civ 1017, [2005] Q.B. 303 (mistake of law; *Pankhania* was a "lucid and trenchant judgment": Maurice Kay L.J. at [10]).

[40] The claim was for damages for loss arising from the purchase of a lot at auction which was described as suitable for redevelopment, and of which a current occupier was represented to hold a licence terminable on three months' notice but which was in fact a tenancy protected by the Landlord and Tenant Act 1954, Pt II. Even if he were wrong on the "misrepresentation of law" rule, the judge would have held that the misrepresentation was within s.2(1) as being a representation as to (a) private rights and (b) the sub-stratum of fact to which the general law had been applied: at [58]. On "private rights", see above, para.3–25. The damages were assessed in a later hearing: [2004] EWHC 323 (Ch), [2004] 1 E.G.L.R. 135.

[41] Above, para.7–10.

[42] For another area in which the courts may seek to re-intepret the statute, in the light of changes to the general law since 1967, see below, para.7–33.

7–12 **Representation must be false.** It is evident that the representation must be false: it must have been a "misrepresentation" within the meaning of section 2(1). The general approach to the interpretation of statements was discussed in Chapter 3[43]: in general terms, a court should adopt a test based on the reasonable interpretation of the representation from the perspective of the representee. This is the approach taken in the tort of deceit, on which the application of section 2(1) is based[44]; and although there does not appear to be direct authority on this point for the purposes of the section, there is authority on another statute, on which the drafting of section 2(1) was itself based, which adopts this objective test.[45]

7–13 **Correction of the misrepresentation.** If, after making a misrepresentation but before the claimant has entered into the contract, the defendant seeks to disclose the truth and therefore to remove the effect the false statement has already had on the claimant's mind, he must do so clearly. An attempt to correct the falsity which does not put the representee in the position of knowing the true facts will not be sufficient.[46]

7–14 **Timing of the falsity: the time of the contract.** Changed facts between statement and contract. For the purposes of a claim under section 2(1) the claimant must show that he entered into the contract after the defendant's misrepresentation had been made, and as a result he has suffered loss. As in the case of other claims based on misrepresentation,[47] the representation must have been false at the time when the representee acted upon it in such a way as to cause

[43] Above, para.3–06.

[44] For the interpretation of the representation in the tort of deceit, see in particular *Smith v Chadwick* (1884) 9 App. Cas. 187, HL; above, para.5–09. The tort of deceit looks also to the meaning which the representor intended, not in ascertaining the meaning of the statement, but in assessing whether the defendant was fraudulent: above, para.5–18; but this is irrelevant for s.2(1).

[45] *Greenwood v Leather Shod Wheel Co.* [1900] 1 Ch. 421, CA, at 433–434, interpreting the Directors Liability Act 1890 s.3; below, para.7–16.

[46] *Peekay Intermark Ltd v Australia and New Zealand Banking Group Ltd* [2006] EWCA Civ 386, [2006] 2 Lloyd's Rep. 511 at [43] (misrepresentation corrected by the terms of the contract which the claimant signed and by which he was bound although he did not read them). See generally above, para.3–11.

[47] Including the tort of deceit, on which the section is itself based: above, para.5–11.

the loss he claims: for section 2(1), this means the time of the contract. So if a statement was false when made but the surrounding facts have changed so that it would be true if repeated at the time of the contract, there is no misrepresentation within the meaning of the section.[48] But a statement which was true when made will be a misrepresentation if it would be false if repeated at the time of the contract, as long as the statement was not limited to refer to the facts only as they stood when it was made.[49]

(c) *Loss*

The claimant must prove his loss. The claimant must show that, having entered into the contract following the defendant's misrepresentation, he has suffered loss as a result.[50] The remedy under section 2(1) is damages; it is therefore natural that the onus should lie on the claimant to prove his loss. This raises a substantial issue as to the nature of the loss which is recoverable under the section: the basis of assessment of damages. This will be discussed in detail below.[51] **7–15**

---

48 There appears to be no direct authority for s.2(1). For the application of this principle in other remedies, see paras 4–27 (rescission), 5–11 (deceit).

49 *Spice Girls Ltd v Aprilia World Service B.V.* [2002] EWCA Civ 15, [2002] E.M.L.R. 27 at [51], [59] (continuing representation by company formed to promote the services of the "Spice Girls" that no member of the group had a declared intention of leaving the group before the end of sponsorship contract; statement that the group was "currently comprising" the five members, taken in context, was not limited to the time at which the statement was made); *British & Commonwealth Holdings Plc v Quadrex Holdings Inc*, unreported, April 10, 1995, CA (true statement falsified by subsequent events, before contract entered into. On facts the representors, though not fraudulent, could not reasonably believe their previous representations were true once they had certain relevant information, and so were liable under s.2(1)). If, before the contract is entered into, the defendant discovers that the facts have changed so as to falsify his earlier statement, or simply discovers that his earlier statement was false, but does not inform the claimant, he may well become fraudulent, and an action can be brought in the tort of deceit, rather than under s.2(1): above, para.5–17. That, however, is a matter of the defendant's state of mind, a different issue from that considered here as to the meaning of the statement.

50 *Spice Girls Ltd v Aprilia World Service B.V. (No.2)* [2001] E.M.L.R. 8 (claimant could recover only for its own loss, not loss suffered by parent company as a result of misrepresentation).

51 Below, paras 7–31 to 7–42.

(d) *The "fiction of fraud"*

7–16 **The role of, and reasons for, the "fiction of fraud" in a claim under section 2(1).** The section uses what at first sight appears to be a curious device. The defendant is liable, notwithstanding that he was not fraudulent, if he "would be liable to damages . . . had the misrepresentation been made fraudulently". That is, the defendant is only liable under the section if he *would* have been liable in damages—in the tort of deceit—*if* he had been fraudulent. This is sometimes referred to as the "fiction of fraud".[52] The reason for this cross-reference to fraud is historical, although in fact it was an unnecessary complication in the drafting of the 1967 Act.

Section 2(1) was enacted to implement the recommendations of the Law Reform Committee[53]; and in making its recommendation, the Committee drew an analogy with the legislation which imposed liability in damages on directors (and others) for a misrepresentation in their company's prospectus seeking subscribers for new shares or debentures, unless the directors could show that they had reasonable ground to believe, and did up to the time of allotment of the shares or debentures believe, that the statement was true.[54] The particular legislation which the Committee had in mind was section 43 of the Companies Act 1948.[55] But that section can itself be traced back to section 3 of the Directors Liability Act 1890 which was enacted to reverse the decision in *Derry v Peek*.[56] That is, it was intended, in the particular context with which *Derry v Peek* was concerned—directors' liability for statements in company prospectuses—to reverse the decision of the House of Lords that the tort of deceit required fraud and did not impose liability on a director who was honest in his belief that his statement was true, but held that belief without reasonable grounds. The Act of 1890 made no change to the tort of deceit itself, which retained the requirement of dishonesty.[57] But a new, statutory claim to damages[58] was

[52] Atiyah and Treitel, "Misrepresentation Act 1967" (1967) 30 M.L.R. 369 at p.373; Treitel, para.9–043. See also Cheshire, Fifoot and Furmston, pp.347–348; *Royscot Trust Ltd v Rogerson* [1991] 2 Q.B. 297, CA, at 305–306.
[53] Above, para.7–04.
[54] Law Reform Committee, Tenth Report, above, para.7–04, n.6, para.18.
[55] For the modern law, see the Financial Services and Markets Act 2000, s.90; below, para.7–51.
[56] (1889) 14 App. Cas. 337, HL; above, para.5–14.
[57] Above, para.5–13.

created, for a particular factual context of misrepresentation, but in effect providing a remedy as for fraud but without the need to prove dishonesty. Indeed, it has been said that[59]:

> "the effect of the section of the original Directors Liability Act was merely to eliminate the element of fraud from the cause of action based in misrepresentation in a prospectus, and to give the same remedy in the statutory conditions for an untrue misrepresentation as for a fraudulent misrepresentation."

Just as the effect of the 1890 Act had been to create a statutory claim to damages, based on the tort of deceit but without the need for the claimant to prove fraud (and, indeed, placing on the defendant the burden of proving that he believed, and had reasonable grounds to believe, that his statement was true in order to exonerate himself), so the Law Reform Committee in its Tenth Report proposed that there should be similarly a general claim for damages for non-fraudulent misrepresentation, with the burden placed on the defendant of proving that he believed, and had reasonable grounds to believe, that his statement was true. And the natural point of reference for the proposed new remedy was again the tort of deceit, not only because the Committee based its thinking on the companies legislation (itself referable to the tort of deceit) but also because at the time the Committee reported, in July 1962, there was not yet any developed tort of negligent misrepresentation. *Hedley Byrne & Co. Ltd v Heller & Partners Ltd*[60] was still to be decided. And it is clear that the Committee did think that its proposed remedy was, in effect, deceit without the fraud[61]:

---

[58] Directors Liability Act 1890 s.3 and Companies Act 1948 s.43, both referred to "compensation" rather than "damages". But there is no difference in the meaning of these words for this purpose: *Clark v Urquhart* [1930] A.C. 28, HL, at 56. Lord Tomlin at 76 referred to the 1890 Act having created a "statutory tort".

[59] *Clark v Urquhart*, above, n.58 at 67 (Lord Atkin). See also Viscount Sumner at 56 and Lord Tomlin at 76. The case involved a claim under the Companies (Consolidation) Act 1908 s.84, into which the Directors Liability Act 1890 s.3 had been consolidated. The implications of the analysis for the measure of damages is discussed below, para.7–33.

[60] [1964] A.C. 465, HL; above, para.6–10.

[61] Tenth Report, above, n.54, para.22. See also Lord Gardiner L.C. in the Second Reading debate in the House of Lords, *Hansard*, HL Vol.274, Col. 924.

> "We appreciate that the independent remedy in damages which we have recommended will be available in any case in which, under the present law, fraud has to be proved. The damages obtainable for misrepresentation will be no less extensive and the plaintiff's burden of proof very much lighter. It may be therefore that, so far as misrepresentations inducing a contract are concerned, actions for fraud will fall into disuse and be replaced by our proposed remedy . . . The tort of deceit will still be needed for those cases where a fraudulent statement has induced a person to act to his detriment otherwise than by entering into a contract . . .."

However, the formulation of the remedy proposed by the Committee[62] did not itself contain a reference to fraud, or the tort of deceit, in its formulation. Nor did the companies legislation, used as a model by the Committee, itself contain such a reference. It simply recited the necessary elements of the action. But the draftsman of section 2(1) of the Misrepresentation Act reinforced the link to the tort of deceit by the incorporation into the text of the "fiction of fraud", which could have been avoided by alternative drafting which would have followed more closely the recommendations of the Committee, or even the language of the companies legislation. If that alternative approach had been adopted, some of the difficulties[63] which have been associated with the "fiction of fraud" in section 2(1) could perhaps have been avoided.

7–17 **The effect of the "fiction of fraud": incorporation of elements of a deceit claim.** The effect of the "fiction of fraud" in section 2(1) is that the claimant must prove all the elements of the tort of deceit in respect of the defendant's statement, *except for* the fraud. This is not onerous, since it is clear that the element of the tort of deceit which is most difficult for the claimant to establish is the defendant's fraud, his lack of honest belief in the truth of his statement. The other elements are[64]: a false representation made to the claimant by or on behalf of the defendant; that the defendant intended the claimant to act on it; and that the representation was an inducement to the claimant's action as a result of which he suffered the loss which he claims. Section 2(1) requires in terms that there be a misrepresentation and that the claimant prove his loss. The

62 Above, para.7–04.

63 In particular, the measure of damages: below, para.7–33. For criticism of the "fiction of fraud" in the Second Reading debate in the House of Lords, see *Hansard*, HL Vol.274, cols 930 (Viscount Colville of Culross), 936 (Lord Reid).

64 Above, para.5–05.

"fiction of fraud" therefore only imports in substance the requirements that the claimant prove that the defendant intended him to act on the statement, and that he did act on it.

The representor's intention that the representation induce the contract. The claimant must show that the defendant intended him to act upon the statement. Under section 2(1) the gist of the claim is that the claimant relied on the representation by entering into the contract, suffering loss as a result.[65] It must therefore be shown that the defendant intended his statement to act as an inducement to the contract. As in all cases, including the tort of deceit,[66] where proof of the defendant's intention is required the court may infer the necessary intention from consideration of the natural consequences of a person's actions: that is, it may look at the natural consequences of the defendant's statement, and the circumstances in which it was made to the claimant, to decide whether it is satisfied, as a matter of fact, that the defendant intended the claimant to rely on his statement in entering into the contract. However, it must be said that it is often easier to infer the representor's intention that the representee act on the representation where there is fraud: once the representor is shown not to have held a positive, honest belief in the statement, his purpose in making the statement is also easier to establish, and it is difficult for him to deny that he intended the representee to act on it. If the incorporation of the rules of deceit into section 2(1) by the "fiction of fraud" has the effect that this aspect of a deceit claim is also incorporated, it might in consequence make it easier for the claimant to establish his claim than if he were driven simply to have to prove that the defendant intended his (non-fraudulent) misrepresentation to be acted upon.[67] 7–18

Reliance by the representee. The claimant must also show that the defendant's statement acted as an inducement to his entering into the contract. This requirement was discussed in general terms 7–19

[65] On the causal link (and the meaning of "as a result thereof" in s.2(1)) see below, paras 7–35, 7–37.

[66] Above, para.5–19.

[67] P.S. Atiyah and G.H. Treitel, "Misrepresentation Act 1967" (1967) 30 M.L.R. 369 at pp.374–375.

in Chapter 3,[68] and in relation to the tort of deceit, which is particularly relevant for a claim under section 2(1), in Chapter 5.[69] The representation must have been *a* cause (not necessarily *the* cause) of the claimant's decision to enter the contract;[70] he must have relied upon it in the meaning that the court is satisfied is false; and it must be proved that he in fact relied on it. Where the representation is "material", in the sense that it is of such a nature that it would be likely to induce a person in the claimant's position to enter into the contract, the courts will infer that the representation induced the claimant so to act, unless the representor can show the contrary.[71]

---

[68] Above, paras 3–50 *et seq*.

[69] Above, paras 5–23 to 5–28.

[70] In *Cassa di Risparmio della Repubblica di San Marino S.p.A. v Barclays Bank Ltd* [2011] EWHC 484 (Comm), [2011] All E.R. (D) 189 (Mar) at [467] Hamblen J. said that it was common ground that for s.2(1) the test of reliance is the "but for" test: "if a representee would have entered into the transaction even had the misrepresentation not been made, there is no inducement". *Cf*., however, the general discussion of the approach to multiple causes, above, para.3–54.

[71] *Gosling v Anderson* [1972] E.G.D. 709, CA, at 714–715 (Lord Denning M.R., applying in the context of a claim for damages under s.2(1) of the Misrepresentation Act 1967 this test from the judgment of Jessel M.R. in *Redgrave v Hurd* (1881) 20 Ch.D. 1, CA, at 21; see also above, para.5–25 (deceit); para.4–33 (rescission)); *Avon Insurance Plc v Swire Fraser Ltd* [2000] 1 All E.R. (Comm) 573 (even if there was on the facts a material misrepresentation, the inference of inducement was rebutted); *Spice Girls Ltd v Aprilia World Service B.V.* [2002] EWCA Civ 15, [2002] E.M.L.R. 27 at [70] (applying in a claim under s.2(1) the inference of reliance from Lord Blackburn in *Smith v Chadwick* (1884) 9 App. Cas. 187 (deceit)); *Cemp Properties (UK) Ltd v Dentsply Research & Development Corp. (No. 1)* [1989] 2 E.G.L.R. 192 at 195–196. *Cf. Infiniteland Ltd v Artisan Contracting Ltd* [2004] EWHC 955 (Ch), [2004] All E.R. (D) 350 at [90]–[91] (share sale agreement: "simply not credible" that contract was entered into in reliance on impression obtained by purchaser's agent "several weeks earlier, from a fairly short conversation over coffee in a hotel"; "a major reason why purchasers of companies carry out due diligence investigations is in order that they do not have to rely on what they have been told by the vendors, but can find things out for themselves before committing themselves to a contract": Park J.). In *Fitzroy Robinson Ltd v Mentmore Towers Ltd* [2009] EWHC 1552 (TCC), [2009] B.L.R. 505 at [111] Coulson J. held that under s.2(1) "reliance needs to be proved to the civil standard" and there is no inference of fact that the representee was induced by a material statement: this is, however, against the authorities set out above.

The representee's ability to discover the truth. In the tort of deceit,[72] as long as it is shown that he relied on the statement, it is not a bar to the claim that the representee could have discovered the truth of the statement. However, such a rule is appropriate in that tort, because contributory negligence is not a defence to a claim in deceit.[73] But it has been held that, since the claim under section 2(1) of the Misrepresentation Act is in substance a claim for negligent misrepresentation, contributory negligence ought to be available as a defence.[74] The strict rule, applied in the tort of deceit, that there can be no issue as to whether the representee should have discovered the truth, may therefore not be imported by the "fiction of fraud" into a claim under the statute. 7–20

Knowledge of representee's agent. Where the representee's agent knows that the representation is false, or otherwise has information about the facts which give the true state of affairs, but does not communicate the relevant information to the representee, the question is whether the knowledge of the agent is to be imputed to the representee. It has been held for the purposes of a claim under section 2(1)[75] that if the information is acquired by the agent in circumstances where he has actual or ostensible authority to receive it on behalf of the representee it will be so imputed, and therefore will prevent the representee from having a successful claim.[76] 7–21

"Non-reliance" clauses. Contractual clauses which attempt to limit or negative the reliance by the representee on a statement made by the representor, or to limit the legal consequences of such reliance, are considered in Chapter 9. 7–22

(2) The Statutory Defence: Honest and Reasonable Belief

The defence. Once the claimant has established the elements of his claim, the defendant is liable "unless he proves that he had reasonable ground to believe and did believe up to the time the 7–23

[72] Above, para.5–26. The same rule has long been adopted in the remedy of rescission: *Redgrave v Hurd*, above, n.71; above, para.4–35.

[73] Above, para.5–31.

[74] Below, para.7–27.

[75] As for the tort of deceit: above, para.5–27.

[76] *Strover v Harrington* [1988] Ch. 390 at 407–410.

contract was made that the facts represented were true." That is, the defendant has the burden of proving that he in fact believed his statement and that he had reasonable ground for believing it—his belief was both honest and reasonable—throughout the period from the statement to the contract.

7–24 **The effect of the defence: limitation of the statutory liability to negligent misrepresentations.** The statute does not in terms define the actionable misrepresentations as being those made negligently: the word "negligent" appears nowhere in the Misrepresentation Act 1967. But in substance the effect of section 2(1), imposing liability for every pre-contractual misrepresentation where the representor cannot prove that he was both honest and reasonable in his belief that it was true, is to impose liability for negligence; or, at least, for statements where the representor cannot prove that he was not negligent. Sometimes, therefore, the liability under section 2(1) is referred to as liability for negligent misrepresentation,[77] but this must always be taken as simply shorthand for the technical requirements of the section, and must not be confused with liability in the tort of negligence.

Indeed, although the statute in substance applies to negligent misrepresentations, there are significant differences between the scope of liability under the statute, and liability in the tort of negligence. In order to establish liability in negligence the claimant must show that the defendant owed him a duty of care, and that he broke that duty.[78] But under section 2(1) the claimant need not establish a duty of care; and the burden is on the defendant to prove that he was honest and reasonable in his belief that his statement

---

[77] e.g. *Howard Marine & Dredging Co. Ltd v A. Ogden & Sons (Excavations) Ltd* [1978] Q.B. 574, CA, at 593, 596, commenting on the trial judge's reference to "negligence" in relation to s.2(1); *HIH Casualty & General Insurance Ltd v Chase Manhattan Bank* [2003] UKHL 6, [2003] 1 All E.R. (Comm) 349 at [5] (Lord Bingham); Atiyah and Treitel, "Misrepresentation Act 1967", above, n.67, at pp.372–373. The terminology was also used as a short-form description of the proposed new remedy by the Law Reform Committee (Tenth Report, above, para.7–04, n.6: see headings to paras 17 and 21), and in the House of Lords in the Second Reading debate on the Bill: *Hansard*, HL Vol.274, Cols 922 (Lord Gardiner L.C.), 950 (Lord Wilberforce, who, in criticising the width of application of the section, went so far as to say that its effect was "to impose generally a duty of care, in relation to all contracts").

[78] Above, para.6–12.

was true—it is not for the claimant to prove his negligence. This[79] makes a claim under section 2(1) much more attractive to a claimant, since it has the result that a defendant may be liable to pay damages under the statute where he could not be held liable in the tort of negligence.[80]

"Reasonable ground to believe". The defendant must show that "he had reasonable ground to believe" that the statement was true. It is not entirely clear whether this is wholly objective, or has a subjective element. But the latter appears to be the more natural reading, since the issue is not the broad one of whether a reasonable person could have believed the statement to be true, but whether the particular defendant had reasonable grounds for his belief: he must prove that "*he had* reasonable ground" to believe it. On this basis, the question is whether a reasonable person could have deduced the truth of the statement from the information available to the defendant.[81] The particular circumstances of the defendant will 7–25

[79] Together with the possibility of a wider recovery in damages in certain cases under s.2(1): below, para.7–33.

[80] *Howard Marine v Ogden*, above, n.77 at 598, where Bridge L.J. held that the representor was liable under the statute even though there was no duty of care in negligence or, if there was such a duty, there was no proof of breach. Lord Denning M.R. at 592, 593 (following the trial judge) held that there was no liability on either basis; Shaw L.J. at 601 held that there was liability both in negligence and under the statute.

[81] In a claim under the companies legislation on which s.2(1) is based (above, para.7–16) it has been held that the defendant must produce in evidence particulars of the grounds of his belief (*Alman v Oppert* [1901] 2 K.B. 576, CA) and that there must be evidence that the particular defendant took steps, using the appropriate means of inquiry available to him, to check the truth of his statement (*Adams v Thrift* [1915] 1 Ch. 557, affd [1915] 2 Ch. 21, CA). The more recent legislation has made explicit this obligation to make reasonable inquiries: the Financial Services Act 1986 ss.151(1) (listed securities), 167(1) (unlisted securities); replaced by the Financial Services and Markets Act 2000 Sch.10, para.1(2). For the particular context of directors' liabilities, see below, paras 7–49 *et seq*. The question of whether the special defence contains an "objective" or "subjective" test was discussed in some detail in the passage of the Bill through the House of Commons: see *Hansard*, HL Vol.274, col.950 (Lord Wilberforce in the Second Reading debate on the Bill in the House of Lords). In the Third Reading debate in the House of Commons Mr Ian Percival said that he had been told by the Solicitor-General by letter that the defendant "will have to establish that there were grounds for his belief and that they were present to his mind, the first part of that being objective and the second subjective": *Hansard*, HC

therefore be relevant.[82] However, it is clear that the courts regard this as an onerous burden for the defendant to discharge.[83]

(3) Other Defences

7–26 **Defences generally available in a claim under section 2(1).** A number of general defences, apart from the specific defence contained in section 2(1) itself, are available to a claim under the section. The most common are the claimant's contributory negligence; expiry of the limitation period barring the claimant's action; the exclusion or limitation of the defendant's liability by a contractual term or a non-contractual notice; and the absence of writing, signed by the defendant, containing the statement (a defence under Lord Tenterden's Act).

The confusion caused by the use of the "fiction of fraud" in the section[84] has given rise to some difficulties in relation to the defences, since at common law the availability and application of certain defences varies according to whether or not the claim is based on fraud. The defendant's liability under section 2(1) depends upon (amongst other things) whether he "would have been liable to damages in respect [of the misrepresentation] had the misrepresentation been made fraudulently." One interpretation[85] would hold

Vol.741, col.1377. The reply of the Solicitor-General (col.1388) in the debate appears to have misunderstood the point as referring to cl.3 of the Bill.

[82] Atiyah and Treitel, above, n.67, p.373 ("a layman may succeed here where an expert would fail").

[83] *Howard Marine v Ogden*, above, n.77 (barge owner's marine manager made misrepresentation to potential hirer of the barge about capacity, relying on his (correct) recollection of an (incorrect) figure in the Lloyd's Register, although he had access to correct information in the ship's documents which he had seen: majority held that the evidence was not sufficient to show that he had an objectively reasonable ground to disregard the figure in the ship's documents and to prefer the Lloyd's figure: see Bridge L.J. at 598). *Cf. Shepheard v Broome* [1904] A.C. 342, HL, a decision on the Directors Liability Act 1890 where a director was liable for non-disclosure of material information even though he had taken "the best advice he could obtain upon the disclosure that should be made in the prospectus": Lord James at 346. For a case in which the defendant discharged the burden, see *Cooper v Tamms* [1988] 1 E.G.L.R. 257 at 262.

[84] Above, para.7–16.

[85] It does indeed appear that in recommending the reform enacted in s.2(1) the Law Reform Committee in its Tenth Report (above, para.7–04) simply had in mind the claim in deceit; and (apart from contractual exclusion clauses) there is no discussion in the Report of how the general defences will operate in a claim

that this requires a complete consideration of the likely success of a claim based on fraud, and therefore it imports into the claim under the section those defences which would be available in the tort of deceit.[86] However, a more satisfactory approach would be to say that the "fiction of fraud" is relevant to the elements of the claim—the cause of action—and not to the larger question of whether the claimant would have had a complete and successful claim, also taking into account such things as the defences which would have been raised had the claim been one in deceit. On this basis, the consequences of the reference in the section to fraud should be limited to importing those elements of the cause of action of the tort of deceit (apart, of course, from the fraud itself), such as the requirement that the defendant should have intended the claimant to rely on the statement, and the claimant's actual reliance.[87] The availability of defences should then be considered on the merits of the claim under section 2(1) itself, unfettered by the link to the tort of deceit.

Contributory negligence. Under the Law Reform (Contributory **7–27**
Negligence) Act 1945[88] the defence of contributory negligence is available where the claimant "suffers damage as a result partly of his own fault and partly of the fault of" the defendant. In relation to the defendant's wrong,[89] "fault" is defined as "negligence, breach of statutory duty or other act or omission which gives rise to liability in tort". On a strict reading this does not in terms cover a claim

under the section. However, the Committee did not itself propose the language of the "fiction of fraud", and it is the apparently closer link to the tort of deceit which was introduced by the draftsman of the Act that has given rise to these difficulties of interpretation. For further discussion of the extent to which the language in the statute should inevitably import the rules of the tort of deceit, in the context of the measure of damages, see below, para.7–33.

[86] On the strongest reading it would be *only* those defences available in deceit, since the section holds the defendant "so liable" [i.e. liable as if in an action of deceit].

[87] Above, para.7–17.

[88] s.1(1).

[89] s.4; *Standard Chartered Bank v Pakistan National Shipping Co. (Nos 2 and 4)* [2002] UKHL 43, [2003] 1 A.C. 959 at [11] (Lord Hoffmann). In relation to the *claimant*, "fault" is defined as "negligence, breach of statutory duty or other act or omission" which gives rise at common law to a defence of contributory negligence: *ibid*.

under section 2(1) of the Misrepresentation Act[90]; and, indeed, if the "fiction of fraud" in the section were held to import the rules of the tort of deceit relating to defences, contributory negligence would not be available since it is not a defence to an action of deceit.[91]

However, the deceit rules have not been applied here, and it has been held that the defence is available to a claim under section 2(1). In *Gran Gelato Ltd v Richcliff (Group) Ltd*[92] Sir Donald Nicholls V.C. held that

> "liability under the Misrepresentation Act 1967 is essentially founded on negligence . . . This being so, it would be very odd if the defence of contributory negligence were not available to a claim based on a breach of a duty to take care in and about the making of a particular representation, but not available to a claim for damages under the Act in respect of the same representation."

Sir Donald Nicholls held that contributory negligence should be available to a defendant in a case where the claimant has concurrent claims against him in negligence in tort and under the Act of 1967. He reached this conclusion by parity of reasoning with the Court of Appeal in *Forsikringsaktieselskapet Vesta v Butcher*[93] regarding

[90] A claim under s.2(1) is not, strictly, for "negligence"; and although the claim is an action under a statute and is in substance a claim in tort, it is not an action for the tort of breach of statutory duty, nor actually a claim in tort. The approach of Sir Donald Nicholls V.C. in *Gran Gelato Ltd v Richcliff (Group) Ltd* [1992] Ch.560, is based on the assumption that this strict reading of the Act should be applied. If, however, it were held that the claim under s.2(1) is for "negligence" *within the meaning of the Act* or that it is liability "in tort", the Act can be held to apply by its express terms to all claims based on s.2(1) without requiring proof of a concurrent potential liability in the tort of negligence. For references in other contexts to the claim under s.2(1) as in "negligence", see above, para.7–24, n.77; and for the suggestion that it is a claim "in tort" for the purposes of the Limitation Act 1980, see *Laws v Society of Lloyds* [2003] EWCA Civ 1887, [2003] All E.R. (D) 392 (Dec) at [92], below, para.7–28, n.101.

[91] Above, para.5–31.

[92] Above, n.90 at 572–575. See also *Alliance & Leicester Building Society v Edgestop Ltd* [1993] 1 W.L.R. 1462 at 1474–1475 (Mummery J., emphasising that the rule in deceit remains intact after *Gran Gelato*); *Standard Chartered Bank v Pakistan National Shipping Co. (Nos 2 and 4)*, above, n.89 at [17] (Lord Hoffmann, noting the decision in *Gran Gelato*; HL confirmed that contributory negligence is not a defence to the tort of deceit).

[93] [1989] A.C. 852 at 858–868, 875, 879 (CA; the question was not pursued in HL).

concurrent claims in negligence and contract. The defence of contributory negligence is available to a claim for breach of contract only where the defendant's liability in contract is the same as his liability in the tort of negligence independently of the existence of any contract: that is, where the claim in contract is based on an act or omission which comprises a breach of a contractual duty concurrent with, and of content equivalent to, a duty in the tort of negligence.[94] On this basis, therefore, before he can employ the defence to a claim based on section 2(1) of the Misrepresentation Act, a defendant will have to show[95] that he owed a concurrent duty in the tort of negligence, on which he could have been sued and in respect of which he could have raised a defence of the claimant's contributory negligence.

Once the defence of contributory negligence is established, the court reduces the damages to such extent as it thinks just and equitable having regard to the claimant's share in the responsibility for the damage. A claimant may be held to be contributorily negligent in relation to his own acts or omissions which, together with his reliance on the defendant's statement, caused his overall loss. But it will generally not be possible to hold the claimant contributorily negligent simply by reason of his reliance on the defendant's statement. Before the defendant can be liable under section 2(1) it must be shown that he intended, or can be taken to have intended, the claimant to act in reliance on his statement in entering into the contract.[96] It will therefore be only in a special case that carelessness by the claimant would make it just and

---

94 Below, para.8–20.

95 This is an odd aspect of this defence, since it involves the defendant admitting that he also owed a duty in negligence in order to raise a defence to a claim under the 1967 Act. For a similar issue in relation to contributory negligence as a defence to a claim for breach of contract, see *Barclays Bank Plc v Fairclough Building Ltd (No.3)* (1995) 44 Con. L.R. 35, CA (duty in tort argued by defendant, and accepted by court, in order to found defence of contributory negligence in contract claim). However, very commonly a claimant under s.2(1) will be owed by the defendant a concurrent duty in the tort of negligence, even though (because it is less easy to prove) he may well not have pleaded it: above, para.7–24. The effect, therefore, is that contributory negligence will generally apply to a claim under s.2(1). A less strict reading of the Law Reform (Contributory Negligence) Act 1945 would avoid the need for finding a concurrent duty in the tort of negligence in relation to s.2(1): above, n.90.

96 Above, para.7–18. This is an aspect of the claim under s.2(1) which is incorporated by the "fiction of fraud".

equitable to reduce the damages payable to compensate him for loss suffered in consequence of doing the very thing which, in making the statement, the defendant intended should happen, that is, that he should rely on the statement.[97] But it appears that, in principle, it is possible for contributory negligence to be found on such a basis.[98]

7–28 **Limitation periods.**[99] An action under section 2(1) of the Misrepresentation Act 1967 cannot normally be brought (that is, a claim form cannot be issued[100]) after the expiration of six years from the date on which the cause of action accrued.[101] The cause of

---

[97] *Gran Gelato Ltd v Richcliff (Group) Ltd*, above, n.90 at 574. For a similar doubt about the applicability of contributory negligence based on the claimant's fault in relying on the defendant's representation, see above, para.6–48 (negligence).

[98] For cases in the tort of negligence, see above, para.6–48, n.320. In *Strover v Harrington* [1988] Ch. 390 at 410 Sir Nicolas Browne-Wilkinson V.C., in the context of a claim under the Misrepresentation Act, s.2(1), thought that "if it is once shown that a misrepresentation has been made, it is no answer for the representor to say that the representee has been negligent and could have found out the true facts if he had acted otherwise"; this was however before the decision in *Gran Gelato* which leaves this possibility theoretically open. *Cf. Infiniteland Ltd v Artisan Contracting Ltd* [2004] EWHC 955 (Ch), [2004] All E.R. (D) 350 at [97] (no reliance; but if there had been reliance, "there would have been a high degree of contributory negligence": Park J.).

[99] In 2001 the Law Commission proposed a general reform of the rules on limitation of actions: Law Com. No.270, *Limitation of Actions* (2001), but in 2009 the Government announced that the limitation reforms would not be taken forward: above, para.6–50, n.330.

[100] Below, para.11–05.

[101] Limitation Act 1980, either s.2 (action founded on tort) or s.9 (action "to recover any sum recoverable by virtue of any enactment"): *Laws v Society of Lloyds* [2003] EWCA Civ 1887, [2003] All E.R. (D) 392 (Dec) at [92] (unnecessary to decide, but "our present view is that it is an action founded on a tort, albeit a statutory tort, and thus within section 2"). See, however, *Hartley v British Railways Board*, unreported, June 25, 1999, in which CA left open for argument in a full hearing the question of whether the limitation period under the Misrepresentation Act 1967, s.2(1), is set by the Limitation Act 1980, s.9, rather than s.2 (tort: six years) or s.8 (action on a specialty: 12 years; but this longer period is surely excluded by s.8(2), and was dismissed in *Laws v Society of Lloyds*, above); and Law Com. No.151, *Limitation of Actions* (1998), para.7.18 which assumes that the action under s.2(1) is founded on tort for the purpose of limitation. For general provisions for extension of limitation periods in cases of the claimant's disability, see s.28, and in cases of deliberate concealment by the defendant or his agent of facts relevant to the claimant's right of action, see s.32(1)(b). For a claim to contribution under the Civil Liability (Contribution) Act

action under section 2(1) will not accrue until the claimant has relied on the representation and suffered the loss which is recoverable under the section.[102]

In an action "based upon the fraud of the defendant" the limitation period does not begin to run "until the plaintiff has discovered the fraud . . . or could with reasonable diligence have discovered it".[103] But, even though the claim under section 2(1) is linked to the tort of deceit by the "fiction of fraud"[104] this provision cannot apply. The action under the statute is not "based on" the defendant's fraud: indeed, it is based on the assumption that there is *no* fraud. And it would not make sense to defer the start of the limitation period to the discovery (or discoverability) of the fraud, given that there is no fraud to discover.[105]

Where the claim under section 2(1) is concurrent with a claim in the tort of negligence the limitation periods of the two claims may generally coincide, since in each of the claims the cause of action normally accrues when the claimant suffers loss, and the limitation period is six years. However, in a claim for negligence, other than a

---

1978, s.1, below, para.7–43 there is special time-limit of two years from the accrual of the right to recover contribution: see the Limitation Act 1980, s.10. For the special time-limit in actions for damages for personal injuries, see s.11.

[102] For the recoverable loss, see below, para.7–34. Commonly the claimant will suffer loss by the very act of entering into the contract in reliance on the statement; but sometimes the loss may only be suffered at a later stage: Chitty, para.28–034; *Toprak Enerji Sanayi A.S. v Sale Tilney Technology Plc* [1994] 1 Lloyd's Rep. 303 (cause of action for misrepresentation inducing contract for supply of goods arose not on contract but only on delivery of the goods). For an analogy under the Directors Liability Act 1890 (above, para.7–16) under which the limitation period began to run not on the preparation or issue of the untrue document but only when the claimant had subscribed for shares and thereby suffered damage, see *Thomson v Lord Clanmorris* [1900] 1 Ch. 718, CA, at 728–729.

[103] Limitation Act 1980, s.32(1)(a).

[104] Above, para.7–16.

[105] However, s.32(1)(b), which defers the start of the limitation period in cases where "any fact relevant to the plaintiff's right of action has been deliberately concealed from him by the defendant" can apply to a claim under s.2(1). For the intepretation of s.32, see *Cave v Robinson Jarvis & Rolf* [2002] UKHL 18, [2003] 1 A.C. 384, above, para.6–50, n.332. Where the defendant's concealment of facts is subsequent to the accrual of the cause of action, the full limitation period begins to run only after the claimant has discovered, or should have discovered, the concealment: *Sheldon v R.H.M. Outhwaite (Underwriting Agencies) Ltd* [1996] A.C. 102, HL.

claim for damages for personal injuries, the limitation period will sometimes be extended where at the time when the cause of action accrues the claimant does not have sufficient knowledge of relevant facts to bring his claim.[106] But no such extension is available for claims under section 2(1), since such claim is not an "action for damages for negligence" within the meaning of the Limitation Act 1980.[107] This is therefore one of the few circumstances in which a claimant, with an action under both section 2(1) and in the tort of negligence, might be driven to pursue the tort claim because it is still available whereas the claim under section 2(1) has become barred by the passage of the period of limitation.

7–29 **Exclusion and limitation clauses.** A defendant may seek to exclude or limit his liability under section 2(1) of the Misrepresentation Act 1967 by a contractual exclusion clause or a non-contractual notice[108] and the clause or notice may seek to achieve this in various ways; for example, by negativing the claimant's reliance on the representation and so preventing a claim arising, or by excluding or limiting the remedy which would otherwise be available. The effect of such clauses and notices, and the limits on their effectiveness through such controls as section 3 of the Misrepresentation Act 1967 and the Unfair Contract Terms Act 1977, are discussed in Chapter 9.

7–30 **Absence of writing: Lord Tenterden's Act.** Under section 6 of the Statute of Frauds Amendment Act 1828 ("Lord Tenterden's Act") no action may be brought on a representation relating to a third party's credit unless the representation is in writing, signed by the person to be charged—that is, the defendant.[109] This rule has

---

[106] Limitation Act 1980, s.14A; above, para.6–50.

[107] *Laws v Society of Lloyds* [2003] EWCA Civ 1887, [2003] All E.R. (D) 392 (Dec) at [84]–[87] (Limitation Act 1980 s.14A, contemplates that an action for damages for negligence will involve the claimant relying upon an "act or omission which is alleged to constitute negligence"; but in a claim under s.2(1) it is not necessary for the claimant to allege that the representation was made negligently).

[108] It should be noted that this is another point on which the "fiction of fraud" is not applied, since an exclusion or limitation clause cannot generally protect the representor against an action in deceit: below, para.9–13.

[109] For further detail on this section, see above, para.5–30.

long been held to apply only to fraudulent representations[110]; but it has also been assumed by the Court of Appeal that the "fiction of fraud" incorporates the rule into a claim under section 2(1) of the Misrepresentation Act from the tort of deceit: since the defendant would not be liable in deceit in respect of such a representation in the absence of the required writing, he cannot be liable under section 2(1).[111] Such reasoning is not, however, necessary. The older cases had held that Lord Tenterden's Act does not cover an action in negligence because such an action is based not on the representation but on the breach of a duty of care[112]: before the Misrepresentation Act 1967 there was no action for damages for representations which were not fraudulent.[113] However, the plain language of Lord Tenterden's Act applies to statements actionable under section 2(1) of the Misrepresentation Act, since it requires a "representation" as to credit to be in writing before an action can be brought.[114]

(4) The Damages Recoverable[115]

Principles of award of damages under section 2(1). After some hesitation in the earlier cases, it has now become clearly established that damages are awarded under section 2(1) on the tort measure. The current authority, at the level of the Court of Appeal, goes further than this: not only are damages awarded on the tort measure, 7–31

[110] *Banbury v Bank of Montreal* [1918] A.C. 626, HL.

[111] *UBAF Ltd v European American Banking Corp.* [1984] Q.B. 713, CA, at 718–719 (this was "common ground" and was not argued before the Court of Appeal).

[112] *Banbury v Bank of Montreal*, above, n.110 at 639, 708, 713.

[113] On the distinction between a claim based on a breach of duty, and a claim based on the misrepresentation, see also above, para.6–12.

[114] Spencer Bower (Misrepresentation), 3rd edn, para.225; confirmed by 4th edn, para.232. Discussion in *Banbury v Bank of Montreal*, above, n.110, to the effect that Lord Tenterden's Act cannot have been intended to apply to innocent (i.e. non-fraudulent) representations must therefore be read with caution: see esp. Lord Atkinson at 669, 691–694. However, a court which wishes to bring the Misrepresentation Act 1967 s.2(1) as far as possible into line with claims in the tort of negligence (see below, para.7–33) might perhaps want to use this as a starting-point for an interpretation of Lord Tenterden's Act so as to limit it not simply to causes of action based on a misrepresentation, but also to claims in deceit for fraudulent misrepresentation.

[115] McGregor, paras 41.041–41.059.

they are the same measure as the damages awarded in the tort of deceit. Even though this link to the tort of deceit appears to have been intended by the draftsman of the 1967 Act, there are some indications that the courts may not be prepared to continue to maintain the link and may in due course reinterpret the remedy under section 2(1) as being equivalent to the tort of negligence. Each of these points will be discussed in detail in the following paragraphs.

7–32 **Damages are assessed on the tort measure.** In some of the earliest cases decided under section 2(1) the courts appeared to assume that damages would be awarded on the same measure as for breach of contract.[116] But it was soon established that the proper measure was the tort measure.[117] This view is consistent with the intentions of the Law Reform Committee whose recommendation was enacted in section 2(1),[118] and with statements in Parliament

---

[116] *Gosling v Anderson* [1972] E.G.D. 709, CA, at 717 (Lord Denning M.R.); *Jarvis v Swans Tours Ltd* [1973] Q.B. 233, CA, at 237 (Lord Denning M.R.; but the claim itself was for damages for breach of contract, not under the 1967 Act); *Davis & Co. (Wines) Ltd v Afa-Minerva (E.M.I.) Ltd* [1974] 2 Lloyd's Rep. 27 at 32 (Judge Fay, following Lord Denning in *Jarvis v Swans Tours Ltd*, although on the facts the damages awarded were in respect of consequential losses which would be recoverable equally in contract and tort); *Watts v Spence* [1976] Ch. 165 (Graham J., following Lord Denning in *Gosling v Anderson* in an attempt to avoid the rule in *Bain v Fothergill* (1874) L.R. 7 H.L. 158; see J. Cartwright, "Damages for Misrepresentation" [1987] Conv. 423 at p.426).

[117] For some of the earlier considered decisions which held that the measure was the tort measure, see *Sharneyford Supplies Ltd v Edge* [1986] Ch. 128 at 149 (disapproving *Watts v Spence*, above, n.116 both on the general question of the measure of damages under s.2(1) and on the impact of a s.2(1) claim on the rule in *Bain v Fothergill*, above, n.116 (the rule in *Bain v Fothergill* was abolished by Law of Property (Miscellaneous Provisions) Act 1989 s.3)); [1987] Ch. 305, CA, at 323; *André & Cie S.A. v Ets Michel Blanc & Fils* [1979] 2 Lloyd's Rep. 427, CA, at 181; *McNally v Welltrade International Ltd* [1978] I.R.L.R. 497; *F. & B. Entertainments Ltd v Leisure Enterprises Ltd* (1976) 240 E.G. 455 at 461; *Chesneau v Interhome Ltd* [1983] C.A.T. 238, CA, reported only briefly at *The Times*, June 9, 1983 and (1983) 134 N.L.J. 341.

[118] Tenth Report, above, para.7–04, n.6, paras 18, 22. The Committee based its recommendation on the analogy of directors' liability for misstatements in prospectuses (above, para.7–16; below, para.7–50), which it is clearly established is liability for damages measured on the tort basis: see esp. *McConnel v Wright* [1903] 1 Ch. 546, CA, at 554; *Clark v Urquhart* [1930] A.C. 28, HL, at 67, 76; below, para.7–62.

during the passage of the Bill,[119] but is based on the wording of the section itself.[120] It is the reference to fraud in the section that has led the courts to hold that the proper measure of damages is as for fraud: that is, the tort measure. In *Royscot Trust Ltd v Rogerson*[121] Balcombe L.J. quoted with approval from an earlier, unreported decision of the Court of Appeal[122] on this point:

> "Eveleigh L.J. said:
>
> '[Damages] should be assessed in a case like the present one on the same principles as damages are assessed in tort. The subsection itself says: 'if the person making the misrepresentation would be liable to damages in respect thereof had the misrepresentation been made fraudulently, that person shall be so liable . . .' By 'so liable' I take it to mean liable as he would be if the misrepresentation had been made fraudulently.'
>
> In view of the wording of the subsection it is difficult to see how the measure of damages under it could be other than the tortious measure."

It now seems to be beyond argument that the measure of damages under section 2(1) is the tortious measure: it has been accepted as correct at first instance[123] and in the Court of Appeal,[124] and has even been assumed to be correct in the House of Lords.[125]

---

[119] For the Second Reading debate in the House of Lords, see *Hansard*, HL Vol.274, cols 930–931 (Viscount Colville of Culross), 936 (Lord Reid), 955 (Lord Gardiner L.C.: "the ordinary measure of damages will be as in tort").

[120] It should be noted that there is no useful guide to the interpretation of s.2(1) elsewhere in the Act. Although there is specific provision in s.2(3) dealing with the situation where an award of damages under s.2(1) overlaps with an award under s.2(2), this gives no assistance to the interpretation of the measure of damages under either provision: J. Cartwright, "Damages for Misrepresentation", above, n.116 at pp.428–429. For the measure of damages under s.2(2), see above, para.4–71.

[121] [1991] 2 Q.B. 297, CA, at 304–305.

[122] *Chesneau v Interhome Ltd*, above, n.117.

[123] In addition to cases listed in n.117, above, see *Cemp Properties (UK) Ltd v Dentsply Research & Development Corp. (No.2)* [1989] 36 E.G. 90 at 97–98 (Morritt J: the words of s.2(1) "must import the measure of damages appropriate to the tort of deceit. Had it been intended to introduce the contractual measure of damages, one would have expected the statutory hypothesis to be that the misrepresentation had become a term of the contract"); *Gran Gelato Ltd v Richcliff (Group) Ltd* [1992] Ch. 560 at 575 (Sir Donald Nicholls V.C.: "that sum of money which will place the plaintiff in the position he would have been in if the misrepresentation had not been made"); *Dodd v Crown Estate Commissioners* [1995] E.G.C.S. 35; *Avon Insurance Plc v Swire Fraser Ltd* [2000] 1 All E.R. (Comm) 573 at [200].

7–33 **Damages on the same measure as the tort of deceit? The relevance of the "fiction of fraud".** A consequence of the logic which led the courts to hold that the basic measure of damages is the tort measure is, however, that the measure of damages is for the tort *of deceit*. It was the reference to the "fiction of fraud"[126] in the subsection which led the courts to hold that the statute necessarily imported the tort measure; and the courts have therefore consistently held, up to the level of the Court of Appeal, that this has the consequence that damages under the statute are measured on the same basis as in deceit.[127] This appears to be the correct conclusion, in the sense that the draftsman of section 2(1) was implementing a proposal which was indeed intended to create a new statutory liability for damages based on the tort of deceit, and in which the remedy would be the same as the tort of deceit but without proof of fraud.[128] At the time when the remedy was proposed,[129] and even when the 1967 Act was passed, it was perhaps not obvious that the remedy in deceit was significantly different from the remedy in negligence. But since then there have been developments of the torts of deceit and negligence which mean that it now appears

---

[124] *Bridgegrove Ltd v Smith* [1997] 2 E.G.L.R. 40, CA, at 42, following *Royscot Trust Ltd v Rogerson*, above, n.121; *Spice Girls Ltd v Aprilia World Service B.V.* [2002] EWCA Civ 15, [2002] E.M.L.R. 27 at [12].

[125] *South Australia Asset Management Corp. v York Montague Ltd* [1997] A.C. 191, HC, at 216 and *Smith New Court Securities Ltd v Scrimgeour Vickers (Asset Management) Ltd* [1997] A.C. 254 at 267, 283. The House of Lords there cast some doubt on the application in this context of the *fraud* measure (below, para.7–33), but did not appear to doubt that the basic measure is as in tort.

[126] Above, para.7–16.

[127] See especially *André & Cie SA. v Ets Michel Blanc & Fils*, above, n.117; *Cemp Properties (UK) Ltd v Dentsply Research & Development Corp. (No.2)*, above, n.123; *Royscot Trust Ltd v Rogerson*, above, n.121; *Chesneau v Interhome Ltd*, quoted above, para.7–32.

[128] Above, para.7–16.

[129] The Law Reform Committee reported in 1962, before *Hedley Byrne & Co. Ltd v Heller & Partners Ltd* [1964] A.C. 465, HL, had extended the tort of negligence to misstatements causing economic loss; there was therefore no direct comparison in the tort of negligence to which the Law Reform Committee could make reference and the tort of deceit was the natural point of comparison—in addition to the fact that the Committee used as its analogy the legislation imposing liability on directors for misstatements in prospectuses, which was also linked to the tort of deceit: above, para.7–16. For further discussion and explanation about this historical background to the 1967 Act, see J. Cartwright, "Damages for Misrepresentation", above, n.116.

curious to hold that a defendant who was, essentially, only negligent[130] should bear the same responsibility as if he had been fraudulent. For example, there have been developments which show that there are significant differences between the torts of deceit and negligence with regard to the rules of remoteness of damage,[131] and in other aspects of the scope of recoverable loss.[132] The modern law of tort seeks explicitly to reflect in its remedies the moral culpability of the defendant, and therefore to impose a higher responsibility on a fraudulent defendant.[133] But the Law Reform Committee had no such approach in mind. Indeed, in its Report it said[134] that "it is not in general the function of the civil law to grade the damages which an injured person may recover in accordance with the moral guilt of the defendant."

The question, then, is whether in this more developed law of tort the courts will be prepared to maintain the link between section 2(1) and the tort of deceit. There have been clear signs in recent judgments in the House of Lords that the question remains open. Most particularly, Lord Steyn has asked "whether the rather loose wording of the statute compels the court to treat a person who was morally innocent as if he was guilty of fraud when it comes to the measure of damages".[135] It appears likely that the Supreme Court,

---

130 Indeed, he may not even be liable in the tort of negligence: he just cannot prove that he had reasonable ground to believe, and did believe, his statement to be true: above, para.7–24.

131 Below, para.7–38.

132 Below, para.7–35.

133 *South Australia Asset Management Corp. v York Montague Ltd*, above, n.125 at 215; *Doyle v Olby (Ironmongers) Ltd* [1969] 2 Q.B. 158 at 167; above, para.5–40; *Smith New Court Securities Ltd v Scrimgeour Vickers (Asset Management) Ltd*, above, n.125 at 279–281.

134 Tenth Report, above, para.7–04, n.6, para.22; *Raiffeisen Zentralbank Österreich A.G. v Royal Bank of Scotland Plc* [2010] EWHC 1392 (Comm), [2011] 1 Lloyd's Rep. 123 at [387].

135 *Smith New Court Securities Ltd v Scrimgeour Vickers (Asset Management) Ltd*, above, n.125 at 283. The question was left open (with less overt criticism of the current state of the law) by Lord Browne-Wilkinson at 267. See also *South Australia Asset Management Corp. v York Montague Ltd*, above, n.125 at 216; *Showan v Yapp*, unreported, November 3, 1998, CA (Robert Walker J. declined to consider whether *Royscot Trust Ltd v Rogerson*, above, n.121, was decided *per incuriam* because of the comments in *Smith New Court* expressly reserving the question); *Bridgegrove Ltd v Smith*, above, n.124 at 42. In *Avon Insurance Plc v Swire Fraser Ltd*, above, n.123 Rix J. applied the fraud measure, as he was bound on the authorities to do, but as a result thought that "where there is room for an

when the opportunity presents itself, will overrule those cases which have held that the remedy is as for deceit, and will instead hold that the measure of damages is the same as in the tort of negligence. In so doing, it will be necessary to reinterpret the language of the section, and to hold that the "fiction of fraud" imports only the elements of the cause of action of tort of deceit, and not all aspects of the claim (such as all rules relating to the measure of remedy). That is, when the statute says:

> "if the person making the misrepresentation would be liable to damages in respect thereof had the misrepresentation been made fraudulently, that person shall be so liable notwithstanding that the misrepresentation was not made fraudulently"

the words "so liable" refer only to a liability in damages, without necessarily importing the consequence that the liability is identical to a claim in deceit.[136] It must be said that such a reinterpretation will produce a new reading which is at variance with what the draftsman intended, and it is not without consequential difficulties.[137] But it would remove a clear anomaly in this area of the law of misrepresentation.

---

exercise of judgment, a misrepresentation should not too easily be found", whereas if *Royscot Trust Ltd v Rogerson* should one day be overruled, "then there would be nothing to be said against adopting a more closely focused approach to the proof of misrepresentation": at [200]–[201]; *Raiffeisen Zentralbank Österreich A.G. v Royal Bank of Scotland Plc*, above, n.134 at [85] (see also at [387]); *cf. Cassa di Risparmio della Repubblica di San Marino S.p.A. v Barclays Bank Ltd* [2011] EWHC 484 (Comm), [2011] All E.R. (D) 189 (Mar) at [223] (Hamblen J.: "this is questionable in principle. The fact that Parliament (as interpreted by the Court of Appeal) has thought it right to provide a broad measure of compensation where a contract has been made as a result of a misrepresentation should not affect the prior question whether there has been a misrepresentation"; but the Judge did consider that there is a real possibility of *Royscot* being overruled: *ibid.*; *Cheltenham BC v Laird* [2009] EWHC 1253 (QB), [2009] I.R.L.R. 621 at [524]). In *Forest International Gaskets Ltd v Fosters Marketing Ltd* [2005] EWCA Civ 700 CA refused permission to appeal in a case where only £28,500 was at issue, and which could only be decided by HL because CA would be bound by *Royscot*; and Tuckey L.J. at [15]–[16] doubted whether HL would necessarily overrule *Royscot*.

136 *Cheltenham BC v Laird* [2009] EWHC 1253 (QB), [2009] I.R.L.R. 621 at [524]. For the alternative interpretation of "so liable" see the judgment of Eveleigh L.J. in *Chesneau v Interhome Ltd*, quoted above, para.7–32.

137 For example, will the directors' liability, on which s.2(1) was modelled, also be similarly reinterpreted?

In the following discussion of the detailed rules for damages under section 2(1) it will be necessary to refer to the rules for the tort of deceit since, on the authorities as they stand, that is the current point of reference for the statutory remedy. However, any relevant differences in the rules for the tort of negligence will be noted.

Proof of loss. Damages are awarded under section 2(1) to compensate the claimant's loss. There is no definition of "loss" in the statute but it can be assumed that, as in the torts of both deceit[138] and negligence,[139] recoverable loss will extend not only to economic loss but also to damage to property, loss of property, physical injury and to some forms of intangible loss. But if the claimant cannot establish loss, he has no claim for damages under the statute. Although in a claim in the tort of deceit the courts are reluctant to conclude that no loss flowed from a fraud which achieved its end of inducing the claimant's reliance on the fraudulent misrepresentation,[140] that approach is there adopted precisely because of the defendant's fraud and, even if damages under section 2(1) are to be measured on the same basis as for fraud, it is not appropriate for the courts to adopt this approach identifying the claimant's losses under the statute since the defendant was not in fact fraudulent. 7–34

Scope of recoverable loss. Under the statute the claim arises 7–35

> "Where a person has entered into a contract after a misrepresentation has been made to him by another party thereto and as a result thereof he has suffered loss."

The scope of the recoverable loss depends upon the interpretation of these words in the section. In particular, to what do the words "as a result thereof" refer? The contract? Or the misrepresentation? This is a very significant issue, since it is a point on which the torts of deceit and negligence diverge. In a case of deceit where the representee's reliance consists of his entering into a contract, the claimant will recover the losses which he suffers as a result of entering into the contract, and the recoverable loss is not limited to

138 Above, para.5–36.
139 Above, paras 6–18, 6–62.
140 Above, para.5–36.

that part of the loss which flows from the fact that the statement was false.[141] But in the tort of negligence it has become established in recent years that the claimant will recover only such loss as he can show falls within the scope of the defendant's duty which he claims to have been broken; and so if the duty was only to take care in giving accurate information, the recoverable loss is limited to that which flows from the information being inaccurate, and does not extend, for example, to other losses which flow from his entering into the contract.[142] Perhaps the most natural reading of the section would be that the recoverable loss is that which the claimant suffers "as a result" of his having "entered into a contract"—that is, the approach in the modern cases in deceit.[143] This is not surprising, since the drafting of the section was based on the assumption that it was creating a remedy analogous to deceit, not negligence.[144] If, therefore, the House of Lords in the future wishes to bring the remedy under section 2(1) more closely into line with that in the tort of negligence, it will have to consider whether the section should instead be interpreted as allowing damages for only the loss which flows from the misrepresentation.[145]

7–36 **Timing of valuation.** There is no rigid rule about the time of valuation of the claimant's loss. Where the loss can be quantified as soon as it is suffered, that will normally be the appropriate time to value it. For example, it is well established in claims at common

---

[141] Above, para.5–37.

[142] Above, para.6–55.

[143] It was assumed by Rix J. in *Avon Insurance Plc v Swire Fraser Ltd*, above, n.123 at [201]–[202] that the fraud rule applies in this respect, on the authority of *Royscot Trust Ltd v Rogerson*, above, n.121. In *Davis & Co. (Wines) Ltd v Afa-Minerva (E.M.I.) Ltd* [1974] 2 Lloyd's Rep. 27 at 33 Judge Fay had, however, assumed that the recoverable loss was that which flowed from the *misrepresentation*.

[144] Above, para.7–16.

[145] Above, para.7–33. In *Smith New Court Securities Ltd v Scrimgeour Vickers (Asset Management) Ltd*, above, n.125 at 279–282 Lord Steyn attributed the rule relating to the losses flowing from the transaction, rather than from the misrepresentation, to the difference in principle between deceit and negligence (and therefore the wider rule applying to deceit on account of the defendant's fraud). Since the claim under s.2(1) is in essence for negligence, it is likely that the House would wish to interpret it as carrying the negligence rule in this respect, rather than the deceit rule.

law[146] that where a claimant purchases defective property in reliance on inaccurate information provided by the defendant, his loss accrues at the moment of acquisition, and that the damages are to be valued by the difference between the market value of the property without the defects and its actual value with the defects at the date as of purchase. So, for example, where the contract into which the claimant enters following the misrepresentation is a contract of purchase which embodies the claimant's loss, one would expect the starting-point to be to assess the loss at the time of the contract. But a court may, where appropriate, take a later date in order properly to compensate the claimant's loss. In *Naughton v O'Callaghan*,[147] for example, the claimant purchased a racehorse for 26,000 guineas in reliance on a misrepresentation about its pedigree; the truth was discovered only two years later, by which time the value of the horse was only £1,500—not because of any general fall in the market value of racehorses, but because the particular horse had failed to win races and so had been shown not to be a valuable racehorse. In a claim under section 2(1) it was held that the claimant's loss should be valued not at the time of the contract[148] but later, when the misrepresentation was discovered.[149] The claimant's decision to keep the horse and race it was precisely what the sellers would have expected,[150] and the loss which flowed from keeping it and later discovering the misrepresentation (taking into account therefore the diminished value of the horse, together with consequential costs of training and keeping the horse up to the time when the misrepresentation was discovered) was a proper measure of the claimant's loss.[151]

---

146 Above, paras 5–37 (deceit), 6–57 (negligence).

147 [1990] 3 All E.R. 191.

148 Which was said to be only the prima facie rule: *ibid.*, at 196.

149 And so the award was for the difference between the price paid (26,000 guineas) and the then actual value (£1,500). Consequential damages were also awarded: below, para.7–38.

150 Where the contract is for the purchase of a commodity which can be expected to be sold on, such as shares or other financial instruments, it is unlikely that a date other than that of the contract will be taken for valuation of the loss: *Naughton v O'Callaghan*, above, n.147 at 196, citing *Waddell v Blockey* (1879) 4 Q.B.D. 678 (contract for purchase of rupee paper: claim in deceit).

151 For the application of this in the tort of deceit, see *Smith New Court Securities Ltd v Scimgeour Vickers (Asset Management) Ltd*, above, n.125; above, para.5–37. Where the change in the value of the loss results from fluctuations in *market value*, the loss may not generally be recoverable; in

Where a claimant suffers recoverable loss only after the time of the contract,[152] or where there is continuing consequential loss[153] after the time of the contract, it is of course possible to value the loss only after it has arisen.

7–37 **Causation.** The normal principles of causation will apply, and so the claimant must show a sufficient causal link between the misrepresentation (or, rather,[154] the contract into which he entered in reliance on the misrepresentation) and the loss which he claims to have suffered as a result of reliance on it. This is a question of fact; and the test used in other contexts[155] will also be used here: the judge will ask whether the claimant's reliance on the representation in entering into the contract was a substantial factor in producing the loss, or whether in common sense terms there is a sufficient causal connection.[156] The defendant will not however be liable for losses caused by a *novus actus interveniens*—where on general principles there was a break in the chain of causation, typically an

negligence such loss is not generally recoverable unless the risk of market fluctuations is undertaken by the defendant within the scope of his duty: above, para.6–55. And in *Naughton v O'Callaghan*, above, n.147 at 198, Waller J. emphasised that the loss was not due to a general fall in the market in racehorses.

152 *Royscot Trust Ltd v Rogerson*, above, n.121 at 308 (misrepresentation by car dealer to hire-purchase financing company about price of car and value of customer's deposit; loss not at date of contract, when it might have been zero since the car sold by dealer to finance company was then worth the amount paid, but later, when customer wrongfully sold the car without paying the sum due under the contract).

153 Below, para.7–38.

154 On the assumption, as the law currently stands, that the deceit test is used for the scope of recoverable loss: above, para.7–35. But the claimant will already have established that he relied on the statement in entering into the contract (above, para.7–19) and so there will in any event be a causal link from the statement to the loss which flows from the contract.

155 e.g. the tort of deceit: above, para.5–38.

156 *Davis & Co. (Wines) Ltd v Afa-Minerva (EMI) Ltd*, above, n.143 at 33 (misrepresentation by company installing burglar alarm about how it would ring on break-in: damage caused by initial break-in not caused by the misrepresentation, but consequential losses (loss of stock, etc.), which resulted from the burglars not being deterred by inadquate alarm after the initial break-in, were recoverable). For difficulties in using a test of "common sense", see above, para.5–38, n.164.

extraneous and unforeseeable event in the causal chain for which the defendant cannot be held responsible.[157]

Remoteness of damage. It is in the context of the rules of remoteness of damage that the link between the claim under section 2(1) and the tort of deceit has been firmly established at the level of the Court of Appeal. In *Royscot Trust Ltd v Rogerson*[158] that court held that the language of the section was clear; it imported the remedy in damages which applies in the tort of deceit, and this carries with it the liability to make reparation for all the actual damage directly flowing from the fraudulent inducement.[159] This contrasts with the rule in the tort of negligence, where the defendant is liable only for losses of a kind which he could reasonable have foreseen at the time he committed his breach of duty.[160] On the facts of *Royscot* it was not necessary to hold that the deceit rule applied, in order to find the defendant liable for the losses claimed, since it was held that the losses were in fact reasonably foreseeable.[161] But the decision, although only of a two-judge Court of Appeal,[162] was clear on the technical answer to the remoteness rule under the statute, and it is probably correct in the sense that it is what the draftsman had in mind.[163] 7–38

The remoteness rule is perhaps the rule relating to damages which highlights most clearly the difference in principle between the appropriate measure of recovery in cases of deceit and negligence. The reason for a wider test of remoteness in deceit is precisely because of the defendant's fraud: "it does not lie in the mouth of the fraudulent person to say that [the losses] could not reasonably have been foreseen".[164] But to hold that this is the appropriate measure of damages under section 2(1) is to "treat a

[157] *Royscot Trust Ltd v Rogerson*, above, n.121 at 307 (Balcombe L.J.). The reasonable foreseeability by the defendant of the event alleged to constitute a *novus actus interveniens* is here relevant, as in all such cases, even though foreseeability is not the test for remoteness of damage: *ibid*.

[158] Above, n.121.

[159] For this rule in the tort of deceit, see above, para.5–40.

[160] Above, para.6–56.

[161] Above, n.121 at 308, 309.

[162] Balcombe and Ralph Gibson L.JJ.

[163] Above, para.7–16; J. Cartwright, "Damages for Misrepresentation", above, n.116.

[164] *Doyle v Olby (Ironmongers) Ltd*, above, n.133 at 167; *Smith New Court Securities Ltd v Scrimgeour Vickers (Asset Management) Ltd*, above, n.125 at

person who was morally innocent as if he was guilty of fraud when it comes to the measure of damages",[165] and it is likely that the Supreme Court will seek to reinterpret the section to allow it to hold that the measure of damages should be the same as in the tort of negligence, rather than the tort of deceit.[166]

7–39 **Mitigation.** The normal rules of mitigation apply to claims under section 2(1), as in other claims for damages in tort[167]: the claimant will be unable to recover from the defendant any part of his loss which he would not have suffered if he had taken such steps as he ought reasonably to have taken in order to avoid or reduce his loss. Since the test of mitigation depends on what a reasonable person in the claimant's position would have done, the duty to mitigate should only arise when the claimant knows that the defendant has made a misrepresentation, and so is in a position to decide how to respond to its consequences. And even if the action taken by a claimant in properly attempting to mitigate his loss in fact results in the loss being increased, that additional loss will still be recoverable.[168]

264–265, 281–282; J. Cartwright, "Remoteness of Damage in Contract and Tort: a Reconsideration" [1996] C.L.J. 488 at pp.508–510.

165 *Smith New Court Securities Ltd v Scrimgeour Vickers (Asset Management) Ltd*, above, n.125 at 283 (Lord Steyn). See also *Kuwait Airways Corp. v Iraqi Airways Co. (Nos 4 and 5)* [2002] UKHL 19, [2002] 2 A.C. 883 at [101] ("The more culpable the defendant the wider the area of loss of which he can fairly be held responsible": Lord Nicholls of Birkenhead, referring to the discussion by Lord Steyn in *Smith New Court*).

166 Above, para.7–33. Textbook writers and other academic writers strongly favour such a reinterpretation: see, e.g. R. Hooley, "Damages and the Misrepresentation Act 1967" (1991) 107 L.Q.R. 547; I. Brown and A. Chandler, "Deceit, Damages and the Misrepresentation Act 1967, s.2(1)" [1992] L.M.C.L.Q. 40; J. Wadsley, "Measures in Misrepresentation: Recent Steps in Awarding Damages" (1992) 55 M.L.R. 698; McGregor, paras 41.047–41.048.

167 Pleas of mitigation were rejected on the facts in *Cemp Properties (UK) Ltd v Dentsply Research & Development Corp. (No.2)* [1989] 36 E.G. 90 and *Bridgegrove Ltd v Smith*, above, n.124 (representees induced to take lease by misrepresentation as to suitability of premises for their business purposes; reasonable for them to carry on the business under monthly tenancy after expiry of lease, and so to continue to make losses, because they found themselves locked into their position and had no resources to move to new suitable premises elsewhere).

168 *Cemp Properties (UK) Ltd v Dentsply Research & Development Corp. (No.2)* [1989] 27 E.G. 126 at 133 (misrepresentation by vendor to property developer as

Lost potential profits. In an action under section 2(1) a claimant cannot recover damages based on the profits that he would have made if the representation had been true: that is the normal measure of damages in contract, not tort.[169] But if he can show that his financial position at the time of assessment is reduced by virtue of the fact that, had he not been misled by the representation, he would in the mean time have used his money, time and energy to make other profits, those hypothetical lost profits (which must be pleaded and proved) are in principle recoverable.[170] And even though the contract into which the claimant was induced to enter in reliance on the defendant's misrepresentation was ultimately profitable, that does not mean that he has no recoverable loss under section 2(1), if he can show that the profit was less than that which he would have made had the misrepresentation not been made.[171] 7–40

Damages for intangible losses. The losses which may be claimed in an action under section 2(1) may extend to intangible losses, such as distress and inconvenience. Although there does not appear to be 7–41

to availability of deeds disclosing neighbouring owners' rights to light and air; on discovery of rights, developer refused (reasonably) to pay £75,000 to neighbouring owners to release rights, thinking it could deal with the issue at a lower cost, although it then incurred costs of £150,000 in redesign and delay of development). If the claimant's conduct was an unreasonable reaction to the predicament in which he found himself, losses caused by that reaction might be irrecoverable on the basis that the conduct broke the chain of causation: *South Australia Asset Management Corp. v York Montague Ltd*, above, n.125 at 218–219; *Bridgegrove Ltd v Smith*, above, n.124 (no break in causation on facts, because representee's conduct was reasonable).

[169] Above, paras 2–08 to 2–09.

[170] *Dodd v Crown Estate Commissioners* [1995] E.G.C.S. 35 (award in respect of loss of use of capital due to delay in building project as a result of defendant's misrepresentation). For a similar principle in the torts of deceit and negligence, see above, paras 5–39, 6–58.

[171] *Cemp Properties (UK) Ltd v Dentsply Research & Development Corp. (No.2)* [1989] 36 E.G. 90 at 98 (Morritt J: "wasted expenditure is still wasted even if the project produces a profit at the end of the day"). Credit must, however, be given for any additional profit which is made by the claimant as a result of action taken in response to the predicament in which he is placed by reason of the defendant's misrepresentation: [1989] 37 E.G. 126 at 132–133. In deceit, see *Clef Aquitaine S.A.R.L. v Laporte Materials (Barrow) Ltd* [2001] Q.B. 488, CA (claimant induced by misrepresentation to enter into profitable contract, but could claim damages based on the different and *more* profitable transaction into which it would have entered but for the fraud).

direct authority in cases decided under the statute, intangible losses can be claimed both in the tort of deceit and in the tort of negligence. However, the courts have been more reluctant to award such damages in the tort of negligence, and have limited them to the distress or inconvenience caused by the *physical* consequences of the defendant's breach of duty.[172] It is arguable that in dealing with claims under section 2(1), which is in essence a claim for negligent misrepresentation,[173] the courts will seek to take an approach which approximates more to the more restrictive approach in the tort of negligence.

7–42 **Damages are compensatory.** Damages under section 2(1) are designed only to compensate the claimant's losses. Even if the damages under the section are to follow the tort of deceit,[174] this should not result in exemplary damages being awarded in a claim under the statute. Although exemplary damages can in principle be awarded for any tort, the criteria for such an award will not generally be satisfied in the case of a defendant liable under section 2(1).[175]

7–43 **Contribution between co-defendants.** Where a representee is liable under section 2(1) jointly or severally with another defendant for damage suffered by the claimant, whether the co-defendant's liability is also under the statute or is based on some other cause of action such as negligence, deceit or breach of contract, the court will, as in all cases of joint or several liability, have jurisdiction under the Civil Liability (Contribution) Act 1978 to apportion between the co-defendants the damages payable.[176]

---

172 Above, para.6–62. For the apparently wider scope of recovery in deceit, see above, para.5–44.

173 Above, para.7–24.

174 Above para.7–31.

175 Exemplary damages are awarded in two categories of case: where there has been oppressive, arbitrary or unconstitutional action by the servants of the Government; and where the defendant's conduct was calculated by him to make a profit for himself which may well exceed the compensation payable to the claimant: *Kuddus v Chief Constable of Leicestershire Constabulary* [2001] UKHL 29, [2002] 2 A.C. 122. *Cf.* the tort of deceit: above, para.5–42 and the tort of negligence: above, para.6–61.

176 Above, para.2–14.

(5) Relationship to Other Remedies for Misrepresentation

The claim under section 2(1) belongs amongst the remedies in tort. The remedy under the section is damages measured on the tort basis.[177] It therefore belongs within the tort remedies in the overall scheme of remedies for misrepresentation, and the advantages and disadvantages of the tort remedies in general will apply—so, as in other tort claims, the claimant must choose whether this measure of remedy rather than, say, damages calculated on the contract measure, will best compensate his loss; but as a tort remedy in damages, the claim under the statute will be available concurrently with a claim for rescission of the contract.[178] 7–44

Comparison with the tort of negligence. Although the section does not use the word "negligence", the claim for damages under section 2(1) is, in substance, a claim for damages for negligent misrepresentation.[179] The obvious point of reference for the statutory claim amongst the other remedies is therefore the clam for damages in the tort of negligence. However, the remedy is not identical to that awarded in the tort of negligence, but, at least on the authorities as they currently stand, is more closely linked to the tort of deceit.[180] Since there will be cases where a claimant has the choice between a claim under the statute and a claim in negligence, it is necessary to be clear about the points of comparison between the two remedies. Where the claimant has such a choice it is generally to his advantage to pursue the remedy under the statute.[181] 7–45

The concurrence of claims under the statute and in negligence. The circumstances in which claims under section 2(1) and in negligence will be concurrently available to a claimant are defined by reference to the availability of the statutory claim: that is, only where the parties to the action are also principal parties to a contract; and where the misrepresentation which founds the claim was made to the claimant (or his agent) by or on behalf of the 7–46

---

[177] Above, para.7–32.
[178] Above, para.2–12. For cumulation of rescission and a claim under s.2(1), see *Archer v Brown* [1985] Q.B. 401 at 415.
[179] Above, para.7–24.
[180] Above, para.7–33.
[181] *Cemp Properties (UK) Ltd v Dentsply Research & Development Corp. (No.1)* [1989] 2 E.G.L.R. 192 at 196.

defendant and was relied on by the claimant in entering into the contract.[182] The tort of negligence is not restricted to pre-contractual misrepresentations, but applies in any context where a duty of care is owed by one person towards another under the principles described in Chapter 6. Where, therefore, the statute does not apply, the claimant must seek to establish a duty of care in the tort of negligence: for example, where the defendant's statement was made outside the contractual context altogether[183]; or in the context of contractual negotiations but where no contract resulted; or where it was made by one contracting party to the other during the course of performance of the contract, rather than during the negotiations for the contract and as an inducement to enter it; or where, though the statement was made during negotiations which resulted in a contract, it was made by an agent of the contracting party and the claimant seeks to hold the agent personally responsible.[184]

But a duty of care can be owed by one contracting party to the other in making statements during the pre-contractual negotiations.[185] This is therefore the point of concurrence of the two remedies. Indeed, where the Act applies there will generally also be a concurrent duty of care in the tort of negligence, since the relationship between the negotiating parties will normally give rise to a duty of care under the general principles of the tort in relation

[182] Above, para.7–05.

[183] *Hedley Byrne & Co. Ltd v Heller & Partners Ltd* [1964] A.C. 465, HL (non-contractual credit reference).

[184] Above, para.7–09.

[185] *Esso v Mardon* [1976] Q.B. 801, CA, was the first case to settle this; above, para.6–28. At the time when the Misrepresentation Act 1967 was enacted it had therefore not yet been established that the tort of negligence could impose liability between contracting parties in respect of pre-contractual representations. *Hedley Byrne & Co. Ltd v Heller & Partners Ltd*, above, n.183 was a recent decision which seems still generally to have been assumed to apply only where there was no contract: see, e.g. the speeches in the Second Reading debate in the House of Lords on the Misrepresentation Bill: *Hansard*, HL Vol.274, cols 921, 923 (Lord Gardiner L.C.: damages at common law only if fraud), 930 (Viscount Colville of Culross). Lord Reid, who had sat in *Hedley Byrne*, did not mention it during the debate (at 932–939); only Lord Wilberforce (at 950) noted the development of the tort of negligence. But this view of the need for the new Act to fill a gap in the remedies for pre-contractual misrepresentations may be a consequence of the timing of events: the Act was designed to implement the Tenth Report of the Law Reform Committee, above, para.7–04, which had made its recommendations in 1962 before the developments in *Hedley Byrne*.

to a statement made by one with a view to inducing the other to enter into the contract.[186] But in most such cases it will be simpler and, indeed, more advantageous in terms of the remedy he may obtain for the claimant to pursue the remedy under the statute. The points relevant to this analysis have been explained in detail earlier in this chapter in their relevant contexts, but are here summarised again for convenience.

Advantages of a claim under section 2(1).[187] The elements of a claim under section 2(1)[188] are simpler for the claimant to establish than the elements of a claim in the tort of negligence.[189] Under the statute, he has the burden of proving matters which are factual and relatively easy to establish: the misrepresentation, the contract which followed it, the loss and that the defendant intended him to rely on it and his actual reliance on it. But even the more difficult of these—the defendant's intention and the claimant's reliance—are not in practice difficult to prove.[190] The burden is not on the claimant to show any wrongful state of mind or failure to take care on the part of the defendant; it is for the defendant to establish his honest and reasonable belief in his statement, which is an onerous burden.[191] By contrast, the claimant in the tort of negligence must show that the defendant owed him a duty of care, failed to take care and that the breach of duty caused him loss. In the context of pre-contractual misrepresentations it may not be difficult to establish a duty of care[192]; and the loss must be shown here, just as in a claim under the statute. But it is clearly more onerous for the claimant to establish the breach of duty—the defendant's failure to take care in making the statement. And it can have a substantively different result from a concurrent claim under the statute, since in a **7–47**

186 *Gran Gelato Ltd v Richcliff (Group) Ltd* [1992] Ch.560; above, para.7–27 (the concurrence is essential for the application of the defence of contributory negligence to a claim under the Act). On the general principles for the establishment of a duty of care in negligence, see Ch.6.

187 *Inntrepreneur Pub Co. (C.P.C.) v Sweeney* [2002] EWHC 1060, [2002] 2 E.G.L.R. 132 at [59] (Park J.).

188 Above, para.7–03.

189 Above, para.6–12.

190 Above, paras 7–18, 7–19. These two elements are incorporated by the "fiction of fraud".

191 Above, para.7–25.

192 Above, para.6–28.

case where there is doubt whether the defendant took sufficient care in checking his statement it is possible for him to be held liable under the statute but not in the tort of negligence.[193] In general, then, a claimant is likely to prefer a claim under section 2(1) where it is available.[194]

Once a claim is established, it can happen that the measure of recovery under the statute is more extensive than in negligence on the assumption that, at least in certain respects, the rules for damages in deceit have been incorporated by the "fiction of fraud" in section 2(1).[195] In particular, the scope of recoverable loss may be more extensive under the statute, and not limited (as in negligence) to the loss within the scope of the duty of care[196]; and the rule of remoteness of damage may be wider, so as to allow recovery of all losses caused by the claimant's reliance on the statement, rather than restricting recovery to losses of a kind which the defendant could reasonably have foreseen.[197] However, it is clear that the courts are not prepared to import all consequences of the "fiction of fraud" and so, for example, the defence of contributory negligence can be raised against a claim under section 2(1) although it is not available as a defence to a claim in deceit.[198]

7–48 **Proposed new remedy for misleading commercial practices.** The Law Commission has provisionally proposed the introduction of new forms of redress for consumers in respect of misleading commercial practices by traders, including a remedy in damages which would overlap significantly with section 2(1) of the Misrepresentation Act 1967.[199] The proposed reform would provide

---

193 *Howard Marine & Dredging Co. Ltd v A. Ogden & Sons (Excavations) Ltd* [1978] Q.B. 574, CA at 598 (Bridge L.J.; Lord Denning M.R. at 592, 593 held there was no liability on either basis; Shaw L.J. at 601 held the defendant liable both in negligence and under the statute).

194 However, a claim under the statute might sometimes be barred by limitation (above, para.7–28) or under Lord Tenterden's Act (above, para.7–30), when a claim in negligence is still available.

195 Above, para.7–33. For doubts about whether the authorities on this will survive scrutiny in the Supreme Court, however, see *ibid.*

196 Above, para.7–35.

197 Above, para.7–38.

198 Above, para.7–27; *cf.* para.5–31 (deceit).

199 Law Com. Consultation Paper No.199, *Consumer Redress for Misleading and Aggressive Practices* (2011). For the proposed "right to unwind", which would overlap with the remedy of rescission, see above, para.4–05, n.16.

limited civil remedies for breach of the Consumer Protection from Unfair Trading Regulations 2008,[200] which prohibits unfair commercial practices, including representations made by traders which are directly connected with the promotion, sale or supply of products to or from consumers, and which contain false information or whose overall presentation in any way deceives or is likely to deceive the average consumer in relation to a range of relevant matters, and cause or are likely to cause the average consumer to take a transactional decision he would not have taken otherwise.[201] The proposal is not that all breaches of the Regulations should give rise to civil redress,[202] but that damages should be awarded to cover indirect economic losses, and for distress and inconvenience, suffered by a consumer who enters into a contract with a trader whose misleading commercial practice (including express and certain implied misrepresentations) was a significant factor in the consumer's decision to enter the contract. Against claims for damages, the trader would have the same due diligence defence as is available to a criminal charge under the Regulations.[203]

The Law Commission acknowledges that the proposed new Act would cover substantially the same ground as the 1967 Act in the more limited areas to which it would apply (business-to-consumer transactions[204]), but prefers to retain the existing Act unamended whilst expecting that consumers would opt for the simpler solution of suing under the new Act.[205] It remains to be seen what becomes of these provisional proposals, which were published for general public consultation during 2011. However, if they are eventually enacted along the lines of the current proposals, they will not only further complicate the remedial picture in the law of

[200] SI 2008/1277, implementing the Unfair Commercial Practices Directive 2005/29/EC; see below, para.7–72.

[201] *ibid.*, regs 2(1), 3(1), (4)(a), 5. The offence is charged under reg.9, and is subject to a due diligence defence under reg.17.

[202] In particular, there should be no remedy for breach of the general prohibition on unfair commercial practices which contravene the requirements of professional diligence under reg.3(3) (Consultation Paper No.199, above, n.199, paras 10.68–10.73), nor should traders be liable for misleading omissions under reg.6 (para.13.70), nor would the Act imposing civil redress make use of the list of 31 banned misleading practices under the Sch.1 of the Regulations (para.13.81).

[203] Above, n.200.

[204] It is also proposed to exclude land transactions and financial services: Law Com. Consultation Paper No.199, above, n.199, paras 13.52 to 13.62.

[205] *ibid.*, paras 13.121 to 13.124.

misrepresentation,[206] but they could have broader significance in the general practice of the law. There would be a certain parallel with the experience in other jurisdictions[207] such as Australia, where section 52 of the Trade Practices Act 1974,[208] by providing that a person must "not, in trade or commerce, engage in conduct that is misleading or deceptive or is likely to mislead or deceive", has established a general norm of conduct governing commercial behaviour and has had a very great impact on the general law of contract, since it also provides remedies for breach of this norm, and a claim under the statute is included in most claims against businesses which would formerly have been governed by the law of misrepresentation alone.[209] New Zealand has adopted a similar provision in section 9 of its Fair Trading Act 1986, and with a similar effect, although there is a specific and generous statutory remedial scheme for misrepresentations which many claimants still prefer to use.[210] The English proposals are more modest, since they are limited to the protection of consumers and the remedial regime

---

[206] In spite of the fact that the Law Commission claims that a major purpose of its reforms is to simplify the current law of misrepresentation which is too complicated for consumers to use: see, e.g. ibid., paras 1.5(1), 1.9, 1.19, 1.21.

[207] The Law Commission considered lessons from other jurisdictions in Pt 11 of its Consultation Paper.

[208] The 1974 Act has been renamed: see now s.18 of the Australian Consumer Law, Sch.2 to the Competition and Consumer Act 2010. There are also corresponding provisions in State and Territory Fair Trading Acts; and although the supply of financial services is excluded from the federal Trade Practices Act, there is an equivalent provision in the Australian Securities and Investments Commission Act 2001 to cover misleading and other conduct by persons in relation to financial services: Seddon and Ellinghaus, para.11.102.

[209] Carter, Peden and Tolhurst, Ch.19, esp. para.19–01 (the legislation has had "a quite dramatic impact on the general law of contract, such that the possibility of remedies based on s.52 must be considered in practically any commercial litigation based on contractual disputes"); Seddon and Ellinghaus, paras 11.102 to 11.136, esp. para.11.104 ("This section (a mere 23 words long) has transformed the law of misrepresentation and, more generally, Australian commercial law"). See also Harland, "The Statutory Prohibition of Misleading or Deceptive Conduct in Australia and its Impact on the Law of Contract" (1995) 111 L.Q.R. 100.

[210] Burrows, Finn & Todd, para.11.3.1, noting that Contractual Remedies Act 1979 s.6 (innocent or fraudulent misrepresentation inducing entry into a contract: damages as if the representation were a term of the contract, i.e. as if it were true, and displacing claim to damages in deceit or negligence) gives a different balance to the picture when compared with Australia.

would be more narrowly circumscribed.[211] However, in cases involving consumers it would be likely that the new remedy would be a focus for development of the law of misrepresentation.

III. SPECIFIC LIABILITIES

(1) Financial Services and Markets Act 2000, Section 90

Liabilities in respect of statements in prospectuses and listing particulars.[212] Section 90 of the Financial Services and Markets Act 2000 imposes liability in damages in respect of untrue or misleading statements, and the omission of matters required to be included,[213] in documents—prospectuses and listing particulars—issued in support of the public issue of a company's securities.[214] 7–49

---

[211] The Australian and New Zealand provisions provide for a general remedy for loss or damage suffered by conduct in contravention of the prohibition on misleading or deceptive conduct, as well as a range of other orders including rescission and variation of the contract. The Queensland Fair Trading Act is (alone) limited to consumers; Seddon and Ellinghaus, paras 11.103, 11.105.

[212] For a similar liability regime in respect of statements in scheme particulars which must be submitted and published by the manager of an authorised unit trust scheme, see s.248. For further discussion of the liabilities in respect of listing particulars or prospectuses, see Gore-Browne, Ch.43; G. Morse and others (ed.), *Palmer's Company Law* (25th edn, 1992 looseleaf), Pt 5. For a general account of the law and practice of the public offering of securities and the production of listing particulars and prospectuses, see Gore-Browne, Pt IX.

[213] In this chapter only untrue and misleading statements are considered. For liability for the omission of matters required to be included in the listing particulars or prospectus, see below, paras 17–43 *et seq.*

[214] An offer of certain "transferable securities" may not be made to the public in the UK, nor may request be made to have such securities listed on on a regulated market in the UK, unless a prospectus, approved by the "competent authority" has been published: Financial Services and Markets Act 2000, s.85, as replaced by the Prospectus Regulations 2005 (SI 2005/1433). For the time being, the functions of the "competent authority" in the UK are exercised by the Financial Services Authority, although this may be changed by the Treasury by statutory instrument: s.72, Sch.8. In June 2011 the Government published a White Paper, *A new approach to financial regulation: the blueprint for reform* (Cm.8083), together with a draft Bill, which proposes to re-structure financial regulation and would rename the Financial Services Authority the "Financial Conduct Authority" and redefine its role and duties as one of the new regulators; the Financial Conduct Authority would become the "competent authority" for the purposes of the 2000 Act.

The competent authority may also in listing rules require listing particulars to be approved and published before other securities are listed: s.79. Prospectuses approved by the competent authorities of other EEA States are treated as equivalent as long as certain conditions are satisfied: s.87H (inserted by the Prospectus Regulations 2005). The form and content of listing particulars and prospectuses are to be specified in listing rules and prospectus rules made by the competent authority: ss.73A, 79(2); 84(1) (as amended by the Prospectus Regulations 2005), and in many respects the listing rules require listing particulars to follow the corresponding requirements for prospectuses in the prospectus rules: see the listing rules, para.4.2. Many of the detailed requirements of the contents of prospectuses are however fixed by reference to the Prospectus Directive Regulation 2004/809, so as to provide common Europe-wide standards: prospectus rules, App.3. Up-to-date copies of the listing rules and the prospectus rules, and information about the exercise by the Financial Services Authority of its functions as competent authority, can be found on the Authority's web site: *http://www.fsa.gov.uk*.

S.90 applies only to prospectuses and listing particulars which are issued prior to listing: *Hall v Cable & Wireless Plc* [2009] EWHC 1793 (Comm), [2010] 1 B.C.L.C. 95 at [20]. The Companies Act 2006 ss.1270, implementing the Transparency Obligations Directive (2004/109/EC), introduced s.90A into the Financial Services and Markets Act 2000 in order to impose civil liability on the issuer for loss caused by reliance on information required to be provided from time to time by issuers already admitted to trading on certain regulated markets where a person discharging managerial responsibilities within the issuer in relation to the publication knew that, or was reckless whether, the statements made were untrue or misleading, or knew an omission from published information was a dishonest concealment of a material fact: Gower and Davies, *Principles of Modern Company Law* (8th edn, 2008), para.26–11; Gore-Browne, para.43[11]. S.90A was replaced by a new s.90A and Sch.10A by the Financial Services and Markets Act 2000 (Liability of Issuers) Regulations 2010 (SI 2010/1192), which widens the potential liability of issuers in relation to both the range of securities (nearly all UK and many overseas quoted companies) and the range of information provided (all official announcements, not just those concerning financial information); but it does not apply to information in respect of which the issuer is liable under s.90: Sch.10A, para.4; see generally Gore-Browne, paras 43[10] to 43[12C]. The scope of s.90A is significantly narrower than s.90 in that it applies only to the issuer, and covers only fraudulent statements and omissions. It is doubtful, however, whether the common law would impose liability for loss suffered in reliance on information to which s.90A applies, either in the tort of deceit (because no sufficient intention that the claimant would rely) or in the tort of negligence (duty of care unlikely in the light of the decision in *Caparo Industries Plc v Dickman* [1990] 2 A.C. 605, HL (above, para.6–33) in relation to auditors): Gower and Davies, para.26–11.

History of the liabilities.[215] These provisions can be traced back to the Directors Liability Act 1890, which was enacted to reverse the decision in *Derry v Peek*.[216] The House of Lords had there held, in a claim for damages in deceit by a person who subscribed for shares in reliance on a misrepresentation in a prospectus issued by directors of the company, that the tort of deceit required fraud and did not impose liability on a director who was honest in his belief that his statement was true but held that belief without reasonable grounds. The Directors Liability Act made no change to the requirements of the tort of deceit, but, for the particular context of company prospectuses or notices inviting persons to subscribe for shares or debentures, provided[217] that directors and others with responsibility for the prospectus or notice should be liable to pay compensation to all who subscribe on the faith of the prospectus or notice for loss or damage they may have sustained by reason of any untrue statement in it, unless one of certain specific defences[218] could be proved. In that context, the claimant needed no longer to prove the defendant's fraud. **7–50**

The provisions of the Directors Liability Act 1890 were reproduced in later successive Companies Acts, and ultimately in

[215] *Possfund Custodian Trustee Ltd v Diamond* [1996] 1 W.L.R. 1351 at 1358–1361.

[216] (1889) L.R. 14 App. Cas. 337, HL above, para.5–14.

[217] s.3.

[218] (1) That (a) (in the case of a statement not purporting to be made on the authority of an expert, of a public official document or statement) the director had reasonable ground to believe and did up to the time of the allotment of shares or debentures believe that the statement was true; and (b) (in the case of a statement purporting to be a statement by or an extract from an expert's report) the statement fairly represented the expert's statement unless it could be proved that the director had no reasonable ground to believe that the expert was competent to make the statement; and (c) (in the case of a statement purporting to be a statement by or an extract from a public official document) the statement correctly and fairly represented the official statement; or (2) the defendant withdrew his consent to being a director before the prospectus was issued and the prospectus was issued without his authority or consent; or (3) the prospectus was issued without the defendant's knowledge or consent, and on becoming aware of its issue he gave reasonable public notice that he had not consented; or (4) after issue of the prospectus but before allotment of the securities, on becoming aware of an untrue statement he withdrew his consent and caused reasonable public notice of such withdrawal, and the reason for it, to be given.

the Companies Act 1985.[219] The Financial Services Act 1986 repealed the relevant provisions of the Companies Act 1985, but in essence retained the same principle: that directors and other persons responsible for the issue of prospectuses and other public documents connected with the issue of shares or other securities should have a liability to compensate investors who suffer loss as a result of misrepresentations contained in those documents, unless the defendants could establish certain statutory defences. However, it made some significant changes to the detail of the liabilities, and set out separate liability regimes for listing particulars issued in respect of listed securities (Part IV of the Act), and prospectuses issued in respect of unlisted securities (Part V).[220] The provisions of Part V, which were never brought into force, were repealed and replaced by the Public Offers of Securities Regulations 1995.[221] Part IV of the Financial Services Act 1986 was replaced by the Financial Services and Markets Act 2000 when it was brought into force on December 1, 2001.[222] Further changes were made in 2005: the Public Offers of Securities Regulations 1995 were revoked and replaced by new provisions inserted into the Financial Services and

[219] Companies (Consolidation) Act 1908 s.84; Companies Act 1929 s.37; Companies Act 1948 s.43; Companies Act 1985 ss.67 and 68. There were, however, changes in the 1948 Act (taken also into the 1985 Act) in that (1) the defendant, if relying on the defence that the statement was made on the authority of an expert, had also the burden of proving that he had reasonable ground to believe that the expert was competent: the earlier Acts had allowed the defence unless it was shown that the defendant had no such reasonable belief; (2) liability was extended to an expert who authorised the issue of the prospectus as regards his own statements in the prospectus made as expert; (3) by s.45, placees who did not subscribe directly but bought through an issuing house were given protection as deemed subscribers. It also first became compulsory under the 1948 Act, s.38, for prospectuses to be issued containing certain specified information whenever there was an invitation to the public to subscribe for shares.

[220] The separate liability regimes for misrepresentations in listing particulars and prospectuses followed from the creation by the Financial Services Act 1986 of separate new regulatory frameworks for the official listing of securities on The Stock Exchange (Pt IV), and for unlisted securities (Pt V).

[221] SI 1995/1537. Regs 13–15 contained the provisions relating to liability for untrue and misleading statements in prospectuses issued in respect of unlisted securities, drawn from the Financial Services Act 1986, ss.166–168.

[222] Financial Services and Markets Act 2000 (Commencement No.7) Order 2001 (SI 2001/3538); Financial Services and Markets Act 2000 (Consequential Amendments and Repeals) Order 2001 (SI 2001/3649), reg.3.

Markets Act 2000.[223] The provisions relating to prospectuses and listing particulars in relation to both listed and unlisted securities are now therefore all contained in the (amended) 2000 Act.[224] Cases decided under the earlier Companies Acts and the Financial Services Act 1986 will still be relevant in so far as they provide authority for the interpretation of provisions which are reproduced in the 2000 Act.

Overview of the claim. Section 90 of the Financial Services and Markets Act 2000 includes the following provisions: **7–51**

> "**90.**—(1) Any person responsible for listing particulars[225] is liable to pay compensation to a person who has—
> (a) acquired[226] securities to which the particulars apply; and
> (b) suffered loss in respect of them as a result of—
> (i) any untrue or misleading statement in the particulars; or
> (ii) the omission from the particulars of any matter required to be included by section 80 or 81.[227]
>
> (2) Subsection (1) is subject to exemptions provided by Schedule 10.
> (3) If listing particulars are required to include information about the absence of a particular matter, the omission from the particulars of that information is to be treated as a statement in the listing particulars that there is no such matter.
> . . .

[223] Prospectus Regulations 2005 (SI 2005/1433), in force from July 1, 2005, implementing the Prospectus Directive 2003/71/EC. The Directive was amended by Directive 2010/73/EU, at the time of writing not yet implemented in the UK.
[224] Unlisted securities are included within the definition of "transferable securities" in s.102A of the 2000 Act (inserted by the Prospectus Regulations 2005 and amended by Companies Act 2006 Sch.15, para.10(3)), above, n.223.
[225] Including supplementary listing particulars issued under s.81 to correct or add to the original listing particulars before commencement of dealings in the securities: s.90(10). The section applies in relation to a prospectus and a supplementary prospectus, as it applies to listing particulars and supplementary listing particulars: s.90(11), inserted by the Prospectus Regulations 2005, above, n.223. Following the language of s.90, this chapter refers generally to listing particulars, although this should be understood to include prospectuses as appropriate.
[226] Or contracted to acquire them or any interest in them: s.90(7).
[227] The duty of disclosure in respect of listing particulars (s.80) and supplementary listing particulars (s.81), and the claim for damages for loss suffered as a result of the defendant's failure to comply with the duty to submit supplementary listing particulars (s.90(4),(5)) are considered below, paras 17–46 *et seq.*

(6) This section does not affect any liability which may be incurred apart from this section."

In general terms the claimant may recover damages under section 90 if he can show that he acquired or contracted to acquire securities[228]; that the listing particulars which applied to those securities contained an untrue or misleading statement, or omitted some required relevant matter; that he has suffered loss in respect of the securities as a result of the statement or omission; and that the defendant is a person responsible for the listing particulars. Once the claimant has established these elements, the burden shifts to the defendant to establish either one of the specific defences, or "exemptions", set out in the statute, or a general defence. The elements of the claim, and the available defences, will be considered in the following paragraphs. Finally the calculation of the damages will be discussed.

7–52 **The claimant.** The liability is owed to a person who has acquired securities to which the listing particulars apply, or has contracted to acquire them or an interest in them, and has suffered the relevant loss.[229] A claimant need not have been registered as owner of the securities: it is sufficient that he has entered into a binding legal obligation to acquire them or an interest in them (such as a contract to subscribe for or purchase the securities or an option to purchase them). The language of the Financial Services and Markets Act 2000[230] is here significantly different from the provisions of the earlier Companies Acts, in that there is no longer a requirement that the claimant must have relied on the misrepresentation in the prospectus in making his acquisition of the securities. The earlier legislation had required the claimant to have subscribed "on the faith of the prospectus".[231] But under the new provisions, the claimant must simply acquire the securities and suffer loss as a

---

[228] There is an issue as to whether the claimant must be the first purchaser: below, para.7–52.

[229] s.90(1),(7). For the loss, see below, para.7–62.

[230] This change was introduced by the Financial Services Act 1986 s.150, and was taken over by the Act of 2000.

[231] This was not, however, a difficult matter to prove: as in the case of other remedies for misrepresentation, if the statements in the prospectus were likely to induce reliance by a subscriber, there was an inference that the subscriber in fact relied: *Arnison v Smith* (1889) 41 Ch.D. 348, CA, at 369; *Greenwood v Leather*

result of the misrepresentation. The misrepresentation is therefore now linked not to the claimant's decision to acquire the securities but only to the causation of his loss, for example because the statement in the prospectus, even though the particular claimant did not read it, has been found to be false and has therefore caused a reduction in the market value of the shares which affects the claimant simply as holder of the shares. This change in the scope of the statutory protection reflects the reality of public share dealings: many subscribers do not read and directly rely on every statement in the prospectus, but they are in a general sense relying on the market which is itself based on the statements made in the listing particulars.

There has been some uncertainty whether the claim under section 90 is available only to a person who acquires the securities as their first acquirer. It was said by Lightman J. in *Possfund Custodian Trustee Ltd v Diamond*[232] that similar language in the Public Offers of Securities Regulations 1995[233] probably referred only to the placee in respect of the shares originally allotted to him, and did not extend to later purchasers of the securities in the market. This view was, however, obiter[234] and is an unnecessarily strict reading of such language, particularly when read with other provisions of the 2000 Act which might suggest that the liability was not intended to be limited to the first acquirer of the securities.[235] In *Hall v Cable and Wireless Plc*[236] Teare J. assumed, without detailed discussion, that the cause of action created by section 90 is for the benefit of all

Shod Wheel Co. [1900] 1 Ch.421, CA, at 433; above, para.3–53. But he must at least be able to show that he read the prospectus, and therefore could have been influenced by it.

232 [1996] 1 W.L.R. 1351 at 1360–1361.

233 Reg.14: "any person who has acquired the securities to which the prospectus relates" (unlisted securities), following the same language in the Financial Services Act 1986, s.166. By contrast, Lightman J. held that the language of the Financial Services Act 1986, s.150, which (in relation to listed securities) identified as a claimant "any person who has acquired any of the securities in question", was wider and covered all who took the securities or an interest in them, including after-market purchasers.

234 The issue in the case was whether a duty was owed in respect of statements in a prospectus in the tort of negligence.

235 Below, para.7–57.

236 [2009] EWHC 1793 (Comm), [2010] 1 B.C.L.C. 95 at [20].

purchasers of listed securities, whether placees or after-market purchasers, and this is certainly the better view.[237]

7–53 **The "untrue or misleading" statement.** The liability is owed in respect of loss which the claimant suffers as a result of any untrue or misleading statement in the particulars, or the omission of certain matters required by the Act to be included in the particulars. The question of omitted matters, which raises issues of duties of disclosure, will be discussed further in Chapter 17. However, for the present purpose it should be noted that section 90(3) provides that, where under the listing rules the listing particulars must provide information about the absence of a particular matter, the omission of the relevant statement will be treated as a statement that there is no such matter: that is, silence is deemed to be a statement which can form the basis of a claim under section 90.

The Act does not further define the types of statement which can give rise to liability. The statute refers to an "untrue or misleading statement": this is not technical language so there is no reason here to imply any of the common law rules as to the meaning of a "misrepresentation", such as a restriction to statements of fact.[238] However, no doubt statements which would at common law be characterised as "misrepresentations" will be included within the scope of the Act.

Whether a statement is "untrue" or "misleading" will be a question of fact, judged objectively. The question is not whether it is untrue in the sense in which it was intended by the persons who issued the listing particulars: that is in issue when fraud is alleged against the defendants, but fraud is not necessary here. The meaning which is important is the meaning which the prospectus conveys to those who read it.[239]

---

[237] Gower and Davies, above, n.214, para.25–32 note that this is a considerable improvement on equivalent provisions in the former Companies Acts which applied only to subscribers, but note that market purchasers who buy after period of time may no longer be able to show that their loss was caused by the prospectus. E.Z. Lomnicka and J.L. Powell, *Encyclopedia of Financial Services Law*, para.2A–190, make a similar point. See also Gore-Browne, para.43[5].

[238] For such an implication in relation to the claim for "misrepresentation" under the Misrepresentation Act 1967 s.2(1), see above, para.7–07.

[239] *Greenwood v Leather Shod Wheel Co*, above, n.231 at 434 (Directors Liability Act 1890 s.3, but the point still holds under the 2000 Act).

The earlier provisions of the Companies Acts relating to prospectus liability[240] had referred only to liability for "untrue" statements. Although the Financial Services and Markets Act[241] adds a liability also for "misleading" statements, this only makes explicit within the statutory formulation what had already been held to be the position under the earlier Acts.[242] It is also consistent with other remedies for misrepresentation, where the courts have often held that a statement is a misrepresentation even if it is not literally untrue, if it is misleading because of what it omits to say (a "half-truth") or because of its context and therefore in substance it communicates a falsehood.[243]

Timing of the falsity. The time at which the truth of the statements in the listing particulars is to be tested is the time when they are submitted to the competent authority.[244] Where, after this time and before the commencement of dealings in the relevant securities, there is a significant change in facts of which the issuer is aware, he is required[245] to submit supplementary listing particulars (the truth of statements in which will again be tested when the supplementary particulars are submitted). If he fails to do so, or if any other person responsible for the listing particulars is aware of relevant change in facts but fails to inform the issuer and so fails to put the issuer on notice of the need to submit supplementary listing particulars, the claimant's claim is based not on the inaccuracy of the listing particulars which have been submitted, but on the failure to submit supplementary particulars.[246] 7–54

[240] Above, para.7–50, n.219.
[241] Following the Financial Services Act 1986 ss.150 and 166.
[242] *Drincqbier v Wood* [1899] 1 Ch. 393 at 407 (Directors Liability Act 1890: statement untrue by reason of suppression of material facts); *Greenwood v Leather Shod Wheel Co*, above, n.231 at 434.
[243] Above, para.3–08.
[244] The Act is not explicit on this, but it follows from the opening words of the exemptions in Sch.10, paras 1(2), 2(2).
[245] s.81. The requirement of a supplementary prospectus is contained in s.87G, inserted by the Prospectus Regulations 2005.
[246] s.90(4).

7–55 **The persons responsible.** The Financial Services and Markets Act, unlike its predecessor Companies Acts[247] and the Financial Services Act 1986,[248] does not define the persons responsible for listing particulars: this is prescribed by regulations made by the Treasury.[249] However, the Treasury in exercising this power[250] has, broadly, carried forward the provisions which were contained in the Financial Services Act 1986. The "persons responsible" for listing particulars[251] under the 2000 Act are[252] the issuer of the securities (that is, in the normal case of an issue of shares by a company, the company itself);[253] each director (unless[254] the particulars are published without his knowledge or consent and when he becomes aware of the publication he gives reasonable public notice of his lack of knowledge and consent); each person who has authorised himself to be named, and is named, in the particulars as a director or as having agreed to become a director; each person who accepts (and is stated in the particulars as accepting) responsibility for, or for specified parts of, the particulars; and each person (such as the issuing house sponsoring the issue, and an expert such as an accountant) who has authorised the contents of, or specified parts of, the particulars. A person who has accepted responsibility or authorised only part of the particulars has responsibility only for that part and only if the part is included in (or substantially in) the form and context to which he agreed.[255] Professional advisers are not responsible for listing particulars simply by virtue of having

---

[247] See, e.g. Companies Act 1985 s.67(2), which defined those liable for statements in a prospectus.

[248] s.152.

[249] s.79(3).

[250] Financial Services and Markets Act 2000 (Official Listing of Securities) Regulations 2001 (SI 2001/2956) Pt 3.

[251] Or prospectuses: above, para.7–51, n.225.

[252] Financial Services and Markets Act 2000 (Official Listing of Securities) Regulations 2001 reg.6. There are also specific provisions in relation to listing particulars issued in support of shares issued as part of an agreed takeover where the target company and its directors accept responsibility for statements relating to the target company (reg.7) and exemption for directors of the issuer of certain specialist securities (reg.9).

[253] This appears from reg.6(1)(b), (c). In the case of derivatives based on existing securities, the issuer is the securities house issuing the derivatives, not the underlying company: Gore-Browne, para.43[9].

[254] reg.6(2).

[255] reg.6(3).

given professional advice as to the contents of the particulars: they will incur responsibility only if they accept it, or authorise the contents of the particulars.[256]

The statutory "exemptions", or defences. The defendant is not liable if he can establish any one of a range of "exemptions", or defences, set out in Schedule 10 to the Act. These follow the broad pattern of the defences which were included in the earlier Companies Acts[257] and the Financial Services Act 1986, although there are some points which clarify the earlier provisions, and some significant changes which reflect the general changes in the liability regime implemented by the 1986 and 2000 Acts. 7–56

Statutory defence of honest and reasonable belief in the truth of the statement. Under paragraph 1 of Schedule 10: 7–57

"(2) A person does not incur any liability under section 90(1) for loss caused by a statement if he satisfies the court that, at the time when the particulars were submitted to the competent authority, he reasonable believed (having made such enquiries, if any, as were reasonable) that—

(a) the statement was true and not misleading, or

(b) the matter whose omission caused the loss was properly omitted,

and that one or more of the conditions set out in sub-paragraph (3) are satisfied.

(3) The conditions are that—

(a) he continued in his belief until the time when the securities were acquired;

(b) they were acquired before it was reasonably practicable to bring a correction to the attention of persons likely to acquire them;

(c) before the securities were acquired, he had taken all such steps as it was reasonable for him to have taken to secure that a correction was brought to the attention of those persons;

---

256 reg.6(4); *Axa Equity & Law Life Assurance Society Plc v National Westminster Bank Plc* [1998] C.L.C. 1177, CA, at 1182 ("at the very least reasonably arguable" that information provided by a company's auditors, which was incorporated in listing particulars in support of issue of debenture stock, was factual and not advice given in a professional capacity so that liability could not be excluded by the Financial Services Act 1986, s.152(8), the predecessor to reg.6(4)).

257 For a summary, see above, para.7–50, n.218.

(d) he continued in his belief until after the commencement of dealings in the securities following their admission to the official list and they were acquired after such a lapse of time that he ought in the circumstances to be reasonably excused."

In substance this requires the defendant to show that he was not negligent: he must show not only that he actually believed that the statement in question was true, but that the belief was reasonable. Moreover, he must have made any relevant reasonable enquiries in forming his belief. The liability regimes under the earlier Companies Acts had a similar defence that the defendant had actual belief, on reasonable grounds, in the truth of the statement,[258] but before the Financial Services Act 1986 there was no explicit requirement that the defendant must have made enquiries. This had, however, been implied by the courts[259] and so the 1986 Act,[260] followed in this respect by the 2000 Act, only makes this explicit.

Although the defendant must show that he individually made such enquiries as were reasonable, this does not require him to verify personally the truth of every statement in the listing particulars. For example, it is usual for the Board of Directors collectively to obtain reports from relevant competent professionals as to the material facts in the particulars, and this will generally be a sufficient enquiry to enable each director to maintain the defence.[261]

---

[258] e.g. Companies Act 1985 s.68(2): "he had reasonable ground to believe, and did up to the time of the allotment of the shares or debentures . . . believe, that the statement was true." This is the formulation (then contained in the Companies Act 1948 s.43(2)) on which the statutory defence in the Misrepresentation Act 1967 s.2(1) was based: above, para.7–16. It was said by Eve J. in *Adams v Thrift* [1915] 1 Ch.557 at 565, a decision on the Companies (Consolidation) Act 1908 s.84, that the test was whether the belief would have been induced "in the mind of a reasonable man, that is to say, a man who stands midway between the careless and easy-going man on the one hand and the over-cautious and straw-splitting man on the other".

[259] It had been held under the earlier statutory formulations that, before a defendant could show that his belief was based on reasonable grounds, he must show that he individually took steps, using the appropriate means of enquiry available to him, to check the truth of the statement: *Adams v Thrift*, above, n.258, affirmed [1915] 2 Ch. 21, CA (Companies (Consolidation) Act 1908, s.84).

[260] s.151(1).

[261] *Adams v Thrift* [1915] 2 Ch. 21, CA, at 24 (Lord Cozens-Hardy M.R.: "it is not necessary that an intending director should play the part of a lawyer or

Sub-paragraphs (3)(a) to (d) of paragraph 1 of Schedule 10 define the period during which the defendant must show that he continued in the actual belief that the statement was true: if not until the time when the claimant acquired the securities (sub-para.(a)), then at least until dealings in the securities began and the time lapse until the claimant's acquisition is such that it would be reasonable now to excuse him from liability (sub-para.(d)). Or if he discovered the falsity of the statement without satisfying those sub-paragraphs, then either he must have taken reasonable steps to bring a correction to the attention of persons likely to acquire the securities (sub-para.(c)) or the claimant must have acquired them before it was reasonably practicable to bring the correction to his attention (sub-para.(b)). The provisions relating to these periods are more complex than under the earlier Companies Acts, but are necessary if under the Financial Services and Markets Act a defendant may be liable to a claimant who is not an original subscriber, but only a later purchaser of the securities in the market.[262] In those circumstances it is insufficient to provide for a defence based on the defendant's belief only up to the time of the allotment of the securities.[263]

Statutory defence of statement made on authority of an expert. 7–58
Under paragraph 2 of Schedule10:

"(2) A person does not incur liability under section 90(1) for loss in respect of any securities caused by a statement [which purports to be made by, or on the authority of, another person as an expert and which is stated to be included in the particulars with that other person's consent] if he satisfies the court that, at the time when the listing particulars were submitted to the competent authority, he reasonably believed that the other person

(a) was competent to make or authorise the statement, and

(b) had consented to its inclusion in the form and context in which it was included,

and that one or more of the conditions set out in sub-paragraph (3) are satisfied.

(3) The conditions are that—

---

accountant by examining into facts or figures, nor that he should act as a patent agent": Companies (Consolidation) Act 1908 s.84).

262 Above, para.7–52.

263 This was the provision of each of the enactments from the Directors Liability Act 1890 s.3, to the Companies Act 1985 s.68(2).

(a) he continued in his belief until the time when the securities were acquired;
(b) they were acquired before it was reasonably practicable to bring the fact that the expert was not competent, or had not consented, to the attention of persons likely to acquire the securities in question;
(c) before the securities were acquired he had taken all such steps as it was reasonable for him to have taken to secure that that fact was brought to the attention of those persons;
(d) he continued in his belief until after the commencement of dealings in the securities following their admission to the official list and they were acquired after such a lapse of time that he ought in the circumstances to be reasonably excused."

An expert is responsible for a statement which he has authorised to be included in the listing particulars.[264] The effect of the defence under paragraph 2 of Schedule 10 is in such a case to exempt from liability others who are responsible for the particulars unless they cannot show that they actually believed, on reasonable grounds, that the "expert" was competent. This will require a defendant to have made any relevant reasonable enquiries to verify the competence of the "expert",[265] but once the defendant has made a proper selection of the expert he is not then responsible for statements which he accepts from him for incorporation in the particulars as long as the defendant satisfies one of the conditions in para.2(3), which define the period during which the defendant must show that he continued in the belief that the expert was competent, provisions which parallel the similar provisions of paragraph 1.[266]

7–59 **Statutory defence of publication of correction.** It is a defence to show that, before the claimant acquired the securities, a correction of an untrue or misleading statement, or a notice that an "expert" was not competent or had not consented to the inclusion of his statement in the listing particulars, had been published in a manner calculated to bring it to the attention of persons likely to acquire the securities, or the defendant had taken all reasonable

264 Above, para.7–55.
265 "Reasonable belief" implies the obligation to make enquiries: *cf.* above, para.7–57, n.259.
266 Above, para.7–57.

steps to try to secure such publication and reasonably believed that the publication had taken place.[267]

Other statutory defences: reliance on public official document; claimant's knowledge of falsity. It is a defence[268] to show that the loss claimed results from a statement made by an official person or contained in a public official document included in the particulars, as long as the statement is shown to be accurately and fairly reproduced. 7–60

The Financial Services Act 1986 also introduced a new defence which is now contained in the Financial Services and Markets Act 2000[269]: that the claimant acquired the securities with knowledge that the statement was false or misleading, or of any omitted matter which would otherwise give rise to liability. Since it is no longer necessary to show a causal link between the statement and the claimant's decision to acquire the securities, and the only question is whether he suffered loss as a result of the misrepresentation in the listing particulars,[270] it is now necessary to make clear that a claimant cannot recover if he knew about the misrepresentation at the time of acquisition. If no such provision were made, a claimant in such a case might still be able to say that he had a claim under the Act, since his loss would be measured by reference to the market value reduction in his securities, whereas he ought not to be able to claim where he acquired the securities in the full knowledge of the matters which when made public would affect that market value.

Other defences. It is not clear whether the defence of contributory negligence would be available to a claim under section 90 of the Financial Services and Markets Act; and there appears to be no authority on this point in cases decided under it or under the 7–61

[267] Sch.10, paras 3 and 4. A defence in these terms is necessary because of the longer period during which a defendant may be liable under the 2000 Act in favour of a market purchaser of the securities. The earlier legislation provided a naturally more limited defence, under which the defendant discovered a falsity, and gave reasonable public notice of his withdrawal of consent to the issue of the prospectus, after the issue but before the allotment of the securities: see, e.g. Companies Act 1985 s.68(1)(c).

[268] Sch.10, para.5, reproducing a similar defence from the earlier Companies Acts.

[269] Sch.10, para.6, reproducing the Financial Services Act 1986 s.151(5).

[270] Above, para.7–52.

provisions of the earlier Companies Acts or the Financial Services Act 1986. In any event, it appears unlikely that facts would often arise in which a defendant to a claim under section 90 could say that the claimant's loss was suffered as a result partly of his own fault and partly of the fault of the defendant.[271] Nor is it clear whether the defendant might exclude or limit his liability by a contractual term—although such a defence would in any event be possible only for a defendant who has a contract with the claimant, and many claims under section 90 will be against persons with whom there is no contractual relationship.[272] In an appropriate case there will be a defence of the expiry of the limitation period: a claim cannot normally be brought under the Act (that is, a claim form cannot be issued[273]) after the expiration of six years from the date on which the cause of action accrued.[274] The cause of action under section 90

---

[271] For arguments about whether the defence of contributory negligence applies to a claim under the Misrepresentation Act 1967, s.2(1), see above, para.7–27.

[272] Above, para.7–55. Unless the courts were to take the view that the liability under s.90, designed as part of the regulatory regime designed to protect investors, is inherently incapable of being excluded, it is difficult to see why such a clause should not be operative under the general law. Under the Financial Service Authority's Conduct of Business Sourcebook, 2.1.2, however, an authorised person must not in any communication relating to designated investment business seek to exclude or restrict, or rely on any exclusion or restriction of, any duty or liability it may have to a client under the regulatory system (which includes the requirements of s.90). For a general discussion of exclusion and limitation clauses, see Ch.9. It should be noted that ss.2–4 of the Unfair Contract Terms Act 1977 do not apply to any contract in so far as it relates to the creation or transfer of securities or of any right or interest in securities: Sch.1, para.1(e); there is, however, no such restriction in relation to the operation of the Unfair Terms in Consumer Contracts Regulations 1999 (SI 1999/2083).

[273] Below, para.11–05.

[274] Limitation Act 1980, either s.2 (action founded on tort) or s.9 (action "to recover any sum recoverable by virtue of any enactment"). On the analagous provision in the Misrepresentation Act 1967 s.2(1), see *Laws v Society of Lloyds* [2003] EWCA Civ 1887, [2003] All E.R. (D) 392 (Dec) at [92]; *Hartley v British Railways Board* unreported, June 25, 1999, and Law Com. No.151, *Limitation of Actions* (1998), para.7.18, discussed above, para.7–28, n.101. For general provisions for extension of limitation periods in cases of the claimant's disability, see s.28, and in cases of deliberate concealment by the defendant or his agent of facts relevant to the claimant's right of action, see s.32(1)(b). For a claim to contribution under the Civil Liability (Contribution) Act 1978 s.1, below, para.7–63 there is special time-limit of two years from the accrual of the right to recover contribution: see the Limitation Act 1980 s.10. For the special time-limit in actions for damages for personal injuries, see s.11. In 2001 the Law

will not accrue until the claimant has acquired the securities and suffered the loss which is recoverable under the section.[275]

7–62 **The damages recoverable.** The defendant is liable under section 90 to compensate the claimant for the loss he has suffered in respect of the securities as a result of the untrue or misleading statement.[276] This language is not materially different from that of the earlier Companies Acts[277]; and there is well-established authority up to the level of the House of Lords under those Acts that the measure of damages is identical to the tort of deceit.[278] This follows from the interpretation of the original Directors Liability Act 1890 having been intended to reverse the effect of *Derry v Peek*[279] and to create by statute a remedy equivalent to the tort of deceit but without requiring the claimant to prove the defendant's fraud. So damages under the Act will be calculated on the tort measure—that is, the amount by which his wealth has been diminished as a result of the untrue or misleading statement in the listing particulars. Typically, this will be the difference between the price he paid to acquire the securities and the actual value of the securities he received, the valuation being made in the light of the discovery of the falsity of

Commission recommended a general reform of the rules on limitation of actions: Law Com. No.270, *Limitation of Actions* (2001), although in 2009 the Government announce that the reforms would not be taken forward: above, para.6–50, n.330.

275 *Thomson v Lord Clanmorris* [1900] 1 Ch.718, CA at 728–729 (claim under the Directors Liability Act 1890, where the remedy was limited to those who subscribed on the faith of the prospectus and suffered loss). For the loss recoverable under the Financial Services and Markets Act 2000 s.90, see below, para.7–62.

276 s.90(1). Or as a result of the omission of a matter required to be included in the listing particulars: below, para.17–46.

277 e.g. Companies Act 1985 s.67: "compensation is payable to all those who subscribe for shares . . . for the loss or damage which they may have sustained by reason of any untrue statement . . .". However, since the claim under the 2000 Act, unlike its predecessor provisions, does not require proof of reliance by the claimant on the untrue statement (above, para.7–52), it is arguable that the measure of damages should be just the basic measure in tort (the difference in price: below) and not any further consequential loss by virtue of having bought the securities: Gore-Browne, para.43[4].

278 See esp. *McConnel v Wright* [1903] 1 Ch. 546, CA at 554; *Clark v Urquhart* [1930] A.C. 28, HL at 67, 76. For the quantification of the damages in a claim in deceit, see above, para.5–35.

279 (1889) 14 App. Cas. 337, HL; above, paras 5–14, 7–16.

the statement in issue. The claim will arise, and the loss will normally be calculated, at the date of the acquisition even though the truth may be discovered only later. However, as in the case of a claim in deceit,[280] a court is likely to hold that the date of acquisition is only a prima facie rule for the time of assessment of damages, and a later time will be taken if that would be just.

The defendant's liability under section 90 is not, of course, for deceit: he is liable for false statements unless he can prove, for example, that he reasonably believed the statements to be true—in substance, liability for negligence. The cases which have held that the measure of damages under the Act is identical to the measure in deceit were decided before the courts focused on the need to distinguish between the rules governing damages for fraud and damages for negligence. In relation to the similar issue under section 2(1) of the Misrepresentation Act 1967 there have been some indications in the cases that the courts are uncomfortable in imposing on a negligent defendant all the rules of damages which were designed for the fraudulent defendant.[281] It is entirely possible that the Supreme Court, reviewing the measure of damages in a claim under section 90 of the Financial Services and Markets Act 2000, will similarly wish to depart from the view that the section imports the measure for deceit, and instead hold that the measure for negligence is appropriate.[282]

7–63 **Contribution between co-defendants.** Where a defendant is liable under section 90 jointly or severally with another defendant for damage suffered by the claimant, whether the co-defendant's liability is also under the statute[283] or is based on some other cause of action such as negligence, deceit or breach of contract, the court will, as in all cases of joint or several liability, have jurisdiction

[280] Above, para.5–37.

[281] Above, para.7–33.

[282] The language of s.90 lends itself more readily to reinterpretation than the Misrepresentation Act 1967 s.2(1). The Misrepresentation Act has an explicit reference to fraud which has been held to incorporate the deceit rules: above, para.7–33. But s.90 simply refers to "compensation" for "loss"; it is only the context of the Directors Liability Act 1890 which has been taken to import the deceit measure; and the cases which have held this were decided before the full modern development of the rules of liability for negligent statements.

[283] Which will commonly happen, given the range of persons responsible for listing particulars: above, para.7–55.

under the Civil Liability (Contribution) Act 1978 to apportion between the co-defendants the damages payable.[284]

Remedies not exclusive. The remedies available under the Financial Services and Markets Act to a person acquiring securities and suffering loss in respect of them are not exclusive. The relevant provisions of the Act[285] make clear that they do not affect any liability which may be incurred apart from those provisions. Where, therefore, a misrepresentation in listing particulars or a prospectus is actionable in contract, or in the tort of deceit, or the tort of negligence,[286] or under section 2(1) of the Misrepresentation Act 1967, a claimant may pursue those other claims as well as (or instead of) a claim under the Act; and he need not pursue all possible defendants using the same cause of action.[287] 7–64

Comparison with other possible claims. Where it is available, however, a claim under the Financial Services and Markets Act is likely often to be advantageous because it provides a precisely formulated claim for the specific context of public documents in support of the issue of securities; it is therefore designed to impose liability on an appropriate range of defendants. A claim in contract will, of course, be available only against a person with whom the claimant has a contract[288]: usually this will be the company issuing the securities,[289] but it will not extend to others who might have had a hand in making the misrepresentation and who are liable under the 7–65

---

284 Above, para.2–14.

285 ss.90(6) (listing particulars and, by virtue of s.90(11), prospectuses), 248(7) (authorised unit trust scheme particulars).

286 *Possfund Custodian Trustee Ltd v Diamond* [1996] 1 W.L.R. 1351; *Axa Equity & Law Life Assurance Society Plc v National Westminster Bank Plc* [1998] C.L.C. 1177, CA.

287 Multiple defendants would be liable to contribution, regardless of the different bases of their liability, as long as they are liable in respect of the same loss: above, para.7–63.

288 The claimant must also show that the statement in a prospectus was incorporated into a contract with the defendant: below, para.8–03; *Re Addlestone Linoleum Co.* (1887) 37 Ch.D. 191, CA.

289 Under Companies Act 2006 s.655 (reversing the rule in *Houldsworth v City of Glasgow Bank* (1880) 5 App. Cas. 317, HL (Sc.)) a person is not debarred from obtaining damages or other compensation from a company by reason only of his holding or having held shares in the company or any right to apply or subscribe for shares or to be included in the company's register in respect of shares.

Act, such as individual directors or the company's experts who took responsibility for providing the information which is now shown to be inaccurate or misleading; nor will it give a claim to an after-market purchaser who might have a claim under the Act[290] but who has no direct contract with the issuer. A claim under section 2(1) of the Misrepresentation Act 1967 will also be available only against the person with whom the claimant has a contract.[291] For a claim in the tort of deceit fraud must be proved: that is difficult,[292] and it was precisely this difficulty in *Derry v Peek*[293] that provoked the enactment of the Directors Liability Act 1890 to which the provisions now contained in the Act can historically be traced.[294] And although the tort of negligence has now[295] developed to the point where it can sometimes be invoked in a case where there is liability under the 2000 Act, it is always necessary in a claim in negligence to show that the defendant owed the claimant a duty of care,[296] which can be more problematic than a claim under the Act, where there is a more straightforward factual question: whether the defendant was a "person responsible for the listing particulars" within the meaning of the Act.[297]

However, sometimes a claimant will see an advantage in pursing a defendant under one of the other possible causes of action. For example, he may claim in contract in order to recover a measure of loss based on the cost of making good the untrue statement,

---

290 Above, para.7–52.

291 Above, para.7–05.

292 Above, para.5–46.

293 Above, n.279; above, para.7–16.

294 Above, para.7–50.

295 Since the tort is dated in the modern law only from *Donoghue v Stevenson* [1932] A.C. 562, HL (Sc.) and, in relation to liability for negligent statements, only from *Hedley Byrne & Co. Ltd v Heller & Partners Ltd* [1964] A.C. 465, HL, it can be seen that the statutory liability for misrepresentations in prospectuses—though imposing, in effect, liability for negligence (above, para.7–57)—has been developed quite independently from the liability in the tort.

296 Above, para.6–12.

297 Above, para.7–55. This is tighter and more closely defined than in a claim in negligence since a defendant can be identified simply by being in a particular class, such as a director of the issuing company. Moreover, a claim in negligence is limited to the recovery of losses of a foreseeable kind (above, para.6–56) whereas under the Act it appears that there is no limit by reference to the defendant's foreseeability: all losses caused by the untrue or misleading statement are recoverable on the analogy of the rules in the tort of deceit: above, para.7–62.

whereas under the Act damages are calculated on the tort measure.[298] And where he believes that he can satisfy the heavy burden of proving the defendant's fraud he may claim in deceit in order to seek to brand the defendant as fraudulent, even though it appears that by so doing the claimant obtains no real advantage in the measure of recovery since the damages awarded under the Act are themselves calculated on the same basis as in the tort of deceit,[299] and he runs real risks in terms of costs if he fails to establish his claim.[300]

(2) Package Travel, Package Holidays and Package Tours Regulations 1992

Liability in respect of misleading information in description of packages. Regulation 4 of the Package Travel, Package Holidays and Package Tours Regulations 1992[301] provides: 7–66

> "**4.**—(1) No organiser or retailer shall supply to a consumer any descriptive matter concerning a package, the price of a package or any other conditions applying to the contract which contains any misleading information.
>
> (2) If an organiser or retailer is in breach of paragraph (1) he shall be liable to compensate the consumer for any loss which the consumer suffers in consequence."

A "package" is[302] the pre-arranged combination of at least two of transport, accommodation and certain other tourist services, sold at an inclusive price and lasting for at least 24 hours or including overnight accommodation. Broadly, therefore, the regulation provides a remedy in damages for a consumer who enters into a package travel, package holiday or package tour contract for loss he suffers in consequence of misrepresentations about the package.

---

298 Above, para.7–62.
299 Above, para.7–62.
300 Above, para.5–49.
301 SI 1992/3288, implementing Council Directive 90/314/EEC. The Directive was under review as part of the Review of the Consumer Acquis: see the European Commission's Green Paper, COM(2006) 744 Final (08.02.2007); however, the Commission's Proposal for a Directive on Consumer Rights did not include this Directive within its scope: COM(2008) 614 Final (8.10.2008). See further below, para.17–54.
302 reg.2(1).

7–67 **The claimant and the defendant.** The claimant under the Regulations is a "consumer": the person who takes or agrees to take the package, together with any other person on whose behalf he agreed to purchase the package or any person to whom the package is transferred.[303] The claim is therefore not restricted to those who contract directly for the package, but extends to anyone who suffers loss as a consequence of the misleading information, such as the individual members of a group where the booking is made by a single representative.

The person liable under the Regulations is the "organiser or retailer" who supplies descriptive matter which contains the misleading information. The "organiser" is a person who, otherwise than occasionally, organises packages and sells or offers them for sale, whether directly or through a retailer, and the "retailer" is the person who sells or offers for sale the package put together by the organiser.[304] The liability is not therefore restricted to those who contract directly with a consumer to provide the package but extends, for example, to both the tour company which organises and markets the package and the person who actually sells the package to the public, as long as he also has supplied the descriptive matter containing the misleading information on which the claim is based.

7–68 **The misleading information.** Liability is imposed under regulation 4 in respect of misleading information[305] which is contained in any descriptive material which is supplied concerning a package, the price of the package or any other conditions applying to the contract for the package. Misleading statements about the nature of the holiday or travel arrangements, the terms of the contract and the price to be paid for it are therefore all within the scope of the Regulations; and the statement need not be a misrepresentation of fact which would give rise to other remedies for misrepresentation: it must only be "misleading."

7–69 **Nature of the remedy.** The remedy under regulation 4 is compensation for loss suffered by the consumer in consequence of

---

303 reg.1(2).
304 reg.1(2).
305 *Mawdsley v Cosmosair Plc* [2002] EWCA Civ 587, [2002] All E.R. (D) 129 (Apr) (statement of accessibility of hotel restaurant).

the misleading information.[306] The Regulations do not indicate how the loss is to be calculated, but it seems likely that a court would hold that the claim is for damages on the tort measure, rather than the contract measure.[307] There is no indication of other rules in relation to an award of damages, such as the test for remoteness of damage, so it appears that a court should simply apply a test of causation of loss from the misleading information.

Relationship to other remedies for misrepresentation. The Regulations provide a specific remedy for misleading information in the particular context of package holiday and travel contracts. This area is singled out for protection of the consumer, and the Regulations were enacted to satisfy the United Kingdom's obligation to implement the Council Directive of 1990 on Package Travel, Package Holidays and Package Tours.[308] The Regulations therefore provide a straightforward remedy in cases to which they apply, but there is nothing in the Regulations to suggest that the remedy is exclusive, and so a claimant who can establish a remedy outside the Regulations in respect of a misrepresentation made by a package organiser or retailer is free to pursue that remedy. **7–70**

[306] There are other provisions within the Regulations for criminal offences for misleading statements or the failure to give prescribed information to the consumer (regs 5, 7 and 8), but the commission of any of these offences is not actionable in civil proceedings (reg.27).

[307] This is the conclusion which has been reached in relation to statutory liability to pay "compensation" for "loss" caused by untrue statements in company prospectuses and listing particulars: above, para.7–62. Moreover, there are other, separate provisions in regs. 6, 9 and 15 governing the terms, contents and form of the contract under which a package is provided, and liabilities arising under it—see, in particular, reg.6 under which there is an implied term in the contract relating to particulars in the brochure, which will give rise to a claim in contract. It therefore seems likely that, had the remedy under reg.4 been intended to be contractual, this would have been explicit. *Cf. Mawdsley v Cosmosair Plc*, above, n.305 (injury caused by falling down steps).

[308] 90/314/EEC.

(3) Liability Under Other Statutes

7–71 **Statutes imposing civil liability for misrepresentations.** Certain statutes impose civil liability for loss suffered by reliance on misrepresentations in defined circumstances.[309] Sometimes a criminal offence[310] or breach of a regulatory requirement is made also actionable in tort. For example, section 150 of the Financial Services and Markets Act 2000[311] provides a general remedy in

[309] e.g. Companies Act 2006 s.463 makes directors liable to their companies for fraudulent untrue or misleading statements in (or omissions consisting in the dishonest concealment of material facts from) the directors' report and directors' remuneration report; only fraud is covered, and directors (and others) are not liable to any other person than the company (even for fraud) resulting from reliance on information in those reports. A number of statutes give the court the power to order the landlord to pay compensation to a statutorily protected tenant who suffers loss where the landlord obtains possession of the premises, or termination of the tenancy, by making a misrepresentation to the court or concealing material facts: see, e.g. Landlord and Tenant Act 1954, ss.14A, inserted by SI 2003/3096 (long residential tenancies), 37A, inserted by SI 2003/3096 (business tenancies); Rent Act 1977, s.102 (protected tenancy or statutory tenancy of dwelling-house); Housing Act 1988, s.12 (private residential assured tenancy); and see Leasehold Reform Act 1967, s.20(5) (notice to obtain enfranchisement of freehold or extended lease). The Consumer Insurance (Disclosure and Representations) Bill, which is expected to be enacted during 2012 (implementing Law Com No.319, *Consumer Insurance Law: Pre-Contract Disclosure and Misrepresentation* (2009): see also below, para.17–06) would place a new statutory duty on a consumer to take reasonable care not to make a misrepresentation to the insurer before a consumer insurance contract is entered into or varied: cl.2(2); this replaces any existing duties, and the insurer's remedies (set out in Sch.1) are limited: there is no general remedy in damages; the insurer may avoid a contract for fraud ("deliberate or reckness") and need not return any of the premiums paid, except to the extent (if any) that it would be unfair to the consumer to retain them; and in the case of a careless misrepresentation the insurer's remedy is designed to put it into the position in which it would have been if the consumer had fulfilled the duty of reasonable care: if the insurer would not have entered into the contract on any terms, it may avoid the contract and refuse all claims, but must return the premiums paid; otherwise, the insurer is limited to a variation of the terms of the contract to reflect the terms on which it would have entered into the contract.

[310] Below, para.7–72.

[311] Providing a general action for breach of statutory duty for loss suffered by any private person as a result of the contravention of most rules in the FSA Handbook: E.Z. Lomnicka and J.L. Powell, *Encyclopedia of Financial Services Law*, para.2A–310; M. Blair, *Blackstone's Guide to the Financial Services and Markets Act 2000* (2nd edn, 2009), paras 12.37 to 12.42. S.150 enables the FSA

damages for many acts (including misrepresentations) and omissions by authorised persons in breach of their duties under the regulatory regime established by the 2000 Act. The Law Commission has also provisionally proposed introducing new civil remedies for consumers in respect of misleading commercial practices by traders, which would constitute additional remedies for misrepresentation.[312]

Statutes imposing criminal liability for misrepresentations: claims for loss. Various statutes impose criminal liability for misrepresentations. For example, section 397 of the Financial Services and Markets Act 2000[313] imposes criminal liability on a person who knowingly or recklessly makes a misleading, false or deceptive statement to induce another person to enter into, or exercise rights under, an investment agreement or certain other specified agreements.[314] Under the Fraud Act 2006 the general offence of fraud[315] includes fraud by false representation, where a 7–72

to choose which of its rules impose civil liability on authorised persons, and Sch.5 of each of the sourcebooks and manuals within the FSA Handbook identifies those rules which may give rise to a claim for damages for breach: G. Morse and others (eds), *Palmer's Company Law* (25th edn, 1992 looseleaf), para.11.057. For consumer redress schemes under which, if it appears to the Financial Services Authority that there may have been widespread or regular failure by authorised firms to comply with the requirements applicable to the carrying on of any activity, and if consumers have suffered or may suffer loss or damage in respect of which relief would be available in legal proceedings, the Authority can require firms to review past business and, if liable, pay compensation to consumers, see Financial Services and Markets Act 2000 s.404, substituted by Financial Services Act 2010 s.14.

312 Below, n.322.

313 Replacing the Financial Services Act 1986, ss.47 (investment agreements) and 133 (insurance contracts) and the Banking Act 1987, s.35 (deposits). For repeal of these earlier provisions, see the Financial Services and Markets Act 2000 (Consequential Amendments and Repeals) Order 2001 (SI 2001/3649), reg.3.

314 The section also contains an offence of doing an act, or engaging in a course of conduct, which creates a false or misleading impression as to the market, which is in substance a misrepresentation by conduct.

315 s.1, replacing more specific offences involving deception (e.g. Theft Act 1968 ss.15 (obtaining property by deception), 15A (obtaining a money transfer by the deception: introduced by the Theft (Amendment) Act 1996 s.1), 16 (obtaining pecuniary advantage by deception), 20(2) (procuring the execution of a valuable security by deception); Theft Act 1978 ss.1 (obtaining services by deception), 2 (evading liability by deception)). S.11 of the 2006 Act introduces the offence of

person dishonestly[316] makes an express or implied representation of fact or law, which is untrue or misleading and which the person making it knows is, or might be, untrue or misleading and intends by making the representation to make a gain for himself or another, or to cause a loss (or risk of loss) to another.[317] Under the Property Misdescriptions Act 1991[318] a person carrying on an estate agency or property development business commits an offence by making certain false or misleading statements in the course of his business. The Business Protection from Misleading Marketing Regulations 2008[319] prohibit misleading advertising, which includes advertising which deceives or is likely to deceive the traders to whom it is addressed or whom it reaches and, by reason of its deceptive nature, is likely to affect their economic behaviour. And the Consumer Protection from Unfair Trading Regulations 2008[320] prohibit unfair commercial practices, which include representations made by

obtaining services dishonestly. Some provisions of Theft Act 1968 remain in force, e.g. s.19 (misleading, false or deceptive statements by company officers with intent to deceive members or creditors),

[316] This is not the concept of dishonesty commonly referred to within the tort of deceit (above, para.5–14), but the test adopted in the criminal law: a defendant is dishonest if (i) according to the ordinary standards of reasonable and honest people what was done was dishonest, and (ii) the defendant must have realised that what was doing was by those standards dishonest: *R. v Ghosh* [1982] Q.B. 1053, CA, at 1064 (a decision under Theft Act 1968).

[317] s.2. Curiously, s.2(2) includes the defendant's knowledge that the statement is untrue within the definition of "false".

[318] s.1; *Lewin v Barratt Homes Ltd* [2000] 1 E.G.L.R. 77, CA, (showing pictures of design, and a show house, constituted statement to prospective purchaser that nothing stood in the way of building houses to that design; following *R. v Sunair Holidays Ltd* [1973] 1 W.L.R. 1005, CA, a decision under Trade Descriptions Act 1968 s.14, where MacKenna J. at 1110 drew an analogy with the tort of deceit).

[319] SI 2008/1276, implementing Directive 2006/114/EC on misleading and comparative advertising, and replacing the Control of Misleading Advertising Regulations 1988, SI 1988/915 (which are revoked by SI 2008/1277, below, n.320). There are defences of due diligence (reg.11) and innocent publication (reg.12).

[320] SI 2008/1277, implementing the Unfair Commercial Practices Directive 2005/29/EC, and replacing more specific offences of deception, e.g. Trade Descriptions Act 1968, ss.1(1)(a), 3(2), 14 (person guilty of an offence who, in the course of a trade or business, applies a false or misleading trade description to goods or knowingly makes a false statement about services); Weights and Measures Act 1985 s.29 (offence to make misrepresentation as to quantity of goods sold). The Regulations also cover "misleading omissions": see below, para.17–55.

traders which are directly connected with the promotion, sale or supply of products to or from consumers, and which contain false information or whose overall presentation in any way deceives or is likely to deceive the average consumer in relation to a range of relevant matters, and cause or are likely to cause the average consumer to take a transactional decision he would not have taken otherwise.[321]

A person who suffers loss as a result of the commission of such a criminal offence by the defendant does not, however, necessarily have a civil right of action for compensation under the statute which creates the offence. Sometimes an Act in creating a criminal offence makes clear that there is no right of action in civil proceedings in respect of any loss suffered by reason only of the commission of the offences[322]: in such a case any claim to damages must be based not on the Act, but on the other general causes of action for misrepresentation discussed elsewhere in this book, or the claimant must rely on the court to exercise its powers under the Powers of Criminal Courts (Sentencing) Act 2000, discussed below.[323]

Sometimes, however, it might be possible for a claim for damages in tort to be based on the commission of a criminal

[321] *ibid.*, regs 2(1), 3(1), (4)(a), 5. The offence is charged under reg.9, and is subject to a due diligence defence under reg.17.

[322] Property Misdescriptions Act 1991 s.1(4); Consumer Protection Act 1987 s.20 (offence to give misleading price indication; no claim under the Act to damages in civil proceedings: s.41(2)); Business Protection from Misleading Marketing Regulations 2008 reg.29 (agreement not void or unenforceable by reason only of a breach of the Regulations).

The Consumer Protection from Unfair Trading Regulations 2008 (following the Unfair Commercial Practices Directive 2005/29/EC, Art.3(2)) give no civil remedy in damages, and reg.29 provides that an agreement shall not be void or unenforceable by reason only of a breach of the Regulations. However, the Law Commission has provisionally proposed that civil remedies should be introduced for certain breaches of the Regulations: Law Com. Consultation Paper No.199, *Consumer Redress for Misleading and Aggressive Practices* (2011); above, para.7–48.

[323] Below, para.7–73.

offence, either if the statute expressly so provides,[324] or if it can be held that the breach of the statutory duty was intended to be actionable in tort.[325]

7–73 **Powers of Criminal Courts (Sentencing) Act 2000, section 130.** Under section 130 of the Powers of Criminal Courts (Sentencing) Act 2000[326] a court convicting a defendant for a criminal offence may make a "compensation order" requiring the defendant to pay compensation for any personal injury, loss or damage resulting from the offence. The measure of compensation is at the court's discretion,[327] although it has been said that[328]

[324] e.g. a claim for damages breach of statutory duty, where the breach is also a criminal offence; see, e.g. the Consumer Protection Act 1987 s.41(1) (civil claim for breach of "safety regulations" made under s.11, which may included provisions relating to inappropriate information: s.11(2)(i)).

[325] For the tort of breach of statutory duty, see Winfield & Jolowicz, Ch.7; Clerk & Lindsell, Ch.9. There is no express provision in relation to the offences under s.397 of the Financial Services and Markets Act 2000 although it seems unlikely that a court would hold there to be civil liability. The Financial Services and Markets Act 2000 contains a range of specific provisions for breach of statutory duty in respect of other offences and other breaches of duties created by the Act: see ss.20(3), 71, 85(4) (replaced by SI 2005/1433), 150(1) (a very general remedy: above, para.7–71, n.311), 202(2), but no such provision in relation to the offence under s.397. The Financial Services Act 1986 s.47, the predecessor of s.397 of the 2000 Act, did not give rise to a claim for breach of statutory duty actionable in tort: *Norwich Union Life Assurance Co. Ltd v Qureshi* [1999] 2 All E.R. (Comm) 707, CA. See also *Hall v Cable & Wireless Plc* [2009] EWHC 1793 (Comm), [2010] 1 B.C.L.C. 95 at [16] (Teare J: range of specific provisions in Financial Services and Markets Act 2000 for actions by private persons indicates that no actions intended where not expressly provided, so no private claim for breach of listing rules or market abuse).

[326] Replacing the Powers of Criminal Courts Act 1973 s.35, as substituted by the Criminal Justice Act 1982 s.67 and the Criminal Justice Act 1988 s.104. For a detailed account of the exercise of the jurisdiction to make compensation orders, see Archbold, *Criminal Pleading Evidence and Practice*, 2010, paras 5–411 to 5–430.

[327] s.130(4).

[328] *R. v Schofield* [1978] 1 W.L.R. 979, CA (a decision under the Powers of Criminal Courts Act 1973 s.35, above, n.326). See also *Bond v Chief Constable of Kent* [1983] 1 W.L.R. 40 at 44 (McCullough J.: "in assessing whether compensation should be awarded under section 35 the court should approach the matter in a broad common sense way and should not allow itself to become enmeshed in the refined questions of causation which can sometimes arise in

> "the word 'loss' should, in that subsection, be given its ordinary meaning and should not be limited or restricted to any particular kind of loss. In the case of financial loss, you look to see what the loss is which the victim has, in fact, suffered at the time the compensation order is made and then, provided the loss results from the offences and is not otherwise too remote in law, the court may, in its discretion, make a compensation order up to that amount."

Accordingly, an order under the Act for compensation for financial loss can include an element for interest.[329]

It has been said that the machinery of the Act is intended only for simple cases; in more complicated cases the claimant should pursue his remedies in the civil courts.[330] However, the only explicit restriction in the Act is in relation to orders by magistrates, where there is a limit of £5,000.[331]

Even if the court makes an order under the 2000 Act, the claimant is not prevented from bringing a civil claim in respect of the same injury, loss or damage. In such a case damages in the civil proceedings are to be assessed without regard to the order under section 130, but the claimant may only recover in the civil action any sum awarded which is in excess of the amount ordered or actually recovered in respect of the compensation order: there cannot, therefore, be double recovery.[332]

Misrepresentation Act 1967, section 2(2). For the sake of completeness the award of damages in lieu of rescission under section 2(2) of the Misrepresentation Act 1967 should be mentioned. This has been already discussed in detail.[333] 7–74

---

claims for damages under the law of contract or tort. The court simply has to ask itself whether the loss or damage can fairly be said to have resulted from the offence").

329 *ibid.*

330 *R. v Daly* [1974] 1 W.L.R. 133, CA, at 134; *R. v Oddy* [1974] 1 W.L.R. 1212, CA, at 1218 (decisions under the Criminal Justice Act 1972, s.1, the predecessor of the Powers of Criminal Courts (Sentencing) Act 2000 s.130); *R. v Liverpool Crown Court Ex p. Cooke* [1997] 1 W.L.R. 700 at 706 (Powers of Criminal Courts Act 1973 s.35). See also Law Com. Consultation Paper No.199, *Consumer Redress for Misleading and Aggressive Practices* (2011), paras 4.17 to 4.22, noting the limited use of compensation orders.

331 Powers of Criminal Courts (Sentencing) Act 2000 s.131.

332 *ibid.*, s.134.

333 Above, paras 4.61 to 4.71. For the relationship between claims under s.2(1) and s.2(2), see above, para.7–32, n.120.

CHAPTER 8

MISREPRESENTATION AS BREACH OF CONTRACT[1]

I. ELEMENTS OF THE CLAIM

Nature of the claim. A breach of contract is the defendant's failure to fulfil an obligation contained in the contract.[2] The typical contractual obligation is one of future performance: that is, the defendant has promised to do or not to do something. We are not here concerned with such obligations. A misrepresentation, as discussed in this book, is a false statement not of the future, but of something in the present. Generally it is a statement of a fact which has induced the claimant to act in such a way as to suffer loss.[3] But there can be circumstances in which a defendant, in making a **8–01**

[1] Chitty, para.12–003; Furmston, paras 3.1 to 3.3; Treitel, paras 9–045 to 9–053; Anson, pp.133–139; Allen, Ch.5.

[2] In the terminology of Lord Diplock in *Photo Production Ltd v Securicor Ltd* [1980] A.C. 827, HL, at 848–849, the express or implied terms (or promises) contained in the contract are "primary obligations"; and "[e]very failure to perform a primary obligation is a breach of contract" giving rise to the remedy of damages (the defendant's obligation to pay damages is a "secondary obligation") and sometimes to the claimant's right to terminate the contract. On the remedies for breach, see below, para.8–23.

[3] Above, para.3–13.

misrepresentation, breaches a contractual obligation which he owes to the claimant. To assert that the defendant's misrepresentation amounts to a breach of contract is therefore to claim that the defendant has broken an undertaking which he gave, in a contract, about his statement.

8–02 **Overview of the elements of the claim.** In general terms, the representee has a claim for breach of contract if he can show that in a contract the defendant made him a promise—either that his representation was true, or that he had taken care in making the representation—which he has broken. The circumstances in which a court will hold that the defendant has made a contractually binding promise of this nature will be discussed in detail in this section. The defences which can be raised by the defendant once the representee has established the elements of his claim, and the remedies which are available to the successful claimant, will be discussed in later sections of this chapter.

(1) The Contractual Promise

(a) Incorporation of the representation

8–03 **The representation must be incorporated into the contract.** Before a claim for breach of contract can be based on a misrepresentation, the claimant must show that the representation was incorporated into the contract: that is, he must show that there was a term of the contract that was broken by virtue of the representation being false. It has often been said in the cases that the representation must have been *warranted* by the defendant, and that the claim is based on breach of warranty.[4] But it is clear that "warranty" in this context simply means a contractually binding

[4] See, e.g. *Pasley v Freeman* (1789) 3 T.R. 51 at 57, 100 E.R. 450 at 453 (Buller J., referring without citation to a statement of Holt C.J. "that an affirmation at the time of a sale is a warranty, provided it appear on evidence to have been so intended", a quotation frequently cited again in the later cases); *Chandelor v Lopus* (1603) Cro. Jac. 4, 79 E.R. 3; *Hopkins v Tanqueray* (1854) 15 C.B. 130, 139 E.R. 369; *Behn v Burness* (1863) 3 B. & S. 751 at 753, 122 E.R. 281 at 282; *Heilbut, Symons & Co. v Buckleton* [1913] A.C. 30, HL, at 36, 43, 49.

promise, and is not used in its narrower, technical meaning in which it is contrasted with a "condition" of a contract.[5]

Not all pre-contractual representations are incorporated. Not every statement made in the course of pre-contractual negotiations becomes a term of the contract. Nor even does every statement made at the time that the contract is concluded.[6] Other remedies for misrepresentation discussed in this book, such as rescission of the contract, or damages in the tort of deceit or under section 2(1) of the Misrepresentation Act 1967, do not hinge upon the statement having become part of the contract.[7] But for a misrepresentation to give rise to a claim for breach of contract requires proof that the defendant did more than simply make a false statement on which the claimant relied in entering into the contract.[8] The defendant must have intended to be bound in the contract with regard to the statement: his promise about the truth of the statement[9] became part of the bargain itself. This distinction between a "mere representation" and a contractually guaranteed (or "warranted") representation has been drawn firmly in the cases. The circumstances in which the courts will hold that a representation has been guaranteed (expressly or impliedly) in the contract will be discussed below.[10] 8–04

[5] *Oscar Chess Ltd v Williams* [1957] 1 W.L.R. 370, CA, at 374 (Denning L.J.: "everyone knows what a man means when he says 'I guarantee it' or 'I warrant it' or 'I give you my word on it'. He means that he binds himself to it"); *Bannerman v White* (1861) 10 C.B.N.S. 844 at 859, 142 E.R. 685 at 691. For the difference between a "warranty" (in the narrower, technical sense) and a "condition" see below, para.8–38.

[6] Below, para.8–11.

[7] But it is not a bar to the availability of those other remedies that the statement became part of the contract: above, paras 4–38, n.167 (rescission), 5–03 (deceit), 7–44 (Misrepresentation Act 1967 s.2(1)).

[8] Dicta in the speeches of the House of Lords in *Schawel v Reade* [1913] 2 I.R. 64 which, abstracted from their context, might have been understood as suggesting this, are not to be taken as dispensing with the requirement of proving the defendant's intention to be bound in the contract to the truth of his statement—there must be *animus contrahendi* with regard to the matter represented: *Turner v Anquetil* [1953] N.Z.L.R. 952 at 954–955 (observing that the decisions in *Schawel v Reade* and *Heilbut, Symons & Co. v Buckleton* were substantially contemporaneous. This point was also made in *Bowers v Grove* (1938) 60 Ll. L. Rep. 172 at 176).

[9] Or, sometimes, his promise that he is taking care in making the statement: below, para.8–14.

[10] Below, paras 8–07 to 8–13.

But from the outset it should be noted that the courts have emphasised that there is no presumption in favour of a contractual guarantee: there must be evidence that the representation was *intended* to be incorporated into the contract as a term. The general approach is still that set out in the speeches of the House of Lords in *Heilbut, Symons & Co. v Buckleton*.[11] It was there argued that statements made by an employee of underwriters of the issue of shares in a new company, which were alleged to have induced the claimant to subscribe for shares in the company, were guaranteed in a contract collateral[12] to the main subscription contract. Rejecting this, Lord Moulton said[13]:

> "The whole case for the existence of a collateral contract therefore rests on the mere fact that the statement was made as to the character of the company, and if this is to be treated as evidence sufficient to establish the existence of a collateral contract of the kind alleged the same result must follow with regard to any other statement relating to the subject-matter of a contract made by a contracting party prior to its execution. This would negative entirely the firmly established rule that innocent misrepresentation gives no right to damages.[14] It would amount to saying that the making of any representation prior to a contract relating to its subject-matter is

[11] [1913] A.C. 30, HL, followed in, e.g. *Oscar Chess Ltd v Williams*, above, n.5; *London County Freehold & Leasehold Property Ltd v Berkeley Property and Investment Co. Ltd* [1936] 2 All E.R. 1039, CA, at 1043, 1049; *Terrene Ltd v Nelson* (1937) 157 L.T. 254 at 256–257; *Routledge v McKay* [1954] 1 W.L.R. 615, CA, at 618, 623, 624; *Kleinwort Benson Ltd v Malaysia Mining Corp. Bhd* [1989] 1 W.L.R. 379, CA, at 391.

[12] For the significance of such a contract being collateral see below, para.8–06.

[13] Above, n.4 at 48.

[14] [At the time of this case there was still no developed law of damages for non-fraudulent misrepresentation: the only generally available claims for damages were in the tort of deceit (fraudulent misrepresentation) or breach of contract (where the representation was incorporated into the contract). However, the later developments in the tort of negligence (above, Ch.6), and in the passing of the Misrepresentation Act 1967 (above, Ch.7), should not detract from the basic point that the courts require evidence of the representor's (express or implied) intention to be bound before they will hold that he has guaranteed his representation in the contract. But for ambivalent statements about whether developments in other remedies since the decision in *Heilbut* have affected the courts' reluctance to find contractual warranties, see *J. Evans & Son (Portsmouth) Ltd v Andrea Merzario Ltd* [1976] 1 W.L.R. 1078, CA, at 1081 (Lord Denning M.R: broader approach to finding collateral contracts now that damages can be awarded for innocent misrepresentation under the Misrepresentation Act 1967); *Esso Petroleum Co. Ltd v Mardon* [1976] Q.B. 801, CA, at 817

> sufficient to establish the existence of a collateral contract that the statement is true and therefore to give a right to damages if such should not be the case."

Objective test of intention. The question, in general terms, is whether the parties intended the statement to be incorporated into the contract as one of its terms; whether, therefore, the defendant intended to make a contractually binding promise about the accuracy of his statement. Although the application of the test is one of fact, the test itself is one of law.[15] And the test of intention here is objective. As in all matters of formation and interpretation of contracts, the question is not simply what the defendant subjectively intended to promise but what he can be taken, objectively, to have intended.[16] There is, however, some difference of opinion in the cases about how the objective test should be applied. Sometimes the judges appear to assume that the test is wholly objective: that is, it does not take any account of the actual intentions of the parties, nor view the facts through the parties' own eyes, but simply asks whether an external observer would think that the parties had intended to include the defendant's warranty about the statement 8–05

(Lord Denning M.R.: "more often than not the court elevated the innocent misrepresentation into a collateral warranty: and thereby did justice—in advance of the Misrepresentation Act").]

[15] The distinction between law and fact in this context was significant in the older cases where matters of fact were decided by a jury. So the jury would properly be asked to decide what statements were in fact made, and the natural meaning to be attributed to the statement, and whether the statement, in the factual context as found by the jury, was intended between the parties to be part of the contract: *Power v Barham* (1836) 4 Ad. & E. 473, 111 E.R. 865; *Bannerman v White*, above, n.5. The role of the court reviewing a jury's verdict was therefore limited to deciding whether, in the language which the jury found to have been used and to amount to a contract, there could as a matter of law be found material upon which the jury could properly decide that there was a contractually binding promise: *Miller v Cannon Hill Estates Ltd* [1931] 2 K.B. 113. But if there was no dispute or doubt as to the words used or their meaning, and it was clear that the words were only statements of fact and not of obligation, then there was no material to submit to a jury: *Heilbut, Symons & Co. v Buckleton*, above, n.4 at 36–37, 43; *Oscar Chess Ltd v Williams*, above, n.5 at 375. The question of the proper construction of the language of a written document is one of law: *Behn v Burness* (1863) 3 B. & S. 751 at 754, 122 E.R. 281 at 282.

[16] *Turner v Anquetil* [1953] N.Z.L.R. 952 at 957.

within the terms of the contract.[17] However, the better approach is to ask whether the claimant in fact believed, and reasonably could in the circumstances believe, that the defendant intended to make a binding promise in the contract as to the accuracy of his statement. This test is still objective in the sense that it does not depend upon whether the defendant intended (subjectively) to warrant his statement, but whether he has so conducted himself as to induce the claimant to believe that he was giving such a warranty. The test has sometimes been used in the cases[18]; and it would be consonant with

[17] In particular, see *Oscar Chess Ltd v Williams* [1957] 1 W.L.R. 370, CA, at 375 (Denning L.J.: "if an intelligent bystander would reasonably infer that a warranty was intended, that will suffice"), referring to the speech of Lord Moulton in *Heilbut Symons & Co. v Buckleton*, above, n.4 at 51 ("the intention of the parties can only be deduced from the totality of the evidence") which however did not go so far as to say how the objective test should be applied. In questions of the interpretation of the communications alleged to form a contract, Lord Denning in a number of cases was a particularly strong proponent of a wholly objective test: see, e.g. *Solle v Butcher* [1950] 1 K.B. 671, CA, at 691; *Frederick E. Rose (London) Ltd v William H. Pim Jnr & Co. Ltd* [1953] 2 Q.B. 450, CA, at 460; *Hornal v Neuberger Products Ltd* [1957] 1 Q.B. 247, CA, at 257; *Dick Bentley Productions Ltd v Harold Smith (Motors) Ltd* [1965] 1 W.L.R. 623, CA, at 627. See also *Wells (Merstham) Ltd v Buckland Sand and Silica Ltd* [1965] 2 Q.B. 170 at 179 (Edmund Davies J., following Denning L.J. in *Oscar Chess Ltd v Williams*); *Harlingdon and Leinster Enterprises Ltd v Christopher Hull Fine Art Ltd* [1991] 1 Q.B. 564, CA, at 585 (Slade L.J. "an independent onlooker"). This approach is also similar to that adopted in deciding whether a term should be implied ("in fact") into a contract: Chitty, paras 13–004 to 13–007; Treitel, paras 6–034 to 6–039; Anson, pp.152–157; see also *Attorney-General of Belize v Belize Telecom Ltd* [2009] UKPC 10, [2009] 1 W.L.R. 1988 at [25] (Lord Hoffmann, discussing however the implication of terms into an *instrument*). However in finding implied terms the courts are not seeking to characterise the legal significance of what the parties did say, but to fill a gap by reference to what the parties did *not* say; in such cases a more distanced objective analysis is perhaps more generally appropriate.

[18] *Gee v Lucas* (1867) 16 L.T. 357 at 358 (Martin B.: "it is not the intention of the defendant in making this written statement, that is the test; but what he thereby induces the plaintiff reasonably to believe to be his intention"); *Dick Bentley Productions Ltd v Harold Smith (Motors) Ltd*, above, n.17 at 629; *Sabena Technics S.A. v Singapore Airlines Ltd* [2003] EWHC 1318 (Comm), [2003] All E.R. (D) 145 (Jun) at [75] (Colman J: "whether in all the circumstances the statement by the representor would be understood by a reasonable representee in the precise position of the actual representee and with his knowledge of the negotiations as being made with the intention that its truth could be relied upon as a matter protected by contractual enforcement"); Benjamin, para.10.017.

the approach generally adopted when an issue arises as to whether and what terms were included in a contract at its formation.[19]

Collateral contracts.[20] Where it is held that the defendant intended to give contractual force to his misrepresentation it will often follow that the misrepresentation became one of the terms of the contract entered into between the claimant and the defendant following the making of the misrepresentation. For example, if the defendant advertises goods for sale in such a way that his statements about the goods, made in the advertisement and/or during the negotiations, are warranted to be true, the statements may simply become terms of the contract of sale.[21] But sometimes it will be held that the contractual warranty is not incorporated into the main contract itself, but is a term of a separate contract, collateral to the main contract. **8–06**

A situation in which the contract containing the warranty must be collateral, is where it is not between the same two parties as the main contract: for example, where a manufacturer makes representations to the claimant about its product which are intended to have contractual force but the claimant then enters into a contract to purchase the product not directly from the manufacturer but from an intermediate supplier. In such a case, a court might hold that there is a contract with the manufacturer, containing the manufacturer's warranty about the product on which the claimant is entitled to sue, collateral to the main contract of purchase. The consideration provided by the claimant for the collateral contract in such a case is his entering into the contract with the supplier.[22]

[19] Below, Ch.13.

[20] K.W. Wedderburn, "Collateral Contracts" [1959] C.L.J. 58.

[21] *Dick Bentley Productions v Harold Smith (Motors) Ltd*, above, n.17 (statements during negotiations); *Turner v Anquetil*, above, n.16 (statements in newspaper advertisement).

[22] *Shanklin Pier Ltd v Detel Products Ltd* [1951] 2 K.B. 854; *Wells (Merstham) Ltd v Buckland Sand and Silica Ltd*, above, n.17. See also *Brown v Sheen and Richmond Car Sales Ltd* [1950] 1 All E.R. 1102; *Andrews v Hopkinson* [1957] 1 Q.B. 229; *Yeoman Credit Ltd v Odgers* [1962] 1 W.L.R. 215, CA (representations by car dealers formed contracts collateral to main contracts with hire-purchase companies). Where the contract is for the sale, transfer, hire or hire-purchase of goods, and the buyer, transferee, bailee or hirer deals as a consumer, then the circumstances which are relevant to determine whether the goods are of satisfactory quality in relation to the condition implied by statute into the contract with the seller, transferor or hirer include any public statements on the specific

Even in a case where the defendant who gave the contractual warranty was also a party to the contract subsequently entered into by the claimant in reliance on the statement, it will sometimes be appropriate to characterise the warranty as a term of a collateral contract, rather than simply a term of the "main" contract. The "collateral" contract is then *concurrent* with the main contract. Such concurrent, collateral contracts will have the effect of adding to or varying, and even sometimes of directly contradicting, the terms of their "main" contracts and so it is natural that the courts have viewed them with some suspicion.[23] But if the defendant's intention

characteristics of the goods made about them by the producer; i.e. public advertisements about the goods by the producer, as well as by the seller, transferor or hirer, are relevant to the seller/transferor/hirer's liability: Sale of Goods Act 1979, s.14(2D) (sale); Supply of Goods and Services Act 1982, ss.4(2B) (transferee), 9 (bailee); Supply of Goods (Implied Terms) Act 1973, s.10(2D) (bailee or hirer under hire-purchase agreement), as amended by Sale and Supply of Goods to Consumers Regulations 2002 (SI 2002/3045), regs 3, 7, 10 and 13 respectively; below, para.8–13. This does not, however, give a direct claim against the producer.

[23] *Heilbut, Symons & Co. v Buckleton*, above, n.4 at 37, 47; *Business Environment Bow Lane Ltd v Deanwater Estates Ltd* [2007] EWCA Civ 622, [2007] 2 E.G.L.R. 51 at [42] (Morritt C.: "The law relating to collateral contracts is well-established but in connection with sales or leases of land needs to be applied with caution if not the suspicion to which Lord Moulton referred in *Heilbut Symons v Buckleton* [1913] A.C. 30 at 47"); *cf. Hanoman v Southwark LBC (No.2)* [2008] EWCA Civ 624, [2009] 1 W.L.R. 374 at [56]. The fact that the general test for incorporation of a misrepresentation as a contractual warranty (above, para.8–04) has developed from this case, which addressed it in the particular context of collateral contracts, may explain in some measure the courts' general concern to require strict proof of the defendant's intention to warrant his statements. It was suggested by Lord Denning M.R. that the courts have become less hostile to finding collateral contracts: see *J. Evans & Son (Portsmouth) Ltd v Andrea Merzario Ltd*, above, n.14 at 1081; *Esso Petroleum Co. Ltd v Mardon*, above, n.14 at 817; *Howard Marine & Dredging Co. Ltd v A. Ogden & Sons (Excavations) Ltd* [1978] Q.B. 574, CA, at 590–591. See also Lord Denning's unusual willingness in *Dick Bentley Productions Ltd v Harold Smith (Motors) Ltd* to infer that pre-contractual representations are intended to be incorporated into the contract: below, para.8–09. See also Chitty, para.12–005, relying however primarily on dicta of Lord Denning. But it is still correct for the courts to require evidence that the defendant intended to make a contractual promise about his statement before he should be held to his promise, whether the promise is in the main contract or in a collateral contract; and it is no less likely that a court today will be reluctant to find a (concurrent) collateral warranty which directly contradicts the terms of another ("main") contract between the same parties.

to warrant his statement in a collateral contract is proved on the facts, it will be given effect.[24] Such a case may arise where there is a formal reason why the representation cannot be part of the main contract: for example, the contract is required to be in, or to be evidenced by, writing and the representation, though intended to be contractually binding, was oral.[25] Or where the parties wish to keep the representation separate from the main contract—for example, where there is a written contract which is to be varied or supplemented by other terms, but the parties wish to keep the variation or supplement private.[26]

---

[24] *Hanoman v Southwark LBC (No.2)*, above, n.23 at [56] (Arden L.J.: "I do not consider that the court needs to interpret a collateral contract so far as possible to bring it *within* s.2 of the [Law of Property (Miscellaneous Provisions) Act 1989]: on the contrary, on general principle the court should so far as possible interpret it so that it can be enforced and party autonomy respected)".

[25] e.g. where the contract is for a sale of land but a pre-contractual representation about the property was not included in the written contract. The enquiry in such a case is not only whether the representation was intended to have contractual force, but also whether it can be enforceable without having to satisfy the formality required of the main contract: *Record v Bell* [1991] 1 W.L.R. 853; *Tootal Clothing Ltd v Guinea Properties Ltd* (1992) 64 P. & C.R. 452, CA; *Lotteryking Ltd v AMEC Properties Ltd* [1995] 2 E.G.L.R. 13; *Grossman v Hooper* [2001] EWCA Civ 615, [2001] 2 E.G.L.R. 82, CA (see esp. Sir Christopher Staughton at [35] doubting statements in the *Tootal Clothing* case); *Kilcarne Holdings Ltd v Targetfollow (Birmingham) Ltd* [2004] EWHC 2547 (Ch), [2005] 2 P. & C.R. 8 at [189] (Lewison J.: "the court should be wary of artificially dividing what is in truth a composite transaction") (Law of Property (Miscellaneous Provisions) Act 1989, s.2), *cf. North Eastern Properties Ltd v Coleman* [2010] EWCA Civ 227, [2010] 1 W.L.R. 2715 (separate contracts, confirmed by entire agreement clauses: below, para.9–06); *Business Environment Bow Lane Ltd v Deanwater Estates Ltd*, above, n.23 at [42]; *Jameson v Kinmell Bay Land Co. Ltd* (1931) 47 T.L.R. 593, CA (Law of Property Act 1925, s.40); *Angell v Duke* (1875) 10 Q.B. 174 (but see also (1875) 32 L.T. 320) (Statute of Frauds, s.4). Where the contract is not required to be in writing, but is in fact reduced to writing by the parties, it is less likely that a court will hold that an oral representation was intended to have force as a collateral contract; and the parol evidence rule has particular force: below, para.8–12. Where the contract is not a written contract, but is oral, or partly oral and partly in writing, it is not generally necessary to separate the terms into those which are in the "main" contract and those which are "collateral": *J. Evans & Son (Portsmouth) Ltd v Andrea Merzario Ltd*, above, n.14 at 1083.

[26] e.g. where the terms of a lease are overridden by agreement of the landlord in favour of a particular tenant, but the lease is to remain enforceable in its unamended form by and against assignees of the tenant: *Erskine v Adeane* (1873) L.R. 8 Ch. App. 756; *City and Westminster Properties (1934) Ltd v Mudd* [1959]

An "entire agreement" clause in a written contract will however normally have the effect of preventing what might otherwise have been a collateral contract from coming into existence.[27]

(b) *Criteria to test incorporation of the representation*

8–07 **Proof of the intention to be bound to the truth of the statement.** The question is whether the parties intended—and, in particular, whether the representor intended[28]—that the statement made during negotiations or at the time of the contract should become one of the terms of the contract, or of a collateral contract. There is no single test for establishing the answer to this question: there are various criteria by which the courts may judge whether there is sufficient evidence of an intention to incorporate the statement into the contract. The criteria which may be (more or less, depending on the circumstances) useful to make this judgment will be outlined in this section.[29]

8–08 **Significance of the statement.** An important factor in determining whether the statement can be taken to have been intended to have contractual force is its significance: its seriousness, or importance. This has a number of interrelated aspects. A representation is not incorporated into the contract simply because the representee relied on it in deciding to contract.[30] Nor is it necessary

Ch. 129. For other cases of landlords making promises which they refused to incorporate in the written lease, but which were held to be binding as collateral contracts, see *Morgan v Griffith* (1871) L.R. 6 Exch. 70; *Angell v Duke*, above, n.25; *De Lassalle v Guildford* [1901] 2 K.B. 215, CA (disapproved as to some of its reasoning in *Heilbut, Symons & Co. v Buckleton* [1913] A.C. 30, HL, at 50). See also *Esso Petroleum Co. Ltd v Mardon*, above, n.14 (warranty, collateral to lease, that representation about the property was made with care).

[27] *Inntrepreneur Pub Co. (G.L.) v East Crown Ltd* [2000] 2 Lloyd's Rep. 611; followed by *Inntrepreneur Pub Co. (CPC) v Sweeney* [2002] EWHC 1060 (Ch), [2002] 2 E.G.L.R. 132. For further discussion of "entire agreement" clauses, see below, para.9–06.

[28] "Intention" being tested objectively: above, para.8–05.

[29] See also Cheshire, Fifoot & Furmston, pp.165–172; Chitty, para.12–003; Treitel, paras 9–046 to 9–050; Anson, pp.134–135; Lewison, para.3.15.

[30] *J.J. Savage & Sons Pty Ltd v Blakney* (1970) 119 C.L.R. 435, HCA, at 442; *Heilbut, Symons & Co. v Buckleton*, above, n.26 at 50 (Lord Moulton, disapproving dicta in *De Lassalle v Guildford*, above, n.26 at 221); *Mahon v Ainscough* [1952] 1 All E.R. 337, CA, at 340. If this were not the case, every pre-contractual representation would give rise to a claim for damages for breach:

that the representee should have relied on the statement before it can be held to have been incorporated into the contract: the question is always whether the representor can be taken to have intended to guarantee his statement in the contract.[31] But the claimant may have made clear that he regards the fact which is stated or confirmed in the statement as particularly significant for his decision to enter into the contract. In such a case, the representor's willingness to make or confirm the statement with knowledge that the claimant is relying on the particular statement more than other, more routine pre-contractual representations may indicate his willingness to be bound to the statement.[32] Or, without prior indication from the

above, para.8–04. Lord Denning M.R.'s (ex tempore) assertion in *Dick Bentley Productions Ltd v Harold Smith (Motors) Ltd*, above, n.17 at 627, that "if a representation is made in the course of dealings for a contract for the very purpose of inducing the other party to act on it, and actually inducing him to act upon it, by entering into the contract, that is prima facie ground for inferring that it was intended as a warranty," must be viewed with caution: even though Lord Denning says that the inference is rebuttable it is too much even to presume incorporation from the representee's reliance on a pre-contractual representation which was intended by the representor: see further below, para.8–09.

[31] *Harlingdon and Leinster Enterprises Ltd v Christopher Hull Fine Art Ltd*, above, n.17 at 584. However, the reliance on the statement can be particularly relevant to determine whether it was incorporated in the circumstances envisaged by the Sale of Goods Act 1979, s.13 (sale of goods by description): *ibid.* at 574, 584; below, para.8–13.

[32] *cf.* the often quoted dictum attributed to Holt C.J. (above, para.8–03, n.4), "an affirmation at the time of a sale is a warranty, provided it appear on evidence to have been so intended." And see, e.g. *Bannerman v White* (1861) (1861) 10 C.B.N.S. 844, 142 E.R. 685 (purchaser of hops made clear he would only contract on basis that sulphur had not been used in their growth or treatment); *Miller v Cannon Hill Estates Ltd* [1931] 2 K.B. 113 (assurance to prospective buyer of house that it would be built with best materials and workmanship); *Couchman v Hill* [1947] K.B. 554, CA (assurance at auction that heifer was unserved); *Holmes v Burgess* [1975] 2 N.Z.L.R. 311 (assurance of soundness of colt in private sale after auction); *Thornalley v Gostelow* (1947) 80 Ll.L.Rep. 507 (buyers of ship made clear they required a vessel suitable for musselling and shrimping); *Dick Bentley Productions Ltd v Harold Smith (Motors) Ltd*, above, n.17 (purchaser of car had told seller in advance that he was looking for "a well vetted Bentley car" and seller had assured him that he was in a position to find out the history of cars: statement about mileage of car held to be a contractual warranty); *Jones v Bright* (1829) 5 Bing. 533 at 544, 130 E.R. 1167 at 1172 (Best C.J.: "the selling, upon a demand for a horse with particular qualities, is an affirmation that he possesses those qualities"; and the affirmation may be implied, as well as express). In the case of a contract of sale or transfer of goods by a seller or transferor in the course of business, there is an implied condition

representee that the represented fact is of particular significance, the representor may himself take the initiative in giving such an assurance in order to clinch the contract.[33] Sometimes, without any such positive assurances, the representor may be held to have guaranteed his statement in the contract simply because the fact stated is obviously so important for the conclusion of the contract.[34]

If, however, the representor makes clear, or it is otherwise shown by the circumstances in which the statement is made, that he is simply giving his opinion on which the claimant cannot rely as a positive assurance of the truth of the fact, he will not be held to have given any such contractual assurance.[35] And if a pre-contractual statement is simply "sales talk", an exaggerated

---

that the goods will be fit for purposes which the buyer or transferee expressly or impliedly makes known: Sale of Goods Act 1979, s.14(3); Supply of Goods and Services Act 1982, s.4(4), (5).

[33] *Andrews v Hopkinson* [1957] 1 Q.B. 229 (statement by salesman of second hand car: "it's a good little bus; I would stake my life on it; you will have no trouble with it"); *Harling v Eddy* [1951] 2 K.B. 739, CA (no bid first received at auction sale of heifer: in order to induce start of bidding auctioneer said there was nothing wrong with her, and he would take her back if she turned out not to be as represented: statement incorporated in spite of printed auction conditions to the contrary).

[34] *Behn v Burness*, above, n.15 (statement in charterparty about the location of the ship: the place "may be the only datum on which the charterer can found his calculations, or the time of the ship's arriving at the port of load. A statement is more or less important in proportion as the object of the contract more or less depends upon it": Williams J. at 759, at 284). The importance of the fact is not, however, conclusive of a contractual guarantee of the statement of it: *Oscar Chess Ltd v Williams*, above, n.17 at 373. For the separate question of whether, once incorporated, the term is to be characterised as a condition or only a warranty (in the narrow sense) or an "intermediate term", see *Bunge Corp., New York v Tradax Export S.A., Panama* [1981] 1 W.L.R. 711, HL, below, para.8–38.

[35] *Jendwine v Slade* (1797) 2 Esp. 572, 170 E.R. 459 (attribution in auction catalogue of authenticity of an artist "some centuries back" could only be a matter of opinion; the painters in question in the case died in 1682 and 1690); *Cf. Power v Barham* (1836) 4 Ad. & E. 473, 111 E.R. 865 (attribution of pictures to Canaletto on receipt at time of contract of sale could properly be held by jury to be contractual warranty: "it may be true that, in the case of very old pictures, a person can only express an opinion as to their genuineness . . . Canaletti is not a very old painter": Lord Denman C.J. at 476, at 866; Canaletto died in 1768). *Gee v Lucas*, above, n.18 (statement in auction catalogue that a mare was in foal to a particular horse was not only opinion, since it was a fact which could be within the seller's knowledge); *Harlingdon and Leinster Enterprises Ltd v Christopher Hull Fine Art Ltd*, above, n.17 (sale by one art dealer to another of paintings

statement puffing the product which would not be taken seriously by a reasonable person, it will not be held to have been incorporated into the contract.[36]

Sometimes guidance can be obtained from a consideration of the type of circumstance in which the statement is made. For example, there may be a general assumption within a market about whether particular kinds of statement will constitute contractual warranties,[37] such as statements made in answer to standard form enquiries in conveyancing transactions,[38] or statements made privately or in public about a lot which is the object of a contract of sale concluded at auction.[39]

---

wrongly described as by Gabriele Münter: but seller made clear he knew little about the paintings and nothing about Gabriele Münter: not incorporated under the Sale of Goods Act 1979, s.13, below, para.8–13); *Terrene Ltd v Nelson* (1937) 157 L.T. 254 at 257 ("everybody knew from the beginning that" the agent for the vendor of property was giving only an "estimate" of income which could be produced from supply to tenants of electricity from owner's plant); *Ecay v Godfrey* (1947) 80 Ll.L.Rep. 286 (statement by seller of boat to purchaser suggesting he have a survey was evidence that he did not intend to warrant his statements about the soundness of the boat); *Ross v Allis-Chalmers Australia Pty Ltd* (1981) 55 A.L.J.R. 8, HCA (statement by agent of seller of harvesting machine about likely rate of harvesting was, on facts, only tentative and so not warranted); *Oscar Chess Ltd v Williams*, above, n.17; *Laureys v Earl* [2005] EWHC 2601 (QB), [2005] All E.R. (D) 96 (Nov) at [37] (classic car broker's expression of opinion to buyer about authenticity of car not a warranty when, on construction, he was doing no more than passing on an assurance received from the owner). A person making an estimate, or giving an opinion, may however in an appropriate case be held to have given a contractual assurance that he has exercised reasonable care in forming his opinion: below, para.8–14.

36 *Turner v Anquetil* [1953] N.Z.L.R. 952 at 957. See above, para.3–14.

37 For a discussion of the circumstances in which warranties are generally given within the art market, relating to the attribution of works of art, see *Harlingdon and Leinster Enterprises Ltd v Christopher Hull Fine Art Ltd*, above, n.17 at 577–578.

38 In domestic conveyancing transactions statements are commonly made by the seller in response to particular pre-contract enquiries from the buyer: such statements will not be incorporated into the contract unless the contract explicitly so provides. See, e.g. *Mahon v Ainscough*, above, n.30 (printed standard form of pre-contract inquiries made clear that answers were not warranties); *Gilchester Properties Ltd v Gomm* [1948] 1 All E.R. 493 (answers on printed form expressed to be given "so far as the vendor knows" were therefore not warranties); *Terrene Ltd v Nelson*, above, n.35 at 256–257 (purchaser of land normally expected to make proper inquiries for himself: vendor does not normally warrant information he provides). Under the Law of Property (Miscellaneous Provisions) Act 1989, s.2, the contract is now required to be in writing, and so attracts the principle

8–09 **Superior position of the representor.** One factor which may be particularly relevant to determine whether a pre-contractual statement was simply a representation or can be taken to have been intended to be incorporated into the contract is the position of the representor vis-à-vis the representee. A representor who is in a position to know about and give assurances about what he says, when speaking to a representee who is not in such a position, may be held to have given a contractual assurance about the statement. This is by no means an absolute rule: the representor's superior position of skill, or access to knowledge about the subject-matter of the contract, may show that the representee was entitled to rely on

---

discussed below, para.8–12. In a transaction under the National Conveyancing Protocol of the Law Society (6th edn, 2011; see below, para.17–30, n.133) information is first volunteered by the seller, but even such statements will be incorporated into the contract only if the contract so provides. The general conditions contained in the Standard Conditions of Sale (5th edn, 2011) do not provide for replies to pre-contract enquiries to be incorporated into the contract, and it is common for special conditions in such contracts to make explicit provision negativing the contractual force of pre-contractual statements, or limiting such force to those statements which are given in a particular form. For precedents, see *Encyclopaedia of Forms & Precedents* (5th edn, vol.36) (2010 reissue), Form 92 cl.10.2 "not in reliance upon any representation or warranty written or oral or implied made by or on behalf of the Seller (save for any representation or warranty contained in written replies given by the Seller's Solicitors to any written preliminary inquiries raised by the Buyer's Solicitors)" and cl.10.4 ("entire agreement" clause: see below, para.9–06). The National Conveyancing Protocol and the Standard Conditions of Sale are reproduced in F. Silverman, *Conveyancing Handbook* (reissued annually).

[39] In order to allow all bidders to bid on an equal basis, it is common for auction sales to be conducted explicitly on the basis that warranties are not given privately, outside the auction itself; see, e.g. *Hopkins v Tanqueray* (1854) 15 C.B. 130, 139 E.R. 369 (the standard course of dealing at Tattersall's auctions was that no horse is sold with a warranty unless it is expressly mentioned at the time of sale); and it will generally be assumed that a statement in the auction catalogue of a fact which is "such as to confer additional value on the article to be sold" will be incorporated into the sale: *Gee v Lucas* (1867) 16 L.T. 357 at 358. These are however only the starting-point for analysing a case, and it is possible for a warranty to be given to an individual bidder outside the auction: *Couchman v Hill*, above n.32 (note the concern expressed by the report's editor at 560 n.1); *Harling v Eddy*, above, n.33 (but the statement was there made generally to induce bids, and not privately to an individual bidder). And for a case where a statement in the catalogue was only one of opinion, and not incorporated into the contract, see *Jendwine v Slade*, above, n.35.

the statement[40]; but that does not of itself show that the statement was incorporated into the contract.[41] But there are cases where the balance of skill or knowledge (or access to knowledge) has been used by the courts as a significant factor in reaching their conclusion that the representor either did, or did not, make a contractual promise about his statement. This general approach was described by Denning L.J. in *Oscar Chess Ltd v Williams*[42]:

> "The question whether a warranty was intended depends on the conduct of the parties, on their words and behaviour, rather than on their thoughts. If an intelligent bystander would reasonably infer that a warranty was intended, that will suffice . . .
>
> It is instructive to take some recent instances to show how the courts have approached this question. When the seller states a fact which is or should be within his own knowledge and of which the buyer is ignorant, intending that the buyer should act on it, and he does so, it is easy to infer a warranty: see *Couchman v Hill*,[43] where the farmer stated that the heifer was unserved, and *Harling v Eddy*,[44] where he stated that there was nothing wrong with her. So also he makes a promise about something which is or should be within his own control: see *Birch v Paramount Estates Ltd*[45] . . . where the seller stated that the house would be as good as the show house. But if the seller, when he states a fact, makes it clear that he has no knowledge of his own but has got his information elsewhere, and is merely passing it on, it is not so easy to imply a warranty. Such a case was *Routledge v McKay*,[46] where the seller 'stated that it was a 1942 model and pointed to the corroboration to be found in the book', and it was held that there was no warranty."

---

40 Above, para.3–18.
41 See cases cited above, n.35.
42 [1957] 1 W.L.R. 370, CA, at 375.
43 [Above, n.32.]
44 [Above, n.33.]
45 [(1956) 16 EG 396, CA. It was there held that a "serious question and answer" between the purchaser of a new house and a representative of the vendor, in which the representative promised that the house would be equivalent in quality to a show house, gave rise to a collateral contract because the negotiations went forward and the sale was concluded on the faith of the statement.]
46 [[1954] 1 W.L.R. 615, CA. Denning L.J. there said at 623: "it is important to remember that the seller, unless he is the first owner, is not the originator of the statement about the year. He does not know for himself, of his own knowledge, what year the car or cycle is. He has to accept it from the book, and he cannot be expected to warrant its accuracy, unless he in express terms makes himself responsible for it. In the ordinary way, therefore, the statement is only a representation and not a warranty."]

In *Oscar Chess Ltd v Williams* the defendant sold a car to the claimants, describing it as a 1948 model; this date was reflected in the car's registration documents, and was the basis on which the defendant's mother had bought the car a year earlier. Eight months later the claimants, who were motor dealers, discovered that the car was in fact a 1939 model, which was not apparent since there had been no change of style of the car between 1939 and 1948. The price they had paid (£290) was higher than the price they would have been prepared to pay for a 1939 model (£175). It was held by a majority[47] of the Court of Appeal that the claimants had no claim for breach of contract. Although the parties had both made a fundamental mistake as to the age of the car, and there was an innocent misrepresentation by the seller, he gave no contractual warranty. He had no personal knowledge of the year when the car was made, and his statement could not be taken as more than a statement of belief, based on the car's registration documents. Indeed, the purchasers also relied on the registration documents for the same information although (unlike the seller) they were in a position to check the details because as motor dealers they had access though the trade to information about vehicles based on the engine number and chassis number.

The emphasis here is on the relative positions of the parties. We have seen in the context of other remedies[48] that a statement which appears at first sight to be one of fact may be held to have been only one of opinion, on which the representee is not entitled to rely, because of the circumstances in which it is made and in particular where the representee is speaking of something of which, as the representee is aware, he has no particular knowledge. The case may be even stronger where it is the representee who is in the better position to know or discover the relevant facts. Similarly, when the

[47] Morris L.J. dissented, on the basis that the statement was definite and unqualified, not a mere expression of tentative or qualified belief; and it was the foundation of the contract (and therefore warranted in the contract) because the price of £290, a figure arrived at by reference to the value of 1948 cars, was the counterpart of the term of the contract that the particular car was a 1948 model. It cannot surely be adequate to say that a representation is incorporated into the contract simply because it was a fact by reference to which the price was fixed; otherwise many more representations will be incorporated. However, the facts of *Oscar Chess* may well be very close to the line between incorporated statements and mere representations.

[48] Above, para.3–18.

question is whether a representation can be taken to have been incorporated into the contract, if the statement is one which the representee was not entitled in the circumstances to treat as more than one of opinion, the courts will be unlikely to hold that the representor intended to give a contractual warranty.[49]

The reverse need not necessarily follow: that is, just because the representor was in a position to know or discover the accuracy of the facts which he stated (and even where the representee was not in as good a position), the representor will not necessarily be held to have warranted the statement.[50] It is not sufficient to show that the representee reasonably relied on the statement. However, it is in cases where the representor was in such a stronger position, vis-à-vis the representee, that a court might more easily hold that he can be taken to have intended to give contractual force to his statement. For example, in *Dick Bentley Productions Ltd v Harold Smith (Motors) Ltd* a motor dealer was held to have given a contractual assurance to the purchaser of a car that it had done only 20,000 miles since it had been fitted with a replacement engine and gearbox. Lord Denning M.R.[51] contrasted the case with *Oscar Chess Ltd v Williams*:

---

[49] In addition to *Oscar Chess Ltd v Williams*, see *Routledge v McKay*, above, n.46; *Ecay v Godfrey*, above, n.35 at 287 ("absurd to suppose that [the defendant], whose sea-going experience has been in the Thames Estuary during the recent war, would warrant this boat as a sea-going boat"); *Ross v Allis-Chalmers Australia Pty Ltd*, above, n.35 (opinion about the harvesting capacity of a machine, even where said to be based on the seller's experience). If a statement is made not by the other contracting party but by another person in that party's employment, the position and authority of the person making the statement may be relevant to decide whether the representee was entitled to believe that the representation was made with contractual intention: see, e.g. *Bowers v Grove* (1938) 60 Ll. L. Rep. 172 at 176 (statements made about ship by seller's foreman and engineer not part of the bargain); *cf. Mahon v Ainscough* [1952] 1 All E.R. 337, CA (vendor's solicitor innocently giving inaccurate information about property to be sold).

[50] The dictum of A.L. Smith L.J. in *De Lassalle v Guildford* [1901] 2 K.B. 215, CA, at 221, that "in determining whether it was intended [as a warranty], *a decisive test* is whether the vendor assumes to assert a fact of which the buyer is ignorant, or merely states an opinion or judgment upon a matter of which the vendor has no special knowledge, and on which the buyer may be expected also to have an opinion and to exercise his judgment" (emphasis added) was expressly disapproved by Lord Moulton in *Heilbut, Symons & Co. v Buckleton* [1913] A.C. 30, HL, at 50.

[51] [1965] 1 W.L.R. 623, CA, at 627–628.

> "If an intelligent bystander would reasonably infer that a warranty was intended, that will suffice. What conduct, then? What words and behaviour lead to the inference of a warranty?
>
> Looking at the cases once more, as we have done so often, it seems to me that if a representation is made in the course of dealings for a contract for the very purpose of inducing the other party to act upon it, and actually inducing him to act upon it by entering into the contract, that is prima facie ground for inferring that it was intended as a warranty. It is not necessary to speak of it as being collateral. Suffice it that it was intended to be acted upon and was in fact acted on. But the maker of the representation can rebut this inference if he can show that it really was an innocent misrepresentation, in that he was in fact innocent of fault in making it, and that it would not be reasonable in the circumstances for him to be bound by it. In the *Oscar Chess* case the inference was rebutted. There a man had bought a second-hand car and received with it a log-book which stated the year of the car, 1948. He afterwards resold the car. When he resold it he simply repeated what was in the log-book and passed it on to the buyer. He honestly believed on reasonable grounds that it was true. He was completely innocent of any fault. There was no warranty by him, but only an innocent misrepresentation. Whereas in the present case it is very different. The inference is not rebutted. Here we have a dealer, Smith, who was in a position to know, or at least to find out, the history of the car. He could get it by writing to the makers. He did not do so. Indeed, it was done later. When the history of this car was examined, his statement turned out to be quite wrong. He ought to have known better. There was no reasonable foundation for it."

Lord Denning's starting-point—that a representation which is intended to be relied on is likely to have been intended to be warranted—is stronger than that which has generally been adopted in the cases.[52] But the approach based on the contrast between the

[52] As noticed by the editors of the judgment reported at [1965] 1 W.L.R. 623 at 628 and [1965] 2 All E.R. 65, the approach of Lord Denning here is not unlike that proposed by the Law Reform Committee, Tenth Report, *Innocent Misrepresentation*, Cmnd.1782 (1962), which was later translated into the Misrepresentation Act 1967 s.2(1): above, para.7–04. The remedy under that section, which also imposes a liability for damages for pre-contractual statements where the representor cannot prove that he had reasonable grounds for believing his statement, is however quite separate from the issues discussed in this chapter and imposes, in effect, a remedy in tort; it should not affect the basic question here: whether there is evidence that the representor expressly or impliedly warranted his statement in the contract. In the Second Reading debate on s.2(1), however, Lord Denning noted that the new provision would avoid the need to "get round [the] old law" which imposed no remedy in damages for non-fraudulent misrepresentation, and find contractual warranties, such as (he said) the court had done in *Dick Bentley*: *Hansard*, HL Vol.274, cols 939–940.

facts of *Oscar Chess* and *Dick Bentley*, looking to the parties' relative skill and access to information, has been used elsewhere to assist a court in deciding whether a representor can be taken to have intended to warrant his representation.[53] The test of intention is objective. And if one applies the objective test from the perspective of the parties[54] this approach is sensible: the question is whether the representee can be taken reasonably to have believed that the representor was intending to make a promise in the contract about the truth of his statement. If, therefore, the representee knows or ought to know that the representor is only giving an opinion, he cannot expect a warranty. But it is more likely that he can expect a warranty where the representor is making apparently authoritative statements.

State of mind of representor. In a claim for damages for breach of contract arising from a pre-contractual misrepresentation the principal issue is whether the defendant can be shown to have intended to make a contractual promise about the statement. But this intention, as explained in the previous paragraph, is tested objectively. Beyond that, in most cases the representor's state of mind as regards the truth of the statement is not formally in issue: that is, the consideration of the representor's state of mind as fraudulent, negligent or innocent in having made a misrepresentation is not normally part of the analysis of his contractual liability. If the representor has given a contractual promise that the statement is true, the mere fact that the statement is false gives rise to a breach, whether or not the representor knew or ought to have known about the falsity.[55] **8–10**

---

[53] *Heilbut, Symons & Co. v Buckleton*, above, n.50 at 50; *Esso Petroleum Co. Ltd v Mardon* [1976] Q.B. 801, CA, at 818, 826, 831 (warranty of care in making statement, not warranty of truth of the statement: see below, para.8–14). See also, for examples where there was no contractual warranty, the cases cited above, n.49.

[54] As, arguably, it should be applied: above, para.8–05.

[55] An exception to this is where the representee does not promise that the statement is true, but simply promises in the contract that he has taken care in making the statement: below, para.8–14. In such cases the liability is, in substance, based on negligence and the claimant must show the defendant's failure to take care in making the statement.

However, in determining whether the representor can be taken to have intended to make a contractual promise about his representation, the courts do take notice of his innocence (or lack of it). If the representor was in a position to know about the subject-matter of his statement, the court may be more likely to hold that his negligence points towards the statement being incorporated as a warranty; whereas if he is innocent it may point towards the statement being simply an expression of opinion and not intended to be warranted. This is not conclusive, and is another aspect of the approach to the interpretation of pre-contractual statements discussed in *Oscar Chess Ltd v Williams* and *Dick Bentley Productions v Harold Smith (Motors) Ltd.*[56]

8–11 **Timing of the statement.** A representation may become part of the terms of the contract even though it was made before the time at which the contract was concluded,[57] but only where it is shown that the earlier statement was intended to continue into the discussions at the time of the contract itself. For example, a statement in an advertisement which caused the claimant to enter negotiations with the representor may be taken to have been intended to continue (though not repeated) throughout the negotiations and become a term.[58] However, it is undoubtedly easier to establish that a representation made at the time of the contract was intended to be

[56] Above, para.8–09. Lord Denning M.R. in *Dick Bentley*, above, n.51 at 627–628 said that the statement is not likely to be a warranty where the representor "can show that it really was an innocent misrepresentation, in that he was in fact innocent of fault in making it, and that it would not be reasonable in the circumstances for him to be bound by it." The representor's superior position of skill and (access to) knowledge is a significant factor in determining whether he has at least given a contractual warranty that he is taking care in making the statement: below, para.8–15.

[57] *Hopkins v Tanqueray* (1854) 15 C.B. 130 at 139, 139 E.R. 369 at 372.

[58] *Beale v Taylor* [1967] 1 W.L.R. 1193, CA (description in newspaper advertisement of car as "Herald Convertible . . . 1961", although it was in fact parts of two cars welded together, only one part being a 1961 model); *Turner v Anquetil*, above, n.36 (newspaper advertisement for piano in "good order").

part of the terms[59] than in the case where there is a time gap between the making of a statement during the negotiations and the later conclusion of the contract.[60]

Contracts in, or recorded in, writing. Where the parties have created a written document containing the terms of their agreement there will be an inference that statements, oral or written, which do not appear in the document were not intended to be incorporated as terms. Such a written document may be expressed to be the formal contract; that is, either the parties decided during the negotiations that a formal document would be required to complete the contract,[61] or there is some overriding rule of law that a contract of that kind is legally effective only if it fulfils a written formality.[62] Or it may be less formal in that the parties, at the conclusion of their discussions, have chosen to record in writing what was agreed.[63] But in any such case the starting-point is the same: representations which were made in the course of the negotiations and which do not appear in the written document are not generally to be taken as intended to form part of the contractual terms; but a representation which does appear in the document was intended to be incorporated into the contract.[64] This is not simply an application of the parol **8–12**

[59] *cf.* the dictum attributed to Holt C.J. and frequently applied in later cases, "an affirmation at the time of a sale is a warranty, provided it appear on evidence to have been so intended": above, para.8–03, n.4.

[60] *Bowers v Grove*, above, n.49 at 175–176 (statement, sent before the negotiations began, had object only of giving the claimants sufficient details of what the defendant had to offer to enable the claimants to decide whether it was worth their while to open negotiations for purchase); *Hopkins v Tanqueray*, above, n.57 (statement about soundness of horse to be sold at auction made on the day before the auction; *cf. Couchman v Hill* [1947] K.B. 554, CA and *Harling v Eddy* [1951] 2 K.B. 739, CA, esp. at 748, where binding statements about the objects of auction sales were made at the time of the sale); *Howard Marine and Dredging Co. Ltd v A. Ogden & Sons (Excavations) Ltd* [1978] Q.B. 574, CA (statements made three months before contract).

[61] *ibid.* at 176.

[62] Such as contracts for the sale or other disposition of an interest in land: Law of Property (Miscellaneous Provisions) Act 1989 s.2(1).

[63] *T. & J. Harrison v Knowles & Foster* [1918] 1 K.B. 608, CA, reversing Bailhache J. who had held ([1917] 2 K.B. 606) that the memorandum signed by the parties was not intended to contain all the terms of the contract.

[64] A statement in a written contract will normally be held to have been intended to be warranted but, even though in the written contract, it might still be held to be merely a descriptive statement about the subject-matter: *Behn v Burness*

evidence rule,[65] but is also an application of the general test for incorporation of pre-contractual representations. It is natural for the courts to infer from a document, agreed by the parties and which appears on its face to be (or to evidence) a complete set of the express contractual obligations, that the parties had chosen not to include within the bargain other terms such as pre-contractual representations.[66] But there is no absolute rule that a written contract, or a written document evidencing the terms of the contract, excludes the possibility of other contractually binding obligations. In the case of a contract in writing, it may be necessary to hold that any such obligation is contained in a separate contract, collateral to the main written contract.[67] Where there is no formal written contract, but only written evidence of the contract, the representation may be held simply to be one of the terms which were therefore not fully recorded in the written document. But in all cases the question remains: even though the parties entered into a formal written contract, or one or both parties recorded their (informal) contract in writing, was a pre-contractual statement, which is not contained in the written document, intended by the parties to be warranted by the representor?[68]

8–13 **Incorporation of representations and classification of terms by statute.** In some cases statute can assist in answering the question whether a pre-contractual representation is incorporated into the contract. Perhaps the clearest such case is a contract for the sale of goods by description, where under s.13 of the Sale of Goods Act

(1863) 3 B. & S. 751 at 754, 122 E.R. 281 at 282–283 (statement in charterparty that ship was "now in the port of Amsterdam").

[65] Where a contract is made wholly in writing, evidence is not admissible to add to, vary or contradict the written terms, although there are significant exceptions to this rule: see Lewison, para.3.11; Furmston, paras 3.4 to 3.6; Chitty, paras 12–096 to 12–133; Treitel, paras 6–013 to 6–030; Anson, pp.138–139; Cheshire, Fifoot and Furmston, pp.157–165; Phipson, Ch.42.

[66] "The common law's mistrust of oral evidence, particularly of the parties themselves, and its reluctance to impugn the certainty of the written word, comes into conflict with the principle that the law should so far as possible give effect to the presumed intentions of the parties": *Esso Petroleum Co. Ltd v Mardon*, above, n.53 at 824 (Ormrod L.J.).

[67] Above, para.8–06. This assumes that there is no claim that the written contract fails properly to record the parties' intentions: in such a case the proper claim will be for rectification of the written contract: below, paras 13–38 to 13–54.

[68] *Oscar Chess Ltd v Williams* [1957] 1 W.L.R. 370, CA, at 376.

1979 there is implied a term that the goods will correspond with the description.[69] However, the Act is here not in substance changing the common law approach to the question of whether a pre-contractual statement of the description of the goods is incorporated as a term of the contract.[70] Its practical effect[71] is rather to make clear that where there is a description of the goods by reference to which the buyer agrees to purchase them, the term which is thereby incorporated into the contract is a condition,[72] which therefore gives the buyer the right to reject the goods.[73] However, the cases which have been decided under s.13 can be very helpful in showing the circumstances in which a pre-contractual statement of description can be held to have been incorporated. Section 13 refers to a sale of goods "by" description: and this has been held to mean that the description will be incorporated under the statute where the

---

[69] Benjamin, paras 11–001 to 11–023. See also similar implied terms as to description in contracts for the transfer, hire or hire-purchase of goods: Supply of Goods and Services Act 1982 ss.3, 8; Supply of Goods (Implied Terms) Act 1973 s.9, amended by the Sale and Supply of Goods Act 1994 s.7, Sch.2. Although at common law there was no automatic warranty by a seller that he had title to goods (see Benjamin, para.4–001), there were certain contracts in which such a warranty was implied from the offer of goods for sale: *Eichholz v Bannister* (1864) 17 C.B.N.S. 708, 144 E.R. 284. For the terms now implied by statute in contracts of sale, transfer and hire of goods, that the seller, transferor and hirer have the right respectively to sell, to transfer the property in the goods, and to transfer possession of the goods by way of hire for the period of the bailment, see the Sale of Goods Act 1979 s.12 (contract for the sale of goods); Supply of Goods and Services Act 1982 ss.2 (contract for the transfer of goods), 7 (contract for the hire of goods). Under the Package Travel, Package Holidays and Package Tours Regulations 1992 (SI 1992/3288), reg.6(1), certain particulars in a brochure are incorporated into a contract to which the particulars relate.

[70] *Taylor v Combined Buyers Ltd* [1924] N.Z.L.R. 627 at 637–638 (discussing the Sale of Goods Act 1908 s.15, the provision in New Zealand which then corresponded with the Sale of Goods Act 1893 s.13); J.N. Adams and H. MacQueen, *Atiyah's Sale of Goods* (12th edn, 2010), pp.143–144.

[71] *Harlingdon and Leinster Enterprises Ltd v Christopher Hull Fine Art Ltd* [1991] 1 Q.B. 564, CA, at 584.

[72] s.13(1A), as inserted by the Sale and Supply of Goods Act 1994 s.7, Sch.2. The wording of s.13(1) of the 1979 Act (and, indeed, its predecessor the Sale of Goods Act 1893, s.13) before the amendments made in 1994 referred directly to the implied term being a condition. The change was made in order to distinguish in a more satisfactory manner between the principles of contract law in Scottish law (in which there is no formal distinction between conditions and warranties) and English law.

[73] Below, para.8–38.

description is influential in the sale, not necessarily alone, but so as to become an essential term; and that typically the buyer's reliance on the description in deciding to contract will indicate that the sale is by description.[74] There will generally be a sale by description where the sale is of unascertained or future goods which are identified by the description[75]; but also where the sale is of specific goods where the buyer relies on the description rather than on his own inspection of the goods. So if the contract is concluded without the buyer seeing the goods it will be relatively easy to show that the seller's words of description, by reference to which the buyer decided to contract, were to be taken as intended to become terms of the contract.[76] And even where the buyer sees the goods, if he still relies on the description,[77] or if it is not possible for him by his inspection of the goods to know whether the description is accurate,[78] the sale may still be one "by description" within the meaning of s.13.[79] Such an approach is entirely consistent with the common law approach to finding the parties' intentions about the incorporation into the contract of statements about the subject-matter of the contract made during the negotiations.[80]

A pre-contractual representation may also indirectly give rise to a claim for breach of contract under statutory provisions, such as s.14 of the Sale of Goods Act 1979,[81] which implies into a contract a condition that goods will be of satisfactory quality: whether the

[74] *Harlingdon and Leinster Enterprises Ltd v Christopher Hull Fine Art Ltd*, above, n.71 at 571, 574, 584. Stuart-Smith L.J. at 597 doubted whether reliance by the buyer is relevant to the question of whether the sale is by description. However, it is surely right to ask whether the buyer relied on the description to decide whether it can be taken to have been promised: "the description must have a sufficient influence in the sale to become an essential term of the contract and the correlative of influence is reliance" (Nourse L.J. at 574).

[75] Benjamin, para.11.008.

[76] *Varley v Whipp* [1900] 1 Q.B. 513.

[77] *Grant v Australian Knitting Mills Ltd* [1936] A.C. 85, PC, at 100; Sale of Goods Act 1979 s.13(3).

[78] *Beale v Taylor*, above, n.58.

[79] For a detailed discussion of cases decided under Sale of Goods Act 1979 s.13, see Benjamin, paras 11.001–11.023; Chitty, paras 43–073 to 43–080; *Atiyah's Sale of Goods*, above, n.70, pp.143–156.

[80] See, e.g. *Dick Bentley Productions v Harold Smith (Motors) Ltd* [1965] 1 W.L.R. 623, CA (oral description of car); *Turner v Anquetil* [1953] N.Z.L.R. 952 (newspaper advertisement describing piano).

[81] s.14(2) (contract of sale of goods by seller in the course of a business). See also the Supply of Goods and Services Act 1982 ss.4(2) (transfer of goods), 9(2)

goods are of satisfactory quality depends on whether they meet the standard that a reasonable person would regard as satisfactory taking account of, amongst other things, any description of the goods. Where the buyer[82] deals as a consumer, the circumstances which are relevant to determine whether the goods are of satisfactory quality include any public statements on the specific characteristics of the goods made about them by the seller, the producer or his representative, particularly in advertising or on labelling.[83] In effect, this brings within the contract between the seller and the consumer not only statements made by the seller but also public statements by the producer, although the seller is not bound by those public statements if he shows that he was not, and could not reasonably have been, aware of the statement in question; or that before the contract was made the statement had been withdrawn in public or, to the extent that it contained anything which was incorrect or misleading, it had been corrected in public; or that the decision to acquire the goods could not have been influenced by the statement.[84]

(c) Contractual duties of care

Promise of care contrasted with promise of truth. A representation must be incorporated in the contract—"warranted"[85]—if it is to give rise to a claim for breach of contract. But the form of the warranty, the nature of the promise which is incorporated into the contract, may vary. In most cases the 8–14

(hire of goods); the Supply of Goods (Implied Terms) Act 1973 s.10(2) (hire-purchase), all as amended by the Sale and Supply of Goods Act 1994 s.7, Sch.2.

82 Or transferee under a contract of transfer of goods, or the bailee/hirer under a contract of hire or hire-purchase.

83 Sale of Goods Act 1979 s.14(2D) (sale); Supply of Goods and Services Act 1982 ss.4(2B) (transferee), 9(2B) (bailee); Supply of Goods (Implied Terms) Act 1973 s.10(2D) (bailee or hirer under hire-purchase agreement), as amended by the Sale and Supply of Goods to Consumers Regulations 2002 (SI 2002/3045) regs 3, 7, 10 and 13 respectively, implementing Directive 1999/44/EC on Sale of Consumer Goods and Associated Guarantees.

84 Sale of Goods Act 1979 s.14(2E) (sale); Supply of Goods and Services Act 1982 ss.4(2C) (transferee), 9(2C) (bailee); Supply of Goods (Implied Terms) Act 1973 s.10(2E) (bailee or hirer under hire-purchase agreement), as amended by the Sale and Supply of Goods to Consumers Regulations 2002, above, n.83.

85 Above, para.8–03, n.5.

claimant may seek to show that the defendant gave a contractual undertaking that his statement was true. But even if he cannot show such a term in the contract, he may still sometimes be able to show that the defendant gave a contractual undertaking that he was exercising reasonable care and skill in making his statement: a contractual duty of care.

8–15 **Test for contractual duty of care in making a statement.** The test for finding a contractual duty of care in making a statement is the same as the test for all terms of the contract: did the parties (expressly or impliedly) intend there to be such a term? The question, therefore, is whether the representor can be taken to have intended to promise in the contract that he was taking care in making his pre-contractual statement. Such a promise may be found in case where the representor holds himself out to the representee as having skill in making the statement, but where the statement is not sufficiently precise to be warranted to be true. For example, in *Esso Petroleum Co. Ltd v Mardon*[86] a representative of Esso gave inaccurate information[87] to Mr Mardon, a prospective tenant of a new petrol station: he overstated the likely throughput of the petrol station, which induced Mr Mardon to agree to take a lease of it. There was no contractual warranty about the throughput, because the representative's statement was not a positive guarantee about what the throughput would be. But it was held that Esso, through their representative, had given a contractual warranty[88] that the information was given with care. The intention to give this warranty was inferred from, principally, the superior position of Esso who made a significant estimate on which Mr Mardon was entitled to

[86] [1976] Q.B. 801, CA, discussed also above, para.6–28.
[87] The estimate of the station's throughput had originally been accurate; but after the estimate was made the local planning authority required the station to be built 'back to front', so that its entrance was not on the main road. But the throughput estimate was not revised and therefore inaccurate information was given to Mr Mardon.
[88] The warranty here would be collateral to the terms of the lease itself: above, para.8–06.

rely—factors which, as has already been seen,[89] are also relevant in the context of other remedies for misrepresentation. Lord Denning M.R. said[90]:

> "it was a forecast made by a party—Esso—who had special knowledge and skill. It was the yardstick . . . by which they measured the worth of a filling station. They knew the facts. They knew the traffic in the town. They knew the throughput of comparable stations. They had much experience and expertise at their disposal. They were in a much better position than Mr Mardon to make a forecast. It seems to me that if such a person makes a forecast, intending that the other should act upon it—and he does act upon it,[91] it can well be interpreted as a warranty that the forecast is sound and reliable in the sense that they made it with reasonable care and skill."

It must also be noted that Esso was held to owe to Mr Mardon a duty of care in the tort of negligence. That duty arose from the very same facts which the court relied upon to hold that there was a contractual warranty of care in making the statement. The two duties, though owed separately in contract and in tort, were concurrent and of similar content.[92] It may well be that a court will

---

[89] Above, para.3–18. For the relevance of the representor's superior position (in terms of skill or access to relevant information) in deciding whether a representation is incorporated into the contract, see above, para.8–09.

[90] Above, n.86 at 818. See also Ormrod L.J. at 826 and Shaw L.J. at 831.

[91] There is similarity here to Lord Denning's approach in *Dick Bentley Productions v Harold Smith Motors Ltd*, above, para.8–09.

[92] *Esso Petroleum Co. Ltd v Mardon*, above, n.86 at 820, below, para.8–18. See also *South Australia Asset Management Corp. v York Montague Ltd* [1997] A.C. 191, HL, at 211. Of course, a misrepresentation made during pre-contractual negotiations where the contract is not in fact entered into can give rise only to liability in tort, and only if loss flows from relying on the misrepresentation. This emphasises a difference in timing: the tort duty is owed (and, in the case of a misrepresentation made without reasonable care, broken) during the negotiations although it becomes actionable only when the representee suffers loss (typically, by entering into a contract which is a bad bargain: above, paras 2–09, 2–10). The contractual duty is not owed during the negotiations since (unless there is a separate, collateral contract) there is not yet a contract to constitute the source of the obligation; when the contract is formed, it contains a warranty that the earlier representations were made with reasonable care.

be relatively easily disposed to find such a contractual duty of care in those cases where there is also a similar duty in the tort of negligence.[93]

8–16 **Implied contractual duties of care.** Under the Supply of Goods and Services Act 1982, s.13, in a contract for the supply of a service where the supplier is acting in the course of a business, there is an implied term that the supplier will carry out the service with reasonable care and skill. This applies[94] to all such contracts for the supply of a service, and so is not aimed in particular at statements. But where the supply of a service involves the provision of information or advice, such as in the case of a valuer, accountant, lawyer or other professional adviser,[95] the statute will imply a term into the contract that the adviser will take reasonable care and skill: an implied contractual duty of care.[96]

93 Above, para.6–29; both the contractual and the tortious duties of care are here based on the representor's assumption of responsibility in favour of the representee: see, e.g. above, para.6–10.

94 Subject to contrary agreement or course of dealing between the parties, or such usage as binds both parties to the contract (s.16); this in turn is subject to statutory controls on the validity of exclusion clauses, such as the Unfair Contract Terms Act 1977.

95 For categories of professional adviser who may incur duties of care in tort, and who may similarly owe duties of care in contract to the person for whom they provide their professional services for reward, see above, paras 6–30 to 6–42. For the concurrence of contract and tort duties of care generally, see above, para.6–29.

96 For an unusual implied term in the contract between a seller of property and his estate agent, to the effect that the seller would not make fraudulent misrepresentations and thus render any contract of sale unenforceable and this prevent a sale (with the effect of depriving the agent of his commission under the contract), see *John D. Wood (Residential and Agricultural) Ltd v Craze* [2007] EWHC 2658 (QB), [2008] 1 E.G.L.R. 17 at [66]–[68]. A professional adviser may go further and undertake a stricter duty in his contract but special facts or clear languate are required: *Platform Funding Ltd v Bank of Scotland Plc* [2008] EWCA Civ 930, [2009] Q.B. 426 at [48] (surveyor has duty of care in relation to valuation, but contractual retainer carries an inherent unqualified obligation to inspect and value the right property).

(2) Breach of Contract

Breach of contractual promise as to the truth of the statement. 8–17
Where the defendant has given in the contract a warranty that his statement was true, the breach of contract is established by simply showing that the statement was false. Similarly, if the defendant gave a warranty that a statement will remain true during the performance of the contract, the breach is established by showing that the statement has become false.[97] The claimant need not show that the defendant was fraudulent or negligent in making the statement, nor will the defendant be able to use evidence of his innocence to avoid liability.[98] Nor, in order to establish breach of contract, is it necessary for the claimant to show that he relied on the statement and suffered loss.[99] It is sufficient to show that the statement was a term of the contract and was broken. The obligation which the defendant has undertaken in the contract is strict; his liability flows from simple non-performance (that is, from his breach of promise that the statement was true).

Breach of contractual promise of care in making the statement. 8–18
Where, however, the warranty was not that the statement was true, but only that the defendant was exercising care in making the statement, it is not sufficient for the claimant to show that the statement was in fact false. The defendant might have taken care, and so fulfilled his duty, but still made a misrepresentation. It is necessary for the claimant to show that in making the statement as he did the defendant failed to exercise the skill and care required of him by the warranty he gave in the contract. Where, therefore, the

---

97 *Quest 4 Finance Ltd v Maxfield* [2007] EWHC 2313 (QB), [2007] 2 C.L.C. 706.

98 See, e.g. *Beale v Taylor* [1967] 1 W.L.R. 1193, CA (innocent misrepresentation warranted by (private) seller of car); *Wells (Merstham) Ltd v Buckland Sand and Silica Ltd* [1965] 2 Q.B. 170 (innocent assurance by representative of seller of sand that the sand complied with a particular analysis).

99 *Turner v Anquetil*, above, n.80 at 957; *Harlingdon and Leinster Enterprises Ltd v Christopher Hull Fine Art Ltd*, above, n.71 at 584. The claimant's reliance on the statement may be relevant in establishing that the representation was incorporated into the contract (above, para.8–08), but not to the question of breach. The tort of negligence, by contrast, is not complete until the claimant suffers loss in reliance on the statement: above, para.6–46. A claim for substantial (as opposed to merely nominal) damages for breach of contract will, however, require proof of loss: below, para.8–24.

defendant had a duty of reasonable care and skill,[100] the question is whether the claimant can establish that the defendant fell below the standard expected of a reasonably competent person making the statement in similar circumstances to that in which the defendant acted. In substance, this is the same test as that applied in deciding whether a defendant has broken his duty of care in the tort of negligence.[101]

II. DEFENCES

8–19 **Defences generally available to a claim for breach of contract.** A number of defences are available to a claim for breach of contract.[102] Those most commonly raised in claims based on misrepresentations are the claimant's contributory negligence; expiry of the limitation period barring the claimant's action; and the exclusion or limitation of the defendant's liability by a contractual term or non-contractual notice.

8–20 **Contributory negligence.**[103] The defence of contributory negligence is available to a claim for breach of contract only where the defendant's liability in contract is the same as his liability in the tort of negligence independently of the existence of any contract: that is, where the claim in contract is based on an act or omission which comprises a breach of a contractual duty concurrent with, and of

---

[100] Such as under the Supply of Goods and Services Act 1982 s.13: above, para.8–16.

[101] Above, para.6–43. The contractual duty may, of course, be set by the parties' agreement at a level other than the duty of "reasonable care" equivalent to that in the tort of negligence. In all cases the content of the duty must first be identified; and then the facts considered to see whether the defendant has discharged the burden of showing that the defendant failed to fulfil that duty.

[102] Some defences, such as contributory negligence, are relevant to claims for damages but not to termination of the contract. For this reason such matters are often treated in the textbooks as simply part of the question of quantification of recoverable damage, rather than under a grouped heading of "defences". See, e.g. Chitty, Ch.26; Anson, Ch.17. However, the relevant defences are here collected together to enable a closer comparison to be made with the method of analysis in the several claims arising from misrepresentation.

[103] Chitty, para.26–049; Treitel, paras 20–123 to 20–129; Anson, pp.561–563; Cheshire, Fifoot and Furmston, pp.784–786.

content equivalent to, a duty in the tort of negligence.[104] The claimant could pursue either the contract claim or the tort claim, but where he elects to pursue the contract claim he will be met by the very same defence by way of contributory negligence by which he could have been met had he instead pursued the tort claim. The development of the defence of contributory negligence to cover such a case appears to be designed to avoid the claimant having an advantage in pursuing the claim in contract.[105] Contributory negligence is not available as a defence to a claim in contract based on breach of a strict contractual duty,[106] nor even to a claim based on breach of a contractual duty of care where the contractual duty is not concurrent with an equivalent duty in tort, although this latter category is likely to be less significant given the development of the tort of negligence in recent years which now more readily accepts concurrent duties of care in tort and contract.[107]

---

[104] *Forsikringsaktieselskapet Vesta v Butcher* [1989] A.C. 852 at 858–868, 875, 879 (CA; the question was not pursued in HL). The CA (whose decision on this point was strictly obiter) relied in particular on the reasoning of Pritchard J. in *Rowe v Turner Hopkins & Partners* [1980] 2 N.Z.L.R. 550 at 555–556, and the earlier decision of the CA in *Sayers v Harlow Urban DC* [1958] 1 W.L.R. 623. The decision has now become well established: see, e.g. *Barclays Bank Plc v Fairclough Building Ltd* [1995] Q.B. 214, CA.

[105] *Forsikringsaktieselskapet Vesta v Butcher*, above, n.104 at 860. See also *A.B. Marintrans v Comet Shipping Co. Ltd* [1985] 1 W.L.R. 1270 at 1288 (Neill L.J., commenting on the unsatisfactory result of the decision which he there reached: that contributory negligence was not a defence in contract, even in a case of a duty concurrent with a tort duty); *Barclays Bank Plc v Fairclough Building Ltd (No.2)* (1995) 44 Con. L.R. 35, CA (duty in tort argued by defendant, and accepted by court, in order to raise the defence of contributory negligence in contract claim. This was a convenient analysis; *cf.*, however, *Robinson v P.E. Jones (Contractors) Ltd* [2011] EWCA Civ 9, [2011] B.L.R. 206 (no tort duty owed by builder to house owner concurrently with contractual duties)).

[106] *Barclays Bank Plc v Fairclough Building Ltd*, above, n.104; see also *Tennant Radiant Heat Ltd v Warrington Development Corp.* [1988] 1 E.G.L.R. 41, CA; *Bank of Nova Scotia v Hellenic Mutual War Risks Association (Bermuda) Ltd* [1990] 1 Q.B. 818, CA, at 904. In the context of misrepresentation, this means that contributory negligence could not even be argued in a claim based on a breach of a guarantee that the defendant's statement was true, such as in *Dick Bentley Productions Ltd v Harold Smith (Motors) Ltd* [1965] 1 W.L.R. 623, CA; above, para.8–09.

[107] Above, para.6–29; *Henderson v Merrett Syndicates Ltd* [1995] 2 A.C. 145, HL. In 1993 the Law Commission recommended reform to extend the defence of contributory negligence to cases of breach of a contractual duty of care where the contractual duty is not concurrent with an equivalent duty in tort: Law Com.

In principle, therefore, it is open to the defendant to plead contributory negligence on the part of the claimant where the claim is for breach of contract arising from a misrepresentation if the contractual duty is concurrent with, and of similar content to, a duty in tort in respect of the misrepresentation, such as a contractual duty of care in relation to the defendant's provision of pre-contractual information,[108] or the duty of a valuer, accountant, lawyer or other professional adviser to take reasonable care and skill in providing information or advice which will generally be owed to his client in contract[109] concurrently with a similar duty in tort.[110]

The possible scope for the application of the defence of contributory negligence in the context of statements made in breach of a duty of care has been discussed in the context of the tort of negligence, and the points made there will be equally applicable here.[111]

8–21 **Limitation of actions.**[112] An action founded on simple contract[113] cannot be brought (that is, a claim form cannot be issued[114]) after the expiration of six years from the date on which the cause of action accrued.[115] In a claim for breach of contract, the

No.219 *Contributory Negligence as a Defence in Contract* (1993). This report was not, however, accepted for implementation by the Government on the ground that "it was thought to have been overtaken by the developing case law": Law Commission Thirty-third Annual Report 1998, Law Com. No.258, para.1.10.

[108] *Esso Petroleum Co. Ltd vMardon*, above, n.86; above, para.8–15.

[109] Above, para.8–16.

[110] For the concurrence (and equivalence) of duties in contract and tort in the particular context of a professional valuer, see *South Australia Asset Management Corp. v York Montague Ltd*, above, n.92 at 211.

[111] Above, para.6–48.

[112] Chitty, Ch.28; Anson, Ch.20; Cheshire, Fifoot and Furmston, pp.806–815. In 2001 the Law Commission recommended a general reform of the rules on limitation of actions: Law Com. No.270, *Limitation of Actions* (2001), although in 2009 the Government announce that the reforms would not be taken forward: above, para.6–50, n.330.

[113] There are particular rules under the Limitation Act 1980 for actions on a contract of loan (s.6) and actions on a specialty (i.e. where the contract is formally executed as a deed) (s.8), and where the claim (including a claim in contract) is for damages for personal injuries (s.11).

[114] Below, para.11–05.

[115] Limitation Act 1980 s.5. For general provisions for extension of limitation periods in cases of the claimant's disability, see s.28, and in cases of deliberate concealment by the defendant or his agent of facts relevant to the claimant's right

cause of action accrues on breach.[116] Where the claim is based on a pre-contractual misrepresentation which is incorporated into the contract, either a contractual promise of the truth of a statement made during negotiations[117] or a promise that care has been taken in making such a statement,[118] the breach will typically occur at the moment when the contract is formed. Where the claim is based on the breach of a duty of care in providing information or advice during the performance of a contract[119] the breach will occur when the information or advice is given carelessly.

Although the claim in contract may often be concurrent with a claim in tort, and particularly in the tort of negligence,[120] the limitation periods may be very different. In negligence the cause of action accrues at the time when the claimant suffers actionable damage,[121] and not (as in contract) at the moment of the act or omission constituting the breach of duty. And in a claim for negligence, other than a claim for damages for personal injuries, the limitation period will sometimes be extended in cases of latent damage.[122] But no such extension is available for claims in contract, even claims for "contractual negligence", that is, where the action in contract is based on the breach of a contractual duty of care, even one concurrent with the duty in tort which does allow such an extension of the limitation period.[123] Where, therefore, a claimant has a choice between possible actions in contract and in tort, it may

of action, see s.32(1)(b). For a claim to contribution under the Civil Liability (Contribution) Act 1978 s.1, below, para.8–34 there is special time-limit of two years from the accrual of the right to recover contribution: see Limitation Act 1980 s.10.

116 *Battley v Faulkner* (1820) 3 B. & A. 288, 106 E.R. 668; *Gibbs v Guild* (1881) 8 Q.B.D. 296 at 302.

117 e.g. *Dick Bentley Productions Ltd v Harold Smith (Motors) Ltd*, above, n.106; *Shanklin Pier Ltd v Detel Products Ltd* [1951] 2 K.B. 854; *Beale v Taylor*, above, n.98.

118 *Esso Petroleum Co. Ltd v Mardon* [1976] Q.B. 801, CA; above, para.8–15.

119 Such as a valuer, accountant, lawyer or other adviser retained by contract to provide professional services: above, para.8–16.

120 Above, paras 6–29, 8–15.

121 Above, para.6–46.

122 Above, para.6–50. Special provision is made for claims for personal injury, whether the claim is in negligence, nuisance or for any other breach of duty (including a claim in contract): Limitation Act 1980, s.11.

123 *Iron Trade Mutual Insurance Co. Ltd v J.K. Buckenham Ltd* [1990] 1 All E.R. 808 at 821–823; *Société Commerciale de Réassurance v ERAS (International) Ltd* [1992] 2 All E.R. 82, CA. Claims in contract for damages for personal

sometimes happen that he is driven to pursue the tort claim because it is still available whereas the contract claim has become barred by the expiry of the period of limitation.[124]

8–22 **Exclusion and limitation clauses.** A defendant may seek to exclude or limit his liability for breach of contract by a contractual clause; and such a clause may seek to do this by varying the contractual obligation with a view to preventing there being a breach of contract, or by excluding or limiting the remedy which would otherwise be available. The effect of such clauses, and the limits on their effectiveness through such controls as the Unfair Contract Terms Act 1977, are discussed in Chapter 9.

III. REMEDIES FOR BREACH OF CONTRACT

8–23 **The usual remedies for misrepresentation: damages and termination of the contract.** A range of remedies is available for breach of contract.[125] The most common remedy, and one which is available as of right to a claimant who establishes a breach by the defendant, is damages. This remedy will be discussed in this section, together with the remedy of "termination" of the contract—a remedy which is sometimes available for breach of contract, and which will be relevant in the context of claims arising from misrepresentation. Other remedies, such as specific performance of the contract and injunction (mandatory or prohibitory) will not be discussed here because they are not generally relevant in the context of misrepresentation.[126]

injuries will, in cases of latent damage, be subject to the longer limitation period under Limitation Act 1980, s.11; above, n.122.

124 *Henderson v Merrett Syndicates Ltd*, above, n.107.

125 A. Burrows, *Remedies for Torts and Breach of Contract* (3rd edn, 2004); McGregor; Furmston, Ch.8; Treitel, Chs 20–22; Anson, Pt 5; Cheshire, Fifoot and Furmston, Ch.21.

126 These are discretionary remedies, by which the court orders or prohibits performance by the defendant. In the context of misrepresentation, they are normally inappropriate because, e.g. a court cannot order a defendant to "perform" his promise that a statement was true or that he had taken or would take care in giving advice. In favour of a consumer buyer or transferee, however, the seller or transferor of goods which do not conform with the express terms of the contract or the conditions as to description, quality, etc., implied by the Sale of Goods Act 1979, ss.13–15 or the Supply of Goods and Services Act 1982, ss.3–5 can be required to repair or replace the goods: below, para.8–25, n.136.

(1) Damages

Principles of award of damages for breach of contract. Proof of damage is not necessary to found a claim for breach: the cause of action accrues at the moment of breach,[127] even though there is not yet any quantifiable loss flowing from the breach. But the claimant must prove his loss if he seeks to recover substantial compensatory damages, rather than simply nominal damages.[128] The purpose of awarding damages for breach of contract is generally to put the claimant, so far as money can do it, in the same position as if the contract had been performed rather than breached.[129] In a case of misrepresentation giving rise to a claim for breach of contract, the question is therefore what loss, within this basic measure, the claimant can establish. This, together with other aspects of the award of damages for breach of contract, will be discussed in the following paragraphs. 8–24

Calculation of loss: breach of contractual promise of truth of the statement. Where the claim is based on a breach of a contractual promise that the defendant's statement was true,[130] the basic measure of recoverable loss will be such sum as is necessary to place the claimant in the position as if the representation had been true. In accordance with the normal principles of assessment of damages for breach of contract, this may sometimes be calculated as the difference between the value of what the claimant received and the value he would have received if the statement had been true; but sometimes it may be calculated as the cost of curing the defect, such as the cost of carrying out work on the subject-matter of the contract to bring its quality up to the standard which complies with the defendant's promise.[131] 8–25

---

[127] Above, n.116.

[128] McGregor, Ch.10; Chitty, para.26–008; *Marzetti v Williams* (1830) 1 B. & Ad. 415, 109 E.R. 842; *Ruxley Electronics and Construction Ltd v Forsyth* [1996] A.C. 344, HL, at 365; *C & P Haulage v Middleton* [1983] 1 W.L.R. 1461, CA (£10 awarded as nominal damages).

[129] *Robinson v Harman* (1848) 1 Exch. 850 at 855, 154 E.R. 363 at 365 (Parke B.). For further discussion of the contrast between the calculation of damages in contract and in tort, see above, paras 2–07 to 2–10.

[130] Above, para.8–17.

[131] Treitel, paras 20–040 to 20–047. Generally, the courts use the "difference in value" quantification in cases of contracts for the sale of goods where the breach

For example, where a seller of a car gives a contractual warranty about the state of the car which is later found to have been broken because the car was not as described, the measure of damages is generally the difference between the actual (market) value of the car at the time of the contract, and the (market) value it would have had if it had answered to the description.[132] But sometimes the courts will award as damages a sum representing what it would cost to repair the subject-matter of the contract to put it in the condition in which it would have been if in accordance with the warranty.[133] Whichever method of calculation is used,[134] the purpose is to give the claimant the financial equivalent of the defendant's promise: he has a car (worth less than it should have been, given the basis on which he bought it) plus a sum by way of damages to make up the difference to the value the car should have had, or to enable him to remedy the defect. The award of damages does not, of course, give the claimant a car of the promised description. But he is placed in the *financial* position as if he had the promised car and, at least in

---

consists of the fact that the goods fall below the contracted quality (the "prima facie" calculation under the Sale of Goods Act 1979, s.53(3)); and the "cost of cure" in cases where the breach consists of failing to do work which was contracted for: Treitel, paras 20–041, 20–042. But these are only the starting-point, and the court will apply whatever method of quantification appears most appropriately to value the loss of "expectation" which results from the breach. The result, though, is that in most cases of misrepresentation, the starting-point will be to assess the damages by reference to the difference in value, rather than the cost of cure.

[132] *Brown v Sheen and Richmond Car Sales Ltd* [1950] 1 All E.R. 1102 at 1104. There is, however, a lack of clarity in the report about the quantification of loss: the judge described the loss as the fact that the buyer "paid a larger sum . . . for the car than it was worth and he would have paid if the warranty had not been given", which points towards damages calculated on the tort measure (how much worse off the claimant is by virtue of relying on the misrepresentation). But the assessment of damages is then said (correctly) to be the difference between the value of the car and the value it would have had if it had answered to the warranty. The report at [1950] W.N. 316 is unambiguous in stating the correct measure. See also *Andrews v Hopkinson* [1957] 1 Q.B. 229 (consequential losses recoverable in addition to the difference in value).

[133] *Thornalley v Gostelow* (1947) 80 Ll.L.Rep. 507 at 513, where the repairs had been carried out.

[134] Sometimes the two methods of calculation will yield the same answer: e.g. in *Brown v Sheen and Richmond Car Sales Ltd*, above, n.132, damages were apparently awarded on the basis of "difference in value", but they were the same amount as the claimant had spent in having the repairs carried out.

theory,[135] he can himself obtain the contractually promised performance by selling the defective car and using the proceeds, together with the damages he has recovered, to buy another car of the quality he originally sought; or, where "cost of cure" damages are awarded, he can remedy the defect so as to obtain the contractually promised performance.[136]

Calculation of loss: breach of contractual duty of care. Where the claim is based on a breach of a contractual duty of care in making the statement[137] damages are, in principle, still awarded to put the claimant, so far as money can do it, in the same position as if the contract had been performed rather than breached. But here there was no promise that the statement was true, so it is not appropriate to quantify the claimant's loss by reference to the value he would have received had the statement been true. Instead, the 8–26

[135] Not necessarily, of course, in practice: there will be transaction costs in moving to the position of having a new, compliant car; and the damages, which will normally have been calculated on the basis of the car's actual and contracted values at the time of the contract, will not necessarily be sufficient if market prices of replacement cars have increased (or the sale value of the non-compliant car has decreased) by the time the transactions are entered into.

[136] Until recently, there was no mechanism in the law of contract by which the defendant could be compelled to give the claimant a car which complied with the description: the defendant could not be compelled by an order of specific performance to make good his promise that the car which is the object of the contract will be of a particular description which, in fact, it is not; and even where it would be possible to undertake work on the car to remedy any defects by which the car failed to fulfil the promised description, at common law the courts would not order the defendant personally to undertake such work but would require the claimant to take damages. And to require the defendant to provide another car which does fulfil the promised description would be to perform another contract, not the one into which the parties actually entered. However, in the case of a contract of sale or transfer of goods where the buyer or transferee deals *as a consumer* the seller or transferor of goods which do not conform with the express terms of the contract or the conditions as to description, quality, etc, implied by the Sale of Goods Act 1979, ss.13–15 (contract of sale) or the Supply of Goods and Services Act 1982, ss.3–5 (contract for transfer of goods) can now be required by the buyer/transferee (inter alia) to repair or replace the goods, as long as it is not impossible or disproportionate in comparison to the other available remedies: Sale of Goods Act 1979, s.48B; Supply of Goods and Services Act 1982, s.11N, both inserted by Sale and Supply of Goods to Consumers Regulations 2002, implementing Directive 1999/44/EC on Sale of Consumer Goods and Associated Guarantees.

[137] Above, para.8–18.

loss is to be valued by reference to the fact that the defendant has broken his promise to take care. In such cases, since the content of the contractual duty is generally the same as the duty owed in the tort of negligence,[138] the courts have awarded damages for breach of contract on the same measure as normally awarded in tort: that is, the claimant is compensated for the out-of-pocket loss flowing from having entered into a contract in reliance on the defendant's careless statement.[139]

8–27 **Lost potential profits.** The claim for damages for breach of contract may[140] include a claim for the profits which the claimant would have made but for the breach. In the case of a breach of a promise that the statement was true, the claim may therefore be for the profits which the claimant would have made had the statement

[138] *South Australia Asset Management Corp. v York Montague Ltd* [1997] A.C. 191, HL, at 211. Indeed, there will very often be *concurrent* duties, of similar content (above, paras 6–29, 8–15) and the courts will not draw a distinction between the two claims in assessing the basic measure of loss: *Esso Petroleum Co. Ltd v Mardon* [1976] Q.B. 801, CA at 820.

[139] *Esso Petroleum Co. Ltd v Mardon*, above, n.138 at 820–821, 834. Ormrod L.J. at 828–829 appeared to contemplate that, had it not been "virtually incapable of proof", the defendant could have claimed for the "loss of income which he could reasonably have expected to earn from the business". But this would in effect give him a warranted return. The better view (as given by Lord Denning at 821) is that any lost profits in such a claim should be based on the profits he would have been able to make in another venture, by the use of his lost capital: see also below, para.8–27.

[140] Typically, where the claimant is deprived of the chance to make on-going profits. In the case of a contract to buy specific goods, the claimant's loss is normally calculated on the basis simply of the difference in value between the goods as promised and as delivered; no additional sum is included to take account of the claimant's lost potential profit in a (lost) subsequent sale contract, although this may, exceptionally, be recoverable where the defendant had actual or imputed knowledge of the loss in question: Benjamin, para.17–028. Any claim for lost potential profits will of course be subject to the rules of remoteness (below, para.8–30) and mitigation (below, para.8–31). See also *Salford City Council v Torkington* [2004] EWCA Civ 1646, [2004] All E.R. (D) 125 (Dec) (warranty by landlord about competition which business would face: damages to reflect decreased value of business at point when reasonable tenant would decide to cease trading, not for on-going lost profits as if claimants had continued to trade indefinitely, which would (a) be beyond the reasonable contemplation of the parties at the time the warranties were given (an issue of remoteness of damage), and (b) ignore the reality that the defendants had decided to dispose of their business rather than continue it).

been true: for example, if the seller of a business gives a warranty as to a fact relevant to the profitability of the business. Where, however, the breach is only of a contractual duty of care—for example, if the lessor of a business gives false information about the profitability of the business, where he has not promised that the information was true but has only promised to take care in giving the information[141]—the claimant is still entitled to say that, as a result of investing his capital in the business in reliance on the defendant's statement, he has lost the opportunity to make profits from that capital. But he cannot then claim the profits which he should have earned from *that* business had the statement been true, since the defendant did not give such a warranty.[142] But, as in similar claims based on the tort measure of damages,[143] he can say that he would have used his money, time and energy to make profits from another business, in which—but for the inducement to enter this contract—he would have been able to invest his capital. In all cases of claims for lost potential profits, however, the claimant must plead and prove the claim, including the basis on which the calculation is made, although such predictions as to what would have been the case are not always easy to make with absolute certainty, and the court will make the best attempt to quantify the loss.[144] If the claimant cannot show that he has lost a particular sum as a result of the breach, but he can establish (and the court can evaluate) a claim that the defendant's breach of contract has deprived him of the *chance* of making that sum, where the chance depends on some contingency outside the claimant's control, the court may award as damages for breach a sum which reflects the value of the chance of which he has been deprived.[145]

Causation. The normal principles of causation apply to a claim for damages for breach of contract, and so the claimant must establish a sufficient continuing causal link between the breach and **8–28**

[141] *Esso Petroleum Co. Ltd v Mardon*, above, n.138.

[142] *ibid.* at 820–821.

[143] Above, paras 5–39 (tort of deceit), 6–58 (tort of negligence).

[144] *Esso Petroleum Co. Ltd v Mardon*, above, n.138 at 821 (Lord Denning M.R.: "the future is necessarily problematical and can only be a rough-and-ready estimate. But it must be done in assessing the loss"), 829 (Ormrod L.J.: on the facts, claim for loss of profits was "virtually incapable of proof"); *South Australia Asset Management Corp. v York Montague Ltd*, above, n.138 at 220.

[145] *Chaplin v Hicks* [1911] 2 K.B. 786, CA.

the loss which is claimed.[146] The question of causation appears to be raised only rarely in the reported cases concerning claims for breach of contract, but similar principles are generally used here as in questions of causation in claims in tort. However, in cases of misrepresentation, the question in contract is not addressed in quite the same way as in a tort claim. In tort,[147] the issue is generally whether the loss was caused by the claimant's reliance on the statement, since reliance is an integral element of the claim in tort. However, in a claim in contract the question is whether the loss flowed from the defendant's breach of promise.

8–29 **Loss within the scope of the duty.** It is not sufficient for the claimant to show that his loss was caused by the act or omission which constituted the defendant's breach of contract; in addition, the loss is recoverable only if the duty which was broken was a duty which encompassed that kind of loss. Since damages for breach of contract are normally calculated as the sum necessary to put the claimant in the same position as if the contract had been performed, to compensate him for his "loss of bargain", it is necessary to ask what it was that he bargained for. That is, what was it that the defendant promised? The defendant is liable only for the loss suffered by the claimant which falls within that "bargain". One context in which this issue has arisen is the duty of a professional adviser: for example, where a claimant receives information or advice from the defendant, acts upon it and suffers losses, the range of recoverable losses will depend on the scope of the duty which the defendant undertook. If the duty was only to provide accurate information, the recoverable loss will be limited to that which flows

146 McGregor, paras 6.137–6.154. The general approach is to apply "the court's common sense" to determine whether the breach was the cause of the loss, rather than merely the occasion for the loss: *Galoo Ltd v Bright Grahame Murray* [1994] 1 W.L.R. 1360, CA, at 1375, discussing both contract and tort. In one case, the CA used the principles of causation to apportion the liability for claimant's losses (90% claimant/10% defendant): *Tennant Radiant Heat Ltd v Warrington Development Corp.* [1988] 1 E.G.L.R. 41. This unorthodox decision (which was apparently reached to remedy the absence of a defence of contributory negligence in a case of a strict contractual duty: above, para.8–20) has however been later doubted by the CA: *Bank of Nova Scotia v Hellenic Mutual War Risks Association (Bermuda) Ltd* [1990] 1 Q.B. 818 at 904, but followed at first instance in *W. Lamb Ltd v J. Jarvis & Sons Plc* (1998) 60 Con L.R. 1.

147 Above, paras 5–38 (tort of deceit), 6–53 (tort of negligence).

from the inaccuracy of the information, and not the wider loss which resulted from the use of the information to enter into a transaction which proved unprofitable for other reasons.[148]

Remoteness of damage. The normal principles governing remoteness of damage in a claim for damages for breach of contract will apply. According to the traditional rule,[149] this means that the claimant is only entitled to recover damages of such a kind as was in the defendant's contemplation, at the time the contract was entered into, as likely to result in the event of such a breach.[150] **8–30**

Mitigation. The normal rules of mitigation apply to claims for breach of contract based on misrepresentation: the claimant will be unable to recover from the defendant any part of his loss which he **8–31**

[148] *South Australia Asset Management Corp. v York Montague Ltd*, above, n.138 at 211, 214, 216. This principle is applicable to the recoverable loss in both contract and tort (*ibid.* at 211); for further discussion in the context of the tort of negligence, see above, para.6–55. For an illustration of the application of the principle in contract, see *Cossey v Lonnkvist* [2000] Lloyd's Rep. P.N. 885, CA (accountant's duty to give information to bank financing claimant's purchase of business did not extend to advising claimant on wisdom of buying the business).

[149] This now has to be read in the light of *Transfield Shipping Inc. v Mercator Shipping Inc. (The Achilleas)* [2008] UKHL 48, [2009] 1 A.C. 61 where Lord Hoffmann sought to redefine the scope of recoverable loss by reference to that for which the defendant could (on a proper construction) reasonably be taken to have accepted liability. This new test appears only to have supplemented, rather than supplanted, the traditional rule: *Supershield Ltd v Siemens Building Technologies F.E. Ltd* [2010] EWCA Civ 7, [2010] 1 C.L.C. 241 at [43]; *Sylvia Shipping Co. Ltd v Progress Bulk Carriers Ltd* [2010] EWHC 542 (Comm), [2010] 2 Lloyd's Rep. 81 at [48].

[150] *Koufos v C. Czarnikow Ltd (The Heron II)* [1969] 1 A.C. 350, HL, explaining the rules first established in *Hadley v Baxendale* (1854) 9 Exch. 341, 156 E.R. 145. For more detailed discussion of the rules relating to remoteness of damage in contract, see Chitty, paras 26–051 to 26–087 and 26–100A to 26–100H (the latter paragraphs discussing the implications of the decision in *The Achilleas*, above, n.149); McGregor, paras 6.155–6.202. The HL in *The Heron II* were at pains to emphasise that the test in contract is more restrictive than that in those torts (such as negligence) which use a test of remoteness based on "reasonable foreseeability": *ibid.* at 385–386, 389, 411, 413–414, 422. For the principles of remoteness of damage in the torts of deceit and negligence, see above, paras 5–40, 6–56; and for a discussion of the principles in both contract and tort, see J. Cartwright, "Remoteness of Damage in Contract and Tort: a Reconsideration" [1996] C.L.J. 488. The recoverable loss is already limited by the principle that the loss must fall within the scope of the duty: above, para.8–29.

would not have suffered if he had taken such steps as he ought reasonably to have taken in order to avoid or reduce his loss.[151] If the action taken by a claimant in properly attempting to mitigate his loss in fact results in the loss being increased, the additional loss will still be recoverable.[152]

8–32 **Damages are compensatory.** Damages in contract are normally awarded only to compensate the claimant, and not to deprive the defendant of a benefit he has obtained by reason of the breach of contract, although the House of Lords has held that in exceptional cases a court may award an account of the defendant's profits as a remedy for breach.[153] There is no question in English law[154] of awarding punitive damages for breach of contract.[155]

---

[151] *British Westinghouse Electric and Manufacturing Co. Ltd v Underground Electric Railways Co. of London Ltd* [1912] A.C. 673, HL, at 689. For detailed discussion of the rules of mitigation, see Chitty, paras 26–101 to 26–124.

[152] *Esso Petroleum Co. Ltd v Mardon*, above, n.138 at 821–822, 829, 833. If the claimant's conduct was an *unreasonable* reaction to the predicament in which he found himself after the breach, losses caused by that reaction might be irrecoverable on the basis that the conduct broke the chain of causation: *South Australia Asset Management Corp. v York Montague Ltd*, above, n.138 at 218–219.

[153] *Attorney General v Blake* [2001] 1 A.C. 268, HL, see esp. at 284–285 (Lord Nicholls); applied in *Esso Petroleum Co. Ltd v Niad* [2001] All E.R. (D) 324 (Nov), although later cases have arisen in the context where the breach is generally of a negative obligation and where the remedy, whilst appearing to be based on the defendant's profit, has been held not to be an account of the profits, but damages to compensate the claimant's loss in being deprived of the opportunity to bargain for a variation or release of the obligation: *Experience Hendrix LLC v PPX Enterprises Inc.* [2003] EWCA Civ 323, [2003] 1 All E.R. (Comm) 830; *WWF–World Wide Fund for Nature v World Wrestling Federation Entertainment Inc.* [2007] EWCA Civ 286, [2008] 1 W.L.R. 445 applying *Wrotham Park Co. Ltd v Parkside Homes Ltd* [1974] 1 W.L.R. 798; *Pell Frischmann Engineering Ltd v Bow Valley Iran Ltd* [2009] UKPC 45, [2010] B.L.R. 73 at [47]–[49]. "*Wrotham Park* damages" can also be awarded for breach of a positive obligation: *Van der Garde v Force India Formula One Team Ltd* [2010] EWHC 2373 (QB), [2010] All E.R. (D) 122 (Sep) at [526]; however, such a claim is not likely to arise in a claim based on misrepresentation.

[154] In Canada, the Supreme Court has accepted that punitive damages are in principle available in contract, but only in "very unusual" circumstances: *Vorvis v Insurance Corp. of British Columbia* (1989) 58 D.L.R. (4th) 193 at 207 (McIntyre J.; Wilson J. at 223–224 gave a wider (minority) view); *Whiten v Pilot Insurance Co.* (2002) 209 D.L.R. (4th) 257 at [36]–[77] (general and comparative review of punitive damages), [78]–[83] (discussion of when punitive damages

Damages for intangible losses. Damages may sometimes be awarded in contract for intangible losses. Where the object (or, at least, an important object[156]) of the contract is to provide enjoyment, peace of mind or freedom from distress, a claim may be made for that distress or absence of peace of mind which resulted from the breach and which was the very loss against which the contract was intended to protect the claimant.[157] But this is the exception: in most cases the contract does not have as an important object the provision of enjoyment, peace of mind or freedom from distress, and damages are not then recoverable for the claimant's distress, inconvenience or frustration even where that was a likely consequence of the breach.[158] However, where the claimant suffers distress or discomfort arising from the *physical* consequences of the breach, the courts have been willing to award modest sums by way of compensation, as in the case of such distress or discomfort arising from the physical consequences of a breach of a duty of care in the tort of negligence.[159] 8–33

can be awarded in contract, emphasising that the defendant's conduct must be independently an "actionable wrong", although not necessarily a tort); Waddams, paras 743–744; Fridman, pp.753–756; Swann, pp.430–451 (criticising the lack of clarity in the case law). In the United States (where punitive damages are awarded in tort) in principle damages for breach of contract are not punitive, but some courts have made such an award, especially in cases where the breach of contract was also tortious: Farnsworth, para.12.8. Punitive damages are not awarded for breach of contract in Australia: Carter, Peden and Tolhurst, para.35–03; Seddon and Ellinghaus, para.23.2.

155 *Perera v Vandiyar* [1953] 1 W.L.R. 672, CA; *Kenny v Preen* [1963] 1 Q.B. 499, CA, at 513; *Ruxley Electronics and Construction Ltd v Forsyth* [1996] A.C. 344, HL, at 373. In *McCall v Abelesz* [1976] Q.B. 585 at 594 Lord Denning M.R. thought that the damages claimed in *Perera* v *Vandiyar* and *Kenny v Preen* would now be recoverable, but not as punitive damages but as (compensatory) damages for mental distress. For the award of exemplary (punitive) damages in tort, see above, paras 5–42 (deceit), 6–61, n.377 (negligence).

156 *Farley v Skinner* [2001] UKHL 49, [2002] 2 A.C. 732.

157 *Bliss v South East Thames Regional Health Authority* [1987] I.C.R. 700, CA, at 717–718; *Jarvis v Swans Tours Ltd* [1973] Q.B. 233, CA (holiday); *Heywood v Wellers* [1976] Q.B. 446 (breach of duty by solicitor retained to obtain injunction against molestation); *Farley v Skinner*, above, n.156 (contract by which a surveyor was engaged to inspect and report on property to be occupied mainly at weekends and holidays, where the property was near an airport and the client had a particular concern about noise).

158 *Johnson v Gore Wood & Co.* [2002] 2 A.C. 1, HL.

159 For discussion of this, and examples of cases (in both contract and tort) in which such awards have been made, see above, para.6–62.

8–34 **Contribution between co-defendants.** Where a defendant in an action for breach of contract is liable jointly with another defendant for damage suffered by the claimant—whether the co-defendant's liability is also in contract or is based on some other cause of action such as deceit or negligence—the court will, as in all cases of joint or several liability, have jurisdiction under the Civil Liability (Contribution) Act 1978 to apportion between the co-defendants the damages payable.[160] Any express provision in the contract regulating or excluding contribution between co-defendants takes effect in place of the rules provided by the Act.[161]

(2) Termination

8–35 **"Rescission" of the contract for misrepresentation contrasted with "termination".** It is necessary first to understand the terminology used here. The remedy of rescission for misrepresentation involves the contract being avoided *ab initio*. It is the remedy by which a voidable contract is avoided.[162] If a contract is rescinded not only are future, unaccrued obligations released but also those obligations which have accrued, and even those which have been performed, are retrospectively unwound and any performance which has taken place by either party must be reversed.

With this must be contrasted the remedy which is generally referred to in this book as *termination* of the contract. This is a remedy which is sometimes available on breach of contract, and involves the future, unaccrued[163] obligations being released without there being any disturbance of those obligations which, at the moment the remedy takes effect, have already accrued. This remedy will sometimes be available arising out of a misrepresentation, where the representation was incorporated into the contract as a

160 Above, para.2–14.

161 s.7(3)(b); and the Act does not affect any express or implied contractual or other right to indemnity: s.7(3)(a). Under the Companies Act 2006 ss.532–538 a company may agree to limit its auditors' liability in such a way as to make them liable for only their own share of the damage, rather than jointly and severally liable for the whole damage: above, para.6–33, n.182.

162 Above, para.4–05.

163 Obligations which have already accrued survive the termination, even if they have not yet been performed: *Bank of Boston Connecticut v European Grain and Shipping Ltd* [1989] A.C. 1056, HL.

term in the manner described in the earlier sections of this chapter, and has given rise to a breach of contract of the kind for which termination is available.[164]

Inconsistent use of terminology in the older cases. There has been some inconsistency in the use of terminology in the cases. Although it has been usual to use the word "rescission" to describe the remedy of avoidance of the contract *ab initio* for misrepresentation,[165] sometimes judges and writers have used the word "rescission" to mean also termination of the contract. The ambiguity has been noticed in a number of cases. In *Mussen v Van Diemen's Land Co.*[166] Farwell J. said: 8–36

> "No doubt the word 'rescission' or the word 'rescind' is capable of two meanings. The rescission of a contract may mean putting an end to it altogether, that is to say, making it null and void ab initio, or it may mean putting an end to it except so far as any obligation or right which arises under the contract if and when so determined."

There is therefore a real danger of confusion about the nature of the remedy being described, if the terminology is unclear and if the context in which the word is used does not sufficiently show the intended meaning.

---

164 Below, para.8–38.

165 Even this has not always been used consistently, however, particularly in older cases; judges have sometimes referred to a representee "repudiating" the contract for misrepresentation: see, e.g. *Selway v Fogg* (1839) 5 M. & W. 83, 151 E.R. 36; *Rogers v Hadley* (1863) 2 H. & C. 227 at 247, 159 E.R. 94 at 103; *Reese River Silver Mining Co. v Smith* (1869) L.R. 4 H.L. 64 at 73; *Aaron's Reefs Ltd v Twiss* [1896] A.C. 273, HL; *Lagunas Nitrate Co. v Lagunas Syndicate* [1899] 2 Ch. 392, CA. This is certainly not "repudiation" in the technical sense in which it is generally used now, to mean a fundamental breach of contract by which one party manifests to the other party his intention no longer to perform the contract, and which then gives the innocent party the right to terminate the contract: *Afovos Shipping Co. S.A. v Pagnan* [1983] 1 W.L.R. 195, HL, at 203; below, para.8–38.

166 [1938] Ch. 253 at 259. See also *Mersey Steel and Iron Co. v Naylor, Benzon & Co.* (1882) 9 Q.B.D. 648, CA, at 671 (Bowen L.J.: "a fallacy may possibly lurk in the use of the word 'rescission'"); *Buckland v Farmar & Moody* [1979] 1 W.L.R. 221, CA, at 232 (Buckley L.J.: there is "no primary meaning" of the word, which is capable of alternative meanings and frequently used in alternative senses); *Heyman v Darwins Ltd* [1942] A.C. 356, HL, at 373, 399.

8–37 **The preferred (but not unanimous) terminology in the modern law.** More recently, the House of Lords has made clear that the potential confusion arising out of this ambiguity is such that the use of the term "rescission" should be restricted to the remedy of avoidance of the contract *ab initio*. In *Photo Production Ltd v Securicor Transport Ltd*[167] Lord Wilberforce recognised that "to plead for complete uniformity may be to cry for the moon", but he urged the use of such words as "discharge" or "termination" to describe the remedy by which the unaccrued obligations under the contract are released by reason of a breach of contract, without the contract being avoided *ab initio*. This has led to a greater consistency of usage of language in the recent cases and by commentators, although sometimes the older terminology can still be found, particularly in contexts where its usage had become well established.[168] However, in this book the word "rescission" is used in the text to refer only to the remedy by which a voidable contract

[167] [1980] A.C. 827, HL, at 844–845, building on his own earlier criticism in *Johnson v Agnew* [1980] A.C. 367, HL, at 392–393 of the "fertile source of confusion" involved in using the words "rescission" to mean two quite different remedies. See also Lord Diplock in *Photo Production* at 850. The Supreme Court of Canada has similarly said that the confusion between the different meanings of "rescission" has "plagued common law jurisdictions for years" and that "to use 'rescission' and 'accepted repudiation' synonymously can lead only to confusion and should be avoided": *Guarantee Co. of North America v Gordon Capital Corp.* (1999) 178 D.L.R. 1 at 14, 18.

[168] In particular, contracts for the sale of land where standard forms have long referred to (and continue to refer to) rescission as a remedy, e.g. for the other party's failure to complete in accordance with a notice to complete: Standard Conditions of Sale (5th edn, 2011), paras 7.4.2, 7.5.2; but see also paras 7.1.1(b), 7.1.2, where "rescission" may be used in the sense of rescission *ab initio* for misrepresentation. See also Emmet, para.7.003; F. Silverman, *Standard Conditions of Sale: A Conveyancer's Guide* (7th edn, 2006), para.19.2; *Buckland v Farmar & Moody*, above, n.166 at 231–232; *Johnson v Agnew*, above, n.167; E. H. Burn and J. Cartwright, *Cheshire and Burn's Modern Law of Real Property* (18th edn, 2011), pp.995–996. Until recently Treitel still preferred to use the term "rescission" in relation to breach, noticing that some judgments of the House of Lords after *Photo Production* have still used that terminology: e.g. *Bunge Corp., New York v Tradax Export S.A, Panama* [1981] 1 W.L.R. 711 at 719, 723, 724; *Gill & Duffus SA v Berger & Co. Inc.* [1984] A.C. 382 at 390, 391: see, e.g. Treitel (11th edn, 2003), pp.759–760. The current editor, however, favours the term "termination": see Treitel (13th edn, 2011), para.18–001; and other books similarly generally avoid the term "rescission" in relation to breach of contract: Chitty, para.24–047; Anson, Ch.15, esp. p.524; Cheshire, Fifoot and Furmston, p.691; Benjamin, para.15.101, n.674.

is avoided[169]; the remedy of discharge of the obligations for breach of contract is here generally referred to as "termination".

Termination available only for breach of a "condition", or a "fundamental breach".[170] Termination is not available as a remedy for every breach of contract. The innocent party is entitled to damages as of right on proving the defendant's breach; but both parties' obligations remain unchanged and enforceable unless *either* the term broken was a "condition" of the contract[171] *or* the breach was "fundamental", in the sense that the effect of the breach was to deprive the innocent party of substantially the whole benefit which it was the intention of the parties that he should obtain from the contract.[172] In such cases the innocent party then has an election to terminate or to affirm the contract.[173] If he elects to terminate, the 8–38

[169] Above, Ch.4.

[170] *Photo Production Ltd v Securicor Transport Ltd*, above, n.167 at 849 (Lord Diplock). See also *Afovos Shipping Co. S.A. v Pagnan*, above, n.165 at 203.

[171] That is, a term which the parties have agreed by express words or by implication of law will give rise to the right to terminate on the occurrence of any breach, whether or not the consequences of the breach are serious for the innocent party: *ibid.* In this sense "condition" is contrasted with "warranty" (which gives rise only to damages for breach) and "intermediate" (or, sometimes, "innominate") term (which gives rise either only to damages or also to the right to terminate, depending on whether the breach is "fundamental"). On "intermediate" ("innominate") terms, see Treitel, paras 18–047 to 18–052. And on the classification of terms as "conditions" see, e.g. *Bunge Corp., New York v Tradax Export S.A.*, above, n.168, HL (time conditions in mercantile contracts usually to be regarded as conditions); Sale of Goods Act 1979, ss.12(5A), 13(1A), 14(6), amended by the Sale and Supply of Goods Act 1994, s.7, Sch.2 (terms as to right to sell goods, description and quality implied into contracts for the sale of goods to be conditions). In the case of a breach by the seller or supplier of a certain conditions implied by statute into contracts with for the sale or supply of goods, the non-consumer buyer or transferee is not permitted to terminate where the breach is so slight that it would be unreasonable for him to reject the goods: Sale of Goods Act 1979, s.15A (sale of goods); Supply of Goods (Implied Terms) Act 1973, s.11A (hire purchase); Supply of Goods and Services Act 1982, ss.5A (transfer of goods), 10A (hire of goods), as amended by the Sale and Supply of Goods Act 1994, ss.4, 7, Sch.2; Treitel, paras 18–054 to 18–055.

[172] A breach which amounts to a repudiation (or "renunciation") of the contract, either at the time at which performance is due or in advance of the time for performance ("anticipatory breach") are examples of fundamental breach: *Afovos Shipping Co. S.A. v Pagnan*, above, n.165 at 203.

[173] *White and Carter (Councils) Ltd v McGregor* [1962] A.C. 413, HL; *Peyman v Lanjani* [1985] Ch. 457, CA; Sale of Goods Act 1979, s.11(2). Sometimes the

unaccrued obligations of both parties are discharged (and, in the case of a breach by the seller under a contract for the sale of goods, the buyer is entitled to reject the goods)[174] but the party in breach must pay damages to compensate the innocent party not only for the loss caused by the particular breach, but also for the loss which results from the fact that the obligations which have been discharged by the termination will no longer now be performed.[175]

8–39 **Termination in the context of a claim for misrepresentation.** Where the breach of contract consists of the non-performance of the defendant's contractual promise about his statement, whether a promise that his statement is true or a promise that he has taken care in making the statement, the availability to the claimant of remedy of termination will depend upon the application of the general rules set out above. The claimant must therefore establish that the term, whether relating to the truth of the statement or the care taken in making the statement, was a condition of the contract; or that the effect of the term being broken is that the claimant has been deprived of substantially the whole benefit of the contract.

Where the contractual term was a promise by the defendant that a particular statement he made about the subject-matter of the

courts will not allow the innocent party to refuse to accept a repudiatory breach of contract where he has no legitimate interest in insisting on performance: *Attica Sea Carriers Corp. v Ferrostaal Poseidon Bulk Reederei G.m.b.H.* [1976] 1 Lloyd's Rep. 250, CA; *Clea Shipping Corp. v Bulk Oil International Ltd* [1984] 1 All E.R. 129, although the category of cases in which this applies is very limited: *Reichman v Beveridge* [2006] EWCA Civ 1659, [2007] 1 P & CR 20 at [17]. And sometimes the innocent party has no practical choice but to accept a fundamental breach and terminate the contract: see, e.g. the facts of *Photo Production Ltd v Securicor Ltd*, above, n.167 (defendant's fundamental breach of contract to provide security services at claimant's factory resulted in factory being burnt down); *Harbutt's "Plasticine" Ltd v Wayne Tank and Pump Co. Ltd* [1970] 1 Q.B. 447, CA, at 472 (defendants, employed to provide equipment at plaintiff's factory, breached contract and whole factory was destroyed).

174 Sale of Goods Act 1979 s.11(3),(4). For detailed discussion, see Benjamin, paras 12–017 to 12–072.

175 *Photo Production Ltd v Securicor Transport Ltd*, above, n.167 at 849. However, the claimant, whilst exercising his election to terminate the contract, need not claim the damages for breach if he prefers instead to claim damages on another measure, e.g. damages under the Misrepresentation Act 1967 s.2(1), where those damages would on the facts be higher than damages for breach of contract. For a general discussion of election between, and cumulation of, remedies, see above, paras 2–11 to 2–13.

contract was true, it may often be possible to show that the term was a condition. If the statement was a description by reference to which goods were sold or supplied, the term implied by statute by which the defendant promises that the goods will correspond with the description will also by statute be a condition.[176] But even if there is no statutory implication that can be relied upon, it may be possible for the claimant to show that the significance he attached to the description was such that the defendant's statement was not only incorporated into the contract as a term[177] but that the term was expressly or impliedly intended by the parties to be a condition giving rise to the right to terminate on breach. Alternatively, even if he cannot show that it was a condition of the contract, he will still be entitled to terminate if he can show that the effects of the particular breach are so serious as to constitute a fundamental breach: for example, a statement about the quality of the subject-matter of the contract where, on the facts, the subject-matter is so seriously defective as to deprive the claimant of substantially the whole benefit of the contract.[178]

---

[176] Sale of Goods Act 1979 s.13(1A), as amended by the Sale and Supply of Goods Act 1994 s.7, Sch.2; Supply of Goods and Services Act 1982 ss.3(2), 8(2).

[177] Above, para.8–08.

[178] *Holmes v Burgess* [1975] 2 N.Z.L.R. 311 (sale of colt, said to be sound but in fact very seriously ill). Under the Marine Insurance Act 1906 s.17, a contract of marine insurance may be avoided by either party for breach by the other of the duty of utmost good faith: this extends to allowing avoidance by the underwriter for post-contract fraud by the insured. However, it is only appropriate to invoke the remedy of avoidance in a post-contractual context in situations analogous to situations where the insurer has a right to terminate for breach. For this purpose (a) the fraud must be material in the sense that the fraud would have an effect on underwriters' ultimate liability and (b) the gravity of the fraud or its consequences must be such as would enable the underwriters, if they wished to do so, to terminate for breach of contract: *K/S Merc-Scandia XXXXII v Lloyd's Underwriters (The Mercandian Continent)* [2001] EWCA Civ 1275, [2001] 2 Lloyd's Rep. 563 at [35]. See also *Agapitos v Agnew (The Aegeon)* [2002] EWCA Civ 247, [2003] Q.B. 556 at [13] (Mance L.J., hoping that HL or Parliament might confine s.17 to the pre-contract stage). The Law Commission is considering the insured's post-contract duty of good faith, and in particular fraudulent claims, within in its review of insurance contract law (below, para.17–06): *Reforming Insurance Contract Law*: Issues Paper 7 (July 2010); and intends to include this topic within a consultation paper planned for late 2011: Law Com No.328, *Annual Report 2010–11*, para.2.7.

CHAPTER 9

EXCLUSION AND LIMITATION OF LIABILITY FOR MISREPRESENTATION

I. DIFFERENT FORMS OF CLAUSE OR NOTICE EXCLUDING OR LIMITING LIABILITY

Varieties of exclusion and limitation clause. A person may, by the use of a contractual term or a non-contractual notice, seek to exclude or limit the liability or the range of remedies to which he would otherwise be exposed by reason of his statements, his acts or his omission to speak or to act. This is not the place to discuss this topic in detail,[1] but this chapter will explore the use of exclusion and limitation clauses and notices in the context of liability for **9–01**

[1] For a fuller discussion of the topic, see Chitty, Ch.14; Furmston, paras 3.53 to 3.119; Treitel, Ch.7; Anson, Ch.6; Cheshire, Fifoot & Furmston, pp.202–257; Clerk & Lindsell, paras 3–118 to 3–127; R. Lawson, *Exclusion Clauses and Unfair Contract Terms* (10th edn, 2011); E. MacDonald, *Exemption Clauses and Unfair Terms* (2nd edn, 2006).

misrepresentation. There is a wide range of types of clause and notice in common use, and a range of techniques available to the courts to control them. A clause in a contract may seek to exclude altogether, or to limit in some way, a liability which arises either under the contract or outside the contract (for example, in tort). And a notice, even if it is not contained in a contract, can in some circumstances have the effect of limiting or excluding non-contractual liability or remedies.[2] The characteristics of a successful clause or notice will therefore vary according to the remedy which the draftsman wishes to exclude or limit. Moreover, the mechanism by which the clause seeks to achieve its object may vary: it may exclude or limit a liability once it has arisen, in substance operating as a defence to a claim once the claim is established; or it may be drafted so as to avoid the claim itself being successful by negativing an element necessary to establish liability in the first place. It may appear by its language not to be an exclusion clause but may still have that effect, by requiring a person (sometimes even the other party) to indemnify against the liability.[3] And a clause or notice may not seek to avoid all liability: it may limit the range of remedies available; or it may limit the full application of one or more particular remedies (for example, by limiting liability to a particular sum of money). Examples of these varieties of clause and notice will be given in this section. The different techniques available to the courts to control such clauses and notices will be discussed in the following sections of this chapter.

---

[2] In general terms, a liability or remedy *under* the contract can be excluded or limited only by a clause *in* that or another contract which binds the claimant and of which the defendant has the benefit: *cf. White v Blackmore* [1972] 2 Q.B. 651, CA, at 667 (occupiers' liability). For a discussion of the courts' approach to contractual clauses and non-contractual notices, see below, para.9–08. Throughout this chapter reference is made to exclusion and limitation *clauses*, but this should be understood to refer also in appropriate cases to exclusion and limitation *notices*.

[3] *Phillips Products Ltd v Hyland* [1987] 1 W.L.R. 659, CA; *cf. Thompson v T. Lohan (Plant Hire) Ltd* [1987] 1 W.L.R. 649, CA.

Clauses which exclude an established liability. A clause might simply exclude a particular liability, or all liability, for misrepresentation. For example, a contractual clause might provide that[4] 9–02

> "all liabilities for and remedies in respect of any representations made are excluded save in so far as provided in this contract."

The clause might be drafted even more widely, and exclude all liability in respect of representations, both liability in respect of pre-contractual representations and liability for breach of contract arising out of an incorporated representation. Or if the only liability which could arise on the facts is for pre-contractual misrepresentation, such as in tort, a non-contractual notice may be so drafted as to purport to exclude all such liability.

Clauses which negative an element necessary to establish liability. A clause or notice may seek to negative one or more of the elements of a claim for misrepresentation. Such clauses will vary according to the claim they are seeking to negative, but in the context of claims for misrepresentation most commonly they assert that the claimant has not relied on the representation in question. For example[5]: 9–03

[4] *Government of Zanzibar v British Aerospace (Lancaster House) Ltd* [2000] 1 W.L.R. 2333. These words were only part of the relevant clause in that case, which also contained an "entire agreement" provision, and a "non-reliance" provision: below, para.9–07.

[5] *Government of Zanzibar v British Aerospace (Lancaster House) Ltd*, above, n.4. See also *E.A. Grimstead & Son Ltd v McGarrigan* [1999] All E.R. (D) 1163, CA ("The Purchaser confirms that it has not relied on any warranty representation or undertaking of or on behalf of the Vendors . . . or of any other person in respect of the subject matter of this Agreement save for any representation or warranty or undertaking expressly set out in the body of this Agreement"); *Thomas Witter Ltd v TBP Industries Ltd* [1996] 2 All E.R. 573 ("the Purchaser acknowledges that it has not been induced to enter into this Agreement by any representation or warranty other than the statements contained or referred to [in a Schedule]"); Standard Conditions of Sale (5th edn, 2011), special condition 6 ("Neither party can rely on any representation made by the other, unless made in writing by the other or his conveyancer, but this does not exclude liability for fraud or recklessness"; *Encyclopaedia of Forms and Precedents* (5th edn), Vol.4(3) (2008 reissue), Forms 27.4 and 27.6.

> "The parties agree that neither party has placed any reliance whatsoever on any representations agreements statements or understandings whether oral or in writing made prior to the date of this contract other than those expressly incorporated or recited in this contract."

Sometimes a clause may go further and seek to negative the representation itself. It is possible for a clause or notice in an appropriate case to make clear that statements made are only opinions on which the claimant is not entitled to rely without making further enquiries: in substance, to provide that, for certain remedies at least, the statement is not a "representation". A clause may, however, simply deny that any representations have been made during the pre-contractual negotiations.[6] There have been some doubts about whether,[7] and (if so) how,[8] such "no

---

[6] See also *Encyclopaedia of Forms and Precedents*, above, n.5, Form 27.5 (in conjunction with an "entire agreement" provision, below, para.9–06: party acknowledges that "no representations or promises not expressly contained in this agreement have been made by [the other party or his agents])"; *William Sindall Plc v Cambridgeshire CC* [1994] 1 W.L.R. 1016, CA, at 1034 (clauses, including National Conditions of Sale (20th edn), condition 14, did not exclude liability for misrepresentation but qualified any representation which would otherwise have been implied under seller's implied covenants for title).

[7] For the courts' reluctance to admit that a clause can effectively provide that what as a matter of fact is a representation is not in law a representation, see *McCullagh v Lane Fox & Partners Ltd* [1996] 1 E.G.L.R. 35, CA (estate agents' standard form disclaimer included a notice: "None of the statements contained in these particulars as to this property are to be relied on as statements or representations of fact. Any intending purchaser must satisfy themselves by inspection or otherwise as to the correctness of each of the statements contained in these particulars"); *Cremdean Properties Ltd v Nash* [1977] E.G.D. 63, CA, at 72 ("Any intending purchaser must satisfy himself by inspection or otherwise as to the correctness of each of the statements contained in these particulars": held not to destroy the representation but to confirm that it is a representation). See also a similarly-worded notice in *Walker v Boyle* [1982] 1 W.L.R. 495 at 501, followed in *Cooper v Tamms* [1988] 1 E.G.L.R. 257 at 263. See also *Lowe v Lombank* [1960] 1 W.L.R. 196, CA, at 204 (Diplock L.J.: "To call it an agreement as well as an acknowledgment by the plaintiff cannot convert a statement as to past facts, known by both parties to be untrue, into a contractual obligation, which is essentially a promise by the promisor to the promisee that acts will be done in the future or that facts exist at the time of the promise or will exist in the future . . . it can give rise to an estoppel: it cannot give rise to any positive contractual obligation"), now explained in *Springwell Navigation Corp. v J.P. Morgan Chase Bank* [2010] EWCA Civ 1221, [2010] 2 C.L.C. 705 at [145]–[153]; A. Trukhtanov, *"Misrepresentation: Acknowledgement of Non-Reliance as a Defence"* (2009) 125 L.Q.R. 648 at 649–651.

representation" and "non-reliance" clauses can take effect, but it is has recently become accepted that the parties can agree in their contract that the contract is entered into on the basis that there has been no reliance on pre-contractual representations, or that no misrepresentations have been made: both parties are then estopped by their contract from raising the (mis)representations, which were in fact made, in order to obtain a remedy.[9]

---

[8] For the suggestion that such a representation of non-reliance might operate as an evidential estoppel, see the judgments of Chadwick L.J. in *E.A. Grimstead & Son Ltd v McGarrigan* [1999] All E.R. (D) 1163, CA, and *Watford Electronics Ltd v Sanderson C.F.L. Ltd* [2001] EWCA Civ 317, [2001] 1 All E.R. (Comm) 696 at [39]–[40]. This would require the defendant to plead and prove the three requirements identified in *Lowe v Lombank Ltd*, above, n.7 at 205: (1) that the representation of non-reliance is clear and unambiguous; (2) that the claimant meant it to be acted upon by the defendant or at any rate so conducted himself that a reasonable man in the position of the defendant would take the representation to be true and believe that it was meant that he should act upon it; (3) that the defendant in fact believed it to be true and was induced by such belief to act upon it. However, as Chadwick L.J. noted, this last requirement may present insuperable difficulties, because it may be impossible for a party who has made representations which he intended should be relied upon to satisfy the court that he entered into the contract in the belief that a statement by the other party that he had not relied upon those representations was true. See also *Quest 4 Finance Ltd v Maxfield* [2007] EWHC 2313 (QB), [2007] 2 C.L.C. 706 ("non-reliance" clause failed where representor could not show it believed declaration of non-reliance to be true and relied on it: *Peekay Intermark Ltd v Australia and New Zealand Banking Group Ltd*, below, n.9, was not cited).

[9] This solution was suggested by Moore-Bick L.J. in *Peekay Intermark Ltd v Australia and New Zealand Banking Group Ltd* [2006] EWCA Civ 386, [2006] 2 Lloyd's Rep. 511 at [57]. A contractual estoppel does not require the representee to have believed the assumed state of facts, and therefore avoids the problems identified by Chadwick L.J. in relation to estoppel by representation (above, n.8), although Moore-Bick L.J. noted that a non-reliance clause may (depending on its terms) also be capable of giving rise to an estoppel by representation if the necessary elements can be established. *Peekay* has been followed in a series of cases at first instance: *Bottin International Investments Ltd v Venson Group plc* [2006] EWHC 3112 (Ch), [2006] All E.R. (D) 111 (Dec) at [154] (non-reliance clause; but would not prevent claim in deceit); *Donegal International v Zambia* [2007] EWHC 197 (Comm), [2007] 1 Lloyd's Rep 397 at [465] (non-reliance clause); *Trident Turboprop (Dublin) Ltd v First Flight Couriers Ltd* [2008] EWHC 1686 (Comm), [2008] 2 Lloyd's Rep. 581 at [36] (no representation; the appeal at [2009] EWCA Civ 290, [2010] Q.B. 86 proceeded on different grounds: below, para.9–20, n.79); *Titan Steel Wheels Limited v Royal Bank of Scotland Plc* [2010] EWHC 211 (Comm), [2010] 2 Lloyd's Rep. 92 at [87]–[88] (clause negativing reliance on advice); *Foodco UK LLP (t/a Muffin Break) v Henry Boot*

Another variation on this is a clause which seeks to ensure that, even if there is a representation which has been relied on, it is not a representation which binds the defendant. A common example is a clause which provides that any statement made by the defendant's agent does not in law bind the defendant as principal, by making clear that the agent has no authority to make such a statement.[10]

Where the claim is in the tort of negligence, a clause might seek to negative the duty of care[11]:

Developments Ltd [2010] EWHC 358 (Ch) at [168]–[171] (non-reliance clause); *Raiffeisen Zentralbank Österreich A.G. v Royal Bank of Scotland Plc* [2010] EWHC 1392 (Comm), [2011] 1 Lloyd's Rep. 123 at [255] (no representation); and has been confirmed by the Court of Appeal: *Springwell Navigation Corp. v J.P. Morgan Chase Bank*, above, n.7 at [169] (non-reliance and no representation), approving [2008] EWHC 1186 (Comm), [2008] All E.R. (D) 167 (Jun) at [538]–[567]. For further cases, now following both *Peekay* and *Springwell*, see *Cassa di Risparmio della Repubblica di San Marino S.p.A. v Barclays Bank Ltd* [2011] EWHC 484 (Comm), [2011] All E.R. (D) 189 (Mar) at [505]; *Bank Leumi (UK) Plc v Wachner* [2011] EWHC 656 (Comm), [2011] All E.R. (D) 278 (Mar) at [184]; *Standard Chartered Bank v Ceylon Petroleum Corp.* [2011] EWHC 1785 (Comm), [2011] All E.R. (D) 113 (Jul) at [527] – [529]. On contractual estoppel contrasted with estoppel by representation and estoppel by convention, see A. Trukhtanov, "Misrepresentation: Acknowledgement of Non-Reliance as a Defence" (2009) 125 L.Q.R. 648; P. Feltham, D. Hochberg and T. Leech, *Spencer Bower: Estoppel by Representation* (4th edn, 2004), para.VIII.8.1); K.R. Handley, *Estoppel by Conduct and Election* (2006), esp. Ch.8. For the operation of s.3 Misrepresentation Act 1967 in relation to "non-reliance" clauses, see below, para. 9–22; and for the Unfair Terms in Consumer Contracts Regulations 1999, below, para.9–37, see *Shaftesbury House (Developments) Ltd v Lee* [2010] EWHC 1484 (Ch) at [67] (Proudman J., obiter: "it would be strange if a contracting party could get round the Regulations by such a device").

[10] *Collins v Howell-Jones* [1981] E.G.D. 207, CA (clause defining actual authority); *Overbrooke Estates Ltd v Glencombe Properties Ltd* [1974] 1 W.L.R. 1335 (clause negativing estate agent's ostensible authority). A clause which defines the authority of the representor may operate in a different way, so as to make clear that the agent does have authority and that the representation is made in such a way as to bind the principal without imposing any personal liability on the agent: *Stewart v Engel* [2000] 2 B.C.L.C. 528 (clause made clear that liquidator acted only for company and had no personal responsibility).

[11] *McCullagh v Lane Fox & Partners Ltd*, above, n.7 at 45, 47. See also *Hedley Byrne & Co. Ltd v Heller & Partners Ltd* [1964] A.C. 465, HL (credit reference given by bank "without responsibility"); *Smith v Eric S. Bush* [1990] 1 A.C. 831, HL (mortgagors in two cases signed forms requesting mortgage which contained terms providing that "no responsibility whatsoever is implied or accepted" by valuer; and "the surveyor's report will be supplied without any acceptance of responsibility on their part to me": different views were however expressed in the

> "All statements contained in these particulars as to this property are made without responsibility on the part of [the estate agent] or the vendors or lessors."

The purpose of such a clause is to negative the assumption of responsibility which might otherwise arise in the circumstances in which the defendant provides information or advice to the claimant.[12]

Clauses which limit the range of remedies available for misrepresentation. A clause or notice might not limit or exclude remedies for misrepresentation generally, but might instead exclude a particular remedy or remedies, and so have the effect of defining the range of remedies which will be available if a misrepresentation is established. For example, it might exclude rescission, without touching on the question of remedies in damages[13]: 9–04

> "This contract is neither cancellable nor voidable by either party."

Or it might exclude claims in respect of pre-contractual misrepresentations, and limit the remedy to damages for breach of contract in respect of representations which are expressly incorporated into the contract.[14]

CA and within the HL as to the effect of these causes—whether they negatived the duty or excluded liability); *De Balkany v Christie Manson and Woods Ltd* [1997] Tr. L. 163 (auction house would owe duty to buyer in respect of negligent statements in catalogue entries but for statements in catalogue which made reasonably clear that they did not assume responsibility); *Hedley Byrne & Co. Ltd v Heller & Partners Ltd* [1964] A.C. 465, HL (non-contractual notice); *I.F.E. Fund SA v Goldman Sachs International* [2007] EWCA Civ 811, [2007] 2 Lloyd's Rep. 449 at [28]; *Titan Steel Wheels Limited v Royal Bank of Scotland Plc*, above, n.9, at [89].

[12] For the duty of care, and "assumption of responsibility", see above, para.6–25. It has been held that the words "without responsibility" attached to a statement are not sufficiently clear to exclude the remedy of rescission for misrepresentation: *Credit Lyonnais Bank Nederland v Export Credit Guarantee Department* [1996] 1 Lloyd's Rep. 200 at 218.

[13] *Toomey v Eagle Star Insurance Co. Ltd (No.2)* [1995] 2 Lloyd's Rep. 88.

[14] See the clause in *Government of Zanzibar v British Aerospace (Lancaster House) Ltd*, quoted above, para.9–02. An "entire agreement" clause has the effect of limiting claims for breach of contract to those arising in the main contract itself, but does not necessarily exclude other remedies for pre-contractual misrepresentation: below, para.9–06. For a clause defining the remedies available

9–05 **Clauses which impose restrictions on the availability of a particular remedy, or which limit the quantum recoverable.** A clause or notice might sometimes seek not to exclude a particular remedy altogether, but to impose conditions on its availability or scope. For example, it might set a limit on the quantum of damages recoverable in respect of misrepresentation, either generally or in a claim for a particular remedy.[15] Or it might require a claim to be made in a prescribed form, or notified to the defendant within a prescribed time period; or it might set a time-limit within which a claim must be initiated by way of litigation, in effect providing for a more restrictive limitation period than would normally apply under the general law[16]:

> "the Vendor shall not be liable (by way of damages or otherwise) in respect of a breach of this Agreement or claim by the Purchaser in respect of a Warranty unless the Vendor shall have been given written notice by the Purchaser of such breach or claim on or prior to 1st January 1992. Such notice shall be in writing and shall contain the Purchaser's then best

---

for misleading or inaccurate pre-contractual or contractual statements in a contract for the sale of land, see Standard Conditions of Sale (5th edn, 2011), cl.7.1; Standard Commercial Property Conditions of Sale (2nd edn, 2004), cl.9. The most recent versions of these Conditions of Sale are printed in the Appendices to F. Silverman, *Conveyancing Handbook* (re-issued annually).

[15] See, e.g. *Deepak Fertilisers and Petrochemicals Corp. v ICI Chemicals & Polymers Ltd* [1999] 1 Lloyd's Rep. 387, CA (but the clause did not there on construction cover all liabilities); *St Albans City and District Council v International Computers Ltd* [1996] 4 All E.R. 481, CA. A clause might seek to exclude the operation of the principles of joint and several liability, above, para.2–14, and so provide that, in the event that the defendant is liable to the claimant for damage in respect of which another person is also liable (whether jointly or severally), the defendant shall be liable only for his own share of the damage. The defendant thereby avoids running the risk of having no valuable claim under the Civil Liability (Contribution) Act 1978 against other such potential co-defendants who are insolvent. For the ability of a company to agree under the Companies Act 2006 ss.532–538 to limit its auditors' liability in this a way, see above, para.6–33, n.182.

[16] *Thomas Witter Ltd v TBP Industries Ltd* [1996] 2 All E.R. 573 at 599: the clause restricted claims for breach of contract, but not in respect of any misrepresentation which induced the contract. See also *Daroga v Wells*, unreported, May 11, 1994, CA (notice of claim in respect of warranties given by seller in share-sale contract to be given to seller within 24 months after completion). For standard form exclusion clauses to protect the vendor in a share-sale agreement, see *Encyclopaedia of Forms and Precedents* (5th edn), Vol.11 (2010 reissue), Form 8, esp. cl.0.4 (time-limit for claim under warranties).

estimate of the amount claimed and the basis on which such estimate is made. Any liability in respect of a breach or claim of which notice is given as aforesaid shall cease unless proceedings in respect of such breach or claim are issued and served within 6 months of the date of the written notice."

A clause might also seek to restrict the mechanisms available to enforce claims for misrepresentation: for example, by excluding a defendant's rights of set-off including, therefore, set-off arising from the claimant's pre-contractual misrepresentations or claims for breach by the claimant of contractual warranties.[17]

"Entire agreement" clauses. It is not uncommon for a commercial contract to contain an "entire agreement" clause: for example, a clause which provides that[18] **9–06**

"this Agreement constitutes the entire agreement between the parties."

Such a clause constitutes an agreement that the full contractual terms to which the parties agree to bind themselves are to be found in the agreement[19] and nowhere else: there cannot be any claim based on a side agreement or collateral contract.[20] But it does not

---

[17] *Stewart Gill Ltd v Horatio Myer & Co. Ltd* [1992] Q.B. 600, CA; *Society of Lloyd's v Leighs* [1997] C.L.C. 1398, CA; *WRM Group Ltd v Wood* [1998] C.L.C. 189, CA; *Skipskredittforeningen v Emperor Navigation* [1998] 1 Lloyd's Rep. 66; below, para.9–16.

[18] *Inntrepreneur Pub Co. (G.L.) v East Crown Ltd* [2000] 2 Lloyd's Rep. 611; followed *Inntrepreneur Pub Co. (CPC) v Sweeney* [2002] EWHC 1060 (Ch), [2002] 2 E.G.L.R. 132.

[19] Whether the clause excludes implied terms will depend on its construction: *Exxonmobil Sales and Supply Corp. v Texaco Ltd* [2003] EWHC 1964 (Comm), [2003] 2 Lloyd's Rep. 686 at [25]–[27] (clause excluded terms implied by usage and course of dealing, but might not exclude implication based on business efficacy).

[20] *Inntrepeneur Pub Co. (G.L.) v East Crown Ltd*, above, n.18 at 614. In *McGrath v Shah* (1987) 57 P. & C.R. 452 at 460, Chadwick Q.C. appeared to accept that such a clause did not necessarily exclude another, collateral, contract. However, he was there focusing on the significance of an entire agreement clause as ensuring that the written contract contained all the terms of a contract for the sale of land and therefore avoiding a challenge based on non-compliance with the Law of Property Act 1925 s.40 (see now the Law of Property (Miscellaneous Provisions) Act 1989 s.2(1)). For the particular approach to finding a collateral contract in the case of contracts for the sale of land, see above, para.8–06, n.25. An entire agreement clause does not, however, exclude a claim to rectify the

preclude a claim in misrepresentation. It only denies contractual force to statements which are not contained in the contract; it does not purport to affect the status of any statement as a (pre-contractual) misrepresentation.[21]

9–07 **Mixed clauses.** Often a contract will contain a clause which is not simply one of the provisions described above, but is a combination of different forms of exclusion and/or limitation of liability. For example, a clause which combines an "entire agreement" provision, an exclusion of liability for misrepresentation and a "non-reliance" clause[22]:

---

contract in which it is contained: *Surgicraft Ltd v Paradigm Biodevices Ltd* [2010] EWHC 1291 (Ch), [2010] All E.R. (D) 249 (May) at [73], following *J.J. Huber (Investments) Ltd v Private D.I.Y. Co. Ltd* (1995) 70 P. & C.R. D33.

[21] *ibid.*; *Deepak Fertilisers and Petrochemicals Corp. v ICI Chemicals & Polymers Ltd*, above, n.15 at 395; *Alman & Benson v Associated Newspapers Group Ltd*, unreported, June 20, 1980; *Thomas Witter Ltd v TBP Industries Ltd*, above, n.16 at 595; *Government of Zanzibar v British Aerospace (Lancaster House) Ltd,* above, n.4 at 2344; *SERE Holdings Ltd v Volkswagen Group UK Ltd* [2004] EWHC 1551 (Ch), [2004] All E.R. (D) 76 (Jul) at [22] (Nugee Q.C.: entire agreement clause negatives intention to create legal relations with respect to pre-contractual statements and collateral agreements); *Sutcliffe v Lloyd* [2007] EWCA Civ 153, [2007] 2 E.G.L.R. 13 at [23]–[28] (clause did not cover understandings between the parties outside the scope of the contract which gave rise to claim based on proprietary estoppel, nor undertandings which arose after the date of the entire agreement clause); *BSkyB Ltd v H.P. Enterprise Services U.K. Ltd* [2010] EWHC 86 (TCC), (2010) 129 Con. L.R. 147 at [382] ("this Agreement and the Schedules shall together represent the entire understanding and constitute the whole agreement between the parties in relation to its subject matter and supersede any previous discussions, correspondence, representations or agreement between the parties with respect thereto …" only prevented representations becoming terms of the agreement: a clause intended to withdraw representations for all purposes would have had to go further), approved in *AXA Sun Life Services Plc v Campbell Martin Ltd* [2011] EWCA Civ 133, [2011] All E.R. (D) 206 (Feb) at [92] (Rix L.J.: clause providing "This Agreement… constitute the entire agreement and understanding between you and us in relation to the subject matter thereof… this Agreement shall supersede any prior promises, agreements, representations, undertakings or implications whether made orally or in writing between you and us relating to the subject matter of this Agreement" did not exclude liability for misrepresentations of any kind). See also *Encyclopaedia of Forms and Precedents* (5th edn), Vol.4(3) (2008 reissue), "Boilerplate Clauses", paras 27.1 to 27.3 and Form 27.1.

[22] *Government of Zanzibar v British Aerospace (Lancaster House) Ltd*, above, n.4. See also *Thomas Witter Ltd v TBP Industries Ltd*, above, n.16 (two separate clauses containing (a) a combination of "entire agreement" and "non-reliance"

> "The parties have negotiated this contract on the basis that the terms and conditions set out herein represent the entire agreement between them relating in any way whatsoever to the [goods] which form the subject matter of this contract and accordingly they agree that all liabilities for and remedies in respect of any representations made are excluded save in so far as provided in this contract. The parties further agree that neither party has placed any reliance whatsoever on any representations agreements statements or understandings whether oral or in writing made prior to the date of this contract other than those expressly incorporated or recited in this contract."

In such a case the separate elements of the clause must be identified and each different form of exclusion or limitation must be applied separately. As will be described in the later sections of this chapter, the controls available to the courts in respect of the separate forms of exclusion or limitation will vary.

II. COMMON LAW CONTROLS OF EXCLUSION AND LIMITATION CLAUSES

(1) The Scope of the Common Law Controls

Common law controls generally limited to questions of incorporation and interpretation of the clause. The courts have no inherent power at common law to control the substantive fairness of contractual clauses and non-contractual notices: there is no rule at common law that a clause will not be given effect if it is unreasonable.[23] There are statutory controls, such as the Unfair Contract Terms Act 1977, which will be discussed in a later section of this chapter. But there is no similar general control at common law. This is not, however, to say that the courts have not developed 9–08

elements, and (b) limitation of claims for breach of contract unless notice given within prescribed period); *Inntrepreneur Pub Co. (G.L.) v East Crown Ltd*, above, n.18 (successive sub-clauses containing (a) entire agreement clause and (b) clause excluding liability for misrepresentation and breach of duty). See also *Encyclopaedia of Forms and Precedents* (5th edn), Vol.4(3) (2008 reissue), Forms 27.2–267.5 ("boilerplate" clauses: entire agreement, non-reliance and no representation); Vol.36 (2010 reissue), Form 92, cl.10 (disclaimer for contract for sale of freehold property: non-reliance and entire agreement), Forms 225–226 (various forms of exclusion of liability for misrepresentation in contract for sale of land).

[23] *Photo Production Ltd v Securicor Transport Ltd* [1980] A.C. 827, HL, at 851; *Grand Trunk Railway Co. of Canada v Robinson* [1915] A.C. 740, PC, at 747.

techniques at common law to regulate exclusion and limitation clauses and notices.[24] Although in the case of contractual exclusion clauses they start from the position that the parties are free to negotiate the terms of their contract, the courts view an onerous clause, such as a clause excluding or limiting a party's potential liability under the contract,[25] with suspicion. They will require evidence that the party who will be adversely affected by the clause intended it to be part of the bargain; and they will examine the language of such a clause very carefully to determine its proper scope.

9–09 **Incorporation of the clause.**[26] The court must be satisfied that the clause was properly incorporated into the contract.[27] In the case of a written contract, signed by both parties, this presents little difficulty. The claimant's signature is taken as his assent to all the written terms of the document he has signed and any other terms which are expressly incorporated by a reference in the signed document.[28] But where the contract is not wholly reduced to

---

24 *Interfoto Picture Library Ltd v Stiletto Visual Programmes Ltd* [1989] Q.B. 433, CA, at 439, 445; *Laceys Footware (Wholesale) Ltd v Bowler International Freight Ltd* [1997] 2 Lloyd's Rep. 369, CA, at 384–385.

25 The approach at common law is not limited to exclusion and limitation clauses, but extends also to other onerous or unusual clauses: *Interfoto Picture Library Ltd v Stiletto Visual Programmes Ltd*, above, n.24. It applies also to non-contractual notices in so far as such notices can operate to exclude or limit liabilities, e.g. in tort: *Ashdown v Samuel Williams & Sons Ltd* [1957] 1 Q.B. 409, CA (notice excluding occupier's liability in negligence towards entrant on land).

26 For further discussion, see Chitty, paras 12–008 to 12–017, 14–002; Furmston, paras 3.8 to 3.18; Treitel, paras 7–004 to 7–013; Anson, pp.173–177; Cheshire, Fifoot and Furmston, pp.203–212.

27 Or that a non-contractual notice was sufficiently brought to the attention of the claimant so as to be binding on him in relation to a claim in tort: *Ashdown v Samuel Williams & Sons Ltd*, above, n.25.

28 *L'Estrange v F. Graucob Ltd* [1934] 2 K.B. 394, CA, at 403 (Scrutton L.J.: "When a document containing contractual terms is signed, then, in the absence of fraud, or, I will add, misrepresentation, the party signing it is bound, and it is wholly immaterial whether he has read the document or not"); *Peekay Intermark Ltd v Australia and New Zealand Banking Group Ltd* [2006] EWCA Civ 386, [2006] 2 Lloyd's Rep. 511 at [43] (misrepresentation corrected by the terms of the contract which the claimant signed and by which he was bound although he did not read them: the terms were "not buried in a mass of small print but appeared on the face of the documents"; the principle applied in *L'Estrange v Graucob* "is an important principle of English law which underpins the whole of

writing, it can sometimes be difficult to decide whether a clause intended by one party to form part of the contract was in fact incorporated. The general approach in such cases is for the courts to ask whether, at the time when the contract was concluded, the defendant had taken such steps as were reasonably necessary to attempt to bring the clause to the claimant's attention.[29] If so, the claimant may be held to have agreed to the clause, even if he had not in fact intended to include it in the contract, and even if he had not seen or read the clause. This is in reality just part of the court's normal enquiry into the terms of a contract.[30] But the fact that the

---

commercial life; any erosion of it would have serious repercussions far beyond the business community": Moore-Bick L.J. at [43]). For cases in Canada where the signature has been held not to show assent to unusual terms, see *Tilden Rent-a-Car Co. v Clendenning* (1978) 83 D.L.R. (3d) 400 (CA Ontario); *Colonial Investment Co. of Winnipeg, Man. v Borland* (1911) 1 W.W.R. 171 (Sup. Ct. Alta, affirmed on different grounds (1912) 6 D.L.R. 211); *Gray-Campbell Ltd v Flynn* [1923] 1 D.L.R. 51 (Sup. Ct. Alta; see Beck J.A., dissenting). In England, see *Lloyds Bank Plc v Waterhouse* [1993] 2 F.L.R. 97, CA (esp. Sir Edward Eveleigh at 123); J. Cartwright, "A Guarantee Signed by Mistake" [1990] L.M.C.L.Q. 338 at pp.340–341; *Amiri Flight Authority v BAE Systems Plc* [2003] EWCA Civ 1447, [2003] 2 C.L.C. 662 at [15] (Mance L.J., not deciding whether there may be contracts in writing to which the principle of *Interfoto Picture Library Ltd v Stiletto Visual Programmes Ltd*, below, n.31, might apply to exclude "a provision of an extraneous or wholly unusual nature"); *Ocean Chemical Transport Inc. v Exnor Craggs Ltd* [2000] 1 Lloyd's Rep. 446 at [48] (Evans L.J.: the *Interfoto* test might apply in "an extreme case, where a signature was obtained under pressure of time or other cirucumstances"); *cf. H.I.H. Casualty and General Insurance Ltd v New Hampshire Insurance Co.* [2001] EWCA Civ 735, [2001] 2 Lloyd's Rep. 161 at [209] (Rix L.J.: *Interfoto* not applicable to signed documents); *J.P. Morgan Chase Bank v Springwell Navigation Corp.* [2008] EWHC 1186 (Comm), [2008] All E.R. (D) 167 (Jun) at [585] (Gloster J.: "Whatever the precise scope of the principle, I conclude that it must, on any basis, have a very limited application to signed contracts between commercial parties operating in the financial markets").

29 *Parker v South Eastern Railway Co.* (1877) 2 C.P.D. 416.

30 The objective test to ascertain what obligations each party by his words and conduct has reasonably led the other to believe he was undertaking: *Hardwick Game Farm v Suffolk Agricultural Poultry Producers Association* [1966] 1 W.L.R. 287, CA, at 339; *Harris v Great Western Railway Co.* (1876) 1 Q.B.D. 515 at 530 (Blackburn J.); *Smith v Hughes* (1871) L.R. 6 Q.B. 597; below, Ch.13, and see esp. para.13–34.

clause in question is an onerous or unusual clause leads the courts to approach this stage of the enquiry with particular care.[31]

9–10 **The general approach to interpretation: construction *contra proferentem*.** This is not the place for a detailed discussion about the interpretation of contracts. There are various canons of construction which are generally employed to assist a court in its interpretation of a contract,[32] but for the purposes of this book it is sufficient to note that where there is doubt about the meaning of a clause it will be construed *contra proferentem*: that is, against the party for whose benefit it was inserted, or who is seeking to rely on it to his advantage.[33] It is for that party to show that the clause clearly and unambiguously confers on him the benefit which he claims. This approach, originally adopted in relation to the interpretation of a grant contained in a deed,[34] was long ago extended to all contracts; and since an exclusion or limitation clause is one which can clearly have the effect of protecting one of the parties to the exclusion of the other, it is in the context of such clauses that in the modern law the courts have most often emphasised the need to construe clauses *contra proferentem*. A defendant who seeks to rely on a clause to exclude or limit his liability must therefore show that by its language the clause clearly and unambiguously applies to the liability in question.[35] If the

[31] "The more unreasonable the clause is, the greater the notice which must be given of it": *J. Spurling v Bradshaw* [1956] 1 W.L.R. 461, CA, at 466 (Denning L.J.); *Thornton v Shoe Lane Parking Ltd* [1971] 2 Q.B. 163, CA, at 170, 172; *Interfoto Picture Library Ltd v Stiletto Visual Programmes Ltd* [1989] Q.B. 433.

[32] Lewison, Ch.7.

[33] *ibid*., para.7.08; E. Peel, "Whither *contra proferentem*" in A. Burrows and E.Peel (eds), *Contract Terms* (2007).

[34] "Verba cartarum fortius accipiuntur contra proferentem": Co. Litt. 36a; Blackstone, *Commentaries*, II.xxiii.380.

[35] *Thomas Witter Ltd v TBP Industries Ltd* [1996] 2 All E.R. 573 at 595–596 (Jacob J: "if a clause is to have the effect of excluding or reducing remedies for damaging or untrue statements then the party seeking that protection cannot be mealy-mouthed in his clause. He must bring it home that he is limiting his liability for falsehoods he may have told"). But the courts will not apply the strict rules of construction appropriate for exclusion clauses where the clause, although it has the effect of excluding liability, does so by defining an element in the claim itself: *McCullagh v Lane Fox & Partners Ltd* [1996] 1 E.G.L.R. 35, CA at 45 (disclaimer of responsibility which negatived duty of care in the tort of negligence; but such a clause is still subject to the control of the Unfair Contract

clause might have been intended to apply to a different liability, or even if it might cover a different liability as well as the kind of liability against which the defendant seeks to protect himself,[36] the clause will be held not to cover the defendant's case.

Modern approaches to construction *contra proferentem*. There have been some indications that the courts might now not make quite so strict an application of the *contra proferentem* rule. There is no doubt that the rule remains that words in a contract must be read *contra proferentem* and that in order to escape from the consequences of one's own wrongdoing clear words are necessary.[37] But before Parliament intervened and provided the statutory controls in relation to unfair terms which will be discussed later in this chapter, the courts sometimes applied the *contra proferentem* rule so strictly that they placed very strained constructions on exclusion clauses to limit their effectiveness. Now, however, the courts are less likely to place strained constructions on clauses, preferring instead to implement the policy in relation to the effectiveness of clauses which is contained in the controls provided by Parliament and only to ask whether the language of the clause is clear and fairly susceptible of only one meaning, giving allowance for the presumption against effective exclusion which is embodied in the notion of construction *contra proferentem*.[38] 9–11

Terms Act 1977: below, para.9–33); *Trade and Transport Inc v Iino Kaiun Kaisha Ltd* (*The Angelia*) [1973] 1 W.L.R. 210 at 230.

[36] e.g. clauses which might cover both negligent and non-negligent breaches of duty: below, para.9–15.

[37] *Photo Production Ltd v Securicor Transport Ltd*, above, n.23 at 846, 850.

[38] *ibid*. at 851 (Lord Diplock: "any need for this kind of judicial distortion of the English language has been banished by Parliament's having made these kinds of contract subject to the Unfair Contract Terms Act 1977"). For a similar point in relation to the effect of the Misrepresentation Act 1967 on the interpretation of clauses excluding liability for pre-contractual misrepresentation, see *Howard Marine and Dredging Co. Ltd v A. Ogden & Sons (Excavations) Ltd* [1978] Q.B. 574, CA, at 594 (Lord Denning M.R., dissenting on the construction of the relevant clause). See also *Thomas Witter Ltd v TBP Industries Ltd,* above, n.35 at 598 (Jacob J.: it is unnecessary after the Unfair Contract Terms Act to adopt artificial construction: "it is not for the law to fudge a way for an exclusion clause to be valid"; this decision has however been doubted in so far as it intepreted a clause widely as covering fraud: below, n.48); *A.E.G. (UK) Ltd v Logic Resource Ltd* [1996] C.L.C. 265, CA, at 277; *Society of Lloyd's v Leighs* [1997] C.L.C. 1012 at 1033 (in the light of the Unfair Contract Terms Act, principles of narrow construction of exclusion and indemnity clauses need not now be extended to

(2) Examples of the Courts' Construction of Clauses

9–12 **"Entire agreement" clauses.** It is well established that a clause in a written contract providing that the contract constitutes the "entire agreement" between the parties normally[39] has the effect that the parties' contractual obligations are to be found only in the written contract itself and not, for example, in any side agreement or collateral contract.[40] But it goes no further than this. This is simply the natural interpretation of the clause: if it were to be intended to have any wider effect, such as to exclude liability for misrepresentation, or even to exclude all remedies which are not expressly provided for in the contract,[41] clear words would have to

---

prevent clause excluding set-off for fraud from being effective). In *H.I.H. Casualty and General Insurance Ltd v Chase Manhattan Bank* [2001] EWCA Civ 1250, [2001] 2 Lloyd's Rep. 483 at [119] Rix L.J. speculated whether this development of the rules of interpretation of exclusion clauses might call into question the strictness of the *Canada Steamship* approach to clauses excluding liability for negligence: below, para.9–15.

[39] The courts have, however, denied this normal effect to an "entire agreement" clause where, properly construed in the context of the formation of the contract, the parties did not intend the written contract to contain all the terms, but intended that the provisions of a letter of offer which enclosed the written contract for signature should continue to have effect notwithstanding the clause: *Fulton Motors Ltd v Toyota (GB) Ltd*, unreported, July 6, 1999, CA. See also *1406 Pub Co. Ltd v Hoare* [2001] 23 E.G. 154 (C.S.) (collateral contract prevailed over entire agreement clause); doubted in *Inntrepreneur Pub Co. (CPC) v Sweeney* [2002] EWHC 1060 (Ch), [2002] 2 E.G.L.R. 132 at [47] (Park J.).

[40] Above, para.9–06. See in particular *Inntrepreneur Pub Co. (G.L.) v East Crown Ltd* [2000] 2 Lloyd's Rep. 611 at 614. On the question of whether it excludes implied terms, See *Exxonmobil Sales and Supply Corp. v Texaco Ltd* [2003] EWHC 1964 (Comm), [2003] 2 Lloyd's Rep. 686, above, n.19.

[41] *Strachan & Henshaw Ltd v Stein Industrie (UK) Ltd* (1997) 87 B.L.R. 52, CA (clause providing that the parties "intend that their respective rights, obligations and liabilities as provided for in the Conditions shall be exhaustive of the rights, obligations and liabilities of each of them to the other arising out of, under or in connection with the Contract or the Works, whether such rights, obligations or liabilities arise in respect or in consequence of a breach of contract or of statutory duty or a tortious or negligent act or omission which gives rise to a remedy at common law" (MF/1 General Conditions, condition 44.4) held to be a comprehensive exclusion clause which excluded, inter alia, a claim under the Misrepresentation Act 1967, s.2(1), since it was a claim "arising . . . in connection with the Contract").

be used.[42] And the courts in construing such a clause have rejected the argument that it is too technical to draw a distinction between misrepresentations and collateral warranties based on the selfsame representations: the words "this contract comprises the entire agreement between the parties" simply do not themselves exclude misrepresentations.[43]

Exclusion of liability for fraudulent misrepresentation. A clause might attempt to limit or exclude a party's liability for fraudulent misrepresentation either by expressly referring to liability for fraud, or by being drafted so wide as apparently to cover fraudulent, as well as non-fraudulent, misrepresentations. It is generally accepted, however, that a clause which expressly excludes or limits a party's personal liability for fraud would be held ineffective at common law.[44] At least until the enactment of the **9–13**

[42] *Thomas Witter Ltd v TBP IndustriesLtd*, above, n.35 at 595–596 (Jacob J: "Unless it is manifestly made clear that a purchaser has agreed only to have a remedy for breach of warranty I am not disposed to think that a contractual term said to have this effect by a roundabout route does indeed do so"); *Alman & Benson v Associated Newspapers Group Ltd*, unreported, June 20, 1980; *Government of Zanzibar v British Aerospace (Lancaster House) Ltd* [2000] 1 W.L.R. 2333 at 2344; *AXA Sun Life Services Plc v Campbell Martin Ltd* [2011] EWCA Civ 133 at [94] (Rix L.J.: "the exclusion of liability for misrepresentation has to be clearly stated. It can be done by clauses which state the parties' agreement that there have been no representations made; or that there has been no reliance on any representations; or by an express exclusion of liability for misrepresentation. However, save in such contexts, and particularly where the word 'representations' takes its place alongside other words expressive of contractual obligation, talk of the parties' contract superseding such prior agreement will not by itself absolve a party of misrepresentation where its ingredients can be proved").

[43] *Deepak Fertilisers and Petrochemicals Corp. v ICI Chemicals & Polymers Ltd* [1999] 1 Lloyd's Rep. 387, CA, at 395.

[44] *S. Pearson & Son Ltd v Dublin Corp.* [1907] A.C. 351, HL, at 353, 362; *Boyd & Forrest v Glasgow and South Western Railway Co.,* 1915 S.C. (H.L.) 20 at 36; *Pan-Atlantic Insurance Co. Ltd v Pine Top Insurance Co. Ltd* [1993] 1 Lloyd's Rep. 496, CA, at 502 (non-disclosure); *H.I.H. Casualty and General Insurance Ltd v New Hampshire Insurance Co.* [2001] 1 Lloyd's Rep. 378 at 388; see also in CA [2001] EWCA Civ 735, [2001] 2 Lloyd's Rep. 161 at [128] (concealment or misrepresentation inducing insurance contract); *H.I.H. Casualty and General Insurance Ltd v Chase Manhattan Bank* [2003] UKHL 6, [2003] 2 Lloyd's Rep. 61 at [16] (Lord Bingham: "it is clear that the law, on policy grounds, does not permit a contracting party to exclude liability for his own fraud in inducing the making of the contract"; see also Lord Hoffmann at [76] ("no doubt") and Lord

Misrepresentation Act 1967[45] the courts used to construe widely-drafted exclusion clauses so that they did not apply to fraud: they presumed that the parties must have intended the clause only to apply to liability arising from honest (non-fraudulent) misrepresentations.[46] It has been said that such a construction is now no longer necessary, since a clause which is sufficiently general to cover liability for fraud can instead be held unreasonable, and therefore to that extent of no effect, under s.3 of the Misrepresentation Act 1967.[47] However, the courts continue generally to adopt an approach to construction which presumes that a clause was not, in the absence of clear words, intended to apply to exclude or limit liability for fraud: not only because this may more closely reflect reality,[48] but also because, if the clause is construed so as to cover fraud, it is for that reason likely to be held unreasonable in its entirety.[49]

Scott at [122]). The position may be different in relation to fraud of agents or employees: HL in *H.I.H. Casualty and General Insurance Ltd v Chase Manhattan Bank* did not decide whether a principal or employer may in law exclude his own liability for the agent/employee's fraud, but held that, if such an exclusion is possible, it must be done "in clear and unmistakeable terms on the face of the contract": see Lord Bingham (with whom Lord Steyn agreed) at [16]; Lord Hoffmann at [76]–[82] (who saw force in the submission that it may be possible to exclude liability for an agent's fraud in *performance* of the contract, but not in its *formation*); Lord Hobhouse at [98] appears to have thought that an exclusion in relation to formation of the contract is not possible (the principal should insure against his agent's fraud); Lord Scott at [122] saw no reason of public policy why a party should not exclude his liability or other remedies, for the agent's fraud in which he is not personally complicit. In *Smith v Chadwick* (1882) 20 Ch.D. 27, CA, at 44–45, Jessel M.R. assumed that an appropriately-drafted clause could negative a claim of deceit by negativing reliance on the fraudulent statement. Such a clause will, however, be viewed with suspicion, given the statement by Lord Loreburn L.C. in *S. Pearson & Son Ltd v Dublin Corp.*at 353–354: "it seems clear that no one can escape liability for his own fraudulent statements by inserting in a contract a clause that the other party shall not rely upon them".

45 Below, para.9–19.

46 *S. Pearson & Son Ltd v Dublin Corp*, above, n.44; *Walker v Boyle* [1982] 1 W.L.R. 495 at 503.

47 *Thomas Witter Ltd v TBP Industries Ltd*, above, n.35 at 598. For the application of Misrepresentation Act 1967, s.3, see below, paras 9–19 to 9–30

48 *Government of Zanzibar v British Aerospace (Lancaster House) Ltd*, above, n.42 at 2346–2347, Judge Jack Q.C. (expressly disagreeing with the approach of Jacob J. in *Thomas Witter Ltd v TBP Industries Ltd*, above, n.35): "even in the contracts of today it surely has the ring of common sense that clauses dealing

Exclusion of liability *except for* fraud. In order to avoid a successful challenge to a clause on the basis that it is sufficiently wide to contravene either the common law rule that a party cannot exclude liability for his own fraud, or that the clause, by extending to claims for fraud, might thereby be held unreasonable within the statutory controls on exclusion clauses, it is not uncommon for a well-drawn exclusion clause to provide expressly that the clause does not seek to exclude or limit the parties' liability for fraud. The precise scope of such a clause depends on the language used, but if it refers generally to "fraud" it is unlikely to leave intact only claims in the tort of deceit, but may well also allow other claims where fraud has been established, such as rescission of the contract on the basis of a fraudulent misrepresentation, or claims in equity for a party's dishonest abuse of his fiduciary position.[50] 9–14

Exclusion of liability for negligence. At common law a clause may have the effect of excluding or restricting liability for negligence, whether the claim be based on the defendant's breach of a duty of care arising in tort[51] or in contract,[52] or a claim based on 9–15

with representations are not intended by the parties to apply where a representation has been fraudulently made"). This general approach is confirmed by *H.I.H. Casualty and General Insurance Ltd v Chase Manhattan Bank*, above, n.44 at [16], [68], [97] (Lord Hobhouse: "Fraud and negligence are different from each other in kind. Commercial men recognize the risk of want of care or skill; they do not contemplate fraud in the making of the contract"); *Bottin International Investments Ltd v Venson Group plc* [2006] EWHC 3112 (Ch), [2006] All E.R. (D) 111 (Dec) at [154] (non-reliance clause would not prevent claim in deceit); *Foodco UK LLP (t/a Muffin Break) v Henry Boot Developments Ltd* [2010] EWHC 358 (Ch) at [166]–[167] ("non-reliance" clause cannot exclude liability for party's own fraud).

49 *ibid*. For the difficulties of severance, see below, para.9–24.

50 *cf. Cavell USA Inc. v Seaton Insurance Co.* [2009] EWCA Civ 1363, [2009] 2 C.L.C. 991 at [24]–[29] (contractual release of claims "whether at law or in equity . . . save . . . in the case of fraud" allowed claim to proceed for at least some cases of dishonesty abuse of fiduciary position: reference to "equity" assisted the argument that it was not referring only to the (common law) tort of deceit, but "fraud" is wider than simply the tort of deceit). The "no-reliance" clause in the *Law Society Standard Conditions of Sale* (5th edn, 2011), special condition 6, "does not exclude liability for fraud or recklessness": a curious provision, since fraud includes "recklessness": above, para.5–15.

51 e.g. *Smith v Eric S. Bush* [1990] 1 A.C. 831, HL.

52 *Alderslade v Hendon Laundry Ltd* [1945] K.B. 189, CA.

negligence brought in equity[53] or under statute.[54] English law does not distinguish for this purpose between negligence and gross negligence: the dividing line is between negligence (which may be excluded by an appropriately-drawn clause) and fraud or dishonesty (which may not[55]).[56] However, the courts are cautious in their construction of a clause on which a defendant seeks to rely to exclude his liability for negligence. If a clause expressly and unambiguously covers the defendant's liability in negligence, the courts will give effect to the exemption at common law.[57] But a clause which is drafted more generally will be held to cover the liability only if the wording of the clause is wide enough on its ordinary meaning to cover negligence and if there is no head of liability, other than negligence, which it might realistically have been intended to cover.[58] This approach to the construction of exclusion clauses is based on the assumption that[59]:

---

[53] *Armitage v Nurse* [1998] Ch. 241, CA, at 253–254 (exclusion of trustee's liability under settlement "unless such loss or damage shall be caused by his own actual fraud").

[54] A claim under the Misrepresentation Act 1967, s.2(1), although in substance relating to misrepresentations made negligently (above, para.7–24) is not a claim in negligence and so is not necessarily effectively excluded by a clause which expressly refers to a "negligent act or omission"; nor is it a claim based on breach of statutory duty. But it can be excluded by an appropriately-drawn clause: *Strachan & Henshaw Ltd v Stein Industrie (UK) Ltd*, above, n.41 at 70. Whether the strict rule of interpretation in the *Canada Steamship* case (below, n.58) applies to a clause purporting to exclude claim under s.2(1) depends on whether it is treated as a claim in "negligence" for the purposes of that rule, a question raised (but not answered) by Rix L.J. in *H.I.H. Casualty and General Insurance Ltd v Chase Manhattan Bank* [2001] EWCA Civ 1250, [2001] 2 Lloyd's Rep. 483 at [117]. *Cf.* however *H.I.H. Casualty and General Insurance Ltd v New Hampshire Insurance Co.* [2001] EWCA Civ 735, [2001] 2 Lloyd's Rep. 161 at [136] (Rix L.J.: "since negligence is not a condition precedent of a right to claim under s.2(1), I do not see why it needs to be expressly or impliedly excluded").

[55] Above, para.9–13.

[56] *Armitage v Nurse*, above, n.53 at 254. Civil law systems, however, generally treat gross negligence (*culpa lata; faute lourde*) in the same manner as fraud: *ibid.*; G.H. Treitel, *Remedies for Breach of Contract* (1988), p.11.

[57] There is of course then a second question: whether the defendant will be prevented from relying on the clause under the statutory rules discussed below, paras 918 *et seq*.

[58] *Canada Steamship Lines Ltd v The King* [1952] A.C. 192, PC, at 208, Lord Morton, applying the law of Canada but basing his analysis on the earlier English case of *Alderslade v Hendon Laundry Ltd*, above, n.52. Lord Morton's judgment has been regularly cited and followed in later English cases: see, e.g. *Smith v*

> "it is inherently improbable that one party to the contract should intend to absolve the other party from the consequences of the latter's own negligence. The intention to do so must therefore be made perfectly clear, for otherwise the court will conclude that the exempted party was only intended to be free from liability in respect of damage occasioned by causes other than negligence for which he is answerable."

If, therefore, the clause does not expressly cover liability in negligence, and if it might have been intended to cover a head of liability other than negligence, the courts will construe it as not excluding negligence. This is again an illustration of the general approach to construction of the contract *contra proferentem*.

Where, however, the remedy sought is one which does not depend on whether negligence is proved (such as rescission of the contract, which is available for all misrepresentations, whether fraudulent, negligent or innocent[60]) it is not appropriate to apply this rule so as to limit the effect of an exclusion clause to only innocent misrepresentations, although it is still necessary to construe the exclusion or limitation clause to check that there is a sufficiently clear intention to exclude the remedy in the circumstances which have occurred.[61]

South Wales Switchgear Co. Ltd [1978] 1 W.L.R. 165, HL, at 167, 172, 178 (applied to indemnity clause); *Gillespie Bros & Co. Ltd v Roy Bowles Transport Ltd* [1973] Q.B. 400, CA, at 419–420, 421–422 (Lord Denning M.R. differed at 413–415); *The Raphael* [1982] 2 Lloyd's Rep. 42, CA; *E.E. Caledonia Ltd v Orbit Valve Co. Europe* [1994] 1 W.L.R. 1515, CA, at 1521. See also *Macquarie Internationale Investments Ltd v Glencore (UK) Ltd* [2008] EWHC 1716 (Comm), [2008] 2 C.L.C. 223 at [70] (Walker J.: clause did not expressly exclude negligence, but "the obvious claim . . . which everyone must have had in mind when clause 6.8 was drafted, was a claim in negligence").

59 *Gillespie Bros & Co. Ltd v Roy Bowles Transport Ltd*, above, n.58 at 419 (Buckley L.J.); *Toomey v Eagle Star Insurance Co. Ltd (No.2)* [1995] 2 Lloyd's Rep. 88 at 92–93.

60 Above, para.4–04.

61 *H.I.H. Casualty and General Insurance Ltd v Chase Manhattan Bank* [2003] UKHL 6, [2003] 2 Lloyd's Rep 61 at [12], [67], [95], [116]; see also *H.I.H. Casualty and General Insurance Ltd v New Hampshire Insurance Co.* [2001] EWCA Civ 735, [2001] 2 Lloyd's Rep. 161 at [126]–[141] (Rix L.J.), disapproving on this point the approach of Coleman J. in *Toomey v Eagle Star Insurance Co. Ltd (No.2)*, above, n.59 at 93, who applied *Canada Steamship Lines Ltd v The King*, above, n.58, and held that a clause which provided that a "contract is neither cancellable nor voidable by either party" successfully excluded the remedy of rescission but only in relation to innocent misrepresentation because it was not sufficiently clear that the clause was intended to cover

9–16 **Limitation clauses.** In construing exclusion and limitation clauses the courts always pay attention to the scope of the clause: in general terms the less wide-ranging the scope, the less strict the approach to its interpretation. This follows from a belief that it is more likely that a clause was intended to have its literal meaning where the impact of the clause on the defendant's liability is more limited. The courts have said, for example, that they will take a less strict approach in construing a clause which does not exclude liability altogether, but only limits liability to a particular sum of money,[62] or limits the range of recoverable losses.[63] Such a clause will be read *contra proferentem* and must be clearly expressed, but there is no reason why it should be judged by the specially exacting standards which are applied to exclusion and indemnity clauses.[64] Similarly, a clause which excludes or limits a party's rights of set-off is not treated as strictly as a clause which excludes liability,[65] and even if a clause excluding liability for fraudulent misrepresentation would be struck down at common law[66] the parties to a contract can exclude the remedy of set-off in relation to fraudulent

---

negligent misrepresentation, and therefore prima facie was to be construed as directed at the non-negligent ground of liability. In *H.I.H. Casualty and General Insurance Ltd v Chase Manhattan Bank* Lord Bingham in HL at [16] said that it was "common ground, and rightly so" that a clause which provided that the insured "shall have no liability of any nature to the insurers for any information provided by any other parties" precluded avoidance of the policy by the insurers on the ground of innocent misrepresentation by the brokers negotiating the policy. *Cf.*, however, the Misrepresentation Act 1967, s.3, which provides for both exclusions of "any liability" and exclusions of "any remedy"; and rescission is a remedy rather than a liability.

62 *Ailsa Craig Fishing Co. Ltd v Malvern Fishing Co. Ltd* [1983] 1 W.L.R. 964, HL; *George Mitchell (Chesterhall) Ltd v Finney Lock Seeds Ltd* [1983] 2 A.C. 803, HL.

63 *E.E. Caledonia Ltd v Orbit Valve Co.Europe*, above, n.58 at 1521 (clause excluding liability for consequential loss in favour of both parties).

64 *Ailsa Craig Fishing Co. Ltd v Malvern Fishing Co. Ltd*, above, n.62 at 970 (Lord Fraser). At 966 Lord Wilberforce said that "Clauses of limitation are not regarded by the courts with the same hostility as clauses of exclusion; this is because they must be related to other contractual terms, in particular to the risks to which the defending party may be exposed, the remuneration which he receives, and possibly also the opportunity of the other party to insure." This may equally be true of exclusion clauses, but a limitation clause is perhaps more likely to be part of a real bargaining and risk allocation process.

65 *The Fedora* [1986] 2 Lloyd's Rep. 441, CA, at 443–444.

66 Above, para.9–13.

misrepresentations.[67] One might also expect that a court would not take as strict an approach in construing a clause which limited the range of available remedies for misrepresentation as they would in the case of a clause excluding all remedies.

Exclusion of vendor's liability for misrepresentation in contracts for the sale of land. The liability of a vendor of land for misrepresentations or non-disclosure of relevant material matters concerning the property which he is selling is subject to certain special rules developed historically by the courts of equity.[68] Similarly, the courts have viewed with particular caution any clause in the contract of sale which seeks to exclude or limit the vendor's liability in this respect. It has therefore been held that a clause which provides that "no error, mis-statement or omission in any preliminary answer concerning the property . . . shall annul the sale"[69] is ineffective in equity to exclude the vendor's liability not only in relation to matters of title where the vendor has failed to disclose defects of which he knew,[70] but also in relation to misrepresentation where the vendor has, albeit innocently, misdescribed the property or made some other misrepresentation about the property when the true facts were within his own knowledge.[71] 9–17

---

[67] *Society of Lloyd's v Leighs* [1997] C.L.C. 1012; *WRM Group Ltd v Wood* [1998] C.L.C. 189, CA; *Skipskredittforeningen v Emperor Navigation* [1998] 1 Lloyd's Rep. 66 at 76.

[68] See below, para.10–09 (misdescription in contract of sale as a defence to specific performance); paras 17–30, 17–41 to 17–42 (vendor's duty to disclose defects in title).

[69] Condition 17(1)(a) of the National Conditions of Sale (19th edn.) The condition was re-drafted in the 20th edition; and now appears in a substantially revised form in condition 7.1 of the Standard Conditions of Sale (5th edn, 2011). See also Emmet, para.4.019. The Standard Conditions of Sale are reproduced in the Appendices in F. Silverman, *Conveyancing Handbook* (re-issued annually).

[70] Which would, in any event, be covered by the rule that a clause cannot normally be held to cover fraud: above, para.9–13.

[71] *Walker v Boyle* [1982] 1 W.L.R. 495, applying the approach taken by Wills J. at first instance in *Nottingham Patent Brick and Tile Co. v Butler* (1885) 15 Q.B.D. 261. The clause in *Walker v Boyle* was also, as an alternative ground, held unreasonable under the Misrepresentation Act 1967, s.3; below, para.9–19. Clauses excluding the buyer's right to rescind or obtain compensation for misdescription have been held ineffective in relation to a "substantial" misdescription: below, para.10–09. For the view that this is a substantive doctrine of fundamental breach, peculiar to conveyancing law, see C. Harpum, "Specific Performance with Compensation as a Purchaser's Remedy" [1981] C.L.J. 47 at

III. STATUTORY CONTROLS OF EXCLUSION AND LIMITATION CLAUSES

9–18 **The range of statutory controls.** Even if a clause is effective at common law to exclude or limit the defendant's liability for misrepresentation, it might still be wholly or partly deprived of that effect by reason of some statutory provision. There are various different forms of statutory control. In this book we are concerned only with those forms which apply, as between the individual parties to a claim based on misrepresentation, to limit the effectiveness of a clause. We are not concerned with other methods of control, such as the administrative powers of the Office of Fair Trading which in some cases can be relevant to the control of contractual exclusion and limitation clauses.[72]

There are various statutory provisions which might limit a defendant's ability to use effectively a clause for the purposes of excluding or limiting his liability for misrepresentation. The Misrepresentation Act 1967 contains a provision directed specifically at clauses excluding or restricting liability for misrepresentation. There are also general controls contained in the Unfair Contract Terms Act 1977 and the Unfair Terms in Consumer Contracts Regulations 1999 which, although not directed specifically at claims for misrepresentation, will often be relevant in such claims. The following sections of this chapter will consider each of these three controls.[73]

---

pp.47–48; Chitty, para.27–057 (which suggests that the rejection, in *Photo Production Ltd v Securicor Transport Ltd* [1980] A.C. 827, HL, of the general doctrine of fundamental breach should lead to the conveyancing cases now also being approached as a matter of construction). The Unfair Contract Terms Act 1977, s.3, does not apply to any contract so far as it relates to the creation or transfer of an interest in land: Sch.1, para.1(b).

[72] e.g. the powers of the Office of Fair Trading and certain other specified bodies under reg.12 of the Unfair Terms in Consumer Contracts Regulations 1999 (SI 1999/2083, amended by the Enterprise Act 2002, s.2) to seek an injunction against any person appearing to be using, or recommending use of, an unfair term drawn up for general use in contracts concluded with consumers. See also Chitty, paras 15–132 to 15–138; Treitel, para.7–125.

[73] For other statutory restrictions on exclusion and limitation clauses (which are not, however, generally relevant to claims for misrepresentation) see Chitty, paras 14–115 to 14–124, 14–126 to 14–131. In February 2005 the Law Commission proposed the repeal of the Unfair Contract Terms Act 1977 and the Unfair Terms in Consumer Contracts Regulations 1999, and their replacement by a new, single

(1) Misrepresentation Act 1967, Section 3[74]

Scope of the provision. Section 3 of the Misrepresentation Act 1967 [75] provides as follows: 9–19

"**3.**—If a contract contains a term which would exclude or restrict—

---

enactment: Law Com No.292, *Unfair Terms in Contracts*. The proposals would retain much of the protection given by the existing law, but in a simplified structure of regimes, covering business liability for negligence; consumer contracts; and non-consumer contracts. Significant proposals for change included (i) the extension of the regulation of terms in consumer contracts to cover not only non-negotiated terms (except the terms defining the main subject-matter and the price), but all such terms; (ii) the abandonment of the language of "good faith" (below, para.9–37) in favour of whether the business can show that the term is "fair and reasonable" (cl.14 of the draft Bill attached to the Report contains the "fair and reasonable" test; *cf*. the "reasonableness" test in the Unfair Contract Terms Act 1977, s.11; below, para.9–25); and (iii) a new concept, a "small business contract", to be given some of the protections afforded to consumer contracts. No change was proposed to the scope of the Misrepresentation Act 1967, s.3, which was not within the scope of the project, although the test of fairness and reasonableness for the 1967 Act would be the new test of the draft Bill: Law Com No.292, para.4.1, n.1. In July 2006 the Government accepted the Report in principle, but legislation in this area was delayed pending the outcome of negotiations in Europe on a proposed new Directive on consumer rights: Law Com No.323, *Annual Report 2009–10*, para.A.21; Lord Chancellor's first *Report on the implementation of Law Commission proposals* (24 January 2011), para.19. The Directive has now been adopted by the European Parliament but in a compromise form which does not cover unfair contract terms: below, para.17–54.

[74] Chitty, paras 6–136 to 6–140; Furmston, paras 3.95 to 3.96; Treitel, paras 9–116 to 9–125; Anson, pp.329–331; Cheshire, Fifoot and Furmston, pp.369–372.

[75] As substituted by Unfair Contract Terms Act 1977, s.8. The original text read:

"**3.**—If any agreement (whether made before or after the commencement of this Act) contains a provision which would exclude or restrict—

(a) any liability to which a party to a contract may be subject by reason of any misrepresentation made by him before the contract was made; or

(b) any remedy available to another party to the contract by reason of such a misrepresentation;

that provision shall be of no effect except to the extent (if any) that, in any proceedings arising out of the contract, the court or arbitrator may allow reliance on it as being fair and reasonable in the circumstances of the case."

The purpose of the substitution was to bring the provision into line with the scheme of the Unfair Contract Terms Act 1977, and to enable a direct cross-reference to be made to the test of "reasonableness" under the 1977 Act. See also below, para.9–25. The Tenth Report of the Law Reform Committee,

(a) any liability to which a party to a contract may be subject by reason of any misrepresentation made by him before the contract was made; or

(b) any remedy available to another party to the contract by reason of such a misrepresentation,

that term shall be of no effect except in so far as it satisfies the requirement of reasonableness as stated in section 11(1) of the Unfair Contract Terms Act 1977; and it is for those claiming that the term satisfies that requirement to show that it does."

Under this provision a contractual term, even if at common law it is effective to exclude or restrict the defendant's liability for misrepresentation or the remedies for misrepresentation which would otherwise be available to the claimant, is only so effective to the extent that the defendant can show that it is reasonable.

9–20 **"If a contract contains a term".** Section 3 only applies to limit the effectiveness of *contractual* terms which exclude or restrict the liability or remedy. It does not therefore apply to a non-contractual notice, such as a disclaimer in the particulars of sale issued by an estate agent which do not themselves form part of the contract of sale.[76] The section does not require the exclusion clause to be in the same contract in respect of which it constitutes an exclusion or limitation of liability,[77] but before the clause can be relied on by the defendant as effective at common law to exclude or limit the particular liability[78] it will have to be sufficiently clear that it is referring to that liability.

The operation of the section is not, however, limited in its effect to consumer transactions or clauses contained in standard terms of

Cmnd. 1782 (1962) paras 23–24, had proposed only to restrict effective exclusion clauses to cases where the representor could not show that he had reasonable grounds for believing the representation to be true.

[76] *McGrath v Shah* (1989) 57 P. & C.R. 452 at 460–461; *Collins v Howell-Jones* [1981] E.G.D. 207, CA, at 212; *Cremdean Properties Ltd v Nash* [1977] E.G.D. 55 at 59, [1977] E.G.D. 63, CA, at 72.

[77] If such a narrow provision had been intended, s.3(a) would have been drafted: "any liability to which a party to *the* contract", rather than "*a* contract". In *Society of Lloyd's v Leighs*, above, n.67 at 1036 Colman J. was rather too hesitant on this issue.

[78] Without which s.3 is unnecessary anyway: above, para.9–10. Notice also the opening words of s.3: "If a contract contains a term *which would exclude or restrict* ..."; i.e. the section presupposes that the common law rules have been satisfied already and the clause will be effective but for the operation of s.3.

business: it applies to *any* contract containing a term which would exclude or restrict liability or remedies arising by reason of a misrepresentation by a party to a contract.[79]

"exclude or restrict any liability . . . or any remedy". Section 3 controls not only clauses which wholly exclude liability, but also clauses which restrict the liability or exclude or restrict any remedy arising from misrepresentation. A clause which imposes a limit on the quantum of damages recoverable for misrepresentation will therefore be covered by the section. So will a clause which excludes a particular remedy for misrepresentation,[80] even though it does not touch on the availability of other remedies. 9–21

Sometimes a clause has to be analysed very carefully to check whether in substance, even if not by its literal language, it excludes or restricts liability or a remedy for misrepresentation.[81] So a clause which seeks to negative an element of a claim for misrepresentation

[79] *British Fermentation Products Ltd v Compair Reavell Ltd* (1999) 66 Con. L.R. 1 at 14. *Cf.* the limits on the operation of the Unfair Contract Terms Act 1977: below, paras 9–32, 9–34. However, s.3 does not extend to exclusions or restrictions of liability or remedies under contracts for the international sale or supply of goods: Unfair Contract Terms Act 1977 s.26; *Trident Turboprop (Dublin) Ltd v First Flight Couriers Ltd* [2009] EWCA Civ 290, [2010] Q.B. 86 at [19] (reference in s.3 to the 1977 Act makes the latter the controlling instrument). Note, however, that other significant exclusions from scope of the 1977 Act (e.g. insurance contracts, contracts relating to creation or transfer of interest in land, intellectual property rights, securities: Sch.1) apply by their terms only to particular sections of the 1977 Act and will not limit the scope of operation of s.3 Misrepresentation Act 1967.

[80] Clauses excluding rights of set-off: *WRM Group Ltd v Wood*, above, n.67; *Skipskredittforeningen v Emperor Navigation*, above, n.67 at 74 (Mance J.: "the right of set-off represents a means of recovery, and so a remedy in any ordinary sense of the word and within section 3(b)", disapproving the contrary view of Colman J. in *Society of Lloyd's v Leighs*, above, n.67 at 1035–1036).

[81] There is no equivalent within the Misrepresentation Act of the provision in the Unfair Contract Terms Act 1977, s.13(1), to the effect that the 1977 Act also prevents "excluding or restricting liability by reference to terms and notices which exclude or restrict the relevant obligation or duty"; and during the passing of the Misrepresentation Bill the Solicitor-General did not give a direct answer to a question about how non-reliance clauses would be caught by s.3: *Hansard*, HC Vol.741, 20 February 1967, cols 1375–1376, 1387–1390. However, even without an equivalent provision the courts have taken an approach by which a clause which *in substance* excludes or restricts a liability or remedy is caught by the Misrepresentation Act 1967 s.3. On the Unfair Contract Terms Act 1977, s.13(1), see below, para.9–33.

might, in substance, be a clause which excludes the liability which would otherwise have existed. Where, therefore, a misrepresentation was made and was in fact relied upon by the claimant, it was held that a clause which sought to negate the claimant's reliance was a term which excluded a liability to which the representor would otherwise be subject by reason of the representation, and therefore was regulated by s.3: otherwise, the section could always be defeated by including an appropriate non-reliance clause in the contract, however unreasonable that might be.[82] This is not to say that an appropriately-drawn clause cannot effectively prevent a claim arising and therefore avoid the operation of s.3. For example, a clause which genuinely prevents there being a misrepresentation at all, by making clear that a statement is only one of the

---

[82] *Government of Zanzibar v British Aerospace (Lancaster House) Ltd* [2000] 1 W.L.R. 2333 at 2347–2348 ("The parties . . . agree that neither party has placed any reliance whatsoever on any representations . . . made prior to the date of this Contract other than those expressly incorporated or recited in this Contract"). See also *Cremdean Properties Ltd v Nash*, above, n.76 at 72–73 (Scarman L.J., rejecting the argument that a clause warning the representee to check the accuracy of a statement was a clause which effectively avoided s.3 by preventing there being a "misrepresentation": "the case for the appellant . . . runs thus: a statement is not a representation unless it is also a statement that what is stated is true. If in context a statement contains no assertion, express or implied, that its content is accurate, there is no representation. *Ergo*, there can be no misrepresentation; *ergo*, the Misrepresentation Act 1967 cannot apply to it. Humpty Dumpty would have fallen for this argument. If we were to fall for it, the Misrepresentation Act would be dashed to pieces which not all the King's lawyers could put together again . . . The note was . . . a warning to the would-be purchaser to check the facts; that is to say, not to rely on it. Such a warning does not destroy the representation; indeed, it is wholly consistent with the statement being a representation. It is because the statement contains the representation that the warning is given. Since the statement was false, there was a false representation; the Act therefore applies"). In *Watford Electronics Ltd v Sanderson C.F.L. Ltd* [2001] EWCA Civ 317, [2001] 1 All E.R. (Comm) 696 at [40] Chadwick L.J. appeared to doubt the approach of applying the "substance" of the clause, which had been adopted by the trial judge in that case, but this was a regrettable departure from the general approach in other cases: E. Peel, "Reasonable Exemption Clauses" (2001) 117 L.Q.R. 545 at pp.548–549. See A. Trukhtanov, "Misrepresentation: Acknowledgement of Non-Reliance as a Defence" (2009) 125 L.Q.R. 648 at 666–670, highlighting the tension which exists in the authorities, and noting at 668 that, since the court now accept "no representation" and "non-reliance" clauses more generally (see above, para.9–03, esp. n.9), "the case for not allowing legislative protection to be defeated by perceived technicalities will be much stronger".

defendant's opinions on which the claimant is not entitled to rely[83] ought to be unaffected by s.3: the cases[84] in which such clauses have been subjected to the section have been ones in which there was in fact a misrepresentation on which the claimant relied, but a clause was being used to seek to deny those facts. It has also been held that a clause by which the defendant limits the authority of his agent, and therefore successfully at common law ensures that he is not liable for his agent's representations outside the scope of that authority, is unaffected by s.3: the section only applies to a provision which would exclude or restrict liability for a misrepresentation made by a party or his duly authorised agent, but does not qualify the right of a principal publicly to limit the otherwise ostensible authority of his agent.[85] It has also been held that an "entire agreement" clause is not covered by s.3, since such a clause does not preclude a claim in misrepresentation: it only defines where the terms of the contract are to be found.[86]

---

[83] Above, paras 3–14 *et seq*; *I.F.E. Fund SA v Goldman Sachs International* [2006] EWHC 2887 (Comm), [2007] 1 Lloyd's Rep. 264 at [67]–[71], distinguishing *Cremdean Properties Ltd v Nash*, above, n.76 (affirmed [2007] EWCA Civ 811, [2007] 2 Lloyd's Rep. 449); *Titan Steel Wheels Limited v Royal Bank of Scotland Plc* [2010] EWHC 211 (Comm), [2010] 2 Lloyd's Rep. 92 at [98].

[84] *Government of Zanzibar v British Aerospace (Lancaster House) Ltd*, above, n.82; *Cremdean Properties Ltd v Nash*, above, n.76; *Raiffeisen Zentralbank Österreich A.G. v Royal Bank of Scotland Plc* [2010] EWHC 1392 (Comm), [2011] 1 Lloyd's Rep. 123 at [287] (Christopher Clarke J.: "there is an important distinction between a provision which makes clear that no (or only a qualified) representation is being made and one which purports to exclude a representation that has been made"); *Springwell Navigation Corp. v J.P. Morgan Chase Bank* [2010] EWCA Civ 1221, [2010] 2 C.L.C. 705 at [181]; *Trident Turboprop (Dublin) Ltd v First Flight Couriers Ltd* [2008] EWHC 1686 (Comm), [2008] 2 Lloyd's Rep. 581 at [48] (the appeal at [2009] EWCA Civ 290, [2010] Q.B. 86 proceeded on different grounds: above, n.79).

[85] *Overbrooke Estates Ltd v Glencombe Properties Ltd* [1974] 1 W.L.R. 1335 at 1342, approved in *Cremdean Properties Ltd v Nash*, above, n.76. Again, this argument holds only if the clause is a genuine limitation on the agent's authority and will not apply if the agent in fact had authority but the clause is an attempt to deny the effect in law of a misrepresentation which the principal has, in fact, made through his agent: see Bridge L.J. in *Cremdean Properties Ltd v Nash* at 70.

[86] *McGrath v Shah*, above, n.76 at 459; *Inntrepreneur Pub Co. (G.L.) v East Crown Ltd* [2000] 2 Lloyd's Rep. 611 at 614. For "entire agreement" clauses, see above, para.9–12.

9–22 **"a party to a contract".** The section only controls clauses which exclude or restrict the liability of (or remedies owed by) a "party to a contract" in respect of pre-contractual misrepresentations made "by him". This will include representations made by the contracting party's agent for which the contracting party is in law responsible,[87] but it only covers the clause in so far as it is used to exclude or restrict the contracting party's liability. In a claim brought in tort against the agent personally, or in any other case where the claim is brought against a person other than the contracting party who is protected by the contractual exclusion or limitation clause, s.3 of the Misrepresentation Act is not an appropriate method of control, although there will often be other controls such as those under the Unfair Contract Terms Act 1977.[88]

9–23 **"by reason of any misrepresentation".** Section 3 only applies in respect of a liability or remedy based on a misrepresentation made by the defendant before the contract was made. This will therefore include rescission,[89] and a claim for damages under s.2(1) of the Misrepresentation Act 1967.[90] A claim in the tort of deceit[91] by one contracting party against the other may be based on a pre-contractual misrepresentation, but the application of s.3 in such a context will be relatively rare since at common law a party cannot normally exclude his liability for his own fraud: s.3 should only therefore be relevant where the exclusion is of the contracting party's liability for his agent's fraud.[92] Some claims which arise out of false statements may not, however, be claims "by reason of [a] misrepresentation made . . . before the contract". A claim in the tort of negligence is based on the representor's failure to fulfil a duty of care in making the representation, not the falsity of the statement: a clause excluding or restricting liability for the tort of negligence does therefore not appear to fall under s.3 of the Misrepresentation

[87] By analogy with the interpretation of similar language in Misrepresentation Act 1967, s.2(1), in *Resolute Maritime Inc v Nippon Kaiji Kyokai* [1983] 1 W.L.R. 857; above, para.7–09.
[88] Below, paras 9–31 to 9–36.
[89] Above, Ch.4.
[90] Above, Ch.7.
[91] Above, Ch.5.
[92] Above, para.9–13.

Act.[93] Nor does a clause which excludes or restricts a liability arising from a false statement, not in its form of a pre-contractual misrepresentation, but as a representation incorporated into the contract and therefore giving rise to a claim for breach of contract.[94] The validity of any clause excluding or restricting the liability or remedy in negligence, or for breach of contract, must instead be tested under the different scheme of the Unfair Contract Terms Act 1977.[95] Nor does s.3 of the Misrepresentation Act 1967 apply to a clause which excludes or limits a contracting party's liability in performance of his contract, such as a clause limiting the liability of a surveyor or accountant for advice given in the performance of his duties: again, the appropriate control in such cases is the Unfair Contract Terms Act 1977 or the Unfair Terms in Consumer Contracts Regulations 1999.

"that term shall be of no effect except in so far as it satisfies". **9–24**
Section 3 provides that a term to which it applies is of no effect except in so far as it satisfies the requirement of reasonableness. This has been interpreted to mean that, if unreasonable, the *whole* term is of no effect, whether or not the basis of the decision that the term is not reasonable is material to the particular case before the court: the court cannot rewrite the term so that it constitutes only a reasonable exclusion or limitation clause, even if (so rewritten) it would then apply to the case in hand.[96] So, for example, a clause

---

[93] Above, para.6–12. In practice, however, claims against the contracting party for negligent pre-contractual misrepresentation will more commonly be brought under the Misrepresentation Act 1967, s.2(1), than in the tort of negligence: above, para.7–47.

[94] An "entire agreement" clause, above, para.9–12, is therefore subject to the Unfair Contract Terms Act 1977, rather than the Misrepresentation Act 1967, s.3.

[95] For the Unfair Contract Terms Act 1977, see below, paras 9–31 to 9–36. S.2 is relevant for claims in the tort of negligence; ss.2, 3, 6 and 7 are relevant for claims in contract. However, if a clause is so drafted that it (inseparably) covers both a claim based on pre-contractual misrepresentation and a claim in negligence or for breach of contract, then even without reference to the Unfair Contract Terms Act the clause will be of no effect in relation to the latter claims if it is struck down by the Misrepresentation Act 1967, s.3, in its applicability to the misrepresentation claim, since s.3 strikes down the whole term: below, para.9–24; Treitel, para. 9–122.

[96] *Skipskredittforeningen v Emperor Navigation* [1998] 1 Lloyd's Rep. 66 at 75 (applying to the Misrepresentation Act 1967, s.3, the decision in *Stewart Gill Ltd v Horatio Myer & Co. Ltd* [1992] Q.B. 600, CA, a decision on the interpretation

which is drafted widely so as to exclude all liability for misrepresentation might be held to be ineffective on the basis that it covered fraudulent misrepresentations,[97] even where the claim against which the defendant seeks to use the clause is based on a non-fraudulent misrepresentation. In drafting an exclusion or limitation clause great care must be taken to ensure that the clause might not be held ineffective because it covers liabilities which render the whole clause unreasonable. Although a court might sometimes be able to sever the provisions of an exclusion clause and so to hold there to be separate "terms" which can be separately upheld or struck down under s.3,[98] the better advice is to review an exclusion or limitation clause carefully to ensure that it covers as precisely as possible the liabilities or remedies which are intended to be excluded or limited, and to structure the clause in such a way

---

of the Unfair Contract Terms Act 1977). Mance J. at 75 expressed reservations about whether this interpretation reflects Parliament's intention; see also *Bacardi-Martini Beverages Ltd v Thomas Hardy Packaging Ltd* [2002] EWCA Civ 549, [2002] All E.R. (Comm) 335 at [26] (Mance L.J.), but the interpretation is binding at the level of CA.

97 *Thomas Witter Ltd v TBP Industries Ltd* [1996] 2 All E.R. 573 at 598. *Cf.*, however, *Government of Zanzibar v British Aerospace (Lancaster House)Ltd*, above, n.82 at 2346–2347, where Judge Jack Q.C. declined to follow the decision of Jacob J. in *Thomas Witter* by construing the clause as not covering fraud; above, para.9–13, n.48; *Six Continents Hotels Inc. v Event Hotels G.m.b.H.* [2006] EWHC 2317 (QB), [2006] All E.R. (D) 101 (Sep) at [53] (Gloster J., preferring the approach in the *Zanzibar* case).

98 *cf. R.W. Green Ltd v Cade Bros Farms* [1978] 1 Lloyd's Rep. 602 (single clause contained severable provisions relating to time within which claims must be brought and limit on quantum of damages: decision under the Sale of Goods Act 1893, s.55 (replaced by the Unfair Contract Terms Act 1977, s.6) but the decision is still relevant because the language of the 1893 Act on this point was similar to that in the Misrepresentation Act 1967, s.3); *Watford Electronics Ltd v Sanderson C.F.L. Ltd* [2001] EWCA Civ 317, [2001] 1 All E.R. (Comm) 696 at [32] (two sentences in clause; each had its own separate and distinct purpose, exclusion of consequential loss and limitation of liability to a specified sum: judge was wrong to treat them as a single provision). However, in *Stewart Gill Ltd v Horatio Myer & Co. Ltd*, above, n.96, a clause disallowing the withholding of payments "by reason of any payment credit set-off counterclaim allegation of incorrect or defective goods or for any other reason whatsoever which the customer may allege excuses him from performing his obligations hereunder" was a single, unreasonable term which could not be severed to provide an enforceable (reasonable) restriction simply of the right of set-off; noted E. Peel (1993) 56 M.L.R. 98.

that it can be treated as severable in the event that any one provision within it is held to be ineffective under s.3.

The reasonableness test. Section 3 incorporates the test of "reasonableness" from the Unfair Contract Terms Act 1977, s.11(1), which provides as follows[99]: 9–25

> "**11.**—(1) In relation to a contract term, the requirement of reasonableness for the purposes of this Part of this Act, section 3 of the Misrepresentation Act 1967 and section 3 of the Misrepresentation Act (Northern Ireland) 1967 is that the term shall have been a fair and reasonable one to be included having regard to the circumstances which were, or ought reasonably to have been, known to or in the contemplation of the parties when the contract was made."

Burden of proof of reasonableness. It is for the defendant to show that clause is reasonable, not for the claimant to show that the clause is unreasonable. Under s.3,[100] the clause is of no effect unless it satisfies the requirement of reasonableness, and it is for the person claiming that it satisfies the requirement to show that it does: that is, the burden of proof of reasonableness is on the person seeking to rely on the clause. 9–26

Pleading and proving reasonableness. Since it is the defendant who must show that the reasonableness test is satisfied, it is he who must plead the circumstances which render the clause reasonable.[101] Where the pleading makes it clear that the defendant will rely upon an exclusion clause, then it is implicit in that pleading that the defendant is asserting that the clause is reasonable. But the better practice is to include in the defence a statement that the standard conditions relied upon are reasonable.[102] 9–27

---

[99] The Law Commission has proposed the replacement of the test of reasonableness under the Unfair Contract Terms Act 1977 by a new "fair and reasonable" test: Law Com. No.292 *Unfair Terms in Contracts*; above, para.9–18, n.73.

[100] The Unfair Contract Terms Act 1977 contains a similar provision for the application of the reasonableness test within that Act: s.11(5).

[101] *Laceys Footwear (Wholesale) Ltd v Bowler International Ltd* [1997] 2 Lloyd's Rep. 369, CA, at 374; *A.E.G. (UK) Ltd v Logic Resource Ltd* [1996] C.L.C. 265, CA, at 278; *Circuit Systems Ltd v Zuken-Redac (UK) Ltd* (1994) 42 Con. L.R. 120 at 143.

[102] *Sheffield v Pickfords Ltd* [1997] C.L.C. 648, CA, at 650.

However, the court will not normally decide the issue of reasonableness on a strike-out application since it cannot decide whether the term was a fair and reasonable one, having regard to all the circumstances, without hearing evidence: the issue is a broad issue of fact which can normally only be dealt with at the trial of the action.[103] An exception to this is made in the case of a clause which seeks to exclude set-off: such a clause, if it is to be effective at all, can only take effect either upon an application for summary judgment or on the subsequent hearing of a preliminary point as to its reasonableness. To give unconditional leave to defend without ordering the hearing of a preliminary point is in effect to render the clause nugatory, and so the judge should reach a decision on the reasonableness of the clause in the light of such evidence as he has.[104]

9–28 **Time for assessing reasonableness.** The time at which the reasonableness of the term is assessed is when the contract was made: the question is whether the term was a fair and reasonable one to be included having regard to the circumstances which were, or ought reasonably to have been, known to or in the contemplation of the parties at that time.[105] The question is not whether it is reasonable to allow reliance on the clause at the time of the action.[106] The fact that the circumstances have changed since the time of the contract, so that the clause would no longer be a reasonable one to include in those changed circumstances, is irrelevant.

---

[103] *Garden Neptune Shipping Ltd v Occidental Worldwide Investment Corp.* [1990] 1 Lloyd's Rep. 330, CA, at 335; *Killick v PricewaterhouseCoopers* [2001] 1 B.C.L.C. 65 at 72; *Daroga v Wells*, unreported, May 11, 1994, CA (clause limiting time within which claim must be made was probably reasonable but should not be decided in a strike-out application where there was no evidence before the court and the issue would have to be dealt with on the basis of a submission and general knowledge).

[104] *Stewart Gill Ltd v Horatio Myer & Co. Ltd*, above, n.96 at 604; *Skipskredittforeningen v Emperor Navigation*, above, n.96 at 77 (clause excluding set-off for fraud). See also below, para.11–17.

[105] Unfair Contract Terms Act 1977, s.11(1).

[106] This was the effect of the original form of s.3, above, para.9–19, n.75, which was replaced by the Unfair Contract Terms Act 1977, s.8. Care must therefore be taken in reading cases on the interpretation of the reasonableness test which were decided under the old form of s.3.

Statutory criteria for assessment of reasonableness. The Unfair Contract Terms Act 1977 contains two provisions which are relevant to the application of the reasonableness test. Under s.11(4): 9–29

> "Where by reference to a contract term or notice a person seeks to restrict liability to a specified sum of money, and the question arises (under this or any other Act) whether the term or notice satisfies the requirement of reasonableness, regard shall be had in particular (but without prejudice to subsection (2) above[107] in the case of contract terms) to—
> (a) the resources which he could expect to be available to him for the purpose of meeting the liability should it arise; and
> (b) how far it was open to him to cover himself by insurance."

This provision applies directly to a determination of the reasonableness of a clause under s.3 of the Misrepresentation Act 1967, since it applies to such questions under the Unfair Contract Terms Act "or any other Act". If, therefore, a clause seeks to limit[108] liability for misrepresentation to a particular sum of money, the matters set out in s.11(4) must be considered.

Section 11(2) of the Unfair Contract Terms Act 1977 also incorporates[109] guidelines for the application of the reasonableness test but this provision only applies, strictly, to claims under certain specific sections of the 1977 Act,[110] and not to the application of the reasonableness test for the purposes of s.3 of the Misrepresentation Act 1967. However, these guidelines—which include such things as the relative strength of the bargaining position of the parties; whether the claimant received an inducement to agree to the term; and whether the claimant knew or ought to have known of the existence and extent of the term—have been treated by the courts as giving criteria which are generally relevant in applying the reasonableness test, and so they are in practice used in the cases

[107] Below.

[108] Section 11(4) by its terms applies only to limitation clauses (clauses which "restrict" liability to a particular sum) and not to clauses which seek wholly to exclude liability: *The Flamar Pride* [1990] 1 Lloyd's Rep. 434 at 438, but no doubt the matters there mentioned would in any event be relevant in determining the reasonableness of an exclusion clauses, on a similar basis to s.11(2), below.

[109] Set out in Sch.2.

[110] ss.6 and 7 (exclusion of certain liabilities arising from breach of contracts for the sale of goods, hire-purchase and other contracts under which possession or ownership of goods passes).

where the issue is whether an exclusion or limitation clause is reasonable for the purposes of s.3 of the Misrepresentation Act.[111]

9–30 **The application of the reasonableness test in the cases.**[112] In determining whether an exclusion or limitation clause is reasonable, the courts ask whether it was a reasonable clause to have been inserted in this particular contract, between these particular parties. It is not relevant that the clause might have been reasonable in another contract between different parties in different circumstances.[113] So it is not sufficient to show that a clause is a standard form exclusion which is commonly used between other parties in similar contracts,[114] unless it can be shown that it is

---

[111] Judge Thornton Q.C. applied the guidelines of Sch.2 in *Watford Electronics Ltd v Sanderson C.F.L. Ltd*: see [2001] EWCA Civ 317, [2001] 1 All E.R. (Comm) 696 at [22]; in CA the reasonableness test (including the Sch.2 guidelines) was applied only in relation to claims under the contract, not claims for misrepresentation: at [51]–[52].

[112] The Act gives a discretion to the judge; the CA is reluctant to interfere with the trial judge's decision on the issue of reasonableness: *Howard Marine and Dredging Co. Ltd v A. Ogden & Sons (Excavations) Ltd* [1978] Q.B. 574, CA, at 599, Bridge L.J., accepting the judge's decision that the clause in question was unreasonable. Lord Denning, however, dissented and would have substituted a decision that the clause was reasonable: at 594. The case was a decision under the original form of s.3 (above, para.9–19, n.75), but nothing turns on this here. See also *George Mitchell (Chesterhall) Ltd v Finney Lock Seeds Ltd* [1983] 2 A.C. 803, HL, at 815–816; *Watford Electronics Ltd v Sanderson C.F.L. Ltd*, above, n.98 at [30].

[113] *South Western General Property Co. Ltd v Marton* [1982] E.G.D. 113 at 122 (clause in contract for sale of land to private individual at auction, disclaiming responsibility for accuracy of statements in auction particulars and directing purchaser to make his own inquiries, held not reasonable although it might have been reasonable in a similar contract with property speculators). For the same point in a case concerned with the reasonableness of a clause for the purposes of the Unfair Contract Terms Act, see *Phillips Products Ltd v Hyland* [1987] 1 W.L.R. 659 at 668. The issue is not, however, whether the clause is reasonable to exclude the particular claim, but whether the clause *as a whole* is a reasonable one: above, para.9–24.

[114] So the courts held that a standard form exclusion (condition 17) in the National Conditions of Sale (19th edn), was unreasonable: *Walker v Boyle* [1982] 1 W.L.R. 495 at 507–508. See also *Sakkas v Donford Ltd* (1982) 46 P. & C.R. 290 at 306. Condition 17 was revised in the 20th edition, but was still held unreasonable in *McCarthy v George*, unreported, January 15, 1991. That provision has now been substantially revised in the Standard Conditions of Sale (5th edn, 2011) (reproduced in the Appendices in F. Silverman, *Conveyancing*

reasonable in the context of the contract in issue. However, where a standard form clause has been evolved by negotiation between trade associations or others who are concerned to protect the rights of their members, and which can be regarded as representing what consensus in the trade regards as fair and reasonable, the courts will be slow to hold the clause to be not fair and reasonable.[115]

In deciding whether a clause satisfies the reasonableness test, the courts consider not only the substance of the clause but also the circumstances in which it was included in the contract, such as the relative bargaining positions of the two particular parties. So, for example, courts have held that a clause fails to satisfy the reasonableness test because it is too widely drafted[116]; or because the circumstances in which the claimant has been induced to agree to the clause render the clause unreasonable.[117] But they have

---

Handbook (re-issued annually)). See also Emmet, para.4.019. In *Cleaver v Schyde Investments Ltd* [2011] EWCA Civ 929, [2011] All E.R. (D) 285 (Jul) CA upheld the trial judge's finding that condition 7.1.3 of the Standard Conditions of Sale (4th edn) was not fair and reasonable within the particular contract between the parties, and so was of no effect under Misrepresentation Act 1967 s.3.

[115] *Walker v Boyle*, above, n.114 at 508. See also *Schenkers v Overland Shoes Ltd* [1998] 1 Lloyd's Rep. 498, CA, at 507 (clause excluding right of set-off was reasonable under the Unfair Contract Terms Act 1977: relevant factors included that the clause was in common use and well known in the trade following comprehensive discussions between reputable and representative bodies mindful of the considerations involved: it reflected a general view as to what was reasonable in the trade concerned).

[116] *Miljus v Yamazaki Machinery UK Ltd* [1997] 1 C.L.Y. 992 (clause too wide, and excluded all loss in all circumstances); *Thompson v Sayed Ali*, unreported, March 21, 1994, CA (clause deeming as inoperative misrepresentations which were intended to induce and did induce the claimant to enter into the contract could not conceivably satisfy the reasonableness test); *Bellamy v Newbold*, unreported, March 5, 1986, CA (clause in post-completion settlement agreement between vendor and purchaser, even if it could be construed as being sufficiently widely drafted to apply to a claim by purchaser in respect of pre-contractual misrepresentations about property boundary, would be ineffective to exclude claim under s.3 of the Misrepresentation Act, because it cannot be reasonable to exclude liability for misrepresentation in respect of a boundary dispute that was not in the contemplation of the parties when the settlement agreement was entered into).

[117] *Inntrepreneur Estates (CPC) Ltd v Worth* [1996] 1 E.G.L.R. 84 at 88 (clause in contract for lease of tied house to effect that tenants had not relied on pre-contract statements and had made their own independent enquiries: unreasonable where landlord knew that tenants were "people of great enthusiasm, excessive optimism and virtually no business experience" and needed help to

indicated that a clause is more likely to be held to be reasonable where it is negotiated between the two contracting parties, especially where the parties are of equal bargaining power and have the benefit of professional advice[118]: in such cases, the parties are likely to prefer commercial certainty, and are likely to have included the existence and enforceability of the exclusion or limitation clause in their assessment of the balance of risk in the contract.[119]

---

write a business plan: the landlords "knew and relied upon the [tenants'] naiveté during their negotiations"). The same clause was held unreasonable in *Inntrepreneur Estates Ltd v Hollard* [1999] N.P.C. 137 (affirmed CA, unreported, July 31, 2000) on a different basis: that the landlord was there in a unique position of having immediate access to the information about which statements were made, and the tenants had no means of obtaining them; since the information was crucial to the tenants' assessment of the viability of the business, it was not reasonable to exclude liability for the statements in question. For a discussion of the factors that may be relevant in deciding whether a clause disclaiming liability in tort for careless advice is reasonable see *Smith v Eric S. Bush* [1990] 1 A.C. 831, HL, at 858–859 (Lord Griffiths: Were the parties of equal bargaining power? Would it have been reasonably practicable to obtain the advice from an alternative source taking into account considerations of cost and time? How difficult is the task being undertaken for which liability is being excluded? What are the practical consequences of the decision on the question of reasonableness?).

[118] The fact that the parties have proper legal advice in entering into the contract does not of itself mean that a clause will be reasonable: *Walker v Boyle*, above, n.114 at 507 (solicitors who were "men of not inconsiderable experience as conveyancing solicitors" could properly use standard form conditions of sale such as the National Conditions of Sale, but this did not prevent a clause to which they had not directed their attention being held unreasonable).

[119] *E.A. Grimstead & Son Ltd v McGarrigan*, unreported, October 27, 1999, CA, referred to in *Government of Zanzibar v British Aerospace (Lancaster House) Ltd* [2000] 1 W.L.R. 2333 at 2345–2346. See also *White Cross Equipment Ltd v Farrell* (1982) 2 Tr. L. 21 (clause which was interpreted as allocating risks between two commercial parties of equal bargaining power held reasonable for the Misrepresentation Act 1967, s.3 (original version)); *Skipskredittforeningen v Emperor Navigation*, above, n.96 at 77 (clause excluding set-off for fraud was reasonable in a contract negotiated between businessmen); *Daroga v Wells*, above, n.103 (clause limiting time within which claim to be brought by purchaser in respect of breach of warranties in share purchase agreement was probably reasonable, given that it is a usual type of clause and both parties were advised by solicitors: final decision on this was not, however, appropriate in a strike-out application); *Watford Electronics Ltd v Sanderson C.F.L. Ltd* [2001] EWCA Civ 317, [2001] 1 All E.R. (Comm) 696 at [54], [63] (clauses excluding indirect loss reasonable where parties of equal bargaining power negotiated price bearing in

(2) Unfair Contract Terms Act 1977

Scope of the provision. The Unfair Contract Terms Act 1977, Pt I,[120] contains a range of provisions aimed at controlling the extent to which liability for breach of contract, for negligence or for other breaches of duty can be effectively excluded or limited by contract terms or non-contractual notices. The only section of the Act aimed directly at clauses or notices which exclude or limit liability for misrepresentation is s.8, which substituted a new form of s.3 of the Misrepresentation Act 1967 and has been discussed in detail in the previous section.[121] Other sections of the Act are however sometimes relevant in claims based on misrepresentation where the cause of action against which the defendant seeks to use the exclusion or limitation clause or notice is in contract or tort. This is not the place for a detailed discussion of the Unfair Contract Terms Act 1977,[122] and the Act will be discussed only in so far as 9–31

mind where the risk of loss would fall); *AXA Sun Life Services Plc v Campbell Martin Ltd* [2011] EWCA Civ 133 at [108] (Rix L.J.: "an entire agreement clause excluding collateral warranties is a common and business-like clause for parties making a carefully worked up agreement of this kind. It was well sign-posted": clause reasonable; see also Stanley Burnton L.J. at [64], and more generally at [55]–[66]). In *Howard Marine and Dredging Co. Ltd v A. Ogden & Sons (Excavations) Ltd*, above, n.112, Lord Denning M.R., dissenting, would have held under the original wording of s.3 (above, para.9–19, n.75) that reliance on a clause was reasonable because its terms were reasonable, and the parties were commercial concerns and of equal bargaining power. The other judges did not discuss this in detail, but simply accepted that the judge had been entitled to hold the clause unreasonable: see at 599 (Bridge L.J.) and 601 (Shaw L.J.).

120 Pt I has been amended by the Sale of Goods Act 1979, s.63, Sch.2, paras 19, 20; Supply of Goods and Services Act 1982, s.17(2), (3); Occupiers' Liability Act 1984, s.2; Sale and Supply of Goods to Consumers Regulations 2002 (SI 2002/3045), reg.14; Regulatory Reform (Trading Stamps) Order 2005 (SI 2005/871), art.6, Sch. Part II relates to Scotland. Part III contains miscellaneous provisions which relate to the whole of the United Kingdom. In this chapter, references to the "Act" are to those Parts which apply to England and Wales.

121 For the text of the Misrepresentation Act 1967, s.3, as substituted by the Unfair Contract Terms Act 1977, s.8(1), see above, para.9–19.

122 Chitty, paras 14–059 to 14–113; Furmston, paras 3.67 to 3.94; Treitel, paras 7–050 to 7–094; Anson, pp.191–206; Cheshire, Fifoot and Furmston, pp.231–253; [1978] C.L.J. 15 (L.S. Sealy); (1978) 41 M.L.R. 312 (B. Coote), p.703 (J.N. Adams); [1978] L.M.C.L.Q. 201 (F.M.B. Reynolds); [1981] C.L.J. 108 (N. Palmer & D. Yates); (1988) 104 L.Q.R. 94 (J.N. Adams & R. Brownsword). The Law Commission has proposed the repeal of the Act and the replacement of it and

necessary to explain the circumstances in which it might generally be relevant in a misrepresentation claim.

9–32 **Exclusion of "business liability".** Most of the relevant sections of the Act[123] apply to control only clauses and notices which exclude or limit a defendant's "*business* liability"; that is, where the liability arises from things done or to be done by the defendant in the course of a business (whether his own business or another's), or from the occupation of business premises.[124] Where, therefore, the claim is made against a defendant acting in his private, non-business capacity, the Act is generally irrelevant.[125]

9–33 **Varieties of exclusion clause.** It has already been noticed[126] that there is a range of different types of clause or notice by which persons may seek to exclude or limit their liability. The clause may simply exclude a particular liability; it might not exclude it but limit it (for example, by placing a limit on the quantum of damages recoverable, or by imposing conditions on recovery, such as time-limits on notification of claims); or it might seek not to exclude or limit the liability itself, but to prevent the liability arising in the first place. In applying the relevant provisions of the Unfair Contract Terms Act 1977 to this range of different types of clause, the courts have a range of available techniques.

In the first place, they have sometimes been able to say that, although a clause has been drafted so that, on its face, it appears not to be caught by the language of the relevant formal provision of the Act, the Act is none the less applicable because *in substance* the

the Unfair Terms in Consumer Contracts Regulations 1999, below, para.9–37, by a new, single enactment: Law Com. No.292, *Unfair Terms in Contracts*; above, para.9–18, n.73.

123 Including ss.2 (negligence: below, para.9–35), 3 (breach of contract: below, para.9–34), and 7 (breach of certain implied term in contracts, other than sale of goods or hire-purchase contracts). But s.6 (breach of certain implied terms in sale of goods and hire-purchase contracts: below, para.9–34) applies to all liabilities, and not only to business liabilities: s.6(4).

124 s.1(3), amended by the Occupiers' Liability Act 1984, s.2.

125 Unlike the Misrepresentation Act 1967, s.3, which applies to contract terms excluding or restricting any liability for misrepresentation, and is not limited to exclusion of business liabilities: above, para.9–21. The exception under the 1977 Act is s.6(4); above, n.123; below, para.9–34.

126 Above, para.9–01.

clause is one to which the provision of the Act is directed: that is, they have applied a "substance rather than form" approach in their application of the Act.[127]

But, secondly, the draftsman of the Act[128] anticipated that a clause might be drafted so as to seek to exclude or limit liability without being, in form, an exclusion clause. There are therefore certain provisions of the Act which are intended to catch such clauses, the most general of which is s.13(1) which provides:

> "**13.**—(1) To the extent that this Part of this Act prevents the exclusion or restriction of any liability it also prevents—
> (a) making the liability or its enforcement subject to restrictive or onerous conditions;
> (b) excluding or restricting any right or remedy in respect of the liability, or subjecting a person to any prejudice in consequence of his pursuing any such right or remedy;
> (c) excluding or restricting rules of evidence or procedure;
> and (to that extent) sections 2 and 5 to 7 also prevent excluding or restricting liability by reference to terms and notices which exclude or restrict the relevant obligation or duty."

Under this provision, the Act applies generally to clauses which impose conditions, or limit remedies or evidential or procedural rules, as much as to clauses which are more straightforward exclusion clauses. And by the closing words of the provision,

---

127 *Phillips Products Ltd v Hyland*, above, n.113 at 666.

128 It appears that the opening words of this section will apply to the Misrepresentation Act 1967 s.3, since the current form of s.3 was amended by (and so is contained within) s.8 of "this Act". However, the most important last part of the section is limited to ss.2 to 5 and 7, and so does not apply to s.8 (and so not to the Misrepresentation Act 1967, s.3) and there is no similar provision in, or which applies to, the 1967 Act. In applying that Act, therefore, the courts have had to rely on the interpretation of a clause as in substance excluding or limiting liability for misrepresentation without the assistance of a statutory provision similar to the Unfair Contract Terms Act 1977, s.13(1): above, para.9–21. Note, however, that Chadwick L.J. in *Watford Electronics Ltd v Sanderson C.F.L. Ltd* [2001] EWCA Civ 317, [2001] 1 All E.R. (Comm) 696 at [40] appeared to doubt the approach of applying the "substance" of the clause: above, para.9–21, n.82. For a discussion of the Unfair Contract Terms Act 1977, s.13, see *Stewart Gill Ltd v Horatio Myer & Co. Ltd* [1992] Q.B. 600, CA, at 605–606 (Lord Donaldson of Lymington M.R.: "It is a trite fact (as contrasted with being trite law) that there are more ways than one of killing a cat. Section 13 addresses this problem"); *Smith v Eric S. Bush*, above, n.117 at 849, 857, 873.

certain particular sections[129] apply where the clause is drafted not to exclude or restrict the liability, but to prevent the liability arising by a recharacterisation of the obligation which, but for[130] the clause, would have been broken and would therefore have given rise to the liability.

9–34 **Claims for misrepresentation based on a breach of contract.** A claim for misrepresentation may sometimes be a claim for breach of contract: for example, where the claim arises from breach of an express contractual promise as to the truth of a representation, or an implied promise that the subject-matter of a contract will comply with its represented description.[131] If a contract contains a clause which seeks to exclude or limit such a claim and which is otherwise effective at common law so to do,[132] the provision of the Unfair Contract Terms Act which is relevant will depend upon the type of contractual liability in question.

Section 3 is relevant in all claims for breach of contract[133] where the defendant is seeking to exclude his "business" liability[134] and where either the claimant is a "consumer"[135] or the contract is made

[129] Including ss.2 (negligence: below, para.9–35), 6 (breach of certain implied terms in sale of goods and hire-purchase contracts: below, para.9–34) and 7 (breach of certain implied term in contracts, other than sale of goods or hire-purchase contracts). S.3 (breach of contract: below, para.9–34) is not included, but contains its own provisions aimed at catching clauses which seek to avoid liability other than by means of simple exclusion clauses: see s.3(2)(b).

[130] *Smith v Eric S. Bush*, above, n.117 at 857.

[131] For detailed discussion of the circumstances in which a misrepresentation may give rise to a claim for breach of contract, see Ch.8.

[132] Above, paras 9–08 *et seq*. To exclude the defendant's liability to the claimant for breach of contract, a clause must be in a contract which binds the claimant and the defendant: above, para.9–01, n.2.

[133] Except contracts excluded from the scope of the Act by Sch.1: for example, contracts of insurance (para.1(a)), and contracts in so far as they relate to the creation or transfer of interests in land (para.1(b)), intellectual property rights (para.1(c)) or securities (para.1(e)). International supply contracts are also excluded: s.26 (and this exclusion applies also to the scope of operation of s.3 Misrepresentation Act 1967: *Trident Turboprop (Dublin) Ltd v First Flight Couriers Ltd* [2009] EWCA Civ 290, [2010] Q.B. 86, above, para.9–20, n.79).

[134] s.1(3); above, para.9–32.

[135] s.12: broadly, where the defendant can show that the claimant is not making the contract in the course of his business.

on the defendant's written standard terms of business.[136] In such cases, the defendant is not permitted to rely on the exclusion or limitation clause to exclude or restrict the liability, or to avoid performance or to claim that he is entitled to render performance substantially different from that which was reasonably expected of him,[137] unless he shows that the clause satisfies the reasonableness test.

Section 6[138] is relevant where the contract in question is a contract for the sale of goods or hire-purchase, and the claim is based on a breach of a term implied by statute relating to the seller's (or creditor's, in a contract of hire-purchase) title, or undertakings as to the conformity of the goods with description or sample, or as to their quality or fitness for a particular purpose. Section 7[139] applies to similar terms implied by operation of law in other contracts under which the possession or ownership of goods passes, such as contracts for work and materials,[140] or contracts for the exchange of goods. This may therefore be relevant in a claim for misrepresentation by the defendant about goods which passed to the claimant under a contract for the sale or hire-purchase or other contract for the transfer of the goods, where the claimant relies not on the misrepresentation as having been incorporated as an express term of the contract, but on the terms implied by law into the contract.[141] Where ss.6 and 7 apply,[142] they provide that liability for

136 An industry standard form contract is only the *defendant's* written standard terms of business if that form is invariably or at least usually used by the party in question: *British Fermentation Products Ltd v Compair Reavell Ltd* (1999) 66 Con. L.R. 1 at 14–15 (Institution of Mechanical Engineers' Model Form of General Conditions of Contract not the *defendant's* standard terms of business for the purposes of the Unfair Contract Terms Act 1977, s.3).

137 These latter provisions (s.3(2)(b)) are aimed at clauses which are drafted not to exclude or restrict the liability but to permit the defendant to perform alternative obligations, or to avoid performance altogether, without technically being in breach: above, para.9–01. They can also apply to an "entire agreement" clause, but only if it is possible to identify both the performance by the defendant that was reasonably expected and that defined by the contract: *AXA Sun Life Services Plc v Campbell Martin Ltd* [2011] EWCA Civ 133 at [50].

138 Amended by the Sale of Goods Act 1979, s.63, Sch.2, para.19.

139 Amended by the Supply of Goods and Services Act 1982, s.17(2), (3).

140 Into which the Supply of Goods and Services Act 1982 implies terms: above, para.8–13, n.69.

141 Above, para.8–13.

breach of the implied statutory terms[143] as to the seller, creditor's or transferor's title to the property cannot be excluded or restricted by reference to any contract term. As regards clauses excluding or limiting the implied terms relating to description, sample, quality and fitness for their purpose, a distinction is drawn: as against a person dealing as a "consumer"[144] the terms cannot be excluded or restricted.[145] But as against a person not dealing as a consumer, the liability can be excluded or restricted only in so far as the term satisfies the requirement of reasonableness.[146]

Where the claim arises from breach of an express or implied contractual promise that the defendant would take reasonable care in making a representation,[147] any clause seeking to exclude or limit the claim is also regulated by s.2 of the Unfair Contract Terms Act 1977, since the liability falls within the definition of "negligence" under the Act.[148]

9–35 **Claims for misrepresentation in tort.** A claim for misrepresentation may be a claim in tort: either the tort of deceit[149] or the tort of negligence.[150] The Unfair Contract Terms Act does not provide for clauses which seek to exclude liability in the tort of deceit, presumably because a clause excluding such liability is in any event not normally effective at common law.[151] But s.2 makes specific

[142] s.7 applies only where the liability sought to be excluded is the defendant's "business" liability, although s.6 has no such restriction on its application: ss.1(3), 6(4); above, para.9–32.

[143] Sale of Goods Act 1979, s.12; Supply of Goods (Implied Terms) Act 1973, s.8; Supply of Goods and Services Act 1982, s.2. The Unfair Contract Terms Act 1977, s.7(4), provides that other implied terms as to the right to transfer ownership or give possession, or the assurance of quiet possession, can be excluded or restricted but only by a term which satisfies the reasonableness test.

[144] Above, n.135.

[145] Unfair Contract Terms Act 1977, ss.6(2) (referring expressly to the terms implied by the Sale of Goods Act 1979, ss.13, 14 and 15; and the Supply of Goods (Implied Terms) Act 1973, ss.9, 10 and 11), 7(2).

[146] ss.6(3), 7(3).

[147] Above, para.8–14; *EssoPetroleum Co. Ltd v Mardon* [1976] Q.B. 801, CA.

[148] s.1(1); below, para.9–35, n.153.

[149] Above, Ch.5.

[150] Above, Ch.6.

[151] Above, para.9–13. For the possible application of the Misrepresentation Act 1967 s.3 to a clause excluding or limiting liability in deceit, see above, para.9–23.

provision for contractual clauses or non-contractual notices[152] which seek to exclude or restrict liability in negligence.[153] A person cannot by such a clause or notice exclude or restrict his liability for death or personal injury resulting from negligence[154]; and in the case of other loss or damage he cannot exclude or restrict his liability for negligence except in so far as the term or notice satisfies the requirement of reasonableness.[155]

The reasonableness test. The test of reasonableness under the Unfair Contract Terms Act has been discussed already in the context of s.3 of the Misrepresentation Act 1967, which applies the requirement of reasonableness as set out in s.11(1) of the Unfair Contract Terms Act.[156] Where a clause or notice is subject to the reasonableness test, it is for the defendant, who seeks to rely on it, **9–36**

---

[152] A non-contractual notice may sometimes be effective at common law to exclude or limit non-contractual liability: above, para.9–08, n.25.

[153] "Negligence" is defined in s.1(1) as the breach of (a) an express or implied contractual duty of reasonable care; (b) a common law duty of reasonable care; and (c) the common duty of care under the Occupiers' Liability Act 1957. In the context of claims for misrepresentation, it therefore covers claims for breach of contract where the contractual obligation was to take reasonable care in making the statement, as well as claims in the tort of negligence arising from careless misrepresentations. A claim under the Misrepresentation Act 1967, s.2(1) (above, Ch.7) is not a claim in "negligence" within the definition of the Unfair Contract Terms Act 1977, s.1(1), but clauses excluding or restricting liability under the Misrepresentation Act 1967, s.2(1) are regulated by the Misrepresentation Act 1967, s.3, above, para.9–23.

[154] s.2(1). Here, as throughout the Act, liability may be direct or vicarious: s.1(4).

[155] s.2(2). For decisions under this section in the context of claims for misrepresentation, see *Smith v Eric S. Bush* [1990] 1 A.C. 831, HL (disclaimer by property valuer ineffective to negative duty of care in tort because unreasonable as against purchaser of dwelling-house of modest value who had no effective power to object); *Omega Trust Co. Ltd v Wright Son & Pepper* [1997] 1 E.G.L.R. 120, CA (similar disclaimer effective because reasonable as against commercial party of equal bargaining power to the valuer); *McCullagh v Lane Fox & Partners Ltd* [1996] 1 E.G.L.R. 35, CA (disclaimer by estate agents effective to negative duty of care in tort because reasonable as against a sophisticated and experienced member of the public who had ample opportunity to regulate his conduct having regard to the disclaimer).

[156] Above, paras 9–25 *et seq*. The only relevant difference here is that, in applying the reasonableness test for the purposes of the Unfair Contract Terms Act 1977, ss.6 and 7, above, para.9–25, the guidelines for the application of the test set out in Sch.2 are applicable directly, rather than by analogy: see above, para.9–29.

to show that it satisfies the test.[157] And it is the whole clause, or a separate and severable part of it, which must be shown to be reasonable.[158]

(3) Unfair Terms in Consumer Contracts Regulations 1999

9–37 **Scope of the provision.** The Unfair Terms in Consumer Contracts Regulations 1999[159] provide that an "unfair term" in a contract concluded between a seller or supplier[160] and a consumer[161] is not binding on the consumer.[162] A term which has not been individually negotiated is "unfair" if, contrary to the requirement of good faith,[163] it causes a significant imbalance in the parties' rights and

---

[157] s.11(5).

[158] *Stewart Gill Ltd v Horatio Myer & Co. Ltd* [1992] Q.B. 600, CA; above, para.9–24.

[159] SI 1999/2083, amended by SI 2001/1186, reg.2; Enterprise Act 2002, s.2; Railways and Transport Safety Act 2003, s.16, Sch.3; Water Act 2003, s.34(3); SI 2003/3182, reg.2; SI 2004/2095, reg.24; SI 2006/523, reg.2; replacing the earlier Unfair Terms in Consumer Contracts Regulations 1994 (SI 1994/3159); Chitty, Ch.15; Furmston, paras 3.97 to 3.119; Treitel, paras 7–095 to 7–122; Anson, pp.206–215. The Regulations were made to implement Council Directive 93/13 on Unfair Terms in Consumer Contracts; the 1994 Regulations were revoked and replaced by the 1999 Regulations in order to reflect more closely the wording of the Directive, as well as to provide improved enforcement mechanisms: see S. Bright, "Winning the Battle Against Unfair Contract Terms" (2000) 20 L.S. 331. On the 1994 Regulations, see E. Macdonald, "The Emperor's Old Clauses: Unincorporated Clauses, Misleading Terms and the Unfair Terms in Consumer Contracts Regulations" [1999] C.L.J. 413. And for notes on the Directive, see H. Collins, "Good Faith in European Contract Law" (1994) 14 O.J.L.S. 229 at pp.238–254; S.A. Smith, *Current Legal Problems Annual Review 1994*, pp.5–14; H. Beale, "Legislative Control of Fairness: the Directive on Unfair Terms in Consumer Contracts" in *Good Faith and Fault in Contract Law* (Beatson and Friedmann eds, 1995), p.231. The Law Commission has proposed the repeal of the Regulations and the replacement of them and the Unfair Contract Terms Act 1977, above, para.9–31, by a new, single enactment: Law Com. No.292, *Unfair Terms in Contracts*; above, para.9–18, n.73.

[160] A natural or legal person acting for purposes relating to his trade, business or profession: reg.3(1).

[161] A natural person acting for purposes outside his trade, business or profession: reg.3(1).

[162] reg.8(1). The contract continues to bind the parties if it is capable of continuing in existence without the unfair term: reg.8(2).

[163] There is no definition of "good faith" in the 1999 Regulations. However, the Directive in its preamble states that "whereas, in making an assessment of good

obligations arising under the contract, to the detriment of the consumer,[164] and the Regulations contain, in Sch.2,[165] an "indicative and non-exhaustive list" of terms which may be regarded as unfair. But, in so far as it is in plain intelligible language, the assessment of fairness of a term does not relate to the definition of the main subject-matter of the contract, or the adequacy of price or remuneration.[166]

Application of the Regulations in the context of misrepresentation. The Regulations do not contain any provision specific to liability for misrepresentation and, indeed, they do not apply only to exclusion or limitation clauses, but more generally to any "unfair term" in a relevant contract. Within their general scope, however, the Regulations will certainly apply to contractual clauses[167] which 9–38

faith, particular regard shall be had to the strength of the bargaining positions of the parties, whether the consumer had an inducement to agree to the term and whether the goods or services were sold or supplied to the special order of the consumer; whereas the requirement of good faith may be satisfied by the seller or supplier where he deals fairly and equitably with the other party whose legitimate interests he has to take into account." The 1994 Regulations, above, n.159, had taken this language from the preamble and set it out (in Sch.2) as a list of matters to which regard was to be had in determining whether a term satisfies the requirement of good faith: (a) the strength of the bargaining position of the parties; (b) whether the consumer had an inducement to agree to the term; (c) whether the goods or services were sold or supplied to the special order of the consumer; and (d) the extent to which the seller or supplier has dealt fairly and equitably with the consumer. Matters (a) to (c) reproduce matters which are included in Sch.2 to the Unfair Contract Terms Act 1977 as relevant to determine whether a clause satisfies the reasonableness test for certain purposes under that Act. For a decision on the application of the 1994 Regulations, see *Director General of Fair Trading v First National Bank Plc* [2001] UKHL 52, [2002] 1 A.C. 481.

164 reg.5(1).

165 This contains a list of *types* of clause which, in effect, are presumed to be unfair.

166 reg.6(2). There is a specific obligation on a seller or supplier to ensure that any written term of a contract is expressed in plain, intelligible language: reg.7(1), and in the case of doubt about the meaning of a written term, the interpretation most favourable to the consumer normally prevails: reg.7(2)—in effect, the *contra proferentem* rule which would, in any event, be applied in interpreting the clause at common law where it is sought to be used against the consumer: above, para.9–10.

167 The Regulations do not deal with non-contractual exclusion or limitation notices.

seek to exclude or limit a consumer's remedies for misrepresentation, whether through excluding or limiting the scope of the seller or supplier's obligations in respect of his statements, or excluding or limiting the remedies themselves.[168] If such a clause is "unfair" within the meaning of the Regulations, it will not be binding on the consumer.

(4) Interrelationship Between the Several Statutory Controls

9–39 **The controls are independent.** The three controls of s.3 of the Misrepresentation Act 1967, the Unfair Contract Terms Act 1977 and the Unfair Terms in Consumer Contracts Regulations 1999 are,

---

[168] The first two types of term listed in Sch.2, para.1, as being terms which may be regarded as unfair, are traditional exclusion or limitation clauses: "terms which have the object or effect of—(a) excluding or limiting the legal liability of a seller or supplier in the event of the death of a consumer or personal injury to the latter resulting from an act or omission of that seller or supplier; (b) inappropriately excluding or limiting the legal rights of the consumer vis-à-vis the seller or supplier or another party in the event of total or partial non-performance or inadequate performance by the seller or supplier of any of the contractual obligations, including the option of offsetting a debt owed to the seller or supplier against any claim which the consumer may have against him." Para.(n) covers clauses "limiting the seller's or supplier's obligation to respect commitments undertaken by his agents". Since, however, the list in Sch.2 is only "indicative", any contractual term excluding or limiting liability or remedies for misrepresentation, contained in a contract between a "consumer" and a "seller or supplier" within the meaning of the Regulations, is subject to their control. The Office of Fair Trading guidance on Unfair Terms in Consumer Contracts (OFT311, revised September 2008), Annexe A, contains details of particular terms it has found to be unfair in particular contracts, such as terms excluding liability for faulty or misdescribed goods (Sch.2, para.1(b) to the Regulations; e.g. "goods sold as seen"; "unless expressly stated in writing to be accurate no representation or warranty is given as to the accuracy . . .") and entire agreement clauses (Sch.2, para.1(n): e.g. "the agreement is the entire agreement between the parties and supersedes all prior understandings and representations . . ."; "the Seller's employees or agents are not authorised to make any representations . . . unless confirmed by the Seller in writing"; "No representations made by the Company, or by its agents, shall be treated as having induced the Customer to enter into the contract unless the same is included in this document". It is not clear how the narrow form of "entire agreement" clause falls within para.1(n)). In *Shaftesbury House (Developments) Ltd v Lee* [2010] EWHC 1484 (Ch) at [67] Proudman J. expressed the view (obiter) that a "non-reliance" clause (above, para. 9–03) would be covered by the Regulations ("it would be strange if a contracting party could get round the Regulations by such a device").

in principle, entirely separate. Each of them, or any relevant combination of them, may be invoked by a claimant in seeking to prevent a defendant from relying on a clause which would otherwise have the effect of excluding or limiting his liability. If any one of these controls prevents the defendant from relying on the clause in relation to any particular claim, that is sufficient to enable the claimant to his remedy in respect of that claim. So, for example, it is sufficient for the claimant to show that under the Unfair Contract Terms Act the defendant cannot exclude the particular liability which he is claiming, without also having to go on and show whether or not the Unfair Terms in Consumer Contracts Regulations would also have the effect of making that clause not binding on him.

Extent of overlap of the three controls. Sometimes there will be overlap between the operation of the controls. For example, where there is a clause in a contract between a private purchaser and a business seller which seeks to exclude or limit liability for breach of a contractual term by which the defendant guaranteed the description he had placed on the subject-matter of the contract, the exclusion clause may be subject to the Unfair Contract Terms Act 1977[169] as well as the Unfair Terms in Consumer Contracts Regulations 1999.[170] But since each of the controls has been devised independently and for separate purposes,[171] sometimes one will be the more appropriate control, or the only control. For example, the Regulations and s.3 of the Misrepresentation Act only 9–40

[169] s.3(2)(a), since the buyer is likely to be a consumer (ss.3(1), 12); the clause would then be subject to the reasonableness test. If the guarantee is an implied condition under the Sale of Goods Act 1979 s.14, s.6 would also apply (and, as against a consumer, would apply without reference to the reasonableness test: s.6(2)); the claimant would then be best advised to rely on s.6 rather than s.3: above, para.9–34.

[170] The term will have to be "unfair"; but Sch.2, para.1(b), is relevant as indicating that it may be unfair if the exclusion or limitation is "inappropriate".

[171] J. Cartwright, "Excluding Liability for Misrepresentation" in A. Burrows and E. Peel (eds), *Contracts Terms* (2007) at p.231 (the original draft of Misrepresentation Act 1967 s.3 was changed during the passage of the Bill, and its scope widened to bring it into line with the developing thoughts of the Law Commission, but when the Unfair Contract Terms Act 1977 was later proposed by the Commission the 1967 Act was not properly integrated into the new statutory regime). Law Com No.292, *Unfair Terms in Contracts* (2005) does not propose to bring the 1967 Act into line: above, para.9–18, n.73.

apply to *contractual* terms which exclude or limit the liability; they do not cover non-contractual notices. Section 2 of the Unfair Contract Terms Act, however, also applies to non-contractual notices which seek to exclude or restrict liability for negligence: where, therefore, the claim is in tort, based on a statement alleged to have been made in breach of a common law duty of care,[172] and the notice on which the defendant relies was not contained in a contract to which he and the claimant were party,[173] only the 1977 Act is relevant. Or again, where the defendant seeks to use a contractual clause to exclude or restrict his liability for a pre-contractual misrepresentation, rather than a liability for breach of contract by reason of the incorporation of the representation into the contract, s.3 of the Misrepresentation Act is relevant[174]; but most of the provisions of the Unfair Contract Terms Act,[175] and the Unfair Terms in Consumer Contracts Regulations,[176] are not.

In considering whether a clause which seeks to exclude or limit liability for misrepresentation can be struck down by reference to one of the statutory controls it is therefore necessary to apply each of the controls to the particular facts, bearing in mind that the application of each varies according to the nature of the claim and the remedy sought: whether the claim is in respect of a pre-contractual misrepresentation (under s.2(1) of the Misrepresentation Act 1967,[177] in the tort of negligence,[178] or for rescission[179])

---

172 Above, Ch.6; para.9–35.

173 Or a contract to which the claimant was party and of which the defendant has the right to enforce the benefit of the term under the Contracts (Rights of Third Parties) Act 1999.

174 Above, para.9–23.

175 ss.3, 6 and 7 only apply to claims for breach of contract. However, s.2 will apply where the claim is in the tort of negligence for pre-contractual misrepresentation: above, para.9–35.

176 "Unfairness" is assessed in relation to the parties' rights and obligations *arising under the contract*: reg.5(1). It is not clear whether this would apply to a clause restricting the right to rescind a contract for pre-contractual misrepresentation. The Misrepresentation Act 1967 s.3, however, clearly covers this and is most likely to be relied on in practice.

177 Above, Ch.7; the Misrepresentation Act 1967 s.3 is relevant (a claim under the Misrepresentation Act s.2(1) is not "negligence" within the Unfair Contract Terms Act 1977 s.1(1)).

178 Above, Ch.6; the Unfair Contract Terms Act 1977 s.2 is relevant (a claim in negligence is not for "misrepresentation" within the Misrepresentation Act 1967 s.3: above, para.9–23).

179 Above, Ch.4; the Misrepresentation Act 1967 s.3 is relevant.

or a misrepresentation incorporated into the contract (breach of contract[180])—and whether the exclusion takes the form of a contractual term or a non-contractual notice.[181]

[180] Above, Ch.8; the Unfair Contract Terms Act 1977 s.2 (breach of contractual duty of care), s.3 (contracts with consumers and on written standard terms), s.6 (sale of goods contracts) and s.7 (other contracts under which property passes) and the Unfair Terms in Consumer Contracts Regulations 1999 are relevant.

[181] Above; the Unfair Contract Terms Act 1977 s.2 applies to non-contractual notices.

CHAPTER 10

MISREPRESENTATION AS A DEFENCE[1]

I. THE DEFENCE OF MISREPRESENTATION DISTINGUISHED FROM A COUNTERCLAIM BASED ON MISREPRESENTATION

Misrepresentation claims raised by a defendant. A claim for misrepresentation will sometimes be made not by the claimant who initiates an action but by the defendant by way of counterclaim. For example, where the seller under a contract of sale seeks to enforce the buyer's obligation to pay the price of the goods the buyer may—whilst perhaps not denying this obligation—seek by way of counterclaim damages in tort or under the Misrepresentation Act 1967 to recover losses which he alleges flow from a pre-contractual misrepresentation in respect of the goods. In such cases, however, it is not generally significant that it is the defendant who has raised the issue of the misrepresentation: he is a claimant in respect of the misrepresentation within the scope of his counterclaim, and the principles discussed in the earlier chapters of this book will apply to determine whether his (counter)claim can succeed and what remedy can be awarded. So if the defendant raises a counterclaim under s.2(1) of the Misrepresentation Act 1967 the normal rules applicable **10–01**

[1] Spencer Bower (Misrepresentation), Ch.18.

to a claim under that section[2] will apply to determine whether the defendant can establish a claim to damages. If he succeeds in his counterclaim, then the damages due under the counterclaim are set against any damages awarded in the claimant's own claim, and the court may order either the claimant or the defendant, as appropriate, to pay the balance to the other.[3] But the elements of the (counter)claim for misrepresentation will be the same as they would have been had the defendant brought a separate action as claimant.[4]

10–02 **Misrepresentation as a defence.** Sometimes, however, the defendant raises an allegation of misrepresentation not as a counterclaim but by way of a defence to the claimant's own action. In such cases, the defendant does not generally seek to establish the elements of a misrepresentation claim with a view to obtaining a remedy which he can enforce independently, but instead seeks to use the plea that the claimant[5] made a misrepresentation in order to explain why the claim itself should not succeed or why the claimant should not be awarded the remedy he claims. It is in this sense that this chapter discusses misrepresentation as a defence to a claim. Sometimes it can seem difficult to disentangle the reliance by a defendant on a misrepresentation as a defence, and his counterclaim: for example, in resisting a claim for specific performance of the contract a defendant may in substance adduce the same evidence to argue that the court should both refuse to grant the order of specific performance and rescind the contract.[6] But the two must

---

[2] Above, Ch.7.

[3] CPR, r.40.13. This is relevant only where the claim and counterclaim both result in judgment for specified amounts (as in the case of damages). Even if the sums awarded by the judgments are set one against the other and the balance ordered to be paid by the party whose judgment is for the lesser amount, the court may make a separate order as to costs against each party: *ibid.*, r.40.13(3).

[4] For most purposes, a counterclaim is treated under the CPR as if it were a claim: CPR, r.20.3 (a counterclaim is an "additional claim": *ibid.*, r.20(2)). For practice and procedure relating to claims for misrepresentation, see Ch.11.

[5] It must be a misrepresentation by the claimant (or one for which he is responsible), because the court is not allowing him to benefit from the misrepresentation or his misleading conduct: *Lloyds Bank Plc v Waterhouse* [1993] 2 F.L.R. 97 at 120 (Woolf L.J.).

[6] Or that he has already rescinded the contract, given that rescission can be effected without an order: above, para.4–18. For examples of the courts treating together the questions of whether specific performance should be refused (defence), and the contract rescinded (counterclaim), see *Redgrave v Hurd* (1881)

be kept separate, since the court may sometimes refuse to order specific performance even where it would not admit that rescission is available. And misrepresentation will be relevant as a defence only in cases where the misrepresentation, or the circumstances in which it was made, bear on the elements of the claimant's own claim. So, in general, a court will not be concerned with the quantification of the defendant's loss flowing from the misrepresentation he raises by way of defence: that is a matter which is relevant only where he is making a substantive (counter)claim for damages.

Misrepresentation and estoppel. Sometimes the defendant relies on the claimant's misrepresentation under the doctrine of estoppel. This is discussed below.[7] 10–03

II. ILLUSTRATIONS OF THE USE OF MISREPRESENTATION AS A DEFENCE

(1) Refusal of Specific Performance

Specific performance not available where contract rescinded.[8] If a defendant obtains rescission of the contract on the grounds of the claimant's misrepresentation, then of course the court will not order specific performance of the contract. A counterclaim for rescission, if successful, necessarily answers the claim for specific performance.[9] Indeed, given that rescission can be effected by act of party rather than by an order of the court,[10] by the time the court hears the claim for specific performance the contract may already have been rescinded by the defendant.[11] These are not however 10–04

20 Ch.D. 1 at 9–10 (Fry J.: no reliance on misrepresentation, so no defence to specific performance and claim for rescission failed), reversed by CA at 12 *et seq.* (reliance on misrepresentation, so specific performance refused and rescission ordered); *Smith v Land and House Property Corp.* (1884) 28 Ch.D. 7, CA.

[7] Below, para.10–18.

[8] Jones and Goodhart, pp.86 *et seq.*

[9] *Redgrave v Hurd*, above, n.6; *Smith v Land and House Property Corp*, above, n.6.

[10] Above, para.4–18.

[11] This is, however, subject to the discretion of the court in the case of a non-fraudulent misrepresentation to declare the contract subsisting and award damages in lieu of rescission under the Misrepresentation Act 1967 s.2(2); above, para.4–61. The remedy under s.2(2) is not specific performance but it allows the court by order to keep the contract alive (or to resurrect a contract which has

cases that we need to consider further. The issue is whether and when the courts will accept the misrepresentation as a defence to an action of specific performance even if the contract is not rescinded. This might arise in a variety of circumstances.

10–05 **Rescission for misrepresentation available but not claimed.** The defendant might not wish to take the positive step of rescinding the contract, but might prefer to allow the contract to remain alive whilst seeking to resist a claim to specific performance of his obligations under it (but not, therefore, necessarily resisting a claim to pay damages for non-performance of his obligations). This may be in his interest where he has other reasons for wishing to keep the contract on foot: for example if he wishes to make counterclaims for breach of the claimant's own obligations under the contract. However, the defendant must be careful not to do anything which can be taken as his affirmation of the contract: otherwise it seems unlikely that he could then rely on the same misrepresentation to resist specific performance.[12]

10–06 **Specific performance refused even though rescission barred.** Sometimes, however, the defendant might wish to resist a claim to specific performance where rescission is not available to him because, although the claimant made a misrepresentation which would once have been sufficient to allow the defendant to rescind the contract, rescission is now barred.[13] Whether this is possible will depend on the circumstances, and on the ground on which rescission has become barred. If the defendant has affirmed the contract after discovering the misrepresentation, and so has indicated that he does not wish to object to the validity of the contract on that ground, he may well not then be entitled to resist specific performance based on that same misrepresentation.[14] But

already been rescinded by the representee) and therefore, in principle, the contract remains specifically enforceable.

[12] For affirmation, see above, para.4–39. Jones and Goodhart, p.93. See *Aaron's Reefs Ltd v Twiss* [1896] A.C. 273, HL (shareholder, defending action for calls on ground of fraud in prospectus, had not done any act to affirm the contract: he "was perfectly justified in waiting the company's attack": at 293 (Lord Macnaghten). See also at 291, 295).

[13] For the bars to rescission, see above, paras 4–38 to 4–71. See Jones and Goodhart, p.93.

[14] Above, para.10–05. But there appear to be no cases on this.

if, for example, the defendant has waited too long before seeking to rescind,[15] or if rescission would now be barred because of the impossibility of making restitution of the property transferred to him under the contract, the defendant should not necessarily be prevented from raising the misrepresentation against the claim for specific performance. Where the court exercises its discretion under s.2(2) of the Misrepresentation Act 1967[16] to declare a contract subsisting and award damages in lieu of rescission in spite of the claimant's misrepresentation, it would be open to the court also to grant specific performance of the contract itself; but the exercise of the discretion under that section does not constitute an order of specific performance,[17] and it would presumably still be open to a court expressly to refuse to grant such an order, on the ground that the contract was induced by the claimant's misrepresentation.

Specific performance refused even though misrepresentation insufficient to found rescission. Even if the claimant's misrepresentation is not sufficient to found a claim for rescission of the contract, the courts will still sometimes allow the misrepresentation to be raised in defence of a claim to specific performance. For example, a representation by the claimant as to his future intentions, where the representation was made without fraud but is not fulfilled by the claimant's later conduct, does not allow the defendant to rescind the contract: the misrepresentation must be of the present, not of future conduct.[18] But it has been held that such a representation, although not sufficient to entitle the defendant to rescind the contract, might still be used to defeat the claim for specific performance of the contract which the defendant was induced by the representation to enter.[19] And where a misrepresentation was not sufficient to found rescission of a contract to 10–07

[15] *Lamare v Dixon* (1873) L.R. 6 H.L. 414, HL, at 424.

[16] Above, para.4–61.

[17] It is described by Jones and Goodhart, p.87, as "a remedy analogous to specific performance with compensation". See also Chitty, para.27–054.

[18] Above, para.3–43.

[19] *Lamare v Dixon*, above, n.15 at 428 (Lord Cairns: statement by claimant to induce defendant to taken tenancy of cellars that he would make the cellars dry: not a guarantee incorporated into the contract nor, probably, a sufficient misrepresentation to cancel the contract but still a "perfectly good defence in a suit for specific performance" when the representation has not been and cannot be fulfilled); *Myers v Watson* (1851) 1 Sim. (N.S.) 523 at 529, 61 E.R. 202 at 204

purchase a lot of land at auction because the misrepresentation related not directly to that lot but to a second lot which the defendant had also purchased at the auction, specific performance of the contract for the first lot was refused because the misrepresentation about the second lot had induced him to purchase the first lot and it would be a hardship to make him take only the first lot.[20] But a court will not use the fact of the claimant's misrepresentation[21] to defeat the claim for specific performance unless it is satisfied that the misrepresentation was a serious statement[22] which induced the defendant to enter into the contract.[23]

(specific performance will be refused where defendant has been induced to enter into contract in consequence of some independent engagement by the plaintiff to do some other act which he has failed to perform, even though it may have been an engagement incapable of being legally enforced); *Beaumont v Dukes* (1821) Jac. 422, 37 E.R. 910.

[20] *Holliday v Lockwood* [1917] 2 Ch. 47; the contract for the second lot was rescinded.

[21] Specific performance might, of course, be refused for other reasons than the fact of the misrepresentation: Jones and Goodhart, Ch.2; Snell, paras 17–012 to 17–046.

[22] That is, it must be a "representation" in the sense that it was sufficiently serious that it could be relied upon: *Higgins v Samels* (1862) 2 J. & H. 460 at 464, 70 E.R. 1139 at 1141 (specific performance refused: statement "went beyond the sort of puffing or speculative commendation which is held excusable in a vendor"). See also above, paras 3–12 *et seq.*

[23] *Fellowes v Lord Gwydyr* (1829) 1 Russ. & My. 83, 39 E.R. 32 (claimant's misrepresentation of his identity not shown to have affected the defendant's decision to enter contract or the terms of the contract); *cf. Archer v Stone* (1898) 78 L.T. 34 (specific performance refused because misrepresentation of identity did induce the contract); *Wall v Stubbs* (1815) 1 Madd. 80 at 81, 56 E.R. 31 at 32 (misrepresentation may be used to resist specific performance, unless the defendant really knew how the fact was); *Walker v Boyle* [1982] 1 W.L.R. 495 at 506 (if the misrepresentation is so trifling that the truth would have had no effect on the purchaser, it will not operate as a barrier to specific performance); *Baker v Potter* [2004] EWHC 1422 (Ch), [2005] B.C.C. 855 at [121] (David Richards J.: "very doubtful whether it would be right to refuse specific performance on the basis of a dishonest statement made in the course of negotiations which did not play a part in inducing the contract. If the contract would have been made on the same terms in any event, a refusal of specific performance does not redress a wrong done to the defendant but simply imposes a penalty on the claimant"). As in a claim for rescission and for other positive remedies for misrepresentation, a court ought to be prepared to infer inducement from the materiality of the representation: above, para.3–53.

Rules for refusal of specific performance independent of the rules for rescission. It is therefore evident that the courts do not apply the same rules to the defence to the claim of specific performance based on the claimant's misrepresentation as to a claim to rescission. Indeed, there are cases in which the judges have said this explicitly and where the courts have used the fact that the claimant made a misrepresentation as a reason for refusing specific performance whilst also refusing rescission or acknowledging that rescission would not have been available.[24] Specific performance is a discretionary remedy, and although the principles on which the discretion is to be exercised are now well established by case law,[25] the courts still regard it as the exceptional remedy which should be granted only in an appropriate case. Misconduct by the party seeking to enforce the contract can lead to the court's refusal to grant him the remedy. The fact that the claimant made a misrepresentation, even one which might for other reasons not necessarily be sufficient to allow the defendant to rescind,[26] can therefore be sufficient to allow a court to refuse to exercise its discretion in his favour. The fact of his misrepresentation means he does not come to the court with "clean hands".[27] 10–08

[24] *Cadman v Horner* (1810) 18 Ves. Jun. 10, 34 E.R. 221; *Re Banister* (1879) 12 Ch.D. 131, CA, at 142 (Jessel M.R.: "the considerations which induce a Court to rescind any contract and the considerations which induce a Court of Equity to decline to enforce specific performance of a contract are by no means the same. It may well be that there is not sufficient to induce the Court to rescind the contract, but still sufficient to prevent the Court enforcing it"); *Re Terry and White's Contract* (1886) 32 Ch.D. 14, CA, at 29; *Holliday v Lockwood*, above, n.20; *Lamare v Dixon*, above, n.15. Jones and Goodhart, p.88, doubt whether *Cadman v Horner* would be followed today, since it involved a trifling misrepresentation.

[25] Jones and Goodhart, p.1; *Holliday v Lockwood*, above, n.20 at 56–57.

[26] Above, para.10–07. This appears more clearly in older cases, in which specific performance was refused on the basis that the claimant had made an innocent misrepresentation even though there was at that time no claim to rescission for a misrepresentation which was not fraudulent. See, e.g. *Cadman v Horner*, above, n.24; *Re Banister*, above, n.24 at 147. For the recognition that rescission was available even for an innocent misrepresentation, see *Regrave v Hurd* (1881) 20 Ch.D. 1, CA; above, para.4–04.

[27] *Cadman v Horner*, above, n.24 at 11 (Grant M.R.).

10–09 **Misdescription (incorporated misrepresentation) as a defence to specific performance.**[28] The courts have developed special rules to deal with the case where the seller under a contract of sale of land has made a misdescription about the property in the contract of sale.[29] Such an incorporated misrepresentation is generally referred to in this context as a "misdescription", to distinguish it from the pre-contractual "misrepresentation". Where a misdescription is the result of a pre-contractual misrepresentation which has been incorporated into the contract, the defendant is still free to rely on the misrepresentation to counterclaim for rescission or damages in accordance with the rules for each remedy set out in the previous chapters of this book.[30] And if he so wishes, he may seek to raise the misrepresentation as a defence to the claim for specific performance on the basis described earlier in this section.[31] But where the seller seeks specific performance of the contract of sale, the buyer may raise the misdescription in the contract either to defeat the claim altogether, or to seek compensation for the misdescription as a condition of the grant of the order of specific performance. This order for compensation is an award not of

---

[28] Emmet, paras 4.017–4.019; Megarry & Wade, *The Law of Real Property* (7th edn, 2008), paras 15.117–15.119; J.T. Farrand, *Contract and Conveyance* (4th edn, 1983), pp.52–55.

[29] The rules do not apply where the misrepresentation has been incorporated only into another contract, collateral to the contract of sale: the remedy then is under the collateral contract: *Rutherford v Acton-Adams* [1915] A.C. 866, PC, at 870. Nor when the misrepresentation was not incorporated into any contract, since such an order would then amount to an award of damages in respect of misrepresentation, for which the rules of the several remedies for damages for misrepresentation must be applied: *Gilchester Properties Ltd v Gomm* [1948] 1 All E.R. 493 at 496–497 (Romer J., noting the law's reluctance at that time to award damages for non-fraudulent misrepresentation; even after the Misrepresentation Act 1967 (above, Ch.7), however, the general point still holds); *Schmidt v Greenwood* (1912) 32 N.Z.L.R. 241, NZCA.

[30] Rescission (above, Ch.4) is not barred simply because the misrepresentation has been incorporated into the contract: Misrepresentation Act 1967, s.1(a). A counterclaim for damages will depend on the application of the rules of deceit (above, Ch.5), negligence (above, Ch.6) or the Misrepresentation Act 1967 s.2(1) (above, Ch.7); or on the establishment of a collateral contract (above, Ch.8).

[31] Above. *Rutherford v Acton-Adams*, above, n.29 at 870 (Viscount Haldane: specific performance with compensation will be ordered "provided that the vendor has not, by misrepresentation or otherwise, disentitled himself to his remedy").

damages for misrepresentation,[32] but of compensation in equity. In exercising their jurisdiction over the remedy of specific performance the courts of equity looked at the substance and not merely the letter of the contract; and if a seller of land sued and was in a position to convey substantially what the purchaser had contracted to get, the courts developed the jurisdiction to decree specific performance with compensation for any small and immaterial deficiency.[33] In the case of a substantial misdescription, the seller cannot insist on specific performance even with compensation, and so the purchaser can raise the misdescription as a bar to the award of specific performance.[34] The jurisdiction to award compensation in equity may also be exercised on the buyer's claim, where it is the buyer who seeks specific performance of the contract together with a claim for an abatement of the purchase price. In such cases, however, the courts will more readily grant compensation, even in

[32] For which a (counter)claim must be made in tort, or under the Misrepresentation Act 1967 s.2(1), or under a collateral contract: above, n.30.

[33] *Rutherford v Acton-Adams*, above, n.29 at 869–870 (but no order there because the description was only a misrepresentation, not incorporated into the contract of sale itself). For examples of the operation of the jurisdiction in response to the seller's claim for specific performance, see *Dyer v Hargrave* (1805) 10 Ves. 505, 32 E.R. 941 (house described as being in good repair, and land described as "in a high state of cultivation"; other misdescriptions irrelevant, because the purchaser had knowledge of their falsity); *Scott v Hanson* (1829) 1 Russ. & My. 128, 39 E.R. 49 (14 acres of land sold as "uncommonly rich water meadow", but two acres not meadow land nor capable of being watered); *King v Wilson* (1843) 6 Beav. 124, 49 E.R. 772 (property represented to be 46ft in depth in fact only 33ft); *Hughes v Jones* (1861) 3 De G. F. & J. 307, 45 E.R. 897 (purchase of property subject to leases at low rents: purchaser did not resist specific performance but claimed compensation as condition of its award); *Shepherd v Croft* [1911] 1 Ch. 521 (natural underground watercourse which could be diverted: compensation ordered notwithstanding condition providing that no compensation should be payable for misdescription).

[34] This is so whether the contract (a) contains a stipulation providing for compensation for misdescription: *Flight v Booth* (1834) 1 Bing. N.C. 370, 131 E.R. 1160; or (b) contains a stipulation providing that no compensation should be payable nor should the contract be annulled for misdescription: *Jacobs v Revell* [1900] 2 Ch. 858; *Re Puckett and Smith's Contract* [1902] 2 Ch. 258, CA; *Lee v Rayson* [1917] 1 Ch. 613; or (c) is silent as to the payment of compensation: *Ridley v Oster* [1939] 1 All E.R. 618 (claim by purchaser for return of deposit). On the question of whether a misdescription is "substantial", see *Lee v Rayson* at 618 (value is not the only or dominant element to be taken into account); *Watson v Burton* [1957] 1 W.L.R. 19 at 25 (question of fact); and generally cases cited above, n.33.

cases where the misdescription is substantial, since the purchaser is allowed to elect to take all he can get under the contract, whilst being compensated for the difference between that and what the seller promised in the contract.[35]

Contracts for the sale of land often make express provision concerning the right to compensation in the event of misdescription. Where the special conditions of the contract allow compensation, the court can simply apply the conditions rather than exercising the inherent equitable jurisdiction.[36] But sometimes the conditions expressly exclude the right to compensation for misdescription, often together with a provision expressly excluding the purchaser's remedy of rescission of the contract for misdescription.[37] Such a

---

[35] *Rutherford v Acton-Adams*, above, n.29 at 870. However, this does not apply where the seller would be in breach of a prior contract with a third party by conveying to the purchaser: *Lipmans Wallpaper Ltd v Mason & Hodghton Ltd* [1969] 1 Ch. 20 at 38; nor where the purchaser knew about the defect in title at the time of the contract: *Castle v Wilkinson* (1870) L.R. 5 Ch. App. 534; *Dyer v Hargrave* (1805) 10 Ves. 505 at 509, 32 E.R. 941 at 942–943; nor where compensation cannot be fairly assessed: *Rudd v Lascelles* [1900] 1 Ch. 815 at 819–820; nor where it would be a great hardship on the vendor to enforce performance: *Rudd v Lascelles*, above, at 820; nor where the difference between what was promised and what is given under the contract is so significant that it is a different contract: *Earl of Durham v Legard* (1865) 34 Beav. 611, 55 E.R. 771. In *Cato v Thompson* (1882) 9 Q.B.D. 616, CA, at 618 Jessel MR thought that "cases of specific performance with compensation ought not to be extended. In many of them a bargain substantially different from that which the parties entered into has been substituted for it and enforced, which is not right." See C. Harpum, "Specific Performance with Compensation as Purchaser's Remedy" [1981] C.L.J. 47 for a general review of this area, arguing that it should no longer be regarded as distinct from the remedy of specific performance with compensation under Lord Cairns' Act (now the Senior Courts Act 1981 s.50), and criticising *Rudd v Lascelles*, above.

[36] *Re Fawcett and Holmes' Contract* (1889) 42 Ch.D. 150, CA, at 157 (misdescription of area of property); *Re Brewer and Hankins's Contract* (1899) 80 L.T. 127, CA (public sewer passing under garden behind property); *Re Belcham and Gawley's Contract* [1930] 1 Ch. 56 (two sewers ran through property); *Leslie v Tompson* (1851) 20 L.J. Ch. 561 (contractual provision for compensation in favour of either party). The current standard form conditions of sale provide for damages to be payable in the event of, inter alia, material misdescription: Standard Conditions of Sale (5th edn, 2011), condition 7.1.1(a), reproduced in the Appendices in F. Silverman, *Conveyancing Handbook* (re-issued annually).

[37] See, e.g. *Jacobs v Revell*, above, n.34; *Re Puckett and Smith's Contract*, above, n.34; *Shepherd v Croft*, above, n.33; *Lee v Rayson*, above, n.34; *Watson v*

clause ought to be subject to the normal rules relating to exclusion and limitation clauses,[38] but it will be held in appropriate cases that the remedy of compensation with specific performance has been effectively excluded.[39]

(2) Defence to Actions for Debt or Damages

Defence based on rescission of the contract under which the debt or damages claim arose. A claim to enforce a debt is, generally speaking, an action to enforce the obligation to pay a liquidated sum which arises out of a contract or other transaction.[40] For example, the claim may be for the payment of the price due under a contract for the sale of goods,[41] or the sum due under an insurance policy when the insured risk has materialised,[42] or calls 10–10

Burton, above, n.34 (Law Society's Conditions of Sale, 1953 edn); *Walker v Boyle*, above, n.23 (National Conditions of Sale, 19th edn). "Rescission" in this context means termination of the contract: above, para.8–35.

[38] Above, Ch.9. There is however a particular restriction on the effectiveness of clauses seeking to exclude the vendor's liability for misrepresentation in contracts for the sale of land: above, para.9–17. The Unfair Contract Terms Act 1977 s.3 does not apply to any contract so far as it relates to the creation or transfer of an interest in land: Sch.1, para.1(b); and the control of exclusion and limitation clauses by the Misrepresentation Act 1967 s.3 (which does apply to contracts for land) only extends to claims for pre-contractual misrepresentation: above, para.9–23.

[39] *Cordingley v Cheesebrough* (1862) 3 Giff. 496, 66 E.R. 504 (property described in particulars of sale as containing "an area of 7683 square feet or thereabouts" in fact contained 4350ft^2; this would have given rise to a claim for compensation but "no allowance shall be made or required either way" if the measurements were inaccurate); *Re Terry and White's Contract*, above, n.24 (misdescription of area of property by a factor of over a third: but "no error, mis-statement or misdescription shall annul the sale, nor shall any compensation be allowed in respect thereof"; the case was however decided on other grounds).

[40] For the distinction between specific performance, debt and damages, see Treitel, paras 21–001 to 21–002.

[41] *Bannerman v White* (1861) 10 C.B.N.S. 844, 142 E.R. 685 (on construction, misrepresentation incorporated into sale as condition).

[42] *Anderson v Thornton* (1853) 8 Exch. 425, 155 E.R. 1415. Where the contract of insurance itself contains provisions which render it void or voidable in the event of misrepresentation, the defence may in substance be under the contract: *Re Marshall and Scottish Employer's Liability and General Insurance Co. Ltd's Arbitration* (1901) 85 L.T. 757; *Kumar v Life Insurance Corp. of India* [1974] 1 Lloyd's Rep. 147.

due under a contract to subscribe for shares.[43] And a claim for damages arises where the defendant has broken his obligations under a contract.[44] Where the defendant seeks to defend the claim to enforce the debt, or the claim for damages for breach, on the basis of the claimant's misrepresentation, he generally bases the defence on the fact that the contract was itself induced by the misrepresentation. In such cases the defendant will have to show not only that the misrepresentation entitles him to rescind the contract,[45] but also that the contract has already been rescinded or that he is electing now to rescind,[46] before he can be heard to raise the misrepresentation as a defence to a claim to enforce payment of a debt or damages due under it. Where the defendant is continuing to take the benefits of the contract he cannot consistently deny his continuing obligation to make payment of the debt or damages.[47]

---

[43] *Burnes v Pennell* (1849) 2 H.L.C. 497, 9 E.R. 1181, HL (Sc.); *Bwlch-y-Plwm Lead Mining Co. v Baynes* (1867) L.R. 2 Exch. 324; *Bentley & Co. Ltd v Black* (1893) 9 T.L.R. 580, CA; *Aaron's Reefs Ltd v Twiss* [1896] A.C. 273, HL.

[44] *United Shoe Machinery Co. of Canada v Brunet* [1909] A.C. 330, PC (contract for lease of machines); *Wharton v Lewis* (1824) 1 Car. & P. 529, 171 E.R. 1303 (breach of promise of marriage; this no longer takes effect as a contract: Law Reform (Miscellaneous Provisions) Act 1970 s.1(1)).

[45] *Bentley & Co. Ltd v Black*, above, n.43 (company's actions to recover calls on shares: no defence because no misstatement of fact in prospectus); *Burnes v Pennell*, above, n.43 (shareholder knew truth and so not induced by statements to purchase shares: counterclaim for reduction or cancellation of shares failed, as well as defence to claim to recover calls on shares).

[46] *Bwlch-y-Plwm Lead Mining Co. v Baynes*, above, n.43 (action for calls: defendant had already repudiated the shares on discovering fraud); *Gordon v Street* [1899] 2 Q.B. 641, CA (promissory note, given to secure loan, induced by fraudulent misrepresentation of identity by creditor: defence to action on the note, because defendant had repudiated the contract within a reasonable time of discovering the fraud). It is sufficient that the contract has been rescinded without the defendant taking positive steps himself to rescind: *Aaron's Reefs Ltd v Twiss*, above, n.43 (call on shares: shares forfeited by failure to pay calls, so defendant became a mere debtor to the company: as long as he had done nothing to affirm the contract, it was not incumbent on him to take active steps to avoid the contract).

[47] *Dawes v Harness* (1875) L.R. 10 C.P. 166 (cheque given by defendant in payment of purchase of business from claimant; defendant could not resist payment under the cheque on the basis of the claimant's fraudulent misrepresentation without disaffirming the contract of sale); *United Shoe Machinery Co. of Canada v Brunet*, above, n.44 (defence to claim for damages under contract for lease of machines failed because defendant had continued to work the machines after discovery of the misrepresentation).

Defence that the contract is void, rather than voidable. The need for the defendant to rescind the contract, before he can defend a claim aimed at enforcing his obligations under the contract, follows from the fact that misrepresentation renders a contract voidable, not void[48]; and the whole contract, and not simply the representee's obligations, must be rescinded.[49] If, however, the defendant can show that the contract was void, rather than simply voidable, he need not have taken any active steps to avoid the contract, and can raise the fact that the contract is void to defend a claim to enforce the obligations he would have had under the contract had it not been void. A contract may be void for mistake, such as a mistake of identity,[50] or on the grounds of *non est factum*.[51] In such cases the mistake may arise from a misrepresentation,[52] but it is the mistake which is relied upon by the defendant in order to resist the enforcement of his obligations under the contract. 10–11

---

[48] Above, para.4–05.

[49] Above, para.4–13. Where misrepresentation is raised as a defence to a claim by the insured under a contract of insurance, and the contract is rescinded by the insurer in order to resist the claim, there is a variation from the usual rule that both parties must make restitution of benefits received under the contract. Where the insurer shows that the claimant induced the contract by a fraudulent misrepresentation, he need not repay the premium in order to raise successfully the misrepresentation to resist performance of his own obligations. The insurer must, however, repay the premiums in a case of non-fraudulent misrepresentation: *Feise v Parkinson* (1812) 4 Taunt. 640, 128 E.R. 482; *Anderson v Thornton*, above, n.42; and it appears that he must also repay where he takes the initiative in rescinding the contract: *Barker v Walters* (1844) 8 Beav. 92, 50 E.R. 36. See also Treitel, para.9–089; but no such limitation appears in the Marine Insurance Act 1906, s.84(3)(a). The terms of the insurance contract may, however, make express provision relating to the retention or repayment of premiums: *Re Marshall and Scottish Employer's Liability and General Insurance Co. Ltd's Arbitration*, above, n.42; *Kumar v Life Insurance Corp. of India*, above, n.42. For reform by the Consumer Insurance (Disclosure and Representations) Bill, expected to be enacted during 2012 (implementing Law Com No.319, *Consumer Insurance Law: Pre-Contract Disclosure and Misrepresentation* (2009)), which will limit the insurer's right to avoid the contract as against a consumer insured, see above, para.4–29, n.137; below, para.17–06.

[50] *Cundy v Lindsay* (1873) 3 App. Cas. 459, HL; *Shogun Finance Ltd v Hudson* [2003] UKHL 62, [2004] 1 A.C. 919; below, Ch.14.

[51] *Saunders v Anglia Building Society* [1971] A.C. 1004; below, paras 13–55 to 13–61.

[52] Above, para.1–03; below, para.12–19.

(3) Defence to the Enforcement of Deeds, Written Contracts and Other Documents

10–12 **Enforceability of deeds and written contracts: the parol evidence rule.** In interpreting the terms set out in a written document, the courts normally apply the objective meaning of the words used and are reluctant to admit evidence that the parties meant their words to be interpreted in any other sense. And where the parties intended a written document to embody the complete express terms of their contract[53] the courts will not normally admit evidence to contradict or add to the terms contained in the written document. The former rule is one of interpretation of written documents[54]; the latter rule is commonly referred to as the "parol evidence rule".[55] Both rules, however, admit of exceptions; and statements made by one party to the other at the time of the contract may be used to vary the meaning or legal effect which would otherwise be given to the written document.

10–13 **Misrepresentation giving rise to collateral contract.** Although the statement might not vary the written contract, it might give rise to a separate, collateral contract which the representee can enforce even though this contradicts the terms of the main contract. So

[53] Or where the contract is one which is required by law to be in writing, such as a contract for the sale or other disposition of an interest in land under Law of Property (Miscellaneous Provisions) Act 1989 s.2.

[54] Chitty, paras 12–117 to 12–126; Lewison, paras 2.06, 5.01; Phipson, Ch.42. For recent decisions of the House of Lords in which the literal, objective interpretation of written contracts and other documents has given way to more commercial, contextual interpretation, see *Mannai Investment Co. Ltd v Eagle Star Life Assurance Co. Ltd* [1997] A.C. 749 at 770–771, 775 and 779–780; *Investors Compensation Scheme Ltd v West Bromwich Building Society* [1998] 1 W.L.R. 896 at 912–913; *Bank of Credit and Commerce International S.A. v Ali* [2001] UKHL 8, [2002] 1 A.C. 251 at [29], [39], [78]; *Chartbrook Ltd v Persimmon Homes Ltd* [2009] UKHL 38, [2009] 1 A.C. 1101 at [14]. See also below, para.13.36.

[55] Chitty, paras 12–096 to 12–112; Furmston, paras 3.4 to 3.6; Treitel, paras 6–013 to 6–030; Anson, pp.138–139; Cheshire, Fifoot and Furmston, pp.157–165; Lewison, para.3.11; Phipson, Ch.42. See also below, para.13–33 and *Chartbrook Ltd v Persimmon Homes Ltd* [2009] UKHL 38, [2009] 1 A.C. 1101 (obiter: HL should not depart from its earlier decision in *Prenn v Simmonds* [1971] 1 W.L.R. 1381 excluding pre-contractual negotiations in interpreting a written document; although they are admissible in support of a claim for rectification or estoppel: at [42]).

where the claimant relies on his rights under the main contract, the defendant might raise the collateral contract by way of defence and, where appropriate, counterclaim. Collateral contracts were discussed in Chapter 8.[56]

Misrepresentation about scope or effect of written term or document. Where a claimant seeks to rely on a written term in accordance with its objective meaning, the defendant may show that the claimant made a statement at or before the time of the contract that the term would not have the effect which the claimant now asserts. Where, therefore, a party makes a misrepresentation to the effect that the defendant will not be bound by an exemption clause which is included in a contractual document, or that the clause is only to have a more limited scope by way of exemption of the claimant's liability than its literal, objective interpretation would provide, then the claimant cannot enforce the clause against the defendant (either at all, or beyond its represented scope, as the case may be).[57] This is so even though the misrepresentation may have been made wholly innocently, and whether made by words or conduct, even if it only created a false impression about the scope of the term and might not be a sufficiently precise and unambiguous representation to give rise to other remedies, such as an estoppel.[58] 10–14

[56] Above, para.8–06.

[57] *Curtis v Chemical Cleaning and Dyeing Co.* [1951] 1 K.B. 805, CA (claimant, on leaving wedding dress for cleaning, signed acknowledgement that "the company is not liable for any damage howsoever arising" after defendant's employee told her it was required only because the defendants would not accept liability for certain specified risks, including risk of damage by or to the beads and sequins with which the dress was trimmed; the clause "never became part of the contract" (Somervell L.J. at 808), or there was a "sufficient misrepresentation to disentitle the cleaners from relying on the exemption, except in regard to beads and sequins" (Denning L.J. at 809): *cf. AXA Sun Life Services Plc v Harry Bennett & Associates Ltd* [2011] EWCA Civ 133 at [105] (Rix L.J.: Somervell L.J.'s judgment is the ratio in *Curtis*)). This principle applies equally to a situation where the misrepresentation is as to the whole of the contents of a document rather than as to the existence of a particular exemption clause: *Lloyds Bank Plc v Waterhouse* [1993] 2 F.L.R. 97 at 120 (Woolf L.J.).

[58] *ibid.* at 808–809 (Denning L.J.). See also *L'Estrange v F. Graucob Ltd* [1934] 2 K.B. 394, CA, at 403 (Scrutton L.J.: a party's signature is binding *in the absence of fraud or misrepresentation*); *Jaques v Lloyd D. George & Partners Ltd* [1968] 1 W.L.R. 625, CA (estate agent's representative misrepresented effect of clause requiring seller to pay commission); *Lee v Lancashire and Yorkshire Railway Co.* (1871) L.R. 6 Ch. App. 527 (injured railway passenger not bound by

10–15 **Misrepresentation in a deed.** Where a deed contains a false statement of fact the deed may sometimes be given effect as between the parties as if the statement were true: this is an application of the doctrine of estoppel.[59] If it is a statement agreed by both parties it will bind them both. But if it is intended to be the statement of one party only, the estoppel is confined to that party,[60] so that the other party may enforce the deed as if the statement were true. However, if the party who made the statement seeks to enforce the deed, the other party may raise as a defence the fact that the statement is false with a view to resisting the enforcement of the deed.[61]

10–16 **Misrepresentation in statutory notices.** Where a claimant seeks to assert a right based on a notice given pursuant to statute it may be open to the defendant to raise by way of defence to the enforcement of the right the fact that the claimant's notice contained a misrepresentation. For example, in *Lazarus Estates Ltd v Beasley*[62]

receipt acknowledging payment made in full satisfaction of his claim where he had been told by the railway company's agent that it would not prevent his recovering future damages if his injuries turned out to be more serious than then supposed); *Hirschfeld v London Brighton and South Coast Railway Co.* (1876) 2 Q.B.D. 1 at 5 (misrepresentation as to effect of deed of release of claim could be defence to enforcement of the deed). For the different question, whether a misrepresentation about the effect of a document is an actionable misrepresentation when it induces the representee to enter into another transaction (i.e. not the transaction whose effect is itself being misrepresented), see above, para.3–24.

[59] *Halsbury's Laws of England*, Vol.16(2) (4th edn, 2003 reissue), paras 954, 1014; it is based on the principle that a party to a deed is not permitted to deny his statements in the deed (i.e. contrary evidence is not admissible). On estoppel more generally, see below, paras 10–18 to 10–28. For the use of contractual estoppel as a means of giving effect to clauses in a contract (not limited to deeds) by which the parties agree that no pre-contractual representations have been made, or that the representee did not rely on any such representations, see above, para.9–03, n.9.

[60] *Greer v Kettle* [1938] A.C. 156, HL, at 170 (recital in guarantee under seal).

[61] *Greenfield v Edwards* (1865) 11 L.T. 663 (injunction granted to prevent party enforcing mortgage deed which contained false representation by him that money had been advanced).

[62] [1956] 1 Q.B. 702, CA. See also *Rous v Mitchell* [1991] 1 W.L.R. 469, CA (notice to quit served under the Agricultural Holdings Act 1986); *Betty's Cafés Ltd v Phillips Furnishing Stores Ltd* [1959] A.C. 20, HL (notice of intention to reconstruct premises given by landlord under the Landlord and Tenant Act 1954 to oppose grant of new tenancy: if the notice had been given fraudulently it would have been voidable: Lord Denning at 50–51).

a landlord gave a statutory notice to raise the rent on the ground that he had carried out repairs to the property, but the tenant was allowed later to resist a claim for the increased rent on the basis that the landlord in the notice had fraudulently overstated the repairs which had been carried out. The cases which have applied this principle have involved fraudulent misrepresentations, and their reasoning has been based on the principle that "fraud unravels everything".[63] However, in the case of a notice containing a (non-fraudulent) misrepresentation, the question whether the misrepresentation can be relied on to deny the validity of the notice ought to be a matter of the interpretation of the statute under which the notice was given.[64] Where, however, the validity of a notice is challenged on the ground of fraud, it is not necessary for the defendant to show that he was deceived by it. The fraud of itself nullifies the notice, without further proof of reliance by the defendant on it.[65]

Court orders obtained by misrepresentation. Where the claimant seeks to enforce a court order, the defendant may also be able to raise as a defence the fact that the order was procured by misrepresentation. Although a party should normally apply to have the judgment set aside in order to avoid being bound by the **10–17**

[63] *Lazarus Estates Ltd v Beasley* [1956] 1 Q.B. 702, CA, at 712–713, 722; *Rous v Mitchell*, above, n.62 at 701.

[64] In *Lazarus Estates Ltd v Beasley*, above, n.63, Morris L.J. dissented on the basis that on a proper construction of the Housing Repairs and Rents Act 1954, under which the notice was given, the defendant should have raised objection to the misrepresentation about the extent of the repairs within a prescribed time, and so it was now too late for her to raise the issue. In *Rous v Mitchell*, above, n.62, the court made clear that legislation could deprive the court of jurisdiction even where fraud was alleged, but such a provision must be clear. *Cf. R. v Registrar of Companies Ex p. Central Bank of India* [1986] Q.B. 1114, CA, at 1177 (if registration of a company charge is procured by fraud, the registrar's certificate of the charge may be conclusive under the Companies Act 1948, s.98(2) [now the Companies Act 2006, s.869(6)], although a court might act in personam against the fraudulent party so as to prevent him taking advantage of the fraudulently obtained certificate).

[65] *Rous v Mitchell*, above, n.62 at 690–691, 701–702. However, in *Betty's Cafés Ltd v Phillips Furnishing Stores Ltd*, above, n.62 at 51 Lord Denning said that a fraudulent notice would be "bad—voidable—liable to be set aside for fraudulent misrepresentation".

judgment under the principles of estoppel by record,[66] it was said in *Lazarus Estates Ltd v Beasley*[67] that if the landlord had procured a court order for increased rent by fraud, the tenant could have refused to pay the increase and if sued could have raised as a defence that the order was obtained by fraud. Where a consent judgment or order[68] embodies an agreement which has been induced by misrepresentation, a party seeking to avoid the estoppel should apply to the court to have the judgment or order set aside.[69]

III. MISREPRESENTATION AND ESTOPPEL[70]

10–18 **Estoppel as a defence.** The defendant may assert that the claimant is precluded from obtaining the relief which he seeks because to grant the relief would be contrary to a representation which the claimant himself made, and which the defendant has relied upon. Such a defence is an application of the doctrine of estoppel by representation.

10–19 **The general concept of estoppel, and its different forms.** The original, core meaning of the verb "to estop" is, simply, "to stop"[71]: a party who is "estopped" is stopped, or prevented, from doing something. The verb, together with the noun ("estoppel") derived

[66] *Jonesco v Beard* [1930] A.C. 298, HL, at 300. See also Spencer Bower and Handley, *Res Judicata* (4th edn, 2009), Ch.16. Foreign judgments may be impeached for fraud: L. Collins (ed.), *Dicey, Morris and Collins, The Conflict of Laws* (14th edn, 2006), paras 14.127–14.140. Where an arbitral award is procured by fraud a party may apply to the court to challenge the award: Arbitration Act 1996, s.68(1), (2)(g).

[67] Above, n.63 at 722; see also at 712.

[68] CPR, r.40.6.

[69] *Parker v Simpson* (1869) 18 W.R. 204 (party's consent to order obtained by fraud); *Wales v Wadham* [1977] 1 W.L.R. 199 (judge appeared to assume that pleas of (innocent) misrepresentation by one of the parties to an agreement which was embodied in a court order should be considered on the same basis as would have been applicable to a simple contract).

[70] Allen, Ch.6.

[71] "The word 'estoppel' only means 'stopped.' You will find it explained by Coke in his Commentaries on Littleton . . . It was brought over by the Normans. They used the old French 'estoupail'. That meant a bung or cork by which you stopped something from coming out. It was in common use in our courts when they carried on all their proceedings in Norman-French . . .": *McIlkenny v Chief Constable of the West Midlands* [1980] Q.B. 283, CA, at 316–7 (Lord Denning M.R.); Co. Litt. 352a.

from it, is used today only in its technical legal sense; and in this context Coke[72] saw as the general link between different forms of estoppel that the party's act or words preclude him from pleading to the contrary: in effect, a rule which stops a party leading evidence to deny his act or words. There are various different forms of estoppel, which have their own separate rules.[73] It is not appropriate to discuss here in detail the whole range of the different forms of estoppel and their effect: the following paragraphs will focus on estoppel by representation, which relates most closely to the general rules of misrepresentation and which can sometimes provide a defence based on the claimant's representation.

The elements of an estoppel by representation. If the defendant can show that the claimant by his words or conduct made a representation of fact on which he intended the defendant to rely, and on which the defendant in fact relied, then the claimant is estopped from asserting facts which contradict the representation. These elements of an estoppel by representation will be discussed in the following paragraphs. It will be seen that, although the doctrine of estoppel is different in its effect from a claim to a remedy based on misrepresentation,[74] there are similarities between their elements. 10–20

The representation: words or conduct. To establish an estoppel by representation the defendant must show that the claimant made a representation on which he relied but, as in claims for misrepresentation,[75] the representation need not be made through the medium of words. As long as the claimant caused the defendant 10–21

---

[72] Co. Litt. 352a: "it is called an estoppel or conclusion, because a man's owne act or acceptance stoppeth or closeth up his mouth to alleage or plead the truth".

[73] Coke, *ibid.*, listed estoppel by record, estoppel by deed and estoppel by matter *in pais*. In the modern law the categories of estoppel (the rules of some of which continue to be developed) include estoppel by record (including issue estoppel and the general principles of *res judicata*); estoppel by representation (including estoppel by deed), estoppel by convention, promissory estoppel and proprietary estoppel. For detailed discussion, see *Halsbury's Laws of England*, Vol.16(2) (4th edn, 2003 reissue), paras 951–1094; Spencer Bower, Turner and Handley, *Res Judicata*, above, n.66; Spencer Bower, *Estoppel by Representation* (4th edn, 2004); K.R. Handley, *Estoppel by Conduct and Election* (2006); Phipson, Ch.5.

[74] Below, para.10–27.

[75] Above, para.3–04.

to believe the fact in question, it may be done by words or by conduct.[76] Mere silence cannot normally amount to a representation.[77]

10–22 **Representation of fact?** Within this form of estoppel,[78] it has generally been said that the representation must be of fact. It is certainly not sufficient that the claimant misrepresented his intentions. If a statement of intention were to be binding by virtue of the representee's reliance on it, it would undermine the requirement that consideration be given to make a promise binding

[76] *Pickard v Sears* (1837) 6 Ad. & E. 469, 112 E.R. 179 (owner of goods stood by and allowed former owner to sell them to defendant: representation to defendant that claimant made no claim to the goods); *Cornish v Abington* (1859) 4 H. & N. 549, 157 E.R. 956 (implied representation to supplier that employee had authority to bind employer).

[77] For estoppel, the representation must be clear and unequivocal, but "it is difficult to imagine how silence and inaction can be anything but equivocal": *Allied Marine Transport Ltd v Vale Do Rio Doce Navegacao S.A.* [1985] 1 W.L.R. 925, CA, at 937. Where, however, there is a duty to disclose silence may become significant and amount to a representation, at least in a case of estoppel by negligence; below, n.87: *Greenwood v Martins Bank Ltd* [1933] A.C. 51 at 58 (Lord Tomlin). Spencer Bower, *Estoppel by Representation*, above, n.73, para.III.5.1, rejects the term "estoppel by negligence" and prefers to see instead the cases of breach of duty to speak as simply examples of estoppel by representation.

[78] A representation of intention may, however, be binding on the representor under the doctrines of promissory or proprietary estoppel. In promissory estoppel, a defendant who has been induced by the claimant to believe that the claimant will not enforce his rights—typically, his contractual rights—against him, and has altered his position on the faith of this assurance, may be able thereby to resist the enforcement of the claim, at least until the claimant has given him the opportunity of again placing himself in the position of being able to perform (a requirement that the claimant give him "reasonable notice" of the withdrawal of the concession), although where the defendant's alteration of position is irrevocable the claimant's concession may itself also be irrevocable: *Ajayi v R.T. Briscoe (Nigeria) Ltd* [1964] 1 W.L.R. 1326, PC, at 1330; Chitty, paras 3–085 to 3–106; Treitel, paras 3–111 to 3–117; Anson, pp.116–126. In proprietary estoppel, the representee who has been led to believe that he has or will receive from the representor an interest in property and who relies to his detriment on the faith of representation so that the court judges it inequitable to deny him a remedy, may be awarded a remedy which (at the court's discretion) may even extend to an order to transfer to him the property right that he believed he had or would obtain: *Crabb v Arun DC* [1976] Ch. 179, CA; Megarry & Wade, *The Law of Real Property* (7th edn, 2008), Ch.16; E.H. Burn and J. Cartwright, *Cheshire and Burn's Modern Law of Real Property* (18th edn, 2011), pp.906–922.

as a contract.[79] It also used to be said that a representation of law cannot give rise to an estoppel.[80] However, since the courts have now abandoned the formal distinction between misrepresentations of law and misrepresentations of fact in relation to restitution and contract[81] it seems likely that they will accept that, in principle, an estoppel may arise by virtue of a representation of law.[82] Whether a particular representation of law is capable of giving rise to an estoppel, however, will depend on whether the other requirements are satisfied.[83]

The representor's state of mind. It is not necessary that the party making the representation should know that it was false.[84] The doctrine of estoppel by representation focuses on the representation, and the representee's reliance on it, and not on the state of mind of the representor. However, before he can be estopped it must be shown that the representor intended (or can be taken to have 10–23

[79] *Jorden v Money* (1854) 5 H.L.C. 185 at 215–216, 10 E.R. 868 at 882, HL (Lord St. Leonards dissenting at 248, at 895); *Maddison v Alderson* (1883) 8 App. Cas. 467, HL, at 473; *Low v Bouverie* [1891] 3 Ch. 82, CA, at 102, 109; *George Whitechurch Ltd v Cavanagh* [1902] A.C. 117, HL, at 130. For a different interpretation of *Jorden v Money*, however, see P.S. Atiyah, *Essays on Contract* (1988; revised edn 1990), pp.233–238. For the similar requirement that a misrepresentation be of fact, not intention, to be actionable, see above, para.3–43.

[80] *Territorial and Auxiliary Forces Association of the County of London v Nichols* [1949] 1 K.B. 35, CA, at 50 (representation that premises fell within the Rent Restriction Acts would be a representation of law). For the difficulty of distinguishing between representations of law and of fact see above, paras 3–22 to 3–27.

[81] For a general discussion of the "mistake of law" and the "misrepresentation of law" rules, and their abandonment by the courts in the contexts of both restitution and contract, see above, paras 3–20 to 3–41.

[82] Spencer Bower, *Estoppel by Representation*, above, n.73, para.II.8.1.

[83] e.g. whether the representee relied on it; whether the representor intended him to rely on it or owed a duty in relation to the representation: below, paras 10–24, 10–25; Spencer Bower, *Estoppel by Representation*, above, n.73, para.I.2.3. This mirrors the position in relation to remedies for misrepresentation: even though there is no longer a firm distinction between a misrepresentation of law and a misrepresentation of fact, misrepresentations of law may not be actionable where it is not reasonable for the representee to rely on the representation: above, para.3–41.

[84] *Jorden v Money*, above, n.79 at 212, at 881; *Carr v London and North Western Railway Co.* (1875) L.R. 10 C.P. 307 at 316–318; *Seton, Laing & Co. v Lafone* (1887) 19 Q.B.D. 68, CA.

intended[85]) that the representee should act on his representation[86] or, if he did not intend the representee so to act, it must be shown that it was the representor's negligent conduct that misled the representee.[87]

10–24 **Interpretation of the representation and the representor's intention.** The representation must be clear and unambiguous.[88] However, as in the case of misrepresentations,[89] the courts apply an objective test in interpreting the representation which is alleged to give rise to an estoppel. In *Freeman v Cooke*[90] Parke B. said of the doctrine of estoppel by representation

---

[85] Below, para.10–24.

[86] *Freeman v Cooke* (1848) 2 Exch. 654 at 663, 154 E.R. 652 at 656, explaining the judgment of Lord Denman C.J. in *Pickard v Sears*, above, n.76 at 474, at 181 ("where one by his words or conduct wilfully causes another to believe the existence of a certain state of things, and induces him to act on that belief, so as to alter his own previous position, the former is concluded from averring against the latter a different state of things as existing at the same time").

[87] This form of estoppel is generally referred to as "estoppel by negligence", and requires that the representor owed the representee a duty to take care in his words or conduct from which the representation was inferred, and that the negligence was the proximate or real cause of the representee being misled: *Carr v London and North Western Railway Co.*, above, n.84 at 318; *Seton, Laing & Co. v Lafone*, above, n.84; *Swan v North British Australasian Co. Ltd* (1862) 7 H. & N. 603, 158 E.R. 611; *Freeman v Cooke*, above, n.86 at 663–664, at 656–657; *London Joint Stock Bank Ltd v Macmillan* [1918] A.C. 777, HL; *Greenwood v Martins Bank Ltd* [1933] A.C. 51, HL; *Moorgate Mercantile Co. Ltd v Twitchings* [1977] A.C. 890, HL, at 912, 925; *Halsbury's Laws of England*, above, n.73, paras 1061–1064; Spencer Bower, *Estoppel by Representation*, above, n.73, para.III.5.1.

[88] *Low v Bouverie*, above, n.79 at 106; *Canada and Dominion Sugar Co. v Canadian National (West Indies) Steamships Ltd* [1947] A.C. 46, PC, at 55, 56; *Woodhouse v A.C. Israel Cocoa Ltd S.A. v Nigerian Produce Marketing Co. Ltd* [1972] A.C. 741, HL, at 755, 768, 771 (promissory estoppel, but approving *Low v Bouverie* on this point generally); *Moorgate Mercantile Co. Ltd v Twitchings*, above, n.87 at 902.

[89] Above, para.3–06.

[90] Above, n.86 at 663, at 656. This is the statement which was used by Blackburn J. in *Smith v Hughes* (1871) L.R. 6 Q.B. 597 at 607 to describe the objective test of interpretation of contractual communications: above, para.3–06; below, para.13–09. For further statements to the effect that the meaning of the representation which gives rise to an estoppel is tested objectively, see *Cornish v Abington*, above, n.76 at 556–557, at 959; *Low v Bouverie*, above, n.79 at 106.

> "if whatever a man's real intention may be, he so conducts himself that a reasonable man would take the representation to be true, and believe that it was meant that he should act upon it, and did act upon it as true, the party making the representation would be equally precluded from contesting its truth."

Reliance by the representee. Before the defendant can rely on the estoppel, he must show that he relied on the representation, and therefore that he acted upon the representation in such a way that he should be entitled to require the claimant to have his legal rights determined on the basis of the facts as stated in the representation.[91] In relation to remedies for misrepresentation, the representee must show that he relied on the misrepresentation in entering into the contract or in otherwise suffering loss: there, the reliance is necessary to show a causal link between the representee's statement and the consequence (the contract or the loss) against which the claimant seeks to be relieved.[92] In the case of estoppel, it is not a matter of showing a link between the representation and a particular loss which is itself the basis of the claim, but rather the reliance is necessary to justify the representee's assertion that he is entitled to have his legal position vis-à-vis the representor decided on the basis as set out in the representation. 10–25

---

[91] *Greenwood v Martins Bank Ltd*, above, n.87; *Peyman v Lanjani* [1985] Ch. 457, CA (representee not estopped by conduct from denying that he had affirmed contract where no detrimental reliance); *Canada and Dominion Sugar Co. v Canadian National (West Indies) Steamships Ltd* above, n.88 at 56 (the representee "cannot be said to rely on the statement if he knew that it was false: he must reasonably believe it to be true and therefore act on it"). The requirement of reliance was an obstacle to analysing the operation of "no representation" and "non-reliance" clauses as being based on estoppel by representation: above, para.9–03, n.8; however, such clauses are now generally thought to be effective under the principles of contractual estoppel which does not require the representee to have believed the assumed state of facts: below, para. 9–03, n.9.

It is often said that the representee must have relied on the representation to his "detriment" or "prejudice", but the real question seems to be whether the representee's action in reliance would render it to his detriment or prejudice if the representor were not estopped: "the real detriment or harm from which the law seeks to give protection is that which would flow from the change of position if the assumption were deserted that led to it": *Grundt v Great Boulder Pty Gold Mines Ltd* (1937) 59 C.L.R. 641, HCA, at 674 (Dixon J.). For examples of action by a representee which amounts to a change of position, see Spencer Bower, *Estoppel by Representation*, above, n.73, paras V.5.2–V.5.6.

[92] Above, para.3–50.

The question is whether the representee actually relied on the representation, and not whether his reliance was reasonable.[93] For the purposes of some of the remedies for misrepresentation the courts have been prepared to infer from the materiality of the representation that the representee relied upon it: once a statement is shown to be material, in the sense that it was likely that a person in the representee's position would rely upon it, the representor will have the burden of adducing evidence to rebut the inference that his representation was relied on by the representee.[94] Although there do not appear to be cases in which this principle has been applied to a claim of estoppel by representation, it has been applied in other forms of estoppel.[95]

10–26 **The representee's own fault.** In claims for misrepresentation, the relevance of the claimant's "fault" varies from one remedy to another, but in general the representor who intended the representee to act on the representation cannot be heard to say that the representee should not have relied on the representation but should have checked its accuracy.[96] Similarly, where a defendant raises an estoppel by representation on the basis that the claimant intended him to rely on the representation the claimant cannot say that the defendant should not have so relied, if in fact he did.[97]

---

[93] *Downderry Construction Ltd v Secretary of State for Transport, Local Government and the Regions* [2002] EWHC 2, [2002] All E.R. (D) 01 (Jan). For the similar requirement that the claimant rely (but not necessarily reasonably) on the representation for the remedy of rescission, see above, para.4–32.

[94] Above, para.3–53. See also paras 4–33 (rescission), 5–25 (deceit), 7–19 (Misrepresentation Act 1967 s.2(1)).

[95] Promissory estoppel: *Brikom Investments Ltd v Carr* [1979] Q.B. 467, CA, at 482–483; proprietary estoppel: *Greasley v Cooke* [1980] 1 W.L.R. 1306, CA, at 1311, 1313 (applying the rule from the misrepresentation cases, and in particular *Smith v Chadwick* (1882) 20 Ch.D. 27, CA, at 44); *Grant v Edwards* [1986] Ch. 638, CA, at 657 (constructive trust); *Coombes v Smith* [1986] 1 W.L.R. 808 at 821 (reliance, but not detriment, is presumed); *Stevens & Cutting Ltd v Anderson* [1990] 1 E.G.L.R. 95, CA, at 97.

[96] Above, para.3–55.

[97] *Bloomenthal v Ford* [1897] A.C. 156, HL, at 162, 168. *Cf.*, however, *George Whitechurch Ltd v Cavanagh*, above, n.79 at 145 (Lord Brampton: where representations are "induced by the concealment of any material fact on the part of those who seek to use them as such; and if the person to whom they are made knows something which, if revealed, would have been calculated to influence the

The consequences of the estoppel. Where an estoppel by representation is established, the legal relationship between the claimant and defendant is to be determined on the basis set out in the representation: that is, the claimant[98] can assert his rights and claim remedies only in so far as they are consistent with the facts as he represented them. In this sense, the party who relies on an estoppel by representation makes a very different use of the representation from the party who seeks positive remedies for misrepresentation of the several kinds discussed in earlier chapters of this book. Remedies for misrepresentation are sought by a party who shows that the statement was false; and that as a result he has suffered some consequence against which he seeks to be relieved: whether some form of loss or having entered into a contract he now regrets.[99] In a case of estoppel, however, the party does not rely on the falsity of the statement. Indeed, it is not an issue as to whether the statement was false: the estoppel precludes the enquiry into the truth of the statement, by preventing the other party from disputing the fact he represented. Rather, the defendant who relies on the claimant's statement of fact under the doctrine of estoppel by representation seeks to have his rights and obligations determined on the basis that the fact is true.[100] 10–27

Estoppel as a cause of action. Estoppel by representation is generally said to be a rule of evidence rather than of substantive law,[101] and as such it does not itself create a cause of action.[102] 10–28

---

other to hesitate or seek for further information before speaking positively, and that something has been withheld, the representation ought not to be treated as an estoppel").

98 Or a person whose claim is based on the claimant's own right, such as a trustee in bankruptcy who can claim no better title to property than the bankrupt where the bankrupt's representation related to his own title to the property: *Freeman v Cooke*, above, n.86.

99 Above, para.3–05.

100 *Low v Bouverie*, above, n.79 at 112 (Kay L.J.); *Burkinshaw v Nicolls* (1878) 3 App. Cas. 1004, HL, at 1026 (Lord Blackburn). For the relationship between estoppel by representation, which operates fully by reference to the facts as represented, and the defence of change of position, which operates *pro tanto*, see *National Westminster Bank Plc v Somer International (UK) Ltd* [2001] EWCA Civ 970, [2002] Q.B. 1286.

101 *Low v Bouverie*, above, n.79 at 101, 105, 112; *Evans v Bartlam* [1937] A.C. 473, HL, at 484; *National Westminster Bank Plc v Somer International (UK) Ltd*, above, n.100 at [36].

However, even if it is right to insist that estoppel is only a rule of evidence, it must be admitted that it has the effect of changing the basis on which the substantive legal rights can be determined as between the representor and the representee.[103] And some judges have resisted classifying estoppel as simply a rule of evidence.[104] It is also clear that some other forms of estoppel can be relied upon by claimants as the basis of a claim to the legal rights which the other party is estopped from denying, and therefore they can be said to give rise to a cause of action.[105] However, estoppel by representation is used defensively to resist the claim which is inconsistent with the facts as the claimant represented them.

---

102 *Seton, Laing & Co. v Lafone* above, n.84 at 70.

103 Estoppel "is hardly a rule of what is called substantive law in the sense of declaring an immediate right or claim. It is rather a rule of evidence, capable not the less on that account of affecting gravely substantive rights": *London Joint Stock Bank Ltd v Macmillan* [1918] A.C. 777, HL, at 818 (Viscount Haldane).

104 "Estoppel is often described as a rule of evidence, as, indeed, it may be so described. But the whole concept is more correctly viewed as a substantive rule of law": *Canada and Dominion Sugar Co. v Canadian National (West Indies) Steamships Ltd*, above, n.88 at 56; "Estoppel is not a rule of evidence. It is not a cause of action. It is a principle of justice and of equity": *Moorgate Mercantile Co. Ltd v Twitchings* [1976] Q.B. 225, CA, at 241 (Lord Denning M.R.).

105 Proprietary estoppel can be relied upon by the representee to claim the property rights he was led to believe he would be granted by the representor: *Crabb v Arun DC*, above, para.10–22, n.78. It is arguable whether estoppel by convention (under which both parties may be estopped from denying that their legal rights are to be determined on the basis of fact which they both assumed) in effect can create new substantive rights: Treitel, paras 3–094 to 3–099. Promissory estoppel "does not create new causes of action where none existed before. It only prevents a party from insisting on his strict legal rights": *Combe v Combe* [1951] 2 K.B. 215, CA, at 219 (Denning L.J.), although the High Court of Australia, reasoning from a unity of principle in the different forms of estoppel, has allowed promissory estoppel to give rise to a claim by a landlord to estop his prospective tenant from denying that he was bound to complete the lease, because it would be unconscionable for him to retreat from his implied promise to complete the contract: *Waltons Stores (Interstate) Ltd v Maher* (1988) 164 C.L.R. 387. The English courts have not unified the different forms of estoppel, and therefore estoppel by representation remains separate and is governed by its distinct rules: *National Westminster Bank Plc v Somer International (UK) Ltd*, above, n.100 at [38]–[39]; see also *Baird Textiles Holdings Ltd v Marks and Spencer Plc* [2001] EWCA Civ 274, [2002] 1 All E.R. (Comm) 737 at [35]–[38], [50]–[55], [83]–[85] (promissory estoppel).

CHAPTER 11

PRACTICE AND PROCEDURE RELATING TO CLAIMS FOR MISREPRESENTATION

I. CIVIL PROCEDURE RULES AND PRACTICE

The Civil Procedure Rules. The Civil Procedure Rules 1998[1] apply to most proceedings in county courts, the High Court and the Civil Division of the Court of Appeal commenced on or after April 26, 1999.[2] The Rules replace the rules formerly contained in the Rules of the Supreme Court 1965[3] and the County Court Rules 1981,[4] although some of those earlier rules are retained in schedules to the Civil Procedure Rules[5] and will apply within the overall framework of the new Rules until they are replaced by newly drafted provisions incorporated within the Civil Procedure Rules themselves.[6] **11–01**

---

[1] SI 1998/3132, as amended. Information on the CPR and up-to-date texts of the Rules and Practice Directions can be found on the website of the Ministry of Justice, *http://www.justice.gov.uk*.

[2] Certain proceedings, such as insolvency proceedings and family proceedings, are covered by other statutes: CPR r.2.1(2). There are transitional provisions for the conduct of proceedings already commenced before April 26, 1999: CPR Pt 51, PD 51.

[3] SI 1965/1776, as amended.

[4] SI 1981/1687, as amended.

[5] Sch.1 contains provisions taken from the RSC, Sch.2 from the CCR, in both cases sometimes with revisions from the original RSC/CCR forms.

[6] For example, the rules (in RSC, Ord.11 and CCR, Ord.8) relating to service out of the jurisdiction were at first revised and retained in Sch.1 to the CPR, but were removed with effect from May 2, 2000 when newly drafted provisions were inserted into CPR Pt 6 by Civil Procedure (Amendment) Rules 2000 (SI 2000/221).

11–02 **Civil practice and procedure.** This is not the place for a detailed discussion of the Civil Procedure Rules or indeed for a detailed discussion of practice and procedure, whether in the courts or in arbitration.[7] This section will simply discuss those Rules and the practice which are of particular relevance to a claim or defence based on misrepresentation. It will also proceed on the basis of the Rules in force at the time of writing, and will discuss earlier provisions, such as the Rules of the Supreme Court, only where they are still relevant to a discussion of the current rules, either because they are still in force within the schedules to the Civil Procedure Rules, or because the earlier provisions cast light on the current Rules.

II. PARTICULAR RULES AND PRACTICE RELEVANT TO MISREPRESENTATION CLAIMS AND DEFENCES

11–03 **Fraudulent misrepresentation.** It should be noted at the outset that the rules and practice relating to misrepresentation will sometimes vary according to whether or not the case involves a claim of fraud. For example, the rules governing the method of trial, the particularity required in the claim and issues of proof all contain distinctions which turn on whether the claim is based on fraudulent or non-fraudulent misrepresentation. However, rather than treating separately the rules and practice relating to fraud, the following paragraphs will discuss misrepresentation claims and defences generally, drawing attention where appropriate to distinctions drawn between cases of fraud and cases where the claim is based only on non-fraudulent misrepresentation.

11–04 **Jurisdiction and the allocation of cases to management tracks.** Under the Civil Procedure Rules the court allocates a claim to one of three management tracks—the "small claims track", the "fast track" and the "multi-track"—using criteria set out in the Rules but based on such things as the court's assessment of the value of the

[7] For the CPR, see *Civil Procedure* (the "White Book"; a new edition is published annually); I. Grainger and M. Fealy, *The Civil Procedure Rules in Action* (2nd edn, 2000); C. Plant (ed.), *Blackstone's Guide to the Civil Procedure Rules* (2nd edn, 1999); D. Greene, *The New Civil Procedure Rules* (1999). For civil procedure and practice generally, see also S. Sime and D. French (eds), *Blackstone's Civil Practice* (a new edition is published annually); D. Salter, P. Sycamore and C. Osborne (eds), *The Litigation Practice* (looseleaf).

claim and any counterclaim, and the complexity and nature of the case.[8] Cases on the small claims track[9] and the fast track[10] are heard in the county court.[11] Cases on the multi-track[12] may be heard in a county court or the High Court: generally claims with an estimated value of less than £50,000 are heard in a county court, but the High Court will be appropriate for certain types of claim, including those falling within specialist lists[13] or where there is a claim of professional negligence or fraud.[14] Misrepresentation claims, and cases where misrepresentation is raised as a defence, may therefore fall in any of the three tracks, depending upon the detail of the claim. But where it is alleged that the claim is based on fraudulent misrepresentation the High Court will normally hear the case on the multi-track procedure.[15]

Starting proceedings. The timing of the start of proceedings can be significant where the defendant seeks to rely on a defence of the expiry of a limitation period under the Limitation Act 1980[16]: the question will be whether the action was brought within the relevant limitation period. Proceedings are started when the court issues a claim form at the request of the claimant,[17] but where the claim 11–05

[8] CPR Pt 26.

[9] Normally claims not exceeding £5,000: CPR r.26.6(3). The detail of the procedure for the small claims track is contained in CPR Pt 27.

[10] Normally claims between £5,000 and £25,000 (or, for proceedings issued before 6 April 2009, £15,000), where the trial is likely to last no longer than one day and with limited expert evidence: CPR r.26.6(4),(5). The detail of the procedure for the fast track is contained in CPR Pt 28.

[11] *Civil Procedure 2011*, para.26.6.7. A claim form to be issued in the High Court must state that the claimant expects to recover more than £25,000: CPR r.16.3(5)(a); PD 16 para.2.1.

[12] Normally claims for which the small claims track or the fast track are not the normal track: CPR r.26.6(6).

[13] Such as commercial and mercantile actions (heard in the Commercial Court of the Queen's Bench Division or a Mercantile Court: CPR Pts 58 and 59) and technically complex cases (allocated to the Technology and Construction Court: CPR Pt 60).

[14] CPR PD 29, paras 2.2, 2.6(1), (3).

[15] Cases involving disputed allegations of dishonesty will not usually be suitable for the small claims track: CPR PD 26, para.8.1(1)(d).

[16] For limitation periods in relation to particular claims, see above, paras 5–34 (deceit), 6–50 (negligence), 7–28 (Misrepresentation Act 1967 s. 2(1)), 7–61 (Services and Markets Act 2000 s.90), 8–21 (contract).

[17] CPR r.7.2(1). For rules for service of the claim form, see r.7.5.

form was received in the court office earlier than the date on which it was issued by the court, the claim is "brought" for the purposes of the Limitation Act on that earlier date.[18]

11–06 **Cases with a foreign element: service out of the jurisdiction.**[19] Where the defendant is outside the jurisdiction, the claimant in some cases has the right to serve his claim form without the court's permission,[20] but in other cases must first obtain permission. The grounds on which permission may be given[21] include that the claim is made "in respect of a contract" where the contract was made within the jurisdiction or by or through an agent trading or residing within the jurisdiction, or is governed by English law, or contains a term to the effect that the court shall have jurisdiction to determine any claim in respect of the contract[22]; or the claim is made in

[18] CPR PD 7A, para.5.1.

[19] CPR Pt 6, s.IV. See also PD 6B. For further details on jurisdiction of the English courts, see Lord Collins of Mapesbury (ed.), *Dicey, Morris and Collins on the Conflict of Laws* (14th edn, 2006), Ch.11 (with cumulative supplements, which reflect the new CPR Pt 6, substituted by SI 2008/2178); A. Briggs and P. Rees, *Civil Jurisdiction and Judgments* (5th edn, 2009); *Civil Procedure* (the "White Book") paras 6.33.1 to 6.33.30, esp. paras 6.33.13 (matters relating to a contract) and 6.33.14 (matters relating to tort). For the broader question of the conflict of laws in cases involving misrepresentation, see the relevant chapters of *Dicey, Morris and Collins* (esp. Ch.32, Contracts; Ch.35, Torts).

[20] CPR r.6.33; in particular, where the case is one in respect of which the court has (pursuant to the Civil Jurisdiction and Judgments Acts 1982 and 1991) jurisdiction under the Brussels or Lugano Conventions and the defendant is domiciled in the UK or in a state to which the Brussels or Lugano Conventions apply; or where the court has jurisdiction under the Judgments Regulation (Council Regulation (EC) No. 44/2001 of 22 December 2000 on jurisdiction and the recognition and enforcement of judgments in civil and commercial matters) and the defendant is domiciled in the UK or any other Member State; or where the case is one in respect of which the court has jurisdiction under any other enactment although the defendant is not within the jurisdiction or the facts giving rise to the claim did not occur within the jurisdiction.

[21] Application is made under CPR r.6.36, and PD 6B, which sets out in para.3.1 the heads of jurisdiction for which permission may be given.

[22] CPR PD 6B, para.3.1(6). A jurisdiction clause, like an arbitration clause (below, para.11–20), is a separable agreement from the agreement as a whole, and disputes about the validity of the contract must be resolved under the terms of the clause, unless the jurisdiction clause is itself under some specific attack (e.g. fraud alleged in relation specifically to the clause, or (perhaps) if the signatures to the agreement were alleged to be forgeries), but not merely if there is a plausible allegation that the contract in which the clause is contained is vitiated by mistake,

respect of a breach of contract committed within the jurisdiction[23]; or the claim is made for a declaration that no contract exists[24]; or the claim is made in tort where the damage was sustained within the jurisdiction or resulted from an act committed within the jurisdiction[25]; or the claim is for restitution where the defendant's alleged liability arises out of acts committed within the jurisdiction.[26] Taken together these grounds will generally provide sufficient basis for application to serve the claim form out of the jurisdiction in cases of misrepresentation, although the appropriate ground will vary according to the remedy sought: whether it is a claim "in respect of a contract" for rescission of the contract or for damages under the contract; or in tort.[27]

---

misrepresentation, illegality, lack of authority or lack of capacity: *Deutsche Bank AG v Asia Pacific Broadband Wireless Communications Inc.* [2008] EWCA Civ 1091, [2008] 2 C.L.C. 520 at [24], [29].

23 CPR PD 6B, para.3.1(7).

24 CPR PD 6B, para.3.1(8). This provision did not appear in the predecessors to CPR Pt 6 (RSC, Ord.11 and CCR, Ord.8). It will however not normally apply to claims of misrepresentation, since the contract is generally at most voidable, not void: above, para.4–05. However, it could apply where the claim is that the misrepresentation gave rise to a mistake which rendered the contract void *ab initio* (above, para.1–03; below, para.12–19); or, perhaps, where the claimant has already rescinded by notice to the defendant (above, para.4–18) and seeks a declaration that his rescission was effective—i.e., that "no contract [now] exists"—although such a claim can in any event be brought within the very wide wording of para.3.1(6) ("in respect of a contract"); below, n.27.

25 CPR PD 6B, para.3.1(9); *Metall und Rohstoff AG v Donaldson, Rufkin & Jenrette Inc.* [1990] 1 Q.B. 391 at 437 (on identical language in the earlier provision, RSC, Ord.11, r.1(1)(f): the court must "look at the tort alleged in a common sense way and ask whether damage has resulted from substantial and efficacious acts committed within the jurisdiction"); *Domicrest Ltd v Swiss Bank Corp.* [1999] Q.B. 548 at 567 (Rix J.: "the place where the harmful event giving rise to the damage occurs in a case of negligent mis-statement is, by analogy with the tort of defamation, where the mis-statement originates", rather than where it is received); followed in *Alfred Dunhill v Diffusion Internationale Moroquinerie De Prestige SARL* [2002] 1 All E.R. (Comm) 950 and *Newsat Holdings Ltd v Zani* [2006] EWHC 342 (Comm), [2006] 1 Lloyd's Rep. 707.

26 CPR PD 6B, para.3.1(16). However, where restitution is sought following rescission of a contract for misrepresentation, it ought to be sufficient to rely on the very wide wording of para.3.1(6) (that the claim is still one "in respect of a contract").

27 A claim to avoid a contract for misrepresentation (i.e. for rescission) is a claim "in respect of a contract": *cf. Agnew v Länsförsäkringsbolagens AB* [2001] 1 A.C. 223, where the HL thought it obvious that an action to avoid a contract for

11–07 **The claim.** The general rule is that the claimant must include in his particulars of claim a concise statement of the facts on which he relies[28] and, where the claim is for money, a statement of the value of the claim.[29] He must also specifically set out any allegation of fraud and the details of any misrepresentation on which he wishes to rely,[30] and he may refer to any point of law on which his claim is based.[31] In a claim based on misrepresentation, therefore, the claimant must include in his particulars the elements necessary to establish the claim to the remedy he seeks. In all cases this will include the details of the relevant misrepresentation[32] and, because this is generally a requirement of the remedies for misrepresentation,[33] any facts necessary to show his reliance on the misrepresentation. If the claim is for damages, whether in tort or under the Misrepresentation Act 1967 or for breach of contract, he

---

misrepresentation or non-disclosure is a matter "relating to a contract" for the purposes of Art.5(1) of the Lugano Convention: see at 239, 246, 252–253 and 262. For the purposes of the Brussels Convention, a claim for damages under the Misrepresentation Act 1967 s.2(1), or at common law for negligent misrepresentation inducing a contract, is a matter relating to tort (within Art.5(3)) and not a matter relating to a contract (within Art.5(1)): *Alfred Dunhill Ltd v Diffusion Internationale de Maroquinerie de Prestige SARL*, above, n.25; *cf.*, however, *Strachan & Henshaw Ltd v Stein Industrie (UK) Ltd* (1997) 63 Con. L.R. 160 at 168, CA (claim under s.2(1) is a claim "in connection with" a contract within the meaning of an exemption clause in a contract). Note, however, that CPR PD 6B, para.3.1(20) allows for a claim under an enactment which allows proceedings to be brought and those proceedings are not covered by any of the other grounds referred to.

[28] CPR r.16.4(1)(a). If he claims interest, or aggravated or exemplary damages, he must also include a statement to that effect: r.16.4(1)(b), (c). For the question of when exemplary damages are recoverable in deceit, see above, para.5–42; *cf.* above, paras 6–61, n.377 (negligence), 7–42 (Misrepresentation Act 1967 s.2(1)).

[29] CPR r.16.3(2).

[30] CPR PD 16, para.8.2.

[31] CPR PD 16, para.13.3.

[32] *Newport (Mon.) Slipway Dry Dock and Engineering Co. v Paynter* (1887) 34 Ch.D. 88, CA; *Seligmann v Young* [1884] W.N. 93 (Field J. affirmed Master's order that plaintiff give particulars of the "nature of the [alleged] false and fraudulent representation, and whether oral or in writing and when and where made"); *Smith v Chadwick* (1884) 9 App. Cas. 187, HL (ambiguity in meaning of statement).

[33] Above, Ch.3.

must include a sufficient case as to the loss he has suffered which is recoverable under the particular head of damages he claims.[34]

The courts are particularly demanding in the requirement that fraud be clearly and sufficiently particularised in the claim if it is to be relied on.[35] Full and specific details must be given of any allegation of fraud or dishonesty, and where an inference of fraud or dishonesty is alleged, the facts on the basis of which the inference is alleged must be listed in the statement of case.[36] And if a party is

---

[34] *SX Holdings Ltd v Synchronet Ltd* [2001] C.P. Rep. 43, CA (case on damages in deceit insufficiently pleaded, but permission given under CPR for amendment to statement of case). See also, on the rules applicable before the CPR, *Smith New Court Securities Ltd v Scrimgeour Vickers (Asset Management) Ltd* [1997] A.C. 254, HL, at 268. For the different measures of loss in contract, deceit and negligence, see above, paras 2–07 to 2–10.

[35] *Bradford Third Equitable Benefit Building Society v Borders* [1941] 2 All E.R. 205 at 218, HL; *Garden Neptune Shipping Ltd v Occidental Worldwide Investment Corp.* [1989] 1 Lloyd's Rep. 305 at 308. It is not necessary to use the word "fraud" in the claim if it is sufficiently clear and unambiguous that fraud is alleged: *Davy v Garrett* (1878) 7 Ch.D. 473, CA, at 489.

[36] Queen's Bench Guide 2007, para.5.6.3; Chancery Guide 2009, para.2.8; Admiralty & Commercial Courts Guide 2011, para.C1.2(c). A general allegation of fraud has never been sufficient: *Wallingford v Mutual Society* (1880) 5 App. Cas. 685, HL, at 697, 701, 705, 709. Old cases which had held that, in a claim against a principal for the fraud of his agent or employee, it was sufficient to plead the fraud as being that of the principal, may not satisfy this rule: *Barwick v English Joint Stock Bank* (1867) L.R. 2 Exch. 259 at 266 (but Spencer Bower (Misrepresentation), para.387 assumes that *Barwick* still applies). Under the Code of Conduct of the Bar (8th edn, 2004), s.704, a practising barrister must not draft any statement of case or other document containing an allegation of fraud unless he has clear instructions to make such allegation and has before him reasonably credible material which as it stands establishes a prima facie case of fraud. A barrister who drafts an allegation of fraud in breach of this requirement may be personally liable to either his own party or to the opposing party for wasted costs. At the hearing, counsel cannot properly make or persist in an allegation unsupported by admissible evidence, but where the allegation is made at the preparatory stage of proceedings it is sufficient if the material before him is of such a character as to lead responsible counsel to conclude that serious allegations could be based upon it: *Medcalf v Mardell* [2002] UKHL 27, [2003] 1 A.C. 120; *Brown v Bennett (No.1)* [2002] 1 W.L.R. 713. The wasted costs jurisdiction applies to all legal representatives, not only barristers: Senior Courts Act 1981 s.51 (substituted by the Courts and Legal Services Act 1990 s.4(1)) and CPR r.48.7. Under CPR Pt 22, there is a requirement that certain documents, including every statement of case and amendments to the statement of case, be verified by a statement of truth signed by the party or his legal representative. See also *Black v Sumitomo Corp.* [2001] EWCA Civ 1819, [2002] 1 W.L.R. 1562 at

accused of fraud, and is called as a witness, the particular fraud alleged must be put specifically so that the witness may answer it.[37] If, however, an allegation of fraud is not sufficiently made it is not fatal to the claimant's case if he can obtain the remedy he seeks without reliance on the fraud: for example, a claim for damages under s.2(1) of the Misrepresentation Act 1967 is for damages on the deceit measure and requires proof of the elements of deceit *except* for fraud.[38] Similarly, if fraud is alleged but not proved, the claimant may still obtain a remedy on another ground which is established without proof of fraud,[39] but only if the claim is sufficiently clearly made and, where the alternative remedy is sought only on appeal, where the case was so argued at first instance.[40]

11–08 **Alternative claims.** Given the range of remedies for misrepresentation, the claimant often has a choice of remedies he might be able to pursue[41]; and he may wish to make claims for remedies in the alternative because before trial it may not be clear to which remedy or remedies he will be able to establish a successful claim. He may include alternative claims in his particulars of claim, even if the alternatives depend on inconsistent facts: he must verify his statement of case by a statement of truth[42] but alternative claims, based on alternative sets of facts, can still be made as long as the claimant is not asserting that he believes that both sets of facts are

---

[54], [57] (court to exercise caution in ordering pre-action disclosure in fraud cases, even where counsel claims disclosure necessary to enable him to sign statement of case).

37 *Haringey LBC v Hines* [2010] EWCA Civ 1111, [2011] H.L.R. 6 at [39]; *Abbey Forwarding Ltd v Hone* [2010] EWHC 2029 (Ch), [2010] All E.R. (D) 24 (Aug) at [47].

38 Above, para.7–16. *Thompson v Sayed Ali*, unreported, March 21, 1994, CA (judge found fraud although not pleaded by claimant; but his decision stood on appeal since the claimant had made out the elements of his claim under the Misrepresentation Act 1967 s.2(1)); *Garden Neptune Shipping Ltd v Occidental Worldwide Investment Corp.* [1990] 1 Lloyd's Rep. 330, CA.

39 *Nocton v Lord Asburton* [1914] A.C. 932, HL.

40 *Connecticut Fire Insurance Co.v Kavanagh* [1892] A.C. 473, PC; *Haringey LBC v Hines*, above, n.37 at [58] (no finding by trial judge on any innocent mispresentation case, and no opportunity for a factual investigation as to whether the proviso to s.2(1) Misrepresentation Act 1967 might be in point).

41 Above, para.2–11.

42 Above, n.36.

true, and is merely affirming his honest belief that on either one set of facts or the other his case is made out.[43]

Counterclaims and raising misrepresentation as a defence. 11–09
Where a defendant raises a misrepresentation by way of *counterclaim* against the claimant, the counterclaim is treated for most purposes of the Civil Procedure Rules as if it were a claim.[44] In a *defence* the defendant must state which of the allegations in the particulars of claim he denies, and give his reasons for doing so[45]: where, therefore, the defendant wishes to raise a misrepresentation by way of defence[46] he must include in his defence particulars of the misrepresentation. As in all cases of allegations of fraud, if the defendant seeks to show that the claimant made a fraudulent misrepresentation, he must make a clear and particularised allegation of fraud in his defence.[47]

Amendment to statements of case. If the statement of case has 11–10
been served, it may be amended only with the written consent of all the other parties, or with the permission of the court.[48] In deciding whether to give permission the court will have regard to the

[43] *Clarke v Marlborough Fine Art (London) Ltd* [2002] 1 W.L.R. 1731. A unified claim which would result in the claimant making inconsistent statements of truth is not possible: *ibid. Cf. Binks v Securicor Omega Express Ltd* [2003] EWCA Civ 993, [2003] 1 W.L.R. 2557 at [8]; *Bleasdale v Forster* [2011] EWHC 596 (Ch), [2011] All E.R. (D) 18 (Mar) at [26] (it is possible for claimant to advance a claim in misrepresentation where the primary case is that the representation in question was never made to him).

[44] CPR r.20.3 (a counterclaim is an "additional claim": *ibid.*, r.20(2)). The requirements for the particulars of claim, above, para.11–07, therefore apply *mutatis mutandis*. For the case where the court gives judgment for specified amounts (e.g. damages) both for the claimant on his claim and against the claimant on a counterclaim, see CPR r.40.13.

[45] CPR r.16.5. Or he may admit allegations, or state which allegations he is unable to admit or deny but which he requires the claimant to prove. If he fails to deal with an allegation, he is taken to admit it. For the claimant's *reply* to the defence, see CPR r.16.7.

[46] Above, Ch.10. For the raising of misrepresentation as a defence to an application for summary judgment in respect of a call under a letter of credit, see *Safa Ltd v Banque du Caire* [2000] 2 Lloyd's Rep. 600, CA.

[47] *Bailey v Munro* [1953] N.Z.L.R. 577; Queen's Bench Guide, para.5.6.3; Chancery Guide, para.2.8; Admiralty & Commercial Courts Guide, para.C1.2.(c); above, para.11–07, n.36.

[48] CPR r.17.1.

overriding objective of the Civil Procedure Rules,[49] but where the limitation period has expired it may allow an amendment whose effect will be to add or substitute a new claim only if the new claim arises out of the same facts or substantially the same facts as a claim in respect of which the party applying for permission has already claimed a remedy in the proceedings.[50] This will depend on a close analysis of the statement of case and the amendment sought. Where, as often in a case involving misrepresentation or non-disclosure, the original claim was based on a breach of duty in contract or in tort, the question whether an amendment raises a new cause of action requires comparison with the unamended claim to determine (a) whether a different duty is alleged; (b) whether the breaches alleged differ substantially and, where appropriate, (c) the nature and extent of the damage of which complaint is made.[51] But if a party relies on

---

[49] CPR Pt.1; *SX Holdings Ltd v Synchronet Ltd* [2001] C.P. Rep. 43, CA (claimant given permission, on terms as to costs and payment of sum into court, to amend statement of claim to plead case on damages recoverable in deceit and defendant's liability as joint tortfeasor for procuring and inducing company to make false representations). However, where the application is to introduce a claim of fraud the court may refuse permission if the application is made only at a late stage, such as during an appeal following trial: *SX Holdings Ltd v Synchronet Ltd*at [26] (permission granted); *Standard Chartered Bank v Pakistan National Shipping Corp. (No.2)* [2000] 1 Lloyd's Rep. 218, CA (permission refused). Before the CPR it was already established that an amendment alleging fraud should be allowed in an appellate court only if the defendant has had the opportunity of defending himself, not only by the arguments of his counsel on appeal, but by giving evidence in his own defence specially directed to the charge made in the amendment: *Bradford Third Equitable Benefit Building Society v Borders* [1941] 2 All E.R. 205, HL, at 218–219.

[50] CPR r.17.4(2); Limitation Act 1980, s.35(4),(5). Before the introduction of the CPR a similar rule, also based on the Limitation Act 1980, s.35, was contained in RSC, Ord.20, r.5. and CCR, Ord.15, r.3.

[51] *Darlington Building Society v O'Rourke, James Scourfield & McCarthy* [1999] Lloyd's Rep. P.N. 33, CA (claim alleging breach of duty and negligence against solicitors in mortgage transaction; permission refused to amend to include different breaches of duty based on solicitors' failure to disclose knowledge of borrowers' fraud). For further examples, see *Hydrocarbons Great Britain Ltd v Cammell Laird Shipbuilders Ltd* (1991) 58 B.L.R. 123 (claim against party who inspected and certified component parts of hydraulic cylinders later found to be defective was pleaded as claim for damages for negligent act: amendment to introduce new cause of action based on negligent misstatement under principles of *Hedley Byrne & Co. Ltd v Heller & Partners Ltd* [1964] A.C. 465, HL, was based on different facts and so was refused); *Brickfield Properties Ltd v Newton* [1971] 1 W.L.R. 862, CA (original claim against architect for negligent

two different and distinct representations in entering into a contract, he will normally have two different causes of action, because the success of each claim, and the remedy available for each, may differ.[52] And a claim based on fraud is a different cause of action from a claim based on negligence.[53] The introduction of a claim based on a different representation, or the introduction of an allegation of fraud, is therefore normally not possible after the expiry of the limitation period where the relevant facts have not already been included in the statement of case.

Burden and standard of proof. The remedies discussed in detail in this book are all remedies for civil actions, whether the action is for rescission of the contract, or for damages in tort or for breach of contract, or under statute. The normal rules of civil law actions therefore govern the burden and standard of proof in all such cases: it is for each party to prove any issue which forms an essential part of his case—that is, broadly, the claimant must prove the elements of his claim on the balance of probabilities, and the defendant must prove any particular or general defence on which he relies to defeat the claim. And where the defendant seeks to rely on a misrepresentation as a defence, it is for him to establish the defence on the balance of probabilities.[54] For each of the remedies the elements of **11–11**

---

superintendence of building works: new claim for negligence in design allowed because "the facts relating to design, execution and superintendence are inextricably entangled until such time as the court succeeds in elucidating the position through evidence": Sachs L.J. at 873); *Howe v David Brown (Tractors) Ltd* [1991] 4 All E.R. 30, CA (amendment allowed to introduce claim for breach of contract where the claim arose substantially from facts already pleaded in relation to claim in negligence); A. McGee, *Limitation Periods* (6th edn, 2010), Chs 22 and 23.

[52] *Government of Zanzibar v British Aerospace (Lancaster House) Ltd* [2000] 1 W.L.R. 2333 at 2350. But this is not the case where, although a new instance of non-disclosure is sought to be pleaded, it is not to allege a new cause of action but is simply a further instance or particular of the breach of a warranty that full disclosure has been made: *Savings and Investment Bank Ltd v Fincken* [2001] EWCA Civ 1639, *The Times*, November 15, 2001.

[53] *Paragon Finance Plc v D.B. Thakerar & Co.* [1999] 1 All E.R. 400, CA (whether the allegation of fraud is for the purposes of a common law claim in deceit, or for an equitable remedy which is the counterpart under the concurrent equitable jurisdiction of a claim at law).

[54] Phipson, paras 6.06, 6.08, 6.54. Similarly, a defendant raising a misrepresentation as a counterclaim must discharge the burden of a claimant.

the claim and any particular or general defences to the claim have been set out in the relevant chapters.[55]

11–12 **Limitation of actions.** The defendant must include in his defence details of the expiry of any relevant limitation period on which he relies.[56] Once the issue is raised, the burden on a plaintiff is to show that, on the balance of probabilities, his cause of action accrued on a day within the period of limitation.[57] The expiry of a limitation period is relevant not only to the commencement of proceedings but also to any amendment to the particulars of claim. Where the limitation period has expired, the court may only allow an amendment whose effect will be to add or substitute a new claim if the new claim arises out of the same facts or substantially the same facts as a claim in respect of which the party applying for permission has already claimed a remedy in the proceedings.[58] The detail of the limitation periods applicable to the different misrepresentation claims have been considered in the relevant chapters.[59]

11–13 **Disclosure of documents.** The Civil Procedure Rules changed the rules on disclosure of documents,[60] with a view to changing the old

---

[55] For particular problems associated with proving reliance, see above, para.3–53; and for proof of fraud, see above, para.5–46.

[56] CPR PD 16, para.13.1.

[57] *London Congregational Union Inc v Harriss & Harriss* [1988] 1 All E.R. 15, CA, at 30. In a case (such as a claim in negligence) where the accrual depends on the claimant suffering actionable damage, and where the claimant has shown that relevant damage was suffered within the requisite period of limitation, the burden may then shift back to the defendant to adduce evidence to show that the apparent accrual within the limitation period was misleading: *ibid.* at 30, 34; *DnB Mortgages Ltd v Bullock & Lees* [2000] Lloyd's Rep. P.N. 290, CA; *Cartlege v E. Jopling & Sons Ltd* [1963] A.C. 758, HL, at 784.

[58] Above, para.11–10.

[59] Above, paras 5–34 (deceit); 6–50 (negligence); 7–28 (Misrepresentation Act 1967 s.2(1)), 7–61 (Financial Services and Markets Act 2000, s.90); 8–21 (breach of contract). There is no statutory limitation period for a claim to rescission for misrepresentation, but a claim may be barred by lapse of time: above, para.4–48.

[60] Note the wide meaning of "document": CPR r.31.4 ("anything in which information of any description is recorded") which includes informal communications, such as e mails (which can be difficult to erase effectively from a computer system), and personal notebooks.

practice of routine very extensive disclosure.[61] Accordingly, in most cases disclosure is to be limited to "standard disclosure": the disclosure of documents which are or have been in that party's control[62] on which the party relies, and those which adversely affect his own or another party's case or support another party's case, or which are required by a relevant practice direction to be disclosed.[63] However, a court may order "specific disclosure" which will be more extensive than standard disclosure.[64]

Method of trial. The remedies discussed in detail in this book are all remedies sought in civil actions. The normal method of civil trial by judge alone, without a jury, is therefore appropriate in most cases.[65] However, claims in the tort of deceit in the Queen's Bench Division or a county court are heard by judge and jury unless the court orders trial by judge alone.[66] **11–14**

Multiple claimants. Where a number of claimants have similar claims arising out of a single misrepresentation, they may bring their claims separately or, where the claims can be conveniently disposed of in the same proceedings,[67] together. Where claims are brought together, each claimant must still establish the elements of his own claim and meet any defences raised against him, although the fact that the claims are heard together will save time and effort. **11–15**

---

[61] "Discovery", in the pre-CPR terminology. See I. Grainger and M. Fealy, *The Civil Procedure Rules in Action* (2nd edn, 2000), Ch.17; S. Sime and D. French (eds), *Blackstone's Civil Practice 2011*, Ch.48.

[62] CPR r.31.8.

[63] CPR rr.31.5, 31.6. The party is required to make a reasonable search for such documents: *ibid.*, r.31.7.

[64] CPR r.31.12. For *pre-action* disclosure, see the Senior Courts Act 1981 s.33(2); CPR r.31.16; *Black v Sumitomo Corp.* [2001] EWCA Civ 1819, [2002] 1 W.L.R. 1562.

[65] Although there is a power for the court to order trial by jury in civil cases in either the Queen's Bench Division of the High Court (Supreme Court Act 1981, s.69(3)) or a county court (County Courts Act 1984, s.66(2)), it is not normally exercised: *H. v Ministry of Defence* [1991] 2 Q.B. 103, CA.

[66] Above, para.5–48.

[67] CPR r.7.3. The former RSC, Ord.15, r.4 contained more detailed provisions for joinder of two or more persons as plaintiffs or defendants with leave of the court. For an example of a single action by multiple claimants, see *Arnison v Smith* (1889) 41 Ch.D. 348, CA (54 claimants, each of whom claimed to have relied on misrepresentations in company's prospectus in subscribing for debenture stock).

In practice, all the claims will involve some identical issues, such as proving the misrepresentation and, where relevant to the claims brought, the defendant's state of mind.[68]

It is also sometimes possible for a representative party to bring a claim on behalf of others who have the same interest in the claim.[69] This has been interpreted as extending to cases where a number of persons have a common grievance, and seek similar relief.[70] Where the claims have some elements which cannot be disposed of in a representative action, such as proof of reliance on the misrepresentation by each separate claimant,[71] it may still be possible for the representative to seek declaratory relief as to the elements which are common to the several claims.[72] In the context of misrepresentation this will mean that a representative action cannot be brought for rescission or damages on behalf of all those who claim separately to have relied on the defendant's misrepresentation, but it might be possible for a representative action to deal with common elements of the claims, such as establishing the meaning of the representation and its falsity, and the defendant's state of mind.

Another method of proceeding, in the case of multiple actions against the same defendant raising the same issues, is for one action to be selected as a "test" case and the other proceedings stayed pending the outcome of that case.[73]

---

68 This will be relevant in claims where the defendant's fraud or negligence is in issue, as well as in the question of whether the defendant can establish the statutory defence to a claim under the Misrepresentation Act 1967 s.2(1). Some issues will naturally vary between claims, such as the quantum of damage suffered by each claimant, and whether each claimant can be shown to have relied on the misrepresentation, although often there will also be common issues of principle even in these elements of the claims.

69 CPR r.19.6, replacing similar provisions in RSC, Ord.15, r.12 and CCR, Ord.5, r.5. For group litigation, see CPR rr.19.10–19.15.

70 *Duke of Bedford v Ellis* [1901] A.C. 1, HL, at 8.

71 *Lord Churchill v Whetnall* (1918) 87 L.J. Ch. 524 at 526.

72 *Prudential Assurance Co. Ltd v Newman Industries Ltd* [1981] Ch. 229 at 254–255 (although the representative may himself obtain substantive judgment on his own claim: *ibid.*).

73 See, e.g. *Amos v Chadwick* (1877) 4 Ch.D. 869. In such a case the decision in the test case is not binding on the parties in the other actions, but it will in practice provide a basis for settling the other actions without further protracted litigation. A judgment or order in a representative action or in group litigation (above, n.69) can however be binding on the parties to the other claims: CPR rr.19.6(4), 19.12.

Multiple defendants. A single claim form may include claims against a number of defendants,[74] even though different relief may be sought against different defendants: for example, a claim against a company and its directors for misrepresentations in a prospectus, where the claim against the directors is only for damages but the claim against the company is also for rescission of the allotment of shares.[75] **11–16**

Summary judgment. Under Pt 24 of the Civil Procedure Rules the court has wide powers to decide a claim or a particular issue without a full trial: the court may give summary judgment against a claimant or a defendant if it considers that the claimant has no real prospect of succeeding on the claim or issue, or that the defendant has no real prospect of successfully defending the claim or issue, and there is no other compelling reason why the case or issue should be disposed of at a trial.[76] The courts may now be more willing to grant summary judgment than under the provisions which the Rules replaced.[77] However, the courts' reluctance to decide without a full trial certain issues which commonly arise in misrepresentation actions may still survive into the procedure to be followed under the new Rules. In particular, it may be relatively rare that a court will be prepared to give summary judgment against a defendant on a claim of fraud.[78] It was also held under the old **11–17**

[74] As with multiple claimants, the basic test is whether the claims can be conveniently disposed of in the same proceedings: r.7.3.

[75] *Frankenburg v Great Horseless Carriage Co.* [1900] 1 K.B. 504, CA.

[76] CPR r.24.2. For a discussion of the relevant principles, see *Doncaster Pharmaceuticals Group Ltd v Bolton Pharmaceutical Co. 100 Ltd* [2006] EWCA Civ 661, [2007] F.S.R. 63 at [10]–[18]; *Easyair Ltd v Opal Telecom Ltd* [2009] EWHC 339 (Ch), [2009] All E.R. (D) 13 (Mar) at [15]; *A.C. Ward & Son v Catlin (Five) Ltd* [2009] EWCA Civ 1098, [2010] Lloyd's Rep. I.R. 301 at [24]; *Mentmore International Ltd v Abbey Healthcare (Festival) Ltd* [2010] EWCA Civ 761, [2010] All E.R. (D) 62 (Jul) at [20]–[23], applied to the context of misrepresentation in *Bleasdale v Forster* [2011] EWHC 416 (Ch), [2011] All E.R. (D) 34 (Mar) at [22]–[24].

[77] In particular, RSC, Ord.14 and 14A: see I. Grainger and M. Fealy, *The Civil Procedure Rules in Action*, above, n.7, Ch.15; S. Sime and D. French (eds), *Blackstone's Civil Practice 2011*, above, n.7, Ch.34.

[78] A court had power to give summary judgment on a claim of fraud under RSC, Ord.14 after the amendment to Ord.14 by SI 1992/638, and there is similarly now nothing in CPR Pt.24, to exclude summary judgment on a claim of fraud. However, there will surely have to be strong and very clear evidence of fraud before summary judgment will be given, particularly since in the Queen's Bench

rules that, where a defendant claimed that a notice he had inserted into sale particulars prevented his statements constituting misrepresentations, or being relied on, the court could not decide the issue without trial: one cannot determine whether there has been a misrepresentation inducing a contract without ascertaining all the facts.[79] Where the case requires a detailed examination of voluminous documentation and oral evidence to determine whether misrepresentations were made and, if so, their content, relevance and effect, summary judgment is not appropriate.[80] And the court cannot normally decide whether a clause which seeks to exclude or limit liability for misrepresentation is fair and reasonable without hearing full evidence: this is a broad issue which can only be dealt with at trial.[81] Where, however, there is an issue of construction of a clause—such as an "entire agreement" clause—or any other issue

---

Division or a county court a claim of fraud is normally tried by jury unless the court otherwise orders: above, para.11–14. For a case where the CA refused summary judgment because there were allegations of fraud, see *Fashion Gossip Ltd v Esprit Telecoms UK Ltd* [2000] All E.R. (D) 1090 ("where . . . there are allegations of fraud, there must be a firm foundation of fact and all the facts, every nuance, needs exploration and needs to be firmly established": Ward L.J.). However, if the other elements of the claim in deceit are made out, summary judgment may be given with damages to be assessed, even if the defence argues that there is no recoverable loss because the loss has been fully recouped or mitigated: such a claim goes only to the assessment of damages and not the cause of action: *4 Eng Ltd v Harper* [2007] EWHC 1568 (Ch) at [50]. Summary judgment was also entered for the claimant on a claim of fraud in *Cheshire Building Society v Dunlop Haywards (DHL) Ltd* [2008] EWHC 51 (Comm), [2008] P.N.L.R. 19. A court may more easily give summary judgment for a *defendant* on a claim of fraud, if the test in CPR r.24.2 is satisfied.

[79] *Cremdean Properties Ltd v Nash* (1977) 241 E.G. 837, affirmed [1977] E.G.D. 63.

[80] *Bleasdale v Forster*, above, n.76 at [26]–[27].

[81] *Garden Neptune Shipping Ltd v Occidental Worldwide Investment Corp.* [1989] 1 Lloyd's Rep. 305 at 335; *Killick v PricewaterhouseCoopers* [2001] 1 B.C.L.C. 65 at 72; *Daroga v Wells*, unreported, May 11, 1994, CA. *Cf.*, however, *Circuit Systems Ltd v Zuken-Redac (UK) Ltd* (1995) 42 Con. L.R. 120 (the Misrepresentation Act 1967 s.3 nullifies an exclusion and limitation clause unless it is shown by the defendant that it satisfies the requirement of reasonableness: defendant must therefore plead and prove that the clause is reasonable if he is to avoid judgment against himself). However, a clause which seeks to exclude set-off, if it is to be effective at all, can only take effect either upon an application for summary judgment or on the subsequent hearing of a preliminary point as to its reasonableness: *Stewart Gill Ltd v Horatio Myer & Co. Ltd* [1992] Q.B. 600, CA, at 604; *Skipskredittforeningen v Emperor Navigation* [1998] 1 Lloyd's Rep.

of law which goes to the heart of the case and can be decided on its own, then as a general rule the necessary steps should be taken under the Civil Procedure Rules to obtain an early and separate trial of that issue to minimise the time and cost spent on the case.[82]

Costs. In most respects the jurisdiction and practice relating to the award of costs in actions for misrepresentation is the same as in all civil cases.[83] However, there are certain particular rules where fraud is alleged: these have already been considered in the chapter on the tort of deceit.[84] **11–18**

Appeals.[85] An appeal court[86] has all the powers of the lower court, but in most cases an appeal is limited to a review of the decision of the lower court and the appeal will be allowed only where the decision of the lower court was wrong or unjust because of a serious procedural or other irregularity in the lower court.[87] This jurisdiction is more restricted than that which was in place before the Civil Procedure Rules; and second appeals are now intended to be available only in exceptional cases.[88] **11–19**

In misrepresentation cases the appeal court will have jurisdiction to review both the directions of law by the trial judge and his

---

66 at 77. For further detail on the reasonableness of exclusion and limitation clauses, see above, paras 9–24 to 9–29, 9–35.

82 *Inntrepreneur Pub Co.v East Crown Ltd* [2000] 3 E.G.L.R. 31 at 35.

83 CPR Pts 43–48; I. Grainger and M. Fealy, *The Civil Procedure Rules in Action*, above, n.7, Ch.24; S. Sime and D. French (eds), *Blackstone's Civil Practice 2011*, above, n.7, Chs 63–68.

84 Above, para.5–49.

85 CPR Pt 52.

86 Appeals may be to the High Court or the CA, depending on the jurisdiction of the decision appealed against, whether the decision was fast track or multi-track, and whether or not the appeal is against a final decision: see the Access to Justice Act 1999 (Destination of Appeals) Order 2000 (SI 2000/1071) as amended by SI 2003/490. For an explanation of the new provisions relating to appeals, see *Tanfern Ltd v Cameron-MacDonald* [2000] 1 W.L.R. 1311, CA; *Lloyd Jones v T-Mobile (UK) Ltd* [2003] EWCA Civ 1162, [2003] 3 E.G.L.R. 55; *Scribes West Ltd v Relsa Anstalt (Practice Note)* [2004] EWCA Civ 965, [2005] 1 W.L.R. 1839.

87 CPR Pt 52, r.52.10, 11.

88 Access to Justice Act 1999, s.55: second-level appeal to the CA is only possible where the CA considers that the appeal would raise an important point of principle or practice, or there is some other compelling reason for the CA to hear it. See also *Tanfern Ltd v Cameron-MacDonald*, above, n.86 at 1319–1320.

findings of fact[89]; this therefore includes such issues of fact as whether the representee relied on the statement,[90] and whether the representor was fraudulent. However, even before the recent changes to the procedure relating to appeals, the Court of Appeal was very reluctant to disturb the findings of the trial judge, and would do so only if convinced that the judge's conclusion from the evidence presented to him was wrong. It is not sufficient for the Court of Appeal to have doubts as to the correctness of the judge's decision.[91] This reluctance to intervene is particularly strong when the issue is whether the defendant was fraudulent and where the defendant himself gave oral evidence at the trial; and where the trial judge acquitted the defendant of fraud.[92]

Similarly, whilst the Supreme Court also has undoubted jurisdiction to review findings of fact, it is particularly reluctant to disturb concurrent findings of fact—where the Court of Appeal reviewed but upheld the judge's finding.[93]

11–20 **Arbitration.**[94] A claim based on misrepresentation may be determined in arbitration, rather than in the courts, where the claim falls within the scope of the parties' agreement to arbitrate.[95] This depends on the construction of the arbitration clause. Until recently,

---

89 *Smith v Chadwick* (1884) 9 App. Cas. 187, HL, at 193–194 (Lord Blackburn, discussing the jurisdiction of an appeal court in a case of deceit to disturb findings of a jury, or of a judge sitting without a jury).

90 *Barton v County Natwest Ltd* [1999] Lloyd's Rep. Bank. 408, CA; *Assicurazioni Generali SpA v Arab Insurance Group* [2002] EWCA Civ 1642, [2003] 1 All E.R. (Comm) 140; *Peekay Intermark Ltd v Australia and New Zealand Banking Group Ltd* [2006] EWCA Civ 386, [2006] 1 C.L.C. 582 at [49]–[53].

91 *Smith New Court Securities Ltd v Scrimgeour Vickers (Asset Management) Ltd* [1997] A.C. 254, HL, at 274–275.

92 *Akerhielm v De Mare* [1959] A.C. 789, PC, at 806; *Armstrong v Strain* [1952] 1 K.B. 232, CA, at 241 (Singleton L.J.); *Henry Ansbacher & Co. Ltd v Binks Stern* [1998] P.N.L.R. 221, CA (where, however, the trial judge's decision that the defendant was not fraudulent was reversed).

93 *Smith New Court Securities Ltd v Scrimgeour Vickers (Asset Management) Ltd*, above, n.91 at 275. The appeal jurisdiction formerly exercised by the Appellate Committee of the House of Lords was taken over by the Supreme Court on 1 October 2009 by the Constitutional Reform Act 2005 s.40, Sch.9.

94 For rules of procedure governing applications to the court relating to "arbitration claims" see CPR Pt 62.

95 M.J. Mustill & S.C. Boyd, *Commercial Arbitration* (2nd edn, 1989), pp.112–113.

the courts had recognised subtle nuances in the interpretation of arbitration clauses, which had led them to conclude that a clause submitting to arbitration disputes arising "in connection with" a contract covered claims for damages in tort or under s.2 of the Misrepresentation Act 1967 in respect of misrepresentations which induced the contract,[96] whereas a clause which provided for arbitration of disputes "arising under" a contract was not wide enough to include disputes which do not concern obligations created by or incorporated in that contract, and therefore did not extend to claims in negligence or under the Misrepresentation Act based on pre-contractual misrepresentations, nor did it cover claims under a collateral contract.[97] However, the House of Lords has now rejected such fine distinctions:[98]

> "the construction of an arbitration clause should start from the assumption that the parties, as rational businessmen, are likely to have intended any dispute arising out of the relationship into which they have entered or purported to enter to be decided by the same tribunal. The clause should be construed in accordance with this presumption unless the language makes it clear that certain questions were intended to be excluded from the arbitrator's jurisdiction."

---

[96] *Ashville Investments Ltd v Elmer Contractors Ltd* [1989] Q.B. 488, CA, at 499, 504–505 and 515, not following dicta in *Blue Circle Industries Plc v Holland Dredging Co. (UK) Ltd* (1987) 37 B.L.R. 40, CA, and in *Monro v Bogdanor Urban DC* [1915] 3 K.B. 167, CA. See also *Strachan & Henshaw Ltd v Stein Industrie (UK) Ltd*, above, para.11–06, n.27 at 168 (claim under the Misrepresentation Act 1967 s.2(1), is a claim "in connection with" a contract within the meaning of an exemption clause in a contract); *Trade Indemnity Plc v Försäkringsaktiebölaget Njord* [1995] 1 All E.R. 796 at 816–817 (Rix J.: in the light of *Ashville Investments, Monro v Bogdanor Urban DC* "must now be regarded as of dubious authority"). For claims based on misrepresentation which are "in respect of" a contract for the purposes of CPR PD 6B, para.3.1(6) (service out of the jurisdiction), see above, para.11–06.

[97] *Fillite (Runcorn) Ltd v Aqua-Lift* (1989) 45 B.L.R. 27, CA. *Cf. Fiona Trust & Holding Corp. v Privalov*, below, n.98, at [11] (Lord Hoffmann, noting that CA in *Fillite (Runcorn) Ltd v Aqua-Lift* did not consider *Mackender v Feldia A.G.* [1967] 2 Q.B. 590, CA, "in which a court which included Lord Denning MR and Diplock L.J. decided that a clause in an insurance policy submitting disputes 'arising thereunder' to a foreign jurisdiction was wide enough to cover the question of whether the contract could be avoided for non-disclosure").

[98] *Fiona Trust & Holding Corp. v Privalov* [2007] UKHL 40, [2007] 4 All E.R. 951 at [13] (Lord Hoffmann); distinguished in relation to an *expert determination clause* by CA in *Barclays Bank Plc v Nylon Capital LLP* [2011] EWCA Civ 826, *The Times*, August 18 2011.

It is, of course, possible (and good practice) to draft an arbitration clause in such a way as to make its scope absolutely clear but, if it they are not clearly excluded, claims based on pre-contractual misrepresentations, including questions of whether the contract which contains the arbitration clause is void or voidable, will be interpreted as being within the scope of the clause.

This construction, together with the provisions in force under the Arbitration Act 1996, furthers arbitration over litigation through the courts where the parties have included an arbitration clause in their contract. If a claim falls within the scope of an arbitration clause, but the claimant seeks a remedy not in arbitration but in the court, the court will generally stay the proceedings on the defendant's application.[99] Sections 85 to 87 of the 1996 Act were designed to provide a separate regime relating to *domestic* arbitration agreement,[100] in respect of which the court would have a wider discretion to refuse a stay where satisfied that there are sufficient grounds for not requiring the parties to abide by the arbitration agreement.[101] These provisions have never been brought into force,

---

[99] Arbitration Act 1996, s.9(4): the court shall grant a stay unless satisfied that the arbitration agreement is null and void, inoperative, or incapable of being performed.

[100] An arbitration agreement to which none of the parties is (a) an individual who is a national of, or habitually resident in, a state other than the UK, or (b) a body corporate which is incorporated in, or whose central control and management is exercised in, a state other than the UK, and under which the seat of the arbitration (if the seat has been designated or determined) is in the UK: Arbitration Act 1996, s.85(2).

[101] Arbitration Act 1996, s.86(2). It seems likely that, in exercising this discretion, the court would apply similar principles to those which it applied under the legislation in force before the Arbitration Act 1996 (Arbitration Act 1950, ss.4 (court's discretion to stay if satisfied that there is no sufficient reason why the matter should not be referred to arbitration), 24(2) (court's power to order that arbitration agreement cease to have effect where dispute involves the question whether a party has been guilty of fraud)): that is, where fraud is charged, and the party charged with the fraud wishes the matter to be heard in court, a stay would be refused; but if it is the party alleging the fraud that seeks to have the case heard in court then a stay would normally not be refused: *Russell v Russell* (1880) 14 Ch.D. 471; *Camilla Cotton Oil Co.v Granadex S.A.* [1976] 2 Lloyd's Rep. 10, HL, at 16; *Cunningham-Reid v Buchanan-Jardine* [1988] 1 W.L.R. 678, CA. It is the fact that a party's character is in issue that points the court to allowing him to have the matter tested in court, rather than in a private arbitration, but only if he is the party requesting it: *Russell v Russell*, above, at 477. And where there is an allegation against a professional which brings into

however, thus reducing the power of the court to refuse to stay its own proceedings and so giving more definitive effect to arbitration clauses in domestic agreements.[102]

Assignment of rights of action. The principles governing the assignment of rights of action in respect of misrepresentation are the principles which govern assignment of rights of action generally.[103] So where the claim in misrepresentation is a claim for damages in contract or in tort[104] the right to assign the cause of action, or the accrued right to damages which flows from the cause of action, depends on the nature of the cause of action, as well as the construction of any contractual term which purports to restrict the assignment.[105] However, what can be assigned is a chose in action, not a particular remedy to enforce the chose in action. So a claim to rescission cannot be assigned separately from the property of which restitution will be made following rescission: a claim to rescission is a right of action but is not itself a chose in action.[106] Where, however, a claimant has both a claim to damages and a **11–21**

---

question his professional reputation, whether or not there is an allegation against him of actual dishonesty, the court may be prepared on his application to exercise its discretion to refuse a stay so that his reputation can be tested in open court: *Radford v Hair* [1971] Ch. 758; *Turner v Fenton* [1982] 1 W.L.R. 52. Under the Arbitration Act 1950, in addition to the general discretion under s.4, special provision was made (in s.24(2)) for claims of fraud. This no longer appears in the 1996 Act: all cases involving domestic arbitration agreements would therefore be dealt with under the general discretion now contained in s.86(2).

[102] R. Merkin, *Arbitration Law* (loose-leaf), para.1.44 (s.88, which is in force, confers on the Secretary of State the power to repeal or amend ss.85–87; it appears that the approach of the Government was to wait and see whether the Act works effectively without ss.85–87; if so, they will doubtless be repealed in due course).

[103] On assignment generally, see Chitty, Ch.19; Furmston, paras 6.249 to 6.335; Treitel, Ch.15; Anson, Ch.22; Cheshire, Fifoot and Furmston, Ch.16.

[104] There appears to be no authority on the assignment of the right to damages under the Misrepresentation Act 1967 s.2(1): in *ANC Ltd v Clark Goldring & Page Ltd* [2001] B.C.C. 479, CA, Robert Walker L.J. preferred not to make any comment on this, since it was not necessary for his decision. But as a chose in action the right should surely in principle be assignable.

[105] *Linden Gardens Trust Ltd v Lenesta Sludge Disposals Ltd* [1994] 1 A.C. 85, HL; applied in relation to a misrepresentation claim in *ANC Ltd v Clark Goldring & Page Ltd*, above, n.104.

[106] *Investors Compensation Scheme Ltd v West Bromwich Building Society* [1998] 1 W.L.R. 896, HL, at 915–917.

claim to rescind arising out of the same misrepresentation, he may assign the claim to damages whilst retaining the claim to rescind. The quantum of damages recoverable by the assignee may be affected by whether or not the claimant exercises his right to rescind the contract, but they are quite separate and the inability to assign the rescission claim does not of itself affect the assignability of the damages claim, which is a separate chose in action.[107]

[107] *ibid.*, at 917: Lord Hoffmann, suggesting that the possible conflict between the two separate claims should be solved by procedural means, such as by trying both claims together.

PART 2

Mistake

CHAPTER 12

INTRODUCTION: CATEGORISING MISTAKES

I. SCOPE OF THIS PART

Mistake in the formation of a contract. This part of the book is concerned with the consequences of mistakes made by one or both parties in the formation of a contract. It will not consider in detail the role played by mistake in other areas of the law, such as in restitution.[1] And the inquiry is limited to the role of mistake in *formation* of the contract: that is, where one party, or both, make a mistake at the moment when the contract is formed. The mistake may be made during the course of the negotiations, or it may be made at the very last stage, when the contract is concluded. But the mistake will have relevance to the formation of the contract only if the mistaken belief was held at the time of formation. If the mistake was made during the negotiations, but was corrected before the time of the contract, there is no relevant mistake in the formation of the contract. And if the "mistake" was made only after the contract was concluded, it may have other consequences for the contract, but it is not a mistake within the scope of this book.[2] **12–01**

The aim of the inquiry is to enable a party to identify the remedies available to him where he has entered into a contract—or

[1] For detail of the role of mistake in restitution, see Goff & Jones, Chs 4–9.

[2] For example, a change of circumstances after the contract has been formed cannot constitute a mistake, but may have the effect of frustrating the contract. For comparison between the doctrines of mistake about the subject-matter and frustration, see below, paras 15–19, 15–22, n.83, 15–28, 15–33, n.175.

what he believes to be a contract[3]—and now claims that he made a "mistake" at the time when the contract was formed. We shall see that English law is reluctant to give remedies for mistake. This chapter will outline some of the concerns which appear to lie behind this reluctance, and the difficulties faced by a party seeking to raise a claim based on mistake. The following chapters of Part II will discuss in some detail the different circumstances in which such claims may be made.

II. WHAT IS A "MISTAKE"?

12–02 **Different meanings of "mistake".** A mistake is a misunderstanding, a misapprehension, a misconception, an erroneous belief.[4] The word "mistake" is in everyday use,[5] and it is important to understand the legal significance of the term. Certain points should be noted from the outset: a mistake requires a positive state of mind, and can be only of the present, not the future; and risk-taking excludes mistake about the subject-matter of the risk.

12–03 **A positive state of mind.** In order to succeed in a claim based on mistake, the claimant must show that, at the moment when he entered into the contract, he held a belief, or understanding, which was incorrect. He "mis-understood" something: that is, he had an understanding about something which was (a) legally relevant to the validity of the contract or the terms on which it was concluded,[6] and (b) in fact relevant to his decision to enter into the contract; and this understanding was incorrect. Such a misunderstanding is a positive state of mind:[7] ignorance and forgetfulness, if they are not reflected in a postive erroneous belief, do not constitute mistake.[8]

---

[3] If the mistake is operative, it may make the contract void, and therefore the contract may be apparent, rather than real: below, para.12–09.

[4] *Great Peace Shipping Ltd v Tsavliris Salvage (International) Ltd (The Great Peace)* [2002] EWCA Civ 1407, [2003] Q.B. 679 at [28].

[5] "Mistake" is defined in the Oxford English Dictionary (3rd edn June 2002 and online version June 2011) as "a. A misconception about the meaning of something; a thing incorrectly done or thought; an error of judgement. b. In generalized use: misapprehension, misunderstanding; error, misjudgement".

[6] For legally relevant mistakes, see generally Chs 14, 15 and 16.

[7] The belief must be "positive" in the sense that he actively held it: he had a conscious belief or understanding. It does not require the content of the belief to

To say that the claimant was labouring under a mistake is to say nothing about the origin of his misunderstanding. It may have been caused by inaccurate information given to him by the other party, or by a third party; or he may have made his own investigations and come to the wrong conclusion; or he may simply have jumped to the wrong conclusion and thereby made a spontaneous mistake. The origin of the mistake may have significance in the range of remedies available to the claimant,[9] and to show the origin may assist the claimant to show that he did indeed make the mistake that he claims. But if the claim is based on mistake, the claimant must at least show that he held the positive, but incorrect, belief or understanding. Only then can he claim that the "mistake" had any significance for his decision to enter into the contract.

---

be positive: it could equally be negative, e.g. not only a belief that the other party is Mrs A.; but equally a belief that the other party is not Mrs B.: *Sowler v Potter* [1940] 1 K.B. 271; below, para.14–24.

[8] *Barrow v Isaacs & Son* [1891] 1 Q.B. 417, CA at 420–421 (Lord Esher M.R., discussing the meaning of "mistake" for the purposes of relief in equity: "Can you, in English, say, 'I forgot,' and is that the same thing as saying, 'I was mistaken'? I think not. Both those questions depend on something happening in the mind of the person, and you have to see what it is that happens in his mind. If he merely forgets, he does not assume that one state of things exists whereas some other state of things exists: it is a mere passive state of mind; he has forgotten—he has not thought that one thing was in existence, whereas something else was in existence. I should say that mere forgetfulness is not mistake at all in ordinary language". Cf. G. Virgo, *Principles of the Law of Restitution* (2nd edn, 2006) at pp.145–6, arguing (and citing authorities in support) that such "passive" mistakes, as much as "active" mistakes, should ground restitutionary claims; against: D. Sheehan, "What is a Mistake?" (2000) 20 L.S. 538 at pp.539–540, 541–549; E.A. Farnsworth, *Alleviating Mistakes* (2004), p.20 ("without a flawed perception, there is no mistake"); but see also Ch.3, esp. p.34 (on the inference of perception from ignorance). See also, in the context of criminal law, R. Williams, "Deception, Mistake and Vitiation of the Victim's Consent" (2008) 124 L.Q.R. 132 at p.146.

[9] If the origin was in inaccurate information given by the other party, there will generally be a separate claim for misrepresentation: above, Pt I. For the reasons why a claimant may wish in such circumstances to pursue the claim for mistake rather than the claim for misrepresentation, see above, para.1–03; below, para.12–19. If the origin was in the claimant's incorrect conclusions based on his own investigations, or his spontaneous misunderstanding, the question may be whether his own fault precludes his relying on the mistake to found a remedy: below, para.12–10.

12–04 **Mistake about the present, not the future.** An incorrect belief or understanding is a "mistake" for the purposes of the remedies discussed in this book only if it relates to the present, and not the future. A mistake is fundamentally different from a misprediction.[10] We have seen[11] that a statement by one party to the other during the negotiations is not a misrepresentation if it is only a statement of what will happen in the future. If the representee wishes to hold the representor to liability in the event that the prediction is not borne out by the facts as the future finds them, he must secure a warranty, in the contract, that the facts will turn out as represented. Similarly, a party cannot rely on his own misprediction of the future to challenge the validity of the contract, or its terms.

Traditionally, therefore, it has been said that to give rise to a remedy in relation to the formation of a contract the mistake must be as to present fact.[12] This mirrors the traditional statement that an actionable misrepresentation must be a false statement of present fact.[13] We shall see that, for certain purposes,[14] this is an adequate starting-point, subject to the qualification that in recent years the courts have accepted that mistakes of law are now in principle to be treated on the same basis as mistakes of fact,[15] again mirroring the developments which allow a misrepresentation of law to be treated on the same footing as a misrepresentation of fact.[16] However, when we consider the different categories of mistake, we shall see that a mistake may be made not only about the facts at the time of the formation of the contract, but also about content of the other party's promises.[17] The law of mistake here becomes entwined with

[10] "A mistake as to the future, a misprediction, does not show that the plaintiff's judgment was vitiated, only that as things turned out it was incorrectly exercised. A prediction is an exercise of judgment. To act on the basis of a prediction is to accept the risk of disappointment. If you then complain of having been mistaken you are merely asking to be relieved of a risk knowingly run": P. Birks, *An Introduction to the Law of Restitution* (1985), p.147, discussing mistake in restitution, rather than contract, but the point holds here. See also W. Seah, "Mispredictions, Mistakes and the Law of Unjust Enrichment" [2007] R.L.R. 93.

[11] Above, para.3–43.

[12] Stoljar, p.2. In *The Great Peace*, above, n.4 at [76] the test stated by CA refers rather to a "common assumption as to the existence of a state of affairs".

[13] Above, para.3–13.

[14] See esp. Ch.16.

[15] Below, para.15–24.

[16] Above, para.3–37.

[17] Below, para.12–07.

the fundamental rules for the formation of the contract—the test for deciding whether the parties have reached a sufficient agreement to form a contract, and the content of that contract.[18] But even here the "mistake" relates to the present, and is not simply a misprediction or a misunderstanding about the future. If the claimant is allowed to say that he made a mistake about the terms of the contract, he is asserting that he misunderstood the other party's proposal for the contract as it stood at the moment when he gave his assent to the formation of the contract. If, on the other hand, his complaint is that, after the contract has been formed, the other party has not *kept* his promise, that is a claim for breach of contract, not for mistake.

Risk-taking contrasted with mistake. A party who takes a risk as to whether a fact is true cannot be heard to say that he made a mistake as long as the facts are within the range of the risk. If a party knows that the facts might be [x] or [y], then as long as they are *either* [x] *or* [y], he simply has not made a mistake. This is so, even if he thinks that the facts are [x], but has a residual doubt about whether they might be [y]: for example, if he buys a painting believing it to be a genuine work by a particular seventeenth century artist, whilst knowing that there is a minority opinion amongst art historians that it might have been painted by another artist of the same school.[19] However, if the party holds a positive belief that the facts are [x] or [y] *and not* [z], he may be allowed to assert that he made a mistake if [z] is shown to be the true state of affairs: to continue the example, if the buyer of the painting has a positive belief that it must at least be a genuine seventeenth century work, but in reality it is a modern forgery.[20] 12–05

[18] Below, Ch.13.

[19] Where a party has a doubt, the question remains whether he can be shown to have taken the risk as to the truth: *Deutsche Morgan Grenfell Group Plc v Inland Revenue Commissioners* [2006] UKHL 46, [2007] 1 A.C. 558 at [26]–[27] (Lord Hoffmann, using the example of a party who enters into a contract of compromise with doubts about his liability to pay); [64]–[65] (Lord Hope: the critical question is one of causation: whether the party would have made the payment if he had known the truth); commenting on *Kleinwort Benson Ltd v Lincoln City Council* [1999] 2 A.C. 349 at 410 (Lord Hope: "A state of doubt is different from that of mistake. A person who pays when in doubt takes the risk that he may be wrong—and that is so whether the issue is one of fact or one of law"). See further below, para.15–17.

[20] However, such a mistake (of the provenance of a work of art) is not legally relevant in English law, whether the buyer alone makes the mistake, or whether it

The risk of a particular fact may be undertaken expressly by one of the parties, or impliedly. Allocation of risk will be discussed further in Chapter 15.[21]

III. CATEGORISING MISTAKES

12–06 **Different ways of categorising mistakes.** The doctrine of mistake presents difficulties in English law for a number of different reasons. First and foremost, there is some difficulty in extracting from the authorities a clear and coherent set of rules to apply to a claim of mistake in relation to the validity of a contract.[22] However, beyond this uncertainty in the law itself—but, no doubt, largely in consequence of it—the treatment of the doctrine of mistake in the cases and in the textbooks is far from uniform. There is some confusion in the terminology used by both the judges and textbook writers.[23] And there is no single, clear view as to how to

is shared by the seller: below, paras 15–04, 15–27. The buyer's remedies (if any) would therefore in practice lie in misrepresentation or breach of contract. This emphasises the narrow practical scope of mistake.

[21] Below, paras 15–04, 15–15 to 15–19.

[22] See, e.g. the difficulties posed by the decisions in *Shogun Finance Ltd v Hudson* [2003] UKHL 62, [2004] 1 A.C. 919, below, paras 14–34 to 14–43; and *Bell v Lever Bros Ltd* [1932] A.C. 161, HL, below, para.15–21.

[23] In particular, in considering whether the mistake was made by only one party or by both, judges and writers have used the same terms to mean quite different things. Sometimes a shared mistake—where both parties make the *same* mistake—is described as "mutual" (*Bell v Lever Bros Ltd*, above, n.22; older editions of *Chitty on Contracts*: Chitty, para.5–001, n.3; older editions of Anson's Law of Contract: Anson, p.251, n.21); sometimes it is "common" (Furmston, para.4.73; Cheshire, Fifoot and Furmston, Ch.8; and many of the cases which were decided after the first edition of Cheshire & Fifoot, *The Law of Contracts* (1945): see, e.g. *Solle v Butcher* [1950] 1 K.B. 671, CA, at 686, 693; *Laurence v Lexcourt Holdings* [1978] 1 W.L.R. 1128 at 1137; *The Great Peace* [2002] EWCA Civ 1407, [2003] Q.B. 679 at [32]). "Common" is now the generally favoured term in this context: Chitty, paras 5–001, 5–017; Treitel, paras 8–001, n.4, 8–002; Anson, pp. 251, 278. But some books use the word "mutual" to describe the very different situation where the parties are at cross-purposes, holding different beliefs or understandings, rather than the same (Cheshire, Fifoot and Furmston, Ch.8. Furmston, para.4.73 uses "mutual" to cover both unilateral mistakes (where one party knows that the other is mistaken) and cross-purposes mistakes (where the party does not know that the other is mistaken)). It is important, therefore, to be clear at the outset about how the terminology will be used in this book; and the confusing use of the word "mutual" in describing types of mistake will generally be avoided here. In the discussion of mistake in the

categorise mistakes. In this book, the discussion in the following chapters of this Part will be organised by reference to what the claimant has made his mistake about—the terms of the contract, the identity of the other party, or the subject-matter—which will show a clear path through the complexities of the subject when advising a claimant about his possible remedies.[24] But other ways in which the subject could be ordered are by reference to whether the mistake was unilateral or shared by the contracting parties[25]; the impact it has on the validity of the contract, or the impact on the parties' consent[26]; how the mistake was made—including the role of the claimant's fault (if any) in having made the mistake; and the different approaches to mistake in formal (written) and informal contracts. In reality, all of these matters are relevant and will be discussed where appropriate in the following chapters.

Categorisation by what the mistake is about. The nature of the claimant's mistake—what he claims to have been mistaken about—can vary; and the nature of the mistake affects the substance of the claim, and the remedy sought. He may claim that he misunderstood what the other party was promising—the *terms of the contract*. This argument may be directed either at avoiding being bound by the contract altogether; or at maintaining the contract, but on the basis of the terms as the claimant understood them. Or the claimant may claim that he misunderstood who he was **12–07**

---

following chapters, it is important to be able to distinguish between two situations: where the rule under discussion requires proof only of the claimant's own mistake; and where the rule requires proof that both parties made the *same* mistake. The former is described as *unilateral*. The latter is described as *shared* or *common*.

[24] Waddams, Ch.11 distinguishes between "mistake as to contractual terms" and "mistake in assumptions" (and the latter includes frustration as well as mistake), following G.E. Palmer, *Mistake and Unjust Enrichment* (Columbus, 1962).

[25] Cheshire, Fifoot and Furmston, Ch.8; G.C. Cheshire, "Mistake as Affecting Contractual Consent" (1944) 60 L.Q.R. 175.

[26] Treitel, para.8–001 (mistakes which "negative consent" and mistakes which "nullify consent", quoting *Bell v Lever Bros Ltd*, above, n.22 at 217 (Lord Atkin): below, para.12–09). In the previous editions of Treitel the chapter on mistake was then structured under these headings, but the 12th edn (2007) and the 13th edn (2011) now use the principal headline distinction between 'common mistake' and 'unilateral mistake'. See also S. Stoljar, "A New Approach to Mistake in Contract" (1965) 28 M.L.R. 265 ("correspondence-mistake" contrasted with "expectation-mistake").

dealing with—the *identity of the other party*—and that, had he known the truth, he would not have been willing to enter into the contract at all, and so he should be released from the contract. Or he may claim that he made a mistake about some fact or circumstance relevant to his decision to enter into the contract, such as the existence of the subject-matter, or its factual characteristics or qualities, or some collateral fact which bears upon the subject-matter of the obligations of one of the parties: a mistake about the *subject-matter of the contract*. He will generally then say that, had he known the truth, he would not have entered into the contract, or at least that he would not have entered into it on those terms.

These different types of mistake—about terms, identity, and subject-matter—will be discussed in Chapters 13, 14 and 15 respectively. In the course of this, we shall see that it can be important to bear in mind the other categorisations mentioned above: whether the mistake was unilateral or shared; how the mistake was made (including the relevance of the claimant's own fault); and whether the contract is in writing or was concluded informally.

12–08 **Unilateral mistake or shared mistake.** For the purpose of some rules, it is significant to establish whether the claimant alone made the mistake, or whether the other party shared it—and so they both made the same mistake. In the case of a mistake of identity, the answer is obvious: the defendant can hardly have misunderstood his own identity, and so the mistake will of its nature be unilateral. Mistakes about the subject-matter, however, may be either unilateral or shared; and, as we shall see,[27] a unilateral mistake about the subject-matter does not normally affect the validity of the contract, whereas a common mistake might. And even a mistake about the terms of the contract may be shared, although it is more common for such a mistake to be unilateral.[28]

---

[27] Below, paras 15–10 to 15–11.

[28] If the parties make the same mistake about the terms of the contract, one would expect that the answer will be that their (shared) understanding of the terms *is* the set of terms on which the contract is formed—that is, there is not really a "mistake" at all; and this is generally true except for a few cases where the courts have been prepared to take an objective test which ignores the subjective, common intentions of the two parties: below, para.13–07. However,

Impact on the validity of the contract and on the parties' consent. We shall see that, if it operates at all, a mistake generally renders the contract void.[29] Until recently, the courts recognised circumstances in which a mistake might make a contract voidable (in equity), as well as circumstances in which it might make the contract void (at common law). This doctrine of mistake in equity appears now to have been rejected, thus simplifying one aspect of the law of mistake. However, there are other equitable rules and doctrines governing mistake, which will be discussed in the appropriate place.[30] 12–09

A further, related distinction that can be drawn between different categories of mistake, and which is used by some writers to determine how they present the subject, is between mistakes which "negative" the parties' consent; and mistakes which "nullify" the consent.[31] A mistake "negatives" consent if it prevents the parties from coming to any agreement: for example, they are at cross-purposes as to the very terms of the contract so that there is never a sufficient agreement for the contract to be formed. A mistake "nullifies" consent if, although the parties reach agreement about the terms of the contract, that agreement was based on a sufficiently serious mistake to allow the mistaken party to say that he should not be bound by it. This difference in language therefore describes different ways in which the mistake operates, and different reasons for the contract being void.

How the mistake was made; the claimant's and defendant's fault. It can be relevant to know how the mistake was made. Was it caused by information given by the other party or a third party, or was its origin just in the claimant himself—either through his own incorrect interpretation of the evidence or even through having made an incorrect assumption without any proper investigation? Did the defendant know that the claimant was making the mistake? Such questions raise issues of causation of the mistake and the 12–10

---

where the contract is in writing, the written document may fail properly to reflect the common intentions, and rectification has to be sought based on the common mistake: below, para.13–38.

29 Below, paras 12–17 to 12–19.

30 e.g. the equitable remedy of rectification for mistake (either common or unilateral) about the terms of a written contract; below, paras 13–38 to 13–54.

31 e.g. Treitel, para.8–001; above, n 26. This language and categorisation is based on *Bell v Lever Bros Ltd*, above, n.22 at 217 (Lord Atkin).

respective fault of the two parties; and for some categories of mistake these are relevant questions. For example, even if there is a shared mistake about the subject-matter sufficient to render the contract void, the courts will not allow such a claim by the party who was at fault in having caused the other party to make the mistake; and perhaps even in having made his own mistake without reasonable grounds.[32] And in order to determine whether there was a mistake about the terms of the contract which entitles the claimant to avoid the contract, or to hold the other party to his own understanding, the courts will ask whether a reasonable person in the claimant's position would have shared his understanding.[33] Where, however, the origin of the mistake is in a misrepresentation made by the other party, the picture changes significantly, and the claimant will often be able to rely on the *misrepresentation* in order to obtain remedies against the other party, rather than being driven to rely on the mistake.[34]

12–11 **Mistake in relation to written contracts and informal contracts.** The courts' approach to a claim of mistake will vary depending on whether the contract is constituted by a formal, written document, or whether it was concluded through informal communications between the parties. Where the contract was formed simply by an exchange of communications between the parties, it is natural that the courts should examine those communications to determine what the parties agreed—including questions about what the parties intended or understood their contract to be about. Issues of mistake may therefore be raised as part of such an analysis. However, where the parties have committed their agreement to a single written form of words, to which they have then each given assent, the document becomes the record of the contract; the words in the document are capable of (objective) interpretation, and the courts are reluctant to allow a party to adduce evidence of the negotiations, or of his own understanding about the document, to add to, vary or contradict the written terms.[35] To allow a claim based on a mistake about the

---

32 Below, para.15–23.

33 Below, para.13–12.

34 For discussion of the relationship between mistake and *misrepresentation*, see above, para.1–03; below, para.15–08.

35 The "parol evidence" rule: Chitty, paras 12–096 to 12–112; Furmston, paras 3.4 to 3.6; Treitel, paras 6–013 to 6–030; Anson, pp.138–139; Cheshire, Fifoot and Furmston, pp.157–165; Lewison, para.3.11; Phipson, Ch.42. See also below,

terms of the contract, or the identity of the contracting parties, will undermine the certainty of the written contract. This is not to say that mistake cannot be raised in relation to a written contract; but the starting-point of the courts will be rather different from a claim in relation to an informal contract.[36]

IV. THE RELUCTANCE TO REMEDY A MISTAKE

Why should mistake give rise to any remedy? At first sight, one might expect that the answer to the question, "why should mistake give rise to any remedy?", is obvious. A contract is based on the agreement of the parties. If one of the parties made a mistake, whether about the terms of the contract, or about the identity of the party with whom he was dealing, or about the subject-matter of the contract, then he did not really, fully agree. But this immediately shows that the role admitted by a legal system for mistake in relation to the validity of a contract is itself a reflection of the very notion of contract within the system. A law of contract which is based on the subjective meeting of minds of the parties will see a very significant role for the doctrine of mistake.[37] **12–12**

---

para.13–33 and *Chartbrook Ltd v Persimmon Homes Ltd* [2009] UKHL 38, [2009] 1 A.C. 1101 (obiter: HL should not depart from its earlier decision in *Prenn v Simmonds* [1971] 1 W.L.R. 1381 excluding pre-contractual negotiations in interpreting a written document; although they are admissible in support of a claim for rectification or estoppel: at [42]).

[36] Below, paras 13–32 *et seq.* (mistakes about the terms of the contract); 14–30 to 14–32, 14–37 to 14–38 (mistake about identity).

[37] So Pothier, in describing the old (pre-Napoleonic Code) law of France could write of mistake about the subject-matter of a contract: "*L'erreur est le plus grand vice des conventions: car les conventions sont formées par le consentement des parties; et il ne peut pas y avoir de consentment, lorsque les parties ont erré sur l'objet de leur convention*" (mistake is the greatest defect that can affect a contract, for contracts are formed by the consent of the parties, and there cannot be consent when the parties have made a mistake about the subject-matter of their agreement): *Le traité des obligations* (Paris, 1761), para.17. The detail has changed in the modern law, but the general approach of French law remains the same: in principle, a contract is based on the subjective agreement of the parties, and so primacy is given to *erreur* (mistake) as a vitiating factor: the consent is not fully valid if it was given through mistake: *Code civil*, Arts 1109, 1110; J. Ghestin, *La Formation du Contrat* (3rd edn, LGDJ, Paris, 1993), paras 490–548. For a comparative discussion, see J. Cartwright, "Defects of Consent and Security of Contract" in P. Birks and A. Pretto (eds), *Themes in Comparative Law In Honour of Bernard Rudden* (2002), Ch.11.

This is not, however, how English law views a contract. As we shall see, English law uses an objective test to determine whether there is a contract and, if so, on what terms. The nature of this objective test will be discussed further below,[38] but at the outset it should be noted that the introduction of a doctrine of mistake into a system of contract based on the objective, rather than the subjective, definition of a contract creates a significant tension.

12–13 **Security of contract generally.** The judges have sometimes shown a reluctance to allow a wide doctrine of mistake because of the potential threat to the security of contract: trust in the system of contracting requires a limit to be placed on the role of mistake in contract. Lord Atkin said in *Bell v Lever Bros Ltd*[39]:

> "it is of paramount importance that contracts should be observed, and that if parties honestly comply with the essentials of the formation of contracts—i.e., agree in the same terms on the same subject-matter—they are bound, and must rely on the stipulations of the contract for protection from the effect of facts unknown to them. . . .
>
> . . . it is of greater importance that well established principles of contract should be maintained than that a particular hardship should be redressed; and I see no way of giving relief to the plaintiffs in the present circumstances except by confiding to the Courts loose powers of introducing terms into contracts which would only serve to introduce doubt and confusion where certainty is essential."

---

38 Below, paras 13–08 to 13–19.

39 Above, n.22 at 224, 229; discussed in detail at para.15–21, below. See also *Associated Japanese Bank (International) Ltd v Crédit du Nord S.A.* [1989] 1 W.L.R. 255 at 257 (Steyn J.: "Throughout the law of contract two themes regularly recur—respect for the sanctity of contract and the need to give effect to the reasonable expectations of honest men. Usually, these themes work in the same direction. Occasionally, they point to opposite solutions. The law regarding common mistake going to the root of a contract is a case where tension arises between the two themes"); *Chartbrook Ltd v Persimmon Homes Ltd* [2009] UKHL 38, [2009] 1 A.C. 1101 at [37] (Lord Hoffmann: "the law of contract is an institution designed to enforce promises with a high degree of predictability", rejecting the use of evidence of pre-contractual negotiations in interpreting a written document because "the more one allows conventional meanings or syntax to be displaced by inferences drawn from background, the less predictable the outcome is likely to be"; even if this involves rejecting evidence which would have changed the courts' interpretation of the document, "a system which sometimes allows this to happen may be justified in the more general interest of economy and predictability in obtaining advice and adjudicating disputes" (at [41])).

This approach emphasises certainty; and sees the risk of admitting mistake too widely as requiring the courts to have a discretion to deal with individual cases which would threaten the certainty of contracts generally.[40] The jurisdiction in relation to the avoidance of contracts on the ground of mistake is distinct from the jurisdiction in relation to the avoidance of voluntary or other unilateral dispositions where the interest of the recipient, whilst of course deserving of the law's protection, is not as strong as the interest of a party whose contractual bargain would be reversed.[41]

[40] Whether this is really so depends, however, on how closely the courts could define actionable mistakes. The particular problem in *Bell v Lever Bros Ltd* involved a mistake about the subject-matter, and is discussed below, para.15–21.
[41] *Ogilvie v Littleboy* (1897) 13 T.L.R. 399 at 400 (Lindley L.J.: "Gifts cannot be revoked, nor can deeds of gift be set aside, simply because the donors wish they had not made them and would like to have back the property given. Where there is no fraud, no undue influence, no fiduciary relation between donor and donee, no mistake induced by those who derive any benefit by it, a gift, whether by mere delivery or by deed, is binding on the donor. ... In the absence of all circumstances of suspicion a donor can only obtain back property which he has given away by showing that he was under some mistake of so serious a character as to render it unjust on the part of the donee to retain the property given to him"); *Gibbon v Mitchell* [1990] 1 W.L.R. 1304 at 1309 (Millett J: voluntary transaction can be set aside for mistake of law or fact, "so long as the mistake is as to the effect of the transaction itself, and not merely as to its consequences or the advantages to be gained by entering into it"); *Smithson v Hamilton* [2007] EWHC 2900 (Ch), [2008] 1 W.L.R. 1453 at [118]–[122] (equitable jurisdiction to set aside voluntary disposition for mistake does not apply to claim to set aside rule of a pension scheme for mistake, particularly since CA decision in *Great Peace Shipping Ltd v Tsavliris Salvage (International) Ltd (The Great Peace)* [2002] EWCA Civ 1407, [2003] Q.B. 679 declared *Solle v Butcher* [1950] 1 K.B. 671, CA, to be bad law: see below, paras 15–29 to 15–32); *Pitt v Holt* [2011] EWCA Civ 197, [2011] 2 All E.R. 450 at [210] (Lloyd L.J.: "for the equitable jurisdiction to set aside a voluntary disposition for mistake to be invoked, there must be a mistake on the part of the donor either as to the legal effect of the disposition or as to an existing fact which is basic to the transaction. (I leave aside cases where there is an additional vitiating factor such as some misrepresentation or concealment in relation to the transaction . . .) Moreover the mistake must be of sufficient gravity as to satisfy the *Ogilvie v Littleboy* test, which provides protection to the recipient against too ready an ability of the donor to seek to recall his gift"; see also at [166], distinguishing this equitable jurisdiction from the common law remedies for mistake in relation to contracts). Cf. Goff & Jones, paras 4–020 to 4–022.

Moreover, and for similar reasons, mistake is a ground of restitution of money paid: the claimant's vitiated consent to a transfer of money may be

12–14 **Security of individual contracts.** A different approach—one which is perhaps more easily justifiable within the general approach to formation of contracts in English law—is the concern that to allow a wide, general doctrine of mistake would defeat the expectations of individual contracting parties. If a party is allowed to plead his own mistake, it allows an escape from the contract which is too easy. There are various aspects to this argument.

First, it is sometimes said that the doctrine of mistake, being in essence a subjective concept, is difficult to prove (or disprove) and so it would be too easy for a party to *claim* that he made a mistake and thereby avoid a contract to which he does not wish to be bound. As James L.J. said in *Tamplin v James*[42]:

> "It is not enough for a purchaser to swear, 'I thought the farm sold contained twelve fields which I knew, and I find it does not include them all,' or, 'I thought it contained 100 acres and it only contains eighty'. It would open the door to fraud if such a defence was to be allowed."

However, whilst a subjective test does indeed present difficulties of proof, this is not sufficient to reject a doctrine of mistake altogether.[43]

A different approach is to say that one of the values underlying the rules of the law of contract is the protection of *reasonable* expectations of the contracting parties. And so—setting aside the argument based on difficulty of proof of the mistake—even if one party can be shown in fact to have made the mistake that he claims, that should still not be sufficient to allow him to escape the contract if it has the effect of defeating the *other* party's reasonable expectations. Why should the other party lose the contract in

---

sufficient to render the recipient's consequential enrichment unjust, without the need to establish that the defendant committed any wrong: Goff & Jones, Ch.4; see esp. para.4–005

[42] (1880) 15 Ch.D. 215 at 221. See also Baggallay L.J. at first instance: *ibid.*, at 219: "he is not entitled to say to any effectual purpose that he was under a mistake, when he did not think it worth while to read the particulars and look at the plans. If that were to be allowed, a person might always escape from completing a contract by swearing that he was mistaken as to what he bought, and great temptation to perjury would be offered"; *Van Praagh v Everidge* [1902] 2 Ch. 266 at 272–273 (Kekewich J.; rvsd on different grounds [1903] 1 Ch. 434, CA).

[43] The test used by the courts for the formation of a contract includes a subjective element: para.13–13, below.

circumstances where—let us say, for the sake of argument—he had no knowledge of the mistake, and himself bore no responsibility for it? In *Tamplin v James*[44] James L.J. said:

> "It is said that it is hard to hold a man to a bargain entered into under a mistake, but we must consider the hardship on the other side. Here are trustees realizing their testator's estate, and the reckless conduct of the Defendant may have prevented their selling to somebody else. If a man makes a mistake of this kind without any reasonable excuse he ought to be held to his bargain."

More recently, Steyn L.J. said in *G. Percy Trentham Ltd v Archital Luxfer Ltd*[45]:

> "English law generally adopts an objective theory of contract formation. That means that in practice our law generally ignores the subjective expectations and the unexpressed mental reservations of the parties. Instead the governing criterion is the reasonable expectations of honest men . . ."

This argument will be explored in relation to the different categories of mistake recognised by English law, in the following chapters of this Part. But it can be taken as a starting-point for understanding the general approach of the judges in dealing with claims based on mistake. Put rather simplistically, it could be said that, when considering mistake, the judge does not begin by assuming that the mistake should release the mistaken party from the contract. He is more inclined to ask: why should the non-mistaken party *lose* the contract?

---

[44] Above, n.42 at 221. The defendant entered into a contract to buy an inn and sadler's shop from trustees of a will, wrongly assuming that the property for sale included certain additional plots of land that he knew had been occupied by tenants of the inn and the sadler's shop. The property was offered for sale at auction, which the defendant attended, and where the auctioneer drew attention to plans that were available; the property was not sold at the auction, but the defendant contracted to buy it immediately afterwards. Specific performance was ordered. See further below, paras 13–25, 13–29. Similarly, a mere unilateral mistake by one party about terms of a written document does not entitle him to rescission or rectification in equity against the other (innocent) party: "If reference be made to principles of equity, it operates on conscience. If conscience is clear at the time of the transaction, why should equity disrupt the transaction?": *Riverlate Properties Ltd v Paul* [1975] Ch. 133, CA, at 141; below, paras 13–31, 13–44.

[45] [1993] 1 Lloyd's Rep. 25 at 27.

12–15 **Protection of individuals who make mistakes.** This approach—emphasising objectivity, certainty and the security of contracts—is not, of course, the whole story. We shall see that there are circumstances in which the courts will still remedy a mistake even where the effect is to undermine a particular transaction; and this involves valuing more highly the protection of the party who has made a mistake. The tension between these different approaches can sometimes explain the divergent views in the case law dealing with mistake.[46]

V. AN OVERVIEW OF THE REMEDIES FOR MISTAKE

12–16 **Types of remedy.** A party claiming mistake is generally seeking either not to be bound at all by the contract, or to hold the other party to the contract but on the basis of the terms as the claimant understood them. The remedies are therefore generally avoidance of the contract, or rectification. Damages are not awarded for mistake.

12–17 **Avoidance of the contract.** A defect in the formation of a contract may result in it being *void* or *voidable*. We have seen that a contract may be voidable, but not void, for misrepresentation.[47] Until recently it was held that a contract might in some circumstances be voidable in equity for mistake,[48] but this has now been disapproved.[49] The contract may therefore be void, but not voidable, for mistake. In the case of mistake about the terms of the contract, or mistake about the identity of the other contracting party,

[46] For example, in *Solle v Butcher* [1950] 1 K.B. 671, CA, at 692 Denning L.J. said: "the court of equity would often relieve a party from the consequences of his own mistake, so long as it could do so without injustice to third parties. The court, it was said, had power to set aside the contract whenever it was of opinion that it was unconscientious for the other party to avail himself of the legal advantage which he had obtained". His approach in this case has however now been disapproved: *The Great Peace* [2002] EWCA Civ 1407, [2003] Q.B. 679; below, para.15–32.

[47] Above, para.4–05. Similarly, a contract may be voidable for duress or undue influence: Chitty, paras 7–053, 7–097.

[48] *Solle v Butcher*, above, n.46 at 693 (Denning L.J.) (common mistake about subject-matter); below, para.15–30. Denning L.J. also there said that a contract should be voidable (and not void) for a unilateral mistake about the terms of the contract or about the other party's identity. This has not been accepted in English law: paras 13–31 (terms), 14–09, 14–28, 14–41 (identity).

[49] *The Great Peace*, above, n.46; below, para.15–32.

in substance this involves saying that there was never a sufficient agreement to form the contract.[50] In the case of mistake about subject-matter the analysis is more difficult, because there was an agreement but in circumstances where the court holds that the mistake was sufficiently serious to allow a party to assert that the contract was void *ab initio*. This is construed very narrowly indeed.[51]

Consequences of the view that a contract is void for mistake. 12–18
The courts have not fully explored the difficulties which flow from the general theory that a contract is void, rather than voidable, for mistake. If there was an operative mistake which was sufficient to render the contract void *ab initio*, then the role of the court[52] is limited to so declaring. It does not set the contract aside. Logically, however, this means that the court could hold the contract to be void of its own motion—or even at the instance of a third party who is before the court in a dispute where the validity of the contract is in issue—even if neither party sought so to argue. Moreover, if the mistake renders the contract void, the party who made the mistake cannot, strictly speaking, affirm it. However, we shall see that there are situations in which the fact that the contract is void is not taken to its apparently logical conclusion, and the courts will limit the circumstances in which one or other party is allowed to rely on the contract being void.[53]

---

50 Below, paras 13–02 (terms), 14–05 (identity).

51 Below, para.15–03.

52 If one party claims that there is a contract which, if it exists, would contain an arbitration clause, the court must determine as a preliminary question whether the contract is void: "If the dispute is whether the contract which contains the clause has ever been entered into at all, that issue cannot go to arbitration under the clause, for the party who denies that he has ever entered into the contract is thereby denying that he has ever joined in the submission. Similarly, if one party to the alleged contract is contending that it is void ab initio (because, for example, the making of such a contract is illegal), the arbitration clause cannot operate, for on this view the clause itself also is void": *Heyman v Darwins Ltd* [1942] A.C. 356 at 366 (Viscount Simon L.C.).

53 e.g. where there is a written contract, only the party who satisfies the conditions for a successful plea of *non est factum* can be heard to say that the contract is void: the plea is designed to protect the party who is incapable of understanding a transaction by virtue of a disability: below, para.13–60; where one party knows that the other party is making a mistake about the terms of the contract, or his identity, only the *other* (mistaken) party can use that mistake to

12–19 **Advantages for the claimant in showing that the contract is void for mistake.** From the claimant's point of view, it can be difficult to show that the contract is void for mistake, given the limited scope of the doctrine, and the reluctance of the courts to find a sufficient mistake. In many cases, where the mistake was caused by information provided by the defendant, the claimant can more easily show that the contract was voidable for misrepresentation. However, even in such a case it may still be in his interest to go further and establish the mistake: for example, if rescission of the (voidable) contract has now become barred.[54] Resorting to a claim for mistake in order to avoid being met by a bar to rescission for misrepresentation may be an attempt to avoid policies, set by the law of misrepresentation, limiting the claimant's rights to escape the contract.[55] However, where the reason that rescission is barred is that an innocent third party would thereby be prejudiced,[56] establishing an actionable mistake can be a way of avoiding the policy underlying the rule which is designed to protect third parties. We shall see that this remains a controversial issue.[57]

Where, however, the claimant's mistake was not induced by the other party's misrepresentation, he will be driven to prove mistake

---

show that the contract was void: and so the rogue who misrepresents his identity can be estopped from denying that *he* was a party to the contract if the mistaken party chooses to hold him to it: below, para.14–11; where there is a sufficient common mistake about the subject-matter, either party can rely on it, but not if he has been at fault in causing or in making the mistake: below, para.15–22. It might be better to recognise openly that the purpose of the rules relating to mistake is to protect the party who makes a mistake; and therefore to lay down as a general rule that only the mistaken party may raise his own mistake as ground of avoidance of the contract. This it not to say that the contract should be only voidable; that is a different question: below, para.12–19. One could retain the position that a contract is void in certain defined circumstances for mistake, yet also provide that only the mistaken party (not the other party, and not third parties) may rely on the contract being void.

[54] Above, para.4–38.

[55] e.g. there is no limitation period for claiming that a contact is void (although some claims for relief consequential on a contract being void for mistake may be subject to limitation periods, which may then be extended by Limitation Act 1980 s.32(1)(c) if mistake is an essential ingredient of the cause of action: Goff & Jones, ch.23; paras 28–088, 43–001 to 43–002, 43–004 to 43–005); by contrast, rescission of a voidable contract may be barred for lapse of time: above, para.4–48.

[56] Above, para.4–59.

[57] Below, para.14–39.

if he wishes to avoid the contract. This will happen where the mistake was based on the claimant's own investigations or assumptions, and not caused by the receipt of inaccurate information; or where it was caused by his reliance on information but where the source of the information was a third party for whom the other contracting party had no responsibility.[58] In such a case, the claimant is not necessarily interested in establishing that the contract was void rather than voidable: he seeks to show that it is void because that is the legal consequence of the mistake, and it is mistake alone on which, on the facts, he can rely.

Rectification of the contract. Sometimes, where the contract is in writing, the claimant will seek to rely on his mistake not to avoid the contract, but to have the contract rectified: rewritten into the terms he had understood them to be, rather than the terms in which they were in fact written. This is an equitable remedy, which applies only to written contracts; but it can be awarded in cases of both unilateral and common mistake.[59] **12–20**

No damages for mistake. Damages cannot be awarded for mistake. An award of damages presupposes that the defendant has committed a wrong, such as a tort or a breach of contract. But a claim of mistake is based on the claimant's defective consent, and does not of itself say anything about the defendant's conduct. If the defendant has caused the mistake by his misrepresentation, there may be a claim for damages for the misrepresentation. But where the mistake is raised *as a mistake*, there can be no claim for damages, although there is no obstacle to the claimant recovering damages *in addition to* showing that the contract is void for mistake, if the claim can be established on the facts and is not inconsistent in law with the contract being void. For example, it is not possible for the claimant to claim damages for breach of contract where it is shown that the contract is void, since there are then no enforceable obligations in the contract (nor, therefore, any breach); nor can he claim damages under s.2(1) of the Misrepresentation Act 1967, even if he can show that the mistake was induced **12–21**

---

[58] A misrepresentation makes the contract voidable only where it is made by or on behalf of the other party: above, para.4–24; or where the other party has notice of a misrepresentation by a third party: above, paras 4–72 to 4–78.

[59] Below, paras 13–38 to 13–54.

by the defendant's misrepresentation, since the Act only applies where the claimant "has entered into a contract"—and this appears to exclude a void contract.[60] But if the claimant can show that the defendant committed a tort, such as deceit[61] or negligence,[62] the claim for damages can be cumulated with the contract being void.

60 But not a voidable contract: above, para.2–11, n.32.
61 Above, Ch.5.
62 Above, Ch.6.

CHAPTER 13

MISTAKES ABOUT THE TERMS OF THE CONTRACT[1]

[1] Chitty, paras 5–067 to 5–087; Furmston, paras 4.93 to 4.94, 4.97 to 4.98; Treitel, paras 8–044, 8–046 to 8–083; Anson, pp.252–268; Cheshire, Fifoot and Furmston, pp.304–309; Cartwright, Pt I; Stoljar, Ch.2.

I. INTRODUCTION: "MISTAKE" ABOUT THE TERMS

13–01 **"Mistake" in this context.** At first sight, the language of mistake fits rather uncomfortably in the topics discussed in this chapter. To say that a party to a contract made a mistake is to say that he misunderstood something: that he had a belief, or understanding, that was incorrect.[2] But how can one party be mistaken about the terms of the contract? If they are the terms of the contract, then he must surely, in law, have agreed to them. If he agreed to them, he did not make a mistake about them. This apparent difficulty does not arise in relation to written contracts, where the document *is* the contract—and one or both of the parties can have misunderstood what the document contained when he gave his assent to it. Such cases are discussed towards the end of this chapter.[3] It is more difficult to speak of "mistake" in relation to contracts which are not reduced to writing, and which are formed though discussions between the parties who exchange communications until there is an expression of final assent by one party to the latest proposal of the other. But even here the enquiry is essentially the same: the communications are to be analysed to determine whether there is a contract, and (if so) on what terms. If, at the end of that analysis the conclusion is that there is a contract on a set of terms [x]; but one of the parties believed either that there was no contract, or that there was a contract but on a set of terms [y], then one can say that that party was mistaken about the terms of the contract.

13–02 **Subjectivity, objectivity and "mistake".** This inquiry into mistake about the terms of the contract is only possible because the test for the formation of a contract is not simply a subjective test of the parties' agreement. If a subjective test were used, there would be a contract if but only if both parties in fact intended to enter into a contract, and on the same terms. A party could not be bound to a contract, or to a set of terms, which he did not intend. But as soon as we admit that a subjective test is insufficient for the formation of a contract, and that the test is at least partly objective, the door is open to holding a party to a contract in spite of his mistake. And, in applying the test for the formation of a contract—in analysing the negotiating parties' communications to see whether they have come

[2] Above, para.12–03.

[3] Below, paras 13–32 *et seq*.

to an agreement, or in interpreting the document which they have accepted as the reduction of their agreement to writing—the language of mistake tends to be used. One party may say: "I agreed to your proposal; but I thought that you were proposing [y]; now I discover that you were in fact proposing [x]". So he made a "mistake". But it is clear that the real issue here is whether there is a contract at all; and, if so, whether it is on terms [x] or [y]. That is, the real search in the area discussed in this chapter is for the test to be used to determine whether the parties have come to an agreement that is sufficient in law to constitute a contract.[4]

Mistake and interpretation. In this area, questions of "mistake" are often intertwined with questions of interpretation. This appears most obviously in relation to written contracts: one cannot determine whether a party was mistaken about the terms of a document without asking not only what *that party* understood them to mean (his mistake), but also what they do *in law* mean (their interpretation).[5] But we shall see that, even in relation to the general rules of formation of contracts, the inquiry is essentially as to the meaning that is to be attributed, *in law*, to the parties' exchanged communications. The so-called objective test of formation of a contract is in fact a rule of interpretation.[6] **13–03**

[4] This explains the differences between textbook writers in placing the topics discussed in this chapter. Most of the books place mistake about the terms in the general chapter on mistake: e.g. Chitty, Ch.5 (but see also paras 5–012, 5–066); Furmston, Ch.4, s.C; Treitel, Ch.8 (but see also para.8–054); Anson Ch.8 (but see p.252); Cheshire, Fifoot and Furmston, Ch.8 (but see p.284). But others recognised that the issue is really one as to the formation of the contract itself: e.g. J.C. Smith, *Smith & Thomas Casebook on Contract* (12th edn, 2009), Ch.5; E. McKendrick, *Contract Law* (9th edn, 2011), Ch.4; S.A. Smith, *Atiyah's Introduction to the Law of Contract* (6th edn, 2006), pp.76–85.
[5] Below, para.13–35.
[6] Below, para.13–11.

II. FORMATION OF THE CONTRACT: THE "OBJECTIVE TEST"

(1) Subjectivity and Objectivity

13–04 **A contract is formed through communication between the parties.** The paradigm case is of a contract formed through an exchange of communications between the parties. The communications may be very simple: an offer which is accepted without further negotiation. Or there may be protracted negotiations, which lead up to the final moment when an agreement is clinched by one party accepting the final proposal of the other. But in most cases, for a contract to be found, there must have been some communications between the parties which can be analysed as ending in an offer by one party which was accepted by the other.[7] The very notion of the "acceptance" of an "offer" means that the communications must be made by reference to each other: cross-offers do not make a contract.[8] An "agreement", at least in the sense understood by English law in relation to a contract, is not just a coincidence of ideas but necessarily requires the *sharing* of those ideas through the communication between the parties to the agreement. For this reason mere silence by either party during the formation of a contract is problematic: "silence and inaction are of their nature equivocal, for the simple reason that there can be more than one reason why the person concerned has been silent and inactive".[9] And so unless the silence can in context communicate meaning sufficiently clearly to the other party, it cannot be treated as part of the communications by which their agreement was formed.

---

[7] *Gibson v Manchester City Council* [1979] 1 W.L.R. 294 at 297 (Lord Diplock: "There may be certain types of contract, though I think they are exceptional, which do not fit easily into the normal analysis of a contract as being constituted by offer and acceptance; but a contract alleged to have been made by an exchange of correspondence between the parties in which the successive communications other than the first are in reply to one another, is not one of these").

[8] *Tinn v Hoffmann & Co.* (1873) 29 L.T. 271 at 277 (Grove J.: "there must be an offer which the person accepting has had an opportunity of considering, and which when he accepts he knows will form a binding contract").

[9] *Allied Marine Transport Ltd v Vale do Rio Doce Navagacao S.A. (The Leonidas D)* [1985] 1 W.L.R. 925, CA, at 941 (Robert Goff L.J.).

Similarly, a communication which was made not to the other party or his agent, but to a third party, is not part of the agreement.[10]

Interpretation of the communications. In most cases there is no dispute between the parties about whether there was a contract, and what were its terms. But once such a dispute arises, it becomes necessary to analyse the communications by which the contract is alleged to have been formed; and, typically, this will require the interpretation of those communications, either as to whether each of the parties intended them to have contractual force (that is, whether there was a common intention to form a contract at all); or as to what the parties understood the contents of the contract to be (that is, whether there was a common intention on the terms of the contract). Or, where the parties' agreement was reduced to writing, and was perhaps even signed by both parties, the dispute centres on the meaning of the written document, one party claiming that it does not reflect what he understood the agreement to be. It is at this stage, the interpretation of the communications, that arguments based on mistake will be raised: one party may allege that he did not understand the other to be proposing that the contract should contain a particular term which the latter is now seeking to enforce; or that he did not mean that the other party should take him as proposing a particular term, or even to be bound at all by way of contract; or that, when he signed it, he did not understand the language of the written document in the sense that the other party claims. The question then becomes: how should the communications between the parties be interpreted? Subjectively or objectively? 13–05

The test is not wholly subjective. It is clear that the test in English law is not wholly subjective. The question is not simply what the person making the communication meant; nor whether he was in fact intending to be bound to a particular term, or to the contract. The problems that a wholly subjective test would bring have been discussed in Chapter 12[11]: it presents difficulties of proof; and—much more importantly—would allow a party to 13–06

[10] *Wood v Scarth* (1858) 1 F & F 293, 175 E.R. 733 (communication of a proposed term by defendant to his own agent, but not to claimant: not part of the contract).

[11] Above, paras 12–12 to 12–15.

escape from a contract simply by showing that he did not in fact intend to be bound by it, or did not intend to be bound by a particular term. This would have a destabilising effect not only on individual contracts, but on the system of contracting generally. It is certainly not the approach taken in the English cases.

13–07 **Different approaches to an "objective" test.** Even if the subjective test for the formation of a contract is rejected, it is not necessarily obvious how the acceptable alternative should be formulated. An objective test involves asking whether a reasonable person would say that the parties have come to an agreement and (if so) on what terms. But such a test could be operated in different ways.

A wholly objective test would ignore the subjective intentions of the parties altogether, and simply ask whether a detached observer, with access to all information that such an observer might know, would conclude that the parties have agreed on the same terms. This would involve a consideration of the communications between the parties and their conduct, and anything else that an external observer might be able to draw upon to interpret the communications and conduct. But it would ignore how each party intended his communications or conduct to be interpreted, and how each party in fact understood the other. This is, broadly, how the courts will approach the interpretation of a written document.[12] And some writers[13] and judges[14] have proposed that such an approach should

[12] Below, para.13–35.

[13] See especially W. Howarth, "The Meaning of Objectivity in Contract" (1984) 100 L.Q.R. 265; criticised J. P. Vorster, "A Comment on the Meaning of Objectivity in Contract" (1987) 104 L.Q.R. 274; reply by Howarth at (1987) 103 L.Q.R. 527. See also O.W. Holmes, *The Common Law* (1881), Lecture IX ("The law has nothing to do with the actual state of the parties' minds. In contract, as elsewhere, it must go by externals, and judge parties by their conduct").

[14] Notably Lord Denning. See, e.g. *Solle v Butcher* [1950] 1 K.B. 671 at 691; *Frederick E. Rose (London) Ltd v William H. Pim Jnr & Co. Ltd* [1953] 2 Q.B. 450, CA, at 460; *Oscar Chess Ltd v Williams* [1957] 1 W.L.R. 370, CA, at 373–374. See also *Butler Machine Tool Co. Ltd v Ex-Cell-O Corp. (England) Ltd* [1979] 1 W.L.R. 401, CA, at 404 (Lord Denning M.R., rejecting the test of offer and acceptance for formation of a contract: "the better way is to look at all the documents passing between the parties—and glean from them, or from the conduct of the parties, whether they have reached agreement on all material points"; repeated in *Gibson v Manchester City Council* [1978] 1 W.L.R. 520, CA, at 523–524, but rejected by HL: above, n.7 at 296–297).

be used more generally to find the agreement between the parties in the formation of a contract. But it could have some curious consequences, even to the extent of holding that the parties are bound to a contract on terms that *neither* of them intended.[15] It is not the approach that is generally used by the cases in English law.[16] Rather, we shall see that the courts adopt an objective test which asks how a reasonable person, placed in the position of the parties themselves, would have interpreted their communications; and that the subjective understandings of the parties are not wholly excluded.

(2) The General Approach in English Law

The "objective" test. The test that the courts will apply in order to ascertain whether there is a contract, and (if so) on what terms, is set out in detail at para. 13–19 below. Broadly speaking, we can say that, where the parties are in disagreement about the existence of a contract, or its terms, and where the contract is alleged to have been formed by successive communications between the parties, the general approach in English law is to interpret the parties' intentions objectively; but to allow a party to rely on a disputed term only if at 13–08

[15] Vorster, above, n. 13; *Upton-on-Severn Rural DC v Powell* [1942] 1 All E.R. 220, CA (neither party thought that there was a contract, but CA held that they must have intended to form a contract; however, this might be better explained as a case of restitution: *William Lacey (Hounslow) Ltd v Davis* [1957] 1 W.L.R. 932 at 938–939; J.R. Spencer [1973] C.L.J. 104 at pp.111–112); *Furness Withy (Australia) Pty Ltd v Metal Distributors (UK) Ltd (The Amazonia)* [1990] 1 Lloyd's Rep. 236, CA, at 243 (Staughton L.J.: "If the parties' correspondence and conduct shows . . . an intention [to make a contract] it will not, or may not, matter that neither privately intended to make a contract").

[16] The High Court of Australia has followed the wholly objective approach of Lord Denning, above, n.14, in the case of a formal written contract, although they "left to another day" the question whether it should properly be accepted as applying in the case of an informal contract or in the case where there is a mistake about the identity of the other party: *Taylor v Johnson* (1982–1983) 151 C.L.R. 422 at pp.430–431 (written contract for sale of land at total price of $15,000; vendor under mistaken belief, known by purchaser, that the contract was at price of $15,000 per acre; held binding at common law; but set aside in equity); Carter, Peden and Tolhurst, para.20–54; *cf* Seddon and Ellinghaus, para.12.51, attributing a wider scope of application to *Taylor v Johnson*; see also below, paras 13–31, n.91; 15–33, n.169.

the moment when the contract was formed he in fact (subjectively) believed that the term was included in the contract. The test is therefore not wholly objective.

13–09 ***Smith v Hughes*** The best starting-point, in order to understand the objective test, is *Smith v Hughes*,[17] and in particular the judgment of Blackburn J.

The case is difficult because the facts are not entirely clear, and its outcome is uncertain, because it was sent back for a new trial. The claimant sought payment of the price of oats which the defendant had agreed to buy from him, but had refused to accept. The claimant was a farmer; the defendant was a trainer of racehorses; and the sale was by sample. The oats which the claimant delivered were new oats; but the defendant wanted—and believed that he was buying—old oats which, unlike new oats, would be suitable for feeding to his horses. Both parties therefore thought that there was a contract. The dispute was over whether there was any basis on which the defendant could refuse to be bound to take the (old) oats tendered by the claimant.

The trial judge misdirected the jury, because he did not make sufficiently clear a fundamental distinction: between a misunderstanding about the *terms* of the contract; and a misunderstanding about the *quality of the subject-matter* of the contract.[18] As we shall see, the approach taken where there is no disagreement about the terms of the contract, but only about the subject-matter, is very

[17] (1871) L.R. 6 Q.B. 597. It is perhaps regrettable that the more recent cases—which, as we shall see, approach the subject in a way which is generally consistent with that in *Smith v Hughes*—do not make more use of this judgment, because it casts light on the proper test for the formation of a contract.

[18] The judge directed the jury to return a verdict for the defendant if either (1) the word "old" had been used by the claimant or the defendant in making the contract; or (2) the claimant "believed the defendant to believe, or to be under the impression, that he was contracting for the purchase of old oats". Direction (1) was correct: (above, n.17) at 602, 607–608. But direction (2) failed to make clear whether the claimant believed (a) that the defendant believed that he was buying under a contract which contained a *term* warranting that the oats were old; or (b) that the defendant believed that the contract was simply for oats, but that *as a matter of fact* the oats which formed the subject-matter of the contract were old: see Cockburn C.J. at 606; Blackburn J. at 608; and Hannen J. at 610–611. The jury did not make clear whether their verdict (which was for the defendant) was given on the basis of direction (1) or (2), and so there had to be a new trial.

different.[19] The Court of Queen's Bench explained the basis on which an alleged mistake about the terms should be approached. Blackburn J. put it most clearly in this way[20]:

> "if one of the parties intends to make a contract on one set of terms, and the other intends to make a contract on another set of terms, or, as it is sometimes expressed, if the parties are not ad idem, there is no contract, unless the circumstances are such as to preclude one of the parties from denying that he has agreed to the terms of the other. The rule of law is that stated in *Freeman v Cooke*.[21] If, whatever a man's real intention may be, he so conducts himself that a reasonable man would believe that he was assenting to the terms proposed by the other party, and that other party upon that belief enters into the contract with him, the man thus conducting himself would be equally bound as if he had intended to agree to the other party's terms."

A first question: were the parties subjectively in agreement? 13–10
There is a danger of losing sight of where one should begin: by asking whether the parties were in fact in agreement about the existence of the contract, and its terms. This first question might seem obvious.[22] Surely if the parties were subjectively in agreement, they have a contract, on their agreed terms; or if they are subjectively in agreement that they have no contract, then there is no contract.[23] Such a question will not normally need to be asked, because disputes of the kind discussed in this chapter tend to arise only when—after the parties have entered into the contract, or what

---

[19] Below, Ch.15; see especially the discussion of *Smith v Hughes* in that context at paras 15–10 to 15–13; see also para.16–04. For confirmation of the distinction drawn in *Smith v Hughes* between mistakes as to the terms of the contract, and mistakes about the facts on which a party bases his decision to enter into the contract, see *Statoil A.S.A. v Louis Dreyfus Energy Services L.P. (The Harriette N)* [2008] EWHC 2257 (Comm), [2008] 2 Lloyd's Rep. 685 at [87]–[88], [96].

[20] Above, n.17 at 607. See also Hannen J. at 609: "It is essential to the creation of a contract that both parties should agree to the same thing in the same sense . . . But one of the parties to an apparent contract may, by his own fault, be precluded from setting up that he had entered into it in a different sense to that in which it was understood by the other party."

[21] (1848) 2 Exch 654 at 663, 154 E.R. 652 at 656.

[22] Glanville Williams, "Mistake and Rectification in Contract" (1954) 17 M.L.R. 154–155; Stoljar, p.11; Vorster, above, n.13, at p.286.

[23] *HSBC Bank Plc v 5th Avenue Partners Ltd* [2007] EWHC 2819 (Comm), [2008] 2 C.L.C. 771 at [117] (Walker J.: no contract of variation because neither party had the intention to vary: "Accordingly the principles of objective analysis are not engaged").

they thought was a contract—one of them discovers that there was in fact *no* subjective agreement, and seeks either to escape the contract on that basis, or to hold the other party to his (the claimant's) own subjective agreement. Sometimes the courts have made clear that they have considered first whether there was an actual (subjective) agreement before moving on to apply the objective test to resolve a subjective disagreement between the parties.[24] But the more recent cases have tended not to mention this first, subjective question and have turned immediately to the "objective" test—which can give the impression that it is the only question, the only test for the formation of a contract.[25] Blackburn J.'s approach however, makes clear in its opening words that he is only dealing with the case where there is in fact no agreement. The objective test is to be used to override the lack of subjective agreement; not to substitute for a subjective agreement which did in fact exist at the time when the contract was formed.

13–11 **The link to estoppel.** If, therefore, we are to hold a party to a term to which he did not, in fact, agree, what is the basis for so doing? The clue to Blackburn J.'s thinking lies not only in the

---

[24] e.g. *Falck v Williams* [1900] A.C. 176, PC, at 178–179 (Lord Macnaghten: "The first question is, Was there a contract? If there was no contract in fact, Was the proposal made on Falck's behalf so clear and unambiguous that Williams cannot be heard to say that he misundertood it?") and 180 ("it is impossible to contend that there was a contract in fact. Obviously the parties were not at one . . ."); *Scriven Bros & Co. v Hindley & Co.* [1913] 3 K.B. 564 at 568 (A.T. Lawrence J.: "the parties were never ad idem as to the subject-matter of the proposed sale; there was therefore in fact no contract of bargain and sale. The plaintiff can recover from the defendants only if they can shew that the defendants are estopped from relying upon what is now admittedly the truth").

[25] e.g. *The Hannah Blumenthal* [1983] 1 A.C. 854, HL, at 914 (Lord Brandon: agreement implied from conduct evinced to the other party and acted upon by him), 924 (Lord Brightman). Lord Diplock's formulation at 915 ("what is necessary is that the intention of each as it has been communicated to and understood by the other (*even though that which has been communicated does not represent the actual state of mind of the communicator*) should coincide": emphasis changed from original) may be assuming a prior subjective test but it is not clear. *The Hannah Blumenthal* is discussed further below, paras 13–14 *et seq*.

Moreover, the strongest version of the objective test would ignore both parties' intentions altogether and be prepared to construct a contract on the basis of objective evidence, even to the point of imposing a contract where neither party intended one; or imposing a contract which is different from that which both parties in fact intended: above, para.13–07.

language of the test itself, but also in the case to which he appealed by way of authority. He said that circumstances may "*preclude* one of the parties *from denying* that he has agreed to the terms of the other", and he referred to the judgment of Parke B. in *Freeman v Cooke*,[26] a decision based on estoppel by representation. The underlying idea therefore appears to be to use estoppel to create a contractual obligation. The language of estoppel does not appear explicitly in *Smith v Hughes*, although it has occasionally been used in the later cases.[27]

Whether this is really an application of the doctrine of estoppel, however, is doubtful. An estoppel by representation requires the representee to have relied on the representation to his detriment.[28] But in *Smith v Hughes* the party who can hold the other to a term to which he did not, in fact, intend to agree, does not "rely" on the other party's misleading conduct beyond giving his agreement, in return, to the contract as he believes it to be.[29] Other judges have

---

[26] Above, n.21; above, para.10–24. Hannen J. did not cite *Freeman v Cooke*, but used language in his judgment which appears to be drawn from the same source: above, n.20.

[27] *Pearl Mill Co. Ltd v Ivy Tannery Co. Ltd* [1919] 1 K.B. 78 at 84 (McCardie J.; but see *Allied Marine Transport Ltd v Vale do Rio Doce Navagacao S.A. (The Leonidas D)* [1985] 1 W.L.R. 925, CA, at 939: Robert Goff L.J., suggesting that *Pearl Mill* concerned repudiation, not the formation of a contract of abandonment, and doubting whether much importance should be attributed to the "obiter dictum" about estoppel. *Pearl Mill* was, however, referred to by Lord Brandon in *The Hannah Blumenthal*, below, para.13–15); *Scriven Brothers & Co. v Hindley & Co.*, above, n.24 at 569 (A.T. Lawrence J.: on the facts, no "contract by estoppel"); *The Hannah Blumenthal*, above n.25 at 916 (Lord Diplock, preferring to use "the broader expression 'injurious reliance' in preference to 'estoppel'"). See also P.S. Atiyah, "The Hannah Blumental and Classical Contract Law" (1986) 102 L.Q.R. 363.

[28] Spencer Bower, *Estoppel by Representation* (4th edn, 2003), para.1.2.2; above, para.10–25.

[29] This appears to be what Blackburn J. might have said if pressed to identify the reliance. He used the authority of *Freeman v Cooke* again in a later case to explain why a party who signs a document that he has not read should be bound by it: *Harris v Great Western Railway Co.* (1876) 1 Q.B.D. 505 at 530 ("by assenting to the contract thus reduced to writing, he represents to the other side that he has made himself acquainted with the contents of that writing and assents to them, *and so induces the other side to act upon that representation by entering into the contract with him*, and is consequently precluded from denying that he did make himself acquainted with those terms": emphasis added). See A. de Moor, "Intention in the Law of Contracts" (1990) 106 L.Q.R. 632 at pp.641–642.

kept estoppel separate from the objective test.[30] The better view is that there is no need to appeal to the doctrine of estoppel in this context, although the rationale underlying the objective test may well be similar to that underlying estoppel.[31] The objective test is simply a rule of interpretation of communications. In entering into a contract, a party is entitled to act on what he honestly, and on reasonable grounds, believes the other party to be agreeing. For the purpose of his claim to enforce the contract, the other party's assent will be interpreted by reference to that honest and reasonable belief.

13–12 **The objective element of the test.** The test set out by Blackburn J. relies heavily on objective criteria. Given that it is to be used in a case where the parties were not, in fact, in agreement, it must be applying an objective test to override a party's lack of subjective agreement. This is seen in the words of the test (with emphasis added):[32]

> "*whatever a man's real intention may be*, he so conducts himself that a reasonable man would believe that he was assenting to the terms proposed by the other party."

---

[30] *Tracomin S.A. v Anton C. Nielsen A/S* [1984] 2 Lloyd's Rep. 195 at 204 (Leggatt J: "defendants have abandoned their claim both because there was an implied agreement [applying the objective test] to abandon the submission of their dispute to arbitration, and because the defendants are estopped from denying that they have abandoned their claim"); *Tankreederei Ahrenkeil G.m.b.H. v Frahuil S.A. (The Multitank Holsatia)* [1988] 2 Lloyd's Rep. 486 at 493 (Phillips J.: applying objective test, there was an agreement to abandon arbitration; but no estoppel because no detrimental reliance); *Collin v Duke of Westminster* [1985] Q.B. 581, CA, at 595 (Oliver L.J.: estoppel separate from mutual release); *The Hannah Blumenthal*, above, n.25 at 914 (Lord Brandon: implied agreement, deduced from the "conduct of each party, as evinced to the other party and acted on by him" is separate from estoppel); *Centrovincial Estates Plc v Merchant Investors Assurance Co. Ltd* [1983] Com. L.R. 158, CA (rejecting the argument, accepted by Harman J. at first instance, that "the general rule that the intentions of an offeror must be judged objectively is based on estoppel. Accordingly, if the person who has accepted the offer has not altered his position in reliance on the offer, no such estoppel arises"; "provided only that the offeree has given sufficient consideration for the offeror's promise, it is nothing to the point that the offeree may not have changed his position beyond giving the promise requested of him").

[31] And, indeed, it is similar to other rules applied in the formation of contracts: for further discussion see Cartwright, Ch.1 and generally.

[32] Above, para.13–09.

The question, therefore, where the claimant seeks to hold the defendant to a contract on terms [x], is whether the conduct of the defendant was such that a reasonable man would believe that he was agreeing to [x] even though the defendant may in fact have intended [y]. It appears that Blackburn J. referred to "conduct" in the most general sense: as later cases have shown, it can be not only actions, but also words and even silence and inactivity in unusual circumstances where silence in fact communicates information.[33] The key question, however, is what a reasonable observer would conclude about the defendant's intentions from the evidence available to him (ignoring, therefore, the unexpressed mental state of the defendant). Two further points about this test should be noted.

First, Blackburn J. said nothing about where the "reasonable man" is to be placed. As we have seen, this can be crucial, because it affects the evidence that can be taken into account in applying the objective test.[34] We shall see that later cases have made clear that the reasonable observer should be placed in the position of the claimant—that is, the question is what the claimant could reasonably have concluded about the defendant's intention.[35]

Secondly, one might ask: who, in practice, will be *caught* by this objective test? That is, what does the nature of the test say about the kind of defendant to whom it will apply—what kind of person intends to contract on a set of terms [y], but will under this test find himself bound to a contract on terms [x]? It is the defendant whose words and actions can reasonably be taken by a person in the other contracting party's position as meaning other than that which the defendant intends. That is, there is a mis-match between what the defendant meant, and what he communicated to the other party. The test catches those negotiating parties who not only fail to

[33] *André et Compagnie S.A. v Marine Transocean Ltd (The Splendid Sun)* [1981] Q.B. 694, CA; *Excomm Ltd v Guan Guan Shipping (Pte) Ltd (The Golden Bear)* [1987] 1 Lloyd's Rep. 330; *Tankreederei Ahrenkeil G.m.b.H. v Frahuil S.A. (The Multitank Holsatia)* [1988] 2 Lloyd's Rep. 486; below, para.13.14, n.42.

[34] Above, para.13–07.

[35] The failure to consider the position of the reasonable man is not really problematic in the context of the *Smith v Hughes* test, however, because the second (subjective) part of the test in any event focuses on the claimant's position and (actual) belief: below, para.13–13. The use of the "detached" reasonable observer can give a fundamentally different result if it is the *only* test: above, para.13–07.

communicate their intentions properly, but in fact communicate something which is *contrary* to their real intentions. A party who communicates clearly what he in fact intends is not at risk.[36]

13–13 **The subjective element of the test.** The test as stated by Blackburn J. is not, however, wholly objective. The subjective element is expressed by the words (with emphasis added):[37]

> "and that other party *upon that belief* enters into the contract with him."

The claimant can only hold the defendant to terms [x] if, in addition to that being the view that a reasonable person would have come to, the claimant also *in fact* so believed. This is an important limitation on the application of the test. In substance, it means that a party can enforce a contract only if that was what he in fact believed when he gave his agreement to it. He cannot intend [y], but later claim to enforce [x] when he discovers, to his advantage, that this would have been a reasonable interpretation. And he must have had a positive belief that the defendant was agreeing to [x]: the objective test is designed to protect the claimant who in fact reasonably relies on what he believes the other party is agreeing to, and if he had formed no view one way or the other as to what the defendant intended, he does not merit that protection.[38] Of course, whether the claimant can show what he in fact believed raises the difficulties of proof that are posed by any subjective test.[39] But in this the claimant will no doubt be assisted by making his claim in circumstances where the court has already been satisfied (in the first, objective, part of the test) that his alleged understanding was reasonable.

---

[36] *The Hannah Blumenthal*, above, n.25 at 916 (Lord Diplock: "The rule that neither party can rely upon his own failure to communicate accurately to the other party his own real intention by what he wrote or said or did, as negativing the consensus ad idem, is an example of a general principle of English law that injurious reliance on what another person did may be a source of legal rights against him").

[37] Above, para.13–09.

[38] *Maple Leaf Macro Volatility Master Fund v Rouvroy* [2009] EWHC 257 (Comm), [2009] 2 All E.R. (Comm) 287 at [228] (Andrew Smith J., approving Chitty, para.2–004, which cites cases both for and against this point; affirmed [2009] EWCA Civ 1334, [2010] 2 All E.R. (Comm) 788).

[39] Above, para.12–14.

The Hannah Blumenthal. The more recent decision which is commonly cited as authority for the objective test is that of the House of Lords in *The Hannah Blumenthal*.[40] There are some difficulties in extracting from this case a unanimous view about the test: their Lordships who discussed it—Lord Brandon, Lord Diplock and Lord Brightman—gave rather different accounts. But the later cases have settled on the statement by Lord Brightman which, as we shall see, is consistent with the test stated by Blackburn J. in *Smith v Hughes*. 13–14

The facts of *The Hannah Blumenthal* were not the paradigm case of the formation of a contract: it concerned the alleged abandonment of an arbitration on the basis that neither party had taken steps in the arbitration for a prolonged period.[41] The claim was therefore based on an alleged contract to abandon the arbitration, where the evidence for the abandonment was silence and inactivity by both parties. The claim failed.[42] The language of the speeches is inevitably tailored to the particular context of the claim. But it is clear that their Lordships thought that they were applying the general rules for the formation of a contract. The three different statements of the test should be considered.

Lord Brandon's test. Lord Brandon put the test in this way[43]: 13–15

> "Where A seeks to prove that he and B have abandoned a contract in this way, there are two ways in which A can put his case. The first way is by showing that the conduct of each party, as evinced to the other party and acted on by him, leads necessarily to the inference of an implied agreement

40 *Paal Wilson & Co. A/S v Partenreederei Hannah Blumenthal (The Hannah Blumenthal)* [1983] 1 A.C. 854, HL.

41 This is not, however, an unusual claim, although the application of the law to the facts can inevitably be difficult, given that it rests on an intepretation of silence and inactivity. For similar cases see below, n.42.

42 So did claims based on frustration and repudiation. For similar cases where the court held there was no agreement to abandon the arbitration, see *Allied Marine Transport Co. Ltd v Vale do Rio Doce Navegacao S.A.*, above n.27; *Food Corp. of India v Antclizo Shipping Corp. (The Antclizo)* [1987] 2 Lloyd's Rep. 130, CA; *Gebr. Van Weelde Scheepvaart Kantor B.V. v Compania Naviera Sea Orient S.A. (The Agrabele)* [1987] 2 Lloyd's Rep. 223, CA. But for cases where there was an agreement to abandon, see *André et Compagnie S.A. v Marine Transocean Ltd (The Splendid Sun)*, above, n.33; *Excomm Ltd v Guan Guan Shipping (Pte) Ltd (The Golden Bear)*, above n.33; *Tankreederei Ahrenkeil G.m.b.H. v Frahuil S.A. (The Multitank Holsatia)*, above, n.33.

43 Above, n.40 at 914.

between them to abandon the contract. The second method is by showing that the conduct of B, as evinced towards A, has been such as to lead A reasonably to believe that B has abandoned the contract, even though it has not in fact been B's intention to do so, and that A has significantly altered his position in reliance on that belief. The first method involves actual abandonment by both A and B. The second method involves the creation by B of a situation in which he is estopped from asserting, as against A, that he, B, has not abandoned the contract: *Pearl Mill Co. Ltd v Ivy Tannery Co. Ltd.*[44]"

This statement appears to envisage either an actual agreement or an estoppel. In broad terms, it is consistent with the approach in *Smith v Hughes* although there are some uncertainties over the nature of the "implied agreement" envisaged by Lord Brandon (is it subjective or objective?)[45]; and its relationship to the estoppel which may be used in the absence of such agreement (if the implied agreement is objective, how does that differ from the estoppel?).[46]

13–16 **Lord Diplock's test.** Lord Diplock put the test in this way[47]:

"To create a contract by exchange of promises between two parties where the promise of each party constitutes the consideration for the promise of the other, what is necessary is that the intention of each *as it has been communicated to and understood by the other* (even though that which has been communicated does not represent the actual state of mind of the communicator) should coincide. That is what English lawyers mean when they resort to the Latin phrase consensus ad idem and the words that I have italicised are essential to the concept of consensus ad idem, the lack of which prevents the formation of a binding contract in English law.

Thus if A (the offeror) makes a communication to B (the offeree) whether in writing, orally or by conduct, which, in the circumstances at the time the communication was received, (1) B, if he were a reasonable man, would understand as stating A's intention to act or refrain from acting in some specified manner if B will promise on his part to act or refrain from acting in some manner also specified in the offer, and (2) B does in fact understand A's communication to mean this, and in his turn makes to A a communication conveying his willingness so to act or to refrain from acting which mutatis mutandis satisfies the same two conditions as respects A, the consensus ad idem essential to the formation of a contract in English law is complete."

44 [1919] 1 K.B. 78; [above, n.27].
45 Above, n.25.
46 Above, n.30.
47 Above, n.40 at 915.

This formulation of the test has been criticised in later cases, but the main lines of Lord Diplock's thinking are absolutely clear. A contract requires an agreement—a *consensus ad idem*. But English law tests this objectively, rather than subjectively.[48] I am bound to what I led the other party reasonably to believe that I intended, not what I in fact intended. Thus, the two elements of the "objective test" set out by Blackburn J. in *Smith v Hughes*[49] are contained in Lord Diplock's statement: a reasonable person, placed in the claimant's position,[50] would believe that the defendant intended [x]; and the claimant must in fact have believed that the defendant intended [x]. The difficulty with Lord Diplock's formulation lies in the example in the second quoted paragraph: because it has to be applied from both parties' perspectives, it has been suggested that it will result in a contract only if the parties are subjectively in agreement.[51] In consequence of this, later courts have tended to prefer the rather simpler formulation in Lord Brightman's speech.[52]

Lord Brightman's test. Lord Brightman put the test in this way[53]: 13–17

> "The test in my opinion is not wholly objective.
>
> The basis of 'tacit abandonment by both parties', to use the phraseology of the sellers' case is that the primary facts are such that it ought to be inferred that the contract to arbitrate the particular dispute was rescinded by the mutual agreement of the parties. To entitle the sellers to rely on abandonment, they must show that the buyers so conducted themselves as to entitle the sellers to assume, *and that the sellers did assume*, that the contract was agreed to be abandoned sub silentio."

[48] The first question, however, should be whether there was in fact subjective agreement: this might be assumed by Lord Diplock, but it is not expressly stated: above, para.13–10, n.25.

[49] Above, paras. 13–12, 13–13.

[50] This was not clear in *Smith v Hughes*; above, para.13–12.

[51] *Allied Marine Transport Ltd v Vale do Rio Doce Navegacao S.A. (The Leonidas D)*, above, n.27 at 936.

[52] *ibid*. This is regarded as binding at the level of the CA: *Excomm Ltd v Guan Guan Shipping (Pte) Ltd (The Golden Bear)*, above n.33 at 338; *Food Corp. of India v Antclizo Shipping Corp. (The Antclizo)*, above, n.42 at 144; *Tankreederei Ahrenkeil G.m.b.H. v Frahuil S.A. (The Multitank Holsatia)*, above, n.33 at 492; *Kvaerner Construction Ltd v Eggar (Barony) Ltd* [2000] All E.R. (D) 1157 at [110]–[112]. In *Collin v Duke of Westminster*, above, n.30 at 596 Oliver L.J. cited Lord Diplock's test.

[53] Above, n.40 at 924 (emphasis in the original).

This statement makes clear that, where the claimant seeks to assert a contract [x] against the defendant, he must show that the claimant was *entitled*, from evidence that was available to him, to believe that the defendant intended [x]; and that the claimant *in fact* so believed. That is, both the objective and the subjective elements of the test as originally stated by Blackburn J. in *Smith v Hughes*.

13–18 **Both parties' perspectives are relevant.** Lord Brightman's test is attractive in its simplicity; but omits to discuss one point which needs to be added. The test considers only the claimant's perspective. What happens if the claimant can show that he was entitled to believe, and in fact believed, that the defendant intended [x], but that, in return, the defendant could show that his own honest belief that the contract was on terms [y] was, from his perspective, the reasonable conclusion? That is, both parties are equally honest and reasonable in their conclusions; and yet are not in fact in agreement. Such an outcome may be uncommon, but is possible because the objective element of the test is considered from the perspective of the party seeking to assert his version of the contract. This limits the range of evidence, in applying the objective test, to that which would have been available to each party when viewing the conduct and communications of the other. And it is possible that each party's dealings vis-à-vis the other are equally misleading. The only sensible conclusion in such a case is that there is no contract, because both the subjective test and the objective test fail to find an agreement.[54] In other words, the objective test will override the lack of subjective agreement where one party, *but only one party*, can show that, from his perspective the reasonable observer would have agreed with his (subjective) understanding.

13–19 **Summary of the test to be applied.** At this stage in the discussion, it will be useful to summarise the test that the courts will apply in order to ascertain whether there is a contract, and (if so) on what terms, in a case where the contract is alleged to have been

[54] J. P. Vorster, "A Comment on the Meaning of Objectivity in Contract" (1987) 104 L.Q.R. 274 at pp.283, 286.

formed by successive communications between the parties.[55] It can be put in the following propositions[56]:

1. The first question is whether the parties were in fact (subjectively) in agreement on the existence and terms of the contract. If they were, that should be determinative.[57]
2. If the parties were not, in fact, in agreement, then—in the case where the claimant is seeking to rely on there being a contract on terms [x], and the defendant is either denying that there is a contract at all, or is asserting that there is a contract on terms [y]—the question becomes whether the claimant can in law hold the defendant to have agreed to a contract on terms [x]. He may do so if:
   (a) the defendant's words, conduct or (exceptionally[58]) silence would have led a reasonable person in the claimant's position to believe that the defendant was agreeing to [x];[59] and
   (b) the claimant in fact believed that the defendant was agreeing to [x].[60]
3. If the claimant succeeds in showing that he can hold the defendant to a contract on terms [x] in accordance with proposition 2, he has established a contract on terms [x] *unless* the defendant can rebut this by showing that the claimant's conduct, words or (exceptionally) silence would have led a reasonable person in his position to believe that the claimant was agreeing to [y], and that the defendant in fact believed that the claimant was agreeing to [y]. In such a case, there is no contract.

In the following section we shall see that in any case where there is a dispute between the parties on the question whether they were sufficiently in agreement on the terms of the contract, or—and this

---

[55] Where the contract is in writing, a different approach is adopted: below, paras.13–32 *et seq*.

[56] See also Vorster, above, n.54, p.286. This paragraph was accepted and applied in *DNA Productions (Europe) Ltd v Manoukian* [2008] EWHC 943 (Ch), [2008] All E.R. (D) 428 (Apr) at [47], [50].

[57] Above, para.13–10.

[58] Above, para.13–12.

[59] Above, para.13–12.

[60] Above, para.13–13.

is substantially the same issue—where one party claims that he was mistaken about the terms of the contract, the dispute can be analysed using the propositions set out above. In other words, we shall now consider the *practical* application of the test contained in these propositions—which we shall call, for convenience, the "objective test".

III. PRACTICAL APPLICATION OF THE OBJECTIVE TEST

(1) Misunderstandings Incapable of Resolution

13–20 **No reasonable interpretation; or no single reasonable interpretation.** It is possible for the parties to be so fundamentally at cross-purposes that their subjective mutual misunderstanding cannot be resolved by the objective test. This will happen in two types of case: where *neither* party's understanding of the other's intention is that which the reasonable observer would hold[61]; or if *both* parties' understandings are, from their several perspectives, reasonable.[62] In the former case, neither party can satisfy proposition 2(a) above; in the latter case both parties can satisfy propositions 2(a) and (b), but the application of proposition 3 leads to the conclusion that there is no contract.

(2) Mistake of One Party, Known (or Ought to be Known) by the Other

13–21 **Mistake of one party known by the other.** Under this test a party cannot enforce a contract on his own terms, even if it appears on the objective evidence to have been concluded, where he knows

[61] *Falck v Williams* [1900] A.C. 176, PC (parties contracted by coded telegrams which each, acting in good faith, interpreted differently: the claimant shipowner understood it to be a contract for the carriage of copra from Fiji to the UK or Europe; the defendant shipbroker believed that it was for the carriage of a cargo of shale from Sydney to Barcelona; there was no conclusive reason pointing in favour of either reading); *Raffles v Wichelhaus* (1864) 2 H. & C. 906, 159 E.R. 375 (sale of cotton "ex 'Peerless' from Bombay": but there were two ships called "Peerless" carrying cotton, in October and December. Claimant could not show it was the cargo he offered (from October sailing). The contract may have been void for unresolved latent ambiguity: *Smith v Hughes* (1871) L.R. 6 Q.B. 597 at 609 (Hannen J.) or valid but on the defendant's understanding: *Van Praagh v Everidge* [1902] 2 Ch. 266 at 269 (Kekewich J.)).

[62] Above, para.13–13.

that the other party was mistaken about the terms. In such a case he cannot show that proposition 2(b) is true.[63] This is the basis on which it is sometimes said that a party will not be allowed to "snap at" an offer[64]: that is, if he receives an offer which he knows contains a mistake about a term—for example, the price stated in the offer is lower than the offeror intended the contract to prescribe—he cannot by accepting the offer before the offeror has discovered his mistake conclude a binding contract at the lower price. The fact that he knew that the offeror made a mistake in his letter of offer means that he cannot show that he in fact believed that it reflected the offeror's true intentions.[65]

Mistake of one party that the other should have known about. 13–22
Similarly, a party cannot enforce a contract on terms which he *should have known* did not reflect the other party's true intentions. In this case, he cannot satisfy proposition 2(a), because a reasonable person in his position would not have believed that the other party was agreeing to those terms.[66] In practice, it may be easier to rely on this ground to avoid the contract, rather than proving that the party actually knew about the mistake, because it is easier to prove what reasonable person would have understood than what the other party actually did understand.[67]

---

[63] *Smith v Hughes*, above n.61 at 609–610 (Hannen J., who focused on this situation in explaining the operation of the objective test). *Cf. Statoil A.S.A. v Louis Dreyfus Energy Services L.P. (The Harriette N)* [2008] EWHC 2257 (Comm), [2008] 2 Lloyd's Rep. 685 at [87] (Aikens J.: where one party knows the other is mistaken about the terms, "the normal rule of looking only at the objective agreement of the parties is displaced and the court admits evidence to show what each side subjectively intended to agree by way of terms").

[64] *Tamplin v James* (1880) 15 Ch.D. 215 at 221 (James L.J., describing the facts of *Webster v Cecil* (1861) 30 Beav. 62, 54 E.R. 812).

[65] *Hartog v Colin & Shields* [1939] 3 All E.R. 566 at 568 (defendant mistakenly offered hare skins at prices "per pound" instead of "per piece"; Singleton J: "I am satisfied . . . from the evidence given to me, that the plaintiff must have realised, and did in fact know, that a mistake had occurred").

[66] *Hartog v Colin & Shields*, above, n.65 at 568 ("I am satisfied that anyone with any knowledge of the trade must have realised that there was a mistake").

[67] In *Hartog v Colin & Shields*, above, n.65, the judge was satisfied on both grounds. See also *Chwee Kin Keong v Digilandmall.com Pte Ltd* [2005] 1 S.L.R. 502 (claimants placed orders on internet site for laser printers which were in error priced at $66 each in place of $3,854. CA Singapore drew a different distinction from that known in the English cases and held that the contract would be void only if the claimants *actually* knew of the defendants' mistake, but in Singapore

13–23 **Burden of proof that the other party knew or ought to have known about the mistake.** Sometimes, where the issue turns on whether the claimant knew or ought to have known about the defendant's mistake, the courts appear to place the burden of proof on the defendant. However, this is only a shift in the evidential burden. In principle, it must be for the claimant to establish his claim; and so if he brings a claim based on a term of a contract which the defendant disputes on the basis that he (the defendant) did not agree to it, it is for the claimant to prove that the defendant is bound by such a term.[68] In practice, however, the courts may require the defendant to bring evidence to negative the validity of the apparent contract where the claim is prima facie good, because there is clear objective evidence to support the contract as alleged by the claimant—such as the fact that the defendant has issued a document which in its language clearly appears to show that he has assented to the contract on the terms alleged by the claimant.[69]

(3) Relevant of the Parties' Fault

13–24 **The parties' fault is not itself a test.** Sometimes it is said that a party cannot rely on a mistake about the terms where he was at fault in making it.[70] This is rather imprecise and is better not stated as a

---

there is a wider jurisdiction to render the contract voidable in equity); discussed at (2005) 121 L.Q.R. 393 (T.M. Yeo); [2005] L.M.C.L.Q. 423 (K.F.K. Low). For cases where there was a mistake by the defendant as to the price, but nothing on the facts to show that the claimant either knew about it or ought reasonably to have known about it, see *Centrovincial Estates Plc v Merchant Investors Assurance Co. Ltd* [1983] Com. L.R. 158, CA (error as to rent payable under lease); *O.T. Africa Line Ltd v Vickers Plc* [1996] 1 Lloyd's Rep. 700 (fax from defendant offered settlement for £150,000; defendant alleged not binding because it intended to make offer of $150,000; held binding).

[68] Phipson, paras 6–02, 6–08.

[69] *O.T. Africa Line Ltd v Vickers Plc*, above, n.67 ("[O]n any objective approach there was an agreement to settle at £150,000 . . . In the light of the dicta in the *Centrovincial* case [(above, n.67)] and *The Antclizo* [[1987] 2 Lloyd's Rep. 130 at 146], I . . . proceed on the basis that Vickers would not be bound if they could show that OTAL, or those acting for OTAL, either knew or ought reasonably to have known that there had been a mistake by Vickers or those acting for Vickers. I put the onus that way round, as it appears so in the authorities, but it would not make any difference in this case if it were the other way round": Mance J. at 702–703).

[70] e.g. *Tamplin v James*, above, n.64 at 222 (Brett L.J.: "the Defendant bought under a mistake, but it was a mistake into which he was led solely by his not

formal test, because the fault of the parties—of either the claimant or the defendant—can be raised in various different circumstances. Rather, it can be seen that cases where one party's fault has been raised can be analysed using the general test set out above at para.13–19.[71]

The defendant's "fault". There are a number of cases in which the defendant might be said to have been at fault—with the consequence that he cannot deny that he is bound to the contract on the claimant's terms, even though he in fact made a mistake. In one sense, the very basis of the "objective test" is the defendant's fault: the reason that the defendant's subjective misunderstanding about the terms of the contract is overridden in favour of the claimant's understanding is that he has behaved in such a way as to entitle the claimant to misunderstand him. If the defendant had not failed properly to communicate his own intentions, the problem would not have arisen. So, typically, where the defendant's misunderstanding about the terms was neither caused by the claimant, nor arose in circumstances where the external observer in the claimant's position would have realised that there was a mistake, the defendant is bound because he has no one to blame but himself. For example, where the defendant bids at auction for the wrong property, and the auctioneer (on behalf of the claimant) has no way of knowing that the defendant did not fully understand what he was doing, there is no basis on which the defendant can be heard to say that he misunderstood which property was the subject-matter of the sale.[72] 13–25

taking reasonable care"); *Smith v Hughes*, above, n.61 at 609 (Hannen J.: "one of the parties to an apparent contract may, by his own fault, be precluded from setting up that he had entered into it in a different sense to that in which it was understood by the other party"); *Denny v Hancock* (1870) L.R. 6 Ch. App. 1 at 12 (James L.J.: "I am also of opinion that the mistake was occasioned by at least *crassa negligentia* on the part of the vendors in respect to what they sent out to the public").

[71] *Tamplin v James*, above, n.64 at 222 (Cotton L.J.: "In one sense he was not bound to look at [the plan of the property which would have shown the defendant the truth], but he cannot abstain from looking at it and say that he bought under a reasonable belief . . .").

[72] *Van Praagh v Everidge*, above, n.61 at 269 (Kekewich J: the defendant, who was somewhat deaf, "made an extraordinary blunder"), revsd on different grounds [1903] 1 Ch. 434, CA (no memorandum within the Statute of Frauds; but Collins M.R. at 436 suggested that the parties were, in any event, not *ad idem*. This should not however have prevented the contract from being binding under

Or where the defendant writes to the claimant in terms which contain a proposal as to price which is clear, and the claimant cannot be expected in the circumstances to realise that the defendant has made a mistake when he wrote the price into the letter, the defendant will be bound to the price he has written.[73] In both of these cases the defendant can be said to be at fault, in failing to take the proper precautions to protect his own interests. But that is not, in fact, the point. Under the objective test, the claimant need not identify in what respect the defendant was at fault. The only question is[74]: did the defendant behave in such a way as to lead a reasonable person in the claimant's position to believe that he was agreeing to buy the property that was actually being auctioned; and did the claimant (directly, or through his agent) in fact so believe?

13–26 **The claimant's "fault".** On the other hand, there are cases in which the claimant might be said to have been at fault—with the consequence that he cannot enforce the contract on the terms as he intended them. But, again, it is better not formally to ask whether the claimant was at fault, but to analyse a claim in terms of the propositions set out above[75]: where the claimant can be said—more or less precisely—to have been at fault, it will be found that he fails to satisfy the objective test, either because in fact he knew about the other party's different intentions as to the terms of the contract,[76] or

---

the objective test); *Malins v Freeman* (1836–1837) 2 Keen 25, 48 E.R. 537 (defendant "placed himself near enough to the auctioneer for a person not deficient in hearing to hear what the auctioneer said", but bid for the wrong property, and "kept bidding in a hasty and inconsiderate manner until the price was raised to £1,400"); *Tamplin v James*, above, n.64 (defendant bought after auction, but had been present and had not bothered to look at plans which would have revealed that he was wrongly assuming that the property for sale included certain additional plots of land that he knew had been occupied by tenants).

[73] *Centrovincial Estates Plc v Merchant Investors Assurance Co. Ltd*, above, n.67 (written proposal by landlord that new rent should be £65,000 a year, instead of (as intended) £126,000. The existing rent was already £68,320, but "in the absence of any proof . . . that the [tenant] either knew or ought reasonably to have known of the [landlord's] error at the time when they purported to accept the [landlord's] offer, why should the [landlords] now be allowed to resile from that offer?" (Slade L.J.)); *O.T. Africa Line Ltd v Vickers Plc*, above, n.67. *Cf. Scott v Littledale* (1858) 8 El. & Bl. 815, 120 E.R. 304 (sale by sample; vendor mistakenly used wrong sample).

[74] Above, para.13–19.

[75] *ibid*.

[76] Above, para.13–13.

because he should have done—and so a reasonable person in his position would not have misunderstood the defendant.[77] Where, for example, his "fault" consists of having induced the mistake in the other party, either deliberately or at least carelessly, he will not be allowed to enforce a contract on his own terms—but in such a case it can be said either that he knew, or at least that he reasonably ought to have known, that the defendant's expression of assent did not accord with his real intentions.[78]

(4) The Consequences at Common Law of a Mistake About the Terms of the Contract

A mistake about the terms can give rise to different remedies. 13–27
There can be various different consequences of a mistake about the terms of a contract. If the defendant's mistake is operative, in the sense that he is allowed to say that he did not agree to the contract on the terms as the claimant asserts them to be, this does not necessarily determine whether there is no contract, or whether there might be an enforceable contract on *other* terms which the defendant might be able to establish. And even if the defendant's

---

[77] Above, para.13–12.

[78] *Denny v Hancock*, above, n.70 (vendor provided misleading plan of the property, and so could not hold purchaser to contract: "It really almost requires to my mind some charity—though I will have the charity—to suppose that he did not prepare his plan with the view of leading a purchaser to suppose the trees to be included . . . It appears to me very clear that the purchaser has been deceived by the plan and the particulars respecting a material point, and that under such circumstances he certainly cannot be compelled to complete the purchase, the mistake having arisen, to say the least of it, through the negligence of the vendors' agents": Mellish L.J. at 14); *Scriven Bros & Co. v Hindley & Co.* [1913] 3 K.B. 564 (sale of tow at auction; purchaser believed it was hemp, from misleading markings on samples at the auction. There was no subjective agreement; and there could be no "contract by estoppel": above, para.13–11: "Such a contract cannot arise when the person seeking to enforce it has by his own negligence or by that of those for whom he is responsible caused, or contributed to cause, the mistake": A.T. Lawrence J. at 569); *Lloyds Bank Plc v Waterhouse* [1993] 2 F.L.R. 97, CA, at 123 (Sir Edward Eveleigh: "in all the circumstances, the manager ought to have known that the defendant was not aware of the extent of the obligation in the guarantee, that the defendant would only be willing to undertake a [less extensive] liability . . . Consequently, in my opinion, the guarantee was signed under a mistake which was negligently induced by the manager and, therefore, the mistake prevents the signature from having a binding effect inter partes: see *Scriven Bros v Hindley & Co.*").

mistake is overridden by the objective test—that is, in a sense, his mistake has been held to be irrelevant as regards the formation of the contract on the claimant's terms[79]—the fact that the defendant made a mistake may still be relevant to the remedies that the claimant will obtain.

13–28 **Mistake by the defendant which is not overridden by the objective test.** Where the claimant fails to satisfy the objective test,[80] he has failed to establish the contract that he alleges. But it is important to recognise the limitations of such a decision. The claimant was seeking to prove that the defendant was bound to a contract on terms [x]. He fails. This only proves that there was no contract on terms [x]. Unless the defendant raises the issue by way of counterclaim, or the court of its own motion discusses it in obiter dicta,[81] it is not necessarily clear whether there was no contract (or, as it is sometimes said, the contract was "void"[82]); or whether there was a contract *but on terms [y]*.[83] Sometimes, however, the facts will give the answer: for example, where the contract, if it exists at all, must be based on a document written by one of the parties, and the claimant fails to establish that the defendant is to be taken (objectively) to have agreed to the terms set out in that document,

---

[79] Above, para.13–01.
[80] Above, para.13–19.
[81] *Falck v Williams* [1900] A.C. 176, PC, at 181 ("If the respondent had been maintaining his construction as plaintiff he would equally have failed").
[82] Above, para.12–18. *Cf. Statoil A.S.A. v Louis Dreyfus Energy Services L.P. (The Harriette N)* [2008] EWHC 2257 (Comm), [2008] 2 Lloyd's Rep. 685 at [87] (Aikens J.: "If it is clear from such evidence that there was not consensus, then there can be no contract, because the parties have not truly agreed on the terms. Some of the cases talk of such a contract being 'void', but I think it is clearer to say that there was never a contract at all").
[83] e.g. *Raffles v Wichelhaus* (1864) 2 H. & C. 906, 159 E.R. 375 (sale of cotton "ex 'Peerless' from Bombay": but there were two ships called "Peerless" carrying cotton, in October and December. Claimant could not show it was the cargo he offered (from October sailing). It is generally assumed that the contract was have been void for unresolved latent ambiguity: *Smith v Hughes* (1871) L.R. 6 Q.B. 597 at 609 (Hannen J.); *The Great Peace* [2002] EWCA Civ 1407, [2003] Q.B. 679 at [29]; Treitel, para.8–049; Anson, p.255. But the judgment is so short (seven words: "There must be judgement for the defendants") that it gives no indication of what would have been held if the defendants had been claiming for breach of the contract as *they* understood it to be. In *Van Praagh v Everidge* [1902] 2 Ch. 266 at 269 Kekewich J., relying on *Pollock on Contracts*, assumed that there was a contract but "not the contract that was sued on".

there can be no contract—for the simple reason that, even though the defendant might have intended the contract to be on a different set of terms, there is no external evidence by which he can say that the claimant in fact agreed to it.[84]

Mistake by the defendant which is overridden by the objective test. Where, however, the claimant succeeds in showing that the defendant is bound to a contract on terms [x], in spite of the fact that the defendant intended either no contract, or a contract on terms [y], he has established a contract on terms [x].[85] But there may still be a question of the remedies that the court will award to support the claim. In particular, although the claimant will always be entitled to damages for breach by the defendant of the contract that has been established, the defendant may be able to resist specific performance on the basis of the mistake —even in a case of a kind where specific performance might normally be expected to be awarded. For example, the courts will normally award specific performance of a contract to purchase land.[86] But where the defendant's mistake consists of contracting to purchase the wrong property,[87] and is a property for which he has no use,[88] the court may be persuaded that it would be "hardship amounting to 13–29

[84] e.g. *Hartog v Colin & Shields* [1939] 3 All E.R. 566 (offer and acceptance to create contract for sale of hare skins were in terms of prices "per pound"; claimant could not hold defendant to that bargain, because he knew (or at least should have known) that the defendant intended to contract at prices "per piece": above, paras 13–21, 13–22. But the defendant could not have shown that there was in fact a contract at prices "per piece", because there was no offer and acceptance on those terms). *Cf* similarly the facts of *Webster v Cecil*, above, n.64.

[85] Above, para.13–19.

[86] Jones and Goodhart, p.128.

[87] *Malins v Freeman*, above, n.72 (specific performance refused; "I think that he never meant to enter into this contract, and that it would not be equitable to compel him to perform it, whatever may be the responsibility [i.e. in damages] to which he is left liable at law": Lord Langdale M.R. at 35, at 541). See also *Webster v Cecil*, above, n.64 (contract to sell property for £1,250 instead of £2,250: specific performance refused, but "the Plaintiff . . . might bring such action at law as he might be advised": Romilly M.R. at 64, at 813). When reading such cases, decided before the fusion of the jurisdictions of law and equity (Judicature Act 1873 Pt.II, esp. ss.24, 25), it is important to remember that, unless the court considers the issue, the claimant's failure to obtain specific performance of the contract he alleges may not establish whether there was no contract on the terms he alleged; or there was such a contract but the remedy is only damages at common law.

injustice"[89] to require him to take the property, and may instead order him to pay damages, which will include the vendor's costs of obtaining a resale, as well as any loss in failing to obtain an equivalent price to that which the defendant had agreed to pay.

(5) Equitable Remedies for a Mistake about the Terms

13–30 **Rescission and rectification.** The courts of equity developed their own responses in favour of a party who could show that he had made a mistake about the terms of the contract. We have already seen that, even though the contract might be valid at common law, the courts of equity might sometimes refuse to award specific performance against a defendant who had entered into the contract under a mistake, and would therefore leave the claimant to his remedies at law.[90] Equity went further, however, and developed remedies which could be invoked by the mistaken party: rescission; and rectification. Rectification is available only for written contracts, and will be considered in the following section. A word must first be said about the use of the remedy of rescission in the modern law.

13–31 **No discretion to rescind a contract for unilateral mistake about the terms.** It has sometimes been said that, although the claimant may succeed in showing, by an application of the objective test, that the defendant is bound to a contract on the terms as the claimant understood them—and so the contract is not void—the contract may be rescinded in equity on account of the defendant's mistake.[91]

---

[88] *Van Praagh v Everidge*, above, n.83 (specific performance ordered: no hardship amounting to injustice, because claimant was a property developer and "there is no reason why having bought this he should not develop it": Kekewich J. at 272), revsd on different grounds [1903] 1 Ch. 434, CA; see also above, para.13–25, n.72. Kekewich J. distinguished *Malins v Freeman*, above, n.72; and preferred to follow *Tamplin v James*, above, n.64, where specific performance was ordered); Jones and Goodhart, pp.106–107.

[89] *Tamplin v James*, above, n.64 at 221.

[90] Above, para.13–29.

[91] *Solle v Butcher* [1950] 1 K.B. 671 at 692–692 (Denning L.J.: "a contract will be set aside if . . . one party, knowing that the other is mistaken about the terms of an offer . . . lets him remain under his delusion and concludes a contract on the mistaken terms instead of pointing out the mistake. That is, I venture to think, the ground on which the defendant in *Smith v. Hughes* would be exempted nowadays"); *O.T. Africa Line Ltd v Vickers Plc* [1996] 1 Lloyd's Rep. 700 at 704

Such statements cannot however be relied upon. The Court of Appeal has held that there is no jurisdiction in equity to rescind a contract for common mistake about the subject-matter, where the mistake is not sufficient to render the contract void at common law.[92] Such a mistake, and the approach of the common law to it, raises different issues from those which we are considering here, but one of the court's grounds for rejecting the argument that a contract could be rescinded in equity where it was valid at law was that this would undermine the policy of the common law: "the premise of equity's intrusion into the effects of the common law is that the common law rule in question is seen in the particular case to work injustice, and for some reason the common law cannot cure itself".[93] The same argument holds in the case of unilateral mistake about the terms. The mistake is either sufficient to prevent the a contract being found under the objective test; or it is not. But if it is insufficient, and so the contract exists at common law, equity should not undermine the certainty provided by the common law by holding that the contract may be rescinded on the ground that it would be inequitable to hold the defendant to the bargain.[94]

This has, indeed, been the effect of the approach taken by the Court of Appeal in relation to the equitable remedy of rescission for

(Mance J.: "I am prepared to proceed on the basis that rescission may be available where it is simply inequitable for one party to seek to hold the other to a bargain objectively made"). Lord Denning's approach was adopted explicitly by the High Court of Australia in *Taylor v Johnson* (1982–1983) 151 C.L.R. 422 at 430–431, but only in relation to formal written contracts; they left open the question whether it should properly be accepted as applying in the case of an informal contract or in the case where there is a mistake about the identity of the other party. *Cf.* D.O'Sullivan, S. Elliott and R. Zakrzewski, *The Law of Rescission* (2008), paras 7.07–7.25, who assume that rescission is available for mistake about the terms of the contract, although they note that the law on this is more developed in Australia through the decision in *Taylor v Johnson*.

[92] *The Great Peace* [2002] EWCA Civ 1407, [2003] Q.B. 679, below, para.15–32.

[93] *ibid.* at [156].

[94] This is not to say that the equitable remedy of specific performance might not be refused on the basis of a mistake made by the defendant even though the mistake is not sufficient to render the contract void at common law: above, para.13–29. But to refuse specific performance does not undermine the contract itself; it only leaves the claimant to his remedies at common law (typically, damages). Similarly, equity may refuse specific performance of a contract on the basis of a misrepresentation even though it is insufficient to avoid the contract either at common law or in equity: above, para.10–07.

unilateral mistakes about the terms of the contract. The clearest statement was made by Russell L.J. giving the judgment of the court in *Riverlate Properties Ltd v Paul*[95]:

> "Is the lessor entitled to rescission of the lease on the mere ground that it made a serious mistake in the drafting of the lease which it put forward and subsequently executed, when (a) the lessee did not share the mistake, (b) the lessee did not know that the document did not give effect to the lessor's intention, and (c) the mistake of the lessor was in no way attributable to anything said or done by the lessee? What is there in principle, or in authority binding upon this court, which requires a person who has acquired a leasehold interest on terms upon which he intended to obtain it, and who thought when he obtained it that the lessor intended him to obtain it on those terms, either to lose the leasehold interest, or, if he wished to keep it, to submit to keep it only on the terms which the lessor meant to impose but did not? In point of principle, we cannot find that this should be so. If reference be made to principles of equity, it operates on conscience. If conscience is clear at the time of the transaction, why should equity disrupt the transaction? If a man may be said to have been fortunate in obtaining a property at a bargain price, or on terms that make it a good bargain, because the other party unknown to him has made a miscalculation or other mistake, some high-minded men might consider it appropriate that he should agree to a fresh bargain to cure the miscalculation or mistake, abandoning his good fortune. But if equity were to enforce the views of those high-minded men, we have no doubt that it would run counter to the attitudes of much the greater part of ordinary mankind (not least the world of commerce), and would be venturing upon the field of moral philosophy in which it would soon be in difficulties."

The court here limited the remedy of rescission of the contract for unilateral mistake to circumstances where the party against whom rescission is sought cannot resist it because his "conscience" is affected; and his conscience is *not* affected where he did not share the mistake, did not know about the claimant's mistake, and did not cause it. This does not undermine the common law; indeed, on this account the approach taken by equity is more restrictive—since the equitable principles are based on "conscience"; and this leads the court to give a remedy only against a party whose conscience is affected by having *actual* knowledge or notice of the mistake,

[95] [1975] Ch. 133 at 140–141; this is followed at 141–145 by a detailed discussion of the cases to establish that there was no binding authority to the contrary.

whereas the objective test will allow a party to raise a mistake where the other party *ought* to have known it.[96]

Since the rules applied by equity to a unilateral mistake about the terms would permit a contract to be rescinded only in circumstances where it is void under the common law test, then the equitable remedy appears to have no place: "It is axiomatic that there is no room for rescission in equity of a contract which is void".[97] Even if the contract is contained in a formal written document, it does not need to be set aside in equity if it is void at law: the declaration by the court that it is void should be sufficient.[98]

[96] Above, para.13–22. See also *Commission for the New Towns v Cooper (Great Britain) Ltd* [1995] Ch. 259, CA, at 280 (Stuart-Smith L.J.): "where A intends B to be mistaken as to the construction of the agreement, so conducts himself that he diverts B's attention from discovering the mistake by making false and misleading statements, and B in fact makes the very mistake that A intends, then notwithstanding that A does not actually know, but merely suspects, that B is mistaken, and it cannot be shown that the mistake was induced by any misrepresentation . . . A's conduct is unconscionable and he cannot insist on performance in accordance to the strict letter of the contract; that is sufficient for rescission [and may be sufficient for rectification: below, paras 13–44 *et seq.*]". Here again the example given would be sufficient to allow B to raise his mistake, which would not be overriden at common law by the objective test, because A both intends B to make a mistake and suspects that he has made the mistake—which would certainly prevent A from relying on the objective test.

[97] *The Great Peace*, above, n. 92 at [96].

[98] *cf.* a contract void at common law under the doctrine of *non est factum*; below, para 13–60. or the written contract declared to be void for mistake of identity; below, para.14–30. The context in which the equitable remedy has generally been discussed—and, historically, granted—is rescission of written contracts, where equity might be invoked to support the common law; for example, where the mistaken agreement is embodied in a formal document which requires to be set aside, and other consequential orders have to be made to give effect to the rights of the parties at common law. *Cf.*, in relation to common mistake about the subject-matter, the explanation in *The Great Peace*, above, n.92 at [99] *et seq.* of *Cooper v Phibbs* (1867) L.R. 2 H.L. 149, HL (lease set aside in equity, and terms imposed; but the mistake was sufficiently serious to render the contract void at common law).

IV. WRITTEN CONTRACTS[99]

(1) The Use of Writing in the Formation of a Contract

13–32 **The significance of writing during the formation of a contract.** A contract may be concluded in various different ways: orally, or by an exchange of written correspondence, or by some combination of oral and written communications. For example, the negotiations may be initiated by one party making a written offer to the other, or one party may respond to a written invitation to treat issued by the other (such as a newspaper advertisement, or an invitation to tender), and may then proceed through oral discussions until agreement is reached—or, in the context of the issues considered in this chapter, until one or both parties *believe* that agreement has been reached, although they later discover that there was in fact some misunderstanding between them as to the terms. In such situations, as we have seen in the earlier sections of this chapter, the courts will construe the communications between the parties, whether oral or written, using the objective test[100] to determine whether the defendant's subjective misunderstanding can be overridden, and so whether he can be held bound to a contract on the claimant's terms. We have also seen that for the purposes of the application of the objective test, a communication by one of the parties in writing can have a greater significance, in the sense that if its language is objectively clear, and if it was addressed to the claimant by the defendant, or if the claimant issued it but the defendant simply agreed to it, it will be easier for the claimant to assert that he reasonably understood the defendant to be agreeing to the terms set out in writing.[101] If the defendant seeks to argue that a document that he issued or to which he gave his assent was not reflective of his true intentions, when an objectively clear meaning

[99] On rectification generally, see Chitty, paras 5–107 to 5–136; Furmston, paras 4.112 to 4.127, Treitel, paras 8–059 to 8–075; Anson, pp.262–265; Cheshire, Fifoot and Furmston, pp.301–304; Cartwright, pp.52–57; Goff & Jones, paras 9–053 to 9–061; D. Hodge, *Rectification: The Modern Law and Practice Governing Claims for Rectification for Mistake* (2010); G. McMeel, *The Construction of Contracts* (2nd edn, 2011), Ch.17.
[100] Above, para.13–19.
[101] Above, para.13–25.

is conveyed by the document, he has in practice[102] a significant burden to explain not only that he had a contrary understanding, but also why the claimant should not hold him to the document.

Contracts in writing. The objective significance of writing is even stronger where the parties have not only used writing as a means of communication during their negotiations, but have, on conclusion of their agreement, decided that the agreement should be put into a written document, to which they will both then give their assent (typically, by signing it[103]). This is common practice not only in negotiated commercial (business-to-business) contracts, but also in contracts between businesses and consumers where the business wishes to obtain the consent of the consumer to a complete set of terms, often on the business's own standard form; and also sometimes even between private individuals.[104] The purpose of such practice is clarity and certainty.[105] If each party has given his assent to a single, written statement of the terms, there is much less room for doubt or argument about the fact that both parties have **13–33**

[102] The burden of establishing the contract rests on the claimant. But the evidential burden in practice shifts to the defendant in such a case: above, para.13–23. This is, in a sense, the opposite end of the spectrum from a contract alleged to have been formed by silence. Where there are neither oral nor written communications between the parties, it is difficult to show that there was a communicated understanding between them about the contract and its terms—silence is inherently equivocal: above, para.13–04. Writing, however, is so much more concrete—even more so than an oral exchange between the parties—and so the objective meaning of written communications tends naturally to be viewed with the most significance.

[103] For the significance of signature as indicating assent to the terms of a document, see also above, para.9–09, n.28.

[104] All contracts for the sale or other disposition of an interest in land, whether between commercial or private parties, are required to take this form: either a single document, containing all the expressly agreed terms, signed by both parties; or two identical documents, each signed by one of the parties and exchanged: Law of Property (Miscellaneous Provisions) Act 1989 s.2.

[105] *A. & J. Inglis v John Buttery & Co.* (1877) 5 R. 58 at 69 (Lord Gifford: "The very purpose of a formal contract is to put an end to the disputes which would inevitably arise if the matter were left upon verbal negotiations or upon mixed communings partly consisting of letters and partly of conversations"), approved on appeal at (1878) 3 App. Cas. 552 at 577 (Lord Blackburn), and quoted in *Chartbrook Ltd v Persimmon Homes Ltd* [2009] UKHL 38, [2009] 1 A.C. 1101 at [3] (Lord Hope) and [29] (Lord Hoffmann), rejecting the argument that evidence of pre-contractual negotiations should generally be admissible in interpreting a written document: below, para.13–36, n.127.

agreed to the contract (their signatures show it); and what they have agreed to (the document is to be conclusive)—all the more so if the written contract makes clear that it is the complete agreement.[106]

It should be noticed that, typically, there are two stages to the formation of a contract in writing. First, the agreement is formed between the parties, generally in the same way as any other contract—and so it may well be done by a mixture of oral and written communications. But the agreement may not yet be complete;[107] and even if it is complete, it is still not yet a contract if the parties intend that the contract should be in writing. This is often shown explicitly in the case of negotiations for contracts relating to land, where the parties may head their correspondence "subject to contract"—which means that they do not intend the agreement to have legal effect until they have put it into the form of a written contract.[108] But any indication will suffice if it negatives the intention to create legal relations until the moment when the written document is executed. At that moment, however, the contract is concluded. And it is the written document, rather than the oral or

---

[106] e.g. by the use of an "entire agreement" clause, above, para.9–06, which is very common in commercial contracts. The same is true, in principle, for contracts for the sale (etc.) of land, since the contract is valid only if it contains all the expressly agreed terms: above, n.104.

[107] For the purposes of rectification for common mistake there must have been an "outward expression of "accord", but this does not require proof of complete agreement on all the terms of the contract in advance of the written document being executed: below, para.13–39.

[108] The use of the words "subject to contract" on a written communication between the parties or on a document signed by the parties was established in the context of negotiations for the sale of land—to ensure that a document (and communications which followed it without the express removal of the "subject to contract" label) did not constitute either a written contract or a memorandum which was sufficient under the Law of Property Act 1925 s.40 to evidence (and therefore make enforceable) an oral contract. Since the replacement of s.40 by the Law of Property (Miscellaneous Provisions) Act 1989 s.2, which requires a contract for the sale (etc.) of land to be *in writing*, the need for a "subject to contract" label has reduced, but its use had already become well established and it remains common practice. The words "subject to contract" have been held to have a similar meaning outside the context of contracts for the sale of land: e.g. *Confetti Recordsv Warner Music UK Ltd* [2003] EWHC 1274 (Ch), [2003] E.C.D.R. 31 at [90]–[94] (Lewison J.: the words "subject to contract" on a fax which contained proposed terms for a copyright licence had the effect of preventing a contract from coming into existence when the recipient replied purporting to accept the terms).

(informal) written agreement which preceded it, that is the contract. As we shall see below, this analysis has certain consequences for the relevance of a claim by one or both parties that they made a mistake about the terms of the contract. The starting-point is inevitably the written contract itself. But it becomes possible to argue that the written contract is defective in the sense that it does not match the agreement which preceded it.

General approach to mistakes about written documents; the use of the objective test. The starting-point for contracts in writing is that the written document contains the agreed terms. The document becomes the exclusive record of the contract, and therefore the only evidence that can be used to prove the existence of the contract and its terms is the document itself.[109] By giving his assent to the written document, each party has agreed that the writing reflects his intentions. The court therefore naturally starts with the document, interprets it and gives it effect. The question, however, is in what circumstances can one of the parties be heard to say that the document does not in fact reflect his true intentions, and that it should therefore not be given effect in accordance with its apparent terms? 13–34

The English courts have taken a particularly strong view of the significance of a party's signature on a written document. The leading case is *L'Estrange v Graucob*,[110] where Scrutton L.J. said[111]:

> "When a document containing contractual terms is signed, then, in the absence of fraud, or, I will add, misrepresentation, the party signing it is bound, and it is wholly immaterial whether he has read the document or not."

[109] Phipson, para.42.01. For the parol evidence rule, see generally Phipson, Ch.42; Lewison, para.3.11; Furmston, paras 3.4 to 3.6; Chitty, paras 12–096 to 12–133; Treitel, paras 6–013 to 6–030; Anson, pp.138–139; Cheshire, Fifoot and Furmston, pp.157–165.

[110] [1934] 2 K.B. 394 (claimant bound by her signature on contract of purchase of games machine for her café which contained terms (on brown paper, in "regrettably small print but quite legible": Maugham L.J. at 405) excluding the terms as to quality, etc., that would have been implied by the Sale of Goods Act 1893 s.14).

[111] *ibid.*, at 403.

This has been followed consistently; for example, Moore-Bick L.J. recently said[112]:

> "It was accepted that a person who signs a document knowing that it is intended to have legal effect is generally bound by its terms, whether he has actually read them or not. The classic example of this is to be found in *L'Estrange v Graucob*. It is an important principle of English law which underpins the whole of commercial life; any erosion of it would have serious repercussions far beyond the business community."

However, the limitations of the principle should be noticed. Scrutton L.J. made clear that the written document is subject to challenge on the grounds that the signature was obtained by fraud or misrepresentation. We have seen this in Part I.[113] But, in addition, it seems that the document should equally be open to challenge on the basis of mistake, either under the principle of *non est factum*,[114] or under the principles discussed in the earlier sections of this chapter.

The rationale of the binding force of written contracts was stated by Blackburn J. as follows[115]:

---

[112] *Peekay Intermark Ltd v Australia and New Zealand Banking Group Ltd* [2006] EWCA Civ 386, [2006] 1 C.L.C. 582 at [43]. See also *H.I.H. Casualty and General Insurance Ltd v New Hampshire Insurance Co.* [2001] EWCA Civ 735, [2001] 2 Lloyd's Rep. 161 at [209] (Rix L.J.); *J.P. Morgan Chase Bank v Springwell Navigation Corp.* [2008] EWHC 1186 (Comm), [2008] All E.R. (D) 167 (Jun) at [585] (Gloster J.)

[113] Above, para.10–14.

[114] Below, paras 13–55 to 13–60; *L'Estrange v Graucob*, above, n.110, at 406 (Maugham L.J.)

[115] *Harris v Great Western Railway Co.* (1876) 1 Q.B.D. 505 at 530; doubted in *McCutcheon v David Macbrayne Ltd* [1964] 1 W.L.R. 125, HL, at 134 (Lord Devlin: "when a party assents to a document forming the whole or a part of his contract, he is bound by the terms of the document, read or unread, signed or unsigned, simply because they are in the contract; and it is unnecessary and possibly misleading to say that he is bound by them because he represents to the other party that he has made himself acquainted with them."). *Cf.*, however, *Hardwick Game Farm v Suffolk Agricultural Poultry Producers Association* [1966] 1 W.L.R. 287, CA, at 339 (Diplock L.J.: "any party to a contract by agreeing that its terms shall be embodied in a written document so conducts himself as to lead the other to believe that he intended the written document to set out all the rights and liabilities of each party towards the other which do not arise by implication of law from the nature of the contract itself").

> "where there is a writing, into which the terms of any agreement are reduced, the terms are to be regulated by that writing. And though one of the parties may not have read the writing, yet, in general, he is bound to the other by those terms, and that, I apprehend, is on the ground that, by assenting to the contract thus reduced to writing, he represents to the other side that he has made himself acquainted with the contents of that writing and assents to them, and so induces the other side to act upon that representation by entering into the contract with him, and is consequently precluded from denying that he did make himself acquainted with those terms."

In substance, this is the same test as that which Blackburn J. had used five years earlier in *Smith v Hughes*.[116] But this opens up the argument that, if the party seeking to enforce the written contract knows, or ought to know, that the signature (or other sign of assent) to the document does not in fact reflect the defendant's assent to the terms which are contained in the document, then under the objective test[117] the claimant should not be entitled to hold the defendant to the document. It may be very rare that a court will be satisfied that the defendant made a mistake about the terms in such circumstances that he can resist enforcement of the contract on this basis,[118] but in an appropriate case the argument can succeed.[119]

---

[116] Above, para.13–09. In *Harris v Great Western Railway Co.,* as in *Smith v Hughes*, he ascribed the principle to the rule laid down by Parke B. in *Freeman v Cooke* (1848) 2 Exch. 654 at 663, 154 E.R. 652 at 656; above, para.13–11.

[117] Above, para.13–19.

[118] The mere fact that the claimant knows that the defendant has not read the document is not sufficient: that may only show that he is taking the risk about what the document contains, or did not care to check. It may also be difficult for the defendant so show that he made a mistake; he may simply not have thought about what the document contained, and did not have a positive but incorrect belief about the terms: above, para.12–03. And if the document is sufficently clear, then the claimant is entitled to believe that the defendant has agreed to it: *Peekay Intermark Ltd v Australia and New Zealand Banking Group Ltd*, above, n.112 at [43]: "the true position appeared clearly from the terms of the . . . contract . . . . Moreover, it was not buried in a mass of small print but appeared on the face of the document".

[119] J.R. Spencer, "Signature, Consent, and the Rule in *L'Estrange v Graucob*" [1973] C.L.J. 104. One case in which one judge in the CA held that the argument did succeed was *Lloyds Bank Plc v Waterhouse* [1993] 2 F.L.R. 97, CA, at 122–123 (Sir Edward Eveleigh: defendant signed guarantee, but claimant's representative ought to have known that he was not aware of the extent of the obligations in the document and would only be willing to agree to a more limited guarantee); J. Cartwright, "A Guarantee Signed by Mistake" [1990] L.M.C.L.Q.

(2) Remedying Mistakes by Interpretation

13–35 **Interpretation of communications, and interpretation of the written contract.** We have seen that it could be said that the objective test is a rule of interpretation of communications; that is, when the question is whether the parties by their communications have come to an agreement, the courts will interpret those communications objectively, from the perspective of the parties. What the defendant is taken to have agreed to is not what he intended his communication to convey, but what it would have conveyed to a reasonable person in the claimant's position—and it is binding if the claimant in fact so understood it.[120] Where the contract is in writing, however, the parties have gone further, and have committed their agreement into a written form, which they have then both agreed as the contract.[121] The focus of the interpretation now shifts to the document itself. And, inevitably, it becomes more a question of the objective meaning of the words in the document. The process by which the parties came to their agreement is irrelevant,[122] because it has been superseded by the written contract, although, as we shall see, it may be possible for the defendant to argue that the contract should be rectified because, on its (objective) construction it fails to embody the terms of the agreement.

---

338 at pp.340–341. See also *Amiri Flight Authority v BAE Systems Plc* [2003] EWCA Civ 1447, [2003] 2 C.L.C. 662 at [15] (Mance L.J., not deciding whether a signature might sometimes not be binding if sufficient notice has not been given as to "a provision of an extraneous or wholly unusual nature"); *Ocean Chemical Transport Inc. v Exnor Craggs Ltd* [2000] 1 Lloyd's Rep. 446 at [48] (Evans L.J.: the absence of sufficient notice might override the signature in "an extreme case, where a signature was obtained under pressure of time or other cirucumstances"). In Canada, see *Tilden Rent-a-Car Co. v Clendenning* (1978) 83 D.L.R. (3d) 400 (CA Ontario: hirer of car not bound by unusual, onerous clause in standard form contract that he had signed in course of hurried transaction where the other party knew that he had not read it); Waddams, para.347 (the principle applied in the decision "may be justified on the basis of protection of reasonable expectations"); *Colonial Investment Co. of Winnipeg, Man. v Borland* (1911) 1 W.W.R. 171 (Sup. Ct. Alta, affirmed on different grounds (1912) 6 D.L.R. 211); *Gray-Campbell Ltd v Flynn* [1923] 1 D.L.R. 51 (Sup. Ct. Alta; see Beck J.A., dissenting).

[120] Above, para.13–11.

[121] Above, para.13–33.

[122] Pre-contractual negotiations are not generally admissible in interpreting a written document: below, para.13–36, n.127.

The modern approach to interpretation of written contracts. 13–36
In a number of cases[123] the House of Lords has re-examined the general approach to the interpretation of written contracts and other written documents, and has emphasised that, whilst the test is *objective*—not taking into account the parties' own subjective intentions or understandings about the meaning of the document—it is nevertheless *contextual*. Lord Hoffmann summarised the modern approach in five principles[124]:

> "(1) Interpretation is the ascertainment of the meaning which the document would convey to a reasonable person having all the background knowledge which would reasonably have been available to the parties in the situation in which they were at the time of the contract.
>
> (2) The background was famously referred to by Lord Wilberforce[125] as the 'matrix of fact,' but this phrase is, if anything, an understated description of what the background may include. Subject to the requirement that it should have been reasonably available to the parties and to the exception to be mentioned next, it includes absolutely anything which would have affected the way in which the language of the document would have been understood by a reasonable man.[126]
>
> (3) The law excludes from the admissible background the previous negotiations of the parties and their declarations of subjective intent. They are admissible only in an action for rectification. The law makes this distinction for reasons of practical policy and, in this respect only, legal interpretation differs from the way we would

---

[123] *Mannai Investment Co. Ltd v Eagle Star Life Assurance Co. Ltd* [1997] A.C. 749; *Investors Compensation Scheme Ltd v West Bromwich Building Society* [1998] 1 W.L.R. 896; *Bank of Credit and Commerce International S.A. v Ali* [2001] UKHL 8, [2002] 1 A.C. 251; *Chartbrook Ltd v Persimmon Homes Ltd* [2009] UKHL 38, [2009] 1 A.C. 1101.

[124] *Investors Compensation Scheme Ltd v West Bromwich Building Society*, above, n.123 at 912–913. See also *Mannai Investment Co. Ltd v Eagle Star Life Assurance Co. Ltd*, above, n.123 at 775 and 779–780 (Lord Hoffmann); *Chartbrook Ltd v Persimmon Homes Ltd*, above, n.123, at [14] (Lord Hoffmann: "There is no dispute that the principles on which a contract (or any other instrument or utterance) should be interpreted are those summarised by the House of Lords in Investors *Compensation Scheme Ltd v West Bromwich Building Society*. They are well known and need not be repeated"). Lewison, Ch.1.

[125] [*Prenn v Simmonds* [1971] 1 W.L.R. 1381 at 1384.]

[126] [Further explained by Lord Hoffmann in *Bank of Credit and Commerce International S.A. v Ali*, above, n.123 at [39].]

interpret utterances in ordinary life. The boundaries of this exception are in some respects unclear. But this is not the occasion on which to explore them.[127]

(4) The meaning which a document (or any other utterance) would convey to a reasonable man is not the same thing as the meaning of its words. The meaning of words is a matter of dictionaries and grammars; the meaning of the document is what the parties using those words against the relevant background would reasonably have been understood to mean. The background may not merely enable the reasonable man to choose between the possible meanings of words which are ambiguous but even (as occasionally happens in ordinary life) to conclude that the parties must, for whatever reason, have used the wrong words or syntax: see *Mannai Investments Co. Ltd v Eagle Star Life Assurance Co. Ltd.*[128]

(5) The 'rule' that words should be given their 'natural and ordinary meaning' reflects the common sense proposition that we do not easily accept that people have made linguistic mistakes, particularly in formal documents. On the other hand, if one would nevertheless conclude from the background that something must have gone wrong with the language, the law does not require judges to attribute to the parties an intention which they plainly could not have had."

There is some debate as to whether this involves a change from the previously established principles of interpretation; and, if so, whether such a change is to be welcomed.[129] But it is clear for our purposes that the approach to the interpretation of a contract that has been reduced to writing is in principle to ignore the mistake of either party as to the meaning of the document and the terms it contains. A mistake is a subjective (mis)understanding.[130] The parties' subjective understandings are not relevant in the process of interpretation of the document itself.

---

[127] [For detailed discussion by HL, and the conclusion that the House should not depart from its earlier decision in *Prenn v Simmonds* (above, n.125) excluding pre-contractual negotiations in interpreting a written document, see *Chartbrook Ltd v Persimmon Homes Ltd*, above, n.123; this discussion was, however, obiter: see *ibid.* at [27] (Lord Hoffmann), [69] (Lord Rodger), [97] (Lord Walker).]

[128] [Above, n.123.]

[129] Lewison, paras 1.02, 1.04.

[130] Above, para.12–03.

The correction of mistakes by construction.[131] In principle, interpretation and rectification fulfil different functions. Interpretation discovers the meaning of the document itself. As we shall see in the following sections of this chapter, rectification admits that the document, as interpreted, fails to reflect the meaning of the underlying agreement as the parties intended it—and remedies this by rewriting the document so that it does reflect the meaning. However, sometimes the courts may solve a problem of mistake through interpretation of the contract. But this can be only where, on an objective interpretation of the contract, the court is persuaded that the contract must contain an error of drafting, and can also see what the correct wording should have been.[132] It is a solution which avoids giving either no meaning, or a plainly wrong meaning, to the 13–37

---

[131] Lewison, Ch.9; D. Hodge, *Rectification* (2010), ch.2; A. Burrows, "Construction and Rectification" in A. Burrows and E. Peel (eds), *Contract Terms* (2007) at pp.77–99; G. McMeel, *The Construction of Contracts* (2nd edn, 2011), paras.17.02 to 17.26.

[132] *East v Pantiles (Plant Hire) Ltd* [1982] 2 E.G.L.R. 111 at 112 (Brightman L.J.): "Two conditions must be satisfied: first, there must be a clear mistake on the face of the instrument; secondly, it must be clear what correction ought to be made in order to cure the mistake. If those conditions are satisfied, then the correction is made as a matter of construction. If they are not satisfied then either the claimant must pursue an action for rectification or he must leave it to a court of construction to reach what answer it can on the basis that the uncorrected wording represents the manner in which the parties decided to express their intention. In *Snell's Principles of Equity*, 27th edn, p.611, the principle of rectification by construction is said to apply only to obvious clerical blunders or grammatical mistakes. I agree with that approach. Perhaps it might be summarised by saying that the principle applies where a reader with sufficient experience of the sort of document in issue would inevitably say to himself, 'Of course X is a mistake for Y'"; *Homburg Houtimport B.V. v Agrosin Private Ltd (The Starsin)* [2003] UKHL 12, [2004] 1 A.C. 715 at [23] (Lord Bingham); *Chartbrook Ltd v Persimmon Homes Ltd*, above, n.123, at [22]–[25] (Lord Hoffmann, approving Brightman L.J.'s statement, subject to qualifications explained by Carnwath L.J. in *KPMG LLP v Network Rail Infrastructure Ltd* [2007] EWCA Civ 363, [2008] 1 P. & C.R. 11 at [45]–[50]); *cf. Bashir v Ali* [2011] EWCA Civ 707, [2011] Ell E.R. (D) 132 (Jun) at [39]–[42] (trial judge at [2010] EWHC 2320 (Ch), [2010] All E.R. (D) 115 (Oct) had been wrong to construe contract to convey ground floor shop with flat above as subject to unexpressed lease-back of part: the contract was very favourable to the purchaser, but not so much that it moved the case into the sphere of irrationality and so no interference with the clear wording of the contract was permissible).

terms of a contract[133]; and can be used to read in words which were clearly mistakenly omitted[134]; or to re-order the words or punctuation of the words which are included in the contract[135]; or even to substitute a word or words for those words which were in fact written in the contract.[136] Lord Hoffmann has said:[137]

> "there is not, so to speak, a limit to the amount of red ink or verbal rearrangement or correction which the court is allowed. All that is required is that it should be clear that something has gone wrong with the language and that it should be clear what a reasonable person would have understood the parties to have meant."

Thus there are examples of the courts correcting mistakes by construction which are very close indeed to rectification of the document—and sometimes the courts have contemplated that the solution could be given equally well by either construction or rectification.[138] But construction is simpler, because it does not require a formal application of the rules under which rectification can be ordered.

---

[133] *Tropwood AG of Zug v Jade Enterprises Ltd (The Tropwind)* [1982] 1 Lloyd's Rep. 232, CA, at 237 (Lord Denning M.R.).

[134] e.g. *Homburg Houtimport B.V. v Agrosin Private Ltd*, above, n.132; *KPMG LLP v Network Rail Infrastructure Ltd*, above, n.132.

[135] e.g. *Investors Compensation Scheme Ltd v West Bromwich Building Society*, above, n.123 ("Any claim (whether sounding in rescission for undue influence or otherwise)" construed as meaning "Any claim sounding in rescission (whether for undue influence or otherwise)").

[136] e.g. *Littman v Aspen Oil (Broking) Ltd* [2005] EWCA Civ 1579, [2006] 2 P. & C.R. 2 (break clause in a lease contained proviso "in the case of a notice given by the Landlord"—which was commercial nonsense, and should clearly have referred to a notice given by the tenant; CA interpreted "Landlord" as "Tenant"). See also *Wilson v Wilson* (1854) H.L.C. 40, 10 E.R. 811 (reference to one party ("John") in indemnity clause in deed of separation construed to refer to the other party ("Mary"): "Whether your Lordships could have seen on the face of the instrument that 'Mary' was meant instead of 'John,' or merely have arrived at the conclusion that it was insensible and had no meaning, it is needless to discuss, because the parties have agreed to other stipulations, which show that the deed must be framed upon the footing that 'Mary' shall be substituted there for 'John'" (Lord Cranworth L.C. at 53, at 817).

[137] *Chartbrook Ltd v Persimmon Homes Ltd*, above, n.123 at [25].

[138] In *Littman v Aspen Oil (Broking) Ltd*, above, n.136, the majority of CA would have ordered the contract to be rectified if they had not been able to remedy the

(3) Remedying Mistakes by Rectification: Common Mistakes[139]

The aim of rectification for common mistake. Rectification for common mistake is designed to bring the written document into conformity with the parties' agreement[140]: 13–38

> "the remedy of rectification is one permitted by the Court, not for the purpose of altering the terms of an agreement entered into between two or more parties, but for that of correcting a written instrument which, by a mistake in verbal expression, does not accurately reflect their true agreement."

It has already been noticed that there are two stages in the formation of a written contract: the creation of the parties' agreement; and then the creation of the contract itself by the execution of a written document which is designed to reflect the agreement.[141] Where, however, it can be shown that the written document failed to contain the terms of the agreement which both parties at the moment of its execution intended—that is, they made a *common mistake* about the document—rectification may be ordered. In *Agip S.p.A. v Navigazione Alta Italia S.p.A.*[142] Slade L.J. set out the requirements as follows:

---

mistake by construction; and in *Chartbrook Ltd v Persimmon Homes Ltd*, above, n.123, HL rested the decision on construction of the contract, but would otherwise have ordered rectification.

[139] D. Hodge, *Rectification* (2010), ch.3. On rectification generally, see also the works cited above, n.99.

[140] *Agip S.p.A. v Navigazione Alta Italia S.p.A. (The Nai Genova and Nai Superba)* [1984] 1 Lloyd's Rep. 353, CA, at 359 (Slade L.J.).

[141] Above, para.13–33.

[142] Above, n.140, referring to *Snell's Equity* (28th edn, 1982) at pp.612–614. See also *Swainland Builders Ltd v Freehold Properties Ltd* [2002] EWCA Civ 560, [2002] 2 E.G.L.R. 71 at [33]: "The party seeking rectification must show that: (1) the parties had a common continuing intention, whether or not amounting to an agreement, in respect of a particular matter in the instrument to be rectified; (2) there was an outward expression of accord; (3) the intention continued at the time of the execution of the instrument sought to be rectified; (4) by mistake, the instrument did not reflect that common intention" (quoted by Lord Hoffmann in *Chartbrook Ltd v Persimmon Homes Ltd*, above, n.123 at [48]).

> "First, there must be a common intention in regard to the particular provisions of the agreement in question, together with some outward expression of accord. Secondly, this common intention must continue up to the time of execution of the instrument. Thirdly, there must be clear evidence that the instrument as executed does not accurately represent the true agreement of the parties at the time of its execution. Fourthly, it must be shown that the instrument, if rectified as claimed, would accurately represent the true agreement of the parties at that time."

13–39 **A common intention in regard to the particular provisions of the agreement.** A claim to rectify a contract on the basis of a common mistake requires proof of a common intention in regard to the terms of the agreement, which are not then reflected in the document itself. The purpose of rectification in such a case is therefore to bring the contract into line with the agreement of the parties. However, it is not necessary that the "common intention" should be contained within an agreement which, even before the document is executed, is a complete and enforceable contract. Some older cases suggested that an "antecedent complete concluded contract" is necessary, but it is now clear that this is not so.[143] If, for example, the written contract fails to reflect accurately the terms of an agreement that was concluded "subject to contract" (and so was complete, but not in law binding),[144] rectification is in principle available. But, more than this, there need not be proof that there was a complete agreement on all the terms of the contract in advance of the document being executed[145]:

> "it is sufficient to find a common continuing intention in regard to a particular provision or aspect of the agreement. If one finds that, in regard to a particular point, the parties were in agreement up to the moment when they executed their formal instrument, and the formal instrument does not

143 *Joscelyne v Nissen* [1970] 2 Q.B. 86, CA, rejecting contrary dicta in a number of cases, including *Mackenzie v Coulson* (1869) L.R. 8 Eq. 368 at 375 (James V.C.); *Lovell and Christmas Ltd v Wall* (1911) 104 L.T. 85, CA, at 88 (Cozens-Hardy M.R.), 91 (Fletcher Moulton L.J.); *Craddock Bros v Hunt* [1923] 2 Ch. 136, CA, at 159 (Warrington L.J.); *United States of America v Motor Trucks Ltd* [1924] A.C. 196, PC, at 200 and *Shipley Urban DC v Bradford Corp.* [1936] Ch. 375 at 395 (Clauson J.). *Joscelyne v Nissen* was approved, and some aspects of the earlier cases explained, by Lord Hoffmann in *Chartbrook Ltd v Persimmon Homes Ltd*, above, n.123 at [59]–[60].

144 *Joscelyne v Nissen*, above, n.143 at 98; above, para.13–33.

145 *Crane v Hegeman-Harris Co. Inc.* [1939] 1 All E.R. 662 at 664 (Simonds J.), approved in *Joscelyne v Nissen*, above, n.144 at 98.

conform with that common agreement, then this court has jurisdiction to rectify, although it may be that there was, until the formal instrument was executed, no concluded and binding contract between the parties."

The exact form of words in which the common intention is to be expressed is immaterial if, in substance and in detail, the common intention can be ascertained.[146]

Subjective or objective common intention? Since the remedy of rectification is designed to bring the written document into conformity with the parties "common continuing intention"—their "agreement up to the moment when they executed their formal instrument"—it is critical to know how that common intention, or agreement, is to be established. For this purpose we must of course disregard the terms written in the document itself; but is the search for the actual, shared (subjective) understanding as to the terms, or for the shared understanding which an (objective) reasonable observer would have attributed to the parties at the moment before the document was executed? Judges[147] and writers[148] have commonly stated, or have used language which appears to suggest, that the test should be subjective. This has, however, been 13–40

[146] *Swainland Builders Ltd v Freehold Properties Ltd*, above, n.142 at [34]; *Co-operative Insurance Society Ltd v Centremoor Ltd* [1983] 2 E.G.L.R. 52, CA, at 54, applying *Jervis v Howle & Talke Colliery Co. Ltd* [1937] 1 Ch. 67 and *Crane v Hegeman-Harris Co. Inc* (1939) [1971] 1 W.L.R. 1390n. at 1399.

[147] See, e.g. *Agip S.p.A. v Navigazione Alta Italia S.p.A.*, above, n.140, at 359 (Slade L.J.: "the true agreement"); *Munt v Beasley* [2006] EWCA Civ 370, [2006] All E.R. (D) 29 (Apr) at [36] (Mummery L.J : "true state of belief"); *Bashir v Ali* [2010] EWHC 2320 (Ch), [2010] All E.R. (D) 115 (Oct) at [53] (Elizabeth Jones QC : "evidence of the parties' subjective intention and knowledge is central"; reversed on different grounds [2011] EWCA Civ 707, [2011] Ell E.R. (D) 132 (Jun)). *Cf.*, however, *PT Berlin Laju Tanker TBK v Nuse Shipping Ltd* [2008] EWHC 1330 (Comm), [2008] 1 C.L.C. 967 at [38] (Christopher Clarke J.: "The court is not concerned with what the parties thought they had agreed or what they thought their agreement meant—a subjective inquiry. What it is concerned with is what the parties said and did, and what that would convey to a reasonable person in their position—an objective question"); *Dunlop Haywards (D.H.L.) Ltd v Erinaceous Insurance Services Ltd* [2009] EWCA Civ 354, [2009] Lloyd's Rep. I.R. 464 at [66] (Rix L.J.: "what needs to be shown, as in any case of mutual agreement, are objective manifestations of intention which the parties demonstrate to one another").

[148] See, e.g. L. Bromley, "Rectification in Equity" (1971) 87 L.Q.R. 532 (going, however, further and rejecting the requirement of an "outward expression of accord"); G. McMeel, *The Construction of Contracts* (2nd edn, 2011), para.3.73,

challenged,[149] and in *Chartbrook Ltd v Persimmon Homes Ltd*[150] Lord Hoffmann considered that the test was objective. The premise for this conclusion is, however, doubtful:

> "Now that it has been established[151] that rectification is also available when there was no binding antecedent agreement but the parties had a common continuing intention in respect of a particular matter in the instrument to be rectified, it would be anomalous if the 'common continuing intention' were to be an objective fact if it amounted to an enforceable contract but a subjective belief if it did not. On the contrary, the authorities suggest that in both cases the question is what an objective observer would have thought the intentions of the parties to be.[152]"

This appears to assume that the test to establish the existence and content of the parties' agreement in a case where the parties have not reduced their agreement to a single, written document, is wholly objective.[153] We have seen, however, that this is not so. If the parties are subjectively in agreement about the existence of the contract and its terms, their subjective agreement determines the matter.[154] If there is no subjective agreement, the objective test for the interpretation[155] of the communications passing between the parties allows the claimant to hold the defendant to the terms which the claimant believed were agreed where the defendant's words or conduct would have led a reasonable person in the claimant's position to believe that the defendant was agreeing. But there is still a subjective element, since the claimant cannot hold the defendant

citing Lord Steyn, "Interpretation: Legal Texts and their Landscape" in B.S. Markesinis (ed.), *The Clifford Chance Millennium Lectures* (2000), pp. 79, 80–81.

149 M. Smith, "Rectification of contracts for common mistake, *Joscelyne v Nissen*, and subjective states of mind" (2007) 123 L.Q.R. 116.

150 [2009] UKHL 38, [2009] 1 A.C. 1101.

151 [*Joscelyne v Nissen*, above, n.143.]

152 ibid., at [60]. The discussion of rectification was *obiter*: see at [58]; but Lord Rodger (at [71]), Lord Walker (at [97]) and Baroness Hale (at [101]) agreed with it.

153 It is perhaps significant that Lord Hoffmann at [60] relied for the "clearest statement" on a dictum of Denning L.J. in *Frederick E. Rose (London) Ltd v William H. Pim Jnr & Co. Ltd* [1953] 2 Q.B. 450 at 461; Lord Denning generally took a wholly detached, objective approach to finding the parties' agreement, which was not in line with the test generally adopted in the cases: above, para.13–07.

154 Above, para.13–10.

155 Above, para.13–11.

to a contract that he (the claimant) did not at the time of the contract in fact believe was agreed.[156] The purpose of the objective test in the formation of a contract is not to ignore, or override, the subjective intentions of the parties, but to protect the party who reasonably relies on what he believes that the other intended.[157] The logic behind Lord Hoffmann's statement, quoted above, should lead to the conclusion not that the test for the parties' "common continuing intention" depends on "what an objective observer would have thought", but on what the claimant could have established the terms of the contract to have been, applying the normal test for the formation of a contract—and therefore at least the claimant must have believed the terms into which he claims the document should be rectified. This line of reasoning suggests that the common mistake in a claim for rectification should also be tested by reference to the subjective, shared agreement of the parties.[158] One can add that there is a sensible rationale in allowing a written document to be overridden by the actual intentions of the parties to that document;[159] it is difficult to see why a document should be rectified to reflect an objective observer's interpretation of outcome of the negotiations which conforms with neither party's

[156] Above, para.13–13. For a summary of the test, see above, para.13–19.
[157] Above, para.13–13.
[158] If the defendant did not in fact (subjectively) share that belief, the mistake would not be a common mistake at all, but a unilateral mistake, which is discussed below, para. 13–44. See also D. McLaughlan, "The 'Drastic' Remedy of Rectification for Unilateral Mistake" (2008) 124 L.Q.R. 608, pp.614–617, 640 (rectification for both common mistake and unilateral mistake ensures that the written contract reflects the true bargain between the parties as determined by the ordinary principles of contract formation).
[159] Any potential prejudice to third parties by allowing the document to be rectified can be dealt with by other rules: below, para.13–53.

undertanding.[160] However, Lord Hoffmann's approach in *Chartbrook* has now been followed,[161] although it has not met with unanimous approval.[162]

Even if the search is for a subjective common mistake—that is, a shared, subjective understanding as to the terms which is not accurately reflected in the document as written—it is still necessary for there to be an evidenced agreement. We have seen that a coincidence of intentions is not an agreement; there must in

[160] *Cf.* above, para. 13–07, n.15. See also *Crossco No. 4 Unlimited v Jolan Ltd* [2011] EWHC 803 (Ch), [2011] All E.R. (D) 13 (Apr) at [253] (Morgan J.: "The law as stated by Lord Hoffmann appears to mean that a court can rectify a contract even though one party to the contract (even the party seeking rectification) fully intended, subjectively, to be bound by that contract, if the court is able to find that the final expression of consensus in the contract as executed differs from an earlier expression of consensus in a communication passing during the negotiations between the parties").

[161] *Daventry DC v Daventry & District Housing Ltd* [2010] EWHC 1935 (Ch), [2010] All E.R. (D) 356 (Jul) at [110]–[111] (the objective test was accepted by both parties in the light of *Chartbrook*); *Surgicraft Ltd v Paradigm Biodevices Inc.* [2010] EWHC 1291 (Ch), [2010] All E.R. (D) 249 (May) at [68]; *Scottish Widows Fund and Life Assurance Society v BGC International* [2011] EWHC 729 (Ch), [2011] All E.R. (D) 352 at [35]; *Woodford Land Ltd v Persimmon Homes Ltd* [2011] EWHC 984 (Ch), [2011] 17 E.G. 70 (C.S.) at [48]–[51]; *Hawksford Trustees Jersey Ltd v Stella Global UK Ltd* [2011] EWHC 503 (Ch), [2011] All E.R. (D) 154 (Mar) at [101].

[162] *Bashir v Ali*, above, n.147 at [53] (where *Chartbrook* was cited; the rectification issue was not raised on appeal [2011] EWCA Civ 707, [2011] Ell E.R. (D) 132 (Jun) at [46]); *Crossco No. 4 Unlimited v Jolan Ltd*, above, n.160 at [253] (Morgan J.: "With considerable diffidence, I feel that I ought to say that I have some difficulty with Lord Hoffmann's description of the principles as to rectification for common mistake"). The subjective test is still preferred by Snell, para.16–015 ("it is difficult to justify why any prior objective agreement should override a later, formal instrument, unless the prior agreement reflects the parties' actual agreement, and continued to do so at the time the instrument was executed"). *Cf.* D. Hodge, *Rectification* (2010), paras 3–48 to 3–76, following Lord Hoffmann's objective approach, but suggesting at para.3–72 that "the proof of an actual consensus should effectively 'trump' the need for proof of the existence of an objective consensus between the parties": that is, there should be no need to prove subjective agreement in order to obtain rectification (objective agreement is sufficient) but the objective interpretation of the agreement should not prevail over proven subjective agreement. G. McMeel, *The Construction of Contracts* (2nd edn, 2011), para.17.63 suggests that the adoption in *Chartbrook* of an objective test for "common mistake rectification" renders it redundant, and the only reason now for including a plea of rectification is to circumvent the exclusionary rule of evidence in the (objective) construction of a written contract.

addition be some sharing between the parties of their intentions. It is not therefore surprising that the courts have required proof of the "common intention" to be based on some outward expression of their accord.[163] However, this has been said to be more a matter of evidence than a strict legal requirement in all cases of rectification for common mistake.[164]

The common intention must have continued up to the time of execution. Typically, the common intention as to the term which is not accurately reflected in the written document will be evidenced by what the parties said and did during the negotiations for the contract[165]—that is, some time before the document was executed. In order to succeed in a claim to rectify the document on the basis of a common mistake the claimant must therefore show not only that there was such a common intention, but that it was still held by both parties at the moment when the document was executed: this is the time at which the "common intention"—and therefore the common mistake—must be established. Otherwise, the fact that the parties then signed a document which provided otherwise will be cogent evidence that, whatever the parties may 13–41

---

163 *Joscelyne v Nissen*, above, n.143 at 98.

164 *Munt v Beasley*, above, n.147 at [36] (Mummery L.J.: "an outward expression of accord" is not "a strict legal requirement for rectification in a case such as this, where the party resisting rectification has in fact admitted that his true state of belief when he entered into the transaction was the same as that of the other party and there was therefore a continuing common intention which, by mistake, was not given effect in the relevant legal document. I agree with the trend in recent cases to treat the expression 'outward expression of accord' more as an evidential factor rather than a strict legal requirement in all cases of rectification: see *Gallaher v Gallaher Pensions Ltd* [2005] EWHC 42 (Ch), [2005] All E.R. (D) 177 (Jan) at [116]–[118]; *Westland Savings Bank v Hancock* [1987] 2 N.Z.L.R. 21 at 29, 30; and *JIS (1974) Ltd v MCP Investment Nominees I Ltd* [2003] EWCA Civ 721 at [33]–[34]; *cf. Frederick E. Rose (London) Ltd v William H. Pim Jnr & Co. Ltd* [1953] 2 Q.B. 450 at 462 per Denning L.J. and *Swainland Builders Ltd v Freeland Properties Ltd* [2002] EWCA Civ 560, [2002] 2 E.G.L.R. 71 at 74"). *Cf.* Smith, above, n.149 at p.127, arguing that the requirement of an outward expression of accord necessarily excludes a subjective test of common intention.

165 Although evidence of pre-contractual negotiations is generally not admissible in interpreting a written document (above, para.13–36, n.127), it can be used to support a claim for rectification: *Chartbrook Ltd v Persimmon Homes Ltd* [2009] UKHL 38, [2009] 1 A.C. 1101 at [42] (rectification is not an exception to the exclusionary rule, but operates outside it, as a "safety net" or "safety device": see at [41] and [47]).

have agreed during the negotiations, they had decided by the end to contract on the basis of the document as written.[166]

13–42 **The instrument must fail to represent the true agreement.** The claimant must show that the written document fails to represent the true agreement: "it is not sufficient to show that the written instrument does not represent their common intention unless positively also one can show what their common intention was".[167] Although in an appropriate case the court can itself draft the form of words which it considers to give effect to the true common intention of the parties, it should not do so without a high degree of certainty that the wording would achieve that aim.[168]

It is important to remember that the comparison is between the *terms* as the parties intended them, and the *terms* as the document records them. If the document accurately records the agreement, but it appears that the parties made a common mistake in their underlying agreement, or about its legal effect, that is not a matter that can be remedied by rectification.[169]

---

[166] An entire agreement clause (above para.9–06) does not exclude a claim to rectify the contract in which it is contained: *Surgicraft Ltd v Paradigm Biodevices Ltd* [2010] EWHC 1291 (Ch), [2010] All E.R. (D) 249 (May) at [73], following *J.J. Huber (Investments) Ltd v Private D.I.Y. Co. Ltd* (1995) 70 P. & C.R. D33; *cf. Phillips Petroleum Co. UK Ltd v Snamprogetti Ltd* [2001] EWCA Civ 889, (2001) 79 Con. L.R. 80 at [32] referring to *Spry on Equitable Remedies* (5th edn, 1997), p.612 (if the parties have included an "entire agreement" clause this may tend to show that "in fact no inconsistent governing intention has subsisted and that hence no basis for rectification has arisen because the parties have intended to be bound by the document in the material respects regardless of prior or other intentions").

[167] *Crane v Hegeman-Harris Co. Inc.* [1939] 1 All E.R. 662 at 664 (Simonds J.).

[168] *Connolly Ltd v Bellway Homes Ltd* [2007] EWHC 895 (Ch), [2007] All E.R. (D) 182 (Apr) at [101] (Stephen Smith Q.C.); *Fairstate Ltd v General Enterprise & Management Ltd* [2010] EWHC 3072 (QB), (2010) 133 Con. L.R. 112 at [93] (particularly important that court should require clarity as to all (and not just some of) the material terms of the transaction where it is asked to rectify a document which is relied on to satisfy formality requirements of s.4 Statute of Frauds 1677: to do otherwise risks undermining the intended protection of the statute). It is not an obstacle to rectification that there are more than one methods of achieving the common intention: *Swainland Builders Ltd v Freehold Properties Ltd*, above, n.164 at [38].

[169] *Frederick E. Rose (London) Ltd v William H. Pim Jnr & Co. Ltd*, above, n.164, CA (parties contracted in writing for sale of "horsebeans", having agreed on the use of that (generic) term which covers a range of beans, although they

Burden and standard of proof. The claimant seeking to obtain rectification of the contract on the basis of a common mistake has the burden of proving the common intention; and that it continued until the document was executed; and that the document does not correctly reflect the terms as the parties both intended. A claim to rectification is a civil claim, and therefore the normal civil standard of the balance of probability applies.[170] But since the document itself is clear objective evidence that the parties did agree it in the form that it was executed,[171] the claimant will inevitably have to overcome this with sufficient contrary evidence:[172] 13–43

> "as the alleged common intention ex hypothesi contradicts the written instrument, convincing proof is required in order to counteract the cogent evidence of the parties' intention displayed by the instrument itself. It is not, I think, the standard of proof which is high, so differing from the normal civil standard, but the evidential requirement needed to counteract the inherent probability that the written instrument truly represents the parties' intention because it is a document signed by the parties."

---

both thought that it referred to a particular kind of horsebean, "feveroles", which they knew the purchaser required in order to fulfil another contract; rectification refused, because the mistake was in the underlying agreement, and the document was an accurate expression of what the parties had in fact agreed). However, "rectification is available not only in a case where particular words have been added, omitted or wrongly written as the result of careless copying or the like. It is also available where the words of the document were purposely used but it was mistakenly considered that they bore a different meaning from their correct meaning as a matter of true construction": *Re Butlin's Settlement Trusts* [1976] Ch. 251 at 260 (unilateral mistake in voluntary deed, applied to common mistake in contract in *Phillips Petroleum Co. UK Ltd v Snamprogetti Ltd* (2001) 79 Con. L.R. 80 at [39]; affirmed on different grounds [2001] EWCA Civ 889, (2001) 79 Con. L.R. 80); *Chartbrook Ltd v Persimmon Homes Ltd*, above, n.165 at [46]. Rectification can be granted in order to give the parties fiscal advantages which they intended as long as the mistake in the terms of the document, and not only in its fiscal effect: *W.G. Mitchell (Gleneagles) Ltd v Jemstock One Ltd* [2006] EWHC 3644 (Ch), [2006] All E.R. (D) 105 (Oct) at [22]; *Ashcroft v Barnsdale* [2010] EWHC 1948 (Ch), [2010] S.T.C. 2544 at [17].

170 *Agip S.p.A. v Navigazione Alta Italia S.p.A.* [1984] 1 Lloyd's Rep. 353, CA, at 359 (Slade L.J.)

171 Above, para.13–32.

172 *Thomas Bates & Son Ltd v Wyndham's (Lingerie) Ltd* [1981] 1 W.L.R. 505 at 521 (Brightman L.J.); see also at 514 (Buckley L.J.); *Agip S.p.A. v Navigazione Alta Italia S.p.A.*, above, n.170 at 359. See also *Ashcroft v Barnsdale*, above, n.169 at [16] (HH Judge Hodge: it may in practice prove easier to discharge the evidential burden of establishing a mistake in the case of an inadvertent *omission* of a word or phrase).

(4) Remedying Mistakes by Rectification: Unilateral Mistakes[173]

13–44 **The aim of rectification for unilateral mistake.** Where a party to a written contract claims rectification on the basis of unilateral mistake, he does not say that he did not agree to the written document[174]; nor that the document fails to reflect the terms as the defendant intended them; but simply that the document does not reflect his own intentions.[175] Given the significance that the law places on written documents as prima facie evidence of the intention of the parties,[176] and given that—unlike in a case of common mistake—the claimant cannot say that the document is itself written in error, failing properly to record the agreement that was reached, it will be evident that the courts are reluctant to rectify a contract where the mistake is only unilateral.

Where there is a written contract on terms [x], and the claimant asserts that he intended it instead to be on terms [y], the court naturally starts from the position that the contract is [x]. That is what the claimant (objectively) agreed to, by giving his assent to the document which contained terms [x]. If we consider the facts through the objective test applied by the common law,[177] the defendant will be able to hold the claimant to the contract as written if the defendant in fact believed that the document reflected the claimant's intentions, and as long as that is the reasonable view for the defendant to have held (which it normally will be, given the fact that the claimant signed the document or otherwise assented to it). Under that test, therefore, the contract is binding on both parties, in

[173] D. Hodge, *Rectification* (2010), ch.4. On rectification generally, see also the works cited above, n.99.

[174] Such a claim may however be made on the basis of *non est factum*; below, para.13–55.

[175] In a claim for rectification on the basis of unilateral mistake, the subjective mistake of the claimant in relation to the written document is in issue (together with such questions as whether the defendant knew of the claimant's mistake: below, para.13–48). Cf. the question of whether, in a claim for rectification on the basis of common mistake, the parties' understanding should be tested subjectively or objectively: above, para.13–40.

[176] Above, para.13–32.

[177] Above, para.13–19.

the terms as written: [x]. A mere unilateral mistake by one party about the terms is not sufficient at common law to disturb the other party's security of contract.[178]

But if the defendant *knew* about the claimant's mistake about the terms, or if (even though he did not in fact know about it) a reasonable person in his position would have realised that the claimant was making a mistake, the common law would say that the defendant is not entitled to hold the claimant to terms [x]. A claim for rectification, however, goes further than this. The claimant who gave his assent to a written document is not simply seeking to avoid the transaction on the basis of his mistake; he is seeking to enforce the transaction on the terms as *he* understood them. He asks the court to rewrite the document into the terms the claimant intended—to change the words that are written in the document and thereby to change the evidence of the agreement.[179] Rectification for unilateral mistake therefore involves depriving the defendant of the terms of the contract that he had intended, and to which the claimant had in fact agreed, and requiring the defendant to submit to a contract on the claimant's own terms. That is, in effect, the rectification remedies the claimant's mistake, but creates an equal and opposite "mistake" in the defendant, since he, rather than the claimant, is now bound to a contract that he did not intend.[180]

The claim for rectification on the basis of unilateral mistake. 13–45
The courts have a well-established jurisdiction to rectify contracts for unilateral mistake, although some elements of the test that should be applied have been the subject of debate in recent years. In

---

[178] Above, para.13–02.

[179] The document, as rectified by the court order, then becomes the exclusive record of the contract: below, para.13–53.

[180] *Agip S.p.A. v Navigazione Alta Italia S.p.A.*, above, n.170 at 360, 365 (Slade L.J.: the "drastic nature" of an order for rectification which has the effect of imposing on defendants a contract which they did not intend); *George Wimpey UK Ltd v VI Construction Ltd* [2005] EWCA Civ 77, [2005] B.L.R. 135 at [75] (Blackburne J.); see also at [51] (it is an "exceptional jurisdiction to rectify for unilateral mistake": Peter Gibson L.J.); *Rowallan Group Ltd v Edgehill Portfolio No.1 Ltd* [2007] EWHC 32 (Ch), [2007] All E.R. (D) 106 (Jan) at [14]. For criticism of the view that the remedy is "drastic", and the argument that the purpose of rectification is simply to bring the written document into line with the parties' agreement as determined by the ordinary test for contract formation, see D. McLaughlan, "The 'Drastic' Remedy of Rectification for Unilateral Mistake" (2008) 124 L.Q.R. 608, p.640.

Thomas Bates & Son Ltd v Wyndham's (Lingerie) Ltd[181] Buckley L.J. set out the requirements as follows:

> "first, that one party A erroneously believed that the document sought to be rectified contained a particular term or provision, or possibly did not contain a particular term or provision which, mistakenly, it did contain; secondly, that the other party B was aware of the omission or the inclusion and that it was due to a mistake on the part of A; thirdly, that B has omitted to draw the mistake to the notice of A. And I think there must be a fourth element involved, namely, that the mistake must be one calculated to benefit B.[182] If these requirements are satisfied, the court may regard it as inequitable to allow B to resist rectification to give effect to A's intention on the ground that the mistake was not, at the time of execution of the document, a mutual [i.e. common] mistake."

13–46 **A unilateral mistake about the terms.** The claim for rectification for unilateral mistake requires proof of the claimant's mistake about the terms of the document. The question, therefore, is whether when he gave his assent to the document, the claimant misunderstood its terms. Although, if he succeeds in showing that a document which in fact contains terms [x] should be rectified to contain instead terms [y], the claimant can in most cases show that before the document was executed the parties had come to an agreement which contained terms [y], there is no requirement to prove this. And, indeed, it has been said that a written contract can be rectified for unilateral mistake when there was no antecedent agreement about the content of the clause to be rectified.[183]

---

181 [1981] 1 W.L.R. 505 at 516; *Agip S.p.A. v Navigazione Alta Italia S.p.A.*, above, n.170 at 361; *Littman v Aspen Oil (Broking) Ltd* [2005] EWCA Civ 1579, [2006] 2 P. & C.R. 2 at [21]; *George Wimpey UK Ltd v VI Construction Ltd* [2005] EWCA Civ 77; [2005] B.L.R. 135 at [38], [73].

182 [This fourth point was doubted by Eveleigh L.J.: *ibid.*, at 521: "It is enough that the inaccuracy of the instrument as drafted would be detrimental to the other party, and this may not always mean that it is beneficial to the one who knew of the mistake".]

183 *Littman v Aspen Oil (Broking) Ltd*, above, n.181 at [26], [32], [33] (obiter, since the decision was based on construction, rather than rectification). Where rectification is granted, however, the claimant will be able to show that terms into which the document is rectified are those to which, at the time when he signed the contract, he was entitled to hold the defendant under the objective test, above, para.13–19: the claimant in fact, and on reasonable grounds, believed that those were the terms of the contract, and that therefore the document would reflect them. So, in that (objective) sense a claim for rectification will be a claim to bring

The defendant's knowledge of the claimant's mistake. The test set out by Buckley L.J. requires proof that the defendant was "aware of the omission or the inclusion and that it was due to a mistake on the part of" the claimant.[184] In later cases the courts have discussed the degree of knowledge which is necessary before the defendant is deprived of relying on the document as it is written. For example, in *Agip S.p.A. v Navigazione Alta Italia S.p.A.*[185] Slade L.J. emphasised that the drastic nature of the remedy of rectification pointed towards it being granted only where the defendant had "actual knowledge of the existence of the relevant mistaken belief at the time when the mistaken plaintiff signed the contract." However, although it is not sufficient to show simply that the defendant ought to have known about the claimant's mistake, or even that the defendant actually knew of facts from which he could have realised it, it is not necessary to show that the defendant had actual knowledge in the narrowest sense. In *Commission for the New Towns v Cooper (Great Britain) Ltd*[186] the Court of Appeal made clear that it extends to those degrees of knowledge that 13–47

the written contract into line with the agreement as the claimant understood it to be; see also McLaughlan (2008) 124 L.Q.R. 608, above, n.180.

[184] Old authorities which suggested that, where the defendant did not know of the claimant's mistake, the court could require the defendant to choose between rescission of the contract, and submission to rectification of the contract on the basis of the terms as they were believed by the claimant to be, were rejected in *Riverlate Properties Ltd v Paul* [1975] Ch. 133. See also above, para.13–31 (unilateral mistake is not of itself sufficient for rescission).

[185] Above, n.170 at 365.

[186] [1995] Ch. 259, CA, at 280–281, 292, accepting for this purpose the first three categories of knowledge or notice listed by Peter Gibson J. in *Baden v Société Générale pour Favoriser le Développement du Commerce et de l'Industrie en France S.A.* [1993] 1 W.L.R. 509 and cited by Millett J. in *Agip (Africa) Ltd v Jackson* [1990] Ch. 265 at 293. It is therefore sufficient if the defendant does not actually know, but merely suspects, that the claimant has made a mistake that the defendant intended him to make: *Commission for the New Towns v Cooper* at 280. See also *George Wimpey UK Ltd v VI Construction Ltd*, above, n.181 at [45], [79] (as stated by Millett J. and accepted by CA in *Commission for the New Towns v Cooper*, categories (ii) and (iii) involve dishonesty, which must therefore be pleaded); *Traditional Structures Ltd v H.W. Construction Ltd* [2010] EWHC 1530 (TCC), [2010] All E.R. (D) 197 (Jun) at [32]–[33] (HH Judge David Grant, following *Commission for the New Towns v Cooper*, and noting that the alternative basis for rectification proposed by McLaughlan (2008) 124 L.Q.R. 608, above, n.180, would involve a change more properly to be effected by an appellate court).

constitute actual knowledge in law: that is, it encompasses "(i) actual knowledge; (ii) wilfully shutting one's eyes to the obvious; and (iii) wilfully and recklessly failing to make such enquiries as an honest and reasonable man would make".

13–48 **Inequity or unconscionability.** It is not sufficient that the defendant knew of the claimant's mistake. In addition, the court must be satisfied that in the circumstances it would be inequitable for the defendant to resist rectification into the terms as the claimant believed them to be. Various different tests have been offered in the cases, which also point to different underlying bases of the principles by which the courts can order rectification for a unilateral mistake. It has been suggested, for example, that rectification in this context is a species of estoppel[187]; or based on the defendant's fraud[188] or "sharp practice"[189] or the "equity of the position".[190] What is clear, however, is that the court looks at the facts to see

[187] Either an "equitable estoppel": Snell, para.16–019 (but stated less enthusiastically than in 31st edn (2005), para.14.15); *A. Roberts & Co. Ltd v Leicestershire CC* [1961] Ch. 555 at 570 (Pennycuick J., commenting on this proposition in *Snell* (25th edn, 1960), p.569: "If the principle is correctly rested upon estoppel it seems to me that it is not an essential ingredient of the right of action to establish any particular degree of obliquity to be attributed to the defendants in such circumstances"); *Thomas Bates & Son Ltd v Wyndham's (Lingerie) Ltd*, above, n.181 at 520–521 (Eveleigh L.J.: "if one party alone knows that the instrument does not give effect to the common intention and changes his mind without telling the other party, then he will be estopped from alleging that the common intention did not continue right up to the moment of the execution of the clause"); *Agip S.p.A. v Navigazione Alta Italia S.p.A.* [1983] 2 Lloyd's Rep. 333 at 342 (Leggatt J.); or estoppel in pais, although this requires proof of a representation by the defendant and reliance by the claimant intended, or at least foreseeable, by the defendant: *Agip S.p.A. v Navigazione Alta Italia S.p.A.* [1984] 1 Lloyd's Rep. 353, CA, at 365 (Slade L.J.: "the proffering of the draft [which purports to give effect to a pre-existing accord between the parties] may, in some circumstances, amount to a representation that the draft gives effect to the accord").

[188] *Blay v Pollard and Morris* [1930] 1 K.B. 628, CA, at 633 (Scrutton L.J.); *May v Platt* [1900] 1 Ch. 616 at 623 (Farwell J.); *A. Roberts & Co. Ltd v Leicestershire CC*, above, n.187 at 570.

[189] *Riverlate Properties Ltd v Paul*, above, n.184 at 140, doubted in *Thomas Bates & Son Ltd v Wyndham's (Lingerie) Ltd*, above, n.181 at 515 (Buckley L.J.) and 520–521 (Eveleigh L.J.), but used by Slade L.J. in *Agip S.p.A. v Navigazione Alta Italia S.p.A.*, above, n.170 at 365. See also *George Wimpey UK Ltd v VI Construction Ltd*, above, n.181 at [79] (Blackburne J.: "by its nature, a successful rectification claim based upon unilateral mistake will usually, if not always, call into question the probity of the defendant").

whether it would be inequitable for the defendant not only to insist on the document as it stands,[191] but also to resist its rectification into the terms that the claimant mistakenly believed the document to contain. This test may be satisfied by proof of unconscionable conduct, or unfair dealing: some positive conduct by the defendant which either causes the mistaken belief about the contents of the document or (without causing the mistake) is calculated to divert the claimant from discovering the truth about it[192]; or it may be less actively taking advantage of the claimant's own misunderstanding about the document, when the defendant knows that he is making such a mistake.[193]

Burden and standard of proof. The claimant seeking to obtain rectification of the contract on the basis of his own unilateral 13–49

190 *Thomas Bates & Son Ltd v Wyndham's (Lingerie)* Ltd, above, n.181 at 515 (Buckley L.J.).

191 That is, he could obtain rescission of the contract; although the reasons for holding that the contract should be rescinded in equity will often be similar, if not identical, to the reasons for ordering rectification: *Commission for the New Towns v Cooper (Great Britain) Ltd* above, n.186, at 280 (Stuart-Smith L.J.); above, para.13–31.

192 *Commission for the New Towns v Cooper (Great Britain) Ltd*, above, n.186 at 280 (Stuart-Smith L.J. (obiter): "where A intends B to be mistaken as to the construction of the agreement, so conducts himself that he diverts B's attention from discovering the mistake by making false and misleading statements, and B in fact makes the very mistake that A intends, then notwithstanding that A does not actually know, but merely suspects, that B is mistaken, and it cannot be shown that the mistake was induced by any misrepresentation, rectification may be granted. A's conduct is unconscionable . . .").

193 *Thomas Bates & Son Ltd v Wyndham's (Lingerie) Ltd*, above, n.181 at 516 (Buckley L.J.); *Agip S.p.A. v Navigazione Alta Italia S.p.A.*, above, n.170 at 365 (Slade L.J. (obiter): "I strongly incline to the view that in the absence of estoppel, fraud, undue influence or a fiduciary relationship between the parties, the authorities do not in any circumstances permit the rectification of a contract on the grounds of unilateral mistake, unless the defendant had actual knowledge of the existence of the relevant mistaken belief at the time when the mistaken plaintiff signed the contract"); *George Wimpey UK Ltd v VI Construction Ltd*, above, n.181 at [61] (Sedley L.J.: "absent . . . a dishonest inducement to contract, one is looking for a mistake on the claimant's own part which the defendant was honour-bound, despite his own legitimate business interests, to point out to him)."

mistake has the burden of proving not only his own mistake,[194] but also the other elements of the claim—that is, that the defendant knew about his mistake, and the defendant's unconscionable conduct or other evidence to show why it would be inequitable for him to resist the rectification of the contract.[195] A claim for rectification for unilateral mistake, just as a claim for rectification for common mistake,[196] is a civil claim, and therefore the normal civil standard of the balance of probability applies.[197] But the claim to rectify for unilateral mistake is a more difficult argument to mount, since not only is the document itself clear objective evidence that the parties did agree it in the form that it was executed,[198] but also the claimant is alleging that the defendant should be bound to a *different* set of terms, in the rectified document, to which he did not in fact agree[199]; and to establish rectification the claimant has to show some form of wrongdoing by the defendant, at least in having taken knowing advantage of the claimant's mistake.[200] In this last point, it will often be necessary to establish the defendant's dishonesty; dishonesty must be pleaded with full particulars and put to the person alleged to be dishonest.[201]

[194] *George Wimpey UK Ltd v VI Construction Ltd*, above, n.181 at [48] (where the decision to enter into the contract is taken by someone other than the negotiatior, it must be shown that the decision-taker made the mistake: and, for this, evidence must be led).
[195] *Fredensen v Rothschild* [1941] 1 All E.R. 430 (claim to rectify gratuitous transaction); Phipson, para.42.46.
[196] Above, para.13–38.
[197] *Thomas Bates & Son Ltd v Wyndham's (Lingerie) Ltd*, above, n.181 at 521 (Brightman L.J.).
[198] Above, para.13–32.
[199] Above, para.13–44.
[200] Even if it is not necessarily "sharp practice": above, para.13–48.
[201] *George Wimpey UK Ltd v VI Construction Ltd*, above, n.181 at [31]. It is not open to the court to infer dishonesty from facts which have not been pleaded, nor from facts which have been pleaded but are consistent with honesty: *ibid*. On the problem of pleading and proving dishonesty, see above, para.5–46.

(5) Limitations on the Remedy of Rectification

The remedy is discretionary, and is subject to certain bars. 13–50
The remedy of rescission was devised by the courts of equity, and its award is subject to the discretion of the court.[202] It may also be barred by lapse of time; or where the order would prejudice an innocent third party; or where there is no issue to be resolved between the parties that requires the intervention of the court[203]; or if the contract is no longer capable of being performed.[204]

Lapse of time: laches. There is no statutory limitation period for 13–51
a claim to rectify a contract, but such a claim may be barred by laches, once the claimant has discovered the mistake,[205] and the delay in pursuing the claim renders it "practically unjust to give a

---

[202] *Re Butlin's Settlement Trusts* [1976] Ch. 251 (voluntary settlement; unilateral mistake); *KPMG LLP v Network Rail Infrastructure Ltd* [2006] EWHC 67 (Ch); [2006] 2 P. & C.R. 7 (rectification in favour of defendant for common mistake not affected by (1) the defendant's "admitted discourtesy" in negotiations which caused additional work to the claimant; nor (2) the fact that the omission was result of the defendant's own carelessness in failing properly to check the draft document. "If it were, many a claim to rectification for mutual mistake would fail since, ex hypothesi, the instrument as executed has failed accurately to express the parties' common intention and this will very often have been as a result of carelessness for which, in part at least, the claimant for relief must share responsibility": Blackburne J. at [195]. The actual decision was however reversed on appeal on the ground that the common intention did not continue up to the time of execution of the document: [2007] EWCA Civ 363, [2008] 1P. & C.R. 11). If a mistake is made in a document legitimately designed to avoid the payment of tax, there is no reason why it should not be corrected: *Re Slocock's Will Trusts* [1979] 1 All E.R. 358 at 363.

[203] *Whiteside v Whiteside* [1950] Ch. 65, CA, at 76.

[204] *Borrowman v Rossel* (1864) 16 C.B. (N.S.) 58, 143 E.R. 1045. See also *Caird v Moss* (1886) 33 Ch.D. 22, CA (agreement for division of proceeds of sale of ship already performed under judgment of the court: too late for rectification, which was also designed to challenge the earlier order).

[205] *Beale v Kyte* [1907] 1 Ch. 564 (mistake discovered four years after conveyance executed: no laches because claim for rectification brought shortly thereafter). *Cf.* lapse of time as a bar to rescission for misrepresentation, where time begins to run from the contract, rather than from discovery of the truth: above, para.4–48. It is arguable that a similar rule ought to apply to rectification: *cf. Bloomer v Spittle* (1872) L.R. 13 Eq. 427; Treitel, para.8–071; or at least that time should run from the time of the contract in the case of a *common* mistake (by analogy with innocent misrepresentation; in the case of fraud time does not run until discovery of the fraud: above, para.4–50).

remedy, either because the party has, by his conduct, done that which might fairly be regarded as equivalent to a waiver of it, or where by his conduct and neglect he has, though perhaps not waiving that remedy, yet put the other party in a situation in which it would not be reasonable to place him if the remedy were afterwards to be asserted".[206]

13–52 **Rectification and third parties.** The right to seek rectification of a contract is an *equity*, which may bind certain third parties, but can also be defeated where the award of rectification would prejudice innocent third parties.[207] If, for example, a party's title to property (other than land)[208] depends upon a document which is sought to be rectified, and where the rectification will prejudice the property rights, rectification will be refused if the party or a predecessor in title acquired the rights in the property in good faith and without notice of the facts giving rise to the defect in the earlier contract.

---

206 *Lindsay Petroleum Co. v Hurd* (1874) L.R. 5 P.C. 221 at 239–240 (Sir Barnes Peacock: laches in relation to claim for rescission for fraud, applied (but misattributed to Lord Selborne L.C.) to rectification in *KPMG LLP v Network Rail Infrastructure Ltd*, above, n.202 at [197], Blackburne J.; but no defence of laches on the facts). Sir Barnes Peacock said at 240: "Two circumstances, always important in such cases, are the length of the delay and the nature of the acts done during the interval, which might affect either party and cause a balance of justice or injustice in taking one course or the other, so far as relates to the remedy". *Cf. Transview Properties Ltd v City Site Properties Ltd* [2008] EWHC 1221 (Ch), [2008] 2 P. & C.R. DG13 at [149] (Briggs J., distinguishing laches ("delay coupled with some form of relevant prejudice to the defendant") and acquiescence ("the non-exercise of a right in circumstances where the obligor may reasonably assume that it will never be exercised")).

207 For the equity to rescind and third parties, see above, para.4–10.

208 In the case of land, the position varies according to whether or not the land is registered. In unregistered land, the equity to rectify is not binding on a purchaser of the legal title or equitable title without notice; a later purchaser of even an equitable interest in the property can therefore defeat the right: *Phillips v Phillips* (1862) 4 De G. F. & J. 208 at 218, 45 E.R. 1164 at 1167; *Latec Investments Ltd v Hotel Terrigal Pty Ltd* (1965) 113 C.L.R. 265, HCA, at 286. Where the title is registered a registered disponee who gives valuable consideration will take free of the equity unless it is protected by entry of a notice in the register, or as an overriding interest: the equity to rectify has effect as an interest capable of binding successors to the registered title: Land Registration Act 2002, s.116(b).

(6) The Mechanics of Rectification

Rectification is effected by the order of the court. The court order of itself effects the necessary change in the terms of the contract.[209] No new contract need be executed.[210] A claimant may obtain rectification, and specific performance of the contract as rectified, in the same action.[211] 13–53

Rectification is retrospective. The contract is rectified *ab initio*, since its terms are rewritten into the form in which they should have been written at the moment the contract was entered into. In consequence, the effect of rectification is retrospective, in the sense that it affects anything that has already been done under the contract.[212] 13–54

[209] Causes and matters relating to "rectification, setting aside or cancellation of deeds or other instruments in writing" are assigned to the Chancery Division in the High Court: Senior Courts Act 1981, s.61, Sch.1, para.1; Chancery Guide 2009, para.18.1. A county court has jurisdiction where the value of the property does not exceed £30,000: County Courts Act 1984, s.23(d); County Courts Jurisdiction Order 1981 (SI 1981/1123). A court with jurisdiction to rectify the contract may treat it under Senior Court Act 1981 s.49(2) as having been rectified without making a formal order for rectification: D. Hodge, *Rectification* (2010), para.1–70.

[210] *White v White* (1872) L.R. 15 Eq. 247. Where, however, the instrument that is rectified was one relating to land pursuant to which an entry was made in the register, it may be necessary for the register to be altered in order to give full effect to the rectification of the instrument. In relation to registered land, the Adjucator to H.M. Land Registry has the power to make any order which the High Court could make for the rectification of certain documents: Land Registration Act 2002, s.108.

[211] *Craddock Bros v Hunt* [1923] 2 Ch. 136, CA; *United States of America v Motor Trucks Ltd* [1924] A.C. 196, PC, at 201–202.

[212] *Malmesbury v Malmesbury* (1862) 31 Beav. 407 at 418, 54 E.R. 1196 at 1200 (rectification retrospectively validated leases granted by tenant for life). Hence, it will not be awarded if it would prejudice innocent third parties: above, para.13–52. Where an agreement for the sale or other disposition of an interest in land is rectified so as to constitute a contract within the Law of Property (Miscellaneous Provisions) Act 1989 s.2(1), the contract comes into being, or is deemed to have come into being, at such time as may be specified in the court order: *ibid.*, s.2(4); this is different from the usual retrospective effect of rectification: *Oun v Ahmad* [2008] EWHC 545 (Ch), [2008] 2 P. & C.R. DG3 at [36].

(7) Non est Factum[213]

13–55 **Non est factum in the modern law.** The modern law relating to the plea of *non est factum* is found in the decision of the House of Lords in *Saunders v Anglia Building Society*.[214] Before this decision, the law had become unclear, and in some respects the previous decisions were contradictory. Lord Wilberforce summarised the problem by reference to the historical development[215]:

> "In medieval times, when contracts were made by deeds, and the deed had a kind of life in the law of its own, illiterate people who either could not read, or could not understand, the language in which the deed was written, were allowed this plea (that is what 'non est factum' is—a plea): the result of it, if successful, was that the deed was not their deed. I think that three things can be said about the early law. First, that no definition was given of the nature or extent of the difference which must exist between what was intended and what was done—whether such as later appeared as the distinction between 'character' and 'contents' or otherwise . . . Secondly, these cases are for the most part as between the original parties to the deed, or if a third party is concerned (for example *Thoroughgood's Case*[216]) he is a successor to the estate granted. Thirdly, there is some indication that the plea was not available where the signer had been guilty of a lack of care in signing what he did: there is no great precision in the definitions of the disabling conduct. If Fleta is to be relied upon, there was an exception of negligentia or imperitia—see *Holdsworth's History of English Law*, Vol.8, p.50, n.2.
>
> In the 19th century, the emphasis had shifted towards the consensual contract, and the courts, probably unconscious of the fact, had a choice. They could either have discarded the whole doctrine on which *non est factum* was based, as obsolete, or they could try to adapt it to the prevailing structure of contract. ('These cases apply to deeds; but the principle is equally applicable to other written contracts': *Foster v. Mackinnon*.[217]) They chose the course of adaptation, and, as in many other fields of the law, this process of adaptation has not been logical, or led to a logical result. The modern version still contains some fossilised elements."

---

213 Chitty, paras 5–101 to 5–106; Furmston, paras 4.107 to 4.111; Treitel, paras 8–076 to 8–083; Anson, pp.259–261; Cheshire, Fifoot and Furmston, pp.321–328.

214 [1971] A.C. 1004; on appeal from *Gallie v Lee* [1969] 2 Ch. 17, by which name the case is also often known.

215 *ibid.*, at 1024.

216 (1582) 2 Co.Rep. 9a.

217 (1869) L.R. 4 C.P. 704 at 712.

The speeches in the House of Lords made clear that they intended to settle the law for the future.[218] In consequence, it can now be said that the party will be successful in the plea—and will therefore be heard to say that he is not bound by the document—if he shows that, at the time when he signed it,[219] he was unable to understand the document; and that the document was "fundamentally", "radically" or "totally" different from the document which he believed himself to be signing; and that he was not careless.

Permanent or temporary inability to understand the document. 13–56
The plea of *non est factum* allows a party to say that, by reason of some disability, he could not understand the document. In the early law, this was applied to parties who were blind or illiterate, and so could not read it themselves, and had to trust someone else to tell them what they were signing—and where they were misled about the document. In the modern law, however, this extends also to other "disabilities", whether from defective education, illness or innate incapacity.[220] The disability may be permanent or temporary: the question is whether it rendered the party incapable of both reading and sufficiently understanding the deed or other document to be signed; that is, incapable of understanding it at least to the point of detecting the fundamental difference between the actual document and the document as he had believed it to be.[221] It is not necessary that the other party to the document knew, or ought to have known, about the disability.[222]

[218] *Saunders v Anglia Building Society*, above, n.214 at 1015 (Lord Reid), 1024 (Lord Wilberforce), 1032 (Lord Pearson).

[219] "The plea of *non est factum* obviously applies where the person sought to be held liable did not in fact sign the document": *ibid.*, at 1015 (Lord Reid). But *cf. ibid.*, at 1025 (Lord Wilberforce: the plea is not needed, or indeed available, in the case of a plain forgery).

[220] *Saunders v Anglia Building Society*, above, n.214 at 1016 (Lord Reid).

[221] *ibid.*, at 1034 (Lord Pearson). In *Saunders v Anglia Building Society* the document was signed by a 78-year-old widow, who was "by no means incapable physically or mentally" (Lord Wilberforce at 1027) although she could not at the time read the document because she had broken her spectacles.

[222] *Lloyds Bank Plc v Waterhouse* [1993] 2 F.L.R. 97, CA, at 115 (Purchas L.J.: party had no duty to disclose that he was illiterate). But the fact that he is illiterate may bear on what he has to do to avoid being careless: at 121 (Woolf L.J.); below, para.13–58. In *Saunders v Anglia Building Society*, above, n.214 at 1035, Lord Pearson reserved the question whether the plea could ever be successful where the signer was able to read and sufficiently understand the document, but

13–57 **The document must be "fundamentally", "radically" or "totally" different.** The speeches of the House of Lords used a variety of words to describe and emphasise the degree of difference that must be shown between the actual document, and the document as the party believed it to be. The question here is the party's subjective understanding,[223] and so we are certainly within the realm of a party's mistake about the terms of the contract.[224] But there must be a "radical difference"[225] between what he signed and what he thought he was signing; or it must be "essentially different in substance or kind"[226]; or the difference must "go to the substance of the whole consideration or to the root of the matter"[227]; or the actual document must be "basically",[228] or "fundamentally",[229] or "seriously",[230] or "very substantially",[231] or "totally"[232] different. In using such a test, the House[233] rejected a tendency in the earlier cases[234] to draw a firm distinction between (a) a difference in character of the document (which had been held to be sufficient for

was induced to sign it without reading it; and at 1016 Lord Reid said: "I do not say that the remedy can never be available to a man of full capacity. But that could only be in very exceptional circumstances: certainly not where his reason for not scrutinising the document before signing it was that he was too busy or too lazy." Although such a case is generally likely to fail on other grounds (in particular, that the signer was careless: below, para.13–58) it would be better to exclude it altogether as a matter of principle, since it would seriously destabilise the certainty of written contracts, a policy which HL in *Saunders* was itself keen to maintain. The extension of disabilities to "defective education" is already rather generous. See further below, para.13–61.

223 *Saunders v Anglia Building Society*, above, n.214 at 1035–1035 (Lord Pearson).

224 It must be a mistake about the character or terms of the contract, or about the identity of the other party; a mistake about its legal effect is insufficient: *ibid.*, at 1016 (Lord Reid).

225 *ibid.*, at 1017 (Lord Reid), 1021 (Viscount Dilhorne), 1026 (Lord Wilberforce), 1039 (Lord Pearson).

226 *ibid.*, at 1026 (Lord Wilberforce).

227 *ibid.*, at 1019 (Lord Hodson).

228 *ibid.*, at 1026 (Lord Wilberforce).

229 *ibid.*, at 1017 (Lord Reid), 1022 (Viscount Dilhorne), 1026 (Lord Wilberforce), 1039 (Lord Pearson).

230 *ibid.*, at 1017 (Lord Reid).

231 *ibid.*, at 1017 (Lord Reid).

232 *ibid.*, at 1039 (Lord Pearson).

233 e.g. *ibid.*, at 1039 (Lord Pearson).

234 The distinction stemmed from *Howatson v Webb* [1907] 1 Ch. 537, affirmed [1908] 1 Ch. 1, CA.

the plea of *non est factum*) and (b) a difference only in contents (which had been held not to be sufficient). This distinction may work in many cases, but it is not a formal part of the test. As Lord Reid said[235]:

> "If a man thinks he is signing a document which will cost him £10 and the actual document would cost him £1,000 it could not be right to deny him this remedy simply because the legal character of the two was the same. It is true that we must then deal with questions of degree, but that is a familiar task for the courts and I would not expect it to give rise to a flood of litigation."

The person signing must not have been careless. In addition to the disability of the party, and the very serious degree of his mistake about the document, it must be shown that he was not careless. Older cases had spoken in terms of the party not being "negligent", and this had led to a misunderstanding that it was a question of whether he owed a duty of care to the person seeking to enforce the document against him.[236] But this is not so: it is a broader question of whether he was careless. Much emphasis is placed on this requirement, and the heavy burden on the party to show that he was not careless. Lord Wilberforce said[237]: 13–58

[235] *Saunders v Anglia Building Society*, above, n.214 at 1017. In *Saunders* an assignment of a leasehold interest in a house to X for £3,000 (which was not, and was not intended by X to be, paid) was not sufficiently different from an intended deed of gift in favour of Y, where the signer knew that X and Y were jointly concerned in a project to raise money on the property. See also *Mercantile Credit Co. Ltd v Hamblin* [1965] 2 Q.B. 242 (actual document had same practical effect as the intended document), discussed in *Saunders v Anglia Building Society* by Lord Pearson at 1031–1032. For cases where the test was satisfied, see *Lewis v Clay* (1897) 67 L.J.Q.B. 224 (deception by which defendant signed promissory notes believing he was merely witnessing a signature), discussed in *Saunders* by Lord Pearson at 1034; *Foster v Mackinnon* (1869) L.R. 4 C.P. 704 (defendant tricked into putting name on back of bill of exchange believing he was signing a guarantee).

[236] *Foster v Mackinnon*, above, n.235; *Carlisle and Cumberland Banking Co. v Bragg* [1911] 1 K.B. 489.

[237] *Saunders v Anglia Building Society*, above, n.214 at 1027. This is not an estoppel, but "an illustration of the principle that no man may take advantage of his own wrong": *Gallie v Lee*, above, n.214 at 48 (Salmon L.J.), approved in *Saunders v Anglia Building Society* at 1038 (Lord Pearson). *Cf.* the rational for the binding force of signature on documents more generally: above, para.13–34.

> "a person who signs a document, and parts with it so that it may come into other hands, has a responsibility, that of the normal man of prudence, to take care what he signs, which, if neglected, prevents him from denying his liability under the document according to its tenor. I would add that the onus of proof in this matter rests upon him, i.e., to prove that he acted carefully, and not upon the third party to prove the contrary."

What is expected of the party by way of care will depend on the facts; and will relate also to the nature of the disability and the nature of the transaction. But it is not easy to establish that sufficient care has been taken. In particular, if a party fails to read the document or to ask for an explanation of it, he will normally be held to have failed to exercise sufficient care.[238]

13–59 **Burden and standard of proof.** The plea of *non est factum* is made in civil proceedings, and therefore the normal civil standard (on the balance of probabilities) applies; but the fact that the party has signed a document which apparently indicates his assent to its contents means that he must produce evidence to rebut this. This is the position that we have seen taken by the courts generally in relation to a party's claim to avoid his signature on a written document.[239] In the case of a plea of *non est factum*, however, the courts have gone further in emphasising that the party raising the plea has the burden of proving all of its elements strictly. Although the plea is designed to protect a party who through some disability has been unable to understand the document, this must be balanced against the fact that the successful plea results in a finding that the contract is void—and therefore third parties are prejudiced. Whilst

---

[238] *ibid.*, at 1035 (Lord Pearson). In *Saunders v Anglia Building Society* a 78-year-old lady, whose spectacles were broken, signed a deed without asking the other intended party to read it to her or to explain it. *Cf Lloyds Bank Plc v Waterhouse*, above, n.222 (Purchas and Woolf L.JJ. disagreed on whether illiterate party was at fault in not asking for the document to be read out or explained). See also *United Dominions Trust Ltd v Western* [1976] Q.B. 513, CA (defendant signed printed form, but left blanks for the other party to complete: held, bound by his signature); *Norwich and Peterborough Building Society v Steed* [1993] Ch. 116 at 125–128 (donee of power of attorney careless in not checking the nature of the document she was asked by donor of the power to sign).

[239] Above, para.13–32.

allowing the plea to succeed in an appropriate case, the courts place the burden squarely on the shoulders of the party seeking to escape the apparent contract[240]:

> "The matter generally arises where an innocent third party has relied on a signed document in ignorance of the circumstances in which it was signed, and where he will suffer loss if the maker of the document is allowed to have it declared a nullity. So there must be a heavy burden of proof on the person who seeks to invoke this remedy. He must prove all the circumstances necessary to justify its being granted to him, and that necessarily involves his proving that he took all reasonable precautions in the circumstances."

The contract is void. A successful plea of *non est factum* involves the party establishing that he did not in fact consent. The contract is therefore void, and not merely voidable.[241] In practice, a plea will involve an allegation that the other party to the transaction fraudulently procured the party's signature to the document, either by mispresenting its contents or by some other artifice which caused the signer to misunderstand fundamentally the nature or contents of the document he was signing.[242] So in many cases where the party wishes to avoid the transaction he can do so *as against the other party* on the basis of misrepresentation; and, as we saw in Chapter 4, he can do so with much less difficulty than is imposed on him in relation to the plea of *non est factum*. But misrepresentation (whether fraudulent or innocent) only renders the contract voidable,[243] and one of the bars to rescission is the fact that it would prejudice innocent third parties.[244] The case in which a party will in practice seek to raise the plea of *non est factum* is therefore where he needs to show that the contract was void, typically so that he can say that it does not bind him as against a 13–60

---

240 *Saunders v Anglia Building Society*, above, n.214, at 1016 (Lord Reid). See also at 1019 (Lord Hodson: "The plea of *non est factum* requires clear and positive evidence before it can be established"), 1027 (Lord Wilberforce).

241 *ibid.*, at 1026 (Lord Wilberforce).

242 The mistake need not have been induced by misrepresentation: "it is the lack of consent that matters, not the means by which this result was brought about": *ibid.* However, if the signer can read the document, or cannot read it but fails to ask the other party what it contains, he will normally be unable to show that he took sufficient care: above, para.13–58.

243 Above, para.4–05.

244 Above, para.4–59.

third party—for example, so that he can deny a third party's claim to have subsequently acquired rights in the property which was the subject-matter of the contract.[245] However, it is not clear how far the courts will press the point that the contract is void.[246] Logically, the claimant cannot affirm it; but if he does not raise the plea he will be bound by his own signature to the document, and can therefore rely on the document as binding if he so chooses. Nor does it appear that the other party to the contract should be able to rely on the contract being void: the plea is designed to protect the party who made a very serious mistake by virtue of his inability to understand the transaction; and, in any event, the other party will often have committed a wrong in procuring the mistaken party's signature and should also for that reason not be able to rely on the mistake he caused in the other party in order to escape the contract.

13–61 **Unresolved tension: the relationship between *non est factum*, mistake, misrepresentation and incapacity.** The doctrine of *non est factum* fits uncomfortably in the English law of contract. It is a based on a combination of a disability—the inability to understand the document—and a very serious mistake about the terms of the document. We have seen that a mistake about the terms of the contract may make a contract void; but that where the party has signed a document the courts are very reluctant to allow the signer to escape the apparent consequences of his signature, although they may do so where the other party knows or ought to know that the signature does not in fact signify consent.[247] In the case of *non est factum*, the claim is more extreme: that the contract is void by reason of the mere disability which gave rise to a mistake about the document, without the other party necessarily knowing it or having caused it. At first sight it appears that the doctrine is designed to protect the disabled party against the consequences of his disability. But again it does not fit comfortably with the general approach of the law to contractual disabilities. Where, for example, a party lacks mental capacity a contract which he enters into is not void; it is voidable—and only if the handicap is known to the other

[245] In *Saunders v Anglia Building Society* the question was whether a building society had obtained a valid mortgage of the property which was the subject-matter of the contract.
[246] Above, para.12–18.
[247] Above, para.13–34.

party.[248] So the defendant can normally hold the claimant to a contract that he has signed, however serious the claimant's mistake may have been about the terms of the document, where the defendant did not know (nor should have known) about the mistake; and the contract is not even voidable for the claimant's mistake or disability unless the defendant caused the mistake (by making a misrepresentation) or knew about the disability. However, the approach taken to a plea of *non est factum* appears to run counter to the policies underlying the law of mistake, misrepresentation and incapacity, and to hold that a contract can be void (not merely voidable) where the other contracting party played no part in the creation of the mistake, nor did he at the time of the contract have actual or constructive notice of the defect of consent. As we have seen, the courts reserve this consequence for the most extreme cases: only where the consequences of the mistake are very serious—the document is "radically" different from the document as it was believed to be; and the party is not at fault. But it is an area of the law of mistake which may merit further review.

[248] *Hart v O'Connor* [1985] A.C. 1000, PC, on appeal from New Zealand, but the decision is applicable to common law jurisdicions generally: at 1017, 1027 (Lord Brightman); Chitty, para.8–068; Treitel, para.12–055; Anson, pp.246–247. Similarly, extreme intoxication can render the contract voidable, but only if the other party knows about it: Chitty, para.8–080; Treitel, para.12–062; Anson, pp.247–8; *Irvani v Irvani* [2000] 1 Lloyd's Rep. 412 at 425.

CHAPTER 14

MISTAKES ABOUT THE IDENTITY OF THE OTHER PARTY[1]

[1] Chitty, paras 5–088 to 5–100; Furmston, paras 4.102 to 4.105; Treitel, paras 8–034 to 8–041, 8–045, 8–050; Anson, pp.268–276; Cheshire, Fifoot and Furmston, pp.309–317; Stoljar, Ch.4; G. Williams, "Mistake as to Party in the Law of Contract" (1945) 23 Can. Bar. Rev. 271, 380; G.L. Williams, "A Lawyer's Alice" (1946) 9 C.L.J. 171; R.A. Samek, "Some Reflections on the Logical Basis of Mistake of Identity of Party" (1960) 38 Can. Bar. Rev. 479; J.C. Hall, "New Developments in Mistake of Identity" [1961] C.L.J. 86.

I. INTRODUCTION: "IDENTITY" AND ITS RELEVANCE IN FORMING A CONTRACT

14–01 **Identifying the contracting parties; a contract is "personal".** A contract is a personal relationship between two or more parties.[2] But to describe a contract as *personal* is ambiguous. It certainly means that the rights and duties created by the contract are rights and duties *in personam*: personal, not proprietary.[3] And this means that the identification of the contracting parties is crucial because it defines who can sue, and who can be sued, under the contract. But the personality of the parties can have a stronger significance, in relation either to the formation of the contract or to its performance. To take performance first: it is often said that whether a contract, or a particular contractual right, is assignable depends on whether it was "personal". Originally the law regarded the *in personam* nature of the contract as of itself sufficient reason to deny that the rights were assignable.[4] But in the modern law the courts will generally allow assignment, but only if "it can make no difference to the person on whom the obligation lies to which of two persons he is to discharge it"[5]; that is, a contract is not assignable if it is "personal" in a narrower, more particular sense.[6]

At the moment of formation, however, the personality of the putative parties can also be of significance—to the point where one party is *only* prepared to enter into a contract if the other party to the negotiations is (or, sometimes, is not[7]) a particular individual. In effect, the contract is to be "personal" in the sense that, if the other party does not fulfil the necessary characteristics by way of identity, the contract cannot be formed at all. In the cases with which we are concerned in this chapter one party generally asserts that the

---

[2] Anson, p.25; P. Birks, "Definition and Division" in *The Classification of Obligations* (P. Birks ed., 1997), Ch.1.

[3] A contract may be a means by which property rights are created or transferred; but the contract itself creates personal rights.

[4] *Linden Gardens Trust Ltd v Lenesta Sludge (Disposals) Ltd* [1994] 1 A.C. 85 at 109.

[5] *Tolhurst v Associated Portland Cement Manufacturers (1900) Ltd* [1902] 2 K.B. 660, CA, at 668 (Collins M.R.). The contract may make this clear by expressly prohibiting assignment: *Linden Gardens Trust Ltd v Lenesta Sludge (Disposals) Ltd*, above, n.4.

[6] Chitty, paras 19–054 to 19–055.

[7] This presents greater difficulty: *Sowler v Potter* [1940] 1 K.B. 271; below, para.14–24.

contract was personal in this last sense; that he would not have entered into the contract if he had known the true identity of the other party:

> "a mistaken belief by A. that he is contracting with B., whereas in fact he is contracting with C., will negative consent where it is clear that the intention of A. was to contract only with B.[8];"

> "when any one makes a contract in which the personality, so to speak, of the particular party contracted with is important, for any reason . . . no one else is at liberty to step in and maintain that he is the party contracted with."[9]

As we shall see, there are significant difficulties in disentangling issues of both fact and law in relation to such a claim. There are difficult questions of fact[10]: for example, in what sense does the claimant refer to the "personality", or "identity", of the other party? What does he really mean by saying that he "would not have entered into the contract" if he had known the truth? And there has been sharp disagreement amongst the judges about the legal significance of such a mistake. The House of Lords in 2003 was divided on this issue in *Shogun Finance Ltd v Hudson*,[11] but its decision now gives us a definitive answer to certain questions. In order to understand the significance of the decision in the *Shogun*

---

[8] *Bell v Lever Bros Ltd* [1932] A.C. 161, HL, at 217 (Lord Atkin).

[9] *Boulton v Jones* (1857) 27 L.J. Ex. 117 at 119 (Bramwell B.). The examples given by Bramwell B. suggest that he may in fact have been thinking of vicarious performance of the contract by a third party, or assignment; see also the report of his judgment at 6 W.R. 107 ("I should not like to lay down as a general proposition that in all cases the person only with whom the contract is made (*although it be performed by another*) can sue"; emphasis added). This is not, however, a case of assignment because the offer was accepted by a person other than the one to whom it was addressed; in the case of assignment or vicarious performance the benefit of the contract is transferred to, or the actual performance is given by, a third party *after* the formation of the contract between the originally intended parties. But this emphasises that the "personal" nature of the contract can have a similar significance both at the point of formation and thereafter. See also A.L. Goodhart, "Mistake as to Identity in Contract" (1941) 57 L.Q.R. 228 at p.234.

[10] In *Fawcett v Star Car Sales Ltd* [1960] N.Z.L.R. 406, NZCA, at 413 Gresson P., dissenting in the result, went so far as to say that "the difficulty in deciding whether a mistake of identity prevents the formation of a concluded contract is a proper assessment of the facts rather than the ascertainment of the law".

[11] [2003] UKHL 62, [2004] 1 A.C. 919.

case, however, it is necessary first to explore some of the practical issues arising from alleged mistakes of identity, and the law as it had developed before *Shogun*.

14–02 **What is "identity"? The use of names.** The inherent ambiguity in the description of a contract as "personal" leads on to a corresponding ambiguity in the use of names. The parties to a contract need to be identified; and names are generally used to do this. But the use of names can be ambiguous[12]:

> "A name is a word, or a series of words, that is used to identify a specific individual. It can be described as a label. Whenever a name is used, extrinsic evidence, or additional information, will be required in order to identify the specific individual that the user of the name intends to identify by the name—the person to whom he intends to attach the label."

The mere fact that one person addresses the other as "Mr Smith" during the course of negotiations which lead to their forming an apparent contract, says nothing about the significance that he attaches to the identity of the other contracting party. "Mr Smith" may be just a label to identify him, because "Mr Smith" is the name which that person gave when they first met. He does not really care with whom he enters into the contract: "Mr Smith" is as good a counterparty as any other. And even if "Mr Smith" is a "false" name, this only means that it is not the name by which he is presently generally known. English law is relatively relaxed about names—the law may care who a person *is* for many reasons, such as to ensure that his income is properly taxed. But it does not restrict him in the use of his name—he is free to choose whatever name he likes, and to change it from time to time, by informal means as well as formally.[13] The motives of the person falsely calling himself "Mr Smith" cannot of themselves change the intentions of the other contracting party—although of course in many cases the very reason that a false name will be given will be because the person believes that his "true" identity would be an obstacle to securing the contract. At that point, he may use a false name in order to practise a deception—and this will have legal consequences, including in the law of misrepresentation. And it

[12] *Shogun Finance Ltd v Hudson*, above, n.11 at [120] (Lord Phillips).
[13] *Halsbury's Laws of England* (4th edn), Vol.35 (1994 reissue), paras 1202, 1272–1279.

may indicate that the other party would not in fact have been prepared to contract with him—that is, his identity is more significant to that party than just his name.

The "identity" of a particular, individual person[14] is more, therefore, than just the name. In order to form a contract one person must intend to contract with the other; his communications, whether written or oral, which constitute the negotiations and the ultimate formation of the agreement must be addressed to the other. But the fact that he uses a particular name in addressing the other party does not necessarily determine whether he was using the name as merely a label; or as a more precise indicator of a particular person with whom (and with whom *alone*) he was prepared to contract. We shall see that this difficulty of reaching beyond the use of a name to the significance of the person's intention in using the name has caused difficulties in some cases.

The difficulty of proving identity. It is worth noticing at the outset that one reason that mistakes of identity can be made is because of the difficulty of proving identity. The name is used as a link to a person's identity. But the freedom to change one's name, and the fact that there is no single, reliable means of establishing the link between a person and his name, opens the door to the misuse of names in a way that cannot always be checked. A person may be able to demonstrate his identity from his passport, if he has one. But there is no requirement for an individual to have a passport; many driving licences are still in the old paper form (without photograph)[15]; and there is no official form of personal identity card.[16] A consequence of this is that a contracting party has no reliable means of verifying that the other person is who he says he **14–03**

[14] Oxford English Dictionary (3rd edn, 2010 and online version June 2011): "Identity", 2.a.: "The sameness of a person or thing at all times or in all circumstances; the condition of being a single individual; the fact that a person or thing is itself and not something else; individuality, personality".

[15] Only photocard driving licences have been issued since July 1, 1998: Road Traffic Act 1988 s.98(1), substituted by the Driving Licences (Community Driving Licence) Regulations 1998 (SI 1998/1402) reg.7(2), implementing Directive 96/47/EC.

[16] The Identity Cards Act 2006 provided for the introduction of identity cards but was repealed by the Identity Documents Act 2010 s.1; identity cards which had already been issued were cancelled (s.2) and all information recorded in the National Identity Register was destroyed (s.3).

is. In *Shogun*, for example, a man calling himself "Mr Durlabh Patel" supported his claim to that identity by producing Mr Patel's (valid) driving licence, which he had obtained improperly, and forging Mr Patel's signature on a hire-purchase agreement.[17]

14–04 **Identity is not a term of the contract.** It should also be noted that the identity of the parties to a contract is not a term of the contract.[18] The parties do not exchange promises about their respective identities. If one is not who he claims to be, it is not a breach of contract. On the other hand it has been suggested that the same approach can be taken to identity and terms. We have already seen that, where the parties are not in fact in agreement about the terms of the contract, the subjective misunderstanding may be overridden by the objective test: but under this test one party cannot hold the other to have agreed to terms where he either knew, or

[17] *Shogun Finance Ltd v Hudson*, above, n.11 at [15], [45], [112]. Presumably it was an old-style paper driving licence, without a photograph. The personal details provided by the rogue painted a picture: "Shogun made a computer search to check Mr Patel's name and address against the electoral register, then to check whether any county court judgments or bankruptcy orders were registered against him, then to check his credit rating with one or more credit reference agencies. In the space of about five minutes they learned how long Mr Patel had lived at his address, where he worked and how long he had worked there, his bank account number and how long he had held the account, his date of birth and his driving licence number. They also learned that he had no adverse credit references": at [114] (Lord Phillips). But none of this guaranteed that the person signing the hire-purchase agreement was the same person as the one identified by those details: see [2001] EWCA Civ 1000, [2002] Q.B. 834 at [12] (Sedley L.J., dissenting).

[18] It is not a primary obligation in the sense used by Lord Diplock in *Photo Production Ltd v Securicor Transport Ltd* [1980] A.C. 827, HL, at 848–849; nor a term which qualifies or defines the primary obligations and their consequences (exclusion or limitation clauses, arbitration clauses, choice of law clauses, etc.). A party may give a warranty about his capacity, such as an agent's warranty of authority, or a company's warranty about its power to enter into an agreement. But these are not issues of identity. *Cf. Homburg Houtimport BV v Agrosin Private Ltd (The Starsin)* [2003] UKHL 12, [2004] 1 A.C. 715 at [175] (Lord Millett: "The identity of the parties to a contract is fundamental. It is not simply a term or condition of the contract. It goes to the very existence of the contract itself. If it is uncertain, there is no contract").

ought reasonably to have known, that the latter was making a mistake.[19] In *Shogun* Lord Phillips said that the same approach is taken to mistakes of identity[20]:

> "Just as the parties must be shown to have agreed on the terms of the contract, so they must also be shown to have agreed the one with the other. If A makes an offer to B, but C purports to accept it, there will be no contract. Equally, if A makes an offer to B and B addresses his acceptance to C there will be no contract. Where there is an issue as to whether two persons have reached an agreement, the one with the other, the courts have tended to adopt the same approach to resolving that issue as they adopt when considering whether there has been agreement as to the terms of the contract. The court asks the question whether each *intended*, or must be deemed to have *intended*, to contract with the other. That approach gives rise to a problem where one person is mistaken as to the identity of the person with whom he is dealing, as the cases demonstrate."

This may well be a good analogy.[21] But it still does not take us far enough to solve the particular difficulties thrown up by a claim of mistake of identity. The core problem—with whom did the party intend to contract?—is left open. Was it the person with whom he was dealing, who happened to use a particular name? Or was it a different person to whom, in the eyes of the contracting party, the name made reference?

Mistakes of identity; failure of offer and acceptance. There are 14–05
different ways of looking at claims of mistaken identity. Sometimes the courts have been presented with an argument that a party's communications were addressed only to X, whereas the person who purported to reply was Y. This bases the mistake of identity on a failure of offer and acceptance, and says that no contract was ever formed because the communications never in fact corresponded. On the other hand, and particularly where there is clearly a verbal correspondence between the communications, a party may sometimes argue not that there was no offer and acceptance, but that the

---

[19] Above, paras 13–19 (the "objective" test); 13–21 to 13–22 (mistakes known or ought to have been known).

[20] Above, n.11 at [125]. This analysis in substance draws on the argument in A.L. Goodhart, "Mistake as to Identity in the Law of Contract" (1941) 57 L.Q.R. 228, although Goodhart asserted at p.231 that the parties' identity *is* a term of the contract, and therefore the objective test applies directly.

[21] See further below, paras 14–17, 14–22, 14–29, 14–30, 14–42.

apparent agreement was vitiated by a mistake of identity.[22] In truth, however, both forms of argument, which tend to depend on the circumstances of the case, are based on the same underlying principle: that for a contract there must be an agreement between the parties. And there is no agreement if the parties were not *ad idem* in their dealings.[23]

14–06 **Subjectivity and objectivity in mistakes of identity.** We have seen that mistake is necessarily a subjective concept.[24] The party seeking to escape the contract alleges that he should do so because he misunderstood something; and that this misunderstanding prevented the contract from being properly formed. In the case of a mistake of identity, he says that he misunderstood who he was dealing with. But it is not sufficient in English law for a party to avoid a contract by simply showing that he made a mistake. In addition, it must be shown why the other party should *lose* the contract; because he caused or contributed to the mistake, or knew or at least ought to have known about it.[25] Judges and writers have criticised the tendency of the English cases on mistaken identity to focus on the subjective misunderstanding of the party seeking relief, without giving sufficient attention to the other party's (objective) understanding. This criticism has centred on the reliance, in a number of cases over an extended period of time, on a statement

---

[22] "The problem is sometimes mentioned in the textbooks in the section which deals with the formation of contract, where the question is whether a contract has been concluded; but it is more usually dealt with in the section which is concerned with the effect of mistake and in particular 'mistaken identity', where the question is said to turn on whether A's identity is (i) 'fundamental' (in which case the contract is completely void) or (ii) 'material' but not 'fundamental' (in which case the contract is merely voidable). In his dissenting judgment in *Ingram v Little* [1961] 1 Q.B. 31 at 64 Devlin L.J. distinguished between the two questions and observed that it was easy to fall into error if one did not begin with the first question, whether there is sufficient correlation between offer and acceptance to bring a contract into existence": *Shogun*, above, n.11 at [58] (Lord Millett).

[23] We saw the same distinction in relation to the formation of the contract and its terms. Sometimes the courts have focused on whether there was an agreement at all: e.g. *The Hannah Blumenthal*, above, para.13–14 (no contract because no offer and acceptance); sometimes on whether the apparent agreement was vitiated by mistake: e.g. *Smith v Hughes*, above, para.13–09 (contract for "oats"; or contract for "old oats").

[24] Above, para.12–03.

[25] Above, para.12–14.

from the French writer Pothier. This will be mentioned further below; and it will be seen that it is indeed misleading to give too much weight to the analogy from French law.[26] But it will also be seen that this criticism in a sense misses the mark. The subjective (mis)understanding of the party seeking relief does indeed have to be examined very carefully, for the reason that we have already discussed: to see what his real intentions were about his contractual counterparty: with whom did he think he was dealing, and with whom did he therefore intend to form the contract? But, in addition, a further question has to be asked: how did the other party (objectively) understand him?—though this may get shorter treatment in cases of mistaken identity because it is almost always answered by virtue of the fact that the other party not only knew that the claimant was making a mistake about his identity, but also caused it: most mistakes of identity are in practice induced by the other party's fraud.

Contracts formed orally or by writing; contracts concluded in writing. In reading the following sections it is important to bear in mind that a contract can be formed in different ways: by the exchange of communications (more or less protracted; and oral, or written, or a mixture of the two) which culminate in an offer by one party that is accepted by the other; or by the parties coming to a (not yet binding) agreement which is then formalised into a written document, and it is the document which is intended by the parties to be the contract. Issues of mistaken identity will arise differently in different circumstances. As we saw in relation to alleged mistakes about the terms of the contract, where the contract is formed by communications between the parties the issue can be resolved by an interpretation of the communications themselves. But where the contract is reduced to writing, there is a different approach: there is a heavy burden on a party who seeks to displace the normal, objective meaning of the written document.[27] So, too, when the claim is based on a written contract, we shall see that the court is less easily persuaded that the party to the contract is not simply the party whose name appears on it. A written contract necessarily imports a greater degree of objectivity in its interpretation. 14–07

[26] Below, para.14–16
[27] Above, para.13–32.

II. THE PRACTICAL SIGNIFICANCE OF A MISTAKE OF IDENTITY: VOID AND VOIDABLE CONTRACTS AND TRANSFERS OF PROPERTY

14–08 **Mistakes of identity are normally unilateral and induced by fraud.** In every reported case the alleged mistake of identity has been unilateral. This is inevitable in the normal case, because A may be mistaken about B's identity; but it is difficult to see how B could be equally mistaken. He may share A's mistake about some of his own characteristics, less than a mistake of identity—such as whether he has authority to enter into the contract. But in the absence of some other factor that would affect the validity of the contract on other grounds (such as mental incapacity[28]) or some very unusual circumstances (such as the fact that one has been brought up by an adoptive family in ignorance of the circumstances of one's birth), it is difficult to see how one can be mistaken about one's own identity.

Moreover, in almost every case[29] the mistake of identity was induced by the other party's misrepresentation; and such a misrepresentation is generally fraudulent.[30] The purpose of misleading another party about one's own identity is commonly to practise some form of deception; and, anyway, the misrepresentation of his own identity by a negotiating party is inevitably fraudulent for the very reason that he knows his own identity and therefore knows that he is making a statement that is not true. The party who is misled about the other's intention by his misrepresentation will therefore have a range of remedies arising from the misrepresentation: the contract is voidable[31]; and damages can be obtained for loss caused by reliance on the misrepresentation of identity—typically, this means that the losses flowing from entering into the contract will be recoverable.[32] The fact that the misrepresentation is fraudulent can

---

[28] Above, para.13–61, n.248.

[29] The exception is *Boulton v Jones* (1857) 27 L.J. Ex. 117; below, para.14–20.

[30] The judges' description of the typical case of mistaken identity reflects this. The counterparty is commonly referred to as a "rogue"; e.g. this appears to be the term preferred by Lords Hobhouse, Millett, Phillips and Walker in *Shogun Finance Ltd v Hudson*, above, n.11. Lord Nicholls chose to use the word "crook". The headnote writer in the Law Reports appears to prefer "fraudster".

[31] Above, Ch.4.

[32] Above, Ch.5.

in some respects strengthen the claim to these remedies.[33] The question, therefore, is why a party needs to establish not only that he was misled by the other party about his identity; but also that the mistake was itself sufficient to give rise to a remedy. In most cases, this is because he needs to show that the contract was not just voidable, but void.

The contract entered into under a mistake of identity is void. 14–09 We shall see that the disagreement amongst judges in recent years over mistakes of identity has focused on this issue. Some have argued that a mistake of identity should not make the contract void, because of the drastic consequences which follow upon such a finding; and that it is better to hold that the effect of the mistake should be no more than to render the contract voidable.[34] However, the majority of the House of Lords in *Shogun* has confirmed the earlier authorities that held that, if the mistake is sufficient to constitute an actionable mistake of identity, the consequence is that the contract is void.[35]

The paradigm claim based on mistake of identity: claiming property from a later purchaser. 14–10 The claim based on a mistake of identity is not generally raised as between the parties themselves. A party who seeks to escape the contract as against the other contracting party can generally do so on the basis of the other's fraudulent misrepresentation, which renders the contract voidable.[36]

---

[33] Rescission is available for non-fraudulent, as well as fraudulent misrepresentations, but in some respects the claimant is better placed if he can base his claim on fraud: above, para.4–30. Damages on the fraud measure can be more advantageous than damages for negligence: above, para.5–40; but are also in practice available for negligence because of the interpretation given to the Misrepresentation Act 1967 s.2(1): above, para.7–38.

[34] See esp. Lord Denning M.R. in *Lewis v Averay* [1972] 1 Q.B. 198, CA; below, para.14–28.

[35] Below, para.14–36.

[36] Above, para.14–08. It would, however, be necessary to rely on the mistake even as against the other party if the mistake about identity arose from a misrepresentation by a *third party* for whom the other party had no responsibility and of which the other party was ignorant, since the contract is voidable for misrepresentation only if it is made by the other contracting party or if it is a mispresentation made by a third party of which the other party has knowledge: above, paras 4–72 to 4–77. In such a case, however, it may also be more difficult to satisfy the test for an actionable mistake of identity.

Indeed, the claim in support of which the mistake issue is raised is not generally a claim in contract at all. It is a claim in tort, against a third party who now has possession of goods which the claimant delivered under the contract which he alleges was void because of the mistake. The normal mechanism to protect and enforce one's rights in personal property is the law of tort—and, in particular, the tort of conversion.[37] But the claimant in an action of conversion must be able to show that he has title to the goods. If he has parted with the goods under a contract which was only voidable, then he loses his right to rescind the contract, and thereby to re-vest the title at common law, when the goods are sold in turn to a purchaser in good faith.[38] But if the apparent contract under which he delivered the goods was void, no title passed.[39]

In the typical case, therefore, the claimant is the original party to the contract which he now claims was void for mistake; and he is seeking return of his property, or its value in damages,[40] against a person who now has possession of the property, and purchased it in good faith. Both the claimant and the defendant are, in some sense, innocent, and the fraudster has disappeared, or at any rate is not worth suing. Lord Cairns set the scene in *Cundy v Lindsay* as follows[41]:

> "My Lords, you have in this case to discharge a duty which is always a disagreeable one for any Court, namely, to determine as between two parties, both of whom are perfectly innocent, upon which of the two the consequences of a fraud practised upon both of them must fall."

---

[37] M. Bridge, *Personal Property Law* (3rd edn, 2002), Ch.3.

[38] Above, para.4–60. Conversion is a (common law) tort, and therefore the claimant must be able to show title at common law: above, para.4–11.

[39] *Cundy v Lindsay* (1878) 3 App. Cas. 459, HL, at 464 (Lord Cairns: "if the property in the goods in question passed, it could only pass by way of contract; there is nothing else which could have passed the property"). See also *Fawcett v Star Car Sales Ltd* [1960] N.Z.L.R. 406, NZCA, at 424 (Gresson P.: "In this case, the delivery which was made purported to be made in performance of the apparent contract; if this was a nullity, there was nothing to support the delivery"). For the view that this is a misinterpretation of the old authorities and that delivery ought to pass the legal title independently of the validity of the contract, see W. Swadling, "Rescission, Property, and the Common Law" (2005) 121 L.Q.R. 123.

[40] Torts (Interference with Goods) Act 1977, s.3; Clerk & Lindsell, paras 17.87 to 17.90.

[41] Above, n.39 at 4–63.

In some of the recent cases there has been a tendency to focus on the plight of the purchaser—the defendant in the action; to regard him as the more deserving of sympathy[42]; and to criticise the current state of the law to the point of arguing that a contract should never be void for mistake of identity but only voidable, thereby guaranteeing protection for the purchaser in good faith. Such a general solution was rejected by the majority in *Shogun Finance Ltd v Hudson*, but was at the heart of the disagreement of principle between the majority and the minority speeches in that case. This is considered further below.[43]

Other consequences of the contract being void. Although in most of the cases the principal significance of the contract being void is the retention of title by the claimant who parted with possession of the property in performance of the apparent contract, 14–11

[42] e.g. *Lewis v Averay* above, n.34, at 207 (Lord Denning M.R.); *Shogun Finance Ltd v Hudson* [2003] UKHL 62, [2004] 1 A.C. 919 at [35] (Lord Nicholls: "As between two innocent persons the loss is more appropriately borne by the person who takes the risks inherent in parting with his goods without receiving payment"), [82] (Lord Millett: "someone has to bear the loss where there is fraud, but it is surely fairer that the party who was actually swindled and who had an opportunity to uncover the fraud should bear the loss rather than a party who entered the picture only after the swindle had been carried out and who had none"); Law Commission, Ninth Programme of Law Reform, Law Com. No.293 (2005), para.3.54 (commenting on the decision in *Shogun*: "by a majority of three to two, the House of Lords found for the finance company, because the contract was 'void' rather than 'voidable'. The result is extremely technical and may be too harsh to the innocent buyer"). But see also *Shogun* at [181]–[182] (Lord Walker: "it would not be right to make any general assumption as to one innocent party being more deserving than the other"); *Ingram v Little* [1961] 1 Q.B. 31 at 73–74 (Devlin L.J.: "For the doing of justice, the relevant question in this sort of case is not whether the contract was void or voidable, but which of two innocent parties shall suffer for the fraud of a third. The plain answer is that the loss should be divided between them in such proportion as is just in all the circumstances. If it be pure misfortune, the loss should be borne equally; if the fault or imprudence of either party has caused or contributed to the loss, it should be borne by that party in the whole or in the greater part". Devlin L.J.'s proposal was considered but rejected by the Law Reform Committee: Twelfth Report, *Transfer of Title to Chattels*, Cmnd. 2958 (1966), paras 9 to 12. The Law Commission included this topic in its list of possible projects for reform in the Ninth Programme of Law Reform, above, paras 1.16, 3.51 to 3.57 but in 2008 it deferred it for reconsideration in the Eleventh Programme: Tenth Programme of Law Reform, Law Com No.311 (2008), paras 4.2 to 4.4. See also below, para.14–39.

[43] Below, para.14–39.

there are also other consequences. Strictly speaking, if the contract is void *ab initio*, neither party can affirm it.[44] It should be noted, however, that the other party to the contract (the "rogue") would not be able to rely on the mistake to avoid the contract; it was his own (mis)representation of identity that induced the contract, and so if the mistaken party chose not to take the point the rogue would be estopped from proving his true identity. And there is some uncertainty over whether the point that it is void may be taken not only by the mistaken party but also by a third party.[45]

III. THE LAW BEFORE SHOGUN FINANCE LTD V HUDSON

14–12 **The development of a theory of mistake of identity.** The law relating to mistakes in the formation of a contract was in a state of development from the mid-nineteenth century onwards, and has been subject to various twists and turns throughout the twentieth century.[46] It should therefore not be surprising to discover that the courts throughout this time were striving to develop a coherent theory about the significance of mistake about the *identity* of the parties to a contract; and that they should have found different ways of exploring the issue, and focused on different key elements of the argument—and, indeed, that they should have disagreed amongst themselves over the proper formulation of the principles applicable

[44] *Fawcett v Star Car Sales Ltd*, above, n.39 at 412 (Gresson P.)

[45] *ibid.* (execution creditor of original owner of car argued that sale of the car was void for mistaken as to identity of purchaser, and so the car remained part of vendor's assets available for distribution; held, by majority, no sufficient mistake of identity, so contract not void; Gresson P. dissented, and said at 411 that "the Court is not precluded from finding that there was no binding contract, even if both the parties to the transaction should contend that there was a binding contract"; but he relied on cases which did not involve claims by third parties, nor claims involving mistakes of identity). At first instance the trial judge had held that a third party could *not* raise the question of mistake about the person: [1959] N.Z.L.R. 952 at 954. See also Chitty, para.5–098; and (on the general question of what it means to say that a contract is "void") above, para.12–18.

[46] D. Ibbetson, *A Historical Introduction to the Law of Obligations* (1999), pp.225–229; J. Gordley, *The Philosophical Origins of Modern Contract Doctrine* (1991), pp.186–187, 197–201; J. Cartwright, "The rise and fall of mistake in the English law of contract" in R. Sefton-Green (ed.), *Mistake, Fraud and Duties to Inform in European Contract Law* (2005).

to this area of the law.[47] In this section, we shall consider many of the cases which were decided on the basis of alleged mistakes as to identity over this period; and in reading the cases it is important always to bear in mind the development of the law that was taking place. We here group the cases in categories which we can now with hindsight see to have been developed, and which are the categorisations which were most recently addressed authoritatively by the House of Lords in *Shogun Finance Ltd v Hudson*[48]; in particular, it has become significant in the analysis of an alleged mistake to know whether the parties communicated at a distance, or face to face; and whether the contract was concluded by oral or written exchanges, or in writing. First, however, we shall consider how the courts have identified what constitutes a sufficient mistake of identity.

(1) The Claimant Must Have Made a Mistake of Identity Which Caused Him to Contract

The claimant must have made a mistake of "identity", not merely "attributes". It is often said that the claimant must have made a mistake about the other party's identity, and not merely his attributes. However this was criticised by Lord Denning M.R.[49]: 14–13

> "it has been suggested that a mistake as to the identity of a person is one thing: and a mistake as to his attributes is another. A mistake as to identity, it is said, avoids a contract: whereas a mistake as to attributes does not. But this is a distinction without a difference. A man's very name is one of his attributes. It is also a key to his identity. If then, he gives a false name, is it a mistake as to his identity? or a mistake as to his attributes? These fine distinctions do no good to the law."

This statement was made as part of an argument that a mistake of identity should never make a contract void, and so must be read with some circumspection. Although the distinction between a person's identity and his attributes is often, on the facts, not easy to make, it is still valid, and relates back to the problem which we

[47] For a historical discussion, and the suggestion that the older cases must be read with an understanding of the contemporary issues in criminal law, see C. MacMillan, *Mistakes in Contract Law* (2010), Ch.8.

[48] Below, paras 14–34 *et seq.*

[49] *Lewis v Averay* [1972] 1 Q.B. 198, CA, at 206. See further below, para.14–28.

have seen already in relation to the use of names.[50] As Lord Denning indicated, a person's name is one of his attributes. And we have seen that the other party's name can have quite different significance to the claimant in negotiating a contract: it might be just a label, an identifier. But, more than that, it might identify the person (and, let us say, the *only* person) with whom he is prepared to enter into the present contract. This is what lies at the heart of the difficulty of establishing whether the claimant really made a mistake of "identity", and sometimes it will help to exclude an alleged mistake by characterising it as only a mistake about the person's attributes.

To say that the claimant made a mistake of identity means, therefore, that the person with whom he was in fact dealing was *a different person* from the person with whom he believed that he was dealing.

14–14 **Identity is not normally fundamental.** In most cases the particular identity of the other party has no fundamental significance to the claimant. Most contracts are not, in this sense,[51] personal. This is certainly so in the case of contracts relating to goods, the context in which mistakes of identity have normally been raised.[52] If a person enters a shop to buy goods,[53] or sends an order to the shop to be executed in return by post,[54] or bids at an auction,[55] the identity of each party is generally immaterial to the other. The buyer's concern relates to the goods themselves, not to

[50] Above, para.14–02.

[51] Above, para.14–01.

[52] One might expect that the courts' approach to this question would vary according to the type of contract in question, some contracts being more easily identified as personal—most obvious, perhaps, contracts for services where the identity of the person providing the services is significant. This distinction has been drawn in cases which have addressed the question of whether a contract, once concluded, can be assigned: above, para.14–01. But the cases in which the question of mistaken identity has been raised have been contracts relating to goods—and usually by the seller, because the context in which it arises is where he seeks to recover the goods from a third party: above, para.14–10.

[53] *Phillips v Brooks Ltd* [1919] 2 K.B. 243.

[54] *Boulton v Jones* (1857) 27 L.J. Ex. 117 where, however, the identity was held to be fundamental.

[55] *Dennant v Skinner and Collom* [1948] 2 K.B. 164 at 167 (Hallett J.: "Mr. Dennant had never seen him before and did not know in the least who he was. He was simply a man there who had made the highest bid").

the personality of the seller; and the seller's concern relates to the buyer's ability to pay the price. In such cases, therefore, the fact that either party misunderstood who the other party was, is not sufficient to make the contract void. If he accurately identified the other party (he believed that he was dealing with X, and was in fact dealing with X), and only misunderstood some attribute (such as X's creditworthiness), then the contract is not void because the mistake was not about the other party's identity. It may be voidable as a result of the fraudulent misrepresentation which induced the mistake, but that is a different matter. However, even if the claimant thought he was dealing with X, and was in fact dealing with Y—that is, he *did* make a mistake of identity—it does not mean that the mistake is sufficient. In most cases he will still have been prepared to contract with anyone who could provide what he wished to obtain under the contract, and so before holding that the mistake is in principle sufficient the court will have to be satisfied that, on the facts, the particular identity of the other party was fundamental to his decision to enter into the contract—a *causa sine qua non*.[56]

(2) A Subjective Mistake is Not Sufficient

The emphasis on the claimant's subjective mistake. The cases have often emphasised that the claimant must show that he made a mistake about the other party's identity: that he did not in fact intend to deal with the other party, but another person; that his offer was intended only for X, and therefore could not be accepted by Y. This places a necessary emphasis on establishing that the claimant (a) made a (subjective) mistake; and (b) made a mistake about the *identity* of the counterparty, rather than about something less than his identity—and the difficulties of establishing this latter fact involves a close analysis of what the claimant's mistake was really about. 14–15

The reference to Pothier in the older cases. The judges of the nineteenth century did not yet have a developed theory of mistake, and sometimes looked across to the civil law, which had recognised 14–16

[56] *Citibank NA v Brown Shipley & Co. Ltd* [1991] 2 All E.R. 690 at 699–700 (the mistake was not as to the "crucial importance" of the person; not a "fundamental mistake").

that mistakes can affect the validity of a contract. From French law, Pothier's influence was felt in relation to other types of mistake, too[57]; but we are here concerned with what he had to say about identity. The following passage[58] was first quoted by Fry J. in *Smith v Wheatcroft*,[59] apparently in the judge's own English translation[60]:

> "Does error in regard to the person with whom I contract destroy the consent and annul the agreement? I think that this question ought to be decided by a distinction. Whenever the consideration of the person with whom I am willing to contract enters as an element into the contract which I am willing to make, error with regard to the person destroys my consent and consequently annuls the contract.... . On the contrary, when the consideration of the person with whom I thought I was contracting does not enter at all into the contract, and I should have been equally willing to make the contract with any person whatever as with him with whom I thought I was contracting, the contract ought to stand."

This extract (and translation) was then further quoted, generally in full and with attribution to its source in the earlier judgment of Fry J., in a number of later cases.[61] But it proved controversial, because it was interpreted as allowing a party to escape too easily from a contract. Some said that the test was too loose, and allowed a

---

[57] For mistakes about the subject-matter, see J. Cartwright, "The rise and fall of mistake in the English law of contract", above, n.46 at pp.65–86. For a general historical account, see C. MacMillan, *Mistakes in Contract Law* (2010); the discussion of Pothier's influence, in particular, is in Ch.5.

[58] R. J. Pothier, *Le traité des obligations* (Paris, 1761), para.19.

[59] (1878) 9 Ch.D. 223 at 230.

[60] J.C. Smith and J.A.C. Thomas, "Pothier and the Three Dots" (1957) 20 L.Q.R. 38 at pp.38–39.

[61] *Gordon v Street* [1899] 2 Q.B. 641, CA, at 647 (A.L. Smith L.J.); *Phillips v Brooks Ltd*, above, n.53 at 248 (Horridge L.J., quoting only the third sentence, following counsel's argument at 245); *Said v Butt* [1920] 3 K.B. 497 at 501 (McCardie J., omitting the first two sentences); *Lake v Simmons* [1927] A.C. 487, HL, at 501 (Viscount Haldane); *Sowler v Potter* [1940] 1 K.B. 271 at 274 (Tucker J., quoting it within a quotation from *Lake v Simmons*); *Dennant v Skinner and Collom*, above, n.55 at 166 (Hallett J., quoting it from *Lake v Simmons* but without attribution to Pothier); *Ingram v Little* [1961] 1 Q.B. 31 at 54–55 (Sellers L.J.) and 68 (Devlin L.J.). See also *Fawcett v Star Car Sales Ltd* [1960] N.Z.L.R. 406, NZCA, at 419–420 (Gresson P., dissenting on the facts, but drawing his test from D.L. McDonnell and J.G. Monroe, *Kerr on the Law of Fraud and Mistake* (7th edn, 1952), p.156, which itself clearly draws on Pothier in Fry J.'s translation, but without attribution).

mistake which was less than one of identity[62]; others that it focused too much on the subjective mistake of the claimant[63]; and that the time had come for Pothier's statement to be "firmly and finally buried".[64] In fact, when viewed in context,[65] Pothier's statement was intended to convey a test of mistake of identity which was quite narrow: the mistake must be as to the actual person with whom the party intended to contract, very much in line with the generally accepted view in English law.[66] However, the difficulty with Pothier's statement, and the danger of its use in English law, was the apparent used of an exclusively subjective test: if the claimant intended to contract with X, but in fact contracted with Y, Pothier would say that the contract was a nullity. Such a test fails to take into account the position of the other party to the contract—to ask what would happen if Y, the recipient of the claimant's communications, reasonably believed that he was the person with whom the claimant intended to contract. It failed to follow the approach of English law to the formation of a contract, which does not allow a party to escape simply on the grounds of his own mistake, but also

---

[62] Smith and Thomas, above, n.60 at pp.40–41, criticising the view then taken by Cheshire and Fifoot.

[63] A.L. Goodhart, "Mistake as to Identity in Contract" (1941) 57 L.Q.R. 228 at pp.235–236.

[64] *ibid.*, at 244, noted in *Ingram v Little*, above, n.61 at 54–55 (Sellers L.J., but without any firm conclusion) and at 55 (Pearce L.J., with approval). *Cf. Solle v Butcher* [1950] 2 K.B. 671, CA, at 692 (Denning L.J.: "the doctrine of French law enunciated by Pothier is no part of English law"); *Lewis v Averay*, above, n.49 at 206 (Lord Denning M.R.: "Pothier's statement has given rise to such refinements that it is time it was dead and buried together").

[65] Smith and Thomas, above, n.60, demonstrating that what was left out by Fry J. in his quotation from Pothier demonstrated a narrower view of actionable mistake than the critics had assumed.

[66] Pothier wrote before the Civil Code of 1804, which, both by its terms and as subsequently interpreted by the French courts, in fact gives modern French law a more generous doctrine of mistake—including mistake about the other party's identity—than Pothier described; and most certainly wider than the English law doctrine. See B. Nicholas, *The French Law of Contract* (2nd edn, 1992), pp.95–98; J. Cartwright, "Defects of Consent and Security of Contract" in P. Birks and A. Pretto (eds), *Themes in Comparative Law In Honour of Bernard Rudden* (2002) at pp.153–164, esp. at p.160.

requires a consideration of whether the mistake should be overridden by the other party's actual and reasonable understanding.[67]

14–17 **Objectivity in relation to mistakes of identity.** In order to be consistent with the general approach to mistakes in the formation of a contract, therefore, any test designed to determine the sufficiency of an alleged mistake of identity should consider not only whether the claimant was in fact (subjectively) mistaken about the other party's identity; but also whether his mistake should be overridden by an objective consideration of the facts: that is, whether he should still be held to the contract, in spite of his mistake, if he so conducted himself that the other party was entitled to believe, and did in fact believe, that he was the person with whom the claimant intended to deal.[68] If the claimant was himself at fault in making the mistake, or in failing to make clear to the other party that he was misunderstanding his identity or that he was not intending to deal with him, the claimant's mistake should not be sufficient. It must be admitted that the courts have not generally emphasised this aspect of the test, but it is submitted that this is for good reason. In most cases, the real difficulty is in establishing the answer to the first part of the test: whether the claimant in fact made a mistake of identity rather than of something less than identity. Many cases will fail at that hurdle. But, if it is established that the mistake was really of identity, then in practice it will often follow that the other party should have realised it, and did in fact know about it—because of the circumstances in which the mistake arose, created by the deception practised by the other party himself. It would be better, however, in cases where the courts find a mistake of identity to be established, if they were to consider explicitly the objective

[67] "The statement [of Pothier] is untrue in English law, for it substitutes for the English test, 'How ought the promisee to have interpreted the promise?' the entirely different one, 'What did the promisor intend when he made his promise?'": Goodhart, above, n.63 at p.236; approved by Pearce L.J. in *Ingram v Little*, above, n.61 at 55. In fact, this analysis fails to do full justice to Pothier, who (in the section omitted by Fry J. in his quotation) also considered that, if the other party to the (non-existent) contract was ignorant of the mistake, and performed his contract, the mistaken party would be required to compensate him, not under the contract (which is void) but under the principle of "equity, which obligates me to indemnify the one whom I have by my fault led into error").
[68] Goodhart, above, n.63.

interpretation of the facts, rather than giving the impression that the test is entirely subjective. In the following section we shall see how these different issues were addressed in the cases before the decision of the House of Lords in *Shogun*.

(3) The Cases: Mistakes of "Identity" Made in Different Circumstances

Categorisation of the cases. The cases in which the courts have considered claims based on mistakes of identity can be divided into three: those where the alleged contract was formed through communications at a distance—that is, where the parties did not meet, but relied on letters or other communications which passed between them; those where the contract was concluded face to face; and those where, however it was initially negotiated, the contract itself took the form of a single, written document. These are different factual situations in which such issues have arisen over the years, although they have hardened into typical cases which have come to be seen as attracting different substantive tests for claims based on mistakes of identity. One issue which was addressed by the House of Lords in *Shogun* is whether such definitive categorisation of cases is appropriate. 14–18

(a) *The parties communicate at a distance*

The significance of the communications. Where the contract is formed by communications exchanged by the parties, the name by which a person is addressed has an evident significance in identifying him. I write a letter to "Mr Smith" at a particular address.[69] I use the name and address to identify him. If I know who the person is to whom I intend to address the letter, and if I believe that his name is "Mr Smith" and that I have his correct address, the name and address are more than just labels—they are the most obvious way of limiting the destination of the letter to the very person to whom I intend to make my communication. Moreover, the fact that the letter bears a particular name and address gives an 14–19

[69] The argument holds in the case of any communication where the person sending the communication has only such identifiers as the name and address to determine the recipient—and so will apply equally to a fax sent to a particular fax number; an email sent to a particular email address; or a text message sent to a particular mobile telephone number.

external sign of the intended recipient. The communications by which the contract was apparently formed lend themselves to objective interpretation—and the interpretation can be made from the perspective of the person to whom they were apparently addressed, and who in fact received them and claims to have been entitled to act on them. Where, therefore, the contract was formed, if it was formed at all, by the exchange of such communications, the evidence is available for the court to establish whether there was contract, or whether the claimant can be allowed to say that there is no contract because he did not intend his communication to be received and acted upon by the person who in fact did so. We have seen above that the question should not be simply whether the claimant intended to contract with (and only with) the particular person to whom he thought he was addressing the communication, but also whether the other party who in fact received it and concluded an apparent contract with him was entitled reasonably to believe that he was the intended recipient.[70] This involves, first, an inquiry into the subjective intentions of the claimant to see whether he really made a mistake of identity. And then how his mistake should be interpreted by the other party.

14–20 **The mistake of identity: where there is an identifiable, distinct person.** Where the person with whom the claimant believes he is dealing is identifiable and distinct from the other party, it will be possible for the claimant to satisfy the first part of this test. He intended to deal with X, but in fact the communication was received, and acted upon, by Y. Before he can claim a mistake, he must of course in fact know of X and therefore intend to deal with X. However, it is still necessary to show that X was intended to be the only authorised recipient. Where, for example, an order for goods is sent to a shop which, unknown to the person sending the order, has recently been sold to a new owner, it is not obvious that the order is addressed only to the old owner: was the purchaser intending to buy (a) the goods in question, without really being concerned about who sold them to him; or (b) from that particular shop (for example, because he knows of the shop's reputation for price or quality); or (c) from the particular owner of the shop? Such a case occurred in *Boulton v Jones*[71] in which Jones sent an order

[70] Above, para.14–17.
[71] (1857) 27 L.J. Ex. 117.

for goods to Brocklehurst. Earlier in the day Brocklehurst had sold his business, including the stock, to Boulton, who sent the goods requested by Jones. When he later received the invoice in the name of Boulton, Jones refused to pay on the basis that he had not entered into a contract with Boulton. He succeeded.[72] Three of the four judgments in the case appear simply to have assumed that Jones' intention was to deal only with Brocklehurst. Certainly, the order was addressed to Brocklehurst by name; and it may well be that the nature of commerce in the mid-nineteenth century was such that the personality of the proprietor of such a shop was self-evidently significant.[73] But the judges found that the use of Brocklehurst's name did, on the facts, show an intention to deal only with him (and therefore not with Boulton).[74] Bramwell B. did not rely only on the fact that the order was addressed to Brocklehurst, but went further and used as evidence that Jones intended to deal only with Brocklehurst the fact that he had a running account with Brocklehurst which was in credit, and therefore he would have a set-off against him (which would not be available against Boulton).[75]

Similarly, in *Cundy v Lindsay*[76] where the claimants, Lindsays, linen manufacturers in Belfast, responded to an enquiry which they

---

[72] He was not liable to pay the price under the contract, because the contract was void. And he was not required to return the goods because they had by then been "consumed". The goods were "three 50-feet leather hose 2½ in.": (1857) 2 H. & N. 564, 157 E.R. 232. There is no detailed discussion of any possible restitutionary claim, although Bramwell B. rejected ((1857) 27 L.J. Ex. 117 at 119) the suggestion that Jones should be required to pay for the goods "upon some contract which he never made". See Goff & Jones, para.23–005 (the mistake that prevented the formation of the contract may equally preclude any inference that the defendant has freely accepted the goods). In *Shogun Finance Ltd v Hudson* [2003] UKHL 62, [2004] 1 A.C. 919 at [96] Lord Millett said "We would classify the case today as an example of a claim in unjust enrichment being defeated by a change of position defence".

[73] Chitty, para.5–090.

[74] The reports of the judgments vary. But see the report at (1857) 27 L.J. Ex. 117: Cotton L.J. at 118: "The point raised was this, whether the order in writing did not import, on the part of the buyer, the defendant, an intention to deal exclusively with Brocklehurst"; Martin B. at 119: "Where the facts prove that the defendant never meant to contract with A alone . . .".

[75] See, e.g. (1857) 27 L.J. Ex. 117 at 119. Bramwell B. rested his judgment on this issue, but it was clearly before the court, and is also mentioned by Pollock C.B.: *ibid*.

[76] (1878) 3 App. Cas. 459.

believed came from a firm of which they had heard (Blenkiron & Co., in London), and entered into a contract of sale of handkerchiefs in favour of "Blenkiron & Co.", the contract was held to be void because the sender of the letter—and the recipient of the handkerchiefs, which had been sold on to the defendant—was a man called Blenkarn, of whom Lindsays had never heard, and with whom they did not intend to deal. The claimants' mistake was here evidenced by the fact that they knew of Blenkiron & Co., and addressed their communications to that name. The use of the particular name was held, on the facts, to be not just a means of identifying the writer of the letter which came from an address in London, but the means of identifying the particular intended recipient.[77] The decision might be criticised, on the basis that it is not self-evident that the identity of the recipient of their handkerchiefs was crucial to the claimants; they were really interested in their "respectability"[78]—that is, their honesty in contracting and their ability to pay the price; and they were not seeking out a particular party with whom to deal, but responding to an enquiry.[79] And the case might be evidence of a tendency for the courts, in cases of contracts by correspondence, to assume too quickly that the use of a name in a letter is more than just an identifier, and points to the only person with whom the contract was intended to be formed. That is, the objective evidence of the communications is taken to determine the (subjective) mistake.[80]

---

[77] *ibid.*, at 471 (Lord Penzance).

[78] See the statement of facts: *ibid.*, at 460.

[79] In this respect, *Boulton v Jones*, above, n.71 is a stronger case because there was a continuing relationship with a known individual, and the claimant initiated the disputed transaction. *Cf. Ingram v Little*, above, n.61 at 61 (Pearce L.J., drawing the same distinction between a claimant who sought out the other party by name, and one who simply responds to the fraudster's approach, in the context of face-to-face transactions).

[80] "What has to be judged of, and what the jury in the present case had to judge of, was merely the conclusion to be derived from that writing, as applied to the admitted facts of the case": Lord Cairns, at 465. However, the directions to the jury by Blackburn J., reported in the statement of facts at 460, do not appear to have focused on this fundamental aspect of the claimants' intention, but rather on the defendant's fraud. The reliance on the objective meaning of the words in a contract reduced to writing, below, paras 14–30 to 14–31, is different from the interpretation of written communications which passed between the parties.

But the principle underlying the decision is sufficiently clear: that the question is, on the facts, to whom did the claimants intend to limit their communications?

The "mistake" where there is no identifiable, distinct person. 14–21
A different situation arises, however, where "X" is simply a name used as an alias by Y. The claimant, who says that he was mistaken in that he believed that he was dealing with X, cannot show a mistake of identity at all—he cannot show that he was intending to deal with another person. In *King's Norton Metal Co. Ltd v Edridge, Merrett and Co. Ltd*[81] the claimant received an order to sell a ton of brass rivet wire to "Hallam & Co.", although there was no such entity separate from the person who was writing the letters—a man called Wallis who had assumed the business name, and used printed notepaper which made him sound more respectable. A.L. Smith L.J. distinguished *Cundy v Lindsay*[82]:

> "The question was, With whom, upon this evidence, which was all one way, did the plaintiffs contract to sell the goods? Clearly with the writer of the letters. If it could have been shown that there was a separate entity called Hallam and Co. and another entity called Wallis then the case might have come within the decision in *Cundy v Lindsay*. . . . There was only one entity, trading it might be under an *alias*, and there was a contract by which the property passed to him."

This does not, of course, say that the contract would have been void if there had been a separate entity; merely that it might have been void. And this is right: the fact that there was a separate entity would open up the possibility of a mistake of identity. But it would still be a question of whether the person with whom the claimant intended to contract was the distinct person with whom it exchanged correspondence. The facts of the case point against such a decision even if there had been a separate entity, since there had been dealings already between the claimants and "Hallam & Co." in respect of which invoices had been paid: it was "nothing more than a long firm fraud"[83]—and the claimants' complaint appears to be

[81] (1897) 14 T.L.R. 98, CA.
[82] *ibid.*, at 99.
[83] *ibid.*, A.L. Smith L.J., quoting Cave J., at first instance. It appears from the statement of facts that "the plaintiffs had been paid for some goods previously

that their counterparty was not creditworthy, rather than that they really intended to deal with a particular individual.

In short, then, there can be a mistake of identity only if the claimant had a positive belief that he was dealing with X, and intended his communications to be addressed to and responded to by X; but in fact the other party was not X, but a distinct and identifiable person, Y.

14–22 **The interpretation of the communications from the other party's perspective.** It is not, however, sufficient for the claimant to show that he made a mistake, even a mistake which was in reality about the other party's identity in the narrow sense. In addition, it is necessary to consider whether he should be bound to the contract in spite of his mistake, because he has led the other party to believe that he was an acceptable counterparty to the transaction. In most cases, as we have noted, the answer to this will be evident because of the fraud of the other party—and so the courts tend not to focus in detail on the issue.[84] However, they do make clear that this is their underlying assumption. In *Cundy v Lindsay*[85] Lord Cairns made clear that Blenkarn could not have held Lindsays to the contract—that is, the contract was void[86]—because by his conduct "he intended to lead [Lindsays] to believe, and they did believe, that the person with whom they were communicating was not Blenkarn, the dishonest and irresponsible man, but was a well known and solvent house of Blenkiron & Co., doing business in the same street". That is, there was a mistake of identity, which was induced by the fraudster; and he could not therefore deny that the contract was not intended to be with him. And in *Boulton v*

ordered by Hallam and Co., by a cheque drawn by 'Hallam and Co.'" For the notion and history of the "long firm fraud", see C. MacMillan, *Mistakes in Contract Law* (2010), p.224.

84 Above, para.14–06.

85 Above, n.76 at 465.

86 The question is not, in fact, whether Blenkarn could hold Lindsays to the contract, but whether he *could have done*, because the validity of the contract is in issue not as between the original parties but in the claim against the third party. The decision is to the effect that there was no contract of sale with Blenkarn, who could therefore not sell the handkerchiefs on to Cundy. But nor, of course, was there a contract with the real Blenkiron & Co, "for as to them the matter was entirely unknown, and therefore the pretence of a contract was a failure": *ibid.*, at 466 (Lord Cairns).

Jones,[87] although the court emphasised that Boulton's intention was to deal only with Brocklehurst, it is clear on the facts that Brocklehurst knew that this was the intention, because he crossed out the name on the order and substituted his own, without notifying Jones about the change of ownership.

(b) *The parties deal face to face*

The significance of the meeting of the parties. When the parties meet to negotiate the contract, the picture changes. This is a different situation from that which arose in *Cundy v Lindsay*, and the decision of the House of Lords in that case does not give a definitive answer to the question of how to deal with it.[88] However, in principle there is no difference in the test that should be applied: did the claimant make a mistake of identity; and can his mistake be overridden by an objective appreciation of the facts from the other party's perspective? But the application of the test is different. The fact that the parties have met means that the claimant is not relying simply on the name and other such objective criteria, in order to identify the person with whom he is dealing. In short, if the claimant met Y, and dealt with him, it is as a matter of evidence more difficult for him to claim that he was intending to deal with X, even if Y gave his name as "X". The difference, therefore, comes principally in the first part of the test: whether the claimant really intended to deal with X *as opposed to Y or any other person*; that is, did he really make a mistake of identity at all? 14–23

[87] Above, para.14–20.

[88] "Hypothetical cases were put to your Lordships in argument in which a vendor was supposed to deal personally with a swindler, believing him to be some one else of credit and stability, and under this belief to have actually delivered goods into his hands. My Lords, I do not think it necessary to express an opinion upon the possible effect of some cases which I can imagine to happen of this character, because none of such cases can I think be parallel with that which your Lordships have now to decide. For in the present case the Respondents were never brought personally into contact with Alfred Blenkarn; all their letters, although received and answered by him, were addressed to Blenkiron & Co., and intended for that firm only; and finally the goods in dispute were not delivered to him at all, but were sent to Blenkiron & Co., though at a wrong address": (1878) 3 App. Cas. 459 at 471–472 (Lord Penzance).

As we shall see, the approach which was eventually developed by the courts was to say that, in a face-to-face transaction,[89] there is a presumption that the claimant did not make a mistake of identity. However, this was not articulated in the earlier cases, where the judges simply asked themselves whether the claimant intended to contract with the person whom he met, or the person with whom, because of the fraud that had been practised on him, he believed he was dealing. This resulted in decisions both in favour of claimants (the contract was void) and against them (the contract was not void—although of course it would generally be voidable by reason of the misrepresentation which had induced the claimant to enter into the contract).

14–24 **Examples from the cases: the contract is void.** In one of the earliest cases, *Hardman v Booth,*[90] the claimant called at the place of business of a firm to which he intended to offer to sell goods; but he was met by a person who was not a member of the firm, and had no authority to contract on behalf of the firm. The court held that the contract under which the claimant supplied goods was void, because he had a positive intention to contract with the firm, but the firm knew nothing of him—and so there could be no contract; but nor could there be a contract with the individual whom he met, because he did not intend to contract with him personally.[91] This case shows that an apparent contract concluded face to face may be

[89] Or, as it is sometimes called in the cases, a contract concluded *inter praesentes*; e.g. *Ingram v Little*, above, n.61 at 57 (Pearce L.J., quoted below, para.14–27).

[90] (1863) 1 H. & C. 803, 158 E.R. 1107.

[91] Three of the four judges sat also in *Boulton v Jones*, above, para.14–20. The firm was Gandell & Co.; the individual was Edward Gandell, who diverted the contract to another firm which he had established with another person. Pollock C.B. said at 806–807, at 1109: "Mr Hawkins contended that there was a contract personally with Edward Gandell, the individual with whom the conversations took place. It is true that the words were uttered by and to him, but the plaintiffs supposed that they were dealing with Gandell & Co., the packers, to whom they sent the goods, the fact being that Edward Gandell was not a member of that firm and had no authority to act as their agent. Therefore at no period of time were there two consenting minds to the same agreement". *Hardman v Booth* was applied in *Cundy v Lindsay*, above, n.76 at 467 (Lord Hatherley) and 471 (Lord Penzance). In *Shogun Finance Ltd v Hudson*, above, n.72 at [130] Lord Phillips noted that, at the time when *Hardman v Booth* was decided, the courts had not yet begun to apply the modern objective test for formation of a contract.

void; but it should be noted that the facts were strong in that the claimant sought out the particular firm to which he wished to offer his goods, and so he could more easily be heard to say that he had that particular firm in mind as his intended counterparty.[92]

Other decisions in which the court held that a contract concluded face to face was void, have been more controversial. In *Sowler v Potter*[93] a woman calling herself Ann Potter took a lease of a room from the claimant with a view to opening a restaurant there. The woman was in fact Ann Robinson, who had been convicted three months earlier of permitting disorderly conduct in a café. During the negotiations she changed her name by deed poll to Ann Potter; and so there was at the outset of the negotiations a misrepresentation by the defendant[94] about her name, but by the time of the contract it was in law her name (but the new name still disguised her old name and therefore her past history). Tucker J. held that there was a mistake of identity; the claimant's agent was aware that there was in existence a Mrs Ann Robinson, a convicted person, and believed that, whoever he was contracting with, it was not the Mrs Ann Robinson who had been convicted. It is a very difficult case, however. Successful cases of mistaken identity typically involve a claim of a positive intention to contract with X. *Sowler v Potter*, however, involved a claim that the person with whom the contract

---

[92] *Ingram v Little*, above, n.61 at 61 (Pearce L.J.). See also *Lake v Simmons*, above, n.61 where Viscount Haldane held at 500–502 that the delivery of jewellery by the jeweller to a person whom he believed to be Mrs Van der Borgh, to take on approval for her husband to decide whether to buy, was not capable of giving rise to a contract because "there was no mutual assent to any contract which would give her even the qualified proprietary right to hold it as a bailee proper. The appellant thought that he was dealing with a different person, the wife of Van der Borgh, and it was on that footing alone that he parted with the goods. He never intended to contract with the woman in question". This has been shown to have been an individual approach, and disapproved: *Ingram v Little* at 69–73 (Devlin L.J.); *Shogun Finance Ltd v Hudson*, above, n.72 at 141 (Lord Phillips).

[93] [1940] 1 K.B. 271.

[94] This is a case in which the issue was the validity of the contract between the parties, rather than the more common case of a contract relating to goods, where the issue arises as against a third-party purchaser of the goods: above, para.14–10. There was also a successful claim in trespass and deceit against Ann Potter, and also in deceit against a third party who wrote a fraudulent reference on Potter's behalf: see the report at [1939] 4 All E.R. 478 at 482–484.

was negotiated was *not Y*. It is much more difficult to establish such a firm negative intention. The decision was later disapproved by the Court of Appeal.[95]

In *Ingram v Little*[96] the Court of Appeal also held, by a majority, that a contract for the sale of a car concluded face-to-face was void because the sellers intended to contract only with P.G.M. Hutchinson, of a particular address (which they checked in the telephone directory), and not with the man (whose identity was never discovered) who answered their newspaper advertisement falsely claiming to be Hutchinson and whom the sellers allowed to take away the car in return for a worthless cheque. This decision, too, was later disapproved on its facts, although we shall see that the modern approach to dealing with face-to-face contracts grows out of it.[97]

14–25 **Examples from the cases: the contract is not void.** Although some courts have been prepared to hold that an apparent contract, concluded face to face, was in fact void for mistaken identity, this is not the usual outcome, particularly in the paradigm case of a contract for the sale of goods. The cases will always turn on the facts, and there is room for disagreement between the judges—even the judges in the same court[98]—as to whether in such a case the

---

[95] *Solle v Butcher* [1950] 2 K.B. 671, CA, at 691–692 (Denning L.J.); *Gallie v Lee* [1969] 2 Ch. 17, CA, at 33 (Lord Denning M.R.), 41 (Russell L.J.), 45 (Salmon L.J.); *Lewis v Averay* [1972] 1 Q.B. 198, CA, at 206 (Lord Denning M.R.); *Shogun Finance Ltd v Hudson* [2001] EWCA Civ 1000, [2002] Q.B. 834 at [33]–[34] (Dyson L.J.). It is not the only case in which such a situation—in effect, a negative mistake—has arisen: see also *Said v Butt* [1920] 3 K.B. 497 (ticket for theatre bought by friend on behalf of a person to whom the theatre had refused to sell the ticket; but the decision turned on the agency relationship); *Gordon v Street* [1899] 2 Q.B. 641, CA (defendant would not have borrowed money from money-lender who advertised under fictitious name, if he had realised identity of lender; but the claim turned on fraud, not mistake). The basis of the decision of Tucker J. in *Sowler v Potter* was the statement of Pothier, above, para.14–16.

[96] [1961] 1 Q.B. 31; below, para.14–27.

[97] Below, paras 14–27 *et seq*.

[98] The court was divided 2–1 in favour of the contract being void in *Ingram v Little*, above, n.96. *Cf. Fawcett v Star Car Sales Ltd* [1960] N.Z.L.R. 406, NZCA, where the court was divided 2–1 in favour of the contract not being void (sale of a car was made to Mr Gould by the (female) agent of a man, Saint-Merat, who had bought it from Mrs Fawcett, fraudulently using Mrs Fawcett's name as if she were the vendor. See at 419–420, Gresson P., dissenting on the facts: "personality

claimant's mistake was really one of identity. However, it is difficult for a claimant who has goods to sell, and who has no particular reason to choose to sell them to X or to Y, to argue successfully that when a person approached him with a view to buying the goods calling himself "X", he really meant to deal with X *and not with Y*, who was in fact the person before him. Even where there is a distinct individual X, and even where the claimant asked for proof of identity before letting "X" take the goods away, is it really the case that he was intending to deal only with X? Such checks on the "identity" appear to be designed more towards reassuring the claimant that deferred payment (such as a cheque) will be made, rather than defining the person to whom the goods are to be sold.[99] This, indeed, is the general approach that the courts have taken. In *Phillips v Brooks Ltd*,[100] for example, the claimant contracted to sell some jewellery to North, who said that he was Sir George Bullough, a name known to the claimant, who checked the address given by North before allowing him to take away some of the jewellery. Horridge J. rejected the application of Pothier's test[101] to these facts, and said that "the seller intended to contract with the person present, and there was no error as to the person with whom he contracted, although the plaintiff would not have made the contract if there had not been a fraudulent misrepresentation".[102]

was important, because Mr Gould believed that in buying from Mrs Fawcett (as he thought he was) he was buying from one who had been the owner of the car for about eighteen months. He was not merely willing to buy the car from any owner whoever he or she might be; he would not have bought the car from Saint-Merat, a one-day owner"; *cf.* at 426, North J.: "The name 'Mrs Fawcett' meant nothing to the purchaser. All he was interested in was to ensure that he was dealing with the true owner, and indeed he was"; and at 431, Cleary J.: "Mr Gould believed that the woman before him was Mrs Fawcett (which she was not) and was the owner of the car (which for present purposes she was). He was in fact dealing with a person able to make title to the car").

99 *Dennant v Skinner and Collom* [1948] 2 K.B. 164 ("In normal times a shopkeeper is not usually concerned with the identity of the customer when deciding whether he is willing to sell his goods to him, although he may be concerned with that matter when deciding whether, having effected the sale, he should give the purchaser credit": Hallett J., drawing analogy with auction sale).

100 [1919] 2 K.B. 243.

101 Above, para.14–16.

102 Above, n.100 at 248–249. It has been suggested that the representation was made only after the contract had been concluded: E.C.S. Wade, "Mistaken Identity in the Law of Contract" (1922) 38 L.Q.R. 201; *Ingram v Little*, above, n.96 at 51 (Sellers L.J.) and 60 (Pearce L.J.), relying on *Lake v Simmons* [1927]

Similarly, in *Lewis v Averay*[103] the contract to sell a car to a person answering a newspaper advertisement was not void when the purchaser used the name and some apparent evidence of identity of another individual. Megaw L.J. said[104]: "it is, I think, clear . . . that there was not here any evidence that would justify the finding that he, Mr. Lewis, regarded the identity of the man who called himself Mr Green as a matter of vital importance".

14–26 **The test to be applied: a presumption against the mistake being one of identity.** The modern test to be applied in the case of claims of mistake about the other party's identity where the contract was concluded face-to-face has developed within the English case law from the decision of the Court of Appeal in *Ingram v Little.*[105] In that case, the court was divided about the result—and the actual decision has been disapproved. But those are matters of the application of the test to the facts of the case. What is important is the test itself—which holds that, if the claimant met the other person with whom he was in fact dealing in entering into the contract, there is a presumption that he intended to contract with the person physically present. As the party seeking to establish that the contract was void, the claimant has the burden of proof. But, more than this, the court will infer from the fact that he met the other party that his intention was to contract with that person, whoever he

A.C. 487, HL, at 501 (Viscount Haldane); but this interpretation was rejected in *Lewis v Averay* [1972] 1 Q.B. 198 at 206 (Lord Denning M.R.). If the identity is questioned only after the contract has been concluded, it can certainly not affect the validity: *Dennant v Skinner and Collom*, above, n.99 (contract at auction, concluded by fall of hammer; question of identity raised only afterwards when memorandum signed).

[103] Above, n.102; below, para.14–28.

[104] *ibid.*, at 209. Phillimore L.J. at 208 also held that there was no evidence to displace the presumption (below, para.14–27) that the claimant was intending to contract with the person physically present. Lord Denning M.R.'s reasoning was rather different, because he declined to accept that a mistake of identity should ever make a contract void: at 204; below, para.14–28.

[105] Above, n.96. See Devlin L.J. at 66, applying the approach already proposed in *Benjamin on Sale* (8th edn, 1950), p.102 and *Corbin on Contracts* (1951), Vol.3, para.602. In *Phillips v Brooks*, above, n.100, Horridge J. had taken a similar approach at 246: "I have . . . to decide what is the proper inference to draw where a verbal contract is made and an article delivered to an individual describing himself as somebody else"; but he did not formulate a presumption as firmly as the later cases.

really was and by whatever name he called himself. The claimant must therefore produce evidence to rebut this presumption: to show that he was in fact intending to deal with a different, identifiable person. However, there was some disagreement about the test amongst the judges in *Ingram v Little*; and it was further discussed by the Court of Appeal in *Lewis v Averay*.[106] We need to establish the outcome of these two cases, in order to see to what extent, if any, it has been changed by the decision of the House of Lords in *Shogun Finance Ltd v Hudson*.[107]

The test as stated in *Ingram v Little*. All three members of the Court of Appeal in *Ingram v Little* agreed that the proper approach in a face-to-face contract is to require the claimant to rebut the presumption that he intended to deal with the person physically present; but there was a significant disagreement as to how this test should be formulated and applied. The majority reasoning is contained in the judgments of Sellers and Pearce L.JJ., whose reasoning was broadly similar. Pearce L.J. said[108]: 14–27

> "An apparent contract made orally inter praesentes raises particular difficulties. The offer is apparently addressed to the physical person present. Prima facie, he, by whatever name he is called, is the person to whom the offer is made. His physical presence identified by sight and hearing preponderates over vagaries of nomenclature. 'Praesentia corporis tollit errorem nominis' said Lord Bacon.[109] Yet clearly, though difficult, it is not impossible to rebut the prima facie presumption that the offer can be accepted by the person to whom it is physically addressed. To take two extreme instances. If a man orally commissions a portrait from some unknown artist who had deliberately passed himself off, whether by disguise or merely by verbal cosmetics, as a famous painter, the impostor could not accept the offer. For though the offer is made to him physically, it is obviously, as he knows, addressed to the famous painter. The mistake in identity on such facts is clear and the nature of the contract makes it obvious that identity was of vital importance to the offeror. At the other end of the scale, if a shopkeeper sells goods in a normal cash transaction to a man who misrepresents himself as being some well-known figure, the transaction will normally be valid. For the shopkeeper was ready to sell goods for cash to the world at large and the particular identity of the purchaser in such a contract was not of sufficient importance to override the

106 Below, para.14–28.
107 Below, paras 14–34 *et seq*.
108 Above, n.96 at 57–58. See also Sellers L.J. at 50.
109 *Law Tracts* (1737), p.102.

physical presence identified by sight and hearing. Thus the nature of the proposed contract must have a strong bearing on the question of whether the intention of the offeror (as understood by his offeree) was to make his offer to some other particular identity rather than to the physical person to whom it was orally offered."

The key points here are that (i) in a face-to-face transaction there is a presumption that the contract is with the person physically present; (ii) this presumption is one of fact, since the question is with whom the claimant intended to contract—and that is itself a question of fact; (iii) the presumption may therefore be rebutted; (iv) but it is a strong presumption and therefore not easy to rebut.

Devlin L.J. took a different approach. He divided the inquiry into two separate stages: first, whether the offer and acceptance met sufficiently to form a contract; and secondly, if it did, whether the resulting contract was void for the mistake of identity.[110] In discussing the first question, he, too, started from the presumption that there is a valid contract in a face-to-face transaction; but he said that the question is not simply one of fact, but requires the application of a *legal* presumption.[111]

"There can be no doubt upon the authorities that this argument must be settled by inquiring with whom Miss Ingram intended to contract: was it with the person to whom she was speaking or was it with the person whom he represented himself to be? It has been pressed upon us that this is a question of fact and that we ought to give great weight to the answer to it provided by the trial judge. It is, I think, a mixed question of fact and law. I am sure that any attempt to solve it as a pure question of fact would fail. If Miss Ingram had been asked whether she intended to contract with the man in the room or with P.G.M. Hutchinson, the question could have no meaning for her, since she believed them both to be one and the same. The reasonable man of the law—if he stood in Miss Ingram's shoes—could not give any better answer. . .

[110] In this second enquiry the test was whether the "mistaken identity would . . . destroy a fundamental assumption and frustrate the object of the contract": above, n.96 at 68, basing the test on the proposition that a mistake of identity should only avoid a contract if it is as serious a mistake as any other mistake; *cf.* Ch.15, below. He held that, on the facts, it did not: the purchaser's identity was immaterial to the vendors; it was only his creditworthiness that was material. Other judges have not separated out the issues of mistaken identity in this manner: if the contract was properly formed (at the stage of the analysis of the offer and acceptance), then the question of the identity of the parties has been answered.

[111] Above, n.96 at 64–67.

> Courts of law are not inexperienced in dealing with this sort of situation. They do so by means of presumptions. . . .
>
> In my judgment, the court cannot arrive at a satisfactory solution in the present case except by formulating a presumption and taking it at least as a starting point. The presumption that a person is intending to contract with the person to whom he is actually addressing the words of contract seems to me to be a simple and sensible one and supported by some good authority. It is adopted in *Benjamin on Sale*, 8th edn (1950), p.102 . . .
>
> I do not think that it can be said that the presumption is conclusive, since there is at least one class of case in which it can be rebutted. If the person addressed is posing only as an agent, it is plain that the party deceived has no thought of contracting with him but only with his supposed principal; if then there is no actual or ostensible authority, there can be no contract. *Hardman v Booth*[112] is, I think, an example of this. Are there any other circumstances in which the presumption can be rebutted? It is not necessary to strain to find them, for we are here dealing only with offer and acceptance; contracts in which identity really matters may still be avoided on the ground of mistake.[113] I am content to leave the question open, and do not propose to speculate on what other exceptions there may be to the general rule. . . ."

On first reading, this may appear to be consistent with the reasoning in the other judgments in the case. But it is significantly different, in that it treats the question of identity as not simply one of fact, to be inferred from the face-to-face dealings (a factual presumption) but capable of rebuttal by evidence from the claimant as of his contrary (factual) intention. Rather, it takes the position that the claimant cannot normally lead evidence of the fact of his intention which will prevail over the (legal) presumption. The intention is inferred as a matter of law from the face-to-face dealings, and this can be overcome only in exceptional types of case, not simply by showing contrary facts.[114]

The ratio of *Ingram v Little*, therefore, is contained in the judgments of Sellers and Pearce L.JJ., who also (contrary to Devlin L.J.) held that, on the facts, the presumption *had* been rebutted. If the purchaser, calling himself "Hutchinson", had paid cash, the contract would have been valid. But because it was not a cash sale, but became a credit sale when he asked to take the car away in

[112] (1863) 1 H. & C. 803, 158 E.R. 1107; above, para.14–24.

[113] [See above, n.110.]

[114] On the difference between presumptions of law and presumptions of fact, see Phipson, para.6.17: a presumption of fact is a "misnomer. It describes the readiness of the court to draw certain repeated inferences as a result of common human experience".

return for a cheque, both the sellers and the buyer "knew that the identity of the purchaser was of the utmost importance"[115]; and this was proved by the fact that one of the sellers checked the name and address of "Hutchinson" in a telephone directory. On this point the decision may be doubted. But although the application of the test to the facts may not survive scrutiny, the test itself remains significant.

14–28 **Development of the test in *Lewis v Averay*.** In *Lewis v Averay*[116] the Court of Appeal again considered the test that should be applied in face-to-face transactions. The case again involved the sale of a car, following a newspaper advertisement, when the purchaser gave the name and other details of another person, and thereby obtained the car in return for a worthless cheque. On this occasion, the contract was held not to be void for mistake of identity. The court was unanimous in the result, although again the reasoning varied.

Lord Denning M.R. rejected the view that a mistake of identity should ever make a contract void[117]:

> "When two parties have come to a contract—or rather what appears, on the face of it, to be a contract—the fact that one party is mistaken as to the identity of the other does not mean that there is no contract, or that the contract is a nullity and void from the beginning. It only means that the contract is voidable, that is, liable to be set aside at the instance of the mistaken person, so long as he does so before third parties have in good faith acquired rights under it.
>
> Applied to the cases such as the present, this principle is in full accord with the presumption stated by Pearce L.J. and also Devlin L.J. in *Ingram v. Little*. When a dealing is had between a seller like Mr. Lewis and a person who is actually there present before him, then the presumption in law is that there is a contract, even though there is a fraudulent impersonation by the buyer representing himself as a different man than he is. There is a contract made with the very person there, who is present in person. It is liable no doubt to be avoided for fraud, but it is still a good contract under which title will pass unless and until it is avoided."

Although this refers to the presumption as stated by Pearce and Devlin L.JJ., we have seen that their judgments were fundamentally different on the nature of the presumption: Pearce L.J. viewed it as a presumption of fact; Devlin L.J. as a presumption of law. Lord

[115] Above, n.96 at 58 (Pearce L.J.). See also at 49 (Sellers L.J., approving the analysis by Slade J. at first instance).
[116] [1972] 1 Q.B. 198, CA.
[117] *ibid.*, at 207.

Denning's view is based on the approach taken by Devlin L.J. in *Ingram v Little*; but he appears to go even further. It is a "presumption in law"; but it appears to be an irrebuttable presumption. Phillimore L.J., by contrast, quoted and applied the presumption of fact in Pearce L.J.'s judgment.[118] Megaw L.J. approached the matter more broadly, and discussed whether, on the facts, the claimant regarded the identity of the other party as a matter of vital importance; he did not speak in terms of a presumption.[119]

It is therefore not easy to find a ratio in *Lewis v Averay* as to the test to apply. But it is clear from the judgments of Phillimore and Megaw L.JJ. that a mistake of identity can make a contract void in a face-to-face transaction; but whether there is a sufficient mistake is a question as to the intention of the claimant; and this is a matter of fact.

The interpretation of the communications from the other party's perspective. As with contracts formed by communications between the parties at a distance, it is not sufficient for the claimant to show that he made a mistake about the other party's identity. In addition, it is necessary to consider whether he should be bound to the contract in spite of his mistake, because he has led the other party to believe that he was an acceptable counterparty to the transaction. It is therefore necessary to ask whether the other party knew, or ought to have known, that he was not the person with whom the claimant intended to deal[120]: 14–29

[118] *ibid.*, at 208.
[119] *ibid.*, at 209.
[120] *Ingram v Little*, above, n.96 at 61 (Pearce L.J.; emphasis added). See also at 53 (Sellers L.J., approving Goodhart (1941) 57 L.Q.R. 228); *Fawcett v Star Car Sales Ltd*, above, n.98 at 418 (Gresson P.: "if it is established that A did not intend to make a contract with B, *and B was aware of this fact*, then the apparent contract is void for mistake . . ."; emphasis added). *Cf.*, however, *Lewis v Averay*, above, n.116 at 208 (Megaw L.J.: "The question of the existence of a contract and therefore the passing of property, and therefore the right of third parties, if this test is correct, is made to depend upon the view which some rogue should have formed, presumably knowing that he is a rogue, as to the state of mind of the opposite party to the negotiation, who does not know that he is dealing with a rogue").

> "Has it been sufficiently shown in the particular circumstances that, contrary to the prima facie presumption, a party was not contracting with the physical person to whom he uttered the offer, but with another individual whom (*as the other party ought to have understood*) he believed to be the physical person present. The answer to that question is a finding of fact."

In most cases, of course, this will be self-evident because of the fraud practised by that other party, and therefore if the claimant did in fact make a mistake *of identity*, the other party will not be able to resist the argument that the contract is void.

(c) *The contract is concluded in a single, written document*

14–30 **The significance of the contract being in writing.** If the contract was formed through successive written communications between the parties, culminating in an offer by one, accepted by the other, the fact that the communications are in writing will mean that the identity of the intended recipient of each communication can be determined objectively, interpreted from the position of the recipient of the communication. But the inquiry is still as to the intentions of the parties in making those communications.[121] However, we have seen in relation to claims based on mistakes as to the terms of the contract that, once the parties have reduced their agreement to a single written document which they agree shall form the basis of their legal relationship, the courts focus on the language of the document itself to ascertain the terms of the contract. In exceptional cases the courts may look beyond the document, but unless it is to rectify the document so that it reflects the terms as they should have been recorded, they will not normally allow one party to assert that the terms were other than the terms recorded in the document, interpreted objectively according to the usual principles of interpretation of contracts.[122] The courts have taken a similar approach in establishing the identity of the parties to a written contract.

---

[121] *Cundy v Lindsay*, above, para.14–22. See Lord Cairns L.C. at 465: "The principal parties concerned, the Respondents and Blenkarn, never came in contact personally—everything that was done was done by writing. What has to be judged of, and what the jury in the present case had to judge of, was merely the conclusion to be derived from that writing, as applied to the admitted facts of the case".

[122] Above, paras 13–32 to13–34.

Establishing the parties' identity in a written contract. In *Hector v Lyons*[123] Sir Nicolas Browne-Wilkinson V.C. made clear that a different approach is taken in relation to alleged mistakes of identity in a written contract as compared with a contract concluded face to face: 14–31

> "[Counsel] relies on the line of cases dealing with unilateral mistake. In those cases, typically goods are sold by a vendor V, to a purchaser P, under the mistake that P is someone else, X. The cases referred to in *Lewis v Averay* typify that type of transcaction. Normally the case is that the purchaser P makes a fraudulent representation to the vendor that he, P, is some other person, X. In the case of a face to face sale, where the sale is over a counter or between two individuals, the law is well established that the mere fact that the vendor V is under a misapprehension as to the identity of the person in front of him does not operate so as to render the contract void for mistake, it being a mere unilateral mistake as to a quality of the purchaser; only in cases where the identity of the purchaser is of direct and important materiality in inducing the vendor to enter into the contract is a mistake of that kind capable of avoiding the contract. . . .
>
> With one exception those cases are entirely concerned with transactions between two individuals face to face entering into oral agreement. In my judgment the principle there enunciated has no application to a case such as the present where there is a contract and wholly in writing. There the identity of the vendor and of the purchaser is established by the names of the parties included in the written contract. Once those names are there in the contract, the only question for the court is to identify who they are."

There are certain difficulties in understanding the actual decision in this case[124]; but the court's approach to the general question of how to establish the identity of the parties to a written contract is clear; and, in consequence, the general approach to claims of mistake about the identity of the other party is also clear. Where a party who has concluded a written contract which records the counterparty as X—assuming that it is clear from the document who "X" is[125]—he

[123] (1989) 58 P. & C.R. 156, CA, at 158–159. See also Woolf L.J. at 160: "This was a contract in writing for sale of land. Parties to the contract are normally to be ascertained from the document or documents containing the contract. There can be limited circumstances where it is possible to allow oral evidence to be given in relation to a written contract, but those circumstances are recognised as being exceptional and should, in my view, be strictly confined".

[124] See, e.g. the discussion in *Shogun Finance Ltd v Hudson* [2003] UKHL 62, [2004] 1 A.C. 919 at [192] (Lord Walker).

[125] Evidence can be properly admitted in order to identify the true party to a written contract, when the description of that party in the contract does not make

will normally be able simply to say that the contract was with X. If in fact the contract was made by Y, pretending to be X, without X's authority and in circumstances where X does not adopt it, the contract is void.[126]

14–32 **Non est factum.** We saw in Chapter 13 that a party who signed a written document may successfully plead *non est factum*—and will therefore be heard to say that he is not bound by the document—if he shows that, at the time when he signed it, he was unable to understand the document; that the document was "fundamentally", "radically" or "totally" different from the document which he believed himself to be signing; and that he was not careless.[127] However, it is clear from the decision in *Saunders v Anglia Building Society*[128] that a mistake about the identity of the transferee does not necessarily make the document of a totally different character from that which the party intended to sign.

(4) Summary of the position before Shogun

14–33 **The law as it stood before *Shogun*.** We can summarise the position of the law as it stood before the decision of the House of Lords in *Shogun Finance Ltd v Hudson*[129] as follows:

---

it clear who is the real contracting party: *Hector v Lyons*, above, n.123 at 160 (Woolf L.J.); Phipson, para.42.29. For criticism of both *Hector v Lyons* and the (related) reasoning of Lord Hobhouse in *Shogun Finance Ltd v Hudson*, above, n.25, see D.W. McLaughlan, "Parol Evidence and Contract Formation" (2005) 121 L.Q.R. 9.

[126] This does not preclude the claimant having other remedies directly against Y: e.g. in the tort of deceit for the loss caused by entering into the contract in reliance on his fraudulent mispprepresentation of identity. If he so chooses, he may also be able to establish a contract with Y, on the basis that by his misrepresentation of identity Y is estopped from denying that he is the party to the contract.

[127] Above, paras 13–55 *et seq*.

[128] [1971] A.C. 1004, HL, at 1018 (Lord Hodson), 1031 (Lord Pearson), approving Russell L.J. in CA: *Gallie v Lee* [1969] 2 Ch. 17 at 41 (assignment of a leasehold interest in a house to X for £3,000 (which was not, and was not intended by X to be, paid) was not sufficiently different from an intended deed of gift in favour of Y, where the signer knew that X and Y were jointly concerned in a project to raise money on the property).

[129] Above, n.124.

1. Where the alleged contract was formed by communications between the parties in circumstances where one ultimately accepted an offer made by the other, the contract will be validly formed if each party intended to deal with the other. Even if one party (A) misunderstood with whom he was dealing, the other (B) is entitled to hold that party to having intended to contract with him, if B could reasonably believe that he was the intended recipient of A's communications, and in fact so believed.
2. Therefore, for A to say that he made a mistake about the other's identity, and did not intend to deal with the person who was in fact communicating with him, he must show (i) that he made a mistake of *identity*, that is, he intended to deal with another, distinct person whom he can identify; and (ii) that his subjective mistake should be allowed to prevail, that is, that B knew about it, or ought to have known about it (in practice, (ii) is often easy to establish because the mistake in most cases is caused by B's deception as to his own identity).
3. Where the alleged contract was formed by communications between the parties who did not meet, the application of (2) depends on a proper construction of the communications themselves in order to determine A's intention. *Where the alleged contract was formed* between the parties in a face-to-face transaction, there is a presumption that A intended to deal with the person physically present, by whatever name or other information he identified himself; but this is rebuttable by A showing that, on the facts, he did make a mistake of identity.
4. Where the alleged contract was formed in writing, by the execution of a single, agreed document, the identity of the parties to the contract is to be determined by the objective construction of the document itself.

We can now consider to what extent the decision of the House of Lords in *Shogun* has confirmed or changed the law.

IV. THE CURRENT LAW: SHOGUN FINANCE LTD V HUDSON

(1) The Issue Decided by the House of Lords

14–34 **The narrow question for decision.** The facts of *Shogun Finance Ltd v Hudson*[130] were different from those in the cases discussed earlier in this chapter; and the precise question which the House of Lords had to answer was very narrow.

A man falsely claiming to be Mr Durlabh Patel, and giving Mr Patel's personal details and producing his (improperly obtained) driving licence, agreed with a dealer to buy a car on hire-purchase. The hire-purchase contract was to be between the buyer and Shogun Finance Ltd. Shogun (who never met the buyer, but to whom a copy of the application form and the stolen driving licence were faxed by the dealer) ran credit checks on Mr Patel, and agreed to the contract. Under the hire-purchase contract, the property in the car was transferred by the dealer to Shogun, who authorised the release of the car to "Mr Patel" after he had signed the contract of hire-purchase. The buyer sold the car on to Mr Hudson by way of a private sale; Mr Hudson's title to the car was in issue. This appears at first sight to raise issues similar to those in the earlier cases involving the sale of cars, obtained by fraudulent representations of identity, to innocent third-party purchasers.[131] But the analysis is fundamentally different. The contract signed by the buyer in the showroom did not purport to give him title to the car; the buyer under a hire-purchase agreement receives only possession of the property which is bailed to him, and (before the eventual transfer of title at the end of the contract) does not have title to pass: *nemo dat quod non habet*. However, there is an exception to the *nemo dat* rule in the Hire-Purchase Act 1964,[132] under which, where

> "a motor vehicle has been bailed under a hire-purchase agreement and, before the property in the vehicle has become vested in the debtor, he disposes of the vehicle to another person"

---

[130] [2003] UKHL 62, [2004] 1 A.C. 919. For discussions of the case, see (2004) 120 L.Q.R. 369 (C. MacMillan); (2004) 67 M.L.R. 993 (C. Hare); (2005) 121 L.Q.R. 9 (D.W. McLaughlan); (2005) 21 *Journal of Contract Law* 1 (D.W. McLaughlan); [2006] L.M.C.L.Q. 49 at pp.69–79 (G. McMeel).

[131] e.g. *Ingram v Little*, above, para.14–27; *Lewis v Averay*, above, para.14–28.

[132] s.27(1), (2), substituted by the Consumer Credit Act 1974, s.192(3)(a), Sch.4, para.22. It applies equally to a motor vehicle that has been agreed to be sold under a conditional sale agreement.

the debtor can pass good title to a private purchaser in good faith without notice of the hire-purchase agreement. The narrow question in *Shogun* was whether this statutory exception to the *nemo dat* rule applied. It did so only if the person who had passed himself off as "Mr Patel" was the "debtor" under a "hire-purchase agreement" under which the car had been bailed to him. Shogun argued that the original hire-purchase agreement was void as a result of their mistake about the buyer's identity; and that therefore the buyer was not a debtor under the hire-purchase agreement, and so Mr Hudson did not acquire title to the car. In order to answer the narrow question, therefore, the House of Lords had to consider the rule that should be applied to determine the validity of the hire-purchase agreement where there was an allegation by the creditor of mistake about the identity of the debtor. And, in this regard, it should be noted that the contract was concluded in writing; and in circumstances where the parties did not meet.[133]

A wider question. The House chose, however, to hear a broader argument about the significance of an alleged mistake of identity in the formation of a contract, not limited to the particular circumstances of the case, and certainly not limited to contracts in writing. Indeed, nearly four months after the close of oral submissions their Lordships invited written submissions from counsel on the point "whether the presumption regarding 'face to face' dealings should apply equally to dealings by correspondence and, if so, whether the House should depart from its decision in *Cundy v Lindsay*".[134] In other words, the whole range of issues discussed in the earlier sections of this chapter were before the House: how to deal with communications by correspondence and face to face; and how to deal with a contract reduced to writing. As we shall see, one of the difficulties with the decision in *Shogun* is that the different speeches concentrated on different issues. 14–35

[133] The car dealer was not acting as agent of Shogun in making the contract, and so it was not a face-to-face contract: at [51] (Lord Hobhouse), [176] (Lord Phillips), [191] (Lord Walker); *cf. Branwhite v Worcester Works Finance Ltd* [1969] 1 A.C. 552 at 573 (whether dealer is agent of finance company for a particular purpose is question of fact; but mere possession of company's forms not sufficient to constute agency: Lord Morris of Borth-y-Gest), 578–580 (dealer not normally acting as agent: Lord Upjohn); Lord Reid and Lord Wilberforce dissented on this point.

[134] See [2004] 1 A.C. 919 at 927.

(2) The Decision

14–36 **The contract was void.** The contract in *Shogun* was void. The majority was formed by Lords Hobhouse, Phillips and Walker, and although a different range of issues was covered in their respective speeches, the reason for their decision is clear, and focused on the fact that the contract was concluded in writing.

14–37 **The majority speeches: the approach to a contract concluded in writing.** Lord Hobhouse (with whom Lord Walker agreed, although he added some observations of his own) rested his decision on the fact that the contract was in writing.[135] There was no ambiguity in the identification of the parties to the written document, and therefore the parties must be Shogun and Mr Patel. Evidence was not admissible to contradict the clear provisions of the contract—although, in fact it was clear that the contracting party was (only) the real Mr Patel, because Shogun had made clear that the customer's identity was fundamental to their agreement to give him credit. The person signing the document was not Mr Patel, and had no authority to sign on his behalf; therefore the contract was void. The delivery of the car to the buyer in the showroom (the "rogue") was therefore made by the dealer without authority, and so it did not create any bailment.[136] Therefore Mr Hudson could not claim title to the car: he was not protected by section 27 of the Hire-Purchase Act 1964[137] because the person from whom he purchased it was not the "debtor" under a "hire-purchase agreement" under which the car had been "bailed" to him.

Lord Hobhouse gave a second ground for his decision: that there was no consensus *ad idem* between Shogun and the rogue.[138] Shogun believed that it was accepting an offer by the real Mr Patel, but was not, and so there was no contract formed. The identity of "Mr Patel" was fundamental to the acceptance by Shogun, because it was a credit agreement; and Shogun had made this clear to the buyer on the face of the documents on which it required him to make his written offer for credit.

[135] Above, n.130 at [47]–[49]; followed (in a different context) to determine the identity of a party to a charterparty in *TTMI Sarl v Statoil ASA* [2011] EWHC 1150 (Comm), [2011] All E.R. (D) 82 (May) at [33].
[136] *ibid.*, at [52].
[137] Above, para.14–34.
[138] Above, n.130 at [50].

These two grounds of decision are related, in that they focus on the fact that the contract was concluded through the medium of writing. The first ground looks at the fact that the contract was the written document—it was a contract *in writing*; and therefore construes the document itself[139]; the second looks at the (written) communications which constituted the offer and acceptance leading up to the conclusion of the contract.[140] On either basis the contract could be with, and only with, the real Mr Patel. Lord Phillips also based his decision on the fact that the agreement was concluded in writing, and therefore the identification of the parties turned upon the construction of the writing.[141] What is clear, however, is that the facts of the case, and its ultimate decision, did not require any discussion of the face-to-face cases, in so far as they may apply any test different from that applied in the case of written contracts, or contracts formed through written communications.[142]

The minority speeches: a unified approach to contracts concluded in writing or face to face. The minority speeches were delivered by Lords Nicholls and Millett. They dissented vigorously, both on the result of the case itself, and on the principles to be applied to a case of mistaken identity. In their view, *Cundy v* **14–38**

139 Above, para.14–30.

140 Above, para.14–19. This dual approach in Lord Hobhouse's speech followed from the fact that there was an "offer and acceptance" clause in the hire-purchase agreement which said: "You [the customer named overleaf] are offering to make a legal agreement by signing this document. We [the creditor] can reject your offer, or accept it by signing it ourselves . . . If we sign this document it will become legally binding at once (even before we send you a signed copy) . . .". Lord Hobhouse said at [46] that the effect of this clause is that "(i) it re-emphasises that the customer/hirer is, and is only, the person *named* on the front of the document; (ii) it makes it clear that the agreement is the written agreement contained in the written document; (iii) the offer being accepted by the creditor is the offer contained in the document and that alone, that is to say, the offer of Mr Durlabh Patel of the address in Leicester and to whom the driving licence was issued; (iv) for a valid offer to be made, the form must have been signed by Mr Durlabh Patel; and, (v) most importantly of all, the question in issue becomes a question of the construction of this written document, not a question of factual investigation and evaluation".

141 Above, n.130 at [178], although it is not entirely clear whether he was following the first or second of Lord Hobhouse's approaches: see at [170] (discussing the approach where "*dealings* are exclusively conducted in writing") and [178] ("*agreement* . . . concluded in *writing*") (emphasis added).

142 Lord Hobhouse put this forcefully at [55].

Lindsay[143] should no longer be followed, but replaced by a rule which would apply equally to written and face-to-face contracts; and which would result generally in the contract being not void for mistake but only voidable for the fraudulent misrepresentation of identity.

The minority took the view that the current law was unprincipled, because of the distinctions drawn between contracts concluded face to face, and contracts concluded through, or in, writing. They approved the approach used in the face-to-face cases, and proposed to extend it to all contracts:

> "a person is presumed to intend to contract with the person with whom he is actually dealing, whatever be the mode of communication.[144]"

As long as there is in fact an offer and acceptance between the parties, and one party has not intercepted a communication directed at another person,[145] there will normally be a contract (albeit voidable for fraud) whether the transaction is negotiated orally or in writing.[146] In essence, this approach adopts the *legal* presumption which was described by Devlin L.J. in *Ingram v Little*,[147] but extends it to all claims of mistake, not only the face-to-face transaction to which it was there applied; and goes so far as to suggest that the presumption may be in practice, or even in law, irrebuttable.[148] It draws no distinction between oral and written contracts, nor between contracts formed by written communications and contracts formed in writing. Even in a case such as that in

---

143 (1878) 3 App. Cas. 459, HL; above, para.14–20.

144 *Shogun*, above, n.130 at [36] (Lord Nicholls). See also at [68]–[70], [76] (Lord Millett).

145 *ibid.*, at [63] (Lord Millett). This is referring only to a physical interception of a communication that was in fact sent to another person, and does not cover the case where B *directs* his communication to A, but (because of the mistake of identity) *intends* it for C: *ibid.*, at [64].

146 "The legal principle applicable in these cases cannot sensibly differ according to whether the transaction is negotiated face to face, or by letter, or by fax, or by e-mail, or over the telephone or by video link or video telephone": at [33] (Lord Nicholls).

147 Above, para.14–27. Devlin L.J.'s approach was approved in *Shogun* at [36] (Lord Nicholls) and [69] (Lord Millett).

148 *Shogun*, above, n.130 at [37] (Lord Nicholls), [67] (Lord Millett). At [61] Lord Millett approved the approach of Lord Denning in *Lewis v Averay*, which appeared to deny that a contract can ever be void for mistake: above, para.14–28.

Shogun itself, where the contract is a single, written document, which identifies one of the parties in a way which objectively refers to a person other than the one who signed it, the contract is normally with the signer, because that was the person with whom Shogun were actually dealing. In consequence, on that analysis, there would have been a hire-purchase agreement *with the rogue*, who would have sold the car to Mr Hudson as "debtor" under that agreement, and Mr Hudson would accordingly have obtained good title.

An underlying disagreement: the impact on third-party purchasers. At the heart of the disagreement between their Lordships in *Shogun* were not only different views about the relevance of one party's intention about the other party's identity in the formation of a contract, and the methods by which such intention can properly be established, but also different views about the relevance of the consequences of holding a contract to be void for mistake of identity. Lord Nicholls and Lord Millett both openly favoured the view that a contract should not be void for mistake, but only voidable for the fraud that induced the mistake, because of the impact on third-party purchasers.[149] In the paradigm case of a mistake of identity the dispute centres on the competing claims to property by the original owner and by the later purchaser of it in good faith.[150] If the contract is void, then the purchaser has acquired **14–39**

[149] *ibid.*, at [13], [35] (Lord Nicholls); [60], [82] (Lord Millett). In *Lewis v Averay* [1972] 1 Q.B. 198, CA, at 207 Lord Denning M.R. also gave this as his reason for holding that the presumption in a face-to-face transaction should be irrebuttable ("As I listened to the argument in this case, I felt it wrong that an innocent purchaser (who knew nothing of what passed between the seller and the rogue) should have his title depend on such refinements. After all, he has acted with complete circumspection and in entire good faith: whereas it was the seller who let the rogue have the goods and thus enabled him to commit the fraud. *I do not, therefore, accept the theory* that a mistake as to identity renders a contract void"; emphasis added). Lord Denning appeared in *Lewis v Averay* to refer to the contract being voidable for mistake; *cf.* also *Solle v Butcher* [1950] 2 K.B. 671, CA, at 692–693. But mistake does not render a contract voidable; either the mistake is sufficient to render the contract void *ab initio*; or it is not void. In the case of a mistake as to identity, if the mistake is not sufficient to render the contract void, the contract is voidable for the fraudulent *misrepresentation* of "identity".

[150] Above, para.14–10.

no title to the property, and is liable to the original owner in conversion. This appears unfair to an innocent purchaser[151]:

> "it is surely fairer that the party who was actually swindled and who had an opportunity to uncover the fraud should bear the loss rather than a party who entered the picture only after the swindle had been carried out and who had none."

On the other hand, the members of the majority in the House did not give weight to this argument. Lord Walker thought it was not right always to assume that the purchaser was more deserving of sympathy than the original owner,[152] and he and Lord Phillips preferred simply to apply the rules relating to the formation of a contract. Lord Hobhouse took an even stronger line, and not only preferred to apply the well-established rules of contract formation, but also firmly rejected any suggestion that concern for third parties should be allowed to undermine the certainty that is provided by the *nemo dat* rule.[153]

Lord Millett, in criticising the consequences of the rule in English law for third-party purchasers, drew attention to the very different approach in other legal systems such as Germany, where a purchaser in good faith from a non-owner can obtain title by taking possession of the goods from him.[154] The fact that a purchaser in

---

[151] *Shogun*, above, n.130 at [82] (Lord Millett). See also R. Goode, *Commercial Law* (4th edn, 2010), pp.481–482.

[152] *ibid.*, at [181]–[182].

[153] *ibid.*, at [49], [55].

[154] *ibid.*, at [84]–[85] ("it would be unfortunate if our conclusion proved to be different [from that in Germany]. Quite apart from anything else, it would make the contemplated harmonisation of the general principles of European contract law very difficult to achieve"). Lord Hobhouse's reply is in the last sentence of his speech at [55]. In English law the purchaser can acquire title to a chattel by virtue of the Limitation Act 1980, s.3(2) (title of owner extinguished where no action brought for six years after the first conversion during which the owner has not recovered possession; in the case of a theft, or obtaining of a chattel by blackmail or by fraud, the time starts to run not from the theft but from the sale to the purchaser in good faith: *ibid.*, s.4, amended by Fraud Act 2006, Sch.1, para.18). See Clerk & Lindsell, paras 32.30–32.33. In modern civil systems, the rule that the purchaser in good faith may obtain title from a non-owner is not based on limitation of actions, but a general rule of the law of property. For comment on the decision in *Shogun* from the perspectives of Dutch, French, Spanish and Portuguese law, see (2005) *European Review of Private Law* 519–552. The Draft Common Frame of Reference, art.II.-7:212 provides for

good faith can be prejudiced by such a void contract, or even a contract which is voidable but which has already been avoided before the time of the transaction in favour of the purchaser in good faith,[155] has often been criticised, and the particular criticisms by Devlin L.J. in *Ingram v Little*[156] caused the Lord Chancellor to refer the question to the Law Reform Committee. The Committee proposed, inter alia, that where goods are sold under a mistake about the buyer's identity, the contract should, so far as third parties are concerned, be voidable and not void.[157] Their Report was not implemented. The solutions found in modern civil law systems are within the law of property; in English law the link between the validity of the contract and the passing of property, taken together with the *nemo dat* rule with its very limited exceptions, places a real significance on the distinction between void and voidable contracts for third-party purchasers. The decision of the House of Lords in *Shogun*, in maintaining the rule that a contract may be void for mistake of identity, has also maintained this potential difficulty for third parties, and if reform is desired, it must now be sought in the law of property.[158] In 2005[159] the Law Commission included this

retrospective avoidance for mistake and fraud, and refers to the rules on the transfer of property the effect of avoidance on the ownership of property which has been transferred under the avoided contract; although avoidance of the contract has retroactive effect (art.VIII.-2:202), the DCFR contains provision in art.VIII.-3:101 for a transferee to acquire ownership of goods in good faith from a person without right or authority to transfer ownership: C. von Bar and E. Clive (eds), *Principles, Definitions and Model Rules of European Private Law: Draft Common Frame of Reference (DCFR), Full Edition* (Sellier, Munich, 2009). The Feasibility Study (May 2011) of the Expert Group established by the Commission to develop a possible instrument of European Contract Law based on the DCFR includes remedies between the parties following avoidance of the contract, but not rules for third party property rights, which would therefore be dealt with under the applicable domestic law. See above, para.1–05 and below, para.17–54 for further details of the European contract law project.

[155] *Car and Universal Finance Co. Ltd v Caldwell* [1965] 1 Q.B. 525; above, para.4–60.

[156] [1961] 1 Q.B. 31 at 73–74; above, para.14–10.

[157] Law Reform Committee, Twelfth Report, *Transfer of Title to Chattels*, Cmnd. 2958 (1966), para.15, noting that this would be in accordance with French and German law, and the Uniform Commercial Code in the US. The Committee rejected as impracticable Devlin L.J.'s suggestion in *Ingram v Little* of a system of apportioning loss between the two innocent parties: paras 9 to 12.

[158] For criticism of the underlying assumption that title cannot pass by delivery pursuant to a void contract, see W. Swadling, "Rescission, Property, and the

issue amongst those which it proposed to review in its Ninth Programme of Law Reform, but in 2008[160] the Commission said that "there appears to be little enthusiasm within Government or industry for reform at this particular time" and that would consider it again in the Eleventh Programe "to see whether the climate has become more conducive to tacking this long-standing problem". This lack of enthusiasm for reform remained the case when the Law Commission published its Eleventh Programme in 2011, and the project was neither taken up nor deferred for consideration. If it is to be taken up again, it will have to be proposed afresh.[161]

(3) The Impact of the Decision in *Shogun* on the Earlier Authorities

14–40 **The narrow ratio of *Shogun*.** The binding ratio of *Shogun* is narrow. It is found in the speeches of the majority; and those speeches focused on the law as it applies to the particular facts of the case—a contract concluded in writing. They also discussed the alternative analysis of the facts—that the contract was formed by written communications, and therefore how such communications are to be interpreted. But the decision says nothing as such about the approach to be taken in a face-to-face transaction. Indeed, Lord Hobhouse declined to discuss such cases because he regarded them as a distraction from the relevant issue.[162] However, Lord Phillips and Lord Walker did discuss the general approach more broadly; and they accepted that, in the case of a face-to-face transaction,

Common Law" (2005) 121 L.Q.R. 123, and reply by B. Häcker at [2006] R.L.R. 106; and for discussion of §2–403(1) of the Uniform Commercial Code (above, n.157) and its comparison with *Shogun*, above, n.130, see S. Thomas, "Mistake of identity: a comparative analysis" [2008] L.M.C.L.Q. 188.

159 Law Commission, Ninth Programme of Law Reform, Law Com. No.293 (2005), paras 1.16, 3.51–3.57: "Transfer of title by non-owners is another area in which English law is markedly different to the laws of many of our continental neighbours and of some other common law jurisdictions. While this does not suggest that our law should be changed, it does suggest that we should review it to ensure that it does actually meet the needs of business and private citizens in the modern world" (para.3.56).

160 Law Commission, Tenth Programme of Law Reform, Law Com. No.311 (2008), paras 4.2–4.4.

161 Law Commission, Eleventh Programme of Law Reform, Law Com. No.330 (2011), paras 3.4–3.6

162 *Shogun*, above, n.130 at [47], [55].

each party is presumed to have intended to deal with the person physically present; but that this is not to be applied in a case where the contract is formed through written communications at a distance, or in a single written document.[163]

The "face to face" presumption after *Shogun*. We have seen that, as it had been developed by the courts before *Shogun*, the presumption in face-to-face transactions was no more than a rebuttable presumption of fact. By the nature of the facts of cases in which it is relevant, the presumption is not easy to rebut: the claimant must produce evidence that he did make a mistake of the other party's identity, which was fundamental in the sense that he was prepared to contract with, and only with, the distinct person with whom he mistakenly believed that he was dealing. But the presumption was in principle rebuttable; and the alternative approaches of Devlin L.J. in *Ingram v Little*[164] and Lord Denning M.R. in *Lewis v Averay*,[165] which held that it was a presumption of law—even (according to Lord Denning) an irrebuttable presumption—had not been adopted. It is arguable whether this is still the case after the decision of the House of Lords in *Shogun*. Both Lord Phillips and Lord Walker made clear that it is a "strong" presumption;[166] but Lord Walker approved in general terms the approach of Devlin L.J. and, whilst accepting that it might be a rebuttable presumption, made clear that it will be rebutted only in exceptional cases, such as a physical impersonation.[167] We have 14–41

[163] *ibid.*, at [154], [170] (Lord Phillips, speaking of the case where the dealing are *exclusively* conducted in writing); [188] (Lord Walker: "It may be that [the presumption] should apply to an oral contract alleged to have been made on the telephone, where the parties are identified by hearing, although not by sight. An alleged oral contract made by telephone might be a case where the presumption applied, but was rebuttable. But to extend the principle to cases where the only contract was by written communication sent by post or by e-mail would be going far beyond identification by sight and hearing. Where there is an alleged contract reached by correspondence, offer and acceptance must be found, if they are to be found at all, in the terms of the documents").

[164] Above, para.14–27.

[165] Above, para.14–28.

[166] *Shogun*, above, n.130 at [170], [187].

[167] *ibid.*, at [185], [187]: "If the principle is no more than a presumption, it is a strong presumption, and exceptions to it would be rare . . ." The only example he gave which he contemplated might rebut the presumption is a deception such as Jacob practised on Isaac (Genesis, Ch.27).

already seen that, in their dissenting speeches, Lord Nicholls and Lord Millett both approved the approach taken by Devlin L.J. in *Ingram v Little* to a legal presumption; and Lord Millett thought that "there might perhaps be something to be said for making the presumption irrebuttable".[168] In a case which comes before the courts in relation to a face-to-face transaction, where there is a claim of mistake about the other party's identity, the courts should still look to the earlier cases, which were settled before *Shogun* in favour of a rebuttable presumption of fact. This has not formally been overridden by *Shogun* itself, although there will no doubt be room for further argument in the higher courts about whether the presumption in such cases should be strengthened in the manner discussed by some of their Lordships in *Shogun*. However, it is submitted that the approach taken by the majority in *Ingram v Little* in relation to the nature of the presumption—as a presumption of fact but one which is inevitably not easy to rebut—is still preferable, because it fits most closely with the general overall approach to the test for mistake about identity, based on the intention of the parties.

14–42 **The test of intention after *Shogun*.** The House of Lords in *Shogun* continued to emphasise that the key question in relation to a claim of mistake is the intention of the parties; and in particular the intention of the claimant who alleges that he made a mistake, but viewed also from the position of the other party. A party is taken to have intended what the other party reasonably believed him to intend; and the intentions concerning the identity of the party to whom communications were addressed will be judged on a proper construction of the communications from the perspective of the recipient.[169] If the other party knows that the party making the communication does not intend to address the communication to him, he cannot rely on it.[170] These propositions are consistent with the general approach as it had been developed before *Shogun*, and should be retained because they are consistent with the general

[168] *ibid.*, at [67].

[169] *ibid.*, at [183] (Lord Walker), [123]–[124] (Lord Phillips).

[170] *ibid.*, at [48] (Lord Hobhouse: "The rogue knew, or at least confidently expected, that the finance company would be prepared to deal with Mr Durlabh Patel but probably not with him, the rogue; and he was, in any event, not willing himself to enter into any contract with the finance company"); [123] (Lord Phillips).

approach in English law to the formation of a contract, and to mistakes allegedly made by one or other party during the negotiations.[171]

The current state of the law on mistake about the identity of the other party. The law as it stood before *Shogun* is summarised above.[172] We have seen that this would have been fundamentally changed if the approach preferred by Lord Nicholls and Lord Millett had been adopted. As it is, the decision of the House is narrow and, strictly, deals only with the case of written contracts; and in this it confirms the earlier position—where a contract is concluded in writing, the identity of the parties is to be determined by the objective construction of the document itself; and where the contract is formed by written communications, the intentions of each party as to the person with whom he is intending to deal is to be determined by the objective construction of the document from the recipient's perspective. The decision in *Shogun* does not formally touch on the approach to face-to-face contracts, but it appears that the presumption should be retained for such cases; and that, although there are some contrary views amongst the speeches in *Shogun*, the better approach is to continue to view the presumption as one of fact, albeit a presumption not in practice easy to rebut. 14–43

[171] *ibid.*, at [125] ("Just as the parties must be shown to have agreed on the terms of the contract, so they must also be shown to have agreed the one with the other. If A makes an offer to B, but C purports to accept it, there will be no contract. Equally, if A makes an offer to B and B addresses his acceptance to C there will be no contract. Where there is an issue as to whether two persons have reached an agreement, the one with the other, the courts have tended to adopt the same approach to resolving that issue as they adopt when considering whether there has been agreement as to the terms of the contract. The court asks the question whether each *intended*, or must be deemed to have *intended*, to contract with the other"); [170] ("*Cundy v Lindsay* exemplifies the application by English law of the same approach to identifying the parties as is applied to identifying the terms of the contract. In essence this focuses on deducing the intention of the parties from their words and conduct") (Lord Phillips). For Lord Phillips' explanation of the test for the terms of the contract, see at [123].

[172] Above, para.14–33.

CHAPTER 15

MISTAKES ABOUT THE SUBJECT-MATTER OF THE CONTRACT[1]

[1] Chitty, paras 5–017 to 5–065; Furmston, paras 4.75 to 4.87; Treitel, paras 8–002 to 8–032, 8–042 (but the cases there described are mistakes about the terms of the contract), 8–043; Anson, pp.276–298; Cheshire, Fifoot and Furmston, pp.286–301; Cartwright, Ch.11; Stoljar, Ch.3; F.H. Lawson, "*Error in Substantia*" (1936) 52 L.Q.R. 79; C. Slade, "The Myth of Mistake in the English Law of Contract" (1954) 70 L.Q.R. 385; P.S. Atiyah and F.A.R. Bennion, "Mistake in the Construction of Contracts" (1961) 24 M.L.R. 421; L.B. McTurnan, "An Approach to Common Mistake in English Law" (1963) 41 Can. Bar. Rev. 1; J. Cartwright, "*Solle v Butcher* and the Doctrine of Mistake in Contract" (1987) 103 L.Q.R. 594; J.C. Smith, "Contracts—Mistake, Frustration and Implied Terms" (1994) 110 L.Q.R. 400. Books and articles on this topic must be read in the light of their contemporary significance, given the development of the law in *The Great Peace* [2002] EWCA Civ 1407, [2003] Q.B. 679; below, paras 15–23, 15–32.

I. INTRODUCTION: THE NATURE OF A MISTAKE ABOUT THE SUBJECT-MATTER

(1) What is a Mistake about the Subject-Matter?

15–01 **Mistake about the subject-matter.** The mistake with which we are concerned in this chapter is rather loosely described as a mistake about the subject-matter of the contract. This means a mistake of fact or law which bears upon the subject-matter of the obligations of one of the parties. Such mistakes may take various forms. In a contract of sale, for example, the mistake may be as to (a) the existence of the goods; (b) their factual characteristics or qualities; (c) the seller's title to sell them; or (d) the lawfulness of the sale. The mistake may be made by one party, or by both parties. But for a party to claim that he made a mistake, he must show that when he gave his assent to the contract he had a relevant positive belief or understanding of fact or law which was incorrect,[2] and which was causally related to his decision to give his assent. So he will show that he believed that (a) the goods were in existence at the time of the sale (but it now turns out that they had been destroyed; or never existed); or (b) the goods possessed certain qualities (which he has now discovered they do not); or (c) the seller had title to the goods, and so could sell them (but it now turns out that the seller had no title; or even that the buyer himself already owned them); or (d) the sale was lawful (but it has now been discovered that it was a type of transaction covered by a statutory prohibition).

15–02 **Mistake about the subject-matter contrasted with a mistake about the terms or identity.** It is evident that a mistake about the subject-matter is very different in nature from a mistake about the identity of the other party. Sometimes the judges refer to mistakes about the "identity of the subject-matter",[3] but this language is chosen to refer to the essential, identifying characteristics of the subject-matter itself. The identity of the parties to the contract is different from both the terms of the contract and the subject-matter of the contract.[4]

[2] Above, para.12–03.
[3] e.g. *Bell v Lever Bros Ltd* [1932] A.C. 161 at 227 (Lord Atkin).
[4] Above, para.14–04.

It is important, however, to distinguish between a mistake about the subject-matter and a mistake about the terms of the contract; there is a danger that they may be confused, since the subject-matter of the contract is inevitably itself prescribed by the terms of the contract. In the case of a claim relating to the subject-matter, the precise mistake must be identified with care. Indeed, we have already seen that the court in *Smith v Hughes*[5] had to order a retrial because the original trial judge's direction to the jury had not sufficiently distinguished between mistake about the terms, and mistake about the subject-matter. Blackburn J. said[6]:

> "I doubt whether the direction would bring to the minds of the jury the distinction between agreeing to take the oats under the belief that they were old, and agreeing to take the oats under the belief that the plaintiff contracted that they were old."

That is, the jury were not instructed to consider whether the buyer of the oats made a mistake about a factual quality of the oats ("the belief that they were old") or a mistake about the terms of the contract ("the belief that the [seller] contracted that they were old"). This is a fundamental distinction. As we have seen, if there is not in fact agreement between the parties about the terms of the contract—the obligations which each party undertakes in favour of the other, and which will constitute a breach of contract if the obligations are not fulfilled—then there is no contract. A lack of subjective agreement about the terms may still be overcome, if one party's misunderstanding can be overridden by the objective test.[7] But, in principle, a failure to agree on the terms of the contract

---

[5] (1871) L.R. 6 Q.B. 597; above, para.13–09.

[6] *ibid.*, at 608. See also Cockburn C.J. at 606: "Both parties were agreed as to the sale and purchase of this particular parcel of oats. The defendant believed the oats to be old, and was thus induced to agree to buy them, but he omitted to make their age a condition of the contract. All that can be said is, that the two minds were not ad idem as to the age of the oats; they certainly were ad idem as to the sale and purchase of them"; and Hannen J. at 611: "In order to relieve the defendant it was necessary that the jury should find not merely that the plaintiff believed the defendant to believe that he was buying old oats, but that he believed the defendant to believe that he, the plaintiff, was contracting to sell old oats" (i.e. it is not sufficient to show that the seller knew that the buyer made a mistake about the age of the oats; he must have known that the buyer made a mistake about the terms on which the seller was selling them).

[7] Above, para.13–19.

prevents the contract from coming into existence. A mistake which is not as to the terms, but only as to the subject-matter of the contract, does not.

15–03 **Mistake about the subject-matter does not negative an agreement.** We shall see later in this chapter that a mistake about the subject-matter of the contract may in certain circumstances render the contract void. However, it is evident that the basis on which it is void is fundamentally different from the basis on which the contract is void for one party's mistake about the terms of the contract or the identity of the other party. In those cases, the contract is void because there has not been a sufficient correspondence of communications between the parties for the agreement to come into existence. The mistake "negatives" the agreement. It may appear that the parties have formed a contract, but their communications masked the absence of essential agreement between two mutually intended parties, about mutually intended obligations. In the case of a mistake about the subject-matter, however, there is not only an apparent agreement between the parties about their respective obligations, but (in law) an actual agreement. In making a contract void, therefore, the mistake must operate in a different way. It was said by Lord Atkin not to "negative" the parties' consent but to "nullify" it[8]:

> "If mistake operates at all it operates so as to negative or in some cases to nullify consent. The parties may be mistaken in the identity of the contracting parties, or in the existence of the subject-matter of the contract at the date of the contract, or in the quality of the subject-matter of the contract. These mistakes may be by one party, or by both, and the legal effect may depend upon the class of mistake above mentioned. Thus a mistaken belief by A. that he is contracting with B., whereas in fact he is contracting with C., will negative consent where it is clear that the intention of A. was to contract only with B. So the agreement of A. and B. to purchase a specific article is void if in fact the article had perished before the date of sale. In this case, though the parties in fact were agreed about the subject-matter, yet a consent to transfer or take delivery of something not existent is deemed useless, the consent is nullified."

[8] *Bell v Lever Bros Ltd*, above, n.3 at 217. Treitel, para.8–001, uses this distinction between mistakes which "negative" consent and mistakes which "nullify" consent as the starting-point for the discussion of mistake, although in the 12th edn (2007) it is no longer the distinction around which the chapter on mistake is structured: above, para.12–06, n.23.

This difference in the underlying theory about why the contract is void gives rise to a different general approach to mistakes about the subject-matter, as compared with mistakes as to terms or identity. Whilst the courts are cautious in admitting mistakes at all, given the overriding reluctance of English law to allow a party to rely on his own mistake in order to avoid his apparent obligations,[9] the starting-point in a case where the parties were not in agreement about the terms, or where one party misunderstood who he was dealing with, is to say that the contract is void unless that failure of essential agreement between two intended parties can be overridden. Where, however, a party claims that the mistake, whilst not sufficient to negative the agreement, should none the less be allowed to nullify it—and have the same legal consequences (the contract is void)—the starting-point is the reverse. The reluctance to allow a mistake of itself to be sufficient to allow a party to escape from his apparent obligations is applied with full force, and the courts take a very restrictive view of the scope of actionable mistake.

(2) Why Should a Mistake about the Subject-Matter be Remedied?

Risk allocation. In considering the legal significance of a mistake of fact or law which bears upon the subject-matter of the contract, it can be difficult to avoid arguments about the allocation of risk. If one party has promised that the goods exist, or are of a particular quality, or that he has title to sell them, or that the transaction is lawful, then the consequences of the inexistence of the goods, their lack of the relevant quality, the defect in the seller's title, or the unlawfulness of the transaction are provided for by the contract. The party who gave such promises in the contract has thereby taken on the risk of those matters, and the contract provides the remedy.[10] A contract contains promises of varying content. Most will be promises of future performance; and the essential function of the law of contract is to give legal force to such promises. A person who makes a statement about his future conduct is not normally held liable for failing to act in accordance with his statement unless he has made a contractually binding promise. An 15–04

[9] Above, para.12–12.
[10] Above, para.12–05; below, para.15–15.

honest statement about one's future conduct is not a misrepresentation.[11] However, a party who makes a statement of the present facts, or the law, which is material to the other party's decision to enter into a contract, thereby opens himself to claims for misrepresentation—for rescission of the contract, and sometimes for damages.[12] One could say that by making the statement to the other he has taken on the risk as to whether his statement is true. Given that the remedy of rescission of the contract may follow from even a wholly innocent misrepresentation,[13] this places the representee in a strong position, and the mere fact that he has made the statement is enough to shift to the representor the risk of truth of the statement. If, however, the law were to allow a party to escape from a contract on the basis of his own mistake relating to the subject-matter of the contract, where he has not requested the other party to undertake the risk of the mistake in the terms of the contract, and where the other party has not taken upon himself the risk by virtue of having made any misrepresentation which induced the mistake in the claimant, it would have the effect of allowing the mistake of itself to shift the risk. This would upset the normal risk allocation which English law attributes to contractual negotiations.

This general approach is seen in the speech of Lord Atkin in *Bell v Lever Bros Ltd*,[14] in a passage to which we shall refer again later in this chapter:

> "A. buys B.'s horse; he thinks the horse is sound and he pays the price of a sound horse; he would certainly not have bought the horse if he had known as the fact is that the horse is unsound. If B. has made no representation as to soundness and has not contracted that the horse is sound, A. is bound and cannot recover back the price. A. buys a picture from B.; both A. and B. believe it to be the work of an old master, and a high price is paid. It turns out to be a modern copy. A. has no remedy in the absence of representation or warranty. A. agrees to take on lease or to buy from B. an unfurnished dwelling-house. The house is in fact uninhabitable. A. would never have entered into the bargain if he had known the fact. A. has no remedy, and the position is the same whether B. knew the facts or not, so long as he made no representation or gave no warranty. A. buys a roadside garage business from B. abutting on a public thoroughfare: unknown to A., but known to B., it has already been decided to construct a byepass road which will divert

[11] Above, para.3–43.
[12] Above, Pt I.
[13] Above, para.4–04.
[14] Above, n.3 at 224.

substantially the whole of the traffic from passing A.'s garage. Again A. has no remedy. All these cases involve hardship on A. and benefit B., as most people would say, unjustly. They can be supported on the ground that it is of paramount importance that contracts should be observed, and that if parties honestly comply with the essentials of the formation of contracts—i.e., agree in the same terms on the same subject-matter—they are bound, and must rely on the stipulations of the contract for protection from the effect of facts unknown to them."

The contract may be void for mistake about the subject-matter. 15–05
The starting-point is therefore clear from Lord Atkin's speech in *Bell v Lever Bros Ltd*: normally a mistake about the subject-matter does not affect the validity of the contract, because a party can generally expect a remedy only if the contract provided for the issue (there was a "warranty"—a contractual allocation of the risk of the mistake) or the other party induced the mistake by making a misrepresentation. However, this does not entirely exclude a remedy for such a mistake. We shall see that Lord Atkin would admit that a contract can be void, in certain narrowly defined circumstances, by reason of a mistake about the subject-matter; and that this continues to be applied in the most recent decision in which the Court of Appeal has discussed the general approach in this area.[15] The common law does recognise that a mistake about the subject-matter may be sufficiently serious to render the contract void. But this narrow approach reflects the underlying policy set out in Lord Atkin's speech.

But a contract is not voidable for mistake about the subject-matter. 15–06
During the second half of the twentieth century an intermediate view developed: that a contract could be voidable (in equity) for mistake about the subject-matter in certain circumstances where the mistake was not sufficiently serious to render the contract void at common law. We shall see that this view had its origins in the judgment of Denning L.J. in *Solle v Butcher*,[16] and was maintained until it was very firmly rejected by the Court of Appeal in 2002 in *The Great Peace*.[17] In essence, the recent decision is based on the same underlying policy as that which was

[15] *The Great Peace* [2002] EWCA Civ 1407, [2003] Q.B. 679. See below, para.15–23.
[16] [1950] 1 K.B. 671 at 693; below, para.15–30.
[17] Above, n.15; below, para.15–32.

set out in Lord Atkin's speech in *Bell v Lever Bros Ltd*; and in the proposition that, if the policy of the common law is to deny a remedy based on mistake which has not been provided for in the contract, nor induced by misrepresentation, and which does not fulfil the very narrow criteria required to make the contract void, it would then undermine that very policy if the court were to allow a contract to be voidable for a less serious mistake. It would be aiming to address the "hardship" of the mistaken party, which Lord Atkin made clear was not a sufficient ground of intervention. Lord Phillips said[18]:

> "A common factor in *Solle v Butcher* and the cases which have followed it can be identified. The effect of the mistake has been to make the contract a particularly bad bargain for one of the parties. Is there a principle of equity which justifies the court in rescinding a contract where a common mistake[19] has produced this result? . . . [T]he premise of equity's intrusion into the effects of the common law is that the common law rule in question is seen in the particular case to work injustice, and for some reason the common law cannot cure itself. But it is difficult to see how that can apply here. Cases of fraud and misrepresentation, and undue influence, are all catered for under other existing and uncontentious equitable rules. We are *only* concerned with the question whether relief might be given for common mistake in circumstances wider than those stipulated in *Bell v Lever Bros Ltd*. But that, surely, is a question as to where the common law should draw the line; not whether, given the common law rule, it needs to be mitigated by application of some other doctrine. The common law has drawn the line in *Bell v Lever Bros Ltd*. The effect of *Solle v Butcher* is not to supplement or mitigate the common law: it is to say that *Bell v Lever Bros Ltd* was wrongly decided."

(3) Categories of Mistake about the Subject-Matter

15–07 **Mistake may arise from the claimant's own misunderstanding.** A party may come to make a mistake about the subject-matter in various ways. He may have made some investigation of the relevant matters of fact or law which impact on his decision whether to give his assent to the proposed contract, and he may have reached the wrong conclusion in the light of that investigation. In such a case, he made the mistake himself, and he may or may not have been at

18 *The Great Peace*, above, n.15 at [155]–[156].

19 [The common law will allow a mistake about the subject-matter to render the contract void only if the mistake was common (shared), and even then only when the mistake satisfies a high threshold of seriousness: below, para.15–25.]

fault in making it—that is, in choosing what questions to ask in the course of his investigation, and in interpreting the answers to his questions, he may have acted as a reasonable person would have done in his position. Or he may have been unreasonable—and so he may have no reasonable grounds for his mistake. On the other hand, he may make a mistake without making any investigations, and without asking any questions, but by just making an assumption about the facts or the law in question. Again, he may not be at fault in so doing; but it may be thought that it was not a reasonable assumption to make in the circumstances without further enquiry.

Mistake may be induced; the relationship between mistake and misrepresentation. A mistake may, however, be caused not by the claimant's own assumptions, or his own interpretation of information that he obtains through his investigations, but by a false statement. If the false statement originates in a third party, for whom the other contracting party has in law no responsibility, it is still generally treated as (and only as) the claimant's mistake. The fact that the claimant was given the incorrect information by a third party may well be relevant to determine whether he was at fault in making the mistake: if the third party was apparently in a position to know the truth of the information he gave, then the claimant will be able to argue that he had reasonable grounds for his (mistaken) belief, if that becomes relevant in the analysis of the remedies he may have for his mistake.[20] And the claimant may have a direct claim against the third party for any loss that flowed from the false information.[21] But the incorrect information provided by a third party does not normally affect the validity of the contract itself.[22] **15–08**

Where, however, the incorrect information is provided by the other party to the contract, the picture changes: there is then a

20 Below, para.15–22.

21 The claim must generally be in tort (either negligence: above, Ch.6; or, if the claimant can establish that the third party was fraudulent, the tort of deceit: above, Ch.5) unless the claimant entered into a contract with the third party under which the information was provided.

22 It is said that there is an exception where the other party knew about the third party's misrepresentation; or, where the contract is a non-commercial bank guarantee, where the creditor ought to have known of the risk of a misrepresentation by a third party because of the relationship between the contracting party and the third party: above, paras 4–72 to 4–78; below, para.15–13.

misrepresentation. And we have seen that a misrepresentation of fact or law renders the contract voidable; this is not restricted to any particular state of mind on the part of the other party (it may be fraudulent, negligent or innocent)[23]; nor to any particular seriousness of misrepresentation (it need not be substantial, or fundamental: it must just be a misrepresentation of fact or law which constituted *an* inducement to the claimant to enter into the contract).[24]

It is very common for mistakes to be induced by representations made by or on behalf of the other party: the other party has information which is relevant to the claimant's decision to enter into the contract, and shares it in order to persuade the claimant to give his assent. In many cases, therefore, the claimant will in practice be able to rely on the fact that his mistake was induced by the other party's misrepresentation, and we have seen that the misrepresentation gives rise to a wide range of potential remedies,[25] including the avoidance of the contract.[26] However, misrepresentation makes the contract only voidable, whereas a mistake—if it operates at all—will make the contract void. Thus, even if he could have established a claim based on the other party's misrepresentation, the claimant will still seek to rely on his mistake if he needs to obtain the advantages that accompany a void contract.[27]

15–09 **Mistake may be unilateral or common.** A mistake about the subject-matter may be unilateral, or common (shared).[28] We have seen that the source of the mistake may be the claimant's own spontaneous assumptions or his incorrect interpretation of the results of his investigations, or incorrect information provided by a third party. In such cases, he may well make a mistake which is not shared by the other party to the contract. The other party may be ignorant of the fact that the claimant is acting under a mistake; but, on the other hand, he may know about the claimant's mistake, but

23 Above, para.4–04.
24 Above, para.4–37.
25 Above, Pt I.
26 Above, Ch.4.
27 e.g. if rescission of a voidable contract would now be barred: above, paras 4–38 to 4–71. See generally above, para.12–19.
28 For difficulties in the terminology, see above, para.12–06, n.23.

may not disabuse him of it; or he may even have caused it by deliberately misleading the claimant. The mistake in all such cases is unilateral.

It is also possible for a mistake about the subject-matter to be common—that is, both parties make the *same* mistake. The sources of such a shared mistake may also vary. Either both parties may independently come to the same incorrect assumption about the relevant facts or law; or they may both be given the same incorrect information by a third party—perhaps the same third party. Or—and this is more common than might at first appear—one party's mistake is caused innocently by the other party. That is, one party first obtained the incorrect information, and then shared it with the other party. Both parties therefore entered into the contract under the same mistake. In other words, an *innocent (non-fraudulent) misrepresentation* will necessarily give rise to a *common mistake*.

We shall see that the response of English law to unilateral and common mistakes about the subject-matter is very different.

II. UNILATERAL MISTAKE

A unilateral mistake about the subject-matter is not sufficient. 15–10
The judgments in *Smith v Hughes* make clear that a unilateral mistake about the subject-matter is not in itself sufficient to allow the mistaken party to avoid the contract. Cockburn C.J. said[29]:

> "I take the true rule to be, that where a specific article is offered for sale, without express warranty, or without circumstances from which the law will imply a warranty . . . and the buyer has full opportunity of inspecting and forming his own judgment, if he chooses to act on his own judgment, the rule caveat emptor applies. If he gets the article he contracted to buy, and that article corresponds with what it was sold as, he gets all he is entitled to, and is bound by the contract. Here the defendant agreed to buy a specific parcel of oats. The oats were what they were sold as, namely, good oats according to the sample. The buyer persuaded himself they were old oats, when they were not so; but the seller neither said nor did anything to contribute to his deception. He has himself to blame."

[29] (1871) L.R. 6 Q.B. 597 at 603. See also *Statoil A.S.A. v Louis Dreyfus Energy Services L.P. (The Harriette N)* [2008] EWHC 2257 (Comm), [2008] 2 Lloyd's Rep. 685 at [88] (Aikens J.: the correctness of the decision in *Smith v Hughes*, and the analysis in it (particularly by Cockburn C.J. at 603, and Blackburn J. at 607, below, n.32) "has never been doubted").

This makes clear that a mistake made by the claimant relating to the factual qualities or characteristics of the subject-matter, which is not provided for expressly or impliedly in the contract, and where the other party has not contributed to the mistake, has no legal consequence. The claimant is simply bound by the contract. *Smith v Hughes* was cited by Lord Atkin in *Bell v Lever Bros Ltd* as one of two cases which are "authoritative expositions of the law" in support of his general proposition that[30]

> "Mistake as to quality of the thing . . . will not affect assent unless it is the mistake of both parties, and is as to the existence of some quality which makes the thing without the quality essentially different from the thing as it was believed to be."

This proposition contains two elements: a mistake about the quality of the subject-matter will not have effect unless it is shared; and, even then, only if the mistake satisfies a particular test about the seriousness of the mistake. That is: however serious the mistake, if it is a mistake only about the qualities of the subject-matter, it is not sufficient that it is unilateral. Moreover, in a passage which has already been quoted,[31] Lord Atkin went on to give examples of mistakes about the subject-matter which are insufficient to render the contract void, including examples where the mistake is, or may be, unilateral:

> "A. agrees to take on lease or to buy from B. an unfurnished dwelling-house. The house is in fact uninhabitable. A. would never have entered into the bargain if he had known the fact. A. has no remedy, and the position is the same whether B. knew the facts or not, so long as he made no representation or gave no warranty. A. buys a roadside garage business from B. abutting on a public thoroughfare: unknown to A., but known to B., it has already been decided to construct a byepass road which will divert substantially the whole of the traffic from passing A.'s garage. Again A. has no remedy."

---

30 [1932] A.C. 161 at 218–219, 220–222. Curiously, in *The Great Peace* [2002] EWCA Civ 1407, [2003] Q.B. 679 at [60] Lord Phillips said "The other case to which Lord Atkin referred was *Smith v Hughes*. On no view did that difficult case deal with common mistake and we are not able to see how it supported the test formulated by Lord Atkin". The other "authoritative" case was *Kennedy v The Panama, New Zealand and Australian Royal Mail Co. Ltd* (1867) L.R. 2 Q.B. 580; below, para.15–21, n.76. The position in relation to *common* mistakes about the subject-matter is considered below.

31 Above, para.15–04.

Even if the other party knows about the mistake, it is not sufficient. It is therefore not sufficient for the claimant to show that he made a unilateral mistake about the subject-matter. And this is the rule even if the other party knows that the claimant is mistaken. This was made clear by Blackburn J. in *Smith v Hughes*[32]: 15–11

> "In this case I agree that on the sale of a specific article, unless there be a warranty making it part of the bargain that it possesses some particular quality, the purchaser must take the article he has bought though it does not possess that quality. And I agree that even if the vendor was aware that the purchaser thought that the article possessed that quality, and would not have entered into the contract unless he had so thought, still the purchaser is bound, unless the vendor was guilty of some fraud or deceit upon him, and that a mere abstinence from disabusing the purchaser of that impression is not fraud or deceit; for, whatever may be the case in a court of morals, there is no legal obligation on the vendor to inform the purchaser that he is under a mistake, not induced by the act of the vendor."

In this passage the judge goes further. Not only is a claimant unable to rely on his unilateral mistake about the qualities of the subject-matter, unless he can show that it was induced by "fraud or deceit", or there was a warranty in the contract; but even the fact that the other party knows about the mistake does not give the claimant a basis on which he can avoid the contract, nor does it impose on the other party any legal obligation to inform him about the mistake. That is, one party's knowledge about the other party's unilateral mistake about the qualities of the subject-matter does not of itself impose a duty of disclosure. Liability for non-disclosure will be discussed in Part III.[33]

No equitable jurisdiction to grant rescission for unilateral mistake of fact. *Smith v Hughes*[34] was a decision of a common law court, before the fusion of the jurisdictions of law and equity.[35] It is not surprising that the question should not have been addressed in that case, but should have arisen since then, as to whether equity 15–12

[32] (1871) L.R. 6 Q.B. 597 at 606–607. This passage was quoted by Lord Atkin in *Bell v Lever Bros Ltd*, above, n.30 at 222.

[33] For the general approach, see below, paras 16–02 to 16–04.

[34] Above, paras 15–10 to 15–11.

[35] Supreme Court of Judicature Act 1873 Pt.II, esp. ss.24, 25; see now Senior Courts Act 1981, s.49.

would give relief for a unilateral mistake in circumstances where the common law refused relief. In one recent case the trial judge appeared to assume that such an equitable jurisdiction might exist.[36] However, this has been firmly rejected by a later judge at first instance,[37] on the basis that the rejection by the Court of Appeal in *The Great Peace*[38] of an equitable jurisdiction in relation to common mistakes of fact strongly suggested that there is no such jurisdiction in the case of a unilateral mistake.

15–13 **A unilateral mistake which is caused by the other party is actionable as a fraudulent misrepresentation, but not as a mistake.** As Blackburn J. made clear in the passage quoted above, however, the claimant will have a remedy—he is "not bound"—if the other party was "guilty of some fraud or deceit upon him". In such a case there will be a misrepresentation. It is clear in the modern law that a contract can be avoided for innocent, as well as fraudulent, misrepresentation,[39] although for the resulting mistake to be unilateral, the misrepresentation will be fraudulent.[40] But it should be remembered that the effect of a misrepresentation, even a fraudulent misrepresentation, is to render the contract voidable, not void. If, therefore, the (unilateral) mistake is induced

[36] *Huyton S.A. v Distribuidora Internacional De Productos Agricolas S.A. de CV* [2002] EWHC 2088 (Comm), [2003] 2 Lloyd's Rep. 780 at [454] (Andrew Smith J., holding, however, at [466] that the mistake was not in the circumstances sufficient to justify a remedy. This issue was not further explored on appeal: [2003] EWCA Civ 1104, [2003] 2 Lloyd's Rep. 780 at [6], [59]). In *Solle v Butcher* [1950] 1 K.B. 671, CA, at 690–693, below, para.15–30, Denning L.J. did not consider rescission in equity for unilateral mistakes of fact.

[37] *Statoil A.S.A. v Louis Dreyfus Energy Services L.P. (The Harriette N)* [2008] EWHC 2257 (Comm), [2008] 2 Lloyd's Rep. 685 at [105] (Aikens J.).

[38] Above, n.30. For the rejection of the equitable doctrine established in *Solle v Butcher* (above, n.36) in relation to common mistakes of fact, see below, para.15–32. The decision of the Court of Appeal in *The Great Peace* was given after completion of the argument in *Huyton*, above, n.36, but before judgment. However, in the light of his findings of fact (and therefore his rejection of any remedy on the basis of unilateral mistake on the facts: above, n.36) Andrew Smith J. did not delay his judgment in order to hear further submissions: see [2002] EWHC 2088 (Comm), [2003] 2 Lloyd's Rep. 780 at [455].

[39] Above, para.4–04. This was not clear at the time when *Smith v Hughes* was decided; and the extension to non-fraudulent misrepresentations was made in equity, whereas the court in *Smith v Hughes* was a common law court. Hannen J. in *Smith v Hughes* spoke more generally of "misrepresentation", at 610–611.

[40] Above, para.15–09.

by a fraudulent misrepresentation, the claimant can avoid the contract—but in so doing he relies upon the misrepresentation, not the mistake. The fraudulent inducement does not change the character of the mistake that it induces. Similarly, where the misrepresentation is made by a third party, but the other party has knowledge of it at the time of the contract, it appears that the claimant can avoid the contract for misrepresentation, although there are unresolved questions about this particular situation.[41]

III. COMMON (SHARED) MISTAKE

A common (shared) mistake about the subject-matter may be sufficient. We shall see in this section that a common (shared) mistake about the subject-matter—a mistake of fact or law which bears upon the subject-matter of the obligations of one of the parties—may be sufficient to render the contract void at common law. This is only the case, however, in very limited circumstances. If the parties have expressly or impliedly made provision in the contract for the so-called mistake—or, in other words, if there is a contractual allocation of the risk of the mistake—then the contract governs. If, however, the contract is silent about the matter, the courts may be persuaded to hold that the contract is void—but only if the mistake is of a degree of seriousness which, as we shall see, is not easy to define, nor (if it can be put into words) is the test for such an operative mistake always easy to apply. We shall also see that, during the second half of the twentieth century the courts were prepared to hold that a common mistake, of a lesser degree of seriousness than that accepted by the common law authorities, could render a contract voidable in equity; but that this has now been rejected. 15–14

[41] *Royal Bank of Scotland Plc v Etridge (No.2)* [2001] UKHL 44, [2002] 2 A.C. 773 at [144] (Lord Scott, discussing both misrepresentation and undue influence by third parties). We have already seen, however, that the courts have not yet considered the relationship between that rule, and the general rule, exemplified by the judgments in *Smith v Hughes*, that a unilateral mistake about the subject-matter is not sufficient, even if it is known by the other party: above, para.4–78.

(1) Risk Allocation in the Contract

15–15 **Risk-taking excludes mistake.** We have seen already that mistake about the subject-matter of the contract inevitably raises questions of the contractual allocation of risk.[42] The courts in discussing cases of alleged mistakes about the subject-matter have not always addressed this question openly,[43] or even at all[44]; but it is clear that this question is logically prior to any analysis based on mistake. If the contract expressly or impliedly provides for the circumstances as they have now been found to be, but were believed by the parties to be otherwise, then the matter is concluded by the provision contained in the contract. There is no "mistake" at all. The common law rules for mistake are, in this sense, rules of last resort which come into play only if there is no solution in the contract itself. In *Associated Japanese Bank (International) Ltd v Crédit du Nord S.A.* Steyn J. said[45]:

> "Logically, before one can turn to the rules as to mistake, whether at common law or in equity, one must first determine whether the contract itself, by express or implied condition precedent or otherwise, provides who bears the risk of the relevant mistake. It is at this hurdle that many pleas of mistake will either fail or prove to have been unnecessary. Only if the contract is silent on the point, is there scope for invoking mistake."

15–16 **The risk may be allocated expressly or impliedly.** The contract may make express provision for the circumstances which turn out to

---

[42] Above, paras 12–05, 15–04.

[43] It was not included expressly as part of the tests for mistake described by Lord Atkin in *Bell v Lever Bros Ltd*, above, n.30. But his insistence on the fact that the solution to mistakes is normally to be found in the fact that the "mistake" formed the subject-matter of a warranty by the other party, above, para.15–04, shows that he had the terms of the contract firmly in mind.

[44] *William Sindall Plc v Cambridgeshire CC* [1994] 1 W.L.R. 1016, CA, at 1035 (Hoffmann L.J.: "I should say that neither in *Grist v Bailey* [1967] Ch. 532 nor in *Laurence v Lexcourt Holdings Ltd* [1978] 1 W.L.R. 1128 did the judges who decided those cases at first instance advert to the question of contractual allocation of risk. I am not sure that the decisions would have been the same if they had").

[45] [1989] 1 W.L.R. 255 at 268; followed in *William Sindall Plc v Cambridgeshire CC*, above, n.44 at 1035 (Lord Hoffmann); *The Great Peace* [2002] EWCA Civ 1407, [2003] Q.B. 679 at [80]; *Graves v Graves* [2007] EWCA Civ 660, [2008] H.L.R. 10 at [27].

have been "mistaken".[46] Or the court may decide from the communications between the parties that they were intending to allocate the risk of certain facts in a particular way. Such an allocation of risk may be express, or it may be implied in fact.[47] In *McRae v Commonwealth Disposals Commission*[48] the Commission invited tenders for "an oil tanker wrecked on Jourmaund Reef approximately 100 miles north Samarai. The vessel is said to contain oil". The claimants submitted a successful tender.[49] There

---

[46] *William Sindall Plc v Cambridgeshire CC*, above, n.44 (sewage pipe discovered under land which had been sold on terms including National Conditions of Sale (20th edn, 1981), condition 14: "Without prejudice to the duty of the vendor to disclose all latent easements and latent liabilities known to the vendor to affect the property, the property is sold subject to any rights of way and water, rights of common and other rights, easements, quasi-easements, liabilities and public rights affecting the same": "In this case the contract says in express terms that it is subject to all easements other than those of which the vendor knows or has the means of knowledge. This allocates the risk of such incumbrances to the buyer and leaves no room for rescission on the grounds of mistake": Hoffmann L.J. at 1035); *Standard Chartered Bank v Banque Marocaine du Commerce Extérieur* [2006] EWHC 413 (Comm), [2006] All E.R. (D) 213 (Feb) at [28]–[29] (contract accepting risk participation in respect of promissory notes clearly allocated risk of non-payment, or of misuse of funds). In the strongest case, the parties may have realised that there was some uncertainty about the subject-matter and may have contracted in clear terms accordingly. In such a case, however, there is clearly no mistake, because the parties do not have a positive belief in incorrect facts; above, para.12–03. In other cases, however, a party may more easily claim to have been contracting under a mistake, because he did not have a positive realisation of the risk being run, although the risk was, in fact, provided for in the contract.

[47] *Associated Japanese Bank (International) Ltd v Crédit du Nord S.A.*, above, n.45 (contract to guarantee lessee's obligations under sale and lease-back of machines which did not in fact exist; held, clause in guarantee contemplated existence of machines, hence express condition precedent as to existence of machines; alternatively, condition precedent implied in fact under *Shirlaw v Southern Foundries (1926) Ltd* [1939] 2 K.B. 206); *Graves v Graves*, above, n.45 at [41] (on the facts, agreement for tenancy contained implied condition that if housing benefit was not payable the tenancy would end: non-payment of benefit did not give rise to actionable mistake or frustration).

[48] (1951) 84 C.L.R. 377, HCA.

[49] The claimants received a sales advice note from the Commission, which said (inter alia) "your offer to purchase, the general conditions contained in Form O, and this acceptance shall constitute the contract". One condition in Form O read: "Condition of property: The property shall be sold as and where it lies, with all faults, (if any), and save as expressly notified to the purchaser no warranty or condition whatsoever is given by the Commonwealth. While every effort shall be

was, however, no tanker at the place indicated, and it appeared that there had never been such a tanker. The claimants sued successfully for breach of contract, having incurred significant expenditure in mounting a salvage expedition.[50] The Commission's defence was that the contract was void for mistake; but this failed. This was not a case of mistake[51]; the Commission had promised that the tanker did exist, and had therefore undertaken the risk of its existence in the terms of the contract. There were certain other risks inherent in the contract: the Commission did not promise that there would be oil in the tanker; nor that such oil as was there would be capable of successful salvage. These risks were on the buyers. But the seller took the risk of the existence of the tanker.[52] This decision can be seen to rest either on the express representations about the tanker,[53] which were given contractual force because, in the circumstances, the Commission can be taken to have been intending to be bound to their truth; or, more simply, on the implied allocation of risk of the

made to describe property correctly, the Commonwealth shall not be liable for compensation or otherwise by reason of any misdescription or alleged variation of property delivered, from sample or property inspected . . .".

[50] This is a case of damages calculated to compensate the claimant's wasted expenditure, rather than his lost expectation: "The fact is that the impossibility of assessing damages on the basis of a comparison between what was promised and what was delivered arises not because what was promised was valueless but because it is impossible to value a non-existent thing. It is the breach of contract itself which makes it impossible even to undertake an assessment on that basis. It is not impossible, however, to undertake an assessment on another basis, and, in so far as the Commission's breach of contract itself reduces the possibility of an accurate assessment, it is not for the Commission to complain": above, n.48 at 414 (Dixon and Fullagar JJ.). An alternative claim in the modern law would be for damages in tort. But this was not then possible; the Commission were "guilty of the grossest negligence" (*ibid.*, at 409), but not fraud; and there was not yet a general liability in tort for economic loss caused by reliance on negligent statements, the case pre-dating by more than a decade the decision in *Hedley Byrne & Co. Ltd v Heller & Partners Ltd* [1964] A.C. 465, above, para.6–10, ((1951) 84 C.L.R. 377 at 410).

[51] The court held that, if their decision was wrong, and the case ought to be treated as one of mistake, the mistake could not be relied upon by the Commission in these circumstances: below, para.15–22.

[52] "The only proper construction of the contract is that it included a promise by the Commission that there was a tanker in the position specified. The Commission contracted that there was a tanker there": above, n.48 at 410 (Dixon and Fullagar JJ.)

[53] Above, n.48 at 409 ("The buyers relied upon, and acted upon, the assertion of the seller that there was a tanker in existence").

existence of the goods that are the subject-matter of any contract of sale of specific goods by description.[54]

This second analysis involves the allocation of risk by implication of law, rather than express promise or implication of fact. In certain contracts there will be typical terms, implied by law, which have the effect of allocating the risk of certain matters to one or other party.[55] For example, in a contract of sale, in the absence of a more limited provision, there is an implied condition that the seller has the right to sell the goods; and where the sale is by description, there is an implied condition that the goods will correspond with the description; and where the seller sells the goods in the course of a business, there is an implied condition that the goods are of satisfactory quality.[56] If the buyer and seller make mistakes about the seller's title, the description of the goods, or their quality, these will not normally[57] be actionable as mistakes because the risk of the "mistake" will be provided for in the terms implied by law into the contract.

Relationship between doubt and implied acceptance of risk. There can be some difficulty in practice in assessing whether a party who has a doubt about the truth of a fact, or a state of affairs, can be held impliedly to have accepted the risk of it (and thereby to 15–17

[54] *ibid.*, at 398; 407 (relying on *Barr v Gibson* (1838) 3 M. & W. 390 at 400, 150 E.R. 1196 at 1200, Parke B.: "The sale in this case of a ship implies a contract that the subject of the transfer did exist in the character of a ship" and *Couturier v Hastie* (1856) 5 H.L.C. 673, 10 E.R. 1065, which was interpreted as involving not a contract void for mistake, but a valid contract under which the seller promised that the goods were in existence; below, para.15–19, n.65).

[55] A contract of compromise, and a consent order which carries out a contract of compromise, will often embody an express or implied allocation of risk, although it may not do so: below, para.15–17; *Huddersfield Banking Co. Ltd v Henry Lister & Son Ltd* [1895] 2 Ch. 273, CA (consent order); *Brennan v Bolt Burdon* [2004] EWCA Civ 1017, [2005] Q.B. 303, below, para.15–24 (risk undertaken in contract of compromise).

[56] Sale of Goods Act 1979, ss.12(1), 13(1), 14(2).

[57] Where the contract is for specific goods, which have perished without the knowledge of the seller, the contract is void: *ibid.*, s.6. This did not apply in *McRae v Commonwealth Disposals Commission*, because the goods had not "perished" but had never existed: above, n.48 at 410. And s.6 is probably only a prima facie rule, which cannot apply where the contract has allocated the risk: *Bell v Lever Bros Ltd*, above, n.30 at 217–218 (Lord Atkin); P.S. Atiyah, "*Couturier v Hastie* and the Sale of Non-Existent Goods" (1957) 73 L.Q.R. 340; *cf.*, however, Treitel, para.8–010.

have excluded a claim for mistake if the fact turns out to be false or the state of affairs is different) by simply entering into the contract without making any express qualification related to his doubt. In *Kleinwort Benson Ltd v Lincoln City Council* Lord Hope said[58]:

> "A state of doubt is different from that of mistake. A person who pays when in doubt takes the risk that he may be wrong—and that is so whether the issue is one of fact or one of law."

However, although proof of the doubt and the fact that the party chose none the less to enter into the contract may constitute evidence that he has accepted the risk, it is not conclusive and the question remains whether, on the facts, the party in entering into the contract took the risk that he might be wrong. In *Deutsche Morgan Grenfell Group Plc v Inland Revenue Commissioners* Lord Hoffmann, discussing the case of a party who enters into a contract of compromise, said[59]:

> "the circumstances in which a payment is made may show that the person who made the payment took the risk that, if the question was fully litigated, it might turn out that he did not owe the money. Payment under a compromise is an obvious example: see *Brennan v Bolt Burdon*.[60] I would not regard the fact that the person making the payment had doubts about his

[58] [1999] 2 A.C. 349 at 410. See also *Perpetual Trustee Co. Ltd v BNY Corporate Trustee Services Ltd* [2009] EWCA Civ 1160, [2010] Ch. 347 at [108] (Longmore L.J.: "Once a party appreciates that an assumption underlying a contract may be legally questionable, that party will usually bear the risk that that assumption will turn out to be false").

[59] [2006] UKHL 46, [2007] 1 A.C. 558 at [27]. At [64]–[65] Lord Hope said that the critical question is one of causation: whether the party would have made the payment if he had known the truth. This case, like *Kleinwort Benson*, above, n.58, was concerned with restitution of money paid under a mistake of law, rather than the validity of a contract entered into under a mistake (*cf.* below, para.15–24). But at [26] Lord Hoffmann saw "a parallel here with the question of whether a common mistake vitiates a contract", and cited the statement by Steyn J. in *Associated Japanese Bank (International) Ltd v Crédit du Nord S.A.* quoted above, para.15–15.

[60] Above, n.55. [That case raises other difficulties, however, since the mistake was not of fact, but about the law as it stood at the time of the compromise but which was later (retrospectively) changed by judicial decision: below, para.15–24. The question of whether a party in entering into such a contract accepts the risk of future change of law may in practice be different from the broader factual question of whether a party who has a residual doubt about the truth of a fact has accepted the risk by entering into the contract.]

> liability as conclusive of the question of whether he took the risk, particularly if the existence of these doubts was unknown to the receiving party. It would be strange if a party whose lawyer had raised a doubt on the question but who decided nevertheless that he had better pay should be in a worse position than a party who had no doubts because he had never taken any advice, particularly if the receiving party had no idea that there was any difference in the circumstances in which the two payments had been made. It would be more rational if the question of whether a party should be treated as having taken the risk depended upon the objective circumstances surrounding the payment as they could reasonably have been known to both parties, including of course the extent to which the law was known to be in doubt."

The term allocating the risk may be positive or negative. The examples of a contractual allocation of risk referred to above are all positive: one party expressly or by implication of fact or law takes on a particular risk (as to the existence of goods, his title to them, their description or quality), and the party will be in breach of contract if the term is not fulfilled. However, the allocation of risk may also be negative: it is established in certain contexts that there is to be no implied undertaking by one party in favour of the other. In *William Sindall Plc v Cambridgeshire CC*[61] Hoffmann L.J., discussing the statement about the allocation of risk by Steyn J., quoted above, said: 15–18

> "When the judge speaks of the contract allocating risk 'by express or implied condition precedent or otherwise' I think he includes rules of general law applicable to the contract and which, for example, provide that, in the absence of express warranty, the law is caveat emptor. This would, in my view, allocate the risk of an unknown defect in goods to the buyer, even though it is not mentioned in the contract.[62] Similarly, the rule in *Hill v*

---

[61] [1994] 1 W.L.R. 1016 at 1035.

[62] [i.e. the implied condition of satisfactory quality in the Sale of Goods Act 1979, s.14(2), which allocates the risk to the business seller, is an exception to the normal rule, which places the risk on the buyer: *ibid.*, s.14(1). See also *Harrison & Jones Ltd v Bunten & Lancaster Ltd* [1953] 1 Q.B. 646 at 658 (Pilcher J.: "When goods, whether specific or unascertained, are sold under a known trade description without misrepresentation, innocent or guilty, and without breach of warranty, the fact that both parties are unaware that goods of that known trade description lack any particular quality is, in my view, completely irrelevant; the parties are bound by their contract, and there is no room for the doctrine that the contract can be treated as a nullity on the ground of mutual mistake, even though the mistake from the point of view of the purchaser may turn out to be of a fundamental character").]

Harris[63] that a lessor or vendor does not impliedly warrant that the premises are fit for any particular purpose means that the contract allocates the risk of the premises being unfit for such purpose."

Therefore, if the contract, either expressly or by implication of fact or law, provides either that there shall, or that there shall not, be a particular remedial consequence in the circumstances on which the claimant bases his claim for mistake, there is no place for the application of the principles of mistake. The risk of those circumstances has been allocated in the contract.

(2) The Common Law Rule: A Contract May be Void for Common Mistake

15–19 **The doctrine of mistake is a rule of law, not based on implied terms.** In the previous section we have seen that, if the contract allocates the risk of the so-called "mistake", the case does not raise an issue of mistake at all. If, however, there is no express or implied allocation of the risk in the contract, it is open for a party to claim that the contract is void for mistake. There have been some suggestions amongst writers[64] and judges[65] that the doctrine of

[63] [1965] 2 Q.B. 601.

[64] J.C. Smith, "Contracts—Mistake, Frustration and Implied Terms" (1994) 110 L.Q.R. 400 (a "formidable argument": Chitty, para.5–016). See also J. Swan, "The Allocation of Risk in the Analysis of Mistake and Frustration," in B.J. Reiter and J. Swan, *Studies in Contract Law* (Butterworth, Toronto, 1980), p.181; C. Slade, "The Myth of Mistake in the English Law of Contract" (1954) 70 L.Q.R. 385; K.O. Shatwell, "The Supposed Doctrine of Mistake in Contract: A Comedy of Errors" (1955) 33 Can. Bar. Rev. 164; P.S. Atiyah, "*Couturier v Hastie* and the Sale of Non-Existent Goods" (1957) 73 L.Q.R. 340.

[65] Some of the earlier cases, which are sometimes categorised as cases of mistake, were decided on the basis of construction of the contract. But these may be cases of contractual allocation of risk, which therefore excludes the operation of mistake; above, para.15–15. See, e.g. *McRae v Commonwealth Disposals Commission*, above, n.48 at 402–410, discussing *Couturier v Hastie*, above, n.54. In *Bell v Lever Bros Ltd* "implied condition" was used as one way of explaining the basis of a contract being avoided for mistake: [1931] 1 K.B. at 557 at 567 (Wright J.), 585 (Scrutton L.J.), 595–596 (Greer L.J. approving Salmond and Winfield's Law of Contract, 1927 edn, p.195); *cf.* [1932] A.C. 161 at 224–225 (Lord Atkin: "The proposition does not amount to more than this that, if the contract expressly or impliedly contains a term that a particular assumption is a condition of the contract, the contract is avoided if the assumption is not true. But we have not advanced far on the inquiry how to ascertain whether the contract

mistake is itself based on the terms of the contract: if the contract is void for "mistake", this is because it is an implied term in the contract that the contract is to be void in these circumstances, and so there is no room for a doctrine of mistake, independent of the construction of the contract. However, this approach has not been followed in the recent authorities; to base the doctrine of mistake on an implied term would be to base it on a fictitious "intention" of the parties. The doctrine is a rule of law[66]:

> "the theory of the implied term is as unrealistic when considering common mistake as when considering frustration. Where a fundamental assumption upon which an agreement is founded proves to be mistaken, it is not realistic to ask whether the parties impliedly agreed that in those circumstances the contract would not be binding. The avoidance of a contract on the ground of common mistake results from a rule of law under which, if it transpires that one or both of the parties have agreed to do something which it is impossible to perform, no obligation arises out of that agreement."

This does not, however, mean that the construction of the contract is irrelevant. Indeed, it is fundamental to the application of the test. Before one can decide whether the performance of the contract *as provided for in the contract* is possible, it is necessary to decide what exactly the contract provided. The circumstances as they turn out to be must then be measured against the contract, to determine whether it is "impossible" to perform[67]:

---

does contain such a condition"; and he proposed at 226–227 to use the same test for "implied conditions" as for "mutual [i.e. shared] mistakes").

[66] *The Great Peace* [2002] EWCA Civ 1407, [2003] Q.B. 679 at [73]. For frustration, *cf. Davis Contractors Ltd v Fareham Urban DC* [1956] A.C. 696, HL, at 715 (Viscount Simonds), 720 (Lord Reid), 728 (Lord Radcliffe: "This approach is in line with the tendency of English courts to refer all the consequences of a contract to the will of those who made it. But there is something of a logical difficulty in seeing how the parties could even impliedly have provided for something which ex hypothesi they neither expected nor foresaw"). See also J. Cartwright, "The rise and fall of mistake in the English law of contract", in R. Sefton-Green (ed.), *Mistake, Fraud and Duties to Inform in European Contract Law* (2005) at pp.73–76. For the doctrine in US law, see Restatement of Contracts (Second), para.152 (mistake must go to a "basic assumption" on which contract was made, have a material effect on agreed exchange of performances, and be not one of which the party seeking avoidance bears the risk); Farnsworth, para.9.3.

[67] *The Great Peace*, above, n.66 at [82]. See, however, at [84]: "Once the court determines that unforeseen circumstances have, indeed, resulted in the contract

"while we do not consider that the doctrine of common mistake can be satisfactorily explained by an implied term, an allegation that a contract is void for common mistake will often raise important issues of construction. Where it is possible to perform the letter of the contract, but it is alleged that there was a common mistake in relation to a fundamental assumption which renders performance of the essence of the obligation impossible, it will be necessary, by construing the contract in the light of all the material circumstances, to decide whether this is indeed the case."

15–20 **Three key cases.** The test which is to be applied to determine whether a contract is void for a common mistake about the subject-matter can be deduced from three key cases. At the centre is the decision of the House of Lords in *Bell v Lever Bros Ltd*[68] which is not easy to interpret, but contains a detailed examination of the law of mistake in the speech of Lord Atkin. In 1988 this whole area was reviewed by Steyn J. in *Associated Japanese Bank (International) Ltd v Crédit du Nord S.A.*,[69] and the test was re stated but in a form which sought to explain and apply the earlier decision in *Bell v Lever Bros Ltd*. The most recent exposition of the law is found in the decision of the Court of Appeal in *The Great Peace*,[70] which approved the test stated by Steyn J., restated it again in slightly different language, but at the same time sought to emphasise that the founding authority remains *Bell v Lever Bros Ltd*. We shall therefore consider these three decisions in turn.

15–21 ***Bell v Lever Brothers Ltd.*** The essential facts of *Bell v Lever Bros Ltd* were deceptively simple. Lever Bros Ltd had paid £30,000 and £20,000 respectively to two employees as severance payments when they became redundant. It later emerged that the employees had committed breaches of duty to the company that would have entitled the company to dismiss them without payment. The company claimed repayment of the money; and the case was

being impossible of performance, it is next necessary to determine whether, on true construction of the contract, one or other party has undertaken responsibility for the subsistence of the assumed state of affairs". This appears to reverse the order of the questions, and is not consistent with the order proposed by Steyn J. in *Associated Japanese Bank (International) Ltd v Crédit du Nord S.A*, above, para.15–15, which was approved by CA in *The Great Peace* at [80].

[68] [1932] A.C. 161.

[69] [1989] 1 W.L.R. 255.

[70] Above, n.66.

decided on the basis that there was a common mistake.[71] Wright J. and the Court of Appeal held that the severance contract was void; the House of Lords by a bare majority held that it was valid. However, this disagreement reflected more of a difference in the application of the principles of mistake to the facts of the case, than a difference in the underlying approach. The judges at every level agreed that a mistake about the subject-matter can render the contract void, but only if the mistake is of a particular degree of seriousness. Lord Atkin, whose speech has generally been relied upon in the later cases, made clear that, if there is no contractual provision to the contrary, a contract will be void where the subject-matter does not exist; or where, even though it does exist, it is so different in quality as to render it an essentially different thing from that which the parties both thought it to be[72]:

> "the agreement of A. and B. to purchase a specific article is void if in fact the article had perished before the date of sale. In this case, though the parties in fact were agreed about the subject-matter, yet a consent to transfer or take delivery of something not existent is deemed useless, the consent is nullified. As codified in the Sale of Goods Act[73] the contract is expressed to be void if the seller was in ignorance of the destruction of the specific chattel. I apprehend that if the seller with knowledge that a chattel was destroyed purported to sell it to a purchaser,[74] the latter might sue for damages for non-delivery though the former could not sue for non-acceptance, but I know of no case where a seller has so committed himself.... Corresponding to mistake as to the existence of the subject-matter is mistake as to title in cases where, unknown to the parties, the buyer is already the owner of that which the seller purports to sell to him. The parties intended to effectuate a transfer of ownership: such a

[71] The judgments refer to the mistake being "mutual", but this meant shared (i.e. common: above, para.12–06, n.23). The jury found that, at the time of the making of the agreement to terminate the employment contracts, the employees did not have the breaches of duty in mind: above, n.68 at 186. Claims based on fraud therefore failed. For discussion of the case, with a historical perspective, see C. MacMillan, *Mistakes in Contract Law* (2010), pp.257–278, who argues that it was the decision of the House of Lords in *Bell v Lever Bros Ltd* that effectively introduced the doctrine of mistake into English law.

[72] Above, n.68 at 217–218.

[73] [Sale of Goods Act 1893 (now 1979), s.6.]

[74] [i.e. there would then be a contractual allocation of risk: the seller would be in breach of the contract, having promised that the goods existed; *cf McRae v Commonwealth Disposals Commission* above, para.15–16.]

transfer is impossible: the stipulation is naturali ratione inutilis.[75] . .

Mistake as to quality of the thing contracted for raises more difficult questions. In such a case a mistake will not affect assent unless it is the mistake of both parties, and is as to the existence of some quality which makes the thing without the quality essentially[76] different from the thing as it was believed to be. Of course it may appear that the parties contracted that the article should possess the quality which one or other or both mistakenly believed it to possess. But in such a case there is a contract and the inquiry is a different one, being whether the contract as to quality amounts to a condition or a warranty, a different branch of the law."

The difficulty in applying this to the facts of the case was that the mistake was not about the existence of the subject-matter (there was an employment contract to terminate) but about its quality (it was a contract that could have been terminated without payment). In the view of the majority of the House, on the facts it was not sufficiently serious mistake.[77]

---

[75] [*Cooper v Phibbs* (1867) L.R. 2 H.L. 149. But the risk as to title will normally be borne by the vendor: above, para.15–16; *cf.* Lord Atkin in *Bell v Lever Bros Ltd*, above, n.68 at 218: "even where the vendor has no title, though both parties think he has, the correct view would appear to be that there is a contract: but that the vendor has either committed a breach of a stipulation as to title, or is not able to perform his contract. The contract is unenforceable by him but is not void".]

[76] [Lord Atkin drew his principles from two cases which were "authoritative expositions of the law": above, n.68 at 218–219; one was *Smith v Hughes* (1871) L.R. 6 Q.B. 597 (which is authority for the proposition that a unilateral mistake of quality is insufficient: above, para.15–10); the other was *Kennedy v The Panama, New Zealand and Australian Royal Mail Co. Ltd* (1867) L.R. 2 Q.B. 580, in which Blackburn J. said "where there has been an innocent misrepresentation or misapprehension, it does not authorize a rescission unless it is such as to show that there is a complete difference in substance between what was supposed to be and what was taken, so as to constitute a failure of consideration". *Cf.* in the lower courts in *Bell v Lever Bros Ltd* [1931] 1 K.B. 557 at 568 (Wright J.: "the mistake or misapprehension here is as to the substance of the whole consideration, and goes 'to the root of the whole matter,' in the words of the Court in Kennedy's case"); 597 (Greer L.J.: "I think the evidence and the findings of the jury in the present case, to use Lord Blackburn's words, establish 'that there was a complete difference in substance between what was supposed to be and what was taken, so as to constitute a failure of consideration"). Other descriptions of the test were the "foundation" of the contract, a "fundamental reason for making it" (Scrutton L.J. at 585, 586); the "fundamental character of the subject matter" (Greer L.J. at 595); "an essential and integral element of the subject-matter" (Lord Thankerton, [1932] A.C. 161 at 235).

[77] The difference of opinion appears to have been over what the parties regarded as the essential quality of the subject-matter. The lower courts and the minority in

Associated Japanese Bank v Crédit du Nord. In *Associated Japanese Bank (International) Ltd v Crédit du Nord S.A.*[78] Steyn J. undertook a detailed review of the law of mistake in contract. He emphasised that the first question is whether the contract expressly or impliedly allocated the risk of the "mistake" to one of the parties, and his decision in the case was based on the finding that the contract did in fact allocate the risk.[79] But he also summarised the approach of the common law to mistake, in five propositions[80]: 15–22

> "The first imperative must be that the law ought to uphold rather than destroy apparent contracts. Secondly, the common law rules as to a mistake regarding the quality of the subject matter, like the common law rules regarding commercial frustration, are designed to cope with the impact of unexpected and wholly exceptional circumstances on apparent contracts. Thirdly, such a mistake in order to attract legal consequences must substantially be shared by both parties, and must relate to facts as they existed at the time the contract was made. Fourthly, and this is the point

---

the House of Lords treated the question as whether there was a *valid and fully binding contract of employment* (there was not, since it could be terminated because of the employee's breach); the majority in the House treated it as whether there was *a contract of employment* (there was). The fact that it was terminable without payment, rather than terminable only on payment, did not make it of an essentially different kind: "on the whole, I have come to the conclusion that it would be wrong to decide that an agreement to terminate a definite specified contract is void if it turns out that the agreement had already been broken and could have been terminated otherwise. The contract released is the identical contract in both cases, and the party paying for release gets exactly what he bargains for. It seems immaterial that he could have got the same result in another way, or that if he had known the true facts he would not have entered into the bargain" ([1932] A.C. 161 at 223–224; Lord Atkin). See also Lord Wright, *Legal Essays and Addresses* (1939), pp.260–262 (as Wright J., he had tried the case at first instance); and *Associated Japanese Bank (International) Ltd v Crédit du Nord S.A.*, below, n.78 at 267 (Steyn J.: "there are indications in the speeches that the so-called 'merits' were not all in favour of Lever Brothers. The company was most anxious, because of a corporate merger, to terminate the two service agreements. There was apparently a doubt as to whether the voidability of the service agreements if revealed to the company at the time of the severance contract would have affected the company's decision").

78 [1989] 1 W.L.R. 255.

79 Above, paras 15–15, 15–16, n.47.

80 Above, n.78 at 268 (the propositions "are valid although not necessarily all entitled to be dignified as propositions of law"). This passage was quoted in full by CA in *The Great Peace* [2002] EWCA Civ 1407, [2003] Q.B. 679 at [90], and approved at [91] "subject to the proviso that the result in *McRae's* case can, we believe, be explained on the basis of construction".

> established by *Bell v Lever Brothers Ltd*, the mistake must render the subject matter of the contract essentially and radically different from the subject matter which the parties believed to exist. While the civilian distinction between the substance and attributes of the subject matter of a contract has played a role in the development of our law (and was cited in speeches in *Bell v Lever Brothers Ltd*), the principle enunciated in *Bell v Lever Brothers Ltd* is markedly narrower in scope than the civilian doctrine. It is therefore no longer useful to invoke the civilian distinction. The principles enunciated by Lord Atkin and Lord Thankerton represent the ratio decidendi of *Bell v Lever Brothers Ltd.* Fifthly, there is a requirement which was not specifically discussed in *Bell v Lever Brothers Ltd*. What happens if the party, who is seeking to rely on the mistake, had no reasonable grounds for his belief? An extreme example is that of the man who makes a contract with minimal knowledge of the facts to which the mistake relates but is content that it is a good speculative risk. In my judgment a party cannot be allowed to rely on a common mistake where the mistake consists of a belief which is entertained by him without any reasonable grounds for such belief: *cf. McRae v Commonwealth Disposals Commission*.[81] That is not because principles such as estoppel or negligence require it, but simply because policy and good sense dictate that the positive rules regarding common mistake should be so qualified."

The key points here are that a mistake can render a contract void at common law if the mistake is a *shared* mistake of *fact*[82]; and if it renders "the subject matter of the contract *essentially and radically different* from the subject matter which the parties believed to exist". These propositions are all consistent with Lord Atkin's statement of the law in *Bell v Lever Bros Ltd* which, indeed, is the authoritative source to which Steyn J. attributed his own statement.[83] The fifth proposition, however, was new in the English cases: "a party cannot be allowed to rely on a common mistake where the mistake consists of a belief which is entertained by him without any reasonable grounds for such belief". Steyn J. drew this

[81] Above, n.48 at 408.

[82] Mistake of law is now included: below, para.15–24.

[83] Lord Atkin said the mistake must make the thing "essentially" different from the thing as it was believed to be. The language of "radical" difference comes not from the mistake cases, but from frustration: *Davis Contractors Ltd v Fareham Urban DC*, above, n.66 at 729 (Lord Radcliffe: "frustration occurs whenever the law recognizes that without default of either party a contractual obligation has become incapable of being performed because the circumstances in which performance is called for would render it a thing radically different from that which was undertaken by the contract"). Steyn J. recognised the links between mistake and frustration: [1989] 1 W.L.R. 255 at 264–265.

from *McRae v Commonwealth Disposals Commission*,[84] and it should be noted that it is a significant limitation on the doctrine of mistake. Under the common law, a contract is void for certain serious mistakes, as long as both parties shared the mistake. In principle, therefore, either party can take the point that the contract is void. However, a party will not be allowed to do so if he was himself unreasonable in making the mistake. This furthers the general policy of English law, which is reluctant to allow a party to use his own mistake in order to avoid an apparent contract. Even if he did in fact make a sufficient mistake about the subject-matter, and the other party shared it, he cannot be allowed to base his claim on the mistake if he had no reasonable grounds for making it—in effect, if he was negligent. The other party (if he did have reasonable grounds) may be able to assert that the contract is void; but not the negligent party.[85]

If he had not found that the contract allocated the risk of the mistake, Steyn J. would have held that the contract was void for mistake at common law. The contract was to guarantee the lessee's obligations under the sale and lease-back of machines which did not in fact exist. Steyn J. said[86]:

> "For both parties the guarantee of obligations under a lease with non-existent machines was essentially different from a guarantee of a lease with four machines which both parties at the time of the contract believed to exist. The guarantee is an accessory contract. The non-existence of the subject matter of the principal contract is therefore of fundamental

[84] Steyn J.'s proposition goes further, however, than was justified by the judgment in *McRae v Commonwealth Disposals Commission* from which he drew it. Dixon and Fullager JJ. said ((1951) 84 C.L.R. 377 at 408): "a party cannot rely on mutual mistake where the mistake consists of a belief which is, on the one hand, entertained by him without any reasonable ground, *and, on the other hand, deliberately induced by him in the mind of the other party*" (emphasis added); that is, that a party is at fault not only in making the mistake, but also in causing the other party to make it. This, in effect, would prevent a party from relying on the mistake when it was caused by his own misrepresentation: above, para.15–08.

[85] This is not saying that the contract is voidable, rather than void; simply that the party to a (void) contract cannot take the point that it is void. *Cf.* the rule that a party may not rely on his own mistake for the purposes of the plea of *non est factum* (even if the mistake fulfils other requirements of the plea) if he was negligent: above, para.13–60.

[86] [1989] 1 W.L.R. 255 at 269.

importance. Indeed the analogy of the classic res extincta cases,[87] so much discussed in the authorities, is fairly close. In my judgment the stringent test of common law mistake is satisfied: the guarantee is void ab initio."

15–23 ***The Great Peace.*** The whole area was reviewed by the Court of Appeal in *The Great Peace*.[88] The defendants agreed to provide salvage services for a vessel, the Cape Providence, which had suffered serious structural damage in the South Indian Ocean. The only available tug would take five or six days to reach the Cape Providence, and since there was a serious concern that the vessel might go down with the loss of her crew the defendants contracted to charter from the claimants a merchant vessel, the Great Peace, in order to escort and stand-by the Cape Providence for the purpose of saving life. The charter was for a minimum of five days, at an agreed daily rate. At the time they made this contract, the defendants thought that the Great Peace was 35 miles away and so could be at the scene within a very short time. In fact, however, the vessels were 410 miles apart. The defendants discovered this within two hours of the contract being concluded, but after the master of the Great Peace had already been instructed to change course towards the Cape Providence. Within two further hours the defendants succeeded in finding a nearer alternative vessel, and cancelled the charter of the Great Peace. They resisted payment under the contract on the basis, inter alia, that the contract was concluded under a mistake about the position of the Great Peace, and was therefore void. Toulson J.[89] and the Court of Appeal rejected this.

Lord Phillips M.R., giving the judgment of the Court of Appeal, reviewed the doctrine of mistake as expounded (by, principally,

[87] [Below, para.15–26.]

[88] *Great Peace Shipping Ltd v Tsavliris Salvage (International) Ltd (The Great Peace)* [2002] EWCA Civ 1407, [2003] Q.B. 679.

[89] [2001] All E.R. (D) 152 (Nov).

Lord Atkin) in *Bell v Lever Bros Ltd*,[90] and preferred to state the test in terms of whether the contract is "impossible" to perform[91]:

> "The avoidance of a contract on the ground of common mistake results from a rule of law under which, if it transpires that one or both of the parties have agreed to do something which it is impossible to perform, no obligation arises out of that agreement."

This is not limited to literal, physical impossibility, although such cases—for example, a contract where, unknown to the parties, the subject-matter no longer exists[92]—will clearly fall within the test. But it extends to cases where the "contractual adventure" is impossible: that is, where the contractual purpose cannot be fulfilled.[93] The court stated the test in this way[94]:

> "the following elements must be present if common mistake is to avoid a contract: (i) there must be a common assumption as to the existence of a state of affairs; (ii) there must be no warranty by either party that that state of affairs exists; (iii) the non-existence of the state of affairs must not be

---

90 Above, para.15–21. Lord Phillips thought at [61] that "the two authorities to which Lord Atkin referred [*Smith v Hughes* (1871) L.R. 6 Q.B. 597 and *Kennedy v The Panama, New Zealand and Australian Royal Mail Co. Ltd* (1867) L.R. 2 Q.B. 580] provided an insubstantial basis for his formulation of the test of common mistake in relation to the quality of the subject matter of a contract", and preferred to follow Lord Atkin's "alternative basis for his test: the implication of a term of the same nature as that which was applied under the doctrine of frustration, as it was then understood". See, however, above, para.15–10, n.30; para.15–21, n.76.

91 Above, n.88, at [73].

92 Below, para.15–26.

93 Above, n.88 at [74] (the "contractual adventure"); [82] ("Where it is possible to perform the letter of the contract, but it is alleged that there was a common mistake in relation to a fundamental assumption which renders performance of the essence of the obligation impossible"). The language of the "contractual purpose" is taken from the judgment of Toulson J., above, n.89 at [163], quoted by Lord Phillips M.R. in CA at [163].

94 *ibid.*, at [76], applying to common mistake a statement made in relation to frustration by Lord Alverstone C.J. in *Blakeley v Muller & Co.* (1903) 19 T.L.R. 186. This test was used in *Standard Chartered Bank v Banque Marocaine du Commerce Extérieur* [2006] EWHC 413 (Comm), [2006] All E.R. (D) 213 (Feb) at [26]–[27]; *Apvodedo NV v Collins* [2008] EWHC 775 (Ch), [2008] All E.R. (D) 246 (Apr) at [43]; *Perpetual Trustee Co. Ltd v BNY Corporate Trustee Services Ltd* [2009] EWCA Civ 1160, [2010] Ch. 347 at [109]; *Acre 1127 Ltd v De Montfort Fine Art Ltd* [2011] EWCA Civ 87, [2011] All E.R. (D) 111 (Feb) at [38].

> attributable to the fault of either party; (iv) the non-existence of the state of affairs must render performance of the contract impossible; (v) the state of affairs may be the existence, or a vital attribute, of the consideration to be provided or circumstances which must subsist if performance of the contractual adventure is to be possible."

This is consistent with the approaches of both the House of Lords in *Bell v Lever Bros Ltd*, and Steyn J. in *Associated Japanese Bank (International) Ltd v Crédit du Nord S.A.*[95] In particular, the court approved two points which were emphasised by Steyn J.: that the first question is whether there has been a contractual allocation of the risk of the facts or circumstances which are alleged to constitute the "mistake"[96]; and that, even if there is a sufficient common mistake, it cannot be relied upon, as avoiding the contract, by a party who induced the mistake by his own fault.[97] Indeed, it appears that the the "impossible to perform" test, and Steyn J's test which asks whether the mistake renders the subject matter of the contract "*essentially and radically different* from the subject matter which the parties believed to exist", amount to much the same thing[98] and, depending on the context, one other test may be more appropriate as the formulation to be applied to determine whether a mistake is sufficient to render a contract void.[99]

---

[95] The court quoted and approved Steyn J.'s test: above, para.15–22.

[96] Above, n.88 at [80], and point (ii) in their general test, above ("there must be no warranty by either party that that state of affairs exists").

[97] *ibid.*, at [79]–[80], referring to *McRae v Commonwealth Disposals Commission*, above, n.48 and point (iii) in their general test above ("the non-existence of the state of affairs must not be attributable to the fault of either party"). Note, however, that the statement by the Court of Appeal is consistent with the narrower statement of the claimant's "fault" in *McRae*, rather than the wider statement by Steyn J. in *Associated Japanese Bank (International) Ltd v Crédit du Nord S.A.*; above, para.15–22, n.84, although the Court of Appeal at [90]–[91] did also approve Steyn J.'s test. The limits of this element therefore remain unclear.

[98] *Kyle Bay (trading as Astons Nightclub) v Underwriters Subscribing Under Policy 019057/08/01* [2007] EWCA Civ 57, [2007] 1 C.L.C. 164 at [24]–[25] (Neuberger L.J.).

[99] *ibid.*, at [25] (settlement of claim under insurance policy under common mistake relating to the terms on which the policy was written); *Brennan v Bolt Burdon* [2004] EWCA Civ 1017, [2005] Q.B. 303 at [22], [59] (common mistake of law in entering into compromise agreement); below, para.15–24. Steyn J.'s test was used (but not satisfied) in *British Nuclear Group Sellafield Ltd v Kernkraftwerk Brokdorf G.m.b.H. & Co. o.Hg.* [2007] EWHC 2245 (Ch), [2007] All E.R. (D) 229 (Oct) at [300]–[307].

In *The Great Peace* the court decided that there was no sufficient common mistake on the facts to render the contract void. Although it was a common assumption by both parties when the contract was concluded that the two vessels were in sufficiently close proximity to enable the Great Peace to carry out the service that she was engaged to perform, the distance between the two vessels was not so great as to confound that assumption and to render the contractual adventure impossible of performance.[100]

Mistake of fact or law. Until recently the cases have spoken in terms which required a common mistake *of fact* which bears upon the subject-matter of the contract. This reflected the view that for most purposes, including the law of mistake in contract, the law would not take into account mistakes of law. Mistake about "fact" was extended to cover mistake about "private rights", such as the question of ownership of property, but mistakes as to the "general law" were not included.[101] 15–24

However, the rejection of the "mistake of law" rule by the House of Lords in the context of the law of restitution[102] acted as a general trigger for the reconsideration of the rule in contract.[103] In *Brennan*

---

100 *ibid.*, at [162]–[165], following the decision of Toulson J., above, n.89 at [56]. It was significant, on the facts, that the defendants had not cancelled the contract immediately when they discovered the true location of the *Great Peace*, and had waited until they found a nearer vessel to assist. "This reaction was a telling indication that the fact that the vessels were considerably further apart than the defendants had believed did not mean that the services that the *Great Peace* was in a position to provide were essentially different from those which the parties had envisaged when the contract was concluded.... The fact that the vessels were further apart than both parties had appreciated did not mean that it was impossible to perform the contractual adventure" (Lord Phillips at [165]).

101 *Cooper v Phibbs* (1867) L.R. 2 H.L. 149 at 170 (Lord Westbury: "It is said, '*Ignorantia juris haud excusat*'; but in that maxim the word '*jus*' is used in the sense of denoting general law, the ordinary law of the country. But when the word '*jus*' is used in the sense of denoting a private right, that maxim has no application. Private right of ownership is a matter of fact; it may be the result also of matter of law; but if parties contract under a mutual mistake and misapprehension as to their relative and respective rights, the result is, that that agreement is liable to be set aside as having proceeded upon a common mistake"); see also above, para.3–25.

102 *Kleinwort Benson Ltd v Lincoln City Council* [1999] 2 A.C. 349; above, para.3–34.

103 Above, para.3–37 (abandonment of *misrepresentation* of law rule).

v Bolt Burdon[104] Morland J. held that a compromise agreement, entered into between litigants on the mistaken assumption that the claim could not proceed because the claim form had not been served in time, could be set aside on the basis of a common mistake about the law. The mistake arose because the parties, in making their compromise agreement, were acting on the basis of case-law authority on the meaning of the Civil Procedure Rules which was later overruled, thereby showing that, at the time when they concluded their agreement, the law had been wrongly stated in the then-existing case law, and therefore wrongly assumed by the parties.[105] However, the decision was reversed by the Court of Appeal.[106] The Court of Appeal affirmed the general proposition that there is no longer a formal distinction between mistakes of law and mistakes of fact within the law of contract[107]; and therefore approached the case on the basis that the common law rule relating to mistake about the subject-matter can now include a common mistake of law, as long as it satisfies the other requirements of the common law test. However, it was held that, on the facts, the case did not involve a mistake of law but a state of doubt about what the law was, and so the parties had contracted their compromise on the basis of this risk.[108]

The case illustrates the difficulty, however, in applying the common law test of common mistake to a mistake of law. Given that a mistake is sufficient to render the contract void only if it makes the performance of the contract, or its purpose, *impossible*,[109] the only situation in which one can say with any confidence that this can apply in the case of a mistake of law is in the very narrow situation where performance of the contract is itself

[104] [2003] EWHC 2493, [2004] 1 W.L.R. 1240.

[105] This follows from the decision in *Kleinwort Benson Ltd v Lincoln City Council*, above, n.102, that a judicial change of a rule of law has a retrospective effect: above, para.3–10.

[106] [2004] EWCA Civ 1017, [2005] Q.B. 303.

[107] *ibid.*, at [10], [26].

[108] The facts of the case were quite particular: the claim had been struck out by the trial judge, on the basis that the it had not been served within time within the meaning of the CPR, as interpreted by another first instance decision. That other decision was being appealed, and was in due course reversed by the CA but the parties had by then compromised their own claim, the claimant having taken no steps either to inquire about any appeal in the other case, or to challenge the interpretation of the CPR by an appeal in her own case.

[109] Above, para.15–23.

illegal.[110] The contract of compromise, however, presents a particular difficulty to the party who seek to challenge it on the basis of a mistake of law, and in particular the kind of mistake of law that was in issue in *Brennan v Bolt Burdon* (a retrospective change by a later judicial decision). Apart from the general policy of the law in favour of finality of compromise agreements,[111] the essence of a compromise is that each party normally takes a risk that the law may change.[112] Moreover, in any case—and not only a compromise agreement—where the mistake is said to have been revealed by a later judicial change in the law, it will be arguable that this was an inherent risk undertaken by each of the parties. As we have seen, the first question in all claims based on common mistake is whether there was an express or implied allocation of the risk of the mistake; and the parties who rely on their interpretation of the current law should always be aware of the fact that any judicial decision is capable of being reassessed. This form of change of law is an inherent risk in the operation of our legal system[113]; and in this respect law is fundamentally different from fact (which cannot be changed retrospectively by any later event or action).[114]

Summary of the common law approach to mistake about the subject-matter. These three cases, together with the other authorities on which they relied and from which they drew their 15–25

[110] [2004] EWCA Civ 1017, [2005] Q.B. 303 at [58]–[59] (Sedley L.J.). See also at [22] (Maurice Kay L.J.). Sedley L.J. suggested at [60] that "a different test may be necessary. The equivalent question needs to be whether, had the parties appreciated that the law was what it is now known to be, there would still have been an intelligible basis for their agreement". See also *Kyle Bay (trading as Astons Nightclub) v Underwriters Subscribing Under Policy 019057/08/01* [2007] EWCA Civ 57, [2007] 1 C.L.C. 164 at [24]–[25] (Neuberger L.J.), above, text to nn.98, 99.

[111] *ibid.*, at [22]; below, para.17–27 (no general duty of disclosure between parties negotiating a compromise).

[112] *ibid.*, at [22], [39].

[113] As shown by *Kleinwort Benson Ltd v Lincoln City Council*, above, n.102.

[114] "This is not to reintroduce the distinction between mistake of fact and mistake of law. It is to require that, where a party wishes to reserve his rights in the event of subsequent judicial decision in a future case to which he is not a party, it is he who should seek and secure a term to that effect, not his opponent who should have to stipulate for protection notwithstanding the possibility of such a subsequent decision": *Brennan v Bolt Burdon*, above, n.106 at [22] (Maurice Kay L.J.).

statements of principle, show a consistent approach taken by the common law to a claim based on mistake about the subject-matter. Where there is a mistake about the circumstances surrounding the formation of a contract, which has an impact on the subject-matter of the contract, it may render the contract void,[115] but only if the contract has not itself made any allocation of the risk of the relevant circumstances; and only if the mistake was shared by the parties, and was of a sufficient degree of seriousness to render the performance of the contract impossible, or essentially different from that which the parties had both contemplated at the time when the agreement was concluded. And a party may not assert that the contract is void if he was himself at fault in having caused the other party to make the mistake.[116]

15–26 **Examples of mistakes that may be sufficient to render a contract void.** It is clear that the test for common mistake at common law will not easily be satisfied. Almost all the cases in which courts have found that the contract has been void have been cases where performance of the contract is literally, physically impossible; and typically where, unknown to the parties and without the fault of either of them, the subject-matter of the contract no longer existed at the time when the contract was concluded.[117] It is always important to ask first whether the contract expressly or

[115] On several occasions Lord Denning said that the proper interpretation of *Bell v Lever Bros Ltd* was that a common mistake, even on a most fundamental matter, does not make a contract void at law: see *Solle v Butcher* [1950] 1 K.B. 671, CA at 691; *Leaf v International Galleries* [1950] 2 K.B. 86, CA, at 89; *Frederick E. Rose (London) Ltd v William H. Pim Jnr & Co. Ltd* [1953] 2 Q.B. 450, CA, at 460; *Oscar Chess Ltd v Williams* [1957] 1 W.L.R. 370, CA, at 373–374; *Magee v Pennine Insurance Co. Ltd* [1969] 2 Q.B. 507, CA, at 514. This was however rejected by both Steyn J. in *Associated Japanese Bank (International) Ltd v Crédit du Nord S.A.* [1989] 1 W.L.R. 255 at 267 ("With the profoundest respect to the former Master of the Rolls I am constrained to say that in my view his interpretation of *Bell v Lever Bros Ltd* does not do justice to the speeches of the majority") and CA in *The Great Peace* [2002] EWCA Civ 1407, [2003] Q.B. 679 at [92] ("We share both the respect and the conclusion"). For further discussion of Lord Denning's approach to mistake, see below, paras 15–30 to 15–34.

[116] Or, perhaps, simply in having unreasonably made the mistake himself: above, paras 15–22, n.84; 15–23, n.97.

[117] Commonly referred to as the "*res extincta*" cases.

impliedly allocates the risk of the non-existence of the subject-matter; but, if it does not, it is relatively easy then to conclude that the contract is void[118]:

> "the agreement of A. and B. to purchase a specific article is void if in fact the article had perished before the date of sale. In this case, though the parties in fact were agreed about the subject-matter, yet a consent to transfer or take delivery of something not existent is deemed useless, the consent is nullified."

By analogy with cases where the subject-matter did not exist, it has been said that a contract for the transfer or property could be void where the transferor does not have the property rights[119]:

[118] *Bell v Lever Bros Ltd* [1932] A.C. 161, HL, at 217 (Lord Atkin). Cases in which this principle is said to have been the basis of the decision (although the reasoning of some of the older cases is not always clear) include *Couturier v Hastie* (1856) 5 H.L.C. 673, 10 E.R. 1065 (sale of a cargo of corn which, unknown to the parties, had already been sold and so no longer existed at the time that the contract was concluded; but this may be better categorised as a contractual allocation of risk: *McRae v Commonwealth Disposals Commission*, above, para.15–16, n.48 at 402–410); *Strickland v Turner* (1852) 7 Exch. 208, 155 E.R. 919 (sale of an annuity on the life of a person who, unknown to the parties, had already died); *Pritchard v Merchant's and Tradesman's Mutual Life Assurance Society* (1858) 3 C.B.N.S. 622, 140 E.R. 885 (life insurance policy renewed in ignorance of the fact that the insured had died); *Galloway v Galloway* (1914) 30 T.L.R. 531 (deed of separation between parties who wrongly believed that they were lawfully married). Lord Atkin said that this principle was codified by the Sale of Goods Act 1893 (now 1979), s.6 ("When there is a contract for the sale of specific goods, and the goods without the knowledge of the seller have perished at the time when the contract is made, the contract is void"); see also *The Great Peace*, above, n.115 at [51]–[53] (Chalmers, who drafted the Sale of Goods Act, cited *Couturier v Hastie, Strickland v Turner* and *Pritchard v Merchant's and Tradesman's Mutual Life Assurance Society* in connection with s.6). In *Associated Japanese Bank International) Ltd v Crédit du Nord S.A.*, above, n.115 at 269, above, para.15–22, Steyn J. would have held the contract void at common law on the "fairly close" analogy of the cases of non-existent subject-matter, if there had not been a contractual risk allocation.

[119] *Bell v Lever Bros Ltd*, above, n.118 at 218 (Lord Atkin); *Cooper v Phibbs*, above, n.101 (which was a decision in equity, but in which the contract was void at common law: *Bell v Lever Bros Ltd* at 218 (Lord Atkin); *Norwich Union Fire Insurance Society Ltd v WMH Price Ltd* [1934] A.C. 455, PC, at 463 (Lord Wright); *The Great Peace* above, n.115 at [118], [126]–[129]. *Cf.*, however, the explanation of *Cooper v Phibbs* by P. Matthews at (1989) 105 L.Q.R. 599: the contract was valid at law, but impugned in equity on the basis that the appellant was beneficially, though not legally, entitled to the property of which he had

> "The parties intended to effectuate a transfer of ownership: such a transfer is impossible: the stipulation is naturali ratione inutilis."

Similarly, it has been held that the contract is void where the parties have contracted for performance which is physically impossible[120]; or impossible as a matter of law[121]; and even where the contract does not in its terms require performance which is impossible, but where the purpose of the contract, as the parties both intended it, is in fact impossible to fulfil.[122]

More difficult, however, are cases where the mistake relates not to the existence of the subject-matter, but to its qualities. This is the point over which debate about the decision in *Bell v Lever Bros Ltd* has centred but, as we have seen, the House of Lords there accepted that such a mistake *can* be sufficient to render a contract void, but

---

agreed to take a lease). In practice, however, such a mistake will rarely render the contract void, since the vendor will normally guarantee his title, either expressly or impliedly, in the contract: above, para.15–16.

[120] *Sheikh Bros Ltd v Ochsner* [1957] A.C. 136, PC (contract to cut and process sisal, with undertaking to manufacture in quantities which the land was in fact incapable of producing; held void under the Indian Contract Act, 1872, s.20: "Where both the parties to an agreement are under a mistake as to a matter of fact essential to the agreement, the agreement is void"; Lord Cohen at 147 rejected counsel's argument that this was insufficient under *Bell v Lever Bros Ltd*: "it was the very basis of the contract that the sisal area should be capable of producing an average of 50 tons a month throughout the term of the licence. It follows that the mistake was as to a matter of fact essential to the agreement"). See also *Re Cleveland Trust* [1991] B.C.C. 33 at 42–44 (issue of bonus shares by company in favour of shareholder is analogous to contract, and issue was void for common mistake under *Bell v Lever Bros Ltd*, above, n.118, where capital profits could not be used in paying up the bonus shares), followed in *EIC Services Ltd v Phipps* [2004] EWCA Civ 1069, [2005] 1 W.L.R. 1377 at [30].

[121] *Nutt v Read* (2000) 32 H.L.R. 761, CA (Chadwick L.J.: "The parties to that agreement thought that the chalet was capable of being sold separately from the land. That was a mistake so fundamental that it led, necessarily, to a conclusion that that agreement was void". The mistake was characterised as one of fact: that the chalet was a chattel, whereas the trial judge held that it was annexed to the land).

[122] *Griffith v Brymer* (1903) 19 T.L.R. 434 (contract to hire room with a view of the coronation procession, when decision had already been reached to operate on the King, which rendered the procession impossible); *Apvodedo NV v Collins* [2008] EWHC 775 (Ch), [2008] All E.R. (D) 246 (Apr) (summary judgment refused because arguable that exclusivity agreement for funding and sub-sale of Ritz Hotel was void for common mistake where agreement was predicated on both parties' assumption that they were dealing with the real vendor of the property rather than with fraudsters).

only if the mistake renders the subject-matter "essentially" different—to the point where the contractual "adventure", or purpose, is not possible. There are few decisions which can point to facts where the test might be satisfied, but it may be sufficient if the effect of the mistake is to give the subject-matter a different identity in commercial terms.[123]

Examples of mistakes that are not sufficient to render a contract void. It is much easier to give examples of the kinds of mistake that will not be sufficient to satisfy the common law test. Indeed, Lord Atkin's speech in *Bell v Lever Bros Ltd*[124] contained a passage in which he gave by way of illustration situations involving mistakes about the quality of the subject-matter which would not render the contract void, including some illustrations of common mistakes: the contract for the sale of a picture, believed by both parties to be the work of an old master, which turns out to be a modern copy[125]; the lease of an unfurnished dwelling-house which 15–27

[123] Lord Atkin stated as one formulation of his test ([1932] A.C. 161 at 227): "Does the state of the new facts destroy the identity of the subject-matter as it was in the original state of facts?" See *Nicholson & Venn v Smith-Marriott* (1947) 177 L.T. 189 (sale of table linen at auction, described as the "authentic property" of Charles I, but in fact Georgian. Held, breach of condition as to description; but (obiter) "Using the language of Lord Atkin, I am disposed to the view that a Georgian relic, if there be such a thing . . . is an 'essentially different' thing from a Carolean relic . . . I should be disposed therefore, though recognising the great difficulties of the point and without any undue confidence in the correctness of any judgment, to hold if necessary that here there was a mutual mistake of the kind or category calculated to vitiate the assent of the parties": Hallett J. at 192); *Sherwood v Walker* (1887) 33 N.W. 919, Sup. Ct. Michigan (sale of cow, believed by both parties to be barren but in fact in calf: "the mistake affected the substance of the whole consideration, and it must be considered that there was no contract to sell the cow as she actually was. The thing sold and bought had in fact no existence. She was sold as a beef creature; she is in fact a breeding cow": Morse J.), discussed Farnsworth, para.9.3. These are the most marginal cases. *Cf. Diamond v British Columbia Thoroughbred Breeders' Society* (1965) 52 D.L.R. (2d) 146, Sup. Ct. British Columbia (mistake as to lineage of racehorse not sufficient: "the 'identity of the subject matter' of the contract, a race horse, was not 'destroyed' by the mistake. Notwithstanding the common mistake as to lineage, the plaintiff acquired a race horse": Aikins J. at [51]).

[124] Above, n.118 at 224, quoted above at para.15–04.

[125] *cf. Leaf v International Galleries*, above, n.115 (argued on the basis of misrepresentation, not mistake; and rescission was barred for lapse of time; see above, paras 4–48 to 4–49).

is uninhabitable.[126] The mere fact that the subject-matter is of a bad, rather than a good quality will not suffice[127]; nor will a mistake be within the scope of the test simply because it has an impact[128]—even a devastating impact—on the value of the subject-matter.[129]

15–28 **The paucity of cases on common mistake.** It is notable that there are relatively few reported cases on common mistake. There are two related explanations for this.

First, although parties may well make common mistakes, the contract will itself very often provide for the risk to be borne by one

---

[126] This example was, no doubt, chosen because at common law the contract for an *unfurnished* dwelling-house does not contain an implied term about its condition: *Robbins v Jones* (1863) 15 C.B.N.S. 221 at 240, 143 E.R. 768 at 776 (Erle C.J.: "fraud apart, there is no law against letting a tumble-down house; and the tenant's remedy is upon his contract, if any); *Cavalier v Pope* [1906] A.C. 428, HL; E.H. Burn and J. Cartwright, *Cheshire and Burn's Modern Law of Real Property* (18th edn, 2011), p.227.

[127] e.g. a horse wrongly believed to be sound: *Bell v Lever Bros Ltd*, above, n.118 at 224 (Lord Atkin; given only as an example based on the buyer's mistake, but a common mistake would have the same result: *Kennedy v The Panama, New Zealand and Australian Royal Mail Co. Ltd* (1867) L.R. 2 Q.B. 580 at 587). The quality of goods is normally within the buyer's implied risk: caveat emptor; above, para.15–17.

[128] *Kennedy v The Panama, New Zealand and Australian Royal Mail Co. Ltd*, above, n.127 (sale of shares: company did not in fact have lucrative contract, so shares were worth less: "there was a misapprehension as to that which was a material part of the motive inducing the applicant to ask for the shares, but not preventing the shares from being in substance those he applied for": Blackburn J. at 589). See also *Kyle Bay (trading as Astons Nightclub) v Underwriters Subscribing Under Policy 019057/08/01* [2007] EWCA Civ 57, [2007] 1 C.L.C. 164 (settlement of claim under policy not void for mistake relating to the terms on which the policy was written: "what was wrongly assumed was a detail, albeit a significant detail, of the basis on which the Policy was written: it did not go to the validity of the Policy, the parties, the property or nature of the business, or even the nature of the risks covered. In addition, if it is appropriate to look at the matter in commercial terms (as I believe it is in this case at any rate), although the claimant received some 33% less than it should have done, which is a significant, even a substantial, reduction on its entitlement, I do not think it can fairly be characterised as an 'essentially or radically' different sum from its entitlement": Neuberger L.J. at [27]).

[129] In *Bell v Lever Bros Ltd* itself, it was not sufficient that £50,000 was paid to achieve an object (the termination of the employment contracts) that could have been obtained without payment.

or other party. This point was made by Lord Phillips in *The Great Peace*, drawing a comparison between mistake and frustration[130]:

> "Circumstances where a contract is void as a result of common mistake are likely to be less common than instances of frustration. Supervening events which defeat the contractual adventure will frequently not be the responsibility of either party. Where, however, the parties agree that something shall be done which is impossible at the time of making the agreement, it is much more likely that, on true construction of the agreement, one or other will have undertaken responsibility for the mistaken state of affairs. This may well explain why cases where contracts have been found to be void in consequence of common mistake are few and far between."

Secondly, whether or not the contract contains an express or implied term allocating the risk of the mistake, the party who seeks to avoid the contract may often be able to do so within the law of misrepresentation. We have already seen that mistakes are very commonly induced by misrepresentations; and that a non-fraudulent misrepresentation gives rise to a common mistake.[131] If such a misrepresentation was made, then unless there is some obstacle to rescission of the contract, or the claimant needs to establish that the contract was void, and not merely voidable,[132] he will more naturally rely on the misrepresentation since he does not have the hurdle of establishing that the mistake that was induced by the misrepresentation was of a particular degree of seriousness, and he may also have other remedies arising from the misrepresentation.[133] Claims will in practice be based on mistake, therefore, only if there is no contractual allocation of risk, and if there is either no misrepresentation on which the claimant can rely to rescind the contract, or if rescission is now unavailable.

130 [2002] EWCA Civ 1407, [2003] Q.B. 679 at [85].
131 Above, paras 15–08 to 15–09.
132 Above, para.12–19.
133 *cf. Leaf v International Galleries*, above, n.115 (mistake about authenticity of work of art would not be sufficient to satisfy test for common mistake; but was induced by misrepresentation, although on facts recission was barred by lapse of time).

(3) Can a Contract be Voidable in Equity for Common Mistake?

15–29 **Equity does not render voidable for common mistake a contract which is valid at common law.** During the second half of the twentieth century the courts accepted that a common mistake, of a lesser degree of seriousness than that required by the common law authorities, could render a contract voidable in equity. This equitable doctrine of common mistake had its origin in the judgment of Denning L.J. in *Solle v Butcher* in 1949.[134] It was applied in a small number of cases at first instance, and by the end of the century it appeared to be accepted at the level of the Court of Appeal, although it was not considered by the House of Lords. In 2002, however, the equitable doctrine was rejected by the Court of Appeal in *The Great Peace*,[135] which held that there is no jurisdiction to grant rescission of a contract on the ground of common mistake where that contract is valid and enforceable on ordinary principles of contract law, and therefore held that *Solle v Butcher* is not good law.

If this latest decision of the Court of Appeal is authoritative,[136] it removes the necessity for a detailed consideration of the cases which developed and applied the equitable doctrine, and which have now been superseded or overruled. However, although we need not discuss those cases in very great detail, it is still appropriate to survey them, to demonstrate the general approach that has been adopted over the last 50 years to common mistake, as well as to consider whether the removal of the equitable doctrine by *The Great Peace* has left a lacuna in the law which requires to be filled.

15–30 **Denning L.J.'s approach in *Solle v Butcher*.** The test given by Denning L.J. in *Solle v Butcher* was[137]:

---

[134] Below, para.15–30. For discussion of the case, with a historical perspective, see C. MacMillan, *Mistakes in Contract Law* (2010), pp.278–290; C. MacMillan, "*Solle v Butcher* (1949)" in C. Mitchell and P. Mitchell (eds), *Landmark Cases in the Law of Restitution* (2006), p.325.

[135] [2002] EWCA Civ 1407, [2003] Q.B. 679 at [157].

[136] Below, para.15–32; and note n.167.

[137] [1950] 1 K.B. 671, CA, at 693.

> "A contract is . . . liable in equity to be set aside if the parties were under a common misapprehension either as to facts or as to their relative and respective rights, provided that the misapprehension was fundamental and that the party seeking to set it aside was not himself at fault."

This appears to be straightforward; a test based on a common (shared) mistake, which requires a particular degree of seriousness ("fundamental"), and which bars a party from relying on his own mistake where he was at fault. These are all elements which resonate with the approach of the common law to mistake about the subject-matter.[138] However, it was controversial because of its relationship to the common-law test, and the interpretation which was later given to the requirements that the mistake be "fundamental".

In order to understand what Denning L.J. might have intended in relation to his test, it is necessary to see it within the context of his judgment[139]:

> "mistake is of two kinds: first, mistake which renders the contract void, that is, a nullity from the beginning, which is the kind of mistake which was dealt with by the courts of common law; and, secondly, mistake which renders the contract not void, but voidable, that is, liable to be set aside on such terms as the court thinks fit, which is the kind of mistake which was dealt with by the courts of equity. Much of the difficulty which has attended this subject has arisen because, before the fusion of law and equity, the courts of common law, in order to do justice in the case in hand, extended this doctrine of mistake beyond its proper limits and held contracts to be void which were really only voidable, a process which was capable of being attended with much injustice to third persons who had bought goods or otherwise committed themselves on the faith that there was a contract. In the well-known case of *Cundy v Lindsay*,[140] Cundy suffered such an injustice. He bought the handkerchiefs from the rogue, Blenkarn, before the Judicature Acts came into operation. Since the fusion of law and equity, there is no reason to continue this process, and it will be found that only those contracts are now held void in which the mistake was such as to prevent the formation of any contract at all.
>
> Let me first consider mistakes which render a contract a nullity. All previous decisions on this subject must now be read in the light of *Bell v Lever Bros Ltd*.[141] The correct interpretation of that case, to my mind, is that, once a contract has been made, that is to say, once the parties,

138 Above, para.15–25.

139 Above, n.137, at 690–693.

140 (1878) 3 App. Cas. 459; [above, para.14–20].

141 [1932] A.C. 161 [above, para.15–21].

whatever their inmost states of mind, have to all outward appearances agreed with sufficient certainty in the same terms on the same subject matter, then the contract is good unless and until it is set aside for failure of some condition on which the existence of the contract depends, or for fraud, or on some equitable ground. Neither party can rely or his own mistake to say it was a nullity from the beginning, no matter that it was a mistake which to his mind was fundamental, and no matter that the other party knew that he was under a mistake. A fortiori, if the other party did not know of the mistake, but shared it. The cases where goods have perished at the time of sale, or belong to the buyer, are really contracts which are not void for mistake but are void by reason of an implied condition precedent, because the contract proceeded on the basic assumption that it was possible of performance. . . .

Let me next consider mistakes which render a contract voidable, that is, liable to be set aside on some equitable ground. Whilst presupposing that a contract was good at law, or at any rate not void, the court of equity would often relieve a party from the consequences of his own mistake, so long as it could do so without injustice to third parties. The court, it was said, had power to set aside the contract whenever it was of opinion that it was unconscientious for the other party to avail himself of the legal advantage which he had obtained: *Torrance v Bolton*[142] per James L.J.

The court had, of course, to define what it considered to be unconscientious, but in this respect equity has shown a progressive development. It is now clear that a contract will be set aside if the mistake of the one party has been induced by a material misrepresentation of the other, even though it was not fraudulent or fundamental; or if one party, knowing that the other is mistaken about the terms of an offer, or the identity of the person by whom it is made, lets him remain under his delusion and concludes a contract on the mistaken terms instead of pointing out the mistake. . . .

A contract is also liable in equity to be set aside if the parties were under a common misapprehension either as to facts or as to their relative and respective rights, provided that the misapprehension was fundamental and that the party seeking to set it aside was not himself at fault."

The essential elements of this passage are as follows. First, the common law and equity have different tests for mistake; at common law a mistake renders a contract void, but in equity the contract is only voidable and liable to be set aside on such terms as the court in its discretion should decide. Secondly, the doctrine of mistake at common law is very narrow: a contract is void only if there is no

[142] (1872) L.R. 8 Ch. 118 at 124.

objectively determinable agreement between the parties[143]; there is no doctrine of common mistake about the subject-matter at common law—decisions in cases involving contracts for non-existent goods are not based on mistake, but on implied terms of the contract. Thirdly, there has been a tendency to allow the common law doctrine to expand, but this is wrong, because a void contract may prejudice third parties.[144] Fourthly, a contract can be voidable in equity on various grounds,[145] including mistake about the subject-matter, but only where it is a shared, fundamental mistake and the claimant was not at fault.

From this it appears that Denning L.J.'s principal concern was to limit the circumstances in which a contract could be held void for mistake, and shift the remedy to rescission of a voidable contract; and that this was motivated by the need to avoid "injustice to third parties". It also, incidentally, gave a power to the court to control the remedy and (where appropriate) impose terms on the award of the remedy of rescission, as in the case of *Solle v Butcher* itself.[146] But, if one simply looks at his judgment, there is nothing to suggest that Denning L.J. intended to expand the width of actionable

143 i.e. cases where the mistake prevents the contract being formed at all: above, Ch.14. Denning L.J. rejected in this passage the theory that a mistake of identity renders the contract void; it, too, should only be voidable: see also above, para.14–28.

144 Above, paras 12–18 to 12–19; 14–39.

145 For criticism of the treatment by Denning L.J. of the earlier authorities, and in particular his use of the judgment of James L.J. in *Torrance v Bolton* (1872) L.R. 8 Ch. 118 to support his arguments about the equitable jurisdiction for common mistake, see J. Cartwright, "*Solle v Butcher* and the Doctrine of Mistake in Contract" (1987) 103 L.Q.R. 594 at pp. 619–623. *Cf.*, however, C. MacMillan, *Mistakes in Contract Law* (2010), Ch.3, discussing the pre-fusion equity cases which exercised a jurisdiction in relation to mistakes including (but only in relatively rare cases) rescission.

146 The case involved the contract for lease of a flat at rent of £250 a year, on the incorrect assumption by landlord and tenant that repairs and improvements after the flat had been damaged during the war made it a different flat and therefore no longer subject to rent control (at £140 a year) under the Rent Restriction Acts. The parties could lawfully have agreed the higher rent, but only by following procedures of the Acts and this was too late after the lease had been entered into. CA held, by a majority, that the tenant could obtain rescission of the contract to pay £250 a year, but on condition that the landlord offered him a new lease at £250. Thus, tenant could leave; but could not stay without paying the full agreed level of rent. Jenkins L.J. dissented on ground that the mistake was of law, not fact. Terms were also imposed in *Grist v Bailey* [1967] Ch.532.

mistakes about the common law: they must still be shared, and fundamental—the very same language which was sometimes used in the common law test.[147]

15–31 **The cases from *Solle v Butcher* to *The Great Peace*.** It may be, therefore, that Denning L.J. sought only to shift the doctrine of mistake relating to the subject-matter from the common law (void) to equity (voidable). This is not, however, how it came to be seen. Very few cases were decided on the basis of the equitable doctrine by way of ratio,[148] or even as alternative grounds of decision,[149] but Denning L.J.'s approach was repeated from time to time by way of

---

147 Above, para.15–21, n.76.

148 *Solle v Butcher*, above, n.137; *Grist v Bailey*, above, n.146 (contract for sale of house for £850, "subject to the existing tenancy thereof"; but there was no protected tenancy, so house was worth £2,250. Rescission in equity, on terms (offered by vendor) that vendor should offer to sell property to puchaser but at the proper vacant possession price. But note that this was a claim for recission by the vendor on the basis of his own mistake about the property he was selling; and *cf. William Sindall Plc v Cambridgeshire CC* [1994] 1 W.L.R. 1016, CA, at 1035, Hoffmann L.J.: "I should say that neither in *Grist v Bailey* nor in *Laurence v Lexcourt Holdings Ltd* [[1978] 1 W.L.R. 1128] did the judges who decided those cases at first instance advert to the question of contractual allocation of risk. I am not sure that the decisions would have been the same if they had"); *West Sussex Properties Ltd v Chichester DC* [2000] All E.R. (D) 887, CA. In *Magee v Pennine Insurance Co.* [1969] 2 Q.B. 507, CA held by majority that contract to settle claim under insurance policy was avoided where the policy itself had been voidable by virtue of misrepresentations on the proposal form. But there is no clear ratio: Lord Denning M.R. applied his test in *Solle v Butcher*, and held the contract not void at law but voidable in equity. Fenton Atkinson L.J. applied *Bell v Lever Bros Ltd.* and (although his judgment is not entirely clear) appears to have held the contract void, not voidable (but see *The Great Peace* [2002] EWCA Civ 1407, [2003] Q.B. 679 at [140]). Winn L.J. dissented (contract valid because facts indistinguishable from those in *Bell v Lever Bros Ltd*).

149 *Laurence v Lexcourt Holdings*, above, n.148 (rescission of contract for lease of property as offices where planning permission for office use did not cover the whole of the premises. Dillon Q.C. held tenant entitled to rescission on basis of landlord's misrepresentation; but in the alternative held voidable in equity for common mistake. *Cf*, however, comment by Hoffmann L.J. in *William Sindall Plc v Cambridgeshire CC*, above, n.148); *Associated Japanese Bank (International) Ltd v Crédit du Nord S.A.* [1989] 1 W.L.R. 255 at 270 (Steyn J. would have held that the guarantee must be set aside on equitable principles if he had not decided in favour of the defendants on construction and common law mistake).

obiter dicta,[150] and it appeared to have become accepted in the Court of Appeal.[151] But the form in which it was accepted was not by way of replacement of the common law doctrine of mistake, but as a supplement to it. The common law doctrine, as defined by the House of Lords' decision in *Bell v Lever Bros Ltd*,[152] was unchanged; the equitable doctrine was interpreted as a lower threshold—a mistake could be sufficiently "fundamental" to satisfy the equitable test, and thereby render the contract voidable, even if it was not sufficient to satisfy the common law test.[153] This was set out explicitly by Steyn J. in *Associated Japanese Bank (International) Ltd v Crédit du Nord S.A.*[154]:

> "Logically, before one can turn to the rules as to mistake, whether at common law or in equity, one must first determine whether the contract itself, by express or implied condition precedent or otherwise, provides who bears the risk of the relevant mistake. It is at this hurdle that many pleas of mistake will either fail or prove to have been unnecessary. Only if the contract is silent on the point, is there scope for invoking mistake. That brings me to the relationship between common law mistake and mistake in equity. Where common law mistake has been pleaded, the court must first consider this plea. If the contract is held to be void, no question of mistake in equity arises. But, if the contract is held to be valid, a plea of mistake in equity may still have to be considered."

That is, if the issue is not determined by the contract itself,[155] the court must first consider the common law test, and decide whether the contract is void at common law. Only if it is not void is the

[150] Denning L.J. repeated it (obiter) in *Leaf v International Galleries* [1950] 2 K.B. 86, CA at 89; *Frederick E. Rose (London) Ltd v William H. Pim Jnr & Co. Ltd* [1953] 2 Q.B. 450, CA, at 460; *Oscar Chess Ltd v Williams* [1957] 1 W.L.R. 370, CA, at 373–374. In *Clarion Ltd v National Provident Institution* [2000] 1 W.L.R. 1888 at 1905–1906 a claim based on the equitable doctrine failed (the mistake was not as to the terms of the contract or as to its subject-matter, but as to the commercial advantage which the contract gave one of the parties).

[151] *William Sindall Plc v Cambridgeshire CC*, above, n.148 at 1042; *Nutt v Read*, above, n.121 at 769 ("the judge was right to reach the conclusion that he had power, in equity, to set aside the . . . agreement. He might have taken the view that the . . . agreement . . . was void in law; but he did not, and there is no appeal on that point": Chadwick L.J.); *West Sussex Properties Ltd v Chichester DC*, above, n.148).

[152] Above, para.15–21.

[153] *Grist v Bailey*, above, n.146 at 537, 541.

[154] Above, n.148 at 268.

[155] Above, para.15–15.

equitable test applied. If, therefore, the contract is found voidable under the equitable test, the court grants rescission of the contract on the basis of a mistake which is not in itself sufficient to satisfy the common law test.

15–32 **Rejection of the equitable doctrine in *The Great Peace*.** The equitable doctrine, as it stood at the start of the twenty-first century, therefore, provided that the court had jurisdiction to grant rescission of a contract for a common mistake which was "fundamental", although not sufficient to satisfy the narrow common law test; this equitable jurisdiction was discretionary and, where appropriate, the court could impose terms on the grant of the remedy. Some judges expressed the view that this state of the law was satisfactory.[156] However, the judges in *The Great Peace*[157] disagreed. Following the lead given by Toulson J. at first instance,[158] the Court of Appeal held that it was impossible to reconcile *Solle v Butcher* with *Bell v Lever Bros Ltd*, and that *Solle v Butcher* is not good law and should no longer be followed.[159]

The court's decision rested on a number of points. First, the claim by Denning L.J. that there was authority for an independent equitable jurisdiction relating to common mistake was wrong[160]:

---

[156] *Associated Japanese Bank (International) Ltd v Crédit du Nord S.A.*, above, n.149 at 267–268 (Steyn J.: "a narrow doctrine of common law mistake (as enunciated in *Bell v Lever Brothers Ltd*), supplemented by the more flexible doctrine of mistake in equity (as developed in *Solle v Butcher* and later cases), seems to me to be an entirely sensible and satisfactory state of the law"); *West Sussex Properties Ltd v Chichester DC*, above, n.148 at [42] (Sir Christopher Staughton: "It is a matter of some satisfaction, in my view, that we can and do regard ourselves as bound by the decision in *Solle v Butcher* [1950] 1 K.B. 671. That decision has now stood for over 50 years. Despite scholarly criticism it remains unchallenged in a higher court; indeed there have been remarkably few reported cases where it has been considered during that long period. As this case shows, it can on occasion be the passport to a just result").

[157] [2002] EWCA Civ 1407, [2003] Q.B. 679.

[158] [2001] All E.R. (D) 152 (Nov).

[159] Above, n.157, at [157], [160]. See also at [126]: "Toulson J described this decision by Denning L.J. as one which 'sought to outflank *Bell v Lever Bros Ltd*'. We think that this was fair comment". For discussion of *The Great Peace*, see (2003) 119 L.Q.R. 177 (F.M.B. Reynolds); [2006] L.M.C.L.Q. 49 at pp. 62–66 (G. McMeel).

[160] *The Great Peace*, above, n.157 at [99]–[118], reviewing in particular the reliance by Denning L.J. on *Cooper v Phibbs* (1867) L.R. 2 H.L. 149.

> "Lord Atkin's test for common mistake that avoided a contract, while narrow, broadly reflected the circumstances where equity had intervened to excuse performance of a contract assumed to be binding in law.[161]"

Secondly, the test which Denning L.J. laid down in *Solle v Butcher*[162] was uncertain: it was unclear what degree of seriousness of mistake was necessary to satisfy the requirement that the mistake be "fundamental", by comparison with the common law test[163]; and the application of the test, based on the court's discretion, was too uncertain, depending on what the court perceives to be "fair".[164] Thirdly, it is inappropriate to invoke a principle of equity which will undermine the policy of the common law in this area[165]:

> "the premise of equity's intrusion into the effects of the common law is that the common law rule in question is seen in the particular case to work injustice, and for some reason the common law cannot cure itself. But it is difficult to see how that can apply here. Cases of fraud and misrepresentation, and undue influence, are all catered for under other existing and uncontentious equitable rules. We are *only* concerned with the question whether relief might be given for common mistake in circumstances wider than those stipulated in *Bell v Lever Bros Ltd*. But that, surely, is a question as to where the common law should draw the line; not whether, given the common law rule, it needs to be mitigated by application of some other doctrine. The common law has drawn the line in *Bell v Lever Bros Ltd*. The effect of *Solle v Butcher* is not to supplement or mitigate the common law: it is to say that *Bell v Lever Bros Ltd* was wrongly decided."

The Court of Appeal held that it had the power in the circumstances to refuse to follow its own earlier decision.[166] This has been

---

161 *ibid.*, at [118].
162 Above, para.15–30.
163 Above, n.157, at [131], [154].
164 *ibid.*, at [138], commenting on the application of the test by Lord Denning M.R. in *Magee v Pennine Insurance Co. Ltd*, above, n.148 at 514–515 ("It is not fair to hold the insurance company to an agreement which they would not have dreamt of making if they had not been under a mistake"); *cf.* at first instance, Toulson J. [2001] All E.R. (D) 152 (Nov) at [120]: "Bluntly, the difficulty about this form of the doctrine is that it puts palm tree justice in place of party autonomy".
165 *ibid.*, at [156].
166 *ibid.*, at [157]–[160].

challenged in commentaries on *The Great Peace*,[167] although the signs are that this point is not being taken, and that the lower courts and the Court of Appeal itself will follow the decision, which is not altogether surprising given the strongly-worded judgments of both Toulson J. and the Court of Appeal.[168]

15–33 **Is there a lacuna after *The Great Peace*?** The question remains whether the removal of the equitable doctrine of common mistake by the decision in *The Great Peace* leaves a lacuna in the law. In other words, has something thereby been lost, which should not have been lost, or which needs to be filled by some other existing doctrine or by reform of the law? We should note that the decision has not been generally welcomed in other common law jurisdictions, principally because, in rejecting the decision in *Solle v Butcher*, it has removed a flexible test which was available to the courts in at least some cases.[169] However, it must be remembered

[167] S.B. Midwinter, "*The Great Peace* and Precedent" (2003) 119 L.Q.R. 180; D. Sheehan, "Vitiation of Contracts for Mistake and Misrepresentation of Law" [2003] R.L.R. 26 at p.33.

[168] See *EIC Services Ltd v Phipps* [2003] EWHC 1507 (Ch), [2003] 1 W.L.R. 2360 at [155]–[158], [176] (*cf.* [2004] EWCA Civ 1069, [2005] 1 W.L.R. 1377 at [26]–[27]); *Champion Investments Ltd v Ahmed* [2004] EWHC 1956; [2004] All E.R. (D) 28 (Aug) at [28], [31]; *Kyle Bay (trading as Astons Nightclub) v Underwriters Subscribing Under Policy 019057/08/01* [2007] EWCA Civ 57, [2007] 1 C.L.C. 164 at [21]; *Islington LBC v Uckac* [2006] EWCA Civ 340; [2006] 1 W.L.R. 1303 at [20]; *Qayyum v Hameed* [2009] EWCA Civ 352, [2009] 3 F.C.R. 545 at [37]; *Smithson v Hamilton* [2007] EWHC 2900 (Ch), [2008] 1 W.L.R. 1453 at [116]–[122]; *Pitt v Holt* [2011] EWCA Civ 197, [2011] 2 All E.R. 450 at [166] (distinguishing the equitable jurisdiction to set aside voluntary transactions for mistake). See also *Statoil A.S.A. v Louis Dreyfus Energy Services L.P. (The Harriette N)* [2008] EWHC 2257 (Comm), [2008] 2 Lloyd's Rep. 685 at [105] (Aikens J., following *The Great Peace* in order to reject the argument that there is an equitable jurisdiction to grant rescission of a contract for *unilateral* mistake of fact: above, para.15–12).

[169] In Singapore, see *Chwee Kin Keong v Digilandmall.com Pte Ltd* [2005] 1 S.L.R. 502, discussed at (2005) 121 L.Q.R. 393 (T.M. Yeo); (2006) 22 J.C.L. 81 (Lee Pey Woan). In Canada, see *Miller Paving Ltd v B. Gottardo Construction Ltd* (2007) 285 D.L.R. (4th) 568 at [26] (Gouge J.A. in CA Ontario: "The loss of the flexibility needed to correct unjust results in widely diverse circumstances that would come from eliminating the equitable doctrine of common mistake would, I think, be a step backward"); Waddams, para.392 (suggesting that Canadian law should retain a flexible power to give relief for fundamental mistake); Swann, p.585 (criticising both *Bell v Lever Bros Ltd* and *The Great Peace* and preferring greater flexibility in the remedy for mistake); Fridman,

that *The Great Peace* was a commercial case, in which both the trial judge and the Court of Appeal took a strong view against intervention by the court in the contract, especially on the basis of a broad general principle such as "fairness". Just as the approach in *Solle v Butcher* had its supporters,[170] it is certainly not inconceivable that the Supreme Court, or even a future Court of Appeal, particularly if faced with a case in which the application of a broader jurisdiction would be desirable, might re-visit the merits of the equitable test which has been rejected.

There are two ways of reading the underlying reasoning in *The Great Peace*. It could be, simply, that *Solle v Butcher* was wrong because it had no legal basis, the court then being bound by the decision in *Bell v Lever Bros Ltd*.[171] Alternatively, it could be based on the proposition that *Solle v Butcher* was wrong in principle: that a test under which the court could in its discretion hold the contract voidable for a less serious common mistake than under the narrow doctrine of the common law is in itself unacceptable. This second view appears to be the principal issue in the minds of both the trial judge and the Court of Appeal in *The Great Peace*, and is reflected in some of the criticisms in the judgments of the test in *Solle v Butcher* based on its inherent uncertainty and unpredictability[172]; in

p.258 (wondering whether the more generous view of mistake will ultimately prevail). In Australia, see *Australia Estates Pty Ltd v Cairns City Council* [2005] Q.C.A. 328 at [52] (Atkinson J.: *The Great Peace* should be followed in CA Queensland); *cf.* Carter, Peden and Tolhurst, para.20–29 (the rationale for *Solle v Butcher* is not mistake *per se*, but unconscionable conduct); Seddon and Ellinghaus, para.12.3 (*Great Peace* was "a most unfortunate development, abandoning after over 50 years a doctrine that provided a flexible and sensible response to the problem of common mistake.... until the High Court says otherwise, the doctrine of mistake in equity is part of the law of Australia"; *Australia Estates Pty Ltd v Cairns City Council*, above, was "an inauspicious occasion to take so radical a step" and is inconsistent with *Taylor v Johnson* (1982–1983) 151 C.L.R. 422, HCA). *Cf.* K.F.K. Low, "Coming to Terms with *The Great Peace* in Common Mistake" in J.W. Neyers, R. Bronaugh and S.G.A. Pitel, *Exploring Contract Law* (2009), p.319 at p.339 ("many of the concerns over *The Great Peace* are either unfounded or overstated").

170 Above, n.156; and for supporters in other common law jurisdictions, see above, n.169.

171 On this point, a future court which sought to circumvent the apparent authority of *The Great Peace* could address itself to the question whether the Court of Appeal had the power to depart from *Solle v Butcher*: above, n.167.

172 Above, n.164. See also [2002] EWCA Civ 1407, [2003] Q.B. 679 at [155] ("A common factor in *Solle v Butcher* and the cases which have followed it can

other words, the way in which the test in *Solle v Butcher* could be applied undermined the certainty which is furthered by the common law test—the policy that contract should not be liable to challenge except in the very narrow circumstances defined in *Bell v Lever Bros Ltd* and the cases which apply it.[173] However, the Court of Appeal itself noted that there might be an argument in favour of law reform to give the court a wider jurisdiction[174]:

> "We can understand why the decision in *Bell v Lever Bros Ltd* did not find favour with Lord Denning M.R. An equitable jurisdiction to grant rescission on terms where a common fundamental mistake has induced a contract gives greater flexibility than a doctrine of common law which holds the contract void in such circumstances. Just as the Law Reform (Frustrated Contracts) Act 1943 was needed to temper the effect of the common law doctrine of frustration, so there is scope for legislation to give greater flexibility to our law of mistake than the common law allows."

It is not clear, however what the basis of such intervention by the court might be.[175] If it is to allow a remedy where the common law

---

be identified. The effect of the mistake has been to make the contract a particularly bad bargain for one of the parties"). The courts in *The Great Peace* appear to have taken the opportunity of the case to reject the principle of *Solle v Butcher*: see, e.g. [2002] EWCA Civ 1407, [2003] Q.B. 679 at [2] ("In the court below Toulson J. used this case as a vehicle to review this difficult area of jurisprudence"); the case was one in which the outcome on the basis of the equitable test of *Solle v Butcher*, as much as the common law test of *Bell v Lever Bros Ltd*, would be to reject the defendants' claim to avoid the contract, since the mistake fell squarely within the scope of the risk allocation on the defendants' part: see also F.M.B. Reynolds, (2003) 119 L.Q.R. 177 at pp.178–179.

173 [2002] EWCA Civ 1407, [2003] Q.B. 679 at [156], quoted above, para.15–32.

174 *ibid.*, at [161].

175 The analogy with the Law Reform (Frustrated Contracts) Act 1943 should not be pressed too far. The Act dealt only with some of the secondary remedial consequences of frustration; it did not redefine test for when a contract is frustrated, nor change the core rule of the common law that a contract is terminated by the frustrating event. See also [2006] L.M.C.L.Q. 49 at 80 (G. McMeel), suggesting that a better analogy would have been the New Zealand Contractual Mistakes Act 1977, which had as its purpose (s.4) "to mitigate the arbitrary effects of mistakes on contracts by conferring on Courts and arbitrators appropriate powers to grant relief" in certain defined circumstances, including a case where "all the parties to the contract were influenced in their respective decisions to enter into the contract by the same mistake", and "The mistake . . . resulted at the time of the contract—(i) In a substantially unequal exchange of values; or (ii) In the conferment of a benefit, or in the imposition or inclusion of

test would not, and on the grounds that the effect of the mistake is a substantive unfairness for one of the parties, it seems that the Court of Appeal would apparently not have welcomed it[176]; and Toulson J. at first instance was particularly forcefully opposed to such an approach[177]:

> "it could be held that Lord Denning's view about the jurisdiction of the court to set aside a valid contract on grounds of mutual [i.e. common] mistake, in the absence of fraud, misrepresentation or unconscionable behaviour by the other party, was over-broad.
>
> Despite the great respect due to Lord Denning, I would respectively adopt as correct the following statement of principle in *Snell's Equity* (30th edn, 2000), para.1.14: 'It is no part of the role of the court to dissolve or vary contracts thought to be harsh on the basis of so-called equitable principles. Its role is to prevent the defendant from insisting on his strict legal rights when, owing to his behaviour, it would be unconscionable or inequitable to allow him to do."

The role of the court in relation to mistakes. The decision in *The Great Peace* highlights a dilemma in the law of contract: the proper resolution of the conflict between the principle of sanctity of contract and the desirability of intervention by the courts to remedy a substantive unfairness in the terms of the contract. The Court of Appeal has taken a strict line, which emphasises certainty for the contracting parties and non-intervention by the courts. This is consistent with the general approach which has been taken in the modern law to the effect that the courts may intervene to remedy a relevant mistake about the subject-matter or the circumstances surrounding the contract where it was caused by the other party's words or conduct—that is, the law provides a range of remedies for misrepresentation[178]—but not generally where the mistaken party cannot attribute it to the other party.[179] This can, however, leave a party bound to a contract where he in fact made a mistake which is 15–34

---

an obligation, which was, in all the circumstances, a benefit or obligation substantially disproportionate to the consideration therefor" and where the risk of the matter in question does not fall on the party seeking relief (s.6). The "relief" may include cancellation or variation of the contract, and restitution or compensation: s.7. For the operation of the New Zealand statute, see Burrows, Finn & Todd, Ch.10.

176 Above, n.172.

177 [2001] All E.R. (D) 152 (Nov) at [121]–[122].

178 Above, Pt II.

179 Above, paras 1–03; 12–12 to 12–15.

relevant to his decision to enter the contract, and where he is in consequence at a significant disadvantage within the balance of terms in the contract. The traditional approach of the common law, which was made explicit by Lord Atkin in *Bell v Lever Bros Ltd*,[180] is that

> "it is of paramount importance that contracts should be observed, and that if parties honestly comply with the essentials of the formation of contracts—i.e., agree in the same terms on the same subject-matter—they are bound, and must rely on the stipulations of the contract for protection from the effect of facts unknown to them."

That is, it is the responsability of each party to check the facts, and if they wish to have an escape route if their understanding of the facts turns out to be mistaken, they should ensure that the contract itself provides it. It is a strict view expecting high standards of each party in relation to their own mistakes. Other systems of contract law take a different approach. However, the supporter of reform of the English law on a particular topic such as mistake in contract cannot simply appeal to the merits of the solutions provided in other legal systems without considering why those other systems naturally contain such different solutions within their broader schemes of law. Mistake in contract is a good example of this. Civil law systems generally have a significantly wider test of actionable mistake, accepting that a unilateral mistake about the subject-matter should in principle be legally relevant, although admitting that such a wide view of actionable mistake needs still to be restrained by other rules to avoid too significant an undermining of the other party's security of contract.[181] However, such a balance, starting from a wider doctrine of mistake, fits naturally in a system where a contract is based on the will or consent of the parties, especially where it is the subjective consent that is the starting-point for assessing the existence and validity of the contractual obligation.[182] English law, however, bases its law of contract on the objective

[180] [1932] A.C. 161, HL at 224; above, para.15–04.

[181] See, e.g. R. Sefton-Green (ed.), *Mistake, Fraud and Duties to Inform in European Contract Law* (2005); H. Kötz and A. Flessner, *European Contract Law*, Vol.1, trans. T. Weir, Ch.10, pp.196–208; J. Cartwright, "*Defects of Consent in Contract Law*" in A. Hartkamp, M. Hesselink, E. Hondius, C. Mak and E. du Perron (eds), *Towards a European Civil Code* (4th edn, 2011), p.537.

[182] Above, para.1–05. The French model is here a particularly good example: J. Cartwright, "*Defects of Consent and Security of Contract: French and English*

assessment of the parties' agreement;[183] and even where this objective test is applied at the level of each party's understanding of the other's intention (rather than simply a detached observer's interpretation of the parties' words and conduct[184]) it still naturally tends to exclude a party's own mistake as a ground of avoidance. What a party (subjectively) understood is not the question. It is what he communicated as his understanding to the other party, and how a reasonable person in the other party's position would have interpreted it. For this reason, the adoption of a wider doctrine of mistake is always going to be more challenging in English law than in the civil law. However, we have seen that other common law jurisdictions[185] have also favoured the more flexible approach to common mistake that was developed by Denning L.J. in *Solle v Butcher*, and such an approach is certainly not incompatible with the fundamental doctrines of the common law. A balance has to be struck, and it is a matter of judgment where to strike that balance. The Court of Appeal in *The Great Peace* re-adjusted the balance within English law against allowing a power for the court to be able to intervene in the contract on the basis of a fundamental shared mistake of fact. Given the narrow scope of the common law test for common mistake,[186] this has reduced the flexibility for future courts. Some English judges, when difficult cases come before them, especially where non-commercial contracts are in issue, may well share the regrets being expressed in other common law jurisdictions about the lack of flexibility which flows from the decision in *The Great Peace*.[187]

Law Compared" in P. Birks and A. Pretto (eds), *Themes in Comparative Law in Honour of Bernard Rudden* (2002), p.153.

183 Above, para.12–14.

184 *Cf.* above, para.13–07.

185 Above, n.169.

186 Above, paras 15–25 to 15–27.

187 The current European project to produce a "Common Frame of Reference" for European Contract Law would introduce a parallel law of mistake into English domestic law if an Optional Instrument were introduced (above, para.1–05). The Commission Expert Group on European Contract Law's, "Feasibility study for a future instrument in European Contract Law" (May 2011), art.45, provided for a party to avoid a contract for mistake of fact or law (other than a mistake about the terms of the contract) if, but for the mistake, he would not have concluded the contract or would have done so on fundamentally different terms (and the other party knew or could be expected to have known it), and as long as the mistake was not inexcusable nor was the risk (nor should it

have been) borne by the mistaken party, where the other party (i) caused the mistake, or (ii) knew or could be expected to have known of the mistake and caused the contract to be concluded under a mistake by not pointing out the relevant information provided that good faith and fair dealing would have required a party aware of the mistake to point it out; or (iii) caused the contract to be concluded in mistake by failing to comply with a specific pre-contractual information duty; or (iv) made the same mistake. This would not allow a party to avoid the contract for simple unilateral mistake of fact where the other party has no responsibility for it, but would give a broader doctrine of common mistake than in the current English law—and, one might say, would be much closer again to the now rejected broader doctrine of common mistake in *Solle v Butcher*.

PART 3

Non-Disclosure

CHAPTER 16

INTRODUCTION: NO GENERAL DUTY OF DISCLOSURE[1]

I. SCOPE OF THIS PART

Duties of disclosure in the formation of contracts. This Part of the book is concerned with the liability of one contracting party to the other party for the failure to disclose information that was relevant to the latter's decision to enter into the contract. Such a liability will necessarily constitute a breach of a duty of disclosure, and therefore our inquiry is into the situations in which the courts recognise duties of disclosure in the formation of a contract. There are other situations in which the law will hold that one party owes a duty to disclose information to the other; for example, during the performance of a contract, or in dealings between them during the currency of a particular relationship between the parties. These are not, however, within the scope of this book and will therefore not be considered in detail. 16–01

II. THE GENERAL RULE: NO LIABILITY FOR NON-DISCLOSURE

The traditional starting-point: no general pre-contractual duty to disclose. English law does not impose on parties who are negotiating for a contract a general obligation to disclose information: that is to say, the starting-point is that each negotiating party may remain silent, even as to facts which he believes would 16–02

[1] On non-disclosure generally, see Spencer Bower (Non-Disclosure); Chitty, paras 1–134, 6–142 to 6–164; Furmston, paras 4.28–4.31; Treitel, paras 9–127 to 9–155; Anson, pp.332–347; Cheshire, Fifoot and Furmston, pp.372–381; A. Duggan, M. Bryan and F. Hanks, *Contractual Non-Disclosure* (Longman, Melbourne, 1994).

be operative on the mind of the other.[2] This does not mean that no party ever has an obligation to disclose information: the circumstances in which the law does recognise a duty to disclose are discussed in Chapter 17. But the burden is on the party who claims a remedy in consequence of the defendant's failure to speak to show that there was, in the circumstances, a duty to disclose.[3]

16–03 **Non-disclosure, misrepresentation and mistake.** This approach to a claim of non-disclosure is in marked contrast to that taken to a claim of misrepresentation. Part I of this book showed that once a misrepresentation is established the claimant has a range of remedies. The more cautious approach to a claim of non-disclosure is a consequence of the distinction between misrepresentation and non-disclosure, viewed in the context of the approach taken by English law to the formation of a contract. A claimant who seeks to avoid a contract on the ground of either non-disclosure or misrepresentation will typically be claiming that he made a mistake, or entered into the contract on the basis of assumptions as to the relevant surrounding circumstances which he now knows were inaccurate; and now that he knows the truth, he says that he would not have entered the contract had he not made the mistake or made those assumptions.[4] In the case of a misrepresentation, he alleges that it was the defendant's misrepresentation that caused him to make the mistake: the defendant's words or conduct communicated information on which the claimant relied in deciding to enter into

[2] *Davies v London and Provincial Marine Insurance Co.* (1878) 8 Ch.D. 468 at 474. The strongest statement is by Blackburn J. in *Smith v Hughes* (1867) L.R. 6 Q.B. 597 at 607; below, para.16–04; see also Cockburn C.J. at 603–604 and Hannen J. at 610–611, statements which are more closely tied to the facts of the case (which involved a sale by sample). For a more recent reaffirmation of this position relying, inter alia, on the judgment of Blackburn J., see *Banque Keyser Ullmann S.A. v Skandia (UK) Insurance Co. Ltd* [1990] 1 Q.B. 665, CA, at 798–799.

[3] *Davies v London and Provincial Marine Insurance Co.*, above, n.2 at 474.

[4] Mistake assumes a positive state of mind about the facts or law: above, para.12–03; a claim for non-disclosure may, however, be based on a less precise state of mind—it can be sufficient to show *forgetfulness* or *ignorance* of the circumstances that would have been relevant if they had been known (sometimes referred to as "passive" mistakes: G. Virgo, *Principles of the Law of Restitution* (2nd edn, 2006) at pp.145–6). However, the gist of the claim in non-disclosure is not the claimant's state of mind (whether "active" or "passive") but the defendant's failure to provide relevant information to the claimant.

the contract.[5] But in the case of non-disclosure the defendant has done nothing to cause the mistake or to give rise to the claimant's assumptions as to the circumstances surrounding the contract; he failed to give the claimant relevant information which would have corrected the mistake or false assumption. A claim of non-disclosure therefore falls between mistake and misrepresentation: the claimant is not simply relying on his own mistake or misunderstanding; but nor does he say that the defendant caused it. He claims that the defendant should have told him something to correct the mistake or to inform him better about the circumstances relevant to his decision to enter into the contract, and that he is entitled to a remedy in consequence of the defendant's failure to fulfil this duty.

The reluctance to impose duties of disclosure. Legal systems differ in their general approach to duties of disclosure; and the contrast in this area between English law and European civil law jurisdictions is particularly sharp. This is therefore an area where a brief comparison with other systems' approaches can illuminate the underlying rationale of the approach taken by English law. Two particular features of the English law of contract, which contrast with the corresponding rules within civil law systems, can be mentioned by way of explanation: the general view of the relationship between parties during the negotiations; and the significance given to a party's mistake in the formation of a contract. 16–04

First, it can be said that English law takes a very narrow view, not only about duties of disclosure, but more generally about liability between negotiating parties during the pre-contractual phase. There is no general heading of "pre-contractual liability" in the English contract law textbooks,[6] whereas continental European jurisdictions generally find a home for such a principle.[7] Although the scope of

---

[5] Above, para.1–04.

[6] Chitty, paras 1–131 to 1–136 is an exception; but that passage is written by way of explanation that the English approach is very different from civil law jurisdictions: see esp. para.1–136.

[7] The place for the principle varies; some legal systems (e.g. France) impose liability in tort for "pre-contractual fault"; others (e.g. Germany) have an autonomous principle of *culpa in contrahendo*; Chitty, para.1–136. For a survey of many common law and civil law jurisdictions, see J. Cartwright and M. Hesselink (eds), *Precontractual Liability in European Private Law* (2009); E.H.

"pre-contractual liability" can extend to other, very different matters[8] it can also encompass the duty of disclosure during the negotiations, because the legal systems which accept a generalised form of pre-contractual liability do so on the basis of a duty of good faith between negotiating parties; and the duty to disclose can be linked to the duty to negotiate in good faith. This is not to say that commercial parties in continental European jurisdictions have onerous altruistic duties from the moment that their negotiations begin, nor that each party has to lay all his (commercially sensitive) cards on the table during the negotiations. All legal systems recognise the independence of the parties negotiating a contract and start from the same position: that each is entitled to look after his own interests during the negotiations. However, although this is not the place to explore the topic in detail,[9] it can be said that European civil law jurisdictions are generally more prepared to recognise that the relationship between negotiating parties—even commercial parties—can change during the negotiations so that each is no longer acting completely at arm's length; and the principle—or, at least, the language—of "good faith" is called upon to explain this. By contrast, the English courts have not admitted a general principle of good faith during the negotiations; indeed, they have

---

Hondius (ed.), *Precontractual Liability* (Kluwer, Deventer, 1990); and for source materials (in English) on several European jurisdictions, see H. Beale, B. Fauvarque-Cosson, J. Rutgers, D. Tallon and S. Vogenauer, *Cases, Materials and Text on Contract Law* (2nd edn, 2010), Ch.9. See also P. Giliker, "A Role for Tort in Pre-Contractual Negotiations? An Examination of English, French and Canadian Law" (2003) 52 I.C.L.Q. 969.

[8] e.g. whether liability can be imposed on a party who negotiated in bad faith and with an ulterior motive, never really intending to conclude the final contract with the claimant; or failed to warn the claimant sufficiently promptly of his decision not to proceed with the final contract and thereby allowed the claimant to continue to run up expenses preparing for the contract; or broke off the negotiations wrongfully in such a way as to inflict loss on the claimant—for example, at the very last moment at the end of detailed and lengthy negotiations, when the contract was about to be signed.

[9] See J. Cartwright and M. Hesselink, *Precontractual Liability in European Contract Law* (2009); R. Sefton-Green, *Mistake, Fraud and Duties to Inform in European Contract Law* (2005); R. Zimmermann and S. Whittaker, *Good Faith in European Contract Law* (2000); Lando and Beale, arts 1.102(1), 1.201, 2.301 and corresponding Comment and Notes; C. von Bar and E. Clive (eds), *Principles, Definitions and Model Rules of European Private Law: Draft Common Frame of Reference (DCFR), Full Edition* (Sellier, Munich, 2009), art.II.-3:301, and corresponding Comments and Notes.

gone further and have rejected the notion of duties between negotiating parties that arise other than from contractually binding promises, or from making misrepresentations[10]:

> "the concept of a duty to carry on negotiations in good faith is inherently repugnant to the adversarial position of the parties when involved in negotiations. Each party to the negotiations is entitled to pursue his (or her) own interest, so long as he avoids making misrepresentations."

Secondly, legal systems, such as those in continental Europe,[11] which in their theory of contract focus on the consent of the contracting party, and which therefore have relatively wide doctrines of mistake, might be expected also to develop quite readily duties of disclosure; or, at least, there is less likely to be resistance to such development.[12] But English law is reluctant to allow a claimant to rely on his mistake to render a contract void,[13] and places more emphasis on the defendant's responsibility in having caused the mistake: misrepresentation. Consistently with this restrictive approach to mistake, English law starts from the strong assumption that there is no general duty of disclosure[14]:

> "whatever be the case in a court of morals, there is no legal obligation on the vendor to inform the purchaser that he is under a mistake, not induced by the act of the vendor."

---

[10] *Walford v Miles* [1992] 2 A.C. 128 at 138 (Lord Ackner). This statement was not made in the context of a claim for non-disclosure, and is a particularly strong statement; some commentators would say, too strong; *cf. Petromec Inc. v Petroleo Brasileiro S.A.* [2005] EWCA Civ 891, [2006] 1 Lloyd's Rep.121 at [121]. But it illustrates the general starting-point of English law, and its contrast with the general approach of the civil law.

[11] Above, para.1–05.

[12] For the duty of disclosure in French law, see J. Ghestin, *La formation du contrat* (3rd edn, L.G.D.J., Paris, 1993), paras 565–571, 593–674; J. Ghestin (French Report), "The Pre-contractual Obligation to Disclose Information" in *Contract Law Today: Anglo-French Comparisons* (D. Harris and D. Tallon, eds, 1989), Ch.4; M. Fabre-Magnan, *De l'Obligation d'Information dans les Contrats: Essai d'une Théorie* (L.G.D.J., Paris, 1992).

[13] Above, para.12–12.

[14] *Smith v Hughes*, above, n.2 at 607 (Blackburn J.); *Walters v Morgan* (1861) 3 De G. F. & J. 718 at 724, 45 E.R. 1056 at 1059 (Lord Campbell L.C.: "simple reticence does not amount to legal fraud, however it may be viewed by moralists").

16–05 **Silence as misrepresentation.** Sometimes what appears to be silence may in fact amount to a misrepresentation. To establish a claim based on misrepresentation the claimant must show that the defendant communicated a falsehood to him: this can be through the defendant's actions, as well as his words; and by the falsehood which is hidden in a true statement. Misrepresentations by conduct and by "half-truth" (statements which are literally true but misleading) have been discussed earlier.[15] The fundamental distinction is between silence which has the effect of misleading the claimant, and silence which simply fails to illuminate the facts or the circumstances surrounding the contract as the claimant already (wrongly) believes them to be. In this Part, we are concerned only with the latter form of silence, that which has not actively misled the claimant. Only if the claimant cannot find a misrepresentation should he seek to establish that the defendant was in breach of a duty to disclose information, because that is generally a more difficult claim and the remedies are less extensive than the remedies for misrepresentation.[16]

16–06 **Non-disclosure as the omission to speak.** Liability for non-disclosure is liability for omission. It is therefore not surprising that the courts have been cautious in imposing liability. We saw earlier[17] that for a long time the courts had difficulty in accepting that there should be liability for non-fraudulent statements where a party had given no contractual warranty about the truth of his statement. In this context words were seen as posing more of a problem than acts; non-fraudulent statements more than fraudulent; claims for economic loss more than claims for physical damage. But at least in such cases the defendant is to be made liable for having actively caused the undesirable state of affairs against which the claimant

---

[15] Above, paras 3–04, 3–08.

[16] Below, Ch.17.

[17] The arguments have varied in relation to different remedies. The courts found particular difficulties in relation to claims for damages for misrepresentation: above, paras 6–01 to 6–05. Rescission was allowed more easily for non-fraudulent misrepresentation, although there was some initial hesitation in moving beyond fraud: above, paras 4–02 to 4–04. We shall see later that the arguments in favour of imposing duties of disclosure also vary according to the remedy sought, and the courts are more reluctant to impose a remedy in damages for non-disclosure than to allow rescission of the contract: below, paras 17–37, 17–38, 17–39.

seeks a remedy. Given, however, that liability for non-disclosure involves a claim that there was not even a positive misrepresentation but only a failure to make a statement which would have avoided the claimant's undesirable state of affairs, one can understand why the courts have required the claimant to show not simply that, had the defendant provided the information in question, the undesirable consequence could have been avoided, but also *why* the defendant *should* have provided it.

Could English law develop more generalised duties of disclosure? One might ask whether there is scope for reform of the law so as to impose more generalised duties of disclosure. In the eighteenth century Lord Mansfield saw the possibility; but also saw it in terms of a generalised principle of good faith between contracting parties[18]: 16–07

> "The governing principle is applicable to all contracts and dealings.
>
> Good faith forbids either party by concealing what he privately knows, to draw the other into a bargain, from his ignorance of that fact, and his believing the contrary.
>
> But either party may be innocently silent, as to grounds open to both, to exercise their judgment upon. *Aliud est celare; aliud, tacere; neque enim, id est celare quicquid reticeas; sed cum quod tu scias, id ignorare emolumenti tui causa velis eos, quorum intersit id scire.*[19]
>
> This definition of concealment, restrained to the efficient motives and precise subject of any contract, will generally hold to make it void, in favour of the party misled by his ignorance of the thing concealed.
>
> There are many matters, as to which the insured may be innocently silent . . .
>
> Men argue differently, from natural phenomena, and political appearances: they have different capacities, different degrees of knowledge, and different intelligence. But the means of information and judging are open to both: each professes to act from his own skill and sagacity; and therefore neither needs to communicate to the other.
>
> The reason of the rule which obliges parties to disclose, is to prevent fraud, and to encourage good faith. It is adapted to such facts as vary the

[18] *Carter v Boehm* (1766) 3 Burr. 1905 at 1909–1910, 97 E.R. 1162 at 1164–1165. For discussion of the case, with a historical perspective, see S. Watterson, "*Carter v Boehm* (1766)" in C. Mitchell and P. Mitchell (eds), *Landmark Cases in the Law of Contract* (2008), p.59.

[19] Cicero, *De Officiis*, Book 3, paras 52, 57: "Concealment is one thing, silence is another. . . . Concealment is not just holding something back in silence, but when, for your own benefit, you intend that those who have an interest in knowing what you know should remain in ignorance of it".

> nature of the contract; which one privately knows, and the other is ignorant of, and has no reason, to suspect.
>
> The question therefore must always be 'whether there was, under all the circumstances at the time the policy[20] was under-written, a fair representation; or a concealment; fraudulent, if designed; or, though not designed, varying materially the object of the policy, and changing the risque understood to be run.'"

In substance, Lord Mansfield argued that there is a general principle of good faith between contracting parties; this does not impose a general duty of disclosure, because it is entirely in accordance with the principle of good faith that one should remain silent and leave it to the other party to discover information for himself. But, depending on the nature of the contract, and the nature of the relationship between the parties and their relative positions of skill and knowledge, the general principle of good faith can lead to a duty on one party to provide certain types of information to the other. And this applies to the particular relationship between insured and insurer[21]:

> "Insurance is a contract upon speculation. The special facts, upon which the contingent chance is to be computed, lie most commonly in the knowledge of the insured only: the underwriter trusts to his representation, and proceeds upon confidence that he does not keep back any circumstance in his knowledge, to mislead the underwriter into a belief that the circumstance does not exist, and to induce him to estimate the risque, as if it did not exist."

From the general principle, a concrete rule is deduced for insurance contracts as a class. The decision in this case is the foundation of the modern law of disclosure in insurance contracts.[22] The reasoning, however, has not survived,[23] and the general duty of disclosure in insurance contracts is seen as a very particular situation, an exception to the general reluctance of English law to find such duties. It would be open to the courts, however, to revisit this. Lord Mansfield's approach—that the relationship between the parties, and their relative positions of skill and knowledge can

---

[20] The case concerned a contract of insurance.

[21] *Carter v Boehm*, above, n.18 at 1909, at 1164.

[22] Below, paras 17–06 *et seq.*

[23] *Pan Atlantic Insurance Co. Ltd v Pine Top Insurance Co. Ltd* [1995] 1 A.C. 501, HL, at 543 (Lord Mustill).

justify the imposition of duties on one (the "stronger") in favour of the other—is not alien to the topics discussed in this book. It is used in the context of various remedies for misrepresentation.[24] And in recent years there has been an increase in the information which parties—in particular, consumers—can by law expect to be given before concluding a contract.[25] European developments play an increasing role in this area.[26] However—as discussed earlier in this chapter—the fundamental difference between misrepresentation, on the one hand, and duties of disclosure, on the other, taken in the context of the general approach to the relationship between the parties during the negotiations for a contract, is likely to lead the English courts to be very cautious in any such development in domestic law.[27]

---

[24] e.g. to determine whether the claimant is entitled to rely on a statement (for the remedy of rescission); whether the defendant owed a duty of care in tort to the claimant; whether a pre-contractual representation was warranted in the contract: above, paras 3–12, 3–46, 3–47.

[25] Below, paras 17–52, 17–53.

[26] Below, paras 17–53, 17–54.

[27] Anson notes at pp.346–347 the increase in regulatory requirements of disclosure and speculates whether legislative intervention might be indicative of the underlying rationale and principle of a duty of disclosure, and therefore lead reform in this area. This is very much the approach that was taken in French law to justify an extension of the duties of disclosure: J. Ghestin, above, n.12. See also M. Fabre-Magnan, above, n.12 and "Duties of Disclosure and French Contract Law" in *Good Faith and Fault in Contract Law* (J. Beatson and D. Friedmann, eds, 1995), p.99; P. Legrand, "Pre-contractual Disclosure and Information: English and French Law Compared" (1986) 6 O.J.L.S. 322; P. Giliker, "Regulating Contracting Behaviour: The Duty to Disclose in English and French Law" (2005) 13 *European Review of Private Law* 621. The underlying principles of contract in civil systems lend themselves more readily to such development: above, para.16–04. For general and comparative discussion see H. Kötz and A. Flessner, *European Contract Law*, Vol.1 (trans. T. Weir), pp.198–205; H. Beale, B. Fauvarque-Cosson, J. Rutgers, D. Tallon and S. Vogenauer, *Cases, Materials and Text on Contract Law* (2nd edn, 2010), section 10.4; R. Sefton-Green, *Mistake, Fraud and Duties to Inform in European Contract Law* (2005), esp. pp.24–30; and for economic arguments see A.T. Kronman, "Mistake, Disclosure, Information, and the Law of Contracts" (1978) 7 J.L.S. 1; R.A. Posner, *Economic Analysis of Law* (7th edn, Aspen, New York, 2007), para.4.7; M. Fabre-Magnan, above, n.12; B. Rudden, "Le juste et l'inefficace, pour un non-devoir de renseignement" (1985) R.T.D.Civ. 91. For possible implications of the current European project to produce a "Common Frame of Reference" for European Contract Law, see above, para.1–05; below, para.17–54.

16–08 **General approach to finding duties of disclosure.** As the law stands today, there is certainly no general duty of disclosure and no single, general test for whether a party owes a duty to disclose information. This does not, however, mean that one cannot categorise the kinds of circumstance in which the courts will impose liability for non-disclosure. Sometimes they will hold that the particular type of contract carries with it a duty on one or both parties to disclose information; and sometimes they will say that, regardless of the type of contract, the type of relationship between the particular parties carries with it the duty on one of them to disclose information to the other. In addition, a party will sometimes be required by statute to disclose information, and in consequence will be liable to the other for failure to disclose it. In Part I we saw that the courts do not take a unitary view of liability for misrepresentation: although there are some general characteristics of a "misrepresentation"[28] the detail varies from one remedy to another. This is true also for non-disclosure: for any remedy the courts will require proof that the defendant had a duty to disclose; but the way in which that duty is found, and its scope, will vary from one remedy to another. In discussing the particular situations in which the courts will find duties of disclosure, and therefore impose liability for non-disclosure, Chapter 17 will therefore follow the pattern of the chapters in Part I and will consider the liability for non-disclosure in the particular context of each of the potential remedies.

[28] Above, Ch.3.

CHAPTER 17

PARTICULAR DUTIES OF DISCLOSURE

I. Rescission of the Contract for Non-Disclosure

Finding a duty of disclosure. We saw in Chapter 4 that rescission is often available as a remedy for misrepresentation: broadly, once the claimant shows that the defendant's false statement induced him to enter into the contract he has a right to rescind subject only to the question of whether the defendant can 17–01 show one or more of the "bars" to rescission. Although some of the rules relating to this remedy are more favourable to a claimant when he can show that the defendant's misrepresentation was fraudulent,[1] the remedy is available even for wholly innocent misrepresentations.[2] So, in a sense, it can be said that rescission is a general remedy for pre-contractual misrepresentation. It is not, however, a general remedy for non-disclosure. It is not sufficient for the claimant to show that the defendant withheld information which, had he known it, would have affected his decision to enter into the contract; it is not even sufficient that he shows that the defendant deliberately withheld information: fraudulent non-disclosure does not of itself give rise to rescission.[3] In addition, the claimant must show that the non-disclosure was in breach of a duty which the defendant owed to him.[4] This duty may arise by virtue of the type of contract in question; or by virtue of the relationship which already exists between the parties at the time they are negotiating for the contract.

17–02 **The nature of rescission for non-disclosure.** The nature of the remedy of rescission was discussed in detail in Chapter 4.[5] In general terms, where rescission is available for non-disclosure in the circumstances described in the following paragraphs of this section, the principles set out in that chapter will apply and so, for example, the contract is voidable (not void); and rescission is barred by affirmation, lapse of time, impossibility of restitution and intervening third-party rights. However, in the case of non-disclosure the court has no discretion to refuse rescission and award damages in lieu under section 2(2) of the Misrepresentation Act 1967 since that subsection applies only where a "misrepresentation has been made to" the representee and therefore covers only cases of active misrepresentation.[6]

---

[1] Above, para.4–30.

[2] Above, para.4–04.

[3] *Smith v Hughes* (1867) L.R. 6 Q.B. 597 at 607; above, para.16–04, n.14.

[4] For the rationale of the distinction between non-disclosure and misrepresentation, see above, para.16–03.

[5] Above, paras 4–01 *et seq*.

[6] *Banque Keyser Ullmann S.A. v Skandia (UK) Insurance Co. Ltd* [1990] 1 Q.B. 665, CA, at 790 on similar wording in the Misrepresentation Act 1967 s.2(1); applied to s.2(2) in *Ramphul v Toole*, unreported, March 17, 1989, CA. For a question whether this interpretation might be revised in the light of the decision

(1) Obligations of Disclosure in Particular Types of Contract

(a) Contracts "uberrimae fidei"

Contracts "uberrimae fidei" carry duties of disclosure. It is generally said[7] that certain types of contract carry for the parties the duty of disclosure because they are contracts "*uberrimae fidei*", of "utmost good faith". This terminology is well established, but its usefulness is questionable. It tends to divert attention from the real question: whether the particular type of contract should carry the duty of disclosure; and, if so, what should be the content of the duty of disclosure. It has been said that the category of contracts accepted as being *uberrimae fidei* cannot be extended, and so is not based on a general principle which can be applied by analogy in new cases.[8] But the courts are not always consistent in their reasoning, and have sometimes said that the reason that a contract cannot be classified as a contract *uberrimae fidei* is because there 17–03

in *Conlon v Simms* [2006] EWCA Civ 1749, [2008] 1 W.L.R. 484, see below, para.17–44. CA has rejected an argument that in the case of insurance contracts, being contracts "*uberrimae fidei*" (below, para.17–03), the court retains some power of equitable intervention to control the exercise of the right to rescind: *Brotherton v Aseguradora Colseguros SA* [2003] EWCA Civ 705, [2003] 2 C.L.C. 629 at [46].

7 Chitty, para.6–142; Treitel, para.9–136; Cheshire, Fifoot and Furmston, p.372; *cf.* Anson, p.334.

8 *L'Alsacienne Première Société Alsacienne et Lorraine d'Assurances contre l'Incendie les Accidents et les Risques Divers v Unistorebrand International Insurance A.S.* [1995] L.R.L.R. 333 at 349 (Rix J., relying on *Bell v Lever Bros Ltd* [1932] A.C. 161, HL, at 227 and 231–232); *H.I.H. Casualty and General Insurance Ltd v Chase Manhattan Bank* [2001] 1 Lloyd's Rep. 30 at 47. There is, however, some doubt about the content of the category: there is no doubt that insurance contracts are included, but cases and textbooks do not always agree on the other members (if any) of the category. The statement of Lord Mansfield in *Carter v Boehm* (1766) 3 Burr. 1905 at 1909–1910, 97 E.R. 1162 at 1164 (insurance contract; above, para.16–07; below, para.17–07), on which the principle of utmost good faith appears to be based, might have led to the acceptance of a general principle of good faith between contracting parties, at least where one party was in a particularly strong position to know the relevant facts. But no such general principle was developed, either a principle of good faith in contractual dealings generally, or in relation to the imposition of duties of disclosure: *Pan Atlantic Insurance Co. Ltd v Pine Top Insurance Co. Ltd* [1995] 1 A.C. 501, HL, at 543; above, para.16–07.

should be no duty of disclosure[9]; sometimes, however, they have accepted some form of disclosure obligation in certain contracts which are not contracts *uberrimae fidei*.[10]

17–04 **Disclosure in formation of the contract contrasted with disclosure in performance.** To use the term "utmost good faith" as the yardstick by which to impose duties of disclosure is unsatisfactory because it fails to distinguish between duties of disclosure in the formation of the contract, and duties of disclosure in the performance of the contract. The term "utmost good faith" is used by section 17 of the Marine Insurance Act 1906[11]:

> "A contract of marine insurance is a contract based upon the utmost good faith, and, if the utmost good faith be not observed by either party, the contract may be avoided by the other party."

This provision, like its common law counterpart in relation to contracts of insurance generally,[12] imposes a more general obligation than simply the duty of disclosure during the formation of the contract[13]: the duty continues through the lifetime of the contract and applies, for example, in relation to claims made and settled under the contract,[14] although the content of the duty after

[9] *Seaton v Heath* [1899] 1 Q.B. 782, CA, at 792 (drawing the distinction between insurance contracts and contracts of guarantee); *The Unique Mariner* [1978] 1 Lloyd's Rep. 438 at 454 (salvage agreement not a contract *uberrimae fidei*: general equitable jurisdiction of the Admiralty Court sufficient to deal with seriously inequitable salvage contracts without imposing duty of disclosure).

[10] e.g. surety contracts: below, para.17–22; contracts for the sale of land: below, para.17–30.

[11] The side-note reads "Insurance is uberrimae fidei", although the Latin formulation does not appear in the section itself. No other UK statute uses either the Latin or the English formulation.

[12] Below, para.17–07. There is no relevant difference between the obligations of disclosure falling on the parties to a contract of non-marine insurance by virtue of the common law and those falling on the parties to a contract of marine insurance by virtue of the Act of 1906: *Banque Keyser Ullmann S.A. v Skandia (UK) Insurance Co. Ltd*, above, n.6 at 770.

[13] *Pan Atlantic Insurance Co. Ltd v Pine Top Insurance Co. Ltd*, above, n.8 at 555.

[14] Clarke, paras 27–1A, 30–6A. However, the duty of good faith no longer applies once the parties are engaged in litigation; the Civil Procedure Rules then govern: *Manifest Shipping Co. Ltd v Uni-Polaris Shipping Co. Ltd (The Star Sea)* [2001] UKHL 1, [2003] 1 A.C. 469 at [77]. See also *Agapitos v Agnew (The*

formation is different.[15] And a contract of partnership is said to be a contract *uberrimae fidei*.[16] It has long been clear that this imposes mutual duties of good faith and disclosure between the partners during the currency of the partnership, but it has now been held that there are also duties of disclosure during the negotiations for the partnership contract.[17]

"Uberrima fides" is an unhelpful test for pre-contractual duties of disclosure. The origin of the terms "*uberrima fides*" and "utmost good faith" in this context seems obscure.[18] The statement by Lord Mansfield which is usually seen as the basis of the principle spoke only of "good faith"[19]; and judges in South Africa have expressed the view that the terms are unhelpful and should be abandoned.[20] In a legal system, such as the South African, which accepts a general principle of good faith in contract it seems curious to add a notion of "utmost good faith"[21]; but even in England, 17–05

Aegeon) [2002] EWCA Civ 247, [2003] Q.B. 556 at [13] (Mance L.J., expressing "the hope that the House of Lords judicially or Parliament legislatively might one day look at" whether s.17 could be confined to the pre-contract stage). The Law Commission is considering the insured's post-contract duty of good faith, and in particular fraudulent claims, within in its review of insurance contract law (below, n.23): *Reforming Insurance Contract Law*: Issues Paper 7 (July 2010) and intends to include this topic within a consultation paper planned for late 2011: Law Com No.328, *Annual Report 2010–11*, para.2.7. By a separate provision the Act imposes duties of disclosure on the insured and his agent: ss.18, 19, below, paras 17–10, 17–13, although these sections can be seen as elaboration and explanation of s.17: *P.C.W. Syndicates v P.C.W. Reinsurers* [1996] 1 W.L.R. 1136, CA, at 1145.

15 *Manifest Shipping Co. Ltd v Uni-Polaris Shipping Co. Ltd*, above, n.14 at [6], [57], [95].

16 *Green v Howell* [1910] 1 Ch. 495, CA, at 504; *Law v Law* [1905] 1 Ch. 140, CA, at 157; *Bell v Lever Bros Ltd* [1932] A.C. 161, HL, at 227.

17 *Conlon v Simms* [2006] EWHC 401 (Ch), [2006] 2 All E.R. 1024 at [196]–[199]; affirmed on this point *Conlon v Simms* [2006] EWCA Civ 1749, [2008] 1 W.L.R. 484 at [127]; below, para.17–20.

18 *Manifest Shipping Co. Ltd v Uni-Polaris Shipping Co. Ltd*, above, n.14 at [5], [44].

19 *Carter v Boehm*, above, n.8 at 1910, at 1164 (contract of insurance).

20 *Mutual and Federal Insurance Co. Ltd v Oudtshoorn Municipality* 1985 (1) S.A. 419 at 433.

21 *ibid.*: "By our law all contract are bonae fidei . . . Yet the duty of disclosure is not common to all types of contract. It is restricted to those contracts, such as contracts of insurance, where it is required *ex lege*. Moreover, there is no magic in the expression *uberrima fides*. There are no degrees of good faith. It is entirely

which has not developed a generalised principle of good faith, the term "utmost good faith" seems unhelpful and unnecessary at least as a tool to determine whether and what duties of disclosure should be imposed on contracting parties. It is preferable to address that substantive question.

(b) *Insurance contracts*[22]

17–06 **Review and reform of insurance contract law.** The Law Commission is undertaking a review of insurance contract law, which includes a number of issues relating to misrepresentation and non-disclosure.[23] Its proposals for reform of the law governing pre-contract disclosure and misrepresentation in relation to *consumer* insurance contracts are likely to be enacted in a new

---

inconceivable that there could be little, more or most (utmost) good faith. The distinction is between good faith or bad faith. There is no room for *uberrima fides* as a third category of faith in our law . . . *uberrima fides* is an alien, vague, useless expression without any particular meaning in law . . . Our law of insurance has no need for *uberrima fides* and the time has come to jettison it." (Joubert J.A., with others concurring. Miller J.A., by contrast, at 443, thought that the words *uberrimae fidei* must not be taken too literally, and had been used in the context of insurance contracts for very many years and so were not potentially misleading).

[22] Clarke, Ch.23; Spencer Bower (Non-Disclosure), Ch.6; Chitty, paras 6–144 to 6–152; Furmston, para.4.29; Treitel, paras 9–136 to 9–141; Anson, pp.333–337; Cheshire, Fifoot and Furmston, pp.372–378; S.Park, *The Duty of Disclosure in Insurance Contract Law* (1996); N. Legh-Jones and others (ed), *MacGillivray on Insurance Law* (11th edn, 2008), Ch.17; P. MacDonald Eggers, S. Picken and P. Foss, *Good Faith and Insurance Contracts* (3rd edn, 2010); H.N. Bennett, "Mapping the doctrine of utmost good faith in insurance contract law" [1999] L.M.C.L.Q. 165; M. Clarke, *Policies and Perceptions of Insurance Law in the Twenty-first Century* (2005).

[23] The project began with a Scoping Paper (January 2006), and has included Issues Papers on Misrepresentation and Non-disclosure (September 2006), Warranties (November 2006), and Intermediaries and Pre-contract Information (March 2007), a Consultation Paper (No.182, *Insurance Contract Law: Misrepresentation, Non-Disclosure and Breach of Warranty by the Insured* (July 2007)) and a Report (Law Com No.319, *Consumer Insurance Law: Pre-Contract Disclosure and Misrepresentation* (December 2009)). A second Consultation Paper, which will include provisional proposals relating to non-disclosure and warranties in business insurance, is planned for late 2011: Law Com No.328, *Annual Report 2010–11*, para.2.7. For up-to-date information see *http://www.lawcom.gov.uk*.

Consumer Insurance (Disclosure and Representations) Act 2012,[24] which will change the law radically. The consumer[25] entering into a contract of insurance will no longer have a duty of disclosure,[26] but will instead have a statutory duty to take reasonable care not to make a misrepresentation to the insurer before a consumer insurance contract is entered into or varied.[27] In consequence, the rule that a consumer insurance contract is one of the utmost good faith[28] is to be modified,[29] and statutory provisions[30] and general rules of law which have hitherto given effect to the duty of good faith and have imposed a duty of disclosure on the insured are to be abolished in relation to consumer insurance contracts.[31] The remedies provided to an insurer against a consumer insured are therefore to be remedies for misrepresentation, rather than for non-disclosure, and are also significantly reformed to take into account the particular context of consumer contracts in light of the Law Commission's review.[32]

---

[24] The Consumer Insurance (Disclosure and Representations) Bill was introduced into the House of Lords on 16 May 2011, and completed its second reading under the new procedure for politically uncontroversial Law Commission Bills on 15 June 2011. In this paragraph references are given to clauses of the Bill as introduced in May 2011.

[25] An individual who enters into the contract wholly or mainly for purposes unrelated to the individual's trade, business or profession, where the insurer is a person who carries on the business of insurance and who becomes a party to the contract by way of that business (whether or not in accordance with permission for the purposes of the Financial Services and Markets Act 2000): cl.1.

[26] Below, para.17–08.

[27] Cl.2(2). A failure by the consumer to comply with the insurer's request to confirm or amend particulars previously given is capable of being a misrepresentation (whether or not it could otherwise be).

[28] Above, para.17–03.

[29] Cl.2(5).

[30] In particular, the Marine Insurance Act 1906 ss.17–20; see below, paras 17–10, 17–12, 17–13.

[31] Cls 2(5)(b), 11.

[32] Above, n.23. The remedies are set out in Sch.1: the insurer may avoid a contract for fraud ("deliberate or reckness") and need not return any of the premiums paid, except to the extent (if any) that it would be unfair to the consumer to retain them; and in the case of a careless misrepresentation the insurer's remedy is designed to put it into the position in which it would have been if the consumer had fulfilled the duty of reasonable care: if the insurer would not have entered into the contract on any terms, it may avoid the contract and refuse all claims, but must return the premiums paid; otherwise, the insurer is limited to a variation of the terms of the contract to reflect the terms on which it

The following paragraphs of this section set out the law relating to the duty of disclosure which applies to all insurance contracts until the reforms are implemented in relation to consumer insurance contracts, and which will continue to apply until any further reform is made in relation to business insurance contracts.[33]

17–07 **The duty of disclosure.** Each party to a contract of insurance has a duty of disclosure towards the other in the formation of the contract.[34] The duty applies in all contracts of insurance,[35] and arises not from a term of the contract itself but as a matter of law.[36] It is said[37] to follow from the categorisation of the contract of

would have entered into the contract. There is therefore to be no longer any general right to rescission of the contract except for fraud; and no remedy (whether rescission or damages) for wholly innocent misrepresentations by consumer insureds.

[33] Proposals relating to business insurance are planned for the second Consultation Paper in late 2011: above, n.23; however, any final Report and its implementation will no doubt take some time.

[34] The duty extends beyond formation: above, para.17–04; *K/S Merc-Scandia XXXXII v Lloyd's Underwriters (The Mercandian Continent)* [2001] EWCA Civ 1275, [2001] 2 Lloyd's Rep. 563; but this goes beyond the scope of this book. The duty is identical on the renewal of an existing policy: *Lambert v Co-operative Insurance Society Ltd* [1975] 2 Lloyd's Rep. 485, CA.

[35] *London Assurance v Mansel* (1879) 11 Ch.D. 363 at 367; *Seaton v Heath* [1899] 1 Q.B. 782, CA, at 790, 792. The duty will be removed in relation to consumer insurance contracts if the Consumer Insurance (Disclosure and Representations) Bill is enacted: above, para.17–06.

[36] Some judges have seen the duty as arising under the contract: *Blackburn, Low & Co. v Vigors* (1886) 17 Q.B.D. 553, CA, at 578, 583; (1887) 12 App. Cas. 531, HL, at 535, 539; but the weight of authority is now against this: e.g. *Bell v Lever Bros Ltd*, above, n.8 at 227 (Lord Atkin); *March Cabaret Club & Casino Ltd v London Assurance* [1975] 1 Lloyd's Rep. 169 at 175; *Banque Keyser Ullmann S.A. v Skandia (UK) Insurance Co. Ltd*, above, n.6 at 779; *H.I.H. Casualty and General Insurance Ltd v Chase Manhattan Bank* [2001] EWCA Civ 1250, [2001] 2 Lloyd's Rep. 483 at [49]. An action to avoid a contract for non-disclosure is, however, a matter "relating to a contract" for the purposes of Art.5(1) of the Lugano Convention: *Agnew v Länsförsäkringsbolagens AB* [2001] 1 A.C. 223, HL. The duty of disclosure may be negatived by a contractual term, but this will not be effective to exclude the duty in circumstances where liability for breach of the duty could not itself be excluded: *H.I.H. Casualty and General Insurance Ltd v Chase Manhattan Bank* [2001] 1 Lloyd's Rep. 30 at [24]–[26] (Aikens J.); *cf.* on appeal [2001] EWCA Civ 1250, [2001] 2 Lloyd's Rep. 483 (Rix L.J.); [2003] UKHL 6, [2003] 2 Lloyd's Rep. 61 at [93] (Lord Hobhouse).

[37] e.g. *Pan Atlantic Insurance Co. Ltd v Pine Top Insurance Co. Ltd*, above, n.8 at 554.

insurance as a contract *uberrimae fidei*, but it has been suggested above[38] that it would be more helpful to consider the substantive question of what duties of disclosure are imposed on the insured and the insurer.

What is an "insurance contract"? Guidance was given by Romer L.J. in *Seaton v Heath*[39] on the general features of an insurance contract: **17–08**

> "Contracts of insurance are generally matters of speculation,[40] where the person desiring to be insured has means of knowledge as to the risk, and the insurer has not the means or not the same means. The insured generally puts the risk before the insurer as a business transaction, and the insurer on the risk stated fixes a proper price to remunerate him for the risk to be undertaken; and the insurer engages to pay the loss incurred by the insured in the event of certain specified contingencies occurring."

The duties are reciprocal. Although the material facts relating to the contract of insurance are generally within the knowledge of the insured, and therefore it is the insured who in practice is most often required to make disclosure in favour of the insurer, the duty of disclosure extends to both parties: not only must the insured disclose to the insurer facts material to the risk to be insured; the insurer is under a reciprocal duty in favour of the insured.[41] **17–09**

The content of the duty: the insured. Section 18 of the Marine Insurance Act 1906 provides as follows: **17–10**

---

38 Above, para.17–05.

39 [1899] 1 Q.B. 782, CA, at 793, drawing a distinction between contracts of insurance and contracts of guarantee: below, para.17–20. See also Clarke, Ch.1. In *H.I.H. Casualty and General Insurance Ltd v Chase Manhattan Bank* [2001] 1 Lloyd's Rep. 30 at [49] Aikens J. drew a distinction between a contract *of* insurance, in which there are duties of utmost good faith, and contracts (such as the line slip facility in that case) which are contracts *for* insurance, which are not contracts of utmost good faith. This was not subject to appeal, but was discussed at [2001] EWCA Civ 1250, [2001] 2 Lloyd's Rep. 483 at [55]–[58].

40 [*Carter v Boehm* (1766) 3 Burr. 1905 at 1909, 97 E.R. 1162 at 1164.]

41 *ibid.* at 1909, at 1164; *Banque Keyser Ullmann S.A. v Skandia (UK) Insurance Co. Ltd*, above, n.6 at 769–773; *Banque Financière de la Cité S.A. v Westgate Insurance Co. Ltd* [1991] 2 A.C. 249, HL, at 268–269, 281–282; below, para.17–17.

"**18.**—(1) Subject to the provisions of this section, the assured[42] must disclose to the insurer, before the contract is concluded, every material circumstance which is known to the assured, and the assured is deemed to know every circumstance which, in the ordinary course of business, ought to be known by him. If the assured fails to make such disclosure, the insurer may avoid the contract.

(2) Every circumstance is material which would influence the judgment of a prudent insurer in fixing the premium, or determining whether he will take the risk.

(3) In the absence of inquiry the following circumstances need not be disclosed, namely:—

(a) Any circumstance which diminishes the risk;

(b) Any circumstance which is known or presumed to be known to the insurer. The insurer is presumed to know matters of common notoriety or knowledge, and matters which an insurer in the ordinary course of his business, as such, ought to know;

(c) Any circumstance as to which information is waived by the insurer;

(d) Any circumstance which it is superfluous to disclose by reason of any express or implied warranty.

(4) Whether any particular circumstance, which is not disclosed, be material or not is, in each case, a question of fact.

(5) The term 'circumstance' includes any communication made to, or information received by, the assured."

Although this provision is by its language limited to contracts of marine insurance, it has been taken to contain principles which apply to contracts of insurance generally.[43]

17–11 **The insured must disclose "material" circumstances.** The insured's duty is to disclose circumstances which would influence the judgment of a prudent[44] insurer in fixing the premium, or

---

[42] ["Assured" (as used in the Act and in some of the cases) and "insured" are interchangeable.]

[43] *P.C.W. Syndicates v P.C.W. Reinsurers* [1996] 1 W.L.R. 1136, CA, at 1140; *Pan Atlantic Insurance Co. Ltd v Pine Top Insurance Co. Ltd*, above, n.8 at 541; *Banque Keyser Ullmann S.A. v Skandia (UK) Insurance Co. Ltd*, above, n.6 at 770. The Act was intended to codify the common law: Sir W. Robson, Solicitor General, in the second reading in the House of Commons: *Hansard*, HC Vol. 155, col.421 (1906). S.18 will be amended by the Consumer Insurance (Disclosure and Representations) Bill 2011 (above, para.17–06) to exclude consumer insurance contracts from its scope, and the equivalent rules at common law are similarly to be abolished in relation to consumer insurance contracts.

[44] Or a "reasonable" insurer, which is often assumed to be the same thing: Clarke, para.23–6; but may not be: "in . . . days of inflation, rising premiums,

determining whether he will take the risk. This does not mean that the non-disclosure would have had a decisive influence, in the sense that full and accurate disclosure would have led the prudent insurer either to reject the risk or at least to have accepted it on more onerous terms. It need only have an effect on the thought processes of the insurer in weighing up the risk.[45] But the test is what the insurer, rather than the insured, would think material.[46] Whether a particular circumstance or fact is material or not is a question of fact.[47]

---

rising costs of claims . . . there may be a tendency, if prudence were the test, for insurers to seek to avoid policies in circumstances which the reasonable insurer test would not permit": *March Cabaret Club & Casino Ltd v London Assurance*, above, n.36 at 176. See also *Drake Insurance Plc v Provident Insurance Plc* [2003] EWCA Civ 1834, [2004] Q.B. 601 at [140]–[141] (Clarke L.J., discussing what characteristics of the *particular* insurer should be taken into account in order to identify what the reasonably prudent insurer would regard as material).

45 *Pan Atlantic Insurance Co. Ltd v Pine Top Insurance Co. Ltd*, above, n.8 at 517, 531. Lord Templeman, at 515, disagreed on the basis that this "would give carte blanche to the avoidance of insurance contracts on vague grounds of non-disclosure supported by vague evidence even though disclosure would not have made any difference"; see also Lord Lloyd at 560. For discussion of *Pine Top*, see *St Paul Fire and Marine Insurance Co. (UK) Ltd v McConnell Dowell Constructors Ltd* [1996] 1 All E.R. 96, CA. For examples of material circumstances, see *London Assurance v Mansel* (1879) 11 Ch.D. 363 (life insurance: failure to disclose that several other insurers had refused to insure proposer's life); *Dunn v Ocean Accident & Guarantee Corp. Ltd* [1933] 37 Ll. L.Rep. 127, CA (motor insurance: proposer's failure to disclose marriage to man who would drive car and who was a dangerous driver and had had a number of accidents); *Lee v British Law Insurance Co. Ltd* [1972] 2 Lloyd's Rep. 49, CA (personal accident insurance: proposer who had not yet been told of cataract discovered by his doctors, in breach of duty to disclose the facts that his eyesight had deteriorated, he had medication, and had been advised to have further tests); *March Cabaret Club & Casino Ltd v London Assurance*, above, n.36 (duty to disclose criminal offence for which insured had been charged and was later convicted: this was material to the "moral hazard"—it went to the moral integrity of the proposer and was vital in respect of the particular insurance, fire insurance of a cabaret club); *Locker and Woolf Ltd v Western Australian Insurance Co. Ltd* [1936] 1 K.B. 408, CA (non-disclosure of previous refusal of motor insurance by other insurers was material in relation to proposal for fire insurance: relevant to the "moral hazard"). Under-insurance is probably not material non-disclosure since it results not in avoidance of the policy but in averaging: *Economides v Commercial Assurance Co. Plc* [1998] Q.B. 587, CA, at 603–604.

46 *March Cabaret Club & Casino Ltd v London Assurance*, above, n.36 at 175–176. Some earlier cases set the test by reference to the reasonable insured's perspective, rather than the reasonable (or prudent) insurer: *Joel v Law Union and*

17–12 **The insured must disclose circumstances he knows or ought to know.** Under section 18(1) of the Marine Insurance Act 1906, the insured is deemed to know every circumstance which, in the ordinary course of business, ought to be known by him: he must therefore disclose not only material circumstances of which he has actual knowledge, but also circumstances which he ought to know in the ordinary course of business.

Crown Insurance Co. [1908] 2 K.B. 863, CA, at 883–884 (Fletcher Moulton L.J.). The Law Reform Committee and the Law Commission both proposed reform of the law to provide that the test of materiality should be viewed from the perspective of a reasonable insured: Law Reform Committee, Fifth Report, Cmnd.62 (1957), para.14; Law Com. No.104, *Insurance Law: Non-Disclosure and Breach of Warranty* (1980), para.4.47. The Court of Appeal in 1975 regretted that the 1957 proposals had not been implemented: *Lambert v Co-operative Insurance Society Ltd,* above, n.34; but nor were the 1980 proposals implemented. In its current project to reform the law of insurance contracts, the Law Commission has recommended the removal of the duty of disclosure in consumer insurance contracts: above, para.17–06; but in relation to business insurance in 2007 it renewed the earlier proposal to replace the current test of materiality for non-disclosure or misrepresentation by a "reasonable insured" test: Consultation Paper No.182, *Insurance Contract Law: Misrepresentation, Non-Disclosure and Breach of Warranty by the Insured* (2007), para.5.83. The consumer insurance proposal is being implemented through the Consumer Insurance (Disclosure and Representations) Bill 2011; a further Consultation Paper (including provisional proposals relating to business insurance) is planned for late 2011: Law Com No.328, *Annual Report 2010–11*, para.2.7.

The Association of British Insurers' *Statement of General Insurance Practice* used to contain a provision to the effect that an insurer would not avoid a policy on grounds of non-disclosure unless it was of a material fact within the knowledge of the proposer which the proposer could reasonably be expected to disclose, but this was replaced by the statutory regulation of general insurance by the Financial Services Authority from January 14, 2005. Now, under the FSA *Insurance: Conduct of Business Sourcebook* (ICOBS) 8.1, an insurer must not unreasonably reject a claim (including by terminating or avoiding a policy); and a rejection of a consumer policyholder's claim is unreasonable, except where there is evidence of fraud, if it is for, inter alia, non-disclosure of a fact material to the risk which the policyholder could not reasonably be expected to have disclosed. The definition of "consumer" is modelled on that in certain European Directives (see, e.g. Directive 2002/65/EC, art.2) and (with specified exceptions) is "any natural person acting for purposes outside his trade, business or profession". See also the *Conduct of Business Sourcebook* (COBS) 17.1.3, which applies similar provisions to long-term care insurance contracts. The failure to disclose a "spent" conviction gives rise to no liability: Rehabilitation of Offenders Act 1974, s.4(2).

[47] *ibid.*, at 176; Marine Insurance Act 1906, s.18(4).

Whether the insured has *actual* knowledge depends on whether he is a natural person or a corporation. In the case of a natural person only the circumstances known personally to him are included[48]; but a corporation will in law have actual knowledge of circumstances known by a director or employee at an appropriate level, such as employees whose business it was to arrange insurance for the company.[49]

Beyond this actual knowledge, the insured is also affected by circumstances of which he is *deemed* to know in the ordinary course of business. Where the insured effects cover as a private individual, he has for the purposes of the contract no "ordinary course of business" and so he is required to disclose only material facts actually known to him: he is not to have ascribed to him any form of deemed or constructive knowledge.[50] But where the insured acts in the course of business, then the question is whether there are material circumstances which he ought in the ordinary course of business to know. In the case of a corporation the test is again whether there are natural persons who ought in the ordinary course of business to know the material circumstances and whether the deemed (constructive) knowledge of those persons is to be attributed to the corporation.[51] This does not extend to the fact that the insured's agent is defrauding him, since that is not information

---

[48] Actual knowledge presupposes, however, that the insured is honest, and has not wilfully shut his eyes to the truth: "that, sometimes called Nelsonian blindness—the deliberate putting of the telescope to the blind eye—is equivalent to knowledge, a very different thing from imputing knowledge of a fact to someone who is in truth ignorant of it": *Economides v Commercial Assurance Co. Plc*, above, n.45 at 601–602 (Simon Brown L.J.); see also at 607 (Peter Gibson L.J.).

[49] *P.C.W. Syndicates v P.C.W. Reinsurers*, above, n.43 at 1142; *Group Josi Re v Walbrook Insurance Co. Ltd* [1996] 1 W.L.R. 1152, CA, at 1169.

[50] *Economides v Commercial Assurance Co. Plc*, above, n.45 at 601, 607; *Joel v Law Union and Crown Insurance Co.*, above, n.46 at 880, 884. Chitty, para.6–148 analyses the cases differently, drawing a distinction between cases of marine insurance (deemed knowledge included, as set out in s.18) and non-marine insurance (only actual knowledge included), although Chitty, para.41–032 appears not to take the same position. For criticism of the decision in *Economides* see A. Bartlett and M. Egan, "Utmost good faith: misrepresentation and non-disclosure" (1997) 141 S.J. 952 ("if it is correct, the duty of good faith is shrinking"); but see M. Clarke [1998] C.L.J. 24.

[51] *Group Josi Re v Walbrook Insurance Co. Ltd*, above, n.49 at 1169–1170 (Saville L.J.).

that the agent would disclose to his principal, whether in the ordinary course of business or otherwise.[52]

17–13 **Duty of the insured's agent to disclose.** Section 19 of the Marine Insurance Act 1906 provides as follows:[53]

> "**19.**—Subject to the provisions of the preceding section as to circumstances which need not be disclosed, where an insurance is effected for an assured by an agent, the agent must disclose to the insurer—
> (a) every material circumstance which is known to himself, and an agent to insure is deemed to know every circumstance which in the ordinary course of business ought to be known by, or to have been communicated to, him; and
> (b) every material circumstance which the assured is bound to disclose, unless it come to his knowledge too late to communicate it to the agent."

This provision applies only to an agent who actually deals with the insurers concerned and makes the contract in question, although if intermediary agents have relevant information which ought in the ordinary course of business to be passed to the agent to insure, that information must be disclosed by the agent to insure and non-disclosure will accordingly render the contract voidable by the insurer.[54] But, like section 18,[55] section 19 does not require an agent to disclose his own fraud.[56] Nor is an agent required under section 19 to disclose a circumstance which the insured would not himself have been required under section 18 to disclose if he had known of it,[57] nor information which he does not hold in his capacity as the insured's agent.[58]

---

52 *P.C.W. Syndicates v P.C.W. Reinsurers*, above, n.43 at 1141; *Group Josi Re v Walbrook Insurance Co. Ltd*, above, n.49 at 1168.

53 S.19 will be amended by the Consumer Insurance (Disclosure and Representations) Bill (above para.17–06) to exclude consumer insurance contracts from its scope.

54 *P.C.W. Syndicates v P.C.W. Reinsurers*, above, n.43 at 1150; *Group Josi Re v Walbrook Insurance Co. Ltd*, above, n.49 at 1169.

55 Above, para.17–11.

56 *P.C.W. Syndicates v P.C.W. Reinsurers*, above, n.43 at 1147.

57 *Société Anonyme d'Intermediaries Luxembourgeois v Farex Gie* [1995] L.R.L.R. 116, CA, at 157 (Saville L.J.). This includes the case where there is an effective waiver of the materiality by the insurer in favour of the insured, or a contractual exclusion of the duty of disclosure which on its construction excludes all claims, including claims against the agent; but a clause may constitute a

Matters that need not be disclosed. Section 18(3) of the Marine Insurance Act 1906[59] sets out certain matters that, even if material, need not be disclosed by the insured unless the insurer makes inquiry about them: circumstances which diminish the risk, or which the insurer knows or can be presumed to know, or as to which the insurer waives information, or which it is superfluous to disclose by reason of any warranty (express or implied) in the contract. These grounds are based on the original formulation of the duty of good faith by Lord Mansfield in *Carter v Boehm*[60]: they are cases of innocent silence, where the insured is not in breach of his duty of good faith by failing to speak. By parity of reasoning, the insurer will not be required to disclose similar matters in order to fulfil his duty of disclosure.[61] 17–14

Time of non-disclosure. The time at which the non-disclosure is tested is the time of the contract. If, after a proposal form has been filled in but before the contract is concluded, material facts change so as to require disclosure, they must be disclosed.[62] 17–15

Inducement. Although the materiality of the non-disclosure is assessed objectively by reference to the prudent insurer, and not the actual insurer, in addition it must actually have induced the insurer to make the contract on the relevant terms. This requirement is 17–16

waiver personal to the principal insured without prejudice to the agent's duty of disclosure: *H.I.H. Casualty and General Insurance Ltd v Chase Manhattan Bank* [2003] UKHL 6, [2003] 2 Lloyd's Rep. 61 at [50]–[55] (Lord Hoffmann).

58 *Group Josi Re v Walbrook Insurance Co. Ltd*, above, n.49 at 1162.

59 Above, para.17–10. The opening words of s.19, above, para.17–13, make clear that the same applies to the insured's agent.

60 (1766) 3 Burr. 1905 at 1910–1911, 97 E.R. 1162 at 1164–1165, discussing the grounds which now appear in s.18(3)(a)–(c).

61 In *Carter v Boehm*, above, n.40 at 1910, at 1164, Lord Mansfield said that "either party may be innocently silent, as to grounds open to both, to exercise their judgment upon".

62 This follows from the Marine Insurance Act 1906 s.18(1) ("before the contract is concluded") and the rule, below, para.17–16, that the insurer must be induced to contract by the non-disclosure. At common law see *Looker v Law Union and Rock Insurance Co. Ltd* [1928] 1 K.B. 554; *Harrington v Pearl Life Assurance Co. Ltd* (1914) 30 T.L.R. 613, CA; and *cf.* the similar rule for misrepresentation, above, para.4–27.

implied into section 18 of the Marine Insurance Act 1906[63] by analogy with the general rules relating to misrepresentation.[64] As in the case of misrepresentation,[65] the burden of proof of inducement is on the insurer[66] but the materiality of the non-disclosure may raise a presumption in fact that it was relied on.[67]

17–17 **The content of the duty: the insurer.** The insurer's duty of disclosure is the counterpart of the insured's duty. Both duties are limited to facts which are material to the risk insured, and so the insurer's duty is to disclose facts which would influence a prudent insured in entering into the contract on the terms proposed by the insurer. Just as any facts which would increase the risk should be disclosed by the insured, any facts known to the insurer but not to the insured, which would reduce the risk, should be disclosed by the insurer.[68] The insurer's duty does not extent to informing the insured of the fraud of the insured's own agent where the agent's fraud is not such as would entitle the insurer to repudiate liability.[69] Nor does it extend to matters other than those relevant to the risks to be covered by the policy.[70]

17–18 **"Basis of contract" clauses.** It has long been common practice for insurers to include in contracts of insurance a clause providing that the accuracy and completeness of information provided by the

[63] And into s.20, which deals with misrepresentation; and (because these provisions of the 1906 Act apply to insurance contracts generally: above, para.17–10, n.43) into the general common law rules relating to non-disclosure.

[64] *Pan Atlantic Insurance Co. Ltd v Pine Top Insurance Co. Ltd* [1995] 1 A.C. 501, HL, esp. at 549–550 (disapproving the approach set out in Spencer Bower (Non-Disclosure), para.3.09).

[65] Above, para.4–33.

[66] *Drake Insurance Plc v Provident Insurance Plc* [2003] EWCA Civ 1834, [2004] Q.B. 601 at [64], [137].

[67] *St Paul Fire and Marine Insurance Co. (UK) Ltd v McConnell Dowell Constructors Ltd*, above, n.45 at 112.

[68] *Banque Financière de la Cité S.A. v Westgate Insurance Co. Ltd* [1991] 2 A.C. 249, HL, at 268–269, 281–282; *Banque Keyser Ullmann S.A. v Skandia (UK) Insurance Co. Ltd* [1990] 1 Q.B. 665, CA at 769–773; *Carter v Boehm* (1766) 3 Burr. 1905 at 1909, 97 E.R. 1162 at 1164.

[69] *Banque Financière de la Cité S.A.*, above, n.68 at 268–269.

[70] *Norwich Union Life Assurance Co. Ltd v Qureshi* [1999] 2 All E.R. (Comm) 707, CA, at 716 (insurer not required to disclose substantial impending losses at Lloyd's, which were not within the risk to be insured against).

proposer is to be the basis of the contract. This goes beyond the general duty of disclosure, in making matters beyond the knowledge of the insured conditions of its validity, and it has been heavily criticised.[71] The courts will apply the usual rules of construction[72] and require the insurer to establish clearly that the insured consented to the accuracy and completeness of his statements being a condition of the validity of the policy before it will give effect to such a clause: ambiguous language will not suffice.[73] In 1980 the Law Commission recommended that such clauses should not have effect,[74] although this was not implemented.[75] However, the Law Commission renewed the recommendation in 2009 in relation to consumer insurance

---

[71] *Joel v Law Union and Crown Insurance Co.* [1908] 2 K.B. 863, CA, at 885.

[72] Above, para.9–08.

[73] *Joel v Law Union and Crown Insurance Co.*, above, n.71 at 886.

[74] Law Com. No.104, *Insurance Law: Non-Disclosure and Breach of Warranty* (1980), para.7.8. Such clauses in consumer contracts may now be subject to control by the courts under the Unfair Terms in Consumer Contracts Regulations 1999 (SI 1999/2083), above, paras 9–37 to 9–38, but only if the clause does not relate to the definition of the main subject-matter of the contract (i.e. the risk undertaken by the insurer): reg.6(2)(a); Treitel, para.7–106; this is doubtful: Clarke, para.19–5A3. The relevant provisions of the Unfair Contract Terms Act 1977 do not apply to insurance contracts: Sch.1, para.1(a). The Law Commission's proposals for the replacement of the 1999 Regulations and the 1977 Act by a new, single enactment would maintain this distinction, including protection for consumer insurance contracts, but excluding insurance contracts from business and small business controls: Law Com. No.292, *Unfair Terms in Contracts* (2005), paras 3.80, 4.84, 5.57.

[75] However, the Association of British Insurers' *Statement of General Insurance Practice* used to contain a provision to the effect that that neither the proposal form nor the policy should contain any provision converting the statements as to past or present fact into warranties, although insurers could require specific warranties about matters material to the risk. This was replaced by the statutory regulation of general insurance by the Financial Services Authority from January 14, 2005. Now, under the FSA *Insurance: Conduct of Business Sourcebook* (ICOBS) 8.1, an insurer must not unreasonably reject a claim (including by terminating or avoiding a policy); and a rejection of a consumer policyholder's claim is unreasonable, except where there is evidence of fraud, if it is for, inter alia, breach of warranty or condition unless the circumstances of the claim are connected to the breach, and the warranty is material to the risk and was drawn to the customer's attention before the conclusion of the contract. See also the *Conduct of Business Sourcebook* (COBS) 17.1.3, which applies similar provisions to long-term care insurance contracts.

contracts,[76] and the Consumer Insurance (Disclosure and Representations) Bill which is passing through Parliament during 2011,[77] if enacted, will give effect to it.

17–19 **Rescission for breach of the duty to disclose.** Where either party to an insurance contract is in breach of the duty of disclosure described in this section the other party has a right to rescind[78] the contract, subject to any bars to rescission which the party in breach of duty may establish.[79] Liability does not depend on proof of fraud or negligence: simply that the duty has been broken.[80] Rescission of

---

[76] Law Com No.319, *Consumer Insurance Law: Pre-Contract Disclosure and Misrepresentation* (2009), paras 6.105–6.112. The Law Commission is considering business insurance contracts separately, and a Consultation Paper is planned for late 2011: above, para.17–06, n.23.

[77] Above, para.17–06.

[78] In *Carter v Boehm* (1766) 3 Burr. 1905 at 1909, 97 E.R. 1162 at 1164, Lord Mansfield said that in the case of non-disclosure "the policy is void", although it now well established that a contract is only voidable: above, para.4–05; *Bell v Lever Bros Ltd* [1932] A.C. 161, HL, at 227. This is an area in which, even before the fusion of the judisdictions by the Judicature Acts, the courts of equity and common law exercised a coordinate jurisdiction; and so an insurer could sue in equity for rescission and delivery up of the policy; the insured's claim under the policy was a matter for suit at law; and each court had jurisdiction to deal with both claim and defence. But the appropriate place for the defence of non-disclosure involving disputed facts was in the common law court hearing (on jury trial) the insured's claim under the policy: *Hoare v Bremridge* (1872) 8 Ch. App. 22.

[79] For an account of the nature of rescission, and the bars, see above, Ch.4; para.17–02. As in the case of rescission for misrepresentation (above, para.4–18; note there n.83), rescission for non-disclosure can be effected by act of party rather than by court order, and there is no special equitable power in the case of insurance contracts to control the exercise of the right to rescind: *Brotherton v Aseguradora Colseguros SA*[2003] EWCA Civ 705, [2003] 2 C.L.C. 629 at [27], [45]–[48], approving *Drake Insurace Plc v Provident Insurance Plc*[2003] EWHC 109 (Comm), [2003] 1 All E.R. (Comm) 759 at [31]; *cf.* Clarke, para.23–181. In the case of a contract of insurance, the contract is still capable of rescission even though the insurer has been on risk in the meantime: Clarke, para.13–12C. But the contract must be rescinded in its entirety unless it is capable of severance, such as a policy which is written so as to separate the risks into separate contracts: above, para.4–14.

[80] *Banque Keyser Ullmann S.A. v Skandia (UK) Insurance Co. Ltd*, above, n.68 at 771; *Carter v Boehm* (1766) 3 Burr. 1905, 97 E.R. 1162 at 1164. The duty of disclosure impose on the insured (and therefore the insurer's right to rescission for the insured's non-disclosure) will be removed in relation to consumer insurance contracts if the Consumer Insurance (Disclosure and Representations)

the contract involves the retrospective avoidance of the obligations under it, and a return of both the premium paid by the insured, and of any sums paid by the insurer under the contract.[81] In practice, this is more commonly a useful remedy for the insurer[82] since he avoids the risk under the insurance policy, although it is also more commonly the insured who will be in breach of the duty of disclosure since the very nature of the contract means that it tends to be the insured, rather than the insurer, who has relevant information which needs to be disclosed.[83]

(c) *Partnership contracts*[84]

Prospective partners have mutual duties of disclosure. It has long been clear that partners owe each other duties of good faith **17–20**

Bill 2011 is enacted, and the insurer's right to avoid a consumer insurance contract will be limited to cases where the insured has made a fraudulent (or, in some cases, careless) misrepresentation: above, para.17–06. See also *Drake Insurance Plc v Provident Insurance Plc* [2003] EWCA Civ 1834, [2004] Q.B. 601 at [83]–[93] (Rix L.J. discussing whether the insurer's right to avoid the contract for non-disclosure by the insured should be limited by the insurer's own duty of good faith; "it may be necessary to give wider effect to the doctrine of good faith and recognise that its impact may demand that ultimately regard must be had to a concept of proportionality implicit in fair dealing" (at [89])). Rix and Clarke L.JJ. did not rest their decision on this ground (at [90], [143]), although Pill L.J. held at [177] that failure to make any inquiry of the insured before taking the drastic step of avoiding the policy was a breach by the insurer of the duty of good faith which invalidated the attempt to avoid the policy).

[81] *Cornhill Insurance Co. Ltd v L. & B. Assenheim* (1937) 58 Ll.L. Rep. 27 at 31. The premium is recoverable on the basis of total failure of consideration; sums paid by the insurer way of loss under the contract were paid under a mistake of fact: Goff & Jones, para.9–014. The general rule for insurance contracts, that the insurer may rescind without repayment of the premium in a case where he raises the insured's *fraudulent* misrepresentation as a defence to a claim under the policy, above, para.10–11, n.49, appears to apply equally in the case of fraudulent non-disclosure: *Anderson v Thornton* (1853) 8 Exch. 425 at 427–428, 155 E.R. 1416 at 1416 (Parke B. in applying this rule referred to both fraudulent misrepresentation and non-disclosure); Marine Insurance Act 1906, s.84(3)(a).

[82] *Banque Keyser Ullmann S.A. v Skandia (UK) Insurance Co. Ltd*, above, n.68 at 777 (but noting that sometimes rescission will not be a sufficient remedy for the insurer, where the non-disclosure has led him to accept a risk at a far lower premium than he would otherwise have charged).

[83] *Carter v Boehm* (1766) 3 Burr. 1905 at 1909, 97 E.R. 1162 at 1164.

[84] R.C. I'Anson Banks, *Lindley & Banks on Partnership* (19th edn, 2010); Chitty, para.6–162 to 6–163; Anson, p.337.

and disclosure during the currency of the partnership. Until recently there was no clear authority on whether the duty extended to the pre-contractual negotiations,[85] but it has now been settled by the Court of Appeal that in negotiating a partnership agreement a party owes a duty to the other negotiating parties to disclose all material facts of which he has knowledge and of which the other negotiating parties may not be aware.[86]

(d) Surety Contracts[87]

17–21 **What is a "surety contract"?** A surety contract (or contract of "guarantee")[88] is a contract under which the surety (or "guarantor") is bound in favour of the creditor to pay the debt of the debtor for whom he stands surety, or to make good to the creditor some other

---

[85] See the first edition of this book (Sweet & Maxwell, London, 2002), para.11.10; Anson (28th edn, 2002), p.272. It is not self-evident that a contract to create a relationship which will contain duties of good faith between the parties must necessarily itself in its formation be subject to obligations of good faith and disclosure. The duty between partners is fiduciary; but it cannot mean that the contract by which every fiduciary relationship is created carries duties of disclosure. A duty of disclosure during the negotiations for a partnership was assumed by Spencer Bower (Non-Disclosure), Ch.10 (admitting that there are no cases and relying at para.10.02, n.1 on a statement in *Lindley on Partnership* (15th edn, p.480) which appeared to be describing not the duty of disclosure in relation to formation of the contract of partnership, but the duty of good faith between partners); Chitty (29th edn, 2004), para.6–157 (citing no case concerning formation); and Lord Atkin in *Bell v Lever Bros Ltd* [1932] A.C. 161 at 227. The Partnership Act 1890 makes consequential provision for a party who rescinds the partnership contract only on the grounds of fraud and misrepresentation, and not non-disclosure: s.41.

[86] *Conlon v Simms* [2006] EWCA Civ 1749, [2008] 1 W.L.R. 484 at [127] (Jonathan Parker L.J.), following Lord Atkin in *Bell v Lever Bros Ltd*, above, n.85 and the trial judge (Lawrence Collins J.) at [2006] EWHC 401 (Ch), [2006] 2 All E.R. 1024 at [196]–[199]. The judge and CA held not only that prospective partners have a duty of disclosure, but also that the fraudulent failure to disclose constitutes the tort of deceit. However, this last point is controversial: below para.17–37.

[87] Spencer Bower (Non-Disclosure), Ch.8; Chitty, paras 6–158 to 6–161, Ch.44; Treitel, para.9–144; Anson, pp.337–338; G. Moss and D. Marks, *Rowlatt on Principal and Surety* (6th edn, 2011); G. Andrews and R. Millett, *Law of Guarantees* (5th edn, 2007); J. O'Donovan and J. Phillips, *The Modern Contract of Guarantee* (2nd English edn, 2010), esp. Ch.4.

[88] The cases discussed in this section use the terms interchangeably, although, strictly, "surety" is the general term, and "guarantee" has a narrower, technical meaning by contrast with an "indemnity": Chitty, paras 44–007, 44–008.

default of the debtor. A surety contract may therefore consist of the guarantee of the debtor's cash obligation to the creditor; or the debtor's obligations of performance under a contract, or some other obligation such as a "fidelity guarantee", a guarantee, usually in favour of an employer, of the debtor's honesty.[89] There is no magic in the word "surety" or "guarantee"; the question is always what obligations the contract creates and therefore whether it carries the duties which are set out in the following paragraphs of this section as being the usual incidents of a surety contract.[90] In particular, there can sometimes be a difficulty in drawing the distinction between a surety contract and an insurance contract. To explain the difference Romer L.J. said in *Seaton v Heath*[91]:

> "On the other hand,[92] in general, contracts of guarantee are between persons who occupy, or ultimately assume, the positions of creditor, debtor, and surety, and thereby the surety becomes bound to pay the debt or make good the default of the debtor. In general, the creditor does not himself go to the surety, or represent, or explain to the surety, the risk to be run. The surety often takes the position from motives of friendship to the debtor, and generally not as the result of any direct bargaining between him and the creditor, or in consideration of any remuneration passing to him from the creditor. The risk undertaken is generally known to the surety, and the circumstances generally point to the view that as between the creditor and surety it was contemplated and intended that the surety should take upon himself to ascertain exactly what risk he was taking upon himself."

Surety contracts are not contracts "uberrimae fidei". It is well established now[93] that surety contracts are not contracts *uberrimae fidei*.[94] The courts have made this clear in order to emphasise that 17–22

[89] For these different kinds of surety contract, see Spencer Bower (Non-Disclosure), paras 8.01, 8.20–8.23; *Levett v Barclays Bank Plc* [1995] 1 W.L.R. 1260 at 1273.

[90] *Seaton v Heath* [1899] 1 Q.B. 782, CA, at 792 (Romer L.J., referring to the question being whether in substance the contract requires "*uberrima fides*"; however, on this see above, para.17–05).

[91] *ibid.*, at 793.

[92] [For the immediately preceding sentences, defining contracts of insurance, see above, para.17–08.]

[93] Contrary to some earlier dicta: see, e.g. *Newton v Chorlton* (1853) 10 Hare 646 at 650, 68 E.R. 1087 at 1089; Spencer Bower (Non-Disclosure), para.8.02.

[94] *Royal Bank of Scotland Plc v Etridge (No.2)* [2001] UKHL 44, [2002] 2 A.C. 773 at [114], [185]; *Barclays Bank Plc v O'Brien* [1993] Q.B. 109, CA, at 127; *Credit Lyonnais Bank Nederland v Export Credit Guarantee Department* [1996] 1 Lloyd's Rep. 200 at 210.

the creditor under a surety contract does not have a general duty of disclosure to the surety. However, a surety contract by its very nature does carry obligations for the creditor to make disclosure to the surety in certain situations, and therefore the creditor under a surety contract has more extensive duties than a party to a normal commercial contract. This is an illustration of the proposition, discussed above,[95] that it is unhelpful to focus on the question of whether a contract is one *uberrimae fidei*: it is preferable to consider the general question of whether by its nature it carries for either party any duty of disclosure and, if so, what duty.

17–23 **The creditor's duty of disclosure.** Although a surety is, in general, expected to inform himself about the risks he is undertaking under the contract, the creditor is under a duty to disclose to the surety any unusual feature of the contract between the creditor and the debtor which makes it materially different in a potentially disadvantageous respect from what the surety might expect.[96] This was established by a speech of Lord Campbell in the House of Lords on an appeal from Scotland in 1845,[97] in terms which have been frequently cited in the English courts:

---

[95] Above, para.17–05. Sometimes it is said that a surety contract is not a contract *uberrimae fidei*, therefore there is no duty of disclosure; therefore the (limited) duty of disclosure (below, para.17–22) must be in fact be liability for implied misrepresentation: see, e.g. *Workington Harbour and Dock Board v Trade Indemnity Co. Ltd* [1934] 49 Ll. L. Rep. 430, CA, at 443–444, 451–453. However, it is preferable to admit that there is a (limited) duty of disclosure: *cf. ibid.*, at 432 (Scrutton L.J.).

[96] *Royal Bank of Scotland Plc v Etridge (No.2)*, above, n.94 at [81], [186]–[188]; *Levett v Barclays Bank Plc*, above, n.89 at 1275.

[97] *Hamilton v Watson* (1845) 12 Cl. & Fin. 109 at 119, 8 E.R. 1339 at 1343–1344, HL (Sc.), cited in, e.g. *Lee v Jones* (1854) 10 Exch. 523 at 534, 156 E.R. 545 at 550; *London General Omnibus Co. Ltd v Holloway* [1912] 2 K.B. 72, CA, at 78, 83; *Cooper v National Provincial Bank Ltd* [1946] K.B. 1 at 5–6; *Credit Lyonnais Bank Nederland v Export Credit Guarantee Department*, above, n.94 at 226; *Levett v Barclays Bank Plc*, above, n.89 at 1274–1275; *Royal Bank of Scotland Plc v Etridge (No.2)*, above, n.94 at [186]; *Palmer v Cornerstone Investments & Finance Co. Ltd* [2007] UKPC 49, 71 W.I.R. 277 at [40]; *North Shore Ventures Ltd v Anstead Holdings Inc.* [2011] EWCA Civ 230, [2011] All E.R. (D) 95 (Mar) at [31] (Morritt C., reviewing the authorities and confirming that the test set out by Lord Campbell in *Hamilton v Watson* and Lord Scott in *Royal Bank of Scotland v Etridge (No.2)*, above, n.94, is still the law; see also Smith L.J. at [57]).

> "I should think that this might be considered as the criterion whether such disclosure ought to be made voluntarily, namely, whether there is anything that might not naturally be expected to take place between the parties who are concerned in the transaction, that is, whether there be a contract between the debtor and the creditor, to the effect that his position shall be different from that which the surety might naturally expect; and, if so, the surety is to see whether that is disclosed to him. But if there be nothing which might not naturally take place between the parties, then, if the surety would guard against particular perils, he must put his question, and he must gain the information which he requires."

Although this case involved a guarantee of a debt the general principle has been held to apply to all surety contracts, although the way in which it applies will vary depending on the nature of the contract.[98] In particular, it has been applied in the context of fidelity guarantees to require an employer to disclose to the surety previous acts of dishonesty by the employee who is the object of the guarantee.[99] Where, however, the creditor makes clear that the surety must ascertain for himself all material facts, no duty of disclosure will arise.[100]

Contrast with the duty of disclosure in insurance contracts. 17–24
The duty of disclosure in surety contracts is clearly much more limited than that in insurance contracts. In insurance contracts, the duty is reciprocal, and extends to the disclosure of all material circumstances; and at least in the case of a corporate insured[101] includes disclosure of matters he ought in the ordinary course of business to know, as well as those he actually knows. In the case of surety contracts, however, the duty is only on the creditor: it is not reciprocal. English cases do not appear to have gone beyond a

---

98 *Levett v Barclays Bank Plc*, above, n.89 at 1273–1275.

99 *London General Omnibus Co. Ltd v Holloway*, above, n.97; see esp. at 85–87 (drawing a distinction between the previous financial dealings of the debtor which, as extrinsic circumstances, need not be disclosed in a guarantee of a debt, and the previous dishonesty of the employee which, as an intrinsic circumstance relevant to the subject-matter of the guarantee (the honesty of the employee) must be disclosed); *Railton v Mathews* (1844) 10 Cl. & Fin. 934, 8 E.R. 993, HL. See also *North Shore Ventures Ltd v Anstead Holdings Inc.*, above, n.97 at [30] (rejecting the trial judge's view that the scope of the duty of disclosure in relation to fidelity guarantees is wider).

100 *Trade Indemnity Co. Ltd v Workington Harbour and Dock Board* [1937] A.C. 1, HL, at 17–18 (performance guarantee).

101 Above, para.17–12.

requirement to disclose information which the debtor actually knows.[102] And, in general, the judges see surety contracts as closer to normal, commercial contracts than contracts *uberrimae fidei*—and therefore they start from the position that the surety should normally inform himself about the risks he is undertaking. There is a real concern to avoid undermining the security of contracts. In *Hamilton v Watson* Lord Campbell, whilst setting out the duty of disclosure which is required of a creditor in favour of a surety, made clear that the required disclosure is limited[103]:

> "I venture to say, if your Lordships were to adopt the principles laid down, and contended for by the appellant's counsel here, that you would entirely knock up those transactions in Scotland of giving security upon a cash account, because no bankers would rest satisfied that they had a security for the advance they made, if, as it is contended, it is essentially necessary that everything should be disclosed by the creditor that is material for the surety to know. If such was the rule, it would be indispensably necessary for the bankers to whom the security is to be given, to state how the account has been kept: whether the debtor was in the habit of overdrawing; whether he was punctual in his dealings; whether he performed his promises in an honourable manner;—for all these things are extremely material for the surety to know."

[102] In *Royal Bank of Scotland Plc v Etridge (No.2)*, above, n.94 at [188] Lord Scott thought that a statement by King C.J. in *Pooraka Holdings Pty Ltd v Participation Nominees Pty Ltd* (1991) 58 S.A.S.R. 184 at 193 that the creditor should disclose unusual features surrounding the transaction between the creditor and the surety (a) of which the creditor is or ought to be aware, (b) of which the surety is unaware, and (c) which the creditor appreciates or ought, in the circumstances, to appreciate might be unknown to the surety and might affect the surety's decision to enter into the guarantee, "may be too wide". For cases where the courts in England have indicated that a creditor would not be required to disclose to the surety matters of which it had only suspicion, and had no duty to enquire into the facts, see *National Provincial Bank of England Ltd v Glanusk* [1913] 3 K.B. 335; *Credit Lyonnais Bank Nederland v Export Credit Guarantee Department*, above, n.94 at 227.

[103] Above, n.97 at 118–119, at 1343. There are similar statements of general principle in *Levett v Barclays Bank Plc*, above, n.89 at 1272; *Commercial Bank of Australia Ltd v Amadio* (1983) 151 C.L.R. 447, HCA, at 456, followed in *Credit Lyonnais Bank Nederland v Export Credit Guarantee Department*, above, n.94 at 226–227. It has been held that the creditor owed no duty to the surety to tell him of his suspicion that the debtor was defrauding him: *National Provincial Bank of England Ltd v Glanusk*, above, n.102; nor to disclose to a surety who guaranteed a bank account that a person who had authority to draw on the account was an undischarged bankrupt and that cheques drawn on the account in the past had not been met: *Cooper v National Provincial Bank Ltd*, above, n.97.

Disclosure to surety wives. However, where the surety contract is one under which a wife guarantees her husband's debts or those of his company, the courts have taken a different approach.[104] Whilst maintaining the position that the surety contract itself imposes no obligation on the creditor in favour of the wife greater than that in any other surety contract,[105] the courts have in effect imposed a higher obligation in circumstances where the creditor has actual or constructive notice that the husband may be making misrepresentations to the wife, or subjecting her to undue influence, in order to induce her to enter into the surety contract. Strictly, therefore, the wife seeks a remedy not on the basis of the bank's failure of disclosure, but of positive misconduct by her husband which affects the validity of her contract with the creditor.[106] But the effect is to impose a duty of disclosure on the surety.[107] In order to minimise the risk that it will be unable to enforce the surety contract, but at the same time to minimise the risk that the surety is entering into the contract in consequence of the debtor's misconduct, the bank which is on notice of the risk of the debtor's misconduct towards the surety is required to take certain steps to satisfy itself that the surety has had brought home to her the practical implications of the surety contract, either by providing the necessary information directly to the surety or by receiving confirmation from a solicitor, acting for her, that he has advised the surety. If the bank is not willing to undertake the task of explanation itself, it must provide the surety's solicitor with the financial information he needs for this purpose. What is required will depend on the facts, but ordinarily it will include information on the purpose for which the loan which is to be guaranteed has been requested by the debtor, the current amount of the debtor's indebtedness, the amount of the current loan facility, and the amount and terms of any new facility.[108] 17–25

[104] The cases have generally involved wives' guarantees of their husbands' (or husbands' companies') debts, although the principles apply to all bank guarantees where the relationship between the surety and the debtor is non-commercial: *Royal Bank of Scotland Plc v Etridge (No.2)*, above, n.94 at [87].

[105] *Royal Bank of Scotland Plc v Etridge (No.2)*, above, n.94 at [81], [114], [189].

[106] See further above, paras 4–72 to 4–77.

[107] M. Fabre-Magnan, "Duties of Disclosure and French Contract Law" in *Good Faith and Fault in Contract Law* (J. Beatson and D. Friedmann eds, 1995), p.107.

[108] *Royal Bank of Scotland Plc v Etridge (No.2)*, above, n.94 at [54]–[55], [79].

17–26 **Rescission for breach of the duty to disclose.** Where the creditor is in breach of his duty to disclose to the surety unusual features of the contract between the creditor and the debtor[109] the surety is entitled to rescission of the surety contract, subject to the usual bars.[110] In many cases rescission will simply involve the avoidance of the surety's obligations. But where necessary, restitution must be made: for example, where the surety has given security against which execution has already been levied to enforce the surety's obligations, the creditor must restore to the surety the proceeds of sale of the security.[111] Where the creditor has notice of misconduct of the debtor against the surety and has not discharged its duty to provide information to the surety or to obtain assurance from the surety's solicitor that she has been properly advised, the bank will be unable to enforce the surety contract.[112]

(e) Compromises, releases and family arrangements[113]

17–27 **No general duty of disclosure on parties to a compromise of disputed claims.** Parties negotiating a contractual compromise of a disputed claim do not in general owe each other duties to disclose information relating to the claim.[114] The courts' policy in favour of settlement of disputes by the parties has led them to be reluctant to interfere.[115]

---

[109] Above, para.17–23.Where the surety knows of the unusual features, even though the creditor does not disclose them, there is no remedy: *North Shore Ventures Ltd v Anstead Holdings Inc.*, above, n.97 at [33] (Morritt C.: "the failure of the creditor to disclose that matter could not have constituted a misrepresentation on which the surety relied").

[110] Above, Ch.4; para.17–02.

[111] *Levett v Barclays Bank Plc*, above, n.89.

[112] *Royal Bank of Scotland Plc v Etridge (No.2)*, above, n.94. Where a guarantee covered the surety wife's own debts in respect of the purchase of her own share in property purchased jointly with the husband, as well as the husband's debts, the court refused to order rescission on the basis of the husband's undue influence unless the surety first discharged her own debts: *Midland Bank Plc v Greene* (1995) 27 H.L.R. 350.

[113] Spencer Bower (Non-Disclosure), Ch.9; Chitty, para.6–164; Treitel, para.9–146; Anson, p.338.

[114] *Turner v Green* [1895] 2 Ch. 205 (claimant's solicitor did not disclose to defendant preliminary hearing of summons by court officer which was adverse to claimant's case but which did not amount to decision that the claim was bad). For discussion of this case, see Spencer Bower (Non-Disclosure), paras 9.05–9.11: the current editors reject Mr Spencer Bower's view that there is a general duty of

Release of claims: duty in respect of known claims? In a release the parties do not settle an existing dispute, but instead release claims which one or both might have against the other or others. A release may be specific to particular claims, or general; it may be unilateral or mutual.[116] It has been suggested that there might be a duty on one party to disclose to the other claims which he knows are to be released but of which he knows the other party is ignorant. In *Bank of Credit and Commerce International S.A. v Ali*[117] Lord Nicholls, whilst not deciding it, spoke in general terms about this: **17–28**

---

disclosure in compromise agreements and his criticism of *Turner v Green*. See also *Silver Queen Maritime Ltd v Persia Petroleum Services Plc* [2010] EWHC 2867 (QB), [2010] All E.R. (D) 202 (Nov) at [131], [137] (Lindblom J., referring to this paragraph at [140]; and "the idea that the negotiation of agreements to settle hostile litigation generally gives rise to a duty of disclosure is misconceived. The existence of such a duty would not be consistent with the general position that parties negotiating for a contract do not owe duties of disclosure to each other. An agreement to settle litigation is not, or at least normally is not, a contract *uberrimae fidei*" (at [131]); and even if there was a fiduciary relationship between the parties, "I cannot see how that duty could have survived the launching of the present proceedings. The parties then found themselves engaged in the hostilities of active litigation. No duty of loyalty exists in that context. And no duty of loyalty arose when the parties set about resolving their differences in that litigation through negotiation" (at [137]); *Manifest Shipping Co. Ltd v Polaris Shipping Co. Ltd (The Star Sea)* [2001] UKHL 1, [2003] 1 A.C. 469 at [77], above, para 17–04, n. 14 (where parties owe duty of good faith, the duty no longer applies once the parties are engaged in litigation; the Civil Procedure Rules then govern).

115 Even if there is no valid claim the compromise will be binding, but if one party knows that his claim is unfounded, he does not provide consideration by agreeing to give it up: *Callisher v Bischoffsheim* (1870) L.R. 5 Q.B. 449; *Cook v Wright* (1861) 1 B. & S. 559 at 569, 121 E.R. 822 at 826; *Wade v Simeon* (1846) 2 C.B. 548, 135 E.R. 1061. For the reluctance of the courts to allow a common mistake to render a compromise void, see *Brennan v Bolt Burdon* [2004] EWCA Civ 1017; [2005] Q.B. 303; above para.15–24.

116 If unilateral, it must be by deed to be enforceable; in the case of mutual releases, each release will generally provide consideration for the other. In the case of unilateral releases, the party agreeing to the release may avoid it more easily on the basis of his mistake, given that there is no bargain to disturb: above, para.12–13, n.41.

117 [2001] UKHL 8, [2002] A.C. 251 at [32]–[33]. On the duty to disclose in the case of releases, see also Spencer Bower (Non-Disclosure), para.9.02, which however states the principle more widely and may be appropriate only to unilateral releases; above, n.116. In *Wales v Wadham* [1977] 1 W.L.R. 199 at 216 Tudor Evans J. held that the transaction was not a release, but also accepted

> "Thus far I have been considering the case where both parties were unaware of a claim which subsequently came to light. Materially different is the case where the party to whom the release was given knew that the other party had or might have a claim and knew also that the other party was ignorant of this. In some circumstances seeking and taking a general release in such a case, without disclosing the existence of the claim or possible claim, could be unacceptable sharp practice. When this is so, the law would be defective if it did not provide a remedy. . ..
>
> That is not the present case . . . This being so, I prefer to leave discussion of the route by which the law provides a remedy where there has been sharp practice to a case where that issue arises for decision. That there is a remedy in such cases I do not for one moment doubt."

Lord Hoffmann[118] was more explicit, both as to the possible principle, and as to its limitations: he would prefer to limit such a duty of disclosure to general releases:

> "A transaction in which one party agrees in general terms to release another from any claims upon him has special features. It is not difficult to imply an obligation upon the beneficiary of such a release to disclose the existence of claims of which he actually knows and which he also realises may not be known to the other party. There are different ways in which it can be put. One may say, for example, that inviting a person to enter into a release in general terms implies a representation that one is not aware of any specific claims which the other party may not know about. That would preserve the purity of the principle that there is no positive duty of disclosure. Or one could say, as the old Chancery judges did, that reliance upon such a release is against conscience when the beneficiary has been guilty of a suppressio veri or suggestio falsi. On a principle of law like this, I think it is legitimate to go back to authority, to Lord Keeper Henley in *Salkeld v Vernon*[119]

---

counsel's submission that there was no separate category of release which requires disclosure: the cases were all examples of family arrangements in which there was an established disclosure obligation: below, para.17–29.

[118] *Bank of Credit and Commerce International S.A. v Ali*, above, n.117 at [69]–[70]. The case involved an agreement by which an employee, on his redundancy, accepted the terms offered by the employer "in full and final settlement of all or any claims . . . of whatsoever nature that exist or may exist" against the employer. The House of Lords dealt with this as a matter of construction: the clause did not extend to claims for "stigma" damages to reflect the employee's difficulty in obtaining employment when the employer later went into liquidation and its corrupt and dishonest business practices were made public. This was not a claim which either party could realistically have had in mind: it was only later established that such a claim was possible in law (*Mahmud v Bank of Credit and Commerce International S.A.* [1998] A.C. 20, HL), so the parties could not have intended the release to cover it.

[119] (1758) 1 Eden 64 at 69, 28 E.R. 608 at 610.

where he said: 'no rule is better established than that every deed obtained on suggestio falsi, or suppressio veri, is an imposition in a court of conscience.'

. . . a person cannot be allowed to rely upon a release in general terms if he knew that the other party had a claim and knew that the other party was not aware that he had a claim. I do not propose any wider principle: there is obviously room in the dealings of the market for legitimately taking advantage of the known ignorance of the other party. But, both on principle and authority, I think that a release of rights is a situation in which the court should not allow a party to do so. On the other hand, if the context shows that the parties intended a general release for good consideration of rights unknown to both of them, I can see nothing unfair in such a transaction."

Duty of disclosure in family arrangements.[120] One type of compromise or settlement in which it is established that there is duty of disclosure is the family arrangement.[121] Where members of a family by contract settle a dispute amongst themselves,[122] such as the division of property, it has been held that there must be "a full and complete disclosure of all material circumstances within the knowledge of any of the parties."[123] Breach of the duty of disclosure entitles a party to the settlement, to whom disclosure was **17–29**

[120] Spencer Bower (Non-Disclosure), paras 9.12–9.15; Chitty, para.6–155; Anson, p.338; Cheshire, Fifoot and Furmston, pp.378–379; *Halsbury's Laws of England*, Vol. 42 (4th edn, reissue 1999), paras 1002–1100, esp. 1016.

[121] It is sometimes said that family arrangements are contracts *uberrimae fidei: Tennent v Tennents* (1870) L.R. 2 Sc. & Div. 6, HL(Sc.) at 10; *Wales v Wadham*, above, n.117 at 216; *Crowden v Aldridge* [1993] 1 W.L.R. 433.

[122] A memorandum between legatees of a will instructing the executors to take steps to vary their legacies so as to confer on the deceased's housekeeper an enhanced legacy was "not a family arrangement, nor a contract of any kind and the executors, although they proposed it, were not parties to it": *Crowden v Aldridge*, above, n.121 at 442.

[123] *Greenwood v Greenwood* (1863) 2 De G. J. & S. 28 at 42, 46 E.R. 285 at 290 (contract between defendant brother and his siblings to divide estate of a deceased brother in advance of knowing of contents of his will, when only defendant had information about value of his estate). See also *Gordon v Gordon* (1819) 3 Swans. 400, 36 E.R. 910 (agreement between brothers to divide family estates, made on basis that elder was illegitimate, rescinded when shown that younger son had not disclosed information relevant to question of legitimacy); *Tennent v Tennents*, above, n.121 (deed between father and two sons: but no failure to disclose); *Cashin v Cashin* [1938] 1 All E.R. 536, PC, at 544 (deed by which sons released doubtful claim against mother; but no failure to disclose).

not made, to rescind it.[124] There are few modern reported cases involving family arrangements.[125]

(f) *Contracts for the sale of land*[126]

17–30 **Vendor's duty to disclose latent defects of title.** Contracts for the sale of land, or of an interest in land, are not contracts *uberrimae fidei*.[127] The vendor under a contract for the sale of land has no general duty of disclosure, and so has no duty to disclose defects in the quality of the property.[128] It is said, however, that he

---

[124] *Gordon v Gordon*, above, n.123. The bars to rescission which are usually operative in cases of rescission for non-disclosure (above, para.17–02) will presumably operate, although *Gordon v Gordon* itself indicates that lapse of time will not normally be a bar: rescission was still available 19 years after the settlement was entered into.

[125] In *Wales v Wadham*, above, n.117, Tudor Evans J. held that there was no duty of disclosure on a wife negotiating a financial settlement on divorce which was to be embodied in a consent order, in circumstances where the parties had negotiated on the basis that neither was making full disclosure; *cf. Livesey v Jenkins* [1985] A.C. 424, HL, at 439, approving Tudor Evans J.'s approach on this point but differing on the basis that, for the court to be properly able to exercise its jurisdiction under the Matrimonial Causes Act 1973, s.25(1), both parties had to have a *duty to the court* to make full and frank disclosure of all material facts to the other party and to the court. Chitty, para.6–155, considers that these decisions "leave it uncertain whether the common law today recognises family settlements as contracts uberrimae fidei": but it is not clear that there is anything in the two cases that justifies this.

[126] Spencer Bower (Non-Disclosure), Ch.7; Treitel, para.9–145; Anson, p.339; E.H. Burn and J. Cartwright, *Cheshire and Burn's Modern Law of Real Property* (18th edn, 2011), pp.950–953.

[127] *Safehaven Investments Inc. v Springbok Ltd* (1996) 71 P. & C.R. 59 at 66 (contract for assignment of landlord's interest under lease not a contract of utmost good faith, so no duty to disclose limited life of sub-tenant as international body, which therefore affected value of lease).

[128] Emmet, para.4.026; J.T. Farrand, *Contract and Conveyance* (4th edn, 1983), pp.67–68; Spencer Bower (Non-Disclosure), paras 7.19–7.20. For the general position, that a purchaser of land is normally expected to make proper inquiries for himself (i.e. *caveat emptor*), even where he has received information from the vendor, see *Terrene Ltd v Nelson* (1937) 157 L.T. 254; and for an extreme case which illustrates the continuing strength of the *caveat emptor* rule, see *Sykes v Taylor-Rose* [2004] EWCA Civ 299, [2004] 2 P. & C.R. 30, above, para.3–07 (vendors of a house, who had recently discovered that a horrific murder been committed in the house some years earlier, had no duty to disclose it). See also D.M. Collins, "The Disclosure of Stigma Events in Property Transactions" [2008] Conv. 50 (contrasting solutions developed in Australian law). A vendor

has a duty to disclose latent defects in the title. This is not, however, a duty breach of which gives rise to rescission of the contract *ab initio* by the purchaser[129]; it may provide a contractual allocation of risk, or may operate as a defence to the vendor's action for specific performance, and is therefore discussed below.[130]

Although the vendor of property has no general duty of disclosure, there are limited specific duties imposed by law,[131] and by internal regulation and practice of the construction industry[132] and the legal profession involved in conveyancing transactions.[133]

who knowingly fails to disclose material defects of quality may, however, be unable to obtain specific performance of the contract: Jones and Goodhart, pp.93–97.

[129] *Faruqi v English Real Estates Ltd* [1979] 1 W.L.R. 963 at 969. In *Carlish v Salt* [1906] 1 Ch. 335 Joyce J. referred to "rescission" for non-disclosure, but probably in the sense of termination for breach, rather than rescission *ab initio*. On the use of this terminology in contracts for the sale of land, see Emmet, paras 7.003; above, para.8–37, n.168.

[130] Below, paras 17–41, 17–42.

[131] Energy Performance of Buildings (Certificates and Inspections) (England and Wales) Regulations 2007, SI 2007/991 (as amended), implementing Directive 2002/91/EC (now recast in Directive 2010/31/EU), imposes duties on sellers and landlords of both commercial and residential property to make available energy performance certificates to prospective buyers and tenants: see F. Silverman, *Conveyancing Handbook* (17th edn, 2010), s.A27. The Housing Act 2004, Pt.5, extended duties of disclosure on sellers of residential property through the requirement to provide a "home information pack" containing documents (some mandatory, some optional) prescribed by regulations. Home information packs were controversial, and the duty to provide them was suspended by the new Government on 21 May 2010 (formal repeal is to be effected by the Localism Bill which is passing through Parliament during 2011). Energy performance certificates were mandatory documents within home information packs.

[132] The Consumer Code for Home Builders (2nd edn, 2010) requires builders and developers of new or newly converted homes for sale to the public, who are registered with an organisation providing home warranties (such as the National House-Building Council: *cf.* below, para.17–41, n.173), to provide enough pre-purchase information to help the home buyer to make suitably informed purchase decisions; an independent dispute resolution scheme is provided, under which an adjudicator can make a performance award or a financial award (with a limit of £15,000).

[133] *Sykes v Taylor-Rose*, above, n.128 at [50] (Peter Gibson L.J.): "Because the *caveat emptor* rule can work harshly on purchasers, whose knowledge of material facts affecting the property they are purchasing is almost certain to be considerably less than that of the vendors, the practice of sending pre-contract enquiries has become standard and the scope of the enquiries has been extended over a period of time. It is for the buyer to decide what enquiries to raise and in

Much information is in practice therefore disclosed, although it is clear that the general legal position remains *caveat emptor*.[134]

17–31 **No duty of disclosure on the purchaser.** The purchaser of land has no duty of disclosure in favour of the vendor. His position is the same as a purchaser of goods: *caveat emptor*—which means that the risks the buyer takes can operate to his advantage as much as to his disadvantage[135]:

> "The case put of the purchase of an estate, in which there is a mine under the surface, but the fact is unknown to the seller, is one in which a man of tender conscience or high honour would be unwilling to take advantage of the ignorance of the seller; but there can be no doubt that the contract for the sale of the estate would be binding."

---

what form". The National Conveyancing Protocol (first introduced in 1990; now 6th edn, 2011) sets out steps to be followed by solicitors acting for seller and buyer, and this includes the provision by the seller of a package of information to the buyer's solicitor, including evidence of the seller's title and the Seller's Property Information Form, which contains answers to standard form pre-contract enquiries. It is specified by the Council of the Law Society as "preferred practice" for solicitors but is not mandatory under the rules of professional conduct.

[134] Even the introduction of home information packs (above, n.131) was not intended to change the *caveat emptor* rule: *Reforming the home buying and selling process in England and Wales: Contents of the home information pack* (Consultation Paper, Office of the Deputy Prime Minister, March 2003), para.7.5: "We do not intend, however, to change the principle of *caveat emptor* (let the buyer beware). We are not suggesting that sellers should be under a legal obligation to answer questions set out in a property information form included in the home information pack.". Much of the information was "authorised" to be included rather than "required", and the buyer's remedies depended on what was, in fact, provided. The failure to provide a home information pack, or any particular required item of information within it, did not entitle the buyer to rescind the contract or to claim damages.

[135] *Smith v Hughes* (1871) L.R. 6 Q.B. 597 at 604. For the same example (and the same answer) see *Fox v Mackreth* (1788) 2 Cox 320 at 321, 30 E.R. 148 at 148–149; *Turner v Harvey* (1821) Jac. 169 at 178, 37 E.R. 814 at 817–818. Non-disclosure by the purchaser could only relate to quality of the property, since he is in no special position as regards information as to the title to the land.

(g) *Other types of contract*

No duty of disclosure in other contracts. Other types of contract[136] do not inherently carry the duty on negotiating parties to make disclosure to each other. There is specific authority that contracts of sale of goods,[137] of employment[138] and of salvage[139] do not carry duties of disclosure. **17–32**

(2) Obligations of Disclosure Arising From Particular Relationships

Duties owed between parties in fiduciary relationships. Parties negotiating for a contract may already be in a relationship which imposes on one or both of them the duty to disclose information during the negotiations. The duties may be mutual—for example, where there are dealings between partners, where the duty of good faith attaches to both parties in their mutual dealings during the **17–33**

[136] As opposed to contracts entered into by persons who, at the time of the negotiations, already have a relationship which carries with it duties of good faith and disclosure: below, para.17–33.

[137] *Jewson & Sons Ltd v Arcos Ltd* [1933] 47 Ll. L. Rep. 93, CA, at 100. The statement by Lord Wynford in *Rothschild v Brookman* (1831) 5 Bli. N.S. 165 at 202, 5 E.R. 273 at 286, that "Between buyers and sellers there must be *uberrima fides*. Each man must know the circumstances under which he is dealing" must be read in context: a contract between principal and agent, below, para.17–34, n.143. However, for the effect of terms implied by statute concerning title and quality of goods as imposing on the seller or supplier a contractual risk which reflects his failure to disclose information, see below, para.17–40.

[138] *Bell v Lever Bros Ltd* [1932] A.C. 161, HL, at 227–228. Nor is there a general duty on the employee during the currency of the contract to disclose his own misconduct or the misconduct of fellow employees. But the terms of the employment contract may be such that there is a contractual duty to disclose the misconduct of other employees: *Sybron Corp. v Rochem Ltd* [1984] Ch. 112, CA; and a director has a duty to disclosure his own misconduct, not by virtue of his contract of employment, but by virtue of his fiduciary duty to the company as director: *Item Software (UK) Ltd v Fassihi* [2004] EWCA Civ 1244, [2005] 2 B.C.L.C. 91 (where Arden L.J. also noted at [55]–[56] that *Bell v Lever Bros Ltd* did not decide that there could never be a duty of disclosure on the part of the employee, nor did it cover the case where there is fraudulent concealment).

[139] *The Unique Mariner* [1978] 1 Lloyd's Rep. 438 at 454–455, interpreting statements to the contrary in *The Kingalock* (1854) 1 Sp. Ecc. & Ad. 263 at 265, 164 E.R. 153 at 154, which however is still regarded as authority by Goff & Jones, para.9–019.

partnership[140]; or unilateral—for example, where there are dealings between a trustee and the beneficiary of the trust, or between a person who owes fiduciary duties and the person to whom he owes those duties.

17–34 **The content of the duty depends on the relationship.** The nature of the relationship between the parties must always be examined, to see what duty is imposed: for example, where the contract is for a trustee to purchase a beneficiary's interest under the trust the contract is voidable by the beneficiary unless the trustee can show that he has taken no advantage of his position and has made full disclosure to the beneficiary, and that the transaction is fair and honest.[141] Where there is a fiduciary relationship the nature of the relationship and its particular circumstances must be examined to decide what duty the fiduciary owes. Sometimes the duty is only one of disclosure; sometimes it goes beyond that and requires a more general fair dealing between the parties.[142] But in various contexts[143] the courts have held that a consequence of characterising the relationship between the parties as fiduciary is

[140] R.C. I'Anson Banks, *Lindley & Banks on Partnership* (19th edn, 2010), Ch.16; see also Partnership Act 1890, s.28. This duty, which may even arise between intending partners who have not yet concluded their partnership agreement, is separate from the duty of disclosure between negotiating partners in respect of the formation of the partnership contract itself: above, para.17–20.

[141] *Tito v Waddell (No.2)* [1977] Ch. 106 at 241. See also *Thomson v Eastwood* (1877) 2 App. Cas. 215, HL, at 236; *Coles v Trecothick* (1804) 9 Ves. Jun. 234 at 246–247; 32 E.R. 592 at 597; J. Mowbray, L. Tucker, N. Le Poidevin, E. Simpson and J. Brightwell, *Lewin on Trusts* (18th edn, 2008), paras 20–135 to 20–140.

[142] Some relationships may raise irrebutable presumptions that one party was in a position to exercise undue influence over the other: *Royal Bank of Scotland Plc v Etridge (No.2)* [2001] UKHL 44, [2002] 2 A.C. 773 at [18]. Other remedies are sometimes available: e.g. account of profits: *Regier v Campbell-Stuart* [1939] Ch. 766; *English v Dedham Vale Properties Ltd* [1978] 1 W.L.R. 93; or compensation in equity: *Longstaff v Birtles* [2001] EWCA Civ 1219, [2002] 1 W.L.R. 470. See generally J.E. Martin, *Hanbury and Martin: Modern Equity* (18th edn, 2009), Ch.21; Snell, Ch.7.

[143] e.g. principal and agent: *Armstrong v Jackson* [1917] 2 K.B. 822; *Rothschild v Brookman*, above, n.137; *Regier v Campbell-Stuart*, above, n.142; *English v Dedham Vale Properties Ltd*, above, n.142 (self-appointed agent); partners: *Law v Law* [1905] 1 Ch. 140, CA, at 157; solicitor and client: *Demerara Bauxite Co. Ltd v Hubbard* [1923] A.C. 673, PC; promoters of company and the company: *Erlanger v New Sombrero Phosphate Co.* (1878) 3 App. Cas. 1218, HL; *Lagunas Nitrate Co. v Lagunas Syndicate* [1899] 2 Ch. 392, CA.

that the party owing the fiduciary duties is required to make full disclose of relevant matters, and that in the event of non-disclosure the other party may avoid the contract. Similarly, even where the relationship does not fall within an established category of fiduciary relationship the court may decide that the relationship on the facts carries duties of confidence and disclosure.[144] For example, where the relationship falls short of partnership, but has elements of joint enterprise or joint venture, there is no hard and fast rule as to whether the parties owe each other duties of good faith, fiduciary duties or duties of disclosure: each case depends on its facts, but the terms of the contract which regulates the relationship will be of primary importance to decide whether one party's actions under the contract can properly be said to have been for the purpose of serving the parties' joint interests, rather than its own separate interest, and therefore the party can be held to have owed a duty of good faith to the other.[145] The scope of the duty of disclosure owed as a result of such a duty of good faith will, however, depend on the facts and on the terms of the contract between the parties.[146]

---

[144] *Tate v Williamson* (1866) L.R. 2 Ch. App. 55 at 66–67 (purchase of property from cousin: "openness and fair dealing were the more necessary when he was negotiating with an extravagant and necessitous young man, deprived at the time of all other advice, eager to raise money, and apparently careless in what manner it was obtained"). For a discussion of the types of relationship to which the courts give particular protection under the doctrine of undue influence, see *Royal Bank of Scotland Plc v Etridge (No.2)*, above, n.142 at [9]–[11], [18], [104]; and for an example of a duty of disclosure arising from a relationship of trust and confidence within the law of undue influence, see *First Plus Financial Group Plc v Hewett* [2010] EWCA Civ 312, [2010] 2 P. & C.R. 22 (husband, asking wife to join him in mortgage of their matrimonial home as security for his separate debts, owed duty to disclose his affair with another woman which, because it carried serious risk of the husband's eventual withdrawal of support, was objectively a material fact calling for disclosure: non-disclosure constituted undue influence, which also affected the mortgagee and therefore the security: *cf.* above, para.17–25).

[145] *Ross River Ltd v Cambridge City Football Club Ltd* [2007] EWHC 2115 (Ch), [2008] 1 All E.R. 1004 at [197]–[199], [229]–[232], following *Hospital Products Ltd v United States Surgical Corp.* (1984) 55 ALR 417 at 454–455, and the approach set out by P. Finn, "Fiduciary Law in the Modern Commercial World" in E. McKendrick (ed.), *Commercial Aspects of Fiduciary Obligations* (1992) p.6 at p.14. The collaboration between co-workout banks does not, in the absence of an express contractual requirement, impose mutual duties of disclosure: below, para.17–36.

[146] *ibid.*, at [233]–[235].

17–35 **Duties of disclosure imposed for reasons of policy.** These duties are imposed in such circumstances for reasons of policy to protect the party in whose favour the duty arises. This area is therefore one in which the general rules of contract formation overlap with the rules for the protection of particular individuals by virtue of the position which they hold, vis-à-vis the other party, independently of the fact that they are entering into the contract; and in such cases the protective rules impose additional duties beyond those which are imposed by the general rules of contract formation. Further discussion of these protective rules is outside the scope of this book.[147]

17–36 **Commercial practice to disclose does not necessarily create legal duty to disclose.** The fact that two parties enter into a contract in a context where it is recognised to be good commercial practice for disclosure of certain information to be made, does not necessarily mean that there will be a legal duty to make such disclosure. It has been held, for example, that although co-workout banks (each working with a common debtor in financial difficulty with a view to minimise the risk of loss to the lending banks) may generally consider it to be good practice to disclose to each other information known to them which related to the assets, liabilities and business of the debtor and which had been obtained for the purposes of the workout, so as to achieve as far as possible common knowledge between co-creditors as to such information, there was no legal duty to adhere to that practice in the absence of an express contractual framework.[148]

---

[147] Spencer Bower (Non-Disclosure), Pts 4 and 5; N. Enonchong, *Duress, Undue Influence and Unconscionable Dealing* (2006), Pt.II; Cartwright, Chs 8 and 9; Chitty, paras 7–056 to 7–139; Furmston, paras 4.137 to 4.156; Treitel, paras 10–012 to 10–044; Anson, pp.359–377; Cheshire, Fifoot and Furmston, pp.379–381, 391–403; Snell, Chs 7 (fiduciaries), 8 (equitable fraud, undue influence and unconscionable transactions); *Hanbury and Martin: Modern Equity*, above, n.142, paras 26.007 to 26.014.

[148] *National Westminster Bank Plc v Rabobank Nederland* [2007] EWHC 1056 (Comm), [2007] All E.R. (D) 186 (May) at [110]–[114] (Colman J., considering at [112]–[113] why such a legal duty of disclosure would be inappropriate and commercially undesirable).

II. LIABILITY IN TORT FOR NON-DISCLOSURE

The tort of deceit. It has generally been said that for the tort of deceit[149] it is not sufficient that a defendant knowingly stood by and allowed the claimant to persevere in his misunderstanding: the tort is committed only if the defendant caused the representee to be deceived, which means that he must have made an active misrepresentation. For example, in *Peek v Gurney* Lord Cairns said:[150] 17–37

> "Mere non-disclosure of material facts, however morally censurable, however that non-disclosure might be a ground in a proper proceeding at a proper time for setting aside an allotment or a purchase of shares, would in my opinion form no ground for an action in the nature of an action for misrepresentation. There must, in my opinion, be some active misstatement of fact, or, at all events, such a partial and fragmentary statement of fact, as that the withholding of that which is not stated makes that which is stated absolutely false."

As we have seen, this can include not only partial statements ("half-truths") but also conduct which communicates a falsehood, such as taking steps to cover up defects in property designed to communicate to a tenant or purchaser that the property is sound.[151]

---

[149] Above, Ch.5.

[150] (1873) L.R. 6 H.L. 377, HL, 403; see also Lord Chelmsford at 390–391. This was obiter, but was followed in *Arkwright v Newbold* (1881) 17 Ch.D. 301, CA, at 318, 320. For further statements that the action of deceit requires a positive misleading of the claimant, see *Aaron's Reefs Ltd v Twiss* [1896] A.C. 273, HL, at 281; *Bradford Third Equitable Benefit Building Society v Borders* [1941] 2 All E.R. 205, HL, at 211, 220. A party can be liable in deceit for failing to correct a statement he has made during the negotiations, where he discovers its falsity before the representee relies on it; but in such a case the defendant is liable for his misrepresentation, not for his silence: *Brownlie v Campbell* (1880) 5 App. Cas. 925 at 950 (Lord Blackburn, who went on however, to make also a wider statement: below, text to n.152). It is sufficient for the tort of deceit that the defendant adopts a representation made by a third party: above, para.5–07; and note that in *Bradford Third Equitable Benefit Building Society v Borders* at 220 Lord Wright said that a person could be liable who learns of another's misrepresentation and "knowingly uses the delusion created by the fraud in the injured party's mind in order to profit by the fraud". But such cases are not simple fraudulent non-disclosure, since it presupposes that a third party made a misrepresentation; but it goes beyond the established core case of deceit where the defendant himself fraudulently deceives the claimant.

[151] *Gordon v Selico Co. Ltd* [1985] 2 E.G.L.R. 79; above, para.5–06.

In *Brownlie v Campbell*,[152] however, Lord Blackburn went further, and suggested rather tentatively that the intentional breach of a duty of disclosure could constitute the tort of deceit:

> "I go on further still to say, what is perhaps not quite so clear, but certainly it is my opinion, where there is a duty or an obligation to speak, and a man in breach of that duty or obligation holds his tongue and does not speak, and does not say the thing he was bound to say, if that was done with the intention of inducing the other party to act upon the belief that the reason why he did not speak was because he had nothing to say, I should be inclined myself to hold that that was fraud also."

In the modern cases, some judges have continued to reject the argument that the tort of deceit can be committed without a positive misrepresentation,[153] but others, without addressing directly the line of authorities[154] against the general proposition, have asserted that deceit does cover non-disclosure. The first such statement made as a necessary part of the reasoning in coming to a decision, was made by Lawrence Collins J. in *Conlon v Simms*:

> "It is clear that where there is a duty to disclose, and the failure to disclose is fraudulent, there will be an action in deceit and damages will be an available remedy. In such cases 'the non-disclosure assumes the character of fraudulent concealment, or amounts to fraudulent misrepresentation, or is otherwise founded on, or characterized and accompanied by, fraud'.[155]"

---

[152] Above, n.150 at 150.

[153] *H.I.H. Casualty and General Insurance Ltd v Chase Manhattan Bank* [2003] UKHL 6, [2003] 2 Lloyd's Rep. 61 at [75] (Lord Hoffmann: "non-disclosure (whether dishonest or otherwise) does not as such give rise to a claim in damages: see *Banque Keyser Ullmann S.A. v Skandia (UK) Insurance Co. Ltd* [1990] 1 Q.B. 665 at 777–781 and 788 ('without a misrepresentation there can be no fraud in the sense of giving rise to a claim for damages in tort') and [1991] 2 A.C. 249 at 280 (per Lord Templeman) and 281 (per Lord Jauncey of Tullichettle)").

[154] Above, n.150.

[155] [2006] EWHC 401 (Ch), [2006] 2 All E.R. 1024 at [202] (the quotation is from Spencer-Bower (Non-Disclosure), para.14.02, although it appears to be taken out of context: J. Cartwright, "Liability in Tort for Pre-Contractual Non-Disclosure" in A. Burrows and E. Peel (eds), *Contract Formation and Parties* (2010), p.137 at p.148). Whether deceit covers non-disclosure had been raised as a question by Rix L.J. in *H.I.H. Casualty and General Insurance Ltd v Chase Manhattan Bank* [2001] EWCA Civ 1250, [2001] 2 Lloyd's Rep. 483 at [48], [164], [168], and assumed to be correct by Lord Bingham in HL: above, n.153 at [21]. Furmston, para.4.66 cites this case as authority for a general proposition that fraudulent non-disclosure constitutes the tort of deceit,

This was confirmed in the same case by the Court of Appeal, where Jonathan Parker L.J. said:[156]

> "Non-disclosure where there is a duty to disclose is tantamount to an implied representation that there is nothing relevant to disclose."

These recent developments, without adequate recognition of contrary authority, and without discussion of the reasons for and against the extension of the law to allow a claim in tort for the intentional breach of a duty of disclosure, or the implications of the decision beyond the tort of deceit, are rather unsatisfactory.[157] However, their effect appears to be that the fraudulent failure to fulfil a duty of disclosure which is imposed by the law, such as the duty of the insured to disclose material facts to the insurer,[158] may now give rise to an action in deceit.[159]

The tort of negligence. Although it is possible for a person to owe a duty of care in the tort of negligence to provide information or advice,[160] the courts have been careful to avoid allowing such 17–38

apparently without even limiting it to the dishonest breach of a duty of disclosure, or noting the authorities against the proposition (above, n.150).

[156] [2006] EWCA Civ 1749, [2008] 1 W.L.R. 484 at [130]. CA reversed the decision of the trial judge on other grounds.

[157] For further discussion, see Cartwright, "Liability in Tort for Pre-Contractual Non-Disclosure", above, n.155; and for the possible consequence of the decision in relation to a claim under Misrepresentation Act 1967 s.2(1), see below, para.17–45. Chitty, para.6–143 regards as "very doubtful" the extension of the tort of deceit in *Conlon v Simms* to cover intentional breaches of duties of disclosure ; Clerk & Lindsell, para.18–09 accepts *Conlon v Simms* but thinks that its application outside fiduciary relations is not entirely clear. The development of the tort of deceit in *Conlon v Simms* is, however, consistent with the extension of criminal liability for fraud by Fraud Act 2006 s.3 to cover fraud by failing to disclose information, which applies to the dishonest failure to disclose information which the defendant was under a legal duty to disclose: below, para.17–55.

[158] Above, paras 17–07 *et seq.*

[159] The approach of Lawrence Collins J. in *Conlon v Simms*, above, n.155, was tentatively followed by Lewison J. in *J.D. Wetherspoon Plc v Ven de Berg & Co. Ltd* [2007] EWHC 1044 (Ch), [2007] P.N.L.R. 28 at [17] (arguable cause of action in deceit for dishonest failure to make disclosure where obligation of disclosure arose from fiduciary obligations). See also *Cavell USA Inc. v Seaton Insurance Co.* [2008] EWHC 3043 (Comm), [2008] 2 C.L.C. 898 at [84], [86].

[160] Above, Ch.6. Such a duty arises where one party assumes a responsibility to the other to provide information or advice: above, para.6–26. The scope of duty

duties to undermine the general principle that there is no obligation to speak within the context of negotiations for an ordinary commercial contract.[161] Even where parties are negotiating for a contract which is a contract *uberrimae fidei* and carries the duty of disclosure,[162] the parties do not thereby undertake a common law duty of care towards each other in the negotiations.[163] This is not to say that there cannot be a duty of care during negotiations for a contract, for example where a person enters into a contract with the one to whom he owes fiduciary duties. Indeed, it was in *Nocton v Lord Ashburton*[164] that the House of Lords recognised a fiduciary's duty of care in giving advice even before they developed the generalised duty to take care.[165] But in such a case the duty arises in

---

undertaken by a professional may go beyond the specific task and carry a duty to keep the client's position under review and inform him of relevant changes in circumstances; see, e.g. *Credit Lyonnais S.A. v Russell Jones & Walker* [2002] EWHC 1310 (Ch), [2003] P.N.L.R. 2 (solicitor); *H.I.H. Casualty & General Insurance Ltd v J.L.T. Risk Solutions Ltd* [2007] EWCA Civ 710, [2007] 2 C.L.C. 62 (insurance broker's post-placement duty).

[161] *Banque Keyser Ullmann S.A. v Skandia (UK) Insurance Co. Ltd* [1990] 1 Q.B. 665, CA, at 798–805. The statements by Slade L.J. at 799–800 to the effect that the courts are reluctant to impose duties which fill contractual gaps because of the decision in *Tai Hing Cotton Mill Ltd v Liu Chong Hing Bank Ltd* [1986] A.C. 80, PC, must be read now in the light of *Henderson v Merrett Syndicates Ltd* [1995] 2 A.C. 145, HL; but nothing in that later case casts doubt on the point made by Slade L.J. that there is no general common law duty of care owed by each party to the other during the negotiations for a contract. See also *Martel Building Ltd v Canada* (2000) 193 D.L.R. (4th) 1, SCC (no general duty of care in conducting commercial negotiations apart from cases within the established categories of duty such as negligent misrepresentation, and no new category should be developed for the conduct of pre-contractual negotiations); *Walford v Miles* [1992] 2 A.C. 128 at 138, HL (Lord Ackner: duty to carry on negotiations in good faith is inherently repugnant to the adversarial position of the parties when involved in negotiations. Each party to the negotiations is entitled to pursue his or her own interest, so long as he avoids making misrepresentations).

[162] Above, para.17–03.

[163] *Banque Keyser Ullmann S.A. v Skandia (UK) Insurance Co. Ltd*, above, n.161 at 800–801; *H.I.H. Casualty and General Insurance Ltd v Chase Manhattan Bank* [2001] EWCA Civ 1250, [2001] 2 Lloyd's Rep. 483 at [59]–[74]. See also *Bank of Nova Scotia v Hellenic Mutual War Risks Association (Bermuda) Ltd* [1990] 1 Q.B. 818, CA, at 900–903 (not discussed on appeal: [1992] 1 A.C. 233, HL).

[164] [1914] A.C. 932, HL; above, para.6–08.

[165] *Hedley Byrne & Co. Ltd v Heller & Partners Ltd* [1964] A.C. 465, HL; above, para.6–10.

tort because there is a particular position held by one party vis-à-vis the other which takes it out of the normal situation of bargaining at arm's length. In effect, the duty in tort reflects the pre-existing relationship between the negotiating parties and imposes a duty to take care in the negotiations entered into within the context of that relationship.[166]

It should be remembered, however, that even if there is a duty in the tort of negligence to speak—to provide information or advice—it is only a duty to take *reasonable care*. Just as liability for negligent statements flows not from the falsity of the statement but from the failure to take reasonable care in making it,[167] so here liability will not be based simply on the failure to disclose information, but on the fact that such failure was a breach of the duty to take reasonable care to provide it.[168]

III. NON-DISCLOSURE AS BREACH OF CONTRACT

No general contractual warranty of disclosure. Given the general position taken by English law that there is no general duty of disclosure between negotiating parties, it follows that there is no general implied contractual promise by each party to the other that material matters have been disclosed. Even where the contract is one *uberrimae fidei* and has associated duties of disclosure in the formation of the contract, there is not thereby any implied contractual warranty that disclosure has been made. The duty of disclosure in the formation of a contract of insurance, for example, **17–39**

[166] Although there are some doubts about the nature and scope of the duty in *Nocton v Lord Ashburton*, and the relationship between the equitable duty of care and the common law duty (above, para.6–08), it seems clear in the light of the developments in *Hedley Byrne* and later cases that the common law will recognise a duty of care by a fiduciary: above, paras 6–09 to 6–11. *Cf. Longstaff v Birtles* [2001] EWCA Civ 1219, [2002] 1 W.L.R. 470 (fiduciary duty owed by solicitor to former client although no common law duty on facts). See, similarly, the duty of disclosure which can give rise to the remedy of rescission in the case of some pre-existing relationships: above, para.17–33.

[167] Above, para.6–12.

[168] The content of the fiduciary duty itself, based on an obligation of loyalty and including the duty of disclosure by the fiduciary in dealings with his beneficiary, is different from the duty of care (whether in equity or at common law): *Bristol and West Building Society v Mothew* [1998] Ch. 1, CA, at 16–18.

arises as a matter of law, and not from a term of the contract; and breach of that duty does not give rise to any claim to damages for breach of contract.[169]

It is, however, possible for a party to give an express warranty that he has made disclosure.[170]

17–40 **Non-disclosure and the contractual allocation of risk.** Sometimes the allocation of risk in a contract can reflect one party's failure to disclose information: for example, by statute a seller or supplier of goods impliedly promises that he has the right to sell or supply the goods free from charges and incumbrances not disclosed or known to the buyer before the contract is made; and a business seller or supplier of goods impliedly promises that they are of satisfactory quality.[171] The fact that these terms will be implied if the seller or supplier fails to provide contrary information provides an incentive for him to draw any defects to the buyer's attention.[172]

---

[169] Above, para.17–07; *Banque Keyser Ullmann S.A. v Skandia (UK) Insurance Co. Ltd*, above, n.161 at 776–781; *H.I.H. Casualty and General Insurance Ltd v Chase Manhattan Bank* [2001] EWCA Civ 1250, [2001] 2 Lloyd's Rep. 483 at [49]; *Bank of Nova Scotia v Hellenic Mutual War Risks Association (Bermuda) Ltd*, above, n.163 at 888–890 (not discussed on appeal: [1992] 1 A.C. 233, HL).

[170] Such as a "basis of contract" clause in an insurance contract: above, para.17–18. There can also be contractual promises, express or implied, to speak in the *performance* of the contract, such as a building contractor's duty to warn his employer of design defects discovered during the course of a building project: *Plant Construction Plc v Clive Adams Associates* [2000] B.L.R. 137, CA. But this is outside the scope of this book.

[171] Sale of Goods Act 1979 ss.12(1), (2)(a), 14(1), (2C)(a). See also the Supply of Goods and Services Act 1982 ss.2(1), (2)(a), 4(2), (3)(a) (transfer of goods), 7(1), (2), 9(2), (3)(a) (hire of goods); Supply of Goods (Implied Terms) Act 1973 ss.8(1)(a), (b)(i), 10(2), (2C)(a) (hire-purchase), all as amended by the Sale and Supply of Goods Act 1994 s.7, Sch.2. For contracts for the sale of land, see below, para.17–41.

[172] In the cases discussed here the defendant's liability is more extensive that it might otherwise be as a result of his failure to disclose information. By contrast, a party sometimes has an incentive to disclose information so that he will himself have a more extensive claim: such as a buyer who wishes to hold a seller liable if goods are not fit for a purpose beyond the normal purpose of the goods in question: Sale of Goods Act 1979 s.14(3); or a party who wishes to be able, in the event of breach of contract, to recover damages to include consequential losses of a kind which arise from special circumstances beyond the normal loss: *Hadley v Baxendale* (1854) 9 Exch. 341, 156 E.R. 145, or to show that the other party can

Contracts for the sale of land. The general position in contracts for the sale of land is *caveat emptor*; and, indeed, the purchaser under a contract for the sale of land is in this respect less protected than the purchaser under a contract for the sale or supply of goods because there are generally fewer implied terms in contracts for the sale of land which reverse the allocation of risk implied by the general *caveat emptor* rule.[173] 17–41

It is said that the vendor under a contract for the sale of land has a duty to disclose latent defects in the title.[174] The purchaser cannot complain where he has actual knowledge of the defects, or where the vendor provides him with sufficient information to enable him to discover them.[175] But for this purpose it is not sufficient that the purchaser has notice of the defects by reason only of their being registered.[176] There is, however, some uncertainty in the cases about the nature and scope of the duty of disclosure. Sometimes it is said that the vendor's duty of disclosure is absolute, and does not depend

be taken to have accepted liability for such losses: *Transfield Shipping Inc. v Mercator Shipping Inc. (The Achilleas)* [2008] UKHL 48, [2009] 1 A.C. 61, above, para.8–30, nn.149–150.

173 In the case of a contract to build and sell a house the builder-vendor impliedly promises that the house will be constructed in a good and workmanlike manner, with good and proper materials, and will be fit for habitation: *Hancock v B.W. Brazier (Anerley) Ltd* [1966] 1 W.L.R. 1317. Builders of new houses may routinely provide express guarantees under schemes run by the National House-Building Council. The starting-point in relation to *leases* is also that "landlord gives no implied warranty as to the fitness or condition of the premises. Caveat lessee": *Southwark LBC v Tanner* [2001] 1 A.C. 1 at 12 (Lord Hoffmann). But there are certain terms implied into certain types of lease, both at common law (e.g. a condition that a furnished house is reasonably fit for habitation) and by statute (e.g. condition that a house let for human habitation at a low rent is fit for human habitation under the Landlord and Tenant Act 1985, s.8). See E.H. Burn and J. Cartwright, *Cheshire and Burn's Modern Law of Real Property* (18th edn, 2011), pp.227–234.

174 Emmet, paras 4.020–4.031; Megarry & Wade, *The Law of Real Property* (7th edn, 2008), paras 15–070 to 15–073; J.T. Farrand, *Contract and Conveyance* (4th edn, 1983), pp.62–75.

175 *Molyneux v Hawtrey* [1903] 2 K.B. 487, CA, at 497. The question is whether the vendor has done enough to draw the attention of an ordinary purchaser to the defect, not whether a trained equity conveyancer would understand it: *Faruqi v English Real Estates Ltd* [1979] 1 W.L.R. 963 at 967. Presumably, though, in an appropriate case notice to the "ordinary" purchaser's (trained) solicitor should be sufficient.

176 *Rignall Developments Ltd v Halil* [1988] Ch. 190 (local land charges register: deemed actual notice under Law of Property Act 1925, s.198(1), insufficient).

on his knowledge of the defect in title.[177] In many cases, however, it is said that the vendor's duty is limited to defects of which he knows, and which are unusual.[178] The most satisfactory interpretation may well be that the vendor's obligation is to convey the property rights which are the object of the contract—and, therefore, in effect there is an implied term in the contract that there are no undisclosed latent defects.[179] The vendor's knowledge of the defect is irrelevant, since he has impliedly promised the complete and unincumbered title. However, when viewed in this way, it may well not add anything to characterise the vendor's duty as one of disclosure, any more than it does in the case of a contract for the sale or supply of goods where by statute a seller or supplier of goods impliedly promises that he has the right to sell or supply the goods free from charges and incumbrances not disclosed or known to the buyer before the contract is made. In effect such a provision imposes on one party a contractual risk which reflects his failure to disclose information, but it is not customarily characterised as a duty of disclosure.[180]

However, it is clear that, for the purposes of some remedies which follow from the discovery by a purchaser of land of a defect in the title, the vendor's knowledge of the defect is relevant.

17–42 **Purchaser's remedies for non-disclosure by vendor of land.** Where the vendor is unable to convey the property without any incumbrance or defect of title, the purchaser may claim damages; or he may defend the vendor's claim to specific performance and seek

---

[177] *Halsbury's Laws of England*, Vol. 42 (4th edn, reissue 1999), para.56, relying on *Re Brewer and Hankins's Contract* (1899) 80 L.T. 127, CA (vendor liable to pay compensation for undisclosed sewer under property of which he had no knowledge).

[178] *Faruqi v English Real Estates Ltd* [1979] 1 W.L.R. 963 at 967 (covenants, copy of which could not be produced); *Re Marsh and Earl Granville* (1883) 24 Ch.D. 11, CA, at 24 (failure to state that deed, to be root of title, was voluntary) *Nottingham Patent Brick and Tile Co. v Butler* (1885) 15 Q.B.D. 261 at 271 (restrictive covenants); *Walker v Boyle* [1982] 1 W.L.R. 495 at 504–507 (misrepresentation); *Rignall Developments Ltd v Halil*, above, n.176 (undisclosed local land charge); *Celsteel Ltd v Alton House Holdings (No.2)* [1986] 1 All E.R. 598 at 607.

[179] Megarry & Wade, above, n.174, para.15–070; C. Harpum, "Selling without title: a vendor's duty of disclosure?" (1992) 108 L.Q.R. 280; Spencer Bower (Non-Disclosure), para.7.15.

[180] Above, para.17–40; Spencer Bower (Non-Disclosure), para.7.15.

the return of his deposit; or although he defends the claim to specific performance, he may (whilst being required to take the property) be awarded compensation in equity. These remedies have already been discussed in relation to misdescription of the property.[181] However, where the vendor knew of the defect, he may not be able to obtain specific performance of the contract[182]; and although the purchaser may have contracted to accept title with the defect, a condition of the contract, worded generally to provide that the property is sold subject to incumbrances entered on the register and that the purchaser is deemed to have notice of them, is insufficient to exclude or discharge the vendor's liability for defects of title of which he knew or ought to have known.[183]

IV. STATUTORY REMEDIES FOR NON-DISCLOSURE

Statutory duties of disclosure. We saw in Chapter 7 that various statutes impose liability for misrepresentation, and that the statutory liability for misrepresentation can be either general, or specific.[184] Section 2(1) of the Misrepresentation Act 1967[185] imposes a general liability for pre-contractual misrepresentation, without restriction to particular kinds of contract or other particular circumstances: in substance, there is a general duty on parties negotiating a contract not to make a false statements which they do not have reasonable ground to believe are true. Other statutes impose specific liabilities in particular circumstances, such as the liability in damages for untrue or misleading statements in prospectuses and listing particulars under section 90 of the Financial Services and Markets Act 2000.[186] Various statutes also impose duties to disclose information, and provide remedies for the party who has entered into a contract in circumstances where the required information has **17–43**

[181] Above, para.10–09. See also Megarry & Wade, above, n.174, para.15–071; Spencer Bower (Non-Disclosure), para.7.16; Emmet, para.4.028; J.T. Farrand, above, n.174, pp.70–71.

[182] G. Jones and W. Goodhart, *Specific Performance* (2nd edn, 1996), pp.93–97.

[183] See cases cited above, n.178; *Weir v Area Estates Ltd* [2010] EWCA Civ 801, [2010] 3 E.G.L.R. 91 at [21], following *Becker v Partridge* [1966] 2 Q.B. 155, CA, and C. Harpum, S. Bridge and M. Dixon, *Megarry and Wade, The Law of Real Property* (7th edn, 2008), para.15–072. See also above, para.9–17.

[184] Above, para.7–01.

[185] Above, paras 7–03 *et seq.*

[186] Above, paras 7–49 *et seq.*

not been disclosed. However, we have already seen that the law is considerably more reluctant to impose duties to disclose information than to impose liability for the disclosure of false information.[187] For example, the tort of deceit creates in substance a general duty to be honest in making representations and therefore not dishonestly to cause another to suffer loss in reliance on false information; yet there is no general duty to provide information that a party knows would prevent the other party suffering loss.[188] It is therefore not surprising that no general duty to disclose has been provided by statute. By contrast, where there are good reasons to require disclosure of particular information in the negotiations for particular kinds of contract or other particular circumstances, statute may impose duties of disclosure. The discussion of statutory duties of disclosure will follow a similar structure to the discussion in Chapter 7: we consider first whether section 2 of the Misrepresentation Act 1967 has any role to play in relation to imposing a general liability for non-disclosure; and then we consider the specific liabilities for non-disclosure under section 90 of the Financial Services and Markets Act 2000, and other specific statutory duties of disclosure.

17–44 **Remedies for breach of statutory duties of disclosure.** Statutes which impose duties of disclosure commonly prescribe remedies which are designed to fulfil the purpose of the duty. As we shall see, this may be a liability to compensate the party who suffers loss as a result of entering into a contract in ignorance of the information which should have been disclosed;[189] but breach of a particular duty of disclosure may render the contract unenforceable,[190] or extend the period during which the party can exercise a right, such as the right to cancel the contract.[191]

[187] Above, paras 16–03, 16–06.

[188] Above, para.17–37, where it was noted that in recent decisions the tort of deceit appears to have been extended to cover non-disclosure, but only where there is a fraudulent breach of a duty of disclosure.

[189] e.g. s.90 of the Financial Services and Markets Act 2000; below, para.17–46.

[190] e.g. s.18 of the Estate Agents Act 1979; below, para.17–52.

[191] e.g. Consumer Protection (Distance Selling) Regulations 2000; below, para.17–53.

(1) Misrepresentation Act 1967, Section 2(1)

Section 2(1) does not by its terms apply to non-disclosure. 17–45
The terms of section 2(1) of the Misrepresentation Act 1967[192] suggest that it requires an active statement: the section imposes liability only for a misrepresentation which has been "made" by the defendant:[193]

> "If section 2(1) is to apply at all, a misrepresentation has to have been 'made' to the complainant by the other party. The expression 'misrepresentation . . . made' (which is repeated in several later sections of the Act of 1967[194]) would, in our judgment, on the ordinary meaning of words be inapt to refer to a misrepresentation which had not been made in fact but was (at most) merely deemed by the common law to have been made. If it had been the intention of the legislature that a mere failure to discharge the duty of disclosure in the case of a contract uberrimae fidei would fall to be treated as the 'making' of a representation within the meaning of the Act of 1967, we are of the opinion that the legislature would have said so."

However, we have seen that in recent decisions the courts have said that the tort of deceit applies to the dishonest breach of a duty of disclosure; and a reason given for this is that in such circumstances non-disclosure is tantamount to an implied representation that there is nothing relevant to disclose.[195] If that is correct, and unless the wording of the statute in requiring a "misrepresentation . . . made" is to continue to be held to be a limiting factor which excludes breach of a duty of disclosure from the scope of section 2(1),[196] it could widen the application of the section so as to render every breach of a duty of disclosure actionable in damages on the tort

---

[192] Above, paras 7–03 *et seq*.

[193] *Banque Keyser Ullmann S.A. v Skandia (UK) Insurance Co. Ltd* [1990] 1 Q.B. 665, CA, at 790 (the point was not discussed on appeal: *Banque Financière de la Cité S.A. v Westgate Insurance Co. Ltd* [1991] 2 A.C. 249, HL); *H.I.H. Casualty and General Insurance Ltd v Chase Manhattan Bank* [2001] EWCA Civ 1250, [2001] 2 Lloyd's Rep. 483 at [51].

[194] [This is the basis for the argument that the court has no discretion under s.2(2) to award damages in lieu of rescission for non-disclosure: above, para.17–02; and that the control by s.3 of contractual clauses excluding or restricting liability and remedies for misrepresentation does not extend to exclusions or restrictions of liability and remedies for non-disclosure: below, para.17–56].

[195] *Conlon v Simms* [2006] EWCA Civ 1749, [2008] 1 W.L.R. 484 at [130] (Jonathan Parker L.J.); above, para.17–37.

[196] *Cf.*, however, above, paras 7–10 and 7–11, noting that the language of s.2(1) ("the *facts* represented were true") does not appear to have deterred the courts

measure[197] unless the statutory defence provided by the section is made out.[198] It is regrettable that the potential for such a wide but uncertain extension of liability for damages for non-disclosure should be made without proper consideration.[199]

(2) Financial Services and Markets Act 2000, Section 90

17–46 **Liability for omissions from prospectuses and listing particulars.** The liabilities under section 90 of the Financial Services and Markets Act 2000 in respect of untrue or misleading statements in prospectuses and listing particulars were discussed in

---

from extending the scope of the section to cover misrepresentations of law, to bring the statute into line with other judicial developments in the meaning of "misrepresentation" at common law.

[197] Until the Supreme Court reconsiders the decision in *Royscot Trust Ltd v Rogerson* [1991] 2 Q.B. 297, CA, this would mean damages on the same measure as the tort of deceit: above, para.7–33.

[198] Above, para.7–03 ("unless he proves that he had reasonable ground to believe and did believe up to the time the contract was made that the facts represented were true"). The question would then be how this formulation, devised for the case of a misrepresentation, would be interpreted in its application to an actionable non-disclosure. It might require the party in breach to establish that he honestly and on reasonable grounds shared the other party's misunderstanding (i.e. erroneously believed the truth) which would have been corrected if he had fulfilled his duty; or, more likely, that he honestly and on reasonable grounds believed that he was entitled not to disclose the information in question. *Cf.* Financial Services and Markets Act 2000 Sch.10, para.1(2) which in relation to liability under s.90 for omissions, as well as untrue or misleading statements, in prospectuses and listing particulars, provides for the defence that the responsible person reasonably believed that (in the case of a statement) "the statement was true and not misleading", and (in the case of an omission) "the matter whose omission caused the loss was properly omitted": above, para. 7–57; below, para.17–50.

[199] Cf, however, *National Westminster Bank Plc v Rabobank Nederland* [2007] EWHC 1056 (Comm), [2007] All E.R. (D) 186 (May) at [112] where Colman J. assumed that, had he found a general duty of disclosure between co-workout banks, s.2(1) would apply to impose liability for damages. See further J. Cartwright, "Liability in Tort for Pre-Contractual Non-Disclosure" in A. Burrows and E. Peel (eds), *Contract Formation and Parties* (2010), p.137; but note that the development of the tort of deceit to cover fraudulent breach of a duty of disclosure is consistent with the development of the crime of fraud in the Fraud Act 2006: below, para.17–55.

Chapter 7.[200] It should be noted, however, that the Act imposes liability not only for loss suffered as a result of misrepresentations in prospectuses and listing particulars, but also for loss suffered as a result of the omission from those documents of certain matters and as a result of the failure to submit a supplementary prospectus or supplementary listing particulars where there is a significant change affecting any matter contained in the original document, or a significant new matter arises which would have been required to be included in it.[201] The account given in Chapter 7 about such matters as who may claim,[202] who is liable,[203] and the nature of the remedy[204] applies generally also to the liabilities for omissions, so mention will be made here only of issues which particularly concern the liability for omissions.

Omission of information from the listing particulars. The relevant provision within section 90(1) reads: 17–47

> "**90.**—(1) Any person responsible for listing particulars[205] is liable to pay compensation to a person who has—
> (a) acquired[206] securities to which the particulars apply; and
> (b) suffered loss in respect of them as a result of—

[200] S.90 applies only to prospectuses and listing particulars which are issued prior to listing: *Hall v Cable & Wireless Plc* [2009] EWHC 1793 (Comm), [2010] 1 B.C.L.C. 95 at [20]. For the liability of the issuers of securities already admitted to trading on regulated markets in respect of *dishonest* concealment of material facts in information provided from time to time, see s.90A and Sch.10A, as inserted by the Financial Services and Markets Act 2000 (Liability of Issuers) Regulations 2010 (SI 2010/1192); above, para.7–49, n.214.

[201] The disclosure obligations contained in the Act, as amended by Prospectus Regulations 2005 (SI 2005/1433), implement European Directives: the Listings Directive (2001/34/EC) and the Prospectus Directive (2003/71/EC).

[202] Above, para.7–52.

[203] Above, para.7–55.

[204] Above, para.7–62.

[205] [Including supplementary listing particulars issued under s.81: s.90(10); below, para.17–48. The section applies in relation to a prospectus and a supplementary prospectus, as it applies to listing particulars and supplementary listing particulars: s.90(11), inserted by the Prospectus Regulations 2005, above, n.201. Following the language of s.90, this chapter refers generally to listing particulars, although this should be understood to include prospectuses as appropriate.]

[206] [Or contracted to acquire them or any interest in them: s.90(7). For further details on the interpretation of this subsection, see above, para.7–52.]

(ii) the omission from the particulars of any matter required to be included by section 80 or 81."

The general duty of disclosure in listing particulars is contained in section 80, which provides as follows:

"**80.**—(1) Listing particulars submitted to the competent authority[207] under section 79[208] must contain all such information as investors and their professional advisers would reasonable require, and reasonably expect to find there, for the purpose of making an informed assessment of—

(a) the assets and liabilities, financial position, profits and losses, and prospects of the issuer of the securities; and
(b) the right attaching to the securities.

(2) That information is required in addition to any information required by—

(a) listing rules, or
(b) the competent authority,

as a condition of the admission of the securities to the official list.

(3) Subsection (1) only applies to information—

(a) within the knowledge of any person responsible for the listing particulars; or
(b) which it would be reasonable for him to obtain by making enquiries.

(4) In determining what information subsection (1) requires to be included in listing particulars, regard must be had (in particular) to—

(a) the nature of the securities and their issuer;
(b) the nature of the persons likely to consider acquiring them;
(c) the fact that certain matters may reasonably be expected to be within the knowledge of professional advisers of a kind which persons likely to acquire the securities may reasonably be expected to consult; and
(d) any information available to investors or their professional advisers as a result of requirements imposed on the issuer of the securities by a recognised investment exchange, by listing rules or by or under any other enactment."

207 [For the time being, the functions of the "competent authority" are exercised by the Financial Services Authority. This may however be changed by the Treasury by statutory instrument: s.72, Sch.8. In June 2011 the Government published a White Paper, *A new approach to financial regulation: the blueprint for reform* (Cm.8083), together with a draft Bill, which proposes to re-structure financial regulation and would rename the Financial Services Authority the "Financial Conduct Authority" and redefine its role and duties as one of the new regulators; the Financial Conduct Authority would become the "competent authority" for the purposes of the 2000 Act.]

208 [Above, paras 7–49, n.214; 7–51, n.225.]

The form and content of listing particulars and prospectuses are to be specified in listing rules made by the competent authority.[209] The effect of section 80 is therefore to impose a general duty of disclosure of relevant information, in addition to the duty to provide specific information required by the listing rules; and section 90 imposes on the persons responsible a liability in damages for loss caused by the non-disclosure. The duty of disclosure is however limited to information of which any person responsible for the particulars knows or which it would be reasonable for him to obtain by making enquiries.[210] The duty may also be more or less extensive depending on the circumstances, such as the nature of the securities, and the nature of the potential claimant and his advisers.[211]

Supplementary listing particulars. Section 81 of the Financial Services and Markets Act 2000 includes the following provisions: 17–48

> "**81.**—(1) If at any time after the preparation of listing particulars which have been submitted to the competent authority under section 79 and before the commencement of dealings in the securities concerned following their admission to the official list[212]—
>
> (a) there is a significant change affecting any matter contained in those particulars the inclusion of which was required by—

[209] ss.73A, 79(2); 84(1) (as amended by the Prospectus Regulations 2005), and in many respects the listing rules require listing particulars to follow the corresponding requirements for prospectuses in the prospectus rules: see the listing rules, para.4.2. Many of the detailed requirements of the contents of prospectuses are however fixed by reference to the Prospectus Directive Regulation (2004/809), so as to provide common Europe-wide standards: prospectus rules, App.3. Up-to-date copies of the listing rules and the prospectus rules, and information about the exercise by the Financial Services Authority of its functions as competent authority, can be found on the Authority's web site: *http://www.fsa.gov.uk*.

[210] s.80(3). It should be noted, however, that the section does not limit liability to information within the knowledge of the particular defendant: any "person responsible for the listing particulars" is liable under s.90; and s.80(3) brings within the duty of disclosure information which any person responsible knew or which it would be reasonable for him to make by making enquiries. A particular defendant may, however, be able to raise a defence that he reasonably believed that matters were properly omitted: below, para.17–50.

[211] s.80(4).

[212] [Or, where the prospectus was submitted in relation to a public offering for unlisted shares, before the end of the offer period: s.87G (inserted by the Prospectus Regulations 2005).]

(i) section 80,
(ii) listing rules, or
(iii) the competent authority, or

(b) a significant new matter arises, the inclusion of information in respect of which would have been so required if it had arisen when the particulars were prepared,

the issuer[213] must, in accordance with listing rules, submit supplementary listing particulars of the change or new matter to the competent authority, for its approval and, if they are approved, publish them.

(2) 'Significant' means significant for the purpose of making an informed assessment of the kind mentioned in section 80(1)."

If supplementary listing particulars are issued but fail to include matters which are required by the general duty of disclosure[214] or by listing rules, then the persons responsible for them will be liable under section 90.[215] However, section 90 makes further provision for the case where a person fails to comply with his obligations under section 81: this will include not only the issuer who fails to issue supplementary listing particulars, but also a person responsible for the particulars who fails to notify the issuer of a change or new matter which requires the submission of supplementary listing particulars.[216] In such cases the liability is to pay compensation to any person who has acquired securities and suffered loss in respect of them as a result of the failure.

17–49 **Omissions authorised by the competent authority.** The competent authority[217] has a general power to dispense with or modify the application of the listing rules in particular cases and by reference to any circumstances.[218] It also has specific power to authorise the omission from listing particulars or supplementary listing particulars of information which would otherwise be required by section 80 or section 81 on the ground that its disclosure would be contrary to the public interest or would be seriously detrimental to the issuer, or (in relation to particular kinds of securities as specified in listing

[213] [If the issuer is not aware of the change or new matter he has no duty to comply unless he is notified of the change or new matter by a person responsible for the listing particulars—and those persons have a duty to inform him if they know of it: s.81(3), (4).]

[214] s.80; above, para.17–47.

[215] s.90(1)(b)(ii); above, para.17–47.

[216] s.81(4).

[217] Above, n.207.

[218] ss.73A (inserted by the Prospectus Regulations 2005), 101(2).

rules) that disclosure is unnecessary for persons of the kind who may be expected normally to buy or deal in securities of that kind.[219] Information may not however be omitted on the ground that it would be seriously detrimental to the issuer, if it is "essential"—that is, information which a person considering acquiring securities of the kind in question would be likely to need in order not to be misled about any facts which it is essential for him to know in order to make an informed assessment.[220]

Statutory defence of honest and reasonable belief that matters were properly omitted. Just as there is a defence within the Act for a person who made an untrue or misleading statement in listing particulars but can show that he reasonably believed it to be true,[221] so there is a similar defence for a person who omits any matter required to be included in the listing particulars, or fails to comply with his duty under section 81 in respect of supplementary listing particulars, but can show that he reasonably believed that the matter whose omission caused the loss was properly omitted[222] or that he reasonably believed that the change or new matter in question was not such as to call for supplementary listing particulars.[223] 17–50

Other statutory defences. It is a defence to show that, before the claimant acquired the securities, notice has been published of the omission[224]; or that the claimant acquired the securities with knowledge of the omitted matter or of the change or new matter.[225] 17–51

[219] s.82(1). The competent authority is entitled to act on a certificate from the Secretary of State or the Treasury to the effect that disclosure would be contrary to the public interest: s.82(3), (4).
[220] s.82(2), (6).
[221] Above, para.7–57.
[222] Sch.10, para.1(2)(b). For conditions which must be satisfied for a defendant to rely on this defence, see *ibid.*, para.3; above, para.7–57.
[223] *ibid.*, para.7.
[224] *ibid.*, para 3; for the notice required, see above, para.7–59.
[225] *ibid.*, para.6(b), (c). See further above, para.7–60. For other possible (non-statutory) defences, see above, para.7–61.

(3) Remedies for Non-Disclosure Under Other Statutes

17–52 **Duties of disclosure in domestic legislation.** We shall see below that in recent years there has been a significant increase in statutory duties of disclosure as a result of the implementation of European Directives, and that there remains significant scope for further development in that context.[226] However, there are also some specific duties of disclosure in legislation of purely domestic origin;[227] for example, under section 18 of the Estate Agents Act 1979 an estate agent must give the client certain specified information before entering into a contract (or the variation of an existing contract) under which the agent will engage in agency work on behalf of the client.[228] Failure to comply with the duty of disclosure does not of itself give the client a general claim in damages, but renders the contract (or the variation) unenforceable without a court order.[229]

17–53 **Duties of disclosure implementing European Directives.** A number of Directives setting particular requirements for disclosure

---

[226] Below, paras 17–53 to 17–54.

[227] See also Consumer Credit Act 1974 s.55, which provided that regulations may require specified information to be disclosed to the debtor or hirer before a regulated agreement is made (s.55(1): and see SI 1983/1553 and SI 2004/1481), and that a regulated agreement was "not properly executed", and therefore enforceable against the debtor only on an order of the court, if the regulations were not complied with (ss.55(2), 65(1)). S.55(2) was amended, and s.55A inserted (to require the creditor to provide further pre-contractual information), by SI 2010/1010 to give effect to Directive 2008/48/EC; below, n.238. See further Housing Act 1985 s.125(4A), inserted by Housing and Planning Act 1986 (where secure public sector tenant has given notice to exercise right to buy or take a lease of the dwelling-house, landlord has duty to inform tenant of any structural defect known to the landlord affecting the dwelling-house or the building in which it is situated or any other building over which the tenant will have rights under the conveyance or lease).

[228] The specified information is set out in s.18(2), consisting of details of the payment arrangements under the contract, but additional required information may be prescribed by Regulations under s.18(4); see SI 1991/856, reg.2, requiring information to be provided as to the services offered by the agent.

[229] s.18(5). Where, however, the court enforces the contract in spite of the breach of the duty of disclosure, it may order that any sum payable by the client under the contract (or under the contract as varied) shall be reduced or discharged so as to compensate the client for prejudice suffered as a result of the agent's failure to comply with his obligation: s.18(6).

of information have been implemented in the United Kingdom.[230] To take one example: under the Consumer Protection (Distance Selling) Regulations 2000[231] the person who supplies goods or services to a consumer under certain types of "distance contract"[232] is required to provide certain information to the consumer in good time prior to the conclusion of the contract, and to provide certain other information in writing either prior to the conclusion of the contract or in good time thereafter. The required information in both cases includes such matters as a description of the main characteristics of the goods or services and the price.[233] The failure to provide the required information does not of itself make the contract void or voidable, or give the consumer a claim in damages. However, the consumer has a right to cancel[234] a distance contract within a period which starts on the day of the contract and normally ends seven working days thereafter or (in a contract for the supply of goods) seven working days after the day on which the consumer received the goods. Where the supplier fails to provide the information required by the regulations the cancellation period is extended, and the right of cancellation is exercisable by the consumer until seven working days after the day on which the supplier provides the information or, if he fails to provide it for three months, the long-stop cancellation period is three months and

230 See generally P. Rott, "Information and Withdrawal Rights" in C. Twigg-Flesner (ed.), *European Union Private Law* (2010), p.187.

231 SI 2000/2334, implementing Council Directive 97/7/EC; amended by (inter alia) SI 2004/2095; SI 2005/689 and SI 2010/2960.

232 A contract concerning goods or services concluded between a supplier and a consumer under an organised distance sales or service provision scheme run by the supplier who, for the purpose of the contract, makes exclusive use of one or more means of distance communication up to and including the moment at which the contract is concluded: reg.3(1). All such distance contracts are included, other than "excepted contracts", such as contracts for the sale or disposition of an interest in land (except rental agreements), and contracts relating to financial services: regs 4, 5 (see, however, Financial Services (Distant Marketing) Regulations 2004, below, n.236); and certain provisions of the Regulations (including the disclosure requirements) do not apply to certain types of contract, such as contracts for home-delivery of food: reg.6.

233 regs 7, 8.

234 reg.10.

seven working days from the day on which the contract was concluded (or the consumer received the goods).[235]

Other Regulations impose duties to provide specific information before or in other types of contract, such as contracts for the distance marketing of consumer financial services,[236] contracts entered into with consumers at their home or workplace ("doorstep selling"),[237] consumer credit,[238] timeshare and other long-term holiday contracts,[239] and package travel, holidays and tours contracts.[240]

[235] regs 11, 12, amended by SI 2005/689 in relation to consequences of the failure by the supplier of services to inform the consumer about his right to cancel.

[236] Financial Services (Distant Marketing) Regulations 2004 (SI 2004/2095), implementing Directive 2002/65/EC, and amended by (inter alia) SI 2010/1010, requiring specified information to be provided to the consumer by the commercial or professional supplier of services in the case of a contract concerning one or more financial services made through distance communication under an organised distance sales or service-provision scheme run by the supplier or an intermediary. Regs 7 and 8 (and Schs 1 and 2) set out the information required prior to the conclusion of the contract (which does not apply if the distance contract is also a consumer credit contract and the supplier has complied with SI 2010/1013, below, n.238), and regs 9 to 11 give the consumer the right to cancel (and the cancellation period is extended where the supplier has not complied with the duty to provide information).

[237] Cancellation of Contracts made in a Consumer's Home or Place of Work etc. Regulations (SI 2008/1816), replacing earlier Regulations and re-implementing Council Directive 85/577/EEC in providing cancellation rights for contracts for goods or services made during a visit by a trader to a consumer's home or place of work (and impose in reg.7 the duty on the trader to inform the consumer of his cancellation right).

[238] Consumer Credit (EU Directive) Regulations 2010 (SI 2010/1010), implementing, together with other Regulations, Directive 2008/48/EC (replacing Council Directive 87/102/EEC) in relation to consumer credit; SI 2010/1010 amends (inter alia) the Consumer Credit Act 1974 to require further pre-contractual information and in relation to rights of withdrawal from a regulated consumer credit agreement; the Consumer Credit (Disclosure of Information) Regulations 2010 (SI 2010/1013) set out pre-contractual information requirements in relation to a range of different types of consumer credit contract, and the Consumer Credit (Agreements) Regulations 2010 (SI 2010/1014) set out requirements of form and content of different types of consumer credit agreement.

[239] Timeshare, Holiday Products, Resale and Exchange Contracts Regulations 2010 (SI 2010/2960), replacing the Timeshare Act 1992 and related regulations, and implementing Directive 2008/122/EC, requiring "key information" to be provided before and in a contract between a trader and a consumer for certain

Potential significance of continuing European developments for duties of disclosure in English law. There are continuing developments within Europe which carry varying potential significance for the law on non-disclosure under English domestic contract law. 17–54

In the first place, following a review of the Consumer Acquis[241] the Commission has sought to bring together Directives, some of which impose duties of information and disclosure, into a single new Directive, with a view to simplify and complete the existing regulatory framework. A proposal in 2008 for a new Directive on Consumer Rights,[242] which would have merged and reformed four of the existing Directives[243] into a single instrument to be implemented with full harmonisation, failed to achieve the

---

holiday contracts. Regs 12 and 13 (and Schs 1 to 4) set out the key information and the form in which it is to be provided, and regs 20 to 21 give the consumer the right of withdrawal (and the withdrawal period is extended where the key information is not provided to the consumer).

[240] Package Travel, Package Holidays and Package Tours Regulations 1992 (SI 1992/3288), implementing Council Directive 90/314/EEC, requiring the organiser or retailer of a package contract for the provision of at least two of transport, accommodation and other tourist services (where the contract is for at least 24 hours or includes overnight accommodation) to provide information to the consumer before and in the contract, and before the start of the journey. However, these Regulations differ from those mentioned in nn.236 to 239, above, in providing criminal offences for breach of the duties of disclosure but without affecting the validity or enforceability of the contract: reg.27; below, para.17–55. *Cf.* the remedy of compensation under reg.4 for loss suffered by the consumer in consequence of misleading information contained in any descriptive matter relating to the package; above, paras.7–66 to 7–70.

[241] Communication: *Updating and simplifying the Community acquis* COM(2003) 71 final (11.2.2003); Communication: *European Contract Law and the revision of the acquis: the way forward* COM(2004) 651 final (11.10.2004); Green Paper on the Review of the Consumer Acquis, COM(2006) 744 Final (08.02.2007).

[242] COM(2008) 614 Final (8.10.2008).

[243] Directive 85/577/EEC on contracts negotiated away from business premises (above, n.237), Directive 93/13/EEC on unfair terms in consumer contracts, Directive 97/7/EC on distance contracts (above, n.231) and Directive 1999/44/EC on consumer sales and guarantees. The review also covered four further Directives which were not included within the proposal for a new Consumer Rights Directive in 2008: Directive 90/314/EEC on package travel, package holidays and package tours (above, n.240); Directive 94/47/EC on timeshare contracts (later replaced by Directive 2008/122/EC; above, n.239); Directive 98/6/EC on price indication; and Directive 98/27/EC on consumer injunctions.

necessary agreement within the Union, and in June 2011 a compromise text, with a significantly reduced scope, was adopted by the European Parliament.[244] It will replace only two Directives (on contracts negotiated away from business premises, and on distance contracts[245]) but in many of its provisions will be a full harmonisation measure. It will set fully harmonised requirements for pre-contractual information to be given to the consumer in the case of distance and off-premises contracts,[246] as well as providing for minimum harmonisation requirements for information to be provided by a trader to a consumer in other contracts (with certain specified exclusions).[247] The information includes such things as the main characteristics of the goods or services, the trader's identity, the price payable, and (in the case of distance and off-premises contracts) the right of withdrawal. The United Kingdom, in common with other Member States, will be required to implement the new Directive within two years after it enters into force: there will therefore be some necessary amendment to some of the the Regulations described in para.17–53.

Secondly, the current European project to produce a "Common Frame of Reference" for European Contract Law[248] may impact upon English law in the longer term. The Feasibility study for a future instrument in European Contract Law, which was published in May 2011,[249] contained a range of mandatory duties to disclose

---

244 Legislative resolution P7_TA-PROV(2011)0293. It is expected to be formally approved by the Council of Ministers in October 2011; publication of the new Directive in the Official Journal will then follow during autumn 2011.

245 Directives 85/577/EEC and 97/7/EC (as amended): above, n.243.

246 Above, n.244, art.9. The formal requirements are set out in arts 10 (off-premises contracts) and 11 (distance contracts), and the common provisions for a 14-day right of withdrawal are in art.12.

247 *ibid.*, art.5. The excluded contracts are listed at art.3.3 (including contracts for financial services; contracts for the creation, acquisition or transfer of rights of or in immovable property; and contracts which fall with the Directives on package travel, package holidays and package tours contracts (above, n.240) and timeshares (above, n.239)). Member States may decide not to apply the Directive to off-premises contracts for which the payment by the consumer does not exceed 50 Euros (or such lower sum as a Member State may define): art.4.

248 Above, para.1–05.

249 Commission Expert Group, "Feasibility study for a future instrument in European Contract Law" (2011), arts 13–22. The remedies for breach of information duties are at art.25. For commentary on the equivalent provisons of the DCFR, from which the Expert Group text is developed, see the Comment in

information,[250] both general duties applicable to all contracts for the supply of goods or services, and duties specific to distance or off-premises contracts, thus drawing largely on the existing duties under the Directives described above, and the current proposals for a new Directive on Consumer Rights. There were also, however, provisions significantly different from those that exist under English law: in particular, a general duty to negotiate in accordance with good faith and fair dealing, breach of which would give rise to liability to pay damages for loss caused to the other party;[251] and provisions allowing a party to avoid a contract for a mistake of fact or law of which the other party knew or could be expected to have known but failed to point out the relevant information where good faith and fair dealing would have required him to point it out, or where he was in breach of one of the pre-contractual information duties;[252] or where there is fraudulent non-disclosure of any information which good faith and fair dealing, or any pre-contractual information duty, required the party to disclose.[253] Such provisions would sit more comfortably with many European civil codes than with the English common law.[254] As we have noted, the

C. von Bar and E. Clive (eds), *Principles, Definitions and Model Rules of European Private Law: Draft Common Frame of Reference (DCFR), Full Edition* (Sellier, Munich, 2009).

[250] *ibid.*, arts 13–23.

[251] *ibid.*, art.27(2), (3); identical to DCFR, II.–3:301(2), (3).

[252] *ibid.*, art.45(1)(b)(ii), (iii); developed from DCFR, II.–7.201(1)(b)(ii), (iii). Criteria are given in art.45(3) to determine whether good faith and fair dealing required a party to point out that the other is mistaken about relevant information: (a) whether the party had special expertise, (b) the cost to the party of acquiring the relevant information, (c) the ease with which the other party could have acquired the information by other means, (d) the nature of the information, and (e) the apparent importance of the information to the other party.

[253] *ibid.*, art.46(1); identical to DCFR, II.–7:205(1). For this purpose the list of criteria to determine whether good faith and fair dealing required a party to disclose information (above, n.252) is expanded to include (f) in contracts between businesses, good commercial practice in the situation concerned.

[254] See, e.g. the Notes contained in von Bar and Clive, *Principles, Definitions and Model Rules of European Private Law: Draft Common Frame of Reference (DCFR)* (above, n.249), vol.1, on each of the provisions mentioned in nn.251 to 253, above, which outline the relationship between the rules presented in the DCFR and national laws. For a comparison between the first published draft of the DCFR and English law, see S. Whittaker, "The 'Draft Common Frame of Reference': An Assessment commissioned by the Ministry of Justice, United Kingdom" (November 2008; available at *http://www.justice.gov.uk/publications/*

impact of such provisions in English law will depend on the form of implementation of the Common Frame of Reference, which is not yet clear [255]; and even if it is introduced as an Optional Instrument, it would be technically separate from the rules of the existing English domestic contract law. It is not, however, inconceivable that English judges might see merit in developing the common law rules on such things as mistake and duties of disclosure in the light of their eventual experience of an Optional Instrument.[256]

17–55 **Statutes imposing criminal liability: claims for loss.** We saw in Chapter 7 that various statutes impose criminal liability for misrepresentations.[257] Given the general distinction between misrepresentation and non-disclosure, and in particular the greater reluctance of the law to sanction non-disclosure than misrepresentation, it is not surprising that fewer statutes impose criminal liability for non-disclosure than for misrepresentations. However, there are examples of criminal liability for failure to provide information, and a significant development has recently been made by the Fraud Act 2006 which includes, within the general offence of

---

docs/Draft_Common_Frame_of_Reference__an_assessment.pdf [Accessed 30 June 2011], and esp. at pp.100–104 (duties to inform and liability for fraud)).

[255] Above, para.1.05. The Commission's working draft of August 2011 made amendments to the Feasibility study, perhaps most significantly removing the general duty to renegotiate in good faith and its associated remedy in damages. See now the Commission's proposal for a Regulation on a Common European Sales Law (COM (2011) 635); Preface, p.vii, above.

[256] For discussion of possible development of duties of disclosure at common law in light of the existing piecemeal statutory duties of disclosure, see Anson, pp.345–347. The recent development of a liability in tort for the fraudulent breach of a duty of disclosure, above, para.17–37, is already consistent with a broader view of the legal wrong involved in not disclosing information in defined circumstances. If the Supreme Court were minded to develop broader general duties of disclosure in English law, this may well be a point at which to start. In the last 40 years French law has developed much broader duties of disclosure than are recognised in English law—and much broader than the former French position, which took a relatively strong line based on *caveat emptor*—using as the springboard cases of fraudulent non-disclosure (*réticence dolosive*): B. Nicholas, *The French Law of Contract* (2nd edn, 1992), pp.102–106; J. Ghestin, "The Pre-contractual Obligation to Disclose Information" in D. Harris & D. Tallon, *Contract Law Today* (1989) at pp.150–166. See also above, para.16–04, n.12.

[257] Above, para.7–72.

fraud, "fraud by failing to disclose information",[258] where a person dishonestly[259] fails to disclose to another person information which he under a legal duty to disclose, and intends, by failing to disclose the information, to make a gain for himself or another, or to cause loss to another or to expose another to a risk of loss. This is a limited offence in the sense that it does not impose liability simply for dishonestly failing to disclose information, but applies only where the information was such that the defendant was under a legal duty to disclose it. The scope of the criminal law matches the general view taken within the civil law that there must first be a reason to impose the duty to disclose.[260] But it appears that, whenever there is under the civil law a duty to disclose information, there is now a potential criminal liability of fraud for dishonestly failing to disclose it with the intention of (inter alia) causing loss to another. The Act imposes only criminal liability, but where loss is in fact caused by the commission of the offence, it seems that (as with criminal offences generally) the victim may be able to seek a remedy under section 130 of the Powers of Criminal Courts (Sentencing) Act 2000.[261] However, as we have seen, the courts have also recently accepted that the fraudulent breach of a duty of

[258] s.3, which falls within the general offence of fraud under s.1. For the offence of fraud by false representation (s.2), see above, para.7–72.
[259] This is not the concept of dishonesty commonly referred to within the tort of deceit (above, para.5–14), but the test adopted in the criminal law: a defendant is dishonest if (i) according to the ordinary standards of reasonable and honest people what was done was dishonest, and (ii) the defendant must have realised that what was doing was by those standards dishonest: *R. v Ghosh* [1982] Q.B. 1053, CA, at 1064 (a decision under Theft Act 1968).
[260] See Law Com. No.276, *Fraud* (2002), paras 7.28, 7.29. Cl.3(3) of the Bill proposed by the Law Commission defined the wrongful failure to disclose as where, inter alia, "(a) D is under a duty under any enactment, instrument or rule of law to disclose the information to P, and (b) D knows that the circumstances which give rise to the duty to disclose the information to P exist or is aware that they might exist". The Explanatory Notes to the Fraud Act 2006, para.18, appear to assume that the simpler formulation in s.3 ("fails to disclose to another person information which he is under a legal duty to disclose") reflects cl.3(3)(a). See also Law Com. Consultation Paper No.199, *Consumer Redress for Misleading and Aggressive Practices* (2011), para.6.5 ("criminal liability for fraud follows the civil law: it is only a criminal offence to fail to disclose information if the defendant was under a 'legal duty' to disclose it"); J. Parry, *Arlidge and Parry on Fraud* (3rd edn, 2007), paras 5–006 to 5–012.
[261] Discussed above, para.7–73.

disclosure can be actionable in the tort of deceit;[262] though controversial, this development is in line with the development in criminal liability for fraud.

A further general criminal liability for omissions by traders in their dealings with consumers is contained in the Consumer Protection from Unfair Trading Regulations 2008,[263] which includes within the definition of an "unfair commercial practice" a misleading omission: this includes the situation where, in its factual context and taking into account a range of defined matters, the commercial practice omits or hides material information and as a result it causes or is likely to cause the average consumer to take a transactional decision he would not have taken otherwise. The Regulations make no provision for a civil remedy in damages, and expressly provide that an agreement shall not be void or unenforceable by reason only of a breach of the Regulations.[264]

There are also more particular criminal offences based on non-disclosure. For example, section 397 of the Financial Services and Markets Act 2000[265] imposes criminal liability on a person who dishonestly conceals any material facts whether in connection with a statement, promise or forecast made by him or otherwise, for the purpose of inducing another person to enter into, or exercise rights under, an investment agreement or certain other specified agreements; it is unlikely, however, that there is any civil claim in respect of an offence under the section.[266] And the Package Travel, Package

---

262 Above, para.17–37.

263 SI 2008/1277, implementing the Unfair Commercial Practices Directive 2005/29/EC. The Regulations also prohibit misleading actions, which include certain misrepresentations: above, para.7–72.

264 *ibid.*, reg.29. The Law Commission, making proposals for the introduction of civil redress for consumers in respect of loss suffered by breach of the Regulations, has rejected the idea that misleading omissions should give rise to liability in damages: Law Com. Consultation Paper No.199, above, n.260 at paras 13.68 to 13.70.

265 Replacing the Financial Services Act 1986, ss.47 (investment agreements), 133 (insurance contracts) and the Banking Act 1987, s.35 (deposits). For repeal of these earlier provisions, see Financial Services and Markets Act 2000 (Consequential Amendments and Repeals) Order 2001 (SI 2001/3649), reg.3. We saw in Chapter 7 that s.150 of the Financial Services and Markets Act 2000 provides a remedy in damages for breaches of the FSA Handbook: above, para.7–71; this will also include actions for omissions by authorised persons in breach of their duties under the regulatory regime established by the 2000 Act.

266 Above, para.7–72.

Holidays and Package Tours Regulations 1992[267] impose criminal liability on organisers for making available to consumers brochures which do not contain prescribed information about the package, and on organisers and retailers of packages for failing to provide certain other information[268]; but these offences under the Regulations do not make the contract void or unenforceable, nor is there any right of action in civil proceedings in respect of any loss suffered.

V. EXCLUSION OF LIABILITY FOR NON-DISCLOSURE

Clauses and notices excluding liability for non-disclosure. The different forms of clause or notice excluding or limiting liability for misrepresentation, and the common law and statutory controls on such clauses and notices, were considered in Chapter 9. The discussion there, except where it concerned remedies or statutory controls which are applicable only to liability for misrepresentation,[269] is equally applicable to clauses or notices which seek to exclude or limit the liability or the range of remedies that would otherwise arise for the defendant's non-disclosure. **17–56**

VI. NON-DISCLOSURE AS A DEFENCE

Non-disclosure may be raised as a defence. Chapter 10 considered the circumstances in which the defendant might raise the claimant's misrepresentation not only by way of counterclaim in order to obtain a substantive remedy but also simply as a defence to deny the claimant the relief he claims. Similarly, where there has been non-disclosure by the claimant in circumstances in which he **17–57**

---

[267] SI 1992/3288. The liability of an organiser or retailer under s.4 of the Regulations to compensate a consumer for misleading information contained in descriptive matter concerning a package travel, package holiday or package tour contract was considered in Ch.7: above, paras 7–66 to 7–70.

[268] *ibid.*, regs 5, 7, 8.

[269] Misrepresentation Act 1967 s.2(1) imposes liability only where a "misrepresentation" has been "made": above, para.17–45; and Misrepresentation Act 1967 s.3, above, para.9–19, only regulates contractual terms which would exclude or restrict liability or remedies in respect of a "misrepresentation made" before the contract. For whether the interpretation of the language of the 1967 Act might be revised in the light of the decision in *Conlon v Simms* [2006] EWCA Civ 1749, [2008] 1 W.L.R. 484, see above, para.17–45.

had a duty of disclosure, the defendant may seek to raise it as a defence, such as a defence to a claim for specific performance.[270]

[270] *Turner v Green* [1895] 2 Ch. 205 at 201. Where the vendor under a contract for the sale of land has failed to disclose defects in the title, the purchaser may defend the vendor's claim to specific performance and seek the return of his deposit or, though he defends the claim to specific performance, he may (though being required to take the property) be awarded compensation in equity: above, paras 17–41 to 17–42.

Index

This index has been prepared using Sweet and Maxwell's Legal Taxonomy. Main index entries conform to keywords provided by the Legal Taxonomy except where references to specific documents or non-standard terms (denoted by quotation marks) have been included. These keywords provide a means of identifying similar concepts in other Sweet and Maxwell publications and online services to which keywords from the Legal Taxonomy have been applied. Readers may find some minor differences between terms used in the text and those which appear in the index. Suggestions to *sweetandmaxwell.taxonomy@thomson.com*.

All references are to paragraph number